Educational Psychology
Windows on Classrooms

Ninth Edition

Paul Eggen
University of North Florida

Don Kauchak
University of Utah

PEARSON

Boston   Columbus   Indianapolis   New York   San Francisco   Upper Saddle River
Amsterdam   Cape Town   Dubai   London   Madrid   Milan   Munich   Paris   Montreal   Toronto
Delhi   Mexico City   São Paulo   Sydney   Hong Kong   Seoul   Singapore   Taipei   Tokyo

Vice President and Editor in Chief:
Jeffery W. Johnston
Vice President and Publisher: Kevin M. Davis
Editorial Assistant: Lauren Carlson
Development Editor: Christina Robb
Vice President, Director of Marketing:
Margaret Waples
Marketing Manager: Joanna Sabella
Senior Managing Editor: Pamela D. Bennett
Senior Project Manager: Sheryl Glicker Langner
Senior Operations Supervisor: Matthew Ottenweller

Senior Art Director: Diane C. Lorenzo
Art Director: Jodi Notowitz
Photo Researcher: Lori Whitley
Permissions Administrator: Rebecca Savage
Media Producer: Autumn Benson
Media Project Manager: Rebecca Norsic
Composition: Element LLC
Printer/Binder: R. R. Donnelley
Cover Printer: Lehigh-Phoenix Color
Text Font: Minion

If you purchased this book within the United States or Canada you should be aware that it has been imported without the approval of the Publisher or the Author.

Credits and acknowledgments borrowed from other sources and reproduced, with permission, in this textbook appear on appropriate page within text.

Every effort has been made to provide accurate and current Internet information in this book. However, the Internet and information posted on it are constantly changing, so it is inevitable that some of the Internet addresses listed in this textbook will change.

Photo Credits: photo credits are on p. xxviii

10 9 8 7 6 5 4 3 2 1

ISBN 10: 0-13-292085-9
ISBN 13: 978-0-13-292085-8

To Judy and Kathy,
teachers who have changed many lives.

preface

Educational Psychology: Windows on Classrooms is the most applied book in the field. Helping you apply the theory and research of educational psychology to increase your students' learning and development has been, and continues to be, our goal. It is the book's identity. If you're looking for a book that gives you a sound theoretical and research-based foundation and then provides specific and concrete illustrations and guidelines for applying this theory and research with your students, this is the book for you.

To accomplish our goal of application, we use an *integrated-case* approach, with "integrated" being the key idea. Most educational psychology textbooks now use case studies, so calling a book "case based" isn't unique. However, fully integrating the case with the content of each chapter *is;* it's what sets our book apart from others, and it's an important way in which we make the book truly applied.

The book's subtitle—*Windows on Classrooms*—reflects this approach. We show you how the theory and research of educational psychology are applied in real classrooms. Our *integrated-case* approach begins each chapter with a case study taken from actual classroom practice. But, instead of stopping there, we then weave the case throughout each chapter— extracting specific illustrations from it, and in some instances even taking dialogue from the lesson—to illustrate classroom applications of the chapter content. To see some examples of this *integrated-case* approach, go to pages 182, 186, and 187 of Chapter 6 or pages 212, 219, 221, and 235 of Chapter 7.

We have spent and continue to spend a great many hours in P–12 classrooms, and we know that the ability to apply a conceptually sound understanding of educational psychology is fundamental to being a great teacher. *Educational Psychology: Windows on Classrooms* can provide you with this practical knowledge, and it can be a resource that you will keep and use as you move into your teaching career.

New to this Edition

In our ongoing effort to provide you with the benefits of the most current findings in educational psychology, we have updated the book to include the latest developments in theory and research while simultaneously retaining our focus on application.

To reach these goals, we have added the following new themes to this edition:

- *Self-regulation:* Learning to monitor and control our thoughts and actions is important, both in classrooms and in our lives. To capitalize on this essential ability, we have made self-regulation a theme for this edition, and detailed discussions of the topic appear in Chapters 1–3, 5, 8, and 12.
- *Technology, learning, and development:* To say that we live in a technological world is a vast understatement. Technology is profoundly influencing the ways in which we communicate and interact, and it is even impacting how we learn. Discussions of technology's influence on cognitive and social/emotional learning and development and on how educators can capitalize on technology to influence both, appear in Chapters 1–3, 5, 6, 8–10, 13, and 14.
- *Student learning and development.* Suggesting that student learning and development is a theme appears self-evident; obviously, an educational psychology text will focus on these factors. However, as you move through your career,

you will teach your students much more than geography, how to write coherent paragraphs, or solve math problems. You will also help them learn to accept responsibility for their actions; develop socially and morally; respect and embrace peers with different ethnic, language, and religious backgrounds; persevere in the face of frustration; and value the acquisition of knowledge and skills that may not be intrinsically interesting to them. These are abilities that will serve your students throughout their lives, and promoting them is also a part of your job. They are essential, and we make all these forms of learning and development a theme to emphasize their importance.

In addition to these themes, we have significantly expanded our discussion of social influences on learning and development. We are social animals, and an expanding body of research helps us understand the social nature of learning and how context impacts who we are. Understanding the implications of this research is essential to education and your work with your students.

We've also created two new chapters for this edition:

- *Principles of Cognitive Learning Theory and the Construction of Knowledge:* To reflect the powerful influence of cognitive learning theory on classroom teaching and learning, we include this new chapter. The chapter is the first of four that focuses explicitly on learning.
- *Classroom Management: Developing Self-Regulated Learners:* To emphasize our theme of self-regulation, we include this new chapter. The chapter emphasizes that classroom management is much more than creating an orderly learning environment; it is a vehicle to teach students essential life skills.

Theory and application exist in a synergistic relationship; theory informs practice, and application demonstrates how theory is put into practice in classrooms. With this in mind we have also added two new features to this edition:

- *Ed Psych and You:* This new feature directly applies the content of each chapter to you, our readers, and shows you how educational psychology impacts your lives right now. For examples of this new feature, see pages 30, 193, 270, and 331.
- *Ed Psych and Teaching:* This feature provides you with specific suggestions for applying the content of each chapter in your teaching.

the most applied educational psychology book in the field

As we said at the beginning of the preface, this is the most applied book in the field, and we described our *integrated-case* approach. Some additional elements that help you apply the content of this text in your teaching include the following:

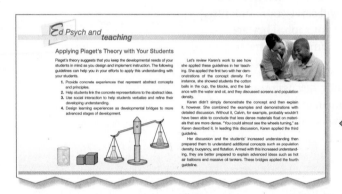

Ed Psych and Teaching. The new *Ed Psych and Teaching* feature helps you apply the content of each chapter by providing specific guidelines for implementing theory and research with your students. The feature also uses the *integrated-case* approach to illustrate the guidelines being applied in classroom settings. For examples see pages 43, 168, 202, and 244.

Summary of Classroom Applications. The applications for each chapter are outlined on each chapter's first page. For examples, see pages 65, 139, 181, and 329.

Classroom Connections at Elementary, Middle School, and High School Levels. These boxed features in each chapter offer suggestions and illustrations for applying content to specific learning and teaching situations at different grade levels. Each strategy is illustrated with a classroom example, derived from our experiences working in classrooms at elementary, middle, and high school levels. For examples see the *Classroom Connections* in Chapter 7 on pages 225, 238, and 244.

clearly identifying and reinforcing key ideas in every chapter

This text is designed to increase your learning with a *guided learning system* that aligns learning objectives with the chapter outline, reinforces main ideas with *Check Your Understanding* questions at the end of every section, and organizes each chapter's summary around the learning objectives.

Clear Alignment of Learning Outcomes and the Chapter Outline. Like previous editions, every chapter in the ninth edition begins with learning outcomes and links these specific learning outcomes to each of the major headings in the chapters. Aligning the learning outcomes and the chapter outline clearly identifies and highlights key ideas to help maximize learning. See pages 251, 363, and 431 for examples.

chapteroutline	learningoutcomes
	After you've completed your study of this chapter, you should be able to:
Concept Learning Theories of Concept Learning Concept Learning: A Complex Cognitive Process	**1.** Define concepts, and describe strategies for helping students learn concepts.
Problem Solving Well-Defined and Ill-Defined Problems Challenges in Teaching Problem Solving Helping Students Become Problem Solvers Creativity in Problem Solving Problem-Based Learning Technology, Learning, and Development: Using Technology to Promote Problem Solving	**2.** Recognize examples of ill-defined and well-defined problems, and describe strategies to teach problem solving in the classroom.
The Strategic Learner Metacognition: The Foundation of Strategic Learning Study Strategies Research on Study Strategies: Implications for You and Your Students Critical Thinking	**3.** Identify applications of study strategies and critical thinking.
Transfer of Learning General and Specific Transfer Factors Affecting the Transfer of Learning	**4.** Analyze applications of the factors that influence the transfer of learning.

Check Your Understanding. *Check Your Understanding* questions at the end of every major section are aligned with the learning outcomes and reinforce the essential ideas of that section. These *Check Your Understanding* questions promote active learning and provide formative feedback to deepen your understanding of chapter content. Check out the *Check Your Understanding* questions in Chapter 8 on pages 256, 269, 279, and 284 for examples. Feedback for all the *Check Your Understanding* questions is provided in Appendix A.

check your understanding

2.1 Your students resist thinking on their own. They expect to find the answer to every question on their homework stated specifically in their textbook. Is this a well-defined or an ill-defined problem? Explain. Using the framework for thinking about problems as a guide, describe how you might try to solve this problem.

2.2 One of the groups in Laura's Monday lesson got an answer of 1,600—more than the total area of the room—for the carpeted portion of their classroom. Accepting this answer illustrates an ineffective application of which stage of problem solving?

2.3 Sample problems with worked solutions (worked examples) are commonly used in math, chemistry, and physics textbooks. You've studied a chapter in a book and see some problems with worked solutions at the end of the chapter. To make your problem solving as meaningful as possible, and using cognitive learning theory as a basis for answering, what should you do before you study the solutions?

To receive feedback for these questions, go to Appendix A.

Summary. The end-of-chapter *summary* links the learning outcomes to a bulleted summary of the topics discussed in each chapter. Organizing the chapter summary around specific learning outcomes highlights and reinforces the key ideas presented in the chapter. For examples, see pages 246, 286, and 426.

Summary

1. Identify the basic components of human memory.
   - The human memory model is composed of memory stores, repositories that hold information; cognitive processes that move information from one store to another; and metacognition, which regulates both memory and cognitive processes.

2. Use the memory stores in the human memory model to explain events in classrooms and the everyday world.
   - Sensory memory is the store that briefly holds stimuli from the environment until they can be processed; working memory is the conscious part of our information-processing system, and its capacity is limited; long-term memory is our permanent information store, and it is where knowledge is stored.
   - When students struggle with complex tasks, lack of prior knowledge stored in long-term memory or skills that haven't been developed to automaticity are often the cause. The memory stores are influenced by development, with older students more effectively accommodating the limitations of working memory and better capitalizing on their experiences to represent information in long-term memory.

3. Describe the cognitive processes in the human memory model, and explain applications in classroom activities.
   - Attention and perception move information from sensory memory to working memory. Attention is the process

of consciously focusing on a stimulus, and perception attaches meaning to a stimulus.
   - Learners use rehearsal to retain information in the phonological loop of working memory, and intensive rehearsal can move information into long-term memory.
   - Encoding represents information in long-term memory. Learners encode information more effectively if it is represented both visually and verbally.
   - Retrieval is the process of pulling information from long-term memory back into working memory for problem solving or further processing.
   - Students' use of the cognitive processes improve as they develop, with older learners better focusing their attention and more effectively using strategies to promote meaningful encoding.

4. Define *metacognition*, and explain how it influences classroom learning.
   - *Metacognition* is individuals' knowledge of, and control over, their cognitive processes.
   - Metacognition influences learning by making learners aware of the way they study and learn, and providing strategies to increase learning.
   - Metacognition is developmental, with young children being less aware of their cognitive activities than their older counterparts.

Expanded content reflecting issues of student diversity has been added, including the implications of student diversity for understanding topics such as development, learning, and motivation as well as increased information on assessing English Learners.

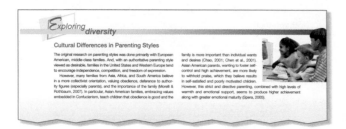

Exploring Diversity. A feature in every chapter, **Exploring Diversity**, shows how diversity influences learning and teaching. This feature illustrates how teachers can capitalize on student diversity to increase learning for all students. For examples, see pages 57, 118, and 123.

Developmentally Appropriate Practice. Children in early childhood programs, elementary schools, middle schools, and high schools think differently and have different social and emotional needs. The *Developmentally Appropriate Practice* feature helps you accommodate developmental differences in your students and provides suggestions for adapting each chapter's content to your students' developmental levels. For examples, see pages 59, 99, and 133.

MyEducationLab

The Power of Classroom Practice

In *Preparing Teachers for a Changing World,* Linda Darling-Hammond and her colleagues point out that grounding teacher education in real classrooms—among real teachers and students and among actual examples of students' and teachers' work—is an important, and perhaps even an essential, part of training teachers for the complexities of teaching in today's classrooms. MyEducationLab is an online learning solution that provides contextualized interactive exercises, simulations, and other resources designed to help you develop the knowledge and skills that teachers need. All of the activities and exercises in MyEducationLab are built around essential learning outcomes for teachers and are mapped to professional teaching standards. Utilizing classroom video, authentic student and teacher artifacts, case studies, and other resources and assessments, the scaffolded learning experiences in MyEducationLab offer you a unique and valuable education tool.

Study Plan and Book Resources Specific to Your Text

A MyEducationLab Study Plan provides students with the opportunity to take a self-assessment after reading each chapter of the text. Self-assessment questions are tied to learning outcomes, so the students are assessed on their knowledge and comprehension of all the concepts presented in each chapter. The quiz results automatically identify areas of the chapter that still need some additional study time. Students are then presented with Review, Practice, and Enrichment exercises to help ensure learning and to deepen understanding of chapter concepts—when just re-reading and studying chapter content is not enough. Flashcards for each chapter help students master definitions of key terms within each chapter. The study plan is designed to help each student perform well on exams and to promote deep understanding of chapter content.

In addition to the study plan, MyEducationLab resources specific to this book include:

- Video examples: These video clips provide real world illustrations of the topics presented in the chapter.

Connection To National Standards

Now it is easier than ever to see how coursework is connected to national standards. Each topic, activity and exercise on MyEducationLab lists intended learning outcomes connected to the appropriate national standards.

Assignments and Activities

Designed to enhance your understanding of concepts covered in class, these assignable exercises show concepts in action (through videos, cases, and/or student and teacher artifacts). They help you deepen content knowledge and synthesize and apply concepts and strategies you read about in the book. (Correct answers for these assignments are available to the instructor only.)

Building Teaching Skills and Dispositions

These unique learning units help users practice and strengthen skills that are essential to effective teaching. After presenting the steps involved in a core teaching process, you are given an opportunity to practice applying this skill via videos, student and teacher artifacts, and/or case studies of authentic classrooms. Providing multiple opportunities to practice a single teaching concept, each activity encourages a deeper understanding and application of concepts, as well as the use of critical thinking skills. Feedback for the final quizzes is available to the instructor only.

IRIS Center Resources

The IRIS Center at Vanderbilt University (http://iris.peabody.vanderbilt.edu), funded by the U.S. Department of Education's Office of Special Education Programs (OSEP), develops training enhancement materials for preservice and practicing teachers. The Center works with experts from across the country to create challenge-based interactive modules, case study units, and podcasts that provide research-validated information about working with students in inclusive settings. In your MyEducationLab course we have integrated this content where appropriate.

Simulations in Classroom Management

One of the most difficult challenges facing teachers today is how to balance classroom instruction with classroom management. These interactive cases focus on the classroom management issues teachers most frequently encounter on a daily basis. Each simulation presents a challenge scenario at the beginning and then offers series of choices to solve each challenge. Along the way students receive mentor feedback on their choices and have the opportunity to make better choices if necessary. Upon exiting each simulation, you will have a clear understanding of how to address these common classroom management issues and will be better equipped to handle them in the classroom.

Teacher Talk

This feature emphasizes the power of teaching through videos of master teachers, who each tell their own compelling stories of why they teach. These videos help you see the bigger picture and consider why the concepts and principles you are learning are important to your career as a teacher. Each of these featured teachers has been awarded the Council of Chief State School Officers Teachers of the Year award, the oldest and most prestigious award for teachers.

Lesson Plan Builder

The **Lesson Plan Builder** is an effective and easy-to-use tool that you can use to create, update, and share quality lesson plans. The software also makes it easy to integrate state content standards into any lesson plan.

Certification and Licensure

The Certification and Licensure section is designed to help you pass your licensure exam by giving you access to state test requirements, overviews of what tests cover, and sample test items.

The Certification and Licensure section includes the following:

- **State Certification Test Requirements:** Here, you can click on a state and will then be taken to a list of state certification tests.
- You can click on the **Licensure Exams** you need to take to find:
    - Basic information about each test
    - Descriptions of what is covered on each test
    - Sample test questions with explanations of correct answers
- **National Evaluation Series™** by Pearson: Here, students can see the tests in the NES, learn what is covered on each exam, and access sample test items with descriptions and rationales of correct answers. You can also purchase interactive online tutorials developed by Pearson Evaluation Systems and the Pearson Teacher Education and Development group.
- **ETS Online Praxis Tutorials:** Here you can purchase interactive online tutorials developed by ETS and by the Pearson Teacher Education and Development group. Tutorials are available for the Praxis I exams and for select Praxis II exams.

Visit www.myeducationlab.com for a demonstration of this exciting new online teaching resource.

supplementary materials

The following instructor supplements to the textbook are available for download on www.pearsonhighered.com/educators. Simply enter the author, title, or ISBN and select this textbook. Click on the "Resources" tab to view and download the available supplements detailed next.

Online Instructor's Resource Manual

The Instructor's Resource Manual (ISBN 0-13-279044-0) includes chapter overviews and outcomes, lists of available PowerPoint® slides, presentation outlines, teaching suggestions for each chapter, and questions for discussion and analysis along with feedback.

Online Test Bank and MyTest Test Bank

The Test Bank (ISBN 0-13-279041-6) provides a comprehensive and flexible assessment package. The Test Bank for this edition has been revised and expanded to make it more applicable to students. To provide complete coverage of the content in each chapter, all multiple-choice and essay items are grouped under the chapters' main headings and are balanced between knowledge/recall items and those that require analysis and application. The computerized test bank software, MyTest (ISBN 0-13-279039-4), is a powerful assessment-generation program that helps instructors easily create and print quizzes and exams. Questions and tests are authored online, allowing ultimate flexibility and the ability to efficiently create and print assessments—any time, anywhere. The Pearson MyTest includes a rich library of assessment items that can be edited to fit your needs. Access Pearson MyTest by going to www.pearsonmytest.com to log in, register, or request access.

Online PowerPoint Slides

The PowerPoint Slides (ISBN 0-13-279040-8) highlight key concepts and summarize text content. "Presentation Guides," now included with the slides, contain detailed outlines of each major section along with "Check Your Understanding" questions to stimulate discussion about chapter content. These guides are designed to provide structure to instructor presentations and give students an organized perspective on each chapter's content.

The Video Package

A video package is offered, including: *Double-Column Addition: A Teacher Uses Piaget's Theory* (ISBN 0-13-751413-1), *Elementary Video Case Studies* (ISBN 0-13-118642-6), and *Secondary Video Case Studies* (ISBN 0-13-118641-8). Instructors should contact their local sales representative to order a copy of these videos.

acknowledgments

Every book reflects the work of a team that includes the authors, the staff of editors, and the reviewers. We appreciate the input we've received from professors and students who have used previous editions of the book, and we gratefully acknowledge the contributions of the reviewers who offered us constructive feedback to guide us in this new edition:

Joel B. Judd, Adams State College; Claire Gonzalez, University of North Florida; Brenda M. Davis, Randolph-Macon College; Pamela K. Kidder, Fort Valley State University; James A. Shuff, Henderson State University; Dylinda Wilson-Younger, Alcorn State University; Amy Hogan, Ottawa University; Michelle Morris, Northwestern State University; and Steven Whitney, University of Missouri.

In addition, we acknowledge with our thanks, the reviewers of our previous editions:

Patricia Barbetta, Florida International University; David Bergin, University of Toledo; Scott W. Brown, University of Connecticut; Kay S. Bull, Oklahoma State University; Barbara Collamer, Western Washington University; Jerome D'Agostino, University of Arizona; Betty M. Davenport, Campbell University; Ronna F. Dillon, Southern Illinois University; Oliver W. Edwards, University of Central Florida; Thomas G. Fetsco, Northern Arizona University; Leena Furtado, California State University, Dominguez Hills; Newell T. Gill, Florida Atlantic University; Charles W. Good, West Chester University; Robert L. Hohn, University of Kansas; Dov Liberman, University of Houston; Hermine H. Marshall, San Francisco State University; Tes Mehring, Emporia State University; Luanna H. Meyer, Massey University–New Zealand; Nancy Perry, University of British Columbia; Evan Powell, University of Georgia; Anne N. Rinn, Western Kentucky University; Jay Samuels, University of Minnesota; Gregory Schraw, University of Nebraska, Lincoln; Dale H. Schunk, Purdue University; Rozanne Sparks, Pittsburgh State University; Rayne A. Sperling, Pennsylvania State University; Robert J. Stevens, Pennsylvania State University; Julianne C. Turner, Notre Dame University; Nancy Vye, University of Washington; Glenda Wilkes, University of Arizona; and Karen M. Zabrucky, Georgia State University.

In addition to the reviewers who guided our revisions, our team of editors gave us support in many ways. Paul Smith and Kevin Davis, our publishers, guided us with their intelligence, insight, and understanding of the field. Shannon Steed and Christie Robb, our development editors, have been available whenever we had questions or needed help and have provided us with invaluable support. Working with them has been a pleasure in every way. Luanne Dreyer Elliott, our copy editor, has been thoroughly professional in her efforts to make the content of the book clear and understandable. Sheryl Langner, our production editor, has been with us for 8 editions; her professionalism and commitment to excellence are appreciated more than we can say.

Our appreciation goes to all of these fine people who have taken our words and given them shape. We hope that all of our efforts will result in increased learning for students and more rewarding teaching for instructors.

Finally, we would sincerely appreciate any comments or questions about anything that appears in the book or any of its supplements. Please feel free to contact either of us at any time. Our e-mail addresses are: peggen@unf.edu and don.kauchak@gmail.com.

Good luck and best wishes.

Paul Eggen

Don Kauchak

brief contents

contents

part 2

learning

part 3

classroom processes

chapter 10

Motivation and Learning   328

chapter 11

A Classroom Model for Promoting Student Motivation   362

chapter 12

Classroom Management: Developing Self-Regulated Learners   390

chapter **13**
Learning and Effective Teaching 430

chapter **14**
Increasing Learning Through Assessment **478**

special features and topics

Exceptional Applications and a Wealth of Classroom Examples

Developmentally Appropriate Practice

Ed Psych and Teaching

Paul Eggen

Paul has worked in higher education for nearly 40 years. He is a consultant for public schools and colleges in his university service area and has provided support to teachers in 12 different states. Paul has also worked with teachers in international schools in 23 different countries in Africa, South Asia, the Middle East, Central America, South America, and Europe. He has published several articles in national journals, is the co-author or co-editor of six other books, and presents regularly at national and international conferences.

Paul is strongly committed to public education. His wife is a middle school teacher in a public school, and his two children are graduates of public schools and state universities.

Don Kauchak

Don has taught and worked in schools and in higher education in nine different states for over 40 years. He has published in a number of scholarly journals, including the *Journal of Educational Research, Journal of Experimental Education, Journal of Research in Science Teaching, Teaching and Teacher Education, Phi Delta Kappan,* and *Educational Leadership.* In addition to this text, he has co-authored or co-edited six other books on education. He has also been a principal investigator on federal and state grants examining teacher development and evaluation practices, and presents regularly at the American Educational Research Association. He currently volunteer-tutors first-, second- and third-graders in a local elementary school. These students have taught him a lot about educational psychology.

photo credits

© Zurijeta/Shutterstock, pp. 1, 159; Digital Vision/Thinkstock, pp. 5, 161, 396, 412; Comstock/Thinkstock, pp. 10, 104, 170, 187, 362, 367, 438; Jack Hollingsworth/Thinkstock, p. 12; © David Young–Wolff/PhotoEdit, pp. 14, 497; FAMILY CIRCUS © 1988 BIL KEANE, INC. DISTRIBUTED BY KING FEATURES SYNDICATE, p. 13; © David Grossman/Alamy, p. 28; © Richard Hutchings/PhotoEdit, pp. 31, 290, 447; © Ian Shaw/Alamy, p. 37; Anthony Magnacca/Merrill, pp. 40 (left and right), 149, 283; © Dmitriy Shironosov/Shutterstock, p. 41; © deanm1974/Fotolia, pp. 46, 64; © Gregory Johnston/Shutterstock, 53; © Karen Struthers/Shutterstock, p. 54; © Blend Images/Alamy, pp. 68, 118, 250, 328; © Monkey Business Images/Shutterstock, pp. 71, 233, 515; © Glenda M. Powers/Shutterstock, p. 76; © Mary Kate Denny/PhotoEdit, pp. 80, 96, 374; © Michael Newman/PhotoEdit, pp. 85, 313, 350, 377, 390, 404, 407, 456; © Mandy Godbehear/Shutterstock, p. 88; © Will Hart/PhotoEdit, pp. 92, 114, 268, 461, 463; Pixland/Thinkstock, p. 97; © Dean Mitchell/Shutterstock, p. 107; Rhoda Sidney/PH College, p. 109; Scott Cunningham/Merrill, p. 119; © Monkey Business Images/Fotolia, p. 124; Punchstock, p. 130; © NovaStock/Purestock/SuperStock, p. 138; Realistic Reflections/Getty Images – Creative Express Royalty Free, p. 150; © Big Cheese Photo LLC/Alamy, p. 151; © Christina Kennedy/PhotoEdit, p. 155; © Tony Freeman/PhotoEdit, pp. 167, 525; Valerie Schultz/Merrill, pp. 180, 353; Tim McCabe, USDA Natural Resources Conservation Service, p. 184; Ken Hammond, USDA Natural Resources Conservation Service, p. 191; © Michael Newman/PhotoEdit, p. 196; © Martin Shields/Alamy, pp. 199, 522; Annie Fuller/Pearson, pp. 210, 237, 430; Tom Watson/Merrill, pp. 216, 266; Lori Whitley/Merrill, pp. 222, 276, 381, 398, 422; David Mager/Pearson Learning Photo Studio, p. 253; © Kablonk Micro/Fotolia, p. 258; © Spencer Grant/PhotoEdit, p. 294; © Getty Images/Comstock Images/Thinkstock, p. 298; © Bonnie Kamin/PhotoEdit, p. 302; © Art Directors & TRIP/Alamy, p. 303; Jupiterimages/Thinkstock, p. 317; © Bill Aron/PhotoEdit, p. 334; © Yuri Arcurs/Fotolia, p. 338; © Ian Shaw/Alamy, p. 343; © Royalty-Free/CORBIS, p. 345; © Bob Daemmrich/PhotoEdit, p. 370; Pearson Scott Foresman, p. 399; SW Productions/Getty Images – Photodisc, p. 402; © Stock Connection Blue/Alamy, p. 419; © Davis Barber/PhotoEdit, p. 446; Image 100, p. 450; © David R. Frazier Photolibrary, Inc./Alamy, p. 478; © Reflekta/Shutterstock, p. 482; David Buffington/Getty Images, Inc. – Photodisc, p. 493; GeoStock/Getty Images, Inc. – Photodisc, p. 495; Spencer Grant/Photo Researchers, Inc., pp. 505, 528; Katy McDonnell/Thinkstock, p. 531; Photos.com, p. 542; George Dodson/PH College, p. 544.prefacespecial features and topics

chapter 1

Educational Psychology
Understanding Learning and Teaching

chapteroutline

learningoutcomes

After you've completed your study of this chapter, you should be able to:

1. Describe the difference between effective and ineffective teaching, and explain how expert teaching influences student learning.

2. Describe the different kinds of professional knowledge that expert teachers possess.

3. Describe different types of student learning and development, and explain how they are related to educational psychology.

4. Explain how case studies make the content of educational psychology more meaningful.

classroomapplications

The following features help you apply the content of this chapter in your teaching

Ed Psych and Teaching:
Applying Professional Knowledge in Your Classroom

Developmentally Appropriate Practice:
Using Knowledge of Learners and Learning to Promote Achievement in Students at Different Ages

You've just opened your textbook, and you're wondering where it's headed and how it will make you a better teacher. So, let's start right off with a couple questions. First, why do children go to school? To learn and develop is the obvious answer. Easy question, right?

Second, which of the following factors contributes the most to children's learning and development?

- *Curriculum and materials available to them*—the content students study and the quality of their textbooks.
- *Facilities and extracurricular activities*—access to a good library, the Internet, and athletics, clubs, and after-school music and drama.
- *Class size*—the number of students in a class.
- *Leadership*—such as the school principal and district superintendent.
- *You*—their teacher.

The unequivocal answer is *you, their teacher*! Unlike our first question, however, this answer hasn't always been obvious to educational leaders. We'll explore the importance of excellent teachers in more detail as the chapter unfolds, but now let's turn to a conversation between Keith Jackson, a struggling, first-year, middle school math teacher and Jan Davis, a four-year "veteran" who has become his confidant. As you read this case study, think about Jan's teaching and how it might influence her students' learning.

As Keith walks into the work room at Lakeside Middle School, Jan looks up and asks, "Hi, Keith. How's it going?"

"My last period class is getting to me," Keith replies. "The students are okay when we just stick to mechanics, but they simply can't do word problems. . . . And they hate them. . . . They just try to memorize formulas and enough stuff to get by.

"I have a good math background, and I was going to be so great when I got here. . . . I'm not so sure any more. . . . I explain the stuff so carefully, but some of the kids just sit with blank looks on their faces. Then, I explain it even more carefully, and . . . nothing.

"And, there's Kelly. She disrupts everything I do. I gave her a referral, and I even called her mother. . . . The only thing that seemed to work was taking her aside and asking her straight out why she was giving me such a hard time."

"Sounds like you're becoming a *teacher*," Jan smiles. "There are few easy answers for what we do. . . . But then, that's what makes it both the toughest and the most rewarding work in the world.

"Like working with Kelly. She might not have another adult she can talk to, and she may simply need someone to care about her.

"As for the blank looks, I'm taking a class at the university. The instructor emphasizes involving the kids, and he keeps talking about research that says how important it is to call on all the kids as equally as possible.

"So, here's an example of how I'm approaching word problems now. We're working on decimals and percents, so I brought in a 12-ounce soft drink can from a machine, a 20-ounce bottle, and a 6-pack with price tags on them.

I put the kids into pairs and told them to figure out a way to determine which one was the best buy. I helped them along, and we created a table, so we could compare the groups' answers. They're beginning to see how math relates to their lives. . . . Some of them even said they think it's important. And, now that they're used to being called on, they really like it. It's one of the most important things I do.

"When I think about it, I realize that I sometimes jump in too soon when they can figure it out themselves, and at other times I let them stumble around too long, and they waste time. So, then I adapt for the next lesson."

"I hate to admit this," Keith says, "but some of my university courses suggested just what you did. It was fun, but I didn't think it was real teaching."

"You couldn't relate to it at the time. You didn't have a class with live students who 'didn't get it.'

"Hang in there," Jan smiles. "You're becoming what teaching needs—a pro."

Now, as you study this chapter, keep the following questions in mind:

1. How was Keith's approach to teaching word problems different from Jan's?
2. Why were their approaches so different, and how will these differences affect their students' learning?

We answer these and other questions about teaching and learning in this chapter. We begin by revisiting the idea we introduced earlier.

The Preeminence of Teachers

We introduced the chapter by asking, "Which of the following factors contributes the most to children's learning and development?" and then we said that the answer hasn't always been obvious to educational leaders. A great deal has been written about this question, and educational reformers have offered a variety of answers, including different organizational structures, such as open classrooms and a variety of curricular and instructional approaches, such as Whole Language or what was commonly described as "New Math." However, none of them were as successful as hoped (Thomas & Wingert, 2010).

The solution, however, is simple (but admittedly not easy). *No organization, system, institution, or enterprise is any better than the people in it,* and the same applies to schools. The quality of a school is determined by the quality of its teachers. *You, you* are the most important factor influencing your students' learning! Surprisingly, only recently have educational researchers and leaders begun to understand and appreciate this fact (Thomas & Wingert, 2010).

How important are teachers? Research provides answers. One widely publicized study found that students who had highly effective teachers in third, fourth, and fifth grades scored more than 50 percentile points higher on standardized math tests than those who had ineffective teachers in the same three grades (Sanders & Rivers, 1996). Another study revealed that five years in a row of expert teaching was nearly enough to close the achievement gap between disadvantaged and advantaged students (Hanushek, Rivkin, & Kain, 2005). Additional research has found that expert teaching in later grades could substantially, but not completely, make up for poor teaching in earlier grades (Rivkin, Hanushek, & Kain, 2001).

The importance of teachers has even caught the attention of the popular press. "The key to saving American education" appeared on the cover of the March 15, 2010, issue of *Newsweek,* identifying teachers as the "key," and the *New York Times* included a lengthy article, "Building a Better Teacher" in its March 7, 2010, issue (Green, 2010). "Teacher quality is now a national priority" (Margolis, 2010, Introduction, para. 1). And, the American people agree. According to an annual poll of the public's attitudes toward public education, "Americans singled out improving the quality of teachers as the most important action for improving education" (Bushaw & Lopez, 2010, p. 15).

Some, including many educational leaders, once believed that expert teaching is essentially instinctive, a kind of magic performed by born superstars. And, some teachers do indeed have more natural ability than others. However, research dating back to the 1960s and 1970s indicates that expert teachers possess knowledge and skills that are not purely instinctive. They are acquired through study and practice (Fisher et al., 1980), and more recent work corroborates these earlier findings (Lemov, 2010). This is true in all domains. Some athletes, for example, have more natural ability than others, but that doesn't prevent the others from becoming superstars in their own right.

We referred to "expert" and "effective" teachers in the preceding paragraphs. **Experts** are people who are highly knowledgeable and skilled in a particular domain, such as teaching, and **effective teachers** are those who produce more learning in their students than would be expected for the students' background and ability. Effective teachers are experts, and their knowledge and understanding of learning and development are what sets them apart. *Effective teachers possess knowledge and skills that their less effective colleagues do not.*

The quality of the teacher is the most important factor influencing student learning.

[handwritten note: Some, a part of it is. The other half has to be built]

Expert. A person who is highly knowledgeable or skilled in a particular domain.

Effective teachers. Teachers who are able to produce more learning in their students than would be expected for the students' background and ability.

This leads us to the reason we wrote this book and the reason you're taking this course. Your goal is to begin acquiring the knowledge and skills that will ultimately lead to expertise and effectiveness, and our goal is to help you in this process. We turn to this topic next.

---

check your understanding

1.1 Describe the essential difference between effective and ineffective teachers.

1.2 Give an example of the impact of expert teaching on student learning.

To receive feedback for these questions, go to Appendix A.

Educational Psychology, Expert Teaching, and Professional Knowledge

Educational psychology. The academic discipline that focuses on human teaching and learning.

Professional knowledge. The body of information and skills that are unique to a particular area of study.

If expertise is so important to effective teaching, how do teachers gain the knowledge needed to become experts? This leads us to the study of **educational psychology (ed psych),** the academic discipline that studies human teaching and learning (Berliner, 2006). Ed psych focuses on the professional knowledge and skills essential for teaching effectiveness and expertise. We discuss this knowledge next.

Ed Psych and You:

How much do you know about teaching and learning? To test your knowledge, complete the following Learning and Teaching Inventory. It will introduce you to the kinds of knowledge you'll need to become an expert teacher.

Professional Knowledge

Professional knowledge refers to the body of information and skills that are unique to an area of study, such as law, medicine, architecture, or engineering. The same applies to teaching, and in this section we focus on how educational psychology can increase your professional knowledge and expertise.

Learning and Teaching Inventory

Look at each of the 10 items, and decide if the statement is true or false.

1. The thinking of children in elementary schools tends to be limited to the concrete and tangible, whereas the thinking of middle and high school students tends to be abstract.
2. Students generally understand how much they know about a topic.
3. Experts in the area of intelligence view knowledge of facts (e.g., "On what continent is Brazil?") as one indicator of intelligence.
4. Effective teaching is essentially a process of presenting information to students in succinct and organized ways.
5. Preservice teachers who major in a content area, such as math, are much more successful than nonmajors in providing clear examples of the ideas they teach.
6. To increase students' motivation to learn, teachers should praise as much as possible.
7. The key to successful classroom management is to stop classroom disruptions quickly.
8. Preservice teachers generally believe they will be more effective than teachers who are already in the field.
9. Teachers learn by teaching; in general, experience is the primary factor involved in learning to teach.
10. Testing detracts from learning, because students who are tested frequently develop negative attitudes and consequently learn less than those who are tested less often.

Let's see how you did. The correct answers for each item are outlined in the following paragraphs. As you read the answers, remember that they describe students or other people in general, and exceptions exist.

1. *The thinking of children in elementary schools tends to be limited to the concrete and tangible, whereas the thinking of middle and high school students tends to be abstract.*
   False: Research indicates that middle school, high school, and even university students can effectively think in the abstract only when they have considerable prior knowledge and experience related to the topic they're studying (Cole, Cole, & Lightfoot, 2009). When you study the development of students' thinking in Chapter 2, you'll see how understanding this research can improve your teaching.

2. *Students generally understand how much they know about a topic.*
   False: Learners in general, and young children in particular, often cannot accurately assess their own understanding (Hacker, Bol, Horgan, & Rakow, 2000). Students' awareness of what they know and how they learn strongly influences understanding, and cognitive learning theory helps us understand why. (You will study cognitive learning theory in Chapters 6, 7, and 8.)

3. *Experts in the area of intelligence view knowledge of facts (e.g., "On what continent is Brazil?") as one indicator of intelligence.*
   True: The Wechsler Intelligence Scale for Children—Fourth Edition (Wechsler, 2003), the most popular intelligence test in use today, has several items similar to this example. Theories of intelligence, which you will study in Chapter 5, examine issues and controversies related to learner intelligence.

4. *Effective teaching is essentially a process of presenting information to students in succinct and organized ways.*
   False: The better we understand learning, the more we realize that simply explaining information to students is often ineffective for promoting understanding (Bransford, Brown, & Cocking, 2000; Mayer, 2008). Learners construct their own knowledge based on what they already know, and their emotions, beliefs, and expectations all influence the process (Bruning, Schraw, & Norby, 2011; Schunk, Pintrich, & Meece, 2008). (You will examine the processes involved in constructing knowledge in Chapter 6.)

5. *Preservice teachers who major in a content area, such as math, are much more successful than nonmajors in providing clear examples of the ideas they teach.*
   False: One of the most pervasive misconceptions about teaching is the idea that knowledge of subject matter is all that is necessary to teach effectively. In a study of teacher candidates, researchers found that math majors were no more capable than nonmajors of effectively illustrating and representing math concepts in ways that learners could understand (U.S. Department of Education, 2008). Knowledge of content is essential, but understanding how to make that content meaningful to students requires additional knowledge (Darling-Hammond & Baratz-Snowdon, 2005). (You will study ways of making knowledge accessible to learners in Chapters 2, 6–9, and 13.)

6. *To increase students' motivation to learn, teachers should praise as much as possible.*
   False: Although appropriate use of praise is effective, overuse detracts from its credibility. This is particularly true for older students, who discount praise if they believe it is invalid or insincere. Older students may also interpret praise given for easy tasks as indicating that the teacher thinks they have low ability (Schunk et al., 2008). Your study of motivation in Chapters 10 and 11 will help you understand this and other factors influencing students' desire to learn.

7. *The key to successful classroom management is to stop disruptions quickly.*
   False: Research indicates that classroom management, one of the primary concerns of beginning teachers, is most effective when teachers prevent management problems from occurring in the first place, instead of responding to problems after they occur

(Brophy, 2006; Emmer & Evertson, 2009; Evertson & Emmer, 2009). (You will study classroom management in Chapter 12.)

8. *Preservice teachers generally believe they will be more effective than teachers who are already in the field.*

   True: Preservice teachers (like you) are often optimistic and idealistic. They believe they'll be effective with young people, and they generally believe they'll be better than teachers now in the field (Feiman-Nemser, 2001; Ingersoll & Smith, 2004). They are also sometimes "shocked" when they begin work and face the challenge of teaching on their own for the first time (Grant, 2006; S. Johnson & Birkeland, 2003). Keith's comments in the opening case study are typical of many beginning teachers: "I was going to be so great when I got here....I'm not so sure anymore." The more knowledge you have about teaching, learning, and learners, the better prepared you'll be to cope with the realities of your first job.

9. *Teachers learn by teaching; in general, experience is the primary factor involved in learning to teach.*

   False: Experience is essential in learning to teach, but it isn't sufficient by itself (Darling-Hammond & Bransford, 2005; Song & Felch, 2009). In some cases, experience results in repeating the same actions year after year, regardless of their effectiveness. Knowledge of learners and learning, combined with experience, however, can lead to high levels of teaching expertise.

10. *Testing detracts from learning, because students who are tested frequently develop negative attitudes and consequently learn less than those who are tested less often.*

    False: In comprehensive reviews of the literature on assessment, experts have found that frequent, thorough assessment is one of the most powerful and positive influences on learning that exist (Rohrer & Pashler, 2010; Stiggins, 2007). (You will study assessment and its role in learning in Chapters 14 and 15.)

The items you've just examined briefly introduce you to the professional knowledge base of teaching, and next we discuss it in more detail. Research indicates that four related types of knowledge are essential for expert teaching (Darling-Hammond & Baratz-Snowdon, 2005; Shulman, 1987). They are outlined in Figure 1.1 and discussed in the sections that follow.

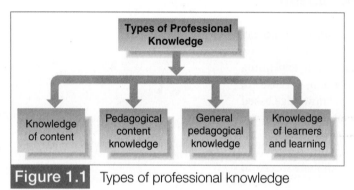

Figure 1.1 Types of professional knowledge

Knowledge of Content

We obviously can't teach what we don't understand. To effectively teach about the American Revolutionary War, for example, a social studies teacher needs to know not only basic facts about the war but also how the war relates to other aspects of history, such as the French and Indian War, the colonies' relationship with England before the Revolution, and the unique characteristics of the colonies. The same is true for any topic in any other content area, and research confirms the relationship between what teachers know and how they teach (Bransford et al., 2000).

Pedagogical Content Knowledge

Pedagogical content knowledge. An understanding of how to represent topics in ways that make them understandable to learners, as well as an understanding of what makes specific topics easy or hard to learn.

Knowledge of content is essential, but—alone—not sufficient for expert teaching. Teachers must also possess **pedagogical content knowledge,** an understanding of how to represent topics in ways that make the content understandable to learners, as well as an understanding of what makes specific topics easy or hard to learn (Darling-Hammond & Bransford, 2005; Shulman, 1986).

Knowledge of content and pedagogical content knowledge are closely related but not identical. For example, understanding the factors that led to the American Revolution reflects knowledge of content; knowing how to illustrate this content so students can understand it reflects pedagogical content knowledge. Expert teachers possess both (Loughran, Mulhall, & Berry, 2004; Segall, 2004).

To illustrate the role of pedagogical content knowledge in expert teaching, think about how you might help students understand the process of multiplying fractions, such as $1/4 \times 1/3 = 1/12$. This is neither easy to understand nor easy to teach. Our experience tells us that the product of two numbers is larger than either (e.g., $6 \times 5 = 30$), but with fractions the product is smaller, so the results are counterintuitive. As a result, students often simply memorize the process with little understanding.

Now, try the following activity. Fold a sheet of plain paper into thirds, and shade the center one third of the paper, as shown:

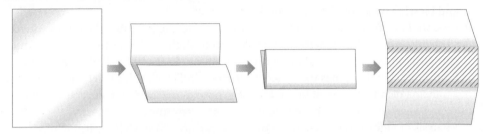

Now, refold your paper so that the shaded third is exposed:

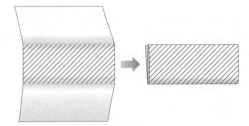

Now fold the paper in half, and in half again, so that one fourth of the shaded one third is visible. Put additional shading on that portion, and then unfold the paper, as shown:

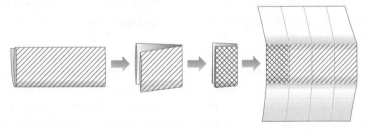

You've just prepared a concrete example demonstrating that $1/4 \times 1/3 = 1/12$ (the cross-hatched portion of the paper). This example helps students see that the product of multiplying two fractions results in a smaller number and also helps them apply their understanding in real-world settings (Mayer, 2008). This is why pedagogical content knowledge is so important. Without examples like this, students grasp what they can, memorize as much as possible, and little understanding develops (Bransford et al., 2000; Donovan & Bransford, 2005).

Depending on the content area, you can represent the topics you teach in several ways:

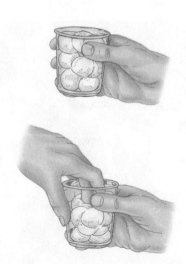

- *Examples.* Examples are useful when you're teaching a well-defined topic. For example, a fourth-grade math teacher has 24 students in her class arranged in 4 rows with 6 students in each row. She uses the students in their rows to illustrate that 6/24 is equivalent to ¼. Similarly, an eighth-grade physical science teacher compresses cotton in a drink cup to illustrate the concept *density,* as you see here. In both instances the example makes abstract ideas easier to understand.

- *Demonstrations.* A first-grade teacher uses water to demonstrate that air takes up space and exerts pressure as you see below.

A middle school teacher demonstrates the concept *force* by pushing on a chalkboard and blowing on an object on his desk.

- *Case studies.* We use case studies throughout this text to illustrate the topics you're studying. Along with vignettes (short case studies), they are effective for illustrating complex topics that are hard to represent with simple examples. For instance, an English teacher illustrates the concept *internal conflict* with this brief vignette:

  > Andrea didn't know what to do. She was looking forward to the class trip, but if she went, she wouldn't be able to take the scholarship-qualifying test.

  Analysis of video cases, such as the ones you can access on MyEducationLab, can also help you think about connections between teaching and student learning (Siegel, 2002).
- *Metaphors.* A world history teacher uses her students' loyalty to their school, their ways of talking, and their weekend activities as metaphors for the concept *nationalism.* Another history teacher uses her class's "crusade" for extracurricular activities as a metaphor for the actual Crusades.
- *Simulations.* An American government teacher creates a mock trial to simulate the workings of our country's judicial system, and a history teacher has students role-play delegates in a simulated Continental Congress to help his students understand forces that shaped our country.
- *Models.* A science teacher uses a model of an atom to help students visualize the organization of the nucleus and electrons, as you see here.

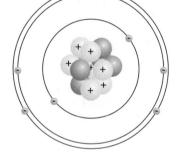

The model in Figure 7.1 (on page 213) helps us think about the ways we process and store information in memory.

This list helps us understand why knowledge of content and pedagogical content knowledge are not identical, and it also helps us understand why item 5 in our Learning and Teaching Inventory ("Preservice teachers who major in a content area, such as math, are much more successful than nonmajors in providing clear examples of the ideas they teach") is false. Earning a degree in a content area, such as math, doesn't ensure that we'll be able to create examples like the one involving the multiplication of fractions, nor does majoring in history ensure that we would be able to think of using a campaign to save a school's extracurricular activities as a metaphor for the Crusades. The ability to represent topics in ways that are understandable to students requires pedagogical content knowledge in addition to understanding content. If we lack either, we commonly paraphrase information in learners' textbooks or provide abstract explanations that aren't meaningful to our students. We need both to become expert teachers.

Expert teachers know how to represent topics in ways that are understandable to learners.

General Pedagogical Knowledge

Knowledge of content and pedagogical content knowledge are domain specific—they're related to knowledge of a particular content area, such as the Crusades, multiplying fractions, or the concepts *density* and *internal conflict.* In comparison, **general pedagogical knowledge** involves an understanding of instructional strategies and classroom management that apply to all subject matter areas and topics (Borko & Putnam, 1996; Darling-Hammond & Bransford, 2005).

Instructional Strategies. Instructional strategies, such as knowing how to plan effective lessons, involve students in learning, and check for understanding, are important regardless of the grade level, content area, or topic. For example, involving all students in a lesson by calling on them as equally as possible is as important if you're teaching first graders, middle school students, or advanced high school students (Good & Brophy, 2008). These strategies are essential aspects of general pedagogical knowledge, and you will study them in detail in Chapter 13.

Classroom Management. Classroom management is a second major component of general pedagogical knowledge. We need to create classroom environments that are safe, orderly, and focused on learning (Emmer & Evertson, 2009; Evertson & Emmer, 2009). Creating these environments requires that we know how to plan, implement, and monitor rules and procedures, organize groups, and intervene when misbehavior occurs. The complexities of these processes help us see why item 7 in the Learning and Teaching Inventory ("The key to successful classroom management is to stop disruptions quickly") is false. It's impossible to maintain an orderly classroom if we wait for misbehavior to occur. Classroom environments must be designed to prevent, rather than stop, disruptions. Chapter 12 describes how to do this in your classroom.

Knowledge of Learners and Learning

Knowledge of learners and learning, the fourth type of professional knowledge, is also essential, "arguably the most important knowledge a teacher can have" (Borko & Putnam, 1996, p. 675). Let's see how this knowledge can influence the way we teach.

Knowledge of Learners. The following items from the Learning and Teaching Inventory all involve knowledge of learners, and each has important implications for the way we teach:

Item 1. The thinking of children in elementary schools tends to be limited to the concrete and tangible, whereas the thinking of middle and high school students tends to be abstract.

Item 2. Students generally understand how much they know about a topic.

Item 6. To increase students' motivation to learn, teachers should praise as much as possible.

For instance, you learned from item 1 that students need to have abstract ideas illustrated with concrete examples, and this is true for older as well as younger students. Chapter 2, which focuses on cognitive development, describes how understanding learners increases your pedagogical content knowledge and helps you provide meaningful representations, such as the example of multiplying fractions.

Item 2 suggests that learners often aren't good judges of either how much they know or the ways they learn. Chapter 7 helps us understand how to guide our students toward becoming more knowledgeable about themselves and more strategic in their approaches to learning (Bruning et al., 2011).

Item 6 has implications for the ways we interact with our students. Intuitively, it seems that providing as much praise as possible is both desirable and effective. However, motivation research, which you will study in Chapters 10 and 11, helps us understand why this isn't always the case.

Knowledge of Learning. As we better understand the different ways people learn, we can understand why item 4 ("Effective teaching is essentially a process of presenting information to students in succinct and organized ways") on the Learning and Teaching Inventory is false. For example, evidence consistently indicates that people don't behave like video recorders; they don't simply remember what they hear or read. Rather, in their attempts to make sense of it, they interpret information in personal and sometimes idiosyncratic ways (Bransford et al., 2000; Mayer, 2002). In the process, meaning can be distorted, sometimes profoundly. For instance, the following statements were actually made by students:

> "The phases of the moon are caused by clouds blocking out the unseen parts."
> "Coats keep us warm by generating heat, like a stove or radiator."
> "A triangle which has an angle of 135 degrees is called an obscene triangle."

Obviously, students didn't acquire these ideas from their teachers' explanations. Rather, they interpreted what they heard, experienced, or read, related it to what they already knew, and attempted to make sense of it all.

These examples help us understand Keith's comments in the case study at the beginning of the chapter: "I explain the stuff so carefully, but some of the kids just sit with blank looks on their faces. Then, I explain it even more carefully, and . . . nothing." Effective teaching is much more than simply explaining, and expert teachers have a thorough understanding of how learning occurs and what they can do to promote it. (We examine learning in detail in Chapters 6 through 9.)

We now understand why item 9 ("Teachers learn by teaching; in general, experience is the primary factor involved in learning to teach") on the Learning and Teaching Inventory is false. Experience is important, but we can't acquire all the knowledge we need to be effective from experience alone. Acquiring this knowledge is the primary reason you're studying educational psychology.

Teacher Knowledge and Reflective Practice

Reflective practice. The process of conducting a critical self-examination of one's teaching.

You will make a staggering number of decisions in your teaching; some historical research suggests as many as 800 per day (P. Jackson, 1968). For example, the following are only a few of the decisions Jan made in her lesson earlier in the chapter:

- The learning objectives for her lesson
- The examples she would use to help students reach the objectives
- Which students she would call on and the order in which she would call on them
- The specific questions she would ask and how she would respond to students if they answered incorrectly

Professionals critically examine their own teaching in efforts to continually improve.

And, no one is there to help you make these decisions; you're essentially on your own. Learning how to make them leads us to the idea of **reflective practice,** the process of conducting a critical self-examination of one's teaching (Clarke, 2006). Every professional decision we make is designed to promote student learning, and research suggests that reflective practice can help us become more sensitive to individual student differences (Berrill & Whalen, 2007), and it can make us more aware of the impact of our instruction on learning (Gimbel, 2008). For example, Jan's comment, "When I think about it, I realize that I sometimes jump in too soon . . . and at other times I let them stumble around too long. . . . So, then I adapt for the next lesson," illustrates the process of reflective practice and its influence on her instruction.

Developmentally appropriate practice

Using Knowledge of Learners and Learning to Promote Achievement in Students at Different Ages

While much of what we know about learners and learning applies to students of all ages, **developmental differences,** changes in students' thinking, personalities, and social skills, exist.

Because the developmental level of your students affects their learning and your teaching, a feature titled "Developmentally Appropriate Practice" appears in each chapter. **Developmentally appropriate practice** refers to instruction that matches teacher actions to the capabilities and needs of learners at different developmental levels. The feature describes ways to adapt each chapter's content to the different learning needs of early childhood and elementary, middle school, and high school students.

Here's how the feature will appear in subsequent chapters:

Developmental differences. Changes in students' thinking, personalities, and social skills that result from maturation and experience.

Developmentally appropriate practice. Instruction that matches teacher actions to the capabilities and needs of learners at different developmental levels.

Working with Students in Early Childhood Programs and Elementary Schools

Young children's thinking differs from the thinking of older students. As an example, look at the accompanying cartoon. Wondering how all the water could fit in the spigot is characteristic of the thinking of young children. Older students would of course realize that a vast reservoir of water exists that we can't see. Young children's personal and social characteristics also differ from those of older students and influence how they interact and learn in classrooms. We examine these differences in each of the chapters in the book.

FAMILY CIRCUS

"How do they fit so much water in that little spigot?"

Source: Family Circus © Bil Keane, Inc. King Features Syndicate.

Working with Students in Middle Schools

As a result of maturation and experience, the thinking and social skills of middle school students differ from those of young children. For example, older students are more likely to realize that they don't understand an idea being discussed in class and raise their hands to ask for an explanation or clarification. In addition middle schoolers are increasingly social and find the opposite sex more interesting. Again, these differences have important implications for how you teach and interact with these students.

Working with Students in High Schools

As with differences between elementary and middle school students, additional differences exist between high school learners and their younger peers. For example, many high school students are quite mature, and speaking to them about personal and social issues on an adult-to-adult level can be effective. They are capable of more abstract thinking than their younger counterparts, although they still need concrete examples to understand new or difficult topics.

"Classroom Connections," an additional feature that appears in Chapters 2 through 15, is also organized by developmental level and is designed to help you appropriately apply chapter topics with the students you'll teach.

Research provides valuable information that teachers can use in their instructional decision making.

Research. The process of systematically gathering information in an attempt to answer professional questions.

Descriptive research. Research that uses tools such as tests, surveys, and observations to describe the status or characteristics of a situation or phenomenon.

The Role of Research in Acquiring Professional Knowledge

So far, we've found that professional knowledge is essential for expert teaching, and we've examined the different types of professional knowledge you need to be an effective teacher. But, where does this knowledge originate, how does it accumulate, and how can we acquire it?

One answer is experience, sometimes called "the wisdom of practice" (Berliner, 2000). Effective teacher education programs help people like you acquire the beginnings of "the wisdom of practice" by integrating clinical experiences in schools with the topics you study in your classes.

Research, the process of systematically gathering information in an attempt to answer professional questions, is a second important source of the knowledge needed for expert teaching. All professions use research to guide their practice (Gall, Gall, & Borg, 2010; Van Horn, 2008). For example, in an effort to answer the question "How does teacher questioning influence student learning?" researchers conducted large numbers of studies examining the numbers and types of questions and the ways they are asked and allocated (Good & Brophy, 2008). The influence of teacher questioning on student learning is part of the professional literature of educational psychology. Jan drew from it when she talked about the changes she made in her teaching based on the class she is taking and her instructor who "keeps talking about research that says how important it is to call on all the kids as equally as possible." Jan is a veteran teacher, but continues to grow professionally by staying up to date on current research.

Research in education exists in several forms, each of which answers different kinds of questions. It includes:

- Descriptive research
- Correlational research ⎫ Quantitative
- Experimental research ⎭
- Qualitative research ⌐
- Action research — by researcher

Descriptive Research

Descriptive research uses tools such as tests, surveys, and observations to describe the status or characteristics of a situation or phenomenon (Gall et al., 2010). For example, "How much are our students learning?" is an important question facing all educators. To answer this question, the *National Assessment of Educational Progress* (NAEP), often called "The Nation's Report Card" administers math and reading tests to samples of fourth, eighth, and twelfth graders every 2 years (Manzo, 2008). Educators use this research to measure the effectiveness of different math and reading programs and make comparisons with other countries (Yeager, 2007).

Surveys, such as the annual *Phi Delta Kappan/Gallup Poll of the Public's Attitude Toward the Public Schools,* (Bushaw & Lopez, 2010), and first-hand observations are also forms of descriptive research. Jean Piaget (1959), a pioneer in the study of cognitive development, used systematic observations of children as his primary research technique. (You will study Piaget's work in Chapter 2.)

Descriptive research provides valuable information about the condition of education, but it doesn't allow us to predict future events, and it doesn't describe relationships. Finding relationships between variables leads us to correlational research.

Correlational Research

Consider the following questions: Does a relationship exist between

- Students' grade-point averages (GPAs) and their scores on the Scholastic Aptitude Test (SAT)?

- Students' absences and their grades in school?
- Students' heights and high school GPAs?

Correlational research is the process of looking for relationships between variables that enables researchers to predict changes in one variable on the basis of changes in another without implying that one variable *causes* the other. A **correlation** is a relationship, either positive or negative, between two or more variables. In our examples, the variables are *grade-point averages* and *SAT scores, absences* and *grades,* and *height* and *high school GPAs.* In the first case, the variables are positively correlated: In general, the higher students' GPAs, the higher their SAT scores. In the second example, the variables are negatively correlated: The more school students miss, the lower their grades. No correlation exists in the third: height and high school GPAs are not related.

It's important to remember that a correlation doesn't imply that one variable *causes* the other. For example, a high GPA—itself—obviously doesn't cause a high SAT score. Rather, time spent studying, effective study strategies, and general intelligence are likely to be causes of both. Similarly, being absent, per se, doesn't *cause* low grades. Instead, missing opportunities to learn topics, not completing homework assignments, and losing chances to interact with peers are likely causes.

Much of what we know about the relationships between teaching and learning is based on correlational research (Springer, 2010).

Experimental Research

Whereas correlational research looks for relationships in existing situations, such as the relationship between teacher questioning and student achievement, **experimental research** systematically manipulates variables in attempts to determine cause and effect (Springer, 2010). To illustrate this process, imagine that researchers randomly assign teachers to two groups (to ensure, as much as possible, that the groups are comparable). The researchers then train teachers in one group to call on their students equally, as Jan did with hers, but the other group receives no training. If the students taught by the trained teachers exhibit higher levels of achievement than the students taught by teachers who receive no training, researchers can then conclude that equal distribution of questions *causes* an increase in achievement (Springer, 2010).

Qualitative Research

Experimental research can be costly, and conducting it can be cumbersome. Training interventions are often time-consuming and expensive, and access to classrooms and teachers may be difficult. **Qualitative research,** which attempts to describe a complex educational phenomenon in a holistic fashion using nonnumerical data, such as words and pictures, is an alternative (B. Johnson & Christensen, 2008). It relies on interviews, field notes, and other descriptive techniques, and then looks for patterns as does quantitative research. The results of qualitative research, however, are published in narrative reports with detailed descriptions of settings and participants, whereas quantitative studies typically result in reports with correlations and other statistical techniques (Gay, Airasian, & Mills, 2009).

A classic qualitative study of teaching, *First-Year Teacher* (Bullough, 1989), illustrates these characteristics. The researcher's goal was to describe what it's like to be a first-year teacher from the teacher's perspective. The researcher spent a year observing a first-year, middle school language arts teacher, interviewing her, and collecting artifacts such as lesson plans and assignments. A realistic account of the triumphs and difficulties encountered by one teacher emerged from the study. As in other qualitative studies, the researcher did not claim that this teacher's experience generalized to *all* first-year teachers' experiences. Instead, the researcher attempted to describe one teacher's experience in as much detail as possible and then allow readers to draw their own conclusions about that teacher's experiences.

Correlational research. The process of looking for relationships between variables that enables researchers to predict changes in one variable on the basis of changes in another without implying that one variable causes the other.

Correlation. A relationship, either positive or negative, between two or more variables.

Experimental research. A type of research that systematically manipulates variables in attempts to determine cause and effect.

Qualitative research. A type of research that attempts to describe a complex educational phenomenon in a holistic fashion using nonnumeric data.

Each of these forms of research contributes to professional knowledge, the body of knowledge expert teachers understand and apply in their work with students.

Action Research

When you teach, and as you gain experience, questions will come up. Some examples include:

- How much homework should I give?
- Should I systematically grade homework, or merely check to see if students have completed it?
- How often should I give quizzes?
- Should I ever give my students free time to socialize with their classmates?

These are merely a few examples, and many others exist. To answer these questions, you might conduct your own studies, which are forms of **action research, applied research designed to answer a specific school- or classroom-related question** (Gay et al., 2009). For example, you might want to compare your students' achievement when you give a quiz every week during one grading period to a previous grading period when you gave only three quizzes for the 9 weeks. In doing so, you are conducting action research.

If carefully organized and systematically conducted, action research can be published in professional journals or presented at conferences just as is research done by professional researchers (Bransford et al., 2000). If you do so, you will also be contributing to the body of professional knowledge that expert teachers possess.

Research and the Development of Theory

As research accumulates, results are summarized and patterns emerge. For instance, after many studies researchers have concluded that the thinking of young children tends to be dominated by their perceptions (Piaget, 1970, 1977; Wadsworth, 2004). For example, when first graders see an inverted cup of water with a card beneath it, as we see in the accompanying picture, they commonly explain that the card doesn't fall because the water somehow holds it against the cup. They focus on the most perceptually obvious aspect of the object—the water—and ignore atmospheric pressure, the actual reason the card stays on the cup.

The statement "The thinking of young children tends to be dominated by their perceptions" is a pattern consistently found in large numbers of research studies. Some additional examples of research-based patterns include:

- Behaviors rewarded some of the time, but not all of the time, persist longer than behaviors rewarded every time they occur.
- People tend to imitate behaviors they observe in others.
- People strive for a state of order, balance, and predictability in the world.

As additional research is conducted, related patterns are found, which in turn generate further studies. As knowledge accumulates, **theories, sets** of related **patterns that researchers** use to explain and predict events in the world, are gradually constructed (Cooper, 2006). In our everyday world, the term is used more loosely. For instance, one person makes a point in a conversation, and a second responds, "I have a theory about that." In this case, the person is merely offering an explanation for the point. In educational psychology, *theory* is reserved for the more systematic collection of data and the forming of patterns over time.

Theories help organize research findings and can provide valuable guidance for our teaching. Let's look at a brief example. One research-based pattern states, "Reinforced behaviors increase in frequency," and a related pattern mentioned earlier indicates that intermittently reinforced behaviors persist longer than those that are continuously reinforced (Baldwin & Baldwin, 2001; Skinner, 1957). Further, too much reinforcement can actually decrease its effectiveness. So, for example, if you reinforce your students for their attempts to answer

Action research. Applied research designed to answer a specific school- or classroom-related question.

Theories. Sets of related patterns, derived from observations, that researchers use to explain and predict events in the world.

why is this?

questions by praising them, they are likely to increase their efforts, but they will persist longer if they are praised for some, but not all, of their attempts (intermittently reinforced). If you praise them too much, they may actually reduce their efforts (Ryan & Deci, 1996).

These related patterns are part of *behaviorism,* a theory that studies the effects of external influences on behavior. Our illustration, of course, is only a tiny portion of the complete theory. (We examine behaviorism in depth in Chapter 9.) The key feature of any theory is the large number of research-based patterns that are integrated into a coherent body of knowledge.

Theories are useful in two important ways. First, they allow us to explain events in our classrooms and the world at large. For instance, look again at the cartoon on page 13. Piaget's theory of cognitive development (1970, 1977), which includes the pattern mentioned earlier ("The thinking of young children tends to be dominated by their perceptions"), helps us explain why the child in the cartoon thinks the way he does. Using Piaget's theory, we can explain this behavior by saying that the child can see only the water and the faucet, and because his thinking is dominated by his perception—what he can see—he concludes that all the water is in the faucet. Similarly, using behaviorist theory, we can explain why casino patrons persist in playing slot machines, though coins infrequently fall into the trays, by observing that they are being intermittently reinforced.

Theories also allow us to predict behavior and events. For instance, based on behaviorism, we would predict that students who periodically receive positive comments on essays will try harder than either students who receive no comments at all, or students who receive effusive positive comments.

In both instances, theories—cognitive development theory and behaviorist theory—help us understand learning and teaching by allowing us to explain and predict our students' behavior and how our actions will influence their learning. Throughout this book, you will study a number of theories, and we will discuss and illustrate ways that you can apply these theories in your teaching. These theories, together with a large body of research, make up the professional knowledge you need to become an expert teacher.

Professional Knowledge: Licensure Exams

As you saw earlier, teacher quality is now a national priority (Margolis, 2010), and, for many, "teacher quality" is synonymous with teacher knowledge. In an attempt to ensure that teachers possess adequate professional knowledge, all states now require prospective teachers to pass one or more tests before they receive a teaching license. These tests commonly measure general knowledge, as well as the types of professional knowledge that we described earlier in the chapter. It is a virtual certainty that you will be required to pass an exam that measures your professional knowledge before you receive your teaching license.

The Praxis™ Exam

The Praxis™ Series, published by the Educational Testing Service, is the test most widely used for teacher licensure (*praxis* means putting theory into practice). Forty-five states plus the District of Columbia, Guam, and the U.S. Virgin Islands use this series (Educational Testing Service, 2010a). Tests in the five states that have created their own—Arizona, Florida, Illinois, Michigan, and Minnesota—are similar to the Praxis in design and content.

The Praxis Series™ tests used for licensing and certification include:

- Praxis I® Pre-Professional Skills Tests (PPST®). These tests measure basic skills in reading, writing and mathematics. In addition to licensure, these tests are often used to qualify candidates for entry into a teacher education program.
- Praxis II® Subject Assessments. These tests measure subject-specific content knowledge, as well as general and subject-specific teaching skills, that you need for beginning teaching (Educational Testing Service, 2010).

• The *Principles of Learning and Teaching (PLT)* tests are important parts of the Praxis II series. The PLT tests are designed for teachers seeking licensure in early childhood or grades K–6, 5–9, and 7–12 (Educational Testing Service, 2008). This book addresses most topics covered on these tests, and a discussion of the Praxis exam and a correlation matrix linking test and text topics appear in Appendix C.

Each of the grade-level–specific PLT tests is 2 hours long and is composed of four case histories, each followed by three short-answer questions. In addition, the test includes 24 multiple-choice questions in two sections of 12 each (Educational Testing Service, 2008. The "case histories" are similar to the case studies you see at the beginning and the end of each chapter of this book. In our "Preparing for Your Licensure Exam" feature, which appears at the end of each chapter, you can practice preparing short-answer responses similar to those you'll encounter on the PLT tests, and we provide feedback for the questions in Appendix B. The multiple-choice questions, to which you will respond as you take quizzes and tests assessing your understanding of the content in this book, also ask you to apply your understanding to the real world of classrooms, and are similar to the multiple-choice questions on the PLT exam.

Applying Professional Knowledge in Your Classroom

Now we'll introduce you to a feature that will appear one or more times in each chapter. As you see in the title, this feature offers suggestions for *applying* the content of educational psychology to your teaching. This is why you're taking this course and studying this book—so you can use your knowledge of learning and teaching to increase your students' achievement.

To begin looking at these applications, let's return to the questions we asked at the beginning of the chapter.

"How was Keith's approach to teaching word problems different from Jan's?"
and
"Why were their approaches so different, and how will these differences affect their students' learning?"

We want to reexamine these questions now, using professional knowledge as a lens. Let's begin by considering the first. Keith's approach to teaching word problems was to ". . . explain the stuff so carefully," and then when the kids sat with blank looks on their faces, to ". . . explain it even more carefully." He was conscientious and sincere in his attempts to help his students learn to solve problems, and his approach—to explain—is the one most commonly used in classrooms. The problem he encountered is also common; explaining—alone—often is ineffective in helping students understand difficult ideas, such as problem solving.

In contrast, Jan built her lesson around concrete and real-world examples—the costs of the 12-ounce soft drink can, the 20-ounce bottle, and the 6 pack.

To promote student involvement, she had them work in pairs to determine which one was the best buy, and she provided them with enough guidance to ensure that they were making progress toward a solution. In contrast with Keith, she didn't use explaining as her primary approach to helping them learn to solve problems.

Now, let's answer the second question. Their approaches were different because Jan possessed more professional knowledge than did Keith, and, as a result, Jan's students are likely to learn more. They both had ample knowledge of content—decimals and percents and the processes involved in problem solving. However, the fact that Keith used explaining—an often ineffective teaching strategy—as his only approach, indicated that he lacked both pedagogical content knowledge and knowledge of learners and learning. He explained, and when that didn't work, all he was able to do was explain some more. In contrast, Jan was able to provide concrete and real-world examples—the different costs of the soft drink can and bottles—of decimals, percents, and problem solving, which demonstrated her pedagogical content knowledge. And, the fact that she knew her students needed the concrete examples and needed to be actively involved in the learning activity indicated her knowledge of learners and learning.

The differences between Jan's and Keith's professional knowledge are not surprising. Keith is a first-year teacher, whereas Jan has four years of experience, and she continues to grow professionally by taking classes that focus on this knowledge.

Also, her study and her commitment to her students' learning are indicators of her professionalism. Because Keith is a rookie, he is less knowledgeable than Jan, but he is no less committed. With study and practice he will learn and grow, and the same applies to you. You won't be an expert immediately, but with effort you can be, and in doing so, you will become a pro.

check your understanding

2.1   Describe and give an example of each of the different kinds of professional knowledge that expert teachers possess.

2.2   Identify the statement Keith made in the opening case study that best indicates his lack of pedagogical content knowledge in trying to teach problem solving to his students. Explain why the statement shows that he lacks this knowledge.

2.3   A life science teacher holds up a sheet of bubble wrap and then places a second sheet of bubble wrap on top of the first to help her students visualize the way that cells are organized into tissue. What kind of knowledge does the teacher's demonstration best indicate? Explain.

To receive feedback for these questions, go to Appendix A.

Themes for this Text

We are developing this text around three themes that capture major trends in educational psychology and that have important implications for you as a prospective teacher. The first of these, student learning and development, is obvious. Promoting as much learning and development in our students as possible is the central focus for both educational psychologists and classroom teachers.

Self-regulation is our second theme. We want our students to become knowledgeable and skilled, of course, but we also want to help them develop into students who can take command of their own learning and guide themselves as they develop throughout their lives.

The growing and pervasive influence of technology on our minds and lives is our third theme. Let's look at these themes in more detail.

Student Learning and Development

Think ahead a year or two, consider your first teaching job, and ask yourself what your primary role will be. If you're like we were when we began teaching, you most likely believe it is to help your students acquire knowledge and skills. When we started out in education, Paul taught chemistry and physics in a high school and Don taught science and American History in a K-8 school. We were young and enthusiastic, we wanted our students to understand the topics we taught, and we didn't think about much else. Helping our students develop into healthy, happy adolescents was implicit in our interactions with students but not uppermost on our minds.

Since those days we have both spent hundreds of hours in classrooms ranging from pre-K through high school, and in urban, suburban, and rural environments. This experience has taught us that helping students understand content is certainly important, but it isn't the whole picture. Let's look at teaching a bit more closely.

David Hicks, a seventh-grade geography teacher, has a rule, the violation of which is "punishable by death" as he mirthfully puts it. It is:

You may not say or do anything at any time to one of your classmates that is sarcastic or hurtful.

"We are in this class to learn as much geography as possible," he asserts the first day. "And, we're in this together. . . . We're going to help each other whenever we can, and we're going to treat each other with kindness and respect. And, this also goes for when we're outside our classroom."

David conscientiously treats his students with courtesy and caring, but at the same time, "Don't mess with Hicks," is a comment his students make to each other.

"I appreciate him," one of his students notes. "He's tough, but fair. He makes us learn, and he helps us if we need it."

What are David's students learning in his class? Hopefully, a considerable amount of geography, but they are also learning lessons that will serve them throughout their lives. Learning to treat others with courtesy and respect, for example, is essential. If you can't get along with your peers, you're unlikely to succeed in business or any other form of work.

As you move through your teaching career, you will teach your students much more than geography, how to write coherent paragraphs, or solve math problems. You will also help them learn to accept responsibility for their own actions; develop socially and morally; respect and embrace peers with different ethnic, language, and religious backgrounds; persevere in the face of frustration; and value the acquisition of knowledge and skills that may not be intrinsically interesting to them. Ideally, you will also help them learn to delay gratification, to forego an immediate pleasure like playing a video game or going out on a Friday night in favor of staying home and studying for an important exam.

That's why we've included topics such as personal and social development, learner diversity, and student motivation in this book. Understanding these topics is part of the professional knowledge you need to become an expert teacher, and these topics may be as—or even more—important than acquiring knowledge of content.

Ed Psych and You:

It's a hot Friday afternoon in August, and you're looking forward to a great weekend. Your boss comes in and says, "I'm not going to pressure you, but I'm in a bit of a jam. If you'll work tomorrow and Sunday, I'll give you a week off with pay in November." What would you do?

Delay of gratification. The ability to forgo an immediate pleasure or reward in order to gain a more substantial one later.

Self-regulation. The ability to direct and control one's own actions and emotions.

Self-Regulation

Back in the 1960s, Stanford University researcher Michael Mischel conducted a series of studies that have become classics in the field of child development. His research focused on **delay of gratification,** the ability to forgo an immediate pleasure or reward in order to gain a more substantial one later. He offered 4-year-olds a marshmallow but told them that if they could wait for the experimenter to return after running an errand, which would take about 15 minutes, they could have two marshmallows. About a third of the children ate the marshmallow right away, another third waited for a few moments, and the final third waited until the experimenter returned.

He followed the children over time, and, years later, the differences between the groups were striking. The children who had initially waited *when they were four years old* were more positive and self-motivated, and they were more persistent in the face of difficulties as they pursued their goals. In adolescence, they earned higher SAT scores and had better emotional coping skills (Mischel, Shoda, & Rodriguez, 1989). They were more successful in their marriages, earned higher incomes and were more satisfied with their careers, were healthier, and even handled interpersonal rejection better than others (Ayduk et al., 2000). This research found that people who are able to delay gratification are not only more successful but are also healthier mentally and emotionally.

So, how did you respond to our "Ed Psych and You" question? We're certainly not suggesting that you are doomed to failure if you chose to take your weekend off. However, as we all look at our lives and how we are living them, this research is indeed food for thought. But what does it have to do with educational psychology and your success as a teacher?

Many aspects of cognitive, personal, and social development, including delay of gratification, fall under the topic of **self-regulation,** the ability to direct and control one's own actions and emotions (Berk, 2010; McDevitt & Ormrod, 2010). These abilities are outlined in Figure 1.2, and studying for this class is an example. You're tired from a long day at school, perhaps combined with work, and one of your friends suggests that you go out for awhile. The last thing you want to do is a homework assignment. Your first thought is to simply bag it and go out with your friend, since the assignment probably won't have a major impact on your grade in the class.

You know that completing the assignment is important, however, so you set the goal of finishing at least half of it before you go to bed, and you get a cup of coffee, sit down, and before too long, you see that you've reached your goal. Rejuvenated, you redouble your efforts and finish the entire assignment.

You have demonstrated several of the dimensions of self-regulation outlined in Figure 1.2. First you demonstrated *impulse control* by resisting the temptation to go out instead of working on your homework, and you *delayed gratification*, since you received little immediate reward for doing your homework; the greater reward is the knowledge or skills you acquire in doing it and the higher grade you earn at the end of the class.

You also displayed both *self-motivation* and *self-regulated learning* by accepting the responsibility for doing the assignment, setting the goal, and completing it.

Researchers have found that self-regulation is associated with a number of factors, such as improved social relationships, including relationships among siblings (Padilla-Walker, Harper, & Jensen, 2010), and the ability to eliminate bad habits (Quinn, Pascoe, Wood, & Neal, 2010). Also, not surprisingly, self-regulated learners perform better on tests (Krebs & Roebers, 2010), achieve higher than their peers, and describe their learning as more satisfying (Zimmerman & Schunk, 2001, 2004).

In many cases, success in school depends more on self-regulation than on native ability (Schunk & Ertmer, 2000). So, if we can help our students learn to be responsible and conscientious, to persevere on challenging tasks, and defer immediate rewards for long-term outcomes, we will make perhaps the greatest contribution possible to their education.

This is the reason we made self-regulation a theme for this text. We will refer to the dimensions of self-regulation throughout the book, and we offer strategies in these chapters that you can use to promote this valuable orientation in your students.

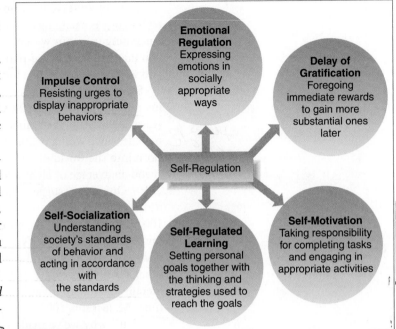

Figure 1.2 Dimensions of self-regulation

Technology, Learning, and Development

Technology is transforming the world and our lives with it. For example, experts believe that technology played an important role in the dramatic and profound events in the Middle East that resulted in the overthrow of the dictators in Tunisia and Egypt in early 2011 (Zakaria, 2011). In our personal lives, computers, the Internet, cell phones, and other forms of technology, such as iPads, are so common that we almost forget that they haven't always been a part of our lives.

Many of these advances in technology are great. For example, Don lives in Utah and Paul lives in Florida, but e-mail allows them to collaborate on their writing almost as easily as if they were in the same town. The ability to Google virtually any subject—we have yet to find a topic Google didn't recognize in some way—provides access to information literally impossible only a few years ago.

Ed Psych and You:
How many times a day do you talk on your cell phone or send a text? You hear the familiar "ping" on your computer telling you that you have new e-mails. Do you immediately check them?

Some of these changes, however, are mixed, and researchers have begun to question how technology is changing our lives (della Cava, 2010). For example, if you're like many people (including us in our weaker moments), you can't resist the "ping" of your computer telling you that you have new e-mails. We take our laptops and BlackBerrys with us on vacations, and we're lost if we're in a location so remote that we don't have cell phone service.

Some researchers suggest that technology is not only changing our lives but also changing our brains (Carr, 2010). One provocative article asked, "Is Google making us stupid?" (Carr, 2008). And, the brains of our students, which are still developing, are particularly vulnerable, since young people are most exposed to new technology (Small & Vorgan, 2008). Born into the world of laptops, cell phones, and texting, some estimates suggest that they spend an average of eight and a half hours each day exposed to digital technology (Hicks, 2010). One survey suggested that a typical American teenager sends and receives 50 or more text messages per day, or 1,500 per month; 31% of teenagers send and receive more than 100 messages per day, or more than 3,000 per month (Pew Charitable Trust, 2010)! All this may be altering children's personal and social development, including the ability to read nonverbal social cues and the ability to empathize with others (Small & Vorgan, 2008). And other researchers argue that, because we're continually bombarded by technology, we've literally lost our ability to pay attention to detail and to concentrate for extended periods of time (M. Jackson, 2009).

That's why we've made the influence of technology on learning and development a theme for our text. As we develop this theme, we don't discuss the technical aspects of technology, such as the use of spreadsheets, databases, and different forms of communication. Rather, we examine their influence on learning and development and the implications for your teaching.

---

check your understanding

3.1 Describe three types of student learning and development that occur in schools.

3.2 Describe and give an example of self-regulation.

3.3 Explain the relationship between the types of learning and development and educational psychology.

To receive feedback for these questions, go to Appendix A.

Case Studies in Educational Psychology

The different forms of knowledge that teachers need for their professional decision making have important implications both for you, who are learning to teach, and for us, as we write this text to help you in this process.

Case Studies and Classroom Applications

Our knowledge of learners and learning reminds us that students of all ages need concrete and real-world representations of the topics they study to make those topics meaningful.

Case studies. Authentic stories of teaching and learning events in classrooms.

Using **case studies**, realistic descriptions of teaching and learning events in classrooms, such as the one at the beginning of this chapter and the one in the previous section, is one of the most effective ways to provide concrete illustrations of the topics you study in educational psychology. Case studies help you prepare for the events that will occur in your own classroom when you begin teaching (Fishman & Davis, 2006; Putnam & Borko, 2000). Long popular in other professions, such as law and medicine, cases are now frequently used in education. Research supports their value in clarifying ideas and showing how the content of educational psychology can be applied in classrooms. Teacher candidates, such as yourself, not only retain more information when it is illustrated in cases, but are more likely to transfer these ideas to their own unique teaching situations (Moreno & Valdez, 2007).

Because of their value in illustrating the complex processes involved in teaching and learning, we employ cases in this text in two ways: (1) We introduce and end each chapter with a case study, and we incorporate other, shorter cases throughout our chapters to illustrate important ideas. (2) We provide access to video cases of real classrooms through MyEducationLab. Our students find the video cases that you can access on MyEducationLab valuable because they realistically portray the complexities of classroom teaching.

Case Studies and Licensure Exams

The introductory and closing cases in each chapter serve two different purposes. The introductory case provides a real-world introduction to the content of the chapter and illustrates the chapter's topics. As we discuss topics, we integrate the cases with the content, in some instances taking dialogue directly from it, to make concepts more meaningful. We also present vignettes (short cases) throughout each chapter to further link the content to real-world examples.

The closing cases, found in the "Preparing for Your Licensure Exam" feature, have an additional purpose. The exams you will be required to pass to assess your professional knowledge before you receive your teaching license all use cases similar to the ones in our "Practicing for Your Licensure Exam" feature. So, these cases and your text can serve as a resource for you later in your program as you prepare for your licensure exam.

We hope this introduction has provided a framework for the rest of your study of this book.

---

check your understanding

4.1 Explain how using case studies to place educational psychology in real-world contexts makes it more meaningful.

4.2 How can the cases found in this text help you prepare for the licensure exams you'll need to take before you teach?

To receive feedback for these questions, go to Appendix A.

Summary

1. Describe the difference between effective and ineffective teachers, and explain how expert teaching influences student learning.
   - Effective teachers can produce learning in their students and do so despite challenging circumstances.
   - Experts are people who are highly knowledgeable and skilled in a particular domain, such as teaching. Effective teachers are experts in their field. Students taught by expert teachers learn more than students taught by teachers with less expertise.

2. Describe the different kinds of professional knowledge that expert teachers possess.
   - Expert teachers thoroughly understand the topics they teach, and their knowledge is reflected in their actions when they use their pedagogical content knowledge to illustrate those topics in ways that make sense to learners.
   - Expert teachers apply general pedagogical knowledge to organize learning environments and use basic instructional skills in ways that promote learning for their students.
   - Expert teachers' knowledge of learners and learning allows them to design learning activities that involve students, promote motivation to learn, and use developmentally appropriate practice.

3. Describe different types of student learning and development, and explain how they are related to educational psychology.
   - During schooling, students acquire knowledge, such as the content of science, literature, and history, and skills, such as the ability to write effectively.
   - Students also learn life skills, such as accepting responsibility, and social skills, such as the ability to work with others.
   - Students also learn self-regulation, the ability to use their own thoughts and actions to reach goals they set for themselves.
   - The content of educational psychology is designed to help teachers acquire the knowledge and abilities to develop each of these forms of learning in their students.

4. Explain how case studies make the content of educational psychology more meaningful.
   - Research indicates that topics embedded in authentic contexts make them more meaningful and easier to learn and also increase the likelihood they will transfer to classrooms.
   - Written and video case studies in this text make the content of educational psychology meaningful by embedding it in real-world classroom contexts.

Understanding Professional Knowledge
Preparing for Your Licensure Exam

You will be required to take a licensure exam before you go into your own classroom. This exam will include information related to the different types of professional knowledge teachers need to become experts, and the following exercises are similar to those that appear on licensure exams. They are designed to help you practice for the exam in your state. This book and these exercises will be a resource for you later in your program as you prepare for the exam.

The following episodes illustrate four teachers at different classroom levels working with their students. As you read the episodes, think about the different types of professional knowledge that the teachers demonstrate in their lessons.

> Rebecca Atkins, a kindergarten teacher, is talking with her children about planting a garden. She sits on a small chair at the front of the room and has the children seated on the floor in a semicircle in front of her.
>
> She begins, "We had a story about gardening the other day. Who remembers the name of the story? . . . Shereta?"
>
> " 'Together,' " Shereta softly responds.

> "Yes, 'Together,' " Rebecca repeats. "What happened in 'Together'? . . . Andrea?"
>
> "They had a garden."
>
> "They planted a garden together, didn't they?" Rebecca smiles. "The boy's father helped them plant the garden."
>
> She continues by referring the children to previous science lessons during which they had talked about plants and soil. She then asks them about helping their parents plant a garden.
>
> "I helped put the seeds in the ground and put the dirt on top of it," Robert offers.
>
> "What kinds of vegetables did you plant? . . . Kim?"
>
> "I planted lots of vegetables . . . tomatoes, carrots."
>
> "Travis?"
>
> "I planted okra."
>
> "Raphael?"
>
> "I planted beans."
>
> She continues, "Tell about the story 'Together.' What did they have to do to take care of the garden? . . . Carlita?"

"Water it."

"Bengemar?"

"Pull the weeds from it."

"Pull the weeds from it," Rebecca smiles. "What would happen if we left those weeds in there? . . . Latangela?"

"It would hurt the soil."

"What's another word for soil?"

"Dirt," several of the children say in unison.

"How many of you like to play in the dirt?"

Most of the children raise their hands.

"So, planting a garden would be fun because you get to play in the dirt," Rebecca says enthusiastically.

"I like to play in the mud," Travis adds.

"You like to play in the mud," Rebecca repeats, attempting to stifle a laugh.

We turn now to Richard Nelms, a middle school science teacher, as he illustrates the concept of *symmetry* for his seventh graders.

Richard begins his discussion of symmetry by holding up a sponge as an example of an asymmetrical object; he demonstrates radial symmetry using a starfish; and he then turns to bilateral symmetry.

"We have one more type of symmetry," he says. "Jason, come up here. . . . Stand up here."

Jason comes to the front of the room and stands on a stool.

"Would you say," Richard begins, "that Jason is asymmetrical—that there is not uniformity in his shape?"

The students shake their heads.

He has Jason extend his arms out from his sides as you see here and then asks, "Would you consider this radial, because he has extensions that go out in all directions? . . . Jarrett?"

"No."

"Why not? Explain that for us."

"There's nothing there," Jarrett says, pointing to Jason's sides.

"There's nothing coming from here, is there, and the arms, legs and head are all different?" Richard adds.

"So, we move to the third type of symmetry," he continues, as Jason continues to stand with his arms extended. "It's called *bilateral* . . . . Bilateral means that the form or shape of the organism is divided into two halves, and the two halves are consistent. . . . If I took a tree saw and started at the top," he says, pointing at Jason's head as the class laughs, "the two halves would be essentially the same."

"Now, tomorrow," he continues, "we're going to see how symmetry influences the ways organisms function in their environments."

Let's look in now at Didi Johnson, a 10th-grade chemistry teacher, as she attempts to help her students understand Charles's law of gases, the law stating that an increase in the temperature of a gas causes an increase in its volume if the pressure on the gas doesn't change.

To illustrate that heat causes gases to expand, Didi prepares a demonstration in which she places three identical balloons filled with the same amount of air into three beakers of water. She puts the first into a beaker of hot water, the second into a beaker of water at room temperature, and the third into a beaker of ice water, as you see here.

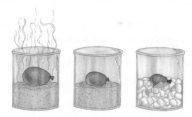

"This water is near boiling," Didi explains as she places the first balloon in the beaker. "This is room temperature, and this has had ice in it, so it is near the freezing point," she continues as she puts the other two balloons into the beakers.

"Today," she continues as she begins writing on the board, "we're going to discuss Charles's law, but before we put it on the board and discuss it, we're going to see what happened to the balloons. . . . Look up here. . . . How is the size of the balloon related to the temperature of the water we placed it in?"

"The balloon in the hot water looks bigger," Chris responds.

"Can you see any difference in these two?" Didi continues, pointing to the other two balloons.

"The one in the cold water looks smaller than the one in the room-temperature water," Shannon adds.

"So, from what we see, if you increase temperature, what happens to the volume of the gas?"

"It increases," several students volunteer.

Didi writes, "Increase in temperature increases volume" on the board, emphasizes that the amount of air and the pressure in the balloons were kept essentially constant, and then asks, "Who can state Charles's law based on what we've seen here?"

"Increased temperature will increase volume if you have constant pressure and mass," Jeremy offers.

Didi briefly reviews Charles's law, writes an equation for it on the board, and has the students solve a series of problems using the law.

Finally, let's look at Bob Duchaine's work with his students. An American history teacher, he is discussing the Vietnam War with his 11th graders.

Bob begins by saying, "To understand the Vietnam War, we need to go back to the beginning. Vietnam had been set up as a French colony in the 1880s, but by the mid-1900s, the military situation had gotten so bad for the French that they only controlled the little city of Dien Bien Phu."

He explains that the French surrendered in the summer of 1954, and peace talks followed. The talks resulted in Vietnam being split, and provisions for free elections were set up.

"These elections were never held," Bob continues. "Ngo Dinh Diem, in 1956, said there will be no free elections: 'I am in charge of the South. You can have elections in the North if you want, but there will be no elections in the South.'"

He continues by introducing the "domino theory," which suggested that countries such as South Vietnam, Cambodia, Laos, Thailand, Burma, and even India would fall into communist hands much as dominos tip over and knock each other down. The way to prevent the loss of the countries, he explains, was to confront North Vietnam.

"And that's what we're going to be talking about throughout this unit," he says. "The war that we took over from the French to stop the fall of the dominos soon was eating up American lives at the rate of 12 to 15 thousand a year. . . . This situation went from a little simple plan—to stop the dominos from falling—to a loss of over 53,000 American lives that we know of.

"We'll pick up with this topic day after tomorrow. . . . Tomorrow, you have a fun day in the library."

Questions for Case Analysis

In answering these questions, use information from the chapter, and link your responses to specific information in the case.

1. What type or types of professional knowledge did Rebecca Atkins primarily demonstrate? Explain.

2. What type or types of knowledge did Richard Nelms demonstrate in his lesson? Explain.

3. What type or types of knowledge did Didi Johnson primarily demonstrate?

4. What type or types of knowledge did Bob Duchaine primarily demonstrate?

To receive feedback for these questions, go to Appendix B.

Your licensure exam will also include multiple-choice questions similar to those your instructor has given you on your quizzes and tests for this course.

Important Concepts

action research (p. 16)
case studies (p. 22)
correlation (p. 15)
correlational research (p. 15)
delay of gratification (p. 20)
descriptive research (p. 14)

developmental
  differences (p. 13)
developmentally appropriate
  practice (p. 13)
educational psychology (p. 6)
effective teachers (p. 5)

expert (p. 5)
experimental research (p. 15)
general pedagogical
  knowledge (p. 11)
pedagogical content
  knowledge (p. 8)

professional knowledge (p. 6)
qualitative research (p. 15)
reflective practice (p. 12)
research (p. 14)
self-regulation (p. 20)
theories (p. 16)

Go to the Topic: Research Methods and Teacher Reflection in the MyEducationLab (www.myeducation lab.com) for *Educational Psychology: Windows on Classrooms,* where you can:

- Find learning outcomes for Teacher Methods and Teacher Reflection along with the national standards that connect to these outcomes.
- Complete Assignments and Activities that can help you more deeply understand the chapter content
- Apply and practice your understanding of the core teaching skills identified in the chapter with the Building Teaching Skills and Dispositions learning units.
- Examine challenging situations and cases presented in the IRIS Center Resources.
- Access video clips of CCSSO National Teachers of the Year award winners responding to the question, "Why Do I Teach?" in the Teacher Talk section.
- See video examples included within the Study Plan that provide concrete and real-world illustrations of the topics presented in the chapter.
- Check your comprehension of the content covered in the chapter with the Study Plan. Here you will be able to take a chapter quiz, receive feedback on your answers, and then access Review, Practice, and Enrichment activities to enhance your understanding of chapter content.

MyEducationLab

chapter 2

Cognitive and Language Development

chapteroutline

learningoutcomes

After you've completed your study of this chapter, you should be able to:

What Is Development?
Principles of Development
Brain Research and Cognitive Development

1. Describe development, and explain why understanding cognitive development is important for teachers.

Piaget's Theory of Cognitive Development
The Drive for Equilibrium
The Development of Schemes
Responding to Experiences: Assimilation and Accommodation
Factors Influencing Development
Stages of Development
Piaget's Stages and Research on Student Thinking
Evaluating Piaget's Theory
Current Views of Cognitive Development

2. Use concepts from Piaget's theory of intellectual development to explain both classroom and everyday events.

Lev Vygotsky's Sociocultural Theory of Cognitive Development
Learning and Development in a Cultural Context
Zone of Proximal Development
Scaffolding: Interactive Instructional Support
Piaget's and Vygotsky's Views of Cognitive Development
Technology, Learning, and Development: Is Technology Interfering with Cognitive Development?

3. Use Vygotsky's sociocultural theory to explain how language, culture, and instructional support influence development.

Language Development
Theories of Language Development
Early Language Development
Language Development in the School Years
Using Language to Learn

4. Use theories of language development to explain language patterns in children.

classroomapplications

The following features help you apply the content of this chapter in your teaching.

Ed Psych and Teaching:
Applying Piaget's Theory with Your Students
Applying Vygotsky's Theory with Your Students
Helping Your Students Develop Language Abilities

Classroom Connections:
Promoting Cognitive Development in Classrooms Using Piaget's Theory
Promoting Cognitive Development in Classrooms with Vygotsky's Work
Promoting Language Development in Classrooms

Developmentally Appropriate Practice:
Promoting Cognitive Development with Learners at Different Ages
Promoting Language Development with Learners at Different Ages

Exploring Diversity:
Language Development for Non-Native English Speakers

*T*he way students think about the world they live in depends on their maturity, and, perhaps more significantly, on the experiences they've had. Think about these factors as you read the following case study, which involves a conversation between two teachers and the frustration one expresses over her students' inability to understand basic science concepts.

On Friday morning Karen Johnson, an eighth-grade science teacher, walks into the teachers' workroom with a discouraged look on her face.

"What's happening?" Ken, one of her colleagues, asks.

"I just had the most frustrating class. . . . You know how I told you the other day that my third-period students are really struggling. Well, today we were working on *density*. They memorize the formula and try to solve problems but don't really get it. And, they're confused about basic concepts such as *mass, weight, volume*—everything. To them, mass, weight, and density are all the same. If it's bigger, it's more dense. The class was a disaster."

"You know how these kids are; they're not used to thinking on their own," Ken responds.

"I guess so, but there's more," Karen nods. "They've never really done anything other than memorize definitions and formulas. So what do we expect?"

We'll return to the conversation between Karen and Ken later in the chapter, but for now, think about these questions:

1. Why did Karen's students struggle with a concept as basic as *density*?
2. What, specifically, can Karen do in response to her students' struggles?
3. How will an understanding of the way students think increase your effectiveness as a teacher?

Theories of cognitive development help answer these questions, and in this chapter you'll see how these theories can be applied to your teaching.

Development. The changes that occur in human beings as they grow from infancy to adulthood.

Physical development. Changes in the size, shape, and functioning of our bodies.

Personal, social, and emotional development. Changes in our personality, the ways we interact with others, and our ability to manage our feelings.

Cognitive development. Changes in our thinking that occur as a result of maturation and experience.

*W*hat Is Development?

Ed Psych and You

Think back to when you were in elementary and middle school. What kinds of things can you do now that you couldn't do then? How about your high school years? How has your thinking changed since you graduated from high school?

The questions in the accompanying "Ed Psych and You" relate to the concept of **development,** the changes that occur in all of us as we grow from infancy to adulthood. **Physical development** describes changes in the size, shape, and functioning of our bodies and explains why we could, for example, run faster as a high school student than we could when we were in the fifth grade. **Personal, social, and emotional development** refers to changes in our personalities, the ways we interact with others, and our ability to manage our feelings.

The term *cognitive* implies thinking, and in this chapter, we focus on **cognitive development,** changes in our thinking that occur as a result of maturation and experience. The question, "How has your thinking changed?" in the accompanying "Ed Psych and You" relates to your cognitive development, and it was an important factor in Karen's students' inability to understand the concept *density*.

Principles of Development

Three general principles apply to all people and describe all forms of development.

- *Development depends on both heredity and the environment.* **Maturation,** genetically controlled, age-related changes in individuals, plays an important role in development. High school students are more cognitively mature than elementary or middle school students, which helps us understand why we don't teach calculus or physics, for example, to younger learners.
- We can't change our students' genes, but we can influence their experiences. Genetics set an upper limit on what may be achieved, but this limit is high, and the environment, through the experiences we provide, determines how close students come to reaching it. *Development proceeds in relatively orderly and predictable patterns.* Development is systematic and predictable (Lerner, 2006). For example, we babble before we talk, crawl before we walk, and learn concrete concepts like *mammal* and *car* before abstract ones like *density* and *democracy.*
- *People develop at different rates.* While progression from childhood to adolescence and ultimately to adulthood is generally orderly, the rate at which we progress varies. We have all heard phrases like, "He's a late bloomer" or "She never quite grew up," which describe individual differences in people's rates of development.

With these principles in mind, we turn now to cognitive development. We begin by considering research on the role of the brain in this process.

Maturation. Genetically controlled, age-related changes in individuals.

A variety of experiences contributes to learners' development.

Brain Research and Cognitive Development

The way we develop depends on physiological changes in our brains, and neuroscience has developed brain imaging techniques that allow scientists to study the way the brain changes as development occurs (Nelson, Thomas, & de Haan, 2006). Understanding these changes can help you better guide the development of your students.

The Learning Physiology of the Brain

The human brain is incredibly complex. Estimates suggest that it is composed of between 100 and 200 billion nerve cells, called **neurons** (Clark, Goldberg, & Rudy, 2009). The neuron is the learning unit of the brain and is central to cognitive development. As you see in Figure 2.1, a neuron is composed of a cell body; **dendrites,** relatively short, branchlike structures that extend from the cell body and receive messages from other neurons; and **axons,** longer branches that also extend from the cell body and transmit messages (Clark et al., 2009).

Neurons don't actually touch one another; instead, signals are sent across **synapses,** tiny spaces between neurons that allow messages to be transmitted from one to another. When an electrical impulse is sent down an axon, it stimulates a chemical that crosses the synapse and stimulates the dendrites of neighboring neurons. Frequent transmission of information between neurons can establish a permanent physical relationship between them, and evidence from animal studies indicates that learning experiences increase the number of synaptic connections per neuron. For example, laboratory rats provided with mazes and objects to manipulate develop and retain 25% more synapses than rats developed in sterile environments (Nelson et al., 2006).

In other words, "What gets fired, gets wired," and this is why experiences are so important for development; they influence the connections between neurons in the brain that stay with us throughout our lives (Berk, 2010).

Neurons. Nerve cells composed of cell bodies, dendrites, and axons, which make up the learning capability of the brain.

Dendrites. Relatively short, branchlike structures that extend from the cell body of neurons and receive messages from other neurons.

Axons. Longer branches that extend from the cell body of neurons and transmit messages to other neurons.

Synapses. The tiny spaces between neurons that allow messages to be transmitted from one neuron to another.

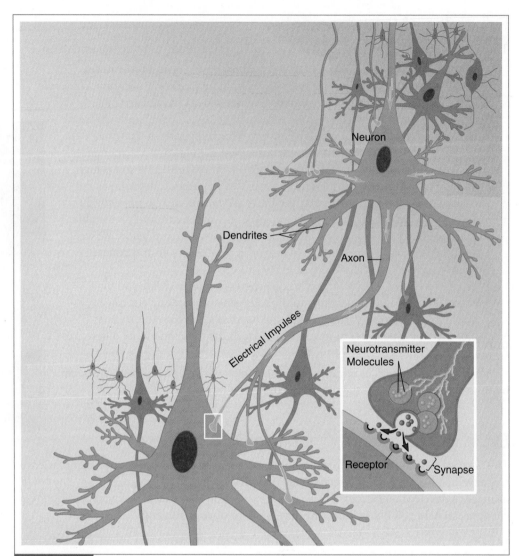

Figure 2.1 The learning physiology of the brain

Each neuron has about 2,500 synapses, and cognitive development involves both creating and eliminating synaptic connections (Spear, 2007). During the first 3 years of our lives, so many new synapses develop that they far exceed adult levels. Psychologists believe that generating more synapses than they will ever need allows children to adapt to the wide variety of circumstances they'll encounter throughout life (Nelson et al., 2006). As we experience patterns in our environment, the large number becomes unnecessary, and two important processes occur in the brain. The first is *myelination.* It occurs when cells grow around neurons to give them structural support, and a fatty coating of myelin develops to insulate axons and enable them to conduct electrical charges quickly and efficiently. The second, *synaptic pruning,* eliminates synapses that are infrequently used. At age 2 or 3 each neuron has around 15,000 synapses, but this number is sharply reduced in adults as a result of synaptic pruning. This "use it or lose it" tendency allows our brains to adjust and respond to the environment.

The Cerebral Cortex

The cerebral cortex, the outer covering of the cerebrum, is the site of much that characterizes human thinking, problem solving, and language (Nelson et al., 2006) (see Figure 2.2).

Not surprisingly, it is proportionately much larger in humans than in other animals, comprising 85% of the brain's total weight and containing the greatest number of neurons and synapses.

The cerebral cortex develops more slowly than other regions of the brain, and its parts mature at different rates. The part controlling physical movement develops first, followed by vision and hearing, and ending with the frontal lobes, which play a major role in decision making and managing risky or impulsive behaviors. This area may not be fully developed until we are in our twenties.

The gradual development in the frontal lobes helps explain several aspects of behavior, such as the temper tantrums of 2-year-olds and the sometimes dangerous behaviors of teenagers, such as drinking and driving, drug use, and unprotected sex. While equipped with the bodies of adults, teenagers' abilities to assess risk and make sound decisions are still developing. Rules and limits that simplify decisions help teenagers through this often confusing period.

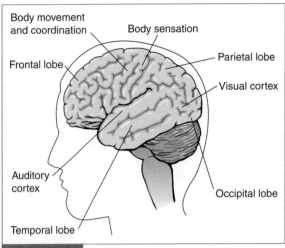

Figure 2.2 The cerebral cortex

The left and right hemispheres of the cortex specialize in different functions (Byrnes, 2007). The right controls the left side of our bodies and vice versa. Also, in most people the left hemisphere controls language and logical thinking, and the right deals with synthesizing information—especially visual images—into meaningful patterns.

not in all? why?

so right-brained research is bullshit?

This hemispheric specialization is commonly misinterpreted, resulting in expressions such as "He's right brained." Despite their separate specialties, the two hemispheres have neural connections and function as an integrated whole, especially with the cognitive tasks found in schools. People are neither right brained nor left brained, and efforts to teach to the left or right brain are both overly simplistic and misguided (Posner & Rothbart, 2007).

Analyzing Brain Research and Its Implications for Teachers

Research on the brain has led to "brain-based learning," a movement in education that attempts to directly apply this research to teaching. This movement is controversial, with proponents (e.g., Jensen, 2005; Walsh & Bennett, 2004) lining up on one side and critics (e.g., Coles, 2004; Willis, 2006, 2007) on the other.

One of the controversies centers on the role of early stimulation for cognitive development. Research on synaptic connections and evidence supporting early stimulation in animals have resulted in some brain-based advocates recommending specialized instruction during the early years. Other experts disagree. Early stimulus deprivation can indeed impede cognitive development, but evidence doesn't support the application of added stimulation, such as expensive toys or computers. In fact, one widely publicized study found that extensive media viewing in young children is associated with reduced language development (Zimmerman, Christakis, & Meltzoff, 2007), and some have criticized the sale of videos and other products designed to promote early stimulation as blatant commercialization (Linn, 2009).

now? stuff like Little Einsteins?

The existence of critical periods for maximum development is a second controversy. For instance, young children who grow up in bilingual homes learn to speak both languages flawlessly, but adults who learn a language later in life struggle to produce certain sounds that are effortless for native speakers (Berk, 2010). Extrapolating from these findings, some educators suggest designing schools around these critical periods, such as introducing foreign languages to preschoolers to take advantage of a critical period in language development.

that would be cool and interesting to witness

Critics acknowledge that critical periods do exist in humans but point out that our brains retain an enormous ability to benefit from stimulation throughout our lives, and they caution against intensive training for young children (Holland, 2004; Willingham, 2006). In addition,

> No evidence exists for a sensitive period in the first few years of life for mastering skills that depend on extensive training, such as reading, musical performance, or gymnastics. To the contrary, rushing early learning harms the brain by overwhelming its neural circuits thereby reducing the brain's sensitivity to the everyday experiences it needs for a healthy start in life. (Berk, 2010, p. 128)

Instruction is a third area of controversy. Brain-based-instruction advocates emphasize the importance of deliberate practice and active learning strategies such as guided discovery, problem solving, and hands-on learning. Critics counter that these are strategies that have been widely accepted for years, and describing them as "brain based" adds nothing new (Byrnes, 2007). To this point, brain research is unable to provide specific guidance to teachers facing the myriad of decisions they make every day (Varma, McCandliss, & Schwartz, 2008).

Research and theory consistently indicate, however, that the stimulation that occurs in a healthy environment is essential for normal cognitive development, and, as teachers, we play major roles in the process. Understanding this research and theory is part of your professional knowledge, and we discuss different ways to promote cognitive development in the next section.

---

check your understanding

1.1 Describe development and explain why understanding cognitive development is important for teachers.

1.2 Describe the basic principles of development. Why are they important for teachers?

1.3 How does the physical development of the brain influence cognitive development?

To receive feedback for these questions, go to Appendix A.

---

*P*iaget's Theory of Cognitive Development

As an introduction to Piaget's theory of cognitive development, consider the following problem:

> You have two identical glasses of water. You then pour the contents of one into a third glass as shown here. Now, are the amounts of water in the first and third glasses the same or different?

The question may seem silly; the amounts are obviously the same. However, when Jean Piaget used a problem such as this to examine children's thinking, he found that 4 and 5 year olds thought that the taller glass had more water. These differences in children's thinking proved fascinating to Piaget and resulted in one of the most widely studied theories of cognitive development (Inhelder & Piaget, 1958; Piaget, 1952, 1959, 1980). We examine his theory in this section.

Ed Psych and You

Are you bothered when something doesn't make sense? Do you want the world to be predictable? Are you more comfortable in classes where the instructor specifies the requirements and outlines the grading practices? For most people, the answer to these questions is "Yes." Why do you think this is the case?

The Drive for Equilibrium

People want their experiences to make sense. They have an intrinsic need for understanding, order, and certainty, and it helps us understand why the answer to the questions we ask here in "Ed Psych and You" is yes. "We inquire about the past, present, and future. We investigate every conceivable subject. Human beings want and need to make sense of things that happen—or don't happen—in the short run as well as over the long haul" (Marinoff, 2003, p. 3).

Piaget (1952, 1959, 1980) described this need for understanding as the drive for **equilibrium,** a cognitive state in which new experiences make sense to us because we're able to explain them using our existing understanding (Berk, 2010). As long as we're able to make sense of new experiences, we remain at equilibrium; when we can't, our equilibrium is disrupted, and we're motivated to reestablish it. Development occurs when our understanding advances as a result of regaining equilibrium.

The drive for equilibrium can be a double-edged sword. Karen's students, for example, were at equilibrium when they thought that *mass* and *density* were the same. This helps us understand why people retain misconceptions and why critical thinking is so difficult for many (Willingham, 2009).

Equilibrium. A cognitive state in which we're able to explain new experiences by using existing understanding.

The Development of Schemes

To make sense of our experiences and reach equilibrium, people construct **schemes,** mental operations that represent our understanding of the world. They are the building blocks of thinking. For instance, when you learned to drive a car, you had a series of experiences with attempting to start the engine, maneuver in traffic, and make routine driving decisions. As you (cognitively) organized these experiences, they became your "driving" scheme.

As suggested by our example with the containers of water, the schemes we construct vary with age. Infants develop psychomotor schemes, such as grasping objects; school-age children develop more abstract schemes like classification and proportional reasoning. Piaget used the idea of schemes to refer to a narrow range of operations, such as children's conservation-of-volume scheme (the idea that the amount of liquid doesn't change when poured into a different-shaped container, as you saw in our example) (Piaget, 1952). However, teachers and some researchers (e.g. Wadsworth, 2004) find it useful to extend Piaget's idea to include content-related schemes, such as *adding-fractions-with-unlike-denominators, creating-a-persuasive-essay,* or *reptile* schemes. As with our driving scheme, each represents our understanding, and they are commonly described as *schemas* rather than schemes. We use this expanded view in our description of Piaget's work. *I've heard this term before*

Schemes. Mental operations that represent our constructed understanding of the world.

Responding to Experiences: Assimilation and Accommodation

Experience is a huge factor in development, and when we have new experiences, we either interpret them with our existing schemes or change our schemes. For instance, suppose you first learned to drive a Honda Civic with an automatic transmission, and later you bought a Toyota Camry, also with an automatic. You were easily able to drive the Camry, because your thinking about driving didn't have to change. You *assimilated* the experience with the Camry into your original driving scheme. **Assimilation** is the process of using existing schemes to interpret new experiences (Berk, 2010).

Now, suppose you buy a Ford Mustang, and it has a stick shift. You must change your thinking about driving, or, in other words you must *accommodate* your driving scheme. **Accommodation** is the process of creating new schemes or adjusting old ones when they can no longer explain new experiences. You modified your original driving scheme, so you can now drive cars with either an automatic or a stick shift.

Assimilation. The process of using existing schemes to interpret new experiences.

Accommodation. The process of creating new schemes or adjusting old ones when they can no longer explain new experiences.

The same processes apply in schools. For instance, if young children are given the problem

$$\begin{array}{r} 47 \\ -\ 23 \\ \hline \end{array}$$

and they get 24 as an answer, their *subtracting-whole-numbers* scheme suggests that they subtract smaller numbers from larger ones. However, if they are then given this problem,

$$\begin{array}{r} 43 \\ -\ 27 \\ \hline \end{array}$$

and they also get 24 as an answer, they have—mistakenly—assimilated the new experience into their existing scheme. Their thinking didn't change and they still subtracted the smaller numbers from the larger ones, ignoring the positioning of the numbers. With modeling, explanation, and practice, children change their thinking and accommodate their scheme, and development advances.

Factors Influencing Development

Experience is essential for development, because new experiences that require accommodation—changes in thinking—advance development. Two forms of experience are important: (1) experience with the physical world and (2) interactions with other people. Let's look at them.

Experience with the Physical World

To see how experience with the physical world influences development, think again about your driving. Because of your experience with stick shifts, you had to accommodate your driving scheme, and your ability to drive developed. For young children, maturation is also important, but for both young and older learners, experience is the primary factor influencing healthy cognitive development (Piaget, 1980).

The essential role experience plays in cognitive development helps us answer our first question at the beginning of the chapter: "Why did Karen's students struggle with a concept as basic as *density*?" Lack of the direct, concrete experiences they needed to understand the concept is the answer. For example, many of us have used the formula Density = Mass/Volume (d = m/v), inserted numbers, and got answers that meant little to us.

To see how Karen responds to this problem, let's sit in on another conversation the Tuesday following their Friday discussion.

> "What's that for?" Ken asks, seeing Karen walking into the teachers' lounge with a plastic cup filled with cotton balls.
>
> "I just had the greatest class," Karen replies. "You remember how frustrated I was on Friday when the kids didn't understand basic concepts like *mass* and *density*. . . . I thought about it over the weekend, and decided to try something different, even if it seemed sort of elementary.
>
> "See," she goes on, compressing the cotton in the cup. "Now the cotton is more dense. And now it's less dense," she points out, releasing the cotton.
>
> "Then, I made some different-sized blocks out of the same type of wood. Some of the kids first thought the density of the big block was greater. But then we weighed the blocks, measured their volumes, and computed their densities, and the kids saw they were the same. They gradually began to get it."

"This morning," she continues, "I had them put equal volumes of water and vegetable oil on our balances, and when the balance tipped down on the water side, they saw that the mass of the water was greater, so water is more dense. I had asked them to predict which was more dense before we did the activity, and most of them said oil. We talked about that, and they concluded the reason they predicted oil is the fact that it's thicker.

"Now, here's the good part. . . . Calvin, he hates science, remembered that oil floats on water, so it made sense to him that oil is less dense. He actually got excited about what we were doing and came up with the idea that less dense materials float on more dense materials. . . . You could almost see the wheels turning. We even got into population density and compared a door screen with the wires close together to one with the wires farther apart, and how that related to what we were studying. The kids were really into it. A day like that now and then keeps you going."

This helps us answer the second question we asked at the beginning of the chapter: "What, specifically, can Karen do in response to her students' struggles?" She responded by providing the specific, concrete experiences they needed to understand the concept. Now, her students are better equipped to explain why people float more easily in the ocean than in lakes, why hot-air balloons rise, and many others. Their thinking is more fully developed because of the experiences she provided.

Social Experience

Piaget also emphasized the role of **social experience,** the process of interacting with other people, on development (Wadsworth, 2004). Social experience allows learners to test their schemes against those of others. When schemes match, we remain at equilibrium; when they don't, our equilibrium is disrupted, we are motivated to accommodate them, and development occurs.

Social experience. The process of interacting with others.

You can provide social experiences for your students in two ways. First, you can guide their developing understanding with your questioning, and second, you can form groups in which students interact. Karen used the former, and many teachers include group work as an integral part of their instruction.

Piaget's Influence on Early Childhood Education

Piaget's emphasis on experience has strongly influenced preschool and kindergarten programs (Berk, 2010). For instance, in many early childhood classrooms, you'll see water and sand tables, building blocks, and other concrete materials that provide young children with concrete experiences.

Maria Montessori, an Italian educator who stressed the importance of exploration and discovery, developed what is probably the best known early childhood program (Dillard, 2007). In her work with children of poverty, Montessori concluded that learning environments in which children simultaneously "worked" on both academic and social activities were needed for development. It wasn't really work, however, because children could freely explore learning centers that provided hands-on activities and opportunities for social interaction with other students. Make-believe was encouraged with dress-up costumes and other accessories like play telephones.

Social experience promotes development by having learners compare their schemes to those of others.

Today, however, early childhood education emphasizes accountability and early reading skills—such as knowing the letters of the alphabet and understanding basic concepts such as *left* and *right*—or math skills—counting, number recognition, and even adding to and taking away, for instance. As a result, child-centered programs have decreased in favor of those more academically oriented. "Despite evidence that formal academic training in early childhood undermines motivation and emotional well-being, preschool and kindergarten teachers have felt increased pressure to take this approach" (Berk, 2010, p. 245). Despite the popularity of Piaget's emphasis on experience with the physical and social worlds, academically oriented early childhood programs are likely to grow.

Stages of Development

Stages of development. General patterns of thinking for children at different ages or with different amounts of experience.

Stages of development—general patterns of thinking for children at different ages or with different amounts of experience—are among the most widely known elements of Piaget's theory. As you examine the stages, keep the following ideas in mind:

- Movement from one stage to another represents a qualitative change in thinking— a difference in the *way* children think, not the *amount* they know. As an analogy, a qualitative change occurs when caterpillar metamorphoses into a butterfly, and a quantitative change occurs as the butterfly grows larger.
- Children's development is steady and gradual, and experiences in one stage form the foundation for movement to the next (P. Miller, 2002).
- All people pass through each stage in the same order but at different rates. Students at the same age may be at different stages, and the thinking of older children and even adults may be similar to that of younger children if they lack experience in that area (Keating, 2004).

The stages are summarized in Table 2.1 and described in the sections that follow.

Table 2.1   Piaget's stages and characteristics

Stage	Characteristics	Example
Sensorimotor (0–2)	Goal-directed behavior	Makes jack-in-the-box pop up
	Object permanence (represents objects in memory)	Searches for object behind parent's back
Preoperational (2–7)	Rapid increase in language ability with overgeneralized language	"We goed to the store."
	Symbolic thought	Points out car window and says, "Truck!"
	Dominated by perception	Concludes that all the water in a sink came out of the faucet (the cartoon in Chapter 1)
Concrete Operational (7–11)	Operates logically with concrete materials	Concludes that two objects on a "balanced" balance have the same mass even though one is larger than the other
	Classifies and serial orders	Orders containers according to decreasing volume
Formal Operational (11–Adult)	Solves abstract and hypothetical problems	Considers outcome of WWII if the Battle of Britain had been lost
	Thinks combinatorially	Systematically determines how many different sandwiches can be made from three different kinds of meat, cheese, and bread

The Sensorimotor Stage (0 to 2 Years)

In the sensorimotor stage, children use their motor capacities, such as grasping objects, to understand the world, and they don't initially represent the objects in memory; the objects are literally "out of sight, out of mind," early in this stage. Later, they acquire **object permanence,** the understanding that objects exist even when out of sight. Children at this stage also develop the ability to imitate, which allows them to learn by observing others.

Object permanence. The understanding that objects exist even when out of sight.

The Preoperational Stage (2 to 7 Years)

The term *preoperational* derives from the idea of "operation," or mental activity. A child who identifies different animals as dogs, cats, and bears, for example, is performing a mental operation.

Perception dominates children's thinking in this stage. For instance, look at the drawing here, which represents an inverted glass filled with water, and a card on the bottom. (Go ahead and try this.) Since they can see the glass, water, and card, preoperational thinkers conclude that the water is holding the card on the glass (atmospheric pressure is what actually holds the card next to the glass).

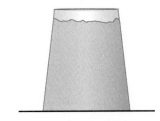

Many cognitive changes occur in children as they pass through this stage. For example, they make enormous progress in language development, reflecting their growth in the ability to use symbols, and they also learn huge numbers of concepts. For example, a child on a car trip will point excitedly and say, "Truck," "Horse," and "Tree," delighting in exercising these newly formed schemes. These concepts are concrete, however, and children in this stage have limited notions of abstract ideas such as *fairness*, *democracy*, and *energy*.

The influence of perceptual dominance is also seen in another prominent idea from Piaget's theory: preoperational thinkers' inability to conserve.

Conservation. **Conservation** refers to the idea that the "amount" of some substance stays the same regardless of its shape or the number of pieces into which it is divided. A number of conservation tasks exist. The example with the glasses of water that we used to introduce our discussion of Piaget's work is one, and two others are outlined in Figure 2.3.

Conservation. The idea that the "amount" of some substance stays the same regardless of its shape or the number of pieces into which it is divided.

In Figure 2.3 we see that preoperational children don't "conserve;" that is, it makes sense to them that the amount of water, the number of coins, or the amount of clay can somehow change without adding or subtracting anything from them. Let's see how this occurs using the example with the water. (You will be asked to explain how this occurs with the coins and clay in "Check Your Understanding," question 2.2.)

First, they tend to *center* on the height of the water in the glass. **Centration** (or centering) is the tendency to focus on the most perceptually obvious aspect of an object or event and ignore other features. The height is most perceptually obvious, so preoperational children conclude that the tall, narrow glass has more water. Second, young children lack **transformation,** the ability to mentally record the process of moving from one state to another, such as pouring the water from the first to the third glass. To them it's a new and different container of liquid. Third, they also lack **reversibility,** the ability to mentally trace the process of moving from an existing state back to a previous state, such as being able to mentally reverse the process of pouring the water from one glass to another. When lack of transformation and reversibility are combined with their tendency to center, we can see why they conclude that the tall, narrow glass has more water in it, even though none was added or removed.

Centration (centering). The tendency to focus on the most perceptually obvious aspect of an object or event, neglecting other important aspects.

Transformation. The ability to mentally record the process of moving from one state to another.

Reversibility. The ability to mentally trace the process of moving from an existing state back to a previous state.

Egocentrism. Preoperational thinkers also demonstrate **egocentrism,** the inability to see objects and events from others' perspectives. In a famous experiment, Piaget and Inhelder

Egocentrism. The inability to see objects and events from others' perspectives.

Figure 2.3	Conservation tasks for number and mass		
Conservation Task	Initial Presentation by Observer	Change in Presentation by Observer	Typical Answer From Preoperational Thinker
Number	The observer shows the child two identical rows of objects. The child agrees that the number in each row is the same.	The observer spreads the bottom row apart while the child watches. The observer then asks the child if the two rows have the same number of objects or if there are more in one row.	The preoperational child typically responds that the row that has been spread apart has more objects. The child centers on the length, ignoring the number.
Mass	The observer shows the child two balls of clay. The child agrees that the amount of clay is the same in each. (If the child doesn't agree that they have the same amount, the observer then asks the child to move some clay from one to the other until the amount is the same.)	The observer flattens and lengthens one of the balls while the child watches. The observer then asks the child if the two have the same amount of clay or if one has more.	The preoperational child typically responds that the longer, flattened piece has more clay. The child centers on the length.

A nonconserver is influenced by appearances, believing that the flat pieces of clay have different amounts than the balls of clay even though they were initially the same.

(1956) showed young children a model of three mountains and asked them to describe how the mountains would look to a doll seated on the opposite side. Preoperational children described the doll's view as identical to their own.

The Concrete Operational Stage (7 to 11 Years)

The concrete operational stage, which is characterized by the ability to think logically when using concrete materials, marks another advance in children's thinking (Flavell, Miller, & Miller, 2002). For instance, when facing the conservation-of-number task, learners in this stage simply say, "You just made the row longer" or "You just spread the coins apart" (so, the number must remain the same).

Concrete operational learners also overcome some of the egocentrism of preoperational thinkers. They are able to understand the perspectives of storybook characters and better understand the views of others, which makes them better able to work effectively in groups.

Classification and Seriation. **Classification,** the process of grouping objects on the basis of common characteristics, and **seriation,** the ability to order objects according to increasing or decreasing length, weight, or volume, are two logical operations that develop during this stage, and both are essential for understanding number concepts (Piaget, 1977). For example, before age 5, children can form simple groups, such as separating black and white circles into two sets. When a black square is added, however, they typically include it with the black circles, instead of forming subclasses of black circles and black squares. By age 7, they can form subclasses, but they still have problems with more complex classification systems.

When children are able to order objects according to some dimension, such as length (seriation), they can master **transitivity,** the ability to infer a relationship between two objects based on their relationship with a third. For example, suppose we have three sticks, you're shown sticks 1 and 2, and you see that 1 is longer than 2. Now, stick 1 is removed, you're shown 2 and 3, and you see that 2 is longer than 3. You demonstrate transitivity when you conclude that 1 is longer than 3, reasoning that since 1 is longer than 2, and 2 is longer than 3, 1 must be longer than 3.

Though concrete operational thinkers have made dramatic progress, their thinking is still limited. For instance, they interpret sayings such as "Make hay while the sun shines" literally, such as concluding, "You should gather your crop before it gets dark."

Let's see how this compares to formal thinkers.

The Formal Operational Stage (Age 11 to Adult)

Although concrete operational learners are capable of logical thought, their thinking is tied to the real and tangible. Formal thinkers, in contrast, can think *abstractly, systematically,* and *hypothetically* (P. Miller, 2002). For example, formal thinkers would suggest that "Make hay while the sun shines" means something

Classification. The process of grouping objects on the basis of common characteristics.

Seriation. The ability to order objects according to increasing or decreasing length, weight, or volume.

Transitivity. The ability to infer a relationship between two objects based on knowledge of their relationship with a third object.

Concrete operational learners can think logically, but they need tangible materials to do so effectively.

abstract, such as "Seize an opportunity when it exists." Their ability to think in the abstract allows the study of courses, such as algebra and physics, to be meaningful.

Formal thinkers also reason systematically and recognize the need to control variables in forming conclusions. For example, if given the following problem,

> You're making sandwiches for a picnic. You have rye and whole wheat bread, turkey, ham, and beef for meat, and Swiss and cheddar cheese. How many different kinds of sandwiches can you make?

formal thinkers attack the problem systematically such as rye, turkey, and Swiss; rye, turkey, and cheddar; rye, ham, and Swiss, and so on. A concrete thinker attacks the problem haphazardly, such as rye, turkey, and Swiss; whole wheat, beef, and cheddar, etc.

Formal operational learners can also think hypothetically. For instance, considering what our country might be like today if the British had won the Revolutionary War requires hypothetical thinking for American history students, as does considering the influence of dominant and recessive genes for biology students.

When students can't think abstractly, systematically, or hypothetically, they revert to memorizing what they can, or, in frustration, give up altogether.

Ed Psych and You

Look at the figure below. The blocks on the balance are solid cubes that aren't compressible. Which of the following statements is true of the relationships between block A and block B?
1. A is bigger than B. 2. The mass of A is greater than the mass of B. 3. A is more dense than B. 4. A is made out of a different material than B. What stage of development is required to respond correctly to each question?

Piaget's Stages and Research on Student Thinking

Let's see how you did answering the "Ed Psych and You" question: Statement 1 is true, and, because we *can see* that A is bigger (greater volume), it is a preoperational task. A first grader, for example, would be able to respond successfully.

Responding correctly to statement 2 requires logical thought. The beam is balanced; therefore, the masses of the two objects are the same, so the statement is false. It requires logical thought with concrete materials, so it is a concrete operational task.

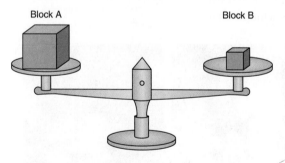

Block A   Block B

Statement 3 is also false. A is larger than B, but the masses are the same, so the density of A is less than B, not greater. Finally, statement 4 is true; if the blocks are solids and have different densities, they must be made of different materials. Statements 3 and 4 require abstract thinking, so they are formal operational tasks.

Don't feel bad if you struggled with one or more of these items. Here's why. Even as adults, *virtually all of us are formal operational thinkers only in areas where we have considerable experience* (Berk, 2010). Research indicates that the thinking of nearly half of all college students isn't formal operational in areas outside their majors (Wigfield, Eccles, & Pintrich, 1996). Many individuals, including adults, never reach the stage of formal operations in a number of content domains.

This creates a dilemma, particularly for those of you who are planning to teach in middle, junior high, and high schools, because understanding numerous topics—and particularly those in high schools—requires formal operational thinking. It was clear that Karen's students' thinking was not formal operational with respect to *density*. Further, while *centering* is viewed as characteristic of young children's thinking, we see it in older students and even adults. Karen's students were eighth graders, but they centered on the "thickness" of cooking oil and concluded that it's more dense than water, and many adults do the same.

These findings have important implications for those of us in middle schools, junior highs, high schools, and even universities. Many of our students come to these settings without the concrete experiences needed to think at the level of abstraction often required. Knowing this, we provide concrete experiences for them, as Karen did with her eighth graders. The many examples that we include in discussions of the topics presented in this book are our efforts to provide you with the concrete experiences needed to understand educational psychology.

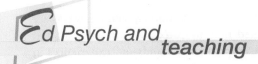

Applying Piaget's Theory with Your Students

Piaget's theory suggests that you keep the developmental needs of your students in mind as you design and implement instruction. The following guidelines can help you in your efforts to apply this understanding with your students.

1. Provide concrete experiences that represent abstract concepts and principles.
2. Help students link the concrete representations to the abstract idea.
3. Use social interaction to help students verbalize and refine their developing understanding.
4. Design learning experiences as developmental bridges to more advanced stages of development.

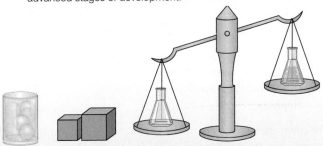

Let's review Karen's work to see how she applied these guidelines in her teaching. She applied the first two with her demonstrations of the concept *density*. For instance, she showed students the cotton balls in the cup, the blocks, and the balance with the water and oil, and they discussed screens and population density.

Karen didn't simply demonstrate the concept and then explain it, however. She combined the examples and demonstrations with detailed discussion. Without it, Calvin, for example, probably wouldn't have been able to conclude that less dense materials float on materials that are more dense. "You could almost see the wheels turning," as Karen described it. In leading this discussion, Karen applied the third guideline.

Her discussion and the students' increased understanding then prepared them to understand additional concepts such as population density, buoyancy, and flotation. Armed with this increased understanding, they are better prepared to explain advanced ideas such as hot air balloons and massive oil tankers. These bridges applied the fourth guideline.

Evaluating Piaget's Theory

As with all theories, Piaget's work has both critics and supporters. Let's look at them, beginning with some of the criticisms.

- Piaget underestimated the abilities of young children. Abstract directions and requirements cause children to fail at tasks they can do under simpler, more realistic conditions (Siegler, 2006).
- Piaget overestimated the abilities of older learners. As you saw in our discussion of student thinking, many middle and high school students are not formal operational thinkers (Flavell et al., 2002).
- Children's logical abilities depend more strongly on prior knowledge and experience in a specific area than Piaget suggested (Alexander, 2006).
- Piaget's descriptions of stages don't adequately describe the changes for all types of tasks (Fischer & Bidell, 2006; Siegler, 2006). For example, the development of concrete operations typically begins with conservation of mass, proceeds through a range of other tasks, and ends with conservation of volume. Instead of discrete stages, many development psychologists now think that general developmental trends best describe the patterns of cognitive development (Halford & Andrews, 2006; Rogoff, 2003).

- Piaget's work was essentially context free and failed to adequately consider the influence of culture on development (M. Cole, Cole, & Lightfoot, 2005; Rogoff, 2003). (We examine the role of culture in development in our discussion of Lev Vygotsky's work in the next section.)

Despite these shortcomings, Piaget's work has been enormously influential. For instance, educators now see learning as an active process in which learners construct their own knowledge, and Piaget strongly contributed to this view.

Piaget's work has also influenced the curriculum (Tanner & Tanner, 2007). Lessons are now organized with concrete experiences presented first, followed by more abstract and detailed ideas. His influence is also evident in the emphasis on "hands-on" experiences in science, in children writing about their own experiences in language arts, and in students beginning social studies topics by studying their own neighborhoods, cities, states, country, and finally those of other nations.

Although some of the specifics of Piaget's theory are now criticized, his emphasis on experience and his idea that learners construct their own knowledge remain unquestioned. He continues to have an enormous influence on curriculum and instruction in this country.

Current Views of Cognitive Development

Neo-Piagetian theory. A theory of cognitive development that accepts Piaget's stages but uses the acquisition of specific processing strategies to explain movement from one stage to the next.

Piaget did his work many years ago, and more recent research has built on and refined his theory. For instance, **neo-Piagetian theory** uses the acquisition of specific information-processing strategies to explain movement from one stage to the next as an alternative to Piaget's global stages (Siegler, 2006). To illustrate this perspective, look at the following list for 15 seconds, cover it up, and see how many items you can remember.

apple	bear	cat	grape
hammer	pear	orange	cow
chair	sofa	chisel	lamp
saw	table	elephant	pliers

Most adults organize the list into categories such as furniture, fruit, tools, and animals, and use the categories to remember specific items (Pressley & Hilden, 2006). Young children tend to use less efficient strategies such as repeating items verbatim. Their ability to gradually begin using more efficient strategies marks an advance in development.

Neo-Piagetian theory also emphasizes the important role that *working memory*, the part of our memory system that holds small amounts of information while we process and attempt to make sense of it, plays in development. As children develop, their working memory capacity increases, which allows them to think about more items of information simultaneously (Case, 1992, 1998).

check your understanding

2.1 The hands-on activities that we see in today's classrooms are applications of Piaget's theory. Explain specifically how hands-on activities apply his theory.

2.2 Use the concepts *centration, transformation,* and *reversibility* to explain why preoperational children don't "conserve" number and mass in the coins and clay tasks.

2.3 Read the following vignette, and explain how it illustrates the concepts *accommodation, assimilation development, equilibrium, experience, organization,* and *scheme.*

You work with the Windows operating system, and you're comfortable performing a variety of operations.

Then, you buy a mini laptop that uses a Linux operating system. Initially, you struggle to use the system, but with some study and practice, you are now able to use the Linux system quite acceptably, and you're even finding that you can learn new operations on it quickly.

To receive feedback for these questions, go to Appendix A.

Classroom connections

Promoting Cognitive Development in Classrooms Using Piaget's Theory

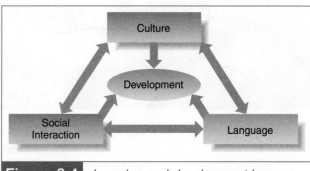

1. Concrete experiences are essential to cognitive development. Provide concrete examples, particularly when abstract concepts are first introduced.

   ■ **Elementary:** A first-grade teacher begins her unit on animals by taking her students to the zoo, and she uses craft sticks with beans glued on them to represent groups of 10 in math.

   ■ **Middle School:** A geography teacher draws lines on a beach ball to represent latitude and longitude. He initially uses the ball so his students aren't distracted by the detail on a globe.

   ■ **High School:** An American government teacher involves his students in a simulated trial to provide a concrete example of the American court system.

2. Social interaction contributes to cognitive development. Use interaction to assess students' development and expose them to more advanced thinking.

   ■ **Elementary:** After completing a demonstration on light refraction, a fifth-grade science teacher asks students to describe their understanding of what they see. He encourages the students to ask questions of each other.

   ■ **Middle School:** An English teacher has her students discuss different perspectives about a character's motives in a novel they've read.

   ■ **High School:** A geometry teacher asks students to explain their reasoning as they demonstrate proofs at the chalkboard. She requires the students to clarify their explanations when their classmates are confused.

3. Development is advanced when learning tasks stretch the developmental capabilities of learners. Provide your students with developmentally appropriate practice in reasoning.

   ■ **Elementary:** A kindergarten teacher gives children in pairs a variety of geometric shapes, asks the students to group the shapes, and then has the pairs explain their grouping while he represents them on a flannel board.

   ■ **Middle School:** An algebra teacher has her students factor this polynomial expression: $m^2 + 2m + 1$. She then asks, "If no 2 appeared in the middle term, would the polynomial still be factorable?"

   ■ **High School:** A history class concludes that people often emigrate for economic reasons. Their teacher asks, "Consider an upper-class family in Mexico. Would they be likely to immigrate to the United States?" The class uses this and other hypothetical cases to examine the generalizations they've formed.

Lev Vygotsky's Sociocultural Theory of Cognitive Development

Piaget viewed developing children as busy and self-motivated individuals who—on their own—explore, form, and test ideas with their experiences.

Lev Vygotsky, a Russian psychologist, provided an alternative view, a **sociocultural theory of development,** which emphasizes the role of social interaction, language, and culture on the child's developing mind (Vygotsky, 1978, 1986). These relationships are outlined in Figure 2.4 and discussed in the sections that follow.

Learning and Development in a Cultural Context

To begin our study of Vygotsky's theory, let's look at two short case studies. As you read them, focus on the social interaction and use of language in each, and consider how culture influences the process.

> Suzanne is reading *The Little Engine That Could* to her 5-year-old daughter, Perri, who sits on her lap. "I think I can, I think I can," she reads enthusiastically from the story.

| **Figure 2.4** | Learning and development in a cultural context |

Culture → Development ← Social Interaction ← Language

Sociocultural theory of development. A theory of cognitive development that emphasizes the influence of social interactions and language, embedded within a cultural context, on cognitive development.

"Why do you think the little engine kept saying, 'I think I can, I think I can'?" Suzanne asks as they talk about the events in the story.

"We need to try . . . and try . . . and try," Perri finally says hesitantly and with some prompting.

Sometime later, Perri is in school, working on a project with two of her classmates.

"I don't get this," her friend Dana complains. "It's too hard."

"No, we can do this if we keep trying," Perri counters. "We need to work a little harder."

Limok and his father look out and see a fresh blanket of snow on the ground.

"Ahh, beautiful," his father observes. "Iblik, the best kind of snow for hunting, especially when it's sunny."

"What is iblik?" Limok wonders.

"It is the soft, new snow; . . . no crystals," his father responds, picking up a handful and demonstrating how it slides easily through his fingers. "The seals like it. They come out and sun themselves. Then, we only need the spear. Our hunting will be good today."

Sometime later, as Limok and his friend Osool hike across the ice, Limok sees a fresh blanket of snow covering the landscape.

"Let's go back and get our spears," Limok says eagerly. "The seals will be out and easy to find today."

> Vygotsky believed that development is a direct result of social interaction.

Cognitive tools. The concepts and symbols (numbers and language) together with the real tools that allow people to think, solve problems, and function in a culture.

Internalization. The process through which learners incorporate external, society-based activities into internal cognitive processes.

Social Interaction and Development

Vygotsky (1978, 1986) believed that social interaction directly promotes development. To see how, let's look again at Perri's and Limok's experiences. First, for example, as she and her mother talked, Perri learned about perseverance, and Limok learned about hunting as he interacted with his father. Vygotsky would say that their thinking developed as a direct result of this interaction.

Second, the interactions were between the children and a *more knowledgeable other*, and as a result, the children developed understanding that they wouldn't have been able to acquire on their own. This understanding exists in the form of **cognitive tools,** the concepts and symbols (numbers and language) together with the real tools that allow people to think, solve problems, and function in a culture. For example, the Yu'pik people, who live in the Bering Sea just west of Alaska, have 99 different ways to describe ice. There are concepts describing wavy ice, shore fast ice, small cakes of ice, and thin ice overlapped like shingles (Block, 2007). These concepts help them function in their culture, just as concepts, such as freedom of speech and managing money, together with real tools, such as computers and the Internet, help us function in ours.

Vygotsky suggested that children need not reinvent the knowledge of a culture on their own; rather, this knowledge has accumulated over thousands of years and should be appropriated (internalized) through social interaction (Leont'ev, 1981). **Internalization** is the process through which learners incorporate external, society-based ideas into internal cognitive structures.

> Every function in the child's cultural development appears twice: first, on the social level, and later on the individual level; first between people . . . and then inside the child. . . . This applies

equally to voluntary attention, to logical memory, and to the formation of concepts. All the higher functions originate as actual relationships between individuals. (Vygotsky, 1978, p. 57)

Perri and Limok both internalized cultural knowledge; Perri learned about perseverance, which is valued in our culture, and Limok learned about the conditions for good hunting. Later, they applied their understanding in a new context. Perri, for example, encouraged Dana, who wanted to quit, to keep trying, and Limok recognized the conditions for good hunting as he and Osool were hiking across the ice. Incorporating understanding into a new context marks an advance in development.

Finally, Perri and Limok were active participants in the interactions. The concept of *activity* is essential in sociocultural theory (Roth & Lee, 2007), and Vygotsky believed that children learn through active involvement with more knowledgeable people.

Language and Development

Social interaction requires the use of language, and sociocultural theory suggests that language plays three important roles in development. First, it gives learners access to knowledge others already possess. Second, as you saw in the previous section, it's a *cognitive tool* that people use to help make sense of their experiences. For example, when Limok learned *iblik*, he didn't just learn the word and how to pronounce it; he also learned that it is soft, fresh, crystal-free snow and something that increases the likelihood of a successful hunt. This is related to the questions we ask in the adjacent "Ed Psych and You." The ability to put our understanding into words marks an advance in both our understanding and development, and it has important implications for us as teachers. We should encourage our students to use language to describe their understanding, and we should guide them in this process. This aids both their thinking and their language skills. Third, language is a means for regulating and reflecting on our own thinking (Winsler & Naglieri, 2003). Let's look at this process in more detail.

Private Speech and Self-Regulation

We all talk to ourselves; we grumble when we're frustrated, and we talk ourselves through uncertain situations. "Oh, no, a flat tire. Now what? I haven't changed a tire in years. I'd better look up how to do it in the owner's guide."

Children also talk to themselves. During free play, for example, you will often hear them muttering to no one in particular, and if you listen closely, you'll notice that they talk as they attempt to complete various tasks. Vygotsky believed this free-floating speech is the precursor of internal, **private speech,** self-talk that guides thinking and action. Private speech provides children with a tool they can use to examine their thinking, help with problem solving and other higher order functions, and control emotions and actions, all of which mark the beginnings of self-regulation.

Private speech provides an *executive function*, the process of monitoring our thoughts and steering them in productive channels, which become increasingly important as we learn complex ideas and solve sophisticated problems. For example, it forms the foundation for cognitive skills such as remembering ("If I repeat the number, I'll be able to remember it") and problem solving ("Let's see, what kind of answer is the problem asking for?") (Winsler & Naglieri, 2003).

As development advances, private speech becomes silent and internalized but remains important for cognitive functioning. Children who use private speech achieve more than their peers, enjoy learning more, and learn complex tasks more effectively than those who don't (Emerson & Miyake, 2003). The absence of private speech, which

talking it out aloud

Private speech. Self-talk that guides thinking and action.

helps monitor learning during reading, math, and complex thinking in other areas, may also be a factor in the problems encountered by students with learning disabilities (Friend, 2011).

Culture and Development

In Vygotsky's sociocultural theory, culture provides the context in which development occurs (Glassman, 2001). The role of culture was illustrated most concretely in the example with Limok and his father. As they interacted, they used the term *iblik*, a concept unique to their culture that provided a cognitive tool they used for both thinking and communication. The same is true for all learners. Perri's development, for instance, was influenced by Suzanne's work ethic, a factor prominent in our culture.

Zone of Proximal Development

Zone of proximal development. A range of tasks that an individual cannot yet do alone but can accomplish when assisted by the guidance of others.

As you saw earlier, children benefit from the experience of interacting with a more knowledgeable other. However, not all forms of interaction are equally effective. A learner benefits most from interaction when working in his **zone of proximal development,** a range of tasks that an individual cannot yet do alone but can accomplish when assisted by others (Glassman & Wang, 2004). Vygotsky (1978) described it as,

> . . . the distance between the actual developmental level as determined by independent problem solving and the level of potential development as determined through problem solving under adult guidance or in collaboration with more capable peers. (p. 86)

Learners have a zone of proximal development for each task they're expected to master, and they must be in the zone to benefit from assistance.

Scaffolding: Interactive Instructional Support

Scaffolding. Assistance that helps children complete tasks they cannot complete independently.

More knowledgeable others, most commonly parents and teachers, play essential roles in helping learners progress through the zone of proximal development for each task they are attempting. For example, as small children learn to walk, their parents often walk behind them, holding onto their hands as they take their tentative steps. As children gain confidence, parents hold only one hand, and later, let the children walk on their own. This help illustrates the concept of **scaffolding,** which is assistance that helps children complete tasks they cannot complete independently (Puntambekar & Hübscher, 2005).

Just as toddlers' development with respect to walking is advanced by their parents' support, learners' development is enhanced by their teachers' support (Rogoff, 2003; Lutz, Guthrie, & Davis, 2006). Without this support, development is impaired. It is important to note, however, that effective scaffolding provides only enough support to allow learners to progress on their own. Doing tasks for learners actually can delay development. Modeling and questioning are two of the most important forms of scaffolding. Our "Ed Psych and Teaching: Applying Vygotsky's Theory" feature provides a concrete illustration of this process.

what do you do when that doesn't work?

Ed psych and teaching

Applying Vygotsky's Theory with Your Students

As with Piaget's work, Vygotsky's theory has important implications for your teaching. The following guidelines can help you apply his ideas in your classroom.

1. Embed learning activities in culturally authentic contexts.
2. Involve students in social interactions, and encourage students to use language to describe their developing understanding.
3. Create learning activities that are in learners' zones of proximal development.
4. Provide instructional scaffolding to assist learning and development.

Let's see how Jeff Malone, a seventh-grade teacher, uses these guidelines as he works with his students.

Jeff begins his math class by passing out two newspaper ads for the same iPod. Techworld advertises "The lowest prices in town"; Complete Computers says, "Take an additional 15% off our already low prices."

Jeff then asks, "So, where would you buy your iPod?"

When the students disagree, Jeff asks, "How can we find out?"

After additional discussion, the students decide they need to find the price with the 15% discount.

Jeff reviews decimals and percentages and then puts students into groups of three and gives them two problems. Here is the first one:

A store manager has 45 video games in his inventory. Twenty-five are out of date, so he puts them on sale. What percent of the video games are on sale?

As he moves around the room, he watches the progress of one group—Sandra, Javier, and Stewart. Sandra zips through the problems. Javier knows that a fraction is needed, but he struggles to compute the decimal, and Stewart doesn't know how to begin.

"Let's talk about how we compute percentages in problems like this," Jeff says, kneeling in front of the group. "Sandra, explain how you did the first problem."

Sandra begins, "Okay, the problem asks what percent of the video games are on sale. First, I thought, how can I make a fraction? . . . Then I made a decimal out of it and then a percent. . . . So here's what I did first," and she then demonstrates how she solved the problem.

"Okay, then let's try this one," Jeff then says, pointing to the second problem.

Joseph raised gerbils to sell to the pet store. He had 12 gerbils and sold 9 to the pet store. What percentage did he sell?

"The first thing," Jeff continues, "I need to find out is what fraction he sold. Why do I need to find a fraction? . . . Javier?"

". . . So we can make a decimal and then a percent."

"Good," Jeff smiles. "What fraction did he sell? . . . Stewart?"

". . . 9 . . . 12ths."

"Excellent. Now, Javier, how might we make a decimal out of the fraction?"

". . . Divide the 12 into the 9," Javier responds hesitantly.

"Good," and he watches Javier get .75. Stewart also begins hesitantly, and then begins to grasp the idea.

After the groups have finished the review problems, Jeff calls the class back together and has some of the other students explain their solutions. When they struggle to put their explanations into words, Jeff asks questions that guide both their thinking and their descriptions.

He then returns to the iPod problem and asks them to apply their knowledge of percentages to it.

Now let's look at Jeff's attempts to apply the guidelines. He applied the first when he began the lesson with a problem that was real for students. iPods are a part of our culture, and shopping is an activity not only familiar but important to middle school students, so his problem was culturally authentic.

Second, his students were involved in social interaction, both with him and each other, and they used language to explain their developing understanding. Jeff then applied the third guideline by conducting his learning activity within each student's zone of proximal development. To illustrate this idea, let's look again at his work with Sandra, Javier, and Stewart, each of whom was at a different developmental level. Sandra could solve the problem without assistance, so Jeff asked her to explain her solution, which is a more advanced task. The task was within Javier's zone of proximal development, because he was able to solve the problems with Jeff's help. But Stewart's zone was below the task, so Jeff had to adapt his instruction to find the zone for him. Stewart didn't initially know how to attack the problem, but with assistance he found the fraction of the gerbils that had been sold to the pet store. By asking Stewart to identify the fraction, Jeff adapted his instruction to find the zone for this task and, as a result of this scaffolding, promoted Stewart's development.

Jeff's instruction seems quite simple, but it was, in fact, very sophisticated. By observing and listening to the students, Jeff assessed their current understanding and then adapted the learning activity so it was within each student's zone of proximal development.

Finally, Jeff applied the fourth guideline by providing scaffolding for Javier and Stewart with his questioning. And, he provided only enough support to ensure that they made progress on their own. Effective scaffolding adjusts instructional requirements to learners' capabilities and levels of performance (Puntambekar & Hübscher, 2005). The relationship between the students' zones of proximal development and the scaffolding Jeff provided is illustrated in Figure 2.5.

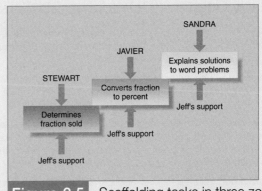

Figure 2.5 Scaffolding tasks in three zones of proximal development

Piaget's and Vygotsky's Views of Cognitive Development

Similarities and differences exist in Piaget's and Vygotsky's perspectives on cognitive development. For example, both views are grounded in the widely accepted idea that learners, instead of passively receiving knowledge from others, actively construct it for themselves. They differ, however, in how the process occurs. Piaget believed that learners construct knowledge essentially on their own, whereas Vygotsky believed that learners first socially construct knowledge and then individually internalize it.

They also differ in their views of the role of language and social interaction in development. For Piaget they are mechanisms for disrupting equilibrium, and people then—individually—reconstruct their understanding, reestablish equilibrium, and development advances. Vygotsky, in contrast, believed that language and social interaction directly advance development (Rogoff, 2003).

The two theories also differ on the role that culture plays in cognitive development (Rogoff, 2003; Siegler & Alibali, 2005). In many respects Piaget ignored culture, viewing development as a universal process that occurs outside of any particular culture. Vygotsky believed that culture provides the cognitive tools that children use to function within their cultures, and all development occurs in a cultural context.

Perhaps most important, both views suggest that we should limit our use of lecturing and explaining and instead use instructional strategies that actively involve students in learning activities. We examine ways to do this in Chapter 6.

---

check your understanding

3.1 You're a math teacher. What does the discussion in the section entitled "Language and Development" suggest your instruction should include as students study math?

3.2 In mainstream American culture, the concept of ice is relatively simple. In contrast, the Yu'pik people have 99 different concepts for ice. Use Vygotsky's theory to explain why this difference exists. How does this difference relate to learner development?

3.3 You are unsuccessfully trying to learn a new word processing program. A friend comes over. You do fine when she helps, but after she leaves, you again run into problems. Explain the difference between your zone of proximal development and your friend's zone. How does this difference relate to development?

To receive feedback for these questions, go to Appendix A.

Classroom connections

Promoting Cognitive Development in Classrooms with Vygotsky's Work

1. Cognitive development occurs within the context of meaningful, culturally embedded tasks. Use authentic tasks as organizing themes for your instruction.

   ■ **Elementary:** A second-grade teacher teaches bar graphing by having students graph the different transportation modes that students in the class use to get to school.

   ■ **Middle School:** A science teacher structures a unit on weather by having her students observe the temperature, barometric pressure, and relative humidity; record and graph the data; and compare the actual weather to that forecasted in the newspaper.

   ■ **High School:** Before a national election, an American government teacher has his students poll their parents and students around the school. Students then have a class election, compare their findings with national results, and discuss differences.

2. Scaffolding is instructional support that assists learners as they progress through their zones of proximal development. Provide enough scaffolding to ensure student success as they progress through each zone.

   ■ **Elementary:** When her students are first learning to print, a kindergarten teacher initially gives them dotted outlines of letters and paper with half lines for gauging letter size. As students become more skilled, she removes these aids.

   ■ **Middle School:** A science teacher helps her students learn to prepare lab reports by doing an experiment with the whole class and writing the report as a class activity. Students use it as a model for writing their own reports.

- **High School:** An art teacher begins a unit on perspective by sharing his own work and displaying works from other students. As students work on their own projects, he provides individual feedback and asks the students to discuss how perspective contributes to each drawing. Later they can use perspective effectively on their own.

3. Vygotsky believed social interaction to be a major vehicle for cognitive development. Structure classroom tasks to encourage student interaction.

- **Elementary:** After fifth-grade students complete writing products, their teacher has them share their assignments with each other. To assist them in the process, she provides them with focusing questions that students use to discuss their work.

- **Middle School:** An English teacher uses cooperative learning groups to discuss the novel the class is studying. The teacher asks each group to respond to a list of prepared questions. After students discuss the questions in groups, they share their perspectives with the whole class.

- **High School:** Students in a high school biology class work in groups to prepare for exams. Before each test, the teacher provides an outline of the content covered, and each group is responsible for creating one question on each major topic.

Developmentally appropriate practice

Promoting Cognitive Development with Learners at Different Ages

As you saw in the sections describing Piaget's and Vygotsky's theories, developmental differences have important implications for the way we teach. We examine these implications here.

Working with Students in Early Childhood Programs and Elementary Schools

Preoperational and concrete operational thinkers are capable of learning a great many concepts, but they need concrete examples that connect abstract ideas to the real world. Those of you who teach early childhood and elementary students should use concrete experiences like squares of candy bars to illustrate fractions, real crabs to demonstrate exoskeletons in animals, and experiences in their neighborhoods to illustrate the concept of *community*.

Elementary students need continual scaffolding to help them progress through their zones of proximal development for each new skill. Provide enough assistance to ensure success, and then reduce scaffolding as development advances.

Working with Students in Middle Schools

Cognitive development varies considerably among students at this age. Some will understand abstract ideas quickly, while others will struggle. Assess frequently to ensure that your instruction is within each student's zone of proximal development. Don't assume that lack of questions means that all students understand an idea.

Though middle school students are chronologically on the border of formal operations, their thinking remains largely concrete operational. As a result, they still need the concrete experiences that make abstract concepts meaningful, such as Karen Johnson provided for her eighth graders when they struggled with the concept *density*.

Middle school students continue to need a great deal of scaffolding when working with topics that are becoming increasingly abstract, such as in prealgebra and algebra. And, the more practice they get with putting their ideas into words, the more effective their learning.

Working with Students in High Schools

Though high school students are chronologically at the stage of formal operations, the ability to think in the abstract depends on their prior knowledge and experiences. When new concepts are introduced, high school students still need concrete examples. Lecture as a teaching method, though widely used, is less effective than instruction that promotes interaction and discussion.

The social dimension of learning assumes a powerful role for high school students; how they look and what other people think of them is very important. They like to socialize, so periodically using small-group work can be effective. Small-group work can easily become a simple gab session, however, so it must be carefully monitored.

This discussion helps answer the third question we asked at the beginning of the chapter: "How will your understanding of the way students think increase your effectiveness as a teacher?" Because you know, for example, that students' thinking depends on their experiences, you will provide as many rich experiences as possible for your students, regardless of the grade level or content area you teach. Also, for those of you planning to be middle or high school teachers, because you realize that the thinking of most students at these levels continues to be concrete, you will initially provide them with the concrete experiences necessary to help them make the transition to abstract thinking. And you will be a more effective teacher as a result.

Technology, Learning, and Development: Is Technology Interfering with Cognitive Development?

Throughout this chapter we've emphasized the importance of experience in cognitive development. As we've moved into the 21st century, technology is providing an increasing amount of this experience, and some experts wonder if it is interfering with healthy cognitive development. For example, in *The Dumbest Generation*, Mark Bauerlein (2008) questions whether our dependence on computers is making us less able to function in the real world. Nicholas Carr (2010) in *The Shallows* goes further, suggesting that, as a result of the Internet, we are more distractible and less able to concentrate on important ideas. Both authors suggest that technology is literally rewiring our brains. "With the exception of alphabets and number systems, the Net may well be the single most powerful mind-altering technology that has ever come into general use" (Carr, 2010, p. 116).

Let's examine these concerns more closely. In *The Shallows*, Carr argues that the amount and accessibility of information on the Internet encourage people to examine ideas superficially, and this shallow processing is having negative effects on our cognitive development. He cautions, ". . . when we start using the Web as a substitute for personal memory, bypassing inner processes of consolidation, we risk emptying our minds of their riches" (Carr, 2010, p. 192). Could easy access to computers actually have an adverse effect on our students' thinking and cognitive development?

Some research suggests that the answer to the question is yes, and it raises some thorny questions. For example, three studies found that the development of computer skills was the only significant educational benefit that resulted from students being supplied with home computers. Achievement in math, language arts, and writing actually declined in some instances, especially for low-income students. Instead of using the computers to access information and provide study aids, kids were instead using them to play video games and socialize (Stock & Fisman, 2010; Stross, 2010).

Not all experts share this pessimistic view of technology's effects on learning and development. Steven Pinker (2007, 2010), a Harvard psychologist, believes that the Internet, when used wisely, can be a valuable resource. In addition, research suggests that viewing children's educational programs is associated with gains in early literacy and math skills as well as academic success in the elementary grades. However, other research suggests that the more time children spend watching prime-time shows and cartoons, the less time they spend reading and interacting with others and the poorer their academic skills (Ennemoser & Schneider, 2007).

Technology supporters also point to the *Flynn Effect*, named after the researcher who discovered it, which concludes that average intelligence test scores have been rising steadily since intelligence testing first began in the early 1900s (Flynn, 1999). Experts believe that exposure to stimulating environments, including technologies like television and the Internet, are contributing factors in this trend (Nettelbeck & Wilson, 2010).

So, is technology interfering with cognitive development? As with many questions about teaching and learning, the answer isn't a simple yes or no. For example, the Internet is, without question, a phenomenal source of information. As we often joke, "You can find anything on Google." On the other hand, used improperly, such as spending inordinate amounts of time playing video games or corresponding on Facebook, instead of studying, is indeed likely to detract from learning and development.

One clear message exists. Merely exposing our students to technology won't produce learning, and it may even detract from it. As with all learning activities and tools, clear learning objectives and careful planning are essential if students are to derive maximum benefit from technology. And we need to work closely with parents to help them understand that technology must be used appropriately to contribute to learning and development.

Some critics believe that too much time spent with technology is interfering with cognitive development.

Language Development

A miracle occurs in kids in their early years. Born with limited ability to communicate, 6-year-olds know between 8,000 and 14,000 words, and by the sixth grade, their vocabulary has expanded to 80,000 (Biemiller, 2005). Perhaps more important, they can use the words to read, talk, and write about the ideas they are studying.

Understanding how language develops is important for three reasons. First, language is the foundation for reading and writing, essential tools for learning. Second, language is a catalyst for all forms of cognitive development; it's the vehicle students use to think and talk about the cognitive changes they're experiencing (Hiebert & Kamil, 2005). Third, language provides a tool for social and personal development, as you'll see in Chapter 3.

Theories of Language Development

Theories of language development differ, and these differences reflect varying emphases experts place on the roles heredity and environment play in development.

Nativist theory, for example, emphasizes heredity and suggests that all humans are genetically wired to learn language. Noam Chomsky (1972, 2006), the father of nativist theory, proposed that an innate, genetically controlled **language acquisition device (LAD)** predisposes children to learn the rules governing language. When children are exposed to language, the LAD analyzes patterns for the rules of grammar—such as the subject after a verb when asking a question—that govern a language.

Other theories more strongly emphasize the influence of the environment. Behaviorism, for instance, suggests that children learn language through reinforcement and practice (Skinner, 1953, 1957). For example, a 2-year-old picks up a ball and says, "Baa." Mom smiles

Nativist theory. A theory of language development that suggests all humans are genetically wired to learn language.

Language acquisition device (LAD). A genetically controlled set of processing skills that enables children to understand and use the rules governing language.

Language development is facilitated by experience and the opportunities to practice language.

broadly and says, "Yes, ball! Good job!" Mom's "Good job!" reinforces the child's efforts, and over time, language is shaped. (We examine behaviorism in detail in Chapter 9.)

Social cognitive theory emphasizes the role of modeling, feedback, and children's imitation of adult speech (Bandura, 1986, 2001, Owens, 2008). For example,

"Give Daddy some cookie."

"Cookie, Dad."

"Good. Jacinta gives Daddy some cookie."

The father modeled an expression, Jacinta attempted to imitate it, and he expanded and refined it when he said, "Good. Jacinta gives Daddy some cookie."

Vygotsky's sociocultural theory provides another perspective. It suggests that children learn language by practicing it in their day-to-day interactions, and adults adjust their speech to operate within children's zones of proximal development. For instance, baby talk and *motherese* use simple words, short sentences, and voice inflections to provide linguistic scaffolding for young children. As their children's language skills advance, parents use bigger words and more complex sentences, which adjusts the process to each child's changing zone of proximal development (Berk, 2010).

Early Language Development

Language development begins in the cradle when adults say "Ooh" and "Aah" and "Such a smart baby!" to encourage the infant's gurgling and cooing. The first words, spoken between ages 1 and 2, are holophrases, one- and two-word utterances that carry as much meaning for the child as complete sentences. For example, "Mama car," means "That's Momma's car."

Children also gradually learn to use intonation and emphasis to convey meaning. For example, "Cookie," means "That's a cookie," but "Cookie!" says "I want a cookie." Differences in intonation signal the beginning of language use as a communication tool.

Overgeneralization. A language pattern that occurs when a child uses a word to refer to a broader class of objects than is appropriate.

Undergeneralization. A language pattern that occurs when a child uses a word too narrowly.

Two patterns emerge and continue with the child through later stages. **Overgeneralization** occurs when a child uses a word to refer to a broader class of objects than is appropriate, such as using the word *car* to also refer to buses and trucks. **Undergeneralization,** which is harder to detect, occurs when a child uses a word too narrowly, such as using "Kitty" for her own cat but not for cats in general (Gelman & Kalish, 2006). Both are normal aspects of language development. In most instances they're corrected through routine interactions, such as a parent saying, "No, that's a truck. See, it has more wheels and a big box on it," and "Oh, look. There's another kitty."

Young children bring to school a healthy and confident grasp of language and how it can be used to communicate with others. The importance of this foundation for learning in general, and particularly for reading and writing, can't be overstated (Tompkins, 2009).

Ed Psych and You

Look at these sentences:

They were too close to the door to close it.
The wind was too strong to wind up the sail.
The bandage was wound around the wound.

What is significant about these sentences, and what do they suggest about language development?

Language Development in the School Years

Cognitive and language development go hand in hand, and two aspects of language development are crucial for cognitive development: *vocabulary* and the *development of syntax and grammar*. We look at them next.

Developing Vocabulary

Before you read this chapter, you may not have understood terms such as *centration*, *object permanence*, and *zone of proximal development*, but hopefully you do now. The concepts represented by these terms are part of the knowledge base that helps you understand cognitive development, and the same is true for any area of study. In addition to subject-specific vocabulary, we also want our students to understand abstract concepts, such as *justice*, *truth*, and *beauty*, that broaden our views of the world and enrich our lives.

Elementary students enter school knowing approximately 10,000 words, but by the time they leave, they have mastered more than eight times that many (Waxman & Lidz, 2006)! They accomplish this prodigious feat in two ways. One is experience with explicit instruction that focuses on key concepts, a strategy widely used by teachers. Explicit instruction is valuable for learning terms that are unlikely to be acquired incidentally, and it's particularly important for abstract, complex, and technical terms with precise definitions (Reutzel & Cooter, 2008). (We use explicit instruction in this text with our "Important Concepts.")

Encountering words in context is a second way new terms are used, and this process relates to **semantics,** a branch of linguistics that examines the meanings of words. To illustrate the process, consider the questions in "Ed Psych and You" at the beginning of this section. In the sentence, "They were too close to the door to close it," the word *close* has two different meanings, and the meanings are determined by the context of the sentence. The other two sentences also contain words with different meanings, and the meanings are also determined by context. These examples illustrate the complexity of language development and help us understand why it's so demanding for young students.

> **Semantics.** A branch of linguistics that examines the meaning of words.

Syntax and Grammar

Vocabulary makes up the building blocks of language, but just as a house is more than a collection of bricks, language development is more than learning words. It also involves an understanding of **syntax,** the rules we use to create meaningful sentences. For example, "I do love you." and "Do I love you?" contain the identical words, but the meanings are very different because of syntax. Grammar, a subcategory of syntax which includes punctuation and capitalization, also aids communication.

> **Syntax.** The set of rules that we use to put words together into meaningful sentences.

Learning syntax and grammar proceeds slowly and with practice (Tomasello, 2006). During the school years children gradually learn more complex language constructions, and this development parallels other aspects of cognitive development. For instance, "Jackie paid the bill" and "She had asked him out" becomes "Jackie paid the bill because she had asked him out." The ability to use more complex sentences reflects the child's developing understanding of cause-and-effect relationships.

[handwritten margin note: Common connective]

Using Language to Learn

Language is the foundation for both learning and communication, and children typically develop the four language skills—*listening, speaking, reading, and writing*—in that order (Berk, 2010). Regardless of the order, however, they have one important feature in common: *They all depend on prior knowledge and experience* (Owens, 2008). When children have visited zoos, for example, listening or reading information about lions, elephants, and giraffes is much more meaningful, as is speaking and writing about them. The same is true for all topics. Now, let's look at these processes in more detail.

Listening. Listening is the first language skill that develops in children, and as all teachers know, students—and especially young ones—are not very good at it. They tend to think that good listening means sitting quietly, and they don't realize that it should be a cognitively active process where they think and ask questions about what they're hearing (McDevitt, Spivey, Sheehan, Lennon, & Story, 1990).

Speaking. Speaking is a naturally occurring process in most students that complements listening and provides a vehicle for organizing thoughts and sharing them with others. As with all language skills, effective speaking depends on background knowledge, but it also requires correct pronunciation and grammar, which is challenging for all students and particularly non-native English speakers (Peregoy & Boyle, 2008).

As with any skill, our ability to speak clearly improves with practice (Tomasello, 2006). In many classrooms, however, teachers do most of the talking, so students don't have many opportunities to practice speaking.

[handwritten note: and it can be a bad thing for them in the future when they must speak in a classroom or other public setting]

Reading. In about second or third grade, the emphasis shifts from *learning to read* to *reading to learn* (Reutzel & Cooter, 2008). As with listening, many students have a tendency to read passively, never realizing that they are understanding little of what they've read (Mayer, 2008). They need help in learning to ask themselves questions, such as, "What am I trying to learn here?" and "What parts of this information are most important?"

Writing. As all of us who have written papers can attest, writing is a cognitively demanding process, which helps us understand why it typically develops more slowly than listening, speaking, and reading.

Writing promotes language development in three ways. First, we can't write about what we don't understand, so it requires even more background knowledge than the other language skills (Cooper & Kiger, 2009). Second, because writing requires the organization of ideas, it requires us to be cognitively active and think deeply about a topic; it's virtually impossible to write passively. And third, because writing encourages us to think about our audience, it helps develop perspective taking, the ability to consider the thoughts and feelings of the reader, an important social skill.

We turn now to strategies for helping our students develop these important language skills.

Ed psych and teaching

Helping Your Students Develop Language Abilities

You can promote language development in your students in several ways:

Vocabulary Development

You can help your students learn vocabulary by emphasizing new terms during instruction, providing examples in context to illustrate the concepts represented by the terms, and encouraging your students to use the new vocabulary in discussions and other classroom activities (Reutzel & Cooter, 2008). For example, if students encounter the term *tarmac* in a story, you can show a picture of an airport, point out the location of the tarmac, and ask students to use the term in a sentence. Effective textbooks assist in the process by putting important concepts in bold print, providing definitions, and listing key concepts at the end of chapters.

Developing Grammar and Syntax

We can promote the development of grammar and syntax by modeling correct grammar and syntax and having our students practice in both speaking and writing. For instance, "Tanya and her," is a grammatically incorrect, but common, response to the question, "Who went downtown?"

When your students use incorrect grammar, you provide the correct response, such as, "Oh, you mean Tanya and she went downtown." Correction without criticism is particularly important for students who aren't native English speakers.

Using Language to Learn: Developing Listening and Reading Skills

We can help students who lack the prior knowledge needed to make listening and reading meaningful, by supplementing our lessons with demonstrations, pictures, and video clips. For example, simply showing students pictures of Native Americans hunting buffalo and pictures of their different dwellings makes listening or reading about their culture much more meaningful. Similarly, simply pushing a ball off a table to demonstrate the transfer from potential to kinetic energy makes reading a science book easier and more enjoyable.

You can also emphasize the importance of active listening, with frequent reminders such as, "Now, listen carefully, because we want to understand this idea." Also, encouraging students to ask questions and reminding them, when reading, to periodically stop and ask themselves if they understand what they've just read can help them develop their reading and listening skills.

Developing Speaking Abilities

To learn to speak effectively, students need practice, just like any other skill. When you ask questions, direct them to the whole class, give students time to think about and organize a response, and then call on an individual to respond. When they struggle, help them put their thoughts into words.

You can also supplement whole-class instruction with small-group work to provide students with additional practice with speaking. Small-group work, however, requires careful planning and monitoring to be sure that students stay on task. For example, using think-pair-share, you ask a question and then ask students to think about an answer and share it with a partner before responding to the whole class. Think-pair-share, where

students think about an answer to a question or problem and share it with a partner before responding to the teacher, is an effective way to combine the benefits of teacher-led discussions with opportunities for developing students' oral language skills.

Developing Students' Writing

Learning to write requires a great deal of practice, and the more your students practice, the better writers they will become. Preparing model paragraphs, short essays, and responses to questions, combined with displaying and analyzing examples of student work, are effective tools to help students develop their writing. Writing assignments that are short and integrated into regular lessons provide an effective way to teach content and to develop students' writing skills.

Language development, as with all forms of development, requires experience, and the suggestions we're offering are, in essence, different ways of providing these experiences for your students.

Exploring diversity

Language Development for Non-Native English Speakers

Ed Psych and You

Have you tried learning a foreign language? What parts of speech did you learn first? Did your understanding of English help you? Which—understanding the language when someone spoke, speaking it yourself, or reading it—was the hardest for you?

Nearly 15% of our school-age population comes from homes where English is not the native language, and this number is increasing (Pew Hispanic Center, 2011). More than half of these students are in the lower elementary grades, where they face the dual tasks of learning to read and write while they're learning a new language (Snow et al., 2005).

As with students in general, not all English language learners (ELs) are alike. Some live in households where books and newspapers are readily accessible, and parents regularly read to and speak with their children; others come from homes where both parents work, and opportunities for language development are limited, making the transition to English challenging (Snow & Kang, 2006).

Many of these children will retain their native language and become bilingual. This is an advantage. Bilingual children better understand the sounds words make, how languages work, and the role language plays in communication (Chen et al., 2004). Bilingual children also tend to perform better on tasks requiring advanced cognitive functions, such as intelligence tests and measures of creativity (Leung, Maddux, Galinsky, & Chiu, 2008).

Learning to pronounce words in a second language such as English is easier for young children than for older ones, especially if the second language is fundamentally different from the first. For example, it is much easier for a native Spanish speaker to learn English than it is for someone whose first language is Chinese. On the other hand, older students have a

greater knowledge of language and have mastered more learning strategies, making second language learning more efficient (Diaz-Rico & Weed, 2009). In short, students of all ages can learn a language when provided with the right kind of instruction.

Effective instruction for students who are ELs doesn't differ fundamentally from language development in general, so the suggestions we offered in "Ed Psych and Teaching: Helping Your Students Develop Language Abilities" also apply to second-language learners. Three additional factors are important, however. First, patience with children who struggle with English is essential. Impatience, and particularly criticism, can create an emotional barrier, making children feel that they are inferior and not welcome in school. Second, the more concrete you can be when promoting language development with second-language learners, the better. For example, when using the term *force,* actually demonstrating the concept, such as pushing a book across a desk, makes the term meaningful. And finally, all children need practice to develop their language skills, and this is especially important for ELs.

Take another look at the questions we asked in our "Ed Psych and You " feature at the beginning of this section. Like infants learning a first language, when we learn a new language, we typically learn nouns first, especially those that are concrete, such as *dog, car,* and *father.* And, just as when we learned our own language, the knowledge we've accumulated about words and how language works helps us in learning a second language.

When learning a second language, listening and reading are easier than speaking, so they commonly develop first. Keep this in mind when you work with your students who are ELs; their reluctance to respond in class may not reflect their knowledge of, or interest in, the topic you're discussing. It may just be due to the difficulty of putting thoughts into word in a second language.

check your understanding

4.1 A child is talking with his friend and says, "Mine is gooder." Which theory of language acquisition best explains the use of "gooder"?

4.2 Is the use of "gooder" an example of under- or overgeneralization? Explain.

4.3 How are vocabulary and syntax development different? Which is more important for school learning?

To receive feedback for these questions, go to Appendix A.

Classroom connections

Promoting Language Development in Classrooms

1. Language development depends on opportunities to hear and use language. Provide students with activities during which they can practice language in the classroom.

   ▪ **Elementary:** A fourth-grade teacher says to a student who has solved a problem involving the addition of fractions with unlike denominators, "Okay, explain to us exactly what you did. Be sure to include each of the terms we've been learning in your description."

   ▪ **Middle School:** An eighth-grade history teacher, in a study of the American Revolution, says to his class, "Now, go ahead and take a few moments to put into words the parallels we've discussed between the American, French, and Russian revolutions."

   ▪ **High School:** A physics teacher, in a discussion of force and acceleration, says, "Describe what we mean by the 'net force' operating on this object."

2. Language development requires that students practice in emotionally supportive environments. Create an emotional climate that makes students feel safe as they practice language.

   ▪ **Elementary:** When a third grader struggles to explain how he solved a problem, his teacher says, "That's okay. We all struggle to express ourselves. The more you practice, the better you'll get at it."

   ▪ **Middle School:** In response to snickers as a student struggles to describe the parallels in the American, French, and Russian revolutions, the teacher states sternly, "We listen politely when a classmate is trying to explain his or her thoughts. We're here to support each other."

   ▪ **High School:** In response to a student who says, "I know what 'net force' is, but I can't quite say it," the physics teacher says, "That's okay. We all struggle. Give it a try, and say as much as you can, and we'll take it from there."

3. Understanding teachers are an essential component of healthy language development. Provide scaffolding when students struggle with language.

   ▪ **Elementary:** When a fifth grader says, "I tried to find for these numbers and, . . ." as he struggles to explain how he found a lowest common denominator, his teacher offers, "You attempted to find the lowest common denominator?"

   ▪ **Middle School:** As the student hesitates in his attempts to describe differences in the American, Russian, and French revolutions, the history teacher says, "First describe one thing the three revolutions had in common."

   ▪ **High School:** In response to the student's struggles, the physics teacher says, "Go ahead and identify two forces that are acting on the block."

Developmentally appropriate practice

Promoting Language Development with Learners at Different Ages

Language is a foundation for understanding and communication regardless of learners' ages. Developmental differences exist however, as we discuss here.

Working with Students in Early Childhood Programs and Elementary Schools

If you're an elementary teacher, language development will be one of your most important goals. Active participation in both whole-group and small-group activities, together with writing about the topics they're learning, provides elementary students with practice that is essential for their development.

Sensitivity to individual differences is important when working with young children. For example, boys' language skills develop less rapidly than girls', and some cultural minorities may not be comfortable interacting with adults as conversation partners (Berk, 2010).

Questioning is one of the most useful tools that you have for promoting language development. When students struggle, you can provide prompts and model responses to questions. Elaborating on responses also provides an opportunity to model correct grammar and syntax as well as clarify content.

Young students' working memories are still developing, which limits their ability to understand complex directions (Nelson et al., 2006). Simplifying directions is important for these students.

Working with Students in Middle Schools

Social interaction becomes increasingly important for middle school students, which presents both opportunities and challenges for their teachers. When well organized, group work can provide opportunities to expose students to different perspectives and to develop their communication skills. Creating groups that are developmentally and culturally diverse provides students with opportunities to learn from each other.

Middle schoolers' listening skills are still developing, so writing definitions and other important ideas on the board or document camera is important.

Middle school students' skills with complex sentence structures and their understanding of figurative speech and metaphorical language are also developing. Jokes based on double meanings, such as "Hey, did you take a bath today? . . . Why, are you missing one?" provide opportunities to talk about language and its central role in communicating with each other (Berk, 2010, p. 317).

Working with Students in High Schools

High school students want to appear grown up and are sometimes hesitant to participate in whole-class activities, so explaining why you call on everyone as equally as possible is important.

Because high school students often want to hide the fact that they don't understand an idea, they are often reluctant to ask questions. So, the fact that no questions are asked doesn't necessarily mean that students understand what you're teaching. Questioning, particularly as a form of informal assessment, is important with these students. Their ability to answer gives you an indication of their understanding.

Providing high school students with practice in writing is important, regardless of your content area. It develops language and thinking skills, encourages deep understanding, and prepares them for college or the world of work, where the ability to write is essential. Despite extensive practice with texting, high school students need instruction in formal conventions of grammar, spelling, and punctuation, and practice with writing is even more important than it has been in the past (Pence & Justice, 2008). Like all of us, high school students get better at writing by practicing, so the more practice you provide, the better writers they'll become.

Summary

1. Describe development, and explain why understanding cognitive development is important for teachers.
   - Development describes the physical, cognitive, social, and emotional changes that occur in people as they grow from infancy to adulthood.
   - Principles of development suggest that development depends on both heredity and environment, that it is continuous and relatively orderly, and that learners develop at different rates.
   - Understanding development helps teachers adapt their instruction to meet the developmental needs and capabilities of their students.

2. Use concepts from Piaget's theory of intellectual development to explain both classroom and everyday events.
   - Concepts from Piaget's theory help explain why people want order and certainty in their lives, and how they adapt their thinking in response to new experiences.
   - According to Piaget, people organize their experience into schemes that help them make sense of their experiences and achieve equilibrium. New experiences are assimilated if they can be explained with existing schemes. Accommodation and a change in thinking are required if new experiences can't be explained with existing schemes.
   - Maturation and experiences with the physical and social world advance development.
   - As children develop, they progress through stages that describe general patterns of thinking, ranging from perceptual dominance in preoperational thinkers to the ability to think logically and hypothetically for formal operational thinkers.

3. Use Vygotsky's sociocultural theory to explain how language, culture, and instructional support influence learner development.
   - Vygotsky describes cognitive development as the interaction between social interaction, language, and culture.
   - Social interaction and language provide the mechanism and tools that help children develop understandings that they wouldn't be able to acquire on their own and advance their development.
   - Social interaction and language are embedded in a cultural context that uses the language of the culture as the mechanism for promoting development.

4. Use theories of language development to explain language patterns in children.
   - Behaviorism describes language development by suggesting that children are reinforced for demonstrating sounds and words, and social cognitive theory focuses on the imitation of language that is modeled.
   - Nativist theory suggests that children are genetically predisposed to language.
   - Sociocultural theory suggests that language is developed through scaffolded practice that occurs within children's zones of proximal development.
   - Children progress from an early foundation of one- and two-word utterances, ultimately to elaborate language that involves complex sentence structures.
   - Language development during the school years focuses on word meanings (semantic), grammar (syntactic) and using language to learn through listening, reading and writing.

Understanding Cognitive and Language Development: Preparing for Your Licensure Exam

Your licensure exam will include information related to cognitive and language development, and we include the following exercises to help you practice for the exam in your state. This book and these exercises will be a resource for you as you prepare for the exam.

In this chapter, you saw how Karen Johnson used her understanding of student development to help her students learn about density. Let's look now at Jenny Newhall, a first-grade teacher, who is working with her children in a lesson on the properties of air. Read the case study, and then answer the questions that follow.

Jenny gathers the children around her on the rug in front of a small table to begin her science lesson. After they're settled, she turns to a fishbowl filled with water and an empty glass and asks students to observe and describe them. She then says, "I'm going to put this glass upside down in the water. What's going to happen? What do you think? . . . Michelle?"

" . . . Water will go in the glass."

"No, it'll stay dry," Samantha counters.

Jenny then says, "Raise your hand if you think it will get water in it. . . . Okay, . . . raise your hand if you think it'll remain dry. . . . How many aren't sure? . . . Well, let's see if we can find out.

She has the students confirm that the glass is dry, and then has the students watch carefully as she pushes the inverted glass under the water, as shown here:

Jenny carefully pulls the glass out of the water, but the students don't agree about whether or not the glass is dry on the

inside, so she wads up a paper towel, pushes it to the bottom of the glass, and asks, "Now if water goes in the glass, what is the paper towel going to look like?"

The class agrees it will be wet and soggy.

The class watches as Jenny pushes the glass into the water again, pulls it back out, and says, "Okay, Marisse, come up here and check the paper towel and tell us whether it's wet or dry."

"Dry," Marisse says, after feeling the towel.

"Why did it stay dry? . . . What do you think, Jessica?"

"'Cause it's inside and the water is outside?"

"But why didn't the water go into the glass? What kept the water out? . . . Anthony?"

"A water seal."

"A water seal," Jenny repeats, fighting back a smile. Hmm. . . . There's all that water on the outside. How come it didn't go inside? . . . How can the towel stay dry?"

A quiet voice volunteers, "Because there's air in there."

"Air. . . . Is that what kept the water out?" Jenny asks.

"Well, earlier Samantha said that when she was swimming in a pool and put a glass under the water,

it stayed dry, but when she tipped it, it got wet inside. Now what do you think will happen if I put the glass under the water and tip it? . . . Devon?"

"It'll get wet."

Jenny removes the paper towel and returns the glass to the fishbowl.

"What's happening?" Jenny asks as she slowly tips the inverted glass, allowing some of the bubbles to escape. " . . . Andrea?"

"There are bubbles."

"Andrea, what were those bubbles made of?"

"They're air bubbles."

Jenny continues to tip the glass, allowing more air bubbles to escape, and asks again, "So, why did the towel stay dry?"

"The air kept the water out," several students respond in unison.

Jenny then divides the class into pairs, and the students use tubs of water, glasses, and paper towels to experiment on their own. After each student has a chance to try the activities, she again calls the children together, and they review and summarize what they have found.

Questions for **Case Analysis**

In answering these questions, use information from the chapter, and link your responses to specific information in the case.

1. At what level of cognitive development were Jenny's students likely to be? What evidence suggests that they were at that level?

2. How, specifically, did Jenny promote cognitive development in her students?

3. What did Jenny do that was essential for helping her students understand that air kept the water out of the glass, so the towel remained dry?

4. Did Jenny conduct the lesson in the students' zones of proximal development? Explain why you do or do not think so. What forms of scaffolding did Jenny provide? How effective was the scaffolding?

For feedback on these responses, go to Appendix B.

Your licensure exam will also include multiple-choice questions similar to those your instructor has given you on your quizzes and tests for this course.

Important **Concepts**

accommodation (p. 36)
assimilation (p. 35)
axons (p. 31)
centration (p. 39)
classification (p. 41)
cognitive development (p. 30)
cognitive tools (p. 46)
conservation (p. 39)
dendrites (p. 31)
development (p. 30)
egocentrism (p. 39)

equilibrium (p. 35)
internalization (p. 46)
language acquisition device
   (LAD) (p. 53)
maturation (p. 31)
nativist theory (p. 53)
neo-Piagetian theory
   (p. 44)
neurons (p. 31)
object permanence (p. 39)
overgeneralization (p. 54)

personal, social, and
   emotional development
   (p. 30)
physical development
   (p. 30)
private speech (p. 47)
reversibility (p. 39)
scaffolding (p. 48)
schemes (p. 35)
semantics (p. 55)
seriation (p. 41)

social experience (p. 37)
sociocultural theory of
   development (p. 45)
stages of development (p. 38)
synapses (p. 31)
syntax (p. 55)
transformation (p. 39)
transitivity (p. 41)
undergeneralization (p. 54)
zone of proximal
   development (p. 48)

Go to the Topic: Cognitive and Linguistic Development in the MyEducationLab (www.myeducation lab.com) for *Educational Psychology: Windows on Classrooms*, where you can:

- Find learning outcomes for Cognitive and Linguistic Development along with the national standards that connect to these outcomes.
- Complete Assignments and Activities that can help you more deeply understand the chapter content.
- Apply and practice your understanding of the core teaching skills identified in the chapter with the Building Teaching Skills and Dispositions learning units.
- Examine challenging situations and cases presented in the IRIS Center Resources.
- Access video clips of CCSSO National Teachers of the Year award winners responding to the question, "Why Do I Teach?" in the Teacher Talk section.
- See video examples included within the Study Plan that provide concrete and real-world illustrations of the topics presented in the chapter.
- Check your comprehension of the content covered in the chapter with the Study Plan. Here you will be able to take a chapter quiz, receive feedback on your answers, and then access Review, Practice, and Enrichment activities to enhance your understanding of chapter content.

MyEducationLab

chapter 3

Personal, Social, and Moral Development

chapteroutline

learningoutcomes

classroom applications

The following features help you apply the content of this chapter in your teaching.

*W*hen we teach, we obviously want our students to learn content and skills, such as the causes of the Revolutionary War and the ability to solve algebraic equations, but we also have other essential goals. We want them to develop a sense of emotional well-being, an ability to get along and work with others, and to be honest and fair. Keep these ideas in mind as you read the following case study, involving a discussion between two middle school teachers as they express their concerns about a student.

> "Ahh," Amanda Kellinger, an eighth-grade English teacher, sighs as she slides into a chair in the faculty lounge.
>
> "Tough day?" her friend, Larry, asks.
>
> "Yes, it's Sean again," Amanda nods. "I can't seem to get through to him. He jumps on other students for no apparent reason, and when I talk to him about it, he says some of them are 'out to get him.' He has a bad attitude about school in general, and when I talked with his mother, she said he's been a handful since birth. Another thing . . . I think it's affecting his academic work."
>
> "I know what you mean," Larry responds. "I had him for English last year. He was a tough one, very distant. At times he would almost open up to me, but then the wall would go up again. . . . And his older brother was so different, eager and cooperative, and he seemed to get along with everyone. . . . Same home, same situation."
>
> "Sean's a bright boy, too," Amanda continues, "I'd love to help him . . . if I can just figure out how."

We'll look back at this conversation as the chapter unfolds, but for now, think about these questions:

1. Is Amanda right? Will Sean's attitude affect his academic work?
2. How might we explain why Sean and his older brother are so different?
3. Why doesn't Sean get along with the other students?

An understanding of personal, social, and moral development can help us answer these and other questions about our students.

Personal development. Age-related changes in personality and the ways that individuals react to their environment.

Personal development refers to age-related changes in people's personality and the ways that individuals respond to their environments, **social development** describes the advances people make in their ability to interact and get along with others, and **moral development** describes advances in people's conceptions of right and wrong and prosocial traits such as honesty, respect for others, and the ability to control one's emotions.

Social development. The advances people make in their ability to interact and get along with others.

Moral development. Advances in people's conceptions of right and wrong, and prosocial behaviors and traits such as honesty, fairness, and respect for others.

These factors begin to answer our first question above. If Sean is consistent with patterns identified by research, Amanda's assessment is indeed accurate; his attitude will detract from his academic achievement. Personal, social, and moral development affect learning and satisfaction with school for all students, including those with exceptionalities (Milsom & Glanville, 2010; Smrtnik-Vitulic & Zupancic, 2010), and they often predict success and fulfillment in later life more accurately than does academic achievement (Obradovic, Burt, & Masten, 2010). These results have important implications for us all. Our jobs involve much more than teaching history, math, or literature. They include helping our students develop the personal, social, and moral characteristics that will help them develop into happy, productive adults. Ways of achieving these goals is our focus in this chapter.

Urie Bronfenbrenner, a psychologist at Cornell University, developed a theory that describes the factors influencing each of these forms of development. We examine his theory in the next section.

Bronfenbrenner's Bioecological Model of Development

Bronfenbrenner's bioecological model offers a comprehensive description of the factors influencing development (Bronfenbrenner & Morris, 2006). Individuals are at the center of Bronfenbrenner's model, and the *bio* in the title reflects genetic influences, such as health and body build. It also includes **temperament,** the relatively stable inherited characteristics that influence the way we respond to our social and physical environments. For example, temperament influences traits such as adventurousness, confidence, and happiness, and differences in individuals persist over time (O'Connor & McCartney, 2007). Siblings raised in the same environments often develop different personalities, and this helps us answer our second question above: "How might we explain why Sean and his older brother are so different?" Even though they were raised in the same family, their genetics resulted in different temperaments.

Temperament. The relatively stable inherited characteristics that influence the way we respond to social and physical stimuli.

Environmental Influences on Development

The *ecological* component in Bronfenbrenner's model suggests that a person's development is influenced by a complex set of systems in the environment, including family, peers, social institutions, such as churches and schools, and individuals' communities and cultures (Bronfenbrenner & Morris, 2006). These relationships are outlined in Figure 3.1. As you see in the figure, each system is nested in a larger system, and each layer is viewed as having a powerful impact on development (Berk, 2010). Let's look at these systems.

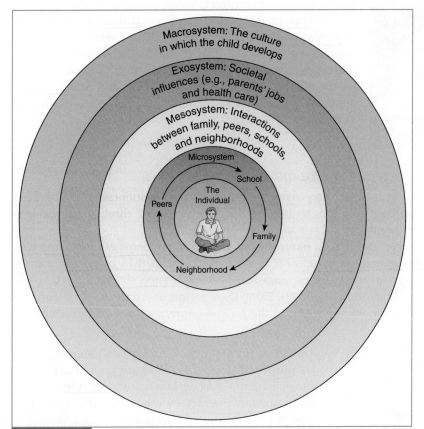

Figure 3.1   Bronfenbrenner's bioecological model of human development

Microsystem. In Bronfenbrenner's bioecological theory, the people and activities in a child's immediate surroundings.

The **microsystem,** the innermost level, is composed of the people and activities in the child's immediate surroundings, such as family, peers, neighborhood, and school (Weigel, Martin, & Bennett, 2005). Some neighborhoods, for example, are safe and nurturant, while others are dangerous and toxic. Similarly, schools can be caring and supportive or sterile and impersonal (Fauth, Roth, & Brooks-Gunn, 2007; Kozol, 2005).

Mesosystem. In Bronfenbrenner's model, the interactions and connections between the different elements of children's immediate settings.

The **mesosystem** consists of the interactions between the elements of the microsystem, and healthy development depends on how effectively the elements work together. For example, parents and schools are two important elements of the microsystem, and effective schools promote high levels of parental involvement (Epstein, 2001).

Exosystem. In bioecological theory, societal influences that affect both the micro- and mesosystems.

The **exosystem** includes societal influences, such as parents' jobs, school systems, and workplace conditions like health care that influence both the microsystem and mesosystem. For example, parents' jobs can affect the amount of time parents have to spend with their children, and wealthy school systems provide nurses, counselors, psychologists, and smaller class sizes.

Macrosystem. Bronfenbrenner's fourth level, which includes cultural influences on development.

The **macrosystem** is the culture in which a child develops, and it influences all the other systems. For example, some cultures focus on the individual and emphasize autonomy, whereas others focus more strongly on social influences and conformity.

Understanding Bronfenbrenner's model has important implications for us as teachers. For example, knowing that neighborhoods, the school system, and the community at large all influence student development, we attempt to involve people at these levels in our students' education. For example, having a member of the police force or community service worker come into our classes and discuss the importance of safe neighborhoods and ways to involve students outside of school can make a difference in the personal and social development of our students. You might even speak at school board meetings to express concerns about district policies that influence schools. Although each system is important for development, elements of the microsystem—particularly parents and peers—are the most significant (Clarke-Stewart & Dunn, 2006). We turn to them next.

Healthy development depends on influences in a child's immediate surroundings, such as parents and teachers, working together.

Parents' Influence on Development

Parents and other immediate caregivers are the most powerful influences on children's development, and they continue to influence our development throughout our lives (Landry, Smith, & Swank, 2006).

Parenting style. General patterns of interacting with and disciplining children.

Research indicates that certain **parenting styles,** general patterns of interacting with and disciplining children, promote more healthy development than others (Baumrind, 1991). Parents' *expectations* and their *warmth* and *responsiveness* characterize these differences (Schaffer, Clark, & Jeglic, 2009). Using these factors as a framework, researchers have identified four parenting styles and the general patterns of personal development associated with them.

Ed Psych and You

How did your parents raise you? How did this compare to your friends' experiences? How did their parenting influence your development? If you plan to have children, how will the way you raise them compare to the way you were raised?

- *Authoritative parents* set high expectations and are warm and responsive. They are firm, caring, and consistent. They explain reasons for rules and frequently interact with their children, who tend to be mature, considerate, confident, secure, and successful in school (Gonzalez & Wolters, 2006).

- *Authoritarian parents* have high expectations but tend to be cold and unresponsive. They expect conformity, they don't explain reasons for rules, and don't encourage verbal give-and-take. Their children tend to be withdrawn, sometimes defiant, and lack social skills (Schaffer et al., 2009).
- *Permissive parents* are warm but hold few expectations for their children, who tend to be immature, compulsive, and unmotivated. Used to getting their own way, the children sometimes have trouble relating to their peers (Walker, 2009).
- *Uninvolved parents* have few expectations for their children and are cold and unresponsive. They have little interest in their children, who tend to lack self-control and long-term goals, and can also be disobedient and easily frustrated.

These parenting styles help you answer the questions we asked in "Ed Psych and You" in this section. We're certainly not suggesting that if your parents were authoritarian, permissive, or uninvolved you are doomed to a life of incomplete development, because these parenting styles describe general patterns, and exceptions will exist. However, an *authoritative* parenting style, one that combines high expectations and high levels of warmth and responsiveness, is most effective for promoting healthy development. Adolescents who characterize their parents as authoritative tend to connect to others who are well-rounded, and they are less likely to be swayed by peer pressure to use alcohol or other drugs (W. A. Collins, Maccoby, Steinberg, Hetherington, & Bornstein, 2000). At the other extreme, students who characterize their parents as uninvolved are more likely to party, use drugs, and reject adult values (Durbin, Darling, Steinberg, & Brown, 1993).

Healthy parent–child relationships promote **attachment,** a strong emotional bond between children and caregivers, and this bond can influence relationships with others throughout life (Thompson & Raikes, 2003). Children with secure attachments tend to be confident in their ability to explore the world, whereas children with insecure attachments can be fearful, anxious, and angry in interactions with caregivers. Some evidence indicates that authoritarian, permissive, and uninvolved parenting styles are related to insecure attachments (Roeser, Peck, & Nasir, 2006).

Attachment. The strong emotional bond that forms between children and caregivers.

Our understanding of effective parenting styles has implications for you as a teacher. The interaction styles of effective teachers are similar to those of effective parents, and the description of authoritative parenting strongly parallels recommended classroom management practices for teachers (Emmer & Evertson, 2009; Evertson & Emmer, 2009). This suggests that you set boundaries for your students, provide reasons for your rules, enforce the rules consistently, and hold students to high standards, both personally and academically. Doing so contributes to their development.

Cultural Differences in Parenting Styles

The original research on parenting styles was done primarily with European American, middle-class families. And, with an authoritative parenting style viewed as desirable, families in the United States and Western Europe tend to encourage independence, competition, and freedom of expression.

However, many families from Asia, Africa, and South America believe in a more collectivist orientation, valuing obedience, deference to authority figures (especially parents), and the importance of the family (Morelli & Rothbaum, 2007). In particular, Asian American families, embracing values embedded in Confucianism, teach children that obedience is good and the

family is more important than individual wants and desires (Chao, 2001; Chen et al., 2001). Asian American parents, wanting to foster self-control and high achievement, are more likely to withhold praise, which they believe results in self-satisfied and poorly motivated children. However, this strict and directive parenting, combined with high levels of warmth and emotional support, seems to produce higher achievement along with greater emotional maturity (Spera, 2005).

A similar pattern is often seen in other cultures, including African American, Middle Eastern, and Hispanic families (Roopnarine & Evans, 2007). In these cultures, parents combine high demands for obedience with close, supportive parent-child relationships.

This research has two implications for you as you work with your students. First, some will be members of cultural minorities, and they'll come from families with parenting styles different from practices typical in this country. As a result, they may react differently to you and your classroom management efforts. Used to direct—and even authoritarian—parenting styles, they might not understand how to respond to a less direct style. So, instead of saying, "Now it's time for math," you might need to say, for example, "Please put away your reading materials and take out your math books. We begin math in one minute." Being sensitive to the possibility

of misinterpretation, you can adjust your directives to communicate more clearly. Carefully explaining classroom rules and why we have them is also important.

In addition, some students might be reluctant to respond, possibly because they lack confidence with English, but also because of home experience, where children are not seen as equal partners in dialogue (Greenfield, Suzuki, & Rothstein-Fish, 2006). Also, for students raised in a culture that tends to deemphasize individualism, effusive praise that singles out a particular student may be undesirable. On the other hand, all students, regardless of culture or background, respond well to patient, caring teachers who are committed to them both as people and as learners. With your support, they will gradually overcome their reluctance to respond, and they will adapt to the culture of your classroom.

Ed Psych and You

Think back to the friends you had in middle and high school. How did your friends influence you then, and do you believe they influenced who you are today?

Peers' Influence on Development

Next to parents and other caregivers, peers are the most powerful influence on development, and the influence of peers increases with age. The influence is minimal in preschoolers, for example, where they largely ignore their classmates, but as students become more aware of and involved in interactions with peers, the influence of a peer culture grows.

Peers influence development in three ways (Rubin, Bukowski, & Parker, 2006). We look at them next.

Attitudes and Values. Peers communicate attitudes and values about topics varying from the importance of school work to definitions of right and wrong (Kidron & Fleischman, 2006). Choice of friends predicts grades, involvement in school, and even behavior problems (Benson, Scales, Hamilton, & Sesma, 2006). If peer groups are academically oriented, they promote hard work, studying, and achievement, but if they reject school values, students are more likely to cut classes, skip school, cheat, and even use drugs. The academic climate in classes in the same school can differ dramatically depending on the dominant peer groups in each room (Rubin et al., 2006).

Opportunities to Practice Social Skills. The extent to which we can make friends and establish meaningful relationships later in life depends on social skills. Peers, and especially close friends, provide opportunities to practice these skills.

A snowballing effect exists. Some students are accepted by others, which gives them even more social experience, whereas those lacking social skills are often rejected by their peers, so they have fewer opportunities to practice and develop their skills (Bukowski, Brendgen, & Vitaro, 2007). Rejected students are often impulsive and aggressive, and over time they tend to withdraw. As a result, their learning and development often suffer (Ladd, 2006).

Emotional Support. Peers, and especially friends, provide both emotional support and a sense of identity, and they also help adolescents understand that they aren't the only ones going through the sometimes confusing changes that occur during this period (Jordan, 2006).

Students tend to select friends and seek emotional support from those who are similar in gender, ethnicity, socioeconomic status, academic orientation, and long-term goals (Maccoby, 2002). This is understandable, since we all like to be around people who are like us. For example, when Paul's kids were in high school, they described themselves as "band nerds," since they tended to hang out with other students in the band. And, Don's daughter, a volleyball player, tended to associate with other athletes.

These influences address the questions we asked in "Ed Psych and You" in this section. As you think about what you've just read, you will realize that your friends' attitudes and values are likely to be similar to yours, you practiced social skills in interacting with them, and they provided you with emotional support.

As with understanding parenting styles and culture, understanding the influence of peers on development has implications for you as a teacher. First, for example, the tendency of students to seek emotional support from others similar to themselves can be limiting, so when you assign students to work together in groups, being sure that the groups are mixed by gender, culture, and achievement provides them with opportunities to learn about peers with different backgrounds. In doing so, they will learn that we're all much more alike than we are different, and stereotypes and barriers tend to break down. Students may initially protest, but if you explain why you're assigning groups in this way, most will understand and cooperate.

Second, try to create a classroom climate in which the students feel as if, "we're all in this together," meaning you and the students are working together to help everyone learn as much as possible. Calling on all students and ensuring that no students are "left out" are two of the most effective ways of creating this climate. The result will be an advance in all forms of development.

Peers influence development through their attitudes and values, opportunities to practice social skills, and emotional support.

Obstacles to Healthy Development

Healthy development is a naturally occurring process in most students. But our modern world can pose challenges to healthy development. They include:

- Obesity
- Alcohol and drugs
- Child abuse
- Peer aggression

We examine them in the following sections.

Obesity

Student obesity has emerged as a major health issue facing our youth. More than one of six children in our country aged 6 to 19 are overweight or obese, triple the proportion in 1980 (Ogden & Caroll, 2010). In addition to immediate health risks, such as high blood pressure and high cholesterol, overweight youth often become heavy adults with additional health issues, such as heart disease and diabetes.

They also face social problems, such as peer rejection and negative perceptions. For example, some research indicates that overweight people are unconsciously perceived as less intelligent than their normal-weight peers (Vedantam, 2010). Several factors contribute to the problem including lack of exercise, unhealthy diets exacerbated by television advertising, and even schools. For instance, elementary school recess has largely been eliminated, only slightly more than 1 of 4 high school students takes physical education, and students spend inordinate amounts of time in front of a computer screen or television, with its ubiquitous advertising of junk foods (Hellmech, 2007). In addition, 6- to 11-year-olds are spending nearly 30 hours a week watching television alone (McDonough, 2009). Also, school districts, which are constantly cash strapped, often sign contracts with corporations to place soft-drink machines in school hallways (Lafee, 2005).

What can you do? Information and your own modeling are your best weapons. For example, some research suggests that students have a limited understanding of what constitutes healthy eating, so teaching them about healthy eating habits can make a difference (Powers, Bindler, Goetz, & Daratha, 2010). Modeling these habits, exercising, and making an effort to control your own weight (which is good for your health as well) can be even more important. Doing so makes a contribution to your students' health and development.

Alcohol and Drugs

Think about the following statistics, which were gathered in 2009 (Centers for Disease Control and Prevention [CDC], 2010a, 2010c):

- More than 4 of 10 high school students used alcohol, and nearly 25% reported binge drinking.
- One of 5 high school students experimented with marijuana.
- Twenty percent of high school students have taken a prescription drug, such as Oxycontin, Ritalin, or Xanax, without a doctor's prescription.
- Nearly 1 of 5 high school students report current use of cigarettes.

The dangers of drug use are well known. Teenagers who abuse alcohol and drugs place themselves at risk for problems, such as damage to their health, car accidents, and even suicide. Alcohol and drug users are less likely to exercise, and academic achievement is decreased. And, they are less likely to develop healthy mechanisms for coping with life's problems (Berk, 2010; Crosnoe & Huston, 2007).

School connectedness—the belief by students that adults and peers in the school care about their learning as well as about them as individuals—is an important protective factor. Young people who feel connected to their school are less likely to smoke, use alcohol and drugs, or initiate sex. They also achieve higher, have better attendance, and are less likely to drop out of school (CDC, 2010b; Finn, Willert, & Marable, 2003).

You can promote feelings of school connectedness by getting to know your students as individuals, calling them by name, and creating classroom environments that are physically and emotionally safe. You can also use teaching strategies that involve students in learning activities, instead of expecting them to listen passively to lectures.

School connectedness. The belief by students that adults and peers in the school care about their learning as well as about them as individuals.

Child Abuse

Denise, one of your students, historically has been a bright, outgoing, and high-achieving girl, but she has changed quite abruptly. She is withdrawn, and she looks down and doesn't respond when you call on her. And, although she is normally well groomed, she has been coming to school looking a bit disheveled. Then, you see a welt on her face, and your concern turns to alarm. You go to your assistant principal and report what you've observed.

Denise's changes in behavior, academic performance, and appearance, and particularly the welt on her face, suggest the possibility of child abuse, and you did precisely what you should have in reporting it.

Teachers in all 50 states are required by law to report suspected child abuse. In addition, you and your school are protected from civil or criminal liability if the report is made honestly and includes behavioral data, such as observations of the symptoms we described (Fischer et al., 2006).

Statistics indicate that in 2007 nearly 170,000 children were physically, sexually, or emotionally abused, and when combined with those who were neglected, the number climbs to nearly three quarters of a million. More than 80% of abuse and neglect is caused by parents with about another 7% committed by other relatives. The remainder occurs in places such as child care centers or foster care (U.S. Department of Health and Human Services, 2009). Because abuse and neglect are often hidden or not reported, reliable figures are difficult to obtain.

so are these stats accurate?

It goes without saying that abuse is an obstacle to development, and you're in a unique position to identify child abuse because you work with children for much of the day, 5 days a week. The probability that you will have abused or neglected children in your classes is low, although it is somewhat higher if you teach in a high poverty area. You need to be aware of the possibility, however, because you could literally save a life.

Peer Aggression

As long as schools have been in existence, aggressive students will attend them, and aggression takes several forms. For example, **instrumental aggression,** the most common, is an action aimed at gaining an object or privilege, such as cutting in line, or a young child grabbing another's toy. Hurting the other student isn't the goal, but it may result. On the other hand **physical** and **relational aggression** are actions intended to hurt others, such as pushing another child down on the playground in the first case (most common in boys), or spreading a rumor about someone else in the second (more common in girls) (Pellegrini, 2002).

Aggression may be **proactive,** where students initiate aggressive acts, or **reactive,** behaving aggressively in response to frustration or an aggressive act (Hanish, Kochenderfer-Ladd, Fabes, Martin, & Denning, 2004).

Highly aggressive students tend to be rejected by peers and do poorly in school. By adolescence, they often seek out peer groups that lead them to delinquency, and at an extreme, criminal behavior as adults (Côté, Vaillancourt, Barker, Nagin, & Tremblay, 2007). Even in less extreme cases, aggressive students often grow up to be aggressive adults who have trouble getting along with others in both the workplace and the world at large (Berger, 2007).

Although genetics can play a role, the home environment is a primary cause of aggression (Côté et al., 2007). Parents are often authoritarian, punitive, and inconsistent, and they commonly use physical punishers, such as slapping, hitting, and spanking for unacceptable behavior. So, aggressive behavior is both modeled and reinforced (Brendgen, Vitar, Boivin, Dionne, & Perusse, 2006). These home environments can result in **hostile attributional bias,** a tendency to view others' behaviors as hostile or aggressive. Aggression is also linked to deficits in perspective taking, empathy, moral development, and emotional self-regulation (Bukowski et al., 2007).

School Violence. School violence is an extreme form of aggression that involves serious bodily injury or death. Because of widely publicized incidents of violence, such as the Columbine massacre in 1999, in which 12 students were killed; the Red Lake, Minnesota, tragedy in 2005 that resulted in the death of 5 students; or, more recently, the incident in Omaha, Nebraska, in 2011, where a suspended student shot and killed the school's assistant principal and wounded the principal, many believe that school violence is a serious problem. In fact, violence in schools has decreased significantly since the mid-1990s (Virginia Youth Violence Project, 2010). For example, in 2010, 14 shootings occurred on school property, resulting in the deaths of 3 students, two of which resulted from self-inflicted wounds (Brady Campaign to Prevent Gun Violence, 2010).

really?

Instrumental aggression. An aggressive act aimed at gaining an object or privilege.

Physical aggression. An aggressive act that can cause bodily injury.

Relational aggression. An aggressive act that can adversely affect interpersonal relationships.

Proactive aggression. A deliberate aggressive act initiated toward another.

Reactive aggression. An aggressive act committed in response to frustration or another aggressive act.

Hostile attributional bias. A tendency to view others' behaviors as hostile or aggressive.

However, even one death is too many, and the threat of violence is much higher than the actual death rate. For instance, in 2007, 10% of male students and 5% of female students were threatened or injured with a weapon on school property (Baum, Dinkes, Kemp, & Snyder, 2010). Obviously, learning and development suffer whenever students don't feel safe in school.

Bullying. A form of peer aggression that involves a systematic or repetitive abuse of power between students.

Bullying. Although incidents of serious crime and violence are rare, **bullying**, a form of peer aggression that involves a systematic or repetitive abuse of power between students (Berger, 2007), is much more common. For example, in a survey of more than 43,000 high school students—the largest ever conducted about the attitudes and conduct of adolescents—half admitted they had bullied someone in the past year, and nearly the same percentage said they were bullied, teased, or taunted in a way that upset them (Josephson Institute Center for Youth Ethics, 2010).

Bullying can exist as either physical or relational aggression, and its victims are often peers who have disabilities or few friends, or are immature and lack self-confidence. Bullying can have long-term negative effects on students, and in the extreme, victims of repeated bullying incidents begin to ask, "Why me?" and "Am I someone who deserves to be picked on?" which can lead to destructive emotions, such as depression and even suicide (Card & Hodges, 2008). In cases of suicide, however, other factors, such as dysfunctional families, easy access to weapons or medications, and social hopelessness, usually also exist (Bonanno & Hymel, 2010).

Historically, bullying has been viewed as a maladjusted reaction from adolescents who are socially marginalized or psychologically troubled, but more recent research suggests that this isn't true. In fact, many students bully to achieve social status, and their bullying tends to escalate until high status is reached, at which time bullying is no longer necessary (Faris & Felmlee, 2011). These researchers found that, over time, students at the very bottom and at the very top of the social hierarchy become the least aggressive youth.

Because of the perceived seriousness of bullying as a school problem, 44 states have passed anti-bullying laws, and many districts have implemented zero-tolerance policies. These laws and policies have been largely ineffective for reducing incidents of bullying, however (Graham, 2010; Walker, 2009).

Peer juries and peer counselors are infrequently used, and their effectiveness is also uncertain, whereas school-wide efforts that include increasing adult supervision, talking with bullies after bullying incidents, and immediate, appropriate, and consistent consequences for bullying have been found to be more effective (Sherer, & Nickerson, 2010).

These findings have important implications for you. First, when you begin teaching, you will almost certainly encounter incidents of bullying. When you do, you should intervene immediately, apply appropriate consequences for the perpetrators, and perhaps more importantly, use the incident as a teachable moment, where you discuss the idea of right and wrong, appropriate treatment of others, tolerance for differences, and abuse of power (Graham, 2010). These discussions obviously won't produce immediate results, but, over the long term, they can make a difference in the development of your students.

Also, the research conducted by Faris and Felmlee (2011) suggests that if you can find appropriate ways to help students achieve social status, such as excelling in sports, academics, or class or school leadership, the likelihood of their displaying bullying behaviors might decrease. Many ways of achieving social status exist, and an approach to dealing with bullying that focuses on social status might be more effective than existing programs with marginal records of success (Shah, 2011).

Technology, Learning, and Development: Cyberbullying

Bullying, in general, is a serious school problem, and, because of the rapidly expanding presence of the Internet in students' lives, **cyberbullying**—a form of bullying that occurs when students use electronic media to harass or intimidate other students—has also become a problem. Cyberbullying has received enormous attention after the suicides of Megan Meier, an eighth grader, who was bullied on MySpace, and Rutgers University freshman, Tyler Clementi, after his roommate streamed video of his sexual encounter with another male student, grabbed headlines. Since then, both school officials and parents have become aware of this growing problem.

> **Cyberbullying.** The use of electronic media to harass or intimidate other students.

sad

Cyberbullying tends to follow the same patterns as traditional forms of bullying; students who are bullied on the playground play similar roles in cyberspace (Raskauskas & Stoltz, 2007). The anonymity of the Internet is what distinguishes cyberbullying from other types, and it can make bullies even less sensitive to the hurtful nature of the bullying incidents (Willard, 2006).

Cyberbullying is hard to measure, but experts estimate that from 1 of 3 to 1 of 10 students are victims of online harassment (Stobbe, 2007). Given the popularity of Internet use among teenagers, cyberbullying is likely to remain a persistent problem (Raskauskas & Stoltz, 2007).

big difference

Because of its anonymity, cyberbullying is also difficult to combat; consequences for perpetrators rarely exist. The best you can do is promote a sense of empathy, fair play, and appropriate treatment of others in your students. We address these issues in the sections that follow.

---

check your understanding

1.1 Describe the components of the bioecological model, and explain how they influence development.

1.2 Describe the different parenting styles and how they influence development.

1.3 Describe three ways in which peers influence development.

To receive feedback for these questions, go to Appendix A.

---

*C*lassroom *connections*

Applying Bronfenbrenner's Theory in Classrooms

1. Bronfenbrenner's bioecological theory describes how development is influenced by different elements, beginning with the individual and extending to family and societal forces. Foster development by connecting to these influences on development.

   ■ **Elementary:** At the beginning of the school year, a third-grade teacher reads her students' files, talks to previous years' teachers, and encourages parents to bring their children with them to parent–teacher conferences. She observes the interaction between parents and their children and uses this information to provide extra structure and emotional support when necessary.

   ■ **Middle School:** Teachers in an urban middle school realize that many of the children on their team do not have adequate medical or dental care. They ask the school psychologist and social worker to come in to talk about possible resources to provide the care.

   ■ **High School:** A history teacher attempts to link course content to students' lives. As she makes these links, she tries to help them understand how societal influences affect their future lives in terms of jobs and schooling.

*P*hysical Development

Ed Psych and You

Are you short or tall? Thin or heavy? Did you go through puberty early or late? How have these factors affected your development as a person?

When we think of development, we tend to focus on its cognitive, personal, social, and moral aspects, and we sometimes tend to forget that children's physical development can influence each of the others. It can even lay the foundation for a lifetime of healthy activity. We examine these issues next.

Early Childhood and Elementary Years

The early childhood and elementary years are marked by gradual but continual growth and change. During this period, children transition from small 3- and 4-year-olds who are working on coordination to large fifth- and sixth-graders who are beginning to go through a myriad of changes.

As young children grow, their balance, agility, and flexibility increase, and fine motor skills such as printing and cutting with scissors also develop. Girls typically have better fine motor skills, but boys are usually better at activities such as throwing and kicking (Berk, 2010).

Size, so important to teenagers, is not a major issue for young children. During the early elementary years, boys and girls are approximately the same size, with wide ranges at each grade level. Some boys are bigger than girls and vice versa, but it largely doesn't matter to them. By the end of about the fifth grade, a growth spurt makes the average girl taller and heavier than her male counterparts.

As young children grow, their developing muscles need exercise, and they also have excess energy that needs to be burned off. This helps explain why younger students are often so fidgety. Boys seem especially ill-suited to the sit-down pace of most elementary classrooms and are much more likely to be identified as needing special help because of hyperactivity and attention problems (Heward, 2009).

Recess and other forms of physical activity provide a healthy outlet for the enormous amounts of energy that young children have.

Recess: An Important Component of Physical Development

Recess provides opportunities for students to practice social skills and burn off excess energy.

As you read earlier, many elementary schools have cut back or eliminated recess time, and developmental psychologists worry that young children are missing an important contribution to physical development. Lack of recess has been linked to childhood problems ranging from obesity to anxiety and hyperactivity (Jacobson, 2008; Samuels, 2009). Through free play during recess, students are also provided with experiences that contribute to cognitive, social, and emotional development (Rathunde & Csikszentmihalyi, 2006).

Given these benefits, why are so many schools cutting back on recess? Time, precious time, is the answer. Many schools are pressured to improve scores on high-stakes tests, so they allocate extra time to the areas covered by these tests, such as reading and math. However, these decisions may be having adverse affects on children's development (Berk, 2010).

Organized Sports

Organized sports, such as soccer and Little League baseball, can contribute to physical development through factors such as conditioning and increased strength and coordination

(Pellegrini, 2005). Participation is also associated with advances in personal and social development, such as lessons in teamwork, competition, and learning to win and lose graciously, all skills important in later life (Daniels & Leeper, 2006).

About half of U.S. children participate in some form of organized sports during the elementary school years, but the ratio of males to females is uneven, with about two thirds of boys participating compared to a little over a third for girls (National Council of Young Sports, 2008). During the high school years, the ratio narrows, with about 4 of 10 girls participating in sports compared to about 6 of 10 boys (National Federation of State High School Associations, 2008).

This disparity gives girls less opportunity to develop both physically and socially. Surveys indicate that neither boys nor girls get enough exercise to stay healthy (defined as an hour of moderate-intensity exercise per day), but the problem is particularly acute for girls. About 40% of boys but only about 11% of girls get sufficient exercise. This trend has long-term ramifications, because physically fit children are more likely to develop into fit adults (Tammelen et al., 2003).

The Adolescent Years

Physical development during adolescence produces young people who are physically, but not mentally or emotionally, ready for parenthood. The growth spurt that occurs during adolescence adds almost a foot in height and 50 to 75 pounds in weight (Berk, 2010). These dramatic increases combined with sexually developing bodies often leave teenagers wondering, "Who am I?"

Between approximately the ages of 10 and 15, the onset of **puberty,** the series of physiological changes that occur during adolescence and lead to reproductive maturation, occurs. It varies widely among adolescents, and girls mature faster than boys, typically reaching puberty 2 years before their male counterparts.

The differences between boys and girls, combined with individual differences within each gender, can strongly influence other aspects of development. For example, early-developing girls tend to be heavier, more curvaceous, and less satisfied with their bodies; less self-confident and less popular; and more likely to get in trouble, both at school and in their communities (Ge et al., 2006; Graber, Brooks-Gunn, & Warren, 2006). On the other hand, early-developing boys are more relaxed and self-confident, and they're more likely to become athletes and hold leadership positions in school. But, like early-maturing girls, they're more prone to antisocial behavior, perhaps because their bodies get ahead of their developing abilities to resist impulses, or because they're thrust into social situations for which they're not ready. Early maturers of both sexes report feeling emotionally stressed by the process and show declines in academic performance (Mendle, Tukheimer, & Emery, 2007).

Interestingly, the opposite occurs for late-developing boys and girls (Lindfors et al., 2007). Late-developing girls are seen as physically attractive (think thin), and they're more lively and sociable, and more likely to be school leaders. Late-developing boys tend to be more anxious, talkative, and prone to attention-seeking behaviors, and they are less athletic, less popular, and less likely to find themselves in leadership positions.

These factors address the questions we asked in "Ed Psych and You" at the beginning of this section. Has your development been consistent with these patterns? For example, if you matured early, how did it influence the other aspects of your development, such as your self-confidence, participation in sports, and leadership positions? Physical development tells us a lot about ourselves.

As a teacher you can play an important role in helping both early and late developers of both sexes by being understanding and, because it is an especially sensitive issue for developing teenagers, by de-emphasizing physical differences in your classroom. You can also help teenagers negotiate this period of uncertainty by establishing an authoritative

Puberty. The series of physiological changes that occur during adolescence and lead to reproductive maturation.

that's with anybody early or not.

classroom environment and providing some of your personal time to talk to students about their uncertainties and their hopes for the future. Other than their parents, and perhaps their friends, you're the most important influence in their lives.

check your
understanding

2.1   Explain how physical development can influence other forms of development.

2.2   Why is physical development important to classroom teachers?

To receive feedback for these questions, go to Appendix A.

The Development of Identity and Self-Concept

Identity. Individuals' self constructed definition of who they are, what their existence means, and what they want in life.

Self-concept. A cognitive assessment of their physical, social, and academic competence.

People's **identity,** their self-constructed definition of who they are, what their existence means, and what they want in life, combines with their **self-concepts,** cognitive assessments of their physical, social, and academic competence, to influence the way they respond to school and life in general. In this section, we consider how identity and self-concept develop, and what they mean for your teaching. We begin with a discussion of Erik Erikson's theory of psychosocial development and how it relates to the concept of identity.

Erikson's Theory of Psychosocial Development

Where are you going with your life? Do you feel you're on a positive career path? Are you in a relationship with someone "special" and do you believe the relationship will last? Erik Erikson (1902–1994), a developmental psychologist and psychoanalyst, addressed questions such as these in his work with clients, and he personally wrestled with them in what he called a "crisis of identity" in his own life (Cross, 2001). Based on these experiences, he developed a theory of "psychosocial" development. The term *psychosocial* derives from the integration of identity (the *psycho* component of the term) and Erikson's belief that a primary motivation for human behavior was social and cultural (the *social* part), reflecting a desire to connect with other people (Erikson, 1968, 1980). His theory is unique in the sense that he viewed developmental changes as occurring throughout our lives.

Erikson believed that all people have the same basic needs. He also believed that personal development occurs in response to those needs and healthy development depends on the quality of support provided by the social environment, particularly parents and other caregivers. Like Piaget, he believed that development proceeds in stages, each characterized by a **crisis,** a psychosocial challenge that presents opportunities for development. Although never permanently resolved, the positive resolution of a crisis at one stage increases the likelihood of a positive resolution at the next. The stages are summarized in Table 3.1.

Crisis. A psychosocial challenge that presents opportunities for development.

While positive resolution of the crisis at one stage better prepares people for resolution at the next, Erikson didn't believe that it is always ideal. For instance, while learning to trust people is a positive resolution of his first stage, we cannot trust all people under all circumstances. However, in a healthy solution to the challenge at each stage, the positive resolution predominates. In addition, when positive resolution doesn't occur at a particular stage, individuals often revisit earlier stages to rework these crises.

Evaluating Erikson's Work

Erikson's work was popular and influential in the 1960s and 1970s, but since then, developmental theorists have taken issue with it on three major points. First, they argue that Erikson didn't adequately address the role of culture in personal and social development. For instance, some cultures discourage autonomy and initiative in children, perhaps as

Table 3.1	Erikson's eight life-span stages
Trust vs. Mistrust (Birth to 1 year)	Trust develops when infants receive consistently loving care. Mistrust results from unpredictable or harsh care.
Autonomy vs. Shame (1–3 years)	Autonomy develops when children use their newly formed mental and psychomotor skills to explore their worlds. Parents support autonomy by encouraging exploration and accepting the inevitable mistakes.
Initiative vs. Guilt (3–6 years)	Initiative, a sense of ambition and responsibility, develops from encouragement of children's efforts to explore and take on new challenges. Overcontrol or criticism can result in guilt.
Industry vs. Inferiority (6–12 years)	School and home provide opportunities for students to develop a sense of competence through success on challenging tasks. A pattern of failure can lead to feelings of inferiority.
Identity vs. Confusion (12–18 years)	Adolescents experiment with various roles in an atmosphere of freedom with clearly established limits. Confusion results when the home environment fails to provide either the necessary structure or when it is overly controlling, failing to provide opportunities for individual exploration with different identity roles.
Intimacy vs. Isolation (Young adulthood)	Intimacy occurs when individuals establish close ties with others. Emotional isolation may result from earlier disappointments or a lack of developing identity.
Generativity vs. Stagnation (Adulthood)	Generativity occurs when adults give to the next generation through child rearing, productive work, and contributions to society or other people. Apathy or self-absorption can result from an inability to think about or contribute to the welfare of others.
Integrity vs. Despair (Old age)	Integrity occurs when people believe they've lived as well as possible and accept the inevitability of death. Remorse over things done or left undone leads to despair.

a way of protecting them from dangers in their environments (Dennis, Cole, Zahn-Waxler, & Mizuta, 2002).

Second, critics point out that some adolescents—and especially girls—establish a sense of intimacy with, or even before, a focus on personal identity (Kroger, 2000). This contrasts with Erikson's description of intimacy following the development of identity.

Third, as you'll see in our discussion of identity development in the next section, many people don't achieve a sense of identity as early as Erikson suggested.

Erikson's work is intuitively sensible, however, and it helps explain behaviors we often see in others. For example, we might explain Sean's contention in the beginning of the chapter that the other students are "out to get him," by saying that he hasn't positively resolved the trust–distrust crisis. This has left him less able to develop a sense of autonomy, initiative, or industry, which helps us understand why it's affecting his academic work. We've all met people we admire because of their positive outlook, openness, and commitment to making the world better. We've also encountered those who believe that others are trying to take advantage of them or are somehow inherently evil. We see good minds sliding into lethargy because of a lack of initiative or even substance abuse. We become frustrated by people's apathy and lack of a zest for living. Erikson's work helps us understand these issues.

Supporting Psychosocial Development

Teachers support psychosocial development in a variety of ways. For example, if you're planning to teach in preschool or early elementary grades, you will want to encourage and reinforce your children's autonomy and initiative. If you're planning to teach in the middle elementary grades, providing challenging experiences and the instructional support that

Early childhood and elementary classrooms should provide opportunities for students to develop autonomy and initiative.

help children develop a sense of competence is important, because it contributes to a positive resolution of the industry–inferiority crisis.

If you're planning to teach in middle school, a classroom structure that sets predictable limits for acceptable behavior, combined with the empathy that helps students negotiate the uncertainties of this period in their lives, is important. You saw that Sean's teachers tried to get him to "open up" to them. Most significant is the sensitivity they demonstrated in their efforts to reach him.

If you're planning to teach in the upper high school levels, you can become an adult that students can turn to as they begin to wrestle with issues such as closer relationships with the opposite sex and plans for their futures. Supporting psychosocial development is one more example that illustrates why your job is much more complex than simply teaching fractions or American history. You're also promoting other essential forms of development.

Contemporary Views of Identity Development

Having examined Erikson's discussion of identity and the social forces that influence it, we now turn to more contemporary views of identity development, views that focus on individuals' efforts to define themselves through their lifestyle and career choices. Parents and a variety of social experiences contribute to this process (Trawick-Smith, 2003). For example, adolescents often identify with a peer group, rigidly adhering to a style of dress or way of wearing their hair (McLeod & Yates, 2006). In time this identification is replaced with a more individual sense of self and an awareness of lifelong goals.

Ed Psych and You

How would you describe yourself on Facebook? What do the following Facebook bios tell us about the authors? (Are the authors male or female?)

Red-haired, left-handed, legally blind, massive consumer of Diet Coke.

The inside of my car is always clean, and I make illustrated lists for everything.

Independent. Dependable. Out of the box. Keeping it interesting.

I surf, therefore I am. (Colman, 2010)

Career Choices in Identity Development

Students' attempts to make career choices also influence their identity development. Let's look at an example.

Four seniors are talking about what they plan to do after high school:

"I'm going into nursing," Taylor comments. "I've been working part-time at the hospital, and it feels good to work with people and help them. I've talked with the counselors, and I think I can do the chemistry and other science courses."

"I'm not sure what I want to do," Sandy comments. "I've thought about veterinary medicine, and also about teaching. I've been working at the vet clinic, and I like it, but I'm not sure about doing it forever. Some of my parents' friends are teachers, so I hear what they say about it. I don't know."

"I wish I could do that," Ramon replies. "But I'm off to the university in the fall. I'm going to be a lawyer. At least that's what my parents think. It's not a bad job, and lawyers make good money."

"How can you just do that?" Nancy wonders. "You've said that you don't want to be a lawyer. . . . I'm not willing to decide yet. I'm only 18. I'm going to think about it for a while."

As adolescents struggle with their identities, two processes occur (Luyckx, Goossens, & Soenens, 2006). The first, *identity formation,* involves the creation of personal commitments based on conviction or belief. This was illustrated in Taylor's comment, ". . . it feels good to work with people and help them." *Evaluation,* the second process, occurs when they consider alternative identities and assess each. For example, before enrolling in this program, you may have asked yourself whether you want to be a teacher or perhaps work instead in the business world. These deliberations are your attempts to evaluate different options.

To study the development of identity, researchers interviewed adolescents and found that young people's decisions can be generally classified into one of four states, which vary in their ability to produce healthy outcomes (Marcia, 1980, 1987, 1999) (see Table 3.2). *Identity moratorium* is a positive state that involves thinking and weighing options and may eventually lead to *identity achievement,* which is also positive. In contrast, *identity diffusion,* common in younger adolescents, reflects haphazard consideration of different career choices. If it persists over time, it can result in apathy and confusion (Berzonsky & Kuk, 2000). *Identity foreclosure,* another less productive path, occurs when adolescents adopt the goals and values of others—usually their parents—without thoroughly examining the implications for their future. Many adolescents experience both identity moratorium and diffusion before arriving at identity achievement. You can help students in this process by openly discussing personal issues with them.

In contrast with the predictions of Erikson's theory, identity achievement more commonly occurs after—instead of during—high school (Berzonsky & Kuk, 2000; Marcia, 1980, 1988). This delay is especially true for college students, who have more time to consider what they want to do with their lives.

identity during college years

The uncertainty adolescents often experience is more likely related to the demands of increased independence than to identity issues (Bettis & Adams, 2005; McLeod & Yates, 2006). Conflict with parents, teachers, and other adults peaks in early adolescence and then declines, as teenagers accept responsibility and adults learn how to deal with the new relationships (Arnett, 2002). The challenges of early adolescence help explain why teaching middle and junior high students can be particularly challenging.

why? trying to retain control of kids but need to learn to give a little responsibility

Sexual Identity

Sexual identity, students' self-constructed definition of who they are with respect to gender orientation, is another important element of identity formation. Sexual identity influences student choices ranging from clothes and friends to the occupations they consider and ultimately pursue (Ruble, Martin & Berenbaum, 2006). **Sexual orientation,** the gender to which an individual is romantically and sexually attracted, is an important dimension of sexual identity.

Sexual identity. Students' self-constructed definition of who they are with respect to gender orientation.

Sexual orientation. The gender to which an individual is romantically and sexually attracted.

Table 3.2	States in identity development

State	Description
Identity moratorium	A state of identity development that occurs when individuals pause and remain in a "holding pattern." Long-range commitment is delayed.
Identity achievement	A state of identity development that occurs after individuals make decisions about goals and commitments.
Identity diffusion	A state of identity development that occurs when individuals fail to make clear choices. The state is characterized by haphazard experimentation with different career options. Individuals may not be developmentally ready to make decisions.
Identity foreclosure	A state of identity development that occurs when individuals prematurely adopt the positions of others, such as parents.

For most students, sexual orientation is not a major issue, but for a portion of the student population—estimates range from 3% to 10%—it is confusing and stressful (Macionis, 2009). Attempts to pinpoint the causes of homosexuality are controversial, with some believing that it is genetic and others attributing it to learning and choice (Gollnick & Chinn, 2009). Most researchers point to genetic causes, however.

"The evidence to date suggests that genetic and prenatal biological influences are largely responsible for homosexuality. In our evolutionary past, homosexuality may have served the adaptive function of reducing aggressive competition for other-sex mates" (Berk, 2010, p. 376). Further evidence exists in studies of twins. If one member of identical twins is homosexual, for example, the other is much more likely to also be homosexual than is the case with fraternal twins (Bailey, 1993).

Research also suggests that homosexuals go through a three-phase sequence in their attempts to understand who they are (Berk, 2010). The first is feeling different, a slowly developing awareness that they aren't like other children. The second is a feeling of confusion, which occurs during adolescence. In this phase, homosexuals attempt to understand their developing sexuality, looking for both social support and role models.

Finally, in the third phase, the majority of gay and lesbian teenagers accept their homosexuality and share it with those who are close to them.

This information is important to you for two reasons. First, you may be one of the people with whom students share this information, and your reaction can have a major impact on students' acceptance of themselves. Second, homosexual students are at greater risk for problems ranging from depression and substance abuse to suicide (Wood, 2005). Peer harassment is a major contributor to these problems, and you play an essential role in setting the moral tone of your classroom, ensuring that it is a safe place for all students.

This discussion also addresses the questions we asked in our "Ed Psych and You" feature for this section. How we describe ourselves to others is a reflection of our identity. In the past this was often a private process. Now with technology and social networks like Facebook and Twitter, we can instantly define and redefine ourselves with the bios we post and the messages we send (Ball, 2010; Colman, 2010). At one level, this can be healthy because it encourages us to think about who we are and what we want to become. At another, it can promote narcissism and preoccupation with ourselves. And, by the way, the first two Facebook postings in "Ed Psych and You" were by females; the last two by males.

Ed Psych and You

How athletic are you? How popular? How "smart" compared to your friends and fellow students? What subject are you best at? What do your responses to these questions tell you about yourself?

The Development of Self-Concept

Your responses to the questions in "Ed Psych and You" here reflect different dimensions of your *self-concept*, which we earlier defined as a cognitive appraisal of your physical, social, and academic competence (Schunk, Pintrich & Meece, 2008). If you believe you're a good athlete, for example, you have a positive physical self-concept, or if you think you're good at getting along with people, you have a positive social self-concept. Self-concepts are formed largely on the basis of experiences and feedback. The formation of a healthy self-concept is central to social and emotional development (Davis-Kean & Sandler, 2001).

Self-Concept and Self-Esteem

Self-esteem (self-worth). An emotional reaction to, or an evaluation of, the self.

The terms *self-concept* and *self-esteem* are often used interchangeably, but they are actually quite different. In contrast with self-concept, which is cognitive, **self-esteem,** or **self-worth,** is an emotional reaction to, or an evaluation of, the self (Schunk et al., 2008). People who have high self-esteem believe that they are inherently worthy people and feel good about themselves. It's important, because low self-esteem during adolescence predicts poor

[handwritten: obesity/weight, overweight, due to excessive eating]

health, criminal behavior, and limited economic prospects as adults (Baumeister, Campbell, Krueger, & Vohs, 2003; Trzesniewski et al., 2006).

Young children tend to have both high self-esteem and positive self-concepts—sometimes unrealistically so—probably because of few social comparisons and the support they receive from parents (Stipek, 2002). Self-esteem tends to drop during the transition from elementary to middle school, probably because of physical changes brought on by puberty and the less personal nature of middle schools. It then rises again during the high school years—to a greater extent for boys than girls (Eccles, Barber, Stone, & Hunt, 2003; Twenge & Campbell, 2001).

[handwritten: don't know yet]

Self-concepts become more realistic as interactions with others give students more accurate measures of their performance compared to their peers (Schunk et al., 2008). As students move into adolescence, self-concept interacts with a developing sense of identity. Each influences the other, and both influence self-esteem.

Self-Concept and Achievement

A positive but weak relationship exists between overall self-concept and achievement, and virtually no relationship exists between achievement and social and physical self-concepts (Marsh & Ayotte, 2003). This makes sense; we've all known socially withdrawn students who do well academically, as well as highly skilled athletes who are modest achievers.

The relationship between achievement and academic self-concept is more robust, and an even stronger relationship exists between specific subject matter self-concepts and achievement in those areas (Choi, 2005). Self-concepts in different subjects, such as math or English, also tend to become more distinct over time (Marsh & Ayotte, 2003). For example, we've all heard people make statements such as, "I'm okay in English, but I'm no good in math."

Extracurricular Activities

[handwritten: nope]

Extracurricular activities are integral components of students' education, and they're important for development (Mahoney, Larson, & Eccles, 2005). A well-established link exists between participation in extracurricular activities, self-concept, and achievement. Students who participate in these activities tend to achieve higher than nonparticipants, even after controlling for social class, gender, and ability. Researchers believe positive identity formation, membership in peer groups, and attachment to adults other than parents are contributing factors in this process (Eccles et al., 2003).

[handwritten: wrong, I did fine without extra curricular activities]

Figure 3.2 illustrates the relationships between the different components of self-concept and achievement.

SMALL CORRELATION WITH ACHIEVEMENT	→	General self-concept		
MODERATE CORRELATION WITH ACHIEVEMENT	→	Academic self-concept	Social self-concept	Physical self-concept
STRONG CORRELATION WITH ACHIEVEMENT	→	Self-concept in math, English, or other subjects	VIRTUALLY NO CORRELATION WITH ACHIEVEMENT	

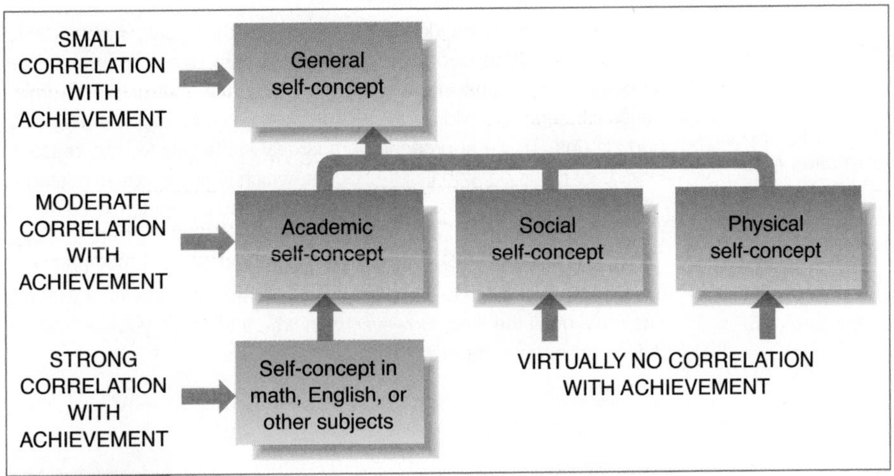

Figure 3.2 The relationships among the different dimensions of self-concept and achievement

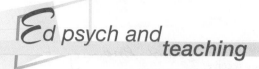

Ed psych and teaching

Supporting Your Students' Identity and Self-Concept Development

As a teacher you can strongly influence your students' developing identity and academic self-concepts. You design the learning activities and assessments and provide the feedback that students use to appraise their academic competence. The following guidelines can help you in your efforts to promote this healthy development.

1. Create a learning-focused classroom.
2. Use an authoritative management style to help your students develop responsibility, and communicate genuine interest in all students.
3. Reward autonomy and initiative in your students.
4. Establish appropriately high expectations for all learners, and provide evidence of increasing competence.
5. Design grading systems that emphasize learning progress and personal growth.

Let's see how John Adler, an eighth-grade English teacher, attempts to implement these guidelines with his students.

> "Here are your papers," John announces on Friday as he hands back a set of quizzes from the day before. "You did a good job and I'm proud of you. Your writing is really improving. . . . I know I expect a lot, but you've always risen to the task.
>
> "Put your scores in your logs, and add your improvement points."
>
> "Who improved the most, Mr. Adler?" Jeremy asks.
>
> "That's not important," John replies. "Remember, we're all in this together. You take responsibility for your learning, I help you as much as I can, and we all try to improve . . . That's why I put your scores on the last page of the quizzes. They're your business, and no one else's.
>
> "Now, I'd like to have a classroom meeting," he continues, changing the direction of the discussion. "Someone came to me after school yesterday, concerned about the way some of you are treating each other outside of class. . . . She didn't name names; she simply expressed a concern, and I like it when someone takes the initiative to make our classroom better.
>
> "I concur with her concern. . . . For instance, I saw one of you get tripped when you walked down the aisle, and another had water splashed on him at the water fountain. . . . I'm also seeing more litter on the floor.
>
> "I'm disappointed at these behaviors. We're here to help one another. . . . So, I want to hear some ideas. What can we do to make our classroom better?"
>
> The students offer comments, with suggestions ranging from kicking perpetrators out of class, to talking to them, to adding some more rules. The students agree that John has been attempting to enforce the rules fairly, but because he expects everyone to be responsible, perhaps he has perhaps been too lenient in some cases.

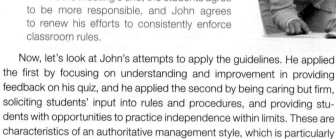

> At the meeting's end, the students agree to be more responsible, and John agrees to renew his efforts to consistently enforce classroom rules.

Now, let's look at John's attempts to apply the guidelines. He applied the first by focusing on understanding and improvement in providing feedback on his quiz, and he applied the second by being caring but firm, soliciting students' input into rules and procedures, and providing students with opportunities to practice independence within limits. These are characteristics of an authoritative management style, which is particularly valuable in middle schools where students are beginning the process of identity development. Students want their teachers to care about them, but they also want their teachers to set limits. For example, when asked about their favorite teachers, students identified qualities such as:

> Caring about them as individuals and seeking to help them succeed as learners. . . . However, students also say that they want teachers to articulate and enforce clear standards of behavior. They view this not just as part of the teacher's job but as evidence that the teacher cares about them. (Brophy, 2010, p. 24)

Third, John realized that no psychosocial challenge is permanently resolved, so, even though his students were eighth graders, he reinforced them for taking the initiative to raise the issue of misbehavior.

John's comment, "You did a good job and I'm proud of you. . . . I know I expect a lot, but you've always risen to the task," communicated high expectations, emphasis on increasing competence, and an attempt to apply the fourth guideline. These efforts also promote a sense of industry and positive academic self-concept.

Finally, he deemphasized competition and applied the fifth guideline, when he said, "That's not important. Remember, we're all in this together," in response to Jeremy's question about who improved the most. Also, by awarding points for improvement, he used his grading system to further emphasize increasing competence.

Research supports John's approach to developing his students' identity and self-concepts. An alternative, more direct approach uses strategies such as having minority students study multicultural learning materials, sending children to summer camps, and implementing support groups. These approaches are largely ineffective for two reasons. First, they focus on global self-concept, which is essentially unrelated to achievement, and second, evidence of increased competence is needed before self-concept will improve (O'Mara, Marsh, Craven, & Debus, 2006).

Helping students develop positive identities and self-concepts isn't easy, and efforts such as John's won't work with all students or with any one student all the time. However, with time and effort, you can make a difference in these important areas of development.

Ethnic Identity

Maria Robles squeezes her mother's hand as they enter her new school. Her mother can tell she is nervous as she anxiously eyes the bigger boys and girls walking down the hallway.

As they enter a kindergarten classroom, Carmen Avilla, her teacher, comes to greet them.

"Hola. ¿Cómo te llamas, niña?" (Hello. What is your name, little one?)

Maria, hiding behind her mother, is still uneasy but feels some relief.

"Dile tu nombre" (Tell her your name), her mother prompts, squeezing her hand and smiling.

" . . . Maria," she offers hesitantly.

Her mother adds quickly, "Maria Robles. Yo soy su madre." (I am her mother.)

Carmen looks on her list, finds Maria's name, and checks it off. Then she invites them, in Spanish, to come into the room and meet the other boys and girls. Music is playing in the background. Maria recognizes some of her friends who are playing with toys in a corner of the room.

"Maria, ven aquí y juega con nosotros." (Maria, come here and play with us.)

Maria hesitates for a moment, looks up at her mother, and then runs over to join her friends.

Ethnicity and Self-Esteem

As you saw earlier, self-esteem (self-worth) is an emotional reaction to, or an evaluation of, the self, and it raises personal questions. Will others like us? Are we perceived as smart? Do people think we're attractive? Culture plays a role in helping us answer these questions, and it is particularly important for members of cultural minorities.

Ethnic identity refers to an awareness of ethnic group membership and a commitment to the values and behaviors of that group, and **collective self-esteem** refers to individuals' perceptions of the relative worth of the groups to which they belong. When these groups are valued by society and perceived as having positive status, personal identities and self-esteem are enhanced. The opposite is also true.

Children as young as Maria know they are part of an ethnic minority, and research dating back to the 1930s indicates that children who are minorities such as African Americans (Clark & Clark, 1939), Mexican Americans (Weiland & Coughlin, 1979), and Chinese Americans (Aboud & Skerry, 1984) evaluate their ethnic reference groups as less worthy than the White majority. As children who are in ethnic minority groups develop, they become increasingly aware of problems with inequality and discrimination.

More recent research suggests that African American children who grow up in supportive environments, both at home and school, actually possess higher levels of self-esteem than their Caucasian American counterparts (French et al., 2006). However, many cultural minorities experience hardships linked to poverty, crime, and drug use, and schools that are unresponsive to the needs of minority children can retard the development of self-concept and self-esteem (Ferguson, 2003; Noguera, 2003). These findings suggest that unique challenges often exist for students who are members of ethnic minorities.

Ethnic Pride and Identity Formation

Students with positive ethnic identities achieve higher and have more positive beliefs about their ability to cope with their environments (French et al., 2006). You can contribute to

Ethnic identity. An awareness of ethnic group membership and a commitment to the attitudes, values, and behaviors of that group.

Collective self-esteem. Individuals' perceptions of the relative worth of the groups to which they belong.

Teachers can help students develop ethnic pride and positive self-esteem by actively acknowledging and valuing the ethnic and cultural strengths different students bring to school.

this process by making every effort to communicate to students that their ethnic heritage and language are both recognized and valued. Like Maria, many students come to school wondering if they will be welcome. The way you react to them, as Carmen did with Maria, has a powerful impact on their developing identities and sense of self-worth. Let's look at another example.

> Because Valdo Ayala, one of his Hispanic students appears withdrawn and emotionally negative in class, David Haughy, an American history teacher, calls Valdo into his classroom early in the school year.
>
> "Where are you from, Valdo?" David asks.
>
> " . . . Puerto Rico."
>
> "Oh, wow!" David exclaims enthusiastically. "My wife and I were in San Juan during the summer, and we loved it. . . . We went down into old San Juan, ate in some of the local restaurants, and listened to some great music. . . . San Juan was great, and we're already talking about going back." (Excerpt based on David Haughy, Personal Communication, January 3, 2011).

As David described it in his personal communication, this simple expression of enthusiasm about being in San Juan resulted in a complete turnaround in Valdo's attitude. We're all emotional beings, and David's affirmation communicated to Valdo that he was welcome and valued in David's classroom.

---

check your understanding

3.1 You are teaching a ninth-grade student whom you can't "get going." He will do what is required of him and no more. He does a good job on his required work, however, and seems to be quite happy. Explain his behavior using Erikson's theory as a basis. What might you do in response to this pattern of behavior?

3.2 Look again at the students' conversation at the beginning of the discussion of identity development. Use their statements to explain the state of identity development for each of the students.

3.3 "I know I can get this down the way I want to say it," a student says to his friend. "I've always been a decent writer. I'm not sure why I'm having a problem." Use the idea of self-concept and/or the idea of self-esteem to explain the student's comments. Describe the relationships between self-concept, self-esteem, and academic achievement.

To receive feedback for these questions, go to Appendix A.

Classroom connections

Promoting Psychosocial and Self-Concept Development

1. Erikson believed that social connections to others play a major role in promoting psychosocial development. Use social connection as an umbrella under which you interact with your students.

   ■ **Elementary:** A kindergarten student, while watering plants, knocks one over on the floor. Her teacher says evenly, "Sweep up the dirt, and wipe up the water with some paper towels." When the student is finished, the teacher hugs her and comments, "Everyone makes mistakes. The important thing is what we do about them."

   ■ **Middle School:** A math teacher designs her instruction so that all students are successful enough to develop a sense of industry. She spends extra time with students after school, and she lets students redo some of their assignments if they make an honest effort the first time. She frequently comments, "Math is for everyone—if you try!"

   ■ **High School:** A biology teacher pays little attention to the attire and slang of his students as long as offensive language isn't used, the rights of others are recognized, and learning occurs.

2. Success on challenging tasks is important for developing a sense of industry in students. Help students understand that effort leads to success and competence.

   ■ **Elementary:** A second-grade teacher carefully teaches a topic and provides precise directions before making seatwork assignments. She conducts "monitored practice" with the first few items to be sure all students get started correctly. When students encounter difficulties, she meets with them separately to provide extra support.

- **Middle School:** A sixth-grade teacher develops a grading system based partially on improvement so that students can succeed by improving their performance. He regularly meets with them to help them monitor their learning progress.

- **High School:** An art teacher uses portfolios and individual conferences to help her students set goals and see their growth over the year. During conferences, she emphasizes improvement and the link between effort and accomplishments.

3. Self-concepts develop from students' experiences. Make students feel wanted and valued in your class. Provide learning experiences that promote success.

- **Elementary:** A fourth-grade teacher starts the school year by having students bring in pictures of themselves and places them on a bulletin board together with personal information that students

volunteer. They list interests and favorite activities and describe what they want to be when they grow up.

- **Middle School:** A homeroom teacher for entering middle schoolers tries to make his classroom a place where students feel safe and secure. He begins the school year with classroom meetings where students get to know one another and form homeroom rules. As the year progresses, he uses these meetings to discuss issues and problems important to students.

- **High School:** A ninth-grade English teacher begins each school year by announcing that everyone is important and that she expects everyone to learn. She structures her classrooms around success and minimizes competition. She also stays in her room after school and invites students who are having problems to come by for help.

Social Development

As you saw at the beginning of the chapter, social development describes the advances people make in their ability to interact and get along with others. The relationship between social development, school success, and success in later life is well established. "There is a growing body of scientifically based research supporting the strong impact that enhanced social and emotional behaviors can have on success in school and ultimately in life" (Zins, Bloodworth, Weissberg, Wang, & Walberg, 2004, p. 19). Understanding social development can help you contribute to this important process.

We turn now to perspective taking and social problem solving, two important dimensions of social development.

Perspective Taking: Understanding Others' Thoughts and Feelings

Perspective taking is the ability to understand the thoughts and feelings of others. Let's look at four fifth graders working on a project to see how Mindy, one of the students, demonstrates this ability.

> Octavio, Mindy, Sarah, and Bill are studying American westward expansion in social studies. They'd been working as a group for 3 days and are preparing a report to be delivered to the class. There is some disagreement about who should present which topics.
>
> "So what should we do?" Mindy asks, looking at the others. "Octavio, Sarah, and Bill all want to report on the Pony Express."
>
> "I thought of it first," Octavio argues.
>
> "But everyone knows I like horses," Sarah counters.
>
> "Why don't we compromise?" Mindy suggests. "Octavio, didn't you say that you were kind of interested in railroads because your grandfather worked on them? Couldn't you talk to him and get some information for the report? And Sarah, I know you like horses. Couldn't you report on horses and the Plains Indians? . . . And Bill, what about you?"
>
> "I don't care . . . whatever," Bill replies, folding his arms and peering belligerently at the group.

Perspective taking. The ability to understand the thoughts and feelings of others.

As with all aspects of development, perspective taking develops slowly (Burack et al., 2006). Before age 8, children typically don't understand events from others' perspectives, and it is often missing even in older children, as illustrated by Octavio's assertion, "I thought of it first," or Bill's angry response. As they mature and acquire social experiences, however, it improves.

People skilled in perspective taking can handle difficult social situations, display empathy and compassion, and are better liked by their peers. Those less skilled tend to interpret others' intentions as hostile, which can lead to conflict, and they don't feel guilty or remorseful when they hurt other people's feelings (Eisenberg, Fabes, & Spinrad, 2006).

This section addresses the third question we asked at the beginning of the chapter: "Why doesn't Sean get along with the other students?" His belief that the other kids are "out to get him" suggests underdeveloped perspective taking. He may also lack social problem-solving skills, the topic of our next section.

Social Problem Solving

Social problem solving is the ability to resolve conflicts in ways that are beneficial to all involved. Students who are good at it have more friends, fight less, and work more efficiently in groups than those who are less skilled (Patrick, Anderman, & Ryan, 2002). Mindy displayed this ability when she suggested a compromise acceptable to everyone.

Social problem solving typically occurs in four sequential steps (Eisenberg et al., 2006).

1. Observe and interpret social cues. ("Bill seems upset, probably because he isn't getting his first choice.")
2. Identify social goals. ("If we are going to finish this project, everyone must contribute.")
3. Generate strategies. ("Can we find different topics that will satisfy everyone?")
4. Implement and evaluate the strategies. ("This will work if everyone agrees to shift their topic slightly.")

Like perspective taking, social problem solving develops gradually and with practice (D. W. Johnson & Johnson, 2006). Young children, for example, are not adept at reading social cues, and they tend to create simplistic solutions that satisfy themselves but not others. Older children realize that persuasion and compromise can benefit everyone, and they're better at adapting when initial efforts aren't successful.

Social problem solving. The ability to resolve conflicts in ways that are beneficial to all involved.

Perspective taking and social problem solving are important aspects of learners' social development.

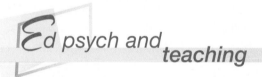 *Ed psych and teaching*

Applying an Understanding of Social Development with Your Students

As with development in general, social development requires experience. You can make important contributions to your students' social development by modeling social skills and by organizing your classroom in ways that provide social experiences. The following guidelines can help you in your efforts to apply this understanding with your students.

1. Model and explicitly teach social skills.
2. Establish rules governing acceptable classroom behavior.
3. Help students understand the reasons for rules by providing examples and rationales.
4. Have students practice social skills, and give them feedback.

Let's see how Teresa Manteras, a first-year teacher, uses these guidelines as she works with her sixth graders.

"How are you doing, Teresa?" Carla Ambergi, a veteran colleague asks as Teresa enters the teachers' lounge.

"A little discouraged," Teresa sighs. "I learned about all those great cooperative learning activities in my university classes, but when I try them with my kids, all they do is snip at each other and argue about who is doing what. Maybe I should just lecture."

"They're not used to working in groups," Carla smiles, "and they haven't learned how to cooperate. They need practice."

"Yes, I know, . . . but I don't even know where to start."

"Would you like me to come in during my planning period? Maybe I can help."

"That would be great!" Teresa replies with a big sense of relief.

Carla comes in the next day, and then she and Teresa sit down together after school. "First, I think you do an excellent job of modeling social skills," Carla comments. "You consider where the kids are coming from, you treat disagreements as an opportunity to solve problems, and you are supportive. . . . But, your modeling goes right over their heads. They don't notice what you're doing. So, I suggest that you be more specific; tell the kids what you're modeling and give them some examples. Then, add a few rules that will help guide their interactions with each other. It will take some time, but it will make a difference."

"Good points," Teresa nods. "I hadn't quite thought about it that way before."

Carla then helps Teresa develop several rules that address behavior in groups:

1. Listen politely until other people are finished before speaking.
2. Treat other people's ideas with courtesy and respect.
3. Paraphrase other people's ideas in your own words before disagreeing.
4. Encourage everyone to participate.

Teresa starts the next day. Before breaking students into groups, she tells them that they are going to work on their social skills, and she models several examples, such as making eye contact, checking perceptions, and listening attentively. Then, she presents and explains the new rules, has volunteers role-play an example for each, and guides a discussion of the examples.

Students then begin their group work. Teresa monitors the groups, intervenes when they have difficulties, and reconvenes the class when she sees a similar problem in several groups. The students are far from perfect, but they are improving.

Now let's look at Teresa's attempts to apply the guidelines. She applied the first by modeling and explicitly teaching her students the social skills she wanted them to develop. Just as learning to write, for example, involves understanding grammar and punctuation together with practice, developing social skills involves both understanding and practice in interactions with others (Elias, 2004).

Teresa applied the second guideline by creating a set of rules designed to support the students as they worked together. She presented only four rules, first because they supplemented her general classroom rules, but also because a small number makes them easier to remember.

Third, Teresa provided concrete examples of the rules by having students role-play social situations and then discussing each to be sure students understood what the role-playing illustrated. Her modeling provided additional examples of desirable social skills and actions.

Finally, Teresa provided opportunities for students to practice their social skills during group work, and she gave them feedback. Students won't become socially skilled after one or two activities, but with time, practice, and explicit instruction, these skills can be developed (D. W. Johnson & Johnson, 2006).

---

check your understanding

4.1 Describe and explain the major components of social development.

4.2 Two kindergarteners are arguing about who gets to play next at the water table. Their teacher approaches them and says, "Hmm. It looks like you both want to play at the water table at the same time. What could we do to make both of you happy?" What dimension of social development is this teacher trying to promote? Why?

To receive feedback for these questions, go to Appendix A.

Classroom connections

Advancing Social Development in Classrooms

1. Perspective taking, the ability to understand the thoughts and feelings of others, is an important part of social development. Provide opportunities for students to consider the perspectives of others.

   ■ **Elementary:** A fourth-grade teacher has her students analyze different characters' motives and feelings when they discuss a story they've read. She asks, "How does the character feel? Why does the character feel that way? How would you feel if you were that person?"

   ■ **Middle School:** A middle school science teacher stays after school to provide opportunities for students to talk both about class work and issues with parents and friends. She listens patiently but encourages students to think about the motives and feelings of the other people involved.

   ■ **High School:** A history teacher encourages his students to consider point of view when they read reports of historical events. For example, when his students study the Civil War, he reminds them that both sides thought they were morally right and asks questions such as, "How did the different sides in the war interpret the Emancipation Proclamation?"

2. Social problem solving is the ability to resolve conflicts in ways that are beneficial to all involved. Provide opportunities for students to engage in social problem solving as they work with others.

   ■ **Elementary:** A third-grade teacher periodically has groups of four students check each others' math homework. When conflicts arise, he encourages students to work out the problems themselves and intervenes only if they cannot resolve the problems.

■ **Middle School:** An eighth-grade English teacher sometimes purposefully leaves decisions about individual assignments up to the groups in cooperative learning activities. When disagreements occur, she offers only enough assistance to get the group back on

track. If the problem is widespread, she calls a whole-class meeting to discuss the problem.

■ **High School:** When art students argue about space and access to materials and supplies, their teacher calls a class meeting and requires them to discuss the problem and suggest solutions acceptable to everyone.

Development of Morality, Social Responsibility, and Self-Control

At the beginning of the chapter, we defined moral development as advances in people's conceptions of right and wrong and prosocial traits such as honesty, respect for others, and the ability to control one's emotions.

Moral issues are common in schools. To see an example, let's revisit Amanda Kellinger, our teacher at the beginning of the chapter, as she works with her eighth graders.

> "I need to go to the office for a moment," Amanda announces as her students work on a seatwork assignment. "Work quietly until I get back. I'll only be gone for a few minutes."
>
> A shuffling of papers can be heard for a few moments, and then Gary whispers, "Psst, what math problems are we supposed to do?"
>
> "Shh! No talking," Talitha says, pointing to the rules posted on the bulletin board.
>
> "But he needs to know so he can do his work," Krystal replies. "It's the evens on page 79."
>
> "Who cares?" Dwain growls. "She's not here. She won't catch us."

What influences our students' interpretation of classroom rules? For example, how might we explain the differences between Talitha's, Krystal's and Dwain's reactions to the rule about no talking? More importantly, as students move through life, how do they think about the laws and conventions that govern our society? These are all moral issues.

Society's Interest in Moral Development

Moral development has always been a priority, and interest in it has increased in recent years, partially due to disturbing trends in our country. For example, you saw earlier in the chapter that nearly half of all students report being bullied (Josephson Institute Center for Youth Ethics, 2010). Also, surveys indicate that as many as three fourths of high school students admit to cheating on tests, and cheating appears to be on the rise from elementary schools through college (Anderman & Murdock, 2007; Bracey, 2005).

Outside of schools, political corruption and scandals that led to the economic downturn in the latter part of the last decade have sent shock waves through the financial community and American society in general. The American public is increasingly looking to education for solutions to problems such as these (Bushaw, & Lopez, 2010).

Moral issues are also embedded in the school curriculum. History is more than a chronology of events; it's the study of people's responses to moral issues, such as human suffering, justice, and whether decisions to go to war are justified. And teachers commonly choose books such as *To Kill a Mockingbird, The Scarlet Letter,* and *A Tale of Two Cities,* not only because they are good literature but also because they examine moral issues.

Moral development is an integral part of development in general, and students' beliefs about right and wrong influence their behavior. For instance, some research suggests that the extent to which adolescents believe the world is fair and just influences their attitudes toward the victims of bullying (Fox, Elder, Gater, & Johnson, 2010), and incidents of cheating and vandalism decrease if students believe they are morally wrong (Murdock, Miller, & Kohlhardt, 2004). Also, the moral atmosphere of a school—democratic and prosocial versus authoritarian, for example—can influence student motivation and the value students place on their learning experiences (Christenson & Havsy, 2004). Understanding moral development helps us better guide our students in this vital area.

Moral, Conventional, and Personal Domains

To understand moral development we need to make distinctions between *moral, conventional,* and *personal* domains (Nucci, 2006; Turiel, 2006), and they relate to the questions we asked in "Ed Psych and You" here. Moral domains deal with basic principles of right, wrong, and justice. Most people believe it's wrong, for example, to pass a parked school bus whether or not children are leaving it, and it's clearly wrong to try to hurt someone by spreading false rumors. (We examine the issue of speeding later in this section.)

Ed Psych and You
Think about these questions:

Is it okay to pass a parked school bus with its stop sign out if no kids are leaving the bus?

Is it okay to drive faster than the speed limit if everyone else is driving about the same speed?

Is it okay to respond in class if your instructor hasn't called on you?

Is it okay to get a tattoo or pierce your nose or eyebrow?

Social conventions, in contrast, are societal norms and ways of behaving in specific situations. For instance, it's likely that your instructors allow students to respond in class without being called on, and it's okay to yell at an athletic event but not in a classroom. Social conventions also vary according to culture and setting. For example, young people addressing adults by their first names is acceptable in some cultures but not in others.

Social conventions. Societal norms and ways of behaving in specific situations.

Finally, the *personal domain* refers to decisions that are not socially regulated and do not harm or violate others' rights. Parents and other adults may think tattoos and body piercing look awful, but they aren't morally wrong, and they aren't usually addressed by social conventions such as dress codes.

Children as young as 2 or 3 begin to make distinctions between moral, conventional, and personal domains (Nucci, 2001, 2006). They understand, for example, that it's wrong to hit and hurt someone regardless of where you are and whether or not rules prohibiting it exist. Some researchers even suggest that we are born with a rudimentary sense of justice that can be observed in the first months of life (Bloom, 2010).

As children acquire experiences and observe the consequences of actions, they gradually develop a more sophisticated understanding of differences in the domains. For example, when children push a classmate down on the playground, they see the impact of their actions on others, and they are often reprimanded or punished by adults. They also begin to realize that conventions are arbitrary and situation specific, which can result in their questioning both school regulations and rules at home.

The lines between the moral, conventional, and personal domains are often blurred and depend on individuals' interpretations. Some preservice teachers, for example, view giving all students the opportunity to participate in class as a moral issue, whereas others are more likely to classify it in the conventional domain (Schellenberg & Eggen, 2008). Further, some researchers view reasoning about social conventions and society's rules as advances in moral development (Kohlberg, 1981, 1984).

Piaget's Theory of Moral Development

Although cognitive development usually comes to mind when we think about Piaget, he also examined the development of morals. He studied cognitive and moral development in much the same way—by observing children, presenting them with problems, and asking questions to probe their thinking (Krebs & Denton, 2005).

Piaget (1965) found that children's responses to moral problems can be divided into two broad stages. In the first, called **external morality,** children view rules as fixed, permanent, and enforced by authority figures. When Talitha said, "Shh! No talking," and pointed to the rules, she was thinking at this stage. It didn't matter that Gary was only asking about the assignment; rules are rules. In responding "Who cares? She's not here. She won't catch us," Dwain demonstrated a similar level of thinking; he was focusing on the fact that no authority figure was there to enforce the rule. External morality typically lasts to about age 10. Piaget believed that parents and teachers who stress unquestioned adherence to adult authority retard moral development and unintentionally encourage students to remain at this level.

When students advance to **autonomous morality,** the second stage, they develop rational ideas of fairness and see justice as a reciprocal process of treating others as they would want to be treated (Turiel, 2006). Children at this stage begin to rely on themselves instead of others to regulate moral behavior. Krystal's comment, "But he needs to know so he can do his work," demonstrates this kind of thinking; she viewed Gary's whispering as an honest request for assistance rather than an infraction of rules.

External morality. A stage of moral development in which individuals view rules as fixed and permanent and enforced by authority figures.

good or bad?

Autonomous morality. A stage of moral development characterized by the belief that fairness and justice is the reciprocal process of treating others as they would want to be treated.

Kohlberg's Theory of Moral Development

Lawrence Kohlberg, a Harvard educator and psychologist, built on and extended Piaget's work. He used **moral dilemmas,** ambiguous, conflicting situations that require a person to make a moral decision, as the basis for his research. Let's look at an example.

Moral dilemma. An ambiguous, conflicting situation that requires a person to make a moral decision.

> Steve, a high school senior, works at a night job to help support his mother, a single parent of three. Steve is conscientious and works hard in his classes, but he doesn't have enough time to study.
>
> Because of his night work and lack of interest in history, he is barely passing. If he fails the final exam, he will fail the course and won't graduate. He isn't scheduled to work the night before the exam, so he has extra time to study. But, early in the evening his boss calls, desperate to have Steve come in and replace another employee who called in sick at the last moment. His boss pressures him, so Steve goes to work at 8:00 p.m. and comes home exhausted at 2:00 a.m. He tries to study but falls asleep on the couch with his book in his lap. His mother wakes him for school at 6:30 a.m.
>
> Steve goes to history, looks at the test, and goes blank. Everything seems like a jumble. Clarice, one of the best students in the class, happens to have her answer sheet positioned so that he can clearly see every answer by barely moving his eyes.
>
> Is he justified in cheating?

This is a moral issue because it deals with matters of right and wrong, and it's a dilemma because any decision Steve makes has positive and negative consequences. If he cheats, he will pass the test, but cheating is wrong. On the other hand, if he doesn't cheat, he will likely fail the course and not graduate.

Kohlberg (1963, 1969, 1981, 1984) used responses to moral dilemmas, such as this one, as a basis for his research, which he later developed into his theory of moral development. Like Piaget, he concluded that moral reasoning exists in stages, and development occurs when people's reasoning advances to a higher stage. On the basis of research conducted in Great Britain, Malaysia, Mexico, Taiwan, and Turkey, Kohlberg concluded that the development of moral reasoning is similar across cultures.

Discussing moral dilemmas provides students with opportunities to examine their thinking about moral issues.

Table 3.3	Kohlberg's stages of moral reasoning
Level 1 Preconventional Ethics (*Typical of preschool and elementary students.*)	The ethics of egocentrism. Typical of children up to about age 10. Called preconventional because children typically don't fully understand rules set down by others.
Stage 1: Punishment–Obedience	Consequences of acts determine whether they're good or bad. Individuals make moral decisions without considering the needs or feelings of others.
Stage 2: Market Exchange	The ethics of "What's in it for me?" Obeying rules and exchanging favors are judged in terms of the benefit to the individual.
Level II Conventional Ethics (*Seen in older elementary and middle school students and many high school students.*)	The ethics of others. Typical of 10- to 20-year-olds. The name comes from conformity to the rules and conventions of society.
Stage 3: Interpersonal Harmony	Ethical decisions are based on concern for or the opinions of others. What pleases, helps, or is approved of by others characterizes this stage.
Stage 4: Law and Order	The ethics of laws, rules, and societal order. Rules and laws are inflexible and are obeyed for their own sake.
Level III Postconventional Ethics (*Rarely seen before college, and the universal principles stage is seldom seen even in adults.*)	The ethics of principle. Rarely reached before age 20 and only by a small portion of the population. The focus is on the principles underlying society's rules.
Stage 5: Social Contract	Rules and laws represent agreements among people about behavior that benefits society. Rules can be changed when they no longer meet society's needs.
Stage 6: Universal Principles	Rarely encountered in life. Ethics are determined by abstract and general principles that transcend societal rules.

Kohlberg originally described moral reasoning as occurring at three levels, consisting of two stages each (Turiel, 2006). They are outlined in Table 3.3 and discussed in the sections that follow. As you read the descriptions, remember that the specific response to a moral dilemma isn't the primary issue; the level of moral development is determined by the *reasons* a person gives for making the decision.

Level I: Preconventional Ethics

Preconventional morality is an egocentric orientation that focuses on the consequences of actions for the self. In the **punishment–obedience** stage, people make moral decisions based on their chances of getting caught and being punished. If a person is caught and punished, an act is morally wrong; if not, the act is right. A person believing that Steve is justified in cheating because he is unlikely to get caught is reasoning at this stage. At Stage 2, **market exchange,** people reason that an act is morally justified if it results in reciprocity, such as "You do something for me, and I'll do something for you."

Level II: Conventional Ethics

When development advances to the **conventional level of morality,** reasoning no longer depends on the consequences for the individual but instead is linked to acceptance of society's conceptions of right and wrong and the creation of an orderly world. In Stage 3, **interpersonal harmony,** people make decisions based on loyalty, living up to the expectations of others, and social conventions. For example, a teenager on a date who believes she should meet a curfew because she doesn't want to worry her parents is reasoning at this stage. A person reasoning at Stage 3 might offer two different perspectives on Steve's dilemma. One could argue that he needs to work to help his family and therefore is justified in cheating.

Preconventional morality. An egocentric orientation lacking any internalized standards for right and wrong.

Punishment–obedience. A stage of moral reasoning in which conclusions are based on the chances of getting caught and being punished.

Market exchange. A stage of moral reasoning in which conclusions are based on an act of reciprocity on someone else's part.

Conventional morality. A moral orientation linked to uncritical acceptance of society's conventions about right and wrong.

Interpersonal harmony. A stage of moral reasoning in which conclusions are based on loyalty, living up to the expectations of others, and social conventions.

Law and order. A stage of moral reasoning in which conclusions are based on following laws and rules for their own sake.

A contrasting view, but still at this stage, would suggest that he should not cheat because people would think badly of him if they found out.

At Stage 4, **law and order,** people follow laws and rules for their own sake. They don't make moral decisions to please other people or follow social norms as in Stage 3; rather, they believe that laws and rules exist to guide behavior and create an orderly world, and they should be followed uniformly. A person reasoning at Stage 4 would argue that Steve should not cheat because "It's against the rules to cheat," or "What kind of world would we live in if people thought cheating was okay."

Stages 3 and 4 relate to the question, "Is it okay to drive faster than the speed limit if everyone else is driving about the same speed?" that we asked in this section's "Ed Psych and You." People reasoning at Stage 3 might conclude that speeding is okay, since everyone else is doing it. On the other hand, they could conclude that it isn't okay, because it isn't safe, and it's wrong to put people in danger. People reasoning at Stage 4 would conclude that the speed limit is the law, and breaking the law is wrong.

Level III: Postconventional Ethics

Postconventional morality. A moral orientation that views moral issues in terms of abstract and self-developed principles of right and wrong.

Postconventional morality, also called *principled morality*, views moral issues in terms of abstract principles of right and wrong. People reasoning at Level III have transcended both the individual and societal levels. They don't follow rules for their own sake, as a person reasoning at Stage 4 would suggest; rather, they follow rules because the rules are principled agreements. Only a small portion of the population attains this level, and most don't reach it until their middle to late 20s.

Social contract. A stage of moral reasoning in which conclusions are based on socially agreed-upon principles.

In Stage 5, **social contract,** people make moral decisions based on socially agreed-upon principles. A person reasoning at Stage 5 would say that Steve's cheating is wrong because teachers and learners agree in principle that grades should reflect achievement, and cheating violates this agreement.

Universal principles stage. A stage of moral reasoning in which conclusions are based on abstract and general principles that transcend or exceed society's laws.

At the sixth and final stage, **universal principles,** the individual's moral reasoning is based on abstract, general principles that transcend society's laws. People at this stage define right and wrong in terms of internalized universal standards. "The Golden Rule" is a commonly cited example. Because very few people operate at this stage, and questions have been raised about the existence of "universal" principles, Kohlberg deemphasized this stage in his later writings (Kohlberg, 1984).

I still don't understand this stage

Evaluating Kohlberg's Theory

As with all theories, Kohlberg's work has strengths and weaknesses. For instance, most people move through the first four stages in the order and rate predicted by his theory. Development is slow and gradual, and reasoning at Stages 1 and 2 decreases in early adolescence. Reasoning at Stage 3 increases in mid-adolescence and then declines. Stage 4 reasoning increases during the teenage years, and by early adulthood, it is the typical response (Nucci, 2006; Turiel, 2006):

Several criticisms have been directed at Kohlberg's work. For example, research suggests that few people move beyond Stage 4 (Gibbs, 2010), so if postconventional reasoning is required for people to be morally mature, few people measure up. Critics also point out that people's thinking, while tending to be at a certain stage, often shows evidence of reasoning at other stages.

Moral reasoning also depends on context (Turiel, 2006), and it relates to our "Ed Psych and You" questions about speeding and passing a parked school bus. For example, people are likely to believe that breaking a traffic law is immoral if it can cause someone harm, and they commonly view passing a parked school bus with the stop sign displayed as unacceptable, but believe exceeding the speed limit on an interstate to be okay.

Although Kohlberg attempted to make his stages content free, thinking about moral dilemmas is influenced by domain-specific knowledge (Nucci, 2006; Turiel, 2006). For example, a medical doctor asked to deliberate about an educational dilemma or a teacher asked to resolve a medical issue would be hampered by their lack of professional knowledge.

Researchers also question the self-reports of individuals' thought processes that Kohlberg used in his data-gathering methods. "Using interview data assumes that participants can verbally explain the workings of their minds. In recent years, this assumption has been questioned, more and more" (Rest et al., 1999, p. 295).

Finally, Kohlberg's work has been criticized for focusing on moral *reasoning* instead of moral *behavior.* People may reason at one stage and behave at another, influenced by context and personal history (Krebs & Denton, 2005). For example, an adolescent trying to decide whether to drink alcohol when out with friends will be influenced by family and cultural values as well as peer pressure. Kohlberg's work ignores these factors.

true!

However, some research supports a connection between moral reasoning and moral behavior. For example, adolescents reasoning at the lower stages are likely to be less honest and to engage in more antisocial behavior, such as delinquency and drug use (Comunian & Gielan, 2000). In contrast, reasoning at the higher stages is associated with altruistic behaviors, such as defending victims of injustice, the rights of minorities, and free speech (Turiel, 2006).

would not consider delinquency and drug abuse/use antisocial but rather immoral; don't have to be alone to be a criminal or a drug

Gender Differences: The Morality of Caring

Some critics of Kohlberg's work also argue that it fails to adequately consider ways in which gender influences morality. Early research examining Kohlberg's theory identified differences in the ways men and women responded to moral dilemmas (Gilligan, 1982, 1998; Gilligan & Attanucci, 1988). Men were more likely to base their judgments on abstract concepts, such as justice, rules, and individual rights; women were more likely to base their moral decisions on interpersonal connections and attention to human needs. According to Kohlberg, these differences suggested a lower stage of development in women responding to moral dilemmas.

Carol Gilligan (1977, 1982), also a Harvard psychologist and Kohlberg's colleague, argued that the findings, instead, indicate an "ethic of caring" in women that is not inferior; rather, Kohlberg's descriptions don't adequately represent the complexity of female thinking. Gilligan suggests that a morality of caring proceeds through three stages. In the first, children are concerned primarily with their own needs. In the second, they show concern for others who are unable to care for themselves, such as infants and the elderly. And in the third, they recognize the interdependent nature of personal relationships and extend compassion to all of humanity. To encourage this development, Gilligan recommends an engaging curriculum with opportunities for students to think and talk about moral issues involving caring.

Nell Noddings (1992, 2002) has also emphasized the importance of caring in schools, especially for teachers. Noddings argues that students should be taught the importance of caring through a curriculum that emphasizes caring for self, family and friends, and others throughout the world.

Gilligan makes an important point about gender differences, but additional research is mixed; some studies have found gender differences whereas others have not (Turiel, 2006). Like cross-cultural studies, Gilligan's research reminds us of the complexity of the issues involved in moral development.

Emotional Factors in Moral Development

Ultimately, we want people to both reason and behave morally. Emotions, including feelings of sorrow and guilt, provide a vital link between our moral reasoning and our actions. Let's see how.

"Are you okay?" her mother asks as Melissa walks in the house after school with a dejected look on her face.

Although unpleasant, feelings of shame and guilt indicate that moral development is advancing.

Shame. The painful emotion aroused when people recognize that they have failed to act or think in ways they believe are good.

Guilt. The uncomfortable feeling people get when they know they've caused distress for someone else.

Empathy. The ability to experience the same emotion someone else is feeling.

Theory of mind. An understanding that other people have distinctive perceptions, feelings, desires, and beliefs.

Emotional intelligence. The ability to understand emotions in ourselves and others.

Emotional self-regulation. The ability to manage our emotions so we can cope with the environment and accomplish goals.

"I feel really bad, Mom," Melissa answers softly. "We were working in a group, and Jessica said something sort of odd, and I said, 'That's dumb. Where did that come from?' . . . She didn't say anything for the rest of our group time. She doesn't get really good grades, and I know saying something about her being dumb really hurt her feelings. I didn't intend to do it. It just sort of came out."

"I know you didn't intend to hurt her feelings, Sweetheart. Did you tell her you were sorry?"

"No, when I realized it, I just sat there like a lump. I know how I'd feel if someone said I was dumb."

"Tell you what," her mom suggests. "Tomorrow, you go directly to her, tell her you're sorry you hurt her feelings, and that it won't happen again."

"Thanks, Mom. I'll do it as soon as I see her. . . . I feel a lot better."

This exchange is about morality, but it doesn't involve reasoning; instead, it deals with emotions. Piaget and Kohlberg focused on cognitive aspects of moral development, but emotions provide an important link between our thoughts and actions (Saarni, Campos, Camras, & Witherington, 2006). For instance, Melissa felt both **shame,** the painful emotion aroused when people recognize that they have failed to act or think in ways they believe are good, and **guilt,** the uncomfortable feeling people get when they know they've caused someone else's distress. Although unpleasant, experiencing shame and guilt indicates that moral development is advancing and future behavior will improve.

When Melissa said, "I know how I'd feel if someone said I was dumb," she was also describing feelings of **empathy,** the ability to experience the same emotion someone else is feeling. Empathy promotes moral and prosocial behavior even in the absence of wrongdoing (Eisenberg, et al., 2006).

As children develop they slowly acquire a **theory of mind,** an understanding that others have distinctive perceptions, feelings, desires, and beliefs. **Emotional intelligence,** the ability to understand emotions, such as shame, guilt, and empathy in ourselves and others is an important part of this theory of mind. The term *emotional intelligence* has been popularized by Daniel Goleman (2006), who asserts that success in life is largely due to our ability to understand the role of emotions in our daily lives. Emotional intelligence is related to positive self-esteem and social skills, and low emotional intelligence and aggression are correlated (Lopes & Salovey, 2004).

Emotional Self-Regulation

Have you ever had a person make a rude remark to you, and you thought, "I'd love to tell him [or her] where to go!"? But, you don't. You have demonstrated **emotional self-regulation,** the ability to manage our emotions so we can cope with the environment and accomplish goals. It's another important component of healthy development, and it includes factors such as:

- controlling impulses to behave in socially unacceptable ways (controlling the impulse to tell the other person where to go)
- managing negative emotions (able to forget about the rude remark after initially feeling angry about it)
- behaving in socially acceptable ways (deciding to talk calmly to the person about the remark, or simply leaving)

Students able to manage their emotions are more personally satisfied and are better able to make and keep friends than those who exhibit less self-control. In addition, they become better students, because they're able to focus their emotions on learning tasks (Saarni et al., 2006).

As we would expect, children differ considerably in their ability to control and regulate their emotions. Older children are better at it than their younger counterparts, significantly because their advanced language development provides a tool they can use to examine and monitor their emotions (e.g., "I know I feel badly about the test, but I'll commit to studying harder for the next one."). Boys have a harder time than girls with controlling negative emotions. Boys tend to act out, whereas girls are more likely to feel sad or guilty, which, if it becomes extreme, can result in moodiness or depression (Berk, 2010). Also, members of Asian cultures, such as Japanese and Chinese, tend to teach emotional restraint instead of the assertive and emotionally expressive patterns common in western cultures (Camras et al., 2006).

You can help students develop emotional self-regulation by openly talking about emotions and discussing strategies for dealing with them. In the process you can remind students that feeling a variety of emotions is normal and okay, but some ways of responding to these emotions are better than others. For example, feeling hurt and angry is normal, but responding calmly is much better than lashing out at a person.

Literature also offers opportunities to focus on emotions by asking questions about characters' motives, feelings, and actions. Our goal is for students to become aware of their emotions, how they influence our behavior, and ultimately how to control them, so they don't control us. As with each of the forms of development discussed in this chapter, if we can meet this goal, our students will have acquired an ability that will serve them well throughout their lives.

You can help students develop emotional self-regulation by openly talking about emotions and discussing strategies for dealing with them.

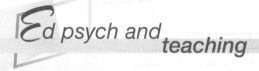

Ed psych and teaching

Promoting Moral Development in Your Students

You have many opportunities to promote moral development in your students. You do so primarily with your modeling, the kind of classroom environment you create, and the way you guide students' interactions with each other. The following guidelines can provide a framework for you as you attempt to promote this essential form of development:

1. Model ethical thinking, behavior, and empathy in your interactions with students.
2. Use classroom management as a vehicle for promoting moral development.
3. Encourage students to understand and respect the perspectives of others.
4. Use moral dilemmas as concrete reference points for discussions of moral issues.

Let's see how Rod Leist, a fifth-grade teacher, uses these guidelines as he works with his students:

> Rod begins language arts by saying, "Let's look in the story we've been reading and talk about Chris, the boy who found the wallet. He was broke, so would it be wrong for him to keep it, . . . and the money in it? . . . Jolene?"
> "No, because it didn't belong to him."
> "Ray?"
> "Why not keep it? He didn't steal it; and . . . "

> "That's terrible," Helena interrupts. "How would you like it if you lost your wallet?"
> "Helena," Rod admonishes, "remember, we agreed that we would let everyone finish their point before we speak."
> "Sorry for interrupting. . . . Please finish your point, Ray," Rod adds.
> " . . . It wasn't his fault that the person lost it. . . . And he was broke."
> "Okay, Helena, go ahead," Rod says.
> "Just . . . how would you feel if you lost something and somebody else kept it? . . . . That's why I think he should give it back."
> "That's an interesting point, Helena. When we think about these issues, it's good for us to try to put ourselves in someone else's shoes. . . . Of course, we would feel badly if we lost something and it wasn't returned.
> "Go ahead, . . . Juan?"
> "I agree. It was a lot of money, and Chris's parents would probably make him give it back anyway."
> "And what if the person who lost the money really needs it?" Kristina adds.

After continuing the discussion for several more minutes, Rod says, "These are all good points. . . . Now, I want each of you to write a short paragraph saying whether or not you would keep the wallet and explaining why you feel it would be right or wrong. Then, we'll discuss your reasons some more tomorrow."

Now, let's look at Rod's attempts to apply the guidelines. He applied the first with his modeling. His simple and brief apology for interrupting the discussion communicated that he also obeyed their classroom rules. Also, he reinforced Helena for being empathic and modeled his own empathy by saying, "That's an interesting point, Helena. When we think about these issues, it's good for us to try to put ourselves in someone else's shoes," Efforts to be fair, responsible, and democratic in dealings with students speak volumes about teachers' values and views of morality (Kohn, 2004).

Rod's management system and his response to Helena applied the second and third guidelines. He stopped her and reminded the class that they agreed to let people finish a point before speaking, and, in doing so he encouraged fairness and tolerance for differing opinions. Understanding these values is an important part of self-regulation, which can only be developed if students understand rules, why they are important, and agree to follow them. This kind of learning environment promotes *autonomous morality* (Murdock et al., 2004).

Rod applied the fourth guideline by using the story of the lost wallet as a concrete reference point for the discussion of a moral issue. During the discussion and in the writing exercise, he encouraged students to articulate and justify their moral positions on the issue.

Research supports this approach. Discussions that encourage students to examine their own reasoning combined with exposure to more advanced thinking promotes moral development (Nucci, 2006).

check your understanding

5.1 Heavy traffic is moving on an interstate highway at a speed limit of 65. A sign appears that says "Speed Limit 55." The flow of traffic continues as before. How might a driver at Stage 3 and a driver at Stage 4 react? Explain each driver's reasoning.

5.2 Think again about the vignette at the beginning of this section. Using Gilligan's views as a basis, how might a woman's response to the problem of Gary not knowing the homework assignment differ from a man's?

5.3 To which of Kohlberg's stages are empathy, prosocial behaviors, and emotional regulation most closely related? Explain.

To receive feedback for these questions, go to Appendix A.

Classroom connections

Supporting Moral Development in Classrooms

1. Moral development is enhanced by opportunities to think about moral dilemmas and hear the positions of others. Openly discuss ethical issues when they arise.

   ■ **Elementary:** The day before a new student with an exceptionality joins the class, a second-grade teacher has students discuss how they would feel if they were new, how new students should be treated, and how they should treat one another in general.

   ■ **Middle School:** A seventh-grade teacher has a classroom rule stating that students may not laugh, snicker, or make remarks of any kind when a classmate is trying to answer a question. She has the students discuss reasons for the rule, emphasizing how people feel when others laugh or snicker at their efforts.

   ■ **High School:** A teacher's students view cheating as a game, seeing what they can get away with. The teacher addresses the issue by saying, "Because you feel this way about cheating, I'm going to decide who gets what grade without a test. I'll grade you on how smart I think you are." This provocative statement precipitates a classroom discussion on fairness and cheating.

2. Moral development advances when students are exposed to moral behavior and moral reasoning at higher levels. Model moral and ethical behavior for students.

   ■ **Elementary:** One election November, fifth-grade students jokingly ask if the teacher votes. The teacher uses this as an opportunity to discuss the importance of voting and each person's responsibilities in our democracy.

   ■ **Middle School:** A science teacher makes a commitment to have students' tests and quizzes scored by the following day. One day, when asked if he has the tests ready, he replies, "Of course. . . . At the beginning of the year, I said I'd have them back the next day, and we can't go back on our agreements."

   ■ **High School:** A group of students finishes a field trip sooner than expected. "If we just hang around a little longer, we don't have to go back to school," one student suggests. "Yes, but that would be a lie, wouldn't it?" their teacher counters. "We said we'd be back as soon as we finished, and we need to keep our word."

Developmentally appropriate *practice*

Personal, Social, and Moral Development with Learners at Different Ages

Important differences exist in the personal, social, and moral development of elementary, middle, and high school students. The following paragraphs outline suggestions that will help you respond to these differences.

Working with Students in Preschool Programs and Elementary Schools

As children enter preschool, they are developing autonomy and taking the initiative to seek out experiences and challenges. "Let me help!" and "I want to do it" are signs of this initiative. Criticism or overly restrictive directions detract from a sense of independence and, in extreme cases, lead to feelings of guilt and dependency. At the same time, children need the structure that helps them learn to take responsibility for their own behavior.

As children move through the elementary years, teachers attempt to help them succeed in learning experiences challenging enough to promote feelings of competence and industry. This is demanding. Activities that are so challenging that students frequently fail can leave them with a sense of inferiority, but success on trivial tasks does little to make students feel competent (Brophy, 2010).

During the elementary years, students need opportunities to practice perspective taking and social problem solving. Discussions and small-group work where students can interact with others and practice these skills are effective learning experiences.

The elementary grades also lay the foundation for students' moral growth and the development of social responsibility and self-control. Teachers who help students understand the impact of their actions on others help them make the transition from preconventional morality, with its egocentric orientation, to conventional morality, at which stage, students understand why rules are important for both classrooms and the world outside of school.

Working with Students in Middle Schools

Adolescence is a time of considerable physical, emotional, and intellectual changes, and adolescents are often uncertain about how to respond to new sexual feelings. They are concerned with what others think of them and are preoccupied with their looks. They want to assert their independence, yet long for the stability of structure and discipline. They want to rebel to assert their independence but need something solid to rebel against.

Most adolescents successfully negotiate this period, however, exploring different roles and maintaining positive relationships with their parents and other adults. Students in middle and junior high school need firm, caring teachers who empathize with them and their sometimes capricious actions while simultaneously providing the security of clear limits for acceptable behavior (Mawhinney & Sagan, 2007). Classroom management provides opportunities to advance moral reasoning from preconventional to conventional thinking. Effective teachers create classroom rules, discuss the reasons for them, and enforce them consistently.

Instruction in middle school classrooms should promote deep understanding of the topics being studied, while simultaneously providing students with opportunities to practice prosocial behaviors, such as tolerance for others' opinions, listening politely, and avoiding hurtful comments. Effective instruction in middle schools is highly interactive, and lecture is held to a minimum.

Working with Students in High Schools

High school students are continuing to wrestle with who they are and what they want to become. Peers become an increasingly important part of students' microsystems and have an important influence on both social and moral development.

Linking content to students' lives is particularly valuable at this age. For example, examining ideas about gender and occupational trends in social studies and showing how math and science can influence their futures are important for these students.

Like younger learners, high school students need opportunities to try out new ideas and link them to their developing sense of self. Discussions, small-group work, and focused writing assignments provide valuable opportunities for students to integrate new ideas into their developing self-identities.

Summary

1. Describe the systems in Bronfenbrenner's bioecological model, and explain how they influence development.
   - The bioecological model includes the individual and the environmental systems that influence each individual's development.
   - The microsystem describes the people and activities in a child's immediate surroundings, and the mesosystem describes interactions among the elements of the microsystem.
   - The exosystem describes societal influences on development, and the macrosystem examines the role of cultural influences.
   - Each system influences development through the experiences they provide for the developing learner.

2. Describe how physical development influences personal, social, and moral development.
   - In elementary schools, differences in size are major factors in development. Girls develop fine motor skills more quickly than do boys.
   - Differences in maturation rates are significant as students move into adolescence. Early-maturing girls experience more uncertainty and tend to be less popular than do girls who mature less rapidly. The opposite is true for boys.

3. Use descriptions of psychosocial, identity, and self-concept development to explain learner behavior.
   - Erikson's psychosocial theory integrates personal and social development. Psychosocial development occurs in stages, each marked by a psychosocial challenge called a *crisis*. Positive resolution of the crisis in each stage prepares the individual for the challenge at the next.
   - The development of identity usually occurs during high school and beyond. Identity moratorium and identity achievement are healthy developmental states; identity diffusion and identity foreclosure are less healthy.
   - Self-concept, developed largely through personal experiences, describes individuals' cognitive assessments of their own physical, social, and academic competence. Academic self-concept, particularly in specific content areas, is strongly correlated with achievement.

   - Attempts to improve self-concept as an outcome of increased achievement in specific areas are often successful, unlike attempts to improve students' self-concepts by direct interventions.

4. Describe major components of social development, and explain how you can promote social development in your students.
   - Perspective taking and social problem solving are major components of social development.
   - Perspective taking allows students to consider problems and issues from others' points of view.
   - Social problem solving includes the ability to read social cues, generate strategies, and implement and evaluate strategies for solving social problems.
   - Teachers promote social development when they provide examples and give students opportunities to practice social skills in the context of classroom learning experiences.

5. Use theories of moral development to explain differences in our responses to ethical issues.
   - Piaget suggested that moral development represents individuals' progress from external morality, the enforcement of rules by authority figures, to autonomous morality, the perception of morality as rational and reciprocal.
   - Kohlberg's theory of moral development is based on people's responses to moral dilemmas. He developed a classification system for describing moral reasoning that occurs in three levels.
   - At the preconventional level, people make egocentric moral decisions; at the conventional level, moral reasoning focuses on the consequences for others; and at the postconventional level, moral reasoning is based on principle.
   - Feeling empathy and even unpleasant emotions such as shame and guilt mark advances in moral development.
   - Teachers promote moral development by emphasizing personal responsibility and the functional nature of rules designed to protect the rights of others.

Understanding Personal, Social, and Moral Development: Preparing for Your Licensure Exam

Your licensure exam will include information related to students' personal, social, and moral development, and we include the following exercises to help you practice for the exam in your state. This book will be a resource for you as you prepare for the exam.

Let's look now at a teacher working with a group of middle school students and how she contributes to these important aspects of development. Read the case study, and answer the questions that follow:

"This is frustrating," Helen Sharman, a seventh-grade teacher, mumbles as she scores a set of quizzes in the teachers' workroom after school.

"What's up?" her friend Natasha asks.

"These students just don't want to think," Helen responds. "Three quarters of them put an apostrophe between the *r* and the *s* in *theirs*. The quiz was on using apostrophes in possessives. I warned them I was going to put some questions on the quiz that would make them think. Not only that, but I had them practice on exercises just like those on the quiz. And I explained it so carefully," she sighs.

"What's discouraging is that some of the students won't even try. Look at this one. It's half blank. This isn't the first time Karl has done this, either. When I talked to him about it last time, he said, 'But I'm no good at English.' I replied, 'But you're doing fine in science and math.' He just shrugged and said, 'But that's different. I'm good at them.' I wish I knew how to motivate him. You should see him on the basketball floor—poetry in motion—but when he gets in here, nothing."

"I've got a few like that myself," Natasha nods.

"What's worse, I'm almost sure some of the kids cheated. I left the room to go to the office, and when I returned, several of them were whispering and had guilt written all over their faces."

"Why do you suppose they did it?" Natasha replies.

"I'm not sure; part of it might be grade pressure, but how else am I going to motivate them? Some just don't see any problem with cheating. If they don't get caught, fine."

"Well," Natasha shrugs, "hang in there."

The next morning, as she returns the quizzes, Helen begins, "We need to review the rules again. You did so poorly on the quiz, and I explained everything so carefully. You must not have studied very hard.

"Let's take another look," she continues. "What's the rule for singular possessives?"

Helen explains the rules for forming possessives, and then asks, "Why didn't you do that on the quiz?"

Hearing no reply she continues, "Okay, look at number 3 on the quiz."

It appears as follows:

The books belonging to the lady were lost.

"It should be written like this," Helen explains, writing, "The lady's books were lost" on the chalkboard.

"Ms. Sharman," Nathan calls from the back of the room. "Why is it apostrophe *s*?"

"Nathan," Helen says evenly. "Remember my first rule?"

"Yes, Ma'am," Nathan says quietly.

"Good. If you want to ask a question, what else can you do other than shout it out?"

"Raise my hand."

"Good."

She then explains the item, also explains other items commonly missed on the quiz, and hands out a review sheet. "Now, these are just like the quiz," she says. "Practice hard on them, and we'll have another quiz on Thursday. Let's all do better. Please don't let me down again.

"One more thing. There was some cheating on this test. If I catch anyone cheating on Thursday, I'll tear up your paper and give you a zero. Now go to work."

Questions for **Case Analysis**

In answering these questions, use information from the chapter, and link your responses to specific information in the case.

1. How might Erikson explain Karl's behavior in Helen's class?

2. Using findings from the research on self-concept, explain Karl's behavior.

3. Using concepts from Kohlberg's theory, analyze Helen's cheating problem. From Kohlberg's perspective, how well did she handle this problem?

4. If you think Helen's teaching could have been improved on the basis of the information in Chapter 3, what suggestions would you make? Again, be specific.

For feedback on these responses, go to Appendix B.

Your licensure exam will also include multiple-choice questions similar to those your instructor has given you on your quizzes and tests for this course.

Important **Concepts**

attachment (p. 69)
autonomous morality (p. 92)
bullying (p. 74)

collective self-esteem (p. 85)
conventional morality (p. 93)
crisis (p. 78)

cyberbullying (p. 75)
emotional intelligence (p. 96)
emotional self-regulation (p. 96)

empathy (p. 96)
ethnic identity (p. 85)
exosystem (p. 68)
external morality (p. 92)

guilt (p. 96)

hostile attributional bias
    (p. 73)

identity (p. 78)

instrumental aggression
    (p. 73)

interpersonal harmony (p. 93)

law and order (p. 94)

macrosystem (p. 68)

market exchange (p. 93)

microsystem (p. 68)

mesosystem (p. 68)

moral development (p. 66)

moral dilemma (p. 92)

parenting style (p. 68)

personal development (p. 66)

perspective taking (p. 87)

physical aggression (p. 73)

postconventional morality
    (p. 94)

preconventional morality
    (p. 93)

proactive aggression (p. 73)

puberty (p. 77)

punishment–obedience
    (p. 93)

reactive aggression (p. 73)

relational aggression (p. 73)

school connectedness
    (p. 72)

self-concept (p. 78)

self-esteem (p. 82)

self-worth (p. 82)

sexual identity (p. 81)

sexual orientation (p. 81)

shame (p. 96)

social conventions (p. 91)

social contract (p. 94)

social development (p. 66)

social problem solving
    (p. 88)

temperament (p. 67)

theory of mind (p. 96)

universal principles (p. 94)

Go to the Topic: Personal, Social, and Moral Development in the MyEducationLab (www.myeducation lab.com) for *Educational Psychology: Windows on Classrooms*, where you can:

- Find learning outcomes for Personal, Social, and Moral Development, along with the national standards that connect to these outcomes.
- Complete Assignments and Activities that can help you more deeply understand the chapter content.
- Apply and practice your understanding of the core teaching skills identified in the chapter with the Building Teaching Skills and Dispositions learning units.
- Examine challenging situations and cases presented in the IRIS Center Resources.
- Access video clips of CCSSO National Teachers of the Year award winners responding to the question, "Why Do I Teach?" in the Teacher Talk section.
- See video examples included within the Study Plan that provide concrete and real-world illustrations of the topics presented in the chapter.
- Check your comprehension of the content covered in the chapter with the Study Plan. Here you will be able to take a chapter quiz, receive feedback on your answers, and then access Review, Practice, and Enrichment activities to enhance your understanding of chapter content.

MyEducationLab

chapter 4

Learner Diversity

chapteroutline

Culture	
Ethnicity	
Culture and Classrooms	
Linguistic Diversity	
English Dialects	
English Learners	
Gender	
School-Related Gender Differences	
Gender Differences in Classrooms	
Gender Stereotypes and Perceptions	
Socioeconomic Status	
Poverty	
How SES Influences Learning	
SES: Some Cautions and Implications for Teachers	
Students at Risk	
Resilience and Students at Risk	

learningoutcomes

After you've completed your study of this chapter, you should be able to:

1. Describe culture and ethnicity, and explain how they can influence learning.

2. Explain why so much linguistic diversity exists in our country, and describe ways that teachers can accommodate this diversity.

3. Explain how gender can influence learning, and describe steps for eliminating gender bias in classrooms.

4. Define socioeconomic status, and explain how it can affect learning.

classroomapplications

The following features help you apply the content of this chapter in your teaching.

Ed Psych and Teaching:
Teaching Students in Your Classes Who Are Culturally and Linguistically Diverse
Responding to Your Students' Gender Differences
Promoting Resilience in Your Students

Classroom Connections:
Working with Students Who Are Culturally and Linguistically Diverse in Classrooms
Eliminating Gender Bias in Classrooms
Effective Teaching Practices for Promoting Resilience in Classrooms

Developmentally Appropriate Practice:
Student Diversity at Different Ages

Exploring Diversity:
Teaching and Learning in Urban Schools

Learner diversity refers to both the group and individual differences in our students, it exists in every classroom, and it can have a powerful effect on learning. As you read the following case study, involving Jay Evans, a third-grade teacher, focus on the diversity in his class and how it influences the way he works with his students.

Jay teaches in a large, urban elementary school. He has 29 students—16 girls and 13 boys—in his class. It includes 8 African Americans, 7 students of Hispanic descent, 3 Asian Americans, and 2 immigrants from Russia. English is not the native language for several, and most of his students come from low-income families.

He smiles as he walks by Katia's desk. She is his "special project," and she is blossoming in response to his efforts. When she first came to school, she was hesitant

Learner diversity. The group and individual differences in our students.

to participate because she came from Mexico, where Spanish was her native language. Initially, she could understand simple English sentences but struggled with speaking and reading English from textbooks. Jay made a point of involving her in learning activities, paired her with students who could help her with English, spent time with her after school, and gave her second-grade books to read at home. Her parents are supportive of Jay's efforts, and home–school communication is very good. Her progress since the beginning of the year has been remarkable.

As he steps past Angelo, his glow turns to concern. Angelo struggles to keep up with the rest of the class, and he is quiet and easily offended by perceived slights from his classmates. Because his parents are Mexican migrant workers, the family moves frequently, and he repeated first grade. His parents are separated, and his mother has settled in this area so the children can stay in the same school.

Jay consults with Jacinta Morales, a colleague who is bilingual, about additional things to try with Angelo. Together they develop a plan to help him with both his English and his academic work.

As you saw in the case study, Jay's students are very diverse. For instance, he has African American, Hispanic, Asian, and Russian students in his class, and 16 are girls and 13 are boys. Cultural background and gender are two types of group differences. English is not the native language for several of the children, and their socioeconomic status (SES) varies. Language and SES are also important group differences. These dimensions of diversity are outlined in Figure 4.1.

When we consider these differences, however, we must remember that they describe only general patterns, and a great deal of variation exists within each group. For instance, both Katia and Angelo come from Mexico, so their cultural backgrounds are similar, and both are native Spanish speakers. However, Katia is thriving in Jay's class, whereas Angelo is struggling. Learner diversity also involves individual differences in our students.

These differences lead to two questions:

1. How might learner diversity influence learning?
2. How should we, as teachers, respond to this diversity?

Research helps answer these and other important questions about our students. We begin by looking at studies examining the impact of culture on learning.

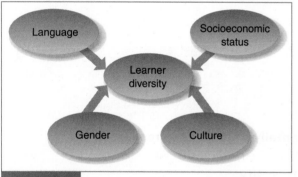

Figure 4.1 Sources of learner diversity

Culture

Ed Psych and You

Think about the clothes you wear, the music you like, and the activities you share with your friends.

Or, even think about food. What, how, and when do you eat? Do you use a knife and fork, or chopsticks, or even your fingers? When is it polite to eat with your fingers?

Culture. The knowledge, attitudes, values, and customs that characterize a social group.

The answers to the questions in "Ed Psych and You" all depend on your **culture,** which includes the knowledge, attitudes, values, and customs that characterize a social group (Banks, 2008). Culture is one of the most important influences in our lives, and it can also influence success in school (see Figure 4.2).

The cultural diversity in our country is rapidly increasing. U.S. Census estimates indicate that members of cultural minorities now make up more than a third of our nation's population (Santa Cruz, 2010), and the 2000 census found, for the first time, that the Hispanic surnames Garcia and Rodriguez are among the 10 most common in our country (Roberts, 2007).

This trend is reflected in our classrooms, where more than 4 of 10 students in the P–12 population are members of cultural minorities. Children of color currently make up the majority of public school enrollments in California, Hawaii, Louisiana, Mississippi, New Mexico, and Texas, and over 90% of the student population in Detroit, New York, Washington, D.C., Chicago, Los Angeles, and Baltimore (Padilla, 2006).

More recently—and significantly—2010 census data indicate that for the first time in history, less than half of 3-year-olds in our country were White (Frey, 2011). This means that White students will no longer be a majority as these children move through school.

Ethnicity

Ethnicity, a person's ancestry and the way individuals identify with the nation from which they or their ancestors came, is an important part of culture (Banks, 2008). Members of an ethnic group have a common history, language (although sometimes not actively used), value system, and set of customs. Experts estimate that nearly 300 distinct ethnic groups live in the United States (Gollnick & Chinn, 2009).

Immigration and other demographic shifts have resulted in dramatic changes in the ethnic makeup of our country's school population. The Immigration Act of 1965, which ended quotas based on national origin, resulted in more immigrants coming to our country from a wider variety of places. For example, while most during the early 1900s came from Europe, nearly 40% of more recent immigrants come from Mexico and Central America, about 25% come from Asia, and 10% come from the Caribbean. Less than 15% now come from Europe (U.S. Bureau of Census, 2010). This helps us understand why Jay's students have such diverse backgrounds.

By the year 2020, the school-age population will see more changes (see Figure 4.3). Researchers predict significant increases in all groups of students except those that are

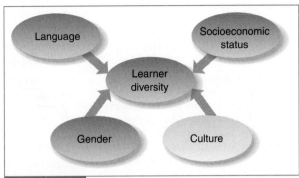

Figure 4.2 Sources of learner diversity: Culture

Ethnicity. A person's ancestry and the way individuals identify with the nation from which they or their ancestors came.

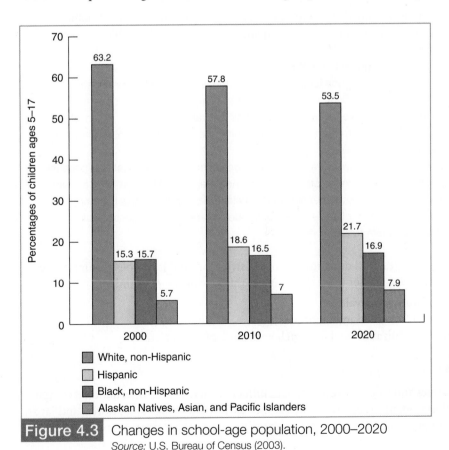

Figure 4.3 Changes in school-age population, 2000–2020
Source: U.S. Bureau of Census (2003).

The diversity in our students is rapidly increasing, and members of cultural minorities are now majorities in several states and large cities.

White and non-Hispanic, who will decrease to a little more than half of the total school population (U.S. Bureau of Census, 2003). By 2050, no one ethnic group will be a majority among adults. Each of these groups brings a distinct set of values and traditions that influences learning.

Race. A socially constructed category composed of people who share biologically transmitted traits considered important.

Race, a socially constructed category composed of people who share biologically transmitted traits considered important, provides another way of classifying people. But its value for understanding the students we teach is limited. First, the idea of race is complex, with the U.S. Census Bureau offering over 60 different options to people describing themselves (Macionis, 2009). In addition, because of immigration and intermarriage—one in seven new marriages is between people of different ethnicities—an increasing number of people are classifying themselves as multiracial or multiethnic (Saulny, 2011). Experts estimate that the mixed-race population has grown by 35% since 2000. So, as we think about culture, ethnicity, and race, it is important to remember that these are simply labels, they are constantly changing, and we teach people, not categories.

Culture and Classrooms

When students enter our classrooms, they bring with them a set of values and beliefs from their home and neighborhood cultures, and these values often complement and reinforce classroom practices. If they don't, however, mismatches that interfere with learning can occur (Greenfield et al., 2006). A **cultural mismatch** is a clash between a child's home culture and the culture of the school that creates conflicting expectations for students and their behavior. Awareness of possible mismatches is a first step in dealing with them.

Cultural mismatch. A clash between a child's home culture and the culture of the school that creates conflicting expectations for students and their behavior.

Let's look at an example.

> Cynthia Edwards, a second-grade teacher in an elementary school in the Southwest, is reading a story. "What do you think is going to happen next? . . . Tony?" Cynthia asks in response to his eagerly waving hand.
>
> "I think the boy is going to meet his friend."
>
> "How do you think the boy feels about meeting his friend?" she continues.
>
> After Tony responds, Cynthia calls on Sharon Nighthawk, one of several Native Americans in her class, even though Sharon has not raised her hand. When Sharon doesn't answer, Cynthia prompts her by rephrasing the question, but Sharon continues to look at her in silence.
>
> Slightly exasperated, Cynthia wonders if Sharon understands her questions, because Sharon seems to be enjoying the story and also understands it. Why won't she answer?
>
> Thinking about the lesson after school, Cynthia realizes that that this has happened before, and that, in fact, her Native American students rarely answer questions in class.
>
> She can't get them to talk.

Why do students respond differently to our instruction, and how does culture influence these differences? We consider these questions in this section as we examine:

- cultural attitudes and values
- patterns of adult–child interactions
- classroom organization and its match with students' home cultures

Cultural Attitudes and Values

Cultural attitudes and values have a powerful influence on learning. International comparisons reveal that students in Asian countries, such as Taiwan, Hong Kong, Korea, and Japan, typically score significantly higher on achievement tests than their counterparts in the

United States (Programme for International Student Assessment, 2006). While structural differences in education probably account for some of these differences (many of these Asian countries have school years that are up to 50 days longer than in the United States), cultural attitudes about the importance of studying and hard work are also likely factors.

These values transfer to Asian American students, who typically score higher on achievement tests and have higher rates of college attendance and completion than do other groups, including European Americans (Greenfield et al., 2006). Asian American parents typically have high expectations for their children and encourage them not only to attend college but also to earn graduate or professional degrees (Gollnick & Chinn, 2009). And they often translate these aspirations into academic activities at home that augment school-assigned homework (Kagitcibasi, 2007). This pattern is symbolized by self-proclaimed "tiger mom" Amy Chua, whose book describing her ultra-strict and, to many, over-the-top expectations for her daughters, received so much publicity that she and her parenting methods were featured in the January 31, 2011, issue of *Time* magazine (Paul, 2011).

In contrast, members of some cultural minorities, such as African American, Native American, and Hispanic American consistently score lower on achievement tests (Aldous, 2006). Sometimes members of these groups form **resistance cultures,** cultures with beliefs, values, and behaviors that reject the values of mainstream culture (Ogbu, 1992, 1999, 2003; Ogbu & Simons, 1998).

To maintain their identity within their chosen group, members of resistance cultures reject attitudes and behaviors that lead to school success, such as doing homework, studying, and participating in class. To become a high achiever is to "become White," and students who study, want to succeed, and become actively involved in school face rejection from their peers. Low grades, classroom management and motivation problems, truancy, and high dropout rates are often the result (Stinson, 2006).

John Ogbu (2003), who was a prominent researcher in the fields of minority education and identity, encourages teachers to help members of cultural minorities adapt to the dominant culture (including schools) without losing their cultural identities, a process he calls "accommodation without assimilation." The challenge is to help students understand the "culture of schooling"—the norms, procedures, and expectations necessary for success—while honoring the value and integrity of students' home cultures.

Minority role models are especially important in this process, as one African American doctor recalls:

> It all started in the second grade. One . . . Career Day at Jensen Scholastic Academy in my teacher, Mrs. F.'s room, an M.D. came to speak to the class about his career as a doctor. . . . I can't remember his name but from that day forward I knew I was destined to be a doctor. From that point on I began to take my work seriously, because I knew to become a doctor grades were very important. Throughout my elementary career I received honors. In the seventh grade I really became fascinated with science, which I owe all to my teacher Mr. H. He made learning fun and interesting. I started to read science books even when it wasn't necessary, or I found myself watching the different specials on Channel 11 about operations they showed doctors performing. (Smokowski, 1997, p. 13)

Minority role models provide learners with evidence that they can both succeed in mainstream culture and retain their cultural identity (Tiedt & Tiedt, 2010).

Stereotype Threat. As minority students struggle to adapt to and compete in schools, they sometimes experience **stereotype threat,** the anxiety felt by members of a group resulting from concern that their behavior might confirm a stereotype (Aronson, Wilson, & Akert, 2010; Huguet & Régner, 2007). It adversely affects performance through heightened anxiety that reduces students' capacity for thinking and problem solving (Okagaki, 2006).

Resistance cultures. Cultures with beliefs, values, and behaviors that reject the values of mainstream culture.

Minority role models help members of cultural minorities understand that they can both succeed in mainstream culture and retain their cultural identity.

Stereotype threat. The anxiety felt by members of a group resulting from concern that their behavior might confirm a stereotype.

Stereotype threat is most pernicious for high-achieving members of cultural minorities, but at some level it's a problem for other groups as well. For instance, it exists when women fear that they will do less well than men on tests involving math or computer science, because they think that these are male domains, or when White males fear they will perform less well on math tests because they're competing with Asian students who they believe are better at math.

You can minimize the negative effects of stereotype threat in three ways. First, communicate positive expectations for all learners from the first days of class. Second, make individual improvement the theme of your teaching, and minimize comparisons among students. And third, model and emphasize the role of hard work and effort in learning. These suggestions increase motivation to learn and lead to increased success for all students (Brophy, 2010).

Cultural Differences in Adult–Child Interactions

Cultural interaction patterns learned in the home also influence student behavior in school (Tyler et al., 2008). For example, Barbara Rogoff found that White children tend to respond comfortably to questions requiring specific answers, such as "What's this story about?" African American children, accustomed to questions that are more "open-ended, story-starter" types, are sometimes confused by the specific questions, because they aren't viewed as information givers in their homes (Rogoff, 2003).

Made aware of these cultural differences, teachers can incorporate more open-ended questions in their lessons, and provide extra support and praise for their minority students' attempts to respond to specific questions. These simple steps build bridges between the students' cultural learning styles and their classrooms.

Cultural mismatches can also occur in interpretations of time and acceptable school-related behaviors. One principal's experience working with Pacific Island students is an example (Winitzky, 1994). The principal had been invited to a community awards ceremony honoring students from her school. She readily accepted, arrived a few minutes early, and was ushered to a seat of honor on the stage. After an uncomfortable (to her) wait of over an hour, the ceremony began. The children received their awards and returned to their seats, which led to an eye-opening experience:

> Well, the kids were fine for a while, but as you might imagine, they got bored fast and started to fidget. Fidgeting and whispering turned into poking, prodding, and open chatting. I became a little anxious at the disruption, but none of the other adults appeared to even notice, so I ignored it, too. Pretty soon several of the children were up and out of their seats, strolling about the back and sides of the auditorium. All adult faces continued looking serenely up at the speaker on the stage. Then the kids started playing tag, running circles around the seating area and yelling gleefully. No adult response—I was amazed, and struggled to resist the urge to quiet the children. Then some of the kids got up onto the stage, running around the speaker, flicking the lights on and off, and opening and closing the curtain! Still nothing from the Islander parents! . . . I suddenly realized then that when these children . . . come to school late, it doesn't mean that they or their parents don't care about learning. . . . that's just how all the adults in their world operate. When they squirm under desks and run around the classroom, they aren't trying to be disrespectful or defiant, they're just doing what they do everywhere else. (Winitzky, 1994, pp. 147–148)

Students from different cultures bring with them ways of acting and interacting with adults that may differ from the traditional teacher-as-authority-figure role (Tyler et al., 2008). Her experience with Pacific Island culture gave the principal insights into the reasons her students often acted as they did.

So, what should we do if we have an experience similar to the principal's? Easy answers don't exist, but we can attempt to apply Ogbu's (2003) idea of "accommodation without assimilation" in situations such as these. We establish the clear classroom norms, procedures, and expectations necessary for success both in school and in life after school, while at the same time communicating that we value and care about all our students and respect their cultural differences.

Classroom Organization and Culture

In many classrooms, teachers emphasize individual performance, which is reinforced by test scores and grades. This can lead to competition, which requires successes and failures, and the success of one student may be tied to the failure of another. Students from other cultures, such as Native American, Mexican American, and Southeast Asian, may experience difficulties in competitive classrooms (Aronson et al., 2010). They may value cooperation and view competition as unnecessary or even distasteful. A cultural mismatch then exists when they come to school and are asked to compete. Raising hands and jousting for the right to answer isn't congruent with the ways they interact at home. In addition, the typical teacher questions–student answers–teacher responds sequence found in most classrooms isn't a normal part of family life in many cultures. Children aren't routinely asked questions adults already know the answer to, instead being expected to quietly observe adult interactions (Greenfield et al., 2006).

This helps us understand the problem with the students who wouldn't respond to Cynthia Edwards' questions. The Native American children sat quietly because doing so was consistent with their culture.

This discussion also helps us answer the first question we asked at the beginning of the chapter: "How might learner diversity influence learning?" When cultural mismatches exist, less learning occurs. Sensitivity to these factors is important for us all.

Multicultural Education

Multicultural education examines ways that culture influences learning and attempts to find ways that students' cultures can be used to enhance achievement (Banks, 2008; Gay, 2005). It attempts to help us become aware of—and sensitive to—the ways that students' cultures can affect their approaches to learning.

Multicultural education. An approach to teaching that examines the influence of culture on learning and attempts to find ways that students' cultures can be used to enhance achievement.

James Banks (2008) has created a comprehensive model of multicultural education that encompasses the entire school. Banks' model emphasizes integration of ideas and experiences from students' cultures, prejudice reduction, and the influence of culture on the way we think about the world. Information adapted from the model is outlined in Table 4.1.

Table 4.1 Dimensions of multicultural education

Dimension	Goal
Prejudice reduction	To modify students' attitudes toward other groups of students
Content integration	To illustrate ideas using content from a variety of cultures
Equity pedagogy	To use instruction that facilitates the academic achievement of students from diverse racial, cultural, and social class groups
Understanding the knowledge-construction process	To investigate and understand how implicit cultural assumptions, frames of reference, perspectives, and biases within a discipline affect the knowledge within that discipline
An empowering school culture and social structure	To examine the total school culture (e.g., grouping, sports, and interactions with faculty and staff) to ensure that it empowers students from diverse racial, ethnic, and cultural groups

Source: Adapted from Banks (2008).

Some Cautions About Culture and Classrooms

When encountering cultural mismatches, teachers sometimes conclude that parents of children who are minorities don't value schooling or support teachers' efforts. This isn't true. Research consistently indicates that these parents care deeply about their children's learning (Greenfield et al., 2006; Lewis & Kim, 2008; Okagaki, 2006). They often don't realize that cultural mismatches exist, however. This isn't surprising; most of us grew up tacitly assuming that all homes were like ours.

Research also reminds us of the need to bridge cultural differences and adapt our instruction to the backgrounds and needs of our students (Greenfield et al., 2006). This begins when we realize that that they often enter our classrooms with different beliefs and behaviors.

Also, we must remember that our discussion of culture has focused on group differences, and individuals within the groups vary, sometimes greatly. For example, our discussion of resistance cultures focused on Ogbu's work with students who were African American. Many African American students very much want to succeed in school and do so. To conclude that they are all members of resistance cultures would be a dangerous form of stereotyping. Similarly, the successes of students who are Asian American do not mean that they are all members of a "model minority," a stereotypic term that many Asian Americans reject. Many encounter difficulties in school, and language and poverty are obstacles for them (Lew, 2006; Ngo & Lee, 2007).

You can help prevent cultural stereotyping by becoming informed about the cultural groups to which your students belong (Castagno & Brayboy, 2008; Kitayama & Cohen, 2007). Reading is helpful, but there is no substitute for direct interaction, both with your students and their caregivers. Parent–teacher conferences, phone calls, and e-mail all help establish and maintain communication.

---

check your understanding

1.1 Describe *culture* and *ethnicity,* and explain how they can influence learning.

1.2 What is a resistance culture? How can teachers effectively deal with it?

1.3 Identify at least one way in which classroom organization can clash with the values of students who are members of cultural minorities. What can teachers do about this problem?

To receive feedback for these questions, go to Appendix A.

Linguistic Diversity

Dialect. A variation of Standard English that is associated with a particular regional or social group and is distinct in vocabulary, grammar, or pronunciation.

One of five students in our country's schools—approximately 14 million—are children of immigrant parents, and they bring with them a variety of languages and dialects (Kober, 2006; Padilla, 2006). Increasingly, these students speak native languages other than English. Let's look at this linguistic diversity and its implications for our teaching (see Figure 4.4).

Ed Psych and You

Have you ever met someone from a different part of the country who talked differently than you do? Have you ever traveled to a different part of the country where you had trouble understanding people or where they had problems understanding you?

English Dialects

Anyone who travels in the United States will notice that our country has many regional and ethnic dialects; experts identify at least 11 that are distinct (Owens, 2005). A **dialect** is a variation of Standard English that is associated with a particular regional or social group and is unique in vocabulary, grammar, or pronunciation. Everyone speaks a dialect, and this addresses the questions we ask in "Ed Psych and You." We merely react to those dialects different from our own, and if they're different enough, we sometimes have trouble understanding them. Dialects are such an integral part of our lives that researchers have found they even appear on Twitter (Eisenstein, O'Connor, Smith, & Xing, 2011). (Guess what part of the country uses "y'all" most?) Some are more accepted than others, however, and language is at the heart of what Delpit (1995) calls "codes of power," the cultural and linguistic conventions that control access to opportunity in our society.

Research suggests that teachers frequently have lower expectations for students who use nonstandard English and assess the students' work accordingly (Godley, Sweetland, Wheeler, Minnici, & Carpenter, 2006). These language patterns are often confused with mistakes during oral reading, and some people believe that dialects, such as Black English, are substandard (Alim & Baugh, 2007; Snow, Griffin, & Burns, 2005). Linguists, however, believe that these variations are just as rich and semantically complex as Standard English (Godley et al., 2006; Labov, 1972).

Figure 4.4 Sources of learner diversity: Language

Dialects in the Classroom: Implications for Teachers

You can effectively respond to diversity by accepting and valuing learner differences, and this is particularly important when working with students who use nonstandard English. Dialects are integral to the culture of students' homes and neighborhoods, and requiring students to eliminate their dialects in your classroom communicates that differences are unacceptable.

Standard English, however, allows access to educational and economic opportunities, which is the primary reason for teaching it (Snow et al., 2005). Students realize this when they interview for a first job or when they plan for admission to college. So, what should you do when a student says, "I ain't got no pencil," or brings some other nonstandard dialect into your classroom? Opinions vary from "rejection and correction" to complete acceptance, but the most culturally sensitive approach is to first accept the dialect and then build on it (Padilla, 2006). For example, when a student says, "I ain't got no pencil," you might say, "Oh, you don't have a pencil. What should you do, then?" Results will take time, but the long-range benefits, both for language development and attitudes toward learning, are worth the effort.

Language differences don't have to form barriers between home and school. **Bidialecticism,** the ability to switch back and forth between a dialect and Standard English, allows access to both (Gollnick & Chinn, 2009). For example, a high school teacher read a series of poems by Langston Hughes and focused on how Hughes used Black English to create vivid images. The class discussed contrasts with Standard English and ways in which differences between the two dialects could be used to accomplish different goals. As time went on, the students learned to use Standard English in school but understood that using different dialects in their home cultures was perfectly acceptable.

Bidialecticism. The ability to switch back and forth between a dialect and Standard English.

English Learners

English learners (ELs) are students whose first or home language is not English. As a result of immigration and high birth rates among immigrant families, the number of students who are ELs and those with limited English have increased dramatically over the last three decades (U.S. Bureau of Census, 2010). In California alone, there are 1.6 million ELs, and they make up a fourth of that state's student population. Projections indicate that by 2015 more than half of all P–12 students in our country will not speak English as their first

English learners (ELs). Students for whom English is not their first or home language.

Increasingly, our students are bringing different native languages to school.

language (Gray & Fleischman, 2005). The diversity is staggering; more than 450 languages other than English are spoken in our schools, with Spanish being the most common (Abedi et al., 2004).

Let's see how this can affect our teaching.

Ellie Barton, a language arts teacher at Northeast Middle School, is the school's EL coordinator. Her job is challenging, as her students vary considerably in their knowledge of English. For instance, one group of Somali-Bantu children just arrived from a refugee camp in Kenya. They can't read or write, because there is no written language for their native tongue. In addition, many have never been in a building with more than one floor, and others find urinals and other aspects of indoor plumbing a mystery. At the other end of the continuum, another of Ellie's students is a girl from India who can read and write in four languages.

To sort out this language diversity, the district uses a placement test that categorizes students into three levels: newcomer classrooms for students who have little or no expertise with English; self-contained EL classrooms, where a primary emphasis is on learning to read and write English; and sheltered English, where students get help in learning academic subjects such as science and social studies. The process is problematic, however, because the school is unable to communicate with some parents, and a few parents don't know the exact ages of their children. Ellie's principal deals with this information void in creative ways; he recently asked a dentist friend to look at a child's teeth to estimate the student's age. (Adapted from Romboy & Kinkead, 2005)

Being an EL creates obstacles for students; they typically lag behind in achievement, they are more often referred for special education services, and they're more likely to drop out of school (Bielenberg & Fillmore, 2005). How do schools respond to this challenge? We address this question in the next section.

Ed Psych and You

Have you ever tried to learn a foreign language? Was it more difficult to learn to speak the language, understand it when spoken, or read it? How proficient were you after 2 or 3 years? How successful would you have been if all the instruction in your other classes were in that language?

Types of EL Programs

Your answers to our questions in "Ed Psych and You" give us some insight into the challenges ELs face. Teaching English is the primary goal of all EL programs, but the way they attempt to reach the goal varies considerably (see Table 4.2).

Immersion programs. English language programs that place students who are ELs in general education classrooms without additional assistance to help them learn both English and academic content at the same time.

Structured immersion. A type of immersion English language program that attempts to assist students who are ELs by teaching both English and academic subjects at a slower pace.

Immersion Programs. **Immersion programs** place students who are ELs in general education classrooms to help them learn both English and academic content (Padilla, 2006). Pure-immersion programs offer no extra assistance to these students; continual exposure is believed to be sufficient to learn English.

Structured immersion, in contrast, attempts to assist students by teaching both English and introducing academic topics at a slower pace. You may have encountered a form of structured immersion in foreign language classes, where your teacher attempted to instruct as much as possible in that language. Several states, including California and Arizona, have mandated a year of structured immersion as the beginning point for EL instruction, which is then followed by complete immersion (Padilla, 2006).

Table 4.2   Types of EL programs

Type of Program	Description	Advantages	Disadvantages
Immersion	Places students in classrooms where only English is spoken, with few or no linguistic aids.	Increased exposure to new language and multiple opportunities to use it.	Sink or swim approach may be overwhelming and leave students confused and discouraged.
Maintenance	Students maintain first language through reading and writing activities in first language while teachers introduce English.	Students become literate in two languages.	Requires teachers trained in first language. Acquisition of English may not be as fast.
Transitional	Students learn to read in first language, and teachers give supplementary instruction in English as a second language. After mastering English, students enroll in regular classrooms and discontinue learning in first language.	Maintains first language. Transition to English is eased by gradual approach.	Requires teachers trained in first language. Literacy skills in first language not maintained and may be lost.
ESL Pullout Programs	Pullout programs in which students are provided with supplementary English instruction along with regular instruction in content classes.	Easier to administer when dealing with diverse language backgrounds because it requires only the pullout teachers to have EL expertise.	Students may not be ready to benefit from content instruction in English. Pullout programs segregate students.
Sheltered English	Teachers adapt content instruction to meet the learning needs of EL students.	Easier for students to learn content.	Requires an intermediate level of English proficiency. Also requires teachers with EL expertise.

Maintenance EL Programs. Maintenance EL programs build on students' native language by teaching in both languages (Peregoy & Boyle, 2009). Found primarily at the elementary level, maintenance EL programs are designed to develop students who can speak, read, and write in two languages. These programs have the advantage of retaining and building on students' heritage language and culture, but they are difficult to implement because they require groups of students with the same native language and bilingual teachers who speak that language.

Transitional EL Programs. Transitional EL programs attempt to use the native language as an instructional aid until English becomes proficient. They begin by teaching reading and writing in the first language and gradually develop learners' English skills. Often, the transition period is too short, leaving students inadequately prepared for learning in English (Echevarria & Graves, 2011). In addition, loss of the first language and lack of emphasis on the home culture can result in communication gaps between children who no longer speak the first language and parents who don't speak English.

ESL Pullout Programs. In English as a second language (ESL) pullout programs, students receive most of their instruction in general education classrooms but are also

Maintenance EL programs. Programs for students who are ELs that build on students' native language by teaching in both languages.

Transitional EL programs. English learner programs that attempt to use the native language as an instructional aid until English becomes proficient.

English as a second language (ESL) pullout programs. Programs for students who are ELs who receive most of their instruction in general education classrooms but are also pulled out for extra help.

pulled out for extra help (Peregoy & Boyle, 2009). Instruction in these programs focuses on English language development, with emphasis on pronunciation, grammar, vocabulary, and oral comprehension. In addition, ESL teachers assist with subject matter content, such as math or social studies, which students are being taught in general education classrooms. The programs require students whose English skills are developed to the point that they can benefit from general instruction. When this isn't the case, sheltered English classes are more effective.

Sheltered English. Sheltered English classrooms modify instruction to assist students in learning content. Also called *specially designed academic instruction in English,* these classes require students with intermediate levels of English proficiency as well as instructors who know both content and EL strategies.

Avoiding overestimating their English proficiency is important when working with students who are ELs (Echevarria, Vogt, & Short, 2004; Padilla, 2006). After about 2 years in language-rich environments, students develop **basic interpersonal communication skills,** a level that allows them to interact socially with their peers (Cummins, 2000). Students often need an additional 5 to 7 years to develop **academic language proficiency,** a level that allows them to handle demanding learning tasks.

Evaluating EL Programs

English learner programs are controversial. For example, advocates of immersion claim that this approach teaches English more rapidly and efficiently; critics question whether this "sink or swim" approach is either effective or humane. Critics also argue that immersion ignores the first language, resulting in a loss of **bilingualism,** the ability to speak, read, and write in two languages.

Maintenance and transitional EL programs are also controversial (Williams, 2009). Critics contend that these programs are:

- Divisive, encouraging groups of nonnative English speakers to remain separate from mainstream American culture.
- Ineffective, slowing the development of English for students who are ELs.
- Inefficient, requiring expenditures for the training of bilingual teachers and materials that could be better spent on quality English programs (Schlesinger, 1992; U.S. English, 2011).

Proponents counter that the programs build on the student's first language and provide a smooth and humane transition to English. They also argue that being able to speak two languages has practical benefits in today's world (Merisuo-Storm, 2007).

Research on these programs is also controversial. For example, advocates of immersion cite research suggesting that students learn English faster when they're given increased opportunities to practice it in classroom activities (Krashen, Rolstad, & MacSwan, 2007). Critics of immersion counter with research suggesting that students in maintenance programs have more positive attitudes toward school and learn more math and reading. They also argue that the knowledge and skills acquired in a native language promote transfer to English (Krashen, 2005; Slavin & Cheung, 2004).

Comparing programs is difficult, because researchers use different criteria for evaluating their merits (Padilla, 2006). Some researchers focus on the speed of English acquisition, whereas others use achievement measures, such as standardized test scores or grades, as criteria. The debate is likely to continue, as the issues are both complex and emotional (Hawkins, 2004).

Sheltered English. An approach to teaching students who are ELs in academic classrooms that modifies instruction to assist students in learning content.

Basic interpersonal communication skills. A level of proficiency in English that allows students to interact conversationally with their peers.

Academic language proficiency. A level of proficiency in English that allows students to handle demanding learning tasks with abstract concepts.

Bilingualism. The ability to speak, read, and write in two languages.

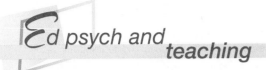

Ed psych and teaching

Teaching Students in Your Classes Who Are Culturally and Linguistically Diverse

It is a virtual certainty that you will teach students who are members of cultural minorities, and it is highly likely that English will not be the first language for some. **Culturally responsive teaching** attempts to understand the cultures of the students we teach, communicate positive attitudes about cultural diversity, and employ a variety of instructional approaches that build on students' cultural backgrounds (Gay, 2005; Leonard, 2008).

Culturally responsive teaching can make your classroom an effective learning environment for all students. The following guidelines can help you in your efforts, and they help answer the second question we asked at the beginning of the chapter: "How should we, as teachers, respond to this diversity?"

1. Communicate that you respect all cultures and value the contributions that cultural differences make to learning.
2. Involve all students in learning activities.
3. Use concrete experiences as reference points for language development.
4. Target important vocabulary, and provide opportunities for all students to practice language.

Let's see how Gary Nolan, a fourth-grade teacher, uses these guidelines as he works with his students.

Culturally responsive teaching. An approach to education that attempts to understand the cultures of the students we teach, communicate positive attitudes about cultural diversity, and employ a variety of instructional approaches that build on students' cultural backgrounds.

Of Gary's 28 students, 9 are Hispanic, 6 are African American, 4 are Asian, and 2 are from Morocco. Eight are ELs.

"You're improving all the time," Gary smiles at his students who are ELs as the rest of the class files into the room. He spends a half hour with them each morning to help them keep up with their classmates.

"Good morning, Tu . . . Nice haircut, Shah," Gary greets the other students as they come in the door.

"Who's up today?" he asks as the students settle down.

"Me," Anna says, raising her hand.

"Go ahead, Anna."

Anna moves to the front of the room. "I was born in Mexico, but my father is from Guatemala, and my mother is from Columbia," she explains, pointing to each of the countries on a map at the front of the room.

Every Friday morning Gary has one of the students make a presentation. They bring food, costumes, art, and music that illustrate their backgrounds, and they place a push pin with their name on it on the map.

Gary frequently comments about how lucky they are to have classmates from so many parts of the world. "Remember when Shah told us about Omar Khayyam?" Gary had asked. "He solved math problems that people in Europe didn't solve until many years later. If Shah wasn't in our class, we would never have learned that."

Gary also has a chart displaying common words and phrases, like "Hello," "Goodbye," and "How are you?" in Spanish, Vietnamese, Arabic, and English. He has labeled objects around the room, like the clock, windows, and chairs, in the students' native languages and English. And, he displays a calendar that identifies holidays in different cultures. Students make special presentations on the holidays, and parents are invited.

"Okay, story time," Gary says when Anna is finished. He reads a story from a book that is liberally illustrated with pictures. As he reads, he holds up the pictures and has students identify the object or event being illustrated. One picture shows a cave in some woods that the boy and girl in the story explore.

"Everyone say 'cave'," Gary directs, pointing at the picture, and the students say "cave" in unison. He does the same with other objects in the picture, such as a tree, rock, and stream.

After finishing, he begins, "Tell us something you remember about the story. . . . Carmela?"

". . . A boy and a girl . . . are lost," Carmela responds in her halting English.

"Yes, good. . . . The story is about a boy and a girl who got lost in a cave," Gary says slowly and clearly, pointing again to each of the objects in the picture.

"Have any of you ever been in a cave?. . . How is a cave different from a hole?" Gary has the students briefly talk to each other and then has them share their personal experiences with digging holes and going into caves. When they struggle with a term, Gary provides it, has the class say it in unison, and he repeats the process with another student.

"Good, everyone," Gary smiles after they've discussed the story for several more minutes. "Let's get ready for math."

Now, let's look at Gary's efforts to apply the guidelines. He implemented the first by having students make presentations about their cultural heritage and emphasizing how lucky they are to have classmates from different parts of the world. His emphasis on the contributions of Omar Khayyam, for example, and comments like, "If Shah weren't in our class, we probably would never have learned that," communicates that students' cultures are respected and valued, which can promote both pride and motivation (Banks, 2008; Gollnick & Chinn, 2009). The personal time he spent before school helping his students who were ELs and his greeting as students enter his room also communicated that he cared for each one. These gestures are subtle but important when working with members of cultural minorities (Gollnick & Chinn, 2009; Suarez-Orozco, Pimentel, & Martin, 2009).

Gary applied the second guideline by calling on all his students as equally as possible. Doing so signaled that he expected each to participate, and when they struggled, he helped them answer.

Effective teachers call on all students, regardless of students' backgrounds.

Some teachers believe that students don't *want* to answer questions. This isn't true. All students, including those who are minorities, want to be called on if they believe they will be able to answer, and you can emphasize that answering incorrectly is simply a part of learning.

Gary further implemented the second guideline by combining whole-class and small-group instruction to accommodate possible differences in learning preferences. (We examine strategies for involving all students in learning activities in Chapter 13.)

By using concrete experiences to facilitate language development, Gary implemented the third guideline. For example, as he read the story he referred to pictures in the book, which provided concrete reference points for vocabulary (Echevarria & Graves, 2011). He also encouraged students to share their personal experiences with the ideas, and he linked language to them.

Gary applied the fourth guideline by specifically targeting key terms. Vocabulary, and especially the technical vocabulary found in many content areas, is challenging for students who are ELs (S. Baker, Gersten, Haager, & Dingle, 2006). Context clues together with specific strategies that differentiate closely related words, such as Gary did with cave and hole, are particularly important. He further applied both the third and fourth guidelines by labeling objects around the room in both English and students' native languages, he spoke slowly and clearly in rephrasing students' responses, and he had the students repeat terms in unison (Peregoy & Boyle, 2009).

Finally, Gary provided all of his students with opportunities to practice language. Language is a skill, and students learn English by using it in their day-to-day lives. Open-ended questions, such as "Tell us something you remember about the story. . . . Carmela?" that allow students to respond without the pressure of giving specific answers are particularly effective (Echevarria & Graves, 2011).

As you saw in Gary's efforts, working with students who are ELs is challenging. However, these students respond very positively to caring and genuine attempts to help them adapt to both school and mainstream American culture. The responses you get from them will be among the most rewarding you will have as a teacher.

Exploring diversity

Teaching and Learning in Urban Schools

Learner diversity and urban schools are interconnected. Members of cultural minorities make up nearly 70% of the student population in urban schools and more than 95% in some. Urban schools also have a disproportionate number of students who speak a first language other than English, as well as a disproportionate number of students who are low-SES; over half of urban students are eligible for free or reduced-price lunch (Macionis & Parillo, 2010).

The term *cultural minority* is often used to refer to non-White cultural groups, but this term is a misnomer in many urban schools. In Adlai Stevenson High School in New York City, for example, nearly all the students are African American or Hispanic; only one half of 1% are White (Kozol, 2005).

In addition, urban schools tend to be larger and less personal than their suburban counterparts. The nation's 100 largest school districts represent less than 1% of all districts in the nation, but they are responsible for the education of nearly one fourth of all students.

Negative stereotypes about urban schools pose another issue. Two of the most common are "Students can't control themselves," and "Students don't know how to behave because the parents don't care" (Goldstein, 2004, p. 43). In response to these stereotypes, urban teachers often "teach defensively, . . . choosing methods of presentation and evaluation that simplify content and reduce demands on students in return for classroom order and minimal student compliance on assignments" (LePage et al., 2005, p. 331).

It doesn't have to be this way. Working with students in urban settings is indeed challenging, but research provides some guidance, suggesting that three factors are important:

- Caring and supportive teachers
- High structure
- Student involvement

Caring and Supportive Teachers

We emphasize the need for caring and supportive teachers throughout this book. Teachers who care are important in all schools but are critical in urban environments. When students perceive their teachers as uncaring, disengagement from school often occurs, and disengaged students are much more likely to be disruptive than are their more-engaged peers (Charles & Senter, 2005; V. F. Jones & Jones, 2010).

High Structure

The need for equilibrium is basic for all of us, and students in urban schools sometimes come from environments lacking the stability that creates a sense of equilibrium. This makes order, structure, and predictability even

Caring teachers are important for all students. In urban environments, they're essential.

more important in urban classrooms. A predictable environment leads to an atmosphere of safety, which is crucial for developing the sense of attachment to school that is essential for learning and motivation. (We discuss ways of creating safe and orderly classrooms in Chapter 12.)

Student Involvement

As you saw earlier, students in urban classrooms are often involved in low-level activities that detract from motivation and lead to feelings of disengagement from school.

> In my chemistry class, the teacher just keeps going and going and writing on the board. She never stops to ask the class, "Is everyone with me?" She's in her own little world. She never turns around, she just talks to the board, not to us. (Cushman, 2003, p. 8)

Exactly the opposite is needed. In a study of elementary teachers, researchers found that highly effective teachers involved their students during more than three fourths of their instructional time, compared to about half their instructional time for less effective counterparts (H. Waxman, Huang, Anderson, & Weinstein, 1997). Involving students is characteristic of good instruction in general; with urban students it is essential (Rosenshine, 2006).

check your understanding

2.1 Explain why so much linguistic diversity exists in the United States, and describe ways that teachers can accommodate this diversity.

2.2 Define English dialects, and explain why understanding them is important for teachers.

2.3 Describe the major approaches to helping students who are ELs. Explain how they are similar and different.

To receive feedback for these questions, go to Appendix A.

Classroom connections

Working with Students Who Are Culturally and Linguistically Diverse in Classrooms

1. Students' cultural attitudes and values can have a powerful effect on school learning. Communicate that you respect and value all cultures, and emphasize the contributions that cultural differences make to learning.

   - **Elementary:** A third-grade teacher designs classroom "festivals" that focus on different cultures and invites parents and other caregivers to help celebrate and contribute to enriching them. He also emphasizes values, such as courtesy and respect, which are common to all cultures.

   - **Middle School:** An art teacher in the Southwest decorates his room with pictures of Native American art and discusses how it contributes to art in general and how it communicates Native American values, such as a sense of harmony with nature and complex religious beliefs.

   - **High School:** An urban English teacher has students read works written by African American and Middle Eastern, South Asian, and far Eastern authors. They compare both the writing approach and the different points of view that the authors represent.

2. Language development is facilitated when teachers use concrete examples to refer to abstract concepts. Begin language development and concept learning activities with experiences that provide a concrete frame of reference.

   - **Elementary:** A fifth-grade teacher, in a unit on fractions, has students fold pieces of paper into halves, thirds, fourths, and eighths. At each point she has them state in words what the example represents, and she writes important terms on the board.

   - **Middle School:** A science teacher begins a unit on the skeletal and muscular systems by having students feel their own legs, arms, ribs, and heads. As they touch parts of their bodies, such as their Achilles tendon, she has them repeat the term *tendon* and has them state in words that tendons attach bones to muscles.

   - **High School:** An English teacher stops whenever an unfamiliar word occurs in a reading passage or discussion and asks for a definition and example of it. He keeps a list of these words on a bulletin board and encourages students to use them in class and in their writing.

3. Learning a second language requires that students use the language in speaking, writing, and reading. Provide students with multiple opportunities to practice language in your classroom.

- **Elementary:** The fifth-grade teacher who had the students fold the papers has them describe each step they take when they add fractions with both like and unlike denominators. When they struggle to put their understanding into words, she prompts them, in some cases providing essential words and phrases for them.

- **Middle School:** A social studies teacher has students prepare oral reports in groups of four. Each student must make a 2-minute presentation to the other three members of the group. After students practice their reports with each other in groups, each person presents a part of a group report to the whole class.

- **High School:** A history teacher calls on a variety of students to provide part of a summary of the previous day's work. As she presents new information, she frequently stops and has other students describe what has been discussed to that point and how it relates to topics discussed earlier.

$\mathcal{G}$ender

Ed Psych and You

Think about this class. What is the ratio of males to females? Is it similar to other classes you're taking? How would the ratio differ if it were an engineering or computer science class?

What Marti Banes sees on the first day of her advanced-placement chemistry class is surprising and disturbing. Of her 26 students, only 5 are girls, and they sit quietly, responding only when she asks them direct questions. Sharing her interest in science is one reason she has chosen teaching as a career, but this situation is giving her little opportunity to do so.

Lori Anderson, the school counselor at an urban middle school, looks up from the desk where she is working on her annual report to the faculty. She knows that boys traditionally outnumber girls with respect to behavioral problems, but the numbers she is seeing are troubling. In every category—referrals by teachers, absenteeism, tardies, and fights—boys outnumber girls by more than 2 to 1. In addition, the number of boys that have been referred to her for special education testing far exceeds referrals for girls.

Why did you choose your current major? Did your gender play a role in the decision? If you are like students in other areas, there's a chance it did. For example, research indicates that over 85% of all elementary teachers are female, as are more than 6 of 10 middle and secondary teachers (National Education Association, 2007). On the other hand, both of Paul's brothers are on computer science faculties at their respective universities, and they report just the opposite—the vast majority of their students are male.

Gender-role identity. Beliefs about appropriate characteristics and behaviors of males and females.

Gender also influences learning. The fact that some of our students are boys and others are girls is so obvious that we tend to not think about it. When we're reminded, however, we notice that they often act and think differently. This is natural and positive in many ways, but problems can occur if societal or school influences limit the academic potential of either girls or boys. Let's look at some of these differences (see Figure 4.5).

Boys and girls *are* different. Girls tend to be more extroverted and anxious, and they're more trusting, less assertive, and have slightly lower self-esteem than boys of the same age and background (Halpern, 2006; Wigfield, Byrnes, & Eccles, 2006). Girls develop faster, master verbal and motor skills at an earlier age, and prefer activities with a social component. Boys are more oriented toward roughhouse play and playing with blocks, cars, or video games—activities that are physical and visual. Both prefer to play with members of the same sex. These tendencies, together with societal expectations, create **gender-role identities,** beliefs about appropriate characteristics and behaviors of males and females.

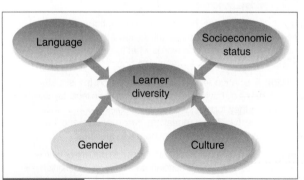

Figure 4.5 Sources of learner diversity: Gender

Experts believe that gender-based differences result from an interaction between genetics and the environment (Halpern et al., 2007). Genes control physical differences such as size and growth rate and probably differences in temperament, aggressiveness, and early verbal and exploratory behaviors. However, girls and boys are treated differently by parents, peers, and teachers, and this treatment influences how they view themselves and their gender roles (Leaper & Freidman, 2007).

The school curriculum also subtly influences gender-role identity (Gay, 2006; Halpern et al., 2007). For example, male characters in stories are typically presented as strong and adventurous, but seldom warm and sensitive (L. Evans & Davies, 2000). Computer software programs and video games are heavily oriented toward boys, with male heroes as the main characters (Comstock & Scharrar, 2006; Newcombe & Huttenlocher, 2006).

How should we respond? Suggestions are controversial, with some believing that most differences between boys and girls are natural and little intervention is necessary, whereas others argue that every attempt should be made to minimize gender differences.

School-Related Gender Differences

Gender differences are real. They include the following (Alperstein, 2005; Perkins-Gough, 2006):

- In the early grades, girls score as high as or higher than boys on almost every standardized measure of achievement and psychological well-being. By the time they graduate from high school or college, they have fallen behind boys.
- Girls score lower on the Scholastic Aptitude Test (SAT) and American College Test (ACT), both of which are important for college admission. The greatest gaps are in science and math.
- Women score lower on all sections of the Graduate Record Exam, the Medical College Admissions Test, and admissions tests for law, dental, and optometry schools.
- Women still lag far behind men in traditionally male college majors, such as mathematics, physics, engineering, and computer science.

On the other hand, boys have a number of issues as well. They include the following (Gurian & Stevens, 2005; Halpern et al., 2007; Sommers, 2008):

- Boys outnumber girls in remedial English and math classes, are held back in grade more often, and are more than twice as likely to be classified as special-needs students.
- Boys receive the majority of failing grades, drop out of school four times more often than girls, and are cited for disciplinary infractions as much as 10 times more often than girls.
- Boys score lower than girls on both direct and indirect measures of reading and writing, and the average 11th-grade boy writes at the same level as an average 8th-grade girl.
- 53% of bachelor's and 59% of master's degrees are earned by women.

To place gender differences in perspective, we should note that the overlap between boys' and girls' performance is much greater than any differences; in any group of boys and girls, we are likely to see students who both struggle and excel. On tests of general intelligence, gender differences are negligible, which we'd expect, because these tests are designed to be gender neutral. There is, however, more variability in boys' performance on achievement tests, with more boys at the upper and lower ends of the spectrum (Halpern, 2006). In addition, boys perform better on visual-spatial tasks, a difference often attributed to the kinds of toys they play with, participation in sports, and greater exposure to computers and computer games.

Although considerable disagreement exists, some researchers explain these differences by suggesting that boys' and girls' brains are wired differently (Gurian & Stevens, 2005; Ruble, Martin, & Berenbaum, 2006). Components of the brain that build word centers and fine-motor skills are a year ahead in girls, which gives them an advantage in reading, using pencils, and other small-motor tasks. Centers in the brain that control emotions are also advanced for girls, making them more able to sit still for the long periods that school often requires (Gay, 2006). Some argue that school systems as a whole are more compatible with girls' genetic characteristics.

Gender Differences in Classrooms

Given these differences, it's not surprising that boys and girls behave and are treated differently in classrooms. Boys participate in learning activities to a greater extent than girls, they are more likely to ask questions and make comments, and are more likely to misbehave (Brophy, 2010; Gay, 2006). Teachers also call on them more often, probably because boys are more verbally assertive (S. Jones & Dindia, 2004).

Gender-related differences are particularly pronounced in science and math (Halpern et al., 2007). Boys are more likely to lead in setting up science experiments, relegating girls to passive roles such as recording data (Sanders & Nelson, 2004). Differences become greater as students move through school, with a significant decrease in girls' participation in science and math activities during the middle school years. In addition, girls are more likely to attribute success in science to luck, and failure to lack of ability. In general, girls are less confident about their abilities, even when aptitude and achievement are comparable (Wigfield et al., 2006).

Although the areas of concern are different, evidence suggests that schools aren't effectively serving the needs of either boys or girls.

Single-gender classes. Classes where boys and girls are segregated for part or all of the day.

The creation of **single-gender classes,** where boys and girls are segregated for part or all of the day, is one response to gender-related issues (Anfara & Mertens, 2008). Proponents argue that they minimize distractions from the other sex. One director of a single-sex school notes, "The boys don't feel like they need to put on a big show for the girls, and the girls feel like they can strive academically without having to dumb down their ability" (Standen, 2007, p. 47). The number of single-gender classrooms in the United States has increased significantly—from less than a dozen in 2000 to 455 in 2009 (Medina, 2009).

Some research indicates that both girls and boys benefit in single-gender schools. Girls in these schools are more apt to assume leadership roles, take more math and science courses, have higher self-esteem, and more strongly believe that they are in control of their destinies (Weil, 2008; Younger & Warrington, 2006). Advocates of all-male schools claim that they promote male character development and are especially effective for males from low-income and minority families.

Single-gender classrooms and schools raise other issues, however. For example, because boys and girls are isolated from one another, stereotypic views of the opposite sex are perpetuated, and these environments fail to prepare students for the "real world" in which males and females must work together (Standen, 2007).

Gender Stereotypes and Perceptions

Society and parents communicate—both directly and unconsciously—different expectations for their sons and daughters (Leaper & Friedman, 2007). The perception that certain areas, such as math, science, and computer science, are male domains can have a powerful effect on career choices. One woman recalled:

It was OK, even feminine, not to be good in math. It was even cute. And so I locked myself out of a very important part of what it is to be a human being, and that is to know all of oneself. I just locked that part out because I didn't think that was an appropriate thing for me to do. . . . [But] it was not OK for the men to not do well in math. It was not OK for them to not take calculus. It was not manly. (Weissglass, 1998, p. 160)

The problem of gender-stereotypic views of math and science-related careers is especially acute for low SES and minority females (Bleeker & Jacobs, 2004). One study found that only 2% of new math faculty at U.S. colleges and universities were minority women (Herzig, 2004).

On the other hand, parents can have a positive influence on girls' attitudes toward math and science, as one female software developer reported:

My mother always engendered in me the attitude that I could do absolutely anything I ever want to do. So she really gave me the confidence that is a big part of success in academics and maybe in other things—sometimes you get to a point where you don't have that much either skill or knowledge, and you have to just go on your guts or your confidence. You have to just kind of push your way through something until you have the time to accumulate the knowledge. And I think that that's something she engendered in me just by always being herself so confident of my abilities, rightly or wrongly. And my father certainly never detracted from that. He always portrayed her as being the smarter of the two. So I was raised in an environment where women were not only capable but were even potentially very well and highly regarded. (Zeldin & Pajares, 2000, p. 229)

What does this information suggest to you as a teacher? We answer this question in the accompanying "Ed Psych and Teaching" section.

Ed psych and teaching

Responding to Your Students' Gender Differences

You can do a great deal to eliminate gender bias and stereotyping in your teaching (Ginsberg, Shapiro, & Brown, 2004). The following guidelines can assist you in your efforts:

1. Communicate openly with your students about gender issues and concerns.
2. Eliminate gender bias in instructional activities.
3. Present students with nonstereotypical role models.

Let's return to Marti's work with her chemistry students to see how she applies these guidelines.

Marti decides to take positive steps to deal with the gender issue in her chemistry class. First, she initiates a discussion. "I almost didn't major in chemistry," she begins. "Some of my girlfriends scoffed, and others were nearly appalled. 'You'll be in there with a bunch of geeks,' some of them said. 'Girls don't major in chemistry,' others added. They all thought science and math were only for guys."

"It is mostly for guys," Amy shrugs. "Look at us."

"It isn't our fault," Shane responds. "Guys didn't try to keep you out of the class."

After several other students add comments, Marti continues. "I'm not blaming either you guys, or the girls. . . . It's a problem for all of us, and I'm not saying that just because I'm a woman. I'd be just as concerned if I were a man, because we're losing a lot of talented people who could be majoring in science."

As they continue, she discusses historical reasons for gender stereotypes and encourages both the boys and the girls to keep their career options open. "There's no rule that says that girls can't be engineers or boys can't be nurses," she emphasizes. "In fact, there's a shortage of both."

She has similar discussions in her other classes. During learning activities, she makes a special effort to encourage both girls and boys to participate equally, and she tells her students why she is doing so. For Career Week, she invites a female chemistry professor from a nearby university to come and talk about opportunities for women in chemistry, and she invites a male nurse from one of the local hospitals to talk about the role of science in his job and his experiences in a female-dominated profession.

Marti also talks with other science teachers and counselors about gender stereotyping, and they work on a plan to encourage both boys and girls to consider career options in nonstereotypical fields.

Openly discussing gender issues can help break down stereotypes and misconceptions about gender-role identity.

Let's look now at Marti's attempts to apply the guidelines in her teaching. She implemented the first by openly discussing the issue of gender and getting responses from both boys and girls. The discussions increased their awareness of stereotyping career choices, and the discussions with her colleagues helped increase their sensitivity to gender issues in the school.

Second, Marti made a special effort to ensure equal treatment of boys and girls, and again she openly communicated why she was making the effort. She called on girls and boys equally, and she expected the same academic behaviors from both girls and boys.

Notice the term *academic behaviors.* Boys and girls are indeed different, and no one is suggesting that they should behave in the same ways. Academically, however, boys and girls should be given the same opportunities and encouragement, just as students from different cultures and socioeconomic backgrounds should be. In this way, Marti applied the second guideline.

She applied the third by inviting a female chemistry professor and a male nurse into her classes to discuss careers in those fields. Seeing that both men and women can succeed and be happy in nonstereotypical fields can broaden the career horizons for both girls and boys (Ruble et al., 2006).

check your understanding

3.1 Explain how gender can influence learning, and describe steps for eliminating gender bias in classrooms.

3.2 Explain the concept of *gender-role identity* and why understanding it is important for teachers.

3.3 You're working with your students in a learning activity. What important factor can help reduce gender bias as you conduct learning activities? Hint: Think about the way Marti interacted with her students.

To receive feedback for these questions, go to Appendix A.

Classroom connections

Eliminating Gender Bias in Classrooms

1. Gender bias often results from a lack of awareness by both teachers and students. Actively attack gender bias in your teaching.

- **Elementary:** A first-grade teacher consciously deemphasizes sex roles and differences in his classroom. He has boys and girls share equally in chores, and he eliminates gender-related activities, such as competitions between boys and girls and forming lines by gender.

- **Middle School:** A middle school language arts teacher selects stories and clippings from newspapers and magazines that portray

men and women in nontraditional roles. She matter-of-factly talks about nontraditional careers during class discussions about becoming an adult.

- **High School:** At the beginning of the school year, a social studies teacher explains how gender bias hurts both sexes, and he forbids sexist comments in his classes. He calls on boys and girls equally, and emphasizes equal participation in discussions.

Socioeconomic Status

The questions in "Ed Psych and You" relate to your **socioeconomic status (SES)**, the combination of parents' income, level of education, and the kinds of jobs they have. Socioeconomic status describes people's relative standing in society and is a powerful factor influencing student achievement (see Figure 4.6).

Researchers divide families into four classes: upper, middle, working, and lower. Table 4.3 outlines characteristics of these classes.

Socioeconomic status consistently predicts intelligence and achievement test scores, grades, truancy, and dropout and suspension rates (Macionis, 2009). It exerts its most powerful influence at the lower income levels. For example, low-SES fourth graders are more than twice as likely as their higher-SES peers to fall below basic levels of reading, and dropout rates for students from the poorest families exceed 50% (Allington & McGill-Franzen, 2003). Students from families in the highest income quartile are much more likely to graduate from high school and college than their low-SES peers (Berliner, 2005; J. Lee & Bowen, 2006).

Ed Psych and You

Were finances ever an important concern in your family? Did your parents go to college? What kinds of jobs do they have?

Socioeconomic status (SES). The combination of parents' income, occupation, and level of education that describes relative standing in society of a family or individual.

Poverty

Some disconcerting statistics exist in our country with respect to SES. The poverty rate in 2009 was nearly 15%, encompassing more than 40 million people, and the percentage of families in our country below the poverty level is five times greater than in other industrialized countries. Minorities and single-parent families are overrepresented; in 2009 the poverty rates for non-Hispanic Whites was nearly 10%, for Asians more than 12%, for both Hispanics and African Americans more than 25% (U.S. Bureau of Census, 2010). In the most recent statistics available, nearly half of students qualify for free or reduced-cost lunches based on their parents' income levels (National Poverty Center, 2008). Children of poverty are likely to experience problems such as substandard housing, an inadequate diet, lack of health and dental care, violence in their communities, few funds for school supplies, and overburdened

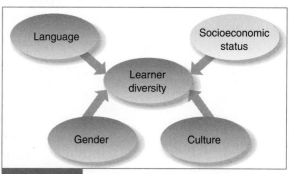

Figure 4.6 Sources of learner diversity: Socioeconomic status

Table 4.3 Characteristics of different socioeconomic levels

	Upper Class	Middle Class	Working Class	Lower Class
Income	$160,000+	$80,000–$160,000 (½) $40,000–80,000 (½)	$25,000–$40,000	Below $25,000
Occupation	Corporate or professional (e.g., doctor, lawyer)	White collar, skilled blue collar	Blue collar	Minimum wage unskilled labor
Education	Attended college and professional schools and expect children to do the same	Attended high school and college or professional schools.	Attended high school; may or may not encourage college	Attended high school or less; cost is a major factor in education
Housing	Own home in prestigious neighborhood	Usually own home	About half own a home	Rent

Source: Macionis, 2009; U.S. Bureau of Census, 2007.

parents who subsist on welfare or work long hours in underpaid jobs (Aikens & Barbarin, 2008; Ashiabi & O'Neal, 2008).

The powerful effect that poverty can have on learning is reflected in integration-by-income programs implemented by a number of school districts in our country (Kahlenberg, 2006). These programs use a variety of ways to integrate students from different SES levels, including magnet schools, vouchers, and even busing. All are based on the belief that high concentrations of students from impoverished backgrounds detract from a school's ability to successfully meet students' needs. Initial results of these programs support their effectiveness; in North Carolina, for example, nearly two thirds of students who are integrated by income passed state-mandated, end-of-course exams compared to less than half of comparable students not participating in the programs (Kahlenberg, 2006).

How SES Influences Learning

SES influences learning in three important ways:

- Basic needs and experiences
- Parental involvement
- Attitudes and values

Let's look at them.

Basic Needs and Experiences

In 2006, over 35 million people in America went hungry, and cultural minorities and single-parent families make up a disproportionate share (U.S. Department of Agriculture, 2007). Over 12 million were children, and the figure didn't include homeless families, because they are hard to identify and count. Further, poor nutrition can affect attention and memory and even lead to lower intelligence test scores (Berk, 2010).

The school nurse in high-poverty schools often serves as a substitute for the family doctor because many families don't have insurance and can't afford to seek medical care. One school nurse reported,

> Mondays we are hit hard. It's not like in the suburbs, where families call the pediatrician. When our kids get sick on the weekends, they go to the emergency room, or they wait. Monday morning, they are lined up, and they have to see the nurse. (F. Smith, 2005, p. 49)

It's hard to learn when you're ill.

Economic problems can also lead to family and marital conflicts, which result in less stable and supportive homes. Children of poverty often come to school without the sense of security that equips them to tackle school-related tasks. Students from poor families have a greater incidence of depression and other emotional problems than do their more advantaged peers (G. Evans & Kim, 2007).

Children of poverty also relocate frequently; in some low-income schools, mobility rates are above 100% (Gruman, Harachi, Abbott, Catalano, & Fleming, 2008). Nearly a third of the poorest students attend at least three different schools by third grade, compared to only 1 of 10 for middle-class students. These frequent moves are stressful for students and a challenge for teachers attempting to develop caring relationships with them.

The problem is particularly acute for the homeless. One of five homeless children fails to attend school regularly, and homeless children are three times more likely to repeat a grade and four times more likely to drop out of school (Macionis & Parillo, 2010).

SES also influences the background knowledge that children bring to school (Aikens & Barbarin, 2008). High-SES parents are more likely to provide their children with educational activities, such as travel and visits to museums and zoos. They also have more computers, books, newspapers, and magazines in the home, and they provide more formal training, such as music and dance lessons—all of which complement classroom learning—outside of school.

Parental Involvement

Higher-SES parents tend to be more involved in their children's schooling (Bolìvar & Chrispeels, 2011). One mother commented, "When she sees me at her games, when she sees me going to open house, when I attend her Interscholastic League contests, she knows I am interested in her activities. Plus, we have more to talk about" (Young & Scribner, 1997, p. 12). Time spent working, often at two jobs or more, is a major obstacle to greater school involvement for low-SES parents (Weiss et al., 2003).

In general, high-SES parents talk to their children more and differently than do those who are low SES. They ask more questions, explain the causes of events, and provide reasons for rules. Their language is more elaborate, their directions are clearer, and they are more likely to encourage problem solving (Berk, 2011; Tomasello, 2006). Called "the curriculum of the home," these rich interaction patterns, together with the background experiences already described, provide a strong foundation for future learning (Aikens & Barbarin, 2008).

Attitudes and Values

The impact of SES is also transmitted through parental attitudes and values. For example, many high-SES parents encourage autonomy, individual responsibility, and self-control, and an expanding body of research indicates that self-control as a child strongly influences success in later life (Moffit et al., 2011). Low-SES parents are more likely to emphasize conformity and obedience (Greenfield et al., 2006; Macionis, 2009).

Values are also communicated by example. For instance, children who see their parents reading and studying learn that reading is valuable and are more likely to read to themselves. And, as we would expect, students who read at home show higher reading achievement than those who don't (Weigel, Martin, & Bennett, 2005).

High-SES parents also tend to have higher expectations for their children and encourage them to graduate from high school and attend college (W. Collins & Steinberg, 2006). They also know how to play the "schooling game," steering their sons and daughters into advanced high school courses and contacting schools for information about their children's learning progress (Englund, Egeland, & Collins, 2008; Davis & Yang, 2005). Low-SES parents, in contrast, tend to have lower aspirations for their children, allow them to "drift" into classes, and rely on the decisions of others. Students get lost in the shuffle, ending up in inappropriate or less challenging classes.

SES: Some Cautions and Implications for Teachers

As with culture, language, and gender, it's important to remember that the patterns we're describing here represent group differences, and individuals within groups will vary widely. For example, many low-SES parents read and talk to their children, encourage their involvement in extracurricular activities, and attend school events. We (Paul and Don) both come from low-SES families, but—fortunately for us—were given all the enriching experiences we've discussed in reference to high-SES parents. Conversely, belonging to a high-SES family doesn't guarantee a child enriching experiences and caring, involved parents (Luthar & Latendresse, 2005).

Second, we know that certain home conditions make it more difficult for students to succeed in school, but we also know that schools and teachers can do much to overcome these problems (Darling-Hammond & Bransford, 2005). Schools that are safe, emotionally supportive, and demanding, and teachers with high expectations who use effective instruction *can* make a significant difference in all students' lives.

Students at Risk

Laurie Ramirez looks over the papers she has been grading and shakes her head. "Fourth grade, and some of these kids don't know what zero means or how place value affects a number. Some can't add or subtract, and most don't understand multiplication. How am I supposed to teach problem solving when they don't understand basic math facts?"

"Reading isn't much better," she thinks. "I have a few who read at a fourth-grade level, but others are still sounding out words like *dog* and *cat*. How can I teach them comprehension skills when they are struggling with ideas this basic?

Students at risk. Students who fail to complete their education with the skills necessary to succeed in today's society.

We find failing learners in every school. Many reasons exist, but some students encounter a combination of obstacles that places them **at risk** of failing to complete their education with the skills necessary to succeed in today's society. Educators used to call these students *underachievers*, but the term *at risk* more clearly reflects the long-term consequences of school failure. Many jobs requiring few specialized skills no longer exist, and others are becoming rare in a world driven by technology. Statistics consistently indicate that high school dropouts earn far less than their more educated peers and also have an increased incidence of crime, alcoholism, and drug abuse (Macionis, 2009).

Students at risk often have the following characteristics:

- *Low SES*. As we saw earlier, poverty creates a number of stress factors that detract from learning (G. Evans & Kim, 2007). For example, students who are eligible for free or reduced-cost lunches because of their family's income consistently score below other students on achievement tests in reading, math, and science (National Assessment of Educational Progress, 2009).
- *Member of Minority*. Being a member of a minority can pose problems when schools are not responsive to cultural or ethnic differences (Borman & Overman, 2004). For example, Figure 4.7 compares the performance of different groups of fourth graders in reading and math, and similar patterns are found in other content areas and grade levels (National Assessment of Educational Progress, 2009).

In addition, risk factors such as poverty, poor health and nutrition, and substandard housing conditions are often found in these populations.

- *Non-native English Speaker*. Learning is demanding for all students; struggling with both language and content can be overwhelming (Bielenberg & Fillmore, 2005; Zwiers, 2005). These struggles are reflected in generally lower achievement for students who are English learners (National Assessment of Educational Progress, 2009).

The combination of these factors can result in a history of low achievement, which makes new learning even more challenging because students lack the background knowledge and skills on which new learning depends (Aikens & Barbarin, 2008). A history of low achievement is compounded by lack of motivation, disengagement from school, and misbehavior (Suh, Suh, & Houston, 2007). The problem can be exacerbated by the fact that students who need quality education the most are often provided

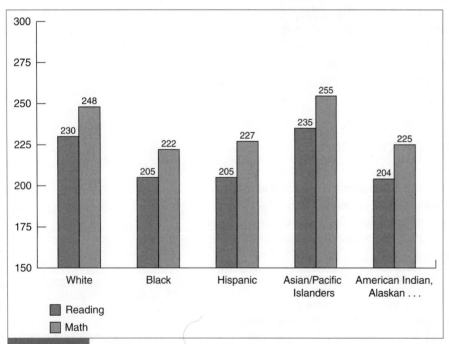

Figure 4.7 Fourth-grade National Assessment of Educational Progress (NAEP) scores in reading and math

Source: National Assessment of Educational Progress, 2009.

with underqualified teachers and substandard buildings and equipment (Crosnoe, 2005; Perkins-Gough, 2004).

How do teachers react to these problems? Some are overwhelmed:

> I just don't know what I'm going to do. Every year, my first grade class has more and more of these kids. They don't seem to care about right or wrong, they don't care about adult approval, they are disruptive, they can't read and they arrive at school absolutely unprepared to learn. Who are these kids? Where do they come from? Why are there more and more of them? I used to think that I was a good teacher. I really prided myself on doing an outstanding job. But I find I'm working harder and harder, and being less and less effective.
>
> Elementary Teacher, Atlanta, Georgia
> (Barr & Parrett, 2001, p. 1)

Our goal in this section is to help you understand how you can help your students respond to the conditions they encounter.

Resilience and Students at Risk

Attempts to assist students at risk now focus on developing **resilience,** a learner trait that, despite adversity, raises the likelihood of success in school and later life (Borman & Overman, 2004; Doll, Zucker, & Brehm, 2004). Researchers have studied young people who have survived and even prospered despite obstacles such as poverty, poor health care, and fragmented support services, and they've found that resilient children have well-developed self-systems, including high self-esteem, optimism, and feelings that they are in control of their destinies. Resilient children set personal goals, expect to succeed, and believe they are responsible for their success. They are motivated to learn and satisfied with school (Masten & Gewirtz, 2006; Masten & Shaffer, 2006).

How do these skills develop? Resilient children come from emotionally supportive environments, and one characteristic is striking. In virtually all cases, these children have one or more adults who have taken a special interest in them and hold them to high moral and academic standards, essentially refusing to let the young person fail (Reis, Colbert & Hébert, 2005). These adults are often parents, but they can also be older siblings or other adults such as teachers who take a young person under their wing (Flores, Cicchetti, & Rogosch, 2005).

Schools also make important contributions to resilience. Let's see how.

Schools That Promote Resilience

Research has identified four school practices that promote resilience:

- *High and uncompromising academic standards.* Teachers emphasize mastery of content and do not accept passive attendance and mere completion of assignments (Tenenbaum & Ruck, 2007).
- *Strong personal bonds between teachers and students.* Teachers become the adults who refuse to let students fail, and students feel connected to the schools (Durlak, Weissberg, Dymnicki, Taylor, & Schellinger, 2011; Werner, 2006).
- *High structure.* The school and classes are orderly and highly structured. Teachers consistently enforce rules and procedures and explain reasons for rules (Emmer & Evertson, 2009; Evertson & Emmer, 2009).
- *Participation in after-school activities.* Activities such as clubs and athletics give students additional chances to interact with caring adults and bond with school (Wigfield et al., 2006).

Effective schools are both demanding and supportive; in many instances, they serve as homes away from home. The emphasis on school-sponsored activities reduces alienation and increases academic engagement and achievement (Christenson & Thurlow, 2004). School-sponsored activities also give teachers the chance to know students in contexts outside the classroom.

Resilience. A learner characteristic that, despite adversity, raises the likelihood of success in school and later life.

Caring teachers promote resilience by forming personal relationships with students and supporting their academic work.

Teachers Who Promote Resilience

Schools are no more effective than the teachers who work in them. Becoming an adult who refuses to let students fail often means spending extra time before or after school and helping students with both their academic work and simply talking to them about issues important in their lives. Spending out-of-class time with students is demanding, but this kind of commitment is at the core of promoting resilience.

What else do we know about teachers who promote resilience? Research indicates that they interact frequently with students, learn about their families, and share their own lives. They maintain high expectations, use interactive teaching strategies, and emphasize success and mastery of content (Doll et al., 2004). They motivate students through personal contacts, instructional support, and attempts to link school to students' experiences (Good & Brophy, 2008).

Let's see what students say about these teachers. One middle school student commented,

> Sometimes a teacher don't understand what people go through. They need to have compassion. A teacher who can relate to students will know when something's going on with them. If like the student don't do work or don't understand, the teacher will spend a lot of time with them. (Wilson & Corbett, 2001, p. 5)

Being the adult who refuses to let a student fail goes the extra mile with students.

Teachers less effective in promoting resilience are more authoritarian and less accessible. They distance themselves from students and place primary responsibility for learning on them. They view instructional support as "babying students" or "holding students' hands." Lecture is a common teaching strategy, and motivation is the students' responsibility. Students perceive these teachers as adversaries, to be avoided if possible, tolerated if not. They also resent the teachers' lack of commitment:

> There's this teacher [over at the regular school] . . . you can put anything down and he'll give you a check mark for it. He doesn't check it. He just gives you a mark and says, 'OK, you did your work.' How you gonna learn from that? You ain't gonna learn nothing.
>
> Student, JFY Academy, Boston, Massachusetts
> (Dynarski & Gleason, 1999, p. 13)

As with culturally responsive teaching, much of promoting resilience lies in teachers' attitudes and commitment to students. Caring teachers are important for all students; for students at risk, they're essential.

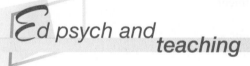

Ed psych and teaching

Promoting Resilience in Your Students

We know that the human element is essential for promoting resilience in students. But what else can you do? Research suggests that the same strategies proven effective for all students promote resilience in students at risk (Good & Brophy, 2008). You don't need to teach in fundamentally different ways, but you do need to do it just that much better. The following guidelines can assist you in your efforts:

1. Create and maintain a classroom environment with predictable routines.
2. Combine high expectations with frequent feedback about learning progress.
3. Use teaching strategies that involve all students and promote high levels of success.
4. Use high-quality examples that provide the background knowledge students need to learn new content.
5. Stress self-regulation and the acquisition of learning strategies.

Let's see how Diane Smith, a fourth-grade teacher, applies the guidelines with her students.

Diane's students are studying adjectives in language arts, and she now wants them to be able to use comparative and superlative forms of adjectives in their writing.

Students file into the room from their lunch break, go to their desks, and begin working on a set of exercises. They identify all the adjectives and the modified nouns in a paragraph displayed on the overhead. As they work, Diane identifies students who have pencils of different lengths and those whose hair color varies.

Diane reviews the passage, has students explain their choices, and provides feedback. When they finish, she directs, "Okay, very good, everyone. Look up here."

"Calesha and Daniel, hold your pencils up so everyone can see. What do you notice?. . . Naitia?"

Diane has the students make observations, among them the fact that Calesha's is longer.

Diane then goes to the board and writes:

Calesha has a long pencil.
Calesha has a longer pencil than Daniel does.

"Now, let's look at Matt and Wesley," she continues. "What do you notice about their hair?. . . Judy?"

Again the students make observations, and after hearing several, Diane asks, "Whose is darker?"

"WESLEY!" several in the class blurt out.

"Good!" Diane again goes to the board and writes three more sentences:

Calesha has a long pencil. Calesha has a longer pencil than Daniel does.	Wesley has black hair. Matt has brown hair. Wesley has darker hair than Matt does.

"Now, how do the adjectives in the sentences compare? . . . Heather?" Diane asks, pointing to the bottom sentences on each list.

". . . The ones at the bottom have an *er* on the end of them," Heather responds hesitantly.

"Yes, good. . . . And, what are we doing in each of the sentences?. . . Jason?"

"We're comparing two things."

"Good thinking, Jason, We call these kinds of adjectives *comparative adjectives,*" Diane smiles.

She then repeats the process with the superlative form of adjectives by having students compare three pencils and three different hair colors, leading them to conclude that superlative adjectives have an *est* on the end of them.

"Very good, everyone. In describing nouns, if we're comparing two, we use the comparative form of the adjective, which has an *er* on the end, and if we have three or more, we have an *est* on the end of the adjective.

"Now," Diane says, pointing to a softball, tennis ball, and golf ball on her desk, "I have a little challenge for you. . . . Write two sentences each that use the comparative and superlative forms of adjectives, and tell about the sizes of these balls."

As the students work, Diane checks on their progress, and when they're finished, says, "Now let's look at your sentences. . . . Someone volunteer, and I'll write it on the chalkboard. . . . Okay, Rashad?"

"The tennis ball is bigger than the golf ball."

"Very good, Rashad. And why did you write *bigger* in your sentence?"

"We're comparing the size of two balls."

They continue discussing the comparative and superlative forms of adjectives, and Diane then directs, "Now, I want you to write a paragraph with at least two sentences that use the comparative form of adjectives and at least two others that use the superlative form. Underline the adjectives in each case."

"And what do we always do after we write something?"

"We read it to be sure it makes sense!" several of the students say simultaneously.

"Very good," Diane smiles. "That's how we become good writers."

As students begin working, Diane circulates among them, periodically stopping for a few seconds to comment on a student's work and to offer brief suggestions.

Now, let's look at Diane's attempts to apply the guidelines. She applied the first by creating a set of well-established routines. For example, when students came in from their break, they went to work on exercises on the overhead without being told to do so. Predictable routines maximize time available for learning and provide the structure that makes classrooms safe and comfortable.

Second, by calling on individuals and requiring that they explain their answers, Diane communicated that she expected all students to participate and learn. Maintaining high expectations is a simple idea but hard to put into practice. Most students initially have trouble putting their understanding into words, and it is even more challenging for students at risk. Many teachers give up, concluding, "They can't do it." They can't because they haven't had enough practice and support. It isn't easy, but it can be done.

Also, Diane provided detailed feedback for the beginning-of-class exercises and the sentences at the end of the lesson. This scaffolding promotes success, minimizes mistakes, and increases motivation (Brophy, 2010). These actions applied the second guideline.

Diane applied the third guideline with questioning that involved all students in the lesson. Open-ended questions such as "What do you notice?" and "How do the adjectives in the sentences compare?" virtually assured student success, an essential factor for both learning and motivation (Brophy, 2010). Promoting involvement is important for all students and essential for students at risk.

Diane applied the fourth guideline by developing her lesson around real-world examples. Teachers who promote resilience attempt to link school to students' lives, and using students' pencils and hair color to illustrate comparative and superlative adjectives was a simple application of this idea (Veralas & Pappas, 2006).

Finally, Diane emphasized self-regulation, and applied the fifth guideline, when she asked, "And what do we always do after we write something?" The fact that the students so quickly replied, "We read it to be sure it makes sense!" suggests that she emphasized student responsibility for their own learning.

Helping them succeed while still presenting challenging activities is our challenge when working with students at risk. It isn't easy. However, seeing these students meet the challenges will be some of the most rewarding experiences you will have.

check your
understanding

4.1 Define *socioeconomic status (SES),* and explain how it can affect learning.

4.2 As you work with your students, what important factor should you keep in mind when considering SES?

4.3 Describe characteristics of schools and teachers that promote resilience in students at risk.

To receive feedback for these questions, go to Appendix A.

Classroom *connections*

Effective Teaching Practices for Promoting Resilience in Classrooms

1. Positive teacher expectations influence both motivation and achievement. Communicate positive expectations to students and their parents.

   ■ **Elementary:** A fourth-grade teacher spends the first 2 weeks of school teaching students her classroom procedures and explaining how they promote learning. She makes short assignments, carefully monitors students to be certain the assignments are turned in, and immediately calls parents if an assignment is missing.

   ■ **Middle School:** A math teacher carefully explains his course procedures. He emphasizes the importance of attendance and effort and communicates that he expects all to do well. He also makes himself available before and after school for help sessions.

   ■ **High School:** An English teacher sends home an upbeat letter at the beginning of the year describing her work requirements and grading practices. She has students help translate the letter for parents whose first language is not English and asks parents to sign the letter, indicating they have read it. She also invites questions and comments from parents or other caregivers.

2. Interactive teaching strategies are essential for students at risk. Use teaching strategies that elicit high levels of student involvement and success.

   ■ **Elementary:** A fifth-grade teacher arranges the seating in his classroom so that students who are and are not minorities are mixed. He combines small-group and whole-class instruction, and when he uses group work, he arranges the groups so they include students who are high and low achievers, students who are and are not minorities, and boys and girls.

   ■ **Middle School:** An earth science teacher gives students a short quiz every day. He provides feedback the following day, and students frequently calculate their averages. The teacher closely monitors these scores and spends time before school to work with students who are falling behind.

   ■ **High School:** An English teacher builds her teaching around questioning and examples. She comments, "My goal is to call on each student in the class at least twice during each lesson. I also use a lot of repetition and reinforcement as we cover the examples."

Developmentally appropriate practice

Student Diversity at Different Ages

While many aspects of diversity are similar across grade levels, important developmental differences exist. The following paragraphs outline suggestions for responding to these differences.

Working with Students in Early Childhood Programs and Elementary Schools

The elementary grades pose developmental challenges for students learning a second language, as they face the dual tasks of learning to read and write while simultaneously learning English. While some research suggests that young language learners may be more adaptable than older ones, they still need special assistance to be successful (Echevarria & Graves, 2011). Instruction that maximizes opportunities for students to practice and use language is essential for these children. The strategies Gary Nolan used in "Ed Psych and Teaching: **Teaching Students in Your Classes Who Are Culturally and Linguistically Diverse**" (p. 117) are effective for learners at all ages but are particularly important for elementary students (O'Donnell, 2006; Tomasello, 2006; S. Waxman & Lidz, 2006). Writing assignments that encourage English learners to use their developing language skills are also important (Graham, 2006).

As you saw earlier, boys develop slower than girls, and girls have more developed language abilities (Halpern, 2006; Ruble et al., 2006). Some experts suggest that developmental lags explain why boys outnumber girls in the number of special education placements (Hardman, Drew, & Egan, 2011; Heward, 2009). Simple strategies such as giving children a chance to get up and move around, providing concrete examples, and interactive instructional strategies proven effective with English learners are also effective with slower-developing boys.

Working with Students in Middle Schools

Developmental changes, such as going through puberty, and the transition to less personal middle schools where students often have five or six teachers, can be problematic for students who come from diverse backgrounds (Chumlea et al., 2003).

Communicating that all students' backgrounds are respected and valued is even more important in diverse middle schools than it is in elementary schools. Safe and predictable classrooms provide both structure and security for middle school students. Well-established routines, consistent enforcement of rules, and emphasis on treating all students with courtesy and respect are essential. Establishing personal relationships with students, emphasizing that learning is the purpose of school, and de-emphasizing competition and differences among students are also important.

Working with Students in High Schools

High school is both the capstone of students' public school experience and an important transition period for both college and careers (New Commission on the Skills of the American Workforce, 2006). Many students who come from low-SES backgrounds or are members of cultural minorities are unaware of the career and higher-education opportunities available to them. Connecting content to students' future lives is particularly important for these students. For example, science teachers can discuss career options in related fields, and social studies and English teachers can examine the impact of technology on our lives.

High school is also an important time for both girls and boys who are trying to reconcile gender-role identities with societal expectations. For example, some high school girls are fearful that being intellectually assertive is not compatible with being feminine, whereas boys are struggling with decisions about whether to go to college or join the workforce. Open discussions with high school students can do a great deal to help them resolve these issues.

Summary

1. Describe culture and ethnicity, and explain how they can influence learning.
   - *Culture* refers to the attitudes, values, customs, and behavior patterns that characterize a social group. The match between a child's culture and the school powerfully influences school success.
   - *Ethnicity* refers to a person's ancestry and the way individuals identify with their ancestors' nation of origin.
   - Culture and ethnicity can influence learning through the cultural attitudes and values that students bring to schools. Some values support learning, whereas others can detract from it.
   - Culture and ethnicity can also influence learning through the interaction patterns characteristic of the cultural group. If the interaction patterns are similar to those found in school, they enhance learning. If they are dissimilar, they can detract from learning.

2. Explain why so much linguistic diversity exists in our country, and describe ways that teachers can accommodate this diversity.
   - Federal legislation, which ended quotas based on national origin, resulted in more immigrants coming to the United States from a wider variety of places. This has resulted in much more cultural, ethnic, and linguistic diversity.
   - Teachers can accommodate this diversity by first communicating that all cultures are valued and respected, involving all students in learning activities, and representing topics as concretely as possible.
   - Teachers also accommodate this diversity by providing students with opportunities to practice language and emphasizing important vocabulary.

3. Explain how gender can influence learning, and describe steps for eliminating gender bias in classrooms.
   - Gender can influence learning if either girls or boys adopt gender-stereotyped beliefs, such as believing that math or computer science are male domains, or believing that girls are inherently better at English and writing than boys.
   - Teachers can attempt to eliminate gender bias by openly discussing gender issues, expecting the same academic behaviors from both boys and girls, and inviting nonstereotypical role models to their classes to discuss gender issues.

4. Define *socioeconomic status (SES)*, and explain how it can affect learning.
   - *Socioeconomic status* describes the relative standing in society resulting from a combination of family income, parents' occupations, and the level of education parents attain.
   - SES can affect learning by influencing students' basic needs. Children of poverty often live in substandard housing and don't have access to medical care.
   - Low-SES children may also lack the school-related experiences they need to be successful, and lower-SES parents tend to be less involved in their children's education than are higher-SES parents.
   - SES can also influence learning through the attitudes and values of parents. Many high-SES parents encourage autonomy, individual responsibility, and self-control, whereas lower-SES parents tend to value obedience and conformity. High-SES parents also tend to have higher expectations for their children than do their lower-SES counterparts.

Understanding Learner Diversity: Preparing for Your Licensure Exam

Because our students are becoming more diverse, your licensure exam will include questions related to learner diversity. To help you practice for the exam in your state, we include the following exercises:

In this chapter, we've seen how culture, language diversity, gender, and SES can influence learning, and how certain combinations of these factors can place students at risk.

Let's look now at another teacher working with students from diverse backgrounds. Read the case study, and answer the questions that follow.

Teri Hall is an eighth-grade American history teacher in an urban middle school. Most of her students are from low-income families, many members of cultural minorities, and some are ELs.

Today, her class is studying the colonization of North America. Teri takes roll as students enter the room, and she finishes entering the information into the computer on her desk just as the bell rings.

"What were we discussing yesterday?" Teri begins immediately after the bell stops ringing. "Ditan?"

". . . The beginning of the American colonies."

"Good. . . . Who can go up to the map, point out where we live, and show us the first British, French, and Spanish colonies. . . . Kaldya?"

After Kaldya walks to the front of the room and points to four different locations on a large map of North America, Teri reviews for a few more minutes and then displays the following on the overhead:

In the mid-1600s, the American colonists were encouraged to grow tobacco, because it wasn't grown in England. The colonists wanted to sell it to France and other countries, but were told no. In return for sending the tobacco to England, the colonists were allowed to buy textiles from England. They were forbidden, however, from making their own textiles. All the materials were carried on British ships.

Early French colonists in the New World were avid fur trappers and traders. They got in trouble with the French monarchy, however, when they attempted to make fur garments and sell them to Spain, England, and others. They were told that they had to buy the manufactured garments from dealers in Paris instead. The monarchy also told them that traps and weapons would be made in France and sent to them as well. One of the colonists, Jean Forjea, complied with the monarchy's wishes but was fined when he hired a Dutch ship to carry some of the furs back to Nice.

"Take a few seconds to read the paragraphs you see on the screen." she begins "Then, with your partner, write down three similarities between the French and English colonists. You have 5 minutes."

Teri does a considerable amount of group work in her class. She sometimes has students work in pairs, and at other times in groups of four. The students are seated together, so they can move into and out of the groups quickly. Students initially protested the seating assignments, because they weren't sitting near their friends, but Teri emphasized that learning and getting to know and respect people different from ourselves were important goals for the class. Teri persisted, and the groups became quite effective.

Teri watches as students work, and at the end of the 5 minutes, she says, "Okay, you've done a good job. . . . Turn back up here, and let's think about this."

As the class quickly turns their attention to the front of the room, Teri asks, "Serena, what did you and David come up with?"

". . . Both of the paragraphs deal with a colony from Europe."

"Okay, Eric, how about you and Kyo?"

". . . The colonies both produced something their countries, England and France, wanted—like tobacco or furs."

"Excellent observation, you two," Teri smiles. "Go on Gustavo. How about you and Pam?"

". . . They sent the stuff to their country," Gustavo responds after looking at his notes.

"And they couldn't send it anywhere else!" Tito adds, warming up to the idea.

"That's very good, all of you. Where do you suppose Tito got that idea?. . . Connie?"

"It says it right in the paragraphs," Connie responds.

"Excellent, everyone! Connie, good use of information to support your ideas."

Teri continues to guide students as they analyze the paragraphs. She guides the class to conclude that, in each instance, the colonies sent raw materials to the mother country, bought back finished products, and were required to use the mother country's ships to transport all materials.

She then tells them that this policy, called *mercantilism,* was a strategy countries used to make money from their colonies. "Mercantilism helps us understand why Europe was so interested in imperialism and colonization," she adds. "It doesn't explain everything, but it was a major factor in the history of this period."

"Let's look at another paragraph. Does this description illustrate mercantilism? Be ready to explain why or why not when you've made your decision," she directs, displaying the following on the screen:

Canada is a member of the British Commonwealth. Canada is a large grain producer and exporter and derives considerable income from selling this grain to Great Britain, France, Russia, and other countries. This trade has also enhanced the shipping business for Greece, Norway, and Liberia, who carry most of the products. Canada, however, doesn't rely on grain alone. It is now a major producer of clothing, high-tech equipment, and heavy industrial equipment.

The class discusses the paragraph and, using evidence from the text, concludes that it does not illustrate mercantilism.

Questions for Case Analysis

In answering these questions, use information from the chapter, and link your responses to specific information in the case.

1. What strategies did Teri use to eliminate gender bias in her classroom? What else might she have done?

2. One of the principles of effective teaching for students at risk uses high-quality examples to supplement students' background knowledge. How well did Teri apply this principle?

3. Success and challenge are essential for effective instruction for students at risk. Evaluate Teri's attempts to provide these components.

4. What strategies did Teri use to actively involve her students?

For feedback on these responses, go to Appendix B.

Your licensure exam will also include multiple-choice questions similar to those your instructor has given you on your quizzes and tests for this course.

Important Concepts

academic language proficiency (p. 116)

basic interpersonal communication skills (p. 116)

bidialecticism (p. 113)

bilingualism (p. 116)

cultural mismatch (p. 108)

culturally responsive teaching (p. 117)

culture (p. 106)

dialect (p. 112)

English as a second language (ESL) pullout programs (p. 115)

English learners (ELs) (p. 113)

ethnicity (p. 107)

gender-role identity (p. 120)

immersion programs (p. 114)

learner diversity (p. 106)

maintenance English learner (EL) programs (p. 115)

multicultural education (p. 111)

race (p. 108)

resilience (p. 129)

resistance culture (p. 109)

sheltered English (p. 116)

single-gender classes (p. 122)

socioeconomic status (SES) (p. 125)

stereotype threat (p. 109)

structured immersion (p. 114)

students at risk (p. 128)

transitional English learner (EL) programs (p. 115)

Go to the Topic: Student Diversity in the MyEducationLab (www.myeducationlab.com) for *Educational Psychology: Windows on Classrooms*, where you can:

- Find learning outcomes for Student Diversity along with the national standards that connect to these outcomes.
- Complete Assignments and Activities that can help you more deeply understand the chapter content.
- Apply and practice your understanding of the core teaching skills identified in the chapter with the Building Teaching Skills and Dispositions learning units.
- Examine challenging situations and cases presented in the IRIS Center Resources.
- Access video clips of CCSSO National Teachers of the Year award winners responding to the question, "Why Do I Teach?" in the Teacher Talk section.
- See video examples included within the Study Plan that provide concrete and real-world illustrations of the topics presented in the chapter.
- Check your comprehension of the content covered in the chapter with the Study Plan. Here you will be able to take a chapter quiz, receive feedback on your answers, and then access Review, Practice, and Enrichment activities to enhance your understanding of chapter content.

MyEducationLab

Learners with Exceptionalities

chapteroutline

learningoutcomes

After you've completed your study of this chapter, you should be able to:

1. Describe different views of intelligence, and explain how ability grouping influences learning.

2. Describe the major provisions of the Individuals with Disabilities Education Act (IDEA) and the amendments to it.

3. Describe the most common learning problems that classroom teachers are likely to encounter.

4. Identify characteristics of students who are gifted and talented, and explain how teachers identify and teach these students.

5. Describe general education teachers' responsibilities in inclusive classrooms.

classroomapplications

The following features help you apply the content of this chapter in your teaching.

Ed Psych and Teaching:
    Applying an Understanding of Students Who Are Gifted and Talented in Your Teaching

Classroom Connections:
    Accommodating Ability Differences in Classrooms
    Teaching Students with Exceptionalities in the General Education Classroom

Developmentally Appropriate Practice:
    Teaching Students with Exceptionalities at Different Ages

Exploring Diversity:
    Pursuing Equity in Special Education

*W*hen you begin teaching, you almost certainly will have students with exceptionalities, such as specific learning disabilities or behavior disorders, in your classroom. Nationally, more than 6.5 million students are diagnosed with exceptionalities, and most of them get help in general education classrooms (Samuels, 2010). They're like all students in many ways but sometimes need extra help to succeed. Think about these issues as you read the following case study.

Celina Curtis, a beginning first-grade teacher in a large elementary school, has survived her hectic first weeks. She is beginning to feel comfortable, but at the same time, some things are bothering her.

"It's kind of frustrating," she admits to Clarisse, a veteran who has become her friend and confidante. "I think I'm teaching, but some of the kids just don't seem to get it.

"For instance, there's Rodney. You've seen him on the playground. He's cute, but his engine is stuck on fast. I can barely get him to sit in his seat, much less work. The smallest distraction sets him off. He can usually do the work if I can get him to stick to it, but it's tough. I've talked to his mother, and he's the same way at home.

"Then there's Amelia; she's so sweet, but she simply doesn't get it. I've tried everything under the sun with her. I explain it, and the next time, it's as if it's all brand new. I feel sorry for her, because I know she gets frustrated when she can't keep up with the other kids. When I work with her one-on-one, it seems to help, but I don't have enough time to spend with her. She's falling farther and farther behind."

"Maybe it's not your fault. You're supposed to do your best, but you're going to burn yourself out if you keep this up," Clarisse cautions. "Check with one of the special ed teachers. Maybe these students need some extra help."

As you begin your study of this chapter, consider these questions:

1. Do Rodney and Amelia have exceptionalities, and if so, what are they?
2. What more can Celina do to help them?

Learners with exceptionalities.
Students who need special help and resources to reach their full potential.

Disabilities. Functional limitations or an inability to perform a certain act.

Gifts and talents. Abilities at the upper end of the continuum that require additional support to reach full potential.

Special education. Instruction designed to meet the unique needs of students with exceptionalities.

Learners with exceptionalities are students who need special help and resources to reach their full potential. They include students with **disabilities**—functional limitations, such as low intelligence, or an inability to perform a certain act, such as walk or listen—as well as students with **gifts and talents**—abilities at the upper end of the continuum that require additional support to reach full potential. Some have both.

Special education refers to instruction designed to meet the unique needs of these students.

Because it plays an important role in understanding and helping students with exceptionalities, we begin by examining the concept of *intelligence*.

$\mathcal{I}$ntelligence

Ed Psych and You

Consider the following questions: On what continent is Brazil? If two buttons cost 15 cents, what would be the cost of a dozen buttons? In what way are a hammer and a saw alike? What do the questions have in common?

Intelligence. The ability to acquire and use knowledge, solve problems and reason in the abstract, and adapt to new situations in the environment.

We all know people we think are "sharp," because they're knowledgeable, perceptive, or learn new ideas quickly and easily. These are intuitive notions of intelligence. Experts define **intelligence** more formally and generally agree that it includes the ability to acquire and use knowledge, solve problems and reason in the abstract, and adapt to new situations in our environments (Garlick, 2010; Gläscher et al., 2010).

The ability to benefit from experience is a simple way to think about intelligence. For instance, if we could hypothetically give two people exactly the same set of experiences, the more intelligent of the two will derive more benefit from them. Intelligence is important for all of us involved in teaching, because it relates to important aspects of learning, such as success in school and behavior problems. For example, high intelligence correlates with academic achievement, whereas low intelligence correlates with higher incidents of delinquent behavior (Laird, Pettit, Dodge, & Bates, 2005).

Now, let's look at the questions we asked in "Ed Psych and You." Similar items appear on the Wechsler Intelligence Scale for Children—Fourth Edition (Wechsler, 2003), the most popular intelligence test in use today (Salvia, Ysseldyke, & Bolt, 2010). These items are significant for two reasons. First, experts believe that general knowledge, such as "On what continent is Brazil?" is one indicator of intelligence, and second, experience obviously influences our ability to answer the questions. In addition, most experts today agree that intelligence is strongly influenced by culture and the unique experiences embedded within it (Ackerman & Lohman, 2006).

Intelligence: One Trait or Many?

Because scores on different measures of intelligence, such as verbal ability and abstract reasoning, are correlated, early researchers believed intelligence was influenced by a single trait (W. Johnson & Bouchard, 2005; Waterhouse, 2006). For example, Charles Spearman (1927) described it as "g," or general intelligence, a basic ability that affects performance on all cognitive tasks. This helps us understand why people who do well on verbal tests also do well on tests in math, but typically do better on one than the other.

A second perspective contrasts **fluid intelligence,** the flexible, culture-free ability to adapt to new situations and acquire knowledge easily, with **crystallized intelligence,** intelligence that is culture specific and depends on experience and schooling (Cattel, 1963, 1987). Fluid intelligence is often related to nonverbal abilities and is influenced by brain development. Some research suggests that people high in fluid intelligence tend to be more curious and interested in learning than counterparts lower in this measure (Silvia & Sanders, 2010). Fluid intelligence tends to be somewhat stable, whereas crystallized intelligence increases throughout our lives as we acquire new knowledge and skills. Current conceptions of intelligence typically include aspects of both (Ackerman & Lohman, 2006; Phelps, McGrew, Knopik, & Ford, 2005).

Fluid intelligence. The flexible, culture-free mental ability to adapt to new situations and acquire knowledge quickly.

Crystallized intelligence. Culture-specific mental ability, heavily dependent on experience and schooling.

A third perspective views intelligence as hierarchical and multifaceted, with general ability at the top, and those more specific, such as language and logical reasoning, at the bottom (Ackerman & Lohman, 2006). This view suggests that some cognitive abilities, such as the inclination to search for evidence in making decisions, generalize to all situations, whereas others are content specific.

Other prominent thinkers view intelligence as composed of several components or traits. We examine two of them in the following sections: Gardner's theory of multiple intelligences and Sternberg's triarchic theory of intelligence.

Gardner's Theory of Multiple Intelligences

Howard Gardner, a Harvard psychologist, analyzed people's performance in different domains and, dismissing the idea of "g", concluded that intelligence is composed of eight relatively independent dimensions (Gardner, 1983; Gardner & Moran, 2006). They're outlined in Table 5.1. Gardner is also considering additional dimensions, but, as yet, has not found sufficient evidence to support them (Gardner & Moran, 2006).

Applications of Gardner's Theory. Gardner recommends that we present content in ways that capitalize on as many different intelligences as possible and help students understand their strengths and weaknesses in each (Denig, 2003; Kornhaber, Fierros, & Veenema, 2004). For example, to develop interpersonal intelligence you might use cooperative learning; you can encourage students to put their thoughts into words to develop linguistic intelligence; and you can have students practice defending their ideas with evidence to capitalize on logical-mathematical intelligence.

Gardner warns, however, that not all topics can be adapted for each intelligence: "There is no point in assuming that every topic can be effectively approached in [multiple] ways, and it is a waste of effort and time to attempt to do this" (Gardner, 1995, p. 206).

Table 5.1	Gardner's theory of multiple intelligences

Dimension	Examples
Linguistic Intelligence Sensitivity to the meaning and order of words and the varied use of language	• Noticing differences in the meanings of words • Putting thoughts into language or writing creatively
Logical-Mathematical Intelligence The ability to reason logically, particularly in mathematics and quantitative sciences	• Making and defending conclusions based on evidence • Solving math problems and generating geometric proofs efficiently
Musical Intelligence Understanding and appreciating music	• Noticing differences in pitch, melody, and tone • Playing a musical instrument or singing
Spatial Intelligence The ability to perceive the visual world accurately	• Generating mental images of objects or creating drawings • Noticing subtle differences in similar objects
Bodily-Kinesthetic Intelligence The ability to skillfully use one's body	• Playing sports, such as basketball, soccer, or tennis skillfully • Performing dances or gymnastic routines
Interpersonal Intelligence The ability to understand other person's behaviors	• Understanding others' needs, desires, and motives • Interacting with others in socially acceptable ways
Intrapersonal Intelligence Understanding one's own thoughts, moods, and needs	• Understanding what influences one's own motivations • Using knowledge of oneself to interact effectively with others
Naturalist Intelligence The ability to recognize patterns in the physical world	• Classifying natural objects, such as animals and plants • Working successfully in naturalistic settings, such as farming, ranching, forestry, or geology

Source: Adapted from Gardner and Hatch (1989) and Checkley (1997).

Evaluating Gardner's Theory. Gardner's theory is controversial. It's popular with teachers, and it makes sense intuitively (Cuban, 2004). We all know people who don't seem particularly "sharp" analytically but who excel in getting along with others, for example. This ability serves them well, and in some instances, they're more successful in life than their "brighter" counterparts. Others are extraordinary athletes or accomplished musicians. Gardner describes these people as high in interpersonal, bodily-kinesthetic, and musical intelligence, respectively.

On the other hand, Gardner's work has a number of vocal critics. For instance, some caution that the theory and its applications have not been validated by research, nor do they have any support from research in cognitive neuroscience (Waterhouse, 2006). Others disagree with the assertion that abilities in specific domains, such as music, qualify as separate forms of intelligence (McMahon, Rose, & Parks, 2004). Some even argue that it isn't truly a theory (Chen, 2004).

Failure to account for the essential role that working memory plays in intelligent behavior is one of the most important criticisms (Lohman, 2001). Research and theories examining the way we process information suggest that a centralized working memory—the part of our memory system that consciously organizes and makes sense of our experiences—plays a special role in intelligence (Shelton, Elliott, Matthews, Hill, & Gouvier, 2010). For example, when we solve word problems, working memory helps keep the problems' specifics in mind as we search our memories for similar problems, select strategies, and find solutions. This cognitive juggling act occurs in all types of intelligent behavior, and Gardner's work ignores this essential role (Lohman, 2001).

Sternberg's Triarchic Theory of Intelligence

Robert Sternberg (Sternberg, 2003a, 2003b, 2004), another multitrait theorist, describes intelligence as existing in three dimensions:

- *Analytical,* which is similar to traditional definitions of intelligence and is used in thinking and problem solving (Sternberg, 2003b).
- *Creative,* or experiential, which involves the ability to deal effectively with novel situations, as well as the ability to solve familiar problems efficiently (Sternberg, 1998a, 1998b).
- *Practical,* or contextual, which is the ability to effectively accommodate the task demands of the environment. Intelligent behavior involves adapting to the environment, changing it if adaptation isn't effective, or selecting a better environment if necessary (Sternberg, 2007).

Sternberg's emphasis on the creative and practical aspects of intelligence sets his theory apart from others. He sees functioning effectively in the real world as intelligent behavior, and because of this emphasis, he believes that individuals considered intelligent in one setting or culture may be viewed as unintelligent in another (Sternberg, 2004, 2006, 2007).

Influenced by Piaget's emphasis on the role of experience in development, Sternberg believes that providing students with experiences in which they're expected to think analytically, creatively, and practically can increase intelligence. Some examples are outlined in Table 5.2.

Table 5.2 Applying analytic, creative, and practical thinking in different content areas

Content Area	Analytic	Creative	Practical
Math	Express the number 44 in base 2.	Write a test question that measures understanding of three different number bases.	How is the base 2 used in our everyday lives?
Language Arts	Why is *Romeo and Juliet* considered a tragedy?	Write an alternative ending to *Romeo and Juliet* to make it a comedy.	Write a TV ad for the school's production of *Romeo and Juliet*.
Social studies	In what ways were the American and the French revolutions similar and different?	What would our lives be like today if the American revolution had not succeeded?	What lessons can countries take away from the study of revolutions?
Science	If a balloon is filled with 1 liter of air at room temperature, and it is then placed in a freezer, what will happen to the balloon?	How would the balloon filled with air behave on the moon?	Describe two common examples where heating or cooling affects solids, liquids, or gases.
Art	Compare and contrast the artistic styles of Van Gogh and Picasso.	What would the Statue of Liberty look like if it were created by Picasso?	Create a poster for the student art show using the style of one of the artists we studied.

Intelligence: Nature and Nurture

No aspect of intelligence has been more hotly debated than the relative influences of heredity and the environment. The extreme **nature view of intelligence** asserts that intelligence is largely determined by genes; in essence, our intelligence is inherited from our parents and determined at birth (Horn, 2008; Toga & Thompson, 2005). The **nurture view of intelligence** emphasizes the influence of the environment and asserts that intelligence is malleable and can be changed by the experiences we encounter. Most experts take a position somewhere in the middle, believing that it's influenced by both (Coll, Bearer, & Lerner, 2004).

Evidence supports the contention that experience strongly influences intelligence, a view you earlier saw Sternberg emphasize. For example, children exposed to enriched learning experiences score higher on intelligence tests than those lacking the experiences (Campbell & Burchinal, 2008), and even school attendance can have a positive influence on intelligence (Ceci, 2003). This perspective is important for you, because it suggests that the experiences you provide can literally increase your students' intelligence.

Ability Grouping

To respond to differences in students' intellectual capabilities, schools often use **ability grouping,** the process of placing students of similar abilities into groups and attempting to match instruction to the needs of each (Chorzempa & Graham, 2006; McCoach, O'Connell, & Levitt, 2006).

Ability grouping in elementary schools typically exists in two forms. **Between-class grouping** divides students in a certain grade into levels, such as high, medium, and low. For example, an elementary school with 75 third graders might have one class of high achievers, one of average achievers, and one with low achievers. **Within-class grouping** divides students in a single class into groups, typically based on reading and math scores, such as a second-grade teacher having two or three different reading groups.

At the middle and high school levels, **tracking,** the process of placing students in different curricula on the basis of aptitude and achievement, is common, and some form of tracking exists in most schools at these levels. For example, high-ability students in high schools study a curriculum intended to prepare them for college—and in some cases even earn college credit—and lower-ability students receive vocational or work-related instruction (Oakes, 2005).

Ability Grouping: What Does Research Tell Us?

Ability grouping is controversial. Advocates defend it, arguing that it allows teachers to keep instruction uniform for groups, which enables them to better meet learners' needs. Most teachers endorse it, particularly in areas such as reading and math.

Critics counter by citing several problems. They argue that within-class grouping creates logistical problems, because different lessons and assignments are required, and improper placements can occur, which tend to become permanent (Good & Brophy, 2008). And members of cultural minorities and students with low socioeconomic status (SES) are underrepresented in high-ability classes and overrepresented in low-ability classes (McDermott, Goldman, & Varenne, 2006; O'Conner & Fernandez, 2006). Members of low-ability groups are often stigmatized by being labeled as low achievers (Oakes, 2005).

Most significantly, research indicates that homogeneously grouped low-ability students achieve less than heterogeneously grouped students of similar ability (Good & Brophy, 2008).

The negative effects of grouping are often related to the quality of instruction. As you would expect, the vast majority of teachers prefer working with high-ability students, and when

---

Nature view of intelligence. The assertion that intelligence is essentially determined by genetics.

Nurture view of intelligence. The assertion that emphasizes the influence of the environment on intelligence.

Ability grouping. The process of placing students of similar abilities into groups and attempting to match instruction to the needs of these groups.

Between-class grouping. Divides students in a certain grade into levels, such as high, medium, and low.

Within-class grouping. Divides students in a single class into groups, typically based on reading and math scores.

Tracking. Placing students in different classes or curricula on the basis of achievement.

assigned to low-ability groups, teachers sometimes lack enthusiasm and commitment and stress conformity instead of autonomy and the development of self-regulation (Chorzempa & Graham, 2006; Good & Brophy, 2008). As a result, self-esteem and motivation to learn decrease, and absenteeism increases. Tracking can also result in racial segregation of students, which has a negative influence on social development and opportunities to form friendships across cultural groups (Oakes, 2005).

Ability Grouping: Implications for Teachers

Suggestions for dealing with the issues involved in ability grouping vary. At one extreme, critics argue that its effects are so negative that the practice should be abolished. A more moderate position suggests that grouping is appropriate in some areas, such as reading and math (Good & Brophy, 2008). Research suggests that the **Joplin plan,** which uses homogeneous grouping in reading, but heterogeneous grouping in other areas, can increase reading achievement without negative side effects (Slavin, 1987). At the middle and secondary levels, between-class grouping should be limited to the basic academic areas.

Joplin plan. Homogeneous grouping in reading, combined with heterogeneous grouping in other areas.

When grouping is necessary, specific measures to reduce its negative effects should be taken. Some suggestions include:

- Keep group composition flexible, and reassign students to other groups when their achievement warrants it.
- Attempt to keep the quality of instruction high for low-ability groups.
- Teach low-ability students learning strategies and self-regulation.
- Avoid stigmatizing and stereotyping low-ability students.

These suggestions are demanding, and they have implications for you. Almost certainly, you will be assigned low-ability students at some point in your career, and maybe in your first year, because teachers with seniority are often given higher-ability groups. Low-ability students are indeed more difficult to teach. That's reality. When assigned to teach these students, make every effort to help them achieve as much as possible. If you do, you have met your professional responsibility.

Learning Styles

Historically, psychologists have used intelligence tests to measure mental abilities and have used concepts such as *introvert* and *extrovert* to describe different personality types. Researchers who study the interface between the two examine **learning styles**—students' personal approaches to thinking and problem solving (Denig, 2003). The terms *learning style, cognitive style, thinking style,* and *problem-solving style* are often used interchangeably, adding to confusion in this area.

Learning styles. Students' personal approaches to learning, problem solving, and processing information.

One description of learning style distinguishes between deep and surface approaches to studying new content (C. Evans, Kirby, & Fabrigar, 2003). For instance, as you studied the Civil War, did you relate it to the geography, economies, and politics of the northern and southern states? If so, you were using a deep-processing approach. On the other hand, if you memorized important dates, locations, and prominent leaders, you were using a surface approach.

As you would expect, deep-processing approaches result in higher achievement if tests focus on understanding, but surface approaches can be successful if tests emphasize fact learning and memorization. Students who use deep-processing approaches tend to be more intrinsically motivated and self-regulated, whereas those who use surface approaches tend to be extrinsically motivated, for example, by attaining high grades and comparing their performance to others (Schunk, Pintrich, & Meece, 2008).

Other perspectives on learning styles contrast analytic and holistic, and visual versus verbal approaches to learning. Analytical learners tend to break learning tasks into their component parts, whereas holistic learners attack problems more globally (Norenzayan, Choi, & Peng, 2007). Visual learners prefer to see ideas, whereas verbal learners prefer hearing them (Mayer & Massa, 2003). In general, an analytic approach is more beneficial for learning and develops as students mature. You can encourage this learning style with the kinds of questions you ask and the kinds of assignments, tests, and quizzes you give. You can also present information in both visual and verbal forms to capitalize on differences in this area.

Learning Styles and Learning Preferences

The idea of *learning styles* is popular in education, and many consultants use this label when they conduct in-service workshops for teachers. These workshops, however, typically focus on students' *preferences* for a particular learning environment, such as lighting and noise level, and consultants encourage teachers to match classroom environments to students' preferences.

Research on these practices is controversial. Advocates claim the match results in increased achievement and improved attitudes (Farkas, 2003; Lovelace, 2005); critics counter by questioning the validity of the tests used to measure learning styles or preferences (Coffield, Moseley, Hall, & Ecclestone, 2004; Kratzig & Arbuthnott, 2006). They also cite research indicating that attempts to match learning environments to learning preferences have resulted in no increases in achievement and, in some cases, even decreases (Pashler, McDaniel, Rohrer, & Bjork, 2008).

Most credible experts in the field question the wisdom of teachers' allocating energy and resources to attempts to accommodate learning styles.

> Like other reviewers who pay close attention to the research literature, I do not see much validity in the claims made by those who urge teachers to assess their students with learning style inventories and follow with differentiated curriculum and instruction. First, the research bases encouraging these urgings are thin to nonexistent. Second, a single teacher working with 20 or more students does not have time to plan and implement much individualized instruction (Brophy, 2010, p. 283).

Others speak more strongly. "I think learning styles represents one of the more wasteful and misleading pervasive myths of the last 20 years" (R. C. Clark, 2010, p. 10).

Learning Styles: Implications for Teachers

While little evidence supports attempts to match instruction to students' learning styles, the concept of *learning style* does have implications for us as teachers. First, it reminds us that we should vary our instruction, because no instructional strategy works for all students, or even the same students all the time (Brophy, 2010). Second, we should help our students understand how they learn most effectively, something that they aren't initially good at (Kratzig & Arbuthnott, 2006). Third, our students differ in ability, motivation, background experiences, needs, and insecurities. The concept of learning style can sensitize us to these differences, help us treat our students as individuals, and help us do everything we can to maximize learning for each student.

check your
understanding

1.1 Describe differences in the way intelligence is viewed.

1.2 Define ability grouping, and describe what research suggests about its potential impact on learning.

1.3 Describe the difference between the *nature view of intelligence* and the *nurture view of intelligence*. What does research say about these views?

To receive feedback for these questions, go to Appendix A.

Classroom connections

Accommodating Ability Differences in Classrooms

1. Performance on intelligence tests is influenced by genetics, experience, language, and culture. Use intelligence test scores cautiously when making educational decisions, keeping in mind that they are only one indicator of ability.

   ■ **Elementary:** An urban third-grade teacher consults with a school counselor in interpreting intelligence test scores, and she remembers that language and experience influence test performance.

   ■ **Middle School:** When making placement decisions, a middle school team relies on past classroom performance and grades in addition to standardized test scores.

   ■ **High School:** An English teacher uses grades, assessments of motivation, and work samples in addition to aptitude test scores in making placement recommendations.

2. Intelligence is multifaceted and covers a wide spectrum of abilities. Use instructional strategies that maximize student background knowledge, interests, and abilities.

   ■ **Elementary:** In a unit on the Revolutionary War, a fifth-grade teacher assesses all students on basic information, but bases 25% of the unit grade on special projects, such as researching the music and art of the times.

   ■ **Middle School:** An eighth-grade English teacher has both required and optional assignments. Seventy percent of the assignments are required for everyone; the other 30% provide students with choices.

   ■ **High School:** A biology teacher provides students with choices in terms of the special topics they study in depth. In addition he allows students to choose how they will report on their projects, allowing either research papers, classroom presentations, or poster sessions.

3. Ability grouping has both advantages and disadvantages. Use ability grouping only when essential, view group composition as flexible, and reassign students when warranted by their performance. Attempt to provide the same quality of instruction for all group levels.

   ■ **Elementary:** A fourth-grade teacher uses ability groups only for reading. She uses whole-class instruction for other language arts topics such as poetry and American folktales.

   ■ **Middle School:** A seventh-grade team meets regularly to assess group placements and to reassign students to different groups based on their academic progress.

   ■ **High School:** A history teacher videotapes lessons to compare his teaching in high-ability compared to standard-ability groups. He continually challenges both types of classes with interesting and demanding questions and assignments.

The Legal Basis for Working with Students Having Exceptionalities

In the past, students with disabilities were often placed in special classrooms or schools. Instruction in these placements was often inferior, achievement was no better than in general education classrooms, and students didn't learn the social and life skills needed in the real world (Karten, 2005; T. E. Smith, Polloway, Patton, & Dowdy, 2008). In response to the problems, a series of federal laws redefined the way teachers assist and work with these students. We exam these laws next.

Ed Psych and You

You have three students in your class that you suspect have exceptionalities. Do you have professional obligations to them that go beyond those for all your students? If so, what are they?

Individuals with Disabilities Education Act (IDEA)

In 1975 Congress passed Public Law 94-142, which made a free and appropriate public education a legal requirement for all students with disabilities in our country (Sack-Min, 2007). This law, named the *Individuals with Disabilities Education Act* (IDEA), has several provisions, which we discuss in detail later in this section.

Amendments to IDEA

Since 1975, Congress has amended IDEA three times (Sack-Min, 2007). The first amendment, passed in 1986, held states accountable for locating young children who need special education. Amendment 1997, known as IDEA 97, attempted to clarify and extend the quality of services to students with disabilities. This amendment clarifies major provisions in the original IDEA, such as protection against discrimination in testing. It also ensures that districts protect the confidentiality of children's records and share them with parents on request.

More recently, Congress enacted IDEA 2004. Its elements include mechanisms for reducing special education paperwork, creating discipline processes that allow districts to remove students who "inflict serious bodily injury" from classrooms, and establishing methods to reduce the number of students with diverse backgrounds who are inappropriately placed in special education. It also makes meeting the "highly qualified teacher" requirements of the No Child Left Behind legislation of 2001 more flexible by allowing veteran teachers to demonstrate their qualifications by means other than a test (Council for Exceptional Children, 2005).

Most controversial is its provision that calls for including students with disabilities in accountability systems, with critics warning that testing students with exceptionalities in the standard ways harms more than helps them (Meek, 2006).

IDEA and its amendments have affected every school in the United States and have changed the roles of teachers in both general and special education. It also relates to the questions we asked in "Ed Psych and You" in this section. The unequivocal answer to the question, "Do you have professional obligations to them [students with exceptionalities in your classroom] that go beyond those for all your students?" is yes. In the following sections we answer our second question: "If so, what are they?"

We turn now to the major provisions of IDEA.

Major Provisions of IDEA

IDEA requires that educators working with students having exceptionalities do the following:

- Provide a free and appropriate public education (FAPE).
- Educate children in the least restrictive environment (LRE).
- Protect against discrimination in testing.
- Involve parents in developing each child's educational program.
- Develop an individualized education program (IEP) of study for each student.

Let's examine them in more detail.

A Free and Appropriate Public Education (FAPE). IDEA asserts that every student can learn and is entitled to a FAPE. Provisions related to FAPE are based on the 14th Amendment to the Constitution, which guarantees equal protection of all citizens under the law. The Supreme Court in 1982 defined an *appropriate education* as one individually designed to provide educational benefits to a particular student (Hardman, Drew, & Egan, 2011).

Least Restrictive Environment: The Evolution Toward Inclusion. Educators attempting to provide FAPE for all students realized that segregated classes and services were not meeting the needs of students with exceptionalities. **Mainstreaming,** the practice of moving students with exceptionalities from segregated settings into general education classrooms, was one of the first alternatives considered. Popular in the 1970s, it began the move away from segregated services and promoted interaction

Mainstreaming. The practice of moving students with exceptionalities from segregated settings into general education classrooms.

between students with and without exceptionalities. However, students with exceptionalities were often placed in classrooms without adequate support (Hardman et al., 2011).

As educators struggled with these problems, they developed the concept of the **least restrictive environment (LRE),** one that places students in as typical an educational setting as possible while still meeting the students' special needs. Broader than the concept of *mainstreaming*, the LRE can consist of a continuum of services, ranging from full-time placement in the general education classroom to placement in a separate facility. Full-time placement in the general education classroom occurs only if parents and educators decide it best meets the child's needs.

The LRE provision ensures that you will have learners with exceptionalities in your classroom, and you will be asked to work with special educators to design and implement programs for these students. The LRE means that students with exceptionalities should participate as much as possible in all aspects of schooling, ranging from academics to extracurricular activities. The form these programs take varies with the capabilities of each student. Figure 5.1 presents a continuum of services for implementing the LRE, starting with the least confining at the top and moving to the most restrictive at the bottom. If students don't succeed at one level, educators move them to the next to provide additional help and support.

The concept of **adaptive fit** is central to the LRE. It describes the degree to which a school environment accommodates each student's needs and the degree to which a student can meet the requirements of a particular school setting (Hardman et al., 2011). As educators examined mainstreaming, LRE, and adaptive fit, they gradually developed the concept of *inclusion*.

Inclusion is a comprehensive approach that advocates a total, systematic, and coordinated web of services for students with exceptionalities (Sailor & Roger, 2005; Sapon-Shevin, 2007). It has three provisions: (1) students with special needs are placed on a general education school campus; (2) these students are placed in age- and grade-appropriate classrooms; and (3) general and special education services are coordinated.

Inclusion is controversial, with criticisms coming from general education classroom teachers, parents, and special educators themselves (Turnbull et al., 2010). Where it works, general and special education teachers closely collaborate (Vaughn & Bos, 2009). Without close collaboration, general education teachers are overwhelmed by trying to provide the services inclusion specifies, and it isn't effective. Some parents, concerned that their children might become "lost in the shuffle," often favor special classrooms (J. Johnson & Duffett, 2002).

In the special education community, advocates of inclusion contend that placement in a general education classroom is the only way to eliminate the

Increasing Numbers of Students →

Student placed in general classroom; IEP implemented with no additional or specialized assistance

Student placed in general classroom with collaborative assistance and consultation

Student placed in general classroom for majority of day; attends special education resource classroom for specialized instruction

Student placed in special education for most of school day; attends general class in subject areas consonant with abilities

Student placed full-time in special education classroom in a general school

Student placed in separate school or residential facility for children with special needs

Placement in a More Restricted Environment →

Figure 5.1 Educational service options for implementing the LRE

Sources: Hallahan, Kauffman, & Pullen, 2009; Hardman et al., 2011; Turnbull, Turnbull, & Wehmeyer, 2010.

Least restrictive environment (LRE). A policy that places students in as typical an educational setting as possible while still meeting the students' special needs.

Adaptive fit. The degree to which a school environment accommodates the student's needs and the degree to which a student can meet the requirements of a particular school setting.

The least restrictive environment helps students develop to their fullest potential.

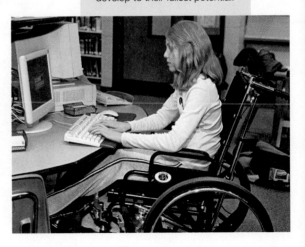

Inclusion. A comprehensive approach to educating students with exceptionalities that advocates a total, systematic, and coordinated web of services.

negative effects of segregation (Turnbull et al., 2010). Opponents counter that inclusion is not for everyone and that some students are better served in special classes, at least for parts of the day. Despite these controversies, inclusion is now widely accepted, and you are almost certain to encounter it in your teaching.

Fair and Nondiscriminatory Evaluation. In the past, students were often placed in special education programs based on invalid information. IDEA requires that any testing used for placement be conducted in a student's native language by qualified personnel, and no single instrument, such as an intelligence test, can be used as the sole basis for placement. More recently, students' classroom performance and general adaptive behavior have been increasingly emphasized (Heward, 2009).

Due process. The guarantee that parents have the right to be involved in identifying and placing their children in special programs, to access school records, and to obtain an independent evaluation if they're not satisfied with the one conducted by the school.

Due Process and Parents' Rights. **Due process** guarantees that parents have the right to be involved in their children's placement in special programs, to access school records, and to obtain an independent evaluation if they're not satisfied with the one conducted by the school. Legal safeguards are also in place for parents who don't speak English; they have the right to an interpreter, and their rights must be read to them in their native language.

Individualized education program (IEP). A written statement that provides a framework for delivering a free and appropriate education (FAPE) to every eligible student with a disability.

Individualized Education Program. To ensure that inclusion works and learners with exceptionalities don't become lost in the general education classroom, educators prepare an **individualized education program (IEP),** a written statement that provides a framework for delivering a FAPE to every eligible student with a disability. The team responsible for developing the IEP will include the students' parents; at least one special education teacher; at least one general education teacher if the student is, or likely will be, participating in the general education environment; and a district representative (Hardman et al., 2011).

The purpose of the IEP is to ensure that special education services are provided for the student on a daily and annual basis, and it is also intended to promote effective communication between the school personnel and the child's family. IDEA 2004 requires that each child's IEP must include the following:

- A statement describing the child's achievement and functional performance, including a description of how the disability affects her progress in the general education curriculum.
- A statement of annual academic and functional goals designed to meet the child's special needs related to his disability.
- A description of how the child's progress toward meeting the goals will be measured and when reports on the child's progress will be provided.
  - A statement of the special education and related services that will be provided for the child.
  - An explanation of the extent, if any, to which the child will not participate with nondisabled children in the general education classroom.
  - A statement of any individual accommodations, such as more time or an interpreter, that are needed to assess the academic achievement and functional performance of the child on state or district-wide assessments.

IEPs sometimes focus on adaptations in the general education classroom, and at others times they provide for outside support, such as a resource room. They are most effective when the two are coordinated, such as when a teacher working on word problems in math asks the resource teacher to focus on the same type of problems.

Teachers and other professionals meet with parents to design an IEP.

Identifying Students with Exceptionalities

Current approaches to identifying students who may need special help are team based, and you, as a general education teacher, will be a key member of the team. Before referring a student for a special education evaluation, you will be asked to document the problem you believe exists and the strategies you're using in attempting to solve it (Hallahan et al., 2009). You will be expected to describe the following:

- The nature of the problem and how it affects classroom performance
- Dates, places, and times problems have occurred
- Strategies you've tried
- Assessment of the strategies' effectiveness

Assessment is an essential part of the identification process. In the past, special educators relied heavily on standardized intelligence tests, but as you saw earlier, the protection-against-discrimination-in-testing provision of IDEA prevents decisions based on an intelligence test alone. Teachers are now increasingly using **curriculum-based assessments,** which measure learners' performance in specific areas of the curriculum and link assessments directly to learning objectives (Vaughn & Bos, 2009).

Discrepancy Versus Response to Intervention Models of Identification

In the past, a **discrepancy model of identification** was used to identify students with learning problems. It looked for differences between (1) intelligence- and achievement-test performance, (2) intelligence-test scores and classroom achievement, or (3) subtests on either intelligence or achievement tests. Inconsistency between any of the two may suggest a learning problem.

Many experts are dissatisfied with the discrepancy model, arguing that it identifies an exceptionality only after—and sometimes long after—a problem surfaces (Brown-Chidsey, 2007). Instead, they argue, educators need early screening measures, so that teachers can intervene before a major problem develops. Critics also contend that the discrepancy model does not provide specific information about the nature of the learning problem and what should be done to correct it (Sternberg & Grigorenko, 2001; Stuebing et al., 2002).

The **response to intervention model of identification** attempts to address both of these problems using a three-tiered approach (Samuels, 2009; Vaughn & Bos, 2009). In the first tier, you use instruction documented as effective for all students. (We examine effective instruction in detail in Chapter 13.) The second begins when a learning problem surfaces, and you provide extra support—such as small-group activities while the rest of the students do seatwork, or help outside of school hours—in an attempt to meet the student's needs. The third tier includes intensive one-to-one help and perhaps a special needs assessment.

The model emphasizes developing skills and study strategies, such as highlighting important vocabulary, reading assignments aloud, or finding a place to study that's free of distractions. If the adaptations don't increase achievement, a learning problem that requires additional help may exist. As you adapt your instruction, you also document what is and is not working, which provides valuable information for later interventions.

Curriculum-based assessment. Measurement of learners' performance in specific areas of the curriculum.

Discrepancy model of identification. One method of identifying students with learning problems that focuses on differences between achievement and intelligence tests or subtests.

Response to intervention model of identification. A method of identifying a learning problem that focuses on the specific classroom instructional adaptations that teachers use and their success.

The response-to-intervention model of identification uses a three-tiered approach with intensive one-on-one help for students in the third tier.

Adaptive Behavior

In addition to academic performance, you will also assess students' *adaptive behavior*, their ability to perform the functions of everyday school life. You observe students to assess the extent to which they perform routine school tasks, such as initiating and completing assignments, controlling their behavior, and interacting effectively with other students.

If your observations suggest that a problem exists, a number of instruments that formally assess the ability to adapt can be used (Heward, 2009). For example, the American Association on Intellectual and Developmental Disabilities Adaptive Behavior Scale—Schools contains 104 items with several questions per item (Pierangelo & Giuliani, 2006). This instrument assesses areas such as students' abilities to understand directions, express themselves, persist on tasks, and make friends.

Referral for Special Services

If you aren't able solve a student's learning problem by adapting instruction, you can then initiate a referral. When considering a referral, you should first check with an administrator or school psychologist to learn about the school's policies.

When the data suggest that a student needs additional help, a prereferral team is formed. The team usually consists of a school psychologist, a special educator, and you as the classroom teacher. The team further evaluates the problem, consults with parents, and begins the process of preparing the IEP.

Parents play an integral role in the process. They can provide valuable information about the student's educational and medical history, and notifying parents is simply the act of a professional, even if it wasn't required by law.

---

check your understanding

2.1 Describe the major provisions of the Individuals with Disabilities Education Act (IDEA).

2.2 Describe the amendments to the Individuals with Disabilities Education Act.

2.3 Explain how mainstreaming and inclusion relate to the FAPE (free and appropriate public education) provision of IDEA.

To receive feedback for these questions, go to Appendix A.

Exceptionalities and Learning Problems

Ed Psych and You

Do you sometimes have trouble paying attention in class or are disorganized and distracted in your studying? Do you feel as if particular areas of the curriculum are extra hard for you? Have you ever joked that you have some sort of disorder?

Almost 7 million students with exceptionalities are enrolled in special programs, two thirds for relatively minor learning problems. About 10% of students in a typical school receive special education services with issues ranging from mild learning problems to physical impairments such as being deaf or blind (U.S. Department of Education, 2009).

Federal legislation has created categories to identify learning problems, and educators use the categories in developing special programs to meet the needs of students in each. We examine the controversies surrounding this process and the specific categories in the sections that follow.

The Labeling Controversy

A number of categories and labels have been created to identify and accommodate learners with exceptionalities (Hardman et al., 2011). *Disorder, disability,* and *handicap* are terms commonly used to describe physical or behavioral differences. **Disorder,** the broadest of the three, refers to a general malfunction of mental, physical, or emotional processes. A **disability** is a functional limitation or an inability to perform a specific act, such as walking or hearing a teacher's voice. A **handicap** is a condition imposed on people's functioning that restricts their abilities, such as being unable to enter a building in a wheelchair. Some, but not all, disabilities lead to handicaps. For example, a student with a visual disability may be able to wear glasses or sit in the front of the classroom; if these measures allow the student to function effectively, the disability isn't a handicap.

The use of categories and their labels is controversial. Advocates argue that categories provide a common language for professionals and encourage specialized instruction that meets students' needs (Heward, 2009). Opponents claim that categories are arbitrary, many differences exist within them, and categorizing encourages educators to treat students as labels instead of people (National Council on Disability, 2000). Despite the controversy, labels are widely used, so you will need to be familiar with them.

Regardless of their position, special educators agree that labels shouldn't focus attention on students' weaknesses, so they endorse **people-first language,** which first identifies the student and then specifies the disability. For example, they use the description *students with a learning disability* instead of *learning-disabled students.* People-first language reminds us that all students are human beings who need to be treated with respect and care.

Categories of Exceptionalities

A range of categories for learners with exceptionalities exist. They include:

- Learning disabilities
- Attention deficit hyperactivity disorder
- Communication disorders
- Behavior disorders
- Intellectual disabilities
- Autism spectrum disorders
- Visual disabilities
- Hearing disabilities

Over 90% of students with disabilities who receive special education services in our country are identified as having *learning disabilities, communication disorders, behavior disorders, intellectual disabilities,* or *autism spectrum disorders.* Ninety five percent of these students receive their education in inclusive programs in general education classrooms, so students with these disabilities are the ones you're most likely to encounter in your work (Hardman et al., 2011; U.S. Department of Education, 2009).

We turn to them now.

Learning Disabilities

Tammy Fuller, a middle school social studies teacher, is surprised when she scores Adam's first quiz. He seemed to be doing so well. He is rarely absent, pays attention, and participates in class. Why is his score so low? Tammy makes a mental note to watch him more closely.

In her second unit, Tammy prepares study guide questions and has students discuss their answers in groups. As she moves around the room, she notices that Adam's sheet is empty, and when she asks him about it, he mumbles something about not having time the night before. Tammy asks Adam to come in after school to complete his work.

Disorder. A general malfunction of mental, physical, or psychological processes.

Handicap. A condition imposed on a person's functioning that restricts the individual's abilities.

People-first language. Language in which a student's disability is identified after the student is named.

He arrives promptly and opens his book to the chapter. When Tammy checks his progress, his page is blank, and it's still empty 10 minutes later.

As she sits down to talk with him, he appears embarrassed and evasive. When they start to work on the questions together, she discovers that he can't read the text.

Learning disabilities. Difficulty in acquiring and using reading, writing, reasoning, listening, or mathematical abilities.

Some students, like Adam, are average or above in intelligence but have **learning disabilities** (also called *specific learning disabilities*), difficulties with reading, writing, reasoning, listening, or math (National Joint Committee on Learning Disabilities, 1994). Problems with reading, writing, and listening are most common, but math-related difficulties also receive attention (S. E. Shaywitz & Shaywitz, 2004). Central nervous system dysfunction—resulting from genetics or adverse environmental conditions, such as malnutrition or alcohol use during pregnancy—are believed to be the cause (Friend, 2008). Learning disabilities often exist together with—but are not caused by—other disabilities such as attention problems. Experts stress that the term *learning disability* is broad and encompasses a range of problems (Berninger, 2006).

The category *learning disabilities* illustrates the labeling controversy we discussed earlier. Critics contend that it's a catchall term for students who have learning problems (Sternberg & Grigorenko, 2001). Part of the criticism results from the rapid growth of the category, nonexistent in the early 1960s, but now estimated to make up close to half of the population of students with disabilities, far and away the largest percentage of all exceptionalities (U.S. Department of Education, 2009).

Characteristics of students with learning disabilities are outlined in Table 5.3. Some of the characteristics are typical of general learning problems or immaturity. Unlike developmental lags, however, problems associated with learning disabilities often increase over time, resulting in lowered achievement and self-esteem and increases in classroom management problems (Heward, 2009).

Identifying and Working with Students Who Have Learning Disabilities. As with all exceptionalities, early identification is important to prevent damaging effects from

Table 5.3 Characteristics of students with learning disabilities

General Patterns
Attention deficits
Disorganization and tendency toward distraction
Lack of follow-through and completion of assignments
Uneven performance (e.g., capable in one area, extremely weak in others)
Lack of coordination and balance

Academic Performance	
Reading	Lacks reading fluency
	Reverses words (e.g., *saw* for *was*)
	Frequently loses place
Writing	Makes jerky and poorly formed letters
	Has difficulty staying on line
	Is slow in completing work
	Has difficulty copying from chalkboard
Math	Has difficulty remembering math facts
	Has trouble with story problems
	Mixes columns (e.g., tens and ones) in computing

accumulating. Identifying these students isn't easy, however, because students with learning disabilities who comply with rules and complete assignments on time are often passed over for referral. This is likely the reason Adam, in Tammy's class, got to middle school before his difficulties with reading were discovered.

You are almost certain to have students with learning disabilities in your classes, and they will need extra structure and support to succeed. For example, you might provide additional study aids, such as content outlines, present information both visually and verbally, and eliminate distractions during seatwork. In addition, systematically teaching study strategies has been proven effective (Mastropieri & Scruggs, 2010).

This section addresses the questions we asked in our "Ed Psych and You" feature at the beginning of this section. Most of us periodically display characteristics similar to those in students with a learning disability—we aren't as efficient as we could be when studying and are often disorganized and distracted. However, unlike students who actually have a disability, our problems typically aren't chronic, and we make appropriate adaptations in our study.

This has implications for our teaching. If we adapt our instruction and provide sufficient emotional and instructional support, students with learning disabilities can learn and succeed.

Attention Deficit Hyperactivity Disorder

Attention deficit hyperactivity disorder (ADHD) is a learning problem characterized by difficulties in maintaining attention. ADHD has long been associated with learning disabilities, and experts estimate an overlap of 25% to 70% in the two conditions (Hardman et al., 2011). It's relatively new as a described exceptionality and isn't listed as a distinct category in IDEA. Students with ADHD may qualify for special education under the "other health impairments" disability category, however.

Attention deficit hyperactivity disorder (ADHD). A learning problem characterized by difficulties in maintaining attention.

Hyperactivity, inattention, difficulty in concentrating, impulsiveness, and an inordinate need for supervision are common characteristics of ADHD. It has received a great deal of media attention, and you will encounter many students who seem to fit the description. However, high activity levels and inability to focus attention are also characteristics of developmental lags, especially in young boys, so you should be cautious about drawing conclusions on the basis of these characteristics alone.

ADHD typically appears early (at age 2 or 3) and usually persists into adolescence or beyond (Purdie, Hattie & Carroll, 2002). Some experts estimate that three to four times as many boys as girls are identified (Hallahan et al., 2009). ADHD can also result in relationship and marital problems in adulthood (Parker-Pope, 2010).

Students with ADHD are impulsive and have difficulty concentrating.

Treatments range from medication, such as the controversial drug Ritalin, to reinforcement programs and structured teaching environments (described later in this chapter). Diagnosis and treatment of ADHD are usually conducted in consultation with medical and psychological experts.

Rodney, in our case study at the beginning of the chapter, displays symptoms of ADHD. He's hyperactive, easily distracted, and has difficulty focusing his attention. Clarisse gave Celina good advice in suggesting that she check with special education experts in their school. However, as you saw earlier in the chapter, Celina will be expected to document the problem, the strategies she has used to solve it, and their effectiveness, before Rodney is referred. For example, simply moving him to quieter part of the room might be a first step. With older students, helping them learn how to break long assignments into smaller components, keep meticulously organized assignment books, and use flash cards and other drills to develop automaticity with basic skills have been proved effective (Vaughn & Bos, 2009).

Communication Disorders

Communication disorders.
Exceptionalities that interfere with students' abilities to receive and understand information from others and express their own ideas.

Speech disorders (*expressive disorders*). Problems in forming and sequencing sounds.

Language disorders (*receptive disorders*). Problems with understanding language or using language to express ideas.

Communication disorders are the second most frequently occurring exceptionality in school-age children, making up nearly 20% of the special education population (Hallan et al., 2011). They exist in two forms. The first is **speech disorders,** sometimes called *expressive disorders*, which involve problems in forming and sequencing sounds. Stuttering and mispronouncing words, such as saying, "I taw it" for "I saw it," are examples. Specialists have identified three kinds of speech disorders (see Table 5.4).

Language disorders, also called *receptive disorders*, make up the second form of communication disorder, and they include problems with understanding language or, more commonly, using language to express ideas. Language disorders are often connected to other problems, such as a hearing impairment, or a learning or intellectual disability (Turnbull et al., 2010).

Because they more strongly detract from learning, language disorders are more serious than speech disorders. The majority of students learn to communicate quite well by the time they start school, but a small number continue to experience problems expressing themselves verbally (Hardman et al., 2011; Heward, 2009). Seldom speaking, even during play, using few words or very short sentences, and overrelying on gestures to communicate are symptoms of language disorders.

Hearing loss, brain damage, learning or intellectual disabilities, severe emotional problems, and inadequate developmental experiences in a child's early years are the most common causes of language disorders.

If you suspect that a student has a speech or language disorder, you should keep cultural diversity in mind. English is not the primary language for many students, and the difficulties these students encounter in learning both content and a second language should not be confused with a communication disorder. Combined with your patience and understanding, English learners will respond to an enriched language environment. Students with communication disorders require the help of a speech and language specialist.

Table 5.4 Types of speech disorders

Disorder	Description	Example
Articulation disorders	Difficulty in producing certain sounds, including substituting, distorting, and omitting	"Wabbit" for *rabbit* "Thit" for *sit* "Only" for *lonely*
Fluency disorders	Repetition of the first sound of a word (stuttering) and other problems in producing "smooth" speech	"Y, Y, Y, Yes"
Voice disorders	Problems with the larynx or air passageways in the nose or throat	High-pitched or nasal voice

Aiding in the process of identification and modeling acceptance and respect for them are your primary tasks in working with these students. As with other exceptionalities, you play an important role in identification because you are in most direct contact with students. And ensuring that students with the disorder are accepted and respected is essential because teasing and social rejection often occur and can cause lasting emotional damage. Being patient as they try to express themselves, refraining from correcting their speech—which calls attention to the problem—and forbidding any form of demeaning comments from peers will do a great deal to help these students accommodate their disability. Cooperative and small-group activities can also provide opportunities for students to practice language in settings that are less threatening than whole-class activities.

Intellectual Disabilities

To begin this section, let's return to Celina's work with her students.

> She watches her children as they work on a reading assignment, and most of the class works quietly. Amelia, in contrast, is out of her seat for the third time, supposedly sharpening her pencil. Celina has reminded her once to get back to work and this time goes over to see what the problem is.
>
> "I can't do this! I don't get it!" Amelia responds in frustration when Celina asks her why she hasn't started her work.
>
> After helping her calm down, Celina works with her for a few moments, but she can tell by Amelia's responses and her facial expressions that she truly doesn't "get" the assignment.

Some students, like Amelia, struggle with learning and become frustrated when they can't keep up with their peers. Unfortunately, this problem often isn't identified until students are several years into school. Many have mild intellectual disability. (You may also encounter the terms *cognitive impairment, educationally* or *intellectually handicapped,* and *intellectual* and *developmental disabilities,* which some educators prefer.) *Mental retardation,* an antiquated term, has been rejected because it's considered offensive and stigmatizing. An intellectual disability is caused by either genetic factors, such as Down syndrome, or brain damage to the fetus during pregnancy (D. Fuchs, 2006).

The American Association on Intellectual and Developmental Disabilities (AAIDD) defines **intellectual disability** as follows:

> Intellectual disability is a disability characterized by significant limitations both in intellectual functioning and in adaptive behavior as expressed in conceptual, social, and practical adaptive skills. This disability originates before the age of 18. A complete and accurate understanding of intellectual disability involves realizing that intellectual disability refers to a particular state of functioning that begins in childhood, has many dimensions, and is affected positively by individualized supports. (American Association on Intellectual and Developmental Disabilities, 2008)

Intellectual disability. A disability characterized by significant limitations both in intellectual functioning and in adaptive behavior.

The AAIDD definition emphasizes limitations in both intellectual functioning and adaptive abilities, such as communication, self-care, and social skills (Turnbull et al., 2010). Functioning in both areas can improve when these students receive services designed to meet their needs.

Students with intellectual disabilities are likely to display some or all of the following characteristics:

- Lack of general knowledge about the world
- Difficulty with abstract ideas
- Poor reading and language skills

- Poorly developed learning and memory strategies
- Underdeveloped motor skills
- Immature interpersonal skills (Hodapp & Dykens, 2006)

Some of these characteristics affect learning directly; others, such as immature interpersonal skills, are less direct but still important, because they affect a student's ability to make friends and develop socially.

Before the 1960s, definitions of intellectual disability were based primarily on below-average scores on intelligence tests, but this approach had three problems. First, tests are imprecise, so misdiagnoses sometimes occurred. Second, disproportionate numbers of minorities and non-English-speaking students were identified as mentally retarded (Hallahan et al., 2009). Third, educators found that individuals with the same intelligence test scores varied widely in their ability to cope with the real world (Heward, 2009). Because of these problems, **adaptive behavior,** the person's ability to perform the functions of everyday living, became more important (Cimera, 2006). Your input is essential in this area.

Programs for students with intellectual disabilities focus on creating support systems to augment existing instruction. Schools often place these students in general education classrooms, so you are likely to work with them at some point in your career. As with other disabilities, you will be expected to adapt your instruction to meet their needs and help them develop socially.

Research indicates that these students often fail to acquire basic learning strategies, such as maintaining attention, organizing new material, and studying for tests (Heward, 2009). Amelia, in Celina's class, is an example. Celina recognized this need and attempted to provide additional support by working with her one-on-one.

Adaptive behavior. A person's ability to perform the functions of everyday living.

Behavior Disorders

Kyle comes in from recess sweaty and disheveled, crosses his arms, and looks at his teacher defiantly. The playground monitor has reported another scuffle, and Kyle has a history of these disturbances. He struggles with his studies but can handle them if provided with enough structure. When he becomes frustrated, he sometimes acts out, often ignoring the rights and feelings of others.

Ben, who sits next to Kyle, is so quiet that his teacher almost forgets he is there. He never causes problems; in fact, he seldom participates in class. He has few friends and walks around at recess by himself, appearing to consciously avoid other children.

Behavior disorders. Serious and persistent age-inappropriate behaviors that result in social conflict, personal unhappiness, and often school failure.

Although very different, Kyle and Ben both display symptoms of **behavior disorders,** serious and persistent age-inappropriate behaviors that result in social conflict and personal unhappiness. School failure is often an outcome. The terms *serious* and *persistent* are important. Many children occasionally fight with their peers, and all children periodically want to be alone. If a child shows a pattern of these behaviors, and if the behaviors interfere with normal development and school success, however, the child may have a behavior disorder.

The term *behavior disorder* is often used interchangeably with *emotional disturbance, emotional disability,* or *emotional handicap,* and you may encounter any of these in your work. Researchers prefer the term *behavior disorder* because it focuses on overt behaviors that can be targeted and changed (Turnbull et al., 2010).

Students with behavior disorders often have the following characteristics:

- Behaving impulsively and having difficulty interacting with others in socially acceptable ways
- Acting out and failing to follow school or classroom rules
- Displaying poor self-concepts

- Lacking awareness of the severity of their problems
- Deteriorating academic performance and frequently missing school (Turnbull et al., 2010)

Students with behavior disorders often have academic problems, some of which are connected with learning disabilities. The combination of these problems results in high absentee rates, low achievement, and a dropout rate of nearly 50%, the highest of any group of students with special needs (U.S. Department of Education, 2009).

Estimates of the frequency of behavior disorders vary. Some suggest that about 1% or 2% of the total school population and close to 10% of the special education population have behavior disorders, but others suggest that, because of identification problems, the percentage is much higher (Hallahan et al., 2009; Hardman et al., 2011). Identification problems are compounded by ethnic and cultural factors. For example, African Americans make up approximately 12% of the general population but 26% of students diagnosed with behavior disorders (Rosenberg, Westling, & McLesky, 2008).

Behavior disorders are classified as either *externalizing* or *internalizing* (Hallahan et al., 2009). Students like Kyle fall into the first category, displaying characteristics such as hyperactivity, defiance, hostility, and even cruelty. Boys are three times more likely to be labeled as having an externalizing behavior disorder than girls, and low SES and membership in a cultural minority increase students' chances of being given this label.

Internalizing behavior disorders can be more destructive, because they don't have the high profile of students who act out, and as a result, they may go unnoticed. They're characterized by social withdrawal, few friendships, depression, and anxiety, problems more directed at the self than others. Like Ben, these children lack self-confidence and are often shy, timid, and depressed, sometimes even suicidal.

Students with internalizing behavior disorders are withdrawn and often experience anxiety and depression.

Suicide. Suicide is the third leading cause of teen death, surpassed only by car accidents and homicide (Kids Health for Parents, 2006). Not every student with a behavior disorder is at risk for suicide, of course, but a combination of factors often connected to behavior disorders, such as depression and substance abuse, stress, and family conflict and rejection, are directly linked to the problem (Berk, 2010). About a half million young people attempt suicide each year, and between 2,000 and 5,000 succeed, although accurate figures are hard to obtain because of the social stigma attached to suicide (Fisher, 2006; Moore, 2007). The suicide rate among adolescents has quadrupled in the last 50 years. Girls are twice as likely as boys to attempt suicide, but boys are four times more likely to succeed. Boys tend to employ more lethal means, such as shooting themselves, whereas girls choose more survivable methods, such as overdosing on drugs.

Potential suicide indicators include

- An abrupt decline in the quality of schoolwork
- Withdrawal from friends or classroom and school activities
- Neglect of personal appearance or radical changes in personality
- Changes in eating or sleeping habits
- Depression, as evidenced by persistent boredom or lack of interest in school activities
- Comments about suicide as a solution to problems (Fisher, 2006; Kids Health for Parents, 2006).

If you observe any of these indicators in a student, contact a school counselor or psychologist immediately, because early intervention is essential.

Bipolar Disorder. **Bipolar disorder** is a condition characterized by alternative episodes of depressive and manic states (Heward, 2009), and the number of children treated for the disorder increased 40-fold from 20,000 in 1994 to 800,000 in 2003 (Carey, 2007). Experts believe that the incidence hasn't actually increased; rather, the numbers reflect a greater tendency to apply the diagnosis to children. The increase is also controversial, with critics claiming the label has become a catchall term applied to any child who is either depressed, the most common symptom, or explosively aggressive.

The symptoms of bipolar disorder are similar to depression or anxiety and are often linked to other issues, especially ADHD. Treatment typically includes powerful psychiatric drugs, which generally succeed in reducing or eliminating symptoms but may have negative side effects, such as a gain in weight. If you encounter students with this disorder, you can expect advice and assistance from special educators and school psychologists.

Teaching Students with Behavior Disorders. Students with behavior disorders require a classroom environment that invites participation and success while providing structure through clearly stated and consistently enforced rules (Swanson, 2005).

Behavior management strategies are often used with these students (Alberto & Troutman, 2009). They include rewarding desired behaviors, such as praising a student for behaving courteously; teaching replacement behaviors, such as helping students learn to express personal feelings verbally instead of fighting; and time-out, isolating a child for brief periods of time.

Teaching self-management skills can also be effective (Heward, 2009). You will see an example when you analyze the case study at the end of the chapter.

Students with behavior disorders can be frustrating, and it's easy to forget that they have unique needs. This is where your sensitivity and acceptance are essential. Communicating to these students that their behaviors are unacceptable but they are innately worthy as human beings, and you care about them and their learning, is crucial. This acceptance and caring can do more for them than any other form of intervention.

Autism Spectrum Disorders

Originally thought of as a single disorder, **autism spectrum disorder** describes a cluster of problems characterized by impaired social relationships and skills and often associated with highly unusual behaviors (Hardman et al., 2011; Heward, 2009).

Autism was added to the IDEA list of disabilities qualifying for special services in 1990, and since that time the term has been expanded to *autism spectrum disorders* to reflect the wide range of disabilities it encompasses. They all involve problems with social relationships, ranging from conditions in which language is severely impaired and normal social relations are virtually impossible, to *Asperger's syndrome*, in which students have average to above-average intelligence and only moderately impaired language abilities and social relationships (Friend, 2008).

In addition to impaired social relationships, characteristics of autism spectrum disorder include

- Communication and language deficits
- Unusual sensitivity to sensory stimuli such as light and sound
- Insistence on sameness and perseveration
- Ritualistic and unusual behavior patterns (Heward, 2009)

Bipolar disorder. A condition characterized by alternative episodes of depressive and manic states.

Autism spectrum disorder. A description of a cluster of disorders characterized by impaired social relationships and skills and often associated with highly unusual behavior.

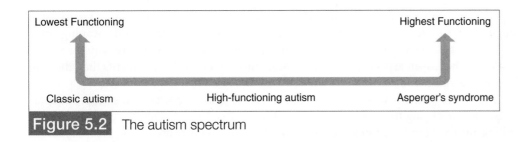

Figure 5.2 The autism spectrum

An orderly and predictable classroom is essential for students with autism spectrum disorders.

Autism spectrum disorders are thought to be caused by abnormalities in the brain. Their incidence has increased significantly in recent years, and they are four times more prevalent in boys than girls (Darden, 2007). Lack of responsiveness to social stimuli and unusual, ritualistic behaviors such as rocking or repeating words or phrases are often the first symptoms. Many children with autism spectrum disorders are in general education classes for part or all of the school day. Figure 5.2 illustrates the concept of the autism spectrum.

Two approaches to working with these students are most effective. One attempts to make the classroom environment as predictable as possible. Routines are helpful for all students; they are essential for children with an autism spectrum disorder. Also, clearly outlined rules and expectations that are consistently applied provide additional support for these students.

A second approach focuses on social skills and attempts to help these students learn to interact with their peers and adjust to the social demands of classrooms. Students with autism spectrum disorders are commonly unaware of the effects of their behaviors on others, so conscious efforts to teach socially acceptable behaviors can be effective.

Visual Disabilities

About 1 in 5 of us have some type of vision loss. Fortunately, most problems can be corrected with glasses, surgery, or therapy. In some situations—approximately 1 child in 3,000—the impairment cannot be corrected (Hardman et al., 2011). People with this condition have a **visual handicap,** an uncorrectable visual impairment that interferes with learning. Many of these students can read with the aid of a magnifying glass or large print books, but others are entirely dependent on the spoken word or Braille.

Visual handicap. An uncorrectable visual impairment that interferes with learning.

Nearly two thirds of serious visual disabilities exist at birth, and most children are given visual screenings when they enter elementary school. Some vision problems appear during the school years as a result of growth spurts, however, so you should remain alert to the possibility of an undetected impairment in your students. Symptoms of these problems include:

- Holding the head in an awkward position or holding a book too close or too far away
- Squinting and frequently rubbing the eyes
- Tuning out or constantly asking about procedures, particularly when information is presented on the board
- Using poor spacing in writing and having difficulty staying on the line

Students with visual disabilities differ from their peers without disabilities in areas ranging from understanding spatial concepts to general knowledge. Word meanings may not be as rich or elaborate because of the students' lack of visual experience with the world. As a result, hands-on experiences are even more important for these students than they are for other learners.

If you have students with visual disabilities in your class, you can make simple adaptations, such as seating them near writing boards and displays on screens, verbalizing while writing on the board, and ensuring that handouts are high contrast and clear (Heward, 2009). You can also supply large-print books and magnifying aids to adapt materials. Peer tutors can provide assistance in explaining and clarifying assignments and procedures.

Hearing Disabilities

Partial hearing impairment. An impairment that allows a student to use a hearing aid and to hear well enough to be taught through auditory channels.

Deaf. A hearing impairment that requires the use of other senses, usually sight, to communicate.

Students with a hearing loss have problems perceiving sounds within the normal frequency range of human speech. Two kinds of hearing disabilities exist. A **partial hearing impairment** allows a student to use a hearing aid and to hear well enough to be taught through auditory channels. For students who are **deaf,** hearing is impaired enough so that these students use other senses, usually sight, to communicate. About 1.5% of students with exceptionalities have a hearing disability (U.S. Department of Education, 2009). Of the students with a hearing loss requiring special services, more than 60% receive instruction in general education classrooms for all or part of the school day, and the numbers have increased in recent years (Shirin, 2007).

Hearing disabilities may result from rubella (German measles) during pregnancy, heredity, complications during pregnancy or birth, meningitis, or other childhood diseases. In almost 40% of cases involving hearing loss, the cause is unknown; this makes prevention and remediation more difficult (Hardman et al., 2011; Heward, 2009).

Testing by a trained audiologist is the best method of identifying students with hearing problems, but not all schools have these programs, and problems can be overlooked if students miss the screening. When such an omission occurs, your sensitivity to possible hearing difficulties is essential. Some indicators of hearing impairment include:

- Misunderstanding or not following directions and displaying nonverbal behaviors, such as frowns or puzzled looks when directions are given
- Asking people to repeat what they've just said
- Articulating words, and especially consonants, poorly
- Turning up the volume when listening to audio recordings, radio, or television
- Showing reluctance to participate in oral activities

Lack of proficiency in speech and language are learning problems that can result from hearing disabilities. These problems affect learning that relies on reading, writing, and listening. You should remember that these language deficits have little bearing on intelligence; these students can succeed if given appropriate help.

Effective programs for students with hearing disabilities combine general education classroom instruction with additional support. Programs for students who are deaf include lipreading, sign language, and fingerspelling. Total communication is the simultaneous presentation of manual approaches, such as signing, and speech (through lipreading and residual hearing), and is increasing in popularity (Hardman et al., 2011).

You can also adapt your instruction by supplementing auditory presentations with visual information, speaking clearly and orienting yourself so students can see your face, eliminating distracting noise, and frequently checking for understanding.

Having peers without disabilities serve as tutors and work in cooperative groups with students who have hearing disabilities can also be helpful. Teaching students without disabilities the elements of American Sign Language and fingerspelling provides an added dimension to their education.

Self-Regulation and Students with Exceptionalities

Don (one of your authors) regularly tutors in a local elementary school in his city. The first-, second-, and third-grade students he works with all struggle academically and are behind in reading and math. When he works with these students and talks with their teachers, two patterns consistently emerge. First, the students are intelligent enough to succeed in school. The second is that they lack self-regulation.

Paul had a set of experiences that corroborated Don's observations. As part of a project a couple years ago, he was making a series of observations of first-grade classes, and he was struck by what he observed when the students were doing silent reading. Some of the students read intently for 45 minutes or more, whereas others spent little time reading, instead gazing around the room, or playing with pencils or other objects. In fact, in one observation he watched a boy work for 45 minutes to make his book stand up on the desk. As the students progress through the grades, the gap between those who did and did not read conscientiously is likely to become wider and wider.

Many students with exceptionalities receive extra help in the form of tutoring but typically don't receive support that helps them develop their **self-regulation,** the ability to direct and control one's own actions and emotions. Self-regulation plays a powerful role in school success, and students who are self-regulated learn more, are happier in school, and have an easier time making friends (Berk, 2010).

Self-regulation. The ability to direct and control one's own actions and emotions.

Students with exceptionalities typically have poorly developed self-regulatory skills (Heward, 2009; Hallahan et al., 2009). They have problems staying on task, completing assignments, and using effective learning strategies, as Don witnessed directly and Paul observed. They also have problems controlling their impulses, such as shouting out in the middle of a teacher's explanation, or interacting with peers in socially acceptable ways.

You can help these students in several ways. First, you can make them aware of their actions and how they affect learning and their ability to get along with their peers. As they become self-aware, they will gradually learn that they have control over their learning success (Turnbull et al., 2010). Second, you can teach them effective learning strategies, such as writing information down, summarizing, and self-questioning. You might even provide checklists that they can use to monitor their progress (Mastropieri & Scruggs, 2010; Vaughn & Bos, 2009). Finally, you need to be patient and provide support and encouragement as they gradually develop their self-regulation.

Technology, Learning, and Development: Using Technology to Support Learners with Disabilities

Julio is partially deaf, barely able to use a hearing aid to understand speech. Kerry Tanner, his seventh-grade science teacher, works closely with the special education instructor assigned to her classroom to help Julio. Seated near the front of the room to facilitate lipreading, Julio takes notes on a laptop computer during teacher presentations. Other students take turns sharing their notes with him so he can compare and fill in gaps. He especially likes to communicate with other students on the Internet, as this levels the communication playing field. When he views video clips on his computer, he uses a special device with earphones to increase the volume.

Jaleena is partially sighted, with a visual acuity of less than 20/80, even with corrective lenses. Despite this disability, she is doing well in her fourth-grade class. Tera Banks, her teacher, has placed her in the front of the room so that she can better see the chalkboard and overhead and has assigned students to work with her on her projects. Using a magnifying device, she can read most written material, but the computer is giving her special problems. The small letters and punctuation on Website addresses and other information make it difficult for her to use the computer as an information source. Tera works with the special education consultant in her district to get a monitor that magnifies the display. She knows it is working when she sees Jaleena quietly working alone at her computer on the report due next Friday.

Assistive technology. A set of adaptive tools that support students with disabilities in learning activities and daily life tasks.

Assistive technology is a set of adaptive tools that support students with disabilities in learning activities and daily life tasks, and it is having a particularly important impact on these students. These tools are required by federal law under IDEA and include motorized chairs, remote control devices that turn machines on and off with the nod of the head or other muscle action, and machines that amplify sights and sounds (Heward, 2009).

Probably the most widespread contribution of assistive technology is in the area of computer adaptations. Let's look at them.

Adaptations to Computer Input Devices

To use computers, students must be able to input their words and ideas. This can be difficult for those with visual or other physical disabilities that don't allow standard keyboarding. Devices that enhance the keyboard, such as making it larger and easier to see, arranging the letters alphabetically to make them easier to find, or using pictures for nonreaders, are adaptations that accommodate these disabilities. A number of software programs that help developing writers by providing spell-check and word-prediction scaffolding currently exist (Roblyer & Doering, 2010). When a student hesitates to finish a word, the computer, based on the first few letters, then either completes it or offers a menu of suggestions. Advocates claim it frees students to concentrate on ideas and text organization.

Additional adaptations bypass the keyboard altogether. For example, speech/voice-recognition software can translate speech into text on the computer screen (Silver-Pacuilla & Fleischman, 2006). These systems can be invaluable for students with disabilities that affect the use of hands and fingers. Other adaptations use switches activated by a body movement, such as a head nod, to interact with the computer. Touch screens also allow students to go directly to the monitor to indicate their responses.

Students with learning disabilities encounter difficulties translating ideas into written words, and speech-recognition technology eases the cognitive bottleneck in working memory by helping to produce initial drafts that are longer and have fewer errors.

Adaptations to Output Devices

Adaptations to output devices also exist. For example, the size of the visual display is increased by using a special magnifying monitor, such as the one Jaleena used. For students who are blind, speech synthesizers can read words and translate them into sounds. In addition, special printers can convert words into Braille and vice versa.

These technologies are important because they reduce the extent to which disabilities become handicaps. As technology becomes a more integral part of classroom instruction, assistive technology will become increasingly important for students with exceptionalities.

Brain Research and Exceptionalities

Technology such as functional magnetic resonance imaging and electroencephalograms is revolutionizing research that examines our brains and how they work.

Using this technology, researchers have learned that many disabilities are caused by brain abnormalities that interfere with normal cognitive functioning. For example, a gene defect may hamper synaptic pruning, the process of eliminating synapses that are infrequently used, which clears the way for efficient information processing (Cook & Cook, 2009).

In addition, researchers have found that blood flow to the cerebellum and frontal lobes is lower than normal, and neural activity, as measure by electrical firings, is different in certain areas of the brains of students with learning disabilities and ADHD (Barkley, 2006). Brain-imaging research also suggests that the cerebral cortex—responsible for executive control of our actions, such as attention and impulse control—develops more slowly in some students with ADHD (Shaw & Rapoport, 2007). These results help us understand why students with ADHD may outgrow the condition in their teen years.

Researchers have also examined the functioning of different parts of our memory systems (Seidman, Valera, & Makris, 2005). For example, students with learning disabilities have trouble holding information in working memory, the component of our memory system in which we consciously organize and combine new information with information from our long-term memories. If we can't retain information in working memory, organizing and making sense of our experiences is very difficult (Geary, 2007).

Research also suggests that difficulties in learning math may be linked to problems holding visual and spatial information in working memory (D'Amico & Guarnera, 2005; Geary, 2007). This prevents struggling students from effectively using visual aids such as pictures, diagrams, or number lines in their problem-solving efforts. Additional research suggests that reading disabilities may be linked to an inability to retrieve the names and sounds of letters and recognize patterns (Katzir & Paré-Blagoev, 2006). So, when first graders are trying to sound out an unfamiliar word, they have trouble remembering that the *s h* combination is "shh."

Brain research is also helping us better understand the influence of educational interventions. For instance, patterns of electrical activity in parts of the brain linked to spatial and motor activity are different for deaf persons who have learned to sign compared to those who haven't developed this ability, suggesting that learning strongly influences brain functioning (Varma, McCandliss, Schwartz, 2008).

Additional research has identified differences in brain activity between good and poor readers. However, after an intensive, 100-hour phonics intervention with the poor readers, researchers found brain activity in them nearly resembling that of the good readers, and the physiological changes still existed a year later (B. Shaywitz et al., 2004).

It's clear that environmental conditions can cause changes in brain functions. For example, we know that prolonged stimulus deprivation during the early years can result in lowered IQ and impaired cognitive function, inattention and difficulty concentrating, hyperactivity, and unruly behavior and lack of self-regulation (Berk, 2010). Brain research is helping us understand how these environmental influences impact the brain's functioning and may eventually offer suggestions as to how to reverse these negative influences.

We also know that a healthy environment can help optimize the brain's potential. In addition, stimulation, in the form of effective instruction, can play a powerful role in helping students with exceptionalities adapt to their disabilities and flourish. This is where you, the classroom teacher, are so important.

---

check your understanding

3.1 Describe the most common learning problems that classroom teachers are likely to encounter.

3.2 Identify at least one similarity and one difference between learning disabilities and an intellectual disability.

3.3 Describe the two major types of behavior disorders, and explain how they influence classroom behavior.

3.4 What are communication disorders, and how do they affect classroom performance?

To receive feedback for these questions, go to Appendix A.

Students Who Are Gifted and Talented

Although we don't typically think of students who are gifted and talented as having exceptionalities, they frequently cannot reach their full potential in general education classrooms. At one time, *gifted* was the only term educators used, but now the enlarged category includes students who do well on IQ tests (typically 130 and above) as well as those who demonstrate talents in a range of areas, such as math, creative writing, and music (G. A. Davis, Rimm, & Siegel, 2011).

Characteristics of Students Who Are Gifted and Talented

Students who are gifted and talented have the following characteristics:

- Learn more quickly and independently than their peers
- Use advanced language, reading, and vocabulary skills
- Display more highly developed learning and metacognitive strategies
- Demonstrate higher motivation on challenging tasks and less on easy ones
- Set high personal standards of achievement

Providing rich learning experiences that help these children develop to their fullest potential is our challenge.

The history of gifted and talented education in the United States began with a longitudinal study conducted by Louis Terman and his colleagues (Terman, Baldwin, & Bronson, 1925; Terman & Oden, 1947, 1959). Using teacher recommendations and IQ scores (above 140 on the Stanford Binet intelligence test), Terman identified 1,500 gifted individuals to be tracked over a lifetime (the study was projected to run until 2010). The researchers found that, in addition to being high academic achievers, these students were better adjusted as children and adults, had more hobbies, read more books, and were healthier than their peers. This study, combined with more current research, has done much to dispel the stereotype of gifted students as maladjusted and narrow "brains."

The current definition used by the federal government describes gifted and talented students as

> Children and youth with outstanding talent who perform or show the potential for performing at remarkably high levels of accomplishment when compared with others of their age, experience, or environment.
>
> These children and youth exhibit high performance capability in intellectual, creative, and/or artistic areas, possess an unusual leadership capacity, or excel in specific academic fields. They require services or activities not ordinarily provided by the schools.
>
> Outstanding talents are present in children and youth from all cultural groups, across all economic strata, and in all areas of human endeavor. (*National Excellence: A Case for Developing America's Talent,* 1993, pp. 54–57)

Because the federal government does not include giftedness as a recognized exceptionality in IDEA, states define it in many ways, but many state departments of education have incorporated components of the National Excellence description into their definitions of giftedness and talent. In addition, depending on the state's definition, the percentage of students served in different states varies from 2% to 22%, with an average figure of about 12% (Friend, 2008).

Another popular definition of giftedness uses three criteria: (1) above-average ability; (2) high levels of motivation and task commitment; and (3) high levels of creativity (Renzulli & Reis, 2003).

More recent work in the area of gifted education has shifted away from the concept of giftedness as a general characteristic and toward talents in specific areas (Colangelo & Davis, 2003; G. A. Davis et al., 2011).

Identifying Students Who Are Gifted and Talented

Meeting the needs of students who are gifted and talented requires early identification and instructional modifications. Failure to do so can result in gifted underachievers with social and emotional problems linked to boredom and lack of motivation (G. A. Davis et al., 2011). Conventional procedures often miss students who are gifted and talented because they rely heavily on standardized test scores and teacher nominations, and females and students from cultural minorities are typically underrepresented in these programs (Gootman & Gebelhof, 2008). When New York City moved from a comprehensive approach to identifying Kindergarten students who are gifted and talented to one based solely on tests, the number of Black and Hispanic students decreased from 46% to 27% (Winerip, 2010). To address this problem, experts recommend more flexible and less culturally dependent methods, such as creativity measures, tests of spatial ability, and peer and parent nominations in addition to teacher recommendations (G. A. Davis et al., 2011).

As with all exceptionalities, you play an essential role in identifying learners who are gifted and talented because you work with these students every day and can identify strengths that tests may miss. However, research indicates that teachers often confuse conformity, neatness, and good behavior with being gifted or talented (Colangelo & Davis, 2003). You might ask yourself questions such as the following as you consider whether or not students are gifted or talented:

- Are they curious and inquisitive?
- Do they think in the abstract and play with abstract symbol systems?
- Do they have advanced vocabularies and language skills?

Acceleration. Programs for students who are gifted and talented that keep the curriculum the same but allow students to move through it more quickly.

Enrichment. Programs for students who are gifted and talented that provide alternate instruction.

Programs for the Gifted and Talented

Programs for students who are gifted and talented are usually based on either **acceleration,** which keeps the curriculum the same but allows students to move through it more quickly, or **enrichment,** which provides alternate instruction (Schiever & Maker, 2003). Educators disagree over which approach is better. Critics of enrichment charge that it often involves busywork and point to research suggesting that students benefit from acceleration (Feldhusen, 1998a, 1998b). Critics of acceleration counter that comparisons are unfair because the outcomes of enrichment, such as creativity and problem solving, are not easily measured. They further argue that the general education curriculum is narrow, and social development can be impaired when younger students who want accelerated content must take classes with older students. The question remains unanswered, and the debate is likely to continue.

Programs for students who are gifted and talented are typically organized in either self-contained classes or pullout programs that occupy a portion of the school day. Self-contained classes usually include both acceleration and enrichment; pullout programs focus primarily on enrichment.

Enrichment activities provide opportunities for gifted students to explore alternative areas of the curriculum.

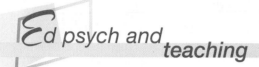

Ed psych and teaching

Applying an Understanding of Students Who Are Gifted and Talented in Your Teaching

If you have students who are gifted and talented in your classes, and they're pulled out for part of the day, you'll be expected to provide enrichment activities during the time they're with you. The following guidelines can assist you as you attempt to adapt instruction to meet these students' needs:

1. Assess frequently to identify areas where students have already mastered essential content.
2. Provide alternative activities to challenge students' abilities and interests.
3. Use technology to provide challenge.

Let's see how the guidelines assist Jared Taylor, a sixth-grade teacher, as he works with his students.

> Jared has three students—Darren, Sylvia, and Gabriella— who have been identified as gifted and talented, and who meet with a teacher of the gifted twice a week in a pullout program. Jared's task is to provide a motivating menu for them while they are in his class.
>
> To accomplish the task, Jared pretests his students before beginning a new unit, and he also closely monitors Darren's, Sylvia's, and Gabriella's homework. When he sees that they have mastered the content, he provides enrichment by first offering alternative learning activities. For instance, in a unit on plants in science, Jared arranges with the librarian to provide resources for a project, and he meets with the students to help them design its goals and scope.
>
> Jared also creates a series of learning centers that are available to all the students. The centers focus on weather, geometry, music, and art, and students can go to them when they have free time. Each center has reading materials and projects that can be completed. When Darren, Sylvia, and Gabriella demonstrate that they have mastered the content the other students are studying, he substitutes projects from the centers for them.
>
> Finally, Jared supplements his curriculum with technology. He works with the district's media coordinator to locate software programs and Websites that provide enrichment and acceleration.

Jared attempted to apply the guidelines by first gathering information to assess each student's understanding of the topics he was teaching. When he found they had mastered a topic, he substituted enrichment activities (guideline 2). Acceleration has benefits, but it is difficult to implement in the general education curriculum. Jared's approach was manageable; it didn't require an inordinate amount of extra work, and it also provided enriching experiences for the students. Finally, he applied the third guideline by providing challenge through technology and by working with the district's media coordinator to supply his students with relevant materials.

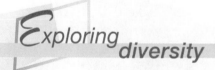

check your understanding

4.1 Identify characteristics of students who are gifted and talented, and explain how the definition of students who are gifted and talented has changed over time.

4.2 Describe methods for identifying students who are gifted and talented. What are some advantages and disadvantages of these methods?

4.3 Describe the two most common methods for teaching students who are gifted and talented. Explain the relative advantages and disadvantages of these methods.

To receive feedback for these questions, go to Appendix A.

Exploring diversity

Pursuing Equity in Special Education

A paradox exists in special education. The very system that was created to provide fair and humane treatment for all students has resulted in one in which culturally and linguistically diverse students are both over- and underrepresented in programs for learners with exceptionalities (Harry & Klingner, 2007). For example, African American students make up less than 15% of the school population but account for 20% of students diagnosed with exceptionalities (Blanchett, 2006). In addition, minority students, especially African American and Hispanic, have been underrepresented in gifted and talented programs (Hardman et al., 2011; Heward, 2009).

These are not recent trends. As far back as 1979, the U.S. Congress recognized these disparities and asked researchers to look for possible reasons (Turnbull et al., 2010). The reasons are complex and range from problems in the students' home and neighborhood environments to factors within schools themselves (O'Conner & Fernandez, 2006). For example, poverty results in poorer prenatal care, nutrition, and health care, all of which can influence both intelligence and school performance. In addition, poverty can result in neighborhoods that are less nurturant, with limited access to early educational resources.

The children of poverty also attend poorer-quality schools. For instance, classes in high-poverty schools are nearly 80% more likely to have an out-of-field teacher than those in more advantaged areas.

Critics also point to the special education placement process itself (O'Conner & Fernandez, 2006). They ask whether or not classrooms are culturally responsive, build on students' existing knowledge, and provide instruction sensitive to the strengths that students from diverse backgrounds possess.

The identification and placement process also depends heavily on culture and language. Tests used to identify students with exceptionalities are culturally based and depend on facility with English (Rogoff, 2003).

As a general education teacher, you can do much to address these issues. For example, culturally responsive teaching that builds on your students' strengths can help you better meet the needs of students with diverse backgrounds. When learning problems exist, you will then be sure that you have done everything possible before referring students for special services. If you conclude that special services are necessary, you will be able to provide the most accurate information available for helping meet these students' needs.

Teachers' Responsibilities in Inclusive Classrooms

As we said at the beginning of the chapter, it's almost certain that you will have students with exceptionalities in your classroom, so it's important to understand how you can best help them learn as much as possible.

You have three responsibilities in working with these students. They're outlined in Figure 5.3 and discussed in the sections that follow. In each area, you should have assistance from special educators who have the expertise to help you.

Ed Psych and You

Did you know any students with exceptionalities when you were in school? Do you have any of these students in your close circle of friends? How were students with exceptionalities treated in the schools you attended?

Modifying Instruction to Meet Students' Needs

Modifying instruction to meet the learning needs of students with exceptionalities is your most important responsibility. Fortunately, instruction that is effective with students in

general is also effective with students having exceptionalities. "In general, the classroom management and instruction approaches that are effective with special students tend to be the same ones that are effective with other students" (Good & Brophy, 2008, p. 223). You will need to provide additional support, however, to help students overcome a history of failure and frustration and to convince them that renewed effort will work. For instance, while the majority of the class is completing a seatwork assignment, you can work with individuals or students or small groups to provide additional support. Strategies

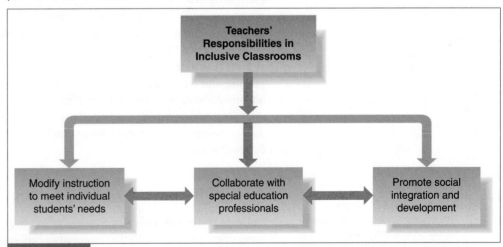

Figure 5.3 Teachers' responsibilities in inclusive classrooms

Instruction proven effective with general education students is also effective for students with exceptionalities.

effective for all students, and particularly important for students with exceptionalities, include:

- Carefully model solutions to problems and other assignments.
- Teach in small steps, and provide detailed feedback on homework.
- Call on students with exceptionalities as equally as possible compared to your other students.
- Provide outlines, hierarchies, charts, and other forms of organization for the content you're teaching.
- Increase the amount of time available for tests and quizzes.
- Use available technology.
- Teach learning strategies.

The last item deserves elaboration. Strategy training is one of the most promising approaches that has been developed for helping students with exceptionalities. A *strategy* is a plan that students use to accomplish a learning goal. Let's look at an example.

In working with Adam (the middle school student with a learning disability in reading that you encountered earlier in the chapter), Tammy Fuller, his teacher, helped him develop a strategy for understanding the content of a chapter in his history book. Tammy first had Adam study the chapter outline so he could see how the chapter was organized, and she had him keep the outline in front of him as he read the chapter. She then modeled reading sections of the chapter aloud, and stopped every few paragraphs and created a summary of the information he had just read. She then had him practice by doing the same. If he wasn't able to create a clear summary, she had him reread the section and again try to summarize it.

This process is admittedly demanding, but students with exceptionalities will need to make extra efforts to accommodate their learning issues, and our role is to teach them the strategies needed to help them succeed.

Because students with exceptionalities tend to approach tasks passively or use the same strategy for all types of content, we must help them actively use strategies, as Tammy did in the example above. Students also must learn to adapt their strategies to the learning task at hand (Vaughn & Bos, 2009). For instance, because Adam was attempting to comprehend the content of the chapter, Tammy taught him a different strategy than he would have used if he was simply learning to spell a list of words. Students with learning problems can use strategies but need to be taught how and provided with supervised practice until they become comfortable with the strategy (Carnine et al., 2006). Your modeling and explanation, together with opportunities for practice and feedback, are essential. (The case study at the end of the chapter, involving Mike Sheppard's work with his students, illustrates a classroom application of these strategies.)

Peer tutoring, which can benefit both the tutor and the person receiving the tutoring, as well as home-based tutoring programs that involve parents, can also be effective (Vaughn & Bos, 2009).

Collaborating with Special Education Professionals

Collaborative consultation. The process of general and special education teachers working together to create effective learning experiences for students with exceptionalities.

Collaborating with other professionals is your second responsibility. Initially, educators viewed inclusion as additive; students with exceptionalities received additional services to help them function in general education classrooms (Turnbull et al., 2010). Gradually, the idea of coordination replaced addition. Today, **collaborative consultation** combines general education teachers and special educators on teams to ensure that experiences for students with exceptionalities are effectively integrated. On these teams, you'll work collaboratively with special educators, reading specialists, English language development teachers, school psychologists, and even school administrators to design and implement instructional programs. One special educator described the process this way: "We actually work together to solve problems. It's not like I have all of the answers or she [the classroom teacher] has all the problems. We really help each other come up with ideas that work" (Vaughn & Bos, 2009, p. 153). The collaborative consultation group, sometimes called a teacher assistance team (TAT), tries to make the classroom teacher's job more effective and efficient. The goal is to create a safety net for students who need extra help to ensure success and guard against failure.

Collaboration is essential for effective inclusion, and typically begins when a learning problem is identified (Karten, 2005; T. E. Smith et al., 2008). In the response-to-intervention model described earlier in the chapter, this occurs when interventions you've tried fail to produce successful learning experiences for a student. Once a learning problem that requires extra services is identified, the team of professionals meets to clarify the problem; design, implement, and evaluate more intense interventions; develop IEPs; and work with parents.

Promoting Social Integration and Development

Promoting the social integration and development of students with exceptionalities is your third important responsibility. Students with exceptionalities often fall behind in their academic work, frequently misbehave, and sometimes lack social skills (Hallahan et al., 2009). As a result, other students develop negative attitudes toward them, which adversely affect their confidence and self-esteem. You'll need to make special efforts to promote the acceptance of these students in your classroom. You can do so in three ways:

- Develop classmates' understanding and acceptance of them.
- Help students with exceptionalities learn acceptable behaviors.
- Use strategies to promote social interaction among students. (Plata, Trusty, & Glasgow, 2005)

Developing Classmates' Understanding and Acceptance

Students' negative attitudes toward their peers with exceptionalities often result from a lack of understanding, and open discussion and information about disabilities can help change these attitudes (Heward, 2009). Emphasizing that people with disabilities want to have friends, be happy, and succeed, just as we all do, can do much to change attitudes. These discussions can reduce stereotypes about learners with exceptionalities and break down the barriers between them and other students. Literature and videos that explore the struggles and triumphs of people with disabilities are also valuable sources of information.

Strategies for Promoting Social Integration and Development

Students with disabilities often lack social skills and the ability to make friends, and they may avoid other students or unknowingly alienate them (Turnbull et al., 2010). Modeling, coaching, and involving students in learning activities can all help them develop social skills. To teach a student how to initiate play, for example, you might say, "Barnell's over there on the playground. I think I'll say, 'Hi, Barnell! Want to play ball with me?' Now you try it, and I'll watch."

You can also model social problem solving. For instance you might ask, "Mary has a toy that I want to play with. What could I do to make her want to share that toy?" Direct approaches such as these have been successful in teaching social skills such as empathy, perspective taking, negotiation, and assertiveness (Vaughn & Bos, 2009).

Calling on students with exceptionalities as frequently as possible in learning activities, and expecting them to be as involved as their classmates are two of the most effective ways to promote their integration and development. Doing so communicates that all students are valued and are expected to participate and succeed.

Cooperative learning can also help students learn social skills (Mastropieri, Scruggs, & Berkeley, 2007). When students work closely in groups, emotional barriers are often broken down and students both with and without exceptionalities learn that they are more alike than they are different.

This discussion addresses the questions we asked in our "Ed Psych and You" feature in this section. Most of us probably were aware that we had classmates with exceptionalities, but we didn't have opportunities to get to know them. This was unfortunate for both them and us, because it didn't give us the chance to learn about—and possibly even become friends with—different kinds of students. As a teacher you can do much to ensure that all students feel welcome in your classroom and have opportunities to learn about each other.

Classroom connections

Teaching Students with Exceptionalities in the General Education Classroom

1. Effective teachers adapt instruction to meet the needs and capabilities of students with exceptionalities. Provide additional instructional scaffolding to ensure success on instructional tasks.

   ■ **Elementary:** A third-grade teacher carefully monitors students during seatwork. She often gathers students with exceptionalities in a small group to provide additional assistance at the beginning of assignments.

   ■ **Middle School:** A sixth-grade math teacher organizes his students in groups of four for seatwork assignments. Each student completes a problem and confers with a partner. When two students disagree, they confer with the other pair in their group. The teacher carefully monitors the groups to be sure that all four are participating and contributing.

   ■ **High School:** A science teacher assesses frequently and provides detailed feedback on all assessment items. She spends time in one-on-one conferences with any students having difficulty.

2. A major obstacle to social integration and growth is other students' lack of understanding. Discuss the subject of exceptionalities in an open and positive manner.

   ■ **Elementary:** A second-grade teacher uses role-playing and modeling to illustrate problems such as teasing and taunting others. She emphasizes treating students who look or act differently with the same respect that other students receive.

   ■ **Middle School:** An English teacher uses literature, such as *Summer of the Swans*, by Betsy Byars (1970), as a springboard for talking about individual differences. He encourages students to reflect on their own individuality and how important this is to them.

   ■ **High School:** An English teacher leads a discussion of students' favorite foods, activities, movies, and music, and also discusses topics and issues that concern them. She uses the discussions as a springboard for helping create a sense of community in the classroom.

3. Students with exceptionalities often pursue learning tasks passively. Use modeling and coaching to teach effective learning strategies.

   ■ **Elementary:** A fourth-grade math teacher emphasizes questions such as the following in checking answers to word problems: Does the solution answer the problem? Does it make sense? Are the units correct? He reinforces this process throughout the school year.

   ■ **Middle School:** A math teacher teaches problem-solving strategies by thinking aloud at the chalkboard while she's working through a problem. She breaks word problems into the following steps and places these on a poster at the front of the room: (1) *Read*: What is the question asking? (2) *Reread*: What information do I need? (3) *Stop and think*: What do I need to do—add, subtract, multiply, or divide? (4) *Compute*: Put the correct numbers in and solve. (5) *Label and check*: What answer did I get? Does it make sense?

   ■ **High School:** An English teacher teaches and models step-by-step strategies. A unit on writing one-paragraph essays teaches students to use four steps: (1) Write a topic sentence, (2) write three sentences that support the topic sentence, (3) write a summary sentence, and (4) reread and edit the paragraph. The teacher models the strategy and provides positive and negative examples before asking the students to write their own.

Teaching Students Who Are Gifted and Talented

4. Students who are gifted and talented need challenging learning activities to motivate them. Provide supplementary enrichment activities to challenge students who are gifted and talented.

   - **Elementary:** A fifth-grade teacher allows students who are gifted and talented to substitute projects of their choice for homework assignments once they have demonstrated that they have mastered the general education curriculum.

   - **Middle School:** A prealgebra teacher pretests students at the beginning of each unit. Whenever a student has mastered the concepts and skills, she receives an honor pass to work on an alterna-

tive activity in the school media center. The activities may be extensions or applications of the concepts taught in the unit, or they may involve learning about mathematical principles or math history not usually taught in the general education curriculum.

   - **High School:** A social studies teacher caps off every unit with a hypothetical problem, such as "What would the United States be like today if Great Britain had won the Revolutionary War?" Students work in groups to address the question, and the teacher gives extra credit to those who want to pursue the topic further in a paper or project.

---

check your understanding

5.1 Describe general education teachers' responsibilities in inclusive classrooms.

5.2 What does research indicate about teaching strategies that are effective for learners with exceptionalities? What implications do these strategies have for you as a classroom teacher?

5.3 Describe three ways that you can promote the social integration and growth of students with exceptionalities in your classroom.

To receive feedback for these questions, go to Appendix A.

Developmentally appropriate practice

Teaching Students with Exceptionalities at Different Ages

Development plays an important role in understanding and dealing with student exceptionalities. Effective practices for students with exceptionalities are influenced by the age and developmental characteristics of students.

Working with Students in Early Childhood Programs and Elementary Schools

Early childhood and lower elementary teachers are in a unique position to help identify learning problems. Pretesting of all students at the beginning of the school year not only provides a baseline for future growth, but can also identify potential learning problems (Reutzel & Cooter, 2008; Vaughn & Bos, 2009). When pretesting data alert teachers to a potential learning problem, detailed records that identify the nature of the problem and records of intervention attempts can provide special educators with the tools they need to create effective interventions.

Sensitivity to the possibility of developmental lags is particularly important with young children. Research on learner development indicates that considerable variation exists in students' rates of development, and developmental lags are often mistaken for more serious learning problems (Lerner, 2006).

Similarly, being aware of the role of culture and language in early school success is important. Many students grow up in homes where English isn't the first language and where newspapers, magazines, and books are not readily available. Ascertaining that problems cannot be traced to cultural or language differences is important before referring a child for special services.

Working with Students in Middle Schools

The middle school years present challenges to all students. These challenges take the form of physical and emotional changes, as well as the move from self-contained elementary classrooms to the less personal environments in middle schools.

Adaptive behaviors, such as keeping track of assignments and taking notes, present special challenges for students with exceptionalities (Vaughn & Bos, 2009). Efforts to help these students acquire learning strategies can be particularly effective.

Peers become increasingly important to middle school students. Helping students with exceptionalities learn acceptable behaviors, together with strategies for promoting interaction and cooperation, are essential. Cooperative learning and peer tutoring can be effective, but students with exceptionalities need extra support to function effectively in these settings.

Working with Students in High Schools

High school—with large schools, less personal attention, and switching classes—can be particularly challenging for students with exceptionalities (Kincheloe, 2004; Schutz, 2004). Peer acceptance continues to be a priority for all high school students.

Special efforts to help students with exceptionalities—who are sometimes painfully aware of their differences—feel welcome in their classrooms are very important for high school students. Teachers set the tone by modeling courtesy and respect and requiring students to treat each other the same way. Cooperative learning and small-group work provide opportunities for students with exceptionalities to interact socially and learn from their peers.

With respect to acquiring a deep understanding of the topics they're studying, helping learners with exceptionalities acquire effective learning strategies is even more effective with high school students than with younger learners.

Summary

1. Describe different views of intelligence, and explain how ability grouping influences learning.
   - Intelligence is the ability to profit from past experiences to solve future problems. It is also often defined as the ability to acquire and use knowledge, solve problems and reason in the abstract, and adapt to new situations in the environment.
   - Some theories suggest that intelligence is a single entity; others describe intelligence as existing in several dimensions.
   - Some experts believe that intelligence is largely genetically determined; others believe it is strongly influenced by experiences. Most suggest that it is determined by a combination of the two.
   - Ability grouping can influence learning through the quality of instruction that learners are provided and through teachers' expectations for students.

2. Describe the major provisions of the Individuals with Disabilities Education Act (IDEA) and the amendments to it.
   - The major provisions of the IDEA require instruction of students with exceptionalities in the least restrictive environment (LRE), parent involvement, protection of learners against discrimination in testing, and individualized education programs (IEPs) for each student with exceptionalities.
   - Amendments to IDEA make states responsible for locating children who need special services and have strengthened requirements for nondiscriminatory assessment, due process, parental involvement in IEPs, and the confidentiality of student records.

3. Describe the most common learning problems that classroom teachers are likely to encounter.
   - The most common learning problems that classroom teachers encounter include learning disabilities, difficulties in reading, writing, reasoning, or mathematical abilities; communication disorders, which may include either speech or language disorders; intellectual disabilities, limitations in both intellectual functioning and adaptive behavior; and behavior disorders, serious and persistent age-inappropriate behaviors.
   - Teachers may also encounter autism spectrum disorders—disabilities that affect communication and social interaction—as well as visual and hearing disabilities.

4. Identify characteristics of students who are gifted and talented, and explain how teachers identify and teach these students.
   - Students who are gifted and talented learn quickly and independently, possess advanced language and metacognitive skills, and are often highly motivated and set high personal standards for achievement.
   - Methods of identifying students who are gifted and talented include intelligence testing and teacher, parent, and peer reports of unique talents and abilities.
   - The two most common methods of teaching students who are gifted and talented include acceleration, which moves students through the general education curriculum at a faster rate, and enrichment, which provides alternative instruction to encourage student exploration.

5. Describe general education teachers' responsibilities in inclusive classrooms.
   - Teachers' roles in inclusive classrooms include working with other professionals on a collaborative consultation team, adapting instruction to meet their needs, and promoting their social integration and growth.
   - Effective instruction for students with exceptionalities is similar to effective instruction in general. Providing additional scaffolding and helping students acquire learning strategies are also helpful.

Understanding Learners with Exceptionalities: Preparing for Your Licensure Exam

Because it's virtually certain that you will have students with exceptionalities in your classroom, your licensure exam will include items related to best practices for working with these students. We include the following exercises to help you practice for the exam in your state.

Let's look now at a junior high math teacher and his efforts to work with students in his class who have exceptionalities. Read the case study, and answer the questions that follow.

Mike Sheppard teaches math at Kennedy Middle School. He has introduced his prealgebra class to a procedure for solving word problems and assigned five problems for homework.

Mike has 28 students in his second-period class, including five with exceptionalities: Herchel, Marcus, and Gwenn, who have learning disabilities, and Todd and Horace, who have difficulty monitoring their own behavior. Herchel, Marcus, and Gwenn each have problems with decoding words, reading comprehension, and writing. Other teachers describe Todd as verbally abusive, aggressive, and lacking in self-discipline.

He is extremely active and has a difficult time sitting through a class period. Horace is just the opposite: a very shy, withdrawn boy.

At Mike's request, Herchel, Marcus, and Gwenn come to class a few minutes early each day so they have extra time to read the problems he has displayed on the document camera and get additional help. (As part of his daily routine, Mike displays two or three problems for students to complete while he takes roll and finishes other beginning-of-class tasks.)

Mike watches as Herchel, Marcus, and Gwenn take their seats, and then he slowly reads the displayed problem:

> On Saturday the Harris family drove 17 miles from Henderson to Newton, stopped for 10 minutes to get gas, and then drove 22.5 miles from Newton through Council Rock to Gildford. The trip took 1 hour and 5 minutes, including the stop. On the way back, they took the same route but stopped in Council Rock for lunch. Council Rock is 9.5 miles from Gildford. How much farther will they have to drive to get back to Henderson?

As Mike reads, he points to each displayed word. "Okay," he smiles after he finishes reading. "Do you know what the problem is asking you?"

"Could you read the last part again, Mr. Sheppard?" Gwenn asks.

"Sure, but make sure that you read along with me," Mike replies and repeats the part of the problem that describes the return trip, again pointing to the words as he reads.

"All right, jump on it. Be ready, because I'm calling on one of you first today," he directs with another smile.

The rest of the class comes in the room, and they're studying the screen as the bell rings. Mike quickly takes roll and then walks to Todd's desk.

"Let's take a look at your chart," he says. "You've improved a lot, haven't you?"

"Yeah, look," Todd responds, proudly displaying the following chart.

	2/9–2/13	2/16–2/20	2/23–2/27
Talking out	ЖЖ ЖЖ ЖЖ ЖЖ	ЖЖ IIII ЖЖ	ЖЖ II
Swearing	ЖЖ ЖЖ	ЖЖ II	IIII
Hitting/ touching	ЖЖ III	ЖЖ IIII	III
Out of seat	ЖЖ ЖЖ ЖЖ III	ЖЖ ЖЖ ЖЖ IIII	ЖЖ ЖЖ ЖЖ III
Being friendly	II	IIII	ЖЖ II

"That's terrific," Mike whispers as he leans over Todd's desk. "You're doing much better. We need some more work on 'out-of-seat,' don't we? I don't like getting after you about it, and I know you don't like it

either. . . . Stop by at the end of class. I have an idea that I think will help. Don't forget to stop. . . . Okay. Get to work on the problem." Mike gives Todd a light thump on the back and returns to the front of the room.

"Okay, everyone. How did you do on the problem?"

Amid a mix of "Okay," "Terrible," "Fine," "Too hard," some nods, and a few nonresponses, Mike begins, "Let's review for a minute. . . . What's the first thing we do whenever we have a word problem like this?"

He looks knowingly at Marcus, remembering the pledge to call on one of the five students first today. "Marcus?"

"Read it over at least twice," Marcus replies.

"Good. . . . That's what our problem-solving plan says," Mike continues, pointing to the following chart hanging on the chalkboard:

PLAN FOR SOLVING WORD PROBLEMS
1. Read the problem at least twice.
2. Ask the following questions:
What is asked for?
What facts are given?
What information is needed that we don't have?
Are unnecessary facts given? What are they?
3. Make a drawing.
4. Solve the problem.
5. Check to see whether the answer makes sense.

"Then what do we do? . . . Melissa?"

"See what the problem asks for."

"Good. What is the problem asking for? . . . Rachel?"

" . . . How much farther they'll have to drive?"

"Excellent. Now, think about this. Suppose I solved the problem and decided that they had $39\frac{1}{2}$ miles left to drive. Would that make sense? Why or why not? Everybody think about it for a moment."

"Okay. What do you think? . . . Herchel?" Mike asks after a moment.

". . . I . . . I . . . don't know."

"Let's look," Mike encourages. "How far from Henderson to Gildford altogether?"

"Thir—," Rico begins until Mike puts his hand up, stopping him in mid-word. He then waits a few seconds as Herchel studies a sketch he has made on his paper:

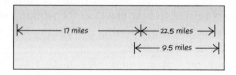

" . . . $39\frac{1}{2}$," Herchel says uncertainly. "Oh! . . . The whole trip was only that far, so they couldn't still have that far to go."

"Excellent thinking, Herchel. See, you could figure it out."

"Now go ahead, Rico. How far do they still have to go?"

"Thirty miles," Rico, one of the higher achievers in the class, responds quickly.

"Okay. Not too bad for the first time through," Mike continues enthusiastically. "Now, let's take a look at your homework."

Mike reviews each homework problem just as he did the first one, asking students to relate the parts to the steps in the problem-solving plan, drawing a sketch on the chalkboard, and calling on a variety of students to supply specific answers and describe their thinking.

With 20 minutes left in the period, he assigns five more problems for homework, and the students begin working. Once the class is working quietly, Mike gestures to Herchel, Marcus, and Gwenn to join him at a table at the back of the room.

"How'd you do on the homework?" Mike asks. "Do you think you get it?"

"Sort of," Gwenn responds, and the other two nod.

"Good," Mike smiles. "Now, let's see what we've got."

When about 5 minutes are left in the period, Mike tells the three students, "Run back to your desks now, and see whether you can get one or two more problems done before the bell rings."

The bell rings, and the students begin filing out of the room. Mike catches Todd's eye, Todd stops, and Mike leads him to a small area in the back of the room where a partition has been set up. The area is partially enclosed but facing the class.

"Here's what we'll do," Mike directs. "When you have the urge to get out of your seat, quietly get up and move back here for a few minutes. Stay as long as you want, but be sure you pay attention to what we're doing. When you think you're ready to move back to your seat, go ahead. All I'm asking is that you move back and forth quietly and not bother the class. . . . What do you think?"

Todd nods, and Mike puts a hand on his shoulder. "You're doing so well on everything else; this will help, I think. You're a good student. You hang in there. . . . Now, here's a pass into Mrs. Miller's class."

Questions for **Case Analysis**

In answering these questions, use information from the chapter, and link your responses to specific information in the case.

1. Describe specifically what Mike did to create a supportive academic climate for his students.

2. How did Mike attempt to ensure success in his teaching?

3. What did Mike do to alter instruction for his students with learning disabilities? How effective were these modifications?

4. What did Mike do to meet the needs of his students with behavior disorders? How effective were these interventions?

To receive feedback for these exercises, go to Appendix B.

Your licensure exam will also include multiple-choice questions similar to those your instructor has given you on your quizzes and tests for this course.

Important **Concepts**

ability grouping (p. 144)
acceleration (p. 167)
adaptive behavior (p. 158)
adaptive fit (p. 149)
assistive technology (p. 164)
attention-deficit/
  hyperactivity disorder
  (ADHD) (p. 155)
autism spectrum disorder
  (p. 160)
behavior disorders (p. 158)
between-class grouping
  (p. 144)
bipolar disorder (p. 160)
collaborative consultation
  (p. 170)

communication disorders
  (p. 156)
crystallized intelligence
  (p. 141)
curriculum-based assessment
  (p. 151)
deaf (p. 162)
disabilities (p. 140)
discrepancy model of
  identification (p. 151)
disorder (p. 153)
due process (p. 150)
enrichment (p. 167)
fluid intelligence (p. 141)
gifts and talents (p. 140)
handicap (p. 153)

inclusion (p. 149)
individualized education
  program (IEP) (p. 150)
intellectual disability
  (p. 157)
intelligence (p. 140)
Joplin plan (p. 145)
language disorders (receptive
  disorders) (p. 156)
learners with exceptionalities
  (p. 140)
learning disabilities (p. 154)
learning styles (p. 145)
least restrictive environment
  (LRE) (p. 149)
mainstreaming (p. 148)

nature view of intelligence
  (p. 144)
nurture view of intelligence
  (p. 144)
partial hearing impairment
  (p. 162)
people-first language (p. 153)
response to intervention model
  of identification (p. 151)
self-regulation (p. 163)
special education (p. 140)
speech disorders (expressive
  disorders) (p. 156)
tracking (p. 144)
visual handicap (p. 161)
within-class grouping (p. 144)

Go to the Topic: Students with Special Needs in the MyEducationLab (www.myeducationlab.com) for *Educational Psychology: Windows on Classrooms*, where you can:

- Find learning outcomes for Students with Special Needs, along with the national standards that connect to these outcomes.
- Complete Assignments and Activities that can help you more deeply understand the chapter content.
- Apply and practice your understanding of the core teaching skills identified in the chapter with the Building Teaching Skills and Dispositions learning units.
- Examine challenging situations and cases presented in the IRIS Center Resources.
- Access video clips of CCSSO National Teachers of the Year award winners responding to the question, "Why Do I Teach?" in the Teacher Talk section.
- See video examples included within the Study Plan that provide concrete and real-world illustrations of the topics presented in the chapter.
- Check your comprehension of the content covered in the chapter with the Study Plan. Here you will be able to take a chapter quiz, receive feedback on your answers, and then access Review, Practice, and Enrichment activities to enhance your understanding of chapter content.

MyEducationLab

chapter 6

Principles of Cognitive Learning Theory and the Construction of Knowledge

chapteroutline

learningoutcomes

After you've completed your study of this chapter, you should be able to:

1. Describe principles of cognitive learning theory, and identify applications of the principles in classrooms and in our personal lives.

2. Describe differences between cognitive and social constructivism, and analyze examples of each.

3. Explain misconceptions, how they occur, and how they can be eliminated.

4. Describe suggestions for classroom practice, and explain how each is grounded in principles of cognitive learning theory.

classroomapplications

The following features help you apply the content of this chapter in your teaching.

Ed Psych and Teaching:
Applying Principles of Learning in Your Classroom

Classroom Connections:
Promoting Conceptual Change in Students
Helping Students Construct Valid Knowledge

Developmentally Appropriate Practice:
Principles of Learning with Students at Different Ages

Exploring Diversity:
The Impact of Diversity on Knowledge Construction

*C*ognitive is in the title of this chapter, and the terms *cognitive* and *cognition* imply "thinking." Because cognitive learning theory has become the predominant framework for examining learning and teaching, we begin our discussion of learning, both in classrooms and in our daily lives, with it.

In the following case study, fourth graders are attempting to identify the variables—weight and distance from the fulcrum—that make beams balance. Because we're focusing on cognition in this chapter, keep the thinking of the students in mind as you read the case study.

Jenny Newhall, their teacher, wants her students to understand that a beam will balance if the weight times the distance on one side of the fulcrum equals the weight times the distance on the other. She begins by dividing her students into groups of four and giving the groups balances with tiles on them that appear as follows:

Jenny tells the students that they are to figure out how to balance the beam, but before adding tiles to the balances, they need to write down possible solutions and explain to their group mates why they think their solutions will work.

As the class begins to work, Jenny circulates around the room and then joins one of the groups—Molly, Suzanne, Tad, and Drexel—as they attempt to solve the problem. During the group discussion Suzanne offers the following solution: "There are 4 on the 8 and 1 on the 2. I want to put 3 on the 10 so there will be 4 on each side."

Here's the solution she proposes:

Molly agrees that Suzanne's arrangement of tiles will make the beam balance but offers a different explanation. "I think we should put 3 on 10, because 4 on the 8 is 32 on one side. And since we only have 2 on the other side, we need to make them equal. So 3 on 10 would equal 30, plus 2, and we'd have 32 on both sides."

We return to this lesson later, but for now, think about these questions.

1. How might we explain the differences in Molly's and Suzanne's thinking?
2. Where did Suzanne get the idea that the beam would balance if the numbers of tiles on each side of the fulcrum were equal?
3. What implications do these differences in thinking have for our teaching?

Principles of cognitive learning theory help answer these questions, and in this chapter you will see how you can apply these principles in both your teaching and your day-to-day living.

Principles of Cognitive Learning Theory

Principles (laws). Statements about an area of study that are generally accepted as true.

Principles, or laws, are statements about an area of study that are generally accepted as true. For example, a prominent science principle (one of Newton's laws of motion) is, "A moving object will keep moving in a straight line unless a force acts on it." This principle helps us understand events in our world, such as why we wear seatbelts while driving.

Principles of cognitive learning theory serve the same function; they help us understand the way people of all ages think, learn, and develop. These principles, outlined in Figure 6.1, provide the framework for **cognitive learning theories,** theories that explain learning in terms of people's thinking and the processes involved in acquiring, organizing, and using knowledge. The arrows in the figure illustrate the interdependence of the principles.

Cognitive learning theories. Theories that explain learning in terms of people's thinking and the processes involved in acquiring, organizing, and using knowledge.

The emergence of cognitive learning theory has been described as the "cognitive revolution," which occurred between the mid-1950s and the early 1970s. Its influence on education has steadily increased since that time (Berliner, 2006).

Learning and Development Depend on Experience

Our experiences, both in and out of classrooms, provide the raw material for learning and development. To see how, let's compare Molly and Suzanne's thinking. Molly was able to

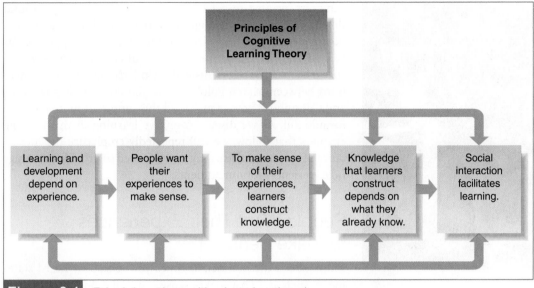

Figure 6.1 Principles of cognitive learning theories

accurately explain why the tiles made the beam balance, "I think we should put 3 on 10, because 4 on the 8 is 32 on one side. And since we only have 2 on the other side, we need to make them equal. So 3 on 10 would equal 30, plus 2, and we'd have 32 on both sides." Suzanne, on the other hand, believed that having an equal number of tiles on both sides of the fulcrum was all that was necessary to make the beam balance; she ignored the distance from the fulcrum.

Ed Psych and You

Do you know how to drive a car with a stick shift? If you do, how did you learn to do so? If you don't, why not?

Our first principle—*learning and development depend on experience*—explains the differences in their thinking, and it also answers our first question at the beginning of this section: "How might we explain the differences in Molly's and Suzanne's thinking?" Molly had prior learning experiences that Suzanne lacked. We don't know how she acquired these experiences, but differences in prior experience influenced their thinking.

Now, think about the questions we asked in the preceding "Ed Psych and You" feature. If you can drive cars with stick shifts, your experiences with them helped you learn how. During your first attempts you probably killed the motor a few times and started in fits and jerks. Then, with some additional experience, your driving smoothed out, and now you can shift gears and maneuver in traffic essentially without thinking about it. On the other hand, if you haven't had these experiences, you are unable to drive with a stick shift, and your driving ability isn't as fully developed.

The same is true for all learning and development. To learn how to write effective essays, we need experiences with writing; to solve problems, we need experiences with problem solving. In a similar way, athletes acquire a great deal of experience as they practice and compete in their sports, and your teaching experiences will help you develop expertise in your field.

Providing experiences for our students is an essential role for us as teachers, and our goal should be to make these experiences as rich and meaningful as possible. **Meaningfulness** describes the extent to which experiences or information are interconnected, and, unfortunately, many learning experiences aren't as meaningful as they could be. For example, as students we all learned about Marco Polo's visit to the Far East, the names of Portuguese explorers, such as Prince Henry the Navigator and Vasco DaGama, and Columbus' trip to the New World in 1492. We usually learned this information as a set of isolated facts and dates, but they are actually closely connected. Because of Marco Polo's travels and the influential book he wrote afterward, many merchants and traders, including the Portuguese

Meaningfulness. The extent to which experiences and information are interconnected with other experiences or information.

Learning and development depend on meaningful learning experiences.

explorers, wanted to get to the Far East. The passage around the tip of Africa and through the Indian Ocean was dangerous, however, so Columbus seized on the idea of getting to the Far East by traveling west (not realizing, of course, that he would run into the Americas instead). Understanding the connections between Marco Polo's travels, the Portuguese navigators and Columbus's voyage makes all this information much more meaningful. As we discuss cognitive learning in this and the chapters that follow, we will repeatedly emphasize the importance of meaningful learning and the need to provide meaningful experiences for our students.

People Want Their Experiences to Make Sense

Think about the number of times you've said or heard statements such as, "That makes sense," or "That doesn't make any sense." They are so common in our everyday lives that we don't even react when we hear them. Why is this the case?

The need to make sense of our experiences may be the most basic cognitive principle. "Human beings want and need to make sense of things that happen—or don't happen—in the short run as well as over the long haul" (Marinoff, 2003, p. 3). NBC newscaster Brian Williams comments, "Our job is to make sense of it all," in referring to the day's news. All societies and cultures, ranging from the ancient Egyptians, Greeks, and Romans, to Native Americans and our own, have constructed systems of beliefs about life, what it means, why we're here and what happens when we die. These belief systems are mechanisms these societies have used to make sense of experiences they couldn't make sense of in any other way.

The same is true in classrooms. Cognitive learning theorists describe students as (cognitively) active beings who continually strive to make sense of their learning experiences (Bransford, Brown, & Cocking, 2000). For example, understanding the relationships between Marco Polo's travels to the Far East and Columbus's voyage makes more sense than a group of isolated facts, such as simply knowing that Columbus reached the New World in 1492.

Information that makes sense is also easier to remember than isolated facts, and this helps us understand why students often recall so little of what we've taught. Too much of what students study isn't meaningful to them, so they memorize enough to pass tests and then promptly forget the information.

Helping our students make sense of what we teach is one of our most important goals. This book is designed to help you reach this goal.

To Make Sense of Their Experiences, Learners Construct Knowledge

Our second question at the beginning of the chapter asked, "Where did Suzanne get the idea that the beam would balance if the numbers of tiles on each side of the fulcrum were equal?" It is highly unlikely that she got this incorrect idea from Jenny, her group mates, or anyone else in the class. Instead, *she constructed it on her own,* and she did so because *it made sense to her.* In fact, to Suzanne, simply focusing on the number of tiles was a more sensible idea than also considering the distance the tiles were from the fulcrum.

Making sense of our experiences is a fundamental cognitive need, and it helps us understand *why* people construct knowledge rather than simply duplicate it as a tape recorder might do. We construct knowledge to make sense of our experiences. This also helps us understand why we develop misconceptions, such as Suzanne did. We construct them because they make sense to us at the time.

The fact that people in general, and students in particular, construct knowledge has important implications for our teaching. If the way we present information isn't meaningful to students—it doesn't make sense to them—they will mentally reorganize it so it does. (We examine misconceptions and discuss strategies to help students construct valid and meaningful ideas later in the chapter.)

Knowledge that Learners Construct Depends on What They Already Know

When we construct knowledge in our attempts to make sense of our world, we rely on what we already know. Consider this problem

$$\frac{1}{3} + \frac{1}{4} =$$

Which answer, 2/7 or 7/12, makes more sense? Initially, for many students it's 2/7. They know how to add numbers, so simply adding the numerators and then adding the denominators is a very sensible idea. Some children, knowing that higher numbers are bigger, even believe that a fraction with a larger denominator, such as 1/5, is greater than one with a smaller denominator, like 1/3. Knowing that 5 is greater than 3, they conclude that 1/5 should be greater than 1/3. Similarly, because we've all had experiences, such as feeling more heat the closer we hold our hand to a hot stove burner or moving closer to a burning fireplace, some people believe that our summers are warmer than our winters because we're closer to the sun in the summer.

Prior knowledge also influenced Molly's and Suzanne's thinking in Jenny's lesson. Because Molly had prior knowledge that Suzanne lacked, she understood what makes beams balance, whereas Suzanne did not.

Social Interaction Facilitates Learning

Ed Psych and You

We've all heard the phrase, "Two heads are better than one." Where do you suppose this phrase originated?

To begin this section, let's look at the following interchange between two students.

> **Devon:** (Holding a spider between his fingers.) Look at the bug.
>
> **Gino:** Yech. . . . Put that thing down. (Gestures toward the spider). Besides, that's not a bug. It's a spider.
>
> **Devon:** What do you mean? A bug is a bug.
>
> **Gino:** Nope. Bugs . . . actually, insects . . . have six legs. See (picking up a beetle). This one has eight. . . . Look (pointing to the spider).
>
> **Devon:** So . . . bugs . . . insects . . . have six legs, and spiders have eight . . . I didn't know that.
>
> **Gino:** Yeah, . . . so, what do you think this is (holding up a grasshopper)?

This brief example illustrates the powerful influence that social interaction has on learning and development. Devon didn't notice that insects and spiders (arachnids) are different until his exchange with Gino, and he probably would have continued to believe they were both "bugs" if they hadn't talked about the beetle and spider.

Social interaction has three important learning benefits for students:

Providing information
Building on others' ideas
Putting thoughts into words

Providing information is arguably the most powerful outcome of social interaction (Thaler & Sunstein, 2008). As they talked, Gino provided Devon with information about spiders and insects, and the new information caused Devon to change his incorrect views about "bugs."

This sharing allows learners to build on each others' ideas (Applebee, Langer, Nystrand, & Gamoran, 2003). In the process, they not only become more knowledgeable but also acquire learning strategies and social skills. For example, in a discussion of reintroducing wolves into northern forests, several students suggested that that the wolves would help balance the ecosystem and would ultimately benefit other animal populations such as beaver, deer, and rabbits. One, however, asked, "Yeah, but what if you were a rancher? Wouldn't you be upset if a wolf came and ate your cattle?" This student modeled the process of *perspective taking*, the ability to understand another person's point of view, and through social interaction, other students gradually acquired this ability (R. Anderson et al., 2001). Perspective taking is an important social skill with life-long benefits both in school and in our day-to-day world.

Social interaction also provides students with practice in articulating their thinking. Putting ideas into words is a cognitively demanding activity, and the better their ability to do so, the deeper their understanding of the topic becomes (Bransford et al., 2000). Even the simple process of Devon saying, "So, . . . bugs . . . insects . . . have six legs, and spiders have eight," helped deepen his understanding. Instead of using the vague term "bug," for example, he used the more precise term "insect" and linked it to having 6 legs. Seemingly minor differences such as these can have long-term positive learning benefits.

Although social interaction is essential for learning, the process isn't as simple as it appears on the surface. For example, as they interact, students may simply be "talking past each other." To illustrate this issue, let's return to the small-group discussion and again focus on Suzanne's thinking.

After Suzanne and Molly offer their solutions and explanations, the group discusses them, and Jenny has the students test their ideas on the balances. She then reassembles the class and has Mavrin, who has solved the problem correctly, come to the board and explain it, using the sketch you see here, which Jenny has drawn on the board.

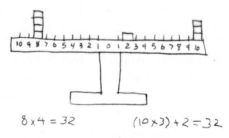

Mavrin explains that $8 \times 4 = 32$ on the left side of the fulcrum equals $(10 \times 3) + 2 = 32$ on the right side, referring to the sketch in his explanation. Jenny reviews it, describes Mavrin's thinking, and concludes by saying, "He has an excellent number sentence here."

An interviewer from a nearby university is observing the class, and following the lesson, he talks with Suzanne, Molly, Tad, and Drexel about their understanding of beam balances. He gives them the problem at right, some time to think about it, and then says, "Suzanne, tell us where you would put tiles to make the beam balance."

Suzanne offers the following solution:

She reasons, "I put 2 here (indicating that she had added 2 tiles to the right side of the fulcrum) so that 2 plus 3 equals 5 . . . and 2 plus 1 plus 2 here, so it will be 5" (indicating that she had put 5 tiles on the left side of the fulcrum)."

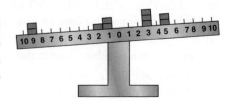

Here we see how the *appearance* of learning through social interaction can be misleading. During the small-group activity, Suzanne heard Molly offer a correct explanation for making the beam balance, and during the whole-group discussion, she heard two more correct explanations—Mavrin's at the board and Jenny's. Yet, Suzanne's thinking didn't change; she continued to believe that having equal numbers of tiles on each side of the fulcrum would make the beam balance. Molly, Mavrin, and Jenny each provided information—an essential benefit of social interaction, but their explanations went right over Suzanne's head. She had an idea that made sense to her, so instead of thinking about what they said, she retained her original idea. This is more common in classrooms than we would like.

This example also illustrates another essential idea about learning: *Wisdom can't be told.* Originally proposed by Charles Gragg (1940) nearly three quarters of a century ago, and emphasized repeatedly by researchers since then (Bransford, Derry, Berliner, Hammerness, & Beckett, 2005), this simple but powerful idea helps us understand why lecturing and explaining, as strategies for promoting learning, are often ineffective. Suzanne's thinking illustrates why this is the case. Although she was part of a group, and appeared to be interacting, *she remained cognitively passive,* and as a result, her thinking didn't change.

So, what can we do about this problem? Let's return to the interview.

Focused and effective social interaction facilitates learning.

> After Suzanne offers her solution, the interviewer asks, "Molly, what do you think of that solution?"
>
> "It won't work," she responds. "It doesn't matter how many blocks there are. It's where they're put."
>
> The interviewer asks Drexel and Tad what they think. Drexel corroborates Molly's answer by saying, "Because of Molly's reasoning. It isn't just the blocks. It's also where you put them."
>
> Tad shrugs with uncertainty.
>
> The students try Suzanne's solution, and the beam tips to the left.
>
> Suzanne suggests taking a block off the 9, reasoning that the blocks near the end of the beam bring it down more, indicating that her thinking is starting to change as a result of seeing the example and interacting with the others.
>
> The interviewer nods but doesn't affirm any explanation, instead giving the students the following problem and asking for solutions:
>
> Molly offers, "Put 1 on the 8 and 4 on the 1."
>
> "What do you think? . . . Tad?" the interviewer asks.
>
> Tad stares at the beam for several seconds, concludes that the solution is correct, and when asked to explain his thinking, says, "Oh, okay, . . . 3 times 4 is 12, . . . and 4 times 1 is 4, . . . and 8 times 1 is 8, and 8 plus 4 is 12."

> The interviewer asks for another solution, and Drexel offers, "1 on the 2 and 1 on the 10."
>
> "Okay, I want you to tell us whether or not that'll work, Suzanne."
>
> ". . . I think it will."
>
> "Okay, explain why you think it will."
>
> "Because, 10 times 1 equals 10, . . . and 2 times 1 equals 2, and 10 plus 2 equals 12. . . . So it'll be even."
>
> Molly, Tad, and Drexel confirm the solution, and the interview is ended.

Why did Suzanne's thinking change during the interview when it hadn't during the lesson? Two factors were operating. First, they tried her solution, and it didn't work; the beam didn't balance. This concrete experience contributed to her change in thinking. Second, as a result of the social interaction during the interview, she became cognitively active; she actually *thought about* the process. The interviewer didn't attempt to help her understand what makes beams balance by explaining it to her. Instead, the group discussed solutions to the problem, and the interviewer *asked her to explain them.*

This process helps us understand why "two heads are better than one," the question we asked in our "Ed Psych and You" feature at the beginning of this section. As two or more people discuss a question or problem, they generate answers and solutions that none of them can create on their own. They can do so because they exchange information, build on each other's ideas, and practice putting their thoughts into words.

Promoting interaction is essential in all effective instruction (Webb, Farivar, & Mastergeorge, 2002). As a rule of thumb, *if we explain an idea, our students may or may not "get" it; if they can explain it to us, we know they have it.*

Using these principles as a framework, in the next section we examine the process of knowledge construction in more detail.

---

check your understanding ▷

1.1 Describe the principles of cognitive learning theories.

1.2 You and a friend are trying to install a sound card in your computer, but you're a little uncertain about how to do it. You open the computer, look inside, and as you talk about how to proceed, she suggests looking to see where the speakers are attached. "Good idea," you say, and you easily install the card. Which principle of learning is best illustrated by this example? Explain how the principle is being applied.

1.3 You and a friend are studying the accompanying drawing, which represents a balance with two containers above it of the same volume. The container on the left is full of water, and the one on the right is full of cooking oil. When the two containers are placed on the balance, you're asked if (a) the left side will go down, (b) the right side will go down, or (c) the balance will remain level.

Your friend erroneously concludes that the right side of the balance will go down. Identify at least three principles of learning that apply in your friend's conclusion. Explain the application of each.

To receive feedback for these questions, go to Appendix A.

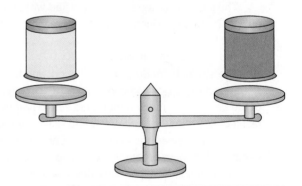

The Process of Knowledge Construction

The need to make sense of our experiences is a basic principle of cognitive learning, and people make sense of their experiences by constructing their own knowledge. Theorists don't completely agree, however, on the process of knowledge construction. We examine two views—*cognitive constructivism* and *social constructivism*—in the following sections.

Knowledge Construction as an Individual Process: Cognitive Constructivism

Cognitive constructivism. A view that describes knowledge construction as an individual, internal process.

Cognitive constructivism, grounded in Piaget's work, focuses on individual, internal constructions of knowledge (Brainerd, 2003; Greeno, Collins, & Resnick, 1996). It emphasizes individuals' search for meaning as they interact with the environment and test and modify their existing understanding. Social interaction influences the process, but primarily as a catalyst for individual cognitive conflict. When one child suggests an idea that causes disequilibrium in another, for example, the second child resolves the disequilibrium by individually reconstructing his or her understanding (Brainerd, 2003).

To illustrate this idea, let's return to the interchange between Devon and Gino earlier in the chapter.

> **Devon:** (Holding a spider between his fingers.) Look at the bug.
>
> **Gino:** Yech. . . . Put that thing down. (Gestures toward the spider). Besides, that's not a bug. It's a spider.
>
> **Devon:** What do you mean? A bug is a bug.
>
> **Gino:** Nope. Bugs . . . actually, insects . . . have six legs. See (picking up a beetle). This one has eight. . . . Look (pointing to the spider).
>
> **Devon:** So . . . bugs . . . insects . . . have six legs, and spiders have eight . . . I didn't know that.
>
> **Gino:** Yeah, . . . so, what do you think this is (holding up a grasshopper)?

Cognitive constructivists interpret this exchange by saying that Devon's equilibrium was disrupted as a result of the discussion, and—individually—he resolved the problem by reconstructing his thinking to accommodate the new evidence Gino offered.

A literal interpretation of this position emphasizes learning activities that are experience-based and discovery oriented. This view suggests, for example, that children learn math most effectively if they discover math ideas while manipulating concrete objects, such as blocks and sticks, rather than having them presented by a teacher or other expert.

One interpretation of this perspective suggests that you should avoid directly teaching or imposing your thinking on your students, but many others question it (e.g., Kirschner, Sweller, & Clark, 2006). As a result, current views of learning focus more strongly on social processes in knowledge construction. To understand how these processes influence learning, let's briefly look at the social world in which we live and how it influences us.

Social Influences in Our Lives

We are social animals (Brooks, 2011). Most of us enjoy the company of others, and we enjoy interacting, both face-to-face and in social networking sites, such as Facebook and Twitter. In fact, people spend an enormous amount of time interacting with others. Research conducted nearly 20 years ago indicates that some of us spend up to 80% of our awake time in the company of others and can average

Ed Psych and You

You notice that your two best friends have gained a considerable amount of weight. Will this influence you in any way? Are you more likely to be careful about what you eat, so the same thing doesn't happen to you?

6 hours or more a day in conversations, mostly with people we know well (Emler, 1994). Because of population increases and urbanization, the figure is probably higher today. A typical American teen sends and receives 50 text messages per day, or 1,500 per month; 31% of teens send and receive more than 100 messages per day (Pew Charitable Trust, 2010)! Some researchers suggest that social behavior is biological in origin, because it increases our likelihood of survival. So we evolved as social animals (Christakis & Fowler, 2009; Gazzaniga, 2008).

Social processes influence our lives in many ways. For example, the answer to the first question in "Ed Psych and You" feature is yes—our friends influence our behavior in many ways. Unfortunately, the answer to the second question is no. Researchers have found that if your friends are overweight, you're also more likely to be overweight. And, if you go out to a restaurant, and your friends are heavy eaters, you're likely to eat more than if your friends order light meals (Thaler & Sunstein, 2008).

Positive social influences exist as well. Programs such as Weight Watchers and Alcoholics Anonymous are based on the influence of social support. For example, researchers found that people with support groups lost 33% more weight than people did alone, and they were more likely to keep the weight off (Wing & Jeffrey, 1999). If you and your friends are smokers, and your friends quit, you're more likely to quit than if your friends continue smoking. Also, you're more likely to be happy if your friends are happy (Christakis & Fowler, 2009). This leads us to a closer examination of social influences in knowledge construction.

Social Processes in Learning and Teaching: Social Constructivism

Social constructivism. A view of constructivism suggesting that learners first construct knowledge in a social context and then individually internalize it.

As with our everyday lives, social forces influence learning. For example, most of us have had the experience of talking to another person about an idea, with neither understanding it completely. As the discussion continues, understanding increases for both of us. This is reflected in the cognitive learning principle *social interaction facilitates learning,* and it also illustrates the basic premise of **social constructivism,** which suggests that learners first construct knowledge in a social context and then individually internalize it. Lev Vygotsky, a Russian psychologist who is often called the father of social constructivism observed,

> Every function in the child's cultural development appears twice: first, on the social level, and later on the individual level; first between people . . . and then inside the child. . . . This applies equally to voluntary attention, to logical memory, and to the formation of concepts. All the higher functions originate as actual relationships between individuals. (Vygotsky, 1978, p. 57)

Social constructivism, strongly influenced by Vygotsky's (1978) work, has become a powerful influence in shaping our thinking about teaching and learning (Martin, 2006).

To illustrate social constructivism in action, think again about the exchange between Devon and Gino. Cognitive constructivists interpret this episode by saying that Devon's equilibrium was disrupted as a result of the discussion, and—individually—he resolved the problem. Social constructivists, in contrast, suggest that the change in Devon's thinking was a direct outcome of the discussion, and the dialogue itself helped Devon more clearly understand the difference between insects and spiders.

Appropriating understanding. The process of individually internalizing understanding after it has first been socially constructed.

Jenny's beam balance lesson also illustrates social constructivism. Tad initially had little understanding about making beams balance, shrugging uncertainly when asked to explain how balance beams worked. Later, however, he was able to offer a correct explanation for the solution that Drexel offered. Social constructivists suggest that his understanding was a direct outcome of the social interaction that occurred during the interview, and he then individually internalized it, a process called **appropriating understanding** (Leont'ev, 1981; Li et al., 2007). In the video of the lesson on which the case study is based, we could almost see the wheels turning in Tad's head as he hesitantly described his developing understanding. As he struggled to articulate his thinking, his understanding also increased.

Social constructivism has important implications for our teaching, and it resolves the dilemma often associated with cognitive constructivism. It doesn't imply that learners should discover everything on their own, nor does it suggest that teachers shouldn't offer their thinking to students, "as Piagetian theory often seemed to imply" (Resnick & Klopfer, 1989, p. 4). Rather, it suggests that teachers consider all the traditional questions related to instruction: how to plan, conduct learning activities, motivate students, and assess learning. The focus, however, is on facilitating students' constructions of knowledge using social interaction as a catalyst, instead of simply standing in front of them and explaining ideas while they listen passively (Fleming & Alexander, 2001). From a social constructivist perspective, creating learning environments in which learners are cognitively active in the process of constructing and internalizing valid ideas is an essential role for us as teachers.

This is a sophisticated and challenging process. For instance, as you saw earlier, in spite of Jenny's use of small-group work and attempts to create a meaningful learning activity for her students, Suzanne initially remained cognitively passive as Molly, Mavrin, and Jenny herself explained how to make beams balance. Not until the interview after the lesson—when the social interaction required Suzanne to become cognitively active—did she understand that both weight and distance from the fulcrum are necessary to make the beam balance.

But, you won't have an interviewer in your classroom, so how can you help your students become cognitively active during your learning activities? We answer this question later in the chapter, but for now, let's take a closer look at social constructivism.

Sociocultural Learning Theory

Just as constructivism, in general, is interpreted differently, theorists emphasize different aspects of social constructivism. **Sociocultural theory,** while still emphasizing the social dimensions of learning, places greater emphasis on the larger cultural contexts in which learning occurs (Mason, 2007). Patterns of interaction in the home provide an example. In some cultures, children are not viewed as legitimate partners in conversation, and as a result, they may be reluctant to raise their hands in attempts to volunteer answers to your questions. And they may even be hesitant to respond when you call on them directly (Au, 1992; Tharp & Gallimore, 1991). Differences also exist in the cultural experiences, attitudes, and values that students bring to school, all of which influence learning (Rogoff, 2003). As teachers, we need to be sensitive to these differences and help our students understand and adapt to the culture of our classrooms.

> **Sociocultural theory.** A form of social constructivism that emphasizes the social dimensions of learning, but places greater emphasis on the larger cultural contexts in which learning occurs.

The Classroom as a Community of Learners

A sociocultural view of learning shifts the emphasis from the individual to the group and from acquiring knowledge, per se, to belonging, participating, and communicating within a community of learners (Mason, 2007). A **community of learners** is a learning environment in which the teacher and students all work together to help everyone learn (A. Brown & Campione, 1994; Palincsar, 1998). This perspective reminds us that our management rules and procedures and the way we interact with students create microcultures in our classrooms, making them cooperative and inviting or competitive and even frightening.

> **Community of learners.** A learning environment in which the teacher and students work together to help everyone learn.

In a learning community:

- All students participate in learning activities. Each student in Jenny's class was involved in trying to identify the variables that make beams balance.
- Teachers and students work together to help one another learn; promoting learning isn't the teacher's responsibility alone. Jenny had her students explain their proposed solutions to their group mates before actually trying them. And, as you saw in the interview that followed the lesson, Suzanne's and Tad's understanding developed as a result of their interaction with Molly and Drexel; the interviewer didn't explain it to them.
- Student–student interaction is an important part of the learning process. As they suggested ideas for making the beam balance work, the interaction was mostly among the students in Jenny's activity.
- Teachers and students respect difference in interests, thinking, and progress. The students in Jenny's classroom listened patiently as their group mates offered solutions, even if the solutions differed from their own.
- The thinking involved in learning activities is as important as the answers themselves. Jenny emphasized that the students verbalize their thinking before they actually tried solutions to the problem.

> In a community of learners, the teacher and all students work together to help everyone achieve.

Each of these characteristics is grounded in the idea that knowledge is first socially constructed before it is appropriated and internalized by individuals.

In attempting to create a community of learners, we are trying to develop a classroom culture where the students feel as if, "We're all in this together." Our role is to try our best to support our students as they struggle to understand the topics we're teaching. Students help each other whenever they can, and scores and grades reflect the extent to which they've mastered the content instead of how well they compete with each other.

Cognitive Apprenticeship

Historically, apprenticeships have helped novices—as they worked with experts—acquire skills they couldn't learn on their own (Black, 2007). Apprenticeships are common in trades such as plumbing, weaving, or cooking, but they are also used in areas such as learning to play musical instruments or creating pieces of art.

Cognitive apprenticeships, influenced by social constructivism, occur when less-skilled learners work alongside experts in developing cognitive skills, such as reading comprehension, writing, or problem solving (Collins, 2006). Cognitive apprenticeships focus on developing thinking and commonly include the following components:

- *Modeling:* Teachers, or other, more knowledgeable students, demonstrate skills, such as solutions to problems, and simultaneously model their thinking by describing it out loud.
- *Scaffolding:* As students perform tasks, teachers ask questions and provide support, decreasing the amount of scaffolding as students' proficiency increases.
- *Verbalization:* Students are encouraged to express their developing understanding in words, which allows teachers to assess students' developing thinking.
- *Increasing complexity:* As students' proficiency increases, teachers present them with more challenging problems or other tasks.

We saw an example of cognitive apprenticeship in the interview following Jenny's lesson. When Molly and Drexel (and later, Tad) offered their explanations, they were *cognitive models,* and this modeling, together with the discussion, *scaffolded* Suzanne's thinking. Then, she verbalized her thinking when she said, "Because, 10 times 1 equals 10, . . . and 2 times 1 equals 2, and 10 plus 2 equals 12. . . . So it'll be even," as she applied her developing understanding to a new problem. Verbalizing understanding helps students put their sometimes fuzzy thoughts into words and helps clarify their thinking (Kastens & Liben, 2007). By participating in a cognitive apprenticeship, Suzanne was able to understand the new content.

Despite consistent evidence that social interaction increases learning (Brophy, 2006c), it is quite rare; teachers spend most of their instructional time lecturing and explaining or having students do seatwork (Pianta, Belsky, Houts, & Morrison, 2007). *Scaffolding* and *verbalization,* two essential components of cognitive apprenticeships, are not possible when teachers simply explain the topics they teach. As you saw earlier: *If we explain an idea, our students may or may not "get" it; if they explain it to us, we know they have it.*

Situated Cognition

Situated cognition (or situated learning), another component of social constructivist learning theory, suggests that learning depends on, and cannot be separated from, the context in which it occurs (J. Brown, Collins, & Duguid, 1989). According to this view, a student who learns to solve subtraction and division problems while determining a car's gas mileage, for example, has a different kind of understanding than one who solves abstract and disconnected subtraction and division problems in school (Rogoff, 2003). Similarly, when you apply your understanding of learning theories to case studies and examples from classrooms, you acquire a different understanding than you would if you studied them in the abstract.

Cognitive apprenticeship. The process of having a less-skilled learner work at the side of an expert to develop cognitive skills.

Situated cognition. A theoretical position in social constructivism suggesting that learning depends on, and cannot be separated from, the context in which it occurs.

Situated cognition, when taken to the extreme, suggests that **transfer,** the ability to apply understanding acquired in one context to a different context, is difficult, if not impossible. It would suggest, for example, that people who learn to drive in rural areas would be unable to drive in big cities with their heavy traffic, because their driving expertise is situated in the rural setting.

Transfer does exist, however, or we would be faced with learning everything anew (Mayer & Wittrock, 2006). For example, the ability to drive in a myriad of contexts occurs, and with practice people become comfortable driving in both rural areas, large cities, and even other countries.

Similarly, we can promote transfer in school by consciously varying learning contexts (Vosniadou, 2007). Math students, for example, should practice solving a variety of real-world problems, and language arts students should practice writing in each of their content areas (Mayer & Wittrock, 2006). Situated cognition reminds us that context is important, and we can accommodate it by asking our students to apply their developing knowledge in a number of different contexts.

Transfer. The ability to apply understanding acquired in one context to a different context.

---

check your understanding

2.1 Describe the primary difference between cognitive and social constructivism.

2.2 In the case study at the beginning of the chapter, is Suzanne's thinking a better example of cognitive or of social constructivism? Explain why you think so.

2.3 A second-grade teacher wants her students to understand diphthongs (speech sounds that begin with one vowel sound and gradually change to another vowel sound within the same syllable, as *oi* in *boil*). She presents her students with this passage:

> A *boy*, Jeremy, walked over by the window of his *house* one evening and *looked* at the full *moon*. It was so bright that he *could* see his shadow on the *floor*. Off in the tree, with a branch that was *bowed,* he heard an *owl* hoot.

She has students make observations of the italicized words and then helps them pronounce each correctly.

Is this is an example of situated cognition? Provide evidence from the example to support your assessment.

To receive feedback for these questions, go to Appendix A.

When Learners Construct Invalid Knowledge: Misconceptions and Conceptual Change

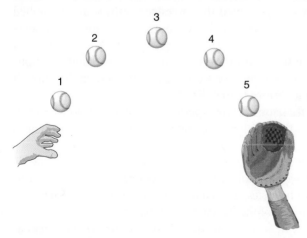

Think about the activity in our "Ed Psych and You" feature. How did you draw the arrows? If you're typical, your drawing will look like the one at the top of the next page.

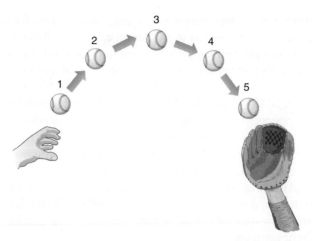

However, when ignoring air resistance, gravity is the only force on the ball, as illustrated below.

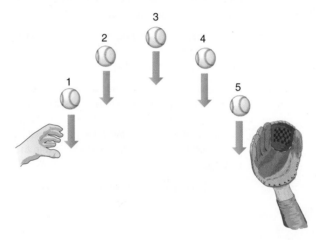

Why did you represent the forces as you did? In all likelihood the answer lies in three of the learning principles discussed earlier in the chapter. First, *Learning and development depend on experience.* Virtually all your experiences suggest that to make an object move in a certain direction, you must exert a force (a push or pull) in that direction. It applies to a myriad of examples, ranging from those as simple as sliding a coffee cup across a table to moving cars down busy streets. (If you represented the forces correctly, you also applied the first principle. You had experiences, perhaps in a physics course, that helped you understand why gravity is the only force operating on the ball.)

If you represented the forces as most people do, you also applied the second principle, *people want their experiences to make sense.* If an object is traveling in a certain direction, it makes sense that some force is making it move in that direction.

Finally, the third principle, *to make sense of their experiences, learners construct knowledge,* suggests you *constructed* the idea that the forces operated as you represented them. It made sense to you.

Misconception. A belief that is inconsistent with evidence or commonly accepted explanations.

However, what makes sense to us is sometimes inconsistent with evidence or commonly accepted explanations. In these cases, we have constructed a **misconception.** Suzanne constructed a misconception about beam balances, mistakenly believing that the beam would balance if the number of tiles on each side of the fulcrum was equal.

Misconceptions are most common in science, but they exist in other content areas as well. For instance, when faced with the following problems:

$$\begin{array}{r} 49 \\ -\ 35 \end{array} \qquad \begin{array}{r} 45 \\ -\ 39 \end{array}$$

many young children get an answer of 14 for both, believing that simply subtracting the smaller from the larger number, regardless of position, is the correct operation. And, you saw earlier that students often try to add fractions by simply adding both the numerators and denominators to each other. Language arts students commonly believe that an adverb is a word that ends in *ly* and adjectives always precede the nouns they modify. And, in social studies many people believe that communism and socialism represent the same ideology. Each is a misconception.

Misconceptions in Teaching and Learning

A number of misconceptions also exist in teaching and learning. For instance, many teachers believe that the most effective way to help students understand a topic is to explain it to them (Cuban, 1993; L. Andrew, 2007). As you saw in the case of Suzanne's thinking, this is a misconception. Suzanne heard three clear and accurate explanations for making beams balance, yet she retained her misconception until it was directly confronted during the interview after Jenny's lesson. And many people, and even some educational leaders, believe that knowledge of content, such as math, English, or history, is all that is necessary to be an effective teacher (Mayer, 2002). This is another misconception. Knowledge of content is essential, of course, but teaching expertise requires much more, such as how to represent content in ways that are understandable to students, how to organize and manage classrooms, and understanding how students learn and develop (U.S. Department of Education, 2008).

Misconceptions about learner development also exist. For example, because middle and high school students' chronological age suggests that they are formal operational in their thinking, some teachers believe they can be taught in the abstract—using words alone to help students understand the ideas they're teaching. This is a common misconception about Piaget's (1970, 1977) developmental theory. If they lack experience related to a topic, learners of all ages need concrete experiences to help them understand the topic.

Now, let's see how misconceptions originate and how they relate to the principles of learning discussed earlier.

The Origin of Misconceptions

Principles of cognitive learning readily explain the origin of misconceptions. Simply, misconceptions are constructed; they're constructed because they make sense to the people who construct them; and they're often consistent with people's prior knowledge or experiences (di Sessa, 2006; Vosniadou, 2007). It makes sense, for example, that the forces on the ball would be in the same direction as the ball's flight, and most of our experiences are consistent with this idea. Also, keeping the numbers of tiles on both sides of the fulcrum equal was simple and made sense to Suzanne.

Prior experiences contribute to misconceptions, but additional factors also exist:

- *Appearances.* People tend to infer cause–effect relationships between two objects or events when they occur together, and one appears to cause the other (Kuhn, 2001). For example, because the beam balanced when the numbers of tiles on each side of the fulcrum were equal, Suzanne concluded that the equal number *caused* the beam to balance.
- *Society.* Commonly held societal beliefs contribute to misconceptions. For instance, many people in the United States think of Africa as a single country, composed primarily of desert, and populated by people with a common culture. It is, of course, a vast continent, with multiple nations and a great deal of geographic and cultural diversity.
- *Language.* Language can contribute to misconceptions. For instance, we describe the sun and moon as "rising" and "setting," which can lead children to believe that they

revolve around the earth, and we refer to lead as a "heavy" metal, which can lead to misconceptions about the relationship between the concepts *weight* (mass) and *density*.

Misconceptions' Resistance to Change

Teachers typically try to correct students' misconceptions by providing information that contradicts the misconception (Alparsian, Tekkaya, & Geban, 2004; Yip, 2004). This often doesn't work, however, as you saw with Suzanne's thinking about the balance beam.

Why are misconceptions so resistant to change? The answer lies in Piaget's concept of equilibrium. Because the misconception makes sense to us, we're at cognitive equilibrium (Sinatra & Pintrich, 2003). Changing thinking requires us to reconstruct our understanding, which is disequilibrating. Assimilating an experience into an existing understanding is simpler and less cognitively demanding.

Knowing that students bring misconceptions to learning experiences and realizing that these misconceptions are resistant to change, what can we do in response? The idea of conceptual change provides answers.

Teaching for Conceptual Change

Conceptual change involves fundamentally altering students' beliefs about a topic. Teaching for conceptual change capitalizes on Piaget's concepts of *disequilibrium, accommodation,* and *assimilation* (Alparsian et al., 2004). Three conditions are required for students to change their thinking:

- The existing conception must become dissatisfying; it must cause disequilibrium.
- An alternative conception must be understandable. Students must be able to accommodate or change their thinking so the alternative conception makes sense.
- The new conception must be useful in the real world; it must reestablish equilibrium, and students must be able to assimilate new experiences into it.

The change in Suzanne's thinking illustrates these conditions. First, the group tried her solution during the interview, and she could see it didn't work (the beam didn't balance). So, her conception became dissatisfying. Encountering convincing evidence that an existing conception is invalid is the first and most important factor leading to conceptual change.

Second, an alternative conception—one involving both the number of tiles and the distance from the fulcrum—was understandable, as indicated by Suzanne's ability to use both in order to explain the solution to a different problem. And third, the alternative conception was productive; she used it to successfully explain an additional example.

Teachers encourage conceptual change with the examples they provide and the discussions they guide.

Even with these conditions in place, conceptual change is not easy, as anyone who has attempted to convince someone to change their thinking will attest. Considerable cognitive inertia exists, requiring us to take an active role in guiding the conceptual change process in our students (Vosniadou, 2007). Questions that reveal and challenge misconceptions and require students to apply their revised thinking to new situations are the most effective tools we have for promoting conceptual change (Yip, 2004).

Conceptual change is grounded in social constructivist learning theory. Suzanne changed her thinking because the new conception made sense to her. And, it made sense because the social interaction in the interview, combined with examples that provided the needed experience, facilitated the change process.

Exploring diversity

The Impact of Diversity on Knowledge Construction

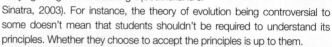

The beliefs that students bring to our classrooms exert powerful influences on what they take away from their learning experiences. For example, Muslim and Jewish students are likely to have very different views about issues in the Middle East, such as the Arab–Israeli conflict and the American interventions in Iraq and Afghanistan. Also, students whose religious beliefs conflict with scientists' description of the earth being four and a half billion years old, or the idea that humans evolved from more primitive species, don't accept the basic tenets of evolution (Southerland & Sinatra, 2003). Students' pre-existing beliefs can have a powerful influence the effectiveness of our instruction.

And students' beliefs are unlikely to change unless compelling evidence indicates that the belief is invalid, like what happened when Suzanne could see that her original suggestion for making the beam balance didn't work. However, in many cases, irrefutable evidence often doesn't exist, as we see with differing political views or even global warming.

So, what can we do when students cling to beliefs that run counter to ideas we are teaching? The most effective approach is to emphasize that students are accountable for *understanding* an idea, theory, or interpretation, but not necessarily agreeing with or believing it (Southerland & Sinatra, 2003). For instance, the theory of evolution being controversial to some doesn't mean that students shouldn't be required to understand its principles. Whether they choose to accept the principles is up to them.

Classrooms as learning communities are important when dealing with diversity of beliefs and understandings. All students should be given the opportunity to share their beliefs, and diversity in thinking should be respected. Recognizing that classmates have beliefs different from their own, and learning to acknowledge and respect those differences, are worthwhile learning experiences in themselves.

check your understanding

3.1 What are misconceptions, and how do they occur?

3.2 Describe four common sources of misconceptions, and provide an example of each.

3.3 Explain how misconceptions can be changed or eliminated.

To receive feedback for these questions, go to Appendix A.

Classroom connections

Promoting Conceptual Change in Students

1. Students construct their own knowledge, and this knowledge is sometimes invalid. Use questions to reveal and challenge students' existing understanding.

   ▪ **Elementary:** When one of his second graders solves the first problem below, and gets 45, the teacher presents the second problem. When the student also gets 45 for this problem, he asks, "We have two very different problems. How can we get the same answer when the numbers are different?"

   $$54 \qquad 59$$
   $$-\,19 \qquad -\,14$$

   ▪ **Middle School:** When one of her eighth graders explains that transparent objects are objects that we can see through, and opaque objects are those we can't see through, ignoring the role of light rays, a physical science teacher asks, "If we can see through a transparent object, why can't we see through it at night?

   ▪ **High School:** When one of his students describes all Native Americans as nomadic hunter gatherers, a history teacher shows pictures of pueblos and other permanent living structures and asks, "If they are nomadic, why would they build dwellings like these?"

2. Conceptual change requires that students are able to apply their revised thinking to new situations. Provide students with tasks that require them to apply reconstructed knowledge to new situations.

   ▪ **Elementary:** The second-grade teacher in suggestion 1 asks his students to solve a series of problems that require regrouping.

   ▪ **Middle School:** The eighth-grade teacher in suggestion 1 asks her students to explain why they can't see a person they hear walking down the hall outside their classroom. She guides them to conclude that the light rays that are reflected from the person won't pass through the opaque wall of the classroom.

   ▪ **High School:** The social studies teacher in suggestion 1 has the students describe the cultural and economic characteristics of different Native American groups, such as plains Indians and those who lived in the Southwest and Northeast.

Principles of Learning in Classrooms

So, what—specifically—do the principles of cognitive learning theory suggest for classroom instruction and helping our students construct valid knowledge? We answer this question in the following sections and examine the implications for your teaching.

The Teacher's Role in Knowledge Construction

Most of your teaching roles—such as specifying learning objectives, preparing learning activities, and designing assessments—are the same when instruction is grounded in these principles as they are in traditional classrooms. The primary difference is a shift in emphasis away from presenting information and toward providing the experiences and promoting the interaction that help students construct valid knowledge (Donovan & Bransford, 2005). This shift results in several suggestions for classroom practice.

Suggestions for Classroom Practice

In applying cognitive learning principles with our students, our goal is to help them construct a valid understanding of the topics we're teaching. The suggestions are outlined in Figure 6.2 and discussed in the sections that follow.

Provide Students with Experiences in the Form of High-Quality Examples

Learning and development depend on experience, and prior experiences contribute to the knowledge students bring to our classrooms. So, what do you do when students lack experiences and come to your classroom with insufficient or even inaccurate prior knowledge? The answer is simple (but admittedly, often not easy): *You supplement existing knowledge with high-quality examples and other representations of the content being taught.*

High-quality examples. Examples that include all the information learners need to understand a topic.

High-quality examples are examples that include all the information learners need to understand the topic, and they serve two essential functions. First, they become the raw material learners use to construct their knowledge (Freeman, McPhail, & Berndt, 2002). Literally, "the example is the experience." For instance, in the natural world, as small children learn about dogs, they see, pet, and play with friendly pooches, and they gradually construct the concept *dog*. The same is true for the myriad of other concepts that children acquire from their natural experiences.

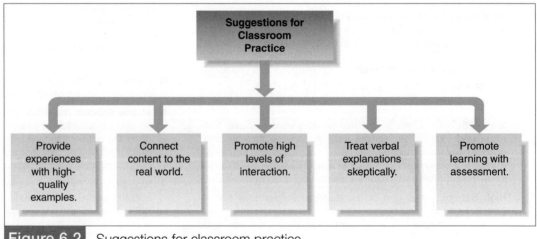

Figure 6.2 Suggestions for classroom practice

To see the power of examples, watch *Sesame Street* with a child some time. Elmo, for instance, jumps above a group of flowers, and says, "I'm *above* the flowers." Then, he pops up below the flowers, and says "Now, I'm *below* the flowers." Elmo is simply providing examples of the concepts *above* and *below*. Everything children's educational programming teaches is through the clever and attractive use of examples.

Using examples in our classrooms models the process children use to construct knowledge in the natural world. You bring parts of the world into your classroom to help your students reach your learning objectives and the standards they are expected to meet.

Promoting conceptual change is the second essential function that examples provide. For instance, the solution that Drexel offered (which you see here) during the interview was a high-quality example that helped Suzanne revise her thinking and construct a valid understanding of the principle that makes beams balance. Without this example, Suzanne would have been unlikely to change her thinking.

Working with high-quality examples provides the experiences students use to construct knowledge.

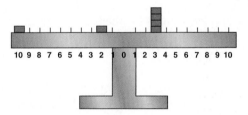

High-quality examples are important for all topics at all grade levels, and they are especially important when learners first encounter a new idea, or for limited-English-proficiency learners who may lack the school-related experiences of their peers (Echevarria & Graves, 2011).

Table 6.1 includes additional examples of ways teachers represent different topics.

Table 6.1   Examples of teachers' representations of content

Topic	Learning Objective	Representations
Decimals and Percents	For students to understand decimals and percents by calculating cost per ounce to determine which product is the best buy	12-ounce soft drink and its cost 16-ounce soft drink and its cost 6-pack of soft drinks and its cost
Properties of Matter	For students to understand the concept *density*	Cotton balls pressed into a drink cup Wooden cubes of different sizes to show that the ratio of weight to volume remains the same Equal volumes of water and vegetable oil on a balance
Parts of Speech	For students to understand comparative and superlative adjectives	Students' pencils of different lengths to show that one is "longer" and another is the "longest" Students' hair color to show that one is "darker" and another is the "darkest"
Longitude and Latitude	For students to understand longitude and latitude	A beach ball with lines of longitude and lines of latitude drawn on it as you see here.

Connect Content to the Real World

To replicate as closely as possible students' natural experiences, we want to connect the topics we teach to the real world whenever possible. This suggestion is supported by social constructivist learning theory and particularly *situated cognition* (J. Brown et al., 1989; Lave, 1997). For example, when geography students connect *longitude* and *latitude* to the location of a favorite hangout, science students relate *inertia* to seatbelts in their cars, or English students write a persuasive essay for their school newspaper, their learning is more meaningful than it would be if they studied the topic in the abstract (van Merriënboer et al., 2003). Jenny created a real-world problem with the beam balances, as did the teachers in Table 6.1. For instance, the first teacher didn't teach decimals and percentages in the abstract; she used different-sized soft-drink containers and their cost to show that understanding decimals and percents not only makes sense in the real world but is also useful for saving money. The teachers in each of the other examples also used realistic examples to link abstract ideas to students' experiences.

Promote High Levels of Interaction

Although essential, high-quality examples won't—by themselves—necessarily produce learning (Moreno & Duran, 2004). Students sometimes misinterpret the examples or may remain cognitively passive, as Suzanne did during Jenny's lesson. If they do, they're likely to retain their misconceptions.

This is why interaction with your students is so important. As you saw earlier, *social interaction facilitates learning* is a principle of cognitive learning theory, and it's vital in the knowledge construction process. Social interaction allows you to check your students' interpretations of your examples, and it promotes conceptual change. It also answers the question we asked earlier in the chapter: "But, since you won't have an interviewer in your classroom, how can you help your students become cognitively active during your learning activities?" The answer is: You promote high levels of interaction.

Your role in this process is crucial. You guide the interaction in whole-group lessons, and you monitor small-group activities to be sure students focus on understanding, instead of simply getting the right answer. You also design assessments that measure students' understanding and hold them accountable for meeting your learning objectives (Blatchford et al., 2006; Webb et al., 2002).

Treat Verbal Explanations Skeptically

Earlier, we introduced the idea, "Wisdom can't be told," and you saw it illustrated in Jenny's lesson. Suzanne heard three clear and accurate explanations for the beam balance problem—Molly's, Mavrin's, and Jenny's—yet at the beginning of the interview, she still believed that the number of tiles was the only factor determining whether the beam would balance. Verbal explanations didn't work, and this is often the case in classrooms. Remember, your students aren't video recorders, storing information in the form in which it's presented. Rather, they either reconstruct the information until it makes sense to them and store it that way or attempt to memorize enough to succeed on tests and then quickly forget it. In spite of this fact, many teachers continue to believe that the best way to help students learn is to lecture to them (Alparsian et al., 2004; Yip, 2004).

We're not saying that you shouldn't explain topics to students, and we're not saying that learners can't construct knowledge from explanations. Rather, we're emphasizing, *don't conclude that your students fully understand an idea because you explained it to them.* Explanations need to be combined with examples and a great deal of social interaction to ensure that learning occurs. This brings us to the essential role of assessment in promoting learning.

Promote Learning with Assessment

If our students behaved like video recorders, teaching and learning would be quite simple. We could merely explain a topic accurately, and learners would record the information in that form. Straightforward, uncomplicated. We know they don't, however. Instead, they construct and store it in a form that makes sense to them, and because they do, individuals' understanding of the topics they study will vary. For example, before the interview following Jenny's lesson, Molly and Drexel understood the principle for making beams balance, but Suzanne and Tad did not, and almost certainly their classmates' understanding also varied.

Perhaps more importantly, how likely is it that Jenny knew this? The answer is, not likely. She had 25 students in her class, so she didn't have the luxury of interacting with each of the groups as did the interviewer with Molly, Suzanne, Tad, and Drexel. She knew that Mavrin understood the principle for making beams balance (the weight times the distance on one side of the fulcrum equals the weight times the distance on the other side), because she saw him explain it at the board, and she picked up snippets of discussion as she moved from group to group. Beyond that, she didn't know about individual students' understanding of the content.

Even when we promote high levels of interaction, we can't involve all students all the time, so we need a mechanism to determine the extent to which our students are learning and their knowledge constructions are valid. This leads us to the role of **assessment,** the process of gathering information and making decisions about students' learning progress. We tend to think of assessment as giving tests and assigning grades, but it is much more than that. It is an essential part of the entire teaching–learning process. "Testing has such a bad connotation; people think of standardized testing or teaching to the test. Maybe we need to call it something else, but this is one of the most powerful learning tools we have" (Carey, 2010, para. 28).

Teachers use two kinds of assessments to gauge learning progress. **Informal assessment,** gathering incidental information during learning activities, allows you to assess learning *while* it is occurring. When Jenny watched Mavrin at the board, for example, and when she listened to students' discussions as she circulated around the room, she was involved in informal assessment. It's important because it allows you to gather information and make decisions during learning activities. For example, if, based on answers to your questions, your students seem to understand a topic, you move on. If they don't, you can provide additional examples or continue the discussion until they are ready to move forward (Hattie & Timperly, 2007; Shute, 2008). Informal assessment helps you make these decisions.

Informal assessment is important but incomplete and potentially misleading. For instance, hearing Mavrin explain the principle, and explaining it herself, could lead Jenny to conclude that all her students understood it. In fact, her informal assessments provided little information about the rest of her students' understanding, as we saw with Suzanne and Tad.

Formal assessment, the process of systematically gathering information about learning from all students, addresses these problems. Jenny, realizing that it was impossible for her to informally assess all her students' understanding, created a formal assessment that she gave the day after the lesson.

The assessment, with Tad's responses, is shown in Figure 6.3. Tad's response suggests that his understanding of the topic is still "a work in progress." He was able to determine that the beam would balance in the first problem, but was unable to draw or write a solution to the second. His experience is not unique; Jenny's assessment revealed that several other students are also still uncertain about solving similar problems. The information she gathered through her formal assessment allowed her to adapt her instruction, which resulted in deeper understanding for all her students.

Assessment. The process of gathering information and making decisions about students' learning progress.

Informal assessment. The process of gathering incidental information during learning activities.

Formal assessment. The process of systematically gathering information about learning from all students.

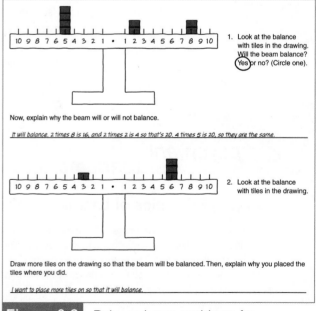

Figure 6.3 Balance beam problems for assessment

Technology, Learning, and Development: Capitalizing on Technology to Promote Knowledge Construction

Promoting knowledge construction is sophisticated and demanding for several reasons; one of the most important is the fact that many of the topics we teach are difficult to represent, and this difficulty is what makes them hard to learn. In these cases technology provides an effective alternative (Roblyer & Doering, 2010). We might simply drop heavy and light objects, for example, to demonstrate that all objects fall at the same rate, regardless of weight, but it's virtually impossible to illustrate the actual acceleration of a falling object. Here, technology can be a powerful tool. For example, Figure 6.4 illustrates the position of a falling ball at uniform time intervals. We see that the distance between the images becomes greater and greater, indicating that the ball is falling faster and faster. This is an example of acceleration that is impossible to represent without the use of technology.

You can also use computer software to capitalize on the power of simulations. For instance, if you're a science teacher, you might use software to simulate a frog dissection rather than using an actual frog. Although the simulation doesn't allow students the hands-on experience of working with a real frog, it's less expensive because it can be used over and over; it's more flexible because the frog can be "reassembled"; and it avoids sacrificing a frog for science (Roblyer & Doering, 2010). As the quality of software improves, representations will become more sophisticated and the simulations will be more interactive, further increasing learner motivation and understanding.

The Internet is also a rich source of examples, all of which can be downloaded and used to represent topics that are hard to illustrate in other ways. For instance, if you want to illustrate the difference between *young mountains* and *mature mountains*, you can simply Google "Rocky Mountains" and "Appalachian Mountains," and beautiful colored pictures of each immediately appear. It requires little effort, and you have examples ready to go. The same applies to a myriad of other topics.

As you saw earlier, assessment should be an integral part of the teaching–learning process, and technology can be a valuable tool for creating, storing, and revising assessment items. For instance, Jenny constructed the pictures she used in the assessment you saw in Figure 6.3, stored them in her computer, and simply pulled them up when she created her assessment. This saved her the time of re-creating them the next time she wanted to prepare her assessment, and it allowed her to efficiently revise the assessment if necessary.

In the process of knowledge construction, technology can never replace you and your teaching expertise. It can, however, be a valuable tool for helping you guide your students' efforts to construct valid knowledge.

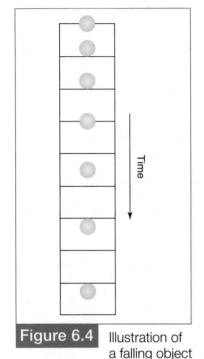

Figure 6.4 Illustration of a falling object

Time

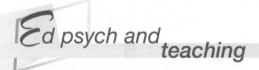

Applying Principles of Learning in Your Classroom

Grounding instruction in the principles of learning, and particularly guiding the social construction of knowledge, can increase learning for all your students. The suggestions for classroom practice that you first saw in Figure 6.2, earlier in the chapter, provide guidelines that can help you apply these principles in your instruction:

1. Provide experiences with high-quality examples.
2. Connect content to the real world.
3. Promote high levels of interaction.
4. Treat verbal explanations skeptically.
5. Promote learning with assessment.

Now, let's examine the extent to which Jenny Newhall applied the guidelines in her lesson.

As with many aspects of instruction, the process isn't as simple as it appears on the surface.

For instance, Jenny didn't quite apply the first. As you saw earlier in the chapter, *a high-quality example is one that includes all the information students need to understand the topic.* The balances and problem were the examples Jenny used, but the balances with the tile arrangement that she initially presented didn't contain all the information the students needed to understand the principle for making beams balance. So, to solve the problem, the students needed prior knowledge that not all of them, such as Suzanne and Tad, possessed. It wasn't until the students suggested putting three tiles on the 10-point on the right side of the fulcrum that the example became "high quality", because it then contained all the information the students needed.

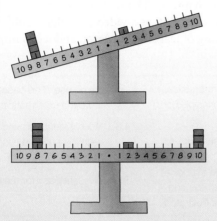

The balances provided a real-world experience, so Jenny applied the second guideline well. But, the experience needed to be supplemented with active instruction to help students understand the principle for making beams balance. This is typical in classrooms; high-quality examples are a solid stating point, but they virtually always need to be supported by teacher guidance.

The learning principle *social interaction facilitates learning,* social constructivism, and particularly cognitive apprenticeships all provide the framework for the third and fourth guidelines. Ideally, the interaction during lessons would be similar to what we saw in the interview that followed Jenny's lesson. In the real world, however, applying them is challenging. The interviewer was working with only four students, so each could describe his or her thinking. This level of interaction is virtually impossible in a whole-group setting, so students often remain cognitively passive. Even in a small group, students can remain passive, as Suzanne did until she was directly involved in the interview.

This helps us understand why formal assessment needs to be an integral part of our teaching. In classrooms with 25 or more students, it's impossible to informally assess the thinking of all learners. Formal assessment is the only way you can determine if each student's constructions are valid. The assessment Jenny gave the day after her lesson was essential and effectively applied the fifth guideline.

Guiding students as they attempt to construct valid knowledge is sophisticated and demanding instruction, but you can learn to do it. The combination of high-quality examples, social interaction, and carefully designed assessments can maximize learning for all your students.

Evaluating Constructivist Instruction

Principles of cognitive learning theory suggest that people construct knowledge and that they do so in attempts to make sense of their experiences. *Constructivism,* the idea that learners construct—rather than record—their knowledge, makes an important contribution to our understanding of learning because it reminds us of how important prior knowledge and social interaction are in the learning process. It also helps us understand why monitoring student thinking is essential (Carver, 2006). Because we know that students want their experiences to make sense, and they construct their own knowledge, we better understand why they don't grasp an idea that's been discussed several times, why they seem to ignore a point that's been emphasized, and why they retain misconceptions.

Constructivism is often misinterpreted, however. For example, rather than focusing on *learning,* which is appropriate, the term *constructivism* is sometimes used to describe teaching, or even educational philosophy, as in *constructivist instruction* or *constructivist philosophy,* which includes the belief that teachers should never tell students anything directly, but rather they should discover it for themselves (Bransford et al., 2000). It also implies that teaching methods, such as small-group discussions, cooperative learning, pure discovery, and hands-on activities are "constructivist," whereas other methods, such as whole-class discussions, are not. This is a misconception. Large-group instruction, effectively done, can promote knowledge construction, and cooperative learning, improperly done, may not.

In addition, confusion sometimes results from a failure to distinguish between students' being *behaviorally* active and being *cognitively* active (Mayer, 2004), and this distinction was illustrated in Jenny's lesson. Jenny used small-group work in her lesson, an approach considered to be "constructivist," but Suzanne remained cognitively passive until the interview after the lesson.

We caution you to treat verbal explanations skeptically, not because it's impossible for students to construct knowledge from an explanation, but rather because explanations are more likely to put students in *cognitively passive* roles than when they're involved in social interaction.

Constructivism, as a description of learning, is also incomplete. It doesn't, for example, take into account the way our human memory systems work, the important role of practice in developing skills, the influence of feedback on learning, and the influence of emotions on motivation and learning. These are topics better explained with other theories (which we examine in later chapters). The idea that learners construct their own knowledge instead of passively recording it, as a video recorder would do, marks an important advance in our understanding of learning, however, and it has important implications for our teaching.

check your understanding

4.1 Describe the suggestions for classroom practice, and explain how each is grounded in principles of cognitive learning theory.

4.2 A language arts teacher wants his students to understand the rules for forming possessive nouns and writes a passage about the school in which he illustrates the rules. Which of the suggestions for classroom practice is best illustrated by his use of his passage about the school to illustrate the grammatical rules?

4.3 Assessments grounded in constructivist views of learning have an essential characteristic. What is this characteristic? Explain.

To receive feedback for these questions, go to Appendix A.

Classroom connections

Helping Students Construct Valid Knowledge

1. Students construct their own knowledge, and the knowledge they construct depends on what they already know. To accommodate differences in prior knowledge, provide a variety of examples and other representations of the content you want students to understand.

   - **Elementary:** A third-grade teacher in a unit on chemical and physical change has students melt ice, crumple paper, dissolve sugar, and break toothpicks to illustrate physical change. She then has them burn paper, pour vinegar into baking soda, and chew soda crackers to illustrate chemical change.

   - **Middle School:** An English teacher presents the following excerpts to illustrate *internal conflict:*

     > Kelly didn't know what to do. She was looking forward to the class trip, but if she went, she wouldn't be able to take the scholarship-qualifying test.
     >
     > Calvin was caught in a dilemma. He saw Jason take Olonzo's calculator but knew that if he told Mrs. Stevens what he saw, Jason would realize that it was he who reported the theft.

   - **High School:** While teaching about the Great Depression, a social studies teacher has students read excerpts from *The Grapes of Wrath,* shows a video of people standing in bread lines, shares statistics on the rash of suicides after the stock market crash, and discusses how a current recession is similar to and different from the Great Depression.

2. Knowledge construction is most effective when learners have real-world experiences. Develop learning activities around realistic problems.

   - **Elementary:** In a lesson relating geography and the way we live, a third-grade teacher has students describe the way they dress for their favorite forms of recreation. She also asks students who have moved from other parts of the country to do the same for their previous locations. She then guides them as they construct an understanding of the effect of geography on lifestyle.

   - **Middle School:** In a unit on percent increase and decrease, a math teacher has students look for examples of marked-down clothes while shopping. He also brings in newspaper ads. The class discusses the examples and calculates the amount saved in each case.

   - **High School:** To help her students understand the importance of persuasive writing, an English teacher brings in three examples of "Letters to the Editor" on the same topic. Students discuss the letters, determine which is most effective, and with the teacher's guidance, identify the characteristics of effective persuasive writing.

3. Social constructivist views of learning emphasize the role of social interaction in the process of knowledge construction. Promote high levels of quality interaction in your classroom, and avoid relying on explanations to promote learning.

   - **Elementary:** A fourth-grade teacher wants his students to understand the concept of *scale* on a map. He places them in groups and has them create a map of their desktops. Then he has them draw a map of their room, and finally, they go outside and draw a map of their playground. When finished, he guides a class discussion to help them understand how the maps are similar and different.

■ **Middle School:** A sixth-grade science teacher has his students take 8 identical wooden cubes and make one stack of 5 and another stack of 3. He has them discuss the mass, volume, and densities of the two stacks. Then, with questioning, he guides them

to conclude that the mass and volume of the stack of 5 are greater than the mass and volume of the stack of 3 but that the densities of the two stacks are equal.

■ **High School:** An algebra teacher "walks" students through the solutions to problems by calling on individuals to provide specific information about each step and explain why the step is necessary. When students encounter difficulties, the teacher asks additional questions to help them understand the step.

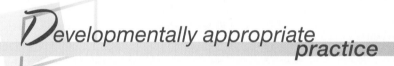

Developmentally appropriate practice

Principles of Learning with Students at Different Ages

Although the principles of cognitive learning theory apply to learners of all ages, a number of developmental differences exist. The following sections outline suggestions for responding to these differences.

Working with Students in Early Childhood Programs and Elementary Schools

Each of the principles of cognitive learning theory applies to working with young students, just as they do with learners of all ages. For example, like all learners, young students want their experiences to make sense, and they also construct knowledge. However, they lack many of the experiences that older students have acquired, so providing concrete learning experiences is crucial in working with early childhood and elementary students.

Young children tend to *center* on the most perceptually obvious aspects of objects and events, and tend to be quite literal in their thinking, which can lead to the construction of many misconceptions. For instance, they tend to equate size with age, believing someone who is bigger is older, and, in social studies they may think that lines of latitude and longitude actually exist on the earth.

As a result, explanations presented in the abstract are almost useless with elementary students, and the notion "Wisdom can't be told," applies even more strongly than it does with older students. When working with young children, concrete, high-quality examples are even more important than with older learners. In addition, interactive instruction allows teachers both to investigate the ideas students currently hold and to assist them as they construct new ones.

Using language to describe their world and communicate with each other not only develops language skills but also promotes meaningful learning. Language is crucial for later learning, and the more opportunities young children have to practice and use language, the better.

Young children also need to learn to accept responsibility for their learning and how to interact positively with their peers. This suggests learning tasks in which young students can interact with their peers in challenging activities. These experiences provide the foundation for later learning.

Working with Students in Middle Schools

Middle school students overcome much of the tendency to interpret events literally, but often, in the process of knowledge construction, they fail to recognize relationships among objects and events. For instance, instead of recognizing that rectangles and squares are subsets of parallelograms, they often classify the figures into different categories.

Middle school students are also developing interaction skills, such as perspective taking and social problem solving. This allows you to use cooperative learning and other small-group strategies to integrate social interaction into your instruction. Cognitive apprenticeships, in which students work with other students in small groups, can provide opportunities for students to think and talk about new ideas. Encourage students to *verbalize* their developing understanding during learning activities to maximize learning. Experts caution, however, that you should carefully structure and monitor small-group activities to ensure that they're cognitively active and remain on task (Ding, Li, Piccolo, & Kulm, 2007).

Working with Students in High Schools

High school students' experiences provide them with a rich store of prior knowledge that increases the validity of their knowledge constructions. However, they continue to construct a variety of misconceptions, particularly when working with symbols and abstract ideas. For instance, in simplifying the expression $2 + 5 \times 3 - 6$, they often get 15 ($2 + 5 = 7$; $7 \times 3 = 21$; $21 - 6 = 15$) instead of the correct answer: 11 ($5 \times 3 = 15$; $15 + 2 = 17$; $17 - 6 = 11$).

As students move to more advanced classes in high school, such as physics, chemistry, and calculus, high levels of interaction become even more important. And, it is in these classes that teachers tend to act more like college instructors, where lecture is the most common instructional strategy. High school teachers sometimes even resist the idea of interaction, believing that lectures are efficient and that students will be subject to lectures in college, so they might as well "get used to it." This is neither valid nor wise. The most effective way to prepare students for advanced studies is to help them acquire the background knowledge needed to understand more abstract and sophisticated topics. And applying the principles of learning—with particular emphasis on high levels of interaction—is the most effective way to help students acquire this background knowledge.

High school students can also participate in and benefit from classroom discussions, which provide opportunities to refine their thinking based on the ideas of others (Hadjioannou, 2007). As with all forms of instruction, high school teachers need to structure and monitor discussions closely to ensure that they are aligned with learning goals.

Summary

1. Describe principles of cognitive learning theory, and identify applications of the principles in classrooms and in our personal lives.
   - *Learning and development depend on experience* is a basic principle of cognitive learning theory. Teachers apply this principle when they provide experiences for their students.
   - *People want their experiences to make sense.* This principle is illustrated in how commonly statements such as "That makes sense" or "That doesn't make any sense" are used both in and outside of school.
   - *To make sense of their experiences, learners construct knowledge.* This explains why we see people generate original ideas, ideas they haven't gotten from any outside source.
   - *Knowledge that learners construct depends on what they already know.* Knowledge isn't constructed in a vacuum. Effective teachers link new knowledge to information learners already possess.
   - *Social interaction facilitates learning.* We are social beings, and social interaction contributes to learning. Effective teachers use questioning and small-group work to encourage students to actively engage with content.

2. Describe differences between cognitive and social constructivism, and analyze examples of each.
   - Cognitive constructivism focuses on individual construction of knowledge. Cognitive constructivists believe that when an experience disrupts an individual's equilibrium, she reconstructs understanding to reestablish equilibrium.
   - Social constructivism emphasizes that individuals first construct knowledge in a social environment and then appropriate it. Knowledge grows directly out of the social interaction.
   - Emphasis on sociocultural theory, communities of learners, cognitive apprenticeships, and situated cognition are all applications of social constructivism to instruction.

3. Explain *misconceptions*, how they occur, and how they can be eliminated.
   - Misconceptions are beliefs that are inconsistent with evidence or commonly accepted explanations.
   - Prior experiences, appearances that lead people to infer cause–effect relationships between two objects or events because they occur together, social forces, and even the misuse of language all can contribute to misconceptions.
   - Changing misconceptions is difficult because the change disrupts individuals' equilibrium, the misconceptions are often consistent with everyday experiences, and individuals don't recognize inconsistencies between new information and their existing beliefs.
   - In order for conceptual change to occur, existing conceptions must become dissatisfying, an alternative conception must be understandable, and the alternative must be useful in the real world.

4. Describe suggestions for classroom practice, and explain how each is grounded in principles of cognitive learning theory.
   - Instruction based on principles of cognitive learning theory emphasizes high-quality examples and other representations of content, student interaction, and connecting content to the real world.
   - Teachers who ground their instruction in the principles of cognitive learning theory realize that lecturing and explaining often fail to promote deep understanding in learners.
   - Basing instruction on principles of cognitive learning theory requires teachers to use ongoing assessment as an integral part of the teaching–learning process.

Understanding Principles of Cognitive Learning Theory: Preparing for Your Licensure Exam

You will be required to take a licensure exam before you go into your own classroom. This exam will include information related to principles of cognitive learning theory, and we include the following exercises to help you practice for the exam in your state. This book and these exercises will be a resource for you as you prepare for the exam.

At the beginning of the chapter, you saw how Jenny Newhall designed and conducted a lesson to help her students construct knowledge about beam balances. In the following case, Scott Sowell, a middle school science teacher, wants his students to understand how to design experiments and control variables.

To do so, he has his students examine factors that influence the frequency of a simple pendulum. Read the case study, and answer the questions that follow.

Scott's students are struggling with the process of controlling variables, even though he has carefully explained the process and has done a whole-class experiment with plants. He decides to give them additional experience with controlling variables with simple pendulums in small groups.

Scott begins by demonstrating a simple pendulum with paper clips attached to a piece of string. He explains that *frequency* means the number of swings in a certain time period and asks students what factors they think will influence the frequency. After some discussion, they suggest length, weight, and angle of release as possible hypotheses. (In reality, only the length of the pendulum determines its frequency.)

"Okay, your job as a group is to design your own experiments," Scott continues. "Think of a way to test how each affects the frequency. Use the equipment at your desk to design and carry out the experiment."

One group of four (Marina, Paige, Wensley, and Jonathan) ties a string to a ring stand and measures its length, as shown:

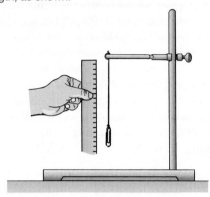

"Forty-nine centimeters," Wensley notes, measuring the length of the string.

The group agrees to use 15 seconds and then do their first test with the 49-centimeter length and one paper clip as weight. Marina counts 21 swings.

A few minutes later, Scott again walks by the group, examines their results, and says, "So you've done one test so far. . . . What are you going to do next? . . . I'm going to come back after your next test and look at it." He then moves to another group.

The group conducts their second test by shortening the string and adding a second paper clip (which violates the principle of altering only one variable at a time).

"Mr. Sowell, we found out that the shorter it is and the heavier it is, the faster it goes," Marina reports to Scott when he returns to the group.

Scott then asks which of the two variables was responsible for the change in the frequency.

Wensley and Jonathan say simultaneously, "They both changed."

"Think about that. You need to come up with a conclusion about length, about weight, and about angle—how each of them influences the frequency of your pendulum," Scott reminds them as he moves from group to group.

As the group investigates the three variables—length, weight, and angle of release—they continue to change two of these at the same time, confounding their results.

"What did you find out?" Scott asks as he returns to check on their progress.

Marina begins, "Okay, Mr. Sowell, we figured out that the shorter it is, the faster the frequency is, . . . and the heavier it is . . . the faster the frequency is."

Scott asks the students to explain their findings about the height.

"In the first one, the height (angle of release) was 56 and the weight was 3, and it came out to 21, and in the second one, the height was higher and the weight was lower, so it was still 21," Marina says, again concluding that the change in weight explains why the frequency was the same even though the angle of release was different.

"Let's do it out loud before you write it. . . . Tell me about length," Scott directs.

"The longer the string is, the slower the frequency is," Wensley says.

"What about weight?" Scott probes.

"The heavier it is, the faster it goes," Marina adds.

"I want to look at these again. . . . Write those down for me."

Scott gives the students a few minutes to write their conclusions, and he then walks to the front of the room and rings a bell to call the class together.

"When I call your group, I want the speaker for your group to report your findings to the class," he says to the class as a whole.

One by one, the spokesperson for each group reports their findings at the front of the room. In general, the groups conclude (erroneously) that each variable—length, weight, and angle—affect the frequency.

In response to this misconception, Scott tries a whole-class demonstration.

"Let's take a look at something here," Scott says, placing a ring stand onto his demonstration table. He attaches a paper clip to the pendulum, puts it in motion, and asks a student to count the swings. He adds a second paper clip and again has the students count, to demonstrate that weight doesn't affect the frequency. He has a student state this conclusion, and he writes it on the board. Then he does a second demonstration to show that angle also has no effect on the frequency and again asks a student to make a conclusion so Scott can write it on the board.

After the demonstrations, he says, "Now I want someone to make a conclusion about what we learned about designing experiments and how we use our variables when we design experiments. . . . Who wants to talk about that? . . . Wensley? Tell me what we learned about how to set up an experiment. What did we learn from this?"

"Each time you do a different part of the experiment, only change one of the variables," Wensley explains.

"Why is that?"

"You're only checking one thing at a time. If you do two, there might be an error in the experiment."

"Okay, if you change more than one thing at one time, why would it be difficult?"

"Because, . . . if you change two different things, you can't tell which one caused the change," Wensley continues.

"Good thinking, Wensley. So, for example, if you were testing weight and length, your group had to

finally decide that we can't change weight at the same time as we change length, because when we test it . . ."

"You couldn't compare them," Marina responds.

"Right, you couldn't compare them. You couldn't tell which one was causing it, could you? . . . It might go faster, but all of a sudden you'd say, well, is it the weight or is it the length?"

Running out of time, Scott then asks if there are any questions, and hearing none, he dismisses the class.

Questions for Case Analysis

In answering these questions, use information from this chapter, and link your responses to specific information in the case study above.

1. Describe the extent to which Scott applied the principles of cognitive learning theory in his lesson.

2. Scott's students had some misconceptions about controlling variables. They failed to keep length constant,

for example, as they changed the weight. How effectively did Scott teach for conceptual change in responding to this misconception? Explain.

For feedback on these responses, go to Appendix B.

Your licensure exam will also include multiple-choice questions similar to those your instructor has given you on your quizzes and tests for this course.

Important Concepts

appropriating understanding (p. 190)

assessment (p. 201)

cognitive apprenticeship (p. 192)

cognitive constructivism (p. 188)

cognitive learning theories (p. 182)

community of learners (p. 191)

formal assessment (p. 201)

high-quality examples (p. 198)

informal assessment (p. 201)

meaningfulness (p. 183)

misconception (p. 194)

principles (p. 182)

situated cognition (p. 192)

social constructivism (p. 190)

sociocultural theory (p. 191)

transfer (p. 193)

Go to the Topics: Knowledge Construction and Planning and Instruction in the MyEducationLab (www.myeducationlab.com) for *Educational Psychology: Windows on Classrooms,* where you can:

- Find learning outcomes for Knowledge Construction and Planning and Instruction along with the national standards that connect to these outcomes.
- Complete Assignments and Activities that can help you more deeply understand the chapter content.
- Apply and practice your understanding of the core teaching skills identified in the chapter with the Building Teaching Skills and Dispositions learning units.
- Examine challenging situations and cases presented in the IRIS Center Resources.
- Access video clips of CCSSO National Teachers of the Year award winners responding to the question, "Why Do I Teach?" in the Teacher Talk section.
- See video examples included within the Study Plan that provide concrete and real-world illustrations of the topics presented in the chapter.
- Check your comprehension of the content covered in the chapter with the Study Plan. Here you will be able to take a chapter quiz, receive feedback on your answers, and then access Review, Practice, and Enrichment activities to enhance your understanding of chapter content.

MyEducationLab

chapter

7

Cognitive
Learning and
Human Memory

chapteroutline

learningoutcomes

After you've completed your study of this chapter, you should be able to:

chapteroutline	learningoutcomes
Human Memory A Model of Human Memory	**1.** Identify the basic components of human memory.
Memory Stores Sensory Memory Working Memory Long-Term Memory Developmental Differences in the Memory Stores The Brain and Human Memory	**2.** Use the memory stores in the human memory model to explain events in classrooms and the everyday world.
Cognitive Processes Attention Technology, Learning, and Development: The Influence of Technology on Attention Perception Encoding and Encoding Strategies Forgetting Developmental Differences in Cognitive Processes	**3.** Describe the cognitive processes in the human memory model, and explain applications in classroom activities.
Metacognition: Knowledge and Control of Cognitive Processes Developmental Differences in Metacognition Unconscious Processing in Human Memory Evaluating the Human Memory Model	**4.** Define *metacognition*, and explain how it influences classroom learning.

classroomapplications

The following features help you apply the content of this chapter in your teaching.

Ed Psych and Teaching:
Applying the Human Memory Model in Your Teaching

Classroom Connections:
Helping Students Store Information Efficiently
Helping Students Capitalize on Cognitive Processes to Increase Their Learning
Promoting Metacognition in Students

Developmentally Appropriate Practice:
The Memory Model with Learners at Different Ages

Exploring Diversity:
The Impact of Diversity on Cognition

As we go through our daily lives, we're inundated by information in a variety of forms—simple sensory stimuli, such as cars passing on the street, people talking, or a dog barking, as well as more organized information, such as e-mails or the morning paper. We pay careful attention to some, but we don't even notice others, such as the whisper of an air conditioner. This chapter focuses on the way we respond to this information, make sense of it, and store and remember it for further use.

Learners' capabilities for handling the enormous amount of information they encounter has important implications for learning and teaching. In the following case study,

David Shelton, a middle school science teacher, is trying to help his students understand our solar system. It begins with David presenting information about the solar system and then focuses on the thinking of three of his students—Juan, Randy, and Tanya. As you read the case study, notice the differences in how Juan attends to and interprets the information compared to Randy and Tanya.

David is beginning a unit on the solar system with his students and has prepared the visuals you see here. He introduces the unit on Monday, displays the visuals on the document camera, notes that they relate to one theory of how the solar system was formed, and asks students for their interpretations of what they see. After some discussion and explanation, David assigns groups to use books and the Internet to gather information about each planet. The students spend the rest of Monday and all period Tuesday collecting and putting information into a matrix (see Table 7.3, p. 232).

On Wednesday, David reviews the information from Monday and Tuesday and poses several questions. The first is, "Why is Pluto's orbital plane different from the planes of the planets?"

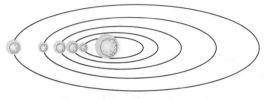

The sun threw off hot spheres of gas which eventually became planets.

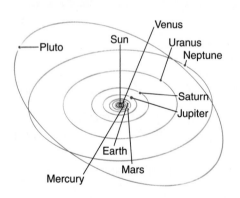

The orbital planes of the planets and Pluto.

"When I try to answer questions like these," David continues, "I first look for a relationship in the parts of the question, like what we know about Pluto compared to the planets? . . . Be sure you write and explain each of your answers."

"I know the answer to the first question," Juan comments to Randy and Tanya in one group as the students go to work. "Pluto was once considered part of the solar system, but it isn't any more. . . . Actually, it's now called a dwarf planet."

"What do you mean?" Randy wonders.

"I was watching *Nova* with my mom, and they said that Pluto was an asteroid, or some other body floating around, and the sun kind of grabbed it. . . . See," he continues, pointing to the visual showing the orbital planes of the planets.

"What's that got to do with it?" Randy asks, still uncertain.

"Look. . . . See how Pluto is up above the rest of them," Juan says, referring to Pluto's orbit.

"Gee, I didn't even notice that," Randy shrugs.

"Oh, I get it, now! . . . Pluto isn't level with the rest of them," Tanya jumps in. "I got kinda lost when Mr. Shelton was explaining all that on Monday, but now it makes sense. . . . And look there," she says, pointing to the chart. "See how small Pluto is? It's the littlest, so it would be easy to capture."

"And it's the last one," Randy adds, beginning to warm to the task. "I better write some of this stuff down, or I'll never remember it."

Now, consider these questions related to the students' thinking.

1. Why was Juan able to make connections in the different items of information that Randy and Tanya were initially unable to make?
2. Why did Tanya get "kinda lost when Mr. Shelton was explaining all that on Monday?"
3. What impact will Randy's decision to "write some of this stuff down" have on his learning?

An understanding of our human memory system helps answer these questions, and in this chapter we'll see how David applies this understanding in his teaching.

Human Memory

People throughout history have been fascinated by memory. We lament our forgetfulness, and comments such as, "Oh yes, I remember that," or "It's on the tip of my tongue," are common. We rack our brains to remember isolated facts, such as William Faulkner's most famous novel (perhaps *The Sound and the Fury*) or the capital of Columbia (Bogotá), and we also solve problems and identify relationships. These examples are related to human memory, the topic of this chapter.

Cognitive learning theories, theories that explain learning in terms of people's thinking and the processes involved in acquiring, organizing, and using knowledge, include the study of human memory (Sawyer, 2006; Schunk, 2008). We store information in our memories, and retrieve and use it to respond to, and make decisions about, new information. For example, when followed too closely by another car, we may speed up or shift lanes, because we know that it takes a certain distance to stop, and the danger of a rear-end collision exists. Knowledge about stopping distance is stored in our memories, and we use it to respond when we drive.

We know that learning and development depend on experience, and we also know that learners construct—rather than record—their knowledge. These ideas raise questions about learning and memory. For example, how do learners acquire the experiences they use to construct their knowledge, and how is prior knowledge combined with new experiences? Also, where is knowledge constructed and how is it stored? The answers to these questions relate to the model of human memory and are the focus of the rest of this chapter. Let's look at this model.

> **Cognitive learning theories.**
> Theories that explain learning in terms of people's thinking and the processes involved in acquiring, organizing, and using knowledge.

A Model of Human Memory

Cognitive learning theorists use a *model* of human memory similar to the one you see in Figure 7.1, which was initially proposed by Atkinson and Shiffrin (1968). Originally described as a framework for **information-processing theory**—a theory that describes how information enters our memory system, is organized, and finally stored—this model has generated a great deal of research and has undergone considerable refinement.

What exactly do we mean by the term *model?* For example, we have model cars and airplanes, models who display clothing on runways and pose for photographers or artists,

> **Information-processing theory.**
> A theory that describes how information enters our memory system, is organized, and finally stored.

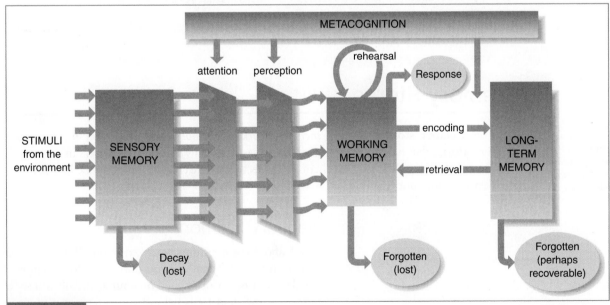

Figure 7.1 A model of human memory

Model. A representation that helps us visualize what we can't observe directly.

and parents and teachers are encouraged to be good "role models." Each is a definition of the term, but **model,** as we use it here, is a representation that helps us visualize what we can't observe directly. It's used in the same way the model of the atom is used in science courses you've taken. Just as we can't directly observe the nucleus or electrons in an atom, we can't look inside our heads to see *working memory* or *encoding,* for example. So, we create a model to help us visualize these components.

The human memory model is composed of three major components:

- *Memory stores*—Sensory memory, working memory, and long-term memory. These are repositories that hold information, in some cases very briefly and in others almost permanently.
- *Cognitive processes*—Attention, perception, rehearsal, encoding and retrieval. These mental processes move information from one memory store to another.
- *Metacognition*—The cognitive mechanism we have for monitoring and regulating both the storage of information and how the information is moved from one store to another.

The model also provides us with additional information. For instance, we see that working memory is smaller than either sensory memory or long-term memory. This reminds us that its capacity is smaller than the other two stores. Also, in Figure 7.1 you see fewer arrows to the right of attention than to its left. This tells us that we don't attend to all the stimuli we encounter; attention is a screen, and realizing that it's a screen helps us understand why we don't notice many of the stimuli we encounter until someone or something reminds us of them.

We will frequently refer back to the model throughout the chapter, and you will see why its components are represented the way they are. As you see in Figure 7.1, the memory stores, cognitive processes, and metacognition are integrated, but we examine them separately for the sake of clarity, beginning in the next section with the memory stores.

---

check your understanding

1.1 Identify the basic components of the human memory model.

1.2 Look again at the memory model in Figure 7.1. You see a curved arrow with the term *response,* which comes out of working memory. Explain what you think this arrow and term are intended to represent.

1.3 Look again at the memory model in Figure 7.1. You see *metacognition* above the model, with arrows pointing down to the cognitive processes. What do you think this information is intended to represent?

To receive feedback for these questions, go to Appendix A.

 **emory Stores**

Memory stores. Sensory memory, working memory, and long-term memory repositories that hold information, both in a raw state and in organized, meaningful form.

The **memory stores**—*sensory memory, working memory,* and *long-term memory*—are repositories that hold information, in some cases in a raw state, and in others in organized, meaningful form. We examine them in this section of the chapter and describe implications they have for your teaching.

Ed Psych and You

Hold your finger in front of you, and rapidly wiggle it. What do you notice? Also, press hard on your arm with your finger, and then release it. What do you feel?

Sensory Memory

Think about the questions we asked in our "Ed Psych and You" feature here. What did you notice and feel when you wiggled your finger or pressed on your arm? Did you see a faint "shadow" that trails behind your finger as it moved? And, did the sensation of pressure remain for an instant after you stopped pressing on your arm? These experiences are related to your **sensory memory,** the information store that briefly holds incoming stimuli from the environment until they can be processed (Neisser, 1967). (Sensory memory is sometimes called the *sensory register* [Schunk, 2008]). The shadow is the image of your finger that has been briefly stored in your visual sensory memory, and your tactile sensory memory stored the pressure of your finger for an instant. Likewise, when you hear someone say, "That's an oxymoron," you retain "Ox see moron" in your auditory sensory memory, even if it has no meaning for you.

Learning and development depend on experience is a principle of cognitive learning theory, and we acquire experiences through our sensory memories. Sensory memory is nearly unlimited in capacity, but if processing doesn't begin almost immediately, the memory trace quickly fades away. Sensory memory retains information for about 1 second for vision and 2 to 4 seconds for hearing (Pashler & Carrier, 1996).

Sensory memory is important because it's the beginning point for further processing. In reading, for instance, it would be impossible to get meaning from a sentence if the words at the beginning were lost from our visual sensory memories before we got to the end. Sensory memory holds the information until we attach meaning to it and transfer it to working memory, the next store.

Sensory memory. The memory store that briefly holds incoming stimuli from the environment until they can be processed.

Working Memory

That we construct knowledge in order to make sense of our experiences is also a principle of cognitive learning theory, and this is where **working memory** comes into play. It is the conscious component of our memory system, it's where our thinking occurs, and it's where we try to make sense of our experiences by linking them to our existing understanding (Paas, Renkl, & Sweller, 2004). It's the workbench of our memory system. We aren't aware of the contents of either sensory memory or long-term memory until they're pulled into working memory for processing.

Working memory. The memory store that holds information as we consciously process and try to make sense of it.

A Model of Working Memory

Figure 7.1 represents working memory as a single unit, and this is how it was initially described (Atkinson & Shiffrin, 1968). However, current views of working memory suggest that it has three components—a *central executive*, a *phonological loop*, and a *visual-spatial sketchpad*—that work together to process information (Baddeley, 1986, 2001). They're outlined in Figure 7.2.

To see how these components work together, try finding the area of the figure you see here.

Central executive. A supervisory component of working memory that controls the flow of information to and from the other components.

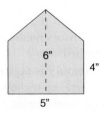

6"

4"

5"

To solve the problem you probably subtracted the 4 from the 6 to determine that the height of the triangular portion of the figure was 2 inches. You recalled that the formulas for the areas of a triangle and a rectangle are $\frac{1}{2}(b)(h)$ and $(l)(w)$, respectively, and you calculated the areas to be $(\frac{1}{2})(5)(2) = 5$ sq. in. and $(5)(4) = 20$ sq. in., making the total area of the figure 25 square inches.

Now, let's see how the components of your working memory executed the task. The **central executive,** a supervisory system, controls the flow of information to and from the other components. For instance, your decision to break the figure into a triangle and

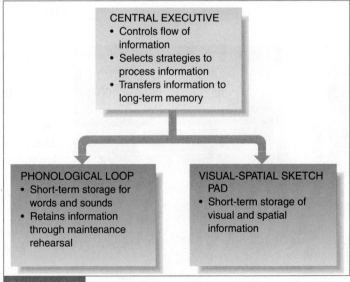

Figure 7.2 A model of working memory

Phonological loop. A short-term storage system for words and sounds in working memory.

Rehearsal. The process of repeating information over and over, either out loud or silently, without altering its form.

Visual-spatial sketchpad. A short-term storage system for visual and spatial information in working memory.

Short-term memory. Historically, the part of our memory system that temporarily holds information until it can be processed.

rectangle, find the area of each, and add the two was a function of your working memory's central executive.

The **phonological loop,** a short-term storage component for words and sounds, temporarily held the formulas and the dimensions of the figure while you made the calculations. Information can be kept in the phonological loop indefinitely through **rehearsal,** the process of repeating information over and over, either out loud or silently, without altering its form. (Rehearsal, as you see it defined here, is often described as *maintenance* rehearsal, because it is used to "maintain" information in working memory.) For example, you look up a phone number, repeat it to yourself until you dial it, and then forget it. The ability to keep information in the phonological loop through rehearsal is represented by the "loop" with rehearsal in it above working memory in Figure 7.1 (We examine rehearsal in more detail later in the chapter.)

The **visual-spatial sketchpad,** a short-term storage system for visual and spatial information, allowed you to visualize the figure and see that it could be broken into a rectangle and triangle. The visual-spatial sketchpad and the phonological loop are independent, so each can perform mental work without taxing the resources of the other (Baddeley, 1986, 2001). They serve the functions that historically have been attributed to **short-term memory.**

The phonological loop can hold about as much information as we can say to ourselves in 1½ to 2 seconds, and the duration of the visual-spatial sketchpad is also limited (Baddeley, 1986, 2001). These limitations have important implications for your work with different types of students. For instance, researchers have found that learners with attention-deficit/hyperactivity disorder (ADHD) rehearse verbal and spatial information as effectively as other children, but their central executive is impaired (Karateken, 2004), whereas learners with reading disabilities have impaired functioning of the phonological loop (Kibby, Marks, & Morgan, 2004). Students with ADHD have trouble controlling their attention and selecting effective learning strategies, and students with reading difficulties have trouble processing verbal information.

Limitations of Working Memory

If you're like most people, at one time or another you've probably thought, or maybe even said, "I'm suffering from mental overload." This feeling is directly related to working memory, and it's because our working memory capacities are severely limited (Sweller et al., 1998). Early research suggested that adult working memories can hold about seven items of information at a time and can hold the items for only about 10 to 20 seconds (Miller, 1956). (Children's working memories are even more limited.) Selecting and organizing information also uses working memory space, so we "are probably only able to deal with two or three items of information simultaneously when required to process rather than merely hold information" (Sweller et al., 1998, p. 252). As you saw in Figure 7.1, working memory is smaller than either sensory memory or long-term memory, which reminds us that its capacity is limited.

The limited capacity of working memory is arguably its most important feature, because working memory is where we make sense of our experiences and construct our knowledge (R. C. Clark & Mayer, 2003). Think about that. The most important process in learning—the construction of meaningful knowledge—takes place in the component of our memory system that is the most limited! Little wonder that students are frequently confused, miss important information, and develop misconceptions.

We see the effects of this limitation played out in different ways in classrooms:

- Students write better essays using computers or word processors if their keyboarding skills are well developed. If not, handwritten essays are superior (Roblyer & Doering, 2010).
- Students' writing often improves more rapidly if they are initially allowed to ignore grammar, punctuation, and spelling (McCutchen, 2000).

Working memory is the "workbench" where students think about and solve problems.

- In spite of research about its ineffectiveness and staff-development efforts to promote more effective forms of instruction, lecturing persists as the most common teaching strategy (Brophy, 2006c; Cuban, 1993).

We can explain the limitations of working memory using the concept of **cognitive load,** which is the amount of mental activity imposed on working memory. Two factors contribute to cognitive load. The first is the number of elements that you must attend to (Paas et al., 2004). For instance, remembering sequences of digits like 7 9 5 3 and 3 9 2 4 6 7 can be thought of as having cognitive loads of 4 and 6, respectively.

The second factor contributing to cognitive load is the extent to which the separate elements of incoming information interact with each other (Paas et al., 2004). This factor helps answer the second question we asked at the beginning of the chapter: "Why did Tanya get 'kinda lost when Mr. Shelton was explaining all that on Monday?'" David's explanations imposed too heavy a cognitive load on Tanya's working memory, and some of the information was lost before she could make sense of it. Similarly, attempting to create a well-organized essay, while at the same time using correct grammar, punctuation, and spelling, imposes a heavy cognitive load on young writers. And using sophisticated teaching strategies, such as guiding students with questioning, imposes a heavy cognitive load on teachers. The load on students is reduced if they're allowed to ignore grammar, punctuation, and spelling, and teachers reduce it by lecturing, a less cognitively demanding instructional strategy.

Temporarily reducing cognitive load in these ways works for awhile, but eventually students need to learn to use correct grammar, spelling, and punctuation in their writing, and you'll need to interact with your students if you're going to maximize learning. So, what can we—both as learners and as teachers—do? We address this question in the next section.

> **Cognitive load.** The amount of mental activity imposed on working memory.

Reducing Cognitive Load: Accommodating the Limitations of Working Memory

We are inundated with an enormous amount of information every day—personal conversations, the Internet, cell phones, television, and other sights and sounds—and they impose an enormous cognitive load on all of us. To cope we reduce the load, and three strategies help.

- Chunking
- Automaticity
- Distributed processing

Ed Psych and You

If you have an electric garage door opener, have you ever wondered whether or not you've put the garage door down and have gone back to check? Or do you ever wonder if you've shut off your coffee pot or failed to complete some other routine task? If so, why might this have happened?

Chunking. **Chunking** is the process of mentally combining separate items into larger, more meaningful units (Miller, 1956). For example, the number 9 0 4 7 5 0 5 8 0 7 is a phone number, but it isn't written as phone numbers typically appear. Now, as normally written, (904) 750-5807, it has been "chunked" into three larger units, which reduces cognitive load by making it both easier to read and to remember. Phone numbers are virtually always chunked, and notice also that, without the area code, they're 7 digits, approximately the capacity of adult working memory.

Chunking is common in our daily lives. For instance, American Express credit cards are 15 digits long chunked into 3 units; Visa cards are 16 digits chunked into 4 units. Drivers' license numbers, memberships in organizations, such as the American Automobile Association, and the long license numbers on purchased computer software are all presented as chunks instead of a continuous string of numbers or numbers and letters.

> **Chunking.** The process of mentally combining separate items into larger, more meaningful units.

Developing Automaticity. **Automaticity** is the ability to perform mental operations with little awareness or conscious effort (Feldon, 2007a), and it helps us answer the question in our "Ed Psych and You" feature. If you answered yes to either of our questions, it was

> **Automaticity.** The ability to perform mental operations with little awareness or conscious effort.

because you put the garage door down or completed the other routine task "automatically." You did so without thinking about it.

As with chunking, automaticity is common in our lives. For instance, most of us develop a number of personal routines, such as always putting our keys in the same place, that we perform automatically. And, automaticity helps us understand why talking on cell phones while driving can be dangerous. Driving is a nearly automatic process, so we don't devote enough attention to it as we talk, increasing the chance of an accident.

Automaticity is a powerful and essential process in reducing cognitive load. Computer keyboarding is an example, and it helps us understand why students compose better essays on computers or word processors, but only if their word processing skills are well developed. If their skills are automatic, they can devote all of their working memory capacities to the essay. If not, they must devote too much to the process of keyboarding, leaving too little for organizing and composing the essay.

Similarly, students' grammar, punctuation, and spelling must eventually become automatic if they are to be good writers, and essential teaching skills, such as questioning, must be nearly automatic for you if you are going to interact effectively with your students.

Using Distributed Processing. Earlier you saw that in working memory the phonological loop and the visual-spatial sketchpad operate independently, so each can perform mental work without taxing the resources of the other. Doing so "distributes" the processing load across the two components, and it suggests that students can learn more if verbal explanations and visual representations are combined in presentations (R. C. Clark & Mayer, 2003; Moreno & Duran, 2004). The visual processor supplements the verbal processor and vice versa.

David capitalized on the independent processing capabilities of these components by combining the visual aspects of his displays with words that explained the information in them. "The integration of words and pictures is made easier by lessons that present the verbal and visual information together rather than separated" (R. C. Clark & Mayer, 2003, p. 38).

Teachers often use words, alone, to present information, which fails to capitalize on working memory's processing capability. If you supplement your verbal presentations with figures, diagrams, and pictures, you will reduce the cognitive load on your students and increase learning.

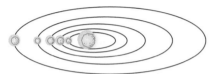

The sun threw off hot spheres of gas which eventually became planets.

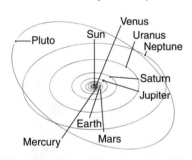

The orbital planes of the planets and Pluto.

Long-term memory. The permanent information store in our human memory system.

Long-Term Memory

Knowledge that people construct depends on what they already know, is another principle of learning, and this is where **long-term memory,** our permanent information store, comes into play. What we already know is stored in long-term memory, and in the process of constructing new knowledge, we retrieve this information, combine it with new information in working memory, conceptually organize it so it makes sense to us, and then place the newly organized information back into long-term memory until it is further needed. For example, when students try to figure out what part of speech *interesting* is in the sentence, "The story was very interesting," they retrieve from their long-term memories the fact that adjectives describe nouns and that "story" is a noun. They combine this information with the sentence, which is temporarily held in working memory, determine that "interesting" describes "story," and conclude (construct the idea) that adjectives sometimes follow the nouns they describe. This new idea is then stored in long-term memory for further use when needed.

Long-term memory is somewhat analogous to a computer hard drive with an enormous number of entries and a network that allows the information to be retrieved for future use. Its capacity is vast and durable, and some experts suggest that information in it remains for a lifetime (Schacter, 2001; Sweller, 2003).

Long-term memory contains three kinds of knowledge: *declarative, procedural,* and *conditional*. **Declarative knowledge** is knowledge of facts, concepts, procedures, and rules, and within this category, some researchers (e.g., Tulving, 2002) distinguish between **semantic memory,** which is memory for concepts, principles, and the relationships among them, and **episodic memory,** which is memory for personal experiences.

To illustrate these ideas, let's look again at some dialogue between Juan and Randy.

> **Juan:** I know the answer to the first question. . . . Pluto was once considered part of the solar system, but it isn't any more. . . . Actually, it's now called a dwarf planet."
>
> **Randy:** What do you mean?
>
> **Juan:** I was watching *Nova* with my mom, and they said that scientists think Pluto was an asteroid, or some other body floating around, and the sun kind of grabbed it.

Juan's comments are forms of declarative knowledge; they are facts he recalled from his experience. Then, when he talked about watching *Nova,* the information came from his episodic memory; it was based on a personal experience.

The lines between episodic and semantic memory are often blurred, but one difference is significant. When people have strong emotional reactions to an event, episodic memories are more enduring. For example, you probably remember exactly where you were and what you were doing when you received word of the terrorist attacks of 9/11. Similarly, you likely recall the events surrounding your first date or kiss. They're stored in your episodic memory. As teachers we can capitalize on episodic memory by personalizing content or teaching it in a way that also has an emotional impact on our students.

Procedural knowledge is knowledge of how to perform tasks, and **conditional knowledge** is knowledge of where and when to use declarative and procedural knowledge (Anderson, 2005). For example, consider the following problems:

$$2/7 + 4/7 =$$
$$1/4 + 2/3 =$$

You know that to add fractions you first must have like denominators. This is a form of declarative knowledge. Recognizing that you must find a common denominator in the second problem but not in the first is a form of conditional knowledge, and actually finding that the answer to the first problem is 6/7 and the answer to the second is 11/12 requires procedural knowledge.

Declarative knowledge can be determined from a person's comments, and most declarative knowledge is *explicit,* meaning we are aware of what we know. On the other hand we infer procedural and conditional knowledge from a person's performance, and this knowledge is often *implicit,* meaning we cannot recall or explain it. For instance, when working at a computer keyboard, you can't recall the knowledge you use as you move your fingers over the keyboard, and you're unable to explain exactly what you're doing. The relationships among these different forms of knowledge are outlined in Figure 7.3.

Now, let's see how these different forms of knowledge are stored in long-term memory.

Representing Declarative Knowledge in Long-Term Memory

Acquiring declarative knowledge involves integrating new information with existing knowledge, such as you saw with the simple example of determining that adjectives don't always precede the noun they modify. We learn more effectively when we have well-developed knowledge to which new information can be related. This knowledge is organized in the form of **schemas** (also called schemata), cognitive structures that represent the way information is organized in long-term memory (J. R. Anderson, 2005; Willingham, 2007). We all

Declarative knowledge. Knowledge of facts, definitions, procedures, and rules.

Semantic memory. Memory for concepts, principles, and the relationships among them.

Episodic memory. Memory for personal experiences.

Procedural knowledge. Knowledge of how to perform tasks.

Conditional knowledge. Knowledge of where and when to use declarative and procedural knowledge.

Schemas. Cognitive structures that represent the way information is organized in our long-term memory.

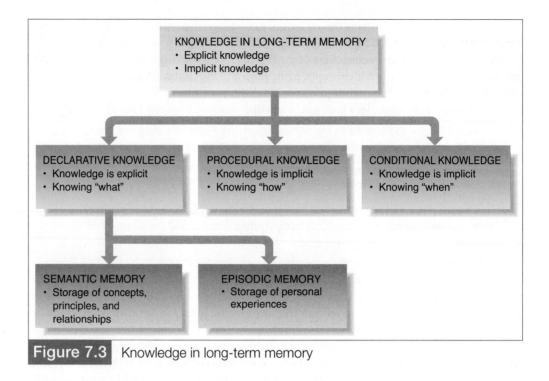

Figure 7.3 Knowledge in long-term memory

have a great many schemas that represent our understanding of our personal, social, and academic worlds. For instance, Paul's wife has several close female friends that she meets socially once a month. Before she goes, she'll make comments, such as, "Sharon will probably be late" and "I'll be home early, since Libby has trouble with her eyes after dark." These comments illustrate the way her knowledge of her friends is represented in her memory. They're organized in a schema and influence how we think about the world. The same is true for much of our understanding.

Meaningful Learning. Consider this question. What state capital was a compromise between the "North Platters" and the "South Platters." Are you stumped? Many people are, since it's an isolated and little known piece of information. One more hint: The term "Platter" relates to the Platte River. Now, if you can identify the capital, it's likely because you know that the Platte River runs through Nebraska, and Lincoln is its capital.

You identified the capital because of the following connections:

$$\text{Platter} \rightarrow \text{Platte River} \rightarrow \text{Nebraska} \rightarrow \text{Lincoln}$$

Meaningfulness. The extent to which information in long-term memory is interconnected with other information.

and they illustrate the concept **meaningfulness,** which describes the extent to which individual items of information are interconnected in long-term memory. The connected items are organized into a simple schema that makes sense to us.

Forming meaningful—interconnected—schemas is one of the most important aspects of the entire learning process, because they represent our understanding of the topics we study. As an example from David's lesson, look at Figure 7.4, which illustrates Randy's and Juan's schemas for the solar system. Remember, these schemas are cognitive structures, which means that Juan and Randy constructed them and they're stored *in the students' heads.* Both Randy's and Juan's schemas organize information into systems that makes sense to them, and they are idiosyncratic to the person who constructed them. If, for instance, you look at Juan's schema in Figure 7.4, and it doesn't appear meaningful to you, it's because you didn't construct it. It *is* meaningful to Juan. The same thing can occur in classrooms when our students construct schemas that make sense to them, but not to us.

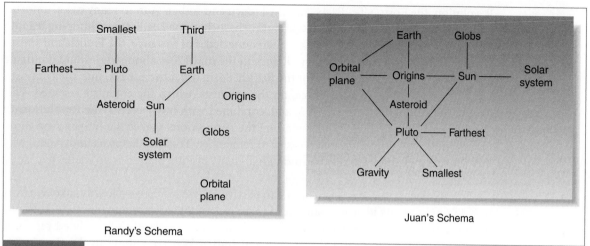

Figure 7.4 Randy's and Juan's schemas

Also, important differences exist between Randy's and Juan's schemas. For instance, even though both contain 10 individual elements, Randy's has only 6 "links" in it, compared to 12 in Juan's. Juan's schema is more organized and meaningful.

Let's use Juan's and Randy's schemas as an illustration to see how meaningfulness can impact further learning. The number of chunks working memory can hold is limited, but the size and complexity of the chunks are not (Sweller et al., 1998). Because the individual items in Juan's schema are all connected, it behaves like a chunk—a single item in working memory (Bransford, Brown, & Cocking, 2000). Because Randy's is less interconnected, it exists as five items: one chunk for the four connected items—*smallest, farthest, Pluto,* and *asteroid;* another for the *third-earth-Sun-Solar system* chunk; and one each for *origins, globs,* and *orbital plane.* Because the information exists as five items, the cognitive load on Randy's working memory is greater than it is on Juan's, making additional processing more difficult for Randy.

Let's look again at their dialogue to see how the organization of their knowledge affects learning.

> **Juan:** Pluto was once considered part of the solar system, but it isn't any more. . . . Actually, it's now called a dwarf planet."
>
> **Randy:** What do you mean?
>
> **Juan:** I was watching *Nova* with my mom, and the person talking said that scientists think Pluto was an asteroid, or some other body floating around, and the sun kind of grabbed it. . . . See.
>
> **Randy:** What's that got to do with it?
>
> **Juan:** Look. . . . See how Pluto is above the rest of them (pointing to the model).
>
> **Randy:** Gee, I didn't even notice that.

Randy didn't "notice," because his background knowledge wasn't organized well enough to facilitate new connections in working memory, making his learning less efficient.

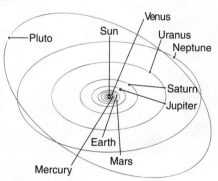

The orbital planes of the planets and Pluto.

Meaningful Learning: Implications for Learners and Teachers. The concept of meaningfulness has important implications for us, both as learners and as teachers. As learners, we should constantly be looking for relationships in the topics we study. For instance, from our study of American history, we know about events, such as the American

Revolution, the Boston Tea Party, and the French and Indian War. In many cases, unfortunately, we only learned specific facts about each, such as the Tea Partiers dumping tea into Boston harbor. They are all, however, interconnected. For instance, the French and Indian War, a conflict between England and France in the mid 1700s about who would dominate colonial America, was very costly for the British. So, in order to raise revenue, they imposed onerous taxes on goods, such as tea, on the colonists, which the colonists resented. This led to the Boston Tea Party in 1773, and, combined with other events, the Revolutionary War, which began in 1775. Understanding the connections makes the information more meaningful, more interesting, and easier to remember. This also helps us understand why memorizing definitions and other individual items of information is an ineffective study strategy.

The same applies from a teaching perspective. As we teach, we should make an effort to help our students identify—and hold them accountable for understanding—the connections among the ideas we teach, rather than teach information in isolated pieces. A question, such as, "How did the French and Indian War contribute to the Boston Tea Party?" is a much better way to promote learning than having students memorize specific facts and dates about each event. Isolated information imposes a heavy load on students' working memories, which helps explain why they seem to retain so little of what they're taught. Connecting ideas reduces the load, makes the information more meaningful, and increases learning by providing more places to attach new information.

Scripts. Schemas for events that guide behavior in particular situations.

Schemas as Scripts. In addition to organizing information, schemas can also guide our actions. For example, when you first enter a college class, you may ask yourself questions, such as:

- What are the instructor's expectations?
- How should I prepare for quizzes and other assessments?
- How will I interact with my peers?

Answers to these questions come from **scripts,** which are schemas for events, developed over years of experience (Nuthall, 2000). You have a script that guides your actions as you prepare for, attend, and participate in your classes. In this regard, scripts also contain procedural knowledge, which we consider next.

To develop procedural knowledge, students need opportunities to practice.

Representing Procedural Knowledge in Long-Term Memory

Our ability to use procedural knowledge depends on both declarative and conditional knowledge (J. R. Anderson, 2005). For example, think back to the problems

$$2/7 + 4/7 =$$
$$1/4 + 2/3 =$$

Your ability to add them depended on your declarative knowledge of the rules for adding fractions and your conditional knowledge, so you knew when finding a common denominator was necessary and when it wasn't.

Our goal in developing procedural knowledge is to reach automaticity, which requires a great deal of time and effort (Taraban, Anderson, & DeFinis, 2007). This suggests that we need to provide students with ample opportunities to practice.

Table 7.1	Characteristics of different memory stores

Store	Characteristics
Sensory Memory	• Virtually unlimited capacity • Holds information in unorganized form • Information is quickly lost if it isn't further processed
Working Memory	• Limited capacity • Conscious component of the memory stores • The workbench where thinking and problem solving occur • A processing bottleneck • Contains a verbal processor and a visual processor that work independently
Long-Term Memory	• Virtually unlimited capacity • Permanent information store • Stores information in the form of schemas and images, encoded from working memory

When we help our students develop their procedural knowledge, the learning context is important (Star, 2004). For example, students should practice their grammar, spelling, and punctuation in the context of their writing, rather than on isolated sentences. And math students should develop their skills in the context of word problems that require a variety of operations, so students learn to identify different conditions and apply the appropriate actions (Bransford et al., 2000).

Table 7.1 outlines the characteristics of the different memory stores and summarizes key similarities and differences between them.

Developmental Differences in the Memory Stores

Our description of the model of human memory suggests that people of all ages process information in essentially the same way, and to a certain extent this is true. For example, small children and adults both briefly store stimuli from the environment in their sensory memories, make sense of it in their working memories, and store it in their long-term memories.

Important developmental differences exist, however. For instance, researchers have found that older children retain sensory memory traces longer than their younger counterparts (Nelson, Thomas, & de Haan, 2006). This means that kindergarten teachers are less likely to have their students understand detailed directions, for instance, than teachers of older children.

In addition, the efficiency of students' working memory components significantly increases as children develop (Gathercole, Pickering, Ambridge, & Wearing, 2004). For example, more of older children's procedural knowledge becomes automatic, so they can process information more quickly and can handle complex tasks more efficiently than younger children (Luna, Garver, Urban, Lazar, & Sweeny, 2004).

Also, because of their experiences, older children bring a broader and deeper store of prior knowledge to learning activities, which increases their ability to make new learning meaningful. Experience can also result in differences in learners who are the same age, and David's students illustrate these differences. Because he had experiences that Randy and Tanya lacked, Juan's understanding of the solar system was more fully developed than theirs, so the information David presented was more meaningful to him.

The Brain and Human Memory

We know that our brains are shaped by our experiences (Blakemore & Frith, 2005). Understanding how our brain functions during cognitive activities can provide us with insights into how to make information processing more effective and efficient.

Information about brain functioning comes from a variety of sources, with functional magnetic resonance imaging (fMRI) being the most recent and promising. fMRI takes a snapshot of brain activity by focusing on the blood flow and oxygen metabolism in different parts of the brain during cognitive activity (Berk, 2010). Using fMRIs, electroencephalograms (EEGs), and other electronic scanning devices, scientists have learned how different types of stimuli influence the workings of the brain.

As a result of this research, we now understand that, at a fundamental level, all cognition is neural, that is, based on neurons. (You will recall that neurons are nerve cells composed of cell bodies, dendrites, and axons, which make up the learning capability of the brain.) Basic mechanisms of thinking involve the interconnections formed between neurons in the brain.

What gets fired gets wired, and what gets fired depends on experience. For instance, a classic study of taxi drivers in London found that navigating its labyrinth-like streets resulted in increased growth of the visual/spatial part of the brain, and the increase was related to how long the drivers had been driving (Maguire et al., 2000).

An additional study compared the brain functions of Chinese and English speakers during problem-solving activities in math, and researchers found interesting cross-cultural differences (Tang et al., 2006). For example, the researchers found that Chinese speakers' brains showed increased activity in the motor or movement area as they thought about math problems, whereas the English speakers showed increases in the language areas of the brain. The researchers concluded that the differences were linked to Chinese speakers' use of the abacus, a calculating tool historically used by Chinese students that requires movement and spatial positioning. Again, we see how different experiences influence the way our brains develop and ultimately the way we think about the world.

Researchers have also found links between patterns of brain activity and students' learning orientations (Delazer et al., 2005). For instance, students who memorized problem solutions had more brain activity in parts of the brain involved in retrieval of verbal information, whereas students who learned and implemented cognitive strategies had more activity in visual and spatial parts of the brain.

This research has two implications for us as teachers. First, our job is to provide students with a rich and varied menu of experiences, experiences that contribute to promoting the neural connections in our students' brains that ultimately lead to the formation of permanent links, such as the brain growth in the London taxi drivers.

Second, neural connections forged by our teaching determine important learning outcomes such as retention and transfer—the ability to apply learning acquired in one context to a new context. For example, as certain synapses are used over and over, "neural commitments" are formed that streamline and speed the transmission of neural messages that ultimately result in automaticity, such as being able to state that $7 \times 8 = 56$ essentially without thinking about it (Kuhl, 2004). Practice over time facilitates this streamlining.

This streamlining can also have drawbacks, however. For instance, it helps us understand why bad habits, such as making the same error while keyboarding, are so hard to break. As some neural connections are streamlined, others atrophy from lack of use. Experts suggest that this is one reason learning to pronounce a second language is often difficult for adult learners; the neural pathways for the first language dominate and overpower new ones (Kuhl, 2004).

Overly tuned neural pathways can also impede transfer. This suggests that we should present new content in a variety of contexts, so that new information will be connected in a number of alternate pathways. For instance, presenting a range of word problems that require different operations, and wording problems differently when the same operation is required, help create these different neural pathways. And, the same processes apply in all content areas.

The way our brains function also helps us understand why meaningful learning is more effective than isolated fact learning. When students study the connections among different ideas, they help form the neural connections that promote both more effective encoding and transfer to new contexts (Mayer, 2008).

Research on brain functioning reinforces much of what we already know about teaching and learning. For instance, it reinforces the importance of a rich and varied set of experiences for learners; it reinforces the need for meaningful learning; and it reinforces the importance of applying content to real-world contexts. It validates the applications we suggest in this chapter.

---

check your understanding

2.1 Some debate exists about whether students should memorize math facts, such as 5 + 4, and 6 × 9. Many teachers believe students should memorize these facts, whereas others believe that students should acquire the facts as they're needed. Using the characteristics of the memory stores as a basis, which side of the debate appears more valid? Explain.

2.2 Use the characteristics of the memory stores to explain why a health club would advertise its telephone number as 2HEALTH rather than 243–2584.

2.3 Procedural knowledge exists in which of our memory stores? Identify an example in the opening case study that illustrates students' being required to demonstrate procedural knowledge. Explain.

To receive feedback for these questions, go to Appendix A.

Classroom connections

Helping Students Store Information Efficiently in Sensory Memory

1. Sensory memory briefly holds incoming stimuli from the environment until they can be processed. To keep students from losing important information, allow them to attend to one message before presenting a second one.

   ■ **Elementary:** A second-grade teacher asks one question at a time and gets an answer before asking a second question.

   ■ **Middle School:** A prealgebra teacher displays two similar problems on the document camera and waits until students have copied them before she starts discussing them.

   ■ **High School:** A geography teacher places a map on the document camera and says, "I'll give you a minute to examine the geography of the countries on this map in the front of the room. Then we'll discuss what you're noticing."

Working Memory

2. Working memory is where learners consciously process information, and its capacity is limited. To avoid overloading learners' working memories, develop lessons with questioning and avoid extended periods of lecturing.

   ■ **Elementary:** A first-grade teacher writes directions for seatwork on the board. He asks different students to repeat and explain the directions before they begin.

   ■ **Middle School:** A teacher in a woodworking class begins by saying, "The density of wood from the same kind of tree varies, depending on the amount of rainfall." He waits a moment, holds up two pieces of wood, and says, "What do you notice about the rings on these pieces?"

   ■ **High School:** An Algebra II teacher "walks" students through the solutions to problems by having a different student describe each step in the solution.

3. Automaticity is the ability to perform tasks with little conscious effort. To develop automaticity in your students, provide frequent practice, and present information in both verbal and visual forms.

   ■ **Elementary:** A first-grade teacher has his students practice their writing by composing two sentences each day about an event of the previous evening. As they practice their letters, he demonstrates how they should look and describes correct procedures verbally.

   ■ **Middle School:** To capitalize on the distributed processing capability of working memory, an eighth-grade history teacher prepares a flowchart of the events leading to the Revolutionary War. As she questions students, she refers to the chart for each point and shows students how to use the chart to organize their notes.

   ■ **High School:** A physics teacher demonstrates the relationship between force and acceleration by pulling a cart along a desktop with a constant force so students can see that the cart accelerates. He then asks to describe what they saw.

Long-Term Memory

4. Information is organized into meaningful schemas in learners' long-term memories. To promote meaningfulness, encourage students to identify relationships between ideas.

■ **Elementary:** During story time, a second-grade teacher uses "how," "when," and "why" questions to encourage students to explain how the events in a story contribute to the conclusion.

■ **Middle School:** In developing the rules for solving equations by substitution, an algebra teacher asks, "How does this process compare to solving equations by addition?"

■ **High School:** To help his students understand cause–effect relationships, a world history teacher asks questions like "Why was shipping so important in ancient Greece?" "Why was Troy's location so important?" and "How do these questions relate to the location of today's big cities?"

Cognitive Processes

Ed Psych and You

Think about a quarter (the coin). What is on one face of the coin? What is on the opposite face for your state?

How does information move from sensory to working memory and from working memory to long-term memory? How can we help our students store the information we want them to learn most efficiently? To answer these questions, let's look at Figure 7.5, which is similar to the model you first saw in Figure 7.1 (on page 213), but this time the cognitive processes—*attention, perception, encoding,* and *retrieval*—are highlighted. As you compare Figure 7.5 to Figure 7.1, focus on the cognitive processes, and remember as you study the following sections that they are responsible for moving information from one information store to another.

Attention

We know that learning and development depend on learners' experiences. These experiences are gathered through everything we see, hear, touch, taste, or smell, and they're represented in Figure 7.5 as arrows to the left of the model. However, we remain unaware of

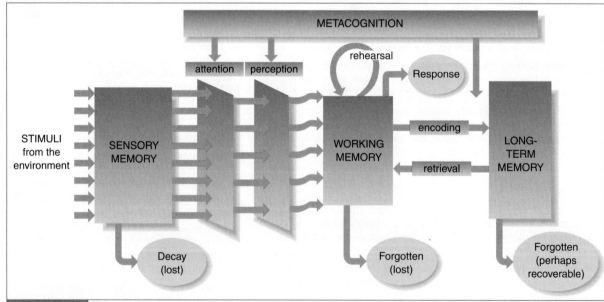

| **Figure 7.5** | Cognitive processes in the model of human memory |

many, if not most, stimuli until we consciously pay **attention** to them. For instance, think about our question in our "Ed Psych and You" feature on the previous page. We're all familiar with quarters, and we handle them all the time. However, many of us don't know what's on either side, and we may not know that each state has developed its own unique face. We don't *pay attention* to this information.

Attention acts as a screen, and this screening function is represented by fewer arrows to the right than to the left of attention in Figure 7.5. Attention is important, because it is impossible to attend to all the stimuli we encounter; to maintain our sanity and focus on the important stimuli that bombard our senses, we filter out some of it.

Attention has two important characteristics that have implications for our teaching. First, while people have individual differences, everyone's attention is limited, both in capacity and duration (Zhou, Hofer, & Eisenberg, 2007). So, our students are likely to pay attention to parts of our explanations but miss other parts.

Second, we are easily distracted; our attention often wanders from one stimulus to another (Zhou et al., 2007). This helps explain why students seem to derive less from our explanations than they should. A myriad of distractions exist in classrooms—other students (especially those of the opposite sex for adolescents), noises both inside and outside the room, and people in the hallway, among others. Any of these can distract students' attention and cause them to miss parts of our lessons.

Attracting and Maintaining Attention

Because attention is where learning begins, attracting and maintaining student attention are essential (Curtindale et al., 2007). You should plan your lessons to help students attend to the important ideas that you're teaching and ignore irrelevant stimuli. If you pull a live crab out of a cooler to begin a lesson on crustaceans, for example, even your most unmotivated students are likely to pay attention. Similarly, if you actively involve your students in learning activities, they are going to be more attentive than if they're passively listening to a lecture (Dolezal, Welsh, Pressley, & Vincent, 2003).

David attempted to attract and maintain his students' attention in two ways. First, his visuals were effective attention getters, and second, the fact that his students were involved in gathering information about the planets and answering the questions he posed helped maintain their attention.

Additional ways to attract student attention are outlined in Table 7.2. Because of its importance, one deserves increased emphasis: *calling on students by name*. The use of students' names is one of the most powerful attention-getters, so we're encouraging you to call on your students as individuals instead of directing questions to the class as a whole. When this becomes a pattern, attention and achievement increase significantly (Good & Brophy, 2008).

Technology, Learning, and Development: The Influence of Technology on Attention

To say that we live in a technological world is a vast understatement. People talk on cell phones as they walk and drive, texting is common, and Facebook and Twitter have literally millions of users.

The impact of this technology on learning and development has become the subject of considerable research, much of it related to people's attention. For instance, studies suggest that drivers are more than 20 times more likely to be involved in an accident if texting while driving, and using cell phones as we drive is comparable to driving while drunk (Virginia Tech Transportation Institute, 2009).

Attention. The process of consciously focusing on a stimulus.

Table 7.2	Strategies for attracting attention
Type	**Example**
Demonstrations	A science teacher pulls a student in a chair across the room to demonstrate the concepts *force* and *work*.
Discrepant events	A world history teacher who usually dresses conservatively comes to class in a sheet, makeshift sandals, and a crown to begin a discussion of ancient Greece.
Charts	A health teacher displays a chart showing the high fat content of some popular foods.
Pictures	An English teacher shows a picture of a bearded Ernest Hemingway as she introduces 20th-century American novels.
Problems	A math teacher says, We want to go to the rock concert on Saturday night, but we're broke. The tickets are $45, and we need about $20 for gas and something to eat. We make $5.50 an hour in our part-time jobs. How many hours do we have to work to be able to afford the concert?"
Thought-provoking questions	A history teacher begins a discussion of World War II with the question, "Suppose Germany had won the war. How might the world be different now?"
Emphasis	A teacher says, "Pay careful attention now. The next two items are very important."
Student names	In his question-and-answer sessions, a teacher asks his question, pauses briefly, and then calls on a student by name to answer.

Maggie Jackson (2009), in her book *Distracted : The Erosion of Attention and the Coming Dark Age,* contends we have developed a form of attention deficit disorder, which limits our ability to remain focused. Immersed in an important writing project, we hear the familiar "ping" telling us we have a new e-mail, and we can't resist checking. We then spend time reading e-mails, responding, and maybe even making a little side sojourn to the Internet. Suddenly we've spent an hour away from our project. Some researchers argue that this constant stimulation appeals to a primitive impulse, provoking excitement—a dopamine squirt—that can be addictive. In its absence, people feel bored (Small & Vorgan, 2008).

Stress can also be a factor. Research indicates that people continually interrupted by e-mails experience increased stress, and stress hormones reduce our brain's efficiency (Mark, Gudith, & Klocke, 2008).

Teachers frequently complain that students, used to the constant stimulation of sophisticated technologies, such as video games, have problems with the mundane in learning, such as listening to detailed explanations. And, phones going off in classrooms are distracting, resulting in schools' and teachers' banning them altogether in many cases.

On the other hand, we all know how powerful a tool technology can be for providing information, making work easier, and communicating instantly across vast distances. Because a digital world is today's reality, we need to adapt to it. Let's look at some suggestions.

First, we need to control potential distractions—both for ourselves and our students. Put your computer speakers on mute, for example, so you won't hear the e-mail "ping," and shut your cell phone off, or put it on vibrate while you're studying. Require students to turn off cell phones, MP3 players, and other electronic gadgets as they enter your classroom, and explain why you are doing so. Encourage parents to eliminate distractions when their children study and do homework (Jackson, 2009).

Second, knowing that technology bombards us with attention-grabbing stimuli, create a to-do work or study list, prioritize the items on it, begin with the first item, complete it, and move on through the list. Cross items off as you finish them, so you experience the satisfaction of completing each task. Avoid the temptation of jumping back and forth. If you have tasks that you can't complete in one work session, do as much as you can before turning to another activity. Avoid multitasking, which, in spite of many people's protests to the contrary, decreases rather than increases efficiency (Hicks, 2010). Explain the same strategy to your students, helping them understand how these actions increase learning.

Third, set time aside during the day to respond to e-mails, text messages, and phone calls. Avoid allowing them to interrupt your work or study. Send as many e-mails and texts as you want late in the evening or any time you're not working.

Finally, make a concerted effort to spend face-to-face time with friends and other people. Our digital world can reduce personal contact with others to the detriment of social development and the intimacy that comes with looking people in the eye as you talk to them (Hicks, 2010).

Technology has revolutionized the way we live. In adapting to this way of life, we want to be sure that it works for us instead of the other way around.

Perception

Look at the picture in the margin. Do you see a young, glamorous woman, or an old, wrinkled one? This classic example illustrates the nature of **perception,** the process people use to find meaning in stimuli. For those of you who "saw" an old woman, for instance, this is the meaning you attached to the picture, and the same is true for those of you who "saw" a young woman. Technically, we were asking, "Do you 'perceive' a young or an old woman?"

Perception. The process people use to find meaning in stimuli.

In our everyday world, the term *perception* is commonly used to describe the way we interpret objects and events (Way, Reddy, & Rhodes, 2007), and it's influenced by our dispositions and expectations (Huan, Yeo, & Ang, 2006). As an example, let's look at the following conversation between two people interviewing for teaching positions at the same school.

"How was your interview?" Lenore asked her friend, Kelly.

"Terrible," Kelly responded. "He grilled me, asking me specifically how I would teach a certain topic and what I would do in the case of two students disrupting my class. He treated me like I didn't know anything. Brenna, a friend of mine who teaches there, told me about him. . . . How was yours?"

"Gosh, I thought mine was good. He asked me the same questions, but I thought he was just trying to find out how we would think about teaching if he hired us."

Kelly and Lenore interpreted their interviews very differently, Kelly viewing hers as being "grilled," but Lenore feeling as if the interviewer only wanted to examine her thinking. Kelly's interpretation was influenced by her friend, Brenna, who created negative expectations for her.

Perceptions are constructed, so they differ among people. The arrows to the right of "perception" in Figure 7.5 are curved to remind us that our students' perceptions will vary. And, because the knowledge learners construct depends on what they already know, learners' perceptions will also depend on their prior knowledge. This helps us understand why Randy didn't "notice" that Pluto's plane differed from those of the planets; his perception of the information in David's visuals was affected by his lack of prior knowledge.

Accurate perceptions in learning activities are essential, because students' perceptions of what they see and hear enter working memory. If these perceptions are inaccurate, the information ultimately stored in long-term memory will also be inaccurate.

The primary way to determine if your students accurately perceive the information you're presenting is to ask them. For instance, if you're a geography teacher and are discussing the economies of different countries, you can check students' perceptions by asking, "What do we mean by the term *economy*?" Students also commonly misperceive questions on homework and tests, which is why discussing frequently missed items and providing feedback is so essential.

Encoding and Encoding Strategies

Encoding. The process of representing information in long-term memory.

After students attend to and perceive information, and organize it in working memory so it makes sense to them, they next **encode** the information, which means they represent it in long-term memory (J. R. Anderson, 2007). The information can be encoded either visually, such as Juan's forming an image of Pluto with a different orbital plane, or verbally, when students construct schemas that relate ideas to each other.

One way to encode information is to rehearse it. *Rehearsal,* described earlier in the chapter, is the process of retaining information in working memory until it is used or forgotten. If rehearsed enough, however, information can be transferred to long-term memory, and this is the strategy learners often use to remember facts, such as $6 \times 9 = 54$, or specific names, dates, and definitions. Using flash cards to remember math facts or definitions is a common form of rehearsal. It is an inefficient encoding strategy, however, because it results in **rote learning,** learning that involves storing information in isolated pieces, most commonly through memorization (Lin, 2007; Mayer, 2002).

Rote learning. Learning that involves storing information in isolated pieces, most commonly through memorization.

In contrast with rote learning, we want important information to be encoded meaningfully—connected to other information in long-term memory. This makes retrieval (remembering it) easier. Juan encoded the information they were studying more meaningfully than did Randy, because the schema he constructed had more connections in it.

Several effective strategies to promote meaningful encoding exist, and we examine four of them in this section:

- Imagery
- Organization
- Schema activation
- Elaboration

These strategies are outlined in Figure 7.6 and discussed in the sections that follow.

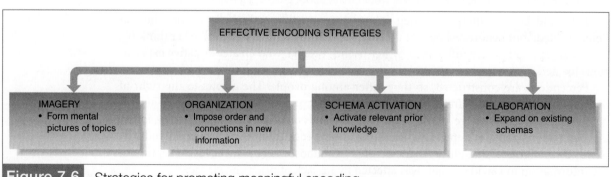

Figure 7.6 Strategies for promoting meaningful encoding

Imagery

How are the two excerpts in our "Ed Psych and You" feature different? The first is rather bland, whereas in the second we can virtually "see" in our mind's eye the woman reading her novel and the student at his computer, and we can almost hear the clicking of rails. It capitalizes on **imagery,** the process of forming mental pictures of an idea (Schwartz & Heiser, 2006), and it's a common strategy novelists and other writers use to make their stories vivid and interesting.

Imagery is also an effective encoding strategy, and its value is supported by **dual-coding theory,** which suggests that long-term memory contains two distinct memory systems: one for verbal information and one for images (Paivio, 1991; Sadoski & Paivio, 2001). According to dual-coding theory, ideas that can be represented both visually and verbally, such as *ball, house,* or *dog,* are easier to remember than abstract ideas that are more difficult to visualize, such as *value, truth,* and *ability* (Paivio, 1986).

As we study human memory, for example, the fact that we can both visualize the models in Figures 7.1 and 7.5 and read about the information in them helps us capitalize on the dual-coding capability of long-term memory. Information in the model becomes more meaningfully encoded than if we had only described it verbally (J. Clark & Paivio, 1991).

Dual-coding theory again reminds us of the importance of supplementing verbal information with visual representations and vice versa (Igo, Kiewra, & Bruning, 2004). Using both capitalizes on both the distributed processing capabilities of working memory and the dual-coding capability of long-term memory.

As you teach, you can take advantage of imagery in many ways (Schwartz & Heiser, 2006). For instance, you can use pictures and diagrams, such as David's visuals of the solar system and the globs of gases coming off the sun; you can ask students to form mental pictures of processes or events; and you can ask students to draw their own diagrams about ideas they are learning.

Imagery can be particularly helpful in problem solving (Kozhevnikov, Hegarty, & Mayer, 1999). It would have been harder for you to solve the area-of-the-pentagon problem that we presented in our discussion of working memory, for example, if you hadn't used the drawing.

Organization

Organization is an encoding strategy that clusters related items of content into categories that illustrate relationships. Because well-organized content contains connections among its elements, cognitive load is decreased, and encoding (and subsequent retrieval) is more effective. Research in reading, memory, and classroom instruction confirms the value of organization in promoting learning (Mayer, 2008). Research indicates that experts in different fields learn more efficiently than novices because their knowledge in long-term memory is better organized, allowing them to access it and connect it to new information (Bransford et al., 2000; Simon, 2001).

We can help our students organize information in several ways:

- *Charts and matrices:* Useful for organizing large amounts of information into categories. David used a matrix to help his students organize their information about the planets. The completed matrix is shown in Table 7.3.
- *Hierarchies:* Effective when new information can be subsumed under existing ideas. For instance, in Figure 7.3 we used a hierarchy to represent the different types of knowledge stored in long-term memory.

Ed Psych and You

Look at the two excerpts below. How are they different?

1. Traveling by rail from the Midwest to California is a pleasant experience. As you sit in the dining car, you might meet interesting people, it's relaxing, and you hear the sound of the train rolling over the rails.

2. At the next table a woman stuck her nose in a novel; a college kid pecked at a laptop. Overlaying all this, a soundtrack: choo-k-choo-k-choo-k-choo-k-choo-k—the metronomic rhythm of an Amtrak train rolling down the line to California (Isaacson, 2009).

Imagery. The process of forming mental pictures of an idea.

Dual-coding theory. A theory suggesting that long-term memory contains two distinct memory systems: one for verbal information and one that stores images.

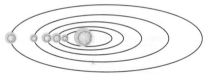

The sun threw off hot spheres of gas which eventually became planets.

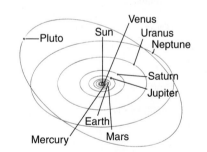

The orbital planes of the planets and Pluto.

Organization. An encoding strategy that involves the clustering of related items of content into categories that illustrate relationships.

| Table 7.3 | David's completed planet matrix |

	Diameter (miles)	Distance from Sun (millions of miles)	Length of Year (orbit)	Length of Day (rotation)	Gravity (compared to Earth's)	Average Surface Temperature (°F)	Characteristics
Mercury	3,030	35.9	88 E.D.[a]	59 E.D. counterclockwise	.38	300 below to 800 above zero	No atmosphere; no water; many craters
Venus	7,500	67.2	225 E.D.	243 E.D. clockwise	.88	900	Thick cloud cover; high winds; no water
Earth	7,900	98.0	365½ E.D.	24 hours counterclockwise	1	57	Atmos. of 78% nitrogen, 21% oxygen; 70% water on surface
Mars	4,200	141.5	687 E.D.	24½ hours counterclockwise	.38	67 below zero	Thin carbon dioxide atmos.; white caps at poles; red rocky surface
Jupiter	88,700	483.4	12 E.Y.[b]	10 hours counterclockwise	2.34	162 below zero	No water; great red spot; atmos. of hydrogen, helium, ammonia
Saturn	75,000	914.0	30 E.Y.	11 hours counterclockwise	.92	208 below zero	Atmos. of hydrogen, helium; no water, mostly gaseous; prominent rings
Uranus	31,566	1,782.4	84 E.Y.	24 hours counterclockwise	.79	355 below zero	Atmos. of hydrogen, helium; no water
Neptune	30,200	2,792.9	165 E.Y.	17 hours counterclockwise	1.12	266 below zero	Atmos. of hydrogen, helium; no water
Pluto	1,423	3,665.0	248 E.Y.	6½ days counterclockwise	.43	458 below zero	No atmos.; periodically orbits closer to sun than Neptune

[a]Earth days.

[b]Earth years.

- *Models:* Helpful for representing relationships that cannot be observed directly. David's model of the solar system and the model of human memory in Figures 7.1 and 7.5 in this chapter are examples.
- *Outlines:* Useful for representing the organizational structure in a body of written material. The detailed table of contents for this book is an example.

Other ways to organize content include graphs, tables, flowcharts, and maps. As a student, you can also use these organizers as aids as you attempt to make the information you're studying meaningful.

A word of caution: We know that people construct knowledge in ways that make sense to them, so if the organizational structure we offer doesn't make sense to our students, they will cope in one of three ways: (1) They will (mentally) reorganize and encode the information in a way that does, whether it's correct or not; (2) they'll memorize as much of it as they can, resulting in rote learning; or (3) they will ignore it altogether.

To ensure that this doesn't happen, we can use questioning and discussion, both to help our students make new information meaningful and to help us determine if their developing understanding is valid. David, for instance, not only organized his content by using various visuals, but he also guided his students' developing understanding with the questions he asked.

Reviews are important for helping students activate their prior knowledge so that new knowledge can be connected to it.

Schema Activation

Think back to some of your most effective teachers. In most cases they probably began their classes with a review, and a long history of research supports the effectiveness of well-structured reviews in promoting learning (Rutter, Maughan, Mortimore, Ousten, & Smith, 1979; Good & Brophy, 2008).

Reviews capitalize on **schema activation,** which is an encoding strategy that involves activating relevant prior knowledge so that new knowledge can be connected to it (Mayer & Wittrock, 2006). Schema activation was illustrated in Juan's comment, "I know the answer to the first question. . . . Pluto was once considered part of the solar system, but it isn't any more." He had a schema related to the solar system that was activated by the discussion. He then connected the new information—explaining why Pluto's orbital plane is different from the planets—to it, which resulted in a deeper understanding of the solar system.

The most effective way of activating students' prior knowledge is to ask them what they already know about a topic or to ask them to provide some personal experiences related to it. Any teaching strategy that helps students form conceptual bridges between what they already know and what they are to learn is a form of schema activation.

Schema activation. An encoding strategy that involves activating relevant prior knowledge so that new knowledge can be connected to it.

Elaboration

You're at a noisy party, and when you miss some of a conversation, you fill in details, trying to make sense of an incomplete message. You do the same when you read a text or listen to a lecture. You expand on (and sometimes distort) information to make it fit your expectations and current understanding. In each case, you are *elaborating* on either the message or what you already know.

Elaboration is an encoding strategy that increases the meaningfulness of new information by connecting it to existing knowledge (Terry, 2009). For example, a student who remembers the location of the Atlantic ocean on the globe because it starts with an "a" and the Americas and Africa also begin with "a", or a student who remembers $6 \times 9 = 54$ because the sum of the digits in the product of a number times 9 always equals $9(5 + 4 = 9)$ is capitalizing on elaboration as an encoding strategy.

When elaboration is used to remember factual information such as the location of the Atlantic Ocean, or $6 \times 9 = 54$, it is often called *elaborative rehearsal.* Research confirms the superiority of elaboration compared to simple rehearsal for long-term retention (Craik, 1979; King-Friedrichs & Browne, 2001). This makes sense, because more connections are formed in long-term memory, increasing the likelihood that information can be retrieved later.

Tanya, in David's class, capitalized on elaboration when she said, "Oh, I get it, now! Pluto isn't level with the rest of them." She linked Pluto to her existing knowledge of the planets, making this new information more meaningful to her.

In addition to elaborative rehearsal, two additional elaboration strategies are effective in encoding new information: (1) the use of examples and analogies, and (2) mnemonics.

Elaboration. An encoding strategy that increases the meaningfulness of new information by connecting it to existing knowledge.

Examples and Analogies. One of the most effective ways of promoting elaboration is through examples and other representations that illustrate the topic being taught. Working with examples—constructing, finding, or analyzing them—is arguably the most powerful elaboration strategy that exists because it also capitalizes on schema activation (Cassady, 1999). When learners create or identify a new example of an idea, they activate their prior knowledge and then elaborate on their understanding of it. Using examples also helps accommodate students' lack of experience. For example, most of David's students had little prior knowledge about the formation of the solar system, and they didn't know how its formation related to the orbital planes of the planets. So, he provided it for them with his visuals.

Our extensive use of examples throughout this book demonstrates our belief in this strategy, and we encourage you to focus on the examples when you study. You can do the same with the concepts you teach.

Analogies. Descriptions of relationships between ideas that are similar in some but not all respects.

When examples aren't available, using **analogies,** descriptions of relationships that are similar in some but not all respects, can be an effective elaboration strategy (Bulgren et al., 2000). As an example, consider the following analogy from science:

> Our circulatory system is like a pumping system that carries the blood around our bodies. The veins and arteries are the pipes, and the heart is the pump.

The veins and arteries are similar, but not identical, to pipes, and the heart is a type of pump. The analogy is an effective form of elaboration because it links new information to a pumping station, an idea learners already understand.

Mnemonic devices. Memory strategies that create associations that don't exist naturally in the content.

Mnemonics. **Mnemonic devices** are memory strategies that create associations that don't exist naturally in the content (Terry, 2009). Mnemonics are used to help remember vocabulary, names, rules, lists, and other kinds of factual knowledge. Mnemonics link knowledge to be learned to familiar information, and they have been proven effective in a variety of content areas and with a wide range of learners (Brehmer & Li 2007; Uygur & Ozdas, 2007). For example, mnemonics have been used to increase cognitive performance of aging adults (Willis et al., 2006), and one study was so successful that it was picked up and discussed in the popular press (Begley, 2010).

Mnemonics can take several forms. We can use acronyms, for example, such as HOMES to remember the names of the Great Lakes (Huron, Ontario, Michigan, Erie, and Superior) and phrases, such as "Every good boy does fine," to remember the names of the notes in the treble clef (E, G, B, D, and F). When learners think of the mnemonic, they link it to the information it represents, which aids the recall of information.

Table 7.4 provides additional examples of mnemonic devices from different content areas.

Ed Psych and You

You and a friend are studying this book. You read and write an answer to each of the "Check Your Understanding" questions in the chapters, and then go to Appendix A to study the feedback. Your friend carefully reads each question and then carefully studies the feedback. Which of you is likely to learn more?

Cognitive Activity: The Essence of Encoding

The answer to our question in this "Ed Psych and You" is, you will learn more, because *you are more cognitively active than your friend.* Writing an answer encourages you to search your long-term memory for connections and actually construct a response. It literally requires you to think carefully about an answer, and *focused thinking* is the essence of cognitive activity. When we simply read the question and the feedback, no matter how hard we try, we aren't likely to focus as clearly and think as deeply about our answer. It is less cognitively active, resulting in fewer connections to information in long-term memory and less meaningful learning. Similarly, asking students to provide or recognize additional examples of an idea places them in more cognitively active roles than providing them with an example (Bransford et al., 2000).

Table 7.4	Types and examples of mnemonic devices	
Mnemonic	**Description**	**Example**
Method of loci	Learner combines imagery with specific locations in a familiar environment, such as the chair, sofa, lamp, and end table in a living room.	Student wanting to remember the first seven elements in order visualizes hydrogen at the chair, helium at the sofa, lithium at the lamp, and so on.
Peg-word method	Learner memorizes a series of "pegs"—such as a simple rhyme like "one is bun" and "two is shoe"—on which to-be-remembered information is hung.	A learner wanting to remember to get pickles and carrots at the grocery visualizes a pickle in a bun and carrot stuck in a shoe.
Link method	Learner visually links items to be remembered.	A learner visualizes *homework* stuck in a *notebook*, which is bound to her *textbook, pencil* and *pen* with a rubber band to remember to take the (italicized) items to class.
Key-word method	Learner uses imagery and rhyming words to remember unfamiliar words.	A learner remembers that *trigo* (which rhymes with *tree*) is the Spanish word for *wheat* by visualizing a sheaf of wheat sticking out of a tree.
First-letter method	Learner creates a word from the first letter of items to be remembered.	A student creates the word *Wajmma* to remember the first six presidents in order: Washington, Adams, Jefferson, Madison, Monroe, and Adams.

Regardless of the encoding strategy we use to help us meaningfully store any new information, putting ourselves in cognitively active roles—thinking carefully about the information—is essential. When we teach, one of the most effective ways to promote cognitive activity is to guide students' processing with questioning. Let's return to David's lesson to see how. We rejoin the class on Thursday.

David begins by saying, "Yesterday, you were supposed to use the information we've gathered to answer a series of questions. Let's see what you've come up with." After Juan, speaking for his group, offers an explanation for the first question, which asked about Pluto's orbital plane, David then asks, "What about the next question—'Why is Mercury so hot on one side and so cold on the other?'"

"We couldn't answer it, Mr. Sheldon," several students respond.

"Okay, let's see if we can figure it out. . . . Look at Mercury's length of day. What do you notice about it? . . . Marcos?"

"It's really long, 59 Earth days. . . . It rotates really slow," Marcos responds after looking at the chart (In Table 7.3) for several seconds.

"Good," David nods. "So, what does that tell us? . . . Serena?"

"One side is . . . facing the sun for a long time," Serena answers hesitantly.

"Aha, . . . I get it," LaToya blurts out. "If one side faces the sun for a long time, it gets really hot, so the other side gets really cold."

"Excellent thinking, LaToya," David smiles. "That's a very good analysis."

David's questions helped his students attend to important information, such as the length of Mercury's day, and to look for a relationship between it and the planet's temperature. And, he structured the discussion around the information in the matrix, so he also capitalized on organization as an encoding strategy. He could have simply explained these relationships, as many teachers do, but the students wouldn't have thought as carefully about them, they would have been less cognitively active, and their learning would have been less meaningful.

David's use of group work also promoted cognitive activity, as you saw in Juan's, Randy's, and Tanya's discussion, but structuring the activity and carefully supervising students while they worked in groups were essential parts of this process. We are sometimes lulled into tacitly concluding that if our students are talking or physically active, they are also cognitively active, but this isn't necessarily the case (Mayer, 2004). They may be talking to each other during group work and hands-on activities but may not be really "thinking about" what they're doing. Group work is popular in schools, but if these activities aren't carefully structured and monitored, they may be no more effective than a dry lecture. Group work and hands-on activities don't, in themselves, ensure "minds-on" learning (Brophy, 2006a; Mayer, 2004).

Forgetting

Forgetting. The loss of, or inability to retrieve, information from long-term memory.

Forgetting is the loss of, or inability to retrieve, information from long-term memory, and it is both a real part of our everyday lives and an important factor in classroom learning.

To understand forgetting, let's look again at the model first presented in Figure 7.1 There we see that information lost from both sensory memory and working memory is unrecoverable. However, information in long-term memory has been encoded. Why can't we find it?

Forgetting as Interference

Interference. The loss of information because something learned either before or after detracts from understanding.

Proactive interference. The loss of new information because of the influence of prior learning.

Retroactive interference. The loss of previously learned information because of the influence of new learning.

The concept of **interference,** the loss of information because something learned either before or after detracts from understanding, is one way to explain forgetting (Howe, 2004). For example, students first learn the rule for forming singular possessives by adding an apostrophe s to the singular noun. If their understanding of this rule for forming singular possessives later interferes with learning the rules for forming plural possessives and contractions, we have **proactive interference,** in which prior learning interferes with new understanding. On the other hand, if the rules for forming plural possessives confuse their prior understanding, **retroactive interference** occurs. Students' understanding of plural possessives and contractions can interfere with their understanding of singular possessives and vice versa.

Teaching closely related ideas—such as adjectives and adverbs, longitude and latitude, and adding fractions with similar and different denominators—together can help reduce interference. In doing so, you help students recognize similarities and differences and identify areas that are easily confused.

You can also reduce interference by using reviews to capitalize on schema activation, comparing the new topic to the closely related information that your students have already studied. This helps students identify easily confused similarities and promotes elaboration.

Forgetting as Retrieval Failure

Retrieval. The process of pulling information from long-term memory into working memory.

Retrieval failure is a second explanation for forgetting. **Retrieval** is the process of pulling information from long-term memory back into working memory, and it's represented in Figures 7.1 and 7.5 by the arrow pointing from long-term memory back to working memory. We've all had the experience of realizing that we know a name or a fact, but we simply can't dredge it up. This is an example of *retrieval failure,* and many researchers believe that "forgetting" is actually our inability to retrieve information from long-term memory (Williams & Zacks, 2001).

Ed Psych and You

Quickly state the months of the year. Now, do the same, but this time list them alphabetically. Why were you so much slower the second time?

Retrieval also depends on context and the way we encode information, and this helps answer the question we asked in our "Ed Psych and You" feature (Williams & Zacks, 2001). The context in which we encode the months of the year is chronological, since that's the way we experience them, and remembering them this way is automatic. Attempting to state them alphabetically presents a different context. We can do it, but we must laboriously go through the process. Similarly, you know a person at school, but you can't remember his name when you see him at a party; his name was encoded in the school context, and you're trying to retrieve it in the context of the party.

Meaningfulness is the key to retrieval. The more interconnected our knowledge is in long-term memory, the easier it is to retrieve. David attempted to make information about the solar system meaningful by using his visuals and cognitively engaging his students with questioning and group work. In doing so, he increased the chance of later retrieval.

Practice to the point of automaticity, such as we've done with the months of the year, also facilitates retrieval (Chaffen & Imreh, 2002). When math facts are automatic, students easily retrieve the facts for use in problem solving, leaving more working memory space to focus on solutions.

Developmental Differences in Cognitive Processes

As with memory stores, developmental differences exist in our cognitive processes (Nelson et al., 2006). One of the most important involves *attention;* older children are better able to focus their attention, are less distracted by irrelevant stimuli, and their attention becomes more purposeful (Dempster & Corkill, 1999; Higgins & Turnure, 1984). Significantly, students with learning disabilities, such as attention deficit hyperactivity disorder, lag developmentally behind their peers (Bental & Tirosh, 2007).

Developmental differences also exist in *perception* and *encoding,* and experience is an important factor. Because older students have more experiences than their younger counterparts, their perceptions are more likely to be accurate, and they can also use more sophisticated encoding strategies. For instance, preschoolers rarely use rehearsal as an encoding strategy, but by the second or third grade, students begin to use rehearsal spontaneously, and as they further develop, they begin to use more advanced encoding strategies, such as imagery, organization, and elaboration, to make their learning more efficient (Pressley & Hilden, 2006).

Teachers can capitalize on learners' differing experiences to increase achievement for all students.

Classroom connections

Helping Students Capitalize on Cognitive Processes to Increase Their Learning

Attention

1. Attention is the beginning point for learning. Begin and conduct lessons to attract and maintain attention.

   ■ **Elementary:** To be sure that all students are attending to the lesson, a third-grade teacher calls on all his students whether they have their hands up or not.

   ■ **Middle School:** A science teacher introducing the concept *pressure* has students stand by their desks, first on both feet and then on one foot. They then discuss the force and pressure on the floor in each case.

   ■ **High School:** To be sure that her students attend to important points, a world history teacher uses emphasis, "Everyone, listen carefully now, because we're going to look at three important reasons that World War I broke out in Europe."

Perception

2. Perception is the process of attaching meaning to the information we attend to, so accurate perceptions are essential for understanding. Check frequently to be certain that students perceive your examples and other representations accurately.

   ■ **Elementary:** In a lesson on living things, a kindergarten teacher holds up a large potted plant, asks, "What do you notice about the plant?" and calls on several children for their observations.

   ■ **Middle School:** A geography teacher downloads colored pictures of different landforms from the Internet and asks students to describe each.

   ■ **High School:** Students are reading an essay and encounter the line, "The revolution often bordered on anarchy; the citizens were out of control." Their teacher stops and asks, "What does the author mean by 'anarchy'?"

Meaningful Encoding

3. Meaningful encoding is the process of connecting new information to information already in long-term memory. To aid encoding, carefully organize the information you present to students, and promote cognitive activity with interactive teaching strategies.

   ■ **Elementary:** A fourth-grade teacher illustrates that heat causes expansion by placing a balloon-covered soft drink bottle in a pot of hot water and by presenting a drawing that shows the spacing and motion of the air molecules. She then guides the students with questioning to understand the relationship between heat, molecular activity, and expansion.

   ■ **Middle School:** A math teacher presents a flowchart with a series of questions students should ask themselves as they solve word problems (e.g., What do I know? What am I trying to find out?). As the class works on problems, he asks them to describe their thinking and tell where they are on the flowchart.

   ■ **High School:** A history teacher presents a matrix comparing different immigrant groups, their reasons for relocating to the United States, the difficulties they encountered, and their rates of assimilation. The students then search for patterns in the information in the chart.

4. Learners elaborate their understanding when they make new connections between the items of information they're studying. Encourage students to relate items of information to each other and form mental images as often as possible.

   ■ **Elementary:** A fourth-grade teacher, after a demonstration at the front of the room, says, "Let's see what we've found out about chemical and physical changes. Give two new examples of each that show the differences between the two."

   ■ **Middle School:** A geography teacher encourages her students to visualize parallel lines on the globe as they think about latitude, and vertical lines coming together at the North and South Poles as they think about longitude. She then asks her students to compare them.

   ■ **High School:** An English teacher asks students to imagine the appearance of the characters in a novel by pretending they are casting them for a movie version. He then asks them to suggest a current actor or actress to play each role.

Retrieval

5. Retrieval occurs when learners pull information from long-term memory back into working memory, and interference can inhibit this process. To prevent interference and aid retrieval, teach closely related ideas together.

   ■ **Elementary:** To teach area and perimeter, a fifth-grade teacher has her students lay squares side by side to illustrate area, and she has them measure the distance around the pieces to illustrate perimeter.

   ■ **Middle School:** An English teacher displays a passage on the document camera that includes gerunds and participles. He then asks the students to compare the way the words are used in the passage to demonstrate that gerunds are nouns and participles are adjectives.

   ■ **High School:** A biology teacher begins a unit on arteries and veins by saying, "We've all heard of hardening of the arteries, but we haven't heard of 'hardening of the veins.' Why not?"

The Impact of Diversity on Cognition

Our students' prior knowledge strongly influences their perceptions and the way they encode new information. For example, Juan's experiences watching *Nova* influenced his perception of information about Pluto. Randy and Tanya lacked this knowledge, so understanding the significance of Pluto's orbit was harder for them.

Differences in background knowledge and experience are particularly important when students come from a variety of socioeconomic and cultural backgrounds. For example, Paul (one of your authors) grew up in a rural, relatively low socioeconomic environment and attended a very small high school. As a result, access to a rich menu of educational experiences, such as advanced math and science courses, foreign languages, and technology, was limited. When he went on to college, he competed with students from larger schools and had to work hard to overcome these deficiencies. Don (your other author), who taught in a low socioeconomic status neighborhood outside of Chicago, found that many of his urban students, because of parental work pressures, family issues, and other factors, never had the chance to capitalize on the educational opportunities available in the city. For instance, although his students lived less than an hour away from world-class museums, a planetarium, and an aquarium, many of his students didn't even know they existed. More advantaged students frequently visited these sites, and their performance in class reflected the educational benefits of these experiences.

In spite of these differences, however, we can do a great deal to accommodate the diversity in our students' background experiences. Research

offers several suggestions (J. R. Anderson, 2005; Huan et al., 2006):

- *Assess students' prior knowledge and perceptions by asking them what they already know about a topic.* For example, because he has several recent-immigrant children in his class, a third-grade teacher begins a unit on communities by saying, "Tell us about the communities where you lived before coming to this country." He then uses the information as a framework for the study of their community.

- *Supplement students' prior experiences with rich examples.* For instance, a middle school science teacher introduces *refraction* by having students put coins in opaque dishes and backing up until they can't see the coins. Partners pour water into the dishes until the coins become visible, and the teacher shows a model illustrating how the light rays are bent when they enter and leave the water.

- *Use students' experiences to augment the backgrounds of others lacking the experiences.* For instance, a teacher whose class is studying modern Europe says, "Celeena, you lived in Europe. Tell us about the thinking of people in countries that were part of the former Eastern Bloc."

In each case, the teacher then uses students' existing knowledge, examples, or background experiences as a launching point for the lesson. The ability to adapt lessons in this way is an important component of teaching expertise.

check your understanding

3.1 Describe the cognitive processes in the human memory model.

3.2 A language arts teacher wants to involve her students in a discussion of plot development in a novel. She begins by asking, "What do we mean by plot development?" To which of the cognitive processes does the teacher's question most closely relate? Explain.

3.3 A third-grade teacher uses flash cards to help her students acquire math facts, such as $6 \times 8 = 48$ and $7 \times 9 = 63$, and she also has her students practice solving word problems by comparing new problems to problems that they have discussed in class. What cognitive process were the students employing when they used the flash cards? What encoding strategies did the students use when they compared and practiced solving problems?

To receive feedback for these questions, go to Appendix A.

Metacognition: Knowledge and Control of Cognitive Processes

Think about the questions we asked in our "Ed Psych and You" feature here. If you answered yes to either, or have had similar thoughts about your learning, you were being *metacognitive*. **Metacognition,** commonly described as "knowing about knowing," is our awareness of and control

Ed Psych and You

Have you ever said to yourself, "I'm beat today. I'd better drink a cup of coffee before I go to class," or, "I better sit near the front of the class so I won't fall asleep." What do these comments suggest about your approach to learning?

Metacognition. Our awareness of and our control over our cognitive processes.

Meta-attention. Our knowledge of and control over our ability to pay attention.

over our cognitive processes, and **meta-attention,** knowledge of and control over our ability to pay attention, is one type of metacognition (Meltzer, Pollica, & Barzillai, 2007; Pressley & Hilden, 2006). You were *aware* of the fact that your drowsiness might affect your ability to attend, and you exercised *control* over it by drinking coffee or sitting near the front of the class.

Metacognition explains a variety of actions in our everyday lives. Paul, for instance, knowing that he is likely to misplace his keys, always immediately puts them in a desk drawer when he comes in from the garage. Don, a self-described absent-minded professor, realizes that he sometimes forgets important dates like his wedding anniversary and kids' birthdays, so he's put them in a computer file. Many of us make to-do lists, and virtually everyone prepares lists when grocery shopping. In all cases we are aware of the limitations of our memories, and we exercise control over them with our lists and other strategies.

Metacognition plays an important role in classroom learning; students who are metacognitive—aware of the way they study and learn and take steps to maximize their strengths—achieve more than those less so (D. Anderson & Nashon, 2007).

Several reasons account for these differences. First, students who realize how important attention is are more likely to create personal learning environments free of distractions, which can be as simple as moving to the front of the class or turning off a cell phone while studying at home. Second, learners who know that they might misperceive information they hear or read attempt to find corroborating information or ask if their understanding is accurate.

Metamemory. Knowledge of and control over our memory strategies.

Third, metacognition helps accommodate the limitations of working memory. For instance, Randy demonstrated **metamemory**—knowledge and control of memory strategies—when he said, "I better write some of this stuff down, or I'll never remember it," and this answers the third question we asked at the beginning of the chapter (What impact will Randy's decision to "write some of this stuff down" have on his future learning?) Realizing that he needed to write some information down, and then doing so will increase his learning, and the more metacognitive he becomes, the greater impact it will have.

Finally, metacognition influences the meaningfulness of encoding. Metacognitive learners consciously look for relationships in the topics they study, which influences their study strategies and ultimately how much they learn. The metacognitive components of the memory model are illustrated in Figure 7.7.

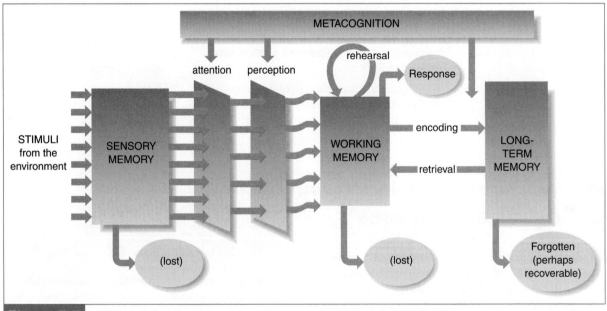

Figure 7.7 Metacognition in the model of human memory

Developmental Differences in Metacognition

Young learners' metacognitive abilities are limited, but they gradually become more strategic about their learning as they mature and gain experience. For example, young children are likely to be aware of the need to pay attention only when reminded to do so by their teacher, but older children are generally aware of the importance of attention and are able to direct it toward important information in a variety of learning tasks (Von der Linden & Roebers, 2006).

These developmental differences also appear in metamemory (Gaskill & Murphy, 2004). Older students use advanced encoding strategies, such as imagery and organization, but younger children do not. And older learners are more aware of their memory limitations, so they use lists and other external aids, while younger children don't (Pressley & Hilden, 2006).

In spite of these developmental differences, older learners and even some college students are not as metacognitive about their learning as they should be (Peverly, Brobst, & Graham, 2003), so, if you're planning to teach in middle or high schools, your students will still need a great deal of guidance and support to develop their metacognitive abilities.

Unconscious Processing in Human Memory

We've described our human information-processing system as logical, sequential, and largely governed by our metacognition. However, aspects of our cognition elude conscious thought and control; we make many decisions and conclusions essentially without thinking about them, a tendency some writers call **unconscious processing** (Vendantam, 2010).

Unconscious Processing. The tendency to make conclusions and decisions without thinking about them.

Over the past few years, geneticists, neuroscientists, psychologists, sociologists, economists, anthropologists, and others have made great strides in understanding the building blocks of human flourishing. And a core finding of their work is that we are not primarily the products of our conscious thinking. We are primarily the products of thinking that happens below the level of awareness. (Brooks, 2011).

For example, think about the questions we asked in our "Ed Psych and You" feature here. Using marketing research, retailers capitalize on this tendency to seduce us into buying certain products. Companies pay big bucks to supermarkets to have their products placed at eye level, so this is the first thing we see when we glance down the aisle. (Children's products are placed at a child's eye level.) The produce section is usually placed at the front of the store, and perhaps slightly to the right, because produce is a high-profit item, and people have a tendency to turn right when they walk into a store. Milk, an item we commonly pick up when we shop, is in the back, so we have to weave our way through the store to find it, making it more likely that we'll pick up other items on the way. The longer we're in the store, the greater the likelihood that we'll spend extra money. When we're bored standing at the checkout line, we reach for a magazine, a pack of batteries, or chewing gum. This section of the store sells almost three times as much merchandise per square foot as the rest of the store, and these are usually high-profit items (SupermarketPage.com, 2010; Underhill, 2009).

Unconscious processing exists at a larger scale as well. For example, international corporations reduce their names to acronyms—it's AT&T, not American Telephone and Telegraph, and it's BP, not British Petroleum—in an effort to create the unconscious impression that companies are generic instead of nation bound. In fact, when president Obama referred to BP as "British Petroleum" after the Gulf oil spill of 2010, many interpreted the term as his effort to shift blame toward Great Britain, which offended many in that country.

Unconscious processing is somewhat analogous to automaticity, a mechanism to overcome the slow and deliberate conscious processing in working memory (Vendantam, 2010). Unlike automaticity, however, which results from practice and repetition, unconscious processing can result in inappropriate and potentially harmful conclusions. For instance, research indicates that people judge obese individuals as less competent and moral than people of average weight (Hebl & Mannix, 2003)!

Unconscious Processing in Classrooms

So how does unconscious processing affect us as teachers? A long history of research indicates that teachers assess physically attractive students as more intelligent and more socially skilled than those who are less attractive. As a result they have different expectations for the attractive students, which can result in differences in achievement for the two groups (Ritts, Patterson, & Tubbs, 1992). In addition, these unconscious evaluations also influence teachers' perceptions of different ethnic and cultural groups. For example, a study examining preservice and practicing teachers' assessments of students' ability found that both groups rated unattractive black males lower in perceived ability and social skills than any other group (Parks & Kennedy, 2007).

College instructors are also influenced by unconscious processing, both as perpetrators and victims. For instance, evidence suggests that college instructors give favored treatment to attractive students, and particularly to attractive, and sometimes scantily dressed, young women (Perlmutter, 2004). On the other hand, the "hotness factor"—how physically attractive instructors are—has been found to result in higher student evaluations of college teachers (Freng & Webber, 2009).

Unconscious Processing and Metacognition

How should we respond to this potential problem? Simply, being aware of our tendencies to make unconscious decisions and taking steps to accommodate them—being metacognitive—can help prevent or overcome many of the potentially destructive aspects of unconscious processing. We can also implement two valuable practices in our teaching to help overcome unconscious tendencies and potential biases. First, we're all human, and we're going to like some of our students more than others, simply because they have better attitudes, more engaging personalities, or are more attractive. To overcome the possibility of unconsciously evaluating their work more positively, assessing students' understanding thoroughly, frequently, and as objectively as possible is essential. This means giving students frequent quizzes and assignments that provide reliable, detailed information about their learning progress.

Frequent and systematic assessment also carries with it a learning bonus. Evidence indicates that assessment is one of the most powerful learning tools at our disposal. "... A combination of study and tests is more effective than spending the same amount of time reviewing the material in some other way, such as rereading" (Rohrer & Pashler, 2010).

Second, we know that social interaction facilitates learning, so when we interact with our students, we should make an effort to call on all of them as equally as possible, a strategy known as **equitable distribution.** Being aware of your questioning patterns and attempting to equitably distribute your questions will help prevent you from unconsciously favoring higher achievers or more attractive and engaging students.

Being aware of our tendencies to process information unconsciously, making assessment an integral part of our instruction, and practicing equitable distribution can help provide all our students with the learning opportunities they deserve.

Equitable distribution. The practice of calling on all students in a class equally.

Developmentally appropriate practice

The Memory Model with Learners at Different Ages

While the implications of cognitive learning theory and the model of human memory apply at all grade levels, important developmental differences exist. The following guidelines outline ways to respond to these differences.

Working with Students in Early Childhood Programs and Elementary Schools

Our attention is limited, and this limitation is even more pronounced in young children. If you're a teacher of young children, you know how important it is to start lessons with an attention-getter and to continually monitor attention during lessons. To maintain the attention of young children, learning activities must be short and frequently changed.

You also need to make directions for every task simple and precise and need to continually check children's perceptions of the task requirements. Complex tasks should be broken into shorter and simpler ones, and each should be completed before moving to the next one.

Young children's thinking tends to be concrete, so abstract ideas need to be illustrated with concrete and personalized examples. Because their language is developing, young children benefit from opportunities to practice putting their developing understanding into words.

Modeling metacognition and helping children develop an awareness of factors that influence their learning is particularly helpful with young students (Meltzer et al., 2007). Children who become aware of how attention influences learning acquire a learning skill that they can use throughout their lifetimes.

Working with Students in Middle Schools

Middle school students are beginning to understand how their metacognitive capabilities influence learning. To capitalize on their increased ability to monitor their own learning, if you're a middle school teacher, helping students develop learning strategies that emphasize metacognition can be effective. For example, encouraging students to ask themselves questions, such as, "How is this idea similar to and different from the previous idea?" and "What would be a real-world example of this idea?" models effective learning strategies that can significantly increase learning.

Much of middle school students' thinking still remains concrete, however, especially when the topic is new or abstract, so you'll need to continue to use concrete examples and analyze them using questioning. And because so much of learning is verbal, guiding students as they put their understanding into words not only increases learning but also promotes language development.

Working with Students in High Schools

High school students can use sophisticated learning strategies, but they are unlikely to use them unless the strategies are modeled and encouraged (Pressley & Hilden, 2006). If you're a high school teacher, modeling the use of encoding strategies, such as organization, elaboration, and imagery is an effective way to promote their use in classrooms. Even high school students are likely to use rehearsal as a strategy when material is difficult for them, however, so practice with other strategies is important.

Teaching strategies like questioning and small-group work that place students in cognitively active roles are important. Unfortunately, many high school teachers tend to rely on lecture in the mistaken belief that "telling" is teaching. High school students are social beings and love nothing more than to sit around and talk about who is dating whom and what's happening that weekend. Carefully structuring and monitoring group work to ensure that students who are socially active are also cognitively active is important.

High school students are capable of abstract thinking and problem solving but may need prompting to do so. They should be encouraged to examine questions in depth, and consider cause-and-effect relationships, such as the questions David asked as they studied the solar system.

Concrete examples continue to be important for introducing abstract and unfamiliar concepts, and questioning continues to be an effective strategy for analyzing new content and developing language skills.

4.1 Define *metacognition,* and explain how it can influence classroom learning.

4.2 As you read this book, you stop and go back to the top of a page and reread one of the sections. Is this an example of metacognition? Explain.

4.3 Note taking is a study strategy. You have a classmate, who, in an attempt to be sure that he doesn't miss anything, writes down virtually everything the instructor says. You write down only the points that you believe are most important. Which of you is more metacognitive in your approach to note taking? Explain.

To receive feedback for these questions, go to Appendix A.

Classroom connections

Promoting Metacognition in Students

1. Metacognition is knowledge of and control over the way we study and learn, and learners who are metacognitive learn more and retain information longer. To capitalize on metacognition, integrate metacognitive strategies into your instruction and model your own metacognition.

   ■ **Elementary:** During a lesson, a fourth-grade teacher holds up a card with the sentence, "If you're paying attention, raise your hand." He acknowledges those who are and encourages them to share their strategies for maintaining attention during class.

   ■ **Middle School:** A social studies teacher emphasizes metamemory by saying, "Suppose you're reading, and the book states that there are three important differences between capitalism and socialism. What should you do?"

   ■ **High School:** An economics teacher models metacognitive strategies by making statements like, "Whenever I read something new, I always ask myself, 'How does this relate to what I've been studying?' For example, how is the liberal economic agenda different from the conservative agenda?"

Ed Psych and teaching

Applying the Human Memory Model in Your Teaching

Applying your understanding of the human memory model in your teaching can increase all your students' learning. The following guidelines can help you in your efforts:

1. Begin lessons with an activity that attracts attention.
2. Conduct frequent reviews to activate students' prior knowledge and check their perceptions.
3. Proceed in short steps, and represent content both visually and verbally to reduce the cognitive load on working memory.
4. Help students make information meaningful, and aid encoding through organization, imagery, elaboration, and cognitive activity.
5. Model and encourage metacognition.

Let's review David's lesson now to see how he applied these guidelines in his teaching. He applied the first when he began the lesson by attracting his students' attention with visuals. He then helped maintain students' attention with his questioning and group work.

He checked his students' perceptions by asking them to describe their interpretations of his visuals, and on Wednesday he reviewed the information in Monday's and Tuesday's lesson. This applied the second guideline.

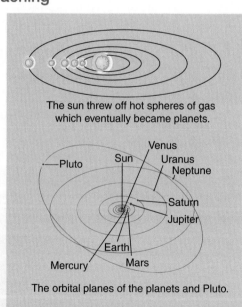

The sun threw off hot spheres of gas which eventually became planets.

The orbital planes of the planets and Pluto.

He applied the third by representing the content both visually and verbally, and when his students struggled, he used information in the matrix combined with questioning to guide students' developing understanding. Both reduced the cognitive load on students' working memories.

His visuals promoted students' use of imagery, and his matrix capitalized on organization to make the information meaningful. The discussion put students in cognitively active roles and also helped them elaborate on their understanding. These processes applied the fourth guideline.

Finally, in saying, "When I try to answer questions like these, I first look for relationships in the parts of the question, like what do I know about Pluto compared to the other planets?" he was modeling metacognition, which applied the fifth guideline.

Applying the memory model in your teaching need not take a great deal of extra effort. For instance, after David first created his materials, he was able to reuse them with little or no further preparation. And checking students' perceptions and guiding their learning with questioning can—with practice—become essentially automatic. This is true for applying all the content of educational psychology: Effective application is more a matter of clear teacher thinking than additional effort.

Evaluating the Human Memory Model

The human memory model makes an important contribution to our understanding of the way we learn and remember. However, the model, as initially presented in Figure 7.1 oversimplifies the nature of human memory. For example, the model presents attention as a filter between sensory memory and working memory, but some evidence indicates that the central executive in working memory influences both our attention and how we perceive that information. So, attending to incoming stimuli and attaching meaning to them are not as simple as the one-way flow of information suggested by the model (Demetriou, Christou, Spanoudis, & Platsidou, 2002). In addition, some researchers question whether working memory and long-term memory are as distinct as the model suggests (Baddeley, 2001; Wolz, 2003).

The memory model has also been criticized for failing to adequately consider the social context in which learning occurs, as well as cultural and personal factors that influence learning, such as students' emotions (Nasir, Rosebery, Warren, & Lee, 2006). Critics also argue that it doesn't adequately account for the extent to which learners construct their own knowledge, a principle of cognitive learning theory (Kafai, 2006).

However, despite these criticisms, virtually all cognitive descriptions of learning accept the basic structure of the human memory model, including a limited-capacity working memory, a long-term memory that stores information in organized form, cognitive processes that move the information from one store to another, and the regulatory mechanisms of metacognition (Bransford et al., 2000). These components help explain learning events that other theories are unable to explain, and the human memory model has important implications for our teaching.

Summary

1. Identify the basic components of human memory.
   - The human memory model is composed of memory stores, repositories that hold information; cognitive processes that move information from one store to another; and metacognition, which regulates both memory and cognitive processes.

2. Use the memory stores in the human memory model to explain events in classrooms and the everyday world.
   - Sensory memory is the store that briefly holds stimuli from the environment until they can be processed; working memory is the conscious part of our information-processing system, and its capacity is limited; long-term memory is our permanent information store, and it is where knowledge is stored.
   - When students struggle with complex tasks, lack of prior knowledge stored in long-term memory or skills that haven't been developed to automaticity are often the cause. The memory stores are influenced by development, with older students more effectively accommodating the limitations of working memory and better capitalizing on their experiences to represent information in long-term memory.

3. Describe the cognitive processes in the human memory model, and explain applications in classroom activities.
   - Attention and perception move information from sensory memory to working memory. Attention is the process of consciously focusing on a stimulus, and perception attaches meaning to a stimulus.
   - Learners use rehearsal to retain information in the phonological loop of working memory, and intensive rehearsal can move information into long-term memory.
   - Encoding represents information in long-term memory. Learners encode information more effectively if it is represented both visually and verbally.
   - Retrieval is the process of pulling information from long-term memory back into working memory for problem solving or further processing.
   - Students' use of the cognitive processes improve as they develop, with older learners better focusing their attention and more effectively using strategies to promote meaningful encoding.

4. Define *metacognition*, and explain how it influences classroom learning.
   - *Metacognition* is individuals' knowledge of, and control over, their cognitive processes.
   - Metacognition influences learning by making learners aware of the way they study and learn, and providing strategies to increase learning.
   - Metacognition is developmental, with young children being less aware of their cognitive activities than their older counterparts.

Understanding the Human Memory Model: Preparing for Your Licensure Exam

Your licensure exam will include information related to human memory and student learning, and we include the following exercises to help you practice for the exam in your state. This book and these exercises will be a resource for you as you prepare for the exam.

In the following case, a teacher helps a group of high school students understand different characters in the novel *The Scarlet Letter*. Read the case study, and then answer the questions that follow.

Sue Southam, an English teacher, decides to use Nathaniel Hawthorne's *The Scarlet Letter* as the vehicle to help her students examine timeless issues, such as moral dilemmas involving personal responsibility and emotions like love, guilt, anger, loyalty, and revenge. The novel, set in Boston in the 1600s, describes a tragic and illicit love affair between the heroine (Hester Prynne) and a minister (Arthur Dimmesdale). The novel's title refers to the letter A, meaning "adulterer," which

the Puritan community makes Hester wear as punishment for her adultery. The class has been discussing the book for several days, and they are now examining Reverend Dimmesdale's character.

To begin, Sue reads a passage from the text describing Dimmesdale and then says, "In your logs, jot down some of the important characteristics in that description. If you were going to draw a portrait of him, what would he look like? Try to be as specific as possible."

She gives the students a few minutes to write in their logs, asking them to describe what they think he looks like and who they might cast in the role of a movie adaptation of the novel.

Then she says, "Let's see if we can find out more about the Dimmesdale character through his actions. Listen carefully while I read the speech he gives in which he confronts Hester in front of the congregation and exhorts her to identify her secret lover and partner in sin."

She reads Dimmesdale's speech, then divides the class into "Dimmesdales" and "Hesters" around the room, and says, "Dimmesdales, in your logs I want you to tell me what Dimmesdale is really thinking during his speech. Hesters, I want you to tell me what Hester is thinking while she listens. Write in your logs in your own words the private thoughts of your character."

After giving the students a few minutes to write in their logs, she organizes them into groups of four, with each group composed of two Hesters and two Dimmesdales. Once students are settled, she says, "In each group, I want you to start off by having Dimmesdale tell what he is thinking during the first line of the speech. Then I'd like a Hester to respond. Then continue with Dimmesdale's next line, and then Hester's reaction. Go ahead and share your thoughts in your groups."

She gives the students 5 minutes to share their perspectives, then calls the class back together: "Okay, let's hear it. A Dimmesdale first. Just what was he thinking during his speech? . . . Mike?"

"The only thing I could think of was, 'Oh God, help me. I hope she doesn't say anything. If they find out it's me, I'll be ruined.' And then here comes Hester with her powerful speech," Mike concludes, turning to his partner in the group, Nicole.

"I wrote, 'Good man, huh. So why don't you confess then? You know you're guilty. I've admitted my love, but you haven't. Why don't you just come out and say it?'" Nicole comments.

"Interesting. . . . What else? How about another Hester? . . . Sarah?"

"I just put, 'No, I'll never tell. I still love you, and I'll keep your secret forever,'" Sarah offers.

Sue pauses for a moment, looks around the room, and comments, "Notice how different the two views of Hester are. Nicole paints her as very angry, whereas Sarah views her as still loving him." Sue again pauses to look for reactions. Karen raises her hand, and Sue nods to her.

"I think the reason Hester doesn't say anything is that people won't believe her, because he's a minister," Karen suggests. "She's getting her revenge just by being there, reminding him of his guilt."

"But if she accuses him, won't people expect him to deny it?" Brad adds.

"Maybe he knows she won't accuse him because she still loves him," Julie offers.

"Wait a minute," Jeff counters. "I don't think he's such a bad guy. I think he feels guilty about it all, but he just doesn't have the courage to admit it in front of all of those people."

"I think he's really admitting it in his speech but is asking her secretly not to tell," Caroline adds. "Maybe he's really talking to Hester and doesn't want the rest of the people to know."

The class continues, with students debating the meaning in the speech and trying to decide whether Reverend Dimmesdale is really a villain or a tragic figure. "Interesting ideas," Sue says as the end of the class nears. "Keep them in mind, and for tomorrow, I'd like you to read Chapter 4, in which we meet Hester's husband," and she then closes the lesson.

Questions for Case Analysis

In answering these questions, use information from the chapter, and link your responses to specific information in the case.

1. Assess the extent to which Sue applied the human memory model in her lesson. Include both strengths and weaknesses in your assessment.

2. Which cognitive process from the memory model was most prominent in Sue's lesson? Explain.

3. Identify at least one instance in Sue's lesson in which she focused on declarative knowledge. Identify another in which she focused on procedural knowledge. Was the primary focus of Sue's lesson the acquisition of declarative knowledge or procedural knowledge?

For feedback on these responses, go to Appendix B.

Your licensure exam will also include multiple-choice questions similar to those your instructor has given you on your quizzes and tests for this course.

Important Concepts

analogies (p. 234)
attention (p. 227)
automaticity (p. 217)
central executive (p. 215)
chunking (p. 217)
cognitive learning theories
    (p. 213)
cognitive load (p. 217)
conditional knowledge
    (p. 219)
declarative knowledge (p. 219)
dual-coding theory (p. 231)
elaboration (p. 233)

encoding (p. 230)
episodic memory (p. 219)
equitable distribution (p. 242)
forgetting (p. 236)
imagery (p. 231)
information-processing
    theory (p. 213)
interference (p. 236)
long-term memory (p. 218)
meaningfulness (p. 220)
memory stores (p. 214)
meta-attention (p. 240)
metacognition (p. 240)

metamemory (p. 240)
mnemonic devices (p. 234)
model (p. 214)
organization (p. 231)
perception (p. 229)
phonological loop (p. 216)
proactive interference
    (p. 236)
procedural knowledge
    (p. 219)
rehearsal (p. 216)
retrieval (p. 236)
retroactive interference (p. 236)

rote learning (p. 230)
schema activation (p. 233)
schemas (p. 219)
scripts (p. 222)
short-term memory
    (p. 216)
semantic memory (p. 219)
sensory memory (p. 215)
unconscious processing
    (p. 241)
visual-spatial sketchpad
    (p. 216)
working memory (p. 215)

Go to the Topic: Memory and Cognitive Processes in the MyEducationLab (www.myeducationlab.com)
for *Educational Psychology: Windows on Classrooms*, where you can:

- Find learning outcomes for Memory and Cognitive Processes along with the national standards that
  connect to these outcomes.
- Complete Assignments and Activities that can help you more deeply understand the chapter content.
- Apply and practice your understanding of the core teaching skills identified in the chapter with the
  Building Teaching Skills and Dispositions learning units.
- Examine challenging situations and cases presented in the IRIS Center Resources.
- Access video clips of CCSSO National Teachers of the Year award winners responding to the question,
  "Why Do I Teach?" in the Teacher Talk section.
- See video examples included within the Study Plan that provide concrete and real-world illustrations
  of the topics presented in the chapter.
- Check your comprehension of the content covered in the chapter with the Study Plan. Here you will
  be able to take a chapter quiz, receive feedback on your answers, and
  then access Review, Practice, and Enrichment activities to enhance
  your understanding of chapter content.

MyEducationLab

chapter 8

Complex Cognitive Processes

chapteroutline

learningoutcomes

After you've completed your study of this chapter, you should be able to:

1. Define *concepts*, and describe strategies for helping students learn concepts.

2. Reognize examples of ill-defined and well-defined problems, and describe strategies to teach problem solving in the classroom.

3. Identify applications of study strategies and critical thinking.

4. Analyze applications of the factors that influence the transfer of learning.

classroomapplications

The following features help you apply the content of this chapter in your teaching.

Ed Psych and Teaching:
Applying Concept Learning Theory with Your Students
Helping Your Students Become Better Problem Solvers
Helping Your Students Become Strategic Learners
Applying an Understanding of Transfer with Your Students

Classroom Connections:
Promoting Concept Learning in Schools
Developing Learners' Problem-Solving Abilities

Promoting Strategic Learning in Classrooms
Promoting Transfer of Learning in Schools

Developmentally Appropriate Practice:
Developing Complex Cognitive Skills with Learners at Different Ages

Exploring Diversity:
Learner Differences in Complex Cognitive Processes

The title of this chapter is "Complex Cognitive Processes," and *cognitive* implies "thinking," so this chapter focuses on complex forms of thinking. But what does "thinking" mean? Definitions vary, but they typically include reasoning, solving problems, or reading and understanding conceptually demanding material (Willingham, 2009b). We focus on these processes in this chapter.

To begin, let's look at fifth graders as they try to solve—what is for them—a complex problem. Keep the students' thinking in mind as you read the case study.

In an attempt to help her students become better problem solvers, Laura Hunter, their teacher, gives them the problem of finding the area of the carpeted portion of their

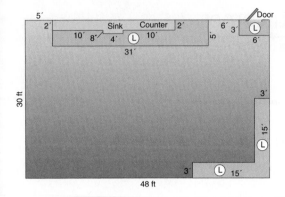

classroom. This portion has an irregular shape because parts of the floor are covered with linoleum, which are marked L in the drawing you see here.

She begins the lesson on Monday by reviewing *area* and *perimeter* and then says, "When we try to solve a problem, we first need to identify what the problem actually is. . . . We're going to get carpeting for this room, but we don't know how much to order, and your job is to figure that out. So, our problem is finding the carpeted area of our room," as she points to different parts of the room.

Having identified the problem, Laura breaks her students into groups and asks them what they will do next. They decide that they first need to know the size of the room, so she has the groups measure the room and the different parts in it. She then gives each group a diagram [the one shown here] showing its dimensions and tells the students that the places marked with an "L" are the parts of the floor covered with linoleum. She also displays the diagram on her document camera and says, "Okay, look at the diagram. . . . It represents our room and the carpeted area. . . . What's your next job?"

Nephi volunteers, "We didn't actually measure the area of the carpeted part; we just measured the perimeter. We need to figure out the area from our measurements."

Laura then tells the groups to work together to select a strategy for finding the carpeted area, and they go to work.

Different groups identify two strategies; one finding the area of the room and subtracting the areas covered with linoleum, and the other finding the area of an interior rectangle and then adding the extra areas of carpeting.

The students work in their groups, and after they're done, she has them report to the whole class. The different groups get the following areas for the carpeted portion: 1,173, 1,378, 1,347, 1,440, 1,169, and 1,600 square feet.

When asked if they are comfortable with the fact that the groups all got different answers, surprisingly, several say yes.

These results and the students' reactions raise the following questions:

1. Why did the groups get such varying answers to the same problem?
2. What should Laura now do to help her students improve their problem solving?
3. Because no group got the correct answer, was the time spent on the activity used wisely, or was it largely wasted?

The students' experiences and our questions help us understand why this chapter is titled "Complex Cognitive Processes." We examine these processes in the sections that follow, beginning with concept learning.

Concept Learning

Ed Psych and You

Look at the first list of 16 words on the right for 10 seconds. Cover up the list, and try to write down as many as you can remember in any order.

Then, do the same with the second list of 16 words. Which list is easier to remember? Why do you think so?

Here is the first list of words related to the exercise described in our "Ed Psych and You" feature:

broom	work	salary	some
sooner	plug	jaw	fastener
jug	president	friend	evening
planet	else	salmon	destroy

Now, here is the second list:

north	blue	cucumber	quarter
celery	west	nickel	purple
red	penny	brown	east
dime	carrot	south	tomato

People instinctively strive to make sense of their experiences, and they begin to do so as infants (Marinoff, 2003; Quinn, 2002). One way of making sense of our experiences is to categorize them into mental classes or sets, an idea pioneered by Jerome Bruner (1960, 1966, 1990), who argued that people interpret the world in terms of its similarities and differences.

This helps us understand your responses to our "Ed Psych and You" feature in this section. If you're like most people, you were able to recall more items from the second list than the first, because it was easy to classify the items into four simple categories—directions, colors, vegetables, and coins. In contrast, the first list is more difficult to categorize, so it is harder to remember.

This process relates to the idea of **concepts,** mental constructs or representations of categories that allow us to identify examples and nonexamples of those categories (Schunk, 2008). The concepts we form are constructed from our experiences and are fundamental building blocks of our thinking (Ferrari & Elik, 2003).

Constructing concepts allows us to simplify the world, and in doing so, helps reduce the cognitive load on our working memories. For example, Laura's students needed to understand that the concept *area* is a physical quantity describing the size of surfaces, such as those in Figure 8.1. *Area* is a mental construct that allows us to think about and compare the surfaces of figures regardless of dimension or orientation.

Concepts represent a major portion of the school curriculum (Brophy & Alleman, 2003; McCleery, Twyman & Tindal, 2003). Table 8.1 includes examples in language arts, social studies, science, and math, and many others exist. For instance, students also study *rhythm* and *tempo* in music, *perspective* and *balance* in art, and *aerobic* and *isotonic exercises* in physical education. Other concepts such as *honesty, bias, love,* and *internal conflict* appear across the curriculum.

Learners simplify and make sense of their experiences by constructing concepts.

Concepts. Mental constructs or representations of categories that allow us to identify examples and nonexamples of those categories.

Theories of Concept Learning

Theorists offer different explanations for how people construct concepts. In this section, we examine *rule-driven, prototype,* and *exemplar* theories, each of which explains concept learning differently.

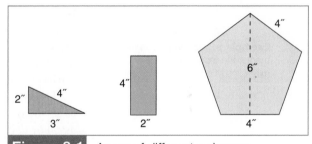

Figure 8.1 Areas of different polygons

Rule-Driven Theories of Concept Learning

Rule-driven theories suggest that we construct concepts based on their attributes or **characteristics**—concepts' essential elements. For some concepts—*square, longitude,* or

Characteristics. A concept's essential elements.

Table 8.1 Concepts in different content areas

Language Arts	Social Studies	Science	Math
Adjective	Culture	Acid	Prime number
Verb	Longitude	Conifer	Equivalent fraction
Plot	Federalist	Element	Set
Simile	Democracy	Force	Addition
Infinitive	Immigrant	Inertia	Parabola

adverb—for instance, these elements are well-defined, such as *closed, equal sides*, and *equal angles* for the concept *square*. When we encounter plane figures with these characteristics, we classify them as squares based on the rule that squares must have these attributes. Other characteristics, such as size or color, aren't essential, so we don't consider them in making our classifications. This rule-driven theory of concept learning was investigated by early researchers (e.g., Bruner, Goodenow, & Austin, 1956), who found that people differentiate concepts on the basis of the defining characteristics of each (Bourne, 1982).

Prototype Theories of Concept Learning

Many concepts don't have well-defined characteristics, however, so creating rules to help differentiate them is difficult. For instance, what are the characteristics of the concepts *Democrat* or *Republican*? Despite their common usage, most people can't define them with any precision. Even common concepts, such as *car*, can have "fuzzy boundaries" (Terry, 2009). For instance, some people describe sport utility vehicles as cars, but others don't. And, how about minivans, crossovers, or railroad "cars"?

Prototype. In concept-learning theory, the best representation of the category.

A second theory of concept learning suggests that people construct a **prototype,** the best representation of the category, for concepts such as *Democrat, Republican,* and even *car* (Medin et al., 2000). Prominent politicians might be prototypes for *Republican* or *Democrat*, for example, and a common passenger car, like a Honda Civic, might be a prototype for *car*.

Prototypes aren't necessarily physical examples. Rather, they can be a mental composite, constructed from the different examples that individuals experience (Reisberg, 2010). For instance, a person who has encountered a number of different dogs might construct a prototype that doesn't look exactly like any particular breed.

Exemplar Theories of Concept Learning

Exemplars. In concept-learning theory, the most highly typical examples of a concept.

A third theory of concept learning holds that learners don't construct a single prototype; rather they store **exemplars,** the most highly typical examples of a concept (Medin et al., 2000). For instance, a child may construct the concept *dog* by storing images of a golden retriever, cocker spaniel, collie, and German shepherd in memory as exemplars.

Each theory explains different aspects of concept learning. For instance, concepts such as *square* or *odd number* are likely constructed based on their characteristics. Others, such as *car* or *dog*, are probably represented with prototypes or exemplars.

Concept Learning: A Complex Cognitive Process

As you've read this section, you might have said to yourself, "Concept learning seems simple enough. Why is it described as a 'complex cognitive process?'" In fact, the thinking required is often more demanding and complex than it appears on the surface. For example, Paul taught a group of fourth graders the concept *arthropods*, animals such as insects, spiders, crabs, and lobsters, which have an *exoskeleton, three body parts,* and *jointed legs* as characteristics. After showing the students examples, such as a crab, beetle, and spider, and helping them identify the characteristics of arthropods, he showed them a clam and asked them if it was an arthropod. Surprisingly, several of the students said yes, reasoning that its hard shell was an exoskeleton. They didn't think about the fact that to be an arthropod an animal must have *all* the essential characteristics. He then asked them if their teacher was an arthropod, and again, some of them said yes, focusing on the fact that she had jointed legs.

Now, consider concepts such as *above, top, west, large, far,* and *right.* These concepts are "relational," meaning they exist only in relation to other concepts. For example, *above* exists only in relation to *below*, and *top* exists only in relation to *bottom*. In spite of the complexity of these concepts, we expect young children to learn them, as anyone who has watched

Sesame Street knows. For example, Murray—the Muppet—sits next to a flowerpot and says, "Now, I'm *near,*" then runs off in the distance and says, "Now, I'm *far.*"

These hard-to-learn concepts are important for future learning. For example, consider these problems:

$$76 \quad \text{and} \quad 74$$
$$-\underline{24} \qquad -\underline{26}$$

If children don't understand relational ideas, they may get 52 for both answers by ignoring their location and simply subtracting the 4 from the 6 in each case.

Other forms of concept learning are also more complex than they appear on the surface. For example, in math, the concept *integer* can be either a negative number, *or* a positive number, *or* zero. A polynomial can be either a single number, such as 4, *or* a number and variable, such as 4*x*, *or* a more complex expression, such as $4x^2 + 2x + 3$. This either–or nature can be confusing for students.

These examples help us understand why concept learning is a complex cognitive process.

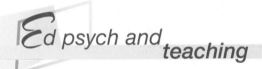

Ed psych and teaching

Applying Concept Learning Theory with Your Students

Regardless of a concept's complexity or the theory that explains concept learning, your students will construct their understanding of a concept based on the examples you present, combined with nonexamples that help them differentiate the concept from others that are closely related. For instance, if you want your students to understand the concept *reptile,* you would use positive examples, such as an alligator, turtle (both sea and land, so your students don't conclude that all reptiles live on land), lizard, and snake. You would also include a *frog* as a nonexample, because many people believe frogs are reptiles. Similarly, if you're teaching the concept *metaphor,* you would include a variety of metaphors, combined with *similes* as nonexamples, because *metaphors* and *similes* are closely related and often confused with each other.

In teaching concepts, some experts argue that we should present a sequence of examples and guide students' constructions of the concept, and this is the approach advocated by Jerome Bruner (1960, 1966). Others suggest that presenting a definition and then illustrating it with examples is more effective, an approach preferred by David Ausubel (1963, 1977). Both Bruner and Ausubel were historically prominent thinkers in the field, and both approaches can be effective.

Based on this information, the following guidelines can support your efforts to help your students learn concepts.

1. Provide a variety of examples and nonexamples of the concept.
2. Present the examples in a real-world context.
3. Sequence the examples beginning with the most typical and ending with those least familiar.
4. Promote meaningful learning by linking the concept to related concepts.

Now, let's see how Carol Lopez, a fifth-grade teacher, applies the guidelines as she attempts to help her fifth graders learn the concept *adjective.*

Carol begins by displaying the following vignette on her document camera:

John and Karen, with her brown hair blowing in the wind, drove together in his old car to the football game. They soon met their very best friends, Latoya and Michael, at the large gate near the entrance. The game was incredibly exciting, and because the team's running game was sparkling, the home team won by a bare margin.

Carol has the students read the vignette and then says, "We've discussed nouns, so let's see what you remember. Identify a noun in the passage. . . . Bharat?"

"John and Karen," Bharat responds.

Carol continues until the students have named each of the nouns, and she then asks, "What do we know about Karen's hair?. . . Jesse?"

"It's brown."

"And what kind of game did they attend?"

"A football game," several students say together.

Carol continues having the students describe the nouns, and she identifies each of the words that describe them as adjectives.

Then she says, "Now let's take a closer look. . . . What's different about *exciting* and *sparkling* compared to others like brown and old? . . . Duk?"

"They . . . don't come in front of the noun . . . like the others do?"

"Very good, Duk. Yes, adjectives don't always come before the noun. . . . Now, what is important about running and football? . . . Sharon?"

"*Running* looks like a verb . . . and *football* looks like a noun."

"Yes they do . . . . but how do we know they're adjectives? . . . Lakesha?"

"They describe nouns . . . like *football* describes *game,* and . . . *running* does too."

"Excellent," Carol smiles. "Now, take a look at the word *the,* like in *the* entrance and *the* game. How do we know that they're not adjectives?"

After several seconds, Yolanda offers, "They don't tell us anything about the noun. . . . It just says, 'the' entrance. It doesn't describe it."

"Very good, Yolanda," Carol nods.

Carol then has her students look at the words *soon, very,* and *incredibly* and explain why they aren't adjectives, and finally, she has them write a paragraph that includes three or more adjectives, with at least one coming after the noun.

Carol collects the paragraphs and displays three of them on the document camera (with the names covered to avoid having the class know whose paragraphs are being analyzed), and discusses them the next day.

Now, let's examine Carol's efforts to implement the guidelines. By embedding a variety of examples and nonexamples in the context of the vignette, she applied both the first guideline (provide a variety of examples and nonexamples) and the second (use a real-world context). She also sequenced the examples so the most obvious ones, such as *brown* and *old* were presented first (guideline 3). And, finally, in discussing the words *soon, very* and *incredibly,* she linked *adjective* to the concept *adverb* in order to make them more meaningful (guideline 4).

Carol also grounded her lesson in cognitive learning theory. Her examples provided the experiences the students needed to construct their knowledge of the concept, and she embedded them in the context of a written passage. (A written passage is more "real world" than words or individual sentences.) The examples in context also helped her students understand that *running,* which looks like a verb, and *football* and *home,* which normally are nouns, functioned as adjectives in this context. And finally, she developed the lesson through questioning, which promoted high levels of social interaction and encouraged students to become cognitively active—to think about what they were doing. Each applies cognitive learning theory, and the nuances of Carol's lesson help us understand why concept learning is a complex cognitive process.

check your understanding

1.1 Define concepts, and explain how young children acquire common concepts, such as *car, truck, dog,* and *cat* as they grow and develop.

1.2 Of the concepts *noun* and *culture,* which should be easier to learn? Which theory of concept learning best explains how each concept is constructed? Explain, basing your answer on the information in this section.

1.3 Carol Lopez taught the concept *adjective,* and she used *very, soon,* and *incredibly*—each an adverb—as nonexamples. Consider the way students typically think, and then explain why *soon* is an essential nonexample in this case.

To receive feedback for these questions, go to Appendix A.

Classroom connections

Promoting Concept Learning in Schools

1. Examples provide learners with the experiences they need to construct concepts. To provide authentic experiences, use realistic examples that include all the information learners need to understand the concept.

   ■ **Elementary:** To illustrate the concept *mammal,* a second-grade teacher brings a hamster to class, and has the students feel and pet it. He also has the students think about themselves, and he shows pictures of a horse, dog, bat, dolphin, and seal. He also includes pictures of an eagle, lizard, and salmon as nonexamples.

   ■ **Middle School:** A geometry teacher presents her students with drawings of similar triangles such as those shown here: She has the students measure the sides and angles of the two triangles. They see that the sides of one are twice as long as the sides of the other, and the angles in the two are equal. She includes additional examples of similar triangles and other pairs of triangles that are not similar.

   ■ **High School:** A tennis coach is helping his students learn how to serve. He videotapes several people, some with good serves and others less skilled. He shows the class the videotapes and asks the students to identify the differences in the serves.

2. To help make concepts meaningful, link new concepts to related concepts.

   ■ **Elementary:** A kindergarten teacher wants her class to understand that living things exist in many different forms. She tells her children that they themselves, as well as pets and plants in their classroom, are living things. In a discussion they identify "the ability to grow and change" and "the need for food and water" as two characteristics the examples have in common.

■ **Middle School:** To help his students understand the relationships between descriptive and persuasive writing, an English teacher displays paragraphs illustrating each and asks the class to identify their similarities and differences.

■ **High School:** A social studies teacher instructs her students to compare cultural revolutions to other revolutions, such as the Industrial Revolution, the American Revolution, and the technological revolution, pointing out similarities and differences in each case.

Problem Solving

To begin this section, consider what the examples in our "Ed Psych and You" feature have in common. They each illustrate a **problem,** which "occurs when a problem solver has a goal but lacks an obvious way of achieving the goal" (Mayer & Wittrock, 2006, p. 288). For instance, the goals are accessing your friend's address, making your relationship more satisfying, and finding more time in your life. Laura's students, in the lesson at the beginning of the chapter, also faced a problem, the goal for which was finding the area of the carpeted portion of their classroom. Defining a *problem* broadly in this way is

Ed Psych and You

What do the following have in common?

• You want to send a birthday card to a friend who has moved to New York, but you don't know her address.

• You're in a romantic relationship with another person, but the relationship isn't very satisfying.

• You're taking classes, but also have a job, and you never seem to have enough time for anything.

helpful because it reminds us that problem solving is a part of our daily lives, and it also allows us to apply general strategies to solve a variety of problems, both in and outside of classrooms (Mayer & Wittrock, 2006).

Problem. The presence of a goal but the absence of an obvious way to achieve it.

Well-Defined and Ill-Defined Problems

Experts distinguish between **well-defined problems,** problems with clear goals, only one correct solution, and a certain method for finding it, and **ill-defined problems,** problems with ambiguous goals, more than one acceptable solution, and no generally agreed-upon strategy for reaching a solution (Mayer & Wittrock, 2006). Our first example in "Ed Psych and You" is well-defined; your friend has only one address, and a straightforward strategy for finding it exists. Many problems in math, physics, and chemistry are well-defined.

On the other hand, your unsatisfactory relationship and lack of time to do anything are ill-defined problems, because your goals aren't clear. For instance, you want your relationship to be more satisfying, but what does that mean? Perhaps you want to communicate more openly, spend more time together, or feel better emotionally when you're together. In our third example, lack of time "for anything" is also vague. Do you want more time to study? To exercise? To simply kick back and relax?

Because the goals in ill-defined problems are ambiguous, no straightforward solutions exist for them. For instance, in the case of your relationship, you might try to talk to your partner about your feelings, consider couples' counseling, or even end the relationship. With respect to your lack of time, you might try to use your time more wisely, cut back on your work hours if possible, drop a class, or even take a semester off from school.

Well-defined problem. A problem that has a clear goal, only one correct solution, and a certain method for finding it.

Ill-defined problem. A problem that has an ambiguous goal, more than one acceptable solution, and no generally agreed-upon strategy for reaching a solution.

Challenges in Teaching Problem Solving

Helping your students become better problem solvers will be among your biggest instructional challenges, for two important reasons. First, your students are likely to lack

Most problems students solve in classrooms are well-defined, but the problems we encounter outside of school are often ill-defined.

experience with problem solving—particularly with ill-defined problems—and they will often lack the prior knowledge needed to solve problems successfully. Second, our students' thinking is sometimes problematic; they have a tendency to use superficial strategies and accept solutions whether or not they make sense. Let's look at these obstacles in more depth.

Experience and Prior Knowledge

A paradox exists in attempting to help people become better problem solvers. Most of the problems we encounter in our everyday living, such as problems with money, careers, social relationships, or personal happiness, are ill-defined, but the vast majority of the problems learners practice solving in schools are well-defined (Mayer & Wittrock, 2006). For instance, students are asked to solve problems similar to the following in the lower elementary grades:

> Jeremy and Melinda are saving up so they can go to iTunes to buy some of their favorite songs. They need 15 dollars. Jeremy has saved 5 dollars, and Melinda has saved 7. How much more money do they have to save to get their 15 dollars?

In high school students solve problems, such as this one:

> Kelsey and Mitch are dating but live in different cities, and they adopt the same cell phone plan. Over one billing period, Kelsey used 45 peak minutes and 50 nonpeak minutes, and her bill was $27.75. Mitch used 70 peak minutes and 30 nonpeak minutes at a charge of $36. What is the peak and the nonpeak rate in their cell phone plan?

Even though the second is more complex, both of these problems are well-defined.

However, even solving well-defined problems can be difficult if we lack experience and prior knowledge (Mayer & Wittrock, 2006). For instance, if we haven't had experience in solving simultaneous equations, finding the cell-phone rates for Mitch and Kelsey will be an ill-defined problem for us, and solving it will be virtually impossible.

Laura's students encountered a similar difficulty. Finding the amount of carpeting necessary for the room is well-defined for most of us, but Laura's students lacked experience in finding areas of irregular shapes; so, for them, the problem was ill-defined. To illustrate this issue, let's look at an interview with four of her students after the lesson. The interviewer showed the students the figures on the left, and then began questioning them. Let's look at the dialogue.

Interviewer: What do we mean by perimeter? . . . Show us on one of these figures. . . . Yashoda?

Yashoda: It's the distance around the figure, like here (moving her finger around the rectangle and then the pentagon).

Interviewer: So, what is the perimeter here (pointing to the rectangle)? . . . Erica?

Erica: . . . 12.

Interviewer: And how did you get that?

Erica: I added 4 and 4 and 2 and 2.

Interviewer: How about the perimeter of this (pointing to the pentagon)? . . . Hasan?

Hasan: . . . 9. . . . I added 3 and 1 and 1 and 2 and 2.

Interviewer: Now, what do we mean by area? . . . Show us. . . . Daniel?

Daniel: It's like if you covered it up with paper or something (moving his hand back and forth over the rectangle). It's how much you need to cover it up.

Interviewer: So, what is the area of the rectangle?

Daniel: . . . 8. I multiplied 4 times 2 because the area is the length times the width.

Interviewer: Good. So, how would you find the area of this (pointing to the pentagon)? . . . Yashoda?

Yashoda: (After thinking for several seconds) I would multiply the 3 times the 1, which would be 3, and then I would take that times 2 (pointing at the 2 in the figure), so the area would be 6.

Interviewer: How do the rest of you feel about that?

The others nod, agreeing Yashoda's strategy makes sense.

The interview helps us answer the first question we asked at the beginning of the chapter: "Why did the groups get such varying answers to the same problem?" Lack of prior knowledge is the obvious answer, but some subtle distinctions exist. For instance, the students had declarative knowledge about the concept *area;* Daniel, for example, explained area by saying, "It's like if you covered it up with paper or something. It's how much you need to cover it up." And, when students were asked to calculate the area of the rectangle, they were quickly able to do so. However, because they hadn't encountered more complex shapes in their problem-solving efforts, they used the same strategy for finding the area of the pentagon. So, because they multiplied 4×2 to find the area of the rectangle, they multiplied $3 \times 1 \times 2$ to find the area of the pentagon.

Cognitive learning theory helps us understand the students' thinking. The knowledge we construct depends on what we already know, so the students—incorrectly—applied what they knew about finding the area of the rectangle to finding the area of the pentagon. This lesson illustrates the complexities of problem solving and suggests that Laura's students need more experience and instructional support before they will be able to successfully solve a problem such as finding the carpeted area of their classroom. Similarly, if you were unable to solve the problem with Mitch and Kelsey's phone rates, you need a variety of experiences in solving problems such as these.

Student Thinking

Now, let's consider the students' thinking in Laura's lesson. As we saw in the diagram, the dimensions of the classroom were 48 feet by 30 feet, which means that the area of the entire room was 1,440 square feet. Yet one of the groups got an answer of 1,600 square feet *for the carpeted portion of the room*—160 square feet more than the entire room, and they were perfectly satisfied with their answer! This tendency of students to accept answers whether they make sense or not is understandably maddening to teachers.

Students also have a tendency to use superficial strategies for solving problems (Mayer & Wittrock, 2006). A common one is the tendency to look for key words, such as *altogether,* which suggests addition, or *how many more,* which implies subtraction. Others include using the operation most recently taught or looking at cues in the chapter headings of the text. These strategies can bypass understanding completely, yet are often quite successful (Schoenfeld, 1991).

So, as teachers we have an ill-defined problem of our own. People in general, and students in particular, are not very good at solving problems (Mayer & Wittrock, 2006), and we want them to be better at it. So, how are we going to solve our problem? We address this question in the next section.

Helping Students Become Problem Solvers

To answer the question of how to help our students become better problem solvers, we'll first examine a general framework for thinking about problems. Then we'll consider how *deliberate practice* can help students acquire expertise in problem solving.

A Framework for Thinking About Problems

Providing a framework for thinking about problems is a first step, because it helps students begin to understand the processes involved in solving problems. This framework helps make sense of problems and allows us to construct effective strategies for solving them. Experts have applied this approach to problems varying as widely as well-defined problems in math and science, to ill-defined problems with school leadership (Canter, 2004), counseling in response to classroom management issues (Dwairy, 2005), and even curbing excessive drinking on college campuses (Biscaro, Broer, & Taylor, 2004).

One popular framework, or model, for thinking about problems appears in Figure 8.2. We discuss this framework in the sections that follow.

Identify the Problem Goal. Earlier, we said that a problem exists when a problem solver has a goal but lacks an obvious way of achieving the goal. Consider the following problem, which was presented to a group of second graders.

There are 26 sheep and 10 goats on a ship. How old is the captain?

In one study, 75% of the children answered 36 (cited in Prawat, 1989)! Obviously, they didn't understand the problem.

In some cases, identifying the problem goal is straightforward, such as it was in Laura's lesson. In other cases, particularly when working with ill-defined problems, it can be one of the most difficult aspects of problem solving (Jitendra et al., 2007). For instance, in solving your less-than-satisfying romantic relationship problem, your goal is ambiguous, making it an ill-defined problem. What exactly do we mean by *satisfying?* You need to first identify one or more tangible goals before you can begin to solve the problem.

When attempting to solve ill-defined problems, identifying subgoals can be a helpful first step. Then, if you succeed in reaching each subgoal, you've solved your problem. For instance, suppose you identify spending more time together, improving communication, and feeling better emotionally as your subgoals. In doing so you've better defined your problem. In general, the first step in solving problems that are ill-defined is to convert them to well-defined problems with clear goals.

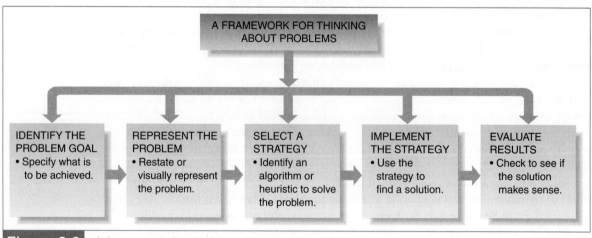

A FRAMEWORK FOR THINKING ABOUT PROBLEMS				
IDENTIFY THE PROBLEM GOAL • Specify what is to be achieved.	REPRESENT THE PROBLEM • Restate or visually represent the problem.	SELECT A STRATEGY • Identify an algorithm or heuristic to solve the problem.	IMPLEMENT THE STRATEGY • Use the strategy to find a solution.	EVALUATE RESULTS • Check to see if the solution makes sense.

Figure 8.2 A framework for thinking about problems

Providing students with practice in identifying problems is the only way they will gradually become good at it. This is a challenge, because, as we said earlier, most of the problems students encounter in schools are well-defined. Mixing the types of problems you're asking students to solve can be a first step for improving problem solving skills in a variety of areas (Taylor & Rohrer, 2010). For instance, when elementary students learn to add fractions, they typically first practice with problems with like denominators, and then practice on problems that require finding a common denominator. When they practice adding fractions with different denominators, simply including some problems that don't require a common denominator can provide students with practice in identifying problems. Then, as you move to multiplication and division, you can do the same, so an assignment might include problems such as the following:

$$\frac{3}{5} - \frac{2}{5} = \qquad \frac{2}{3} + \frac{3}{4} = \qquad \frac{4}{7} \div \frac{3}{4} = \qquad \frac{5}{6} \times \frac{2}{3} =$$

This strategy won't immediately make students expert problem solvers, but it's a good first step.

Represent the Problem. If a problem is complex, it can be helpful to represent it in ways that make it more meaningful, such as stating it in more familiar terms, relating it to problems you've previously experienced, or representing it visually, as Laura did for her students. For instance, consider the following problem:

> Find the area of a pentagon with a base of 3 inches, a vertical height of 2 inches, and a total height of 4 inches.

At first glance, this might be fairly demanding for some students, but a diagram, such as the one shown at right, makes it solvable.

Now, having represented the problem in this way, solving it is straightforward.

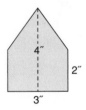

Select a Strategy. After identifying and representing the problem, we need to select a strategy for solving it. If a problem is well-defined, an **algorithm,** a specific step or set of steps for finding the solution, can be used. For example, to find the area of a rectangle, we follow a simple algorithm—multiply the length times the width—and we use other simple algorithms when we solve problems such as adding fractions with unlike denominators or finding the percent decrease of a marked-down retail item. In a similar way, computer experts use complex algorithms to solve sophisticated, but well-defined, programming problems.

Algorithm. A specific step or set of steps for finding the solution to a problem.

Many problems can't be solved with algorithms, because they don't exist for ill-defined problems or for many that are well-defined. In those cases, problem solvers use **heuristics,** general, widely applicable problem-solving strategies (Chronicle, MacGregor, & Ormerod, 2004). The more complex and unfamiliar the task, the greater the need for heuristics (Lee & Reigeluth, 2003).

Heuristics. General, widely applicable problem-solving strategies.

A number of heuristics exist. Trial and error is one. It's primitive and inefficient, but it provides learners with experience in grappling with problems, and many people use it as a first step in trying to solve problems that are unfamiliar (Davidson & Sternberg, 2003).

Means–ends analysis, a strategy that breaks the problem into subgoals and works successively on each, is another heuristic that is effective for solving ill-defined problems, and this is what we used in attempting to solve our dissatisfying-romantic-relationship problem.

Means–ends analysis. A heuristic that breaks the problem into subgoals and works successively on each.

Drawing analogies, a strategy used to solve unfamiliar problems by comparing them with those already solved, is a third heuristic (Mayer, 2002). It can be difficult to implement, however, because learners often can't find problems in their memories analogous to the one they want to solve, or they may make inappropriate connections between the two problems.

Drawing analogies. A heuristic that is used to solve unfamiliar problems by comparing them with those already solved.

Teaching heuristics can improve problem-solving ability even with early elementary students (Hohn & Frey, 2002), but ultimately, prior knowledge and experience with problem solving are essential for successfully selecting a strategy, and no heuristic can replace them (Pittman & Beth-Halachmy, 1997).

Implement the Strategy. Having identified the problem goal, represented the problem, and selected a strategy, problem solvers are now ready to implement it. This is where Laura's students ran into difficulties. They likely struggled for three major reasons:

- Even though the problem goal appeared to be straightforward, some students didn't fully understand it.
- As the interview after the lesson revealed, the students didn't understand how to find areas of irregular figures.
- The students lacked important skills, such as accurately measuring the dimensions of the room.

Each of these factors can be explained with cognitive learning theory. First, the students lacked the experiences necessary to solve a problem as complex as the one Laura presented. Second, the knowledge they constructed depended on what they already knew, such as using the same algorithm to find the area of the pentagon that they used to find the area of the rectangle. They also applied inappropriate algorithms in solving the carpeted-area problem, and as a result, they got widely varying answers. We'll see how Laura adapted her instruction to address these issues in our "Ed Psych and Teaching" feature later in this discussion.

Evaluate the Results. Evaluating results is the final step in effective problem solving, and it requires that our students think about their results (Mayer & Wittrock, 2006). As we saw in Laura's lesson, students will sometimes accept virtually any answer they get, whether it makes sense or not.

You can help your students do a better job of evaluating their results by emphasizing problem solving as a *sense-making* process instead of focusing simply on getting an answer (Mayer, 2002). Having students practice making estimates before they solve the problem and requiring them to justify their answers are two effective ways to promote sense making. Unrealistic estimates indicate a lack of understanding, so estimating can also be an informal assessment tool. As with all abilities, learning to estimate requires practice, but the effort and time needed to help your students make reasonable estimates is well spent. How can we provide this practice without wasting large amounts of class time? This leads us to a discussion of *deliberate practice*.

Developing Problem-Solving Expertise: The Role of Deliberate Practice

Experts. Individuals who are highly knowledgeable or skilled in a specific domain, such as math, history, chess, or teaching.

Experts are individuals who are highly knowledgeable or skilled in a specific domain, such as math, history, chess, or teaching. The term *specific domain* is important. An expert in math, for example, may be a novice in teaching or history, because a great deal of time and effort are required to develop expertise, and acquiring this experience is difficult to accomplish in more than a small number of areas. "Experts are made, not born. This is not to say that intellectual ability and talent do not exist, or are unimportant, but that effort, deliberate practice, and feedback from experts are essential to the development of high-level expertise" (Schraw, 2006, p. 255).

Deliberate practice has the following components (Ericsson, 2003):

- The practice is goal directed. Individuals identify the skills they want to improve and practice those skills extensively.
- The practice focuses on understanding and sense making rather than rote drill and practice.

- The practice is systematic, requiring learners to practice frequently until they have overlearned the idea.
- Learners practice in real-world settings.
- Learners receive extensive feedback.

Research also suggests that **interspersed practice,** the process of mixing the practice of different skills, is superior to **blocked practice,** practicing one skill extensively and then moving to a different skill (Taylor & Rohrer, 2010). For instance, if elementary students are practicing subtraction problems that require regrouping, such as $45 - 27$, their learning will be accelerated if they are also given subtraction problems that don't require regrouping, such as $74 - 43$, as well as addition problems that do and do not require regrouping, such as $76 + 18$ and $25 + 33$. The process applies in all domains. For example, basketball practice is more effective if players practice jump shots for a few minutes, dribbling for a few more, free throws for an additional time, and then return to each skill instead of massing practice on a particular skill and then turning to a different one.

Worked Examples. **Worked examples** are problems with completed solutions that provide students with one way of solving problems. Using worked examples is effective in implementing deliberate practice.

Let's look at a math teacher guiding his students through a worked example.

> Ben Griffin is introducing the process of solving simultaneous equations with his algebra students, and he writes the following on the board:
>
> $$4x + 3y = 17$$
> $$2x + 2y = 10$$
>
> "So, what is the goal in our problem here . . . Sancha?"
>
> ". . . To find x and y."
>
> "Good. . . . Now, look everyone," and Ben writes the following on the board.
>
> $$4x + 3y = 17 \qquad (2)\,4x + (2)\,3y = 2(17)$$
>
> "What did I do here?. . . Sai?"
>
> ". . . You multiplied both sides of the equation by 2."
>
> "And, why can I do that? . . . Nikki?"
>
> "An equation is like a balance. It will stay equal if whatever you do to one side, you also do to the other side."
>
> "Very good," Ben responds. "So, what do we get when we do that? . . . Berto?"
>
> ". . . Eight x plus six y equals 34."
>
> "Good!" Ben replies as he writes $8x + 6y = 34$ on the board, so it now appears as follows.
>
> $$4x + 3y = 17 \qquad (2)\,4x + (2)\,3y = 2(17)$$
> $$8x + 6y = 34$$
>
> "Now let's look at our second equation," Ben directs, and he writes the following on the board.
>
> $$2x + 2y = 10 \qquad (3)\,2x + (3)\,2y = 3(10)$$
>
> "What did I do here? . . . Felipe?"
>
> "You did the same thing. Only this time you multiplied both sides by 3."
>
> "And what do we get? . . . Talia?"
>
> "Six x plus six y equals 30."
>
> "Good, everyone," Ben smiles, and he writes the information on the board, so it appears as follows:
>
> $$4x + 3y = 17 \qquad (2)\,4x + (2)\,3y = 2(17)$$
> $$8x + 6y = 34$$

Interspersed practice. The process of mixing the practice of different skills.

Blocked practice. The process of practicing one skill extensively and then moving to a different skill.

Worked examples. Problems with completed solutions that provide students with one way of solving problems.

$$2x + 2y = 10 \qquad\qquad (3)\,2x + (3)\,2y = 3(10)$$
$$6x + 6y = 30$$

"Now, look at this," he continues, and he writes the following on the board.

$$8x + 6y = 34$$
$$6x + 6y = 30$$
$$2x + 0y = 4$$

"Think carefully," Ben directs. "What did I do here?"

"It looks like you subtracted the bottom equation from the top one," Adelio volunteers.

"Good thinking. . . . Now look," and Ben writes the following on the board.

$$\frac{2x}{2} + \frac{0y}{2} = \frac{4}{2}$$
$$x = 2$$

Ben has the students explain what he did and why, has them replace the x in the first equation with 2, and they find that the value of y is 3.

"We put x into the first equation to find y," he continues. "Would it have worked if we had used the second equation?"

Some students are still uncertain, so Ben has them try it to confirm that it didn't matter which equation he used. He continues the discussion and helps the students understand that multiplying the first equation by 2 and the second by 3 made the coefficient of y the same for each equation, so the value for y would be zero when they subtracted the second from the first.

As they continue the discussion, Zach raises his hand uncertainly and asks, "Wouldn't it have been simpler to just multiply the second equation by 2 and just subtract the first one from it?"

"Excellent thinking, Zach," Ben responds energetically. "See, this is what problem solving is all about. What we do here should make sense, and often we have more than one approach that will work," and he has Zach go to the board to demonstrate and explain his thinking.

Research with learners ranging from lower elementary to university students indicates that worked examples can make problem solving more meaningful than traditional instruction, particularly when students are first learning a procedure (Crippen & Earl, 2007; Shen & Tsai, 2009). Ben's lesson with his algebra students helps us understand why. The students could see, precisely, what each step involved, and Ben required that they verbalize their understanding in each case.

Using worked examples in this way applies cognitive learning theory. The worked examples provided Ben's students with the experiences they needed to help them construct their understanding of the procedure; each step made sense to the students; and Ben used high levels of social interaction to walk them through the process.

Students often prefer worked examples to traditional instruction (Renkl, Stark, Gruber, & Mandl, 1998), and Ben's lesson helps us understand why. Students prefer learning experiences that make sense to those where they memorize a set of steps with little understanding.

As with all forms of learning, problem solving will be easier for some students than for others, but using deliberate practice combined with worked examples can help most students become competent problem solvers. Our next "Ed Psych and Teaching" feature illustrates how Laura applies these ideas with her students.

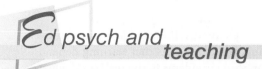

Ed psych and *teaching*

Helping Your Students Become Better Problem Solvers

Your understanding of cognitive learning theory and the components of deliberate practice provide a framework for helping your students develop their problem-solving abilities. The following guidelines can help you apply this understanding in your teaching.

1. Present problems in real-world contexts, and take students' prior knowledge into account.

2. Capitalize on social interaction to engage students, and monitor their learning progress.

3. Provide scaffolding for novice problem solvers, and emphasize understanding and making sense of problems.

4. Teach general problem-solving strategies.

You saw how Laura's students struggled with her problem, as indicated by their widely varying answers. Now, let's return to her class the next day to see how she modifies her instruction while applying these guidelines.

Laura begins Tuesday's lesson by saying, "Let's look at our diagram again," as she displays the following diagram on the document camera.

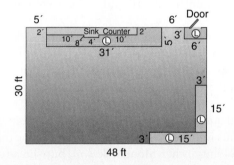

The class agrees to try the first strategy: Find the area of the room, and subtract the parts with the linoleum (marked "L"). So, Laura first has them calculate the area of the room.

She watches to see that they get 1,440 square feet and then asks, "What do we do next?"

The students agree that they must subtract the parts marked "L," and they suggest starting at the top of the diagram.

"How will we find the area of this part? . . . Fred?" Laura asks.

". . . Multiply 31 times 5."

Laura has Fred explain his thinking, the students calculate the area, and she checks to be sure they all get 155 square feet. She then has them repeat the process with the portion by the door, where they get 18 square feet.

Laura then points to the linoleum at the lower right. She asks the students for suggestions, and finding that several are uncertain, she goes to the board and writes:

$$15 \times 3 = 45 \text{ square feet}$$
$$12 \times 3 = 36 \text{ square feet}$$
$$45 + 36 = 81 \text{ square feet}$$

She waits for several seconds and then says, "Someone explain where these numbers came from."

"The 15 is the length of that part," Nephi offers, pointing to the bottom of the diagram. "And the 3 is how wide it is . . . so, the area is 45."

"Forty-five what?" Laura probes.

"Square feet," Nephi adds quickly.

"Now, let's be good thinkers. How do we know the second statement must be 12 times 3 instead of 15 times 3?"

". . . I've got it!" Anya shouts.

"Come up and show us."

Anya goes to the document camera and alters the diagram, as shown here:

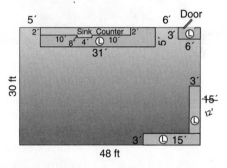

"See, we already have this," she says, pointing to the lower right corner of the drawing. "So, this length is 12, not 15. . . . So, it's 12 times 3."

Laura asks the class if Anya's thinking makes sense, they agree that it does, and she then asks them what they need to do next. They agree that they must add the 45 and 36 to get 81 square feet.

After adding the 115, 18, and 81, to get a total of 254 square feet, the class concludes that they must subtract the 254 from 1,440. Laura asks them to explain why, and they then find that the carpeted portion is 1,186 square feet.

She then says, "For your homework, I want you to figure out what the area of the carpeted portion is using the second strategy," she hands them another diagram showing the dimensions of the inside area, and asks, "Now, what do we always ask ourselves when we try a strategy?"

"Does it make sense?" Shayna answers after thinking for several seconds.

"Yes, exactly," Laura smiles. You'll need to be ready to explain how you got your answers when we start. . . . We'll look for that tomorrow."

Productive social interaction is an important part of problem solving.

Now, let's review Laura's lesson to see how she implemented these guidelines. Cognitive learning theory, and particularly situated cognition, which suggests that learning depends on the context in which it occurs, emphasizes connecting problems to the real world whenever possible. By building her lesson around the problem of finding the carpeted area of their classroom, Laura applied this idea and implemented the first guideline.

Cognitive learning theory also emphasizes social interaction, which was prominent in both her lessons. Her first lesson, however, demonstrates that not all social interaction is effective. Much of the interaction wasn't productive, as was indicated by her students' widely varying answers. She was more direct on Tuesday, but she still maintained high levels of interaction, which effectively applied the second guideline.

Laura scaffolded her students and applied the third guideline in three ways. First, she developed the lesson entirely with questioning, and she asked her students to explain their thinking in each case. The more students use language—both verbal and written—to describe their understanding, the deeper it becomes, and requiring students to explain their thinking emphasizes sense making in problem solving (Leinhardt & Steele, 2005). Second, she gave her students the diagram so they had a visual representation of the problem, and third, she wrote simple, worked examples on the board and asked Nephi and Anya to explain them.

Finally, Laura applied the fourth guideline by providing a general framework for solving problems. General strategies in the absence of domain-specific knowledge have limited value, but they can be effective within specific domains, such as math, because they help students become more aware of the processes involved in solving problems (Mayer & Wittrock, 2006).

This section helps answer our second question from the beginning of the chapter: "What should Laura now do to help her students improve their problem solving?" She didn't provide the students with sufficient scaffolding in her Monday lesson, but she adapted her instruction and provided more on Tuesday—without reverting to simply explaining each step. In doing so, her Tuesday lesson applied social constructivist learning theory and cognitive apprenticeships as she guided her students to a solution.

This leads us to our third question at the beginning of the chapter: "Was the time spent on the activity [Monday's lesson] used wisely, or was it largely wasted?" A clear answer doesn't exist. For example, the students spent valuable class time floundering, so Laura had to spend a full additional lesson guiding them to a solution for the problem. On the other hand, a basic principle of cognitive learning theory states that learning and development depend on experience, and the students acquired considerable experience with designing and implementing problem-solving strategies and working cooperatively. Also, research on a successful math program from Singapore, one of the countries that consistently scores high on international math tests, suggests that examining problems from different perspectives—as Ben Griffin did with his algebra students, and Laura did with her students—is one key to successful math instruction (Hu, 2010).

And, as all of us who have tried to solve ill-defined problems realize, problem solving isn't always successful, and even when it is, it proceeds in fits and starts. Also, having students get the right answer is one goal of problem solving, of course, but helping them to understand the process of problem solving is also important. Whether or not the experiences Laura's students acquired in her Monday lesson were valuable enough to warrant the time spent on them is a matter of professional judgment.

Creativity in Problem Solving

Creativity is the ability to produce original works or solutions to problems that are productive, and it can be an important component of solving ill-defined problems (Plucker, Beghetto, & Dow, 2004). *Original* implies that the action is not learned from someone else, and *productive* means that the product or solution is useful in our culture. One middle school teacher used the following creative example to help her science students learn about cells and tissues:

> Suzanne Schellenberg is struggling to help her students understand how cells, tissues, and organ systems interrelate. After considerable thought, she brings in a piece of bubble wrap and uses the individual bubbles as analogies for cells and the organization of the air pockets as an analogy for tissue (S. Schellenberg, Personal Communication, February 15, 2008).

This simple teaching example meets the criteria for creativity. Suzanne's idea was original—she didn't get it from anyone else—and it was productive because it helped her solve the problem with her students' understanding.

Divergent thinking, the ability to generate a variety of alternate, original solutions to questions or problems, is an important component of creativity (Davis, Rim, & Siegle, 2011). People who think divergently have two important characteristics. First, they possess a great deal of domain-specific knowledge. It's impossible to think creatively in the absence of knowledge, and people who are creative in one domain, such as art, may not be in another, such as writing or music (von Károlyi, Ramos-Ford, & Gardner, 2003). Second, divergent thinkers are intrinsically motivated. They're curious and committed, and they have a passion for the task. Creativity, instead of being an innate talent, is developed through years of practice and commitment (Elder & Paul, 2007).

Creativity. The ability to produce original works or solutions to problems that are productive.

Divergent thinking. The ability to generate a variety of alternate, original solutions to questions or problems.

Measuring Creativity

Creativity is usually measured by giving students a picture or object and asking them to generate responses, such as listing as many uses for a brick as possible (e.g., doorstop, bookshelf, paperweight, weapon, building block), or suggesting ways to improve a common object such as a chair (Davis et al., 2011). Methods of measuring creativity are controversial, with critics charging that existing tests are too narrow and fail to capture its varying aspects (Tannenbaum, 2003).

Fostering Creativity in Learners

Research offers several suggestions for fostering creativity in our students. They include:

- Creating a safe environment where students feel free to risk offering unique ideas and opinions (Md-Yunus, 2007).
- Communicating that creativity is valued, expressing enthusiasm in response to unusual ideas, and rewarding students for original thinking (Runco, 2004).
- Helping learners develop their domain-specific knowledge, which provides the raw materials for creativity (Elder & Paul, 2007).
- Avoiding social comparisons when assessing learning, increasing the number of assessments to reduce the pressure on any single assessment, and emphasizing the role of assessment in promoting learning (VanDeWeghe, 2007).

Teachers sometimes complain that the emphasis on standards and high-stakes testing reduces opportunities to work creatively with students. This doesn't have to be the case. Creativity in teaching is the ability to find, or develop, original examples and representations of the topics being taught, regardless of the emphasis on standards and accountability. Suzanne's use of the bubble wrap is an example. It was both original and productive, so it met the criteria for creativity, but perhaps more importantly, it was simple, and she didn't

Problem-based learning uses problems as the focus for teaching content and for developing skills and self-regulation.

Problem-based learning. A teaching strategy that uses problems as the focus for developing content, skills, and self-regulation.

have to spend any time preparing it. Similarly, fostering creativity in students depends more on the kind of learning environment in which they work than on whether or not they're expected to meet certain standards (Kaufman & Sternberg, 2007).

Problem-Based Learning

Laura's lessons also illustrate **problem-based learning,** a teaching strategy that uses problems as the focus for developing content, skills, and self-regulation (Hmelo-Silver, 2004; Serafino & Cicchelli, 2005). Problem-based learning activities have the following characteristics (Gijbels et al., 2005; Krajcik & Blumenfeld, 2006):

- Lessons begin with a problem, and solving it provides focus for the lesson.
- Students are responsible for designing strategies and finding solutions to the problem. Groups need to be small enough (typically 3 or 4), so that all students are actively involved in the process.
- The teacher guides students' efforts with questioning and other forms of scaffolding.

As we saw in Laura's lessons, the third characteristic is essential. Because her students floundered on Monday, she provided considerably more scaffolding the next day. Some would argue that she should have intervened sooner and more specifically, whereas others would suggest that the experience the students gained through their struggles was a worthwhile goal in itself.

Some evidence indicates that content learned in problem-based lessons is retained longer and transfers better than content learned with direct instruction approaches (Mayer & Wittrock, 2006; Sungur & Tekkaya, 2006). Additional evidence indicates that learners are more motivated in problem-based lessons than in traditional activities (Luft, Brown, & Sutherin, 2007). On the other hand, most of the research has been conducted with older or advanced students, and additional evidence indicates that lack of guidance from teachers in problem-based learning lessons can be ineffective (Kirschner, Sweller, & Clark, 2006). Laura's Monday lesson illustrates why teacher guidance is so important for effective instruction.

Technology, Learning, and Development: Using Technology to Promote Problem Solving

As we've noted, students get little experience in solving ill-defined problems. Often, problems presented in textbooks are well-defined and routine, and only the information needed to solve the problem is typically included. In addition, the operation is often suggested by the wording, such as asking "how many more?" which suggests subtraction (Jitendra et al., 2007). This lack of experience helps explain why students are not better problem solvers.

To address these issues, experts have capitalized on technology to present engaging and real-world problems. One of the best known is the series, *The Adventures of Jasper Woodbury,* created by the Cognition and Technology Group at Vanderbilt (1992). The series consists of 12 videodisc-based adventures that focus on problem finding and problem solving.

To access information about the Jasper series go to http://peabody.vanderbilt.edu/projects/funded/jasper/Jasperhome.html.

The following is an abbreviated version of one of the problems called "Journey to Cedar Creek":

> Jasper has just purchased a new boat and is planning to drive it home. The boat travels 8 mph and consumes 5 gallons of gas per hour. The tank holds 12 gallons of gas. The boat is at mile marker 156, and Jasper's dock is at marker 132. There are two gas stations on the way home. One is at mile marker 140.3 and the other is at mile marker 133. They charge $1.109 and $1.25 per gallon, respectively. They don't take credit cards. Jasper started the day with $20. He bought 5 gallons of gas at $1.25 per gallon (not including a discount of 4 cents per gallon for paying cash) and paid $8.25 for repairs to his boat. It's 2:35. Sundown is at 7:52. Can Jasper make it home before sunset without running out of fuel?

The problems in the series are purposely made complex and left ill-defined to give students practice in identifying problem goals, and they include extraneous material, so students learn to separate relevant from irrelevant information. Because the problems are complex, students also gain experience in identifying subgoals, such as finding out how much money Jasper has left for the trip home. Students work on these problems in teams over several class periods (ranging from a few days to more than a week). They share their ideas, receive feedback to refine their thinking, and present their solutions to the class.

Software designers have developed problem-solving simulations in other areas, as well. In geometry, for example, programs such as *The Geometric Supposer* (http://www.cet.ac.il/math-international/software5.htm) allow students to electronically manipulate figures as they attempt to solve geometry problems. Another program, *Interactive Physics* (http://www.interactivephysics.com), provides problems and tools to help students solve problems involving concepts such as force, acceleration, and momentum.

Some research indicates that these simulations produce as much learning as hands-on experience with concrete materials (Spector, 2008), but additional research is needed to confirm these conclusions. A second issue involves helping students make the transition from traditional to more open-ended problems; students who are used to straightforward, well-defined problems often struggle and become frustrated in attempting to solve problems such as those in the Jasper series. If you use this technology, your role will be demanding. You'll need to provide enough scaffolding to help your students make progress, but not so much that you rob them of experience with solving ill-defined problems. This is very sophisticated instruction.

---

check your understanding

2.1 Your students resist thinking on their own. They expect to find the answer to every question on their homework stated specifically in their textbook. Is this a well-defined or an ill-defined problem? Explain. Using the framework for thinking about problems as a guide, describe how you might try to solve this problem.

2.2 One of the groups in Laura's Monday lesson got an answer of 1,600—more than the total area of the room—for the carpeted portion of their classroom. Accepting this answer illustrates an ineffective application of which stage of problem solving?

2.3 Sample problems with worked solutions (worked examples) are commonly used in math, chemistry, and physics textbooks. You've studied a chapter in a book and see some problems with worked solutions at the end of the chapter. To make your problem solving as meaningful as possible, and using cognitive learning theory as a basis for answering, what should you do before you study the solutions?

To receive feedback for these questions, go to Appendix A.

Classroom connections

Developing Learners' Problem-Solving Abilities

1. Constructivist learning theory and situated cognition suggest that real-world problems enhance students' problem-solving efforts. Use high levels of interaction to actively engage students in analyzing real-world problems.

   ■ **Elementary:** A fourth-grade teacher breaks her students into pairs and gives each pair a chocolate bar composed of 12 square pieces. She gives them problems 1/4 and 1/3 and has students break off certain numbers of pieces to represent the numbers as fractions of the whole bar. She has them explain their thinking in each case.

   ■ **Middle School:** A middle school teacher has a "problem of the week." Each student is required to bring in one real-world problem each week that relates to the topics they are studying. The teacher selects from among them, and the class solves them.

   ■ **High School:** A physics teacher gives students problems such as, "If you're shooting a free throw and launch it at a 45-degree angle, what velocity will you need to put on the ball in order for it to go through the hoop?" After students attempt the problem, she uses questioning to guide them to a solution.

2. Cognitive apprenticeships provide opportunities for students to learn problem-solving skills from more knowledgeable others. As students practice solving problems, provide students with scaffolding and encourage them to put their understanding into words.

   ■ **Elementary:** A second-grade teacher begins a lesson on graphing by asking students how they might determine their classmates' favorite jelly bean flavor. She guides them as they identify the problem and how they might represent and solve it.

   ■ **Middle School:** A prealgebra teacher uses categories such as "We Know" and "We Need to Know" as scaffolds for analyzing word problems. His students then use the scaffolds to solve at least two word problems each day.

   ■ **High School:** In a unit on statistics and probability, a teacher requires her students to make estimates before solving problems. They then compare the solutions to their estimates.

The Strategic Learner

Ed Psych and You

As you sit in your university classes, what do you typically do to learn from the instructor's presentation?

You're studying this textbook. What do you commonly do to try to better understand the content?

Strategies. Cognitive operations that exceed the normal activities required to carry out a task.

How did you answer the questions in our "Ed Psych and You" feature here? If you're like most students, "take notes," is probably the answer to the first question, and "highlight" is the likely answer to the second. If you do, you're using **strategies,** cognitive operations that exceed the normal activities required to carry out a task (Pressley & Harris, 2006). Highlighting is a strategy, because it goes beyond simply reading, the normal activity involved in trying to understand a written passage. A variety of general learning strategies exists, including note taking, highlighting, summarizing, self-questioning, and concept mapping (P. Alexander, 2006). Each can enhance learning.

Regardless of the strategy, students' ability to use it effectively depends on their metacognition.

Metacognition: The Foundation of Strategic Learning

Metacognition. Our awareness of and control over our cognitive processes.

As you first saw in Chapter 7, **metacognition** is our awareness of and control over our cognitive processes. It is the mechanism we use to match a strategy to a goal, and students who are metacognitive perform better than their peers who are less aware (Veenman & Spaans, 2005).

When taking notes, for example, metacognitive learners ask questions such as:

- Am I writing down important ideas or trivial details?
- Am I taking enough notes, or am I taking too many?
- When I study, am I simply reading my notes, or do I search for examples to elaborate on them?

Without this kind of metacognitive monitoring, strategies are largely worthless.

Effective strategy users, in addition to being metacognitive, also have extensive prior knowledge and a repertoire of strategies.

Prior Knowledge

Prior knowledge is important for all learning, and it's equally true when using strategies (Coiro & Dobler, 2007). Learners with extensive prior knowledge can use effective strategies such as self-questioning, creating images, and thinking analogically. Without this knowledge base, strategy use is difficult (Sternberg, 2009). Prior knowledge allows students to make better decisions about what is important to study and helps them efficiently allocate their mental resources to the task (Verkoeijen, Rikers, & Schmidt, 2005).

A Repertoire of Strategies

Just as expert problem solvers draw on a wealth of experiences with problems, effective strategy users have a variety of strategies at their disposal (P. Alexander, 2006). For instance, they take notes, skim, use outlines, take advantage of bold and italicized print, capitalize on examples, and create concept maps. Without this repertoire, it is difficult to match strategies to different tasks.

Becoming a strategic learner takes time and effort, and even after strategy instruction, many students use them only when prompted to do so by their teachers (Pressley & Harris, 2006). Also, most students, including those in college, tend to use primitive strategies, such as rehearsal, regardless of the difficulty of the material (Peverly, Brobst, & Graham, 2003).

Study Strategies

Study strategies are specific techniques students use to increase their understanding of written materials and teacher presentations. The most widely used include the following:

- Note taking
- Using text signals
- Summarizing
- Elaborative questioning
- Concept mapping

Study strategies. Specific techniques students use to increase their understanding of written materials and teacher presentations.

Note Taking

Note taking is probably the most common study strategy, and it's been examined extensively. But despite its popularity, many students, including those in college, are poor note takers (Austin, Lee, & Carr, 2004; Peverly et al., 2007). Paul, one of your authors, is an example. Because he came from a small, rural high school, he was quite insecure when he first went to college, so he tried to write down as much of what the instructor said as possible. (You'd be amazed at how fast a person can learn to write.) He wasn't initially strategic in his note taking. As he acquired experience and confidence, it improved, and with it, his achievement. Note taking can significantly increase learning, especially when it encourages students to actively process information (Igo, Bruning, & McCrudden, 2005). Effective notes include both the main ideas presented in lectures or texts and details that support those ideas (Peverly et al., 2007).

Our understanding of cognitive learning theory and human memory help us explain the positive effects of note taking. First, taking notes helps maintain attention and encourages students to be cognitively active, and second, the notes provide a form of external storage (Igo et al., 2005). Because memory is unreliable, we may fail to encode information accurately, or we may reconstruct our understanding in a way that makes sense to us but isn't valid. Notes provide a source of information against which we can check our understanding.

---

1. Give an example of how each of the following influences climate:

Latitude _____

Wind direction _____

Ocean currents _____

Land forms _____

2. Describe each climate, and identify at least one state that has this climate. Then identify one type of plant that lives in this climate and two different animals that are typically found in the climate.

The Mediterranean Climate _____

_____ State _____

Plant _____ Animals _____

The Marine West Coast Climate _____

_____ State _____

Plant _____ Animals _____

The Humid Subtropical Climate _____

_____ State _____

Plant _____ Animals _____

The Humid Continental Climate _____

_____ State _____

Figure 8.3 A guide for note taking in U.S. geography

Guided notes. Teacher-prepared handouts that "guide" students with cues and space available for writing key ideas and relationships.

We can help our students improve their note taking with **guided notes,** teacher-prepared handouts that "guide" students with cues combined with space available for writing key ideas and relationships. Using guided notes increases achievement in students ranging from those with learning disabilities (Hamilton, Seibert, Gardner, & Talbert-Johnson, 2000) to college students (Austin et al., 2004). Figure 8.3 illustrates a guided-notes form used for different climate regions of the United States by a seventh-grade geography teacher.

Guided notes also model the organization and key points of a topic. And as students acquire experience, they gradually develop organizational skills that they can apply on their own.

Using Text Signals

Text signals. Elements included in written materials that communicate text organization and key ideas.

Text signals are elements in written materials that communicate the organization of the content and key ideas. Common text signals include:

- *Headings.* For example, in this chapter, *note taking, using text signals,* and *summarizing* are subheadings under the heading *study strategies,* so this organization signals that each is a study strategy.
- *Numbered and bulleted lists.* For instance, the bulleted list you're reading now identifies different text signals.
- *Underlined, bold, or italicized text.* Each of the important concepts in this text, for example, is emphasized in bold print.
- *Preview and recall sentences.* For instance, we introduced our discussion of metacognition in this chapter by saying, "As you first saw in Chapter 7, metacognition is. . . ." This signal links the concept to a discussion in an earlier chapter and suggests that you reread that section if you are uncertain about the topic.

Strategic learners use these signals to develop a framework for the topic they're studying (Vacca, Vacca, & Mraz, 2011). You can encourage the use of this strategy with your students by discussing the organization of a topic and reminding them of other text signals that can help make the information they're studying more meaningful.

Summarizing

Summarizing is the process of preparing a concise description of verbal or written passages. It's effective for **comprehension monitoring**—checking to see if we understand what we've read or heard. If we can prepare a summary of a topic, it indicates that we understand it.

Learning to summarize takes time and effort, but with training, students can become skilled at it (P. Alexander, 2003, 2006). Training usually involves walking students through a passage and helping them construct general descriptions, generate statements that relate ideas to each other, and identify important information (Pressley & Harris, 2006).

For instance, we might summarize the problem-solving section of this chapter as follows:

> To solve problems, we must identify the problem goal, represent the problem, select and implement a strategy to solve it, and check to see if the solution makes sense. We can help our students become better problem solvers by presenting a general framework for solving problems and providing them with opportunities for deliberate practice.

Research suggests that summarizing increases both students' understanding of the topics they study and their metacognitive skills (Thiede & Anderson, 2003). Having your students generate key terms that capture the essence of a text passage is a modified form of summarizing that can also increase comprehension (Thiede, Anderson, & Therriault, 2003).

Elaborative Questioning

Elaborative questioning is the process of drawing inferences, identifying examples, and forming relationships. It is an effective comprehension-monitoring strategy because it encourages students to create connections in the material they're studying. Three elaborative questions are especially effective:

- What is another example of this idea?
- How is this topic similar to or different from the one in the previous section?
- How does this idea relate to other ideas I've been studying?

For example, as you were studying the section on problem solving, you might have asked the following questions:

What is another example of a well-defined problem in this class?

What is an example of an ill-defined problem?

What makes the first well-defined and the second ill-defined?

How are problem-solving and learning strategies similar? How are they different?

Questions such as these create links between new information and knowledge in long-term memory, making the new information more meaningful.

Concept Mapping

A **concept map** is a visual representation of the relationships among concepts that includes the concepts themselves, sometimes enclosed in circles or boxes, together with relationships among concepts indicated by lines linking them to each other. Words on the line, referred to as *linking words* or *linking phrases,* specify the relationship between the concepts (Novak & Cañas, 2006). A concept map is somewhat analogous to the way a road map represents

Summarizing. The process of preparing a concise description of verbal or written passages.

Comprehension monitoring. The process of checking to see if we understand what we have read or heard.

Elaborative questioning. The process of drawing inferences, identifying examples, and forming relationships.

Concept map. A visual representation of the relationships among concepts that includes the concepts themselves, sometimes enclosed in circles or boxes, together with relationships among concepts indicated by lines linking the concepts.

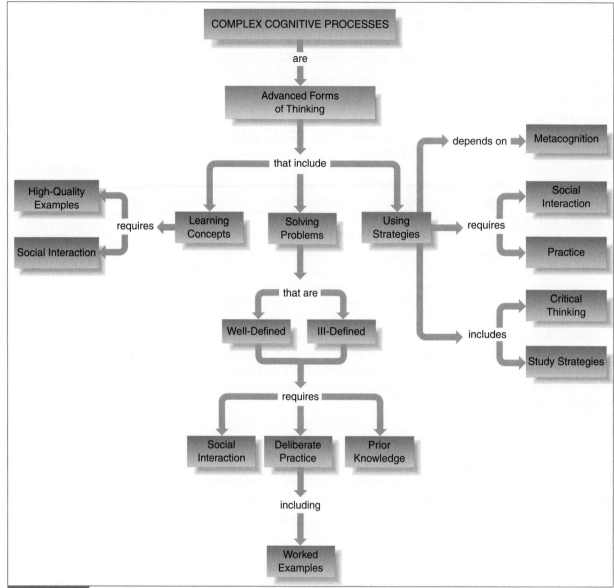

Figure 8.4 Concept map for complex cognitive processes

locations of highways and towns or a circuit diagram represents the workings of an electrical appliance. Figure 8.4 is a concept map for the complex cognitive processes that we've discussed to this point in the chapter.

Concept mapping is an effective study strategy that puts students in cognitively active roles and employs dual-coding theory—the process of encoding information in both visual and verbal form (De Simone, 2007; Nesbit & Adesope, 2006). It also capitalizes on effective encoding strategies (Nesbit & Adesope, 2006). A concept map visually represents relationships among concepts, so it uses *imagery,* and preparing the map itself requires *organization.* As learners' understanding increases, maps can be modified and expanded, which is a form of *elaboration.* Research indicates that the strategy makes initial learning more effective and conceptual change more durable (Kakkarainen & Ahtee, 2007).

Conceptual hierarchies are concept maps that visually illustrate superordinate, subordinate, and coordinate relationships among concepts. The relationships among the concepts are clear in a conceptual hierarchy, because each subordinate concept is a subset of

Conceptual hierarchies. Types of concept maps that visually illustrate superordinate, subordinate, and coordinate relationships among concepts.

the one above it. As a result, linking words or phrases aren't used. A conceptual hierarchy for the concept *closed-plane figures* is illustrated in Figure 8.5. *Closed-plane figures* is superordinate to all the other figures in the hierarchy; *four-sided figures, three-sided figures,* and *curved figures* are subordinate to *closed-plane figures* (they are all subsets of *closed-plane figures*); and *four-sided figures, three-sided figures,* and *curved figures* are coordinate to each other. Similar relationships exist among the other concepts in the hierarchy.

Many concepts, such as our number system, the animal and plant kingdoms, parts of speech, and figurative language, are organized hierarchically.

Concept mapping can be used to measure conceptual change in learners, and it's also an effective assessment tool (Hilbert & Renkl, 2008; MacNeil, 2007). For example, the student who created the conceptual hierarchy in Figure 8.5 didn't include figures with more than four sides or curved shapes other than circles. If you use a concept map as a form of assessment, and you see that your students' understanding is incomplete, you can then provide additional examples, such as pentagons, hexagons, and ellipses in the case of closed-plane figures.

The type of concept map students use should be the one that best illustrates relationships among the concepts. Hierarchies often work best in math and science; in other areas, such as reading or social studies, a traditional concept map may be more effective.

Most students can learn study strategies, and strategy instruction is especially valuable for younger students and low achievers, because they have a smaller repertoire of strategies and are less likely to use them spontaneously (Bruning, Schraw, & Norby, 2011). However, the effectiveness of any strategy depends on learners' motivation, their ability to activate relevant prior knowledge, and their metacognition (Huber, 2004). If one or more of these factors is missing, no strategy is effective.

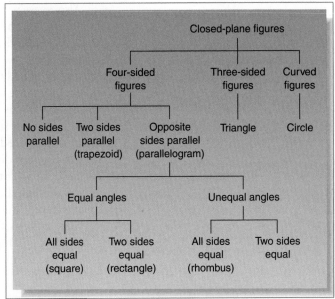

Figure 8.5 Conceptual hierarchy for the concept *closed-plane figures*

Research on Study Strategies: Implications for You and Your Students

Think about the questions we ask in our "Ed Psych and You" feature here. Conventional wisdom suggests that we should study a topic until we thoroughly understand it and then move on to a second topic. It also suggests

Ed Psych and You

How do you study? Do you study one topic thoroughly and then move on to the next? Do you have a designated place in your home where you usually do your studying? Do you study in large chunks of time, or shorter ones? In your estimation, how effective are your study strategies?

that we should have a designated place to study that is free of distractions. However, some of this conventional wisdom is misguided. For example, in a classic study, S. M. Smith, Glenberg, and Bjork (1978) found that simply varying the environment in which students studied resulted in more recall of information than studying the same information in a single environment. This suggests that studying at home some of the time, in the library at other times, and even in a coffee shop is more effective than always studying in your home. Research also indicates that studying different but related topics in one sitting is more effective than focusing intensely on a single topic (Kornell, Castel, Eich, & Bjork, 2010; Taylor & Rohrer, 2010). For example, your study of the human memory model is likely to be more effective if you also study cognitive learning principles and the relationships between the two in a single study session, rather than studying the human memory model in one session and cognitive learning principles in another. "Forcing the brain to make multiple associations with the same material may, in effect, give the information more neural scaffolding" (Carey, 2010, para. 11).

Also, as we've known for decades, spacing study is vastly superior to intense periods of cramming. So, an hour of study tonight, another hour two days from now, and a third hour over the weekend will result in more learning than three hours in any one of the sessions. Cognitive scientists even suggest that seeming to forget something and then remembering it later can actually benefit learning. You don't literally forget it, and the relearning results in deeper and more thorough understanding (Kornell et al., 2010). This helps us understand why spacing study results in more learning than cramming.

Research also suggests that we, as teachers, have a powerful learning tool—assessment—at our immediate disposal. Assessment not only measures knowledge but changes it, and the change is in the direction of deeper understanding (Roediger & Karpicke, 2006). "Testing has such a bad connotation; people think of standardized testing or teaching to the test. Maybe we should call it something else, but this is one of the most powerful learning tools that we have" (Quoted in Carey, 2010, p. 5).

This suggests that we should frequently and thoroughly assess our students' understanding of the topics they study, and these assessments should do more than measure recall of factual information. When they do, they can significantly increase the amount our students learn.

Critical Thinking

Critical thinking is becoming increasingly important in today's world because of the large amounts of information on the Internet, along with the advertising, conscious distortions, and even propaganda that we must constantly sift through. **Critical thinking** has been defined in various ways, but most definitions include an individual's ability and inclination to make and assess conclusions based on evidence (van Gelder, 2005; Willingham, 2009). For example, an advertisement says, "Doctors recommend . . . more often," touting a health product. A person thinking critically is wary because the advertisement provides no evidence for its claims. Similarly, a critical thinker listens to another person's argument with guarded skepticism because people are known to have unconscious biases.

Critical thinking. An individual's ability and inclination to make and assess conclusions based on evidence.

The Challenge of Critical Thinking

Asking students to provide evidence for their conclusions promotes critical thinking.

Consider the following question: Which do people fear more: flying or driving? terrorism or the flu? sharks or dogs? In an overwhelming majority of cases, it is the first of each pair, i.e., flying, terrorism, and sharks. Now, let's look at some statistics. In 2005, 321 people died in airline crashes, whereas more than 34,000 died in auto accidents. In 2008, 33 Americans were killed in terrorist attacks around the world, whereas more than 36,000 people a year die from the flu. And, in 2009 there were 28 shark attacks around the world, whereas an average of more than 4 and a half million people a year are bitten by dogs (Kalb & White, 2010). How can we explain these irrational fears, particularly when reason is supposed to be the highest achievement of the human mind?

Making and assessing conclusions based on evidence, in general, and avoiding irrational emotional reactions, in particular, are more difficult than they appear, and most people are not good at them (Willingham, 2009). For example, when asked to justify an opinion,

to provide some evidence to back it up—more than half the population flounder. . . . The problem is that they do not have a general grasp of the notion of evidence and what would properly count as providing evidence in support of their view. (van Gelder, 2005, p. 42)

Some experts suggest that humans are not naturally disposed to think critically. "Humans don't think very often because our brains are designed not for thought, but for the avoidance of thought" (Willingham, 2009, p. 4). Why is this the case? First, thinking has three properties: It is *slow*, it requires *effort*, and the results are *uncertain*. Second, thinking occurs in working memory, which we know is limited. We function much more efficiently when we perform tasks automatically, essentially without conscious thought (Willingham, 2009).

Belief preservation, the tendency to make evidence subservient to belief, rather than the other way around, and **confirmation bias,** the tendency to focus only on evidence that supports our beliefs, pose additional challenges to critical thinking (Douglas, 2000). When we strongly believe an idea, or desire it to be true, we tend to seek evidence that supports the belief and avoid or ignore evidence that disputes it, or we retain beliefs in the face of overwhelming contrary evidence if we can find some minimal support for the belief. Young children's belief in Santa Claus is an example. Virtually no evidence supports the existence of Santa Claus, but young children cling to the belief, sometimes for years, and give it up only reluctantly.

Cognitive learning theory and Piaget's work help us understand these tendencies. We want our experiences to make sense, so we construct knowledge that makes sense to us. When experiences do make sense, even if they're illusory or distorted, we are at equilibrium, so we have no need to pursue a matter further. And this tendency often applies as much to high achievers as it does to lower achievers (Macpherson & Stanovich, 2007).

In addition, people sometimes have a personal investment in existing beliefs. They feel that changing their beliefs reflects negatively on their intelligence or their resolve, so the change threatens their sense of self-worth (Linnenbrink & Pintrich, 2003). Also, beliefs are sometimes integral to their culture or religion (Southerland & Sinatra, 2003). Meeting these challenges is at the heart of instruction that promotes critical thinking, and experts recommend that it should be integrated into the regular curriculum (Burke, Williams, & Skinner, 2007).

Belief preservation. People's tendency to make evidence subservient to belief, rather than the other way around.

Confirmation bias. People's tendency to focus only on evidence that supports their beliefs.

Promoting Critical Thinking

With awareness and planning, critical thinking can become an integral part of your instruction (Macpherson, & Stanovich, 2007). The following guidelines can help you in this process:

- Model thinking dispositions, such as the use of evidence in making conclusions, a sense of curiosity, a desire to be informed, and a willingness to respect opinions different from your own. Your own modeling is probably the most powerful contribution you can make to your students' inclination to think critically.
- Ask questions such as, "How do you know?" and "Why do you say that?" frequently and make them an integral part of your teaching. These questions require students to provide evidence for their conclusions, and, in many cases, they follow naturally from other questions.
- Promote metacognition by helping students become aware of their own thinking.

To illustrate these guidelines, let's go back to Laura's Tuesday lesson. She had shown the diagram you see here and had written the following on the board:

$$15 \times 3 = 45 \text{ square feet}$$
$$12 \times 3 = 36 \text{ square feet}$$
$$45 + 36 = 81 \text{ square feet}$$

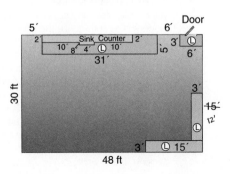

Now, look again at some of the dialogue.

Laura: Someone explain where these numbers came from.

Nephi: The 15 is the length of that part (pointing to the bottom of the diagram). And the 3 is how wide it is . . . so, the area is 45.

Laura: Forty-five what?

Nephi: Square feet.

Laura: Now, let's be good thinkers. How do we know that the second statement must be 12 times 3?

Anya: . . . I've got it!

Laura: Come up and show us.

Anya: See, we already have this (pointing to the lower right corner of the drawing). So, this length is 12, not 15. . . . So, it's 12 times 3.

Laura then completes the activity and assigns homework.

Laura: Now, what do we always ask ourselves when we try a strategy?

Shayna: Does it make sense?

Laura: Yes, exactly. You'll need to be ready to explain how you got your answers.

In this exchange, Laura asked students to justify their thinking, and she promoted metacognition by asking, "What do we always do when we try a strategy?" With practice, students improve, and you can incorporate these processes into your instruction with little additional effort.

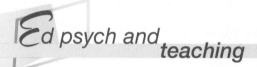

Helping Your Students Become Strategic Learners

Cognitive learning theory offers suggestions for helping your students become better strategy users. The following guidelines can help you in your efforts (Pressley & Harris, 2006):

1. Describe the strategy, and explain why it is useful.
2. Explicitly teach the strategy by modeling both the strategy and metacognition.
3. Provide opportunities for students to practice the strategy in a variety of contexts.
4. Provide feedback as students practice.

Let's see how Donna Evans applies these guidelines in her middle school geography class.

> Donna begins her geography class by directing her students to a section of the text that describes the low-, middle-, and high-latitude climates, and says, "One way to become more effective readers is to summarize the information we read in a few short statements. This makes the information easier to remember, and it will help us understand how one climate region compares with another. You can do the same thing when you study different classes of animals in biology or parts of the court system in government. . . . Now read the section on page 237, and see if you can identify the features of a low-latitude climate."
>
> The class reads the section, and Donna continues, "As I was reading, here's how I thought about it." She then displays the following information on the document camera and describes her thinking as she writes it.

> Low latitudes can be hot and wet or hot and dry. Close to the equator, the humid tropical climate is hot and wet all year. Farther away, it has wet summers and dry winters. In the dry tropical climate, high-pressure zones cause deserts, like the Sahara.

> She then says "Now, let's all give it a try with the section on the middle-latitude climates. Go ahead and read the section, and try to summarize it the way I did. . . . Write your summaries, and we'll share what you've written."
>
> After they finish, Donna asks a student to volunteer a summary.
>
> Kari volunteers, displays her summary on the document camera, and Donna and other students add information and comments to what Kari has written. Donna then has two other students display their summaries, and then the class practices again with the section on the high-latitude climates.
>
> Throughout the school year, Donna continues to have her students practice summarizing once or twice a week.

Now let's look at Donna's efforts to apply the guidelines. She began by describing the process of summarizing and explaining why it is useful. For instance, she said, "One way to become more effective readers is to summarize the information we read in a few short statements. This makes information easier to remember, and it will help us understand how one climate compares with another. . . ." This applied the first guideline.

She then applied the second guideline by modeling both the skill and her thinking when she commented, "As I was reading, here's how I thought about it. . . ." Research indicates that young children's metacognitive awareness can be increased with explicit instruction such as this (J. M. Alexander, Johnson, & Leibham, 2005).

Donna then applied the third and fourth guidelines by having her students practice reading a passage, preparing a summary, and providing them with feedback. She displayed an example on the document camera, so everyone would be responding to the same information. And, she continued the process throughout the school year. As with all complex cognitive processes, become a strategic learner requires a great deal of deliberate practice.

Classroom connections

Promoting Strategic Learning in Classrooms

Study Strategies

1. Students use study strategies to increase their understanding of written materials and teacher presentations. Teach study strategies across the curriculum and throughout the school year to make them most effective.

   - **Elementary:** A second-grade teacher models elaborative questioning and encourages her children to ask themselves what each lesson was about and what they learned from it.

   - **Middle School:** A sixth-grade teacher introduces note taking as a study skill. He then provides note-taking practice in his social studies class by using skeletal outlines to organize his presentations and by having his students use them as a guide for their note taking.

   - **High School:** A biology teacher closes each lesson by having her students provide summaries of the most important parts of the lesson. She adds material to summaries that are incomplete.

Critical Thinking

2. Helping students learn to make and assess conclusions based on evidence promotes critical thinking. Integrate critical thinking into the regular curriculum.

   - **Elementary:** A fourth-grade teacher makes it a point to ask questions, such as (1) What do you observe? (2) How are these alike or different? (3) Why is A different from B? (4) What would happen if . . . ? (5) How do you know?

   - **Middle School:** A seventh-grade geography teacher develops her topics with examples, charts, graphs, and tables. She develops lessons around students' observations, comparisons, and conclusions related to the information they see, and she requires students to provide evidence for their conclusions.

   - **High School:** An English teacher helps his students analyze literature by asking questions such as, "How do you know that?" and, "What in the story supports your idea?"

check your understanding

3.1 You read this chapter carefully in an effort to understand the content. Does your effort illustrate strategic learning? Explain why or why not.

3.2 Three students are discussing the use of highlighting as a study strategy.

"I highlight the first sentence of nearly every paragraph, because that's supposed to be the topic sentence," Alexie comments. "Sometimes I highlight other sentences if they seem to be the topic sentence."

"I highlight passages that I think are important," Ruiz adds. "I look for key terms and lists and examples."

"I highlight practically whole chapters," Will offers. "I read along with it as I'm highlighting."

Which student is using the most effective strategy? Whose strategy is least effective? Explain.

3.3 Mrs. Solis's students are analyzing a table illustrating the average global temperature for the years 1960 to 2000. They conclude that the table shows a general increase. "What have we done here?" Mrs. Solis asks.

"We've found a pattern in the data," Francisco responds.

What important aspect of critical thinking is Mrs. Solis promoting with her question? Explain.

To receive feedback for these questions, go to Appendix A.

Exploring diversity

Learner Differences in Complex Cognitive Processes

The basic processes involved in concept learning, problem solving, and strategic learning are essentially the same for all students. However, their cultural knowledge, approaches to problem solving, and attitudes and beliefs will vary. For example, the Yu'pik people living in the Bering Sea just west of Alaska have 99 different concepts for ice (Block, 2007). This is knowledge important to their culture as they travel and hunt, but it's alien to most of us.

Cultural differences also exist in the way people approach concept learning. For example, adults in western cultures tend to classify items taxonomically, such as putting animals in one group, food items in another, and tools in a third. However, adults in some other cultures classify items into functional categories, such as putting a shovel and potato together, because a shovel is used to dig up a potato (Luria, 1976).

Attitudes and beliefs are also influenced by cultural differences. For instance, learning-related attitudes are offered as an explanation for the impressive problem-solving achievements of Japanese students. "Attitudes toward achievement emphasize that success comes from hard work (not from innate ability). . . . Teachers examined a few problems in depth rather than covering many problems superficially; children's errors were used as learning tools for the group" (Rogoff, 2003, pp. 264–265).

In view of their impressive academic achievements, the fact that early childhood education in Japan focuses on social development instead of academics may be surprising (Abe & Izzard, 1999). Some experts believe this emphasis helps children feel part of a group and responsible to it, which results in greater attention to the topics being taught and fewer classroom-management problems (Rogoff, 2003).

Culture also influences strategic learning. For example, students use more effective comprehension-monitoring strategies when exposed to written materials consistent with their cultural experiences (Pritchard, 1990). Once again we see how important background knowledge is to thinking.

Interestingly, fewer cultural differences are found when tasks are embedded in real-world contexts. For example, when people such as vendors, carpenters, or dieters use math for practical purposes, they rarely get answers that don't make sense. "However, calculations in the context of schooling regularly produce some absurd errors, with results that are impossible if the meaning of the problem is being considered" (Rogoff, 2003, p. 262). This was illustrated in Laura's lesson. Even though finding the carpeted area of the classroom was a real-world task for her students, some were willing to accept widely varying answers to the problem, even answers that didn't make sense. This demonstrates the need to promote metacognition and provide a great deal of scaffolding for all learners, regardless of their cultural backgrounds.

Experiences and cultural and religious beliefs can also influence critical thinking. Learners whose early school experiences involve a great deal of memory-level tasks are more likely to use primitive study strategies, such as rehearsal, and they are less equipped to be critical thinkers than are their peers who have opportunities to practice higher-order thinking. Memory-level tasks are common in urban schools, and urban schools typically have large numbers of minorities. This results in fewer opportunities to think about and practice complex mental processes for members of cultural minorities (Kozol, 2005). Also, members of cultures who have been taught to respect elders, and learners with strong authoritarian religious beliefs, may be less disposed to critical thinking (Kuhn & Park, 2005).

These differences all point to the need to be aware of the differences students bring to our classrooms. Despite these differences, the need to embed learning experiences in real-world contexts, promote high levels of interaction, and provide the scaffolding that helps learners make sense of those experiences is essential for all students, regardless of their cultural backgrounds.

Transfer of Learning

Ed Psych and You

You're studying for a quiz in one of your classes with a friend, and after a considerable amount of discussion, you comment, "Talking it over this way sure helps. I get it better than when I study by myself."

What idea from your study of ed psych does your comment best illustrate?

Transfer. The ability to take understanding acquired in one context and apply it to another.

How did you answer the question in our "Ed Psych and You" feature here? If you concluded that your comment illustrates an application of the cognitive learning principle *social interaction facilitates learning,* you have demonstrated **transfer,** the ability to take understanding acquired in one context and apply it to a different one (Mayer & Wittrock, 2006). Because we can't teach our students everything they need to know, the ability to transfer is essential. Recognizing or providing a new example of a concept, solving a unique problem, or applying a learning strategy to a new situation are all examples of transfer (De Corte, 2007).

Recalling information doesn't involve transfer. If, for example, your instructor had previously discussed the example in our "Ed Psych and You" feature here, you merely remembered the information.

Transfer can be either positive or negative. Positive transfer occurs when learning in one context facilitates learning in another, whereas negative transfer occurs when learning in one

chapteroutline

learningoutcomes

After you've completed your study of this chapter, you should be able to:

1. Use classical conditioning to explain events in and outside of classrooms.

2. Identify examples of operant conditioning in classroom activities.

3. Use concepts from social cognitive theory to explain examples of people's behaviors. Include the nonoccurrence of expected consequences, reciprocal causation, and vicarious learning.

4. Identify examples of social cognitive theory in people's behaviors. Include the types of modeling, modeling outcomes, effectiveness of models, and self-regulation.

classroomapplications

The following features help you apply the content of this chapter in your teaching.

Ed Psych and Teaching:
    Applying Classical Conditioning with Your Students
    Applying Operant Conditioning with Your Students
    Using Social Cognitive Theory to Increase Your Students' Learning

Classroom Connections:
    Developing a Positive Classroom Climate with Classical Conditioning
    Using Operant Conditioning Effectively in Classrooms
    Capitalizing on Social Cognitive Theory in Classrooms

Developmentally Appropriate Practice:
    Applying Behaviorism and Social Cognitive Theory with Learners at Different Ages

Exploring Diversity:
    Capitalizing on Behaviorism and Social Cognitive Theory with Learners from Diverse Backgrounds

*H*ave you ever tried harder after someone praised your efforts, or attempted something, such as a new dance, after watching others do it? If the answer is yes, you will be able to explain why after studying this chapter. Our experiences and observations of others strongly influence the way we act and think, and you will see their effects on Tim Spencer, a 10th grader, in the following case study. As you read it, think about how Tim is influenced by his experience on a math quiz and by observing his friend Susan.

Tim has been doing well in Algebra II—getting mostly B's on the weekly quizzes. On the last one, however, something inexplicably went wrong. He became confused, panicked, and failed it. He was devastated.

Now, on the next quiz, he's so nervous that when he starts, the first few answers he circles have wiggly lines around them from his shaking hand. "I'm not sure I can do this," he thinks. "Maybe I should drop algebra."

His hand also shakes when he takes chemistry tests, but fortunately, he isn't nervous in world history, where he is doing fine.

Tim mentions his troubles to his friend Susan, who always does well on the quizzes.

"They're tough," she comments, "so I really study for them. . . . Let's get together."

Tim is skeptical but agrees, and the night before the next quiz, he goes to Susan's home to study. He sees how she selects several problems from the book and solves them completely, rather than simply reading over the sample problems and explanations. As she begins working on her third problem, he asks her why she is doing another one.

"I try to do as many different kinds as I can to be sure I don't get fooled," she explains. "So, I'm more confident when I go into the quiz. . . . See, this one is different.

"I even make a little chart. I do at least three problems of each type and then check them off as I do them, so I can see that I'm making progress. If I get them all right, I might treat myself to a dish of ice cream."

"Good idea," Tim nods. "I usually do a couple, and if I get them, I quit."

Tim adopts Susan's study habits and sets his own goal of doing three of each type of problem, selecting those with answers at the back of the book.

He does much better on the next quiz. "What a relief," he says to himself.

He's less anxious for the following week's quiz, and his efforts are paying off; he makes his highest score so far.

"Maybe I can do this after all," he says to himself.

To begin our discussion, consider these questions:

1. How can we explain Tim's nervousness on the quiz following his bad experience?
2. Why did his nervousness later decrease?
3. Why did he change his study habits and sustain his efforts?

Behaviorism and social cognitive theory help answer these questions, and in this chapter you'll see how you can apply these theories as you work with your students.

ehaviorist Views of Learning

Behaviorism: A theory that explains learning in terms of observable behaviors and how they're influenced by stimuli from the environment.

Learning (behaviorism). A relatively enduring change in observable behavior that occurs as a result of experience.

Behaviorism is a theory that explains learning in terms of observable behaviors and how they're influenced by stimuli from the environment. It defines **learning** as a relatively enduring change in observable behavior that occurs as a result of experience (Schunk, 2008; Skinner, 1953). Notice—in contrast with cognitive theorists—this definition doesn't include any references to thinking or thought processes, such as expectations, beliefs, insights, desires or goals, or permanent changes in behavior that result from maturation. Behaviorism, as the name implies, focuses exclusively on observable behavior. This narrow focus is controversial, but behaviorism continues to be widely applied in schools, especially in the area of classroom management (Freiberg & Lamb, 2009).

Behaviorism has two major components: *classical conditioning*, which focuses on emotional and physiological responses to stimuli from the environment, and *operant conditioning*, which examines changes in behaviors in response to consequences. We begin with a discussion of classical conditioning.

Classical Conditioning

Think about the questions we ask in our "Ed Psych and You" feature here. If you answered yes to any of them, we can explain your reactions using **classical conditioning,** a component of behaviorism that explains how we *learn* involuntary emotional or physiological responses that are similar to instinctive or reflexive responses (Baldwin & Baldwin, 2001).

Tim experienced what we commonly call *test anxiety,* and let's see how we can explain it using classical conditioning. As a result of his experience—failing the quiz—he was devastated. Tim didn't choose to feel this way; it was involuntary, that is, the feeling of devastation was out of his control. Tim associated the algebra quiz with his failure, and as a result, he was nervous when he took subsequent algebra quizzes. His nervousness was similar to the devastation he felt in response to his original failure. He *learned* to be nervous when he took later algebra quizzes; he learned an emotional response that was similar to his original instinctive response.

We usually think of learning as acquiring knowledge, such as knowing the causes of the War of 1812, or skill, such as finding 42% of 65, but emotions can also be learned, and we saw how in Tim's experience.

Classical conditioning.
A component of behaviorism that explains how we *learn* to display involuntary emotional or physiological responses that are similar to instinctive or reflexive responses.

Stimuli and Responses in Classical Conditioning

Ivan Pavlov, a Russian scientist, originally discovered classical conditioning while investigating salivation in dogs. As a part of his research, he had his assistants feed dogs meat powder so their rates of salivation could be measured. As the research progressed, however, the dogs began to salivate at the sight of the assistants, even when they weren't carrying meat powder. This startling phenomenon caused a turn in Pavlov's work and opened the field of what is now known as classical conditioning.

Let's see how Pavlov's research applies to Tim. The original failure he experienced was an **unconditioned stimulus,** an object or event that causes an **unconditioned response,** the instinctive or reflexive (unlearned) physiological or emotional response caused by the unconditioned stimulus. The devastation Tim felt was the unconditioned response in his case.

Tim associated his algebra quiz with his failure, so the tests became **conditioned stimuli,** formerly *neutral stimuli* that become associated with the unconditioned stimulus (Tim's original failure). A **neutral stimulus** is an object or event that doesn't initially affect behavior one way or the other. The algebra quizzes originally had no impact on Tim until they became associated with his failure; in other words, they were neutral.

As a result of associating algebra quizzes with failure, the quizzes produced a **conditioned response,** a *learned* physiological or emotional response similar to the unconditioned response.

Association is the key to learning in classical conditioning. To form the association, the unconditioned and conditioned stimuli must be *contiguous,* that is, they must occur at the same time. Without this contiguity, an association can't be formed, and learning through classical conditioning can't take place.

Both real-world and classroom examples of classical conditioning are common (Schunk, Pintrich, & Meece, 2008), and the questions in our "Ed Psych and You" feature are examples. Let's consider the last question. You're on a date that turns out to be special, and you feel the attraction and sense of romance that can occur between two people. The encounter is an unconditioned stimulus, and the romantic feeling is the unconditioned response. Now, if a particular song is playing while you're on the date, the song can become associated with the encounter. So, because of the association, it becomes a

Unconditioned stimulus. An object or event that causes an instinctive or reflex (unlearned) emotional or physiological response.

Unconditioned response. The instinctive or reflexive (unlearned) physiological or emotional response caused by the unconditioned stimulus.

Conditioned stimulus. A formerly neutral stimulus that becomes associated with an unconditioned stimulus.

Neutral stimulus. An object or event that doesn't initially impact behavior one way or the other.

Conditioned response. A learned physiological or emotional response that is similar to the unconditioned response.

Table 9.1	Classical conditioning in our lives	
Example	**Stimuli**	**Responses**
Tim	UCS *Failure*	UCR *Devastation* (involuntary and unlearned)
	CS *Quizzes* (associated with failure)	CR *Anxiety* (involuntary but learned; similar to the original devastation)
Us	UCS *Encounter with another person*	UCR *Feeling of romance* (involuntary and unlearned)
	CS *Song* (associated with the encounter)	CR *Feeling of romance* (involuntary but learned; similar to the original romantic feeling)

Abbreviations: UCS, unconditioned stimulus; UCR, unconditioned response; CS, conditioned stimulus; CR, conditioned response.

An understanding of classical conditioning helps teachers see how supportive classroom environments and warm and caring teachers result in positive feelings toward schools and learning.

Generalization. The process that occurs when stimuli similar, but not identical, to a conditioned stimulus elicit the conditioned responses by themselves.

Discrimination. The process that occurs when a person gives different responses to related but not identical stimuli.

Extinction (classical conditioning). The process that occurs when the conditioned stimulus occurs often enough in the absence of the unconditioned stimulus so that it no longer elicits the conditioned response.

conditioned stimulus that produces a romantic feeling, similar to the original feeling, as a conditioned response. The mechanisms involved in Tim's case and in the romantic encounter are outlined in Table 9.1.

As other examples, we probably react warmly when we smell Thanksgiving turkey; and we may be uneasy when we enter a dentist's office. And most of us have experienced test anxiety to some degree. In each of these examples, we learned an emotional response through classical conditioning. (In the "Check Your Understanding" exercises at the end of this section, we ask you to explain these reactions as well as the other examples in the preceding "Ed Psych and You.")

Classical conditioning is also the theoretical framework for a considerable amount of contemporary research in areas ranging as widely as preschoolers' preferences for certain tastes (Lumeng & Cardinal, 2007) to couples' therapy (Davis & Piercy, 2007) and the relationships between personal power and self-esteem (Bogdan & Struzynska-Kujalowicz, 2007).

Generalization and Discrimination

You saw in the opening case study that Tim was also anxious in chemistry tests. His anxiety had generalized to chemistry. **Generalization** occurs when stimuli similar—but not identical—to a conditioned stimulus elicit conditioned responses by themselves (Jones, Kemenes, & Benjamin, 2001). Tim's chemistry tests were similar to his algebra quizzes, and they elicited the conditioned response—anxiety—by themselves.

Generalization can also work in a positive way. Students who associate a classroom with the warmth and respect demonstrated by one teacher may generalize their reactions to other classes, club activities, and the school in general.

Discrimination, the opposite of generalization, is the process of giving different responses to related but not identical stimuli (Hill, 2002). For example, Tim wasn't nervous in world history tests. He discriminated between world history and algebra.

Extinction

After working with Susan and changing his study habits, Tim's performance began to improve on the quizzes. As a result, he was a little less nervous on each subsequent quiz. In time, if he continues to succeed, his nervousness will disappear, that is, the conditioned response will become extinct. **Extinction** in classical conditioning results when the conditioned stimulus occurs often enough in the absence of the unconditioned stimulus that it no longer elicits the conditioned response (Myers & Davis, 2007). As Tim took additional quizzes (conditioned stimuli) without experiencing failure (the unconditioned stimulus), his anxiety (the conditioned response) gradually disappeared.

Ed psych and teaching

Applying Classical Conditioning with Your Students

Some researchers suggest that emotions impact our lives even more strongly than does reason (Brooks, 2011), and others assert that students' emotional reactions to their school experiences are among the most important outcomes of schooling (Gentile, 1996; Noddings, 2001). Many examples exist. For instance, students are often uneasy about attending a new school or even moving to a new grade with an unfamiliar teacher. They may also be uncomfortable with a particular content area, such as math. In each of these cases, their uneasiness can have a negative effect on their feelings about school and even their achievement.

Classical conditioning is a tool that you can use to prevent problems such as these from occurring. The following guidelines can help you in your efforts:

1. Consistently treat your students with warmth and respect.
2. Personalize your classroom to create an emotionally safe environment.
3. Require that your students treat each other with courtesy and respect.

To see these guidelines in practice, let's look in on Sharon Van Horn, a second-grade teacher.

> Sharon greets each of her students with the same routine each morning: As they come in the classroom, they give her a handshake, hug, or high five, whichever they prefer. During the school day, Sharon simultaneously treats her students with a warm, even manner, while requiring that they behave appropriately and are diligent in their work. She forbids students from making any demeaning or hurtful comments to their classmates. They have a classroom meeting once a week, when they discuss the importance of treating others as they would like to be treated.
>
> Sharon has taken digital pictures of her students and displayed them on a large bulletin board. The students have written short paragraphs about themselves, displayed below the pictures.
>
> Sharon periodically displays posters and other artifacts from the heritage countries for her students who are not native English speakers. For example, colorful prints from Mexico

are displayed on one wall, and vocabulary cards in both Spanish and English are hung around the room.

> Alberto, who has immigrated from Mexico, comes in for extra help three mornings a week, and this morning Mariachi music is playing in the background.
>
> "Buenos días, Alberto. How are you today?" Sharon asks before Alberto gives her a hug, which he prefers.
>
> "Buenos días. I'm fine," Alberto responds, as he goes to his desk to take out his homework.

Now, let's look at how Sharon implemented the guidelines with her students. She applied the first with her consistently warm and inviting manner, which acted as an unconditioned stimulus, and the safe and secure feelings that her students experienced were unconditioned responses. Because she was consistently warm and supportive, they gradually began to associate her classroom with her emotional support, so the classroom became a conditioned stimulus that produced similar feelings of safety as conditioned responses. In time the classroom could even generalize to their school work, producing similar positive emotions. Ideally, we all want our students to have positive emotional reactions to us, our classrooms, and the work they do.

Sharon applied the second guideline with the students' photos, personal descriptions, and, in Alberto's case, the music and pictures of his native Mexico. And she did the same with all of her students who weren't native English speakers.

Requiring that her students treat each other with respect and holding periodic classroom meetings to discuss the way the students treat each other applied the third guideline. Through her rules Sharon made her classroom a safe place where students could learn.

Our goal in all our decisions is to promote learning, and students learn more in classrooms that are emotionally safe and secure. Classical conditioning is one tool we can use to promote these feelings.

Classroom connections

Developing a Positive Classroom Climate with Classical Conditioning

1. Classical conditioning explains how individuals learn emotional responses through the process of association. To elicit positive emotions as conditioned stimuli in your students, create a safe and welcoming classroom environment, so your classroom elicits feelings of security.

   - **Elementary:** A first-grade teacher greets each of her students with a smile when they come into the room in the morning. She makes an attempt to periodically ask each of them about their family or some other personal part of their lives.

   - **Middle School:** A seventh-grade teacher enforces rules that forbid students from ridiculing each other in any way. He makes respect a high priority in his classroom.

   - **High School:** A geometry teacher attempts to reduce anxiety by specifying what students are accountable for on tests. She provides sample problems for practice and offers additional help sessions twice a week.

1.1 Identify the unconditioned and conditioned stimuli and the unconditioned and conditioned responses in Pavlov's original experiments.

1.2 Answer the first two questions we asked at the beginning of this section: "How can we explain Tim's nervousness on the quiz following his bad experience?" and "Why did his nervousness later decrease?"

1.3 Think about the following examples: (1) our test anxiety, (2) our fear of spiders and snakes, (3) reacting warmly to the smell of Thanksgiving turkey, and (4) feeling uneasy when we enter a dentist's office. Identify the unconditioned and conditioned stimuli,

the unconditioned and conditioned responses, and describe the association involved in each of these examples.

1.4 Consider again the romantic encounter we described in this section. Suppose the song we hear is a Latin rhythm, and later we discover that all romantic Latin music arouses the same emotion. Later, we hear some rock music and find that it doesn't have the same effect. What concepts are illustrated by our reaction to Latin music but not to rock music?

To receive feedback for these questions, go to Appendix A.

Operant Conditioning

Operant conditioning. A behaviorist form of learning that occurs when an observable behavior changes in frequency or duration as the result of a consequence.

Consequences. An event (stimulus) that occurs following a behavior that influences the probability of the behavior recurring.

In the previous section, we saw how classical conditioning can explain how people learn involuntary emotional and physiological responses to classroom activities and events in our lives. However, people don't simply respond to stimuli; instead, they often "operate" on their environments by initiating behaviors. This is the source of the term **operant conditioning,** which describes learning in terms of observable responses that change in frequency or duration as the result of **consequences,** events that occur following behaviors. B. F. Skinner (1953, 1954), the most influential figure in operant conditioning, argued that behaviors are controlled primarily by consequences. For example, being stopped by a highway patrol for speeding is a consequence, and it decreases the likelihood that you'll speed in the near future. A teacher's praise after a student's answer is also a consequence, and it increases the likelihood of the student trying to answer other questions. A myriad of consequences exist in classrooms, such as high test scores, attention from peers, and reprimands for inappropriate behavior. Each can influence students' subsequent behaviors.

Operant and classical conditioning are often confused. To help clarify important differences, we compare the two in Table 9.2. As you see in the table, learning occurs as a result of experience for both, but the type of behavior differs, and the behavior and stimulus occur in the opposite order for the two.

Table 9.2 A comparison of operant and classical conditioning

	Classical Conditioning	Operant Conditioning
Behavior	Involuntary (person does not have control of behavior) Emotional Physiological	Voluntary (person has control of behavior)
Order	Behavior follows stimulus.	Behavior precedes stimulus (consequence).
How learning occurs	Neutral stimuli become associated with unconditioned stimuli.	Consequences of behaviors influence subsequent behaviors.
Example	Learners associate classrooms (initially neutral) with the warmth of teachers, so classrooms elicit positive emotions.	Learners attempt to answer questions and are praised, so their attempts to answer increase.
Key researcher	Pavlov	Skinner

Now, let's see how different consequences involved in operant conditioning affect behavior. They're outlined in Figure 9.1 and discussed in the following sections.

Reinforcement

Consider the first question in this "Ed Psych and You" feature. Probably, you will be even more likely to try to make similar comments in the future. Your instructor's comment is a **reinforcer,** a consequence that increases the likelihood of a behavior recurring, and **reinforcement** is the process of applying reinforcers to increase behavior. It exists in two forms: positive and negative.

Ed Psych and You

During a class discussion, you make a comment, and your instructor responds, "Very insightful idea. Good thinking." How are you likely to behave in later discussions? On the other hand, if you tend to be a little sloppy, your significant other or roommate may nag you to pick up after yourself. What will you probably do to get them to stop?

Positive Reinforcement. Positive reinforcement is the process of increasing the frequency or duration of a behavior as the result of *presenting* a reinforcer. Your instructor *presented* you with the comment, "Very insightful idea. Good thinking." In classrooms, we typically think of positive reinforcers as something desired or valued, such as your instructor's praise, high test scores, "happy faces," tokens that can be cashed in for privileges, and stars on the bulletin board for young children.

However, any increase in behavior as a result of being presented with a consequence is positive reinforcement, and teachers sometimes unintentionally reinforce undesirable behavior. For instance, if a student is acting out, his teacher reprimands him, and his misbehavior increases, the reprimand is a positive reinforcer. His teacher intended to decrease the behavior, but inadvertently reinforced it instead; the student's behavior *increased* as a result of being *presented* with the reprimand.

Teachers also use positive reinforcement when they take advantage of the **Premack principle** (named after David Premack, who originally described it in 1965), which states that a more-desired activity can serve as a positive reinforcer for a less-desired activity. For example, suppose you say to yourself, "After I clean up the mess in my room, I'll watch a movie." The movie serves as a reinforcer for cleaning up your room.

You can also use the Premack principle in your work with students. If you're a geography teacher, for example, and you know your students like map work, you might say, "As soon as you've finished your summaries, you can start working on your maps." The map work serves as a positive reinforcer for completing the summaries.

Our students also—probably unintentionally—reinforce us when we teach. Their attentive looks, nods, and raised hands are positive reinforcers, and they increase the likelihood that we'll call on them. High student test scores and compliments from students or their parents are also positive reinforcers for all of us.

Negative Reinforcement. Now, think about the second question we asked in our "Ed Psych and You" feature at the beginning of this section. We likely pick up our stuff to make our significant other or roommate stop nagging us. We might even pick up our stuff before we're nagged to avoid it in the first place. This is an example

Reinforcer. A consequence that increases the likelihood of a behavior recurring.

Reinforcement. The process of applying reinforcers to increase behavior.

Positive reinforcement. The process of increasing the frequency or duration of a behavior as the result of *presenting* a reinforcer.

Premack principle. The principle stating that a more-desired activity can serve as a positive reinforcer for a less-desired activity.

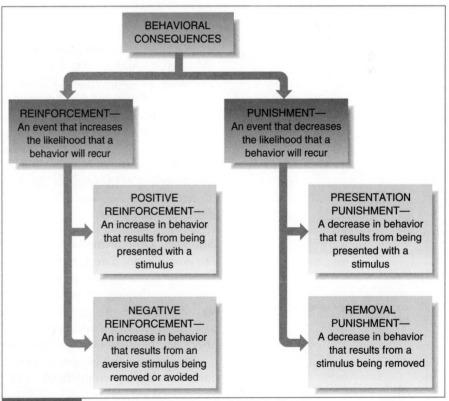

Figure 9.1 Consequences of behavior

Praise, high test scores, and other positive reinforcers can increase desired student behavior.

Negative reinforcement. The process of increasing behavior by removing or avoiding an aversive stimulus.

of **negative reinforcement,** the process of increasing behavior by removing or avoiding an aversive stimulus (Baldwin & Baldwin, 2001; Skinner, 1953). Being nagged is an aversive stimulus, so our *picking-up-our-stuff* behavior increases to eliminate or avoid the nagging. The nagging stopping is the negative reinforcer.

Negative reinforcement is common in the real world, and many examples exist. For instance:

- You get into your car, and the seatbelt buzzer goes off, so you buckle the belt. You have been negatively reinforced for buckling the belt. The noise stopping is the negative reinforcer.
- You're sitting through a terrible movie. The movie is so bad, in fact, that you can't stand it, so you get up and leave. You are being negatively reinforced for leaving the movie, and escaping the bad movie is the negative reinforcer.
- You are melting in the heat of an extraordinarily hot summer. You're out, and you rush home to get into air conditioning. You are being negatively reinforced for rushing home, and escaping the heat is the negative reinforcer.

Negative reinforcement is also common in classrooms. For example, you say to your students, "If you're all sitting quietly when the bell rings, we'll go to lunch. If not, we'll miss 5 minutes of our lunch period." In this case avoiding the aversive stimulus—missing some lunch time—acts as a negative reinforcer for the desired behavior—sitting quietly.

As with positive reinforcement, we sometimes negatively reinforce our students unintentionally.

Kathy Long is discussing the skeletal system with her science students.

"Why do you suppose the rib cage is shaped the way it is? . . . Jim?" she asks.

He sits silently for several seconds and finally says, "I don't know."

"Can someone help Jim out?" Kathy continues.

"It protects our heart and other internal organs," Athenia volunteers.

"Good, Athenia," Kathy smiles.

Later, Kathy calls on Jim again. He hesitates briefly and says, "I don't know."

In this example, Kathy inadvertently negatively reinforced Jim for failing to respond. When she called on Athenia after Jim said, "I don't know," she removed the potentially anxiety-provoking question. We have evidence that he was being negatively reinforced, because he said, "I don't know" more quickly after being called on the second time. If students struggle to answer our questions, being called on can be aversive, so they're likely to try and "get off the hook" as Jim did, or avoid being called on at all by looking down and not making eye contact with us.

This example has important implications for our teaching. We want to reinforce students *for* answering, as Kathy did with Athenia, instead of *for not* answering, as she did with Jim. Instead of turning the question to another student, prompting Jim to help him provide an acceptable answer would have been more effective, and she could then have positively reinforced the answer.

Shaping. The process of reinforcing successive approximations of a behavior.

Shaping. Operant conditioning can also be used to gradually develop desired behaviors. For example, you have a student who is so shy and reluctant to interact with his peers that he rarely speaks. Acquiring social skills is an important part of students' development, and you can use **shaping,** the process of reinforcing successive approximations of a behavior, as a tool. For instance, you might first reinforce the student for any interaction with others, such as a simple smile or sharing a pencil. Later, you reinforce him for greeting other students as they enter the classroom. Finally, you reinforce him only for more prolonged interactions.

Shaping can also be used to develop complex learning behaviors. When students are initially struggling with difficult ideas, you can reinforce their efforts and partially correct responses. For example,

"I start out praising every attempt," Maria Brugera comments to one of her colleagues. "Then, as they improve, I praise them only for better, more complete answers, until finally they have to give well thought-out explanations before I'll say anything."

Although Maria was ultimately seeking correct answers, she considered student effort a beginning step and a partially correct response an approximation of the desired behavior. Through shaping, she hoped to eventually get complete and thoughtful answers from her students.

Reinforcement Schedules. As you saw in the example involving shaping, Maria initially praised her students for every answer, but later praised them only for answers that were better and more complete. Maria's strategic use of praise illustrates an important principle of operant conditioning: *The timing and spacing of reinforcers have different effects on learning.* These effects are illustrated in **reinforcement schedules,** patterns in the frequency and predictability of reinforcers (Baldwin & Baldwin, 2001).

For example, Maria initially praised every answer, but later praised answers only some of the time. Her reinforcement schedule was initially **continuous**—every desired behavior was reinforced—but later she turned to an **intermittent schedule,** where some, but not all, of the desired behaviors are reinforced.

Two types of intermittent schedules exist, and they influence behavior differently. **Ratio schedules** depend on the number of individual behaviors, and **interval schedules** depend on time. Both can be either fixed or variable. In fixed schedules, the individual receives reinforcers predictably; in variable schedules the reinforcers are unpredictable. For instance, when playing slot machines, you insert a coin, pull the handle, and other coins periodically drop into the tray. Receiving coins (reinforcers) depends on the number of times you pull the handle—not on how long you play—and you can't predict when you'll receive coins, so it is a variable-ratio schedule.

Numerous examples of variable-ratio schedules exist in classrooms, such as teacher praise and comments on papers. The praise and comments depend on students' behaviors—not on time, and they usually cannot predict when they will receive either. Fixed-ratio schedules are uncommon in classrooms, except for some forms of drill-and-practice computer software. For instance, a student signs on to the program, receives a personalized greeting, and solves three problems. The program then replies, "Congratulations, Antonio, you have just correctly solved three problems." If the program then gives a similar response for every three problems answered correctly, it is using a fixed-ratio schedule.

Now, suppose you're in a class that meets Mondays, Wednesdays, and Fridays, you have a quiz each Friday, and your instructor returns the quiz each Monday. You study on Sunday, Tuesday, and particularly on Thursday evenings, but you aren't reinforced for studying until the following Monday, when you receive your score. Reinforcement for your studying occurs at a predictable interval—every Monday—so it is a *fixed-interval schedule.* On the other hand, if some of your instructors give "pop" quizzes, they are using a *variable-interval schedule,* because you can't predict when you will be reinforced.

Reinforcement schedules affect behavior differently, and each has advantages and disadvantages. For instance, a continuous schedule yields the fastest rates of initial learning, so it is effective when students are acquiring new skills such as solving equations in algebra (Lee, Sturmey, & Fields, 2007). However, when teachers eliminate reinforcers, the frequency of continually reinforced behaviors decreases more quickly than behaviors reinforced using intermittent schedules (Costa & Boakes, 2007).

Intermittent schedules create more enduring behaviors but also have disadvantages (Lee et al., 2007). With fixed schedules, behavior increases rapidly just before the reinforcer is given and then decreases rapidly and remains low until just before the next reinforcer is given. Giving Friday quizzes is an example; students often study carefully just before the quiz and then don't study again until just before the next quiz.

Reinforcement schedules. Patterns in the frequency and predictability of reinforcers that have differential effects on behavior.

Continuous reinforcement schedule. A schedule of reinforcement in which every desired behavior is reinforced.

Intermittent reinforcement schedule. A schedule of reinforcement in which some, but not all, of the desired behaviors are reinforced.

Ratio schedule of reinforcement. An intermittent reinforcement schedule where specific behaviors are reinforced either predictably (fixed) or unpredictably (variable).

Interval schedule of reinforcement. An intermittent reinforcement schedule in which behaviors are reinforced after a predictable (fixed) or unpredictable (variable) time interval.

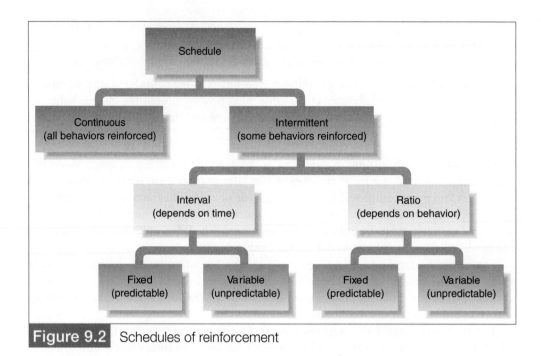

Figure 9.2 Schedules of reinforcement

The relationships among the different types of reinforcement schedules are illustrated in Figure 9.2, and additional classroom examples are outlined in Table 9.3.

Extinction. **Extinction** (in operant conditioning) occurs when a behavior ceases as a result of nonreinforcement. For example:

> Renita, a tenth-grader, enjoys school and likes to respond in her classes. She is attentive and eager to answer questions.
>
> When Mr. Frank, her world history teacher, asks a question, Renita raises her hand, but someone usually blurts out the answer before she can respond. This happens repeatedly.
>
> Now Renita rarely raises her hand and often catches herself daydreaming in class. For Renita, being called on reinforced both her attempts to respond and her attention. Because she wasn't called on, she wasn't reinforced, so her behaviors (raising her hand and paying attention) became extinct.

Table 9.3 Reinforcement schedules and examples

Schedule	Example
Continuous	A teacher "walks students through" the steps for solving simultaneous equations. Students are liberally praised at each step as they first learn the solution.
Fixed-ratio	The algebra teacher announces, "As soon as you've done two problems in a row correctly, you may start on your homework assignment so that you'll be able to finish by the end of class."
Variable-ratio	Students volunteer to answer questions by raising their hands and are called on at random.
Fixed-interval	Students are given a quiz every Friday.
Variable-interval	Students are given unannounced quizzes.

This example has important implications for our teaching. Student involvement and learning are closely related (Good & Brophy, 2008), and Renita's experience helps us understand why. When students are involved, their interest and attention increase, and more learning results. When they aren't, their attention wanes, and learning decreases.

Satiation. Behaviors decrease when they are punished (we examine punishment in the next section) or inadequately reinforced, but they can also decrease when they are reinforced too often. If teachers give too much praise, for instance, **satiation,** the process of using a reinforcer so frequently that it loses its ability to strengthen behaviors, can occur. Effective teachers use their praise and other reinforcers strategically to avoid this problem.

Satiation. The process of using a reinforcer so frequently that it loses its ability to strengthen behaviors.

Punishment

Positive and negative reinforcers are consequences that increase behavior. Other consequences, called **punishers,** *weaken* behaviors—decrease the likelihood of the behaviors' recurring (Mazur, 2006). The process of using punishers to decrease behavior is called **punishment,** and two kinds exist. As you saw in Figure 9.1, **presentation punishment** occurs when a learner's behavior decreases as a result of being presented with a punisher. For example, when a teacher puts her fingers to her lips, signaling "Shh," and students stop whispering, the students are presented with the teacher's signal, and their behavior—whispering—decreases.

Removal punishment occurs when a behavior decreases as a result of removing a stimulus, or the inability to get positive reinforcement. For example, if students are noisy and their teacher keeps them in the room for 5 minutes of their lunch period, he is using removal punishment. Under normal conditions, they go to lunch at the scheduled time, and he takes away some of that free time.

Punishers. Consequences that weaken behaviors, or decrease the likelihood of the behaviors' recurring.

Punishment. The process of using punishers to decrease behavior.

Presentation punishment. The process of decreasing a behavior that occurs when a stimulus (punisher) is presented.

Removal punishment. The process of decreasing a behavior that occurs when a stimulus is removed or when an individual cannot receive positive reinforcement.

Using Punishment Effectively. Some critics suggest that punishment should never be used (e.g., Kohn, 1996). And because punishment decreases undesirable behaviors but doesn't affect desirable ones, systems based on reinforcement are superior to those using punishment (Alberto & Troutman, 2009). However, because some students can become disruptive when all punishers are removed, punishment is sometimes necessary (Pfiffner, Rosen, & O'Leary, 1985; Rosen, O'Leary, Joyce, Conway, & Pfiffner, 1984). A more practical approach is to use punishment sparingly and judiciously, combined with appropriate reinforcement for good behavior (Maag, 2001).

Some effective punishers include:

- *Desists.* **Desists** are verbal or nonverbal communications that teachers use to stop a behavior (Kounin, 1970). A simple form of presentation punishment, such as a teacher putting her fingers to her lips, signaling "Shh," as you saw earlier, is a desist. When administered immediately, briefly, and unemotionally, they can be effective for reducing or eliminating inappropriate behaviors (Emmer & Evertson, 2009; Evertson & Emmer, 2009).

- *Timeout.* **Timeout** involves removing a student from the class and physically isolating him in an area away from classmates. Typically used with young children, the isolation eliminates the student's opportunities for positive reinforcement, so it is a form of removal punishment. It is effective for a variety of disruptive behaviors, and it's also commonly used by parents to eliminate undesirable behaviors in their young children (Alberto & Troutman, 2009).

- *Detention.* Similar to timeout, and typically used with older students, detention involves taking away some of the students' free time (typically a half hour or more) by keeping students in school either before or after school hours. While somewhat controversial (L. Johnson, 2004), it is widely used and generally viewed as effective (Gootman, 1998). It is most effective when students are required to sit quietly and do nothing, because the possibility of positive reinforcement is eliminated (imagine

Desists. Verbal or nonverbal communications that teachers use to stop a behavior.

Timeout. The process of isolating a student from classmates so he or she cannot get positive reinforcement.

Desists are appropriate uses of punishment in classrooms.

Response cost. The process of removing reinforcers already given.

sitting doing absolutely nothing for a half hour). When a parent "grounds" a teenager for inappropriate behavior, the parent is using a form of detention.

• *Response cost.* **Response cost** involves the removal of reinforcers already given (Zhou, Goff, & Iwata, 2000). For example, some teachers design systems where students receive tokens or other reinforcers for desirable behavior, which they can then use to purchase items from a school store, or redeem for free time and other privileges. Taking them away in reaction to inappropriate behavior is a form of response cost.

Ineffective Forms of Punishment. While judicious use of punishment can be effective, some forms are unacceptable and should never be used. They include:

• *Physical punishment.* Physical punishment, such as "swats" or even a slap with a ruler can result in individuals' later demonstrating similar behaviors as undesirable side effects (Bandura, 1986), becoming even more defiant after receiving the punishers (Nilsson & Archer, 1989), or learning more sophisticated ways to avoid getting caught. Students avoid teachers who frequently use punishment, and a number of states forbid physically punishing students (Zirpoli & Melloy, 2001).

• *Embarrassment and humiliation.* Embarrassment and humiliation can lead to some of the same negative side effects as physical punishment (Walker, Bauer, & Shea, 2004).

• *Class work.* Using class work as a form of punishment can teach students that it is aversive and may, through classical conditioning, cause negative emotional reactions to it (Baldwin & Baldwin, 2001). Learners may generalize their aversion to their assignments, other teachers, and the school as well.

As with using reinforcers, the use of punishers requires sound judgment. For example, if you use desists with your students, but your students are reinforced by the attention they receive, then the desists are ineffective, and you should try a different strategy, such as timeout. On the other hand, if being in the regular class is aversive, timeout—instead of being an effective punisher—may be a negative reinforcer. In either case, a change in strategy is needed.

So, we now see that behavior can be decreased in three ways: extinction, satiation, and punishment. Table 9.4 summarizes and compares them.

The Influence of Antecedents on Behavior

Antecedents. Stimuli that precede and induce behaviors.

To this point, we have discussed the influence of consequences—reinforcers and punishers—on behavior. But we can also influence behavior through **antecedents,** stimuli that precede and induce behaviors. The two most common types of antecedents are (1) environmental conditions and (2) prompts and cues. Let's look at them.

Environmental Conditions. Think about the questions in our "Ed Psych and You" feature here. Most likely, "turn on the light" is the answer. The darkness is an environmental antecedent that causes us to flip the light switch. The light coming on is a reinforcer for flipping the switch, so we continue to do so. On the other hand, a traffic light turning red is an antecedent that causes us to stop, because running the light increases the likelihood of being punished by getting a ticket or being hit by another car.

Some teachers dim the lights when students come in from recess. The dim light is an environmental antecedent, reminding students that they are inside and need to use inside voices and behaviors. We can use classroom environments as antecedents for desirable behaviors, which we can then reinforce.

Table 9.4 A comparison of extinction, satiation, and punishment

Concept	Description	Effect on Behavior	Example
Extinction	A behavior is not reinforced.	Behavior decreases	A student raises his hand, to answer questions, but his teacher doesn't call on him. Eventually he stops raising his hand.
Satiation	A behavior is over-reinforced.	Behavior decreases	A teacher effusively praises every answer students give. Eventually, they decrease their efforts to answer.
Presentation punishment	An individual is presented with a stimulus that decreases behavior.	Behavior decreases	A student is whispering, his teacher puts her finger to her lips signally "Shh." The student stops whispering.
Removal punishment	A stimulus is removed or the individual cannot get positive reinforcement.	Behavior decreases	A student is acting out in class and the teacher moves him to the back of the room. When the student is allowed to join the class, he no longer acts out.

Prompts and Cues. Prompts and cues are specific actions and questions you can use to elicit desired behaviors in students, particularly in learning activities. For example:

> Alicia Wendt wants her students to understand the concept *adverb*. She writes this sentence on the board:

> John quickly jerked his head when he heard his name called.

> She then asks, "What is the adverb in the sentence? . . . Calvin?"
>
> " . . . "
>
> "How did John jerk his head?"
>
> ". . . Quickly."
>
> "Okay, good. . . . So, what is the adverb in the sentence?"
>
> ". . . Quickly."
>
> "Yes, . . . well done, Calvin."

When Calvin didn't respond to Alicia's question, "What is the adverb in the sentence?" she prompted him by asking, "How did John jerk his head?" Calvin responded, "Quickly," which Alicia reinforced by saying, "Okay, good." She prompted him again when she asked, "So, what is the adverb in the sentence?" and after Calvin responded, she again reinforced him by saying, "Yes, well done, Calvin."

A variety of cues exists. For instance, when you move to the front of the class or walk among students as they do seat work, you are cuing them to turn their attention toward you or to remain on task. In each case, you can then reinforce the desired behaviors.

Applied Behavior Analysis

Applied behavior analysis (ABA) is the process of systematically implementing the principles of operant conditioning to change student behavior (Baldwin & Baldwin, 2001). (It is also called *behavior modification*, but this term has a negative connotation for some

Applied behavior analysis (ABA). The process of systematically implementing the principles of operant conditioning to change student behavior.

Teacher questions can serve as antecedents to elicit desired responses from students.

people, so experts prefer the term we use here.) ABA has been used successfully to help people increase their physical fitness, overcome fears and panic attacks, learn social skills, and stop smoking. It is widely used in working with students who have exceptionalities (J. B. Ryan, Katsiyannis, & Peterson, 2007).

Steps in ABA

The application of operant conditioning principles in ABA typically involves the following steps:

1. Identify target behaviors.
2. Establish a baseline for the target behaviors.
3. Choose reinforcers and punishers (if necessary).
4. Measure changes in the target behaviors.
5. Gradually reduce the frequency of reinforcers as behavior improves.

To see how to implement these steps, let's look in on Mike Sheppard, a middle-school math teacher, as he works with his students.

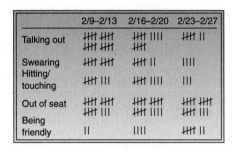

> Mike has 28 students in his second-period class, including, as do most teachers, some with exceptionalities. Todd in particular has difficulty controlling his behavior, and other teachers describe him as verbally abusive, aggressive, and lacking in self-discipline. He is extremely active, and sitting through a class period is hard for him.
>
> As the bell rings, most students are studying the screen at the front of the room as they begin a warm-up problem that Mike displays as part of his beginning-of-class routine. He quickly takes roll and then walks to Todd's desk.
>
> "Let's take a look at your chart," he says. "You've improved a lot, haven't you?"
>
> "Yeah, look," Todd responds, proudly displaying the chart you see here.
>
> "That's terrific," Mike whispers as he leans over the boy's desk. "You're doing much better. We need some more work on out of seat, don't we? I don't like getting after you about it, and I know you don't like it either. . . . Stop by at the end of class. I have an idea that I think will help. . . . Okay. Get to work on the problem." Mike taps Todd on the shoulder and then returns to the front of the room.
>
> Mike then discusses the warm-up exercise with the class, conducts the lesson that focuses on word problems, and gives the students five problems for homework. "Go ahead and get started now," he directs with 15 minutes left in the period.
>
> The bell rings, and the students begin filing out of the room. Todd stops by Mike's desk, and Mike leads him to a small area in the back of the room where a partition has been set up. The area is partially enclosed but facing the class.
>
> "Here's what we'll do," Mike directs. "When you have the urge to get out of your seat, quietly get up and move back here for a few minutes. Stay as long as you want, but be sure you pay attention to what we're doing. When you think you're ready to move back to your seat, go ahead. All I'm asking is that you move back and forth quietly and not bother the class. . . . What do you think?"
>
> Todd nods, and Mike comments, "You're doing so well on everything else; this will help, I think. You're a good student. You hang in there. . . . Now, here's a pass into Mrs. Miller's class."

Now, let's see how Mike implemented the steps in ABA.

Identify Target Behaviors. Identifying the specific behaviors you want to change is the first step in ABA. As you saw in the chart, Mike identified five target behaviors: talking out, swearing, hitting/touching other students, being out-of-seat, and being friendly. Some experts might argue that Mike included too many target behaviors and might further suggest that "being friendly" isn't specific enough. As with most teaching–learning applications, these decisions are a matter of professional judgment.

Establish a Baseline. A baseline is established when the target behaviors are initially measured to provide a reference point for later comparison. For instance, during the baseline period (the week of 2/9 to 2/13), Todd talked out in class 20 times, swore 10 times, hit or touched another student 8 times, was out of his seat 18 times, and was friendly to other students twice. The teacher or an objective third party typically makes observations to determine the baseline. Mike created the behavior tally for the first week.

Choose Reinforcers and Punishers. Before attempting to change behavior, you'll need to identify the reinforcers and punishers that are likely to work for an individual student. Ideally, an ABA system is based on reinforcers instead of punishers, and this is what Mike used with Todd. If punishers are necessary, they should also be established in advance.

Mike used personal attention and praise as his primary reinforcers, and they were effective, as indicated by the positive changes in Todd's behavior. And Todd could see concrete evidence that his behavior was improving, which was, in itself, reinforcing. If the undesirable behaviors had not decreased, Mike would need to modify his system by trying some additional reinforcers and perhaps some punishers as well.

Measure Changes in Behavior. After establishing a baseline and identifying reinforcers and punishers, you then measure the target behaviors for specified periods to see if changes occur. For example, Todd talked out 20 times the first week, 14 times the second, and only 7 times the third. Except for "out of seat," improvement occurred for each of the other behaviors during the 3-week period.

Because Mike's first intervention didn't change Todd's out-of-seat behavior, he designed an alternative. To help Todd satisfy his need to move around, yet not disturb the class, Mike prepared a place at the back of the room where Todd could go when the urge to get out of his seat became overwhelming. He was free to move back and forth at his own discretion, which was also reinforcing for him.

Reduce Frequency of Reinforcers. As Todd's behavior improved, Mike gradually reduced the frequency of reinforcers. Initially, you might use a continuous, or nearly continuous, schedule and then move to an intermittent one. Reducing the frequency of reinforcers helps maintain the desired behaviors and increases the likelihood of the desired behavior generalizing to other classrooms and everyday activities.

Functional Analysis

In the preceding sections we focused on measuring changes in behavior based on the use of reinforcers and punishers when necessary. However, some experts recommend expanding the focus to identify antecedents that trigger inappropriate behaviors (Miltenberger, 2008). For example, Mike found that Todd's abusive behavior most commonly occurred during class discussions, and he believed that the attention Todd received for the outbursts was reinforcing. Similarly, Todd was out of his desk most often during seat work, probably because it allowed him to avoid the tasks with which he struggled. Class discussions were antecedents for abusive behavior, and seat work was an antecedent for leaving his seat. The strategy used to identify antecedents and consequences that influence behavior is called **functional analysis** (Miltenberger, 2008). These relationships in Todd's case are outlined in Figure 9.3.

Functional analyses are useful for creating effective interventions, and attempts to reduce undesirable behaviors are usually coupled with reinforcing behaviors that are more appropriate (Kahng & Iwata, 1999; Lalli & Kates, 1998). For example, Mike's positively

Functional analysis. The strategy used to identify antecedents and consequences that influence behavior.

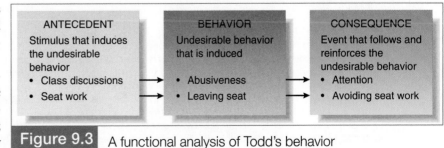

Figure 9.3 A functional analysis of Todd's behavior

reinforcing Todd for "being friendly" was a form of attention, so it served the same purpose that being abusive had previously served. This process of using interventions that replace problem behaviors with appropriate behaviors that serve the same purpose for the student is called **positive behavior support.**

Positive behavior support.
Interventions that replace problem behaviors with appropriate behaviors that serve the same purpose for the student.

Like all interventions, ABA won't work magic, and it is labor intensive (Kaff, Zabel, & Milham, 2007). For example, you can't assume that a student will accurately measure the target behaviors, so you have to monitor the behaviors yourself. This makes managing an already busy classroom even more complex.

Also, personal attention and praise were effective reinforcers for Todd, but if they hadn't been, Mike would have needed others. Finding a reinforcer that is simple to administer yet consistent with school procedures can be challenging. However, it can provide you with an additional tool if conventional classroom management methods, such as a basic system of rules and procedures, aren't working.

Ed psych and teaching

Applying Operant Conditioning with Your Students

Although cognitive learning theory is the framework for most of our instruction, behaviorism can also be used as a tool to promote the development of basic skills, and it is widely used in classroom management (Freiberg & Lamb, 2009). The following guidelines can help you use this tool effectively in your work with your students.

1. Use antecedents to elicit desired behaviors, which can then be reinforced.
2. Reinforce students for genuine accomplishments.
3. Employ drill-and-practice technologies to help students develop basic skills.
4. Use reinforcers and punishers appropriately to help maintain an orderly classroom.

To see these guidelines in practice, let's look in on Sonia Kormell, a fifth-grade teacher, who is working with her students on rounding numbers.

Sonia introduces the topic of rounding numbers by having her students count to 100 by 10s, and then says, "Okay, keeping 10s in mind, let's think about the numbers 34 and 36. To which 10 are they the closest? . . . Juan?"

". . . 34 is closest to 30, and 36 is closest to 40," Juan responds after thinking for a couple seconds.

"Good," Sonia nods. "That's what we mean by *rounding*. Rounding helps us when we estimate answers, and we'll be using it throughout the school year." She does two more examples similar to the first one and then says, "Now, think about 128. . . . Let's round this off to the nearest 10," as she walks down the aisle, touches Henry on the shoulder, and shakes her head, signaling "No," in response to his tapping Gretchen's desk with his foot.

Henry stops.

"A hundred," Andrea volunteers.

"Count from 100 to 200 by 10s," Sonia directs.

Andrea counts 100, 110, and so on until she reaches 200.

"Good. So which 10 is 128 closest to?

". . . One hundred . . . thirty," Andrea hesitantly responds.

"Very good," Sonia nods. "Yes, 128 is closer to 130 than it is to 120. . . . Good thinking."

Sonia then continues the process by having the students count to 1,000 by hundreds, and to 10,000 by thousands, and

she gives them additional examples, such as 462, which they round to the nearest hundred, and 6,457 which they round to the nearest thousand.

"Now, let's be good thinkers," she continues. "Let's round 6,457 to the nearest 10. Everyone write your answer on your chalkboard and hold it up when you're finished. (Sonia's students have small individual chalkboards at their desks which they use to write and display answers to math problems.)

Seeing 6,460 on Michael's chalkboard, Sonia says, "Michael, explain to everyone how you arrived at your answer."

Michael explains that because they're thinking about 10s, 6,457 is closer to 6,460 than it is to 6,450.

"That's excellent thinking, Michael," Sonia smiles. "You showed a very good understanding of the problem."

Sonia continues the process with several more examples, and she then assigns 10 problems for homework, "Go ahead and get started. You should be able to get most of the problems finished before we have our break."

As she checks on the students while they work, she sees that Andrea, David, Gus, and Suzanne are still struggling with the process. To provide them with additional practice, she sends them to four of the computers at the back of her room, has them log on to a "Rounding Numbers" program, and has them practice until the end of their allocated time for math.

As the students approach the end of their math time, Sonia kneels down by Jon's desk and quietly says, "Jon, I'm very proud of you today. You were paying attention, and I didn't have to remind you even once all period. How many checks did you give yourself?"

"Four," Jon responds.

"Very good, you earned them. . . . Keep it up," Sonia says, smiling warmly. Jon has ADHD and has trouble concentrating and controlling his behavior. Sonia has him keep a "behavior" chart, and for each 10 minutes that he is attentive, he gives himself a check. Sonia had to give him a great deal of guidance as they began the process, but he's now much improved.

Now, let's look at Sonia's efforts to apply the guidelines. She applied the first in her interaction with Andrea. When Andrea incorrectly responded, "100," to the problem of rounding 128 to the nearest 10, Sonia had her count from 100 to 200 by 10s and asked, "Which 10 is 128 closest to?" Her directive and question were antecedents (cues) that helped Andrea correctly answer, "One hundred thirty," which Sonia positively reinforced with her response, "Very good. . . . Good thinking."

Sonia's response to Andrea, as well as her comment, "That's excellent thinking, Michael. You showed a very good understanding of the problem," applied the second guideline. Praise for genuine accomplishment can increase both learning and motivation, so reinforcement, in the form of praise used appropriately, can be a valuable instructional tool (Brophy, 2010; Schunk et al., 2008).

Sonia applied the third guideline when she used technology to provide extra practice for students who were still struggling with rounding numbers. (We offer some examples in "Technology, Learning, and Development" in the next section.) And, she applied the fourth when she quickly stopped Henry from tapping on Gretchen's desk, and when she praised Jon for his good behavior. Shaking her head at Henry was an effective application of a punisher—his behavior stopped—and her praise reinforced Jon.

Behaviorism can be used to help students acquire basic skills, and employed judiciously, it can promote an orderly classroom environment and even increase motivation. In the next section we see how technology incorporates operant conditioning to help students develop basic skills.

Technology, Learning, and Development: Capitalizing on Technology to Teach Basic Skills

Behaviorism, and particularly operant conditioning, has historically had a strong influence on the use of technology in classrooms. At the turn of the 21st century, experts estimated that 85% of existing educational software emphasized skill learning based on behaviorist principles (Jonassen, Howland, Moore, & Marra, 2003), and the figure was nearly as high 10 years later (Tamim, Bernard, Borokhovski, Abrami, & Schmid, 2011).

Technology has since become more sophisticated, but drill-and-practice software based on operant conditioning continues to be an effective tool to develop students' basic skills. You saw how Sonia used it to provide her students with practice in rounding numbers in our "Ed Psych and Teaching" feature titled "Applying Operant Conditioning with Your Students." Let's examine this application a bit further with the following example (adapted from Math.com, 2010).

You open the program, and the following appears:

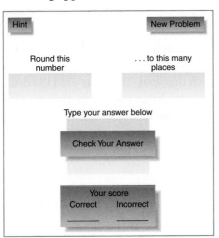

When you click on "New Problem," a problem, such as you see here, is displayed.

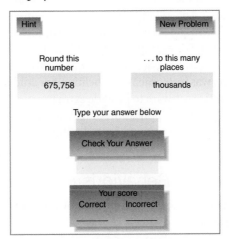

You type in 675,000, as you see here.

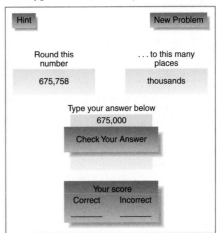

When you click on "Check Your Answer," "No, try again," pops up in a separate box. A bit uncertain about why your answer is incorrect, you click on "Hint" which tells you, "Look to the digit to the right of the rounding place. Is it 5 or greater?" Using the hint, you type in 676,000, and "Correct!" pops up. Had you answered incorrectly a second time, "Sorry, here is the answer," would have been displayed, and you would have been given the answer.

Let's see how this is an application of behaviorism. Your responses (behavior) changed from giving the incorrect answer, 675,000, to the correct answer, 676,000, as a result of: (1) being told your first answer was incorrect ("No, try again"); (2) the information you received in the hint; and (3) being told that your second answer was correct ("Correct!"). "No, try again," is a punisher, and "Correct!" is a reinforcer. The likelihood of your repeating the first answer decreases, whereas the likelihood of repeating the second answer increases.

With your students, you can use software applications such as these in a variety of areas; the most common are drill-and-practice exercises in math and science.

Many programs provide more detailed feedback than simple hints, such as "Look to the digit to the right of the rounding place. Is it 5 or greater?" and they can also be designed to increase learner interest and motivation. Some software asks students to enter information about themselves, such as their names, friends, parents, and their teacher into the program, and it then personalizes problems. For instance, consider this problem designed for elementary students in math:

> There are four objects, and each one is cut in half. In all, how many pieces will there then be?

Now, compare it to the one below, personalized for a student named Josh, whose teacher is Mrs. Gonzalez.

> Mrs. Gonzalez surprised Josh with a treat for his good behavior by giving him four small candy bars. He wanted to share them with his friend, Zach, so he cut each one in half. How many pieces does Josh now have?

The program took the information Josh had previously entered and used it in the problem. Personalizing problems in this way can increase both learning and motivation (Kartal, 2010).

Drill-and-practice software based on behaviorist principles is controversial, with critics describing it as little more than "electronic flashcards" (Inan, Lowther, Ross, & Strahl, 2010). However, when used strategically, it can be a valuable tool to promote learning. As you saw in the examples with rounding, it provides students with individualized practice and increases time on task, because the student must answer every question. Learners using the software also report that they feel more comfortable because they can set their own pace (if the software allows), and their answers and feedback received are private (Inan et al., 2010). And a computer, unlike a human, can be programmed to have unlimited patience.

Drill-and-practice software can supplement your teaching, but it isn't designed to replace you. For example, instead of having her students simply memorize a set of steps for rounding numbers, Sonia's goal was for rounding to make sense to them, and she, not the software, was instrumental in helping her students reach that goal. Then, she used the drill-and-practice software to provide extra practice for students who continued to struggle. This is an appropriate application of technology grounded in behaviorism, and used this way, it can contribute to your students' learning.

Evaluating Behaviorism

Like any theory, behaviorism has both proponents and critics. Criticisms focus on the following areas:

- The ineffectiveness of behaviorism as a guide for instruction
- The inability of behaviorism to explain higher-order functions
- The impact of reinforcers on intrinsic motivation
- Philosophical positions on learning and teaching

Let's look at these criticisms in more detail.

First, instruction based on behaviorism requires specific items of information that allow learners to display observable behaviors, such as the examples with rounding that you saw earlier. However, most of what we learn doesn't exist as specific, decontextualized items of information. For example, we learn to write by practicing writing, not by responding to isolated grammar or punctuation exercises such as we often find in workbooks.

Also, behaviorism, with its focus on observable behaviors, fails to address what's going on in learners' heads. For example, learners often hold misconceptions and sometimes "off-the-wall" ideas for which they haven't been reinforced. These ideas are better explained by cognitive theories, theories that focus on learners' thought processes.

Second, behaviorism cannot adequately explain higher-order functions, such as language development. For instance, Chomsky and Miller (1958) demonstrated that even people with small vocabularies would have to learn sentences at a rate faster than one per second throughout their lifetimes if their learning was based on specific behaviors and reinforcers.

Third, research suggests that offering reinforcers for engaging in intrinsically motivating activities, such as solving puzzles or playing video games, can actually decrease interest in those activities (R. Ryan & Deci, 1996), and finally, some critics hold the philosophical position that schools should attempt to promote learning for its own sake rather than learning to gain rewards (Anderman & Maehr, 1994). Other critics argue that behaviorism is essentially a means of controlling people, instead of a way to help students learn to control their own behavior (Kohn, 1993).

Proponents counter that behaviorism works; reinforcers and punishers can and do influence the way we behave. For example, research indicates that sincere compliments can increase both student motivation and the way students feel about themselves (Brophy, 2010), and teachers' experiences corroborate these findings. Further, supporters of behaviorism ask if we would continue working if we stopped receiving paychecks, and do we lose interest in our work merely because we get paid for it (Gentile, 1996)?

Also, research indicates that reinforcing appropriate classroom behaviors, such as paying attention and treating classmates well, decreases misbehavior. And behaviorist classroom management techniques are often effective when others are not (A. Smith & Bondy, 2007). And finally, as you saw in Sonia's use of technology, drill-and-practice software based on behaviorism can provide students with valuable practice in basic skills.

No learning theory is complete, and this is particularly true of behaviorism. However, if judiciously applied by knowledgeable professionals, it can be a useful tool for creating environments that optimize opportunity to learn for all students.

Classroom connections

Using Operant Conditioning Effectively in Classrooms
Reinforcers and Punishers

1. Reinforcers are consequences that increase behavior, and punishers are consequences that decrease behavior. Use positive reinforcement if possible, and removal punishment if necessary.

   ■ **Elementary:** After assigning seatwork, a first-grade teacher gives tickets to students who are working quietly. Students exchange the tickets for opportunities to play games and work at learning centers.

   ■ **Middle School:** A seventh-grade teacher gives students "behavior points" at the beginning of the week. If students break a rule, they lose a point. At the end of the week, the students may use their remaining points to purchase special privileges such as talking with friends or listening to music with headphones.

   ■ **High School:** A math teacher increases the effectiveness of grades as reinforcers by awarding bonus points for quiz scores that are higher than students' personal averages.

Reinforcement Schedules

2. Reinforcement schedules influence both the acquisition of responses and their extinction. Continuous schedules increase behavior most rapidly, but intermittent schedules result in the most enduring behavior. Select a schedule that is most effective for meeting your goals.

   ■ **Elementary:** At the beginning of the school year, a first-grade teacher plans activities that all students can accomplish successfully. He praises liberally and rewards frequently. As students' capabilities increase, he requires more effort.

   ■ **Middle School:** A sixth-grade teacher only compliments students when they demonstrate thorough understanding. She also praises students when they demonstrate extra effort.

   ■ **High School:** A geometry teacher gives frequent announced quizzes to prevent the decline in effort that can occur after reinforcement with a fixed-interval schedule.

Shaping

3. Shaping is the process of reinforcing successive approximations of a desired behavior. Capitalize on the process to develop complex skills.

   ■ **Elementary:** A second-grade teacher openly praises a student whose behavior is improving. As improvement continues, longer periods of acceptable behavior are required before the student is praised.

   ■ **Middle School:** As a language arts teacher scores students' paragraphs, she is initially generous with positive comments, but as the students' work improves, she is more critical.

   ■ **High School:** An Algebra II teacher liberally praises students as they make the initial steps in solving equations. As their skills improve, he reduces the amount of reinforcement.

Antecedents

4. Antecedents are signals that induce desired behaviors, which can then be reinforced. Provide cues to elicit appropriate behaviors.

   ■ **Elementary:** Before students line up for lunch, a first-grade teacher reminds them to stand quietly while waiting to be dismissed. When they do so, she compliments them on their good behavior.

   ■ **Middle School:** After assigning seat work, a seventh-grade English teacher circulates around the room, reminding students to stay on task.

   ■ **High School:** When a chemistry teacher's students respond incorrectly, or fail to respond, he prompts them with additional questions that help them respond acceptably.

---

check your understanding

2.1 Judy is off task in your class, and you admonish her. In about 10 minutes, she's off task again, and again you admonish her. About 5 minutes later, she's off task a third time. Use operant conditioning to explain Judy's behavior.

2.2 "This test was too long," Rick's students complain as he finishes a discussion of a test he just handed back. Rick reduces the length of his next test, but halfway through a discussion of it, his students again grumble about the length. Rick reduces the length of his third test even more, and as he is turning the test back, his students begin, "What's going on, Mr. Kane? Is writing long tests the only thing you do?" Use operant conditioning to explain Rick's behavior—the lengths of tests he gives, and also use operant conditioning to explain the students' complaining.

2.3 To encourage on-task behaviors, Mrs. Emerick uses a beeper randomly set to beep every few minutes. If students are on task when the beeper goes off, the class earns points toward a classroom party. What reinforcement schedule is Mrs. Emerick using? Explain.

2.4 As part of her routine, Anita Mendez has a warm-up exercise displayed on the overhead each day when students enter her room. They immediately begin working on the exercise as she takes roll. She frequently compliments them on their conscientiousness and good behavior as they work. Identify the antecedent, the behavior, and the reinforcers in this example.

To receive feedback for these questions, go to Appendix A.

Social Cognitive Theory

"What are you doing?" Jason asks Kelly as he comes around the corner and catches her swinging her arms back and forth.

"I'm trying to swing at a ball like the pros do, but I haven't been able to quite do it," Kelly responds. "I was watching a game on TV last night, and the way those guys swing looks so easy, but they hit it so hard. I think I can do that if I work at it."

Three-year-old Jimmy crawls up on his dad's lap with a book. "I read too, Dad," he says as his father puts down his own book to help Jimmy up.

"I really like the way Juanita has quickly put away her materials and is ready to listen," Karen Engle, a second-grade teacher, comments as the students are making the transition from one activity to another.

The other students quickly put away their materials and turn their attention to Karen.

These examples are similar in two ways. First, each involved learning by observing the behavior of others; Kelly tried to imitate the swing of professional baseball players she observed on TV, and Jimmy saw his dad reading and wanted to imitate him. The second graders in Karen's class observed the consequence of Juanita's putting her materials away—being reinforced by Karen's praise—so they did the same.

Second, behaviorism can't explain them. It focuses on changes in behavior that have direct causes outside the learner. For instance, in our chapter-opening case study, taking algebra quizzes directly caused Tim's hand to shake. And in these vignettes, Karen's comment directly reinforced Juanita. But nothing directly happened to Kelly, Jimmy, or the other second graders in Karen's class; observing others caused them to change their behavior.

Social cognitive theory, a theory of learning that focuses on changes in behavior that result from observing others, emerged from the work of Albert Bandura (1925–) (Bandura, 1986, 1997, 2001). Because behaviorism and social cognitive theory both examine changes in behavior, let's compare the two.

> **Social cognitive theory.** A theory of learning that focuses on changes in behavior that result from observing others.

Comparing Behaviorism and Social Cognitive Theory

As you begin this section, you might be asking yourself, "If behaviorists focus on observable behavior, and the term *cognitive* implies memory and thinking, why is a cognitive learning theory included in the same chapter with behaviorism?"

Here's why: Social cognitive theory has its historical roots in behaviorism, but, as the name implies, it has evolved over the years into a more cognitive perspective (Kim & Baylor, 2006). Even today, many authors continue to include aspects of social cognitive theory in books focusing on behavioral principles (e.g., Baldwin & Baldwin, 2001). In addition, behaviorism and social cognitive theory are similar in three ways:

- They focus on experience as an important cause of learning (and an important principle of cognitive theory is that learning and development depend on learners' experience).
- They include the concepts of reinforcement and punishment in their explanations of learning.
- They target feedback as an important aspect of the learning process.

Three important differences exist between the two, however. First, they define learning differently, and second, social cognitive theory emphasizes the role of cognitive processes—beliefs, perceptions, and expectations—in learning. Third, social cognitive theory suggests that the environment, personal factors, and behavior are interdependent, a concept called *reciprocal causation.* Let's look at these differences.

Definition of Learning

Behaviorists define learning as a change in observable behavior, whereas social cognitive theorists view **learning** as a change in mental processes that creates the capacity to demonstrate different behaviors (Hill, 2002). So, learning may or may not result in immediate behavioral change. The role of mental activity (cognition/thinking) is illustrated in our examples. Kelly, for instance, didn't try to imitate the baseball swing until the next day, so her observations had to be stored in her memory or she wouldn't have been able to reproduce the behaviors. Also, nothing directly happened to Kelly, Jimmy, or Karen's second graders—other than observing Juanita. They were reacting to mental processes instead of reinforcers and punishers that directly influenced them.

> **Learning (cognitive).** A change in mental processes that creates the capacity to demonstrate different behaviors.

The Role of Expectations

Instead of viewing reinforcers and punishers as directly causing behavior, as behaviorists do, social cognitive theorists believe that reinforcers and punishers create *expectations*, cognitive processes that then influence behavior. For instance, you study for an exam for several days, but you aren't reinforced until you receive your score. You sustain your efforts because you *expect* to be reinforced for studying. And, Karen's students expected to be praised for following Juanita's example. Behaviorists don't consider the role of expectations in learning, but they are central to social cognitive theory.

The fact that people respond to their expectations means they are aware of which behaviors will be reinforced or punished. This is important because, according to social cognitive theory, reinforcement changes behavior only when learners know what behaviors are being reinforced (Bandura, 1986). Tim, for instance, expected his changed study habits to improve his math scores, so he maintained those habits. If he had expected some other strategy to be effective, he would have used it. He wasn't merely responding to reinforcers; he was actively assessing the effectiveness of his strategy.

The importance of student cognition has two implications for you as a teacher. First, you should clearly specify the behaviors you will reinforce, so students can adapt their behavior accordingly, and second, you should provide students with specific feedback so they know what behaviors have been reinforced. If a student receives full credit for an essay item on a test, for instance, but doesn't know why she received it, she may not know how to respond correctly the next time.

Reciprocal Causation

Reciprocal causation. The interdependence of the environment, behavior, and personal factors in learning.

Behaviorism suggests a one-way relationship between the environment and behavior; the environment influences behavior, but the opposite doesn't occur. Social cognitive theory's explanation is more complex, suggesting that behavior, the environment, and personal factors, such as expectations, are interdependent, meaning each influences the other two. The term **reciprocal causation** describes this interdependence.

For instance, Tim's low score on his algebra quiz (an environmental factor) influenced both his expectations (a personal factor) about future success on algebra quizzes and his behavior (he changed his study habits). His behavior influenced the environment (he went to Susan's home to study) and his later expectations (he became more confident about his capability in algebra). And the environment (his initial low score) influenced both his expectations and his behavior. Figure 9.4 outlines the process of reciprocal causation, illustrated with Tim's example.

We turn now to core concepts in social cognitive theory.

Modeling. A general term that refers to behavioral, cognitive, and affective changes deriving from observing the actions of others.

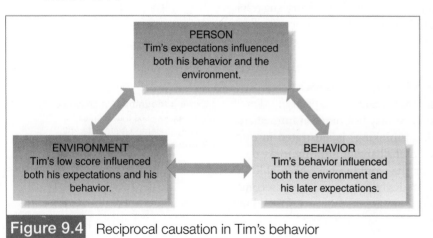

Figure 9.4 Reciprocal causation in Tim's behavior

Modeling

Modeling is a general term that refers to behavioral, cognitive, and affective changes deriving from observing the actions of others (Schunk, 2008). It is the central concept of social cognitive theory. Tim, for example, observed that Susan was successful in her approach to studying for exams. As a result, he imitated her behavior; direct imitation is one form of modeling, and it resulted in a behavioral change in Tim.

Modeling plays an important role in our everyday lives. Children learn acceptable ways of behaving by observing their parents and other adults. Teenagers' hair and dress are influenced by characters on television and in movies, and even as adults, we pick up cues from others in deciding how to dress and act.

Modeling is also important in schools. Teachers demonstrate a variety of skills, such as solutions to math problems, effective writing techniques, and critical thinking (Braaksma et al., 2004). You will also use modeling to teach courtesy and respect for others, tolerance for dissenting opinions, motivation to learn, and other attitudes and values. Coaches demonstrate techniques for correctly hitting a serve in volleyball, making a corner kick in soccer, and other skills, and through modeling, also teach important ideas such as teamwork, a sense of fair play, humility in victory, and graciousness in defeat. As teacher educators, we are urged to be models for our students (Lunenberg, Korthagen, & Swennen, 2007).

When teachers or coaches model intellectual or physical skills, they are *direct models*. Videotaped examples, as well as characters in movies, television, books, and plays are *symbolic models*, and combining different portions of observed acts represents *synthesized modeling* (Bandura, 1986). Table 9.5 outlines these different forms of modeling.

Teacher modeling can help students develop a variety of abilities.

Cognitive Modeling

Cognitive modeling, the process of performing a skill combined with verbalizing the thinking behind the actions, can also be a powerful teaching tool (Schunk, 2008). For example:

> "Wait," Jeanna Edwards says as she sees Nicole struggling with the microscope. "Let me show you. . . . Watch closely as I adjust it. The first thing I think about is getting the slide in place. Otherwise, I might not be able to find what I'm looking for. Then, I want to be sure I don't crack the slide while I lower the lens, so I watch from the side. Finally, I slowly raise the lens until I have the object in focus. You were trying to focus as you lowered it. It's easier and safer if you try to focus as you raise it. Go ahead and try it."

Cognitive modeling. The process of performing a demonstration combined with verbalizing the thinking behind the actions.

Table 9.5 Different forms of modeling

Type of Modeling	Description	Examples
Direct modeling	An individual attempts to imitate the behavior or thinking of a live model.	Tim imitated Susan's study habits. A first grader forms letters in the same way that the teacher forms them.
Symbolic modeling	People imitate behaviors and thinking displayed by characters in books, plays, movies, television, or the Internet.	People adopt fashion patterns displayed by influential people, such as movie stars or the First Lady of the United States. Teenagers adopt slang and slogans displayed by characters in a popular movie or television show oriented toward teens.
Synthesized modeling	People combine behaviors observed in different acts.	A child uses a chair to get up and open a cupboard door after seeing her brother use a chair to get a book from a shelf and seeing her mother open the cupboard door.

As Jeanna demonstrated how to use the microscope, she also described her thoughts: "The first thing I think about is getting the slide into place. Otherwise. . . ." When you put your thinking into words, and when you encourage your students to verbalize their understanding, you provide them with concrete examples of how to think about and solve problems (Braaksma et al., 2004).

Vicarious learning. The process of observing the consequences of others' actions and adjusting our own behavior accordingly.

Vicarious Learning

Think about your behavior in "Ed Psych and You" here. Nothing directly happened to you; you simply observed the consequence of the other driver's actions (he got pulled over), and you adjusted your behavior accordingly, a process called **vicarious learning** (Gholson & Craig, 2006). When you saw the sports car pulled over and you slowed down, you were *vicariously punished*, and when a student is publicly reprimanded for leaving his seat without permission, other students in the class are also vicariously punished.

On the other hand, Tim saw how well Susan did on quizzes, so he was *vicariously reinforced* by her success. And, when Karen Engle said, "I really like the way Juanita has quickly put away her materials and is ready to listen," Juanita's classmates were also vicariously reinforced.

The influence of expectations helps us understand vicarious learning. Tim expected to be reinforced for imitating Susan's behavior, and the other students in Karen's class expected to be reinforced for putting their materials away. You expected to be punished if you continued speeding, so you slowed down.

Nonoccurrence of Expected Consequences

Expectations are also important because they influence behavior when they *are not* met. For example, your instructor gives you a homework assignment, you work hard on it, but he or she doesn't collect it. The nonoccurrence of the expected reinforcer (credit for the assignment) can act as a punisher; you are less likely to work as hard on the next assignment.

Just as the nonoccurrence of an expected reinforcer can act as a punisher, the non-occurrence of an expected punisher can act as a reinforcer (Bandura, 1986). For example, students expect to be reprimanded (punished) for breaking rules, so if they break rules and aren't reprimanded, they are more likely to break rules in the future. The nonoccurrence of the expected punisher (the reprimand) acts as a reinforcer for the misbehavior.

The nonoccurrence of expected consequences is common in our everyday world. For example, if you send an e-mail to an acquaintance, you expect a reply, and receiving the reply is reinforcing. If the person doesn't reply, you're likely to stop sending e-mails to her. Sports fans buy season tickets to see their local team play, but if the team consistently loses, they're less likely to buy tickets in the future. Seeing the team win is reinforcing, and its nonoccurrence decreases fans' season-ticket-buying behavior.

Now, because modeling is central to social cognitive theory, we examine it in more detail in the following sections as we discuss:

- The outcomes of modeling
- The processes involved in learning from models
- The effectiveness of models

check your
understanding

3.1 Teachers who do cooperative learning activities sometimes give all the students in the group the same grade. Research indicates that this practice is ineffective (Slavin, 1995). Using the information in this section, explain why the practice is ineffective.

3.2 Mike was taking chemistry from an instructor who only lectured and then assigned problems for practice. Mike found he often "drifted off" during class. Because he felt he wasn't learning, he managed (with the help of his parents) to get switched to Mr. Adams's class. "If he sees you aren't paying attention, he calls on you," Mike comments. "So, I don't sleep in his class, and I'm getting to where I really understand the stuff now." Explain how reciprocal causation is illustrated in this example.

3.3 Coach Jeffreys emphasizes hard but fair play with his soccer team. Seeing one of his players cut an opposing team member's legs out from under him, Coach Jeffreys benches the player, explaining to him (and the rest of the team) why he did so. He doesn't see another incident of this type of foul for the rest of the year. Explain why this occurred, including the role of expectations in your explanation.

3.4 Answer the third question we asked at the beginning of the chapter: "Why did he [Tim] change his study habits and sustain his efforts?"

To receive feedback for these questions, go to Appendix A.

Outcomes of Modeling

Modeling can result in behavioral change, but it can also affect the way we think and feel. We outline these influences in Figure 9.5 and discuss them in the sections that follow.

Learning New Behaviors. Through imitation, people can acquire abilities they didn't have before observing the model. Solving an algebra problem after seeing the teacher demonstrate a solution, making a new recipe after seeing it made on television, or learning to write a clear paragraph after seeing an exemplary one are all examples. Kelly's comment, "I'm trying to swing at a ball like the pros do, but I haven't been able to quite do it," indicates that she was attempting to learn a new behavior by watching players on television.

Facilitating Existing Behaviors. You're attending a concert, and at the end of one of the numbers, someone stands and begins to applaud. You, and others, join in to create a standing ovation. You already know how to stand and applaud, so you didn't learn a new behavior. Instead, observing the model facilitated your behavior.

This outcome is also illustrated in Tim's behavior. He practiced solving problems before quizzes but admitted, "I usually do a couple, and if I get them, I quit." After observing Susan,

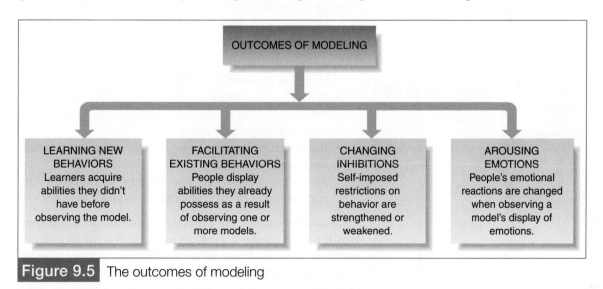

LEARNING NEW BEHAVIORS	FACILITATING EXISTING BEHAVIORS	CHANGING INHIBITIONS	AROUSING EMOTIONS
Learners acquire abilities they didn't have before observing the model.	People display abilities they already possess as a result of observing one or more models.	Self-imposed restrictions on behavior are strengthened or weakened.	People's emotional reactions are changed when observing a model's display of emotions.

Figure 9.5 The outcomes of modeling

he changed the way he studied. Her approach to preparing for quizzes facilitated Tim's studying behavior.

Inhibition. A self-imposed restriction on one's behavior.

Changing Inhibitions.
An **inhibition** is a self-imposed restriction on one's behavior, and observing a model and the consequences of the model's behavior can either strengthen or weaken it. Unlike actions that facilitate existing behaviors, changing inhibitions involves socially unacceptable behaviors, such as breaking classroom rules (Schunk et al., 2008).

For example, students are less likely to break a rule if one of their peers is reprimanded; their inhibition about breaking the rule has been strengthened. Jacob Kounin (1970), a pioneer researcher in the area of classroom management, called this phenomenon the *ripple effect*. On the other hand, if a student speaks without permission and isn't reprimanded, other students are more likely to do the same. The inhibition is weakened.

Vicarious learning and the nonoccurrence of expected consequences help explain changed inhibitions. For instance, if students see a peer reprimanded for breaking a rule, they are vicariously punished; they expect the same result if they break the rule, and their inhibition about breaking rules is strengthened. However, if the student is not reprimanded, the nonoccurrence of the expected punisher acts as a reinforcer, and both the student and the rest of the class are more likely to break the rule. Their inhibition about breaking rules has been weakened.

Arousing Emotions.
Finally, a person's emotional reactions can be changed by observing a model's display of emotions. For example, observing the uneasiness of a diver on a high board may cause an observer to become more fearful of the board. On the other hand, observing teachers genuinely enjoying themselves as they discuss a topic can generate similar enthusiasm in students (Brophy, 2010).

Earlier, we said that modeling describes "behavioral, cognitive, and affective changes deriving from observing the actions of others," and these examples help us better understand why modeling is defined this way. For example, we see behavioral changes when behaviors are learned or facilitated, cognitive changes in strengthening or weakening inhibitions, and affective changes when emotions are aroused.

Processes Involved in Learning from Models

Four processes are involved in learning from models: *attention, retention, reproduction,* and *motivation* (Bandura, 1986). They're illustrated in Figure 9.6 and summarized as follows:

- *Attention:* A learner's attention is drawn to the essential aspects of the modeled behavior.
- *Retention:* The modeled behaviors are transferred to memory. Storing the modeled behavior allows the learner to reproduce it later.
- *Reproduction:* Learners reproduce the behaviors that they have stored in memory.
- *Motivation:* Learners are motivated by the expectation of reinforcement for reproducing the modeled behaviors.

With respect to these processes, three factors are important for us as teachers. First, to learn from models, learners' attention must be drawn to the essential aspects of the modeled behavior (Bandura, 1986). For example, preservice teachers often go into schools and observe veterans in action, but if

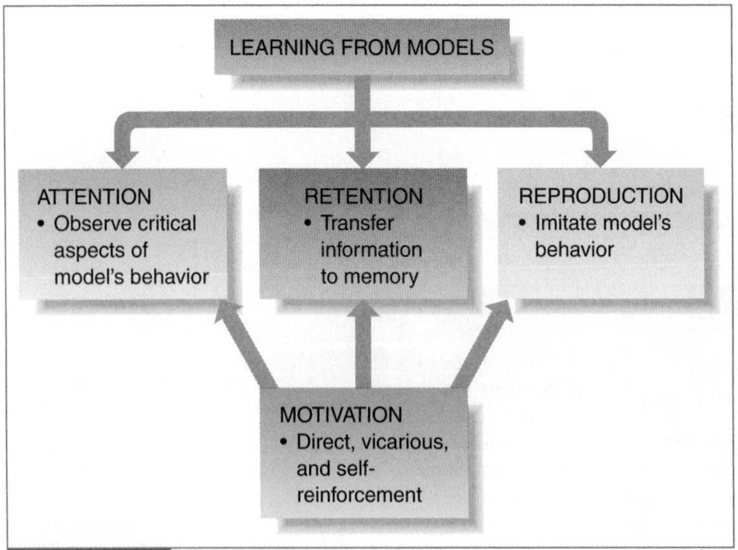

Figure 9.6 Processes involved in learning from models

(Figure contents:)
LEARNING FROM MODELS

ATTENTION
- Observe critical aspects of model's behavior

RETENTION
- Transfer information to memory

REPRODUCTION
- Imitate model's behavior

MOTIVATION
- Direct, vicarious, and self-reinforcement

they don't know what they're looking for, they miss essential aspects of effective teaching, and the observations aren't as valuable as they could be. As teachers, we need to call attention to the important aspects of each skill or process we're demonstrating.

Second, attending to the modeled behaviors and recording them in memory don't ensure that learners will be able to reproduce them. Additional scaffolding and practice with feedback are often required. (We examine this issue in more detail in our "Ed Psych and Teaching" feature titled "Using Social Cognitive Theory to Increase Your Students' Learning," later in the chapter.)

Third, although motivation appears as a separate component in Figure 9.6, it is integral to each of the other processes. Motivated learners are more likely to attend to a model's behavior, to remember it, and to reproduce it. This is illustrated by the arrows from "motivation" pointing to each of the other processes.

Perceived similarity is an important factor in a model's effectiveness.

Effectiveness of Models

The effectiveness of a model influences the likelihood that the behavioral, cognitive, or affective changes derived from observing models will occur. A model's effectiveness depends on three factors:

- Perceived similarity
- Perceived competence
- Perceived status

When we observe a model's behavior, we are more likely to imitate him if we perceive the model as similar to us. This helps us understand why presenting nontraditional career models and teaching students about the contributions of members of cultural minorities are important. Either gender can effectively demonstrate that engineering presents career opportunities, for example, but girls are more likely to believe that it is a viable career if they observe a female rather than a male engineer, just as boys are more likely to consider nursing as a potential career if they observe male rather than female nurses. Similarly, Hispanic students are more likely to believe they can accomplish challenging goals if they see the accomplishments of a successful Hispanic adult than one from another cultural group.

Perception of a model's competence, the second factor influencing a model's effectiveness, interacts with perceived similarity. People are more likely to imitate models they perceive to be competent, regardless of similarity. Tim believed Susan was competent because she was a successful student. Although Tim and Susan are similar—they are classmates—he wouldn't have imitated her study habits if she hadn't been successful.

Perceived status is the third factor. Status is acquired when individuals distinguish themselves from others in their fields, and people tend to imitate models they perceive as having high status, such as professional athletes, stars in entertainment, and world leaders. At the school level, athletes, cheerleaders, and in some cases even gang leaders have high status.

High-status models enjoy an additional benefit. They are often tacitly credited for competence outside their own areas of expertise. This is why you see professional athletes (instead of nutritionists) endorsing breakfast cereal, and actors (instead of engineers) endorsing automobiles and motor oil.

You will also be a high-status model for your students. Despite concerns expressed by educational reformers and teachers themselves, you will enjoy perceived status, particularly if you teach effectively and if your students believe you're fair and care about them.

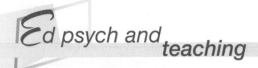

$\mathcal{E}d$ psych and *teaching*

Using Social Cognitive Theory to Increase Your Students' Learning

Social cognitive theory has a wide range of classroom applications. The following guidelines can help you apply the theory with your students.

1. Model desirable behaviors for students.
2. Place students in modeling roles, and use cognitive modeling to share their strategies.
3. Capitalize on the effects of modeling and on the processes involved in modeling to promote learning.
4. Use guest role models.

Let's see how Sally Campese, an eighth-grade algebra teacher, applies these guidelines with her students. Sally has several students in her class who are cultural minorities.

"We'd better get going," Arthur says to Tameka, as they approach Sally's room. "You know how she is. She thinks algebra is sooo important."

As Sally begins her class, she comments, "Just a reminder. I've invited a man named Javier Sanchez to speak on Friday. He is an engineer, and he's going to tell you how he uses math in his career.

"Okay, look here," Sally says, turning to the day's topic. "We're having a little difficulty with simultaneous equations, so let's go over a few more examples.

"Try this one," she says, writing the following on the board:

$$4a + 6b = 24$$
$$5a - 6b = 3$$

Sally watches, and seeing that Gabriela has solved the problem successfully, says, "Gabriela, come up to the board and describe your thinking for us as you solved the problem."

Gabriela explains that she added the two equations to get $9a + 0b = 27$, and as she writes the new equation on the board, Sally then asks, "What is the value of a? . . . Chris?"

". . . Three."

"And how did you get that?"

"Zero b is zero, and I divided both sides by 9, so I have $1a$ equals 3."

"Good! . . . Now, let's find the value of b. What should we do first? . . . Mitchell?"

Now, let's look at Sally's attempts to apply the guidelines with her students. First, Arthur's comment, "She thinks algebra is sooo important," resulted from Sally's modeling her own genuine interest in the topic. Modeling won't make all students enthusiastic learners, but it can make a difference in student motivation, as we saw in Arthur's comment (Brophy, 2010).

Sally applied the second and third guidelines by having Gabriela explain her thinking (cognitive modeling) and guiding her students through the solution with questions rather than simply explaining the solution. Seeing and hearing a classmate's thinking during problem solving made students more likely to attend to the demonstrated behavior, retain it, and reproduce it later. And, Gabriela was an effective model because of perceived similarity.

Finally, Sally applied the last guideline by inviting Mr. Sanchez to her class. Because he was Hispanic, he would, through perceived similarity, be an effective model for her students who are members of cultural minorities. Inviting someone like Mr. Sanchez even once or twice a year can do much to capitalize on the influence of minority role models.

Self-Regulated Learning

In our chapter-opening case study, you saw that Tim, in an effort to improve on his algebra quizzes, and knowing that Susan was a successful student (perceived competence), went to her home to study. There, he observed her in action, and he adopted study strategies similar to hers as a result of her modeling.

Self-regulated learning. The process of setting personal goals, combined with the motivation, thought processes, strategies, and behaviors that lead to reaching the goals.

The changes in Tim's approach to studying were accomplished through **self-regulated learning,** the process of setting personal goals, combined with the motivation, thought processes, strategies, and behaviors that lead to reaching the goals (Schunk, 2008; Zimmerman & Schunk, 2001). Self-regulated learning is the mechanism that allows students like Tim to capitalize on what they learn from observing models (Greene & Azevedo, 2007).

Choice is an essential element of self-regulated learning (Schunk, 2008). When learners have choices, they decide who to observe and how they will integrate the modeled behaviors into their own lives. Tim, for example, *chose* to go to Susan's house and work with her and, based on the behaviors she modeled, he *chose* his own goals. The development of self-regulated learning is difficult, if not impossible, when all aspects of a task are controlled. For example, if a teacher requires that students write 5 typewritten pages on an assigned topic, in a given format, that includes a minimum of 10 references, opportunities to develop self-regulated learning are reduced.

Self-regulated learning includes the following components:

- Goal setting
- Self-monitoring
- Self-assessment
- Strategy use (Meichenbaum, 2000; Paris & Paris, 2001)

Goal Setting

Goals provide direction for our actions and benchmarks for measuring progress. The goals and actions we select are often outcomes of behaviors we see modeled by others. For instance, Susan set the goal of working at least three of each type of algebra problem, and Tim imitated her behavior by setting a similar goal of his own. As a result of seeing other people exercise or succeed in losing weight, you might set the goal of jogging 25 miles a week, or limiting your food intake to 1,800 calories per day, for example.

Goal setting is at the heart of self-regulated learning, and it is one of the most difficult aspects of the process to implement with students. For it to work, students must be committed to challenging but realistic goals, and they are more likely to commit to goals they set for themselves than to goals set by others (Schunk et al., 2008; Stipek, 2002). This is often problematic, because many students aren't motivated to set goals in the first place, and when they do, the goals are often simple and low level.

Self-Monitoring

Once they've set goals, self-regulated learners continually monitor their actions. For instance, you can keep track of the number of miles you've jogged during a week, or monitor the number of calories you consume each day. Susan said, "I sometimes even make a little chart. I try to do at least three problems of each type we study, and then I check them off as I do them."

Students can be taught to monitor a variety of behaviors. For example, they can keep a chart and make a check every time they catch themselves "drifting off" during an hour of study, whenever they blurt out an answer in class, or when they compliment a classmate. Self-observation combined with appropriate goals can improve concentration, study habits, and even social skills (Alberto & Troutman, 2009).

Self-Assessment

Self-assessment helps us determine the extent to which our goals are being met. For example, if you jog 5 miles on Sunday, 3 on Monday, 5 on Tuesday, and 5 more on Thursday, you know that you'll need to get in 7 more miles by Saturday to reach your goal of 25 miles for the week. Similarly, if you've consumed 1,200 calories but still haven't had your evening meal, you might forgo dessert.

Students can also learn to assess their own work (Stiggins, 2008). For example, they can determine the quality of their solutions to word problems by comparing their answers with estimates and asking themselves if the answers make sense. Tim's comparing his answers to those in the back of the book is a form of self-assessment.

Self-assessment can also contribute to motivation and personal satisfaction. For instance, when you realize that you need 7 more miles to reach your goal for the week, you will be motivated to go out for a run. The satisfaction associated with reaching goals often leads to a form of self-reward (Schunk, 2008). For instance, if you've reached your weekly calorie goals for a month straight, you may reward yourself with a nice dinner out with your friends, a new outfit, or a couple days off from dieting. Susan, for example, commented, "If I get them [the problems] all right, I might treat myself with a dish of ice cream." Reaching the goal is satisfying, and the more challenging—within reason—the goal, the more satisfying reaching it will be. In fact, the more times you reach your weekly goal, the more motivated you'll be to attain it in the future.

Self-assessment can also help solve the problem of students' not wanting to set goals or wanting to set trivial and easily-attainable goals. As they see progress toward reaching their goals, their motivation will increase, and they're more likely to commit to other goals in the future.

Strategy Use

Strategy use connects actions to our goals. To be effectively self-regulated, learners must be able to match effective strategies to their goals. For example, Tim initially worked a couple practice problems, and if he was able to do them, he quit. But, because of Susan's modeling, he selected a wider variety of problems. This simple change was a more effective strategy.

Even young children can use strategies. For example, if a first grader practices more on spelling words he doesn't know than on those he can already spell, he is being strategic.

Helping students become self-regulated learners is powerful but demanding. For example, students need a great deal of help in setting challenging but realistic goals, and students won't initially be good at monitoring their own progress, conducting self-assessments, and selecting appropriate strategies (Yell, Robinson, & Drasgow, 2001). **Cognitive behavior modification,** a procedure that promotes behavioral change and self-regulation in students through self-talk and self-instruction, is a tool that you can use to help your students develop these abilities (Meichenbaum, 2000). The procedure begins with cognitive modeling. If a student is disorganized and scattered, for example, you model both the actions and the thinking involved in setting an appropriate goal, such as bringing a pencil, notebook paper, textbook, and completed homework assignment to class each day. You also model the process of monitoring progress and assessing the extent to which your student is meeting the goal. For example, the student can use a simple checklist that includes each of the items, and you can demonstrate how the items are checked off each day.

After observing the cognitive modeling, your students practice the skill with your support and then use self-talk as a guide when performing the skills without supervision. Cognitive behavior modification strategies are particularly effective with students having exceptionalities (Turnbull, Turnbull, & Wehmeyer, 2010).

In spite of your best efforts, not all of your students will become self-regulated learners, but for those with whom you succeed, you will have made a life-long contribution to their success as a student and in life in general.

Evaluating Social Cognitive Theory

Like all theories, social cognitive theory has limitations. The following are some of them:

- Social cognitive theory can't explain why learners attend to some modeled behaviors but not others, and it can't explain why learners can reproduce some behaviors they observe but can't reproduce others.
- It doesn't account for the acquisition of complex abilities, such as learning to write (beyond mere mechanics).
- It can't explain the role of context and social interaction in complex learning environments. For example, research indicates that student interaction in small groups facilitates learning (Fernandez-Berrocal & Santamaria, 2006). The processes involved in these settings extend beyond simple modeling and imitation.

Cognitive behavior modification. A procedure that promotes behavioral change and self-regulation in students through self-talk and self-instruction.

On the other hand, social cognitive theory has important strengths. For example, modeling is one of the most powerful factors influencing both our behavior and classroom learning, and social cognitive theory provides us with suggestions about how to use modeling effectively in our teaching. Social cognitive theory also overcomes many of the limitations of behaviorism by helping us understand the importance of learner cognitions, and particularly expectations, on our actions (Schunk et al., 2008). It provides us with additional tools that we can use to maximize learning for all our students.

Classroom connections

Capitalizing on Social Cognitive Theory in Classrooms

1. Cognitive modeling involves verbalizing your thinking as you demonstrate a skill. Use cognitive modeling in your instruction, and act as a role model for your students.

   - **Elementary:** A kindergarten teacher helps her children form letters by saying, "I start with my pencil here and make a straight line down," as she begins to form a b.

   - **Middle School:** A seventh-grade teacher has a large poster at the front of his room that says, "I will always treat you with courtesy and respect, you will treat me with courtesy and respect, and you will treat each other with courtesy and respect." He models, reinforces, and calls attention to this rule throughout the school year.

   - **High School:** A physics teacher solving acceleration problems writes F = ma on the board and says, "First, I know I want to find the force on the object. Then, I think about what the problem tells me. Tell us one thing we know about the problem, . . . Lisa."

2. Effective modeling requires that students attend to a behavior, retain it in memory, and then reproduce it. To capitalize on these processes, provide group practice by walking students through examples before having them practice on their own.

   - **Elementary:** A fourth-grade class is adding fractions with unlike denominators. The teacher displays the problem 1/4 + 2/3 = ? and then asks, "What do we need to do first? . . . Karen?" She continues guiding the students with questioning as they solve the problem.

   - **Middle School:** After showing students how to find exact locations using longitude and latitude, a seventh-grade geography teacher says to his students, "We want to find the city closest to 85° west and 37° north. What do these numbers tell us? . . . Josh?" He continues to guide students through the example until they locate Chicago as the closest city.

   - **High School:** After demonstrating several proofs, a geometry teacher wants her students to prove that angle 1 is greater than angle 2 in the accompanying drawing.

     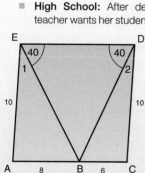

     She begins by asking, "What are we given?" After students identify the givens in the problem, she asks, "What can we conclude about segments BE and BD?" and continues to guide students to a completion of the proof with her questions.

3. When learners observe a classmate being reinforced, they are vicariously reinforced. Use vicarious reinforcement to improve behavior and increase learning.

   - **Elementary:** As students in a reading group move back to their desks, a first-grade teacher comments, "I like the way this group is quietly returning to their desks. Karen, Vicki, Ali, and David each get a star."

   - **Middle School:** An eighth-grade English teacher displays examples of well-written paragraphs on the overhead and comments, "Each of these has excellent paragraph structure, and each shows some imagination. Let's look at them more closely."

   - **High School:** An art teacher displays several well-done pottery pieces and comments, "Look at these, everyone. These are excellent. Let's see why. . . . "

     The English and art teachers accomplished three things. First, the students whose paragraphs or pottery were displayed were directly reinforced, but they weren't put on the spot, because the teachers didn't identify them. Second, the rest of the students in the classes were vicariously reinforced. Third, the teachers gave their classes feedback and provided concrete models for future imitation.

4. Self-regulated learning is the process of students' taking responsibility for their own understanding. Teach students to be self-regulated learners by providing opportunities for them to set goals, use strategies and monitor progress towards those goals.

   - **Elementary:** A third-grade teacher helps his students, who are having problems staying in their seats, design a checklist that they can use to monitor their behavior. The teacher initially reminds them to make a check when they are out of their seats, and later he monitors the students to see if they've given themselves checks when appropriate.

   - **Middle School:** A prealgebra teacher helps her students create a rating scale to assess their progress on homework. For each assignment, they circle a 3 if they complete the assignment and believe they understand it, a 2 if they complete it but are uncertain about their understanding, and a 1 if they do not complete it.

   - **High School:** An English teacher helps his students set individual goals by asking each to write a study plan. He returns to the plan at the end of the unit and has each student assess his or her progress.

4.1 An American history teacher, wanting to inspire students to commit themselves to making our country a better place, shows a DVD of Martin Luther King's famous speech in which he said, "I have a dream that my four little children will one day live in a nation where they will not be judged by the color of their skin but by the content of their character." What type of modeling is being illustrated, how effective is the modeling likely to be, and what is the most likely modeling outcome? Explain.

4.2 You're in a large city waiting to cross the street. No cars are coming from either direction, so a person who is standing beside you crosses against the red light. You and the rest of the people then also cross. Explain why you cross the street. Include all relevant concepts in your explanation.

4.3 To develop a deeper understanding of the topics you're studying in this text, you decide that you're going to answer each of the "Check Your Understanding" questions in writing. You make a chart with the question number on it, and you make a check mark on the chart when you've answered and believe you understand the question. Then, you go to Appendix A to compare your answers to those in the feedback section. If you answer incorrectly, you reread the section and look for examples that illustrate the topic being measured by the question. Identify each of the components of self-regulation in your behavior.

To receive feedback for these questions, go to Appendix A.

Developmentally appropriate practice

Applying Behaviorism and Social Cognitive Theory with Learners at Different Ages

While many applications of behaviorism and social cognitive theory apply at all grade levels, some important developmental differences exist. The following paragraphs outline some of these differences.

Working with Students in Early Childhood Programs and Elementary Schools

The emotional environment we create for our students is important at all levels but is crucial when we work with young children. This explains why preschool, kindergarten, and first-grade teachers make a special effort to connect with students by, for example, giving hugs or "high fives" when children come into their classrooms.

Young children bask openly in positive reinforcement, and it is virtually impossible to satiate them with praise. On the other hand, they respond to punishment quite differently. Because their moral reasoning tends to be external, they conclude that they must be "bad" if they're punished, so punishment should be used sparingly and judiciously. Physical punishment and humiliation should never be used in classrooms, and they are particularly destructive with young children.

When using modeling, attention is important. Because young children's attention wanders, modeling can be problematic; children often don't attend to the modeled behavior. This means that modeling must be very explicit and concrete.

Working with Students in Middle Schools

A warm and supportive classroom environment continues to be important with middle school students, and, because they are going through many physical, intellectual, and emotional changes, consistent enforcement of rules and procedures is essential to help them maintain their sense of equilibrium. Middle school students become increasingly sensitive to inconsistent treatment by their teachers, and fairness is very important to them.

Middle school students evaluate the praise they receive and may even react negatively to praise they view as insincere or unwarranted.

Because of improved language skills, cognitive modeling becomes a valuable instructional tool. They are capable of developing self-regulation but are unlikely to do so without extensive guidance and support.

Working with Students in High Schools

Classroom climate remains important with high school students, but the focus turns more to treating students with respect and communicating that you're genuinely committed to their learning. These students continue to be sensitive to perceptions of fairness and teachers' favoring some students over others (Emmer & Evertson, 2009).

Praise that communicates that their understanding is increasing is very effective and can increase these students' intrinsic motivation (Deci & Ryan, 2002).

High school students are increasingly self-regulated, and they're capable of setting and monitoring goals and using sophisticated learning strategies. However, they—and particularly lower achievers—are unlikely to use strategies effectively without extensive monitoring and support (Pressley & Hilden, 2006). Modeling effective strategy use becomes particularly important, and cognitive modeling can be a very effective tool for promoting self-regulation.

Exploring diversity

Capitalizing on Behaviorism and Social Cognitive Theory with Learners from Diverse Backgrounds

For some students, schools can seem cold and uninviting, and this can be particularly true for members of cultural minorities. Let's look at an example.

> Roberto, a fourth grader, shuffles into class and hides behind the big girl in front of him. If he is lucky, his teacher won't discover that he hasn't done his homework—12 problems! How can he ever do that many? Besides, he isn't good at math. Roberto hates school. It seems strange and foreign. His teacher sometimes frowns when he speaks because his English isn't as good as the other students'. And, often he has trouble understanding what the teacher is saying.
>
> Even lunch isn't much fun. If his friend Raul isn't there, he eats alone. One time when he sat with some other students, they started laughing at the way he talked and made fun of the tortillas he was eating. He can't wait to go home.

The way teachers and other students treat members of cultural minorities has a strong impact on their emotional reactions to school. School wasn't associated with positive feelings for Roberto, and he didn't feel comfortable, safe, or wanted.

It doesn't have to be this way. You saw how Sharon Van Horn treated her students each morning in the "Ed Psych and Teaching" feature titled "Applying Classical Conditioning with Your Students," earlier in the chapter. Let's look again.

> Sharon greets each of her students with the same routine each morning; as they come in the classroom, they give her a handshake, hug, or high five, whichever they prefer. . . .
>
> Sharon periodically displays posters and other artifacts from the heritage countries for her students who are not native English speakers. For example, colorful prints from Mexico are displayed on one wall, and vocabulary cards in both Spanish and English are hung around the room.
>
> Alberto, who has immigrated from Mexico, comes in for extra help three mornings a week, and this morning Mariachi music is playing in the background.

> "Buenos días, Alberto. How are you today?" Sharon asks before Alberto gives her a hug, which he prefers.
>
> "Buenos días. I'm fine," Alberto responds, as he goes to his desk to take out his homework.

Alberto had an instinctive emotional reaction to Sharon's warmth, and in time, her classroom became associated with her manner. We can explain his reaction with classical conditioning, and we can capitalize on it to help all our students feel safe in our classrooms. This is particularly important for students who are members of cultural minorities.

When students struggle, we can use antecedents in the form of prompts to encourage them, and then use praise when they succeed. While these efforts are effective with all students, they are particularly important for members of cultural minorities.

Finally, you saw that Sally Campese (in the "Ed Psych and Teaching" feature titled "Using Social Cognitive Theory to Increase Your Students' Learning") planned to bring Javier Sanchez into her class to discuss the importance of math. Mr. Sanchez's presence would provide clear evidence that a person of Hispanic background can succeed in a demanding academic field. Using role models in this way sends a powerful message to minority youth.

In their efforts to provide role models for members of cultural minorities, teachers often overlook the opportunity to use symbolic models from society at large. For example, a number of syndicated editorial columnists in major newspapers are members of cultural minorities, and they frequently express opinions about prosocial values, such as the need to accept responsibility for personal behavior and success. Their pictures always appear with their columns, so you merely need to skim the newspapers and clip columns that are relevant to your goals. This strategy requires little effort on your part, and again, sends minority youth a powerful message.

Summary

1. Use classical conditioning to explain events in and outside of classrooms.
   - Classical conditioning occurs when a formerly neutral stimulus, such as a teacher's room, becomes associated with a naturally occurring (unconditioned) stimulus, such as the teacher's warm and inviting manner, to produce a response similar to an instinctive or reflexive response, such as feelings of safety.

2. Identify examples of operant conditioning in classroom activities.
   - Operant conditioning focuses on voluntary responses that are influenced by consequences. Consequences that increase behavior are reinforcers, and consequences that decrease behavior are punishers. Teachers' praise is a common reinforcer, and reprimands are common punishers. The schedule of reinforcement influences both the rate of initial learning and the persistence of the behavior.
   - Antecedents precede and induce behaviors that can then be reinforced. They exist in the form of environmental stimuli, prompts and cues, and past experiences.

3. Use concepts from social cognitive theory to explain examples of people's behaviors. Include the nonoccurrence of expected consequences, reciprocal causation, and vicarious learning.
   - Social cognitive theory considers, in addition to behavior and the environment, learners' beliefs and expectations. According to social cognitive theory, each can influence the other in the process of reciprocal causation.
   - The nonoccurrence of expected reinforcers can act as punishers, and the nonoccurrence of expected punishers can act as reinforcers.
   - Modeling is the core concept of social cognitive theory, and vicarious learning occurs when people observe the consequences of others' actions and adjust their own behavior accordingly.

4. Identify examples of social cognitive theory in people's behaviors. Include the types of modeling, modeling outcomes, effectiveness of models, and self-regulation.
   - Modeling can be direct (from live models), symbolic (from books, movies, and television), or synthesized (combining the acts of different models).
   - The effectiveness of models depends on perceived similarity, perceived status, and perceived competence.
   - Social cognitive theory also helps explain why cognitive modeling, teachers' describing their thought processes as they demonstrate skills, is effective, and why students who set goals, monitor progress toward the goals, and assess the extent to which the goals are met learn more than peers who don't.

Understanding Behaviorism and Social Cognitive Theory: Preparing for Your Licensure Exam

Your licensure exam will include information related to behaviorism and social cognitive theory, and we include the following exercises to help you practice for the exam in your state.

You've seen how you can use behaviorism and social cognitive theory to explain student learning. Let's look now at a teacher attempting to apply these theories in his work with his middle school students. Read the case study, and answer the questions that follow.

Warren Rose's seventh graders are working on a unit on decimals and percentages. He begins class on Thursday by saying, "Let's review what we did yesterday."

Hearing some mumbles, he notes wryly, "I realize that percentages and decimals aren't your favorite topic, and I'm not wild about them either, but they'll be on the state exam, so we might as well buckle down and learn them.

"Let's start by looking at a few examples," he continues, displaying the following problem on the document camera:

You are at the mall, shopping for a jacket. You see one that looks great, originally priced at $84, marked 25% off. You recently got a check for $65 from the fast-food restaurant where you work. Can you afford the jacket?

"Now, . . . when I see a problem like this, I think, 'What does the jacket cost now?' I have to figure out the price, and to do that I will take 25% of the $84. . . . That means I first convert the 25% to a decimal. I know when I see 25% that the decimal is understood to be just to the right of the 5, so I move it two places to the left. Then I can multiply 0.25 times 84."

Warren demonstrates the process as he talks, working the problem to completion. He has his students work several examples at their desks and discusses their solutions. He then continues, "Okay, for homework, do the odd problems on page 113."

"Do we have to do all eight of them?" Robbie asks.

Several other students chime in, arguing that eight word problems are too many. "Wait, people, please," Warren holds up his hands. "All right. You only have to do 1, 3, 5, 7, and 9."

"Yeah!" the class shouts.

"Yikes, Friday," Helen comments to Jenny as they walk into Warren's room Friday morning. "I got caught off guard when Mr. Rose sent me to the board last week, and I felt like an idiot. Now, I get so nervous when he makes us go up to the board, and everybody's staring at us. If he calls me up today, I'll die."

Warren discusses the day's homework and then says, "Okay, let's look at this problem."

A bicycle selling for $145 is marked down 15%. What is the new selling price?

"First, let's estimate, so that we can see whether our answer makes sense. About what should the new selling price be? . . . Pamela?"

". . . I'm not sure," Pamela says.

"Callie, what do you think?"

"I think it would be about $120."

"Good thinking. Describe for everyone how you arrived at that."

"Well, 10% would be $14.50, . . . so 15% would be about another $7. That would be about $21, and $21 off would be a little over $120."

"Good thinking," Warren nods. "Now, let's go ahead and solve it. What do we do first? . . . David?"

". . . We make the 15% into a decimal."

"Good, David. Now, what next? . . . Leslie?"

"Take the 0.15 times the 145."

"Okay. Do that everybody. . . . What did you get?"

". . . $200.17," Cris volunteers. "Whoops, that can't be right. That's more than the bicycle cost to start with. . . . Wait. . . . $21.75."

"Good," Warren smiles. "That's what we're trying to do. We are all going to make mistakes, but if we catch ourselves, we're making progress. Keep it up. You can do these problems. Now what do we do?" he continues.

"Subtract," Matt volunteers.

"All right, go ahead," Warren directs.

Warren finishes guiding students through the problem, has them do two additional problems, and then begins to assign five problems for homework. But just as he starts, several students chime in, "How about just four problems tonight, Mr. Rose. We always have so much math to do."

"Okay," Warren shrugs, "numbers 2, 6, 7, and 8 on page 114."

Warren continues monitoring students until 2 minutes are left in the period. "All right, everyone, the bell will ring in 2 minutes. Get everything cleaned up around your desks, and get ready to go."

Questions for Case Analysis

In answering these questions, use information from the chapter, and link your responses to specific information in the case.

1. Describe where classical conditioning occurred in the case study. Identify the classical conditioning concepts in your description.

2. Warren's behavior was influenced by punishment in two different places in the case study. Explain where they occurred, and describe their likely impact on learning.

3. Warren inadvertently negatively reinforced the students at two points in the lesson. Identify and explain both points.

4. Warren's modeling was both effective and ineffective. Identify and explain one effective and one ineffective aspect of his modeling.

5. Warren capitalized on the effects of vicarious learning and perceived similarity in the case study. Explain where and how this occurred.

For feedback on these questions, go to Appendix B.

Your licensure exam will also include multiple-choice questions similar to those your instructor has given you on your quizzes and tests for this course.

Important Concepts

antecedents (p. 302)
applied behavior analysis (ABA) (p. 303)
behaviorism (p. 292)
classical conditioning (p. 293)
cognitive behavior modification (p. 320)

cognitive modeling (p. 313)
conditioned response (p. 293)
conditioned stimulus (p. 293)
consequences (p. 296)
continuous reinforcement schedule (p. 299)
desists (p. 301)

discrimination (p. 294)
extinction (classical conditioning) (p. 294)
extinction (operant conditioning) (p. 294)
functional analysis (p. 305)
generalization (p. 294)

inhibition (p. 316)
intermittent reinforcement schedule (p. 299)
interval schedule of reinforcement (p. 299)
learning (behaviorism) (p. 292)

learning (cognitive) (p. 311)
modeling (p. 312)
negative reinforcement
  (p. 297)
neutral stimulus (p. 293)
operant conditioning
  (p. 296)
positive behavior support
  (p. 306)

positive reinforcement
  (p. 297)
Premack principle (p. 297)
presentation punishment
  (p. 301)
punishers (p. 301)
punishment (p. 301)
ratio schedule of
  reinforcement (p. 299)

reciprocal causation (p. 312)
reinforcement (p. 297)
reinforcement schedules
  (p. 299)
reinforcer (p. 297)
removal punishment (p. 301)
response cost (p. 302)
satiation (p. 301)
self-regulated learning (p. 318)

shaping (p. 298)
social cognitive theory (p. 311)
timeout (p. 301)
unconditioned response
  (p. 293)
unconditioned stimulus
  (p. 293)
vicarious learning (p. 314)

Go to the Topics: Behaviorist Perspectives and Social Cognitive Perspectives in the MyEducationLab (www.myeducationlab.com) for *Educational Psychology: Windows on Classrooms,* where you can:

- Find learning outcomes for Behaviorist Perspectives and Social Cognitive Perspectives along with the national standards that connect to these outcomes.
- Complete Assignments and Activities that can help you more deeply understand the chapter content.
- Apply and practice your understanding of the core teaching skills identified in the chapter with the Building Teaching Skills and Dispositions learning units.
- Examine challenging situations and cases presented in the IRIS Center Resources.
- Access video clips of CCSSO National Teachers of the Year award winners responding to the question, "Why Do I Teach?" in the Teacher Talk section.
- See video examples included within the Study Plan that provide concrete and real-world illustrations of the topics presented in the chapter.
- Check your comprehension of the content covered in the chapter with the Study Plan. Here you will be able to take a chapter quiz, receive feedback on your answers, and then access Review, Practice, and Enrichment activities to enhance your understanding of chapter content.

MyEducationLab

chapter 10

Motivation and Learning

chapteroutline

learningoutcomes

After you've completed your study of this chapter, you should be able to:

What Is Motivation?
Extrinsic and Intrinsic Motivation
Motivation to Learn
Theoretical Views of Motivation

1. Define motivation, and describe different theoretical explanations for learner motivation.

The Influence of Needs on Motivation to Learn
Maslow's Hierarchy of Needs
The Need for Self-Determination
The Need to Preserve Self-Worth

2. Describe learners' needs and how they influence motivation to learn.

The Influence of Beliefs on Motivation to Learn
Expectations: Beliefs About Outcomes
Beliefs About Intelligence
Self-Efficacy: Beliefs About Capability
Beliefs About Value
Attributions: Beliefs About Causes of Performance

3. Explain how learners' beliefs can influence their motivation to learn.

The Influence of Goals on Motivation to Learn
Mastery and Performance Goals
Social Goals
Work-Avoidance Goals
Goals and Motivation: Implications for Teachers

4. Describe how learners' goals can influence their motivation to learn.

The Influence of Interest and Emotion on Motivation to Learn
Personal and Situational Interest
Emotion and Motivation

5. Explain how teachers can capitalize on learners' interests and emotions to increase motivation to learn.

classroomapplications

The following features help you apply the content of this chapter in your teaching.

Ed Psych and Teaching:
Using the Influence of Needs to Increase Your Students' Motivation to Learn
Using Beliefs, Goals, and Interests to Increase Your Students' Motivation to Learn

Classroom Connections:
Capitalizing on Students' Needs to Increase Motivation in Classrooms
Using Students' Beliefs to Increase Their Motivation

Capitalizing on Goals to Increase Student Motivation
Using Students' Interests and Emotions to Promote Motivation in Classrooms

Developmentally Appropriate Practice:
Motivation to Learn in Students at Different Ages

Exploring Diversity:
Student Differences in Motivation to Learn

*W*hy do you like some of your classes more than others? And why do you enjoy certain activities, such as games, sports, listening to music, or reading? The answers to these questions involve motivation, arguably the greatest influence on learning for all of us. Understanding student motivation is an essential part of your professional knowledge, and in this chapter we examine how you can use this knowledge to increase learning in your classroom.

As you read the following case study involving a world history class, think about the students' motivation and how Kathy Brewster, their teacher, influences it.

"We'd better get moving," Susan urges Jim as they approach the door of Kathy's classroom. "The bell's gonna ring, and you know how Brewster is about this class. She thinks it's sooo important."

"Did you finish your homework?" Jim asks and then stops himself. "What am I talking about? You always do your homework."

"Actually, I've always liked history and knowing about the past, . . . and I'm pretty good at it. My dad helps me. He says he wants to keep up with the world," Susan laughs.

"In some classes, I just do enough to get a decent grade, but not in here," Jim responds. "I used to hate history, but I sometimes even read ahead a little, because Brewster makes you think. She's so gung ho, and it's kind of interesting the way she's always telling us about the way we are because of something that happened a zillion years ago—I never thought about this stuff in that way before."

"Gee, Mrs. Brewster, that assignment was impossible," Harvey grumbles as he enters her classroom.

"That's good for you," Kathy smiles. "I know it was a tough assignment, but you need to be challenged. It's hard for me, too, when I'm studying and trying to put together new ideas, but if I hang in, I always feel like I can get it."

"Aw, c'mon, Mrs. Brewster. You know everything."

"I wish. I study every night to keep up with you people, and the harder I study, the smarter I get. . . . And I feel good about myself when I do."

"But you make us work so hard," Harvey continues.

"Yes, but look how good you're getting at writing," Kathy smiles again. "I think you hit a personal best on your last paper. You're becoming a very good writer."

"Yeah, yeah, I know," Harvey replies on his way to his desk, "and being good writers will help us in everything we do in life," echoing a rationale the students often hear from Kathy.

"Just a reminder," Kathy says after the students are settled in their desks, "group presentations on the Renaissance are on Thursday and Friday. You decide what groups will present on each day. Remember, we're all doing our best; we're not competing with each other. . . . Also, for those who chose to write the paper on the Middle Ages, we agreed that they're due on Friday."

We'll return to Kathy's lesson later in the chapter, but for now let's consider three questions:

1. How is Susan's general orientation toward school different from Jim's?
2. How does Jim's motivation in Kathy's class differ from his other classes?
3. How has Kathy influenced Jim's motivation?

Understanding motivation helps us answer these and other questions, as we examine the relationship between motivation and learning in this chapter.

What Is Motivation?

Motivation. The "process whereby goal-directed activity is instigated and sustained" (Schunk, Pintrich & Meece, 2008, p. 4).

"**Motivation** is the process whereby goal-directed activity is instigated and sustained" (Schunk, Pintrich & Meece, 2008, p. 4). Other authors, such as Jere Brophy (2010), provide more elaborate definitions, but they also focus on initiating and continuing behaviors in an effort to reach goals. If we work hard to solve a math problem or attempt to perfect a golf swing, for example, we say we are motivated in each case. Solving the problem and perfecting the swing are the goals, and motivation helped us initiate and sustain our efforts to reach each one.

Motivation is a powerful factor influencing learning and achievement. Motivated students

- Have positive attitudes toward school and describe it as satisfying.
- Persist on difficult tasks and cause few management problems.
- Process information in depth and excel in classroom learning experiences (Perry, Turner, & Meyer, 2006).

Simply, motivated students learn more than their less motivated peers, and this is the reason our chapter is titled *Motivation and Learning.*

Extrinsic motivation. Motivation to engage in an activity as a means to an end.

Intrinsic motivation. Motivation to be involved in an activity for its own sake.

Extrinsic and Intrinsic Motivation

Motivation is often classified into two broad categories. **Extrinsic motivation** is motivation to engage in an activity as a means to an end, whereas **intrinsic motivation** is motivation to be involved in an activity for its own sake (Schunk et al., 2008). If you answered the questions in "Ed Psych and You" by saying that you study primarily to get good grades, you are extrinsically motivated, whereas if you said understanding the course content is more important, you're intrinsically motivated. This difference helps answer our first question (How is Susan's general orientation toward school different from Jim's?). Jim's comment, "In some classes, I just do enough to get a decent grade," reflects extrinsic motivation, whereas Susan's comment, "I've always liked history and knowing about the past" suggests intrinsic motivation. As you would expect, intrinsic motivation is preferable because of its focus on learning and understanding (Brophy, 2010).

Motivation is also contextual and can change over time (Wigfield et al., 2004). For example, we saw that Jim is extrinsically motivated in his other classes, but saying "I sometimes even read ahead a little," and "it's kind of interesting . . ." suggests that he is intrinsically motivated in Kathy's. This helps answer our second question (How does Jim's motivation in Kathy's class differ from his other classes?).

We can also begin to answer the third question (How has Kathy influenced Jim's motivation?) by looking at intrinsic motivation in more detail. Learners are intrinsically motivated by experiences that:

- *Present a challenge.* Meeting challenges is emotionally satisfying, and challenge exists when goals are moderately difficult and success isn't guaranteed (R. Ryan & Deci, 2000; Stipek, 2002).
- *Promote autonomy.* Learners are more motivated when they feel that they have influence over and can control their own learning (R. Ryan & Deci, 2000).
- *Evoke curiosity.* Novel, surprising, or discrepant experiences arouse our curiosity and increase intrinsic motivation (Brophy, 2010).
- *Involve creativity and fantasy* (Lepper & Hodell, 1989). All we have to do is watch a small child mesmerized by *Curious George, Sesame Street,* or other children's programming, or notice the success of the *Harry Potter* stories to see that people are motivated by fantasy.

Ed Psych and You

Think about your classes. Do you study primarily to get good grades, or is understanding the course content more important to you? Do you believe understanding the content is important, even if you're not terribly interested in it?

Learning tasks that evoke curiosity increase learners' intrinsic motivation.

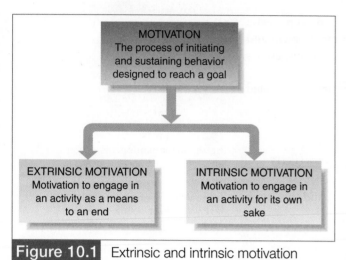

| MOTIVATION |
| The process of initiating and sustaining behavior designed to reach a goal |

| EXTRINSIC MOTIVATION | INTRINSIC MOTIVATION |
| Motivation to engage in an activity as a means to an end | Motivation to engage in an activity for its own sake |

Figure 10.1 Extrinsic and intrinsic motivation

Some researchers suggest that aesthetic experiences associated with beauty that evoke emotional reactions may be intrinsically motivating as well (R. Ryan & Deci, 2000).

Jim's comments suggest that Kathy capitalized on two of these factors. "Brewster really makes you think," suggests he was reacting to the challenge in her class, and "It's kind of interesting the way she's always telling us about the way we are because of something that happened a zillion years ago," suggests her teaching aroused his curiosity.

People tend to think of extrinsic and intrinsic motivation as two ends of a single continuum, meaning the higher the extrinsic motivation, the lower the intrinsic motivation and vice versa, but they are actually on separate continua (Schunk et al., 2008). For example, we asked you earlier if you study to understand the content or primarily to get good grades. You may want good grades but also want to understand the content, as many students do. This suggests that you're high in both intrinsic and extrinsic motivation. People may be high in both, low in both, or high in one and low in the other.

The relationships between extrinsic and intrinsic motivation are outlined in Figure 10.1.

Motivation to Learn

We want our students to be intrinsically motivated, and we are sometimes led to believe that if our instruction is stimulating enough they always will be. This is a worthwhile ideal, but it isn't realistic for all, or even most, learning activities. Here are some reasons why (Brophy, 2010):

- School attendance is compulsory, and content reflects what society believes students should learn, not necessarily what students would choose for themselves.
- Teachers work with large numbers of students and can't always meet individual needs.
- Students' performances are evaluated and reported to parents and other caregivers, so students focus on meeting external demands instead of on personal benefits they might derive from the experiences.

Motivation to learn. Students' "tendencies to find academic activities meaningful and worthwhile and to try to get the intended learning benefits from them" (Brophy, 2010, p. 11).

Jere Brophy (2010) offers an alternative. "I believe that it is realistic for you to seek to develop and sustain your students' **motivation to learn:** their tendencies to find academic activities meaningful and worthwhile and to try to get the intended learning benefits from them" (p. 11).

Motivation to learn is related to the second question we asked in "Ed Psych and You," earlier: "Do you believe understanding the content is important, even if you're not terribly interested in it?" If you answered yes, your *motivation to learn* is high. Motivation to learn will be our focus in this chapter, and if students' intrinsic motivation also increases in the process, so much the better.

Theoretical Views of Motivation

As with learning, different theoretical orientations help us understand students' motivation to learn (Brophy, 2010; Schunk et al., 2008). They are outlined in Figure 10.2 and discussed in the sections that follow.

Behaviorist Views of Motivation

Behaviorism views learning as a change in observable behavior that occurs as a result of experience, and it treats motivation the same way. An increase in the amount of time spent

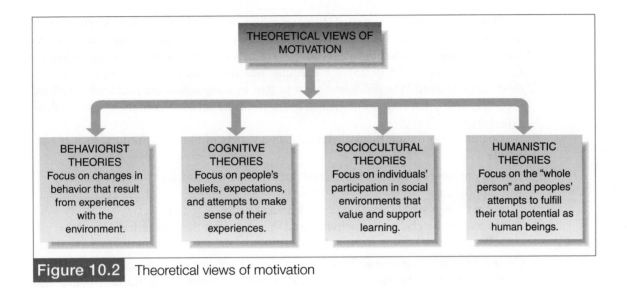

| Figure 10.2 | Theoretical views of motivation |

studying, for example, is viewed as evidence of motivation, so reinforcers, such as praise, comments on homework, and good grades are motivators (Schunk et al., 2008).

Critics argue that using rewards sends students the wrong message about learning, and some research suggests that rewards actually decrease interest when tasks are already intrinsically motivating (R. Ryan & Deci, 1996).

Critics also suggest that behaviorism cannot adequately explain motivation (Perry et al., 2006). For instance, if a student believes he can't complete a difficult assignment, he will be unlikely to work hard on it despite being reinforced for completing past assignments. His motivation is influenced by his beliefs, a cognitive factor not considered by behaviorists.

In spite of these criticisms, rewards are commonly used as motivators in classrooms. For example, teachers in elementary schools use praise, candy, and entertainment, such as computer games, as rewards, and middle and secondary teachers use high test scores, comments on written work, free time, and quiet compliments in attempts to motivate students.

Also, research suggests that judicious use of rewards can be effective. For instance, praise for genuine achievement and rewards that recognize increasing competence can increase intrinsic motivation (Cameron, Pierce, & Banko, 2005). We revisit this issue later in the chapter.

Cognitive Theories of Motivation

"C'mon, let's go," Melanie urges her friend Yelena as they're finishing a series of homework problems.

"Just a sec," Yelena mutters. "I'm not quite getting this one."

"Let's work on it tonight. Everybody's leaving," Melanie urges.

"Go ahead, I'll catch up to you in a minute. I know that I can figure this out. . . . I just don't get it right now."

How might we explain Yelena's persistence? Behaviorism doesn't provide much help. Although getting the right answer would be reinforcing, it doesn't account for her attempt to understand why the problem made sense but still came out wrong. Also, behaviorism doesn't consider cognitive factors in motivation, so it can't explain her saying, "I know that I can figure this out," which indicates that she believes she can resolve the discrepancy and expects to do so.

People's desire to make sense of their experiences is at the heart of both cognitive learning theory and cognitive motivation theory: "Children are seen as naturally motivated to learn when their experience is inconsistent with their current understanding" (Greeno, Collins, & Resnick, 1996, p. 25). For example, why do young children so eagerly explore their environments? Why did Yelena want to stay until she solved the problem? Cognitive theorists suggest that both are motivated by the need to understand and make sense of their experiences.

Cognitive motivation theory helps explain a variety of human behaviors, such as why people

- Try to solve crossword and Sudoku puzzles and other problems with no practical application.
- Are curious when something occurs unexpectedly.
- Persevere on challenging activities and then quit after they've mastered the tasks.
- Want feedback about their performance.

These tendencies all involve an innate desire to make sense of our experiences.

Social cognitive theories elaborate on these views by emphasizing learners' beliefs and expectations and the influence of observing others on our motivation (Schunk & Pajares, 2004). They help explain Jim's comment, "She's so gung ho, and it's kind of interesting the way she's always telling us about the way we are because of something that happened a zillion years ago." His motivation in Kathy's class increased as a result of observing her model her enthusiasm and interest in the topic she was teaching.

Sociocultural Views of Motivation

Motivational zone of proximal development. The match between a learning activity and learners' prior knowledge and experiences that is close enough to stimulate interest and perceived value in the activity but not so familiar that learners are satiated by it.

Sociocultural theories emphasize the powerful role of social interaction in motivation and focus on individuals' participation in classroom communities where all students participate in learning activities and where the teacher and students work together to help everyone learn (Hickey & Zuiker, 2005). These theories suggest that students will be more motivated in classrooms that are cooperative and supportive than in competitive environments, and they help us understand why people are more motivated to engage in an activity if others in the social group are participating in it.

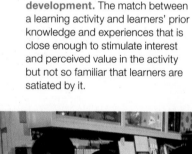

Some experts suggest that a **motivational zone of proximal development** exists (Brophy, 2010). It describes the match between a learning activity and learners' prior knowledge and experiences that is close enough to stimulate interest and perceived value in the activity but not so familiar that learners are satiated by it. For example, multiplying 243 × 694 would not be a motivating task for us, nor would calculating the effects of the moon's perigee and apogee on the earth's tides. The first is so familiar that it's trivial, and the second is too complex and difficult for us to understand or appreciate. Neither falls within our motivational zone of proximal development.

From a sociocultural perspective, our task is to design learning experiences that are familiar enough so our students see their potential value, but not so familiar that they are no longer challenging.

Sociocultural views of motivation suggest that participating in communities of learners can increase students' motivation to learn.

Humanistic Views of Motivation

In the mid-20th century when the "cognitive revolution" in learning was in full swing, a parallel movement called *humanistic psychology* also began. It focuses on the "whole person" and views motivation as people's attempts to fulfill their total potential as human beings and become "self-actualized" (Schunk et al., 2008). According to this view, understanding motivation requires an understanding of people's thoughts, feelings, and actions. Understanding behaviors or even thinking—alone—is not sufficient to understand our students; we need to focus on the total picture, including who they are as human beings (Schunk & Zimmerman, 2006). This perspective remains popular both in schools and in the workplace.

Carl Rogers, a psychologist who founded "person-centered" therapy, and Abraham Maslow, famous for his hierarchy of needs (we discuss his hierarchy in the next section of the chapter), were the two most prominent leaders in the humanistic movement, and both emphasized people's attempts to become self-actualized (Maslow, 1968, 1970; Rogers, 1963).

Rogers believed this actualizing tendency is innately oriented toward competence and autonomy, but experiences in our environment can foster or hinder growth (Rogers & Freiberg, 1994). Important in fostering growth is **unconditional positive regard,** treating students as if they are innately worthy, regardless of their behavior (Rogers & Freiberg, 1994).

Unconditional positive regard. Treating individuals as if they are innately worthy regardless of their behavior.

Unconditional positive regard isn't as simple as it appears. Parents usually feel it for their small children, but as they get older, their regard often becomes "conditional" and depends on factors such as high grades or choosing the right partner or career (Kohn, 2005a). Outside the home, regard is almost always conditional, and in schools, high achievers are regarded more positively than their lower-achieving peers, as are students who are well behaved and who excel in extracurricular activities such as music or sports.

According to Rogers (1963), conditional regard hinders personal growth, and more recent work corroborates his views.

> Students who felt unconditionally accepted by their teachers were more likely to be interested in learning and to enjoy challenging academic tasks, instead of just doing schoolwork because they had to and preferring easier assignments at which they knew they would succeed. (Kohn, 2005b, p. 21)

To see these ideas applied in classrooms, let's return to Kathy's work with her students.

> As she is working after school, Harvey, one of her students, pokes his head into the room.
>
> "Come in," she smiles. "How's our developing writer?"
>
> "I just came by to say I hope you're not upset with me, complaining so much about all the work."
>
> "Not at all. . . . I haven't given it a second thought."
>
> "You already know how much you've done for me. . . . You believed in me when the rest of the world wrote me off. . . . My drug conviction is off my record now, and I'm okay. I couldn't have made it without you. You made me work, and you put in all kinds of extra time with me. You wouldn't let me give up on myself. I was headed for trouble, and now . . . I'm headed for college."
>
> "We all need a nudge now and then," Kathy smiles. "That's what I'm here for. I appreciate your kind words, but I didn't do it; you did. . . . Now, scoot. I'm working on a rough assignment for you tomorrow."
>
> "Mrs. Brewster, you're relentless," Harvey waves as he heads out the door.

Caring teachers who are committed to their students both as people and as learners are essential for motivation and learning (Cornelius-White, 2007). Asking a student to stop by after class because she doesn't seem to be herself is an example, as was separating Harvey's drug conviction from his innate worth as a human being. And research suggests that caring teachers may be particularly important for boys; ". . . boys need to *feel* their teachers—their warmth, their mastery, their inspiration—before opening up to invest themselves in learning" (Reichert, 2010, p. 27).

Kathy also demonstrated that she cared about her students as learners by maintaining high expectations. As you saw in her conversation with Harvey, she pushed him (and all her students), offered evidence of his progress, and emphasized the value of what they were studying.

In the real world, you won't turn every student into a motivated learner. You can make a difference with many, however, and for them, you will have made an immeasurable contribution to their lives.

The theoretical views you've seen here provide the conceptual framework for examining motivation in more detail. Using this framework, we examine the following topics in the next sections:

- *Needs,* such as the need to feel safe, respected by others, and smart.
- *Beliefs* about ourselves and our capacity to learn.
- *Goals,* outcomes we hope to attain.
- *Interests,* our affinity or attraction to certain topics or activities.
- *Emotions,* such as anxiety, fear, pride, or joy.

Each influences motivation to learn, and each is grounded in the theoretical views we've discussed in this section. We begin by examining needs.

---

check your understanding

1.1 Define motivation, and explain how it influences learning.

1.2 Describe how each of the theoretical views explain learner motivation.

To receive feedback for these questions, go to Appendix A.

The Influence of Needs on Motivation to Learn

Ed Psych and You

Think about the number of times you've said something like, "I need to get organized," "I need to lose weight," or simply, "I need to pick up some milk at the store." What role do statements like these play in your own motivation?

Need. An internal force or drive to attain or to avoid a certain state or object.

The notion of *needs* is so pervasive in our lives, and we use the term so often, that we don't think about it, as you see in "Ed Psych and You" here. In motivation theory a **need** is an internal force or drive to attain or to avoid a certain state or object (Schunk et al., 2008), and it makes sense that responding to these needs influences our motivation. For instance, when we say, "I need to get organized," the need pushes us to the desired state—being organized.

Food, water, and sex are considered to be the most basic needs in all species, because they're necessary for survival. Getting them is the force, and survival is the desired state.

In this section we examine the influence of three sets of needs on motivation to learn:

- Maslow's hierarchy of needs
- The need for self-determination
- The need to preserve self-worth

Maslow's Hierarchy of Needs

Earlier we said that humanistic views of motivation emphasize the *whole person*—physical, social, emotional, intellectual, and aesthetic. Maslow's (1968, 1987) hierarchy of needs is grounded in this holistic view of human motivation. As we look at Maslow's hierarchy, outlined in Figure 10.3, we see the needs of the whole person reflected in it. For instance, we see the *physical* person in survival and safety needs, the *social* person in belonging needs, the *emotional* person in self-esteem needs, and the intellectual and aesthetic person in the need for self-actualization.

Let's look at these needs more closely.

Deficiency and Growth Needs

Maslow (1968, 1970) described human needs as existing in two groups. The first, **deficiency needs,** energize people to meet them if they're unfulfilled. *Survival, safety, belonging,* and *self-esteem* are the deficiency needs in the hierarchy, and, according to Maslow, people won't move to a higher need unless the one below it is met. So, for example, if people's safety needs are not being met, they won't move to the need for belonging or any need above it. The arrows extending from one need to another in Figure 10.3 are intended as a visual reminder of this idea.

After all their deficiency needs are met, people can then move to **growth needs,** needs in intellectual achievement and aesthetic appreciation that increase as people have experiences with them. Ultimately, growth can lead to **self-actualization,** reaching our full potential and becoming all that we are capable of being. In contrast with deficiency needs, the need for self-actualization is never satisfied. For instance, as we develop a greater understanding of a certain area, such as literature, our interest in it increases rather than decreases. This helps explain why some people seem to have an insatiable desire for learning or why individuals never tire of fine art or music. Engaging in these activities responds to their need for personal growth, gives them pleasure, and can lead to *peak experiences,* a concept that originated with Maslow.

Evaluating Maslow's Work

Maslow's work has been criticized because little research evidence exists to support his description of needs, and because his work is unable to consistently predict people's behavior (Schunk et al., 2008). For instance, we've all heard about people who have serious illnesses or disabling conditions, suggesting that their survival and safety needs are not being met, yet who accomplish significant intellectual or aesthetic achievements. Maslow's work would predict that this could not happen, because he suggested that people will not move to growth needs unless deficiency needs are met.

On the other hand, Maslow's work is intuitively sensible and appealing. For example, after you first meet someone, you're likely to say, "He seemed really nice," (hopefully not, "Wow, what a jerk"), rather than "He sure seemed smart." We first react to how friendly, outgoing, and "human" people are, not how bright or successful they seem to be. The same likely applies to your instructors; you first notice how personable, supportive, and helpful they are. Maslow's work suggests that personal, social, and emotional needs always precede intellectual ones, and our day-to-day experiences corroborate this suggestion.

Perhaps most important, it makes sense that students are going to learn less if they're hungry or tired, and schools respond by providing free or reduced-cost breakfasts and lunches for them. And research supports the contention that students need to feel safe—both physically and emotionally—if they are to learn as much as possible (Perry et al., 2006). Maslow's work reminds us that the human side of teaching is essential and ignoring it will have a negative impact on both motivation and learning.

The Need for Self-Determination

Self-determination is the need to act on and control one's environment, and having choices and making decisions are intrinsically motivating (R. Ryan & Deci, 2000). According to self-determination theory, people have three innate psychological needs: *competence, autonomy,* and *relatedness* (Levesque, Stanek, Zuehlke, & Ryan, 2004; R. Ryan & Deci, 2000). We examine them next.

THE NEED FOR SELF-ACTUALIZATION
(intellectual achievement, aesthetic appreciation, and reaching one's full potential)

THE NEED FOR SELF-ESTEEM
(recognition and the approval of others)

THE NEED FOR BELONGING
(love and acceptance from others)

THE NEED FOR SAFETY
(freedom from physical and emotional threat)

THE NEED FOR SURVIVAL
(shelter, food, water, warmth)

Figure 10.3 Maslow's hierarchy of needs

Source: Adapted figure from "Maslow's Hierarchy of Needs" from MOTIVATION AND PERSONALITY, 3rd Edition by Abraham H. Maslow, Edited by Robert D. Frager and James Fadiman. Copyright © 1978 by Abraham H. Maslow, Robert D. Frager, and James Fadiman. Printed and Electronically reproduced by permission of Pearson Education, Inc., Upper Saddle River, New Jersey.

Deficiency needs. Needs that energize people to meet them if they're unfulfilled.

Growth needs. Needs in intellectual achievement and aesthetic appreciation that increase as people have experiences with them.

Self-actualization. Reaching one's full potential and becoming all that we are capable of being.

Self-determination. The need to act on and control one's environment.

Meeting challenges provides evidence that competence is increasing and helps meet students' need for self-determination.

Competence. The ability to function effectively in the environment.

Autonomy. Independence and the ability to alter the environment when necessary.

The Need for Competence

As you interact with people, think about the number of times they attempt to demonstrate how much they know about a topic or how good they are at some skill. We all want to be "smart." Self-determination theory explains these efforts by saying that we are attempting to meet our need for **competence,** the ability to function effectively in the environment. The need for competence was originally described by Robert White (1959) in a paper that has become a classic. He suggested that people acquire proficiency and skill "because it satisfies an intrinsic need to deal with the environment" (p. 318).

Our need for competence can be explained at several levels. Most basic, for instance, if an organism can't function effectively in its environment, it isn't likely to survive (Schunk et al., 2008). Competent people succeed and grow in their careers, whereas those less competent languish and stagnate, and competent students are successful learners who find school satisfying and rewarding (Morgan & Fuchs, 2007).

Evidence that their knowledge and skills are increasing is the most important factor influencing students' perception of competence, and this helps explain why praise for genuine accomplishment, high teacher expectations, challenging activities and those that evoke curiosity are intrinsically motivating. The praise, meeting expectations and challenges, and understanding novel or puzzling experiences provide evidence that our competence is increasing. In contrast, completing trivial tasks, solving predictable problems, and receiving grades that haven't been earned provide little evidence about competence, so they often detract from motivation.

The Need for Autonomy

Do you prefer to study at home, in the library, or perhaps in a coffee shop? Would you rebel if someone dictated to you the number of hours you had to study and where you had to do your studying? These questions relate to **autonomy,** independence and the ability to alter the environment when necessary. It is the second innate need described by self-determination theory, and lack of autonomy reduces intrinsic motivation and causes stress. For instance, it is widely believed that the stress of assembly line work results from workers' having little control over their environments (Lundberg, Granqvist, Hansson, Magnusson, & Wallin, 1989).

Giving our students choices is the simplest way that we can increase their perceptions of autonomy. For example, Kathy gave her students the choice of writing a paper on the Middle Ages or making a presentation on the Renaissance, and she also let them decide the order of their presentations. Providing choices often isn't possible, however, but we can enhance perceptions of autonomy in other ways, such as the following:

- Solicit student input in creating classroom rules and procedures.
- Encourage students to set and monitor their own learning goals.
- Emphasize the impact of effort and strategy use, and deemphasize the influence of ability on achievement.
- Use assessments that provide feedback and focus on learning progress.
- Create high levels of involvement in learning activities so students have opportunities to express opinions and contribute ideas.

Autonomy and competence are strongly related. As learners' competence increases, so do their perceptions of autonomy (Bruning, Shraw, & Norby, 2011). So, if we can help students feel competent, we also help them feel autonomous, and we increase both motivation and learning.

The Need for Relatedness

Relatedness, the feeling of being connected to others in one's social environment and feeling worthy of love and respect, is the third innate need described by self-determination theory. Relatedness and Maslow's concept of *belonging* are often treated synonymously (Juvonen, 2006), and the need for relatedness is also similar to the need for *affiliation* as described by early motivational researchers (e.g., Exline, 1962; Terhune, 1968).

The need for relatedness can sometimes have unintended consequences when students develop an unhealthy **need for approval,** the desire to be accepted and judged positively by others (Urdan & Maehr, 1995). Children in elementary schools generally seek the approval of their teachers, but older students with a strong need for approval often have low self-esteem and engage in activities primarily to get praise (Davis, 2003). If the need becomes excessive, they often fear rejection and easily submit to peer pressure. These efforts can be counterproductive, however, because students with excessive needs for approval tend to be unpopular with their peers (Rudolph, Caldwell, & Conley, 2005).

We can help meet students' needs for relatedness and approval by communicating unconditional positive regard and a genuine commitment to their learning. Students are more engaged—behaviorally, cognitively, and emotionally—in classroom activities when they believe their teachers understand, like, and empathize with them. They also report more interest in their class work, behave in more socially responsible ways, and are more likely to seek help when they need it (Cornelius-White, 2007; Marchand & Skinner, 2007).

Self-determination theory explains a number of school-related phenomena. As students' perceptions of self-determination increase, they are more likely to be intrinsically motivated and finish school (Eisenman, 2007), their literacy improves (Crow, 2007), and they even develop a more active lifestyle (Bryan & Solmon, 2007). As teachers, we can contribute to our students' sense of self-determination through our assessment practices, the topic of the next section.

Assessment and Learning: The Role of Assessment in Self-Determination

As we have emphasized throughout this book, assessment is an essential part of the learning–teaching process. This raises an issue, however, because some people believe that evaluating students detracts from their self-determination and intrinsic motivation. And research supports this view if students view assessments as punitive or controlling (Deci & Ryan, 1987).

If assessment is handled properly, however, precisely the opposite is true; assessments that provide information about increasing competence enhance both learning and motivation (Rohrer & Pashler, 2010).

Some suggestions for using assessments to increase self-determination include the following (Schunk et al., 2008; Stipek, 2002):

- Provide clear expectations for students, and ensure that assessments are consistent with the expectations.
- Assess frequently and thoroughly, and emphasize the assessments' learning benefits.
- Provide detailed feedback about responses to assessments, and emphasize the reasons for answers as much as the answers themselves.
- Avoid social comparisons in communicating assessment results.
- Drop one or two of students' lowest test or quiz scores for purposes of grading.

Perceptions of autonomy are increased when expectations are clear and assessments are consistent with them. Assessing frequently, providing detailed feedback about increasing competence, avoiding social comparisons, and dropping one or two quizzes for purposes of grading all communicate that learning is the primary purpose of assessment. Establishing a climate that focuses on learning and increased competence should be our goal when we assess student achievement (Stiggins, 2007).

Relatedness. The feeling of being connected to others in one's social environment and feeling worthy of love and respect.

Need for approval. The desire to be accepted and judged positively by others.

The Need to Preserve Self-Worth

The need to preserve our self-worth provides us with another perspective on motivation. For example, consider the following.

> "I'm a genius; I'm a genius," Andrew, an eighth grader enthusiastically shouts to his mom as he bounces into the house after school. "I got a 97 on my history test, and I didn't study a lick. I'm a genius; I'm a genius."

Self-worth. An emotional reaction to or an evaluation of the self.

We can explain Andrew's behavior using the concept of **self-worth** (or self-esteem, as it is more commonly called), which is an emotional reaction to or an evaluation of the self (Schunk et al., 2008). Self-worth theorists suggest that people have an innate need to protect their sense of self-worth and accept themselves as they are. As you saw earlier, we all have a basic need for competence, which is often reflected in our efforts to "look smart." We appear to have higher ability—look smarter—if we're able to accomplish tasks without having to work hard (Covington, 1992). So, by emphasizing that he got his high score without studying, Andrew was attempting to communicate that he had high ability, which enhanced his feelings of self-worth.

Some interesting developmental patterns in learners' perceptions of effort and ability exist. For instance, when asked, most kindergarteners say they're smart. Young children assume that people who try hard are smart, and people who are smart try hard (Stipek, 2002). However, as students move through school, they begin to equate effort with low ability, and simultaneously their need to appear "smart" increases. For instance, we've all heard statements such as, "He isn't all that sharp, but he really works hard."

Because of their need to be perceived as high ability, older students may hide the fact that they've studied hard for a test, for example, so if they do well, they can, at least in the eyes of their peers, attribute their success to being smart. Others engage in "self-handicapping" strategies to protect their self-worth, such as procrastinating ("I could have done a lot better, but I didn't start studying until after midnight"), making excuses ("This test was so tricky"), anxiety ("I understand the stuff, but I get nervous in tests"), or making a point of not trying. If they didn't try, failure isn't evidence of low ability (Covington, 1998; Wolters, 2003). Self-handicapping behaviors have been found in a range of academic areas including even physical education (Standage, Treasure, Hooper, & Kuczka, 2007). They are most common in low achievers, who often choose to not seek help when it's needed (Marchand & Skinner, 2007).

We examine ways that you can respond to these tendencies in our next "Ed Psych and Teaching" feature, "Using the Influence of Needs to Increase Your Students' Motivation to Learn."

Ed psych and teaching

Using the Influence of Needs to Increase Your Students' Motivation to Learn

Understanding learners' needs has important implications for us as we attempt to increase our students' motivation. The following guidelines can help you in your efforts to apply this understanding with your students.

1. To meet students' needs for belonging and relatedness, treat them as people first.
2. Help meet students' needs for competence by maintaining high expectations and providing evidence of increasing competence.
3. Address students' needs for autonomy by giving them input into decisions and offering them choices when possible.
4. Model and emphasize the belief that effort increases both ability and a sense of self-worth.
5. Avoid all social comparisons among students.

Let's review Kathy's work with her students to see how she applied these guidelines. She applied the first two in the way she interacted with Harvey before her class. First, she treated him with the unconditional positive regard that helped him meet his needs for belonging and relatedness, and second, her comment, "Look how good you're getting at writing. . . . You're becoming a very good writer," provided evidence that his competence was increasing. This evidence is particularly significant because Harvey viewed the assignment as difficult. Success on trivial tasks does little to increase learners' perceptions of competence or self-actualization.

Third, Kathy gave her students the choice of writing a paper or making a group presentation and deciding the order of the presentations. These choices, combined with their increasing competence, contributed to their perceptions of autonomy.

Kathy applied the fourth guideline with her modeling. When she said, "I study every night to keep up with you people, and the harder I study, the smarter I get. . . . And I feel good about myself when I do," she modeled the belief that effort increased both ability and a sense of self-worth.

Finally, when she said, "Remember, we're all doing our best; we're not competing with each other," she emphasized effort and competence, de-emphasized social comparisons, and applied the fifth guideline.

As with all suggestions, these guidelines won't work all the time or with all students. However, the applications can make a difference, which increases the likelihood of increased motivation and learning for many.

---

check your understanding

2.1 Explain how learners' needs, as described in Maslow's hierarchy, can influence their motivation to learn.

2.2 Explain how learners' needs for competence, autonomy, and relatedness can influence their motivation to learn.

2.3 Explain how learners' need to preserve their sense of self-worth can influence their motivation to learn.

To receive feedback for these questions, go to Appendix A.

Classroom connections

Capitalizing on Students' Needs to Increase Motivation in Classrooms

Maslow's Hierarchy of Needs

1. Maslow described people's needs in a hierarchy with deficiency needs—survival, safety, belonging, and self-esteem—preceding the growth needs. Address students' deficiency and growth needs both in instruction and in the way you interact with students.

   ■ **Elementary:** A fourth-grade teacher calls on all students to promote a sense of belonging in his classroom. He makes them feel safe by helping them respond correctly when they are unable to answer.

   ■ **Middle School:** To help meet learners' belonging needs, a seventh-grade teacher asks two of the more popular girls in her class to introduce a new girl to other students and to take her under their wings until she gets acquainted.

   ■ **High School:** To address learners' growth needs, an American government teacher brings in a newspaper columnist's political opinion piece, comments that it was interesting to her, and asks students for their opinions on the issue.

Learners' Needs for Self-Determination

2. Self-determination theory suggests that people have innate needs for competence, autonomy, and relatedness. Design challenging tasks that, when completed, can provide evidence for increasing competence, and emphasize these accomplishments when students succeed.

   ■ **Elementary:** A fifth-grade teacher drops an ice cube into a cup of water and a second cube into a cup of alcohol. He guides students' efforts until they solve the problem and then praises them for their thinking.

   ■ **Middle School:** A math teacher has students bring in a challenging "problem of the week." He helps them solve the problem and comments on how much their problem solving is improving.

   ■ **High School:** A biology teacher guides a discussion of our skeletal system until the students understand the function of the skull, rib cage, and other bones, and then comments on how good the students are getting at analyzing our body systems.

3. Learners' perceptions of autonomy increase when teachers ask them for input into classroom procedures, involve them in learning activities, and give them feedback on assessments. Create a classroom environment that helps meet learners' needs for autonomy.

   ■ **Elementary:** A fourth-grade teacher holds periodic class meetings in which she encourages students to offer suggestions for improving the classroom environment.

   ■ **Middle School:** A prealgebra teacher returns all tests and quizzes the following day and discusses frequently missed problems in detail. He comments on students' continually improving skills.

   ■ **High School:** A world history teacher asks students to identify specific archeological evidence for sites that represent different civilizations. She comments that the students' ability to link evidence to conclusions has improved significantly.

4. Learners' needs for relatedness are met when teachers communicate a commitment to students both as people and as learners.

   ■ **Elementary:** A first-grade teacher greets her students each morning at the door with a hug, "high five," or handshake. She tells them what a good day they're going to have.

■ **Middle School:** A seventh-grade teacher calls a parent to express concern about a student whose behavior and attitude seems to have changed.

■ **High School:** A geometry teacher in an urban school conducts help sessions after school on Mondays through Thursdays. She also encourages students to talk about their personal lives and their hopes for the future.

Learners' Needs to Preserve Self-Worth

5. Self-worth theory suggests that people link self worth to high ability. Emphasize that ability can be increased with effort.

■ **Elementary:** When her second graders succeed with word problems during their seatwork, a teacher comments, "You're really understanding what we're doing. The harder we work, the smarter we get."

■ **Middle School:** A life-science teacher comments, "You're really seeing the connections between animals' body structures and their ability to adapt. I'm sure you're feeling good about yourselves."

■ **High School:** As students' understanding of balancing equations increases, a chemistry teacher comments, "You people are really getting good at this stuff."

The Influence of Beliefs on Motivation to Learn

Student beliefs about their abilities in different academic areas can also influence their motivation to learn. To see how, look at the following statements and think about what they tell us about each person's motivation.

1. "If I study hard for the next test, I'm going to do well."
2. "Learning a foreign language doesn't come naturally for me, but with some more work, I'm going to be good at it by the end of the year."
3. "I'm not that crazy about algebra, but I need to get good at it. I want to major in engineering in college, and I know I'll need it."

Belief. A cognitive idea we accept as true without necessarily having definitive evidence to support it.

Each of these statements describes a **belief,** a cognitive idea we accept as true without necessarily having definitive evidence to support it. In this section we examine the influence of the following beliefs on motivation to learn:

- Expectations: Beliefs about future outcomes
- Beliefs about intelligence
- Self-efficacy: Beliefs about our capabilities
- Beliefs about the value of an activity
- Attributions: Beliefs about the causes of our performance

Ed Psych and You

Do you like to play games? Do you like playing all games or only certain ones? Why do you enjoy playing some and not others? Is succeeding in some games more important to you than succeeding in others?

Expectations: Beliefs About Outcomes

Look again at our first statement: "If I study hard for the next test, I'm going to do well." It describes an **expectation,** a belief about a future outcome (Schunk & Zimmerman, 2006). The influence of expectations on motivation can be described using **expectancy × value theory,** which states that people are motivated to engage in a task to the extent that they expect to succeed on the task *times* the value they place on the success (Wigfield & Eccles, 1992, 2000). (We examine the influence of task value on motivation later in this section.) The × is important because anything times zero is zero. So, if learners don't expect to succeed, their motivation will be low regardless of how much they value the activity (Tollefson, 2000). This relates to the questions in our "Ed Psych and You" feature here. Most people don't enjoy all games, and the games they enjoy the most are the ones in which they generally succeed, winning more often than not. Their expectations for success are quite high, or they quit playing. It's a unique person who continues to play a game he or she rarely wins.

Students with high expectations for success persist longer on tasks, choose more challenging activities, and achieve more than those whose expectations are lower (Eccles et al., 1998; Wigfield, 1994).

Past experience is the primary factor influencing expectations. Students who usually succeed expect to succeed in the future, and the opposite is true for those who are unsuccessful. This helps us understand why promoting motivation to learn is such a challenge when working with low achievers. Because they have a history of failure, their motivation to learn is low as a result of low expectations for success. This, combined with learners' needs to preserve their sense of self-worth, creates a problem that is doubly difficult for teachers.

The only way you can increase motivation to learn in students whose expectations for success are low is to design learning experiences so they're successful. This is, of course, an enormous challenge, but in time, and with effort, it can be done.

Beliefs About Intelligence

To begin this section, let's look at the words of an eighth-grader, Sarah, as she talks about her ability in math:

> My brother, I, and my mom aren't good at math at all, we inherited the "not good at math gene" from my mom and I am good at English, but I am not good at math. (K. E. Ryan, Ryan, Arbuthnot, & Samuels, 2007, p. 5)

Sarah is describing an **entity view of intelligence**, the belief that intelligence is essentially fixed and stable over time (Dweck, 2006). According to Sarah, "some have it and some don't," and there is little she can do about it.

Compare this view with our second statement at the beginning of this section: "Learning a foreign language doesn't come naturally for me, but with some more work, I'm going to be good at it by the end of the year." This statement reflects an **incremental view of intelligence**, the belief that intelligence, or ability, can be increased with effort.

Beliefs about intelligence help us understand why learners sometimes engage in self-handicapping behaviors to protect their self-worth. Failure suggests a lack of ability, so if they believe it's fixed, they protect their self-worth by avoiding situations that reflect negatively on their ability, and motivation and learning decrease.

On the other hand, if learners believe that ability can be increased with effort, difficulty and failure merely suggest that more effort or better strategies are needed. As a result, their motivation and learning increase, and their success provides evidence that their ability is increasing (Schunk & Zimmerman, 2006).

Emphasizing and modeling incremental views of intelligence are the most effective strategies we have for changing students' beliefs about ability. For example, in the opening case study, Kathy commented to Harvey, "I wish. I study every night to keep up with you people, and the harder I study, the smarter I get."

Self-Efficacy: Beliefs About Capability

To begin this section, let's look again at the conversation between Melanie and Yelena, which introduced the discussion of cognitive theories of motivation.

Expectation. A belief about a future outcome. The influence of expectations on motivation is often described using expectancy × value theory.

Expectancy × value theory. A theory that explains motivation by saying that learners will be motivated to engage in a task to the extent that they expect to succeed on a task *times* the value they place on the success.

Entity view of intelligence. The belief that intelligence is essentially fixed and stable over time.

Incremental view of intelligence. The belief that intelligence, or ability, is not stable and can be increased with effort.

Students are more likely to believe that ability can be increased with effort if teachers model incremental views of intelligence.

"C'mon, let's go," Melanie urges her friend Yelena as they're finishing a series of home-work problems in math.

"Just a sec," Yelena mutters. "I'm not quite getting this one."

"Let's work on it tonight. Everybody's leaving," Melanie urges.

"Go ahead, I'll catch up to you in a minute. I know that I can figure this out. . . . I just don't get it right now."

Self-efficacy. The belief that one is capable of accomplishing a specific task.

Yelena's statement illustrates **self-efficacy,** the belief that one is capable of accomplishing a specific task (Bandura, 1997, 2004). Yelena believes she is capable of solving this problem if she perseveres. *Self-efficacy, self-concept,* and *expectation for success* are closely related, but they aren't synonymous (Schunk, 2008). For example, if Yelena believes she is generally competent in math, we would say that she has a positive math self-concept. Self-efficacy is more specific. She believes she can solve this problem and those similar to it, but it doesn't mean that she believes she will succeed in all forms of math or in other domains, such as writing essays. Also, believing she can solve problems such as this one isn't identical to her expectations for success. For example, even though she believes she can solve problems like this one, she won't expect to succeed on her next math quiz if she doesn't do her homework and study.

Self-efficacy depends on four factors (see Figure 10.4). Past performance on similar tasks is the most important. If you have a history of success giving oral reports in your classes, for example, your self-efficacy in this area will be high. Modeling, such as seeing others deliver excellent reports, can also increase your self-efficacy by raising expectations and providing information about the way a skill should be performed (Bandura, 1997; Kitsantas, Zimmerman, & Cleary, 2000).

Although limited in effectiveness, verbal persuasion, such as a teacher's comment, "I know you will give a fine report," can increase self-efficacy by encouraging students to attempt challenging tasks, which increases efficacy if they succeed.

Finally, students' emotional state as well as physiological factors, such as fatigue or hunger, can also influence self-efficacy. If they're anxious, for example, their working memories might be filled with thoughts of failure, so they're less likely to succeed, and self-efficacy then decreases. Or, if they're too tired to study, their self-efficacy is likely to be temporarily reduced.

Self-efficacy strongly influences motivation to learn. Compared to low-efficacy students, high-efficacy learners accept more challenging tasks, exert more effort, persist longer, use more effective strategies, and generally perform better (Bandura, 1997; Schunk & Ertmer, 2000).

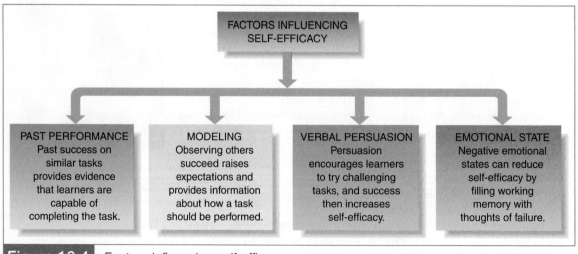

Figure 10.4 Factors influencing self-efficacy

Because of its influence on motivation, increasing our students' self-efficacy is one of our most important goals, and modeling and effective instruction are our most effective tools. When we model effective study strategies, involve students in learning activities, thoroughly assess understanding, and provide detailed feedback, we promote the success that contributes to self-efficacy. Ultimately, we ". . . help them to appreciate that they are developing their abilities by accepting challenges and applying consistent effort" (Brophy, 2010, p. 53).

Beliefs About Value

Value refers to the benefits, rewards, or advantages that individuals believe can result from participating in an activity, and it is the second component of expectancy × value theory.

Three types of values influence motivation (Wigfield & Eccles, 2000, 2002):

- Attainment value
- Utility value
- Cost

Value. The benefits, rewards, or advantages that individuals believe can result from participating in an activity.

Attainment Value. To understand attainment value, let's think about the last question we asked in our "Ed Psych and You" feature earlier: "Is succeeding in some games more important to you than succeeding in others?" The answer is almost certainly "yes," and success is more important to you if you believe you're good at the game. This relates to **attainment value,** the importance an individual attaches to doing well on a task (Wigfield & Eccles, 2000, 2002). For example, it's important to Don that he swims his laps in a certain amount of time, because he believes he's a good swimmer, and winning in tennis is important to Paul because he (perhaps naively) believes he's a good tennis player. Succeeding validates their beliefs about their ability (Anderman & Wolters, 2006). On the other hand, winning at chess isn't important to them, since neither believes he's a good chess player.

Attainment value. The importance an individual attaches to doing well on a task.

Utility value. The belief that a topic, activity, or course of study will be useful for meeting future goals, including career goals.

Cost. The consideration of what a person must give up to engage in an activity.

Utility Value. Now, think about your study of educational psychology and this book. We hope you view it as interesting for its own sake, but perhaps more importantly, we want you to believe that understanding its content will make you a better teacher. If you do, it has high **utility value,** the belief that a topic, activity, or course of study will be useful for meeting future goals, including career goals (Wigfield & Eccles, 1992). Believing that studying educational psychology will make you a better professional increases its utility value and your motivation to study educational psychology.

Believing that a topic, activity, or course of study will be useful for meeting future goals can increase motivation to learn.

Cost. Have you ever dropped a class because your workload was too heavy? Many of us have, and we can explain why using the concept of **cost,** the consideration of what a person must give up to engage in an activity (Wigfield & Eccles, 2002). In the case of an impossible workload, the cost is too high, so you're not motivated to continue in the class.

Beliefs about outcomes (expectations), intelligence, capability (self-efficacy), and value help us understand why our students are likely to engage in and persevere on tasks. Their beliefs about their performances and why they perform the way they do can also influence their motivation. This leads us to a discussion of attributions.

Attributions: Beliefs About Causes of Performance

When you succeed on a task, why are you successful? If you don't succeed, why not? The explanations we offer for our successes and failures influence our motivation, and to see how, let's look at four students' reactions to the results of a test.

"How'd you do, Bob?" Anne asks.

"Terrible," Bob answers sheepishly. "I just can't do this stuff. I'm no good at essay tests. . . . I'll never get it."

"I didn't do so good either," Anne replies, "but I knew I wouldn't. I just didn't study hard enough. I won't let that happen again."

"Unbelievable!" Armondo adds. "I didn't know what the heck was going on, and I got a B. I really lucked out. I don't think she read mine."

"I think the test was too tough," Ashley shakes her head. "I looked at the test, and just went blank. All I could think of was, 'I've never seen this stuff before. Where did it come from?' I thought I was going to throw up."

Attributions. Explanations, or beliefs, related to the causes of performance.

Attribution theory. A cognitive theory of motivation that attempts to systematically describe learners' beliefs about the causes of their successes and failures and how these beliefs influence motivation to learn.

The students are offering **attributions,** explanations, or beliefs related to the causes of their performance. Bob, for example, believed that his poor performance resulted from lack of ability, whereas Ann believed that lack of effort caused hers. Armondo believed he was successful because he was lucky, and Ashley thought the test was too hard. **Attribution theory** attempts to systematically describe learners' beliefs about the causes of their successes and failures and how these beliefs influence motivation to learn. *Ability, effort, luck,* and *task difficulty* are the attributions learners most commonly offer for school success and failure, but others, such as effective or ineffective learning strategies, lack of help, interest, unfair teacher practices, or clarity of instruction are also cited (Weiner, 1992, 2001).

Attributions influence learners in three ways (Weiner, 2000, 2001):

- Emotional reactions to success and failure
- Expectations for future success
- Future effort

To see how these influences work, let's look at Anne's and Bob's attributions again. Anne attributed her poor score to lack of effort. She was responsible for her effort, so guilt was her emotional reaction. Her comment, "I won't let that happen again," suggests that she will increase her effort. As a result, she will expect to succeed, and improved achievement is likely.

Bob attributed his failure to lack of ability. He has an entity view of intelligence, as indicated by his comment, "I'm no good at essay tests. . . . I'll never get it." So, instead of guilt, his emotional reaction is embarrassment and shame, since he views himself as having low ability. His comment, "I'll never get it," suggests that he doesn't expect future success, so both his effort and achievement are likely to decrease (We ask you to analyze Armondo's and Ashley's reactions in "Check Your Understanding," question 3.3 at the end of this section.)

Motivation tends to increase when students attribute failure to lack of effort, as Anne did, or ineffective strategies, because effort and strategy use can be controlled, whereas it tends to decrease when they attribute failure to causes they can't control, such as luck or ability if they believe ability is fixed (Weinstock, 2007).

Learned Helplessness

Learned helplessness. The debilitating belief that one is incapable of accomplishing tasks and has little control of the environment.

If attributing failure to lack of ability becomes a pattern, **learned helplessness,** the debilitating belief that one is incapable of accomplishing tasks and has little control of the environment, can result. Bob's comment, "I just can't do this stuff. . . . I'll never get it," indicates that he is a potential candidate for learned helplessness. Concluding, "I'll never get it," can result in overwhelming feelings of shame and self-doubt and giving up without trying.

Learned helplessness has both an affective and a cognitive component. Students with learned helplessness have low self-esteem and often suffer from anxiety and depression (Graham & Weiner, 1996). Cognitively, they expect to fail, so they exert little effort and use ineffective strategies, which result in less success and an even greater expectation for failure (Dweck, 2000). Fortunately, efforts to intervene through attribution training have been successful.

Attribution Training

Learners can improve the effectiveness of their attributions with training (Robertson, 2000). In a pioneering study, Carol Dweck (1975) provided students who demonstrated learned helplessness with both successful and unsuccessful experiences. When the students were unsuccessful, the experimenter specifically stated that the failure was caused by lack of effort or ineffective strategies. Comparable students were given similar experiences but no training. After the training, learners responded more positively to failure by persisting longer and adapting their strategies more effectively. More recent research has corroborated Dweck's findings (Schunk et al., 2008).

You can promote productive attributions in all your students by encouraging them to attribute their successes to effort and competence and their failures to lack of effort or ineffective strategies. You can also teach and model effective strategies, which is particularly effective for students who believe they are already trying hard. And, as students see their competence increase, their motivation to learn will also increase.

This section also suggests that we should examine our own beliefs about teaching and learning. If, for example, we believe that students respond primarily to reinforcers and punishers, we will design learning experiences that allow us to reinforce our students. On the other hand, if we believe that our students are thinking beings, we will design learning experiences that allow them to see that their competence and self-efficacy are increasing, and we will encourage healthy attributions for their successes and failures.

---

check your understanding

3.1 Explain how learners' beliefs can influence their motivation to learn.

3.2 Look again at the third example that introduced our discussion of beliefs, "I'm not that crazy about algebra, but I need to get good at it. I want to major in engineering in college, and I know I'll need it." Explain how this statement influences motivation to learn, and what theory of motivation it best illustrates.

3.3 Look again at the conversation among the four students at the beginning of our discussion of attribution theory. Explain Armondo's emotional reactions, expectations for future success, future effort, and achievement, based on attributing his success to luck. Then, explain Ashley's reactions based on attributing her failure to task difficulty.

To receive feedback for these questions, go to Appendix A.

Classroom connections

Using Students' Beliefs to Increase Their Motivation

1. Expectations are beliefs about future outcomes, and self-efficacy describes beliefs about our capability to accomplish specific tasks. Develop expectations for success and self-efficacy by providing enough scaffolding to ensure that students make progress on challenging tasks.

   ■ **Elementary:** A fourth-grade teacher presents students with a word problem, has them try it, and then provides enough guidance so they are successful in solving it.

   ■ **Middle School:** A seventh-grade English teacher has his students write paragraphs, and he then displays some of them on the document camera and makes suggestions for improvement.

■ **High School:** An art teacher has students keep a portfolio of their work. She periodically asks them to review their products to see evidence of progress.

2. Learners with incremental views of intelligence believe that ability can increase with effort. Emphasize incremental views of intelligence with your students.

■ **Elementary:** After her students have solved a series of word problems, a second-grade teacher comments, "See how our work is paying off. When we work hard, we get smarter."

■ **Middle School:** A seventh-grade geography history teacher says, "Your efforts to understand how geography influences countries' economies and politics are really helping. I tell the other teachers what geography experts I have in my class."

■ **High School:** A chemistry teacher emphasizes that he studies every night. "The harder I work, the smarter I get," he smiles. "And, you can do the same thing."

3. Utility value is the belief that a topic or activity will be useful for meeting future goals. Emphasize the utility value of the topics students study.

■ **Elementary:** A fifth-grade teacher emphasizes the importance of understanding our bodies so we can make good decisions about keeping our bodies healthy.

■ **Middle School:** A seventh-grade math teacher working on percentage problems brings in newspaper advertisements for marked-down products. The class determines the actual reduction in cost, and the teacher then emphasizes the value of understanding how much people save in promotions.

■ **High School:** An English teacher displays examples of well-written (and not so well-written) attempts to make and defend an argument. She uses the examples to emphasize the value of being able to express oneself clearly.

4. Attributions describe beliefs about causes of performance. Model and encourage students to attribute success to increasing competence and failure to lack of effort or ineffective strategies.

■ **Elementary:** As his students initially work on word problems, a second-grade teacher carefully monitors student effort during seatwork. When he sees assignments that indicate effort, he makes comments to individual students, such as "Your work is improving all the time."

■ **Middle School:** A sixth-grade English teacher comments, "I wasn't good at grammar for a long time. But I kept trying, and I found that I could do it. You can become good too, but you have to work at it."

■ **High School:** A chemistry teacher comments, "The way we're attacking balancing equations is working much better, isn't it? You tried to memorize the steps before, and now you're understanding what you're doing."

The Influence of Goals on Motivation to Learn

To begin this section, let's examine the thinking of several of Kathy's students as they prepare their group presentations on the Renaissance.

Susan: This should be interesting. I don't know much about the Renaissance, and it began a whole new emphasis on learning all over the world. Mrs. Brewster has given us a lot of responsibility, so we need to come through. We need to make a presentation she'll like.

Damien: I'll get my Dad to help us. He's really up on history. Our presentation will be the best one of the bunch, and the class will be impressed.

Sylvia: Yikes! Everyone in my group is so smart. What can I do? They'll think I'm the dumbest one. I'm going to just stay quiet when we're working together.

Charlotte: This should be fun. We can get together to work on this at one of our houses. If we can get the project out of the way quickly, I might have time to get to know Damien better.

Antonio: I don't know anything about this. I'd better do some studying so my group will think I'm pulling my weight.

Patrick: I like group activities. They're usually easy. Somebody is always gung ho and does most of the work.

Goal. An outcome an individual hopes to attain.

Each of the students' thinking reflects a **goal,** an outcome an individual hopes to attain (Anderman & Wolters, 2006). Susan's was to understand the Renaissance and please Mrs. Brewster, Charlotte wanted to socialize, and Patrick simply wanted to do as little work as possible. These different goal orientations will influence both their motivation and learning, as we'll see in the next section.

Mastery and Performance Goals

Much of the research examining goals has focused on differences between **mastery goals** (sometimes called *learning goals*)—goals that focus on accomplishing tasks, improving, and increasing understanding—and **performance goals**—goals that focus on ability and how learners compare to others (Midgley, 2001). For instance, Susan's desire to understand the Renaissance is a mastery goal. Students with a mastery orientation persist in the face of challenge and difficulty, attribute success to effort, use effective strategies (such as self-questioning), and maintain their interest and effort even after formal instruction is finished (Wolters, 2003).

In comparison, the questions in "Ed Psych and You" here relate to performance goals, and if you answered yes to the first one, you're typical. Because ability becomes increasingly important to students as they get older, they want to know how they perform compared to others, which explains why you want to know. Teachers often contribute to this orientation by posting distributions of scores on tests, or using course management systems that display class averages. While some performance orientation in students is inevitable, performance goals are less effective than mastery goals. Let's see why.

Performance goals exist in two forms (Elliot & Thrash, 2001). **Performance-approach goals** emphasize looking competent and receiving favorable judgments from others. Damien's wanting to make the best presentation and impress the class is an example. Students with performance-approach goals tend to be confident and have high self-efficacy, but they may exert only minimal effort or use superficial strategies, such as memorization, to reach them. When goals become challenging, they may engage in self-handicapping behaviors, such as not trying when they're not sure they can meet the goals, or even cheat (Brophy, 2010; Midgley, Kaplan, & Middleton, 2001).

Sylvia's thinking, "They'll think I'm the dumbest one. I'm going to just stay quiet when we're working together," reflects a **performance-avoidance goal,** an attempt to avoid looking incompetent and being judged unfavorably, and this is the most detrimental for motivation and achievement (K. E. Ryan et al., 2007). Students who attempt to avoid looking incompetent tend to have low self-efficacy, lack self-confidence, and experience anxiety about tests and other assessments (Midgley et al., 2001). They often try to avoid tasks that will help them master new skills. For example, Sylvia only wanted to avoid looking "dumb" to the other students; learning was essentially irrelevant to her.

Students with an entity view of intelligence tend to adopt performance goals, whereas those with incremental views are more apt to adopt mastery goals (Dweck, 1999, 2006). This makes sense. For example, making the best presentation in the class—a performance goal—could be interpreted as an indicator of high ability, which is important for individuals who view intelligence as fixed. This can be a problem, however, because we all periodically fail, and failure is an indicator of low ability. In contrast, individuals with an incremental view are more likely to seek challenge and persevere, because failure merely indicates that more work is required, and, as competence increases, so does intelligence.

Social Goals

Let's look at the students' thinking again. Charlotte, for example, thought, "If we can get the project out of the way quickly, I might have time to get to know Damien better," and Antonio decided, "I don't know anything about this. I'd better do some studying so my group will think I'm pulling my weight." Both are **social goals,** goals to achieve particular

Mastery goal. A goal that focuses on accomplishing a task, improving, and increasing understanding.

Performance goal. A goal that focuses on demonstrating ability and competence and how learners compare to others.

Performance-approach goal. A goal that emphasizes looking competent and receiving favorable judgments from others.

Performance-avoidance goal. A goal that emphasizes attempts to avoid looking incompetent and being judged unfavorably.

Social goals. Goals to achieve particular social outcomes or interactions.

Motivation and achievement are highest when students have both mastery and social-responsibility goals.

social outcomes or interactions (Wentzel, 2002). More specifically, Antonio had a *social-responsibility* goal. Other social goals include

- Forming friendships.
- Gaining teacher or peer approval.
- Meeting social obligations.
- Assisting and supporting others.
- Underachieving to make others feel better (Davis, 2003; Wentzel, 2000).

Social goals can both increase and decrease motivation to learn (Horst et al., 2007). For instance, Charlotte's wanting to "get the project out of the way quickly," detracted from her motivation. As we would expect, low achievers report this orientation more often than do high achievers (Wentzel, 1999). On the other hand, social-responsibility goals, such as Antonio's, are associated with both high motivation and achievement (Wentzel, 1996).

Motivation to learn is highest when mastery and social-responsibility goals are combined (Wentzel, 2000). This is illustrated in Susan's thinking, "This should be interesting. I don't know much about the Renaissance" (a mastery goal) and, "Mrs. Brewster has given us a lot of responsibility, so we need to come through. We need to make a presentation she'll like" (a social-responsibility goal).

Work-Avoidance Goals

Patrick's comment, "I like group activities. They're usually easy. Somebody is always gung ho and does most of the work," indicates a work-avoidance goal. Students with these goals feel successful when tasks are easy or can be completed with little effort (Dowson & McInerney, 2001). They also tend to use ineffective learning strategies, make minimal contributions to group activities, ask for help even when they don't need it, and complain about challenging activities. Not surprisingly, students like Patrick are a source of frustration for teachers.

Table 10.1 summarizes the different types of goals and their influence on motivation and achievement.

Goals and Motivation: Implications for Teachers

You obviously can't adapt to each student's goal orientation, and, unfortunately, as students progress through school, their performance orientation tends to increase while their mastery orientation decreases (Elliot & McGregor, 2000). Because parents focus on grades, and grade-point averages are part of the reality of applying for colleges, you won't be able to completely eliminate students' performance orientation, particularly as they get older, but you can take steps to avoid an unhealthy emphasis on performance goals:

- Model a mastery orientation and incremental view of intelligence by describing how much you learn when you prepare for your classes and how much smarter you get in the process.
- Emphasize that learning is the goal of schooling and that grades will take care of themselves if we understand the topics we study.
- Create assessments that measure deep understanding of content, and avoid focusing on factual information.
- Avoid all forms of social comparisons, such as public displays of grades.

Table 10.1 Goals, motivation, and achievement

Type of Goal	Example	Influence on Motivation and Achievement
Mastery goals	Understand the influence of the Renaissance on American history.	Leads to sustained effort, high self-efficacy, willingness to accept challenges, and high achievement.
Performance-approach goals	Produce one of the best essays on the Renaissance in the class.	Can lead to sustained effort and high self-efficacy for confident learners. Can increase achievement. Can detract from willingness to accept challenging tasks, which decreases achievement.
Performance-avoidance goals	Avoid the appearance of low ability in front of peers and teachers.	Detracts from motivation and achievement, particularly for learners lacking confidence.
Social goals	Be perceived as reliable and responsible.	Can either increase or decrease motivation and achievement. *Social-responsibility goals* enhance motivation and achievement, particularly when combined with mastery goals.
	Make friends and socialize.	Can detract from motivation and achievement if social goals compete for time with mastery goals.
Work-avoidance goals	Complete assignments with as little effort as possible.	Detracts from effort and self-efficacy. Strongly detracts from achievement.

You can make some additional symbolic gestures by writing students' scores on the last page of their tests and telling them that they are not to share their scores with each other. You won't be able to enforce the "don't share" policy, but it symbolizes a focus on learning instead of performance. You can also combine small-group work, which helps meet students' social goals, with whole-class instruction, which is often preferred by students with a performance-approach orientation (Bong, 2001).

Exploring *diversity*

Student Differences in Motivation to Learn

The theory and research we've examined in this chapter describe general patterns in motivation to learn, and, in many ways they are true for most students. For instance, all students, regardless of culture, gender, or socio-economic status, have needs for competence, autonomy, and relatedness; they all have particular goal orientations, and they all offer attributions for their successes and failures.

How these factors influence motivation to learn can vary among groups and individuals, however (Rogoff, 2003). For instance, research

indicates that some Native American groups give young children more autonomy in decision making than do parents in mainstream Western culture (Deyhle & LeCompte, 1999), whereas African American parents give their students less autonomy, possibly to protect them in potentially dangerous environments (Smetana & Gettman, 2006). Also, while being allowed to make choices increases learner autonomy,

Asian students may prefer letting people they trust, such as parents or teachers, make choices for them (Vansteenkiste, Zhou, Lens, & Soenens, 2005).

Differences in learners' need for relatedness also exist. Some Asian students, for example, meet this need by excelling in school and gaining the approval of their parents and teachers (Li, 2005), whereas members of other minorities meet the need for relatedness by not achieving. "Indeed, many students from minority groups experience peer pressure discouraging them from adopting attitudes and behaviors associated with achieving good grades" (Rubinson, 2004, p. 58).

Differences also exist in the types of goals learners set. For instance, some research indicates that both Asian American and African American students tend to focus on mastery goals, whereas European American students focus more on performance goals (Qian & Pan, 2002). Asian American students are also more likely to attribute their successes to effort and their failures to lack of effort than are Caucasian students (Lillard, 1997; Steinberg, 1996).

Gender differences also exist. For example, the stereotypical belief that some domains, such as English, are more suited for girls, whereas others, such as math and science, are for boys, still exists (Pajares & Valiante, 1999), so motivation to learn in these domains can vary because of different perceptions of utility value (Jacobs et al., 2002). Further, boys' self-efficacy is higher than girls' in spite of the fact that girls get higher grades (Eccles et al., 1998), and girls are more easily discouraged by failure than are boys (Dweck, 2000). These gender differences may be due to attributions; boys tend to attribute success to high ability and failure to lack of effort, whereas girls show a reverse pattern—the tendency to attribute success to effort and failure to lack of ability (Vermeer, Boekaerts, & Seegers, 2000).

As you apply this information with your students, it's important to remember that individuals within groups vary significantly. For instance, many European American students set mastery goals, and many Asian American students set performance goals. Many girls have high efficacy, and the self-efficacy of some boys is low. As teachers, we want to avoid thinking that can result in stereotyping any group.

check your understanding

4.1 Explain how learners' goals can influence their motivation to learn.

4.2 Which combination of goal orientations is likely to result in the highest level of motivation and achievement? Explain.

To receive feedback for these questions, go to Appendix A.

Classroom connections

Capitalizing on Goals to Increase Student Motivation

1. Goals are outcomes learners hope to achieve. Emphasize mastery goals in your work with your students.

  ■ **Elementary:** As a fifth-grade teacher begins a writing project, he comments, "Our goal is to improve our writing. If it improves, the grade you get will take care of itself."

  ■ **Middle School:** An eighth-grade history teacher puts her students' test scores on the last page of their tests and says, "Our scores are our own business. We're here to learn, not compete with each other."

  ■ **High School:** In response to students asking how many A's were on the last test, a biology teacher says, "We don't care about that. Instead, ask yourself if your understanding is increasing."

2. A combination of mastery goals and social-responsibility goals can lead to the highest levels of motivation to learn. Emphasize social responsibility with your students.

  ■ **Elementary:** A third-grade teacher instructs her students to work in pairs to solve a series of math problems. "Work hard," she emphasizes, "so you can help out your partner if he or she needs it."

  ■ **Middle School:** An eighth-grade English teacher is discussing *To Kill a Mockingbird* with her students. "In order for us to get the most out of the book, we're all responsible for making a contribution to the class discussions," she emphasizes.

  ■ **High School:** An American history teacher asks her students to work in groups of four to prepare a project comparing the American, French, and Russian revolutions. "Remember, the quality of your project depends on all of you doing your parts to contribute to the final product," she emphasizes.

The Influence of Interest and Emotion on Motivation to Learn

"Because it's interesting" is an intuitively sensible answer to why a learner would be motivated to engage in an activity. Students are obviously more motivated to study topics they find interesting, and we commonly attempt to capitalize on student interest in our instruction (Anderman & Wolters, 2006; Brophy, 2010). Let's examine interest in more detail.

Ed Psych and You

Have you ever wondered why there are so many "cop" shows on TV? Or, why barely concealed sexual overtones are such a big part of movies and television?

Personal and Situational Interest

Let's go back to the conversation at the beginning of the chapter between Susan and Jim as they entered Kathy's classroom. Susan commented, "I've always liked history and knowing about the past, . . . and I'm pretty good at it," to which Jim replied, "In some classes I just do enough to get a decent grade, but not in here. . . . It's kind of interesting the way she's always telling us about the way we are because of something that happened a zillion years ago."

Susan's and Jim's comments suggest that they're both interested in Kathy's class, but the nature of their interest differed. Susan expressed **personal interest,** "a person's ongoing affinity, attraction, or liking for a domain, subject area, topic, or activity" (Anderman & Wolters, 2006, p. 374), whereas Jim demonstrated **situational interest,** a person's current enjoyment, pleasure, or satisfaction generated by the immediate context (Schraw & Lehman, 2001).

Personal interest is relatively stable, and it depends heavily on prior knowledge (Renninger, 2000). This stability and knowledge are illustrated in Susan's comment, "I've always liked history, . . . and I'm pretty good at it." Situational interest, in contrast, depends on the current situation and can change quickly. As a person's expertise develops, however, situational interest can lead to personal interest.

Teachers focus more on situational interest, because they have more control over it (Schraw, Flowerday, & Lehman, 2001), and some topics, such as death, danger, power, money, romance, and sex, seem to be universally interesting (Hidi, 2001). This helps us answer the questions we asked in our "Ed Psych and You" feature in this section. For younger students, scary stories, humor, and animals also seem to generate situational interest.

We can't build our instruction around danger, money, romance, and sex, but we can increase situational interest in several ways (Schraw & Lehman, 2001):

- Focus on real-world applications in learning activities.
- Personalize content by linking topics to students' lives.
- Promote high levels of student involvement.
- Provide concrete examples.
- Make logical and coherent presentations.
- Give students choices whenever possible.

In addition, modeling mastery goals and your own interest in the topics you teach can also increase students' interest (Brophy, 2010). It won't increase motivation to learn in all situations or for all students, but you have nothing to lose by being enthusiastic about the topics you teach and emphasizing a mastery goal orientation (Schweinle, Meyer, & Turner, 2006).

We examine strategies for increasing student interest in more detail in Chapter 11.

Personal interest. "A person's ongoing affinity, attraction, or liking for a domain, subject area, topic, or activity" (Anderman & Wolters, 2006, p. 374).

Situational interest. A person's current enjoyment, pleasure, or satisfaction generated by the immediate context.

Expert teachers capitalize on situational interest to increase students' motivation to learn.

Emotion and Motivation

To begin this section, consider how you would react to the following experiences:

- You've just solved a challenging problem.
- Your instructor brings a newspaper clipping to class that graphically describes atrocities occurring on the African continent.
- You've studied carefully for a test in one of your classes, and you still didn't do well.

In each case, the experience likely aroused an emotion. In the first, you probably felt a sense of accomplishment and pride. The second may have caused feelings of outrage and left you thinking about it for an extended period. The third likely left you feeling discouraged and frustrated.

Emotions are complex and range from guilt, shame, and anxiety, to more positive feelings such as pride, joy, and relief, and each can influence motivation to learn (Do & Schallert, 2004; Zeelenberg, Wadenmakers, & Rotteveel, 2006). For instance, both feelings of pride and feelings of guilt can increase motivation, whereas feelings of shame, and particularly if the shame is associated with beliefs about lack of ability, usually decrease motivation.

Motivation and Anxiety

In the conversation that introduced our discussion of attributions, Ashley commented,

> "I looked at the test, and just went blank. All I could think of was, 'I've never seen this stuff before. Where did it come from?' I thought I was going to throw up."

Anxiety. A general uneasiness and feeling of tension relating to a situation with an uncertain outcome.

Ashley experienced **anxiety,** a general uneasiness and feeling of tension relating to a situation with an uncertain outcome. We've all experienced it at one time or another, and it's one of the most studied emotions in teaching and learning.

The relationship between anxiety, motivation, and achievement is curvilinear; some is good, but too much can be damaging (Cassady & Johnson, 2002). For example, some anxiety makes us study hard and develop competence, and relatively high anxiety improves performance on tasks where our expertise is well developed (Covington & Omelich, 1987). Too much, however, can decrease motivation and achievement, and classrooms where the evaluation threat is high are particularly anxiety producing (Hancock, 2001). Our understanding of human memory helps explain its debilitating effects (Cassady & Johnson, 2002). First, anxious students have difficulty concentrating, and because they worry about—and even expect—failure, they often misperceive the information they see and hear. In addition, test-anxious students often use superficial strategies, such as memorizing definitions, instead of strategies that are more productive, like self-questioning (K. E. Ryan et al., 2007). In essence, highly test-anxious students often don't learn the content very well in the first place, which increases their anxiety when they're required to perform on tests. Finally, during assessments, they often waste working memory space on thoughts similar to Ashley's, "I've never seen this stuff before. Where did it come from?" leaving less available for focusing on the task.

Effective instruction—instruction that emphasizes high-quality examples, student involvement, specific feedback on assessments, and outside help—is more effective than any other strategy for helping students cope with anxiety. When understanding increases, poor performance decreases, and, in time, the anxiety it produces will also decrease.

Some interesting and highly applicable research also addresses the issue of anxiety. Researchers Gerardo Ramirez and Sian Beilock found that simply writing about test-related worries for 10 minutes immediately before taking an exam improves test scores in classroom settings, and particularly when high-stakes tests are involved (Ramirez & Beilock, 2011). The researchers concluded that writing about their worries unloaded the thoughts that were occupying students' working memories, thereby making more working memory space available to devote to the task. This suggests that simply offering your students the opportunity to write about their worries for a few minutes before they take a test might increase their performance.

Also, remember that our descriptions of learner anxiety represent general patterns, and individuals will vary. For instance, some high achievers continue to experience anxiety in spite of a long history of success. In all cases, we teach individuals and not groups, and we want to treat our students in the same way.

Ed Psych and teaching

Using Beliefs, Goals, and Interests to Increase Your Students' Motivation to Learn

An understanding of learners' beliefs, goals, and interests has important implications for the way we work with our students. The following guidelines can help you in your efforts to apply this understanding with your students.

1. Increase learner self-efficacy by providing students with evidence of accomplishment and modeling your own self-efficacy.
2. Encourage internal attributions for successes and controllable attributions for failures.
3. Emphasize the utility value of increased skills.
4. Promote student interest by modeling your own interest, personalizing content, providing concrete examples, involving students, and offering choices.
5. Emphasize mastery and social-responsibility goals, effective strategies, and metacognition.

We return once again to Kathy's classroom and her work with her students to see how she applies the guidelines in the second day of a unit focusing on the Crusades.

"We began our discussion of the Crusades yesterday. . . . How did we start?" she asks.

"We imagined that Lincoln High School was taken over by people who believed that extracurricular activities should be eliminated," Carnisha volunteers.

"Good. . . . Then what?"

"We decided we'd talk to them. . . . We'd be on a 'crusade' to change their minds and save our school."

"Very good. . . . Now, what were the actual Crusades all about?. . . Selena?"

"The Christians wanted to get the Holy Land back from the Muslims."

"And why? . . . Becky?"

"The holy lands were important to the Crusaders because they were Christians."

The class then discusses reasons for the actual Crusades, such as religion, economics, the military threat posed by the Muslim world, and the amount of territory they held.

"Excellent analysis. . . . In fact, we'll see that these factors also influenced Columbus's voyage to the New World and its exploration. . . . Think about that. The Crusades nearly 1,000 years ago have had an influence on us here today," she continues energetically.

"Now, for today's assignment, you were asked to write an analysis answering the question, 'Were the Crusades a success or a failure?' and we emphasized the importance of providing evidence for your position, not the position itself. Remember, the ability to make and defend an argument is a skill that goes way beyond a specific topic.

"So, let's see how we did. Go ahead. . . . Nikki?"

Kathy asks several students to present their positions and then closes the discussion by saying, "See how interesting this is? Again, we see ourselves influenced by people who lived hundreds of years ago. . . . That's what history is all about."

"Brewster loves this stuff," David whispers to Kelly.

Kathy then tells the students to revise their analyses based on their discussion.

"Remember," she emphasizes, "when you make your revisions, ask yourself, 'Do I have evidence here, or is it simply an opinion?' . . . The more aware you are when you write, the better your work will be. When you're done, switch with a partner and critique each other's paper. We made a commitment at the beginning of the year to help each other when we give feedback on our writing. . . . So, I know that you'll come through."

Now, let's look at Kathy's attempts to apply the guidelines. Her interaction with Harvey in the case study at the beginning of the chapter illustrates the first three. She applied the first (increase learner self-efficacy) when she said, "Yes, but look how good you're getting at writing. I think you hit a personal best on your last paper." She also commented, "It's hard for me, too, when I'm studying and trying to put together new ideas, but if I hang in, I always feel like I can get it." Her first comment provided Harvey with evidence of his accomplishment, and the second modeled her own developing self-efficacy.

She applied the second guideline (encourage internal attributions for successes) when she responded to Harvey's comment, "But you make us work so hard," by saying, "Yes, but look how good you're getting at writing." Her response encouraged him to attribute his success to effort and increased ability, both of which are internal attributions. His comment, "Yeah, yeah, I know, and being good writers will help us in everything we do in life," reflected her emphasis on the utility value of what they were learning, which applied the third guideline.

Kathy applied the fourth guideline (promote student interest) in three ways. First, she modeled her own interest in saying, "Think about that. The Muslims and the Crusades nearly 1,000 years ago have had an influence on us here today," and "See how interesting this is. . . ." Her statements' impact on students was reflected in David's comment, "Brewster loves this stuff."

She also increased students' interest by personalizing the topic with the analogy of "crusading" to prevent the school from eliminating extracurricular activities, using the analogy as a concrete example of a crusade, and involving students throughout the activity.

Finally, as you saw in the case study at the beginning of the chapter, Kathy allowed the students to choose either a presentation on the Renaissance or a paper on the Middle Ages, to decide which groups would present on certain days, and to negotiate the due date for the papers ("Remember . . . we agreed that they're due on Friday").

Kathy applied the last guideline (emphasize mastery and social-responsibility goals, effective strategies, and metacognition) by encouraging students to be metacognitive about their writing: "Remember, . . . Ask yourself, 'Do I actually have evidence here, or is it simply an opinion?' . . . The more aware you are when you write, the better your work will be," and she emphasized social-responsibility goals when she said, "We made a commitment . . . to help each other when we give feedback on our writing. . . . So, I know that you'll come through." The combination of social-responsibility goals and mastery goals increases motivation and achievement more than either alone.

At the beginning of the chapter, we said that with effort teachers can increase motivation in many of their students. This is what Kathy tried to do as she worked with hers.

check your understanding

5.1 Identify four ways in which teachers can increase students' interest in their learning activities.

5.2 Explain how teachers can capitalize on emotions to increase students' motivation to learn.

5.3 Describe three ways teachers can reduce anxiety in their students.

To receive feedback for these questions, go to Appendix A.

Classroom connections

Using Students' Interests and Emotions to Promote Motivation in Classrooms

1. Promote interest in your learning activities by using personalized, concrete examples and promoting high levels of student involvement.

   ■ **Elementary:** A fourth-grade teacher puts his students' names into word problems. He is careful to be sure that all students' names are used over a 3-day period.

   ■ **Middle School:** A geography teacher begins the study of longitude and latitude by asking the students how they would tell a friend the exact location of one of their favorite hangouts.

   ■ **High School:** A physics teacher creates problems using the velocity and momentum of soccer balls after they've been kicked, and she asks students to determine the acceleration and speed players must run to intercept the kicks.

2. To reduce anxiety, emphasize understanding the content of tests instead of grades, provide opportunities for practice, and give students ample time to finish assessments.

   ■ **Elementary:** A second-grade teacher monitors his students as they work on a quiz. When he sees their attention wander, he reminds them of the work they have done on the topic and to concentrate on their work.

   ■ **Middle School:** An eighth-grade algebra teacher gives her students extensive practice with the types of problems they'll be expected to solve on their tests.

   ■ **High School:** An AP American history teacher knows that her students are nervous about passing the end-of-year exam. She frequently reminds them, "If you thoroughly understand the content, you'll be fine on the test. So, as you study, try to connect the ideas, and don't just memorize information."

*D*evelopmentally appropriate *practice*

Motivation to Learn in Students at Different Ages

Many applications of motivation theory apply to learners at all grade levels, such as using high-quality and personalized examples, involving students, and creating safe and orderly learning environments. Developmental differences exist, however. The following paragraphs outline suggestions for responding to these differences.

Working with Students in Early Childhood Programs and Elementary Schools

In contrast with older students, young children bask openly in praise, and they rarely evaluate whether or not the praise is justified. They also tend to have incremental views of intelligence and set mastery goals. Because of these factors, emphasizing that all students can learn, avoiding social comparisons, praising students for their effort, and reminding them that hard work "makes us smart" can increase motivation to learn.

Working with Students in Middle Schools

As learners grow older, their mastery orientation tends to decrease, while their performance orientation increases. Modeling the belief that intelligence is incremental, and emphasizing the relationship between effort and increased competence and ability are important. Middle school students increasingly meet their needs for belonging and relatedness with peer experiences, so social goals tend to increase in importance. Combining whole-group with small-group activities can help students meet these needs and goals.

Middle school students' need for autonomy also increases, so involving them in activities that increase their sense of autonomy, such as asking them to provide input into classroom rules, can be effective.

Working with Students in High Schools

High school students are beginning to think about their futures, so emphasizing the utility value of the topics they study and the skills they develop can increase their motivation to learn.

Because of the many experiences that high school students can access, such as video games and the Internet, generating interest in school topics can be a challenge. However, using concrete and personalized examples and promoting high levels of interaction remain effective.

Evidence that their competence is increasing is important to high school students, so sincere praise and other indicators of genuine accomplishment can increase motivation to learn.

Summary

1. Define motivation, and describe different theoretical explanations for learner motivation.
   - Motivation is a process in which goal-directed activity is instigated and sustained.
   - Extrinsic motivation is motivation to engage in an activity as a means to an end; intrinsic motivation is motivation to be involved in an activity for its own sake.
   - Behaviorism describes motivation and learning in the same way; an increase in behavior is evidence of both learning and motivation.
   - Cognitive theories of motivation focus on learners' beliefs, expectations, and the desire to make sense of their experiences.
   - Sociocultural views of motivation focus on individuals' participating in learning communities.
   - Humanistic views of motivation are grounded in the premise that people are motivated to fulfill their total potential as human beings.

2. Describe learners' needs and how they influence motivation to learn.
   - A need is an internal force or drive to attain or avoid certain states or objects.
   - According to Maslow, all people have needs for survival, safety, belonging, and self-esteem. Once these needs are met, people are motivated to fulfill their potential as human beings.
   - According to self-determination theory, all people have needs for competence, autonomy, and relatedness. Helping students meet these needs increases motivation.
   - Self-worth theory suggests that all people have the need to protect their sense of self-worth, which depends on maintaining the perception that they have high ability.

3. Explain how learners' beliefs can influence their motivation to learn.
   - A belief is an idea we accept as true without necessarily having definitive evidence to support it.
   - Learners' motivation increases when they expect to succeed.

   - Learners who believe that intelligence can be increased with effort tend to have higher motivation to learn than learners who believe intelligence is fixed.
   - Students who believe they are capable of accomplishing specific tasks have high self-efficacy and are more motivated to learn than students whose self-efficacy is lower.
   - Believing that increased understanding will help them meet future goals increases students' motivation to learn.
   - Students who believe that effort and ability are the causes of their success, or that lack of effort is the cause of failure, are likely to be motivated to learn.

4. Describe how learners' goals can influence their motivation to learn.
   - A goal is an outcome an individual hopes to attain.
   - Learners whose goals focus on mastery of tasks, improvement, and increased understanding have higher motivation to learn than do learners whose goals focus on social comparisons.
   - Social goals can decrease motivation to learn if they focus exclusively on social factors. Social-responsibility goals, however, and particularly social-responsibility goals combined with mastery goals, can lead to sustained motivation and achievement.

5. Explain how teachers can capitalize on learners' interests and emotions to increase motivation to learn.
   - Teachers can increase students' interest by using concrete and personalized examples, emphasizing real-world applications, and promoting high levels of student involvement in learning activities.
   - Teachers can capitalize on emotions to increase motivation to learn by emphasizing the emotional component of topics when opportunities present themselves.
   - Teachers can decrease learner anxiety by clarifying and specifying expectations about learning and student assessment, by using teaching strategies that promote understanding, and by providing students with opportunities to receive outside help.

Understanding the Relationship Between Motivation and Learning: Preparing for Your Licensure Exam

Your licensure exam will include information related to students' motivation, and we include the following exercises to help you practice for the exam in your state. This book and these exercises will be a resource for you as you prepare for the exam.

You saw in this chapter how Kathy Brewster applied an understanding of the relationship between motivation and learning in her teaching. We look in now at another world history teacher who is also teaching about the Crusades. Read the case study, and then answer the questions that follow.

Damon Marcus watches as his students take their seats, and then announces, "Listen, everyone, I have your tests here from last Friday. Liora, Ivan, Lynn, and Segundo, super job on the test. They were the only A's in the class."

After handing back the tests, Damon writes the following on the chalkboard:

$$A \, 4 \qquad D \, 4$$
$$B \, 7 \qquad F \, 3$$
$$C \, 11$$

"You people down here better get moving," Damon comments, pointing to the D's and F's on the chalkboard. "This wasn't that hard a test. Remember, we have another one in 2 weeks. Let's give these sharp ones with the A's a run for their money.

"Now let's get going. We have a lot to cover today. . . . As you'll recall from yesterday, the Crusades were an attempt by the Christian powers of Western Europe to wrestle control of the traditional holy lands of Christianity away from the Muslims. Now, when was the First Crusade?"

"About 1500, I think," Clifton volunteers.

"No, no," Damon shakes his head. "Remember that Columbus sailed in 1492, which was before 1500, so that doesn't make sense. . . . Liora?"

"It was about 1100, I think."

"Excellent, Liora. Now, I know that learning dates and places isn't the most pleasant stuff, but you might as well get used to it, because that's what history is about. Plus, they'll be on the next test."

He continues, "The First Crusade was in 1095, and it was called the 'People's Crusade.' There were actually seven in all, starting in 1095 and continuing until enthusiasm for them ended in 1300.

Damon continues presenting factual information about the Crusades, and then, seeing that about 20 minutes are left in the period, he says, "Now, I want you to write a summary of the Crusades that outlines the major people and events and tells why they were important. You should be able to finish by the end of the period, but if you don't, turn your papers in at the beginning of class tomorrow. You may use your notes. Go ahead and get started."

As he monitors students, he sees that Jeremy has written only a few words on his paper. "Are you having trouble getting started?" Damon asks quietly.

"Yeah, . . . I don't quite know how to get started," Jeremy mumbles.

"I know you have a tough time with written assignments. Let me help you," Damon nods.

He takes a blank piece of paper and starts writing as Jeremy watches. He writes several sentences on the paper and then says, "See how easy that was? That's the kind of thing I want you to do. Go ahead—that's a start. Keep that so you can see what I'm looking for. Go back to your desk, and give it another try."

Questions for Case Analysis

In answering these questions, use information from the chapter, and link your responses to specific information in the case.

1. Assess the extent to which Damon capitalized on learners' needs to promote motivation to learn.

2. Assess the extent to which Damon capitalized on goals to promote motivation to learn.

3. How effectively did Damon promote interest in the topic?

To receive feedback for these questions, go to Appendix B.

Your licensure exam will also include multiple-choice questions similar to those your instructor has given you on your quizzes and tests for this course.

Important Concepts

anxiety (p. 354)
attainment value (p. 345)
attribution (p. 346)
attribution theory (p. 346)
autonomy (p. 338)
belief (p. 342)
competence (p. 338)
cost (p. 345)
deficiency needs (p. 337)
entity view of intelligence (p. 343)

expectancy × value theory (p. 343)
expectation (p. 343)
extrinsic motivation (p. 331)
goal (p. 348)
growth needs (p. 337)
incremental view of intelligence (p. 343)
intrinsic motivation (p. 331)
learned helplessness (p. 346)
mastery goal (p. 349)

motivation (p. 330)
motivation to learn (p. 332)
motivational zone of proximal development (p. 334)
need (p. 336)
need for approval (p. 339)
performance-approach goal (p. 349)
performance-avoidance goal (p. 349)
performance goal (p. 349)

personal interest (p. 353)
relatedness (p. 339)
self-actualization (p. 337)
self-determination (p. 337)
self-efficacy (p. 344)
self-worth (p. 340)
situational interest (p. 353)
social goals (p. 349)
unconditional positive regard (p. 335)
utility value (p. 345)
value (p. 345)

Go to Topic: Motivation and Affect in the MyEducationLab (www.myeducationlab.com) for *Educational Psychology: Windows on Classrooms*, where you can:

- Find learning outcomes for Motivation and Affect along with the national standards that connect to these outcomes.
- Complete Assignments and Activities that can help you more deeply understand the chapter content.
- Apply and practice your understanding of the core teaching skills identified in the chapter with the Building Teaching Skills and Dispositions learning units.
- Examine challenging situations and cases presented in the IRIS Center Resources.
- Access video clips of CCSSO National Teachers of the Year award winners responding to the question, "Why Do I Teach?" in the Teacher Talk section.
- See video examples included within the Study Plan that provide concrete and real-world illustrations of the topics presented in the chapter.
- Check your comprehension of the content covered in the chapter with the Study Plan. Here you will be able to take a chapter quiz, receive feedback on your answers, and then access Review, Practice, and Enrichment activities to enhance your understanding of chapter content.

MyEducationLab

chapter 11

A Classroom Model for Promoting Student Motivation

chapteroutline

learningoutcomes

After you've completed your study of this chapter, you should be able to:

Creating A Mastery-Focused Classroom
A Model for Promoting Student Motivation

1. Describe the differences between a mastery-focused and a performance-focused classroom.

The Teacher: Personal Qualities That Increase Motivation to Learn
Personal Teaching Efficacy: Beliefs About Teaching and Learning
Modeling and Enthusiasm: Communicating Genuine Interest
Caring: Meeting Needs for Belonging and Relatedness
Teacher Expectations: Promoting Learning and Achievement

2. Describe the personal qualities of teachers who increase students' motivation to learn.

Learning Climate: Creating A Motivating Environment
Order and Safety: Classrooms as Secure Places to Learn
Success: Developing Self-Efficacy
Challenge: Increasing Perceptions of Competence
Task Comprehension: Increasing Feelings of Autonomy and Value

3. Identify the learning climate variables that increase students' motivation to learn.

Instructional Variables: Developing Interest In Learning Activities
Introductory Focus: Attracting Students' Attention
Personalization: Links to Students' Lives
Involvement: Increasing Situational Interest
Feedback: Information About Learning Progress
Assessment and Learning: Using Feedback to Increase Interest and Self-Efficacy

4. Describe instructional variables that increase students' motivation to learn.

classroomapplications

The following features help you apply the content of this chapter in your teaching.

Ed Psych and Teaching:
Demonstrating Personal Qualities that Increase Your Students' Motivation to Learn
Applying the Climate and Instructional Variables to Increase Your Students' Motivation to Learn

Classroom Connections:
Demonstrating Personal Characteristics in the Model for Promoting Student Motivation
Promoting a Positive Learning Climate in Classrooms
Using Instructional Variables to Promote Motivation to Learn

Developmentally appropriate practice:
Applying the Model for Promoting Student Motivation with Learners at Different Ages

Exploring Diversity:
Personalizing Content to Increase Motivation to Learn in Students from Diverse Backgrounds

*W*hen we work with our students, both as individuals and in groups, we can do a great deal to influence their motivation to learn. We focus on these influences in this chapter.

Let's begin by looking in on DeVonne Lampkin, a fifth-grade teacher, who wants her students to understand the concept *arthropod*. As you read the case study, think about her students' motivation and how DeVonne influenced it.

DeVonne begins her day's science lesson by reaching into a cooler and taking out a live lobster.

The students "ooh" and "aah" at the wriggling animal, and DeVonne asks Stephanie to carry it around the room so her classmates can observe and touch it.

She then says, "Look carefully, because I'm going to ask you to tell us what you see. . . . Okay, what did you notice?"

"Hard," Tu observes.

"Pink and green," Saleina comments.

"Wet," Kevin adds.

The students make additional observations; DeVonne lists them on the board, and prompts the students to conclude that the lobster has a hard outer covering, which she labels an exoskeleton; three body parts; and segmented legs. She identifies these as essential characteristics of arthropods.

Reaching into her bag again, DeVonne pulls a cockroach out from a baggie. Amid more squeals, she walks around the class holding it with tweezers, and then asks, "Is this an arthropod?"

After some discussion to resolve uncertainty about whether the cockroach has an exoskeleton, the class concludes that it is.

DeVonne next takes a clam out of her cooler, and asks, "Is this an arthropod?"

Some students conclude that it is, reasoning that it has a hard shell.

A.J. comments, "It doesn't have any legs," and, following additional discussion, the class decides that it isn't an arthropod.

"Now," DeVonne asks, "Do you think Mrs. Sapp [the school principal] is an arthropod? . . . Tell us why or why not."

Amid more giggles, some students conclude that she is, because she has segmented legs. Others disagree because she doesn't look like a lobster or a roach. After some discussion, Tu observes, "She doesn't have an exoskeleton," and the class finally agrees that she is not an arthropod.

DeVonne then instructs the students to form pairs, passes out shrimp for examination, calms the excited students, and asks them to observe the shrimp carefully and decide if they're arthropods.

During the whole-group discussion that follows, she discovers that some of the students are still uncertain about the idea of an exoskeleton, so she has them peel the shrimp and feel the head and outer covering. After seeing the peeled covering, they conclude that the shrimp does indeed have an exoskeleton.

As you study this chapter, keep the following questions in mind:

1. How did DeVonne's personal qualities contribute to her students' motivation to learn?
2. How did the classroom environment DeVonne created help motivate her students to learn?
3. What impact did DeVonne's instruction have on her students' motivation?

Classroom applications of both learning and motivation theories help answer this and other questions about student motivation. We examine these applications in this chapter.

Creating a Mastery-Focused Classroom

We begin answering our question by considering two types of classrooms. A **mastery-focused classroom** emphasizes effort, continuous improvement, and understanding, whereas a **performance-focused classroom** stresses high grades, public displays of ability, and performance compared to others (Anderman & Wolters, 2006).

DeVonne attempted to create a mastery-focused classroom in three ways: (1) She created high levels of interest by using concrete examples—a real lobster, cockroach, and shrimp—to teach the concept *arthropod*, and she promoted high levels of involvement throughout the learning activity; (2) she emphasized understanding; and (3) she promoted cooperation instead of competition as students studied the topic. Differences in mastery-focused compared to performance-focused classrooms are summarized in Table 11.1 (Anderman & Wolters, 2006; Pintrich, 2000).

A Model for Promoting Student Motivation

Within this mastery-oriented framework, in this chapter we present a Model for Promoting Student Motivation, which synthesizes learning and motivation theory and research. It is outlined in Figure 11.1 and has three components:

1. *The teacher:* Demonstrates personal qualities that increase student motivation to learn.

Mastery-focused classroom. A classroom environment that emphasizes effort, continuous improvement, and understanding.

Performance-focused classroom. A classroom environment that emphasizes high grades, public displays of ability, and performance compared to others.

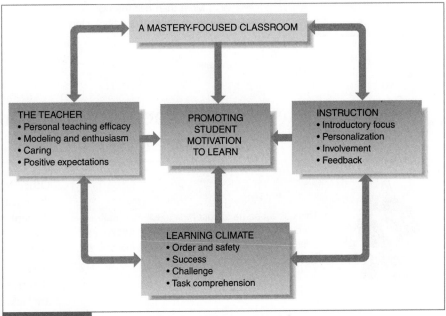

Figure 11.1 A model for promoting student motivation

Table 11.1 Mastery-focused and performance-focused classrooms

	Mastery Focused	Performance Focused
Success defined as . . .	Mastery, improvement	High grades, doing better than others
Value placed on . . .	Effort, improvement	High grades, demonstration of high ability
Reasons for satisfaction . . .	Meeting challenges, hard work	Doing better than others, success with minimum effort
Teacher oriented toward . . .	Student learning	Student performance
View of errors . . .	A normal part of learning	A basis for concern and anxiety
Reasons for effort . . .	Increased understanding	High grades, doing better than others
Ability viewed as . . .	Incremental, alterable	An entity, fixed
Reasons for assessment . . .	Measure progress toward preset criteria, provide feedback	Determine grades, compare students to one another

2. *Learning climate:* Creates a motivating environment for learning.

3. *Instruction:* Develops interest in learning activities.

Each component contains four variables, and the components and variables in the model are interdependent; a single variable cannot be effectively applied if the others are missing. The arrows connecting each of the components are intended to remind you of this interdependence.

check your
understanding

1.1 Describe the differences between a mastery-focused and a performance-focused classroom.

1.2 A teacher says, "Excellent job on the last test, everyone. More than half the class got an A or a B." Based on descriptions of mastery-focused versus performance-focused classrooms, how effective is this comment for promoting motivation? Explain.

To receive feedback for these questions, go to Appendix A.

The Teacher: Personal Qualities that Increase Motivation to Learn

Ed Psych and You

Think about some of your best teachers. What were they like? What kind of learning environment did they create? What did they do that made their classes interesting and worthwhile?

Other than their parents and home environment, you—their teacher—are the most important influence on your students' learning and motivation. You create the emotional climate for your students, implement instruction, and establish mastery-oriented or performance-oriented classrooms. None of the other components of the model are effective if the teacher qualities highlighted in Figure 11.2 are lacking.

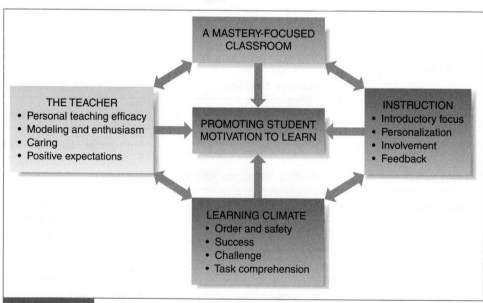

Figure 11.2 Teacher qualities in the Model for Promoting Student Motivation

Personal Teaching Efficacy:
Beliefs About Teaching and Learning

Self-efficacy describes individuals' beliefs about their capability of accomplishing specific tasks. **Personal teaching efficacy** —teachers' believing that they're capable of getting all students to learn, regardless of prior knowledge, ability, or personal backgrounds—is an extension of the concept of self-efficacy (Woolfolk Hoy, Davis, & Pape, 2006).

Teachers high in personal teaching efficacy take responsibility for student learning. They are demanding but fair, they maximize time available for instruction, praise students for their increasing competence, and persevere with low achievers (Ware & Kitsantas, 2007). In contrast, low-efficacy teachers are more likely to blame low achievement on lack of intelligence, poor home environments, or other causes outside the classroom. They have lower expectations, spend less time on learning activities, give up on low achievers, and are more critical when students fail. They are also more controlling and value student autonomy less than do high-efficacy teachers.

Not surprisingly, students taught by high-efficacy teachers learn more and are more motivated than those taught by teachers with lower efficacy (Tschannen-Moran, Woolfolk Hoy, & Hoy, 1998).

All students benefit from **collective efficacy,** beliefs that the faculty as a whole can have a positive effect on student learning, and it is particularly important for students from diverse backgrounds (Hoy, Tarter, & Hoy, 2006). In schools where collective efficacy is high, low-socioeconomic status (SES) students have achievement gains almost as high as those of high-SES students from schools with low collective efficacy (Lee, 2000). Teachers in these schools reduce the achievement gap between advantaged and disadvantaged students.

You can help promote collective efficacy by remaining positive when other teachers become cynical or pessimistic, and you can remind your colleagues of research that confirms the importance of teachers in promoting motivation and learning in all students.

> **Personal teaching efficacy.** Teachers' beliefs that they can help all students learn, regardless of their prior knowledge, ability, or personal backgrounds.

> **Collective efficacy.** Beliefs that the faculty as a whole in a school can have a positive effect on student learning.

Modeling and Enthusiasm:
Communicating Genuine Interest

> Enthusiastic teachers increase student motivation by modeling their own interest in the subjects they teach.

Social cognitive theory explains why teacher modeling is one of the most powerful influences on student interest. Increasing student motivation is virtually impossible if teachers model distaste or disinterest with statements such as, "I know this stuff is boring, but we have to learn it," or "This isn't my favorite topic, either."

In contrast, your students' motivation to learn can significantly increase if you model your own interest in the topics you're teaching. For instance, if you're a geography teacher, and you say, "Geography is interesting because it strongly influences our lives. For example, most of our major cities, such as New York, Chicago, or San Francisco became important because of their geography," your students are more likely to also be interested in the topic. You don't need pep talks, theatrics, or efforts to entertain students. Rather, your genuine interest can induce in your students the feeling that the information is valuable and worth learning (Brophy, 2010).

You can also influence your students' motivation by modeling effort attributions and incremental views of intelligence. If you say, for example, "The harder I study, the smarter I get," you communicate that effort is desirable and leads to higher ability. In doing so, you're increasing the chance that students will adopt these same beliefs (Bruning, Schraw, & Norby, 2011).

Caring: Meeting Needs for Belonging and Relatedness

A first-grade teacher greets each of her children every morning with a hug, handshake, or "high five."

A fifth-grade teacher immediately calls parents if one of his students fails to turn in a homework assignment or misses more than 2 days of school in a row.

An algebra teacher learns the name of each student in all five of her classes by the end of the first week of school, and she stays in her room during her lunch hour to help students who are struggling.

Caring. A teacher's empathy and investment in the protection and development of young people.

Each of these teachers is demonstrating **caring,** which refers to a teacher's empathy and investment in the protection and development of young people (Noddings, 2001; Roeser, Peck, & Nasir, 2006). Caring teachers help meet students' need for belonging, a need preceded only by safety and survival in Maslow's (1970) hierarchy of needs. In addition, relatedness is one of the three innate needs described by self-determination theory (Ryan & Deci, 2000).

> Students who perceived that teachers cared about them reported positive motivational outcomes such as more prosocial and social responsibility goals, academic effort, and greater internal control beliefs. It appears that students want teachers to care for them both as learners and as people. (Perry, Turner, & Meyer, 2006, p. 341)

Caring is particularly important for boys (Reichert & Hawley, 2010) and newcomer immigrant youth (Suarez-Orozco, Pimentel, & Martin, 2009). This might be surprising, particularly for boys, because on the surface they want to appear tough, resilient, and unemotional. Research suggests that exactly the opposite is true; all students, and especially boys, need to feel wanted and cared about.

Communicating Caring

How can you communicate that you care about your students? Concrete suggestions include the following (Alder, 2002; Brophy, 2010):

- Learn students' names quickly, and call on students by their first names.
- Get to know students as individuals by commenting on and asking about personal items, such as a new hairdo, family member, or activity.
- Make eye contact, smile, lean toward them when talking, and demonstrate relaxed body language.
- Use "we" and "our" rather than "you" and "your" in reference to class activities and assignments.
- Spend time with students.
- Demonstrate respect for students as individuals.

The last two items deserve special emphasis. We all have exactly 24 hours in our days, and the way we choose to allocate our time is the truest measure of our priorities. Choosing to allocate some of our time to an individual student communicates caring better than any other single factor. Helping students who have problems with an assignment or calling a parent after school hours communicates that you care about students. Spending your personal time to ask a question about a baby brother or compliment a new hairstyle communicates caring about a student as a human being.

Showing respect is also essential. You can do so in a variety of ways, but maintaining standards—for both behavior and learning—is one of the most important:

> One of the best ways to show respect for students is to hold them to high standards—by not accepting sloppy, thoughtless, or incomplete work, by pressing them to clarify vague comments, by encouraging them not to give up, and by not praising work that does not reflect genuine effort. Ironically, reactions that are often intended to protect students' self-esteem—such as accepting low quality work—convey a lack of interest, patience, **or caring** [emphasis added]. (Stipek, 2002, p. 157)

Research corroborates this view. When junior high students were asked, "How do you know when a teacher cares about you?" they responded that paying attention to them as human beings was important, but more striking was their belief that teachers who care are committed to their learning and hold them to high standards (Wilson & Corbett, 2001).

Respect is a two-way street, of course. You should model respect for students, and in turn you have the right to expect students to respect you and one another. "Treat everyone with respect" is a rule that should be universally enforced. An occasional minor incident of rudeness can be overlooked, but you should clearly communicate that chronic disrespect will not be tolerated, and you then need to follow through to be certain it isn't.

Teacher Expectations: Promoting Learning and Achievement

Communicating positive expectations is the last of the four teacher qualities in our Model for Promoting Student Motivation (Figure 11.2). Positive teacher expectations are consistently linked to increased achievement in a long history of classroom research (Brophy, 2006c; Stipek, 2002).

> Teacher expectations about students' learning can have profound implications for what students actually learn. Expectations affect the content and pace of the curriculum, the organization of instruction, assessment, instructional interactions with individual students, and many subtle and not-so-subtle behaviors that affect students' own expectations for learning and thus their behavior. (Stipek, 2002, p. 210)

Teachers' expectations influence their interactions with students; teachers treat students they perceive to be high achievers differently from those they perceive to be low achievers (Weinstein, 2002). This differential treatment typically occurs in four ways (Good & Brophy, 2008):

- *Emotional support:* Teachers interact more with perceived high achievers; their interactions and nonverbal behaviors are more positive; and they seat these students closer to the front of the class.
- *Effort:* Teachers are more enthusiastic when working with high achievers, their instruction is more thorough, and they require more complete and accurate student answers.
- *Questioning:* Teachers call on perceived high achievers more often, they allow these students more time to answer, and they provide high achievers with more prompts and cues when they're unable to answer.
- *Feedback and assessment:* Teachers praise perceived high achievers more, criticize them less, and they offer perceived high achievers more complete feedback on assessments.

Teachers communicate positive expectations by calling on all their students as equally as possible.

Self-fulfilling prophecy. A phenomenon that occurs when a person's performance results from and confirms beliefs about his or her capabilities.

At an extreme, teachers' expectations for students can become **self-fulfilling prophecies,** phenomena that occur when people's performance results from and confirms beliefs about their capabilities (Weinstein, 2002).

Let's see how this works. Communicating positive expectations suggests to students that they will be successful. When they are, their self-efficacy and motivation increase, and increased motivation results in increased achievement. The reverse also occurs. Communicating low expectations can result in students exerting less effort, so they perform less well, which confirms perceptions about their abilities.

Children of all ages are aware of teachers' expectations (Stipek, 2002). In one study, researchers concluded,

> After ten seconds of seeing and/or hearing a teacher, even very young students could detect whether the teacher talked about or to an excellent or a weak student and could determine the extent to which that student was loved by the teacher. (Babad, Bernieri, & Rosenthal, 1991, p. 230)

Because they are usually unconscious, we often don't realize that we have different expectations for our students, so our goal in writing this section is to remind you of the powerful influence expectations have on student learning and motivation. With awareness, we are more likely to maintain appropriately high expectations for all students, such as calling on our lower achievers as much as our high achievers. The experience of Elaine Lawless, a first-grade teacher, is an example. When she began calling on her students as equally as possible, she saw immediate benefits: "Joseph made my day. He said to one of the other kids, 'Put your hand down. Mrs. Lawless calls on all of us. She thinks we're all smart'" (Elaine Lawless, personal communication, February 19, 2002).

This discussion helps answer the first question we asked in "Ed Psych and You" at the beginning of the section, What were your best teachers like? Most likely they cared about you both as a person and as a student, they communicated their beliefs in your ability to succeed and learn, they were enthusiastic, and they had high expectations for all your work. These are the qualities you will also want to display in your work with your own students.

Ed psych and *teaching*

Demonstrating Personal Qualities That Increase Your Students' Motivation to Learn

Personal qualities that promote motivation to learn can be applied in a number of ways. The following guidelines can help you in your efforts to demonstrate these qualities with your students.

1. Strive to maintain high personal teaching efficacy.
2. Maintain appropriately high expectations for all students.
3. Model responsibility, effort, and interest in the topics you're teaching.
4. Demonstrate caring and commitment to your students' learning by spending time outside of class with them.

Let's see how the guidelines guide DeVonne as she continues to work with her fifth graders.

"Wow, you're here early," Karla Utley, another teacher in the school, says to DeVonne early one morning.

"I've got kids coming in," DeVonne replies. "I did a writing lesson yesterday, and we evaluated some of their paragraphs as a whole class." (DeVonne's writing lesson is the case study at the end of this chapter.) "Several of the kids, like Tu and Saleina, did really well . . . but some are behind. So, Justin, Picey, and Rosa are coming in before school this morning, and we're going to practice some more. They aren't my highest achievers, but I know I can get more out of them than I am right now. They're good kids; they're just a little behind."

A half hour before school is to start, DeVonne is waiting as Justin, Picey, and Rosa come in the door. She smiles and says, "We're going to practice a little more on our writing. I know that you can all be good writers. It's the same thing for me. I've practiced and practiced, and now I'm good at it. You can do the same thing. . . . Let's look at your paragraphs again."

She displays Justin's paragraph on the overhead again (his was one of the papers evaluated in class the day before) and asks, "What did we suggest that you might do to improve this?"

There was a boy named Josh. He lives in a house with the roof falling in and the windows were broke. He had holes in the wall and the ceiling leaked when it rained. But then again it always rained and thunder over his house. No one ever goes to his gate because he was so weird. They say he is a vampire.

"He needs to stay on either the boy or the house," Rosa offers.

"Good," DeVonne nods. "Staying focused on your topic sentence is important." Together, the group looks at each student's original paragraph and makes specific suggestions for improvement.

DeVonne then says, "Okay, now each of you rewrite your paragraphs based on our suggestions. When we're finished, we'll look at them again."

The students rewrite their paragraphs, and the four of them again discuss the products.

"Much improvement," DeVonne says after they've finished. "If we keep at it, we're going to get there. . . . I'll see you again tomorrow at 7:30."

Now, let's look at DeVonne's efforts to apply the guidelines. First, in saying to Karla, "I know I can get more out of them than I am right now. They're good kids; they're just a little behind," she demonstrated both high personal teaching efficacy and high expectations, and applied the first two guidelines. Her comment suggested that she expects all students to learn, not just high achievers like Tu and Saleina.

As she worked with the small group, she applied the third guideline by modeling responsibility and effort with her comment, "I have practiced and practiced, and now I'm good at it. You can do the same thing. . . . Let's look at your paragraphs again."

Finally, and perhaps most significantly, DeVonne demonstrated caring and commitment by arriving at school an hour early to devote extra time to helping students who needed additional support. She kept the study session upbeat and displayed the respect for the students that is essential for promoting motivation to learn.

These personal qualities won't turn all your students into motivated learners, but you can impact many, and for those, you will have provided an invaluable service to their education.

Classroom connections

Demonstrating Personal Characteristics in the Model for Promoting Student Motivation

Caring

1. Caring teachers promote a sense of belonging and relatedness in their classrooms and commit to the development of students both as people and as learners. Demonstrate caring by respecting students and giving them your personal time.

- **Elementary:** A first-grade teacher greets each of her students every day as they come into the classroom and makes it a point to talk to each student about something personal several times a week.

- **Middle School:** A geography teacher calls parents as soon as he sees a student having academic or personal problems. He solicits parents' help and offers his assistance in solving problems.

- **High School:** An Algebra II teacher conducts help sessions after school three nights a week. Students are invited to attend to get help with homework or to discuss any other concerns about the class or school.

Modeling and Enthusiasm

2. Teachers demonstrate enthusiasm by modeling their own interest in the content of their classes. Communicate interest in the topics you're teaching.

- **Elementary:** During individual reading time, a fourth-grade teacher comments on a book she's interested in, and she reads while the students are reading.

- **Middle School:** A life science teacher brings science-related clippings from the local newspaper to class and asks students to do the same. He discusses the clippings and pins them on a bulletin board for students to read.

- **High School:** A world history teacher frequently describes connections between classroom topics and their impact on today's world.

Positive Expectations

3. Teacher expectations strongly influence motivation and learning. Maintain appropriately high expectations for all students.

- **Elementary:** A second-grade teacher makes a conscious attempt to call on all her students as equally as possible.

- **Middle School:** When his students complain about word problems, a prealgebra teacher reminds them of how important problem solving is for their lives. Each day, he guides a detailed discussion of at least two challenging word problems.

- **High School:** When her American history students turn in sloppily written essays, the teacher displays a well-written example on the document camera and requires the students to revise their original products.

check your understanding

2.1 Describe the personal qualities of teachers who increase students' motivation to learn.

2.2 Research indicates that high-efficacy teachers adopt new curriculum materials and change strategies more readily than do low-efficacy teachers (Roeser et al., 2002). Using personal teaching efficacy as a basis, explain why this is likely to be the case.

2.3 Based on the information in this section, what is the most effective way to communicate your enthusiasm to students? Explain.

2.4 Explain why not being called on by a teacher communicates to students that the teacher has low expectations for them.

To receive feedback for these questions, go to Appendix A.

Learning Climate: Creating a Motivating Environment

Positive learning climate. A classroom climate in which the teacher and students work together as a community of learners to help everyone achieve.

As students spend time in school, they can sense if the classroom is a safe and positive place to learn. These feelings reflect the learning climate. In a **positive learning climate,** the teacher and students work together as a community of learners to help everyone achieve. In this climate our goal is to promote students' feelings of safety and security, together with a sense of success, challenge, and understanding (see Figure 11.3).

Let's see how we can create a positive learning climate.

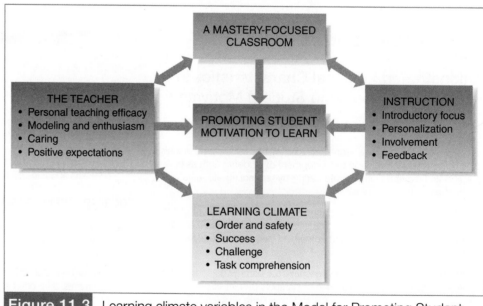

Figure 11.3 Learning climate variables in the Model for Promoting Student Motivation

Order and Safety: Classrooms as Secure Places to Learn

Order and safety together make up a climate variable that creates a predictable learning environment and promotes feelings of physical and emotional security. The importance of order and safety for promoting motivation can be explained at three levels:

- *Establishing equilibrium.* A safe, orderly, and predictable environment helps students meet their desire for equilibrium (Piaget, 1977).
- *Students' needs.* Safety is a deficiency need preceded only by survival in Maslow's (1970) hierarchy, and learners feel more autonomous—an innate need according to self-determination theory—in a safe environment (Brophy, 2010: Deci & Ryan, 2000).
- *Human memory.* A safe environment allows learners to focus working memory space on learning tasks. In environments that aren't safe, students use working memory space to think about ways to avoid criticism, ridicule, or threat.

You set the tone for this essential variable by communicating your expectations, establishing routines that create an orderly environment, modeling respect and courtesy, and requiring students to treat you and everyone else in your classroom in the same way (Blum, 2005).

> **Order and safety.** A learning climate variable that creates a predictable learning environment and supports learner autonomy together with a sense of physical and emotional security.

Success: Developing Self-Efficacy

Promoting our students' beliefs in their capabilities of accomplishing specific tasks—their self-efficacy—is one of our most important goals. Success is the most significant factor that contributes to this belief, so, once you've established a safe and orderly classroom environment, success becomes essential for student motivation. This success, however, needs to indicate learning progress and accomplishing tasks, not just high grades and performing better than others. Praise and other rewards communicate that students' understanding is increasing, and mistakes and periodic uncertainty are a normal part of learning.

You can promote success in several ways:

- Begin lessons with open-ended questions that assess learners' current understanding and promote their involvement. (We discuss open-ended questions later in the chapter).
- Use a variety of high-quality examples that develop background knowledge and promote understanding.
- Develop lessons with questioning, and prompt students when they have difficulty answering.
- Provide scaffolded practice before expecting students to work independently.
- Make assessment an integral part of the teaching–learning process, and provide detailed feedback about learning progress.

However, even with continuous progress, success won't increase motivation to learn if tasks aren't challenging, another component of an effective learning climate.

Challenge: Increasing Perceptions of Competence

Ed Psych and You

Think about how you feel when you solve a difficult problem, make a computer application work, or figure out a puzzling event. Why do you feel this way?

According to self-determination theory, developing a sense of competence is an innate need in all of us, and seeing our competence increase is intrinsically motivating (Deci & Ryan, 2000). This helps us answer the question we ask here in "Ed Psych and You." Solving difficult problems or figuring out a computer application or puzzling event increases our perception of competence. Further, successfully responding to challenges can provide a dopamine-reward rush in the pleasure sensors of our brains (Carey, 2010).

Learners' self-efficacy increases when they succeed on challenging tasks.

This suggests that success, alone, is not sufficient for promoting student motivation. Students can successfully memorize lists of facts and rules or solve routine problems, but this success does little to increase their perceptions of self-efficacy and competence, and it is not emotionally satisfying. They need to experience success in activities they perceive as challenging. In addition, students' beliefs about both attainment value and utility value are increased when they succeed on challenging tasks (Lam & Law, 2007).

You can capitalize on the motivating characteristics of challenge by helping your students identify relationships in the topics they study and the implications of these relationships for new learning (Brophy, 2010). For example, DeVonne didn't immediately tell her students that arthropods had an exoskeleton, three body parts, and segmented legs. Instead, with her guidance they identified these characteristics for themselves. Then, she had them observe and decide if a cockroach, clam, and even Mrs. Sapp (the school principal) were arthropods. Her approach was challenging for students, because some of them initially concluded that both the clam and Mrs. Sapp were arthropods.

We can readily see how this approach was richer and more motivating for the students than memorizing the characteristics of arthropods. And, when tasks are challenging, students will sometimes complain, but when they finally do succeed, their sense of accomplishment will be just that much greater.

Task Comprehension: Increasing Feelings of Autonomy and Value

Understanding what they are expected to learn and why it's important also influence motivation. To see how, let's return to DeVonne's work with her students the day after her lesson.

"Now, let's review for a few minutes," she begins. "What were the characteristics of arthropods that we identified yesterday?"

"Exoskeleton," Seleina volunteers.

"Three body parts," Tu adds.

"Jointed legs," Kevin offers.

"Good. . . . And, what are some examples of arthropods?"

The students offer crabs, lobsters, roaches, beetles, spiders, and others as examples, and DeVonne then asks, "Why is it important to study arthropods?"

After hesitating for a moment, Stephanie says, "We eat them, like shrimp and stuff."

"Good," DeVonne smiles. "Indeed, they're an important food source. In fact, did you know that insects are as nutritious as meat, and they're eaten both cooked and raw in many cultures?"

Amid, "Eeww," "Yuk," "Gross," and other reactions from students, DeVonne adds, "More than 80% of all animal species are arthropods, and there are more than a million different species. . . . Think about that. More than 8 out of 10 animals on this earth are arthropods. . . . And, they're essential for pollinating our plants. Without them, we wouldn't have enough food. We really do need to understand our most abundant, and one of our most important, neighbors."

Task comprehension. Learners' awareness of what they are supposed to be learning and an understanding of why the task is important and worthwhile.

This discussion reflects DeVonne's attempts to capitalize on **task comprehension,** learners' awareness of what they are supposed to be learning and an understanding of why the task is important and worthwhile (Eggen & Kauchak, 2002). Task comprehension also includes decisions about time allocated to tasks, pace of instruction, and provisions for extra help if needed.

As with success, a challenging task won't increase motivation to learn if students don't perceive it as meaningful and worth understanding (Vavilis & Vavilis, 2004). DeVonne could have simply said, "Be sure you know the characteristics of arthropods and some examples of them, because they will be on our next test," and statements such as this are common in classrooms. Instead, she suggested that the reason they were studying arthropods is because they have an impact on our lives today.

The need for task comprehension can be explained with both beliefs about value and the need for self-determination. First, it contributes to perceptions of utility value, the belief that understanding is useful for meeting future goals. Second, understanding what they're learning and why they're learning it increases students' feelings of autonomy, an essential need according to self-determination theory.

As with teacher qualities, climate variables are interdependent. A challenging assignment is motivating, for example, only if students feel safe. If they're worried about negative consequences for making mistakes, the motivating effects of challenge are lost. Similarly, if students don't understand why they study a topic, or the point in an activity, neither success nor challenge will increase motivation to learn. And each of the climate variables depends on the extent to which teachers care about students and hold them to high standards.

Classroom connections

Promoting a Positive Learning Climate in Classrooms

Order and Safety

1. Order and safety create a predictable learning environment and support learner autonomy and security. Create a safe and secure learning environment.

   - **Elementary:** A first-grade teacher establishes and practices daily routines until they're predictable and automatic for students.

   - **Middle School:** An eighth-grade American history teacher leads a discussion focusing on the kind of environment the students want to work in. They conclude that all "digs" and discourteous remarks should be forbidden. The teacher consistently enforces the agreement.

   - **High School:** An English teacher reminds her students that all relevant comments about a topic are welcome, and she models acceptance of every idea. She requires students to listen courteously when a classmate is talking.

Success and Challenge

2. Succeeding on challenging tasks promotes self-efficacy and helps students develop a sense of competence. Structure instruction so students succeed on challenging tasks.

   - **Elementary:** A fourth-grade teacher comments, "We're really getting good at fractions. Now I have a problem that is going to make us all think. It will be a little tough, but I know that we'll be able to do it." After students attempt the solution, he guides a discussion of the problem and different ways to solve it.

   - **Middle School:** A sixth-grade English teacher has the class practice two or three homework exercises as a whole group each day

and discusses them before students begin to work independently.

   - **High School:** As she returns their homework, a physics teacher gives her students worked solutions to the most frequently missed problems. She has students put solutions in their portfolios to study for the weekly quizzes.

Task Comprehension

3. Task comprehension reflects students' awareness of what they are supposed to be learning and an understanding of why the task is important and worthwhile. Promote task comprehension by describing rationales for your learning activities and assignments.

   - **Elementary:** As he gives students their daily math homework, a third-grade teacher says, "We know that understanding math is really important, so that's why we practice word problems every day."

   - **Middle School:** A seventh-grade English teacher carefully describes her assignments and due dates and writes them on the board. Each time, she explains why the assignment is important.

   - **High School:** A biology teacher displays the following on the document camera:

     We don't just study flatworms because we're interested in flatworms. As we look at how they've adapted to their environments, we'll gain additional insights into ourselves.

     He then says, "We'll return to this idea again and again to remind ourselves why we study each organism."

check your
understanding

3.1 Identify the learning climate variables that increase students' motivation to learn.

3.2 "I try to keep my assignments basic," a seventh-grade life science teacher comments. "So, in one activity, I give them a drawing of a skeleton, and they can look up the names in their books. They need to succeed, and they do succeed on this activity." Analyze this teacher's approach for promoting her students' motivation to learn. Explain using the climate variables in the Model for Promoting Student Motivation as a basis for your explanation.

3.3 "I have an inviolable rule in my classroom management system," a middle school teacher comments. "They may make no sarcastic or demeaning comments of any kind when one of their classmates is trying to answer a question. I explained why this is so important, and they agreed. They slip now and then, but mostly they're quite good."

Which two learning climate variables in the Model for Promoting Student Motivation is this teacher attempting to address? Explain.

To receive feedback for these questions, go to Appendix A.

$\mathcal{I}$nstructional Variables: Developing Interest in Learning Activities

Teacher qualities and climate variables form a general framework for motivation. Within this context, we can do much with our learning activities to enhance motivation to learn. From an instructional perspective, a motivated student is someone who is actively engaged in the learning process (Brophy, 2010; Stipek, 2002). To promote motivation, we must initially capture—and then maintain—students' attention and engagement throughout a learning activity. Different ways of doing this are outlined in Figure 11.4.

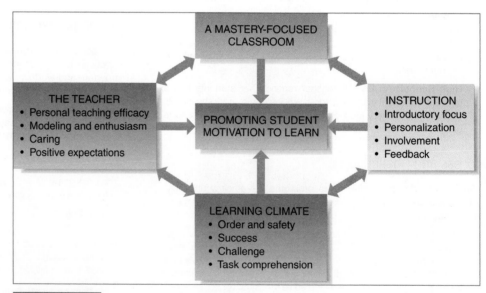

Figure 11.4 Instructional variables in the Model for Promoting Student Motivation

Introductory Focus: Attracting Students' Attention

Our understanding of human memory reminds us that all information processing begins with attention. **Introductory focus** is a lesson beginning that attracts student attention and provides a conceptual framework for the lesson (Marzano, 2003). It also attempts to capitalize on the effects of curiosity and novelty, which are characteristics of intrinsically motivating activities (Brophy, 2010). For example, DeVonne began her lesson on arthropods by bringing a live lobster to class, and the study of arthropods was its conceptual framework. The squeals and "oohs" and "aahs" clearly indicated that she had attracted their attention. Let's look at another example.

> As an introduction to studying cities and their locations, Marissa Allen, a social studies teacher, hands out a map of a fictitious island. On it are physical features such as lakes, rivers, and mountains. Information about altitude, rainfall, and average seasonal temperature is also included.
>
> Marissa begins, "The name of this activity is Survival. Our class has just been sent to this island to settle it. We have information about its climate and physical features. Where should we make our first settlement?"

You can attract your students' attention with unique problems, such as Marissa's survival task; by asking paradoxical questions ("If Rome was such a powerful and advanced civilization, why did it collapse?"); by using demonstrations with seemingly contradictory results (e.g., dropping two balls of different weights and seeing that they hit the floor at the same time); or with eye-catching examples, such as DeVonne's lobster (Hidi & Renninger, 2006).

Teachers use effective lesson introductions less often than is desirable (Brophy, 2010). Providing for effective introductory focus need not be difficult, however. All that is required is an effort to connect the content of the lesson to students' prior knowledge and interests. Some additional examples for providing introductory focus are outlined in Table 11.2.

Once your students are paying attention, and you've provided a conceptual framework for the lesson, it has to maintain their attention and provide information about learning progress. Personalization, involvement, and feedback can help meet this goal.

Introductory focus. A lesson beginning that attracts student attention and provides a conceptual framework for the lesson.

Effective teachers use introductory focus to capture students' attention and draw them into the lesson.

Personalization: Links to Students' Lives

> Sue Crompton, a second-grade math teacher, introduces the topic of graphing by measuring her students' heights. She continues by giving them a length of construction paper and has them place their strip of paper on the spot on a graph that corresponds to their height. After discussing the results, she does a similar activity with hair color to reinforce the idea of graphing.
>
> Chris Emery, a science teacher, begins a unit on genetics by saying, "Reanne, what color are your eyes?"
>
> "Blue," Reanne responds.
>
> "And how about yours, Eddie?"
>
> "Green."
>
> "Interesting," Chris smiles. "When we're done with this unit, we'll be able to figure out why Reanne's are blue and Eddie's are green, and a whole bunch of other things related to the way we look."

Table 11.2 Tools and techniques for providing introductory focus

Tool/Technique	Example
Problems and questions	• A literature teacher shows a picture of Ernest Hemingway and says, "Here we see 'Papa' in all his splendor. He seemed to have everything—fame, adventure, romance. Yet he took his own life. Why would this happen?" • A science teacher asks the students to explain why two pieces of paper come together at the bottom (rather than move apart) when students blow between them. • An educational psychology instructor introducing social cognitive theory displays the following vignette: *You're driving 75 mph on the interstate—with a posted speed limit of 65—when another car blazes past you. A minute later, you see the car stopped by the highway patrol. You immediately slow down. How would behaviorism explain your slowing down?*
Inductive sequences	• An English teacher displays the following: *I had a ton of homework last night! I was upset because I had a date with the most gorgeous girl in the world! I guess it was okay, because she had on the ugliest outfit ever!* The students find a pattern in the examples and develop the concept *hyperbole*. • An educational psychology instructor begins a discussion of development with these questions: Are you bothered when something doesn't make sense? Do you want the world to be predictable? Are you more comfortable in classes when the instructor specifies the requirements, schedules the classes, and outlines the grading practices? Does your life in general follow patterns more than random experiences? The class looks at the pattern and arrives at the concept of *equilibrium*.
Concrete examples	• An elementary teacher begins a unit on amphibians by bringing in a live frog. • A geography teacher draws lines on a beach ball to demonstrate that longitude lines intersect at the poles and latitude lines are parallel to each other. • An educational psychology instructor introduces the concept *negative reinforcement* by describing his inclination to take a pain killer to reduce his discomfort after a demanding workout.
Objectives and rationales	• A math teacher begins, "Today we want to learn about unit pricing. This will help us decide which product is a better buy. It will help us all save money and be better consumers." • A world history teacher says, "Today we're going to look at the concept of *mercantilism*. It will help us understand why, throughout history, Europe came to the New World and went into South Asia and Africa." • An educational psychology instructor says, "We know that learners construct, rather than record, understanding. Today we want to see what that principle suggests about the way we should teach most effectively."

Personalization. The process of using intellectually and/or emotionally relevant examples to illustrate a topic.

Sue and Chris both attempted to increase their students' interest through **personalization,** the process of using intellectually and/or emotionally relevant examples to illustrate a topic. DeVonne also capitalized on personalization when she helped her students understand why they were studying arthropods and how these animals affect their lives.

Personalization is a valuable motivation strategy for several reasons. First, it is widely applicable and intuitively sensible. Experienced teachers describe it as one of the most important ways to promote student interest in learning activities (Schraw & Lehman, 2001; Wortham, 2004). Second, personalized content is meaningful because it encourages students to connect new information to structures already in long-term memory (Moreno & Mayer, 2000). Third, students feel a sense of autonomy when they study topics to which they can personally relate (Iyengar & Lepper, 1999). Additional examples of teachers' attempts to personalize the topics they teach are outlined in Table 11.3.

Table 11.3 Teachers' efforts to personalize examples

Topic	Example
Creating bar graphs	A second-grade teacher uses her students' favorite flavor of jelly beans to create a large bar graph at the front of her classroom.
The concept *population density*	A teacher uses masking tape to create two identical areas on the classroom floor. She then has three students stand in one area and five students stand in the other to demonstrate that the population density of the second is greater. The class then looks up the population density of their city and other cities in their state.
Comparative and superlative adjectives	A language arts teacher has students hold up different length pencils and writes on the board: Devon has a long pencil. Andrea has a longer pencil. Steve has the longest pencil. She then has students identify the characteristics of comparative and superlative adjectives.
Finding equivalent fractions	A math teacher arranges the 24 desks in his classroom into 4 rows of 6 desks each with two rows close together and the other two rows close together. He then guides the students to conclude that two rows are 12/24ths of the desks. He next guides students to conclude that the two rows together are also 1/2 of the desks, so 12/24ths is equivalent to 1/2.
The Crusades	A World History teacher uses the class's "crusade" to prevent extracurricular activities from being eliminated at the school as an analogy for the actual Crusades in history.

Exploring diversity

Personalizing Content to Increase Motivation to Learn in Students from Diverse Backgrounds

Jack Seltzer, a high school biology teacher in the Navajo Nation reservation, uses his students' background experiences to illustrate hard-to-understand science concepts. He uses Churro sheep, a local breed that Navajos use for food and wool, to illustrate genetic principles. When they study plants, he focuses on local varieties of squash and corn that have been grown by students' ancestors for centuries. Geologic formations in nearby Monument Valley are used to illustrate igneous, sedimentary, and metamorphic rocks (Baker, 2006).

We know that belonging and relatedness are needs that strongly influence students' motivation to learn (Baumeister & DeWall, 2005), and students who don't develop a sense of belonging or identify with their schools have high dropout rates (Juvonen, 2006, 2007). This problem is particularly acute among members of cultural minorities and students who are disadvantaged (Wentzel & Wigfield, 2007). Further, minority students' disengagement is often exacerbated by the school curriculum, much of which is oriented toward mainstream, middle-class, nonminority students (Anderson & Summerfield, 2004).

Gender differences in interest also exist (Buck, Kostin, & Morgan, 2002). For instance, males tend to be more interested in topics such as war, politics, hard science, and business, whereas females are more interested in human relationships, arts, literature, marginalized groups, and social reform. Some researchers even link these interests to performance differences on standardized exams, such as advanced placement tests in high school (Halpern, 2006).

Now, let's look back to Jack Seltzer and his work with his Navajo students. He attempted to create a sense of belonging and interest in his class by capitalizing on the motivating effects of personalization. This variable is important for all students, but it can be particularly effective with members of cultural minorities, who commonly say they don't belong or don't feel welcome in school (Rubinson, 2004). When these students are presented with examples and experiences that directly relate to their lives, as Jack did, their interest and sense of belonging can significantly increase.

Involvement. The extent to which people are actively participating in an activity.

Open-ended questions. Questions for which a variety of answers is acceptable.

Involvement: Increasing Situational Interest

The questions in "Ed Psych and You" address the idea of **involvement,** the extent to which people are directly participating in an activity. For instance, when you're talking and actively listening (involved), you pay more attention to the conversation and your interest in it is higher than when you're on its fringes. The same applies in classrooms. Involvement increases situational interest, and it puts students in cognitively active roles. And, we know from our study of human memory that cognitive activity is essential for meaningful learning (Blumenfeld, Kempler, & Krajcik, 2006).

Let's look now at two strategies for increasing student involvement: open-ended questioning and hands-on activities.

Using Open-Ended Questioning to Promote Involvement

Questioning is your most generally applicable tool for increasing involvement. Students' attention is high when they're answering questions, but it drops during teacher monologues. We discuss questioning in detail in Chapter 13, but we introduce open-ended questioning here because it is particularly effective for promoting involvement (Brophy, 2006c). **Open-ended questions** are questions for which a variety of answers is acceptable.

One type of open-ended question simply asks students to make observations. Let's look at an example from DeVonne's lesson.

> **DeVonne:** Okay, what did you notice [about the lobster]?
>
> **Tu:** Hard.
>
> **Saleina:** Pink and green.
>
> **Kevin:** Wet.

Virtually any answer to her question would have been acceptable, making the question accessible and nonthreatening. As another example, a teacher in a lesson on Shakespeare's Julius Caesar might ask questions such as:

> "What has happened so far in the play?"
> "What are some of the major events?"
> "What is one thing you remember about the play?"

Like DeVonne's question, they are easy to answer, activate prior knowledge, and draw students into the lesson.

A second type of open-ended question asks for comparisons. For instance, a teacher in a lesson on amphibians and reptiles might ask questions such as the following:

> "How is a frog similar to a lizard?"
> "How are the frog and a toad similar to or different from each other?"

In the lesson on Julius Caesar, the teacher might ask:

> "How are Brutus and Marc Antony similar? How are they different?"
> "How does the setting for Act I compare with that for Act II?"

Because many answers are acceptable, open-ended questions are safe and ensure success—two of the learning climate variables we discussed earlier. By combining safety and success, you can encourage even the most reluctant student to respond without risk or fear of embarrassment. Also, because open-ended questions can be asked and answered quickly, you can use them to involve a large number of students during a single lesson.

Finally, open-ended questions provide you with insights into your students' thinking, allowing you to build on their prior knowledge (Powell & Caseau, 2004).

Using Hands-On Activities to Promote Involvement

Hands-on activities are another way of promoting involvement and student interest. For example, when students work with manipulatives in math, concrete materials in science, maps and globes in geography, or computers in language arts, their level of interest increases significantly. The involvement in DeVonne's lesson, for example, was at its highest when students in groups worked with the shrimp. In addition, hands-on activities add variety to learning activities, which increases learner interest (Perry et al., 2006).

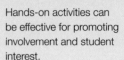

Hands-on activities can be effective for promoting involvement and student interest.

Additional strategies for promoting involvement and situational interest are outlined in Table 11.4, and each promotes cognitive engagement. Improvement drills add an element of game-like novelty to otherwise routine activities, and personal improvement increases self-efficacy. Having students use chalkboards in individual work spaces is similar to having them solve problems on paper at their desks, but the chalkboards allow sharing and discussion, and students often will use them to attempt problems they wouldn't try on paper.

Group work, in which students work together toward common learning goals, can also increase involvement (D. W. Johnson & Johnson, 2006). Group work provides opportunities for students to interact and compare their ideas with others.

A word of caution. We often tacitly assume that students who are behaviorally active in hands-on activities and group work are also cognitively active, but this may not be the case. A hands-on activity may be interesting to students but not produce meaningful learning, and group work may do nothing more than help students meet social goals. You must carefully monitor both hands-on and group-work activities to ensure that students are *learning*, not just enjoying an activity (Brophy, 2010; Mayer, 2004).

Feedback: Information About Learning Progress

We all want information about our current understanding, because it helps us make sense of our experiences. Feedback contributes to motivation by providing this information. Its value can be explained in a variety of ways (Hattie & Timperley, 2007):

* *Self-determination theory.* Feedback indicating that competence is increasing contributes to self-efficacy and self-determination.

Table 11.4   Strategies for promoting involvement

Technique	Example
Improvement drills	Students are given a list of 10 multiplication facts on a sheet. Students are scored on speed and accuracy, and points are given for individual improvement.
Games	The class is divided equally according to ability, and the two groups respond in a game format to teacher questions.
Individual work spaces	Students are given their own chalkboards on which they solve math problems and identify examples of concepts. They hold the chalkboards up when they've solved the problem or when they think an example illustrates a concept. They also write or draw their own examples on the chalkboards.
Student group work	Student pairs observe a science demonstration and write down as many observations of it as they can.

• *Attribution theory.* Feedback helps us understand why we perform the way we do, which attribution theory considers an important need.

• *Self-regulated learning.* Feedback gives us information about progress toward goals, and when they're met, our self-efficacy increases. If they're not met, we can then increase our effort or change strategies.

The type of feedback is important (Hattie & Timperley, 2007). When it provides information about learning progress, motivation increases, but if it has a performance orientation, such as emphasizing high grades, competition, and social comparisons, it can detract from motivation to learn (Brophy, 2010; Schunk et al., 2008). Performance-oriented feedback has a particularly detrimental effect on less-able students and detracts from intrinsic motivation for both low and high achievers.

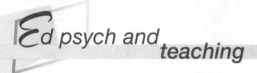

Ed psych and teaching

Applying the Climate and Instructional Variables to Increase Your Students' Motivation to Learn

Throughout the chapter, we've emphasized that the variables in the Model for Promoting Student Motivation are interdependent. This is particularly true for the climate and instructional variables. The following guidelines can help you capitalize on this interdependence as you attempt to apply the model in your classroom:

1. Establish rules and procedures that maintain a safe, orderly learning environment.
2. Create links between topics and students' personal lives.
3. Explain the reasons for studying particular topics, and provide evidence for increasing competence.
4. Establish and maintain high levels of student involvement in learning activities.
5. Provide specific and detailed feedback on student work.

Let's see how David Crawford, a world history teacher at Baker County High School, attempts to apply these guidelines as he works with his students.

As the bell rings, the students are in their seats and have their notebooks on their desks. David moves to the front of the room and begins, "Okay, everyone, let's think about some of the technology that we have in today's world. Go ahead. . . . Brenda?"

The students offer examples such as computers, cell phones, and iPods, and then David continues, "Good examples. . . . Now, we tend to think of technology as something recent, but it's existed throughout history, and we can tell a great deal about a civilization by looking at its artifacts.

He clarifies the term *artifact* and then says, "Today we're going to examine some artifacts to see what they might tell us about the people who left them behind. This will give us the thinking tools to understand the civilizations we study as we look at the history of the world."

David reaches into a box, pulls out two animal skulls, a piece of woven fabric, and a stone spear point that is ground to a fine edge, and puts them on the table at the front of the room. Then, he puts another stone spear point that is also sharp but chipped, two small animal bones, and a fragment from an animal skin on the table next to the first group.

"We'll call this Civilization A, and this one Civilization B," he says, pointing to the sets of materials.

The class observes the artifacts and with David's guidance concludes that the two skulls are from a cow and a sheep and the bones are leg and rib bones from an antelope or deer.

"Now," David smiles, "We're archeological teams, and we found these sites. . . . I want you to work with your partners and write down as many conclusions as you can about the people from each, and any comparisons between the two, such as which one you believe was more advanced. In each case, provide evidence for your conclusions."

At the end of their allotted time, David says, "Okay, what did you come up with?"

"We think those are newer," Lori says, pointing at the chipped spear points.

"No way," Rodney interjects.

"Rod," David says firmly, "remember that we can disagree, but we extend the courtesy of listening to what others have to say."

"Sorry."

"Go ahead, Lori."

"The points are sharp, and they're sort of like art."

"Okay, Rod, go ahead," David says after Lori finishes.

"Those look like they're ground," Rodney responds, referring to the points with fine edges. "Grinding would be a more advanced technology than chipping."

The class continues discussing the artifacts, and from the cow and sheep skulls and the cloth, the students conclude that Civilization A had domesticated animals and the ability to weave. And, they decide that the antelope bones and skin indicate that Civilization B probably consisted of hunter-gatherers.

After completing the discussion, David says, "Okay, for tonight, I want you to read about the Old, Middle, and New Stone Ages on pages 35 to 44 of your books and decide what ages these artifacts probably belonged to. . . . You did a great job today. You made some excellent conclusions and supported them in each case."

Now, let's look at David's attempts to apply the guidelines. First, his classroom was safe and orderly. For instance, all the students were in their desks with their notebooks out when the bell rang, indicating a well-established routine. In addition, David admonished Rodney for interrupting Lori, which suggests he was attempting to create an emotionally safe environment. These were all applications of the first guideline.

He attempted to personalize the activity, applying the second guideline, by beginning the lesson with examples of today's technology and by placing students in the role of archeologists.

Then, in displaying the artifacts and saying, "This will give us the thinking tools to better understand the civilizations we study, . . ." he provided a rationale for the activity and capitalized on introductory focus and task comprehension. Also, his comment, "You did a great job today. You made some excellent conclusions and supported them in each case," provided further evidence of their increasing competence. Each of these factors helped apply the third guideline.

Finally, David's students were highly involved in the lesson, and success was enhanced because the task—making conclusions—was open-ended and challenging. Any conclusion that the students could support was acceptable.

Next, we discuss the topic of assessment, feedback, and motivation to learn—the fifth guideline.

Assessment and Learning: Using Feedback to Increase Interest and Self-Efficacy

To examine the role of assessment and its influence on learning and motivation, let's return to David Crawford's work with his students.

The next day, David begins by saying, "One of our goals for yesterday and throughout the year is to be able to provide evidence for the conclusions we make. . . . You did a good job on this, but we need a little more practice. . . . I'm going to display the conclusions and evidence that some of you offered. . . . Now, remember the spirit we're doing this in. It's strictly for the sake of learning and improvement. It's not intended to criticize any of you. . . . I've covered up your names, so everyone can remain anonymous. . . . Let's take a look at what two groups wrote," as he displays the following on the document camera:

Conclusion: The people had cloth.

Evidence: There is cloth from Civilization A.

Conclusion: The people in Civilization A were more likely to survive.

Evidence: They had cows and sheep, so they didn't have to find wild animals. The cloth piece suggests that they wove cloth, so they didn't have to use animal skins.

"What comments can you make about the two sets of conclusions?"

"The first one isn't really a conclusion," Shantae offers. "You can see the cloth, so it really doesn't say anything."

"Good observation, Shantae. . . . Yes, a conclusion is a statement based on a fact; it isn't the fact itself."

The class then discusses the second example and agrees that the conclusion is based on evidence.

"This is the kind of thing we're looking for," David comments. "I know that you're all capable of this kind of thinking, so let's see it in your next writing sample."

He then brings out a can of soup and asks students to make conclusions about the civilization that might have produced such an artifact and to give evidence that supports each conclusion.

The class, beginning to understand the process, makes a number of comments, and David writes the students' conclusions and evidence on the board.

Assessment with detailed feedback is essential for learning, and collecting and reading the students' papers was a type of assessment. Because they had limited experience with forming conclusions based on evidence, without the assessment and accompanying feedback, David's students were unlikely to understand the difference between good and poor conclusions. The same is true for all forms of learning beyond simple memory tasks.

Feedback is important for motivation because it helps students improve the quality of their work. As they see that the quality is increasing, their perceptions of competence, self-determination, and intrinsic motivation also increase. None of this is possible without ongoing assessment and feedback.

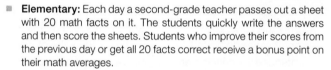

Classroom connections

Using Instructional Variables to Promote Motivation to Learn

Introductory Focus

1. Introductory focus attracts students' attention and provides a conceptual umbrella for the lesson. Plan lesson introductions to capitalize on this variable.

   ■ **Elementary:** A fifth-grade teacher introduces a lesson on measuring by bringing in a cake recipe and ingredients that have to be modified if everyone in the class is going to get a piece of cake. He says, "We want to make enough cake so we can all get a piece. This is what we're going to figure out today."

   ■ **Middle School:** A physical science teacher begins her lessons with a simple demonstration, such as whirling a cup of water suspended on the end of a string around her head. "Why doesn't the water fly out of the cup? . . . Let's try to figure this out," she says in beginning the lesson.

   ■ **High School:** An English teacher introduces *A Raisin in the Sun* (Hansberry, 1959) by saying, "Think about a Muslim family in Detroit. How do you think they felt after the events of 9/11? Keep those questions in mind as we read *A Raisin in the Sun*."

Personalization

2. Personalization uses intellectually or emotionally relevant examples to illustrate a topic. Personalize content to create links between content and students' lives.

   ■ **Elementary:** A fourth-grade teacher begins a lesson comparing animals with exoskeletons and those with endoskeletons by having students squeeze their legs to demonstrate that their bones are inside. He then passes out a number of crayfish and has the students compare the crayfish to themselves.

   ■ **Middle School:** A seventh-grade teacher begins a lesson on percentages by bringing in an ad for computer games and products from a local newspaper. The ad says "10% to 25% off marked prices." The class works problems to see how much they might save on popular computer games.

   ■ **High School:** As her class studies the Vietnam War, a history teacher asks students to interview someone who served in the military at the time. The class uses the results of the interviews to remind themselves of the "human" dimension of the war.

Involvement

3. Involvement describes the extent to which students are actively participating in a lesson. Promote high levels of involvement in all learning activities.

   ■ **Elementary:** Each day a second-grade teacher passes out a sheet with 20 math facts on it. The students quickly write the answers and then score the sheets. Students who improve their scores from the previous day or get all 20 facts correct receive a bonus point on their math averages.

   ■ **Middle School:** A seventh-grade pre-algebra teacher assigns students to work in pairs to complete seatwork assignments. He requires them to work each problem individually, then check with each other, and ask for help if they can't agree on the solution.

   ■ **High School:** An English teacher randomly calls on all students as equally as possible, whether or not they raise their hands. At the beginning of the year, he explains that his intent is to encourage participation, and that students will soon get over any uneasiness about being "put on the spot." He prompts students who are unable to answer until they give an acceptable response.

Feedback

4. Feedback provides students with information about their learning progress. Provide prompt and informative feedback about learning progress.

   ■ **Elementary:** A fourth-grade teacher discusses the most frequently missed items on each of her homework assignments and quizzes, providing detailed information about each of the items.

   ■ **Middle School:** A seventh-grade teacher writes on a student paper, "You have some very good ideas. Now you need to rework your essay so that it is grammatically correct. Look at the notes I've made on your paper."

   ■ **High School:** A world history teacher displays an "ideal answer" on the document camera for each of the items on his homework assignments and essay items on his tests. Students compare their answers to the ideal and take notes with suggestions for improving their responses.

check your
understanding

4.1   Describe instructional variables that can increase students' motivation to learn.

4.2   Identify where DeVonne used personalization in her lesson.

4.3   Provide an example of "mastery-oriented" and another example of "performance-oriented" feed-back, using the topic of writing an effective para-graph. Explain the difference between the two.

To receive feedback for these questions, go to Appendix A.

Developmentally appropriate practice

Applying the Model for Promoting Student Motivation with Learners at Different Ages

The components of the Model for Promoting Student Motivation apply to learners at all grade levels. For example, caring teachers, a safe and orderly environment, success, and high levels of student involvement are essential for all students. Developmental differences exist, however. We outline these differences in this section.

Working with Students in Early Childhood Programs and Elementary Schools

Elementary students enter school wide-eyed and optimistic, with only vague ideas about what they will do or learn. However, school is often the first time they are separated from their homes and parents, and anxiety about the unfamiliar may result. Taking extra time to make classrooms inviting places to learn is important with these children.

Interest can be a powerful motivating factor for elementary students (Hidi, Renninger, & Krapp, 2004). Topics such as animals, cartoon characters, sports, dinosaurs, and fan-tasy are interesting for most children. Incorporating these topics into reading, writing, and math assignments can be effective.

Elementary students' ability to set goals and use learning strategies are largely unde-veloped, but the beginnings of self-regulation can be established with conscious efforts to model and teach metacognition (Paris, Morrison, & Miller, 2006).

Working with Students in Middle Schools

Middle school students have become savvy about rules and procedures and the school-ing "game." However, the transition to middle school can be challenging for adolescents, and both motivation and learning often suffer (Wigfield, Byrnes & Eccles, 2006). Classes are usually larger and less personal, and students leave the security of one teacher for a schedule that sends them to different classes. Caring teachers who take the time to form personal relationships with their students are essential at this age.

Peers become increasingly important during the middle school years, and coopera-tive learning and group work become effective vehicles for increasing involvement and motivation. However, the growing influence of peers can result in off-task behaviors during group work, so structuring it carefully, monitoring students during activities, and holding students accountable for a product are important.

Variables such as challenge and task comprehension become more important than they were with elementary students. Middle schoolers also begin to assess the relevance and value of what they're studying, so personalization also becomes an increasingly important variable.

Working with Students in High Schools

While more mature, many high school students still have not reached a high level of self-regulation. Modeling self-regulation and conscious efforts to teach more sophisticated and effective learning strategies can help these students meet their needs for self-determination (Pressley & Hilden, 2006).

High school students are also self-aware and are thinking about their futures after high school, so they assess the value of the topics they study. In addition, high school stu-dents' needs for competence and autonomy are prominent. As a result, climate variables, such as challenge and task comprehension, and instructional variables, such as personal-ization and feedback, become increasingly important.

Summary

1. Describe the differences between a mastery-focused and a performance-focused classroom.

   - Mastery-focused classrooms emphasize effort and increased understanding. Performance-focused classrooms emphasize demonstrating high ability and comparisons among students.
   - Mastery-focused environments increase student motivation to learn, whereas performance-focused environments can detract from motivation to learn for all but the highest achievers.

2. Describe the personal qualities of teachers who increase students' motivation to learn.

   - Teachers who are high in personal teaching efficacy believe they can help students learn, regardless of students' prior knowledge or other factors.
   - Modeling courtesy and respect is essential for motivation, and communicating genuine interest in the topics they teach demonstrates teacher enthusiasm.
   - Teachers demonstrate that they care about their students by spending personal time with them and demonstrating respect for each individual. Holding students to high standards is one of the most effective ways to simultaneously show respect and communicate that teachers expect all students to succeed.

3. Identify the learning climate variables that increase students' motivation to learn.

   - Motivating environments are safe, secure, and orderly places that focus on learning.
   - Success on tasks students perceive as challenging increases motivation to learn. Meeting challenges provides evidence that competence is increasing and leads to feelings of autonomy.
   - In motivating environments, students understand what they're expected to learn. Understanding what they're learning and why increases perceptions of autonomy and contributes to task value.

4. Describe instructional variables that increase students' motivation to learn.

   - Teachers can increase motivation to learn by beginning lessons with examples, activities, or questions that attract students' attention and provide frameworks for information that follows.
   - Students maintain their attention and interest when teachers make content personally relevant to them and keep them involved in learning activities.
   - Teachers increase student motivation to learn by providing feedback about learning progress. When feedback indicates that competence is increasing, self-efficacy and self-determination both improve, and intrinsic motivation increases.

Understanding Student Motivation: Preparing for Your Licensure Exam

Your licensure exam will include information related to students' motivation, and we include the following exercises to help you practice for the exam in your state. This book and these exercises will be a resource for you as you prepare for the exam.

You saw at the beginning of the chapter how DeVonne Lampkin taught the concept *arthropod*. Now read about a language arts lesson on the construction of paragraphs that DeVonne taught later that same day. After reading the case study, answer the questions that follow.

> DeVonne is working with her fifth graders on their writing skills. She plans to have them practice writing paragraphs and conduct self-assessments using criteria in a 3-point rubric.

> She begins, "Today, we're going to practice some more on composing good paragraphs. . . . Now, we know the characteristics of a good paragraph, but let's review for a moment. . . . What do we look for in a well-composed paragraph?"

> "Topic sentence," several students say immediately.

> "Okay, what else?"

> "Sentences that go with the topic," others add.

> "Yes, 'go with the topic' means that the sentences support your topic sentence. You need to have at least four supporting sentences."

> DeVonne reminds students that they also need to use correct grammar and spelling, and then displays the following paragraphs:

Computers come in all shapes and sizes. One of the first computers, named UNIVAC, filled a room. Today, some large computers are as big as refrigerators. Others are as small as books. A few are even tiny enough to fit in a person's pocket.

Ann's family bought a new color television. It had a 54-inch screen. There were controls for color and brightness. Ann likes police stories. There were also controls for sound and tone.

After some discussion, the class concludes that the first example meets the criteria for an acceptable paragraph, but the second one does not, because the topic sentence doesn't have four supporting sentences and the information "Ann likes police stories" doesn't pertain to the topic.

She then says, "Now, you're going to write a paragraph on any topic that you choose, and then the class is going to grade your paper." DeVonne smiles as she hears several calls of "Woo, hoo" from the students.

The students go to work, and when they've finished, DeVonne says, "Okay, now we're going to grade the paragraphs." She reviews the criteria from the 3-point rubric, and then says, "Okay, who wants to go first?"

"Me!" several of the students shout.

"I should have known that," DeVonne smiles. "Okay, Tu, come on up."

Tu displays his paragraph and reads it aloud:

Quidditch is a wizard sport that is famous in the wizard world. There is 7 people allowed on each team. On the field there are 4 balls. The Quaffle is a red soccerball. The two bludgers try to knock players of their brooms. Finally, the Golden Snitch is very small and when caught the team gets 150 points. And that team mostly always win. Therefore, Quidditch is very exciting.

The class discusses his paragraph, agrees that it deserves a 3, and then several students call out, "I want to go next! I want to go next!"

DeVonne asks Justin to display his paragraph:

There was a boy named Josh. He lives in a house with the roof falling in and the windows were broke. He had holes in the wall and the ceiling leaked when it rained. But then again it always rained and thunder over his house. Noone every goes to his gate because he was so weird. They say he is a vampire.

She asks students to raise their hands to vote on the score for this paragraph. About half give it a 2, and the remainder give it a 1.

"Samantha, why did you give it a 2?" DeVonne asks, beginning the discussion.

"He didn't stay on his topic. . . . He needs to stay on either the boy or the house," Samantha notes.

"Haajar? . . . You gave him a 1. . . . Go ahead."

"There was a boy named Josh, and then he started talking about the house. And then the weather and then the boy again," Haajar responds.

A few more students offered comments, and the class agrees that Justin's paragraph deserves a 1.5. Justin takes his seat.

"Me, me! I want to do mine!" several students exclaim with their hands raised. DeVonne calls on Saleina to display her paragraph, the students agree that it deserves a 3, and DeVonne then says, "I am so impressed with you guys. . . . Your work is excellent."

"Okay, let's do one more," DeVonne continues. "Joshua."

"No! No!" the students protest, wanting to continue the activity and have theirs read.

"Okay, one more after Joshua," DeVonne relents with a smile. The class assesses Joshua's paragraph and one more, and just before the end of the lesson, several students ask, "Are we going to get to do ours tomorrow?"

DeVonne smiles and assures them that they will get to look at the rest of the paragraphs the next day.

Questions for Case Analysis

In answering these questions, use information from the chapter, and link your responses to specific information in the case.

1. In spite of the fact that they were having their paragraphs publicly evaluated, DeVonne's students were enthusiastic about displaying their work. Offer an explanation for their enthusiasm, including as many of the variables in the Model for Promoting Student Motivation as apply.

2. DeVonne's students' backgrounds are very diverse, and she teaches in an urban school. Assess her classroom environment for learners with diverse backgrounds.

For feedback on these responses, go to Appendix B.

Your licensure exam will also include multiple-choice questions similar to those your instructor has given you on your quizzes and tests for this course.

Important Concepts

caring (p. 368)
collective efficacy (p. 367)
introductory focus (p. 377)
involvement (p. 380)
mastery-focused classroom (p. 365)

open-ended questions (p. 380)
order and safety (p. 373)
performance-focused classroom (p. 365)

personal teaching efficacy (p. 367)
personalization (p. 378)
positive learning climate (p. 372)

self-fulfilling prophecy (p. 370)
task comprehension (p. 374)

Go to Topics: Motivation and Affect, Classroom Management, and Planning and Instruction in the MyEducationLab (www.myeducationlab.com) for *Educational Psychology: Windows on Classrooms*, where you can:

- Find learning outcomes for Motivation and Affect, Classroom Management, and Planning and Instruction, along with the national standards that connect to these outcomes.
- Complete Assignments and Activities that can help you more deeply understand the chapter content.
- Apply and practice your understanding of the core teaching skills identified in the chapter with the Building Teaching Skills and Dispositions learning units.
- Examine challenging situations and cases presented in the IRIS Center Resources.
- Access video clips of CCSSO National Teachers of the Year award winners responding to the question, "Why Do I Teach?" in the Teacher Talk section.
- See video examples included within the Study Plan that provide concrete and real-world illustrations of the topics presented in the chapter.
- Check your comprehension of the content covered in the chapter with the Study Plan. Here you will be able to take a chapter quiz, receive feedback on your answers, and then access Review, Practice, and Enrichment activities to enhance your understanding of chapter content.

MyEducationLab

chapter 12

Classroom Management: Developing Self-Regulated Learners

chapteroutline

learningoutcomes

After you've completed your study of this chapter, you should be able to:

Goals of Classroom Management
Developing Learner Self-Regulation
Creating a Community of Caring and Trust
Maximizing Time for Teaching and Learning

1. Describe the goals of classroom management, and identify applications of the goals.

Planning for Classroom Management
The Interdependence of Management and Instruction
Classroom Organization
Planning for Classroom Management in Elementary Schools
Planning for Classroom Management in Middle and Secondary Schools
Planning for the First Days of School

2. Identify characteristics of elementary, middle, and secondary school students and how they influence planning for classroom management.

Communicating with Parents
Benefits of Communication
Strategies for Involving Parents

3. Describe effective communication strategies for involving parents.

Intervening When Misbehavior Occurs
Emotional Factors in Interventions
Cognitive Interventions
Behavioral Interventions
An Intervention Continuum

4. Use cognitive and behavioral learning theories to explain effective interventions.

Serious Management Problems: Defiance and Aggression
Responding to Defiant Students
Responding to Fighting
Responding to Bullying

5. Describe your legal and professional responsibilities in cases of aggressive acts and steps you can take to respond to defiance and aggression.

classroomapplications

The following features help you apply the content of this chapter in your teaching.

Ed Psych and Teaching:
Creating and Teaching Your Classroom Rules
Responding Effectively to Misbehavior in Your Students

Classroom Connections:
Preparing Rules and Procedures in Classrooms
Communicating Effectively with Parents
Intervening Successfully in Classrooms

Developmentally Appropriate Practice:
Classroom Management with Learners at Different Ages

Exploring Diversity:
Classroom Management with Students from Diverse Backgrounds

*C*lassroom management consists of "actions teachers take to create an environment that supports and facilitates both academic and social–emotional learning" (Evertson & Weinstein, 2006, p. 4). As these authors imply, classroom management is much more than simply creating an orderly environment; effectively done, it also promotes learning, motivation, and a sense of safety and security in students (Emmer & Evertson, 2009; Evertson & Emmer, 2009). Keep these ideas in mind as you read the following case

Classroom management.
"Actions teachers take to create an environment that supports and facilitates both academic and social–emotional learning" (Evertson & Weinstein, 2006, p. 4).

study and see how Judy Harris, a middle school teacher, handles the classroom management incidents illustrated in it.

Judy's seventh-grade geography class is involved in a cultural unit on the Middle East.

As the students enter the room, they see a large map, together with the following directions displayed on the document camera.

Identify the longitude and latitude of Damascus and Cairo.

Judy's students begin each class by completing a review exercise while she takes roll and returns papers. They also pass their homework forward, each putting his or her paper on top of the stack.

Judy waits for the students to finish, and then begins, "About what latitude is Damascus. . . . Bernice?" as she walks down one of the rows.

". . . About 34 degrees north, I think," Bernice replies.

As Judy walks past him, Darren reaches across the aisle and pokes Kendra with his pencil. Her 30 students are in a room designed for 24, so the aisles are narrow.

Darren watches Judy from the corner of his eye.

"Stop it, Darren," Kendra mutters loudly.

Judy turns, comes back up the aisle, stands near Darren, and continues, "Good, Bernice. It is close to 34 degrees.

"So, would it be warmer or colder than here in the summer? . . . Darren?" she asks, looking directly at him.

". . . Warmer, I think," Darren responds after Judy repeats the question for him, because he didn't initially hear it.

"Okay. Good. And why might that be the case? . . . Jim?"

As she waits for Jim to answer, Judy leans over Rachel, who has been whispering and passing notes to Deborah, points to the rules displayed on a poster, and says quietly but firmly, "We agreed that it was important to listen when other people are talking, and you know that we all have to honor our agreements. . . . We can't learn when people aren't paying attention, and I'm uncomfortable when my class isn't learning."

"Damascus is south of us and also in a desert," Jim responds.

"Good, Jim. Now let's look at Cairo," Judy responds as she watches to ensure that Rachel is looking at the map.

Now, as you read this chapter, keep the following questions in mind:

1. What, specifically, did Judy do to create an environment that was orderly and simultaneously promoted student learning and development?
2. How can you establish and maintain a similar environment in your own classroom?

We answer these questions in this chapter.

Goals of Classroom Management

Ed Psych and You

As you anticipate your first teaching position, what is your greatest concern? Why do you feel that way?

Classroom management is a topic of ongoing concern for teachers, administrators, and the public, and it directly relates to the first question we ask here in "Ed Psych and You." If you're typical, the answer is classroom management. It was for both of us (Paul and Don) as we started our first jobs, and most beginning teachers perceive it as their most serious challenge (Kaufman & Moss, 2010). It's also a major cause of teacher burnout and job dissatisfaction for veteran teachers (Evertson & Weinstein, 2006). Public opinion polls identify it as one of schools' most challenging problems, with only inadequate funding ranked higher (Bushaw & Lopez, 2010).

Beginning teachers are often uncertain about their ability to manage classrooms, and the complexities of teaching and learning help us understand why (Doyle, 2006). For example, Judy had to deal with Darren's and Rachel's misbehavior while simultaneously maintaining the flow of her lesson. And, to prevent the incident between Darren and Kendra from escalating, she needed to immediately react to Darren while simultaneously deciding if she should intervene in the case of Rachel's whispering and note passing. Also, had she reprimanded Kendra instead of Darren—the perpetrator of the incident—it would have communicated that she didn't know what was going on in her class.

To accommodate this complexity and to create a classroom that facilitates the "academic and social–emotional learning" you saw specified in the definition, we have three major classroom management goals:

- Develop learner self-regulation.
- Create a community of caring and trust.
- Maximize time for teaching and learning.

We discuss them next.

Developing Learner Self-Regulation

Teachers frequently lament students' lack of effort and willingness to take responsibility for their own learning.

> My kids are so irresponsible," Kathy Hughes, a seventh-grade teacher, grumbles in a conversation at lunch. "They don't bring their books, they forget their notebooks in their lockers, they come without pencils.... I can't get them to come to class prepared, let alone get them to read their assignments."
>
> "I know," Mercedes Blount, one of Kathy's colleagues, responds, smiling wryly. "Some of them are totally spacey, and others just don't seem to give a rip."

The solution to this problem, while not simple or easy, is the development of student **self-regulation,** which is the ability to direct and control our actions and emotions (Berk, 2010; McDevitt & Ormrod, 2010). Self-regulation is multifaceted and includes:

- *Self-motivation*—taking responsibility for completing tasks and engaging in appropriate activities
- *Delay of gratification*—forgoing immediate rewards to gain more substantial ones later
- *Impulse control*—resisting urges to display inappropriate behaviors
- *Emotional regulation*—expressing emotions in socially appropriate ways
- *Self-socialization*—understanding society's standards of behavior and acting in accordance with those standards
- *Self-regulated learning*—setting personal learning goals together with the thinking and strategies used to reach the goals

Self-regulation. The ability to direct and control one's own actions and emotions.

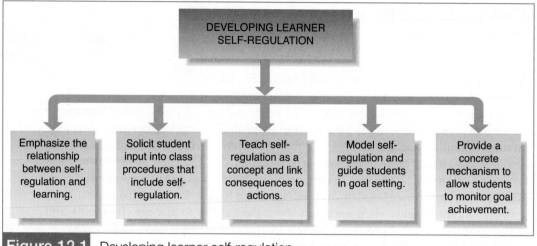

| Figure 12.1 | Developing learner self-regulation |

Developing self-regulation takes time and effort, and you will need to initially assist student efforts in the process (Bohn, Roehrig, & Pressley, 2004). Suggestions for providing your students with assistance in developing self-regulation are outlined in Figure 12.1 and illustrated in the case study that follows:

Let's see how Sam Cook, a seventh-grade math teacher, attempts to apply the suggestions in Figure 12.1 with his students.

Sam begins the first day of school by welcoming the students, having them introduce themselves, and then says, "To learn as much as possible, we need to work together and support each other in all our efforts. For instance, I need to plan for what we're trying to accomplish, and I need to bring the examples and materials that will help you understand our topics. . . . That's my part. . . . So, what is your part?"

With some guidance from Sam, the students conclude that they should bring their books and other materials to class each day, they need to be in their seats when the bell rings, and they need to understand their homework instead of merely getting it done. They also decide that they need to listen until their classmates finish talking, and they need to be supportive of their classmates' efforts.

"Now, who is responsible for all this?" Sam asks.

"We are," several students respond.

"Yes. . . . I'm responsible for my part, and you're responsible for your parts."

"Now, let's see what happens when people aren't responsible," Sam says, displaying the following on the document camera:

Josh brings all his materials to school every day, and he carefully does his homework. He has a list that he checks off to be sure that he has each of the items and that he understands his homework. If he's uncertain about any part, he asks the next day. He participates in class discussions and is supportive when his classmates talk.

Josh is learning a lot, and he says his classes are interesting. His teachers respect his effort.

Andy gets in trouble with his teachers because he often forgets to bring his book, notebook, or pencil to class. He sometimes forgets his homework, so he doesn't get credit for the assignment, and he isn't learning very much. Andy also snaps at his classmates in discussions, and sometimes hurts their feelings. Now, some of the other students don't want to talk to him.

Andy's teacher called his mom to discuss his behavior and lack of responsibility, and now Andy can't watch TV for a week.

"What are some differences you notice between Josh and Andy?" Sam asks after giving students a minute to read the vignettes.

The students make several comments, and in the process, Ronise concludes, "It's his own fault," in response to someone pointing out that Andy isn't learning very much and not getting along with the other students.

"Yes," Sam nods, "if we don't take responsibility for ourselves and control our own actions and emotions, whose fault is it if we don't learn?"

"Our own," several students respond.

"Yes," Sam emphasizes. "We're all responsible for ourselves."

With Sam's guidance, the students set goals that will help them take responsibility and control themselves, and the next day, he distributes a monitoring sheet (see Figure 12.2), which he has prepared based on the discussion. He has them put the sheet in the front of their notebooks and check off the items the first thing each morning. As the sheets accumulate, the students have a "self-regulation portfolio" that gives them a record of their progress.

Sam then asks the students how they will determine whether they understand their homework, and they agree that they will either explain it in class or to their parents. Finally, they decide that each week the students who get 18 or more checks for the self-regulation goals and 8 or more for the learning goals will have free time on Fridays. Those with fewer than 15 checks on the self-regulation goals will spend "quiet time" alone during that period, and those with fewer than 8 checks for the learning goals will work with Sam on areas that need improvement.

Now, let's see how Sam attempted to apply the suggestions in Figure 12.1. First, he emphasized from the beginning of the year that they were there to learn and that self-regulation was necessary if they were to learn as much as possible. Second, he asked for students' input into class procedures, which increases the likelihood that students will follow them and also contributes to their feelings of autonomy, a basic need according to self-determination theory (R. Ryan & Deci, 2000).

Figure 12.2 Monitoring sheet

Week of _____ Name _____

Self-Regulation Goals	Monday	Tuesday	Wednesday	Thursday	Friday
Bring sharpened pencil					
Bring notebook					
Bring textbook					
In seat when bell rings					
Listen while a classmate is speaking					
Extend courtesy and respect					
Learning Goals	**Monday**	**Tuesday**	**Wednesday**	**Thursday**	**Friday**
Finish homework					
Understand homework					

Self-regulated learners take responsibility for completing tasks and engaging in appropriate activities.

Third, Sam treated self-regulation as an abstract concept, an idea that needed to be understood and formally taught. He did so by illustrating it with an example (Josh) and nonexample (Andy). Students often aren't self-regulated simply because they aren't aware that they're behaving irresponsibly or are failing to control their impulses and emotions. Also, they often don't see the relationship between their actions and the consequences of those actions. By illustrating the consequences of being—or not being—self-regulated, Sam helped promote this awareness and understanding (Charles & Senter, 2012).

Fourth, in saying, "I need to plan for what we're trying to accomplish, and I need to bring the examples and materials that will help you understand our topics. . . . That's my part," he personally modeled responsibility. He also guided students as they set goals. And fifth, he prepared a concrete structure (the sheet) to help students monitor progress toward their goals. We want our students to gradually accept responsibility for following these procedures and also learn to make decisions that will increase their own learning. Doing so marks progress on the path to self-regulation.

Sam's students initially met goals to receive rewards (free time) and avoid punishers (quiet time alone during the free period). As self-regulation develops, his students hopefully will begin setting their own goals because they see that setting and monitoring goals increase learning.

Regardless of how hard you try, some of your students will misbehave and fail to accept responsibility, as you saw with Darren and Rachel in Judy's class. However, for students who do become self-regulated, you will have made a lifelong contribution to their learning and overall well-being.

Creating a Community of Caring and Trust

Community of caring and trust. A classroom environment in which learners feel physically and emotionally safe and their needs for belonging and relatedness are met.

As you saw in the definition, classroom management should support both academic and social–emotional learning. We can promote social-emotional learning by creating a **community of caring and trust,** a classroom environment in which learners feel physically and emotionally safe and their needs for belonging and relatedness are met (Watson & Battistich, 2006). "This requires a school and classroom climate in which students can afford to be emotionally vulnerable, and in which that vulnerability extends to the student's willingness to risk engagement in acts of kindness and concern for others" (Nucci, 2006, p. 716). In addition, we want our students to feel emotionally connected to us and their classmates and worthy of love and respect (O'Connor, Dearing, & Collins, 2011).

Caring teachers are at the core of communities of caring and trust. We demonstrate caring by spending time with our students; demonstrating that we're committed to them both as learners and as people; and modeling prosocial behaviors, such as courtesy, respect, and fairness, and expecting the same in return. And systematically teaching self-regulation, as you saw with Sam Cook and his students, creates an environment in which community and caring can develop (Watson & Ecken, 2003).

Maximizing Time for Teaching and Learning

As students' self-regulation develops and a community of caring and trust is created, disruptions and misbehavior will decrease, so you will have more time to devote to teaching and learning, the third important goal of classroom management.

But, "time" isn't as simple as it appears on the surface, and different types exist (Weinstein, Romano, & Mignano, 2011). They include:

- *Allocated time*—the amount of time a teacher or school designates for a content area or topic, such as elementary schools' allocating an hour a day to math or middle and secondary schools' having 55-minute periods.
- *Instructional time*—the amount of time left for teaching after routine management and administrative tasks are completed.
- *Engaged time*—the amount of time students are paying attention and involved in learning activities.
- *Academic learning time*—the amount of time students are successful while engaged in learning activities.

When reformers suggest lengthening the school day or year, they're suggesting an increase in allocated time. Its value, however, depends on how efficiently it's used. For instance, the benefits of increased allocated time are reduced if instructional time is spent dealing with student misbehavior. Engaged time is lost if students aren't paying attention, and academic learning time decreases if students are confused and unsuccessful.

The different types of time help us understand why classroom management is so essential for learning. In classrooms where students are engaged and successful, achievement is high, learners feel a sense of competence and self-efficacy, and interest in the topics increases (Good & Brophy, 2008).

The ideal we strive for is to maximize instructional, engaged, and academic learning time so that all our allocated time is devoted to learning. Although we must spend some time on routine activities, such as taking roll and collecting homework, we try to come as close as possible to this ideal. For example, Judy gave her students a review exercise to complete while she took roll and handed back papers. The exercise activated students' prior knowledge, focused their attention on the day's topic, and eliminated noninstructional time when disruptions are most common. This begins to answer the first question at the beginning of the chapter: "What, specifically, did Judy do to create an environment that was orderly and simultaneously promoted student learning and development?"

She maximized the time available for learning.

---

check your understanding

1.1 Describe the goals of classroom management.

1.2 Identify strategies that teachers can use to increase learner self-regulation, and explain how Sam Cook implemented these strategies with his students.

1.3 Sam's students initially attempted to meet goals to receive rewards and avoid punishment. Offer an example that would illustrate a move toward greater self-regulation.

1.4 A teacher tries to call on all students in her classes as equally as possible. To which component of time—allocated time, instructional time, engaged time, or academic learning time—is this suggestion most closely related? Explain.

To receive feedback for these questions, go to Appendix A.

Planning for Classroom Management

Some of the earliest research examining classroom management was conducted by Jacob Kounin (1970), who found that the key to orderly classrooms is the teacher's ability to prevent management problems before they occur, rather than focusing on **discipline**, responses to misbehavior after they happen. His findings have been consistently corroborated over the years (Brophy, 2006b).

Discipline. Teachers' responses to student misbehavior.

Our goal should be to prevent as many management problems as possible, leaving fewer incidents of misbehavior to deal with later. This requires planning, and beginning teachers tend to underestimate the amount of time and energy it takes. Because they don't plan carefully enough to prevent problems, they often find themselves responding to misbehavior, which increases their uncertainty about classroom management (Reupert & Woodcock, 2010). We discuss planning for classroom management in the sections that follow.

Ed Psych and You

Think about your experiences as a student. In which classes are you most likely to drift off, perhaps text a friend, or even chat with the person next to you?

Classroom management and effective instruction are interdependent.

The Interdependence of Management and Instruction

Think about the questions we ask here in "Ed Psych and You" and also about Judy's work with her students. We're most likely to drift off, text, or talk to a neighbor if our instructor stands at the front of the class droning on in a boring lecture. This was certainly true when we—Paul and Don—were students. In Judy's case, it would have been virtually impossible for her to maintain an orderly and learning-focused classroom if her instruction had been ineffective.

The close link between management and instruction has been consistently corroborated by research, and it is true whether you plan to teach in elementary, middle, or high schools (Gay, 2006).

> Without question, the most essential classroom management tool is a rigorous and relevant curriculum. Walk the halls of any school, and you'll find that it's not the strictest teacher with the most rules, but the personable teacher with the most interesting and challenging lesson plan that has the best behaved students. (Kraft, 2010, p. 45)

So, what this suggests is clear: As you plan for classroom management, you need to simultaneously plan for effective instruction (Good & Brophy, 2008). (We discuss planning for instruction in detail in Chapter 13.)

Classroom Organization

We've probably all said at some point in our lives, "I need to be better organized." This usually means that we don't have routines for where we put personal items, such as our keys, being able to easily access important papers and other materials, or wasting time.

The same idea applies in classrooms. **Classroom organization** is a professional skill that includes:

- Preparing materials in advance
- Starting classes and activities on time
- Making transitions quickly and smoothly
- Creating well-established routines

It is essential for effective classroom management, and it's one of the first aspects you'll consider as you plan.

Judy, for example, was well organized. She had an exercise prepared and waiting for her students as they entered the room, so instruction began the instant the bell rang. By planning a warm-up activity as Judy did, having your materials prepared in advance, and beginning your instruction immediately, you can eliminate "dead" time, when disruptions are most likely to occur.

Classroom organization. A professional skill that includes preparing materials in advance, starting classes and activities on time, making transitions quickly and smoothly, and creating well-established routines.

Transitions from one activity to another, such as from whole-class instruction to group work and back again, are also important. Providing clear and precise directions for group work helps make transitions quick and smooth and reduces the opportunities for disruptions.

Well-established routines, such as procedures for turning in papers, going to the bathroom, and lining up for lunch, are essential as well. When students perform routines, such as turning in papers, automatically, management problems are reduced and opportunities for teaching and learning are maximized, because you don't have to spend time and cognitive energy explaining or reminding students of what to do.

We turn now to the process of planning for classroom management in both elementary and in middle and secondary schools.

Planning for Classroom Management in Elementary Schools

If you're preparing to teach in an elementary school, your planning will be different than if you're working with older students. Let's look at one intern's experience with first graders.

> Jim Cramer, an elementary education major, is beginning his internship in a first-grade classroom. It's a disaster. Students get up from their seats and wander around the room. They begin playing with materials at their desks while he is trying to explain a topic. They argue about their roles in cooperative learning activities. Reminders to pay attention have no effect. They're not destructive or intentionally misbehaving; they're little kids. His directing teacher has a rather laissez faire approach to classroom management, and the lack of focus in her classroom doesn't seem to bother her.

Characteristics of Elementary Students

As we know, young children's thinking tends to focus on the concrete and tangible, and their attention spans are limited (Piaget, 1970; Zhou, Hofer, & Eisenberg, 2007). Socially and emotionally, they are eager to please their teachers and are vulnerable to criticism and harsh treatment (K. Carter & Doyle, 2006).

Developing a sense of personal autonomy as they move from their family to the school setting is one of the most important tasks young children face. An orderly and predictable school environment is important, because it mirrors the stability they—hopefully—experience in the home. For children who don't have this experience, an orderly classroom can be a stabilizing force that helps build a sense of trust and security (Watson & Ecken, 2003).

Young children need enough freedom to develop initiative but sufficient structure to maintain their sense of equilibrium. As they progress through the elementary grades, they continue to need acceptance and the recognition that helps them develop a sense of industry and self-assurance. This is a challenge. "It is difficult to meet the misbehaving child's needs for autonomy, belonging, and competence, and also maintain a safe and productive classroom" (Watson & Ecken, 2003, p. 3).

You can meet this challenge by creating a system of **rules,** standards for acceptable behavior, and **procedures,** guidelines for accomplishing recurring tasks, such as turning in papers and making transitions from one activity to another. As with all aspects of cognitive learning, the rules and procedures for elementary students must make sense to children if

Rules. Descriptions of standards for acceptable behavior.

Procedures. Guidelines for accomplishing recurring tasks.

The developmental characteristics of students influence planning for classroom management.

they are to be effective. To help your students make sense of your classroom rules and procedures, you must concretely teach, practice, monitor, and discuss them to help students develop self-regulation.

Rules and Procedures in Elementary Classrooms

Rules and procedures are especially important for young children, and evidence suggests that effective rules and procedures support both academic and social-emotional learning (Evertson & Emmer, 2009). For example, researchers found that implementing a rule preventing the exclusion of classmates promoted social acceptance to a greater extent than did individual efforts to help the excluded children (Harriet & Bradley, 2003).

One first-grade classroom had these rules:

- We raise our hands before speaking.
- We leave our seats only when given permission by the teacher.
- We stand politely in line at all times.
- We keep our hands to ourselves.
- We listen when someone else is talking.

Another elementary teacher stated her rules more broadly.

- We treat everyone with respect.
- We listen politely.
- We wait our turn to speak.
- We leave our seats only when given permission.

Now, let's look at these two sets of rules in more detail. First, we see that the teachers both kept the number small—five rules for the first teacher and four for the second. This makes them easier to remember, which is particularly important for young children.

Second, providing reasons for rules is essential, even for very young children. People want their experiences to make sense, and this applies as much to classroom management as to any other form of learning. Explaining the reasons for rules helps students make sense of them, helps them understand why they're important, and increases the likelihood that they will contribute to student self-regulation.

Third, when working with young children, rules and procedures need to be concretely taught and illustrated (Evertson & Emmer, 2009). Let's look at an example.

Martha Oakes, a first-grade teacher, is helping her students understand the procedure for putting away worksheets.

"I put each of their names, and my own, on cubby holes on the wall of my room. Then, while they were watching, I did a short worksheet myself and walked over and put it in my storage spot, while saying out loud, 'I'm finished with my worksheet. . . . What do I do now? . . . I need to put it in my cubby hole. If I don't put it there, my teacher can't check it, so it's very important. . . . Now, I start on the next assignment.'

"Then I gave my students the same worksheet, directing them to take it to their cubbies, quietly and individually, as soon as they were finished. After everyone was done, we spent a few minutes discussing the reasons for taking the finished work to the cubbies immediately, not touching or talking to anyone as they move to the cubbies and back to their desks, and starting right back to work. Then I gave them another worksheet, asked them what they were going to do and why, and had them do it. We then spent a few more minutes talking about what might happen if we didn't put papers where they belong.

"We have a class meeting nearly every day just before we leave for the day. We discuss classroom life and offer suggestions for improvement. Some people might be skeptical about whether or not first graders can handle meetings like this, but they can. This is also one way I help them keep our rules and procedures fresh in their minds."

Martha's approach is grounded in cognitive learning theory. She modeled the process for taking worksheets to the cubbies, used cognitive modeling in verbalizing what she was doing, and had the students practice doing the same. Being specific and concrete was essential for Martha's students because they're first graders, and these actions provided the concrete examples they needed to construct their understanding of the process and promote self-regulation. With enough practice, the procedure will become automatic, which will reduce the cognitive load on both Martha and the children.

Finally, rules and procedures need to be taught and reinforced throughout the school year. You can capitalize on examples that occur during the natural course of classroom activities, explain how an incident relates to one of the rules, and provide specific feedback to your students (K. Carter & Doyle, 2006). Over time, your students will construct an understanding of the rules' meanings and how they are expected to behave (Murphy, 2007). We illustrate these processes with a concrete example in our "Ed Psych and Teaching" feature later in this section.

Arranging the Physical Environment in Elementary Classrooms

The physical environment in elementary classrooms plays an important role in management (Weinstein et al., 2011). Tables, chairs, cubbies, carpeted areas, plants, easels, building blocks, and shelves should physically accommodate whole-group, small-group, and individual study and should be flexible and adaptable to various instructional formats.

While everyone's classroom will look different, some guidelines can be helpful (Evertson & Emmer, 2009):

- Be sure that all students can see the writing board, document camera or overhead projector, and other displays. If students have to move or crane their necks to see, disruptions are more likely.
- Design your room so you can see all your students. Monitoring their reactions to instruction is important for both learning and classroom management.
- Make sure that students can easily access commonly used materials without disrupting their classmates.
- Keep high-traffic areas free from obstructions, and provide ample space for student movement.

Figure 12.3 illustrates the physical arrangement of one elementary classroom. Note how it is designed to maximize these guidelines. This is merely an example, and you may choose to arrange your classroom differently.

Planning for Classroom Management in Middle and Secondary Schools

Middle and secondary classes are populated by adolescents, who have unique developmental characteristics, and they will influence your planning. Let's take a look.

Characteristics of Middle and Secondary Students

As students move through school, several developmental trends become significant:

- The influence of peers increases.
- Needs for belonging and social acceptance increase.
- Search for a sense of identity begins.
- Desire for autonomy and independence increases.

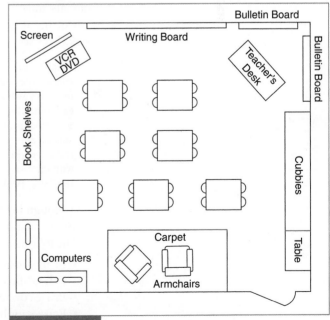

Figure 12.3 The physical arrangement of an elementary classroom

As students move through school, the influence of peers and the need for belonging and social acceptance increase.

Learning and motivation theories help us understand the implications of these developmental changes for classroom management. For example, social cognitive theory helps us understand how peers influence student behavior. Peers become important models, and students tend to imitate peers who are accomplished in academics, athletics, or even delinquency (Kidron & Fleischman, 2006). Vicarious reinforcement and punishment can be effective if peers believe that the reinforcers and punishers are fairly administered. Judy's interventions with Darren and Rachel are examples. Their classmates could see that they were breaking rules the class had agreed upon and that Judy was enforcing the rules fairly.

Second, belonging and relatedness are important to all students, and the need to be accepted by peers increases as students move into adolescence. This helps us understand why they tend to be conforming in their speech, dress, and behavior even if seemingly bizarre by adult standards. Peer rejection can lead to academic, personal, and social problems, which can then result in disruptive behavior (Wentzel, 2003). You can promote feelings of belonging and relatedness by communicating a genuine commitment to students, both as people and as learners, calling on all students as equally as possible, and enforcing rules forbidding students from mistreating each other (Kraft, 2010).

Third, adolescents are beginning their search for identity, and their needs for autonomy and independence increase. This can result in attempts at rebellious and seemingly capricious behavior, which may frustrate you. However, while attempting to exercise their newfound independence, adolescents need the stability and equilibrium that result from the firm hand of a caring teacher who sets clear limits for acceptable behavior.

Rules and Procedures in Middle and Secondary Classrooms

As students move into middle school, perceptions of fairness, inequitable treatment, and teachers having "favorites" increase. As a result, clear rationales for rules are essential, and students must perceive the rules as fair and consistently enforced. Allowing students to provide input into the rules is more important than it is with elementary students. Does it work? Let's see what one middle school teacher had to say.

> I began with my first-period class. We started slowly, with my asking them about what it would take for the class to work for them. I then told them what it would take for the class to work for me. I was amazed at the overlap. . . . We talked about respect and the need to respect ideas and each other, to listen to and be willing to be an active participant without [verbally] running over other people in the class or being run over. . . . Well, this was five months ago and I was amazed at the level of cooperation. . . . I didn't believe it would make a difference; the students really surprised me with their level of maturity and responsibility and I surprised myself with my own willingness to change. This has been a great year and I am sorry to see it end. (Freiberg, 1999, p. 169)

Although involving students in management decisions won't solve all problems, it is an important first step in gaining middle and secondary students' cooperation.

The following are rules from one seventh-grade class:

- Be in your seat and quiet when the bell rings.
- Follow directions the first time they're given.
- Bring covered textbooks, notebook, pen, pencils, and planner to class every day.
- Raise your hand for permission to speak or leave your seat.
- Keep hands, feet, and objects to yourself.
- Leave class only when dismissed by the teacher.

As in elementary classrooms, the specific rules you create will depend on your professional judgment. For example, some teachers suggest that the third rule is too specific, but this teacher noted that the specifics were necessary to ensure that her students actually brought the materials to class (J. Holmquist, Personal Communication, January 14, 2008).

As students move into high school, their behavior tends to stabilize, they communicate more effectively at an adult level, and they respond generally well to clear rationales.

The following are rules taken from a tenth-grade class:

- Do all grooming outside of class.
- Be in your seat before the bell rings.
- Stay in your seat at all times.
- Bring all materials daily. This includes your book, notebook, pen/pencil, and paper.
- Give your full attention to others in discussions, and wait your turn to speak.
- Leave when I dismiss you, not when the bell rings.

In both cases the rules are designed to accommodate the characteristics of the students. For example, older students sometimes obsess about their looks and decide, for example, to brush their hair in the middle of a class discussion, which explains, "Do all grooming outside of class."

As with rules in elementary classrooms, they vary in specificity, but the number of rules is small. Both the seventh-grade teacher and the tenth-grade teacher provided clear rationales for the rules, and they applied the rules consistently throughout the school year.

Arranging the Physical Environment in Middle and Secondary Classrooms

The physical environment in middle and secondary classrooms tends to be the more nearly traditional arrangement of desks in rows or in a semicircle facing the front of the room. Figures 12.4 and 12.5 illustrate these arrangements.

If you use a combination of whole-group and small-group instruction, you may want to arrange the room as you see in Figure 12.6, which helps simplify making transitions back and forth. Students are seated with their group mates so they don't have to move to get into their groups. Then, when the learning activity moves from small to whole group, students merely have to turn their heads to see you, the board, and the overhead or document camera.

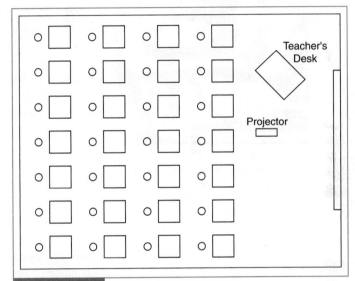

Figure 12.4 Classroom arrangement in traditional rows

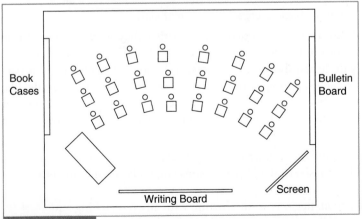

Figure 12.5 Classroom arrangement in a semicircle

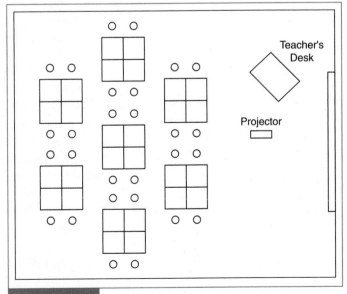

Figure 12.6 Sample seating arrangement for group work

Classrooms decorated with personal items and student work create inviting learning environments.

No single room arrangement works for all situations. For example, one study found that behavior improved when learners were seated in rows (Bennett & Blundel, 1983), but another found that a semicircle was most effective (Rosenfield, Lambert, & Black, 1985). You should experiment and use the arrangement that works best for you.

Personalizing Your Classroom

Many classrooms, and particularly those in middle and secondary schools, are quite impersonal, and they reveal little about the people who spend time in them (Emmer & Evertson, 2009).

Your classroom will be more inviting if you post personal items such as individual or class pictures, artwork, poetry, and other products prepared by students, on bulletin boards or posters. A section of a bulletin board can display names of students who improved from one test to another or some other form of recognition so all students have an equal chance of being honored.

You can also personalize your classroom by involving students in decisions about its arrangement. If they know that the goal is promoting learning, and if self-regulation is stressed, their input provides a sense of ownership that increases their security and sense of belonging.

Planning for the First Days of School

Research consistently indicates that the patterns of behavior for the entire year are established in the first few days of school (Gettinger & Kohler, 2006; V. Jones & Jones, 2010). Let's look at two examples.

> Donnell Alexander is waiting at the door for her eighth graders with prepared handouts as students come in the room. As she distributes them, she says, "Take your seats quickly, please. You'll find your name on a desk. The bell is going to ring in less than a minute, and everyone needs to be at his or her desk and quiet when it does. Please read the handout while you're waiting."
>
> She is standing at the front of the room, surveying the class as the bell rings. When it stops, she begins, "Good morning, everyone."
>
> Vicki Williams, who also teaches eighth graders across the hall from Donnell, is organizing her handouts as the students come in the room. Some take their seats while others mill around, talking in small groups. As the bell rings, she looks up and says over the hum of the students, "Everyone take your seats, please. We'll begin in a couple minutes," and she turns back to organizing her materials.

In these first few minutes, Donnell's students learned that they were expected to be in their seats and ready to start at the beginning of class, whereas Vicki's learned just the opposite. Students quickly understand these differences, and unless Vicki changes this pattern, she will soon have problems, perhaps not dramatic, but chronic and low grade, like nagging sniffles that won't go away. Problems such as these cause more teacher stress and fatigue than any other (Friedman, 2006). Some suggestions for the first few days include the following:

- *Establish expectations.* Hand out a description of the class requirements and grading system the first day. Emphasize that all the decisions you make are intended to promote learning.
- *Plan structured instruction.* Begin your instruction with an eye-catching and motivating learning activity, and avoid group work for the first few days.

- *Teach rules and procedures.* Begin teaching your rules and procedures the first day of class, and discuss and practice the rules with extra frequency the first few days.
- *Begin communication with parents.* Write a letter to parents, which includes a description of the class requirements and rules and procedures, hand it out the first day, and have students return the letter with parents' signatures the following day.

Establishing expectations and communicating with parents immediately demonstrates that you're in charge of your classroom and that you have your act together. Combined with effective instruction, nothing does more to prevent classroom management problems.

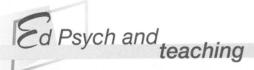

Creating and Teaching Your Classroom Rules

Rules are essential for creating an orderly and learning-focused class-room. The following guidelines can help in your efforts to create and teach rules effectively:

1. State rules positively.
2. Minimize the number.
3. Solicit student input.
4. Emphasize rationales.
5. Use concrete examples to illustrate rules and procedures.

(We focus on rules in this section, but the guidelines apply equally well to procedures.)

Let's flash back to the beginning of the year to see how Judy Harris created and taught her rules:

Judy begins by having students introduce themselves, including any personal items they would like to share, and she does the same.

When they're finished, she says, "Our goal for this class is to learn as much as possible about the geography of our world and how it impacts the way we live. In order to learn as much as possible, we need some rules that will guide the way we operate. So, think about some rules that make sense and are fair to all of us. . . . Go ahead, Jonique."

". . . We should listen," Jonique offers after pausing for several seconds.

The class agrees that the rule makes sense, Judy writes it on the board, and then asks, "Why is this rule so important?"

". . . It's rude if we don't listen to each other or if we interrupt when someone is talking," Enita offers.

"Of course," Judy smiles. "What's the very most important reason?"

"To learn," Antonio responds, remembering what Judy said at the beginning of the discussion.

"Absolutely, that's what school is all about. We learn less if we don't listen. . . . And, we're all responsible for our own behavior, so this will also help us meet that goal. . . . And listening attentively is a part of treating everyone with courtesy and respect."

The students agree that they all want to be treated courteously, Judy

writes it on the board, and she continues to lead the discussion until the rules you see here appear on the list.

In each case she emphasizes why the rule is important, how it will increase learning, and their ability to take responsibility for their own behavior.

Throughout the year, and particularly during the first few weeks of school, when an incident occurs, such as one student interrupting another, Judy stops what they are doing, reminds the class of the rule, and again asks the students why it's important. The students gradually adapt to the rules and become acclimated to the classroom environment.

Let's look now at Judy's attempts to apply the guidelines. The first two are illustrated in the rules themselves: She stated the rules positively and created only five. Positively stated rules promote a supportive emotional climate, and keeping the number small reduces the amount students must remember. Students most commonly break rules—particularly in elementary schools—because they simply forget!

Judy applied the third guideline—soliciting student input—when she said, "In order to learn as much as possible, we need some rules that will guide . . . us. . . . Go ahead, Jonique." Being asked for input creates social contracts that can increase moral development, students' feelings of autonomy, and motivation to learn (Brophy, 2010; R. Ryan & Deci, 2000). This guideline is more important at the middle and secondary level than in elementary schools, and some teachers choose to create effective rules and procedures without student input (K. Carter & Doyle, 2006). We endorse the process, particularly at the middle and secondary levels, because it reinforces the message that students are responsible for their actions.

Applying the fourth, and perhaps most important, guideline, Judy provided a careful rationale for each rule. Students are more likely to accept a rule, even when they disagree with it, if they understand why it's important.

Finally, Judy applied the fifth guideline by using incidents as concrete examples that illustrated the rules during the normal course of learning activities. Earlier, you saw how Martha Oakes had her first graders practice the procedure for putting worksheets in their cubbies. Concrete examples such as these help students construct their understanding of the rules, just as they construct understanding of any concept.

Classroom connections

Preparing Rules and Procedures in Classrooms

1. Effective classroom management begins with planning. Carefully plan your rules and procedures before you meet your first class.

   ■ **Elementary:** A third-grade teacher prepares a handout for his students and their parents and gives it to his students the first day of school. The students take the handout home, have their parents sign it, and return it the next day.

   ■ **Middle School:** A prealgebra teacher prepares a short written list of rules before she starts class on the first day. She plans to ask her students to suggest additional rules that will increase everyone's opportunity to learn.

   ■ **High School:** An English teacher prepares a description of his procedures for the way writing drafts will be handled and how his class will use peer comments to improve essays. He displays and discusses the procedure the first day of class.

   ■ **Elementary:** At the beginning of the school year, a first-grade teacher takes a few minutes each day to have her students practice procedures such as turning in materials and lining up for lunch. She continues having them practice until students follow the procedures without being reminded.

   ■ **Middle School:** A sixth-grade teacher has a rule that says, "Treat everyone with respect." She offers specific examples, and asks students to discuss whether or not the example illustrates treating everyone with respect.

   ■ **High School:** A chemistry teacher takes a full class period to teach safe lab procedures. She models correct procedures, explains the reasons for them, and carefully monitors students as they work in the lab.

Teaching Rules and Procedures

2. The developmental characteristics of students influence teachers' management strategies. Consider the developmental level of your students when teaching rules and procedures.

check your understanding

2.1 Identify characteristics of elementary, middle, and secondary students, and explain how they influence planning for classroom management.

2.2 In the examples presented in this section, we see "We keep our hands to ourselves" in the first-grade list and we see a similar rule—"keep hands, feet, and objects to yourself"—in the seventh-grade list, but not in the tenth-grade list. Explain the likely reason for this difference.

2.3 Using your understanding of cognitive learning theory as a basis, explain why using examples to teach rules and procedures is so important.

To receive feedback for these questions, go to Appendix A.

Communicating with Parents

Students' home environments have a powerful influence on both learning and classroom management, so involving parents in their children's life at school is essential (O'Connor et al., 2011). Classrooms with large numbers of students from diverse backgrounds present unique communication challenges (J. M. Walker & Hoover-Dempsey, 2006). Lower parent participation in school activities is often associated with families who are members of cultural minorities, are lower in socioeconomic status, or have a child enrolled in either special education or programs for students who are English learners (ELs) (Hong & Ho, 2005). You will need to make special efforts to initiate and maintain home–school communication with these parents (Zaragoza, 2005).

Benefits of Communication

Students benefit from home–school cooperation in several ways, such as more positive attitudes and higher long-term achievement, better attendance, greater self-regulation, and increased enrollment in postsecondary education (Hong & Ho, 2005; Sheldon, 2007).

These outcomes likely result from parents' participation in school activities, higher expectations for their children, and teachers' increased understanding of learners' home environments. Deciding how to respond to a student's disruptive behavior is easier, for example, if you know that his mother or father has lost a job, his parents are going through a divorce, or there's an illness in the family.

Parent–teacher collaboration can also have benefits for you as a teacher. For example, teachers who encourage parental involvement report more positive feelings about teaching and their school and rate parents higher in helpfulness and follow-through (Weinstein et al., 2011).

Strategies for Involving Parents

All schools have formal communication channels, such as open houses—usually occurring within the first 2 weeks of the year—when teachers introduce themselves and describe their policies; interim progress reports, which tell parents about their youngsters' achievements at the midpoint of each grading period; parent–teacher conferences; and, of course, report cards. These processes are school-wide and necessary, but you can go well beyond them. Let's see how Jacinta Escobar attempts to increase communication with her students' parents.

Students benefit from home–school cooperation in a number of ways, including higher achievement and increased motivation to learn.

> Every year Jacinta prepares a letter to parents, which states that she expects to have a productive and exciting year, outlines her expectations and classroom procedures, and solicits parents' support. She shares and discusses it with her students the first day of class, and explains why having their parents involved is so important. She also asks for their suggestions for rules and procedures to include in the letter. She then takes the letter home, revises it, and brings a final copy to school the next day. She sends the letters home with her students, reminding them that the letters must be signed and returned. She follows up on those that aren't returned with e-mails and phone calls. Her letter appears in Figure 12.7.
>
> Every week throughout the year, Jacinta sends assignments and graded homework home to be signed by parents—to indicate that the parents have looked at them. She also encourages parents to contact her if they have any questions about the packets.
>
> During the evening, Jacinta periodically calls parents to let them know about their children's progress. If students miss more than one assignment, she calls immediately and expresses her concern. She also makes a point of e-mailing parents to report positive news, such as a student's exceeding requirements, overcoming an obstacle, or showing kindness to a classmate.

Jacinta attempted to promote communication with parents in three ways. The first was her letter. (Her letter is simply an example. You will tailor your letter to best meet your students' needs.) It began the communication process, expressed positive expectations, specified class rules (described as "guidelines"), and outlined procedures for homework, absences, and extra credit.

The letter also asked for the parents' signature, which makes it a contract soliciting their support. Signatures aren't guarantees, but they symbolize a commitment and increase the likelihood that parents and students will attempt to honor it. Also, because students have input into the content of the letter, they feel greater ownership of the process.

Notice also that the letter is free from grammar, punctuation, and spelling errors. Teachers sometimes send communications home with errors in them. Don't. First impressions are important and lasting. Your first letter creates a perception of your competence, and errors detract from your credibility.

Figure 12.7 Letter to parents

August 22, 2012

Dear Parents,

I am looking forward to a productive and exciting year, and I am writing this letter to encourage your involvement and support. You always have been and still are the most important people in your youngster's education. We cannot do the job without you.

For us to work together most effectively, some guidelines are necessary. With the students' help, we prepared the ones listed here. Please read this information carefully, and sign where indicated. If you have any questions, please call me at Southside Middle School (441-5935) or at home (221-8403) in the evenings.

Sincerely,

Jacinta Escobar

AS A PARENT, I WILL TRY MY BEST TO DO THE FOLLOWING:

1. I will ask my youngsters about school every day. (Evening meal is a good time.) I will ask them about what they're studying and try to learn about it.

2. I will provide a quiet time and place each evening for homework. I will set an example by also working at that time or reading while my youngsters are working.

3. Instead of asking if their homework is finished, I will ask to see it. I will have them explain some of the information to see if they understand it.

Parent's Signature _____

STUDENT SURVIVAL GUIDELINES:

1. I will be in class and seated when the bell rings.

2. I will follow directions the first time they are given.

3. I will bring covered textbook, notebook, paper, and two sharpened pencils to class each day.

4. I will raise my hand for permission to speak or leave my seat.

5. I will keep my hands, feet, and objects to myself.

HOMEWORK GUIDELINES:

1. Our motto is I WILL ALWAYS TRY. I WILL NEVER GIVE UP.

2. I will complete all assignments. If an assignment is not finished or ready when called for, I understand that I get no credit for it.

3. If I miss work because of an absence, it is my responsibility to come in before school (8:15–8:45) to make it up.

4. I know that I get one day to make up a test or turn in my work for each day I'm absent.

5. I understand that extra credit work is not given. If I do all the required work, extra credit isn't necessary.

Student's Signature _____

In her second attempt to enhance communication, Jacinta sent packets of students' work home every week and asked parents to sign and return them. In addition to creating a link between home and school, these packets give parents an ongoing record of their child's progress.

Third, she periodically called and e-mailed parents, which is very effective for maintaining communication and enlisting cooperation (Anderson & Minke, 2007). Allocating some of your personal time to call or e-mail parents communicates caring better than any other way. Also, talking to a parent allows you to be specific in describing a student's needs and gives you a chance to again solicit support. If a student is missing assignments, for example, you can find out why and can encourage parents to more closely monitor their child's study habits.

When we talk to parents, we need to establish a positive, cooperative tone that lays the foundation for joint efforts. Consider the following:

"Hello, Mrs. Hansen? This is Jacinta Escobar, Jared's geography teacher."

"Oh, uh, is something wrong?"

"Not really. I just wanted to call to share with you some information about your son. He's a bright, energetic boy, and I enjoy seeing him in class every day. But he's missing some homework assignments."

"I didn't know he had geography homework. He never brings any home."

"That might be part of the problem. He just might forget that he has any to do. I have a suggestion. I have the students write their homework assignments in their folders each day. Please ask Jared to share his folder with you every night, and make sure that his homework is done. Then, please initial it so I know you and he talked. I think that will help a lot. How does that sound?"

"Sure. I'll try that."

"Good. We don't want him to fall behind. If he has problems with the homework, have him come to my room before or after school, and I'll help him. Is there anything else I can do? . . . If not, I look forward to meeting you soon."

This conversation was positive, created a partnership between home and school, and offered a specific plan of action.

Decisions about when to call parents about a management issue depend on your professional judgment. The question, "To what extent does this issue influence learning?" is a good guideline. For instance, you should probably handle an incident where a student slips and uses a cuss word in class. On the other hand, if the student's language or behaviors are detracting from other students' learning, you should probably contact the parents.

Finally, emphasizing accomplishments should be uppermost in all types of communication with parents. When you call about a problem, first try to describe accomplishments and progress if possible. You can also initiate communication for the sole purpose of reporting good news, as Jacinta did in her e-mails. All parents want reasons to feel proud of their children, and sharing accomplishments can further improve the home–school partnership.

As it continues to expand, technology will provide an ever more important channel for improving communication. For example, you can create an electronic template and involve your students in inserting information into it. As it becomes a routine you can maintain communication with parents efficiently and with a minimum of time and effort.

Classroom connections

Communicating Effectively with Parents

1. Communication with parents is an essential part of effective classroom management. Begin communication during the first few days of school, and maintain it throughout the year.

   ■ **Elementary:** A kindergarten teacher calls each of her students' parents during the first week of school, tells them how happy she is to have their children in her class, learns as much as she can about them, and encourages them to contact her at any time.

   ■ **Middle School:** Each week, a sixth-grade social studies teacher sends home a "class communicator," describing the topics his students will be studying, and giving suggestions parents can follow in helping their children. Students write notes to their parents on the communicator, describing their personal efforts and progress.

   ■ **High School:** A geometry teacher sends a letter home at the beginning of the school year, describing his homework and assessment policies. He calls parents when more than one homework assignment is missing.

2. Effective communication with parents is positive, clear, and concise. Communicate in nontechnical language, and make specific suggestions to parents for working with their children.

   ■ **Elementary:** A third-grade teacher asks all her parents to sign a contract agreeing that they will (a) designate an hour each evening when the television is shut off and children do homework; (b) ask their children to show them their homework assignments each day; and (c) look at, ask their children about, and sign the packet of papers that is sent home every other week.

   ■ **Middle School:** A sixth-grade teacher discusses a letter to parents with his students. He has them explain what each part of the letter says and then asks the students to read and explain the letter to their parents.

   ■ **High School:** A ninth-grade basic math teacher makes a special effort at the beginning of the school year to explain to parents of students with exceptionalities how she'll modify her class to meet their children's needs. She strongly encourages parents to monitor homework and assist if they can.

3. Take extra steps to communicate with the parents of children who are members of minorities.

   ■ **Elementary:** A second-grade teacher in an urban school enlists the aid of teachers who are bilingual. When he sends messages home, he asks them for help in translating notes for parents.

   ■ **Middle School:** At the beginning of each grading period, a sixth-grade teacher sends a letter home, in each student's native language, describing the topics that will be covered, the tests and the approximate times they will be given, and any special projects that are required.

   ■ **High School:** A biology teacher, who has many students with parents who speak little English, holds student-led conferences in which the students report on their progress. She participates in each conference and has students serve as translators.

check your understanding

3.1 Describe effective communication strategies for involving parents.

3.2 Explain how Jacinta's letter home helped to meet the classroom management goals discussed earlier in the chapter.

3.3 In this section, we said that calling or e-mailing parents communicates caring better than any other way. Explain how calling or e-mailing parents communicates caring. (Hint: Think about your study of time earlier in the chapter.)

To receive feedback for these questions, go to Appendix A.

Intervening When Misbehavior Occurs

Our focus to this point has been on preventing management problems. We have emphasized the interdependence of classroom management and effective instruction, the importance of planning, and the central role rules and procedures play in creating a classroom environment that promotes both academic and social–emotional learning. Despite your best efforts, however, your students will periodically misbehave or fail to pay attention. For example, Judy, in our opening case study, had carefully planned her rules and procedures, she was well organized, and she promoted high levels of student involvement in her teaching, but she still had to intervene with Darren and Rachel. This is common in classrooms.

In the following sections, we discuss interventions from emotional and humanistic, cognitive, and behaviorist perspectives. Each helps guide us as we make decisions about how to intervene most effectively.

Emotional Factors in Interventions

From our study of humanistic views of motivation and Maslow's work, we understand that safety—including emotional safety—is an important need for all of us. This need relates to the questions we ask in "Ed Psych and You." We all want to avoid being humiliated in front of our peers, and the same applies in classrooms. The emotional tone of your interventions influences both the likelihood of students complying with them and their attitudes toward you and the class afterward. Loud public reprimands, criticism, and sarcasm reduce students' sense of safety and are particularly destructive in elementary schools, where children are vulnerable and strongly seek the approval of their teachers. In middle and secondary schools, they create resentment, detract from classroom climate, and lead to students finding creative ways to be disruptive without getting caught.

Ed Psych and You

Have you ever been chewed out in front of other people or have been in an argument in public? How did it make you feel? How did you feel afterward?

Similarly, arguing with students about the interpretation of a rule or compliance with it also detracts from the emotional climate of classrooms. You never "win" an argument with students. You can exert your authority, but doing so is not sustainable throughout a school year, resentment is often a side effect, and the encounter may expand into a major incident (Pellegrino, 2010).

Consider the following incident that occurred after a teacher directed a chronically misbehaving student to move:

> **Student:** I wasn't doing anything.
>
> **Teacher:** You were whispering, and the rule says listen when someone else is talking.
>
> **Student:** It doesn't say no whispering.
>
> **Teacher:** You know what the rule means. We've been over it again and again.
>
> **Student:** Well, it's not fair. You don't make other students move when they whisper.
>
> **Teacher:** You weren't listening when someone else was talking, so move.

The student knew what the rule meant and was simply playing a game with the teacher, who allowed herself to be drawn into an argument. In contrast, consider the following.

> **Teacher:** Please move up here (pointing to an empty desk in the first row).
>
> **Student:** I wasn't doing anything.
>
> **Teacher:** One of our rules says that we listen when someone else is talking. If you would like to discuss this, come in and see me after school. Please move now (turning back to the lesson as soon as the student moves).

This teacher maintained an even demeanor and didn't allow herself to be pulled into an argument or even a brief discussion. She handled the event quickly and efficiently, offered to discuss it with the student, and immediately turned back to the lesson.

Students' inclination to argue with teachers strongly depends on the emotional climate of the classroom. If rules and procedures make sense to students, and if they're enforced consistently and fairly, students are less likely to argue. When students break rules, simply reminding them of the rule and why it's important, and requiring compliance, as Judy did with Rachel, are as far as minor incidents should go. (We examine serious management issues, such as defiance and aggression, later in the chapter.)

When interventions make sense to students, the likelihood of management problems is reduced.

Withitness. A teacher's awareness of what is going on in all parts of the classroom at all times and communicating this awareness to students.

Cognitive Interventions

The term *cognitive* implies thinking, and the desire for our experiences to make sense is arguably the most fundamental principle of cognitive learning theory. We said earlier that rules and procedures should make sense to students, and we want our interventions to make sense to them as well. If they do, the likelihood of serious management problems is sharply reduced. Also, rules, procedures, and interventions that make sense contribute to students' self-regulation. When students understand the impact of their behavior on others and on learning, they are more likely to begin regulating their own actions and emotions. Keep these ideas in mind as you examine the following interventions.

Demonstrate Withitness

Withitness, a teacher's awareness of what is going on in all parts of the classroom at all times, and communicating this awareness to students, is an essential component of successful interventions (Kounin, 1970). Withitness is often described as "having eyes in the back of your head." Let's compare two teachers.

> Ron Ziers is explaining the process for finding percentages to his seventh graders. While Ron illustrates the procedure, Steve, in the second desk from the front of the room, is periodically poking Katilya, who sits across from him. She retaliates by kicking him in the leg. Bill, sitting behind Katilya, pokes her in the arm with his pencil. Ron doesn't respond to the students' actions. After a second poke, Katilya swings her arm back and catches Bill on the shoulder. "Katilya!" Ron says sternly. "We keep our hands to ourselves! ... Now, where were we?"
>
> Karl Wickes has the same group of students in life science. He puts a drawing displaying a flowering plant on the document camera. As the class discusses the information, he notices Barry whispering something to Julie, and he sees Steve poke Katilya, who kicks him and loudly whispers, "Stop it." As Karl asks, "What is the part of the plant that produces fruit?" he moves to Steve's desk, leans over, and says quietly but firmly, "We keep our hands to ourselves in here." He then moves to the front of the room, watches Steve out of the corner of his eye, and says, "Barry, what other plant part do you see in the diagram?"

We can see why demonstrating withitness is a cognitive intervention. In Ron's class, being reprimanded when she was completely innocent didn't make sense to Katilya, whereas seeing Karl immediately respond to Steve's misbehavior did. This is why withitness is so important.

Karl demonstrated withitness in three ways:

- He identified the misbehavior immediately, and quickly responded by moving near Steve. Ron did nothing until the mischief had spread to other students.
- He correctly identified Steve as the cause of the incident. In contrast, Ron reprimanded Katilya, leaving students with a sense that he didn't know what was going on.
- He responded to the more serious infraction first. Steve's poking was more disruptive than Barry's whispering, so Karl first responded to Steve and then called on Barry, which drew him back into the activity and made further intervention unnecessary.

Withitness goes further (Hogan et al., 2003). It also involves watching for evidence of inattention or confusion and responding with questions, such as "Some of you look puzzled. Do you want me to rephrase the question?" And it includes approaching or calling on inattentive students to bring them back into lessons.

Lack of withitness is often a problem for beginning teachers because of the heavy cognitive load on their working memories, making the process of continually monitoring student behavior difficult (Wubbels, Brekeimans, den Brok, & van Tartwijk, 2006). You can best address this issue by creating well-established routines and carefully planning your instruction, which reduce the cognitive load during teaching and contribute to your own self-confidence. As you acquire experience, you will learn to be sensitive to students and make adjustments to ensure that they are as involved and successful as possible.

Be Consistent and Follow Through

"Be consistent" is recommended so often that it has become a cliché, but it is essential nevertheless. If one student is reprimanded for breaking a rule and another is not, for example, students are unable to make sense of the inconsistency. They are likely to conclude that the teacher doesn't know what's going on or has "pets," either of which detracts from classroom climate.

Although consistency is important, achieving complete consistency in the real world is virtually impossible, and you should adapt your interventions to both the student and context. For example, most classrooms have a rule about speaking only when recognized by the teacher, and as you're monitoring seatwork, one student asks another a question about the assignment and then goes back to work. Failing to remind the student that talking is not allowed during seatwork is technically inconsistent, but an intervention in this case is both unnecessary and counterproductive. On the other hand, a student who repeatedly turns around and whispers becomes a disruption, and intervention is necessary. Students understand the difference, and the "inconsistency" is appropriate and effective.

Following through means doing what you've said you'll do. Without follow-through, your management system will break down because students learn that you aren't fully committed to maintaining an orderly environment. This is confusing and leaves them with a sense of uncertainty. Once again, the first few days of the school year are important. If you follow through consistently during this period, enforcing rules and reinforcing procedures will be much easier during the rest of the year.

Keep Verbal and Nonverbal Behaviors Congruent

For interventions to make sense to your students, your verbal and nonverbal behaviors must be congruent (Doyle, 2006). Compare the following interventions:

> Karen Wilson's eighth graders are working on their homework as she circulates among them. She is helping Jasmine when Jeff and Mike begin whispering loudly behind her.
>
> "Jeff. Mike. Stop talking, and get started on your homework," she says, glancing over her shoulder.
>
> The two slow their whispering, and Karen turns back to Jasmine. Soon, the boys are whispering as loudly as ever.
>
> "I thought I told you to stop talking," Karen says over her shoulder again, this time with irritation in her voice.
>
> The boys glance at her and quickly resume whispering.
>
> Isabel Rodriguez is in a similar situation with her prealgebra students. As she is helping Vicki, Ken and Lance begin horseplay at the back of the room.
>
> Isabel excuses herself, turns, and walks directly to the boys. Looking Lance in the eye, she says evenly and firmly, "Lance, we have plenty to do before lunch, and noise during seat work detracts from learning. Begin your work now." Then, looking directly at Ken, she continues, "Ken, you, too. Quickly now. We have only so much time, and we don't want to waste it." She waits briefly until they are working quietly and then returns to Vicki.

The teachers had similar intents, but the impact of their actions on students was very different. When Karen glanced over her shoulder as she was telling the boys to stop whispering, and then failed to follow through, her communication was confusing; her words said one thing, but her body language said another. When messages are inconsistent, people attribute more credibility to tone of voice and body language than to spoken words (Aronson, Wilson, & Akert, 2010).

In contrast, Isabel's communication was clear and consistent. She responded immediately, faced her students directly, explained how their behavior detracted from learning, and made sure her students were on-task before she went back to Vicki. Her verbal and nonverbal behaviors were consistent, so her message made sense. Characteristics of effective nonverbal communication are outlined in Table 12.1.

Use I-Messages

Successful cognitive interventions should both focus on the inappropriate behavior and help students understand the effects of their actions on others. To illustrate, let's look again at Judy's encounter with Rachel in the case study at the beginning of the chapter. Judy pointed to the rule and then said:

> We agreed that it was important to listen when other people are talking, and you know that we all have to honor our agreements. . . . We can't learn when people aren't paying attention, and I'm uncomfortable when my class isn't learning."

I-message. A nonaccusatory communication that addresses a behavior and describes the effects on the sender and the feelings it generates in the sender.

In this encounter, Judy sent an **I-message,** a nonaccusatory communication that addresses a behavior and describes the effects on the sender and the feelings it generates in the sender (Gordon, 1981).

Judy's I-message reminded Rachel that her behavior was unacceptable while simultaneously communicating that she was still valued as a person. Judy also described the behavior's effect on the sender—herself—and the feelings it generated: "We can't learn when people aren't paying attention, and I'm uncomfortable when my class isn't learning." The intent of an I-message is to promote understanding, as it always is in cognitive interventions. Judy wanted Rachel to understand the effects of her actions on others, and if successful, this becomes a step toward self-regulation.

Assertive discipline. An approach to classroom management that promotes a clear and firm response style with students.

Judy was also assertive in her directive to Rachel. Lee and Marlene Canter, founders of **assertive discipline,** an approach to classroom management that promotes a clear and firm response style, suggest that teachers are often ineffective because their responses to students

| **Table 12.1** | Characteristics of effective nonverbal communication |

Nonverbal Behavior	Example
Proximity	A teacher moves close to an inattentive student.
Eye contact	A teacher looks an off-task student directly in the eye when issuing a directive.
Body orientation	A teacher directs himself squarely to the learner, rather than over the shoulder or sideways.
Facial expression	A teacher frowns slightly at a disruption, brightens her face at a humorous incident, and smiles approvingly at a student's effort to help a classmate.
Gestures	A teacher puts her palm out (Stop!) to a student who interjects as another student is talking.
Vocal variation	A teacher varies the tone, pitch, and loudness of his voice for emphasis and displays energy and enthusiasm.

are either passive or hostile (Canter, 1996). For example, a passive response to Rachel might be, "Please. How many times do I have to remind you of our rule about paying attention?" A hostile response would be, "Your whispering is driving me up the wall," which implies a weakness in students' characters and detracts from the classroom's emotional climate. In comparison, an assertive response style signals that you know what you're doing and you're in charge of your class.

Apply Logical Consequences

Logical consequences are outcomes that are conceptually related to misbehavior; they help learners make sense of an intervention by creating a link between their actions and the consequences that follow. For example:

> Allen, a rambunctious sixth grader, is running down the hall toward the lunchroom. As he rounds the corner, he bumps Alyssia, causing her to drop her books.
>
> "Oops," he replies, continuing his race to the lunchroom.
>
> "Hold it, Allen," Doug Ramsay, who is monitoring the hall, says. "Go back and help her pick up her books and apologize."
>
> Allen walks back to Alyssia, helps her pick up her books, mumbles an apology, and then returns. As he approaches, Doug again stops him.
>
> "Now, why did I make you do that?" Doug asks.
>
> "Cuz we're not supposed to run."
>
> "Sure," Doug says evenly, "but more important, if people run in the halls, they might crash into someone, and somebody might get hurt. . . . Remember that you're responsible for your actions. Think about not wanting to hurt yourself or anybody else, and the next time you'll walk whether a teacher is here or not. . . . Now, go on to lunch."

Doug applied a logical consequence in this incident. Having to pick up Alyssia's books after bumping her and causing her to drop them made sense to Allen, and this is the goal in applying logical consequences. They help students understand the effects of their actions on others and promote the development of self-regulation (Watson & Battistich, 2006).

Behavioral Interventions

While interventions that make sense and lead to learner understanding and self-regulation are the ideals we strive for, in the real world, some students seem either unable or unwilling to direct and control their actions and emotions. In these cases, behavioral interventions—applying the concepts of reinforcement and punishment to manage student behavior—may be necessary (Fabiano, Pelham, & Gnagy, 2007; J. B. Ryan, Katsiyannis, & Peterson, 2007). Experts recommend using behavioral interventions as short-term solutions to specific problems, with development of self-regulation remaining the long-term goal (Emmer & Evertson, 2009; Evertson & Emmer, 2009).

Let's see how Cindy Daines, a first-grade teacher, uses a behavioral intervention with her students:

> Cindy has a problem with her students' making smooth and orderly transitions from one activity to another. In an attempt to improve the situation, she makes "tickets" from construction paper, gets local businesses to donate small items to be used as prizes, and displays the items in a fishbowl on her desk. She then explains, "We're going to play a little game to see how quiet we can be when we change lessons. . . . Whenever we change, I'm going to give you 1 minute, and then I'm going to ring this bell," and she rings the bell to demonstrate. "Students who have their books out and are waiting quietly when I ring the bell will get one of these tickets. On Friday afternoon, you can turn them in for prizes you see in this fishbowl. The more tickets you have, the better the prize will be."

Logical consequences. Outcomes that are conceptually related to misbehavior; they help learners make sense of an intervention by creating a link between their actions and its consequences.

During the next few days, Cindy moves around the room, handing out tickets and making comments such as "I really like the way Merry is ready to work," "Ted already has his books out and is quiet," and "Thank you for moving to math so quickly."

She realizes her strategy is starting to work when she hears "Shh" and "Be quiet!" from the students, so she is gradually able to space out the rewards as the students become more responsible.

Cindy used concepts from both behaviorism and social cognitive theory in her system. Her tickets and prizes were positive reinforcers for making quick and quiet transitions, and her comments, such as, "I really like the way Merry is ready to work" and "Ted already has his books out and is quiet" were vicarious reinforcers for the other children.

Reinforcement is more effective for changing behavior than is punishment, and this principle applies when using behavioral interventions (Landrum & Kaufman, 2006). However, punishment may be necessary in some cases. Desists, timeout, and detention can be effective punishers. However, physical punishment, embarrassment or humiliation, and class work are ineffective, and you should never use them. The following are guidelines for using punishment as management alternatives:

- Use punishment as infrequently as possible.
- Apply punishers immediately and directly to the behavior.
- Apply punishers only severe enough to eliminate the behavior.
- Apply punishers dispassionately, and avoid displays of anger.
- Explain and model alternative desirable behaviors.

Designing and Maintaining a Behavioral Management System

Clear rules and expectations followed by consistently applied consequences (reinforcers and punishers) are the foundation of a behavioral management system. Designing a management system based on behaviorism involves the following steps:

- Prepare a list of specific rules that clearly define acceptable behavior.
- Specify reinforcers for obeying each rule and punishers for breaking the rules, such as the consequences in Table 12.2.

Table 12.2 Sample consequences for breaking or following rules

Consequences for Breaking Rules

First infraction	Name on list
Second infraction	Check by name
Third infraction	Second check by name
Fourth infraction	Half-hour detention
Fifth infraction	Call to parents

Consequences for Following Rules

A check is removed for each day that no infractions occur. If only a name remains, and no infractions occur, the name is removed.

All students without names on the list are given 45 minutes of free time Friday afternoon to do as they choose. The only restrictions are that they must stay in the classroom, and they must not disrupt the students who didn't earn the free time.

- Display the rules, and explain the consequences.
- Consistently apply consequences.

A behavioral system doesn't preclude providing rationales or creating the rules with learner input. The primary focus, however, is on clearly specifying behavioral guidelines and applying consequences, in contrast with a cognitive approach, which emphasizes learner understanding and self-regulation.

In designing a comprehensive management system, you probably will combine elements of both cognitive and behavioral approaches. Behavioral systems have the advantage of being immediately applicable; they're effective for initiating desired behaviors, particularly with young students; and they're useful for reducing chronic misbehavior. Cognitive systems take longer to produce results but are more likely to develop learner self-regulation.

Positive Behavior Support

When you begin teaching, you will almost certainly have students in your class who have exceptionalities, such as students with specific learning disabilities or behavior disorders. You will be expected to create a classroom environment that meets the needs of all of your students, including those with exceptionalities. Let's look at an example.

> You have a student named Tanya in your class who has been diagnosed with a mild form of autism. She displays behaviors typical of the disorder, such as underdeveloped social skills, highly ritualistic behavior, and a strong emotional attachment to a particular adult—you in this case. For example, she is sometimes abusive to other students when you do group work, so you remove her from the group. And she frequently becomes upset and will even periodically shout and run out of the room when you have your students begin their homework for the next day.
>
> With the help of your school's special education specialist, you analyze Tanya's behavior and conclude that her abuse and running out of the room serve two purposes: (1) they allow her to escape social situations in which she is uncomfortable, and (2) they get your attention.
>
> Based on the analysis, you both work with Tanya to help her learn to make appropriate comments and ask questions during group work, and you design a system so she earns points that she can trade for treats of her choosing when she behaves appropriately. You also spend extra time helping her with her seat work, and you create a private area in the back of the room where she can go whenever she feels she needs a break from academic tasks.

Your interventions are examples of **positive behavior support,** interventions that replace problem behaviors with alternative, appropriate actions that serve the same purpose for the student (D. R. Carter & Van Norman, 2010). For example, Tanya was negatively reinforced for behaving abusively (she was allowed to escape the uncomfortable situation), and when she was taught some specific interaction skills, the negative reinforcer was replaced with a positive reinforcer (the points). Similarly, the attention she received when she shouted and ran out of the room was replaced with your attention when you worked with her one-on-one.

Positive behavior support. Interventions that replace problem behaviors with appropriate actions that serve the same purpose for the student.

Positive behavior support is widely used and is commonly implemented on a school-wide basis (Scott, Gagnon, & Nelson, 2008). Research suggests that it is generally effective for dealing with problems that traditional classroom management systems can't solve (Scott, Alter, Rosenberg, & Borgmeier, 2010). You are likely to be involved in positive behavior support when you begin teaching, and you will be provided with extensive staff development experiences that will help you implement it in your classroom.

Despite the most thorough planning and implementation, the need for periodic teacher intervention is inevitable. Keeping both cognitive and behavioral approaches in mind, we next consider intervention options.

An Intervention Continuum

Disruptions vary from isolated incidents, such as a student's briefly whispering to a neighbor, to chronic infractions, such as a student's repeatedly poking other students or even fighting. Because infractions vary, your interventions should also vary, and they will include both cognitive and behavioral elements.

To maximize instructional time, interventions should be as unobtrusive as possible. A continuum of interventions is outlined in Figure 12.8 and discussed in the following sections.

Praising Desired Behavior. Because promoting desired behaviors is an important goal, praising students for displaying them is a sensible first intervention. Praise occurs less often than might be expected, so efforts to "catch 'em being good" are worthwhile, especially as a method of prevention. Elementary teachers praise openly and freely, and middle and secondary teachers often make private comments such as, "I'm extremely pleased with your work this week. . . . Keep it up," or write private notes to students praising them for their work and behavior. Some research suggests that praising middle school students in notes significantly reduces discipline referrals (Nelson, Young, Young, & Cox, 2010).

Reinforcing behaviors that are incompatible with misbehavior is an extension of this idea (Alberto & Troutman, 2009). For instance, participating in a learning activity is incompatible with daydreaming, so calling on a student and reinforcing any attempt to respond are more effective than reprimanding a student for not paying attention.

Ignoring Inappropriate Behavior. Behaviors that aren't reinforced become extinct. The attention students receive when they're admonished for minor misbehaviors is often reinforcing, so ignoring the behavior can eliminate the reinforcers you might inadvertently provide (Landrum & Kaufman, 2006). This is effective, for example, when two students briefly whisper but soon stop. A combination of praising desired behaviors, reinforcing incompatible behaviors, and ignoring misbehavior can be effective with minor disruptions.

Using Indirect Cues. You can also use indirect cues—such as proximity, methods of redirecting attention, and vicarious reinforcers—when students display behaviors that can't be ignored but can be stopped or diverted without addressing them directly (V. Jones & Jones, 2010). For example, Judy moved near Darren and called on him after she heard Kendra mutter. Her proximity stopped his misbehavior, and calling on him directed his attention back to the lesson.

Vicarious reinforcement can also be effective. If you plan to be an elementary teacher, you can use students as models and vicariously reinforce the rest of the students with statements such as, "I really like the way Row 1 is working quietly" or "Elisa has already started the assignment."

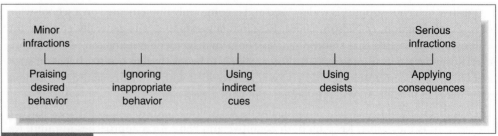

Minor infractions				Serious infractions
Praising desired behavior	Ignoring inappropriate behavior	Using indirect cues	Using desists	Applying consequences

Figure 12.8 An intervention continuum

Using Desists. A **desist** is a verbal or nonverbal communication a teacher uses to stop a behavior (Kounin, 1970). "Glenys, we leave our seats only when given permission," "Glenys!" and a finger to the lips, or a stern facial expression are all desists. They are the most common teacher reactions to misbehavior.

Clarity and tone are important when using desists. For example, "Randy, what is the rule about touching other students?" or "Randy, how do you think that makes Willy feel?" are more effective than "Randy, stop that," because they link the behavior to a rule or to the behavior's effects. Students react to these subtle differences and prefer rule and consequence reminders to teacher commands (Brophy, 2006b).

The tone of desists should be firm but not angry. Kounin (1970) found that kindergarten students managed with rough desists actually became more disruptive, and older students are uncomfortable in classes where harsh desists are used. In contrast, firm, even reprimands, the suggestion of alternative behaviors, and questioning that maintains student involvement in learning activities can reduce off-task time in most classrooms.

Clear communication, including congruence between verbal and nonverbal behavior, an awareness of what is happening in the classroom (withitness), and effective instruction are essential in using desists. However, even when these elements exist, desists sometimes aren't enough.

Desists are effective for stopping many common misbehaviors.

Desist. A verbal or nonverbal communication used to stop a behavior.

Applying Consequences. If you've tried all other options on the intervention continuum, and they simply aren't working, you'll then need to apply consequences. Logical consequences are most desirable and should be tried first, but classrooms are complex and busy, so it isn't always possible to solve problems with them. In these cases behavioral consequences—simply intended to change a behavior quickly and efficiently—can be effective (Murphy, 2007). Let's look at a classroom example.

> Jason is an intelligent and active fifth grader. He loves to talk and seems to know just how far he can go before Mrs. Aguilar becomes exasperated with him. He understands the rules and the reasons for them, but his interest in talking seems to take precedence. Ignoring him isn't working. A call to his parents helped for a while, but soon he's back to his usual behavior—never quite enough to require a drastic response, but always a thorn in Mrs. Aguilar's side.
>
> Finally, she decides to give him only one warning. At a second disruption, he's placed in timeout from regular instructional activities. She meets with him and explains the rules. The next day, he begins to misbehave almost immediately.
>
> "Jason," she warns, "you can't work while you're talking, and you're keeping others from finishing their work. Please get busy."
>
> He stops, but a few minutes later, he's at it again.
>
> "Jason," Mrs. Aguilar says quietly as she moves back to his desk, "Please go back to the timeout area."
>
> Now, a week later, Jason is working quietly with the rest of the class.

Behavior such as Jason's is common, particularly in elementary and middle schools, and it causes more teacher stress than do highly publicized threats of violence and bodily harm (Friedman, 2006). The behavior is disruptive, so it can't be ignored; praise for good work helps to a certain extent, but students get much of their reinforcement from friends; desists work briefly, but teachers tire of constant monitoring. Mrs. Aguilar had little choice but to apply behavioral consequences with Jason.

Overlapping. The ability to intervene in cases of misbehavior without disrupting the flow of a lesson.

Consistency is the key to promoting change in students like Jason. He understood what he was doing, and he was capable of controlling himself. When he could predict the consequences of his behavior with certainty, he quit. He knew that his second infraction would result in a timeout, and when it did, he quickly changed his behavior. There was no argument, little time was used, and the class wasn't disrupted.

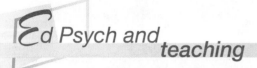

Ed Psych and teaching

Responding Effectively to Misbehavior in Your Students

Incidents of misbehavior will inevitably occur in your classroom. The following guidelines can help you intervene effectively.

1. Maintain the flow of instruction while intervening in cases of misbehavior.
2. Protect students' emotional safety when intervening.
3. Use cognitive interventions when possible; revert to behavioral interventions when necessary.
4. Move along the intervention continuum only as far as necessary.

Let's look again at Judy's work with her students to see how she applied these guidelines.

First, she maintained the flow of the lesson while intervening in each case. Let's review her actions:

> **Judy:** About what latitude is Damascus, . . . Bernice?
>
> **Bernice:** . . . About 34 degrees north latitude, I think.
>
> **Judy:** Good, Bernice. It's close to 34 degrees. . . .
> So, would it be warmer or colder than here in the summer?
> . . . Darren? (seeing that Darren has poked Kendra with his pencil, and walking near him).
>
> **Judy:** And, why might that be the case? . . . Jim? (moving over to Rachel and telling her to move to a different desk).

In this brief episode Judy intervened with both Darren and Rachel without disrupting the flow of her lesson, an ability called **overlapping** (Kounin, 1970).

Second, Judy maintained an even demeanor in her interventions, which helped her students feel emotionally safe, and third, her interventions were primarily cognitive. For example, she was "withit" in recognizing that Darren was the perpetrator of the incident with Kendra; she was consistent and followed through to be sure Rachel complied; she kept her verbal and nonverbal behavior consistent (e.g., looking directly at Darren when she called on him, and leaning over Rachel's desk when talking to her); and she responded to Rachel with an I-message.

Finally, she only had to go as far along the intervention continuum as using indirect cues with both Darren and Rachel. She simply moved over near Darren and called on him, and she referred Rachel to the class rule and ensured that she complied. Neither action disrupted the flow of her lesson.

Careful planning for classroom management combined with efforts to promote self-regulation can prevent many management problems from occurring in the first place, and applying these guidelines can quickly eliminate most others.

Once in a great while, however, serious problems occur. We discuss them in the next section of the chapter.

Classroom connections

Intervening Successfully in Classrooms

1. Cognitive interventions target learners' need to make sense of their experiences. Use logical consequences to help students develop responsibility. Hold discussions regarding fairness or equity after class and in private.

   - **Elementary:** During daily classroom chores, two first graders begin a tug-of-war over a cleaning rag and knock over a potted plant. Their teacher talks to them, they agree to clean up the

   mess, and they write a note to their parents explaining that they will be working in the classroom before school the next week to pay for a new pot.

   - **Middle School:** A social studies teacher makes her interventions learning experiences by identifying rules that were broken

and explaining why the rules exist. In cases of uncertainty, she talks privately to students.

■ **High School:** After having been asked to stop whispering for the second time in 10 minutes, a ninth grader protests that he was asking about the assigned seat work. His teacher reminds him of the incidents, points out that his behavior is disruptive, and reprimands him without further discussion. His teacher talks to him after class, explaining why rules exist, and reminding him that he is expected to accept responsibility for his behavior.

2. Positive reinforcement can be used to increase appropriate behavior. Use positive reinforcers to initiate and teach desirable behaviors.

■ **Elementary:** A first-grade teacher, knowing that the time after lunch is difficult for many students, gives students 1 minute after a timer rings to settle down and get out their materials. When the class meets the requirement, they earn points toward free time.

■ **Middle School:** To encourage students to clean up quickly after labs, a science teacher offers 5 minutes of free time to talk in their seats if the lab is cleaned up in time. Students who don't clean up in time are required to finish in silence.

■ **High School:** A ninth-grade basic math teacher is encountering problems getting his students to work quietly in small groups. He discusses the problem with the class and then closely monitors the groups, circulating and offering praise and reinforcement when they are working smoothly.

3. Linking consequences to behaviors helps students see the connection between their actions and their effects on others. To help students see the logical connection between behaviors and consequences, follow through consistently in cases of disruptive behavior, and explain your actions.

■ **Elementary:** A second-grade teacher finds that transitions to and from lunch and bathroom breaks are sometimes disruptive. She talks with the class about the problem, initiates a "no-talking" rule during these transitions, and carefully enforces the rule.

■ **Middle School:** A teacher separates two seventh graders who disrupt lessons with their talking, telling them the new seat assignments are theirs until further notice. The next day, they sit in their old seats as the bell is about to ring. "Do you know why I moved you two yesterday?" the teacher says immediately. After a momentary pause, both students nod. "Then move quickly now, and be certain you're in your new seats tomorrow. You can come and talk with me when you believe you're ready to accept responsibility for your talking."

■ **High School:** An eleventh-grade history teacher reminds students about being seated when the bell rings. As it rings the next day, two girls remain standing and talking. The teacher turns to them and says, "I'm sorry, but you must not have understood me yesterday. To be counted on time, you need to be in your seats when the bell rings. Please go to the office and get a late-admit pass."

---

check your understanding

4.1 What is the framework on which all cognitive interventions are based? Use cognitive learning theory to explain why verbal–nonverbal congruence, I-messages, and logical consequences are effective interventions.

4.2 Use behaviorism and/or social cognitive theory to explain why each of the points on the intervention continuum (Figure 12.8) is an effective intervention.

4.3 One of your students is talking without permission. Describe an I-message that would be effective as a response.

4.4 A teacher sees a seventh grader spit on the door to the classroom. According to the information in this section, which is the more appropriate response: put the student in after-school detention (which is part of the school's management policy), or have the student wash the door? Explain.

To receive feedback for these questions, go to Appendix A.

Serious Management Problems: Defiance and Aggression

Ed Psych and You

We've all heard about highly publicized incidents of school shootings and other stories about teachers being assaulted by students. Do you worry about these possibilities as you anticipate your first teaching job?

If you answered yes to our question in this "Ed Psych and You," you're like many other beginning teachers. Many preservice teachers think—and worry—about incidents of school violence and even the possibility of being assaulted by a student. However, incidents of defiance and aggression toward teachers is rare in schools, with research indicating that the assault rate is slightly over 3 per 1,000 teachers (Moriarity, 2009). However, these incidents do happen, and you need to be aware of the possibility and be prepared to deal with an incident in the unlikely event that it occurs.

Serious management problems require both short-term interventions and long-term strategies.

Responding to Defiant Students

Tyrone, one of your students, has difficulty maintaining attention and staying on task. He frequently makes loud and inappropriate comments in class and disrupts learning activities. You warn him, reminding him that being disruptive is unacceptable, and blurting out another comment will result in timeout.

Within a minute, Tyrone blurts out again.

"Please go to the timeout area," you say evenly.

"I'm not going, and you can't make me," he says defiantly. He crosses his arms and remains seated at his desk.

What do you do when a student like Tyrone says, "I'm not going, and you can't make me?" Experts offer two suggestions (Moriarity, 2009; A. Smith & Bondy, 2007). First, remain calm to avoid a power struggle. A teacher's natural tendency is to become angry and display a show of force to demonstrate to students that they "can't get away with it." Remaining calm gives you time to control your temper, and the student's mood when facing a calm teacher is likely to change from anger and bravado to fear and contrition (Good & Brophy, 2008).

Second, if possible, give the rest of the class an assignment, and then tell the student calmly but assertively to please step outside the classroom so you can talk. Communicate an assertive, but not threatening, tone.

Defiance is often the result of negative student–teacher relationships, and they occur most often with students who display externalizing behavior problems, such as aggression, temper tantrums, or impulsive and hyperactive behavior (Henricsson & Rydell, 2004). When a problem occurs with such a student, it's important to let the student say everything that is on his or her mind in a private conference, such as outside the classroom, before responding. Finally, arrange to meet with the student before or after school, focus on the defiance as a problem, and attempt to generate solutions that are acceptable to both of you.

In the case of a student who refuses to leave your classroom, or one who becomes physically threatening, immediately send someone to the front office for help. Defiance at this level likely requires help from a mental health professional.

Responding to Fighting

As you work with a small group of your fourth graders, a fight suddenly breaks out between Trey and Neil, who are supposed to be working on a group project together. You hear sounds of shouting and see Trey flailing at Neil, who is attempting to fend off Trey's blows. Trey is often verbally aggressive and sometimes threatens other students.
What do you do?

Incidents of student aggression toward each other are much more common than threats to teachers. Information from the National Center for Educational Statistics indicates that that about 10% of all public schools had one or more serious violent crimes, such as sexual battery, suicide, or physical attack, with the vast majority of the incidents being physical attacks or fights without a weapon (Kelly, 2011).

Negligence. The failure of teachers or schools to exercise sufficient care in protecting students from injury.

In a situation such as the one between Trey and Neil, you are required by law to intervene. If you don't, you and the school can be sued for **negligence,** the failure to exercise sufficient care in protecting students from injury (Fischer, Schimmel, & Stellman, 2006). However, the law doesn't require you to physically break up the fight; immediately reporting it to administrators is acceptable.

An effective response to fighting involves three steps: (1) Stop the incident (if possible), (2) protect the victim, and (3) get help. For instance, in the case of the classroom scuffle, a loud noise, such as shouting, clapping, or slamming a chair against the floor, will often surprise the students enough so they'll stop (Evertson & Emmer, 2009). At that point, you can begin to talk to them, check to see if the victim is all right, and then take the students to the main office, where you can get help. If your interventions don't stop the fight, you should immediately send an uninvolved student for help. Don't attempt to separate the students unless you're sure you can do so without danger to yourself or them. You are responsible first for the safety of the other students and yourself, second for the involved students, and finally for property (Good & Brophy, 2008).

Responding to Bullying

Matt, one of your seventh graders, is shy and a bit small for his age. As he comes into your class this morning, he appears disheveled and depressed. Concerned, you take him aside and ask if anything is wrong. With some prodding he tells you that he repeatedly gets shoved around on the school grounds before school, and two boys have been taunting him and calling him gay. "I hate school," he comments.
      How do you respond?

Bullying, a form of peer aggression that involves a systematic or repetitious abuse of power between students, is a serious management problem in our schools. In a survey of more than 43,000 high school students, half admitted they had bullied someone in the past year, and nearly the same percent said they had been bullied, teased, or taunted (Josephson Institute Center for Youth Ethics, 2010). Forty-four states have passed anti-bullying laws, and many districts have implemented zero-tolerance policies. Unfortunately, these laws and policies have been largely ineffective in reducing incidents of bullying (Graham, 2010; D. Walker 2009).

Bullying is a serious management issue because it threatens the safety and security of schools and classrooms, making it difficult to create communities of caring and trust. In addition, it carries with it serious psychological problems for both perpetrators and victims. Bullies learn maladaptive ways of relating to others, and victims often suffer from anxiety and depression (Hyman et al., 2006). It is difficult to concentrate on your learning and development when you fear for your safety.

Teachers are central to schools' efforts to eliminate bullying, so you will play an important role in the process. "[C]hildren's school behavior is greatly shaped by their school's culture, climate, and more specifically, the attitudes and behaviors of teachers" (Hyman et al., 2006, p. 869). The most effective responses to bullying are school-wide and include communication with parents, close adult supervision, talking with bullies after bullying incidents, and immediate, appropriate, and consistent consequences for bullying acts (Sherer, & Nickerson, 2010). Near term, when you see a case of bullying, you should intervene immediately and apply appropriate consequences—cognitive if possible or behavioral if necessary—for the perpetrators. Trey, for example, must understand that his aggressive actions are unacceptable and won't be tolerated.

Long-term, you can use the incident as a teachable moment, in which you discuss ideas about right and wrong, appropriate treatment of others, tolerance for differences, and abuse of power (Graham, 2010). These discussions may not produce immediate results, but in time they can make a difference. For the students you reach, the results can be increased self-regulation and healthier social development.

Bullying. A form of peer aggression that involves a systematic or repetitious abuse of power between students.

Culturally responsive classroom management. Classroom management that combines cultural knowledge with teachers' awareness of possible personal biases.

Exploring diversity

Classroom Management with Students from Diverse Backgrounds

Working with learners from diverse backgrounds will present a unique set of challenges for you. A long history of research suggests that discrepancies exist in disciplinary referrals and punishment for students who are members of cultural minorities (Gay, 2006). For example, African American boys are referred for behavior problems at a much higher rate than their peers, and they also receive harsher punishments (Skiba, Michael, Nardo, & Peterson, 2002). Also, European American students are often disciplined for observable infractions, such as smoking, leaving school without permission, or profanity, whereas African American students are more often disciplined for infractions that require a teacher's interpretation, such as disrespect, defiance, or class disruptions.

Additional evidence suggests that communication breakdowns between teachers and students who are ELs sometimes result in students' being punished for what teachers thought they heard and not for what children actually said (Kirylo, Thirumurthy, & Spezzini, 2010). Some researchers believe this miscommunication occurs because most teachers are middle class, female, and White, whereas students who are ELs are cultural minorities and are often from families with lower socioeconomic status.

Culturally responsive classroom management, which combines cultural knowledge with teachers' awareness of possible personal biases, can help overcome some of these problems. A culturally responsive classroom management model designed to address this problem has five elements:

- Become personally aware of possible cultural biases.
- Learn about students' cultural heritage.
- Learn about student's neighborhoods and home environments.
- Create caring learning environments.
- Develop culturally responsive classroom management strategies. (Milner & Tenore, 2010)

As you become aware of your own possible fears and biases and come to understand your students' interaction patterns, you will realize that student responses that appear threatening or disrespectful often are not intended that way. Increased awareness and knowledge, combined with culturally responsive classroom management strategies, can contribute a great deal toward overcoming racial discrepancies in classroom management issues (McCurdy, Kunsch, & Reibstein, 2007). The strategies, to a large extent, include those we've discussed in this chapter, such as promoting student responsibility and self-regulation, creating communities of caring and trust, and establishing clear expectations for behavior. Combined with conducting highly interactive lessons and providing students with specific and nonjudgmental feedback about their behavior and learning progress, these strategies are effective with all students, and they're particularly important for students from diverse backgrounds. As with all strategies, they won't solve every problem, but they will contribute to your students' academic and social-emotional learning.

check your understanding

5.1 Describe your legal responsibilities in the event of a fight or other aggressive act in your classroom.

5.2 If you encounter two students fighting, or you see a smaller student being bullied by other students, what steps should you take?

5.3 Describe the focus of a long-term cognitive approach to bullying and other acts of aggression.

To receive feedback for these questions, go to Appendix A.

Developmentally appropriate practice

Classroom Management with Learners at Different Ages

While many aspects of classroom management, such as creating a caring classroom community, developing learner responsibility, and careful planning apply across the K–12 continuum, developmental differences exist. The following paragraphs outline suggestions for responding to these differences.

Working with Children in Early Childhood Programs and Elementary Schools

Earlier in the chapter we discussed the importance of teaching rules and procedures to elementary students. These children are often unaware of rules and procedures and may not understand how they contribute to learning. Because their cognitive development is likely to be preoperational, special efforts to explain the importance of rules and their connection to personal responsibility and learning can be helpful.

Young children are trusting and vulnerable, so criticism and harsh reprimands and desists are particularly harmful (K. Carter & Doyle, 2006). They respond well to praise, but ignoring inappropriate behavior and using indirect cues are likely to be less effective with them than with older students. Behavioral interventions, such as timeout for chronic interruptions, can be effective if they are not overdone. Developing personal responsibility for behavior is an important long-term goal.

Working with Students in Middle Schools

As students develop, they become more cognitively, personally, and socially aware. As a result, consistency and logical consequences become increasingly important and effective. Middle school students continue to need a caring teacher; clear boundaries for acceptable behavior and consistently enforced boundaries are indicators of caring for these students. Timely and judicious praise continues to be important, but ignoring inappropriate behavior and using indirect cues can also be effective for minor rule infractions.

The increasing importance of peers presents both challenges and opportunities in middle schools. Whispering, note passing, and general attempts to socialize become problems, and clear, consistently applied rules are essential. Middle school students appreciate being involved in rule setting, and periodic class meetings are effective in enlisting student commitment to and cooperation with classroom rules and procedures.

Working with Students in High Schools

High school students react well to being treated as adults. Developing personal responsibility is important, and private conferences that appeal to their sense of responsibility can be effective. Peers continue to exert a powerful influence on behavior, so avoiding embarrassing students in front of their peers is important. Often, a simple request to turn around or get busy is all the intervention needed.

High school students are also becoming increasingly skilled at reading social and nonverbal cues, so congruence between verbal and nonverbal channels is important. Honest interventions that directly address the problem and leave students' dignity intact, but still communicate commitment and resolve, are very effective.

A positive teacher–student relationship remains the foundation of an effective management system, and high school students react well to personal comments, such as a compliment about a new outfit or hairstyle, or questions, such as asking about an ill parent's progress or how a new brother or sister is doing.

Summary

1. Describe the goals of classroom management, and identify applications of the goals.
   - Promoting student self-regulation, the ability to control one's actions and emotions, is a primary goal of classroom management.
   - When students learn to behave in acceptable ways and control their impulses, communities of caring and trust, classroom environments where students feel safe to share their thinking without fear of humiliation or ridicule, are developed.
   - In classrooms where learners are self-regulated and communities of caring and trust are created, time available for learning is maximized.

2. Identify characteristics of elementary, middle, and secondary school students and how they influence planning for classroom management.
   - Young children's thinking is perceptual and concrete; they are eager to please their teachers and are vulnerable to criticism and harsh treatment.
   - Effective teachers in elementary schools teach rules and procedures and provide concrete opportunities to practice them, which create orderly and predictable environments that build trust and develop autonomy.
   - Middle school students are increasingly influenced by peers, and needs for social acceptance and independence increase.
   - Effective teachers in middle schools treat students with unconditional positive regard and provide the firm hand of a caring teacher who sets clear limits for acceptable behavior.
   - As students move into high school, they communicate more effectively at an adult level, and they respond well to clear rationales for rules and procedures that make sense to them.

3. Describe effective communication strategies for involving parents.
   - Effective communication with parents begins with early communication and maintains links throughout the school year.
   - Home–school cooperation increases students' achievement, increases willingness to do homework, improves attitudes and behaviors, and increases attendance and graduation rates.

4. Use cognitive and behavioral learning theories to explain effective interventions.
   - Cognitive learning theory is grounded in the premise that people want their experiences to make sense.
   - Demonstrating withitness—being consistent, keeping verbal and nonverbal messages congruent, using I-messages, and applying logical consequences—are cognitive interventions.
   - Praising desired behavior, ignoring inappropriate behavior, using desists, and applying consequences all capitalize on behavioral concepts, such as reinforcement, extinction, and punishment to maintain an orderly classroom.

5. Describe your legal and professional responsibilities in cases of aggressive acts and steps you can take to respond to defiance and aggression.
   - Teachers are required by law to intervene in cases of violence or aggression.
   - Stopping the incident, protecting the victim, and seeking assistance are the first steps involved in responding to fighting.
   - Responding immediately and applying appropriate consequences are the most effective responses to incidents of bullying.

Understanding Classroom Management: Preparing for Your Licensure Exam

States realize that classroom management is essential for successful teaching, so your licensure exam will include information related to it. We include the following exercises to help you practice for the exam in your state.

In the opening case study, you saw how Judy Harris maintained an orderly and learning-focused classroom. In the following case study, Janelle Powers, another seventh-grade geography teacher, also has her students working on a lesson about the Middle East. Analyze Janelle's approach to classroom management, and answer the questions that follow.

In homeroom this morning, Shiana comes through the classroom doorway just as the tardy bell rings.

"Take your seat quickly, Shiana," Janelle directs. "You're just about late. . . . All right. Listen up, everyone," she continues. "Ali?"

"Here."

"Gaelen?"

"Here."

"Chu?"

"Here."

When Janelle finishes taking the roll, she walks around the room, handing back a set of papers.

"You did quite well on the assignment," she comments. "Let's keep up the good work. . . . Howard and Manny, please stop talking while I'm returning papers. Can't you sit quietly for 1 minute?"

The boys, who were whispering, turn back to the front of the room.

"Now," Janelle continues, returning to the front of the room, "we've been studying the Middle East, so let's review for a moment. . . . Look at the map, and identify the longitude and latitude of Cairo. Take a minute, and jot these down right now. I'll be collecting these in a few minutes."

The students begin as Janelle goes to her file cabinet to get out some materials to display on the document camera.

"Stop it, Damon," she hears Leila blurt out behind her.

"Leila," Janelle responds sternly, "we don't talk out like that in class."

"He's poking me, Mrs. Powers."

"Are you poking her, Damon?"

". . ."

"Well?"

"Not really."

"You did, too," Leila complains.

"Both of you stop it," Janelle warns. "Another outburst like that, Leila, and your name goes on the board."

As the students are finishing their work, Janelle looks up from the materials on her desk to check an example on the overhead. She hears Howard and Manny talking and laughing at the back of the room.

"Are you boys finished?"

"Yes," Manny answers.

"Well, be quiet then until everyone is done," Janelle directs and goes back to rearranging her materials.

"Quiet, everyone," she again directs, looking up in response to a hum of voices around the room. "Is everyone finished? . . . Good. Pass your papers forward. . . . Remember, put your paper on the top of the stack. . . . Roberto, wait until the papers come from behind you before you pass yours forward."

Janelle collects the papers, puts them on her desk, and then begins, "We've talked about the geography of the Middle East, and now we want to look at the climate a bit more. It varies somewhat. For example, Syria is extremely hot in the summer but is actually quite cool in the winter. In fact, it snows in some parts.

"Now, what did we find for the latitude of Cairo?"

"Thirty," Miguel volunteers.

"North or south, Miguel? . . . Wait a minute. Howard? . . . Manny? . . . This is the third time this period that I've had to say something to you about talking, and the period isn't even 20 minutes old yet. Get out your rules, and read me the rule about talking without permission. . . . Howard?"

". . ."

"It's supposed to be in the front of your notebook."

". . ."

"Manny?"

"'No speaking without permission of the teacher,'" Manny reads from the front page of his notebook.

"Howard, where are your rules?"

"I don't know."

"Move up here," Janelle directs, pointing to an empty desk at the front of the room. "You've been bothering me all week. If you can't learn to be quiet, you will be up here for the rest of the year."

Howard gets up and slowly moves to the desk Janelle has pointed out. After Howard is seated, Janelle begins again, "Where were we before we were rudely interrupted? . . .

Oh, yes. What did you get for the latitude of Cairo?"

"Thirty North," Miguel responds.

"Okay, good. . . . Now, Egypt also has a hot climate in the summer—in fact, very hot. The summer temperature often goes over 100 degrees Fahrenheit. Egypt is also mostly desert, so the people have trouble making a living. Their primary source of subsistence is the Nile River, which floods frequently. Most of the agriculture of the country is near the river."

Janelle continues presenting information to the students for the next several minutes.

"Andrew, are you listening to this?" Janelle interjects when she sees Andrew poke Jacinta with a ruler.

"Yes," he responds, turning to the front.

"I get frustrated when I see people not paying attention. When you don't pay attention, you can't learn, and that frustrates me because I'm here to help you learn." Janelle continues with her presentation.

Questions for Case Analysis

In answering these questions, use information from the chapter, and link your responses to specific information in the case.

1. Analyze Janelle's planning for classroom management.

2. Evaluate the effectiveness of Janelle's management interventions.

3. The chapter stressed the interdependence of management and instruction. Analyze the relationship between management and instruction in Janelle's class. Include both strengths and weaknesses in your analysis.

To receive feedback for these questions, go to Appendix B.

Your licensure exam will also include multiple-choice questions similar to those your instructor has given you on your quizzes and tests for this course.

Important Concepts

assertive discipline (p. 414)
bullying (p. 423)
classroom management
   (p. 392)
classroom organization
   (p. 398)

community of caring and
   trust (p. 396)
culturally responsive
   classroom management
   (p. 423)
desist (p. 419)

discipline (p. 397)
I-message (p. 414)
logical consequences
   (p. 415)
negligence (p. 422)
overlapping (p. 420)

positive behavior support
   (p. 417)
procedures (p. 399)
rules (p. 399)
self-regulation (p. 393)
withitness (p. 412)

Go to Topic: Classroom Management in the MyEducationLab (www.myeducationlab.com) for *Educational Psychology: Windows on Classrooms*, where you can:

- Find learning outcomes for Classroom Management along with the national standards that connect to these outcomes.
- Complete Assignments and Activities that can help you more deeply understand the chapter content.
- Apply and practice your understanding of the core teaching skills identified in the chapter with the Building Teaching Skills and Dispositions learning units.
- Examine challenging situations and cases presented in the IRIS Center Resources.
- Access video clips of CCSSO National Teachers of the Year award winners responding to the question, "Why Do I Teach?" in the Teacher Talk section.
- See video examples included within the Study Plan that provide concrete and real-world illustrations of the topics presented in the chapter.
- Check your comprehension of the content covered in the chapter with the Study Plan. Here you will be able to take a chapter quiz, receive feedback on your answers, and then access Review, Practice, and Enrichment activities to enhance your understanding of chapter content.

MyEducationLab

chapter 13

Learning and Effective Teaching

chapteroutline

learningoutcomes

After you've completed your study of this chapter,
you should be able to:

Planning for Instruction
Identifying Topics
Specifying Learning Objectives
Preparing and Organizing Learning Activities
Planning for Assessment
Instructional Alignment
Planning in a Standards-Based Environment
The Common-Core State Standards Initiative

1. Describe the steps in planning for instruction, including planning in a standards-based environment.

Implementing Instruction
Teacher Beliefs and Behaviors
Organization
Review
Focus
Questioning
Feedback
Closure
Communication

2. Describe essential teaching skills, and explain why they're important.

Models of Instruction
Direct Instruction
Lecture–Discussion
Guided Discovery
Cooperative Learning
Differentiating Instruction
Technology, Learning, and Development: Using Powerpoint Effectively

3. Explain the relationships between models of instruction and essential teaching skills, and describe how the components of different models contribute to learning.

Assessment and Learning: Using Assessment as a Learning Tool

4. Identify the essential characteristics of effective assessments.

classroomapplications

The following features help you apply the content of this chapter in your teaching.

Classroom Connections:
Planning Effectively in Classrooms
Demonstrating Essential Teaching Skills in Classrooms
Using Models of Instruction Effectively in Classrooms

Developmentally Appropriate Practice:
Effective Instruction with Learners at Different Ages

Exploring Diversity:
Using Cooperative Learning to Capitalize on Your Students' Diversity

*I*magine you're sitting in the back of a classroom observing a teacher working with students. How would you know if the teacher is "good" or "effective?" What would you look for? What would you expect to see? Keep these questions in mind as we follow the work of Scott Sowell, a seventh-grade science teacher, through this chapter.

As Scott is working on a Saturday afternoon to plan his next week, he looks at his textbook and his state's standards for middle school science. One standard says: *The student knows that if more than one force acts on an object, then the forces can reinforce or cancel each other, depending on their direction and magnitude.* (Florida Department of Education, 2007, p. 2)

As he plans, he also thinks about his past experience with the topic and decides that he will incorporate the standard into lessons on Bernoulli's principle, the law that helps explain how different forces enable airplanes to fly. "The kids like it," he remembers, "because it's both interesting and has a lot of real-world applications."

He decides that he has three objectives for his Monday lesson. First, he wants his students to know that a force is a push or a pull, and his second is for the students to be able to identify examples of force. He thinks about simple demonstrations he can use, such as pulling a student's chair across the floor, pushing on the chalk board, and having the students lift their books off their desks. Then, he thinks, "My third objective is for them to determine what will happen to an object when different forces act on it (the net effect of forces on an object). "So," he smiles to himself, "I'll demonstrate it with a little tug of war with one of the kids. I'll let him pull me to show that because his force is greater, we'll move that way. It'll help them understand the part of the standard that says, 'forces can reinforce or cancel each other, depending on their direction and magnitude.'"

Finally, he decides to teach Bernoulli's principle on Tuesday and Wednesday with a review Thursday and a quiz on Friday.

Effective teaching. Instruction that promotes as much learning as possible in all students.

We have made "Learning and Effective Teaching" the title of this chapter because, simply, **effective teaching** is instruction that promotes as much learning as possible in all students. Our purpose in writing this chapter is to help you identify what effective teachers do to maximize their students' learning, how their actions relate to cognitive learning theory, and how you can become an effective teacher when you have your own classroom. We'll use Scott's work with his students as the framework for our discussion.

Effective teaching can be summarized in three phases, which are outlined in Figure 13.1. As you see in the figure, the phases are interdependent and cyclical. The process begins with planning, and we turn to it next.

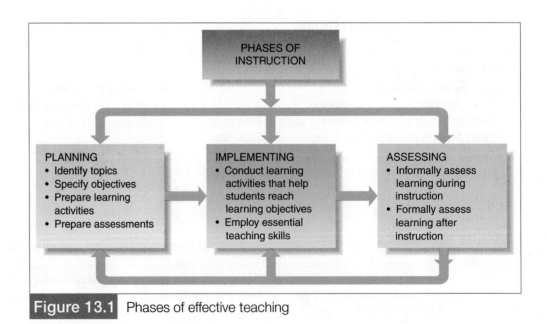

Figure 13.1 Phases of effective teaching

Planning for Instruction

Think about the questions we ask in "Ed Psych and You" here. After identifying the project, such as redecorating the living room in your apartment, you'll then probably ask yourself a series of questions, the first being the project's purpose, or objective. Maybe you want it to be more comfortable, perhaps you want it to be warmer and more inviting for guests, you might simply want to use the space more efficiently, or maybe all three. Then, you'll ask yourself how you'll achieve your objective, such as repainting the room, rearranging the furniture, or adding some art work. And, when you're finished, you'll consider some way of determining whether or not you did indeed achieve your purpose.

As you plan for your teaching, you'll go through a similar process. You will ask yourself a series of questions, and you'll make decisions that answer them, just as you did with your redecorating project (Anderson & Krathwohl, 2001; Lemov, 2010). The questions and related decisions that Scott made as he planned are outlined in Table 13.1.

We examine these planning decisions in more detail next.

Ed Psych and You
You have a personal project that you want to complete, such as redecorating the living room in your house or apartment. What is the first thing you think about? What else do you consider?

Identifying Topics

"What is important to learn?" is the first question you'll ask yourself when you begin planning (Lemov, 2010). In answering the question, you'll rely on textbooks, curriculum guides, and standards, such as the one Scott used. Students' interests in the topic and the availability of real-world applications will also influence your decisions. Scott, for example,

Table 13.1 Planning for instruction

Question	Planning Decision	Example
What is important for students to learn?	Identify topic(s)	Scott decided that his students should understand • the concept *force* and relationships among forces • Bernoulli's principle.
What, specifically, do I want students to know or be able to do with respect to the topic?	Specify learning objective(s)	Scott wanted his students to: • know that a force is a push or a pull • identify examples of forces • understand that objects move in the direction of the greater force (the net effect of two forces on an object) • understand that the greater the speed of air over a surface, the less force it exerts (Bernoulli's principle)
What will I do to help students reach the learning objective(s)?	Prepare learning activity	Scott decided he would: • pull a student across the floor to demonstrate force • conduct a "tug of war" to demonstrate relationships among forces • conduct a series of demonstrations of Bernoulli's principle (illustrated on pp. 443–444)
How will I determine the extent to which students have reached the learning objective(s)?	Design assessment	Scott decided he would: • have students sketch and describe the relationship between speed of air and force (illustrated on pp. 471–472)

identified *force* and relationships among forces as his Monday topic and Bernoulli's principle for his Tuesday and Wednesday topic. He decided that *force* is important because it's a basic science concept, and Bernoulli's principle is important because it can help us understand real-world events, such as how airplanes are able to fly.

More content appears in textbooks than can be learned in depth. So, instead of teaching a topic simply because it's the next one that appears in your textbook, you'll need to make decisions about whether or not a topic is important enough to teach. Your knowledge of content and your state standards will guide you in this process (Bereiter & Scardamalia, 2006).

Specifying Learning Objectives

Learning objective. A statement that specifies what students should know or be able to do with respect to a topic.

After identifying a topic, you will specify your **learning objectives,** what you want students to know or be able to do with respect to the topic. Clear learning objectives are essential because they guide the rest of your planning decisions. For example, designing learning activities—what you will do to help your students reach your learning objectives—is impossible if you're not clear about the objectives in the first place, and the same is true for designing assessments. Unsuccessful lessons are often the result of teachers not being clear about their objectives.

Objectives in the Cognitive Domain

Cognitive domain. The area of learning that focuses on knowledge and higher cognitive processes, such as applying and analyzing.

Scott had three objectives for his Monday lesson. He wanted his students to (1) know that a *force* is a push or a pull, (2) identify examples of forces, and (3) determine what will happen to an object when different forces act on it (the net effect of forces on an object). These are learning objectives in the **cognitive domain,** the area of learning that focuses on knowledge and higher cognitive processes such as applying and analyzing.

Let's take a historical look at objectives in this domain. In his classic work, *Basic Principles of Curriculum and Instruction,* Ralph Tyler (1950) suggested that the most useful form for stating objectives is "to express them in terms which identify both the kind of behavior to be developed in the student and the content or area of life in which this behavior is to operate" (p. 46). Applications of his ideas, such as management-by-objectives in the business world, became popular in the 1950s and 1960s. Some approaches, such as Robert Mager's in his highly readable book, *Preparing Instructional Objectives* (1962), expanded Tyler's original conception to include the conditions under which learners would demonstrate the behavior and the criteria for acceptable performance. Mager's work also strongly influenced teaching and remains popular today (Mager, 2000). Examples of objectives using Mager's approach are outlined in Table 13.2.

Table 13.2 Objectives using Mager's approach

Objective	Condition	Performance	Criteria
Given 3 examples of *force* in a real-world problem, students will identify each.	Given 3 examples of force in a real-world problem	Identify	Each
Given 10 problems involving subtraction with regrouping, students will correctly solve 7.	Given 10 problems involving subtraction with regrouping	Solve	7 of 10
Using a topic of their choice, students will write a paragraph that includes at least two examples each of metaphors, similes, and personification.	Using a topic of their choice	Write	A paragraph including 2 examples each of metaphors, similes, and personification

Table 13.3 Objectives using Gronlund's approach

General Objective	Specific Learning Outcome
Understands *force*	1. Identifies examples of force in problems 2. Gives examples of forces
Understands fractions with grouping	1. Recognizes need for regrouping 2. Performs operations 3. Solves problems
Uses figurative language in writing	1. Gives written examples 2. Puts examples into written context

Norman Gronlund (2004) offered a popular alternative to Mager's approach that includes the statement of a general objective, such as *know, understand,* or *apply,* which is then followed by specific learning outcomes. Table 13.3 includes examples of objectives written according to Gronlund's guidelines.

These approaches to preparing objectives were influenced by behaviorism. Tyler (1950) used *behavior* and content in his description of objectives, Mager (1962, 2000) also used the term *behavior* in his, and Gronlund emphasized that each specific learning outcome, "starts with an action verb that indicates observable student responses; that is, responses that can be seen by an outside observer" (Gronlund, 2004, p. 23). These behaviorist views of planning have evolved, as you'll see in the next section.

Taxonomies for Cognitive Objectives

Let's look again at Scott's objectives. For example, his first was for his students to "*know that force is a push or a pull,*" his second was for them to "*identify examples of force,*" and his third was for them to "*determine what will happen to an object when different forces act on it (the net effect of forces).*"

Each of these objectives is in the cognitive domain, and they all involve the concept *force,* but the cognitive processes required of learners are quite different. To respond to these differences, experts developed a system to classify objectives, questions, and assessment items. The result was the famous "Bloom's Taxonomy," which has been a cornerstone of education for more than a half century (Bloom, Englehart, Furst, Hill, & Krathwohl, 1956). The categories in the system include:

- *Knowledge:* Knowledge of facts, definitions, and other forms of memorized information, such knowing that *force* is a push or a pull (Scott's first objective).
- *Comprehension:* Understanding information, such as the ability to state a problem in one's own words or identify an original example of a concept, such as identifying examples of force (Scott's second objective).
- *Application:* Using what one knows to solve an original problem, such as determining the net effect of two forces on the same object (Scott's third objective).
- *Analysis:* The ability to break information into component parts and provide evidence to support conclusions, such as explaining how one knows that one force is greater than another.
- *Synthesis:* Combining information to create an original process or product, such as constructing a unique process for finding a solution to a problem.
- *Evaluation:* Making judgments about validity or quality of work based on a set of criteria, such as determining which of two approaches to solving a problem is more efficient.

To reflect our increased understanding of teaching and learning since the middle of the 20th century, when the original taxonomy was published, it has been revised and now more nearly reflects the influence of cognitive learning theory on education (Anderson & Krathwohl, 2001). This new taxonomy describes objectives in terms of students' cognitive processes instead of behaviors, and uses the term *knowledge*—which behaviorists initially frowned upon because it wasn't observable—to reflect what students should know or acquire (Anderson & Krathwohl, 2001). For example, in Scott's first objective: "Know that force is a push or a pull," *force* is the knowledge, and *know* is the cognitive process.

The result is a matrix with 24 cells that represent the intersection of four types of knowledge with six cognitive processes (Anderson & Krathwohl, 2001). The revised taxonomy appears in Figure 13.2.

To understand this classification matrix, let's look at Scott's three objectives again:

- To know that force is a push or a pull
- To identify examples of force
- To determine what will happen to an object when different forces act on it (the net effect of forces).

The first two objectives focus on the concept *force,* and the first involves memory, so the objective would be classified into the cell where *conceptual knowledge* intersects with *remember.* Because being able to identify examples of force requires understanding, the second objective would be classified into the cell where *conceptual knowledge* intersects with *understand.* The third objective, determining what will happen to an object when different forces act on it, belongs in the cell where *procedural knowledge* intersects with *apply,* because making this determination requires the application of procedural knowledge.

The taxonomy helps us understand the complexities of learning, and it also reminds us that we want our students to do more than remember factual knowledge. Unfortunately, schooling often focuses more on this most basic type of learning than it does on the other 23 cells combined. These other forms of knowledge and more advanced cognitive processes are even more important now in the 21st century, as student thinking, decision making, and problem solving are increasingly emphasized.

The Knowledge Dimension	The Cognitive Process Dimension					
	1. Remember	2. Understand	3. Apply	4. Analyze	5. Evaluate	6. Create
A. Factual knowledge						
B. Conceptual knowledge						
C. Procedural knowledge						
D. Metacognitive knowledge						

Figure 13.2 A taxonomy for learning, teaching, and assessing

Source: "A Taxonomy for Learning, Teaching, and Assessing" from A TAXONOMY FOR LEARNING, TEACHING, AND ASSESSING: A REVISION OF BLOOM'S TAXONOMY OF EDUCATIONAL OBJECTIVES by ABRIDGED EDITION, 1st Edition by Anderson ET AL. Copyright © 2001 by Anderson/Krathwohl/Cruikshank/Mayer/Pintrich/Raths/Wittrock. Printed and Electronically reproduced by permission of Pearson Education, Inc., Upper Saddle River, New Jersey.

Preparing and Organizing Learning Activities

Once Scott had specified his learning objectives, he then prepared and organized his learning activities. This process involved four steps:

1. Identify the components of the topic—the concepts, principles, and relationships among them—that students should understand.
2. Sequence the components.
3. Prepare examples that students can use to construct their knowledge of each component.
4. Order the examples with the most concrete and obvious presented first.

Scott used task analysis to accomplish these steps. Let's look at this planning tool.

Task Analysis: A Planning Tool

Task analysis is the process of breaking content into component parts and sequencing the parts. While different forms of task analysis exist, a subject matter analysis, such as Scott used, is most common in classrooms (Alberto & Troutman, 2009).

During task analysis, we first identify the specific concepts and principles included in the general topic, then sequence them in a way that will be most understandable to students, and finally identify examples to illustrate each.

Scott knew that his students needed to understand the concept *force* and the effect of different forces on an object in order to understand Bernoulli's principle. So, he first planned to teach *force* and the relationships among forces on Monday and Bernoulli's principle on Tuesday and Wednesday. Scott's task analysis is outlined in Table 13.4.

Task analysis. The process of breaking content into component parts and sequencing the parts.

Planning for Assessment

Because formal assessments, such as quizzes and tests, are typically given after students complete a learning activity, you might assume that thinking about assessment also occurs after learning activities are conducted. This isn't true; thinking about assessment is an essential part of planning (Martone & Sireci, 2009). As you saw in Table 13.1, effective assessments answer the question, "How can I determine if my students have reached the learning objectives?" (We examine Scott's assessment in detail later in the chapter.)

Assessment decisions are important during planning because they help us align our instruction. Let's look at this idea.

Table 13.4 A task analysis for teaching *force* and Bernoulli's principle

Task-Analysis Step	Example
1. Identify components of the topic.	Scott identified the concept *force,* the influence of two different forces on an object, and *Bernoulli's principle* as different components of the topic.
2. Sequence the components.	Scott planned to teach the (1) concept of *force;* (2) the effect of different forces on an object; and (3) *Bernoulli's principle,* in that order.
3. Prepare examples of each.	Scott prepared examples of each, such as pulling a student in a chair, pushing on the chalkboard, and having a "tug of war" with a student.
4. Order the examples.	Scott first planned to pull a student in his chair because it was the best attention getter, then push on the chalkboard, and later have his "tug of war" with a student.

Expert teachers are careful to ensure that their learning activities and assessments are aligned with their objectives.

Instructional alignment. The match between learning objectives, learning activities, and assessments.

Standards. Statements that describe what students should know or be able to do at the end of a prescribed period of study.

Instructional Alignment

Instructional alignment is the match between learning objectives, learning activities, and assessments, and it is essential for promoting learning (Martone & Sireci, 2009).

> Without this alignment, it is difficult to know what is being learned. Students may be learning valuable information, but one cannot tell unless there is alignment between what they are learning and the assessment of that learning. Similarly, students may be learning things that others don't value unless curricula and assessments are aligned with . . . learning goals. (Bransford, Brown, & Cocking, 2000, pp. 151–152)

Maintaining alignment isn't as easy as it appears. For instance, if our objective is for students to be able to write effectively, yet our learning activities focus on isolated grammar skills, our instruction is not aligned. It is similarly out of alignment if the objective is for students to apply math concepts to the real world, but learning activities have students practicing computation problems.

Scott's instruction was aligned. His objectives were for students to understand the concept *force,* the effect of different forces on an object, and Bernoulli's principle; his learning activity focused on those objectives, and his assessment measured the extent to which students understood these ideas.

Planning in a Standards-Based Environment

Over the last several years, a great deal has been written about American students' lack of knowledge. For example, one survey found that more than half of high school students identified Germany, Japan, or Italy, instead of the Soviet Union, as America's World War II ally (Bauerlein, 2008), and another found that most 18- to 24-year-olds couldn't find Iraq on a map of the Middle East (Manzo, 2006).

Similar concerns have been raised about math and science, where international comparisons indicate that American students lag behind many of their counterparts in other countries (National Center for Education Statistics, 2007).

In response to concerns about students' lack of knowledge, educators have established academic **standards,** statements that describe what students should know or be able to do at the end of a prescribed period of study. All states and the District of Columbia have established standards, and your school will be held accountable for the extent to which students meet the standards prescribed by your state. So, you will need to be able to design learning activities to help students reach them.

Standards are essentially statements of objectives, but, because they vary in specificity, you often will first need to interpret the meaning of the standard and then construct your own specific learning objectives based on your interpretation.

For instance, this is the standard that Scott used as a basis for planning his lesson:

> The student knows that if more than one force acts on an object, then the forces can reinforce or cancel each other, depending on their direction and magnitude.

Based on this standard, he specified the following objectives, the first three for Monday, and the fourth for Tuesday and Wednesday:

1. Students will know that a force is a push or a pull.
2. Students will identify examples of forces.
3. Students will determine the net effect of different forces on an object.
4. Students will understand that where the speed of air over a surface increases, the force it exerts on the surface decreases (Bernoulli's principle).

He then prepared his learning activities and assessments based on his objectives. Scott's lesson plan appears in Figure 13.3.

Scott's lesson was in middle school science. Let's look at an example from 10th-grade World History in the state of California.

> Students analyze the effects of the Industrial Revolution in England, France, Germany, Japan, and the United States.
>
> 1. Analyze why England was the first country to industrialize.
>
> (California State Board of Education, 2008)

Figure 13.3 Scott's lesson plan in middle school science

Topics: Force and Bernoulli's principle

Standard:

The student knows that if more than one force acts on an object, then the forces can reinforce or cancel each other, depending on their direction and magnitude.

Learning Objectives:

Students will: (1) know that force is a push or a pull; (2) identify examples of forces; (3) determine the net effect of two forces on an object; and (4) understand that where the speed of air over a surface increases, the force the air exerts on the surface decreases.

Content:

Any push or pull is a force. Objects move in the direction of the greater net force. When the speed of a fluid (most commonly air) increases over a surface, the force and pressure that it exerts on the surface decrease.

Learning Activities:

Monday:

1. Define *force* as a push or a pull and show examples of forces, such as pulling a student across the room in a desk and pushing on the board.
2. Have students identify additional examples of forces.
3. Tug objects back and forth to demonstrate the net effect of different forces on an object. Emphasize that objects will move in the direction of the greater force.

Tuesday and Wednesday:

4. Have students blow over a piece of paper, ask for observations, and guide them to observe that the paper rises. Have them blow between two pieces of paper and observe that the papers come together.
5. Have students blow through the neck of a funnel with a ping-pong ball in the mouth and observe that the ball stays in the mouth of the funnel.
6. Sketch the examples on the board, and have the students identify where the force was greater in each case. Guide them to conclude that the force under the paper, on the outside of the two papers, and in front of the ball was greater than the force on top of the paper, between the papers, and behind the ball.
7. Have the students identify where the speed of the air was greater in each case.
8. Guide the students to conclude that where the speed of the air was greater, the force it exerted on the papers or ball was less (the force was greater on the opposite side). Label this relationship "Bernoulli's principle."

Assessment:

1. Have the students sketch the flow of the air over the surface for each of the examples and prepare a written description of the relationship between speed of air and the force it exerts.
2. Ask students to use Bernoulli's principle to explain how airplanes are able to fly.

An objective based on this standard might appear as follows:

Students will identify the economic and political factors existing in England and in other countries that contributed to its being the first country to industrialize.

Finally, let's look at an example from the state of Texas in third-grade math.

(3.2) Number, operation, and quantitative reasoning. The student uses fraction names and symbols to describe fractional parts of whole objects or sets of objects. The student is expected to:

(A) construct concrete models of fractions;

(B) compare fractional parts of whole objects or sets of objects in a problem situation using concrete models (Texas Education Agency, 2008)

An objective related to the standard as an interpretation of part (B) could be:

Students will identify fractional parts in sets of objects.

States often provide sample assessments to help guide teachers as they plan. For instance, the following item is similar to one that appears on the 2009 *Texas Assessment of Knowledge and Skills* for third-grade math and is designed to assess the preceding standard (Texas Education Agency, 2009).

Which of the following groups shows that 3/5 of the shapes are circles? Mark your answer.

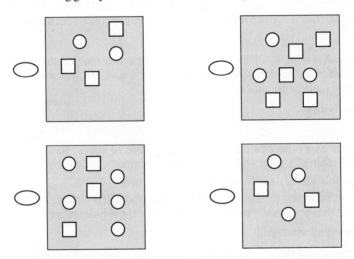

We encourage you to look at sample assessment items if your state provides them. They help you understand how your students will be assessed and help you better prepare them for the high-stakes tests they'll be required to take.

Keep in mind that the objectives we've offered here are merely examples based on individuals' interpretations of the standards. Based on your knowledge of content and your students, your interpretations might differ from the examples you see here.

Becoming comfortable with the idea that you can—and should—use your professional judgment in interpreting standards and constructing lessons is important. As you acquire experience, you will put less information on paper as you plan, but you will be no less clear about your learning objectives, how you will help your students reach them (learning activities), and how you will determine the extent to which they have been reached (assessments).

The Common Core State Standards Initiative

In spite of progress in the standards movement, American students still remain behind other nations in terms of academic achievement and readiness to succeed in life after school. Inconsistency among the states and the charge that some states have lowered their standards to meet federal mandates are often offered as reasons (Ginsburg, Leinwand, & Decker, 2009).

In response to these issues, the **Common Core State Standards Initiative (CCSSI),** a state-led effort to establish a single set of clear educational standards for all states in English-language arts and mathematics—that states can share and voluntarily adopt—was launched in 2009 (Common Core State Standards Initiative, 2010a). The CCSSI is coordinated by the National Governors Association Center for Best Practices (NGA Center) and the Council of Chief State School Officers (CCSSO). By early 2011 the standards had been formally adopted by 41 of the 50 states (Common Core State Standards Initiative, 2011). The standards are designed to ensure that students graduating from high school are prepared to go to college or enter the workforce and that parents, teachers, and students have a clear understanding of what is expected of them. The standards are also linked to international benchmarks to hopefully ensure that American students are competitive in the emerging global marketplace (Ginsburg et al., 2009; C. D. Lee & Spratley, 2010).

The following is an example from first-grade math.

> First grade:
> Number—Operations and the Problems They Solve
> Addition and subtraction
>
> 1. Understand the properties of addition.
>   a. Addition is commutative. For example, if 3 cups are added to a stack of 8 cups, then the total number of cups is the same as when 8 cups are added to a stack of 3 cups; that is, $8 + 3 = 3 + 8$.
>   b. Addition is associative. For example, $4 + 3 + 2$ can be found by first adding $4 + 3 = 7$ then adding $7 + 2 = 9$, or by first adding $3 + 2 = 5$ then adding $4 + 5 = 9$. (Common Core State Standards Initiative, 2010b, p. 13).

An example in writing for middle and high school looks like this.

> Writing Standards for History/Social Studies and Science 6–12
> Grades 9–10 students:
>
> 1. Write informative/explanatory texts, including the narration of historical events or scientific procedures/experiments, in which they:
>   a. Introduce a topic and organize information under concepts and into categories, making clear the connections and distinctions between key ideas; use formatting and graphics (e.g., headings, figures, tables, graphs, illustrations) as useful to clarify ideas.
>   b. Develop a topic that has historical or scientific significance using well-chosen, relevant, and sufficient facts, data, details, quotations, examples, extended definitions, or other information. (Common Core State Standards Initiative, 2010c, p. 60)

As you see, these standards are similar to many of the existing state standards. The consistency that the standards provide—both among states in our country and internationally—is the primary advantage of the CCSSI, and overall, the standards are endorsed by most professional groups (Gewertz, 2010). The standards movement, in general, will be part of your teaching life, the trend is certain to continue, and the common core standards are likely to be a part of your teaching future.

Common Core State Standards Initiative (CCSSI). A state-led effort to establish a single set of clear educational standards for English-language arts and mathematics that states can share and voluntarily adopt.

---

check your understanding

1.1 Describe the four essential steps involved in planning for instruction.

1.2 Planning in a standards-based environment involves an additional task beyond the planning components described in this section of the chapter. Identify this additional step.

1.3 Consider the following learning objective: *Students will learn to search for relevant and irrelevant information in applications of all the topics they study.* Classify the objective into one of the cells of the taxonomy matrix in Figure 13.2, and explain your classification.

To receive feedback for these questions, go to Appendix A.

Classroom connections

Planning Effectively in Classrooms

1. Knowledge can vary from factual to metacognitive, and cognitive processes range from remembering to creating. Consider the level of your instruction, and prepare objectives that require students to do more than remember factual knowledge.

   ■ **Elementary:** A fourth-grade teacher wants her students to understand the different functions of the human skeleton, such as why the skull is solid, the ribs are curved, and the femur is the largest bone in the body. "This is better than simply having them label the different bones," she thinks.

   ■ **Middle School:** A seventh-grade geography teacher wants his students to understand how climate is influenced by the interaction of a number of variables. To reach his objective, he gives students a map of a fictitious island, together with longitude, latitude, topography, and wind direction and has students make and defend conclusions about the climate of the island.

   ■ **High School:** A biology teacher wants her students to understand the relationships between an organism's body structure and its adaptation to its environment. She has her students identify the characteristics of parasitic and nonparasitic worms and the differences between them. Students then link the differences to the organisms' abilities to adapt to their environments.

2. Instructional alignment ensures that learning activities are congruent with learning objectives, and assessments are consistent with both. Prepare assessments during planning, and keep the need for alignment in mind as you plan.

   ■ **Elementary:** The fourth-grade teacher in her unit on the skeletal system prepares the following as an assessment: "Suppose humans walked on all fours, as chimpanzees and gorillas do. Describe how our skeletons would be different from our skeletons now."

   ■ **Middle School:** To assess his students' developing knowledge, the geography teacher gives them another map of a fictitious island with different mountain ranges, wind directions, ocean currents, and latitude and longitude. He then asks them to identify and explain where the largest city on the island would most likely be.

   ■ **High School:** The biology teacher describes two organisms, one with radial symmetry and the other with bilateral symmetry. She asks her students to identify the one that is most advanced with respect to evolution and to explain their choices.

Implementing Instruction

Ed Psych and You

You have thought about and made the necessary decisions about redecorating your living room. Now, what do you do?

Implementing instruction. The process of putting decisions made during planning into action.

Think again about the questions we asked in "Ed Psych and You" in the first section of the chapter, "You have a personal project that you want to complete, such as redecorating the living room in your house or apartment. What is the first thing you think about?" and "What else do you consider?" We then said that you'll think about the purpose (objective) of the project, how you will achieve the purpose, and how you will know if you've achieved it.

Now consider the question we ask in "Ed Psych and You" here, "Now, what do you do?" The answer is simply, *implement your plans*. For example, you actually will do the painting, rearranging the furniture, or adding some artwork to your room.

Again, teaching is similar. **Implementing instruction** is the process of putting the decisions made during planning into action. Planning is primarily a series of thought processes, whereas implementation involves action. A great deal of thinking is involved during implementation as well, but if you've planned carefully, the load on your working memory during implementation will be significantly reduced.

Effectively implementing instruction is a systematic process that involves a number of sophisticated abilities and skills. To illustrate, let's return to Scott's work with his students. Scott had taught the concept of *force* and the net effect of forces on an object (objects move in the direction of the greater force) on Monday. We join him as he begins class Tuesday with a review:

"Let's go over what we did yesterday," he begins just as the bell stops ringing. "What is a force? . . . Shantae?"

" . . . A push or a pull," she responds, after thinking for a second.

"Good, Shantae," Scott smiles and then reviews the concept of force by pushing on the board, blowing on an object sitting on his desk, and asking students to explain why they are forces.

He continues by holding a stapler and having Damien pull it away from him to review the idea that objects move in the direction of the greater force.

Reminding students to "keep these ideas in mind" and raising his voice to emphasize his points, he gives each two pieces of paper, picks up a similar piece, and blows over it, as you see here.

He directs students to do the same, and then asks, "What did you notice when we blew over the top? . . . David?"

"The paper moved."

"How did the paper move? . . . Let's do it again."

David again blows over the surface of the paper, and Scott repeats, "What did the paper do?"

" . . . It came up."

"Yes," Scott waves energetically. "When you blow over it, it comes up."

He then has students pick up both pieces of paper and demonstrates how to blow between them, as shown here.

"What did you notice here? . . . Sharon?" Scott asks after they've done the same.

" . . . The papers came together."

"Okay, good. Remember that, and we'll talk about it in a minute," Scott smiles. "Now, let's look at one more example. . . . I have a funnel and a ping-pong ball. . . . I'm going to shoot Tristan in the head when I blow," he jokes, pointing to one of the students.

He blows through the funnel's stem, and to the students' surprise, the ball stays in the funnel.

Scott has students repeat the demonstration and make observations, and he then draws sketches of the three examples on the board and says, "Let's look at these."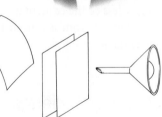

Referring to the first sketch, Scott asks, "Was I blowing on the top or the bottom? . . . Rachel?"

"The top."

"And what happened there? . . . Heather?"

"The paper rose up."

Referring to the second sketch, he asks, "What did we do here, . . . Shantae?"

"We blew in between them."

"And what happened there? . . . Ricky?"

"They came together."

Scott does a similar analysis with the ball and funnel and then says, "Let's think about the forces here. . . . What forces are acting on the paper? . . . Colin?"

"Gravity."

"And which direction is gravity pulling?"

"Down."

Scott draws an arrow pointing downward, indicating the force of gravity, and labels it "A."

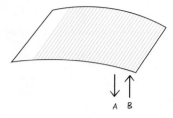

"What other force is acting on the paper? . . . William?" he continues.

"Air," William says, pointing up.

"How do you know it's pushing up?"

"The paper moved up."

"Exactly. You know there's a force pushing up, because objects move in the direction of the greater force, and the paper moved up." Scott then draws an arrow pointing up and labels it "B."

Scott guides the students through a similar analysis of the second and third examples, leading them to conclude that the forces pushing the two papers together were greater than the forces pushing them apart, and the force pushing the ball into the funnel was greater than the force pushing the ball out.

"Now let's look again at the forces and where we blew," Scott continues, as he moves back to the first sketch. "Study the drawings carefully, and see what kind of relationship exists between the two."

After several seconds, Heather concludes, "It seems like wherever you blew, the force was stronger on the opposite side."

Seeing that the bell is going to ring in a minute, Scott continues, "Yes, excellent, Heather. . . . A person named Bernoulli discovered that every time you increase the speed of the air over a surface, the force goes down. . . . So, when I speed up the air over the top of the paper (holding up the single sheet of paper), the force goes down and this force takes over (motioning underneath the paper to illustrate a force pushing up).

He summarizes the other two examples in the same way, finishing just as the bell ending the period begins to ring.

Essential teaching skills. Basic abilities that all teachers, including those in their first year of teaching, should possess to maximize student learning.

As Scott implemented his plans, he demonstrated a number of **essential teaching skills,** basic abilities that all teachers, including those in their first year of teaching, should possess to maximize student learning. They are equally important for working with learners having exceptionalities, students who are members of cultural minorities, and those in urban, suburban, and rural environments. In short, essential teaching skills apply to all students and teaching situations.

Essential teaching skills are analogous to what is commonly referred to as *basic skills,* the skills in reading, writing, math, and technology that all people need in order to function effectively in today's world. You will be expected to understand and demonstrate these skills regardless of the content area or grade level that you're planning to teach.

Derived from a long line of research (Brophy, 2006c; Good & Brophy 2008), these essential teaching skills are outlined in Table 13.5 and discussed in the sections that follow.

Teacher Beliefs and Behaviors

Admittedly, beliefs are not skills, but the effectiveness of your teaching will substantively depend on your beliefs about learning, teaching, and students. For instance, if you believe that you are capable of getting all students to learn (high personal teaching efficacy), you will work harder, expect more from your students (high expectations), demonstrate your own interest in the topics you're teaching (modeling and enthusiasm), and commit yourself to your students, both as learners and as people (caring). These beliefs are fundamental for effective teaching. Each is linked to increased achievement and student motivation (Brophy, 2010; Bruning, Schraw, & Norby, 2011).

Scott's interactions with his students suggest that he held these beliefs. He was energetic and enthusiastic, he demonstrated the respect for students that indicates caring, and his questioning suggested that he expected all students to participate and learn. These are the beliefs and behaviors we hope to see in all teachers.

Table 13.5 Essential teaching skills, components, and cognitive learning theory applications

Essential Teaching Skill	Essential Teaching Skill Components	Application of Cognitive Learning Theory
Teacher beliefs and behaviors	• Personal teaching efficacy • High and positive expectations • Modeling and enthusiasm • Caring	Models desired behaviors, increases self-efficacy and helps students meet their need for relatedness.
Organization	• Starting instruction on time • Having materials ready • Creating well-established routines	Reduces the cognitive load on teachers' and students' working memories and helps establish and maintain students' equilibrium.
Review	• Beginning-of-lesson review • Interim reviews	Activates prior knowledge retrieved from long-term memory, to which new knowledge is attached.
Focus	• Capture attention • Maintain attention	Attracts learners' attention and provides a conceptual umbrella for the lesson.
Questioning	• Questioning frequency • Equitable distribution • Prompting • Wait-time	Encourages learners to become cognitively active. Provides scaffolding.
Feedback	• Immediate • Specific • Corrective information • Positive emotional tone	Provides students with information they use to determine whether the knowledge they've constructed is valid.
Closure	• End-of-lesson summary	Contributes to schema construction and meaningful encoding.
Communication	• Precise terms • Connected discourse • Transition signals • Emphasis	Makes information understandable and meaningful. Maintains learner attention.

Organization

To teach effectively, you first must be well organized. This means that you will (1) prepare the materials you need in advance, (2) start your instruction on time, (3) make transitions from one activity to another quickly and smoothly, and (4) develop well-established classroom routines. These components both increase achievement by maximizing instructional time and help prevent classroom management problems (Good & Brophy 2008).

Scott was well organized. He began his lesson as soon as the bell finished ringing, he had the sheets of paper, balls, and funnels ready to hand out, and he made the transition from his review to the learning activity quickly and smoothly. This organization was the result of clear thinking and decision making during his planning.

Review

Implementing instruction is a systematic process, and it begins with a **review,** a summary that helps students link what they've already learned to the new information you're planning to teach them. It can occur at any point in a lesson, although it is most common at the beginning and end.

Review. A summary that helps students link what they've already learned to new information in the learning activity.

Focus helps capture and maintain students' attention throughout a lesson.

Focus. The essential teaching skill teachers use to capture and maintain students' attention and interest throughout the lesson.

Questioning frequency. Refers to the number of questions teachers ask during a learning activity.

An important cognitive learning principle says that the knowledge learners construct depends on what they already know, and beginning reviews help students activate the prior knowledge needed to construct their new understanding.

Scott's beginning review on Tuesday was one of the most effective aspects of his lesson. He didn't just ask the students to recall the definition of *force* and the influence of different forces on an object; he illustrated the ideas with examples. Though it may seem redundant to use additional examples, because he had shown examples on Monday, it's often necessary. Providing students with concrete examples during the review increases its effectiveness by providing additional links in long-term memory. And Scott's review was essential because his students had to understand force and the influence of different forces on an object in order to understand Bernoulli's principle.

Focus

We know from our understanding of human memory that all learning begins with attention, so we need a mechanism to capture students' attention and interest and maintain both throughout the lesson. **Focus** provides this mechanism, and some authors use the label "hook" to describe this function (Lemov, 2010).

Scott provided focus for his students by beginning his lesson with his demonstrations. They attracted students' attention and provided a context for the rest of the lesson. Scott's demonstrations and sketches on the board also helped maintain his students' attention throughout his learning activity. Concrete objects, pictures, models, materials displayed on the overhead or document camera, or even information written on the board can all act as focus during a lesson.

Questioning

You've begun your lesson with a review, and you've used a form of focus to attract your students' attention. Your next challenge is to involve them in the lesson and make them cognitively active. Doing so is supported by a long history of research.

> Teachers who elicit greater achievement gains spend a great deal of time actively instructing their students. Their classrooms feature more time spent in interactive lessons featuring teacher–student discourse and less time spent in independent seatwork. . . . Most of their instruction occurs during interactive discourse with students rather than during extended lecture-presentations. (Brophy, 2006c, p. 764)

Questioning is the most widely applicable and effective tool we have for promoting this involvement (Leinhardt & Steele, 2005; Lemov, 2010). Skilled questioning is sophisticated, but in our work with teachers we've seen that with practice and experience they've become expert at it, and you can, too (Eggen & Kauchak, 2012; Kauchak & Eggen, 2012). To avoid overloading your working memory, you need to practice questioning strategies until they're essentially automatic, which leaves working memory space available to monitor students' thinking and assess learning progress (Feldon, 2007a). Once you master this ability, you'll find that using questioning to guide your students' increasing understanding will be some of your most rewarding professional experiences.

The features of effective questioning are outlined in Figure 13.4 and discussed in the sections that follow. The connections in the figure remind us that the features are interconnected and interdependent.

Questioning Frequency

Questioning frequency refers to the number of questions we ask during a learning activity, and Scott developed his entire lesson with questioning. As with many aspects of teaching, questioning frequency isn't as simple as it appears on the surface. To maximize learning, questions must largely remain focused on the learning objectives, and this is another reason careful planning is so important. If you're clear about your objectives, deciding what questions to ask will be much easier.

Equitable Distribution

Equitable distribution is the process of calling on all the students in a class as equally as possible (Kerman, 1979), and it is intended to reverse teachers' tendencies to call on high-achieving or more outgoing students more often than their peers. To emphasize that we should call on students whether or not they have their hands raised, some experts use the term "cold call" when describing equitable distribution (Lemov, 2010).

To illustrate this idea, let's return to Scott's lesson:

Questioning allows teachers to guide student learning while also gauging learning progress.

> **Scott:** (Referring to the sketch of the single piece of paper.) Was I blowing on the top or the bottom? . . . Rachel?
>
> **Rachel:** The top.
>
> **Scott:** And what happened there? . . . Heather?
>
> **Heather:** The paper rose up.
>
> **Scott:** (Referring to sketch of the two pieces of paper.) What did we do here . . . Shantae?
>
> **Shantae:** We blew in between them.
>
> **Scott:** And what happened there . . . Ricky?
>
> **Ricky:** They came together.

In this short episode, Scott called on four different students, and he first asked the question and then identified who he wanted to respond. Equitable distribution makes everyone responsible for generating an answer and creates the expectation that all learners are capable of responding and should be paying attention (Good & Brophy, 2008).

Equitable distribution. The process of calling on all the students in a class as equally as possible, whether or not they have their hands raised.

> Students benefit from opportunities to practice oral communication skills, and distributing response opportunities helps keep them attentive and accountable. Also, teachers who interact primarily with a small group of active (and usually high-achieving) students are likely to communicate undesirable expectations and be generally less aware and less effective. (Good & Brophy, 2008, p. 322)

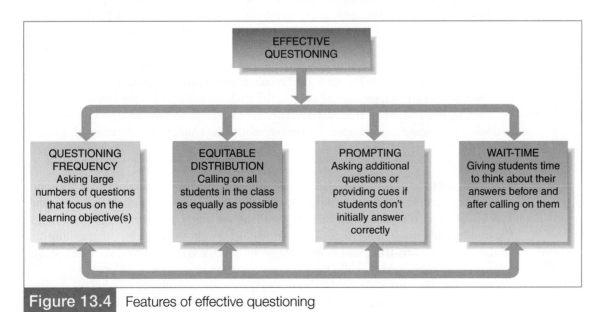

EFFECTIVE QUESTIONING

QUESTIONING FREQUENCY	EQUITABLE DISTRIBUTION	PROMPTING	WAIT-TIME
Asking large numbers of questions that focus on the learning objective(s)	Calling on all students in the class as equally as possible	Asking additional questions or providing cues if students don't initially answer correctly	Giving students time to think about their answers before and after calling on them

Figure 13.4 Features of effective questioning

Equitable distribution is a simple but demanding idea because it requires careful monitoring of students and a great deal of your energy. This is another reason why you should practice questioning to the point of automaticity to reduce the cognitive load it imposes (Feldon, 2007a).

Prompting

In attempting to equitably distribute your questions, you might wonder, What do I do when the student I call on doesn't answer or answers incorrectly? Ideally, **prompting**—an additional question or statement used to elicit an appropriate student response after a student fails to answer correctly—is the answer. Its value to both learning and motivation is well documented (Brophy, 2006c).

To illustrate, let's look again at Scott's work with his students.

Scott: What did you notice when we blew over the top? . . . David?

David: The paper moved.

Scott: How did the paper move? Do it again.

(David again blew over the surface of the paper.)

Scott: What did the paper do?

David: It came up.

David didn't initially give the answer necessary to help him understand the relationship between force and the movement of the paper, so having him repeat the demonstration was a form of prompting.

As another example, Ken Duran, in a language arts lesson on adjectives, displays the following on his document camera:

The girl was very athletic.

Let's look at some brief dialogue:

Ken: Can you identify an adjective in the sentence . . . Chandra?

Chandra: . . .

Ken: What do we know about the girl?

Chandra: She was athletic.

Ken's prompt, which elicited an acceptable response, kept Chandra involved in the activity and helped her be successful. She hadn't arrived at the answer Ken wanted, but the question kept her active and in the zone of proximal development, allowing her to make learning progress.

You will need to be strategic as you prompt. For instance, if the question calls for factual knowledge, such as "What is 7 times 8?" or "Who was our president during the Civil War?" and a student doesn't answer, prompting isn't useful; students either know the fact or they don't. It's effective, however, when studying conceptual, procedural, and metacognitive knowledge, and when using cognitive processes beyond remembering (Anderson & Krathwohl, 2001).

Wait-Time

For questions to be effective, we need to give our students time to think. And, if we wait a couple seconds and survey the room after asking a question, we alert all students that they may be called on. Then, after identifying a student, we wait a couple more seconds to give the student additional "think" time. This period of silence, both before and after calling on a student, is called **wait-time,** and in most classrooms, it is too short, often less than 1 second (Rowe, 1974, 1986; Stahl et al., 2005).

Increasing wait-time, ideally to about 3 to 5 seconds, communicates that all students are expected to answer, results in longer and better answers, and contributes to a positive classroom climate (Kastens & Liben, 2007; Rowe, 1974, 1986).

As with prompting, we should use wait-time strategically. For example, if students are practicing basic skills, such as multiplication facts, quick answers are desirable, and wait-times should be short (Good & Brophy, 2008). Also, if a student appears uneasy, you may choose to intervene earlier. However, if you expect students to think—using cognitive processes such as apply, analyze, or evaluate—wait-times should be longer, sometimes exceeding the 3- to 5-second rule of thumb.

Cognitive Levels of Questions

The kinds of questions we ask also influence learning, and the merits of low- and high-level questions have been widely researched. The results are mixed, however. Both low-level questions, such as remembering factual information, and high-level questions that require students to apply knowledge to a new situation, can increase achievement, depending on the teaching situation (Good & Brophy, 2008).

The appropriate level for a question depends on your learning objective, and you should think about asking logical sequences of questions instead of questions in isolation. You saw this illustrated in Scott's lesson. After completing the demonstrations, Scott first asked the students to describe how the papers and the ball acted, which he followed with questions asking them to identify the relationship between the speed of the air and the forces it exerted on the objects.

As you teach, you should focus on your learning objectives and not on the level of questions you choose to ask. If your thinking about your objectives is clear, the levels of questions you ask will take care of themselves.

Feedback

As you teach your lesson, students need information that will help them determine whether or not the knowledge they're constructing is accurate and valid. **Feedback** provides this information, and its value for promoting learning is well documented (Hattie & Timperley, 2007). It also contributes to motivation because it provides learners with information about their increasing competence (Brophy, 2010).

> **Feedback.** Information teachers provide to students that helps students determine whether or not the knowledge they're constructing is accurate and valid.

Effective feedback has four characteristics:

- It is immediate or given soon after a learner response.
- It is specific.
- It provides corrective information for the learner.
- It has a positive emotional tone (Moreno, 2004).

To illustrate these characteristics, let's compare three examples.

Mr. Dole: What kind of figure is displayed on the document camera, . . . Jo?

Jo: A square.

Mr. Dole: Not quite. Help her out, . . . Steve?

Ms. West: What kind of figure is shown on the overhead, Jo?

Jo: A square.

Ms. West: No, it's a rectangle. What is the next figure, . . . Albert?

Ms. Baker: What kind of figure is shown on the overhead, Jo?

Jo: A square.

Ms. Baker: No, remember, we said that all sides have the same length in a square. What do you notice about the lengths of the sides in this figure?

Each teacher gave immediate feedback, but neither Mr. Dole nor Ms. West gave Jo any corrective information. Ms. Baker, in contrast, provided Jo with specific information that helped her understand the concept, which is the most important feature of effective feedback (Hattie & Timperly, 2007).

Although these examples don't illustrate the emotional tone of each teacher's responses, it is important. Harsh, critical, or sarcastic feedback detracts from students' feelings of safety and relatedness, which decreases both motivation and learning (Schunk, Pintrich, & Meece, 2008).

Praise

Praise is the most common form of positive feedback, and a study examining college students' reactions to praise is revealing. The researchers found that the desire for praise, and the boost to self-esteem that comes with it, trumped other desires and needs, including alcohol, money, or even sex (Bushman, Moeller, & Crocker, 2010).

Other research examining the use of praise in K-12 classrooms has found the following patterns:

- Praise is used less often than most teachers believe—less than five times per class.
- Praise for good behavior is quite rare; it occurs once every 2 or more hours in the elementary grades and even less as students get older.
- Praise tends to depend as much on the type of student (e.g., high achieving, well behaved, and attentive) as on the quality of the student's response.
- Teachers praise students based on the answers they expect to receive as much as on those they actually hear (Good & Brophy, 2008).

Using praise effectively is complex. For instance, young children tend to accept it at face value even when overdone, whereas older students assess the validity of the praise and what they believe it communicates about their ability. Young children bask in praise given openly in front of a class, whereas adolescents often react better if it's given quietly and individually (Stipek, 2002). Experts suggest that praise delivered to older students should reflect genuine accomplishment and be delivered simply and directly using a natural voice (Good & Brophy, 2008). Highly anxious students and those from low socioeconomic status environments tend to react more positively to praise than students who are confident or come from more advantaged backgrounds (Good & Brophy, 2008).

Finally, although research indicates that specific is more effective than general praise, if every desired answer is praised specifically, it can sound stilted and artificial and may disrupt the flow of a lesson. Experts suggest that praise for student answers that are correct but tentative should provide additional, affirming information, whereas praise for answers delivered with confidence should be simple and general (Rosenshine, 1987).

Closure. A summary that occurs at the end of lessons.

Praise given quietly and individually is effective with adolescents.

Written Feedback

Much of the feedback we provide occurs during lessons, but students also need feedback on their written work. Because writing detailed comments is enormously time-consuming, providing each student with individual, written feedback is a nearly impossible job.

One solution to this problem is to provide model responses to written assignments. For instance, to help students evaluate their answers to essay items, you can write ideal answers, display them, and encourage students to compare their answers with the model. Combined with discussion and time available for individual help, the model provides informative feedback that is manageable in terms of time and effort.

Closure

Closure is a summary that occurs at the end of lessons. Closure helps students conceptually organize what they've learned into a meaningful schema; it pulls the different aspects of the topic together and signals the end of a lesson. When students are involved in higher-level learning, a summary statement combined with having them identify additional examples of a concept, or apply a principle, generalization, or rule to a new situation is an effective form of closure. When teaching problem solving, summarizing the thinking involved in solving the problem is also effective.

Communication

Throughout all your lessons—your reviews, forms of focus, questioning, the feedback you provide, and the way you bring lessons to closure—clear and concise communication is important. Clear communication increases student achievement, and students are more satisfied with instruction when their teachers communicate clearly (Good & Brophy, 2008; Weiss & Pasley, 2004). In a sense, clear communication is an umbrella under which the other essential teaching skills fall.

Effective communication has four characteristics:

- Precise language
- Connected discourse
- Transition signals
- Emphasis

Precise language omits vague terms—such as *perhaps, maybe, might, and so on,* and *usually*—from explanations and responses to students' questions. For example, if you ask, "What do high-efficacy teachers do that promotes learning?" and your instructor responds, "Usually, they use their time somewhat better and so on," you're left with a sense of uncertainty about the idea. In contrast, if the instructor says, "They believe they can increase learning, and one way they do this is by using their time efficiently," you're given a clear picture, which makes the idea more understandable.

Precise language. Teacher language that omits vague terms from explanations and responses to students' questions.

Connected discourse refers to instruction that is thematic and leads to a point. If the point of the lesson isn't clear, if it's sequenced inappropriately, or if incidental information is interjected without indicating how it relates to the topic, the discourse becomes disconnected or scrambled. This means we should keep our lessons on track and minimize time spent on matters unrelated to the topic (Burbules & Bruce, 2001; Leinhardt, 2001).

Connected discourse. Instruction that is thematic and leads to a point.

Transition signals are verbal statements indicating that one idea is ending and another is beginning. For example, an American government teacher might signal a transition by saying, "We've been talking about the Senate, which is one house of Congress, and now we'll turn to the House of Representatives." Because not all students are cognitively at the same place, a transition signal alerts them that the lesson is making a conceptual shift—moving to a new topic—and allows them to prepare for it.

Transition signals. Verbal statements indicating that one idea is ending and another is beginning.

Emphasis consists of verbal and vocal cues that alert students to important information in a lesson. For example, Scott used a form of vocal emphasis—raising his voice—when he said, "Keep these ideas in mind," as he moved from his review to the lesson itself. Whenever you say something such as, "Now remember, everyone, this is very important" or "Listen carefully now," you're using verbal emphasis.

Emphasis. Verbal and vocal cues that alert students to important information in a lesson.

Repeating a point is another common form of emphasis. Asking students, "What did we say these problems have in common?" stresses an important feature in the problems and helps students link new to past information. Redundancy is particularly important when reviewing abstract rules, principles, and concepts (Brophy & Good, 1986; Shuell, 1996).

Knowledge of content is essential for clear communication. If we clearly understand the topics we teach, we'll use clearer language, our lessons will be more thematic, and we will remain focused on our learning objectives to a greater extent that we would if we're uncertain (Brophy, 2006c; Staples, 2007). This suggests that, as we plan, we should carefully study any topics about which we're uncertain.

check your understanding

2.1 Describe essential teaching skills, and explain why they are important.

2.2 We try to model with our writing the content that we're discussing in each chapter. What are we doing to provide focus for each chapter's contents?

2.3 Identify at least two other essential teaching skills that we utilize in each of the chapters of this book.

To receive feedback for these questions, go to Appendix A.

Classroom connections

Demonstrating Essential Teaching Skills in Classrooms

Teacher Beliefs and Behaviors

1. Personal teaching efficacy, high expectations, modeling and enthusiasm, and caring are teacher beliefs and behaviors associated with increased student achievement. Try to demonstrate these beliefs during lessons to increase student motivation and achievement.

 - **Elementary:** A third-grade teacher communicates her personal efficacy and caring by calling a student's parents and soliciting their help as soon as the student fails to turn in an assignment or receives an unsatisfactory grade on a quiz or test.

 - **Middle School:** A seventh-grade teacher commits himself to being a role model by displaying the statement, "I will always behave in the way I expect you to behave in this class," on the bulletin board. He uses the statement as a guiding principle in his class.

 - **High School:** A geometry teacher, knowing that her students initially have problems with proofs, conducts help sessions twice a week after school. "I would much rather help them than lower my expectations," she comments.

Organization and Communication

2. Effective organization helps teachers begin classes on time, have materials prepared, and maintain well-established routines. Carefully plan and organize materials and communicate clearly to maximize instructional time.

 - **Elementary:** A first-grade teacher has several boxes filled with frequently used science materials, such as soft drink bottles, balloons, matches, baking soda, vinegar, funnels, and a hot plate. The day before a science demonstration, he spends a few minutes selecting his materials from the boxes and sets them on a shelf near his desk so that he'll have everything ready at the beginning of the lesson.

 - **Middle School:** An eighth-grade American history teacher asks a member of her team to visit her class to provide feedback about her instruction. She also asks her colleague to check if she clearly emphasizes the important points in the lesson, sequences the presentation logically, and communicates changes in topics.

 - **High School:** A biology teacher begins each class with an outline of the day's topics and activities on the board. As she makes transitions from one activity to the other, she calls students' attention to the outline so students can understand where they've been and where they're going.

Focus and Feedback

3. Lesson focus helps maintain student attention, and feedback provides students with information about their learning progress. Use problems, demonstrations, and displays to provide focus during lessons. Provide feedback throughout all learning experiences.

 - **Elementary:** A fourth-grade teacher beginning a study of different groups of animals brings a live lobster, a spider, and a grasshopper to class and builds a lesson on arthropods around these animals. After making a list of arthropods' characteristics on the board, she asks students if a clam is an arthropod. When some say it is, she provides feedback by referring them to the list and asking them to identify each characteristic in the clam. After a short discussion, they conclude that the clam isn't an arthropod.

 - **Middle School:** A science teacher dealing with the concept of kindling temperature soaks a cloth in a water–alcohol mix, ignites it, and asks, "Why isn't the cloth burning?" He provides feedback during the class discussion by asking guiding questions to help students develop their understanding.

 - **High School:** A physical education teacher shows students a videotape of a professional tennis player executing a nearly perfect backhand. She then videotapes the students as they practice backhands, and they attempt to modify their swings to more nearly imitate the pro's.

Questioning and Review

4. Reviews help activate and consolidate students' prior knowledge, and questioning puts them in cognitively active roles. Begin and end each class with a short review, and guide the review with questioning.

 - **Elementary:** A fifth-grade teacher whose class is studying different types of boundaries says, "We've looked at three kinds of boundaries between the states so far today. What are these three, and where do they occur?"

 - **Middle School:** An English teacher begins, "We studied pronoun–antecedent agreement yesterday. Give me an example that illustrates this idea, and explain why your example is correct."

 - **High School:** An art teacher says, "Today we've found that many artists use color to create different moods. Let's summarize some of the features that we've learned about. Go ahead, offer one, someone."

Models of Instruction

As you saw in the previous section, demonstrating essential teaching skills will increase your students' learning regardless of the content area or grade level in which you expect to teach. By comparison, **models of instruction** are prescriptive approaches to teaching designed to help students acquire a deep understanding of specific forms of knowledge. Each is grounded in cognitive learning theory and supported by research. Each also includes sequential steps designed to help students reach specified learning objectives.

Essential teaching skills support each model. For instance, just as students use reading in all their content areas, organization, questioning, and the other essential teaching skills are important regardless of the model being used.

Research tells us that no single model is most effective for all students or for helping students reach all learning objectives (Knight, 2002; Kroesbergen & van Luit, 2002; Marzano, 2003). In this section we examine four of the more widely used:

- Direct instruction
- Lecture–discussion
- Guided discovery
- Cooperative learning

> **Models of instruction.** Prescriptive approaches to teaching designed to help students acquire a deep understanding of specific forms of knowledge.

Direct Instruction

Direct instruction is a teaching model designed to help students acquire well-defined knowledge and skills needed for later learning. Examples of these skills include young students' using basic operations to solve math problems, students' using grammar and punctuation in writing, and chemistry students' balancing equations. Direct instruction is useful when skills include a sequence of specific steps, and it is particularly effective in working with low achievers and students with exceptionalities (Flores & Kaylor, 2007; Turnbull, Turnbull, & Wehmeyer, 2010).

Direct instruction ranges from a highly structured, nearly scripted, and somewhat behaviorist approach (Carnine, Silbert, Kame'enui, Tarver, Jongjohann, 2006) to one that is more flexible and cognitive (Eggen & Kauchak, 2012; Kauchak & Eggen, 2012). We discuss the latter here, which typically occurs in four phases:

- Introduction and review
- Developing understanding
- Guided practice
- Independent practice

Table 13.6 outlines the phases in direct instruction and their relationships to cognitive learning theory.

> **Direct instruction.** A teaching model designed to help students acquire well-defined knowledge and skills needed for later learning.

Table 13.6 The phases in cognitive-based direct instruction

Phase	Cognitive Learning Component
Introduction and Review: Teachers begin with a form of introductory focus and review previous work.	• Attract attention. • Access prior knowledge from long-term memory.
Developing Understanding: Teachers describe and model the skill or explain and present examples of the concept. Teachers emphasize understanding.	• Acquire declarative knowledge about the skill or concept. • Encode declarative knowledge into long-term memory.
Guided Practice: Students practice the skill or identify additional examples of the concept, and the teacher provides scaffolding.	• Move through the associative stage of developing procedural knowledge.
Independent Practice: Students practice on their own.	• Develop automaticity with the skill or concept.

Let's look at how these phases contribute to learning in a second-grade math lesson taught by Sam Barnett, a teacher in a large elementary school in Illinois. Sam has 24 students in his class; Cathy, Josh, and Jeremy have learning disabilities in math; and six of his students are not native English speakers. The standard Sam is addressing in his lesson is:

6.B.1 Solve one- and two-step problems with whole numbers using addition, subtraction, multiplication and division. (Illinois State Board of Education, 2008)

Sam begins his lesson on the addition of two-digit numbers by saying, "Today we are going to go a step further with our work in addition so that we'll be able to solve problems like this," as he displays the following on the document camera:

Jana and Patti are saving special soda cans to get a free CD. They can get the CD if they save 35 cans. Jana had 15 cans and Patti had 12. How many did they have together? [Jana and Patti are two students in Sam's class.]

After giving students a few seconds to read the problem, he asks what the problem calls for, and why it's important.

The students have boxes of interlocking cubes that they can connect to represent 10s and single-digit numbers, and Sam uses computer software to project the same numbers on the screen at the front of his room.

Sam reviews single-digit addition with problems, such as 8 + 7 and 9 + 5, and has the students represent the numbers with their cubes, and then turns back to the problem on the document camera. He has the students demonstrate 15 and 12 with their cubes, and next displays on the screen the image of grouped cubes that you see here.

He then writes the following on the board:

$$\begin{array}{r} 15 \\ + \ 12 \\ \hline \end{array}$$

"Now, watch what I do here," he continues. "When I add 5 and 2, what do I get? Let me think about that. . . . 5 and 2 are 7. Let's put a 7 on the board," he says as he walks to the board and adds a 7 so his problem appears as follows:

$$\begin{array}{r} 15 \\ + \ 12 \\ \hline 7 \end{array}$$

"Now show me that with your cubes," and he watches as the students group 5 cubes with 2 cubes on their desks.

"Now, we still have to add the tens. What do we get when we add two tens? . . .

Let's see. One ten and one ten is two tens. Now, look where I've put the 2. It is under the tens column because the 2 means two tens." With that, he writes the following on the chalkboard:

$$\begin{array}{r} 15 \\ + \ 12 \\ \hline 27 \end{array}$$

"So, how many cans did Jana and Patti have together? . . . Alesha?"

After a short pause, Alesha offers 27.

"Good. They have 27 altogether."

Sam has the students explain and demonstrate with their cubes what the 7 and the 2 in 27 mean, and then asks, "Now, we saw that I added the 5 and the 2 before I added the two 10s. Why do you suppose I did that? . . . Anyone?"

". . . You have to find out how many ones you have to see if we can make a 10," Callie offers.

"Good, Callie."

"So, let's look again," he continues. "There's an important difference between this 2," he says, pointing to the 2 in 27, "and this 2," pointing to the 2 in the 12. "What is this difference? . . . Katrina?"

"That 2 . . . is two groups of 10, . . . and that one is just 2 by itself."

"Good, Katrina. Good work, everyone. . . . Show me this 2," Sam directs, pointing to the 2 in 27.

Students hold up two groups of 10 cubes connected to each other as you see here.

"Good, and now show me this 2." He points to the 2 in the 12, and the students hold up two cubes.

"Great," Sam smiles. He has the students demonstrate their answers to three additional problems, discusses each in detail, and then says, "When we've had enough practice with our cubes to be sure that we understand these problems, we'll start practicing with the numbers by themselves. We're going to get so good at these problems that we'll be able to do them without even thinking about it."

He assigns five more problems and watches carefully as the students work at their desks.

Now, let's look at Sam's use of direct instruction with his students.

Introduction and Review. Learning begins with attention, and Sam used an attention-getting real-world problem to begin his lesson. He then checked students' perceptions by having them describe what the problem asked and reviewed what they had already done to retrieve prior knowledge from long-term memory. The value of checking and reviewing is well established (Brophy, 2006c; Kirschner, Sweller, & Clark, 2006). Although its importance seems obvious, many classroom lessons begin with little or no attempt to attract attention or activate relevant prior knowledge (Brophy, 2010).

Developing Understanding. An essential part of learning procedural knowledge involves recognizing when and how to use a skill. Sam addressed this need when he modeled the skill and said, "Now, watch what I do here," and he used cognitive modeling when he said, "When I add 5 and 2, what do I get? Let me think about that . . . . 5 and 2 are 7. Let's put a 7 on the board."

During this phase, students acquire the declarative and conditional knowledge that allows them to adapt when applying their procedural knowledge in different situations. If they fail to do so, students apply procedures mechanically or use superficial strategies, such as subtracting when they see the words "how many more" in a math problem (Jitendra et al., 2007; Mayer, 2008).

To see how Sam emphasized understanding, let's look at some dialogue from his lesson:

Sam: So, let's look again. There's an important difference between this 2 (pointing to the 2 in 27) and this 2 (pointing to the 2 in the 12). What is this difference? . . . Katrina?

Katrina: That 2 . . . is two groups of 10, . . . and that one is just 2 by itself.

Sam: Good, Katrina. Good work, everyone. . . . Show me this 2 (pointing to the 2 in 27).

The students held up groups of 10 cubes connected to each other.

Sam: Good, and show me this 2 (pointing to the 2 in the 12).

The students then held up two cubes.

The students had concrete examples (the cubes) and Sam used questioning to guide them through this phase of the lesson, both of which are important for making the topic

The developing understanding phase of direct instruction is highly interactive.

meaningful. Students fail to fully develop understanding in this phase if we emphasize memorization, don't ask enough questions, or move too quickly to practice (Rittle-Johnson & Alibali, 1999). Or we may involve learners in hands-on activities but then fail to establish the connection between the materials, such as the cubes, and the abstractions they represent (the numbers in the problem) (Ball, 1992). By asking students to explain and demonstrate the difference between the 2 in 27 and the 2 in 12 with their cubes, Sam helped them make this connection.

Guided Practice. Once students have developed an understanding of the procedure, they begin practicing as you monitor their progress. Initially, you will use questioning to provide enough scaffolding to ensure success, but not so much that challenge is reduced. As students practice, they gradually develop automaticity and become confident with the new content (Péladeau, Forget, & Gagné, 2003). Sam had his students work a problem, and they discussed it afterward, so he could ensure that they understood the process. He continued with guided practice until he believed that most students were ready to work on their own.

Independent Practice. In this final phase of direct instruction, you reduce scaffolding and shift responsibility to the students. Our goal is for students to perform the skill automatically, so working memory space can be devoted to higher-level applications (Feldon, 2007a).

Monitoring students' progress continues to be important. Expert teachers carefully monitor students to assess their developing understanding; their less-effective counterparts are more likely to merely check to see that students are on task (Brophy, 2006c; Safer & Fleischman, 2005).

Homework. Homework is a common form of independent practice, and, perhaps surprisingly, it is somewhat controversial. Some authors argue that it is ineffective and even destructive (Kohn, 2006a, 2006b). Others note that American students are assigned more homework than students in other developed countries, yet score lower in comparisons of international achievement (Baines, 2007).

Research, however, consistently indicates that homework, properly designed and implemented, increases achievement, and, because learners must take responsibility for completing it, it also develops self-regulation (Cooper, Robinson, & Patall, 2006; Marzano & Pickering, 2007). *Properly designed and implemented* is essential. Simply assigning homework doesn't increase achievement, and more isn't necessarily better. Increasing the amount of homework in the name of raising expectations or increasing academic requirements is ineffective at best and, at worst, can decrease both motivation and achievement (Baker & Letendre, 2005; Marzano & Pickering, 2007).

The amount of cognitive effort—thinking—students apply in completing homework is the primary factor influencing its effectiveness, and cognitive motivation theory helps us understand how to increase effort (Trautwein, Ludtke, & Schnyder, 2006). Three factors are involved. The first is perceived value. If students believe that homework will increase their understanding, they're more likely to make a conscientious effort to complete it (Trautwein & Ludtke, 2007). Homework perceived as busywork or unnecessary, particularly for older students, detracts from motivation and does little to promote learning. Assigning more exercises than necessary for maximizing learning can be counterproductive, and older students are unlikely to complete homework assignments for which they receive no credit (Marzano & Pickering, 2007).

Table 13.7	Characteristics of effective homework at different developmental levels

Level	Characteristic
All Levels	• Aligned with learning objectives and learning activities • Clear directions • High success rates • Feedback provided • Parental involvement
Elementary	• A quiet place, free from distractions, to do homework • Part of the regular class routine
Middle and Secondary	• Clear reasons for the importance of the homework • Credit, such as points toward an overall grade

Second, students must be generally successful on homework assignments, so their perceptions of competence and self-efficacy are increased. Third, students are much more likely to do homework if their parents expect it and monitor the extent to which it is done.

The characteristics of effective homework are summarized in Table 13.7, together with developmental differences between elementary and middle/secondary students (Brophy, 2006c; Cooper et al., 2006; Marzano & Pickering, 2007).

Lecture–Discussion

Lecture–discussion is an instructional model designed to help students acquire organized bodies of knowledge. **Organized bodies of knowledge** are topics that connect facts, concepts, and generalizations, and make the relationships among them explicit (Eggen & Kauchak, 2012; Rosenshine, 1987). For example, students acquire organized bodies of knowledge when they examine the relationships among plot, character, and symbolism in a novel such as *To Kill a Mockingbird* in literature; study landforms, climate, and economy in different countries in geography; or compare parasitic and nonparasitic worms and how differences between them are reflected in their body structures in biology.

Because lecture–discussions are modifications of traditional lectures, and because lecturing is so prevalent in classrooms today, we briefly examine lectures before turning to a discussion of lecture–discussions.

Lecture–discussion. An instructional model designed to help students acquire organized bodies of knowledge.

Organized bodies of knowledge. Topics that connect facts, concepts, and generalizations, and make the relationships among them explicit.

Lectures

The prevalence of the lecture as a teaching method is paradoxical. Although the most criticized of all teaching methods, it continues to be the most commonly used (Cuban, 1993; Friesen, 2011). Reasons for its popularity include:

• Lectures help students acquire information not readily accessible in other ways; they can be effective if the goal is to provide students with information that would be time-consuming to find on their own (Ausubel, 1968; Friesen, 2011).
• Lectures assist students integrate information from a variety of sources.
• Lectures expose students to different points of view.

If you're trying to accomplish one or more of these goals, lecturing can be effective.

Lectures have three other advantages. First, because planning time is limited to organizing content, they're efficient. Second, they're flexible—they can be applied to virtually any content area. And, third, they're seemingly simple. The cognitive load on teachers is low, so all of their working memory space can be devoted to organizing and presenting content. Even novice teachers can learn to deliver acceptable lectures.

Despite their ease, efficiency, and widespread use, lectures have disadvantages:

- They put learners in cognitively passive roles. This is inconsistent with cognitive views of learning and is arguably their primary disadvantage.
- They often fail to attract and maintain students' attention. We've all sat through mind-numbing lectures with a goal of simply getting the time to pass as quickly as possible.
- They don't allow teachers to determine if students are interpreting information accurately.
- While lowering the cognitive load for teachers, they often impose a heavy cognitive load on learners, so information is frequently lost from working memory before it can be encoded into long-term memory.

Lectures are especially problematic for young students because of their short attention spans and limited vocabularies, and they're also ineffective if higher-order thinking is a goal. In seven studies comparing lecture to discussion, discussion was superior in all seven on measures of retention and higher-order thinking. In addition, discussion was superior in seven of nine studies on measures of student attitude and motivation (McKeachie & Kulik, 1975).

Overcoming the Weaknesses of Lectures: Lecture–Discussions

Lecture–discussions help overcome the weaknesses of lectures by interspersing systematic teacher questioning between short presentations of information.

Lecture–discussions exist in four phases:

- Introduction and review
- Presenting information
- Comprehension monitoring
- Integration

Table 13.8 outlines these phases in lecture–discussion and how they relate to cognitive learning theory.

Table 13.8 Phases of lecture–discussion and cognitive learning components

Phase	Cognitive Learning Component
Introduction and Review: The teacher begins with a form of introductory focus and reviews previous work.	• Attract attention. • Access prior knowledge from long-term memory.
Presenting Information: The teacher presents information. The teacher keeps presentations short to prevent overloading learners' working memories.	• Acquire declarative knowledge about the topic.
Comprehension Monitoring: The teacher asks a series of questions to check learners' understanding.	• Check students' perceptions. • Put students in cognitively active roles. • Begin schema construction.
Integration: The teacher asks additional questions to help learners integrate new and prior knowledge.	• Construct integrated schemas that organize information and reduce cognitive load.

Let's see how Diane Anderson, a 10th-grade American history teacher, implements these phases with her students.

Diane wants her students to understand the events leading up to the American Revolutionary War, and she begins with a review. "Where are we now?" she asks, pointing to a timeline above the chalkboard.

"About there," Adam responds, pointing to the middle of the 1700s.

"Good," Diane smiles. "We're leading up to the Revolutionary War, but we want to understand what happened before that time, so we're going to go back to the early 1600s. When we're finished today, we'll see that the Revolutionary War didn't just happen; there were events that led up to it that made it almost inevitable.

"For instance, the conflicts between the British and the French in America became so costly for the British that they began policies in the colonies that ultimately led to the Revolution. That's what we want to look at today."

She then begins, "We know that the British established Jamestown in 1607, but we haven't really looked at French expansion into the New World. Let's look again at the map. Here we see Jamestown, but at about the same time, a French explorer named Champlain came down the St. Lawrence River and formed Quebec City, here. . . . Over the years, at least 35 of the 50 states were discovered or mapped by the French, and they founded several of our big cities, such as Detroit, St. Louis, New Orleans, and Des Moines," she continues, pointing to a series of locations she had marked on the map.

"Now, what do you notice about the location of the two groups?"

". . . The French had a lot of Canada, . . . and it looks like this country, too," Alfredo offers as he points to the north and west on the map.

"It looks like the east was British, and the west was French," Troy adds.

"Yes, and remember, this was all happening at about the same time," Diane continues. "Also, the French were more friendly with the Native Americans than the British. The French had what they called a seigniorial system, where the settlers were given land if they would serve in the military. So, . . . what does this suggest about the military power of the French?"

"Probably powerful," Josh suggests. "The people got land if they went in the army."

"And the Native Americans probably helped, because they were friendly with the French," Tenisha adds.

"Now, what else do you notice here?" Diane asks, moving her hand up and down the width of the map.

"Mountains?" Danielle answers uncertainly.

"Yes, exactly. . . . Why are they important?"

". . . The British were sort of fenced in, and the French could do as they pleased."

"Good. And now the plot thickens. The British needed land and wanted to expand. So they headed west over the mountains, and guess who they ran into? . . . Sarah?"

"The French?" Sarah responds.

"Right! And conflict broke out. Now, when the French and British were fighting, why do you suppose the French were initially more successful than the British? . . . Dan?"

"Well, they had that sig . . . seigniorial system, so they were more eager to fight, because they owned land or were going to get it."

"Other thoughts? . . . Bette?"

"I think that the Native Americans were part of it. The French got along better with them, so they helped the French."

"Okay, good, now let's think about some of the advantages of the British."

Let's look now at Diane's application of the lecture–discussion model. She introduced the lesson with a review and attempted to capture students' attention by creating a link between the French and Indian war and the Revolutionary war. Then, she presented information about Jamestown, Quebec, and French settlements in the present-day United States. After this brief presentation, she used questioning to involve her students in the comprehension-monitoring phase. To illustrate, let's review a brief portion of the lesson.

Diane: Now, what do you notice about the location of the two groups?

Alfredo: The French had a lot of Canada, . . . and it looks like this country, too (pointing to the north and west on the map).

Troy: It looks like the east was . . . British, and the west was French.

Diane's questions were intended to put students in cognitively active roles, check their perceptions, and begin the process of schema production. Satisfied that her class was with her, she returned to presenting information when she said, "Yes, and remember, this was all happening at about the same time." She continued by briefly describing the French seigniorial system and pointing out the friendly relations between the French and the Native Americans.

Then she again turned back to the students.

Diane: So, . . . what does this suggest about the military power of the French?

Josh: Probably powerful. The people got land if they went in the army.

Tenisha: And the Native Americans probably helped, because they were friendly with the French.

The two segments appear similar, but there is an important distinction. In the first, Diane was monitoring comprehension; students' responses to the question, "Now, what do you notice about the location of the two groups?" helped her assess their understanding of what she had presented in the first segment. In the second, she used questions to promote schema production by helping students integrate the seigniorial system with French military power and the relationship between the French and the Native Americans.

After completing this cycle of presenting information, monitoring comprehension, and integration, she would repeat the process, with the second integration being broader than the first. Diane's goal for the entire lesson was the development of a comprehensive schema that would summarize students' understanding of the cause–effect relationships between the French and Indian Wars and the American Revolutionary War.

The quality of lecture–discussion lessons depends on how effectively we guide the discussions that help students correctly perceive and integrate the information we present. Because students construct their own knowledge, the schemas they construct won't necessarily mirror the way we organize the body of knowledge. Our discussions allow us to assess the validity of students' schema constructions and help them reconstruct their understanding when necessary. This is a primary reason lecture–discussion is more effective than traditional lecture.

Guided Discovery

Guided discovery. A model of instruction that involves teachers' scaffolding students' constructions of concepts and the relationships among them.

Guided discovery is an instructional model that involves teachers' scaffolding students' constructions of concepts and the relationships among them (Eggen & Kauchak, 2012; Mayer, 2008). When using the model, you identify your learning objectives, arrange information so that patterns can be found, and guide students to the objectives.

When using guided discovery, teachers sometimes believe that students should be left essentially on their own to "discover" the ideas being taught (Kirschner et al., 2006). This is a misconception. Guided discovery—and other forms of learner-centered instruction, such as inquiry and problem-based learning—is highly scaffolded, and you play an essential role in guiding your students' learning progress (Hmelo-Silver, Duncan, & Chinn, 2007).

Unstructured discovery consists of learning activities in which students receive limited scaffolding. Doing so allows misconceptions to form, wastes time, and often leaves students frustrated (Kirschner et al., 2006; Mayer, 2004). As a result, unstructured discovery is rarely seen in today's classrooms, except in student projects and investigations.

When done well, guided discovery is highly effective. "Guided discovery may take more or less time than expository instruction, depending on the task, but tends to result in better long-term retention and transfer than expository instruction" (Mayer, 2002, p. 68).

When using guided discovery, you will spend less time explaining and more time asking questions, so students have more opportunities to share their thinking and put their developing understanding into words. Also, because of the high levels of student involvement, guided discovery tends to increase students' intrinsic interest in the topic being studied (Lutz, Guthrie, & Davis, 2006).

Guided discovery occurs in five phases:

- Introduction and review
- The open-ended phase
- The convergent phase
- Closure
- Application

Guided discovery can increase students' intrinsic interest in the topics being studied.

Table 13.9 outlines these phases of guided discovery and how they influence learning.

Scott's lesson on Bernoulli's principle on pages 443 and 444 is an application of guided discovery. You might want to read it again before studying the following sections. Let's see how Scott applied the phases in his lesson.

Introduction and Review. Scott began his lesson by reviewing the concept of *force* and the influence of different forces on an object (objects move in the direction of a greater force). The review activated students' prior knowledge, and the examples he used in his review, such as pushing on the board, and tugging on the stapler, attracted students' attention.

Table 13.9	The phases of guided discovery and cognitive learning components

Phase	Cognitive Learning Component
Introduction and Review: The teacher begins with a form of introductory focus and reviews previous work.	• Attract attention. • Activate prior knowledge.
The Open-Ended Phase: The teacher provides examples and asks for observations and comparisons.	• Provide experiences from which learners will construct knowledge. • Promote social interaction.
The Convergent Phase: The teacher guides students as they search for patterns in the examples.	• Begin schema production. • Promote social interaction.
Closure: With the teacher's guidance, students state a definition of the concept or a description of the relationship among concepts.	• Complete schema production.
Application: The teacher has students use the concept or principle to explain another (ideally) real-world example.	• Promote transfer.

The Open-Ended Phase. Scott implemented the open-ended phase when he had students blow over the pieces of paper, between the papers, and through the necks of the funnels. Each example illustrated Bernoulli's principle. After his students worked with the examples, Scott asked for observations, such as, "What did you notice when we blew over the top? . . . David?" and "What did you notice here? . . . Sharon?" The open-ended questions promoted involvement and helped students begin the process of schema production.

The Convergent Phase. The convergent phase continues to capitalize on social interaction to promote schema construction. Scott began the transition to the convergent phase when he drew the sketches on the board and had students restate the observations and conclusions. Let's look again at some dialogue that illustrates this process.

> **Scott:** Was I blowing on the top or the bottom? . . . Rachel? (Referring to the first sketch)
>
> **Rachel:** The top.
>
> **Scott:** And what happened there? . . . Heather?
>
> **Heather:** The paper rose up.

Scott did a similar analysis with the second and third example and then guided the students as they formed conclusions.

> **Scott:** Let's think about the forces acting on these (turning back to the first sketch). What forces are acting on the paper? . . . Colin?
>
> **Colin:** Gravity.
>
> **Scott:** And which direction is gravity pulling?
>
> **Colin:** Down.
>
> **Scott:** What other force is acting on the paper? . . . William?
>
> **William:** Air (pointing up).
>
> **Scott:** How do you know it's pushing up?
>
> **William:** The paper moved up.

Scott guided a similar analysis of the second and third examples, and the lesson then moved to closure. Your guidance in the form of questions and prompts is essential in this phase (Moreno, 2004; Moreno & Duran, 2004).

Closure. Closure completes the process of schema construction. Scott's lesson came to closure when he said, "Now let's look at the forces and where we blew. Study the drawings carefully, and see what kind of relationship exists between the two." When you are moving a lesson to closure, your questioning will provide scaffolding for your students as they attempt to put their understanding into words.

Closure is particularly important when using guided discovery because the direction of the lesson is less obvious than it is with either direct instruction or lecture–discussion. Articulating the definition of a concept or stating the principle, as was the case in Scott's lesson, helps eliminate uncertainty that may remain in students' thinking.

Application. Application is essential for transfer. Scott, for example, attempted to promote transfer by having students use Bernoulli's principle to explain how airplanes can fly. He showed his students the accompanying drawing and then guided the class to conclude that the curvature of the wing made the air flow more rapidly over the top, so the pressure above the wing was lower than the pressure below the wing, enabling planes to fly.

Cooperative Learning

Cooperative learning is a set of instructional strategies in which students work in mixed-ability groups to reach specific cognitive and social development objectives. Cooperative learning strongly emphasizes social interaction, and research suggests that groups of learners co-construct more powerful understanding than individuals do alone (Hadjioannou, 2007; Li et al., 2007). This co-constructed knowledge can then be internalized and used by individuals.

Cooperative learning can also increase motivation. When implemented effectively, it involves all students, which can be difficult in whole-class activities where less confident learners have fewer chances to participate. If students aren't involved, they're more likely to drift off (Brophy, 2010).

Cooperative learning has become one of the most widely used approaches to instruction in schools today; one study found that over 90% of elementary teachers used some form of cooperative learning in their classrooms (Antil, Jenkins, Wayne, & Vadasy, 1998). However, some teachers equate any form of getting students into groups with cooperative learning, and they tend to ignore research about essential components that promote learning (Cohen, 1994).

Cooperative learning activities encourage knowledge construction through social interaction.

Although a single view doesn't exist, most researchers agree that cooperative learning consists of students working together in groups small enough (typically two to five) so that everyone can participate in a clearly assigned task (Cohen, 1994; D. W. Johnson & Johnson, 2006; Slavin, 1995). Cooperative learning also shares four other features:

- Learning objectives direct the groups' activities.
- Learning activities require social interaction.
- Teachers hold students individually accountable for their understanding.
- Learners depend on one another to reach objectives.

Cooperative learning. A set of instructional strategies in which students work in mixed-ability groups to reach specific cognitive and social development objectives.

The last characteristic, called *positive interdependence* (D. W. Johnson & Johnson, 2006) or *reciprocal interdependence* (Cohen, 1994), is important because it emphasizes the role of peer cooperation in learning. Accountability is also essential because it keeps students focused on the objectives and reminds them that learning is the purpose of the activity (Antil et al., 1998; Slavin, 1995).

Unlike direct instruction, lecture–discussion, and guided discovery, cooperative learning activities don't follow a specific set of steps, which is why we describe them as "strategies" instead of "models." However, successful implementation of cooperative learning activities requires as much thought and planning as does using any model.

Introducing Cooperative Learning

Your students won't automatically be good at cooperative learning, and some—particularly those in middle schools—may view cooperative activities more as opportunities to socialize than to meet your learning objectives. To get your students started, the following suggestions can be helpful.

- Seat group members together, so they can move back and forth from group work to whole-class activities with little disruption.
- Have materials ready for easy distribution to each group.
- Introduce students to cooperative learning with short, simple tasks, and make objectives and directions clear.
- Specify the amount of time available to accomplish the task (and keep it relatively short).

- Monitor groups while they work.
- Require that students produce a product, such as written answers to specific questions, as an outcome of the activity.

These suggestions are designed to minimize the likelihood of distruptions and maximize the likelihood of students remaining on task, particularly when you first introduce them to cooperative learning activities.

Cooperative Learning Strategies

Social constructivism provides the framework for all cooperative learning strategies, and those most widely used are outlined in Table 13.10. Other forms of cooperative learning exist, and although they differ in format, all incorporate the suggestions described earlier. As with all forms of instruction, no single cooperative learning strategy can reach all learning objectives, and cooperative learning should not be overused.

Evaluating Cooperative Learning

Research examining cooperative learning suggests that it can increase student achievement, and it can also improve problem-solving abilities, motivation, and interpersonal skills (Gao, Losh, Shen, Turner, & Yuan, 2007; Roseth et al., 2007).

On the other hand, simply putting students into groups doesn't ensure either increased achievement or motivation. For instance, when students are organized into mixed-ability groups, those with higher ability often feel they are being exploited by slackers and, in fact, frequently prefer to work alone instead of in groups (Cohen, 1994; Su, 2007). Further, average-ability students often do not take advantage of learning in mixed-ability groups because high-ability students tend to dominate the group interaction (Saleh, Lazonder, & Jong, 2007).

Table 13.10	Cooperative learning strategies	
Strategy	**Description**	**Example**
Think–Pair–Share	Individuals in a pair answer a teacher question and then share it with their partner. The teacher calls on pairs to respond to the original question.	A world history teacher says, "Identify two factors or events that the Russian Revolution, which began in 1917, had in common with the French Revolution that began in 1789. . . . Turn to your partner, see what both of you think, and we'll discuss your answers in a minute."
Reciprocal Questioning	Pairs work together to ask and answer questions about a lesson or text.	Teacher provides question stems, such as "Summarize . . ." or "Why was . . . important?" and students use the stems to create specific questions about the topic.
Scripted Cooperation	Pairs work together to elaborate on each other's thinking.	Math: First member of a pair offers a problem solution. The second member then checks the answer, asks clarifying questions, and the process is repeated. Reading: Pairs read a passage, and the first member offers a summary. The second edits and adds to it, and the process continues.
Jigsaw II	Individuals become expert on subsections of a topic and teach it to others in their group.	One student studies the geography of a region, another the economy, a third the climate. Each attends "expert" meetings, and the "experts" then teach the content to others in their group.
Student Teams Achievement Divisions (STAD)	Social interaction helps students learn facts, concepts, and skills.	The independent practice phase of direct instruction is replaced with team study, during which team members check and compare their answers. Team study is followed by quizzes, and individual improvement points lead to team awards.

These results have two implications for us if we want to use cooperative learning. First, careful planning is essential. For instance, when we tell students that we expect them to collaborate, such as ensuring that they solicit comments from everyone in the groups, interaction improves (Saleh et al., 2007). Second, group grading (grading in which all students in groups receive the same grade) should be avoided; individual accountability is crucial (Su, 2007).

A final reminder about cooperative learning. They are strategies, and only strategies, which means you use them to help you reach different learning goals; they are never goals in themselves. If you believe you can best reach learning goals with a cooperative learning strategy, using it is appropriate. However, putting students into groups for its own sake is never an appropriate goal.

Also, cooperative learning strategies, like all strategies and models, have both strengths and weaknesses, and overusing any one is not effective. Used judiciously and thoughtfully, however, cooperative learning can be effective for adding variety to your instruction, increasing student interest, and improving the social skills so important for students' overall education. We examine this idea in more detail in the accompanying "Exploring Diversity" feature.

Using Cooperative Learning to Capitalize on Your Students' Diversity

Although important for constructing knowledge, effective social interaction doesn't always occur easily, especially in classrooms with diverse student populations. People tend to be wary of those different from themselves, and this tendency also occurs in classrooms. Students of specific ethnic groups tend to spend most of their time together, so they don't learn that all of us are much more alike than we are different (Juvonen, 2006; Okagaki, 2006).

You can't mandate tolerance, trust, and friendship among your students. Classroom activities that encourage mixed-group cooperation are needed, and the benefits are clear; students working in cooperative groups improve their social skills; develop friendships and positive attitudes toward others who differ in achievement, ethnicity, and gender; and increase their acceptance of students with exceptionalities (D. W. Johnson & Johnson, 2006; Vaughn & Bos, 2009).

Let's see how Olivia Costa, an eighth-grade math teacher, attempts to reach these goals in her classroom.

As Olivia watches her students work, she is both pleased and uneasy. They've improved a great deal in their math, but there is little mixing among her minority and nonminority students She worries about six children from Central and South America who are struggling with English and three students with exceptionalities who leave her class every day for extra help.

To promote a more cohesive atmosphere, Olivia spends time over the weekend, organizing students into groups of four, with equal numbers of high- and low-ability students in each group. She also mixes students by ethnicity and gender, and she makes sure that no group has more than one student for whom English is a second language or more than one student with an exceptionality.

On Monday she explains how they are to work together. To introduce the process, she sits with one group and models cooperation and support for the others. After she finishes a lesson on problem solving, she sends the groups to different parts of the room to practice the skills she's been teaching. All students in each group solve a problem and then share their answers with group-mates. If they cannot solve the problem, or resolve differences about the correct answer, Olivia intervenes. She carefully monitors the groups to be sure that each student first attempts the problems before conferring with others.

Monitoring the groups is demanding, but her first session is fairly successful. "Phew," she thinks to herself at the end of the day. "This isn't any easier, but it already seems better."

Let's look at Olivia's efforts in more detail. First, because her objective was to promote interpersonal relationships, she organized the groups so that high- and low-ability students, boys and girls, members of minorities and nonminorities, and students with and without exceptionalities were represented equally. Letting students form their own groups is one of the most common mistakes beginning teachers make.

Second, knowing that effective interaction must be planned and taught, she modeled desired behaviors, such as being supportive, listening, asking questions, and staying on task. You can also directly teach interaction strategies or use role-plays and video recordings of effective groups to help students learn cooperation skills (Blatchford et al., 2006; Vaughn & Bos, 2009). These skills are especially important for students from minority groups, who are often hesitant about seeking and giving help.

Third, she carefully monitored students while they worked. Initial training, alone, won't ensure cooperation. Groups need constant monitoring and support, particularly with young children and when cooperative learning is first introduced (Vaughn & Bos, 2009). If problems persist, you may need to reconvene the class for additional training.

The benefits of student cooperation stem primarily from three factors:

- Students with different backgrounds work together.
- Group members have equal status.
- Students learn about each other as individuals (Slavin, 1995).

As students work together, they frequently find that they have more in common than they would expect. They all want to succeed and to get along with their peers and to be accepted and respected. Having students work together to achieve common goals can be one of the most effective tools you have for helping students meet these needs.

Differentiating Instruction

Differentiating instruction. The process of adapting instruction to meet the needs of students who vary in background knowledge, skills, needs, and motivations.

Our students are more diverse than ever before in our nation's history. Because of this diversity, they all respond a bit differently to both the essential teaching skills and the teaching models we've discussed in this section. **Differentiating instruction,** the process of adapting instruction to meet the needs of students who vary in background knowledge, skills, needs, and motivations, is a response to this diversity.

Two factors related to differentiated instruction are important. First, differentiated instruction is not individualized instruction (Tomlinson & McTighe, 2006). In essence, tutoring is the only true form of individualization, and it's literally impossible for you to tutor every one of your students.

Second, much of what you do when you plan carefully and effectively implement your instruction, in general, will include forms of differentiation. For example, differentiation experts suggest the following (Hall, Strangman, & Meyer, 2003).

- Plan thoroughly, and carefully teach the essential knowledge and skills needed for further learning. This is part of all forms of effective instruction and lays the foundation for future learning.
- Use assessment as a tool to extend rather than simply measure learning. (We discuss assessment as a learning tool in the next section of the chapter.) Emphasize critical thinking by requiring students to provide evidence for their conclusions. This goal is often neglected in instruction with students who are lower achievers or members of cultural minorities.
- Actively engage all learners. Equitable distribution and cooperative learning are two effective ways to reach this goal.
- Vary your instruction. For example, using direct instruction in one lesson, guided discovery in another, and cooperative learning in a third, or in combination with the other models, helps meet students' varying needs and interests.

In addition to the preceding suggestions, some specific differentiation strategies can be effective (Kauchak & Eggen, 2012). They include

- Small-group support
- Mastery learning
- Personalizing content

Small-Group Support. Providing extra instructional support for small groups of students is one of the most applicable and practical forms of differentiation. For instance, when Sam's students began independent practice in his lesson on adding whole numbers, he called Cathy, Josh, and Jeremy to the back of the room, where he provided additional assistance to help them better grasp the ideas. Because he was working with only three students, his instruction in the small group was nearly one-on-one.

Effectively implementing the *developing understanding* and *guided practice* phases of direct instruction are crucial for this form of differentiation. The rest of the class must be working quietly and successfully. If you have to get up to help other students or deal with off-task behavior, your small-group support will be much less effective.

Mastery Learning. **Mastery learning** is a system of instruction that allows students to progress at their own rate through a unit of study (Tanner & Tanner, 2007). Objectives specify the essential learning outcomes for the unit, and frequent formative quizzes provide feedback about learning progress. When students master a learning objective, they continue; when they don't, they are provided with alternative learning activities.

Mastery learning can be effective, particularly for low achievers (Verdinelli & Gentile, 2003), but it is logistically demanding (Good & Brophy, 2008).

Personalizing Content. Much of what is written about differentiating instruction focuses on cognitive objectives. However, responding to differences in individual students' needs and motivations are also important.

Personalizing content is another way to differentiate instruction. For example, Sam implemented a simple form of personalization by putting two of his students' names in the original problem he presented. Doing so took no additional effort, and it can significantly increase student interest and motivation (Schraw & Lehman, 2001).

Personalizing content primarily requires awareness and some imagination. If you're aware of the need to link content to students' lives, and you make attempts to do so, you will find the process gets easier and easier. The result will be your students' improved interest and motivation.

Other ways of differentiating instruction exist, such as varying learning objectives, learning materials, and assessments, but they are demanding and difficult to implement (O'Meara, 2011). Most beginning teachers begin with the strategies we've outlined here and, as they gain experience and confidence, experiment with different ways to adapt their instruction to meet individual student needs and interests.

Technology, Learning, and Development: Using PowerPoint Effectively

Earlier in the chapter you saw how Diane Anderson used the lecture–discussion model to help her students understand events leading up to the American Revolution.

Let's look now at Jack Wilson, another American history teacher, and how he covers similar information with his students.

Jack introduces the topic and then comments, "We need to know why the colonists in our country originally fought the war," he says. . . . There were several causes, and we're going to look at them today."

He then brings PowerPoint up on his computer, and displays the following information:

> • The French and Indian War (1754–1763)
>   The war was costly for the British, who looked to the colonies to help pay some of the costs.

"This is where it all started," he comments, pointing to the display on the screen. "The French and Indian War was incredibly costly for the British, so they needed to figure out a way to make additional money to pay for the debt that resulted from the war."

As Jack watches, his students quickly write down the information they see, and he then displays the following slides, making brief comments after each one, and allowing students time to copy the information on them.

Mastery learning. A system of instruction that allows students to progress at their own rate through a unit of study.

- The British impose new taxes (1764)

  The British felt they were spending a great deal of money to protect the colonists, so they imposed new taxes to cover the costs of stationing British troops in North America.

- Boston Massacre (1770)

  In response to taunts by colonists, British soldiers killed five colonists. The event turned colonists' opinions against the British.

- Boston Tea Party (1773)

  In response to an act granting a monopoly on tea trade, colonists dumped tons of tea into Boston harbor, one of the most famous events leading up to the Revolutionary War.

After he has displayed his PowerPoint slides, made comments, and allowed the students time to copy the information, he summarizes the lesson by saying, "Keep these events in mind as we begin our discussion of the Revolutionary War. . . . We'll start our discussion of the war itself tomorrow."

Look familiar? We've all sat through PowerPoint presentations where an instructor or presenter displayed bullet points, often read them to us, or gave us time to copy the information.

Jack fell into this pattern. Instead of involving his students in a discussion of the historical events before the American Revolution and how they contributed to it, he reduced the causes to a series of bullet points, and the students simply copied the information, a cognitively passive process. This isn't an effective use of PowerPoint.

Teachers are using significantly more technology in their work with students, with PowerPoint presentations being one of the most popular, particularly in middle and secondary schools (Adams, 2006; Isseks, 2011). However, some experts, school administrators, and teachers themselves have begun to question the effectiveness of PowerPoint presentations, suggesting that they are inconsistent with efforts to involve students in learning activities and teach higher-order thinking (Adams, 2006). Others go even further and suggest that the technology is an impediment to using student-centered forms of instruction, such as guided discovery and problem-based learning (Langenegger, 2011).

PowerPoint, itself, is not the issue, however.

> The root problem of PowerPoint presentations is not the *power* or the *point*, but the *presentation*. A presentation, by its very nature, is one-sided. The presenter does everything—gathers information, eliminates extraneous points, and selects the direction and duration of the presentation (Isseks, 2011, pp. 74–75.)

From a learning perspective, PowerPoint presentations can be problematic because they tend to put learners in even more cognitively passive roles than do standard lectures. Students can ask questions, but usually only to clarify information on a slide.

The allure of PowerPoint is understandable. Information can be easily copied onto PowerPoint slides, and the slides organize the lecture, which dramatically reduces the cognitive load on teachers. Further, in an era of high-stakes testing, PowerPoint presentations are effective for "covering" content and creating the illusion that doing so equals teaching (Isseks, 2011).

Criticisms of PowerPoint presentations have also come from outside education. For example, they are common in the business world, and members of the military complain that the near universal use of the presentation format oversimplifies military objectives and the complexity of military missions (Bumiller, 2010).

Using PowerPoint Effectively

None of the criticisms we've outlined above suggest that you shouldn't use PowerPoint in your teaching. The issue is *how* you use it. Combined with information you can get from the Internet, it can be a powerful learning tool. Two suggestions can be helpful.

First, reduce the number of bullet points, and include pictures, videos, diagrams, and maps that stimulate student interest and thought. For example, Jim Norton, an earth science teacher, simply Googled the Rocky and Appalachian mountains and downloaded detailed, colored pictures onto PowerPoint slides, which he used to illustrate the characteristics of young and mature mountains. He did the same with other landforms, such as young and old rivers and used them to provide detailed, concrete examples of each of the concepts.

Second, make your presentations interactive. Jim, for instance, displayed the slides of the Rockies and Appalachians, had his students make observations to identify differences between them, and then suggest possible reasons for the differences. Instead of passively looking at a series of bullet points and attempting to remember the information displayed with them, his students were involved in a form of inquiry.

Used effectively, PowerPoint has the potential to enhance learning experiences, as you saw in the example with Jim Norton and his students. Jim was also able to store everything on a thumb drive, making it simple and efficient for him to retrieve, revise, and improve the presentation for the next time he teaches the topic.

As with many aspects of teaching and learning, the issue isn't whether to use or not use a strategy or tool; it's *how* to use it. How effectively you use any strategy depends on your professional knowledge and judgment.

---

check your understanding

3.1 Using the essential teaching skills as a basis, explain why the introduction phase is important in direct instruction, lecture–discussion, and guided discovery.

3.2 Which phase of direct instruction is most important for ensuring successful independent practice? Explain.

3.3 We said, "When done well, guided discovery is highly effective." What is necessary for instruction to be "done well"? Explain.

3.4 A teacher places her third graders in groups of three and gives each group magnets and a packet including a dime, spoon, aluminum foil, rubber band, wooden pencil, paper clip, and nails. She tells the groups to experiment with the magnets and items for 10 minutes and write three differences between objects that are and are not attracted to magnets. As they work, she answers questions and makes comments. The class as a whole group discusses the results. How effectively did the teacher introduce cooperative learning to her students? Cite evidence from the example to support your conclusion.

To receive feedback for these questions, go to Appendix A.

Classroom connections

Using Models of Instruction Effectively in Classrooms

Direct Instruction

1. Direct instruction includes an introduction and review, a phase for developing understanding, and guided and independent practice. Emphasize understanding, and provide sufficient practice to develop automaticity.

   ▪ **Elementary:** A fourth-grade teacher, in a lesson on possessives, first explains the difference between singular and plural possessives and then asks students to punctuate the following sentences.

The students books were lost when he forgot them on the bus.

The students books were lost when they left them on the playground.

Who can describe the boys adventure when he went to the zoo?

Who can describe the boys adventure when they swam in the river?

He then has students write paragraphs that incorporate both singular and plural possessives.

- **Middle School:** In a unit on percentages and decimals, a math teacher comments that the star quarterback for the state university completed 14 of 21 passes in last Saturday's game. "What does that mean? Is that good or bad? Was it better than the 12 of 17 passes completed by the opposing quarterback?" she asks. She then explains how to calculate the percentages with the class and then has the students practice finding percentages in other real-world problems.

- **High School:** A ninth-grade geography teacher helps his students locate the longitude and latitude of their city by "walking them through" the process, using a map and a series of specific questions. He then has them practice finding the longitude and latitude of other cities, as well as finding the major city nearest sets of longitude and latitude locations.

Lecture–Discussion

2. Lecture–discussions include an introduction and review, a phase where information is presented, and questions that check comprehension and help students integrate ideas. Keep presentations short, and use high levels of interaction to maintain students' attention and promote schema production.

- **Elementary:** A first-grade teacher wants her students to know similarities and differences between farm animals and pets. To do this, she constructs a large chart with pictures of both. As they discuss the two groups of animals, she continually asks students to identify similarities and differences between the two groups.

- **Middle School:** An American history teacher discussing immigration in the 19th and early 20th centuries compares immigrant groups of the past with today's Cuban population in Miami, Florida, and Mexican immigrants in San Antonio, Texas. He asks students to summarize similarities and differences between the two groups with respect to the difficulties they encounter and the rates of assimilation into the American way of life.

- **High School:** A biology teacher is presenting information related to transport of liquids in and out of cells, identifying and illustrating several of the concepts in the process. After about 3 minutes, she stops presenting information and asks, "Suppose a cell is in a hypotonic solution in one case and a hypertonic solution in another. What's the difference between the two? What would happen to the cell in each case?"

Guided Discovery

3. When teachers use guided discovery, they present students with examples and guide students' knowledge construction. Provide examples that include all the information students need to understand the topic, and guide student interaction.

- **Elementary:** A fifth-grade teacher begins a unit on reptiles by bringing a snake and turtle to class. He includes colored pictures of lizards, alligators, and sea turtles. He has students describe the animals and pictures and then guides them to an understanding of the essential characteristics of reptiles.

- **Middle School:** A seventh-grade English teacher embeds examples of singular and plural possessive nouns in the context of a paragraph. She then guides the discussion as students develop explanations for why particular sentences are punctuated the way they are, for example, "The girls' and boys' accomplishments in the middle school were noteworthy, as were the children's efforts in the elementary school."

- **High School:** A world history teacher presents students with vignettes, such as this one:

  You're part of an archeological team, and at one site you've found some spear points. In spite of their ages, the points are still quite sharp, having been chipped precisely from hard stone. You also see several cattle and sheep skulls and some threads that appear to be the remains of coarsely woven fabric.

  He then guides the students to conclude that the artifacts best represent a New Stone Age society.

Cooperative Learning

4. Cooperative learning requires that students work together to reach learning objectives. Provide clear directions for groups, and carefully monitor students as they work.

- **Elementary:** A second-grade teacher begins the school year by having groups work together on short word problems in math. When students fail to cooperate, she stops the groups and immediately discusses the issues with the class.

- **Middle School:** A life-science teacher has students create and answer questions about the characteristics, organelles, and environments of one-celled animals. He periodically offers suggestions to the pairs to help them ask more meaningful questions.

- **High School:** A geometry teacher has pairs use scripted cooperation to solve proofs. When they struggle, she offers hints to help them continue to make progress.

5. Because of its emphasis on group interdependence, cooperative learning can promote healthy interactions between students from different backgrounds. Use cooperative learning groups to capitalize on the richness that learner diversity brings to classrooms, and design tasks that require group cooperation.

- **Elementary:** A second-grade teacher waits until the third week of the school year to form cooperative learning groups. During that time, she observes her students and gathers information about their interests, talents, and friendships. She then uses the information in making decisions about group membership.

- **Middle School:** A sixth-grade math teacher uses cooperative learning groups to practice word problems. He organizes the class into pairs, forming, whenever possible, pairs that are composed of a minority and nonminority student, a student with and a student without an exceptionality, and a boy and a girl.

- **High School:** An English teacher has students work in groups of four to provide feedback on one another's writing. The teacher organizes all groups so that they're composed of equal numbers of boys, girls, minorities and nonminorities, and students who do and do not have exceptionalities.

Assessment and Learning: Using Assessment as a Learning Tool

Think about our question in "Ed Psych and You" here. The most likely answer is, *Have I accomplished my purpose?* For instance, you'll ask yourself if the room really is more comfortable and inviting, or if you really are using the space more efficiently. In other words, you'll assess the extent to which you've achieved your objective.

Again, the process you're going through is analogous to teaching. Having conducted a learning activity—or series of activities—you'll want to assess the extent to which your students have reached your learning objectives. Assessment is the third step in the planning–implementing–assessing cycle.

Let's see how Scott assessed his students' understanding of Bernoulli's principle. The following is an item on his Friday quiz and students' responses to it.

> Look at the drawing that represents the two pieces of paper that we used in the lesson. Explain what made the papers move together. Make a sketch that shows how the air flowed as you blew between the papers. Label the forces in your sketch as we did during the lesson.

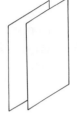

Shown here are two students' sketches of the flow of air between the papers:

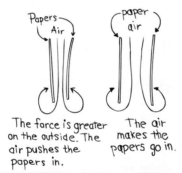

The students' responses illustrate an essential characteristic of effective assessments: *Assessments must provide information about students' thinking* (Stiggins, Arter, Chappuis, & Chappuis, 2010). For instance, the sketches show that the students correctly concluded that the force (pressure) on the outside of the papers pushing in was greater than the force (pressure) between the papers pushing out. This doesn't provide a great deal of evidence about their understanding, however, because the lesson emphasized this conclusion.

The students' explanations of their sketches of the air flow are more revealing. They concluded that the moving air curled around the bottoms of the papers and pushed the papers together, which indicates a misconception. (The papers moved together because increasing the speed of the air over a surface [in this case over the surface of the papers] decreases the pressure the air exerts on the surface [the papers], and the still air on the outside of the papers pushes them together, as illustrated in the sketch here. This is an application of Bernoulli's principle.)

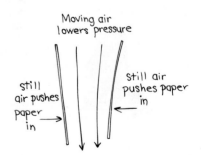

If Scott's assessment hadn't asked for both an explanation and a drawing, he might not have learned that his students left the lesson with misconceptions. Assessments such as these provide opportunities to directly address student misconceptions, which you can then correct to increase your students' understanding (which is why "Using Assessment as a Learning Tool"

is the subtitle of this section). A detailed discussion of these responses together with additional examples (demonstrating that air exerts pressure in all directions and that all objects, including air particles, move in a straight line unless a force acts on them) would greatly expand the students' understanding of basic principles in science. In fact, teaching these principles after the assessment likely produces more learning than trying to teach them beforehand, because the students' responses to the assessment provide both motivation and context for learning. Ideally, all assessments provide similar opportunities to extend learning.

The same is true for much of classroom learning. We tend to think of assessment as giving tests and assigning grades, but it is much more than that; it's an essential part of the entire teaching–learning process. "Testing has such a bad connotation; people think of standardized testing or teaching to the test. Maybe we need to call it something else, but this is one of the most powerful learning tools we have" (Carey, 2010, para. 28).

---

check your understanding

4.1 Identify two essential characteristics of effective assessments.

4.2 Identify the essential teaching skill that teachers must use in conjunction with assessments to increase student learning.

4.3 An English teacher wants his students to use figurative language, such as similes, metaphors, and personification, in their writing. He gives them several examples of each, and then he gives them a quiz on which they identify additional examples of figurative language. Evaluate his assessment with respect to its effectiveness.

To receive feedback for these questions, go to Appendix A.

Developmentally appropriate practice

Effective Instruction with Learners at Different Ages

Essential teaching skills are important at all developmental levels, and the models of instruction discussed in this section can be used at all levels as well. But when using the models, some adaptations are necessary to accommodate developmental differences in students. The following paragraphs outline suggestions for responding to these developmental differences.

Working with Students in Early Childhood Programs and Elementary Schools

Because it is effective for teaching basic skills, direct instruction is probably the most widely used instructional model in the lower elementary grades. When using direct instruction with young children, the developing understanding and guided practice phases are crucial because they lay a foundation for independent practice. Monitoring learner progress during guided practice and spending extra time with lower achievers while the majority of the students are practicing independently is an effective adaptation with young children.

Lecture–discussions should be used sparingly with young children because of their short attention spans and lack of prior knowledge. Verbal explanations must be kept short and combined with frequent episodes of comprehension monitoring for young children. Models other than lecture–discussion are often more effective with young students.

Guided discovery can be particularly effective with young children if the goal is for them to understand topics that you can illustrate with concrete examples, such as crustaceans, fractions, or parts of speech. When using guided discovery with young children, you should verbally link examples to the concept being taught and emphasize new terms.

Young children need a great deal of scaffolding and practice to work effectively in groups. Clearly describing procedures for turning in materials and participating in the activities is also crucial.

Working with Students in Middle Schools

In middle schools, direct instruction is an effective model for learning procedural skills that require practice, such as in pre-algebra, algebra, and language arts. As with younger students, the developing understanding and guided practice phases are essential for the success of the activity.

Guided discovery is one of the most effective models with middle school students, but establishing rules about treating each other with courtesy and respect during the activities is important with these students. If you use high-quality examples, middle school students are capable of learning more abstract concepts such as symmetric and asymmetric body structures in life science or culture in social students. Guided discovery continues to be an effective model for teaching concepts that can be represented with concrete examples.

Cooperative learning can be effectively used to complement direct instruction, as Olivia Costa did with her eighth graders. Cooperative learning can also help middle school students develop social and communication skills, perspective taking, and collaboration.

Lecture–discussion can be effective for teaching organized bodies of knowledge in science, literature, and social studies.

Working with Students in High Schools

High school students typically pose fewer management challenges than younger students, but their greater willingness to sit passively can be a problem. Using lecture–discussions as an alternative to pure lectures is desirable.

Each of the other models can also be effective as instructional alternatives, depending on your goals. High school students are often familiar with the other models, as they've encountered them in earlier grades. Frequent monitoring is still needed to keep lessons on track and aligned with learning objectives.

Summary

1. Describe the steps in planning for instruction, including planning in a standards-based environment.
   - When planning for instruction, teachers first identify topics that are important for students to learn, specify learning objectives, prepare and organize learning activities, and design assessments.
   - When using standards to plan for instruction, teachers first need to interpret the standard and then design learning activities to help students meet the standard and assessments to determine whether the standard has been met.

2. Describe essential teaching skills, and explain why they're important.
   - Essential teaching skills are the abilities and attitudes that all effective teachers possess. These attitudes include high personal teaching efficacy—the belief that they are responsible for student learning and can increase it. These attitudes also include caring, modeling, enthusiasm, and high expectations for student achievement and behavior.
   - Essential teaching skills include the ability to organize efficiently, communicate clearly, attract and maintain student attention, provide informative feedback, and deliver succinct reviews.
   - Effective questioning is an important essential teaching skill and should include high frequency and equitable distribution, prompts when students can't answer, and sufficient wait-time for students to think about their answers.

3. Explain the relationships between models of instruction and essential teaching skills, and describe how the components of different models contribute to learning.
   - Essential teaching skills support and are incorporated in all models of instruction.
   - Direct instruction is an instructional model designed to teach knowledge and essential skills that students need for later learning. Teachers conduct direct instruction in four phases: (a) introduction and review, to attract students' attention and activate prior knowledge; (b) developing understanding, to acquire declarative knowledge about the skill; (c) guided practice, to begin the development of

procedural knowledge; and (d) independent practice, to further develop the skill to automaticity.
   - Lecture–discussion is an instructional model designed to help students acquire organized bodies of knowledge. It consists of (a) an introduction and review, to attract attention and activate prior knowledge; (b) presenting information, to provide knowledge; (c) comprehension monitoring, to check students' perceptions; and (d) integration, to promote schema production.
   - Guided discovery is an instructional model that helps students learn concepts and the relationships among them. It consists of (a) an introduction and review, to attract students' attention and activate prior knowledge; (b) an open-ended phase in which students make observations of examples; (c) a convergent phase in which teachers identify patterns and begin schema production; (d) closure, when teachers complete schema production and clarify the learning objective; and (e) application, which helps promote transfer.
   - Cooperative learning is a set of instructional models that uses group interaction to reach specified learning objectives. Teachers hold learners individually accountable for understanding, and learners must depend on each other to reach the objectives.
   - Differentiating instruction is the process of adapting instruction to meet the needs of students who vary in background knowledge, skills, needs, and motivations.

4. Identify the essential characteristics of effective assessments.
   - Productive learning environments are assessment centered. This means that assessment is an integral part of the learning–teaching process and that assessments are aligned with objectives and learning activities.
   - Effective assessments provide teachers with information about students' thinking, which both teachers and students can use as feedback about learning progress.
   - Effective assessments provide opportunities for increasing students' understanding through detailed feedback and discussion. Discussion following assessments often increases understanding as much as or more than the learning activity itself.

Understanding Effective Teaching: Preparing for Your Licensure Exam

Your licensure exam will include information related to effective teaching, and we include the following exercises to help you practice for the exam in your state. This book and these exercises will be a resource for you as you prepare for the exam.

In the chapter, you saw how Scott planned his lesson, demonstrated essential teaching skills, and assessed his students' learning. Let's look now at a teacher working with a class of ninth-grade geography students. As you read the case study, consider the extent to which the teacher applied the information you've studied in this chapter in her lesson. Read the case study, and answer the questions that follow.

Judy Holmquist, a ninth-grade geography teacher, has her students involved in a unit on climate regions of the United States. The class has worked in groups to gather information about the geography, economy, ethnic groups, and future issues in Florida, California, New York, and Alaska, and students have entered the information on a matrix. The first two columns of the matrix are shown at right.

In today's lesson, Judy wants her students to understand how the geography of each region influenced its economy.

As the bell signaling the beginning of the class stops ringing, Judy refers students to the matrix, hung at the front of the classroom. She reminds them they will be looking for similarities and differences in the information about the states, organizes students into pairs, and begins, "I want you to get with your partner and write down three differences and three similarities that you see in the geography portion of the chart."

As groups begin their work, Judy moves around the classroom, answering questions and making brief suggestions.

A few minutes later, she calls the class back together. "You look like you're doing a good job. . . . Okay, I think we're ready."

"Okay, go ahead Jackie," Judy begins, pointing to the chart.

"Mmm, they all have mountains except for Florida."

"Okay, they all have mountains except for Florida," Judy repeats and writes the information under "Similarities" on the chalkboard.

"Something else. . . . Jeff?"

"They all touch the oceans in places."

"What else? . . . Missy?"

"New York and Florida both have coastal plains."

The class continues identifying similarities for a few more minutes, and Judy then says, "How about some differences? . . . Chris?"

"The temperature ranges a lot."

"All right. . . . John?"

"Different climate zones."

"Alaska is the only one that has an average low temperature below zero," Kiki puts in.

"Carnisha, do you have anything to add?"

"All except Alaska have less than 4 inches of moisture in the winter," Carnisha adds.

After students offer several more differences, Judy asks, "Okay, have we exhausted your lists? Anyone else have anything more to add?"

	Geography		Economy
	Geography		**Economy**
	Coastal plain		Citrus industry
F	Florida uplands		Tourism
L	Hurricane season		Fishing
O	Warm ocean currents		Forestry
R			Cattle
I	Dec. 69 1.8		
D	March 72 2.4		
A	June 81 9.3		
	Sept 82 7.6		
C	Coastal ranges		Citrus industry
A	Cascades		Wine/vineyards
L	Sierra Nevadas		Fishing
I	Central Valley		Lumber
F	Desert		Television/Hollywood
O	Temp. Moisture		Tourism
R	Dec. 54 2.5		Computers
N	March 57 2.8		
I	June 66 T		
A	Sept. 69 .3		
N	Atlantic Coastal Plain		Vegetables
E	New England uplands		Fishing
W	Appalachian Plateau		Apples
	Adirondack Mts.		Forestry
Y	Temp. Moisture		Light manufacturing
O	Dec. 37 3.9		Entertainment/TV
R	March 42 4.1		
K	June 72 3.7		
	Sept. 68 3.9		
	Rocky Mountains		Mining
	Brooks Range		Fishing
A	Panhandle area		Trapping
L	Plateaus between mountains		Lumbering/forestry
A	Islands/treeless		Oil/pipeline
S	Warm ocean currents		Tourism
K	Temp. Moisture		
A	Dec. −7 .9		
	March 11 .4		
	June 60 1.4		
	Sept. 46 1.0		

Judy waits a couple seconds and then says, "Okay, now I want you to look at the economy, and I want you to do the same thing; write down three similarities and three differences in the economies of the different states. Use the economy column of our matrix like you did with geography. You have 3 minutes."

The students again return to their groups, and Judy monitors them as she had earlier.

After they finish, she again calls for and receives a number of similarities and differences based on the information in the matrix.

She then shifts the direction of the lesson, saying, "Okay, great. . . . Now, let's see if we can link geography and economics. For example, why do they all have fishing?" she asks, waving her hand across the class as she walks toward the back of the room. "John?"

"They're all near the coast."

"And, why do they all have forestry? . . . Okay, Jeremy?"

"They all have lots of trees," Jeremy replies as the rest of the class smiles at this obvious conclusion.

"So, what does this tell you about their climate?"

"They all have the right temperature . . . and soil . . . and enough rain for trees."

"Good, Jeremy," Judy smiles, and then says, "Now, let's look again at our chart. We have the citrus industry in California and Florida. Why do these states have a citrus industry?"

" . . . It's the climate," Jackie answers hesitantly.

"All right, what kind of climate allows the citrus industry? . . . Tim?"

" . . . Humid subtropical."

"Humid subtropical means that we have what? . . . Go ahead."

" . . . Long humid summers. . . . Short mild winters," he replies after thinking for a few seconds.

"Now let's look at tourism. Why is tourism a major factor in each state's economy?" Judy continues. "Okay, Lance?"

"Because they're all spread out. They're each at four corners, and they have different seasons that they're popular in."

"Good, Lance," Judy nods, and then seeing that they are near the end of the period, Judy says, "Okay, I want you to describe in a short summary statement what effect climate has on the economy of those regions."

She gives the class a couple minutes to work again in their pairs, and then says,

"Let's see what you've come up with. "Braden, go ahead."

"If you have mountains in the area, you can't have farmland," he responds.

"Okay, what else? . . . Becky?"

"The climate affects what's grown and what's done in that area."

"Okay, great. Climate affects what's grown, and what was the last part of that?"

With Judy's guidance, the class makes a summarizing statement indicating that the climate of a region is a major influence determining the economy of the region, and she then dismisses the class.

Questions for Case Analysis

In answering these questions, use information from the chapter, and link your responses to specific information in the case.

1. Describe three planning decisions that Judy made as she planned her lesson.

2. Analyze Judy's instructional alignment. Offer any suggestions that you might have that would have increased the alignment of the lesson.

3. Analyze Judy's application of the essential teaching skills in her lesson. Which did she demonstrate most effectively? Which did she demonstrate least effectively?

To receive feedback for these questions, go to Appendix B.

Your licensure exam will also include multiple-choice questions similar to those your instructor has given you on your quizzes and tests for this course.

Important Concepts

closure (p. 450)
cognitive domain (p. 434)
Common Core State Standards Initiative (CCSSI) (p. 441)
connected discourse (p. 451)

cooperative learning (p. 463)
differentiating instruction (p. 466)
direct instruction (p. 453)
effective teaching (p. 432)
emphasis (p. 451)

equitable distribution (p. 447)
essential teaching skills (p. 444)
feedback (p. 449)
focus (p. 446)

guided discovery (p. 460)
implementing instruction (p. 442)
instructional alignment (p. 438)

learning objective (p. 434)
lecture–discussion (p. 457)
mastery learning (p. 467)
models of instruction (p. 453)

organized bodies of
    knowledge (p. 457)
precise language (p. 451)
prompting (p. 448)

questioning frequency
    (p. 446)
review (p. 445)
standards (p. 438)

task analysis (p. 437)
transition signals (p. 451)
wait-time (p. 448)

Go to Topic: Planning and Instruction in the MyEducationLab (www.myeducationlab.com) for *Educational Psychology: Windows on Classrooms,* where you can:

- Find learning outcomes for Planning and Instruction along with the national standards that connect to these outcomes.
- Complete Assignments and Activities that can help you more deeply understand the chapter content.
- Apply and practice your understanding of the core teaching skills identified in the chapter with the Building Teaching Skills and Dispositions learning units.
- Examine challenging situations and cases presented in the IRIS Center Resources.
- Access video clips of CCSSO National Teachers of the Year award winners responding to the question, "Why Do I Teach?" in the Teacher Talk section.
- See video examples included within the Study Plan that provide concrete and real-world illustrations of the topics presented in the chapter.
- Check your comprehension of the content covered in the chapter with the Study Plan. Here you will be able to take a chapter quiz, receive feedback on your answers, and then access Review, Practice, and Enrichment activities to enhance your understanding of chapter content.

MyEducationLab

chapter 14

Increasing Learning Through Assessment

chapteroutline

learningoutcomes

After you've completed your study of this chapter,
you should be able to:

Classroom Assessment
Assessment *for* Student Learning
Validity: Making Accurate Assessment Decisions
Reliability: Consistency in Assessment

1. Describe assessment *for* learning, and explain how validity and reliability are related to it.

Informal Assessment
Informal Assessment During Learning Activities
Reliability of Informal Assessments

2. Describe informal assessment, and explain how it is an important part of assessment *for* learning.

Formal Assessment
Paper-and-Pencil Items
Commercially Prepared Test Items
Performance Assessments
Portfolio Assessment: Involving Students in the Assessment Process
Evaluating Formal Assessment Formats

3. Identify differences between formal and informal assessment, and analyze formal assessment items.

Effective Assessment Practices
Planning for Assessment
Preparing Students for Assessments
Administering Assessments
Analyzing Results

4. Explain how effective assessment practices increase student learning.

**Grading and Reporting:
The Total Assessment System**
Formative and Summative Assessment
Designing a Grading System
Assigning Grades: Increasing Learning and Motivation
Technology, Learning, and Development: Using Technology to Improve Your Assessment System

5. Describe the components and decisions involved in designing a total assessment system.

classroomapplications

The following features help you apply the content of this chapter
in your teaching.

Ed Psych and Teaching:
Increasing the Quality of Your Assessments

Classroom Connections:
Capitalizing on Informal Assessment in Classrooms
Creating Valid and Reliable Classroom Assessments
Conducting Effective Classroom Assessment Practices
Designing Effective Classroom Assessment Systems

Developmentally Appropriate Practice:
Assessment of Learning with Students at Different Ages

Exploring Diversity:
Effective Assessment Practices with Students from
Diverse Backgrounds

You've taught a lesson, and it went well. The students were involved and seemed interested. But, you're missing some essential information: To what extent did the kids "get it," and how can you find out? Answering these questions is a fundamental part of the learning–teaching process.

As you read the following case study, consider how DeVonne Lampkin, a fifth-grade teacher, answers the questions, and more importantly, how she uses the information she gathers to increase her students' learning.

DeVonne is beginning a unit on fractions. She knows that fractions were introduced in the fourth grade, but she isn't sure how much her students remember, so she gives them a pretest. When she scores it, here's what she finds:

Draw a figure that will illustrate each of the fractions.

3/4   3/8   1/3

You need 3 pieces of ribbon for a project. The pieces should measure 2 5/16, 4 2/16, and 1 3/16 inches. How much ribbon do you need in all?

$7\frac{10}{16}$

The students seem to understand the basic idea of a *fraction*, and how to add fractions with like denominators. But the following responses suggest they struggle with adding fractions when the denominators are different.

Latoya made a punch recipe for a party.

Punch Recipe
3/4 gallon ginger ale   1/2 gallon grapefruit juice
1 2/3 gallon orange juice   2/3 gallon pineapple juice

a. Will the punch she made fit into one 3-gallon punch bowl? Explain why or why not.

No because when added correctly it is more.

b. How much punch, if any, is left over?

None

On Saturday, Justin rode his bicycle 12 ½ miles. On Sunday, he rode 8 3/5 miles.

a. How many miles did he ride altogether?

21

b. How many more miles did Justin ride on Saturday than on Sunday?

4 miles more.

Based on these results, DeVonne plans to focus on *equivalent fractions* in her first lesson, because her students need to understand this concept to be able to add fractions with unlike denominators.

She begins the lesson by passing out chocolate bars divided into 12 equal pieces, and with her guidance, the students show how 3/12 is the same as 1/4, 6/12 is equal to 1/2, and 8/12 equals 2/3. In each case she has them explain their answers.

DeVonne then goes to the board and demonstrates how to create equivalent fractions using numbers. At the end of the lesson, she gives a homework assignment that includes the following problems:

Write two equivalent fractions for each shaded part.

1.   2.   3.   4.

____   ____   ____   ____

When she scores the homework, she sees that some students are still having difficulties.

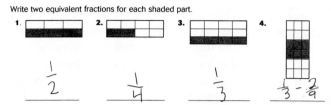

Write two equivalent fractions for each shaded part.

$\frac{1}{2}$ $\frac{1}{4}$ $\frac{1}{3}$ $\frac{1}{3} = \frac{2}{9}$

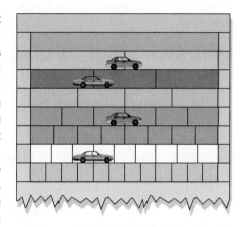

So, she designs another activity for the next day to further illustrate equivalent fractions. She begins the activity by having students construct a model fraction city with equivalent-length streets divided into different parts:

When the students are finished making their strips, she has them move cars along the different streets to illustrate equivalent fractions such as 1/2 = 3/6 and 1/3 = 3/9. Then, she illustrates adding fractions with like denominators, using the cars and strips as concrete examples. Next she uses the same cars and strips to illustrate adding fractions with unlike denominators.

Finally, DeVonne goes to the board and demonstrates how to perform the same operations using numbers, and gives her students a homework assignment on adding fractions with unlike denominators.

At the end of the week, she gives a cumulative test on fractions. Her students' answers suggest that they seem to understand equivalent fractions and how to add fractions with unlike denominators.

To begin your study of this chapter, consider these questions:

1. What is classroom assessment?
2. What was the primary purpose of DeVonne's assessments?
3. What different kinds of assessments did DeVonne use in her teaching?

Research on classroom assessment helps us answer these questions and suggests ways to make our assessments more effective. In this chapter we examine how you can apply this research with your students.

Classroom Assessment

Classroom assessment includes all the processes involved in making decisions about our students' learning progress (Nitko & Brookhart, 2011). Our observations of students' written work, their answers to questions in class, and their performance on teacher-made and standardized tests are types of classroom assessment. It also includes performance assessments, such as watching first graders print or observing art students create a piece of pottery.

Assessment also involves decisions about reteaching a topic or assigning grades, such as DeVonne's deciding to begin her unit with a lesson on equivalent fractions, to teach a second lesson on the topic, and to give her unit test at the end of the week. This answers our first question above, "What is classroom assessment?"

Classroom assessment. All the processes involved in making decisions about students' learning progress.

Assessment *for* Student Learning

Think about the questions we ask in "Ed Psych and You" here. If you're typical, it's classes in which you're frequently and thoroughly assessed. Students sometimes protest that they would learn as much or more if they weren't assessed, but this assertion isn't supported by research. In fact, quite the opposite is true (Carey, 2010; Rohrer & Pashler, 2010). "Testing has such a bad connotation; people think of standardized testing or teaching to the test. Maybe we need to call it something else, but this is one of the most powerful learning tools we have" (Carey, 2010, para. 28).

This captures the essence of **assessment *for* learning,** the idea that assessment is a continual, ongoing process designed to support and increase student learning (Stiggins & Chappuis, 2012). Instead of assessment occurring at the end of a unit or course of study to determine the amount students learned—assessment *of* learning—assessment *for* learning becomes an integral part of the teaching–learning process.

Assessment *for* learning also helps us answer our second question at the beginning of the chapter: "What was the primary purpose of DeVonne's assessments?" Assessments are used in assigning grades, of course, but *promoting learning* is their primary purpose.

Effective assessments serve four functions, each of which contribute to learning. They are:

- Measuring current understanding
- Increasing motivation to learn
- Developing self-regulation
- Measuring achievement

We examine them next.

Assessment *for* learning. Assessment that is a continual, ongoing process designed to support and increase learning.

Assessment is one of the most powerful learning tools that we, as teachers, have.

Diagnostic Assessment: Measuring Current Understanding

To begin this section, let's look again at DeVonne's work with her students. Before she began her unit on fractions, she gave a pretest to determine her students' current level of understanding. She found that they understood the concept *fraction* and could add fractions with like denominators, but they had misconceptions about adding fractions when the denominators were different. As a result, her first learning objective was for her students to understand the concept *equivalent fraction,* and the second was for them to be able to add fractions with unlike denominators.

Diagnostic assessment. A form of assessment designed to provide information about students' prior knowledge and misconceptions before beginning a learning activity.

DeVonne's pretest was a form of **diagnostic assessment,** an assessment designed to provide teachers with information about students' prior knowledge and misconceptions before beginning a learning activity (Burns, 2005). Diagnostic assessment helps us identify our students' zones of proximal development, so we can provide the scaffolding that helps them progress through their zones.

DeVonne's homework assignment was also a form of diagnostic assessment. For example, in scoring her students' papers, she saw responses such as those at left to her first four items:

Their responses suggested that they retained misconceptions about the concept *equivalent fraction,* because they wrote only one fraction for the first three problems and answered the fourth problem incorrectly. As a result, she designed a second learning activity to teach *equivalent fractions.*

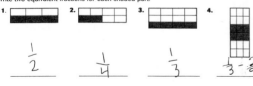

Write two equivalent fractions for each shaded part.

1. $\dfrac{1}{2}$ 2. $\dfrac{1}{4}$ 3. $\dfrac{1}{3}$ 4. $3 - \dfrac{2}{9}$

Increasing Motivation to Learn

Part of the reason you learn more in classes where you're frequently and thoroughly assessed is that you're motivated: you're more likely to study when you know you're going to be held accountable for understanding the content. Initially, you're probably extrinsically motivated—you study to get a good grade—but as your understanding increases, your intrinsic motivation often increases as well. These tendencies are confirmed by research (Stiggins & Chappuis, 2012).

Assessments that increase motivation to learn have the following characteristics (Brookhart, Walsh, & Zientarski, 2006; Schunk, Pintrich, & Meece, 2008):

- They are aligned with learning objectives.
- They focus on content mastery and improvement.
- They avoid social comparisons.
- They measure higher level learning.
- They include detailed feedback.

Assessments aligned with learning objectives provide students with the information they need to focus their efforts and also increase the likelihood of success. When students are successful and attribute their success to effort, motivation to learn increases. Focusing on content mastery and improvement, eliminating social comparisons, and measuring higher-level outcomes also promote feelings of autonomy and competence, which increase motivation to learn. "Setting high standards for student achievement and holding students accountable for reaching them can motivate students to excel" (Schunk et al., 2008, p. 371).

Finally, feedback on all assessments—including homework—is essential. We all want and need information about our learning progress. Effective assessments combined with feedback tell us if our study efforts are paying off and what we still need to work on. The opposite is also true. Your worst classes are likely those in which assessments are infrequent or murky, leaving you wondering about how you're doing and whether or not you're on the right path to mastering course content.

Developing Self-Regulation

Self-regulated learning occurs when we set goals and monitor progress toward those goals. High-quality assessments contribute to this process by providing us with information that can help us focus our efforts. For example, if assessments require that we do more than memorize factual information, we quickly adapt our study habits and focus on deeper understanding. Many experts believe that assessment has more influence on the way students study and learn than any other aspect of the teaching–learning process (Carey 2010; Popham, 2011a; Stiggins, 2007).

You contribute to learner self-regulation by making your expectations clear, emphasizing that assessments are designed to increase learning, aligning assessments with learning objectives and learning activities, and providing detailed feedback on all assessments (Stiggins, 2007; Stiggins & Chappuis, 2012).

Measuring Achievement

In addition to increasing motivation and helping students develop self-regulation, assessment also provides students and their parents, teachers, and school leaders with information about learner achievement (McMillan, 2007). This has historically been the role of assessment, but as you've seen in this section, assessment *for* learning expands this role to also include making students more motivated and efficient learners. The relationships among these processes are outlined in Figure 14.1.

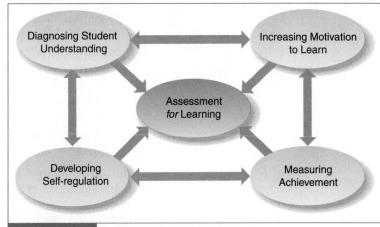

Figure 14.1 Assessment *for* learning

Validity: Making Accurate Assessment Decisions

Validity is the degree to which an assessment actually measures what it is supposed to measure (M. Miller, Linn, & Gronlund, 2009). In teaching, our assessments are valid if they are aligned with learning objectives. For example, if our objective is for students to understand the causes of the Revolutionary War, but a quiz asks them to recall names, dates, and places, it would be invalid. Based on the quiz results, we might decide students had met the objective, when in fact we would have gathered little information about their understanding of the war's causes.

Assessment decisions are also invalid if they're based on personality, appearance, or other factors unrelated to our learning objectives, such as giving lower scores on essay items because of messy handwriting (M. Miller et al., 2009). These actions are usually unconscious; without realizing it, teachers sometimes base their assessments on appearance rather than substance.

Creating valid assessments is challenging but not impossible. If you continually look for ways to improve your tests, quizzes, and other assessments, analyze trends and patterns in student responses, and conscientiously revise your assessments, validity will improve.

Reliability: Consistency in Assessment

In addition to being valid, we also want our assessments to be reliable. **Reliability,** an intuitively sensible concept, describes the extent to which assessments are consistent and free from errors of measurement (M. Miller et al., 2009). For instance, if your bathroom scale is reliable, and your weight doesn't change, the readings shouldn't vary from one day to the next. Hypothetically, if we could repeatedly give a student the same reliable test, and if no additional learning or forgetting occurred, the scores would all be the same. Unreliable assessments cannot be valid, even if they are aligned with teachers' learning objectives, because they give inconsistent information.

Ambiguous wording on test and quiz items, directions that aren't clear, and inconsistent scoring, which is common on essay items, are three factors that detract from reliability. For example, different instructors with similar backgrounds, ostensibly using the same criteria, have awarded grades ranging from excellent to failure on the same essay (Gronlund & Waugh, 2009). If scoring is inconsistent, lack of reliability makes the grades and feedback we give invalid.

The following are some ways to increase reliability:

- Use a sufficient number of items or tasks on assessments. For instance, a quiz of 15 items is likely to be more reliable than a quiz that has only 5 items.
- Clearly explain requirements for responding to assessment items.
- Identify criteria for scoring students' essay items in advance. Score all students' responses to a particular item before moving to a second one.
- To prevent being influenced by your expectations of students, score assessments anonymously, particularly if you're scoring essay items or solutions to problems where partial credit is given. Have students put their names on the last page of the quiz, for example, so you won't know whose quiz you're scoring until you're finished.

Visualizing a target is one way to think about the relationship between validity and reliability (M. Miller et al., 2009). A valid and reliable shooter consistently clusters shots in the target's bull's-eye. A reliable but invalid shooter clusters shots, but the cluster is not in the bull's-eye. And a shooter who scatters shots randomly over the target is analogous to an assessment instrument that is neither valid nor reliable. These relationships are illustrated in Figure 14.2.

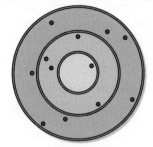

TARGET 1
(reliable and valid shooting)

TARGET 2
(unreliable and invalid shooting)

TARGET 3
(reliable but invalid shooting)

Figure 14.2 The relationships between validity and reliability
Source: "The Relationships Between Validity and Reliability" adapted from
MEASUREMENT AND ASSESSMENT IN TEACHING, 10th Edition by Miller et al.
Copyright © 2009 by David M. Miller; Robert L. Linn; Norman E. Gronlund. Printed
and Electronically reproduced by permission of Pearson Education, Inc., Upper Saddle
River, New Jersey.

*check your
understanding*

1.1 Describe assessment *for* student learning and how validity and reliability are related to it.

1.2 An eighth-grade history teacher reminds his students that correct grammar and punctuation are important parts of writing, and he gives his students two scores on their history essay items: one for the history content and a second for grammar and punctuation. Is his assessment valid? Explain why or why not.

1.3 A high school science teacher wants her students to be able to design effective experiments. After discussing the process with them, she has them complete a lab assignment in which they are required to design an experiment. On Friday she gives a quiz that requires students to list the steps, in order, for designing an experiment. Is her assessment valid? Explain why or why not. Is her quiz likely to be reliable? Explain why or why not.

To receive feedback for these questions, go to Appendix A.

Informal Assessment

When we see or hear the term *assessment* we typically think of tests and quizzes. But we want to continually gather assessment information as we interact with our students. For example, consider the following:

- You see some of your students drifting off during an explanation, so you stop and ask a series of questions to review what you've covered so far.
- You're circulating around the room as your students work on a seat-work assignment in math, and you see that several students have made the same error on three similar problems.

Your observations combined with the related decisions are part of **informal assessment,** the process of gathering incidental information about learning progress and making decisions based on that information. In the examples, you didn't plan to gather the information in advance, and you didn't get the same information from each of your students. Several of your students' making an error, for instance, doesn't mean that *all* students in the class have made the same error.

Informal assessment. The process of gathering incidental information about learning progress and making decisions based on that information.

Your experience with your preowned car in our "Ed Psych and You" feature in this section is also an example of informal assessment. Your experiences with your air conditioning, brakes, and differential howl are all incidental information that you gathered during the normal course of operating your car. And, you made the decision to never own another Brand X based on that information.

Informal assessment is an essential part of the total assessment process because it helps us make the many decisions required every day (Black, Harrison, Lee, Marshall, & William, 2004). Let's look at this process in more detail.

Informal Assessment During Learning Activities

Let's return to DeVonne's work with her students. The class has added fractions with unlike denominators using their cars, and she now wants them to be able to add fractions having unlike denominators without the support of the concrete example.

"Let's review what we've done," she begins. "Look at your cars again, and move one of your cars to First Street and Fourth Avenue and your other car to First Street and Eighth Avenue. . . . How far have your two cars moved altogether? . . . Write the problem on your paper using fractions."

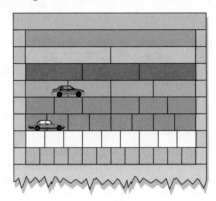

She sees that Jeremy has written the following on his paper:

$$\frac{1}{4} + \frac{1}{8} = \frac{2}{8}$$

She also sees that Juanita, Michael, and Cassie have written 1/4 + 1/8 = 2/12 on their papers.

$$\frac{1}{4} + \frac{1}{8} = \frac{2}{12}$$

$$\frac{1}{4} + \frac{1}{8} = \frac{2}{12}$$

$$\frac{1}{4} + \frac{1}{8} = \frac{2}{12}$$

"I'll work with them when I assign seat work," she thinks to herself.

She waits for the students to finish and then, seeing that Nikki has a clear solution, says, "Nikki, please come up and show us how you solved the problem."

Nikki goes to the board and writes:

$$\frac{2}{2} \times \frac{1}{4} = \frac{2}{8}$$

"Explain why Nikki could write 2/2 times 1/4 to get 2/8. . . . Amir."

". . ."

"What does 2/2 equal?"

". . . One," Amir responds.

"Good, . . . and whenever we multiply something by one, we don't change the value. . . . So, now what can Nikki do? . . . Thelicia?"

". . . Add the 2/8 and 1/8 to get 3/8."

"Good, Thelicia," DeVonne smiles. "Now, let's try this one," and she gives the students another problem, again watches as they attempt to solve it, and discusses it as they discussed the first one. After two more problems, she gives a seat-work assignment and then calls Jeremy, Juanita, Michael, and Cassie to a table at the back of the room to provide additional help.

In this brief episode, DeVonne used informal assessment in three ways:

- She observed that Jeremy, Juanita, Michael, and Cassie had misconceptions about adding fractions with unlike denominators and decided to give them extra help while the rest of the class did seat work.
- She could have demonstrated the solution to the problem herself, but she decided to use Nikki as a peer model instead.
- Instead of asking Nikki to explain why she could multiply 1/4 by 2/2, she decided to call on Amir and also decided to prompt him when he was unable to answer instead of turning the question to another student.

Each of DeVonne's decisions was a part of informal assessment, each was designed to promote learning, and each was based on incidental information she gathered during the learning activity.

Students' personal, written products can also be sources of informal assessment information. Some examples include:

- *Response journals.* Have students respond to a specific event in a work of literature or a controversial topic in social studies.
- *Personal diaries.* Ask students to share their current thinking about topics.
- *Learning Logs.* Have students evaluate their own learning progress by responding to specific questions. (Stiggins & Chappuis, 2012).

These products provide us with another source of information. They also give us insights into our students' thinking and encourage them to become more reflective and self-regulated about their own learning. To be most effective, however, we should respond to students' entries, which can become enormously time-consuming. You must decide if the time invested in the process is worth the extra learning that might result.

Reliability of Informal Assessments

While informal assessments are essential in the day-to-day functioning of classrooms, they provide an incomplete picture of learning, and they're often unreliable. For example, concluding that all students understand an idea on the basis of responses from only a few (who usually have their hands up) is a common mistake. Further, evidence indicates that students who are physically attractive or have engaging personalities are awarded higher grades than their less fortunate peers (Parks & Kennedy, 2007; Ritts, Patterson, & Tubbs, 1992), so important decisions, such as assigning grades should not be made on the basis of informal assessments (M. Miller et al., 2009).

Similarly, suppose you see a student push another down on the playground. Concluding that the student is a bully on the basis of one playground incident is unreliable, and accusing the student of bullying could be emotionally damaging.

Your experience with your preowned car in our "Ed Psych and You" feature at the beginning of this section is another example of issues with informal assessment reliability. For instance, because your Brand X turned out to be a lemon doesn't mean that all Brand X cars are lemons.

Because informal assessments are always potentially unreliable, we need additional information. This leads us to a discussion of formal assessment, our next topic.

check your understanding

2.1   Describe informal assessment, and explain how it is an important part of assessment *for* learning.

2.2   Which aspects of students' learning and development depend almost totally on informal assessment? Explain why this is the case.

2.3   Identify a weakness that often exists with informal assessment. Why is it important that teachers are aware of this weakness?

To receive feedback for these exercises go to Appendix A.

*C*lassroom *connections*

Capitalizing on Informal Assessment in Classrooms

Informal assessment is the process of gathering information during learning activities and other school events and making instructional decisions on the basis of that information. Attempt to make your informal assessments as systematic as possible.

- **Elementary:** A first-grade teacher notices that one of her students appears listless and sometimes falls asleep during learning activities. She watches the student for several days, and then contacts the school counselor.

- **Middle School:** A sixth-grade math teacher sees that one of her students has incorrectly solved a word problem involving decimals. He tells the student to recheck his answer, and then checks several other

students' answers to see if the class appears to have the same misconception.

- **High School:** An American history teacher wants his students to understand the relationships among Marco Polo's visit to the far east, the Portuguese explorers, and Columbus's trip to the new world. A few students respond to open-ended questions, but most sit silently. Adapting, he changes the direction of the lesson and provides a short presentation on the main idea, followed by a discussion in which he asks students to use the facts involved in each individual case to examine the relationships among the ideas.

*F*ormal Assessment

In the previous section you saw how DeVonne used informal assessment as an integral part of her instruction. This is only one aspect of the assessment process, however. For instance, DeVonne also used:

- A diagnostic pretest, which gave her information about her students' understanding of fractions and how to add them.
- Homework assignments that measured their understanding of *equivalent fractions* and adding fractions with unlike denominators.
- A unit test that covered all aspects of adding fractions.

Each was a **formal assessment,** the process of systematically gathering the same kind of information from every student and making decisions based on the information. And,

Formal assessment. The process of systematically gathering the same kind of information from every student and making decisions based on that information.

this discussion addresses the third question we asked at the beginning of the chapter: "What different kinds of assessments did DeVonne use in her teaching?" DeVonne also used formal assessments to provide a comprehensive picture of her students' learning. For instance, when DeVonne gave her students the items shown here for homework, every student responded to the same problems. Formal assessments overcome the reliability issues that often accompany informal assessment, so the combination of the two increases the likelihood of gathering accurate information for instructional decision making.

Formal assessments most commonly occur in three forms:

- Paper-and-pencil items, such as multiple-choice and essay.
- Performance assessments, such as observing students making a presentation.
- Portfolios, collections of students' work that measure progress over time.

Let's look at them.

Write two equivalent fractions for each shaded part.

Paper-and-Pencil Items

Paper-and-pencil items are commonly classified as either *selected-response formats,* such as multiple-choice, true–false, and matching, because they require learners to select the correct answer from a list of alternatives, or *supply formats,* such as completion or essay, because they require learners to supply their answers. Items can also be classified as *objective,* such as multiple-choice, where scorers don't have to make decisions about the quality of an answer, or *subjective,* such as essay, where scorer judgment is a factor (M. Miller et al., 2009).

Regardless of whether the format is selected-response or supply, objective or subjective, two factors are important for making the items valid and reliable. First, to be valid, the items must be aligned with your learning objectives and standards. The best way to ensure alignment is to write the items during planning. Second, students' responses to the items should be analyzed, and items should be modified when necessary to make them more effective.

Let's look now at the most common paper-and-pencil formats.

Multiple-Choice Items

Multiple-choice is an assessment format that consists of a *stem* and a series of answer choices called *distractors.* The **stem** is the beginning part of the item. It presents the item as a problem to be solved, a question to be answered, or an incomplete statement. The item also includes options—typically four or five. One option is the correct or best choice, and the rest are **distractors,** because they are designed to distract students who don't understand the content the item is measuring (M. Miller et al., 2009). The stem should pose one question or problem to be considered, and distractors should address students' likely misconceptions. You can then identify and discuss the distractors when giving your students feedback (Ciofalo & Wylie, 2006).

People often think that multiple-choice items measure only factual information that students memorize, but this is a misconception. Multiple-choice, when items are well designed, is a valid and highly effective format for assessing a range of thinking levels. The fact that most standardized tests use this format is evidence of its effectiveness. Guidelines for preparing effective multiple-choice items are summarized as follows (Gronlund & Waugh, 2009):

1. Present one clear problem or question in the stem.
2. Make all distractors plausible to students with an incomplete understanding of the content.
3. Vary the position of the correct choice, and avoid overusing choice *c.*
4. Avoid using similar wording in the stem and the correct choice.
5. Avoid using more technical wording in the correct choice than in the distractors.
6. Keep the correct choice and the distractors similar in length. A longer or shorter answer should be an incorrect choice.

Multiple-choice. A paper-and-pencil format that consists of a question or statement, called a stem, and a series of answer choices that include one correct—or best—answer and a series of distractors.

Stem. The beginning part of a multiple-choice item that presents the item as a problem to be solved, a question to be answered, or an incomplete statement.

Distractors. Incorrect choices in multiple-choice items.

7. Avoid using absolute terms, such as *always* or *never*, in incorrect choices.
8. Keep the stem and distractors grammatically consistent.
9. Avoid including two distractors with the same meaning.
10. Emphasize negative wording by underlining, italicizing, or putting it in bold print.
11. Avoid using "all of the above" as a choice, and use "none of the above" with care.

Items may be written so that only one choice is correct, or they may be in a best-answer form, in which two or more choices are partially correct but one is clearly better than the others. The best-answer form is more demanding, promotes higher-level thinking, and measures more complex understanding. Many of the multiple-choice questions that assess your understanding of the material in this text use the best-answer form.

Many problems with faulty multiple-choice items involve clues in distractors that allow test-wise students to answer the question correctly without fully understanding the content. "Check Your Understanding" item 3.2 at the end of this section asks you to identify features of test items that are inconsistent with these guidelines.

Assessing Higher-Level Learning. In the previous section we said that multiple-choice items can be effective for assessing higher-order thinking. *Interpretive exercises* are useful for this process. These exercises present information covered in class in a different context, and the distractors represent different "interpretations" of it (Gronlund & Waugh, 2009). The material may be a graph, chart, table, map, picture, or written vignette.

Figure 14.3 contains an example in science. In this case, the goal is for students to apply information about heat, expansion, mass, volume, and density to a unique situation. This type of exercise promotes transfer, helps develop critical thinking, and can also increase

Look at the drawings above. They represent two identical soft drink bottles covered with identical balloons sitting side-by-side on a table. Bottle A was then heated. Which of the following is the most accurate statement?

a. The density of the air in Bottle A is greater than the density of the air in Bottle B.
*b. The density of the air in Bottle A is less than the density of the air in Bottle B.
c. The density of the air in Bottle A is equal to the density of the air in Bottle B.
d. We don't have enough information to compare the density of the air in Bottle A to the density of the air in Bottle B.

Figure 14.3 Interpretive exercise using the multiple-choice format

learner motivation. Most of the higher-order multiple-choice items that you will respond to as you take this class are interpretive exercises.

Matching Items

The multiple-choice format is inefficient if all of the items require the same set of answer choices, as in the following (asterisk indicates correct answer):

1. The statement "Understanding is like a lightbulb coming on in your head" is an example of
   *a. simile
   b. metaphor
   c. hyperbole
   d. personification
2. "That's the most brilliant comment ever made" is a statement of
   a. simile
   b. metaphor
   *c. hyperbole
   d. personification

These assessments can be made more efficient by using a **matching format,** which requires learners to classify a series of examples using the same alternatives. The following is an example based on the multiple-choice items above.

> Match the following statements with the figures of speech by writing the letter of the appropriate figure of speech in the blank next to each statement. You may use each figure of speech once, more than once, or not at all.

    _____ 1. Understanding is like a lightbulb coming on in your head.
    _____ 2. That's the most brilliant comment ever made.
    _____ 3. His oratory was a bellow from the bowels of his soul.
    _____ 4. Appropriate attitudes are always advantageous.
    _____ 5. Her eyes were limpid pools of longing.
    _____ 6. He stood as straight as a rod.
    _____ 7. I'll never get this stuff, no matter what I do.
    _____ 8. The colors of his shirt described the complex world in which he lived.

a. alliteration
b. hyperbole
c. metaphor
d. personification
e. simile

This example illustrates four characteristics of effective matching items. First, the content is homogeneous; all the statements are figures of speech, and only figures of speech appear as alternatives. Other topics for which the matching format is effective include people and their achievements, historical events and dates, terms and definitions, and authors and their works (M. Miller et al., 2009). Second, the item includes more statements than possible alternatives (to prevent getting the right answer by process of elimination). Third, students may use the alternatives more than once or not at all, as specified in the directions. Finally, the entire item includes 8 statements. As a rule of thumb, if a matching item involves more than 10 statements, you should create two separate items to prevent confusion.

True–False Items

True–false is an assessment format that includes statements that learners judge as being correct or incorrect. Because true–false items usually measure lower-level outcomes, and because students have a 50–50 chance of guessing the correct answer, the format should be used sparingly (M. Miller et al., 2009). We don't recommend that you use the format, and we include no true–false items in the test bank that accompanies this text.

Matching. A paper-and-pencil format that requires learners to classify a series of examples using the same alternatives.

True–false. A paper-and-pencil format that includes statements that learners judge as being correct or incorrect.

If you choose to use the format, however, the following guidelines can improve the effectiveness of these items:

- Write more false than true items. Teachers tend to do the reverse, and students tend to mark items they're unsure of as "true."
- Make each item one clear statement.
- Avoid clues that allow students to answer correctly without fully understanding the content. Examples of clues include the term *most,* which usually indicates a true statement, or *never,* typically suggesting a false statement.

Completion Items

Completion. A paper-and-pencil format that includes a question or an incomplete statement that requires the learner to supply the answer.

Completion is an assessment format that includes a question or an incomplete statement that requires the learner to supply the answer.

The following are two examples.

1. What is an opinion? _____
2. _____ is the capital of Canada.

Items that consist of questions, such as the first example, are sometimes called short-answer items. This format is popular with teachers, probably because the questions seem easy to construct. This is misleading, however, because completion items have two important disadvantages. First, it is difficult to phrase a question so that only one possible answer is correct. A number of defensible responses could be given to item 1, for example. Overuse of completion items can put students in the position of trying to guess the answer the teacher wants instead of giving the one they think is correct.

Second, unless the item requires solving a problem, completion items usually measure recall of factual information, as in item 2. Because of these weaknesses, experts recommend that you use completion formats sparingly (Gronlund & Waugh, 2009). Table 14.1 presents guidelines for preparing completion items.

Essay Items: Measuring Complex Outcomes

Essay. A paper-and-pencil format that requires students to make extended written responses to questions or problems.

Essay is an assessment format that requires students to make extended written responses to questions or problems. Essay items make three valuable contributions to our assessment efforts. First, they can assess dimensions of learning, such as creative and critical thinking, that can't be measured with other formats. Second, the ability to organize ideas, make and defend arguments, and describe ideas in writing is an important goal across the curriculum, and the essay format is an effective way to measure progress toward this goal (Stiggins

Table 14.1 Guidelines for preparing completion items

Guideline	Rationale
1. Use only one blank, and relate it to the main point of the statement.	Several blanks are confusing, and one answer may depend on another.
2. Use complete sentences followed by a question mark or period.	Complete sentences allow students to more nearly grasp the full meaning of the statement.
3. Keep blanks the same length. Use "a(an)" at the end of the statement, or eliminate indefinite articles.	A long blank for a long word or a particular indefinite article commonly provides clues to the answer.
4. For numerical answers, indicate the degree of precision and the units desired.	Degree of precision and units clarify the task for students and prevent them from spending more time than necessary on an item.

& Chappuis, 2012). Third, essay items can improve the way students study. If they know an essay format will be used, for example, they are more likely to look for relationships in what they study and to organize information in a meaningful way.

Essay items also have disadvantages, however. Because essay tests require extensive writing time, it isn't possible to assess learning across as broad a spectrum, so breadth of coverage can be a problem. In addition, scoring them is time-consuming and, as discussed earlier, sometimes unreliable. Scores on essay items are also influenced by writing skill, including grammar, spelling, and handwriting (Nitko & Brookhart, 2011).

Essay items appear easy to write, but they can be ambiguous, leaving students uncertain about how to respond. As a result, students' ability to interpret the question is often the outcome measured. Figure 14.4 presents guidelines for preparing and scoring essay items (Stiggins & Chappuis, 2012). In addition to these suggestions, rubrics can help improve the reliability of scoring essays. We examine them next.

Teachers use essay items to assess complex outcomes that other formats can't assess.

Using Rubrics

A **rubric** is a scoring scale that explicitly describes criteria for grading (Stiggins & Chappuis, 2012). Originally created to increase reliability and validity when scoring essays, rubrics are also used when assessing performances, such as a student presentation, or products other than essays, such as a science lab report.

Rubric. A scoring scale that explicitly describes criteria for grading.

Rubrics provide guidance for your planning by providing targets to focus on during instruction; you can share them with your students during learning activities to help them understand what you're looking for; and they're essential for assessment. The following steps are useful when constructing rubrics:

- Establish criteria based on elements that must exist in students' work.
- Decide on the number of levels of achievement for each criterion.
- Develop clear descriptors for each level.
- Determine a rating scale for the entire rubric.

Figure 14.5 contains a rubric for assessing paragraph structure. In it, we see that the teacher has identified a topic sentence, supporting sentences, and summarizing sentence as essential components of an effective paragraph. These elements appear in a column along

---

1. Elicit higher-order thinking by using such terms as *explain* and *compare*. Have students defend their responses with facts.

2. Write a model answer for each item. You can use this both for scoring and for providing feedback.

3. Require all students to answer all items. Allowing students to select particular items prevents comparisons and detracts from reliability.

4. Prepare criteria for scoring in advance.

5. Score all students' answers to a single item before moving to the next item.

6. Score all responses to a single item in one sitting if possible. This increases reliability.

7. Score answers without knowing the identity of the student. This helps reduce the influence of past performance and expectations.

8. Develop a model answer complete with points, and compare a few students' responses to it, to see if any adjustments are needed in the scoring criteria.

Figure 14.4 Guidelines for preparing and scoring essay items

	Levels of Achievement		
Criteria	**1**	**2**	**3**
Topic Sentence	Not present; reader has no idea of what paragraph is about	Present but does not give the reader a clear idea of what the paragraph is about	Provides a clearly stated overview of the paragraph
Supporting Sentences	Rambling and unrelated to topic sentence	Provides additional information but not all focused on topic sentence	Provides supporting detail relating to the topic sentence
Summarizing Sentence	Nonexistent or unrelated to preceding sentences	Relates to topic sentence but doesn't summarize information in paragraph	Accurately summarizes information in paragraph and is related to topic sentence
Overall Score (9 Possible)			

Figure 14.5 Sample rubric for paragraph structure

the left side of the matrix. Then, the rubric describes levels of achievement for each element. Clear descriptors guide students as they write and also provide reference points for you when you score student products. As a final planning step, you make decisions about grading criteria. For example, you might decide that 9 points would be an A, 7–8 points a B, and 5–6 points would be a C. So, a student would be required to be at a level of achievement of 3 on all three criteria to earn an A, for example, and would have to be at level 2 on two of the three elements and at level 3 on the third to earn a B.

Rubrics are essential for increasing reliability when assessing students' work. If you were using this rubric to score students' paragraphs, for example, the descriptions of the dimensions and levels of achievement in Figure 14.5 help maintain consistency in evaluating each student's work. Without the rubric as a guide, the likelihood of inconsistent scoring and unreliable assessments are much higher.

Commercially Prepared Test Items

Because you will be very busy when you begin teaching, you are likely to use test items included in the ancillary materials for your textbooks. Although using these items saves time, you should use them with care, for three reasons (Nitko & Brookhart, 2011; Popham, 2011a):

1. *Compatibility of learning objectives:* The learning objectives of the curriculum developers may not be the same as yours. If items don't reflect the objectives in your lesson or unit, they are invalid.
2. *Uneven quality:* Textbook authors often don't prepare the test items included with ancillary materials, and, as a result, many commercially prepared tests are poor quality.
3. *Emphasis on lower-level items:* Commercially prepared items typically measure at a knowledge-recall level.

The time and labor you save in using commercially prepared items are important advantages, however. The following guidelines can help you capitalize on these benefits:

- Select items that are consistent with your learning objectives, and e-file them for editing later.
- Using feedback from students and analysis of test results, revise ineffective items.
- Create additional items that help you accurately assess your students' understanding.

Only you know what your objectives are, and you are the best judge of the extent to which commercially prepared items assess them.

Performance Assessments

Critics argue that traditional paper-and-pencil assessments, most commonly in the form of multiple-choice tests, lack validity, and fail to assess higher level outcomes (Corcoran et al., 2004; French, 2003). In response to these criticisms, the use of **performance assessments,** direct examinations of student performance on tasks relevant to life outside of school, have been emphasized, especially in the language arts (Frey & Schmitt, 2005; Popham, 2011a). The term *performance assessment* originated in content areas like science and the performing arts, where students were required to demonstrate an ability in a real-world situation, such as a laboratory demonstration or recital.

Let's look at two examples.

A high school auto mechanics teacher wants his students to be able to troubleshoot and diagnose what is wrong with a car engine that won't start. He provides an overview of common starting problems along with actual examples of auto engine malfunction. Students discuss the problems in each example; with the assistance of the teacher, they arrive at steps and criteria for troubleshooting unresponsive engines and then use these to guide their work on other engines.

A health teacher reads in a professional journal that the biggest problem people have in applying first aid is not the mechanics per se, but knowing what to do and when. In an attempt to address this problem, the teacher periodically plans "catastrophe" days. Students entering the classroom encounter a catastrophe victim with an unspecified injury. In each case, they must first diagnose the problem and then apply first aid. The teacher observes them as they work and uses the information she gathers in discussions and assessments.

Designing performance assessments involves three steps, each designed to make them as valid and reliable as possible (Marion & Pellegrino, 2006; M. Miller et al., 2009).

1. Specify the type of performance you are trying to assess.
2. Structure the evaluation setting, balancing realism with safety and other issues.
3. Design evaluation procedures with clearly identified criteria.

Specifying the Performance Components

Specifying the components you're attempting to measure is the first step in designing any assessment. A clear description of the performance helps students understand what is required and assists you in designing appropriate instruction. An example of component specification in the area of persuasive writing is outlined in Figure 14.6.

In some cases the performance components will be processes—what students actually do—and in others they will be the final products. The initial focus is typically on processes,

Teachers use performance assessments to measure abilities similar to those required of students in the real world.

Performance assessments. Direct examinations of student performance on tasks that are relevant to life outside of school.

Persuasive essay

1. Specifies purpose of the essay
2. Provides evidence supporting the purpose
3. Identifies audience
4. Specifies likely counterarguments
5. Presents evidence dispelling counterarguments

Figure 14.6 Performance outcomes in persuasive writing

Table 14.2   Processes and products as components of performance

Content Area	Product	Process
Math	Correct answer	Problem-solving steps leading to the correct solution
Music	Performance of a work on an instrument	Correct fingering and breathing that produce the performance
English Composition	Essay, term paper, or composition	Preparation of drafts and thought processes that produce the product
Word Processing	Letter or copy of final draft	Proper stroking and techniques for presenting the paper
Science	Explanation for the outcomes of a demonstration	Thought processes involved in preparing the explanation

with the emphasis shifting to products after procedures are mastered (Gronlund & Waugh, 2009). Examples of how processes and products are interrelated components of performance assessments are shown in Table 14.2.

Structuring the Evaluation Setting

Performance assessments are valuable because they emphasize real-world tasks. However, time, expense, or safety often prevent performance in the real world, so intermediate steps are necessary. For example, in driver education, the goal is to produce safe drivers. However, putting beginning drivers in heavy traffic is both unrealistic and dangerous. So, teachers might begin by having students respond to written case studies, progress to using a simulator, then to driving on roads with little traffic, and finally to driving in all kinds of conditions. As students' driving skills develop, they progress to higher degrees of realism.

Simulations provide opportunities to measure performance in cases where high realism is not feasible, and a driving simulator is an example. As another example, a geography teacher wanting to measure students' understanding of the impact of climate and geography on the location of cities might display the information shown in Figure 14.7. This simulation asks students to identify the best location for a city on the island and the criteria they use in determining the location. Their criteria provide insights into their thinking.

Designing Evaluation Procedures

Designing evaluation procedures is the final step in creating effective performance assessments. Scoring rubrics, similar to those used with essay items, can increase both reliability and validity (Stiggins & Chappuis, 2012).

Strategies that can be used to assess learner performance include (1) systematic observation, (2) checklists, and (3) rating scales.

Systematic Observation. Teachers routinely observe students in classroom settings, but these informal observations usually are not systematic, and records are rarely kept. **Systematic observation,** the process of specifying criteria for acceptable performance in an activity and taking notes based on the criteria, attempts to solve these problems. For example, if you're a science teacher assessing your students' ability to use the scientific method, you might establish the following:

1. States problem or question
2. States hypotheses

Systematic observation. The process of specifying criteria for acceptable performance in an activity and taking notes based on the criteria.

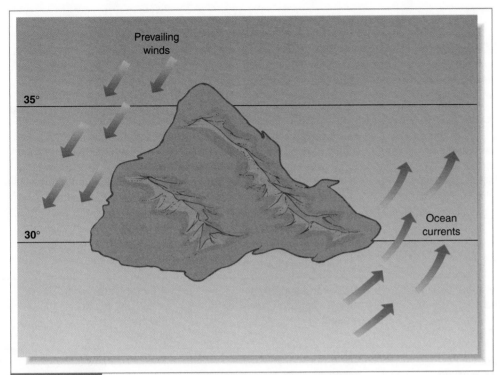

Figure 14.7 Simulation in geography

3. Specifies independent, dependent, and controlled variables
4. Gathers and displays data
5. Evaluates hypotheses based on the data

Your notes then refer directly to the criteria, making them consistent for all groups. You can also use these notes to give learners feedback and provide information for use in future planning.

Checklists. Checklists, written descriptions of dimensions that must be present in an acceptable performance, extend systematic observation by specifying important aspects of performance and by sharing them with students. During the assessment, you check off the desired dimensions rather than describing them in notes, as in systematic observation. For instance, in the preceding example you would check off each of the five criteria for effective use of the scientific method as they appeared in students' reports.

Checklists are useful when you can clearly determine whether a student did or did not meet a criterion, such as "States hypotheses." In other cases, however, such as "Evaluates hypotheses based on the data," the results aren't cut-and-dried; some evaluations will be more thorough and precise than others. Rating scales address this problem.

Rating Scales. Rating scales are written descriptions of the dimensions of an acceptable performance and scales of values on which each dimension is rated. They can be constructed in numerical, graphic, or descriptive formats and are similar to the scoring rubrics we discussed earlier in the chapter. An example of a rating scale using a descriptive format is illustrated in Figure 14.8.

Checklists. Written descriptions of dimensions that must be present in an acceptable performance of an activity.

Rating scales. Written descriptions of the dimensions of an acceptable performance and scales of values on which each dimension is rated.

Systematic observations, checklists, and rating scales help increase the reliability of performance assessments.

Effectiveness Concept	1	3	5
Lesson scope	No learning objective is apparent. The focus and scope of the lesson are uncertain.	Learning objective is unclear. The lesson covers too much or too little content.	A clear learning objective is apparent. The scope of the lesson is effective for reaching the objective.
Organization	Materials are not prepared and ready prior to the lesson. Routines are not apparent. Instructional time is wasted.	Some materials are prepared in advance, and some routines are apparent. Instructional time used reasonably well.	Instructional time is maximized with materials prepared in advance and well-established routines apparent.
Quality of examples/ nonexamples	Examples/nonexamples are not used.	Examples/nonexamples are used but are inadequate to accurately represent the topic.	A variety of high-quality examples in context are used to represent the topic.
Review	No review of previous work is conducted.	A brief and superficial review of previous work is present.	A thorough review of ideas necessary to understand the present topic is conducted.
Questioning frequency	Teacher lectured. Few questions were asked.	Some questions were asked. Much of the content was delivered through lecture.	The lesson was developed with questioning throughout.
Equitable distribution of questions	Questions were not directed to specific students.	Some questions were directed to individual students. Volunteers were called on most frequently.	All students in the class were called on as equally as possible, and questions were directed to students by name.
Wait-time and prompting	Little wait-time was given. Unanswered questions were directed to other students.	Intermittent assistance was provided as well as adequate wait-time in some-cases.	Students were consistently given wait-time and were prompted when they were unable to answer correctly.
Closure	Lesson lacked closure.	The teacher offered a summary and closure of the lesson.	The teacher guided students as they stated the main ideas of the lesson.
Instructional alignment	Learning objectives, learning activities, and assessment are out of alignment.	Objectives, learning activities, and assessment are partially aligned.	Learning objectives, the learning activity, and assessment are clearly aligned.

Figure 14.8 Rating scale for teaching effectiveness

Source: "Rating Scale for Teaching Effectiveness" adapted from AN EXAMINATION OF THE RELATIONSHIPS BETWEEN ELEMENTARY TEACHERS' UNDERSTANDING OF EDUCATION PSYCHOLOGY AND THEIR PEDAGOGICAL PRACTICE, Paper presented at the annual meeting of the American Education Research Association, Chicago, April 2007.

Portfolio Assessment: Involving Students in the Assessment Process

Portfolio assessment is the process of selecting collections of student work that both you and your students evaluate using preset criteria (Popham, 2011a; Stiggins & Chappuis, 2012). The portfolio is the actual collection of works, such as essays written over the school year, projects, samples of poetry, lab reports, video recorded performances, and quizzes and tests. The use of portfolios is common in areas varying as widely as measuring readiness in children at risk for school failure to assessing biology students' developing understanding of complex life forms (Dickson, 2004; Smith, Brewer, & Heffner, 2003). As the use of technology advances, electronic portfolios are becoming increasingly popular. Table 14.3 contains examples of portfolio assessments in different content areas.

Portfolio assessment has two valuable features. First, because it involves the collection of work samples over time, it reflects learning progress. For instance, writing samples can document improved skills that have developed over a period of time.

Second, portfolio assessment involves students in the design, collection, and evaluation of the materials to be included in the portfolio. Involving students in evaluating their own work encourages them to be more metacognitive about their approaches to studying and can increase self-regulation.

The following guidelines make portfolios more effective learning tools:

- Integrate portfolios into your instruction, and refer to them as you teach.
- Provide examples of portfolios when introducing them to students.
- Involve students in the selection and evaluation of their work.
- Require students to provide an overview of each portfolio, a rationale for the inclusion of individual works, criteria they use to evaluate individual pieces, and a summary of progress.
- Provide students with frequent and detailed feedback about their decisions.

Student-led conferences can be an effective way to communicate with parents about portfolio achievements. Researchers have found that these conferences increase students' sense of responsibility and pride and improve both home–school cooperation and student–parent relationships (Stiggins & Chappuis, 2012). Time constraints and logistics are obstacles to full-scale implementation of student-led conferences, but the educational benefits of learner involvement and initiative help balance these limitations.

Portfolio assessment. The process of selecting collections of student work that both students and teachers evaluate using preset criteria.

Table 14.3	Portfolio samples in different content areas
Content Area	**Example**
Elementary Math	Homework, quizzes, tests, and projects completed over time.
Writing	Drafts of narrative, descriptive, and persuasive essays in various stages of development. Samples of poetry.
Art	Projects over the course of the year collected to show growth in an area perspective or in a medium painting.
Science	Lab reports, projects, classroom notes, quizzes, and tests compiled to provide an overview of learning progress.

Evaluating Formal Assessment Formats

Each type of formal assessment format—paper-and-pencil items, performance assessments, and portfolios—is controversial in different ways. For instance, critics of paper-and-pencil items argue that they focus on low-level knowledge and skills, fail to measure learners' ability to apply understanding in the real world, and measure only outcomes, so these assessments provide no insight into students' thinking (Solley, 2007). Advocates of performance and portfolio assessment contend that these formats tap higher-level thinking and problem-solving skills, emphasize real-world applications, and focus on the processes learners use to produce their products (DiMartino & Castaneda, 2007). However, education is in an era of accountability, and multiple-choice, often combined with a writing component, is by far the most common format used on high-stakes tests. Faced with the demands of standards-based accountability, you will feel pressure to prepare your students for these tests.

Reliability is also an issue with performance assessments and portfolios, and, in practice, obtaining acceptable levels of reliability has been a problem (Barnes, Torrens, & George, 2007; Tillema & Smith, 2007). In response to these issues, several states have reduced their use of portfolios, particularly for English language learners (Zehr, 2006).

At the classroom level, allowing students to determine portfolio content creates additional problems. For example, when students choose different items to place in their portfolios, cross-student comparisons are difficult, which decreases reliability. To address this issue, experts recommend supplementing portfolios with traditional measures to obtain the best of both processes (Stiggins & Chappuis, 2012).

As with all aspects of learning and teaching, assessment is complex, and your knowledge, skill, and professional judgment will be crucial in designing assessments that will maximize learning in your students.

---

check your understanding

3.1   Identify differences between formal assessment and informal assessment.

3.2   Each of the following items has flaws in them that might allow students to identify the correct answer without fully understanding the content. Identify the flaw in each case.

---

1. Which of the following is a function of the circulatory system?
   a. to support the vital organs of the body
   *b. to circulate the blood throughout the body
   c. to transfer nerve impulses from the brain to the muscles
   d. to provide for the movement of the body's large muscles
2. Of the following, the definition of *population density* is:
   a. the number of people who live in your city or town.
   b. the number of people who voted in the last presidential election.
   *c. the number of people per square mile in a country.
   d. the number of people in cities compared to small towns.
3. Of the following, the most significant cause of World War II was:
   a. American aid to Great Britain.
   b. Italy's conquering of Ethiopia.
   c. Japan's war on China.
   *d. the devastation of the German economy as a result of the Treaty of Versailles.

4. Which of the following is the best description of an insect?
   a. It always has one pair of antennae on its head.
   *b. It has three body parts.
   c. None lives in water.
   d. It breathes through lungs.
5. The one of the following that is not a reptile is a:
   a. alligator.
   b. lizard.
   *c. frog.
   d. turtle.
6. Which of the following illustrates a verb form used as a participle?
   a. Running is good exercise.
   *b. I saw a jumping frog contest on TV yesterday.
   c. Thinking is hard for many of us.
   d. All of the above.

3.3   Describe how you would create a rating scale to assess someone's performance in creating high-quality multiple-choice test items. Provide an example.

3.4   Are essay items performance assessments? Defend your answer using the information from this section.

To receive feedback for these questions, go to Appendix A.

Classroom *connections*

Creating Valid and Reliable Classroom Assessments

1. Validity describes the extent to which an assessment measures what it is supposed to measure. Increase validity through careful planning before assessment.

   ■ **Elementary:** A third-grade teacher compares items on her quizzes, tests, and graded homework to the standards in the curriculum guide and the objectives in her unit plan to be sure all the appropriate objectives are covered.

   ■ **Middle School:** A social studies teacher writes a draft of one test item at the end of each day to be certain the emphasis on his tests is consistent with his instruction. When he puts the test together, he checks to be sure that all content areas and difficulty levels are covered.

   ■ **High School:** After composing a test, a biology teacher rereads the items to eliminate wording that might be confusing or too advanced for her students.

2. Performance assessments directly examine students' ability to perform tasks similar to those they will be expected to perform in life outside of school. Increase the validity of your assessments by using performance assessment when appropriate.

   ■ **Elementary:** A first-grade teacher uses a rating scale to assess his students' oral reading ability. While he listens to each student read, he uses additional notes to help him remember each student's strengths and weaknesses.

   ■ **Middle School:** A math teacher working on decimals and percentages brings in store ads from three local supermarkets and asks students to compare prices on five household items. Students must determine which store provided the best bargains and the percentage difference between the stores on each item.

   ■ **High School:** A teacher in business technology has students write letters in response to job notices in the newspaper. The class then critiques the letters in terms of format, grammar, punctuation, and clarity.

3. Portfolio assessments involve students in the assessment process. Use portfolios to develop learner self-regulation.

   ■ **Elementary:** A fourth-grade teacher uses portfolios as an organizing theme for his language arts curriculum. Students collect pieces of work during the year and evaluate and share them with other members of their writing teams.

   ■ **Middle School:** A math teacher asks each student to compile a portfolio of work and present it at parent–teacher conferences. Before the conference, the teacher meets with students and helps them identify their strengths and weaknesses.

   ■ **High School:** An auto mechanics teacher makes each student responsible for keeping track of the competencies and skills each has mastered. Each student is given a folder and must document the completion of different shop tasks.

Effective Assessment Practices

To this point, we have examined basic assessment concepts such as validity and reliability as well as informal and formal assessment using different formats. To maximize learning, however, you will need to combine individual items into tests, include performance assessments and portfolios where appropriate, administer and score assessments, and analyze and discuss assessment results. In this section we offer suggestions for completing these tasks as we discuss:

- Planning for assessment
- Preparing students
- Administering assessments
- Analyzing results

Planning for Assessment

As with all aspects of teaching, planning is essential for effective assessment. To ensure that your assessments are aligned with your learning objectives, you should think about your assessments as you plan for instruction. Teachers commonly wait to prepare assessments until after they completed a chapter or unit of instruction, and, as a result, they might give little emphasis to a topic in class but have several items on a quiz related to it, or emphasize a topic in class but give it minimal coverage on a quiz. Also, teachers often emphasize application in learning activities but write test items that merely require recall of factual information. Doing so reduces the validity of the assessments.

Tables of Specifications: Increasing Validity Through Planning

Table of specifications. A matrix that helps teachers organize learning objectives by cognitive level or content area and links instruction and assessment to objectives and standards.

A **table of specifications** is a matrix that helps you organize your learning objectives by cognitive level or content area and links instruction and assessment to objectives and standards. Preparing a table of specifications is one way to ensure that learning objectives and assessments are aligned (Notar, Zuelke, Wilson, & Yunker, 2004). For example, a geography teacher based her instruction in a unit on the Middle East on the following list of objectives:

Understands location of cities

1. Identifies locations of major cities
2. Explains historical factors in settlements

Understands climate

1. Identifies major climate regions
2. Explains factors that influence existing climates

Understands influence of physical features

1. Describes topography
2. Relates physical features to climate
3. Explains impact of physical features on location of cities
4. Analyzes impact of physical features on economy

Understands factors influencing economy

1. Describes economies of countries in the region
2. Identifies major characteristics of each economy
3. Explains how economies relate to climate and physical features

Table 14.4 contains a table of specifications for a content-level matrix based on these objectives. The teacher had a mix of items, with greater emphasis on physical features than other topics. This emphasis reflects the teacher's objectives, which stressed the influence of physical features on the location of cities, the climate, and the economy of the region. It also reflects the time and effort spent on each area. A table of specifications such as this increases validity by ensuring a match between objectives, instruction, and assessment.

For performance assessments, establishing criteria serves a function similar to that of a table of specifications. The criteria identify the performance, determine emphasis, and help ensure congruence between learning objectives and assessments.

Table 14.4   Sample table of specifications

Content	Outcomes			
	Knowledge	Comprehension	Higher-Order Thinking and Problem Solving	Total Items in Each Content Area
Cities	4	2	2	8
Climate	4	2	2	8
Economy	2	2	—	4
Physical features	4	9	7	20
Total items	14	15	11	—

This information addresses the questions we asked in "Ed Psych and You" at the beginning of this section. We've all experienced the frustration of trying to prepare for a test but not knowing how to study because we didn't know what would be on it. Effective assessment should not be a guessing game between us and our students. They should know what is expected of them, so they know how to study and prepare. We eliminate any guesswork by being clear about our objectives and ensuring that assessments are aligned with them. Using the objectives listed previously, for instance, geography students know that they need to know the locations of major cities, understand the causes of the climates in the Middle East, and how the economies of the countries relate to the climates and physical features of each. Now, they know how to study.

Preparing Students for Assessments

Preparing students for assessments is important for validity because we want our assessments to accurately reflect what students actually know and can do. To illustrate this idea, let's look again at DeVonne's work with her students the day before she gives her unit test.

"Get out your chalkboards," she directs, referring to individual chalkboards each student has to show their work on math problems.

"We're having a test tomorrow on finding equivalent fractions and adding fractions, and the test will go in your math portfolios. . . . I have some problems on the test that are going to make you think. . . . But you've all been working hard, and we've been practicing, and you're getting good at this, so you'll be able to do it. You're my team, and I know you'll come through," she smiles.

"To be sure we're okay, I have a few problems that are just like ones on the test, so let's see how we do. Write these on your chalkboards."

$$\frac{1}{3} + \frac{1}{4} = ? \qquad \frac{2}{7} + \frac{4}{7} = ?$$

DeVonne watches as they work on the problems and hold up their chalkboards when they finish. Seeing that three students miss the first problem, she reviews it with the class, and then displays the following three:

$$\frac{2}{3} + \frac{1}{6} = ? \qquad \frac{4}{9} + \frac{1}{6} = ? \qquad \frac{2}{9} + \frac{4}{9} = ?$$

Two students miss the second one, so again she reviews it carefully.

"Now, let's try one more," she continues, displaying the following problem on the overhead:

You are at a pizza party with 5 other people, and you order 2 pizzas. The 2 pizzas are the same size, but one is cut into 4 pieces and the other is cut into 8 pieces. You eat 1 piece from each pizza. How much pizza did you eat in all?

Again, she watches the students work and reviews the solution with them when they finish, asking questions such as "What information in the problem is important?" "What do we see in the problem that's irrelevant?" and "What should we do first in solving it?" in the process.

After discussing two more word problems, she tells students, "The problems on the test are like the ones we practiced here today," asks if they have any additional questions, and finishes her review by saying, "All right, when we take a test, what do we always do?"

"We read the directions carefully!" they shout in unison.

"Okay, good," DeVonne smiles. "Now, remember, what will you do if you get stuck on a problem?"

"Go on to the next one so we don't run out of time."

"And what will we be sure not to do?"

"We won't forget to go back to the one we skipped."

In preparing students for tests, we have both long-term and short-term goals. Long term, we want our students to develop effective test-taking strategies and enter testing situations with confidence. Short term, we want them to understand the format and the content being tested. Preparing students helps reach both of these goals.

Teaching Test-Taking Strategies

You can help your students improve their test-taking skills by teaching them the following strategies:

- Read directions carefully.
- Use time efficiently and pace themselves.
- Identify the important information in questions.
- Understand the demands of different testing formats.
- Determine how questions will be scored.

To be most effective, you should explicitly teach these strategies and illustrate them with concrete examples. Students also need practice with a variety of formats and testing situations. Research indicates that strategy instruction improves performance and that young, low-ability students and students who are minorities or who have limited test-taking experience benefit the most (Pressley & Hilden, 2006).

Reducing Test Anxiety

Think about the questions we ask in "Ed Psych and You" here. If you answered yes to the first two questions—and most of us have had this experience—you experienced classic **test anxiety,** an unpleasant emotional reaction to testing situations that can lower performance. Usually, it is momentary and minor, but for a portion of the school population (estimates run as high as 10%), it can be a serious problem (Putwain, 2007; Whitaker, Lowe, & Lee, 2007).

Test anxiety is triggered by testing situations that (1) involve pressure to succeed, (2) are perceived as difficult, (3) impose time limits, and (4) contain unfamiliar items or formats (Schunk et al., 2008). Unannounced quizzes and tests are particularly powerful triggers for test anxiety.

Research suggests that test anxiety consists of both an emotional and a cognitive component (Schunk et al., 2008). Its emotional component can lead to physiological symptoms, such as increased pulse rate, dry mouth, upset stomach and headache, as well as feelings of dread and helplessness and sometimes "going blank." Its cognitive, or worry, component involves preoccupation with test difficulty, thoughts of failure and other concerns, such as parents being upset by a low score. These thoughts take up working memory space, which leaves less time and energy to think about specific items.

Now, let's look again at the third question we asked in "Ed Psych and You," "What can you do about it?" The most effective way to deal with test anxiety is to study and prepare to the point that your understanding is so thorough that you succeed in spite of feeling nervous. Students, including those in college, often fail to study as thoroughly as necessary, and they tend to believe they understand a topic better than they do (Bembenutty, 2009). As a result their anxiety spikes when they're faced with a test, and particularly if the test measures understanding beyond recall of factual information. On the other hand, if we thoroughly understand the content, some anxiety can actually increase performance (Bembenutty, 2009).

In addition, an interesting piece of research published in 2011 suggests that simply writing about worries a few minutes before taking a test unloads anxieties and frees working memory space that can then be devoted to the test itself (Ramirez, & Beilock, 2011).

As teachers we can do much to reduce test anxiety in our students, and the most successful efforts focus on the worry component (Schunk et al., 2008). Suggestions include:

- Discuss test content and procedures before testing, and give clear directions for responding to test items.
- Give more, rather than fewer, quizzes and tests to lessen the effects of any one assessment.
- Use criterion measures to minimize the competitive aspects of tests, and avoid social comparisons, such as public displays of test scores. (We discuss criterion referencing in the next section.)
- Teach test-taking skills, and give students ample time to take tests.
- Use a variety of assessments to provide opportunities for students to demonstrate their understanding and skills.

Let's look now at specific test-preparation procedures.

Ed Psych and You

Have you ever felt that you were prepared for a big test and "blanked" when you turned it over? Have you ever felt like you knew the test content but did not do well on it because of being nervous? What can you do about it?

Test anxiety. An unpleasant emotional reaction to testing situations that can lower performance.

Teachers can reduce test anxiety by increasing the number of assessments and by providing clear explanations of content.

Specific Test-Preparation Procedures

Before any test, you'll want to ensure that your students understand test content and procedures as thoroughly as possible and expect to succeed on the exam. To reach these goals you can:

- Specify what will be on the test.
- Give students a chance to practice similar items under test-like conditions.
- Establish positive expectations and encourage students to link effort and success.

Clarifying test formats and content provides structure for students, which reduces test anxiety. Knowing what will be on the test and how items will be formatted leads to higher achievement for all students and particularly those who are struggling with the content.

Specifying test content often isn't enough, however, particularly with young learners, so giving students practice exercises and presenting them in a format that parallels their appearance on the test is important. In learning math skills, for instance, DeVonne's students first practiced adding fractions with like denominators, then learned to find equivalent fractions, and finally added fractions with unlike denominators, each in separate lessons. On the test, however, the problems were mixed, so DeVonne gave students a chance to practice integrating these skills before the test.

Finally, DeVonne communicated that she expected students to do well on the test. The motivational benefits of establishing positive expectations have been confirmed by decades of research (Schunk et al., 2008; Stipek, 2002). She also emphasized student effort and the role of hard work and studying on success by saying, "But you've all been working hard, and you're getting good at this, so you'll be able to do it." Encouraging students' belief that ability is changeable and not permanent and can be improved through effort benefits both immediate performance and long-term motivation.

Administering Assessments

When we administer assessments, we want to ensure as much as possible that results accurately reflect what students know and can do. To see an example, let's return to DeVonne's classroom.

At 10:00 Thursday morning, DeVonne shuts a classroom window because of noise from delivery trucks outside. She considers rearranging the desks in the room but decides to wait until after the test.

"Okay, everyone, let's get ready for our math test," she directs, as students put their books under their desks.

She waits a moment, sees that everyone's desk is clear, and says, "When you're finished, turn the test over, and I'll come and get it. Now look up at the board. After you're done, work on the assignment listed there until everyone is finished. Then we'll start reading." As she hands out the tests, she says, "If you get too warm, raise your hand, and I'll turn on the air conditioner. I shut the window because of the noise outside."

"Work carefully," she says after everyone has a copy. "You've all been working hard, and I know you will do well. You have as much time as you need."

As students begin working, DeVonne stands at the side of the room, watching them. After several minutes, she notices Anthony doodling at the top of his paper and glancing around the room. She goes over and says, "It looks like you're doing fine on these problems," pointing to some near the top of the paper. "Now concentrate a little harder. I'll bet you can do most of the others." She smiles reassuringly and again moves to the side of the room.

DeVonne goes over to Hajar in response to her raised hand. "The lead on my pencil broke, Mrs. Lampkin," she whispers.

"Take this one," DeVonne responds, handing her another. "Come and get yours after the test."

As students finish, DeVonne picks up their papers, and they begin the assignment on the board.

Now let's see how DeVonne's actions in administering the test helped maximize her students' performance. First, she arranged her classroom to be comfortable, free from distractions, and similar to the way it was when students learned the content. Distractions can depress test performance, particularly in young or struggling students.

Second, she gave specific directions for taking the test, turning in the papers, and spending time afterward. These directions helped maintain order and prevented distractions for late-finishing students.

Finally, she carefully monitored students as they worked on the test. This not only allowed her to encourage those who were distracted but also discouraged cheating. In the real world some students will cheat if given the opportunity (Bracey, 2005). However, an emphasis on learning versus performance and efforts to create a supportive learning environment decrease the likelihood of cheating (Kohn, 2007; Murdock & Anderman, 2006). In addition, external factors, such as your leaving the room, influence cheating more than whether students are inclined to do so.

In DeVonne's case, monitoring was more a form of support than of being a watchdog. For example, when she saw that Anthony was distracted, she quickly intervened, encouraged him, and urged him to increase his concentration. This encouragement is particularly important for students who are underachieving or test-anxious (Danner, 2008).

Analyzing Results

"Do you have our tests finished, Mrs. Lampkin?" students ask Friday morning.

"Of course!" she smiles, returning their papers.

"Overall, you did well, and I'm proud of you. I knew all that hard work would pay off. . . . There are a few items I want to go over, though. We had a little trouble with number 13, and you all made nearly the same mistake, so let's take a look at it."

She waits a moment while students read the problem and then asks, "Now, what are we given in the problem?. . . Saleina?"

"Mr. El had two dozen candy bars."

"Okay. Good. And how many is that?. . . Kevin?"

"Umm . . . two dozen is 24."

"Fine. And what else do we know?. . . Hajar?"

DeVonne continues the discussion of the problem and then goes over two others that were frequently missed. In the process, she makes notes at the top of her copy, identifying the problems that were difficult. She writes "Ambiguous" by one and underlines some of the wording in it. By another, she writes, "Teach them how to draw diagrams of the problem." She then puts her copy of the test in a folder, lays it on her desk to be filed, and turns back to the class.

DeVonne's assessment efforts didn't end with administering the test. She scored and returned it the next day, discussed the results, and provided students with feedback as quickly as possible. Feedback helps learners correct misconceptions, and knowledge of results increases student motivation. Because student attention is high during discussions of missed items, many teachers believe that students learn more in these sessions than they do in original instruction (Brookhart, 2007/2008).

Finally, DeVonne made notes on her copy of the test before filing it. Her notes reminded her that the wording on one of her problems was confusing, so she would need to revise it before using again. This, plus other information taken from the test, would assist her in future planning for both instruction and assessment.

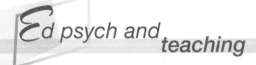

Ed psych and teaching

Increasing the Quality of Your Assessments

Assessment is one of the most important components of the teaching–learning process, but creating quality assessments is demanding. The following guidelines can help you make the assessment process as efficient as possible:

1. Create an item file of paper-and-pencil items. Use the best items from tests that are included as part of your textbook's ancillary materials, and supplement these items with items you construct yourself. E-file the items, and create future tests and quizzes from the file.
2. Provide students with detailed feedback about frequently missed paper-and-pencil items and results of performance measures.
3. Write model responses to essay items, and display them for students as part of the feedback you provide.
4. Collect all tests and quizzes after you've returned them to your students and have provided them with detailed feedback. Then, keep them on file, so you can again discuss them with students if they so desire.
5. Revise both paper-and-pencil and performance items to increase their quality.

Next we provide more detail to help you implement these guidelines.

For our first guideline, on creating paper-and-pencil assessments, keep in mind that it's impossible to continually create new assessment items at levels above recall of factual information from scratch; you simply won't have the time. However, over time you can gradually develop an item file of high-quality items and then create your individual assessments from the item file. Doing so saves you time and contributes to quality assessments. Our second guideline suggests thoroughly discussing items after assessments are returned. Items measuring learning at the application,

analysis, and evaluation of conceptual and procedural knowledge are challenging, and students will initially struggle with these items, because they won't be used to assessments at these levels. Discussing these items and receiving feedback both increases students' understanding of the content and helps them learn how to respond to higher level items. This is the essence of assessment *for* learning, and the instructional time spent on it is very worthwhile (Stiggins & Chappuis, 2012).

Third, providing model responses for essay items saves you the time of trying to provide detailed feedback to individual students. As you display the response you can identify its important features, and students can compare their responses to it.

Fourth, after giving tests and quizzes, collect them and put them on file for students, so you can reuse the items. As we said, it's impossible to continually create new high-quality test items, so you need to be able to reuse items. Keeping them on file allows students to come in and review them before end-of-quarter and semester exams. Encourage students to come in and go over their quizzes and tests.

Finally, items written above the recall of factual information will need to be interpretive exercises, and some students will misinterpret the items. Discussion and feedback will help you identify wording in your items that can be misinterpreted. You can then revise the items to make them clearer and reuse them. As a result your assessments will continually improve. This process takes time and effort, but once you have created a file of high-quality items, your assessments truly will be designed *for* learning.

check your understanding

4.1 Explain how effective assessment practices increase learning.

4.2 Creating tables of specifications for assessments is considered to be an effective assessment practice. Explain the primary purpose of a table of specifications. When should it be created?

4.3 Effective assessment practices suggest that students should be taught test-taking strategies. Identify three test-taking strategies that DeVonne emphasized with her students as she prepared them for their test.

To receive feedback for these questions, go to Appendix A.

Classroom connections

Conducting Effective Classroom Assessment Practices

1. Preparing assessments during planning for instruction helps ensure that assessments are aligned with learning objectives. Create your assessments during planning.

   ■ **Elementary:** A third-grade teacher, as part of an extended unit on reading comprehension, is planning lessons focusing on cause-and-effect relationships. As he plans, he identifies passages that he will use for practice and as the basis for assessing his students' abilities in this area.

   ■ **Middle School:** A middle-school social studies teacher is planning a unit focusing on the relationships between technological events, such as the Industrial Revolution, and changes in societies. As she plans, she writes a series of short essay questions that she will use to assess the students' understanding of the relationships.

   ■ **High School:** A geometry teacher is planning a unit on the construction of segments and angles, angle bisectors, and parallel and perpendicular lines. As he plans, he creates problems that he will use to assess his students' understanding of these processes.

2. Providing students with specific test-preparation procedures both increases achievement and decreases test anxiety. Provide students with practice on items similar to those that will appear on the assessment, and state positive expectations about their performance.

   ■ **Elementary:** The third-grade teacher gives his students reading passages and has them identify cause-and-effect relationships in the passages.

   ■ **Middle School:** The middle-school social studies teacher presents examples of responses to essay questions similar to those she plans to use for her assessment. With her guidance, students identify both well-written and poorly written responses and explain differences between the two.

   ■ **High School:** The geometry teacher has his students practice creating constructions similar to those that they will have to prepare on the assessment.

3. Feedback and discussion of assessment items increases students' understanding of the topics they are studying. Provide detailed feedback on frequently missed items.

   ■ **Elementary:** The third-grade teacher returns students' papers and discusses each of the items in detail.

   ■ **Middle School:** The social studies teacher creates ideal responses to the essay items and helps the students identify the characteristics that made those responses ideal.

   ■ **High School:** The geometry teacher demonstrates how each of the constructions of the items on the test could be created. He guides a discussion of alternate ways the constructions could be accomplished.

Grading and Reporting: The Total Assessment System

To this point, we have discussed formal and informal assessment and the assessment process itself, which includes preparing students, administering assessments, and analyzing results. Designing a total assessment system raises additional questions, such as:

- Should I give grades to all assignments and quizzes, or use some primarily for feedback?
- How many tests and quizzes should I give?
- How will I use performance assessments?
- How will I count homework?
- How will I assess and report affective dimensions, such as cooperation and effort?

Making the decisions that answer these questions will be your responsibility, a prospect that may seem daunting, because you have little experience to fall back on. However, knowing that the decisions are yours removes some of this uncertainty. We discuss these issues in this section.

Formative and Summative Assessment

Although we often think that the purpose of giving tests and quizzes is to assign grades, its most important function is to provide information about learning progress (Stiggins & Chappuis, 2012). Assessment *for* learning includes diagnosing students' existing understanding, assessing their learning progress, and providing feedback. You will often use assessments to increase learning but not include the results in decisions about grading, a process called **formative assessment** (Popham, 2011b).

Virtually all forms of informal assessment are formative. For example, when you use students' responses to questions to provide feedback in a learning activity, the primary purpose is to promote learning and clear up misconceptions, rather grading students. Pretests, work samples, and writing assignments that can be rewritten are other common forms of formative assessment. Providing students with feedback, which is essential for increasing motivation and helping students learn to monitor their own progress, is its primary purpose. In this respect, formative assessment is a form of instructional scaffolding that assists students during learning (Shepard, 2005).

Summative assessment is the process of assessing after instruction and using the results for grading decisions. Although used for grading, feedback on summative assessments is as essential as it is with formative assessments, and summative assessments can also be effective for promoting learning. In classrooms, most assessments are used for summative purposes; however, used properly, both formative and summative assessments can be useful for making instructional decisions and increasing student motivation.

Formative assessment. The process of using assessments to provide students with feedback about learning progress, but not using the assessment information to make decisions about grading.

Summative assessment. The process of using assessment results for making grading decisions.

Designing a Grading System

An effective grading system provides feedback to students, helps them develop self-regulation, and can increase motivation. It also aids communication between teachers and parents. The following guidelines can help you design an effective grading system in your own classroom:

- Create a system that is clear, understandable, and consistent with school and district policies.
- Design your system to support learning and instruction by gathering frequent and systematic information from each student.
- Base grades on observable data.
- Assign grades consistently regardless of gender, class, race, or socioeconomic status.

You should be able to confidently defend your system to a parent or administrator if necessary (M. Miller et al., 2009).

Ed Psych and You

Do you want to know the criteria for an A, B, and so on at the beginning of the term? After taking a test, do you want to know how you did compared to the other students in your class?

Norm-Referenced and Criterion-Referenced Grading Systems

Assigning value to students' work is an integral part of assessment. Norm-referenced and criterion-referenced systems are two ways to assign value to student performance. When **norm-referenced grading** is used, assessment decisions are based on an individual's performance compared to the performance of peers. The following is an example of a norm-referenced system:

A   Top 15% of students

B   Next 20% of students

C   Next 30% of students

D   Next 20% of students

F   Last 15% of students

Norm-referenced grading. A grading system in which teachers base assessment decisions about an individual's performance on comparisons to the performance of peers.

When using **criterion-referenced grading,** you make assessment decisions according to a predetermined standard, such as 90–100 for an A, 80–89 for a B, and so on. The specific standards vary among school districts, and even schools. They are often established by the school or district, but in some cases the decision will be yours.

Criterion-referenced systems have two important advantages over norm-referenced ones (Stiggins & Chappuis, 2012). First, because they reflect the extent to which learning objectives are met, they more accurately describe content mastery, an important consideration in this era of accountability. Second, they deemphasize competition. Competitive grading systems can discourage students from helping each other, threaten peer relationships, and decrease motivation to learn. While norm-referencing is important in standardized testing, it is rarely used in classroom assessment systems.

This section addresses the questions we asked in "Ed Psych and You" in this section. If you're like most students, you will want to know the criteria for earning grades at the beginning of the semester. On the other hand, while we don't want to openly compete with our classmates, most of us want to know how we've done on a quiz or test compared to others in the class. So, we prefer explicit criterion-referenced assessment systems, but we retain a tendency to compare our performance to others.

Paper-and-Pencil and Performance Assessments

For those of you who will teach in upper elementary, middle, and high schools, paper-and-pencil assessments will likely be the cornerstones of your grading system. Some teachers add tests and quizzes together and count them as a certain percentage of the overall grade; others weigh them differently in assigning grades.

If you're using performance assessments or portfolios as part of your assessment system, you should include them in determining grades. To do otherwise communicates that they are less important than the paper-and-pencil measures you're using. If you rate student performance on the basis of well-defined criteria, scoring will have acceptable reliability, and performance assessments and/or portfolios can then be an integral part of your total assessment system.

Homework

Properly designed homework contributes to learning, but to be most effective, you must collect, score, and include homework in your grading system. Students, and particularly older students, tend to exert little effort on homework for which they receive no credit (H. Cooper et al., 2006; Marzano, 2007). Beyond this point, however, research provides little guidance as to how you should manage homework. Accountability, feedback, and your own workload will all influence this decision. Table 14.5 outlines some homework-assessment options.

As you can see, each option has advantages and disadvantages. The best strategy is one that results in learners making the most consistent and conscientious effort on their homework without costing you an inordinate amount of time and effort.

Assigning Grades: Increasing Learning and Motivation

Having made decisions about paper-and-pencil and performance assessments, portfolios, and homework, you are now ready to design your total grading system. At this point, you need to make two decisions: (1) what to include and (2) the weight to assign each component.

In addition to paper-and-pencil assessments, performance measures, and homework, some teachers include affective factors, such as effort, class participation, and attitude. Assessment experts discourage this practice, although it is common in classrooms (M. Miller et al., 2009). Gathering systematic information about affective variables is difficult, and assessing them is highly subjective. In addition, a high grade based on effort suggests to both students

Criterion-referenced grading. A grading system in which you make assessment decisions according to a predetermined standard.

Table 14.5 Homework-assessment options

Option	Advantages	Disadvantages
Grade it yourself	Promotes learning. Allows diagnosis of students. Increases student effort.	Is very demanding for the teacher.
Grade samples	Reduces teacher work, compared with first option.	Doesn't give the teacher a total picture of student performance.
Collect at random intervals	Reduces teacher workload.	Reduces student effort unless homework is frequently collected.
Change papers, students grade	Provides feedback with minimal teacher effort.	Consumes class time. Doesn't give students feedback on their own work.
Students score own papers	Also provides feedback with minimum teacher effort. Lets students see their own mistakes.	Is inaccurate for purposes of evaluation. Lets students not do the work and copy in class as it's being discussed.
Students get credit for completing assignment	Gives students feedback on their work when it's discussed in class.	Reduces effort of unmotivated students.
No graded homework, frequent short quizzes	Is effective with older and motivated students.	Reduces effort of unmotivated students.

and parents that important content was learned when it may not have been. Factors such as effort, cooperation, and class attendance should be reflected in a separate section of the report card.

Let's look at two teachers' systems for assigning grades:

Kim Sook (Middle school science)		Lea DeLong (High school algebra)	
Tests and quizzes	50%	Tests	45%
Homework	20%	Quizzes	45%
Performance assessment	20%	Homework	10%
Projects	10%		

We see that these two grading systems are quite different. Kim, an eighth-grade physical science teacher, emphasizes both homework and **alternative assessments,** which include projects and performance assessments. Traditional tests and quizzes count only 50% in his system. Lea emphasizes tests and quizzes more heavily; they count 90% in her system. The rationale in each case is simple. Kim, an experienced middle school teacher, believes that homework is important to student learning, and has found that unless it is emphasized, students won't do it. He also includes projects as an important part of his system, believing they involve his students in the study of science. He uses performance assessments to chart students' progress as they work on experiments and other lab activities. Lea, a secondary Algebra II teacher, believes that students understand the need to do their homework in

Alternative assessment. Assessment measures that include projects and performance assessment.

order to succeed on tests and quizzes, so she deemphasizes this component in her grading system. Instead, she gives a weekly quiz and three tests during a 9-week grading period.

A recent development, **standards-based grading,** targets specific standards that students have learned (Deddeh, Main, & Fulkerson, 2010). By focusing solely on mastery of content, standards-based grading eliminates factors such as effort or credit for homework. Teachers who implement this system claim that it simplifies communication with both students and parents because it specifically identifies content and skills that students have learned and provides students with clear messages about important ideas that still need additional work and effort.

To promote learning, students need to understand your assessment system. Even young students can understand the relationship between effort and grades if they are assessed frequently and if their homework is scored and returned promptly. Conversely, even high school students can have problems understanding a grading system if it is too complex.

Parents also need to understand your assessment system if they are to be involved in their children's learning (Guskey, 2002). Parent–teacher conferences and graded examples of their child's work together with report cards are valuable sources of information parents use to gauge their children's learning progress. An understandable assessment system is essential in this process.

> **Standards-based grading.** A grading system that is based on a student's mastery of specific standards.

Points or Percentages?

In assigning scores to assessments, you have two options. In a percentage system, you convert each score to a percentage and then average the percentages as the marking period progresses. In a point-based system, students accumulate raw points, and you convert them to a percentage only at the end of the marking period.

A percentage-based system has one important weakness. If a student misses 1 item on a 10-item quiz, for example, the student's score is a 90%. If you give another short quiz, and the student gets 3 of 5 items correct, the student's score on the second quiz is 60%, and the average of the two quizzes is 75%. This process gives the two quizzes equal weight, even though the first had twice as many items. The student got 12 of 15 items correct, which is 80%, so a point system more accurately reflects the student's performance.

If averaging percentages is flawed, why is it so common? The primary reason is simplicity. It is both simpler for teachers to manage and easier to communicate to students and parents. Many teachers, and particularly those in elementary and middle schools, have attempted point systems and later returned to percentages because of pressure from students.

As with most aspects of teaching, the design of a grading system is a matter of your professional judgment. A percentage system is fair if assignments are similar in length, tests are also similar in length, and tests receive more weight than quizzes and assignments. On the other hand, a point system can work if students keep a running total of their points and you tell them the number required for an A, a B, and so on at frequent points in the marking period.

Technology, Learning, and Development: Using Technology to Improve Your Assessment System

Because of its ability to store large amounts of data and process it quickly, technology is proving to be especially valuable in classroom assessment. Technology, and particularly computers, can serve three important and time-saving assessment functions (Roblyer & Doering, 2010):

- Planning and constructing tests
- Analyzing test data, especially data gathered from objective tests
- Maintaining student records

Let's look at them.

Planning and Constructing Tests

As you saw in our "Ed Psych and Teaching" feature earlier in the chapter, we advocate collecting assessments after you've given them and revising and storing the individual items to be reused in the future. Doing so will increase the quality of your assessments. And, because multiple-choice is the most common format for high-stakes tests, you will need to provide your students with practice in responding to this type of item.

You will likely have access to software programs that can assist in this process. These programs have the following capabilities:

- Develop a test file in multiple-choice and other formats that can be stored in the system. Within a file, items can be organized by topic, chapter, objective, or by difficulty.
- Revise items to eliminate misleading wording and ineffective distractors.
- Select items from the file to generate the complete assessment and create multiple versions of a test if so desired.
- Produce student-ready copies and an answer key.

You can also store model answers to essay items on your computer, which can be repeatedly used. So, once you've written a model answer, you need only revise it to make it clearer; you don't need to re-create the answer every time you use the item.

Analyzing Test Data

Once administered, tests need to be scored and analyzed. If you're a middle or high school teacher with 5 sections of 30 students and you've given a 40-item test, for example, you face an overwhelming logistical task: $5 \times 30 \times 40 = 6,000$ individual items!

Most schools now have technology that can machine-score or scan your tests if they're in multiple-choice, true–false, or matching formats, and a number of software programs exist that can machine-score tests. These programs can:

- Score objective tests and provide descriptive statistics such as mean, median, mode, range, and standard deviation.
- Identify the number of students who selected each response, the percentage of students who didn't respond to an item, and the correlation of each item with the total test.
- Sort student responses by score, grade/age, or gender.

Your school will most likely also have a technology expert who can help you with each of these tasks.

Maintaining Student Records

To be used as a tool for promoting learning, assessments need to be frequent and thorough, and you need to be able to easily access the information you gather about each student. In addition, your students need to know where they stand in the course to make the best use of their time and resources. Computers provide an efficient way of storing, analyzing, and reporting student assessments.

Let's see what one teacher has to say.

> I use an electronic gradebook in my teaching, and the program allows me to set it up either by total points or percentages. It also allows me to decide the amount of weight I want to assign to tests, quizzes, homework, and anything else, such as projects, for students' final averages. The program is very user friendly, and it's an enormous time saver. (Nicole Yudin, Personal Communication, April 18, 2011)

Your school will have access to one or more electronic gradebook programs, and you will be provided with technical support in setting up and using this software. Paul's wife is a teacher and is self-proclaimed as "low tech." However, in spite of lacking advanced technical expertise, she comments that technology is invaluable in the assessment process. And, as it continues to improve, it will become an even more useful tool to make your teaching more efficient.

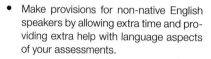

Exploring diversity

Effective Assessment Practices with Students from Diverse Backgrounds

Learner diversity influences teaching and learning in a number of ways, and the process of assessment is one of the most important.

The current reform movement, with its emphasis on standards and the achievement of all students, has heightened awareness of the problem of educating students from diverse backgrounds. The problem is particularly acute in urban settings, where diversity is the most pronounced (Macionis & Parillo, 2010).

Student diversity influences classroom assessment in three important ways. First, learners from diverse backgrounds may lack experience with general testing procedures, different test formats, and test-taking strategies. Second, because most assessments are strongly language based, language may be an obstacle (Solorzano, 2008). Third, learners may not fully understand that assessments promote learning and instead view them as punitive. The following recommendations respond to these issues (Popham, 2011a):

- Attempt to create a learning-focused classroom, in which you emphasize that assessments are used to promote learning, provide feedback, and measure learning progress.

- Increase the number and frequency of assessments, and provide detailed and corrective feedback for all items. Encourage students to ask questions about test items, and when they answer incorrectly, ask them to explain their answers. Emphasize that mistakes are part of learning, and continually present students with evidence of their learning progress.

- Deemphasize grades, and keep all assessment results private. Establish a rule that students may not share their scores and grades with each other. (This is impossible to enforce, but as a symbolic gesture it attempts to protect students who want to succeed but face peer pressure not to.)

- Drop one or two quizzes a marking period for purposes of grading. This practice reduces test anxiety and communicates to students

that you are "on their side" and want them to succeed. It also contributes to a positive classroom climate.

- Make provisions for non-native English speakers by allowing extra time and providing extra help with language aspects of your assessments.

Of these suggestions, feedback and discussion are the most beneficial. While important in all environments, they are essential for effective assessment with learners from diverse backgrounds. In many cases, students' explanations for their answers can reveal misconceptions, which you can then address. In addition, feedback can help you identify content bias in your questions (Popham, 2011a). For example, some students may have limited experiences with electrical appliances such as an iron or vacuum cleaner, summertime activities such as camping and hiking, or musical instruments like a banjo. If assessment items require knowledge or experiences with these ideas, you are measuring both the intended topic and students' general knowledge, which detracts from validity. The only way to identify these potential sources of bias is to discuss assessment items afterward. Then, you can revise and more carefully word your assessments to help eliminate bias.

The possibility of content bias is even more likely if you have nonnative English speakers in your classes. Suggestions for supporting these students include the following (Solorzano, 2008; Wright, 2006):

- Provide extra time to take tests.

- Allow a translation glossary or dictionary to be used during the test.

- Read directions aloud. (It is even better if you can read the students the directions in their native languages.)

- Allow them to take the test at a different time, and read it to them, clarifying misunderstandings where possible.

Detailed feedback on assessments is important for all students, and particularly for members of cultural minorities.

Learners with exceptionalities pose special grading challenges; research indicates that large numbers of these students receive below-average grades in their general education classes (Heward, 2009). The effects of these low grades can be devastating to students who already experience frustration in attempting to keep up with their peers. In addition, federal legislation in the form of the Individuals with Disabilities Education Act (IDEA) mandates that schools make appropriate accommodations for students with physical, mental, social, or emotional disabilities. This requirement applies to both instruction as well as assessment practices.

To address this problem, teachers often adapt their grading systems by grading on improvement, assigning separate grades for process and for products, and basing a grade on meeting the objectives of an individualized education program (IEP). The dilemma for teachers is how to increase motivation to learn while providing an accurate indicator of learning progress (Vaughn & Bos, 2009).

The primary function of assessment in general, and with diverse learners in particular, is to provide evidence of increasing competence. And, evidence of learning progress can then be an important source of motivation to learn. The accommodations you make in your own classroom to help learners perform at the highest levels on your assessments will exert a powerful influence on how your students view themselves as well as your classroom.

---

check your
understanding

5.1 Describe the components and decisions involved in designing a total assessment system.

5.2 Describe differences between formative and summative assessment.

5.3 Describe the advantages and disadvantages of a percentage compared to a point system for grading.

To receive feedback for these questions, go to Appendix A.

Classroom connections

Designing Effective Classroom Assessment Systems

1. Formative assessment is used primarily to provide feedback to students; summative assessments are used for grading. Use both to promote learning in your assessment system.

   ■ **Elementary:** A second-grade teacher discusses math problems that several students missed on their homework and then asks them to rework the problems. If students are still having problems with the content, she re-teaches it before she gives them a graded assessment.

   ■ **Middle School:** A sixth-grade science teacher has created and e-filed an item pool. He uses some of the items to create a "practice test," which the class discusses immediately after they've taken it. He then uses additional items on a summative assessment.

   ■ **High School:** A tenth-grade English teacher provides extensive individual comments on students' papers. In addition, he identifies problem areas common to the whole class and uses anonymous selections from students' papers to discuss and provide feedback to the whole class.

2. Frequent and thorough assessments, combined with feedback, promote learning. Design your assessment system so that gathering systematic information from each student is part of your routines.

   ■ **Elementary:** A second-grade teacher has his students solve two problems each morning that focus on the previous day's math topic. The class discusses the solutions before he moves to the topic for the day.

   ■ **Middle School:** A geography teacher gives a weekly quiz and three tests during each 9-week grading period with the majority of the items written above the recall of factual information level. She provides detailed feedback on each of the items and then collects the quizzes and tests, so she can reuse the items.

   ■ **High School:** A history teacher gives at least one quiz a week in which students must respond to items such as: "Before the Civil War the South was primarily agricultural rather than industrial. Explain how this might have influenced the outcome of the Civil War." The day after each quiz, she displays an ideal answer to the item and a second, lower-quality response, and the class discusses differences between the two.

3. Effective grading systems are understandable to both students and their parents. Create a grading system that is understandable and consistent with school policies.

   ■ **Elementary:** A fourth-grade teacher's school uses a 70–79, 80–89, and 90–100 grading system for a C, B, and A, respectively. She explains the system in a letter to her students' parents, and routinely sends home packets of student papers that indicate the students' learning progress.

   ■ **Middle School:** A math teacher displays his grading system on a wall chart. He explains the system and what it requires of students. He emphasizes that it is designed to promote learning and returns to the chart periodically to remind students of their learning progress.

   ■ **High School:** A history teacher in a school with high percentages of minority students takes extra time and effort during parent–teacher conferences to explain how she arrives at grades for her students. She saves students' work samples and shares them with parents during conferences.

Developmentally appropriate practice

Assessment of Learning with Students at Different Ages

While many aspects of assessment, such as aligning assessments with learning objectives, attempting to ensure that they are valid and reliable, and using them to promote learning, apply at all developmental levels, important differences exist. The following paragraphs outline suggestions for responding to these differences.

Working with Students in Early Childhood Programs and Elementary Schools

Young children are just learning to play the school game, and assessment is often one of its more puzzling aspects (Berk, 2010). They come from environments where play and informal social interaction are integral parts of their daily lives, and sit-down formal assessments are often foreign to them.

This suggests that informal assessments such as systematic observation, checklists, and rating scales can be used to provide valuable sources of information about achievement. In addition, performance assessments that gauge young students' abilities to perform tasks such as counting and classifying are also useful. When formal assessments are used, structure and support in the form of detailed directions and ample opportunities to practice with immediate feedback will be necessary.

In addition to gathering accurate information about progress in learning and development, one of our major assessment goals at the P–K level should be to begin the process of helping students understand how effort and assessment influence learning. Motivation to learn is starting to crystallize at this early age, and positive experiences with assessment tasks can lay a firm foundation for future classroom learning (Schunk et al., 2008).

Lower elementary grades strongly emphasize reading and math, and performance assessments are widely used. For example, first graders are asked to identify sounds of vowels and consonant diagraphs in printed words, decode words, and print letters. In math, they are asked to write numbers, order whole numbers up to 100 or more, and represent numbers on a number line. Each task suggests a performance assessment.

Informal assessment and assessment of affective outcomes, such as "Gets along well with others" are also more prominent in elementary report cards than with older students. Because of these emphases, being aware of the possibility that assessments may be unreliable or invalid is important. Attempting to gather the same information from all students and increasing the frequency of assessments are important when assessing young children's knowledge and skills.

Working with Students in Middle Schools

The cognitive demands on middle school students increase significantly, and teachers use paper-and-pencil assessments to a much greater degree than elementary teachers. For example, in social studies, eighth graders are expected to understand ideas such as the ways in which architecture, language, and beliefs have been transmitted from one culture to another; in science they are expected to understand the difference between weight and mass, and the relationships between the temperature and the motion of particles; in math they are expected to solve systems of linear equations; and in language arts they are expected to understand literary devices, such as meter and figurative language.

These are all abstract ideas, and instructional alignment is the key to effective assessment of these topics. If topics are taught in the abstract, they won't be meaningful to students, and the students will memorize what they can in order to perform acceptably on the assessments. Instruction that includes high-quality examples and a great deal of discussion is necessary to make the topics meaningful. Then, assessments that also employ examples, such as the interpretive exercise in Figure 14.3, are effective for promoting learning.

Working with Students in High Schools

Standards for high school students typically require a great deal of abstract thinking. For instance, in language arts they are expected to understand how strategies such as hyperbole, rhetorical questioning, and glittering generalities are used as persuasive techniques; in science they are required to understand atomic theory, and in social studies they are asked to understand why ancient civilizations such as those in Mesopotamia, Egypt, and the Indus Valley evolved and were successful. As with middle school students, unless these topics are meaningfully taught, students will try memorizing enough information to survive assessments, and then information will be promptly forgotten. To make the information meaningful, teachers need to use a variety of ways to represent topics, such as vignettes, timelines, and artifacts in history, and well-designed models and simulations in science. If the topics are meaningfully taught, and assessments are aligned with the instruction, assessment *for* learning can be accomplished.

Summary

1. Describe assessment *for* learning, and explain how validity and reliability are related to it.
   - Assessment *for* learning makes assessment an integral part of the teaching–learning process, designed to support and increase learning.
   - All forms of assessment must be valid, meaning that they measure what they're supposed to measure.
   - All forms of assessment must also be reliable, meaning they produce consistent assessment results. Assessments that are unreliable cannot be valid.

2. Describe informal assessment, and explain how it is an important part of assessment *for* learning.
   - Informal assessment is the process of gathering information and making decisions during learning activities and other classroom activities.
   - Informal assessment is essential for the many instructional decisions that teachers make each day, such as how quickly to move a learning activity, who to call on, what questions to ask, how long students should be given to respond, and many others. Without informal assessment, making these decisions would be impossible.

3. Identify differences between formal and informal assessment, and analyze formal assessment items.
   - Informal assessment is the process of gathering information and making decisions during learning activities and other classroom activities. Formal assessment is the process of systematically gathering the same kind of information from each student.
   - Paper-and-pencil items, performance assessments, and portfolios can all be used as formal assessments.
   - Formal assessments can be analyzed using specific criteria that exist for each assessment format.

4. Explain how effective assessment practices increase student learning.
   - Teachers use effective assessment practices when they design assessments that are congruent with learning objectives and instruction, communicate what will be covered on assessments, allow students to practice on items similar to those that will appear on tests, teach test-taking skills, and express positive expectations for student performance.
   - Effective assessment practices also include attempts to reduce test anxiety, such as increasing testing frequency, using criterion referencing, providing clear information about tests, and giving students ample time.
   - Effective assessment practices increase learning by making expectations clear, providing students with opportunities to practice, and providing detailed feedback.

5. Describe the components and decisions involved in designing a total assessment system.
   - A total assessment system includes creating traditional and alternative assessments, preparing students, administering assessments, analyzing results, and assigning grades.
   - Decisions involved in designing a total assessment system include the number of tests and quizzes; the uses of alternative assessments; the level of assessment items, such as knowledge, application, or analysis; the role of homework in assigning grades; and the assessment and reporting of affective dimensions, such as cooperation and effort.

Understanding Effective Assessment Practices: Preparing For Your Licensure Exam

Your licensure exam will include information related to classroom assessment, and we include the following exercises to help you practice for the exam in your state. This book and these exercises will be a resource for you as you prepare for the exam.

At the beginning of the chapter, you saw how DeVonne Lampkin used assessment to help increase her students' achievement.

Let's look now at Ron Hawkins, an urban middle school English teacher, who is involved in assessing his students' understanding of pronoun cases. Read the case study, and answer the questions that follow.

"Today we're going to begin studying pronoun cases," Ron announces as he starts the lesson.

"Everybody turn to page 484 in your text. . . . This is important in our writing because we want to be able to write and use standard English correctly, and this is one of the places where people get mixed up. So, when we're finished, you'll all be able to use pronouns correctly in your writing."

He then writes the following on the board:

Pronouns use the nominative case when they're subjects and predicate nominatives. Pronouns use the objective case when they're direct objects, indirect objects, or objects of prepositions.

"Let's review," Ron continues, briefly discussing direct and indirect objects, predicate nominatives, and objects of prepositions.

"Now let's look at some additional examples," he continues, as he displays the following sentences on the overhead:

1. Did you get the card from Esteban and (I, me)?
2. Will Meg and (she, her) run the concession stand?
3. They treat (whoever, whomever) they hire very well.
4. I looked for someone (who, whom) could give me directions to the theater.

"Okay, look at the first one. Which is correct? . . . Omar?"

"*Me.*"

"Good, Omar. How about the second one? . . . Lonnie?"

"*Her.*"

"Not quite, Lonnie. . . . Suppose I turn the sentence around and say, 'Meg and her will run the concession stand.' That doesn't sound right, does it? 'Meg and she' is a compound subject, and when we have a subject, we use the nominative case. . . . Okay?"

Lonnie nods and Ron continues, "Look at the third one. . . . Cheny?"

"I'm not sure . . . *whoever,* I guess."

"This one is a little tricky," Ron nods. "When we use *whoever* and *whomever, whoever* is the nominative case and *whomever* is the objective case. In this sentence, *whomever* is a direct object, so it is the correct form."

After he finishes, Ron gives students another list of sentences in which they are to select the correct form of the pronoun.

On Tuesday, Ron reviews the exercises the students completed for homework and discusses several additional examples that use *who, whom, whoever,* and *whomever.* He then discusses the rules for pronoun–antecedent agreement (pronouns must agree with their antecedents in gender and number). He again has students analyze examples as he did with pronoun cases.

He continues with pronouns and their antecedents on Wednesday and begins a discussion of indefinite pronouns as antecedents for personal pronouns—*anybody, either, each, one, someone*—and has students analyze examples as before.

Near the end of class on Thursday, Ron announces, "Tomorrow, we're going to have a test on this material: pronoun cases, pronouns and their antecedents, and indefinite pronouns. You have your notes, so study hard. . . . Are there any questions? . . . Good. I expect you all to do well. I'll see you tomorrow."

On Friday morning as students file into class and the bell rings, Ron picks up a stack of tests from his desk. The test consists of 30 sentences, 10 of which deal with case, 10 with antecedents, and 10 with indefinite pronouns. The final part of the test directs students to write a paragraph. The following are sample items from the test:

Part I. For each of the items below, mark A on your answer sheet if the pronoun case is correct in the sentence, and mark B if it is incorrect. If it is incorrect, supply the correct pronoun.

1. Be careful who you tell.
2. Will Renee and I be in the outfield?
3. My brother and me like water skiing.

Part II. Write the pronoun that correctly completes the sentence.

1. Arlene told us about _____ visit to the dentist to have braces put on.
2. The Wilsons planted a garden in _____ backyard.
3. Cal read the recipe and put _____ in the file.
4. Each of the girls on the team wore _____ school sweater to the game.
5. None of the brass has lost _____ shine yet.
6. Few of the boys on the team have taken _____ physicals yet.

Part III. Write a short paragraph that contains at least two examples of pronouns in the nominative case and two examples of pronouns in the objective case. (Circle and label these.) Include also at least two examples of pronouns that agree with their antecedents. Remember!! The paragraph must make sense. It cannot be just a series of sentences.

Ron watches as his students work, and seeing that 15 minutes remain in the period and that some students are only starting on their paragraphs, he announces, "You only have 15 minutes left. Watch your time and work quickly. You need to be finished by the end of the period."

He continues monitoring students, again reminding them to work quickly when 10 minutes are left and again when 5 minutes are left.

Luis, Simao, Moy, and Rudy are hastily finishing the last few words of their tests as the bell rings. Luis finally turns in his paper as Ron's fourth-period students are filing into the room.

"Here," Ron says. "This pass will get you into Mrs. Washington's class if you're late. . . . How did you do?"

"Okay, I think," Luis says over his shoulder as he scurries out of the room, "except for the last part. It was hard. I couldn't get started."

"I'll look at it," Ron says. "Scoot now."

On Monday, Ron returns the tests, saying, "Here are your papers. You did fine on the sentences, but your paragraphs need a lot of work. Why did you have so much trouble with them, when we had so much practice?"

"It was hard, Mr. Hawkins."

"Not enough time."

"I hate to write."

Ron listens patiently and then says, "Be sure you write your scores in your notebooks. . . . Okay, you have them all written down? . . . Are there any questions?"

"Number 3," Enrique requests.

"Okay, let's look at 3. It says, 'My brother and me like water skiing.' There, the pronoun is part of the subject, so it should be *I* and not *me*."

"Any others?"

A sprinkling of questions comes from around the room, and Ron responds, "We don't have time to go over all of them. I'll discuss three more."

He responds to the three students who seem to be most urgent in waving their hands. He then collects the tests and begins a discussion of adjective and adverb clauses.

Questions for Case Analysis

In answering these questions, use information from the chapter, and link your responses to specific information in the case.

1. How well were Ron's objectives, instruction, and assessment aligned? Explain specifically. What could he have done to increase curricular alignment?

2. In the section on effective assessment practices, we discussed preparing students for assessments, administering them, and analyzing results. How effectively did Ron perform each task? Describe specifically what he might have done to be more effective in these areas.

3. Ron teaches in an urban environment, so his students likely had diverse backgrounds. How effective were his teaching and assessment for urban students?

4. What were the primary strengths of Ron's teaching and assessment? What were the primary weaknesses? If you think Ron's teaching and assessment could have been improved on the basis of information in this chapter, what suggestions would you make? Be specific.

To receive feedback for these questions, go to Appendix B.

Your licensure exam will also include multiple-choice questions similar to those your instructor has given you on your quizzes and tests for this course.

Important Concepts

alternative assessment (p. 512)

assessment *for* learning (p. 482)

checklists (p. 497)

classroom assessment (p. 481)

completion (p. 492)

criterion-referenced grading (p. 511)

diagnostic assessment (p. 482)

distractors (p. 489)

essay (p. 492)

formal assessment (p. 488)

formative assessment (p. 510)

informal assessment (p. 485)

matching (p. 491)

multiple-choice (p. 489)

norm-referenced grading (p. 510)

performance assessment (p. 495)

portfolio assessment (p. 499)

rating scales (p. 497)

reliability (p. 484)

rubric (p. 493)

standards-based grading (p. 513)

stem (p. 489)

summative assessment (p. 510)

systematic observation (p. 496)

table of specifications (p. 502)

test anxiety (p. 505)

true–false items (p. 491)

validity (p. 484)

Go to Topic: Assessment in the MyEducationLab (www.myeducationlab.com) for *Educational Psychology: Windows on Classrooms*, where you can:

- Find learning outcomes for Assessment along with the national standards that connect to these outcomes.
- Complete Assignments and Activities that can help you more deeply understand the chapter content.
- Apply and practice your understanding of the core teaching skills identified in the chapter with the Building Teaching Skills and Dispositions learning units.
- Examine challenging situations and cases presented in the IRIS Center Resources.
- Access video clips of CCSSO National Teachers of the Year award winners responding to the question, "Why Do I Teach?" in the Teacher Talk section.
- See video examples included within the Study Plan that provide concrete and real-world illustrations of the topics presented in the chapter.
- Check your comprehension of the content covered in the chapter with the Study Plan. Here you will be able to take a chapter quiz, receive feedback on your answers, and then access Review, Practice, and Enrichment activities to enhance your understanding of chapter content.

MyEducationLab

Standardized Testing and Learning

classroomapplications

The following features help you apply the content of this chapter in your teaching.

Ed Psych and Teaching:
Your Role in Standardized Testing

Classroom Connections:
Using Standardized Tests Effectively in Classrooms
Eliminating Test Bias in Classrooms

Developmentally Appropriate Practice:
Standardized Testing with Learners at Different Ages

*A*ccountability is being emphasized more in education today than at any point in our nation's history, and as a result, standardized testing will be an ongoing part of your professional life. As you read the following case study, consider how standardized testing influences the work of Mike Chavez, a fourth-grade teacher, and think about how it will influence your teaching.

"Hello, Mrs. Palmer. I'm glad you could come in," Mike says, offering his hand in greeting.

"Thank you," Doris Palmer responds. "I'm a little confused by a report that was sent home with David after he took the Stanford Achievement Test."

"Well, let's take a look," Mike replies as he offers Mrs. Palmer a seat next to his desk.

"Here's what we received," Mrs. Palmer offers, and she shows Mike the chart that appears on the following page.

"I'm not sure what this information means," she continues. "For instance, it says 'Total Reading' and then this number 70. And, then there's this information in the box."

"I understand completely," Mike smiles in response. "Let me try to clarify the information. . . . First, the PR stands for percentile rank. That means he scored as well as or better than 70% of the students who took this test around the country. . . . You already know he's in our top reading group, and these results suggest that he's properly placed."

"And what about these 'percentile bands' that we see here?" she continues, pointing to the information on the paper.

		NATIONAL GRADE PERCENTILE BANDS							
NATIONAL	PR	1	10	30	50	70	90	99	
Total Reading	70					▬			
Total Math	64					▬			
Language	66					▬			
Spelling	80						▬		
Science	55				▬				
Social Science	85						▬		
Listening	40			▬					
Complete Battery	64					▬			

Source: "National Grade Percentile Bands" adapted from STANFORD ACHIEVEMENT TEST SERIES, TENTH EDITION (STANFORD 10). Copyright © 2003 by NCS Pearson, Inc. Reproduced with permission. All rights reserved.

"A percentile band shows a range in which a student's *true score* is likely to fall. Because a possibility of some measurement error always exists in a test, the test manufacturers use the percentile band to accommodate this possibility."

"Is all this testing really necessary?" Mrs. Palmer queries. "Every time we turn around, David seems to be taking another test."

"That's a good question, and a lot of people question the amount of testing that goes on in schools. . . . They do give us some valuable information, however. For example, they give us an objective, outside measure to help us understand how our students are doing compared to others around the country. And, we, the teachers, receive some additional and more detailed information about our students' performance, so the tests help us provide extra instructional support if it should be necessary. . . . Here, let me share some of this information about David with you."

We will examine this information as the chapter unfolds, and as you study, keep the following questions in mind:

1. How have standards and accountability changed standardized testing?
2. What is the purpose of standardized testing?
3. How can you use standardized tests to increase your students' learning?

Research helps us answer these and other questions. We examine this research throughout the chapter.

Accountability and Standardized Testing

A great deal has been written over the last several years about American's lack of knowledge. For example, a report from the National Assessment of Educational Progress found that only 12% of American 12th graders scored well enough to be considered "proficient" in American history (National Center for Education Statistics, 2010), a result significant enough to be covered on the national news in June of 2011 (Murray, 2011). And, *Newsweek* magazine gave 1,000 Americans the U.S. Citizenship test. Nearly 40% failed (Romano, 2011). The results are no better in science and math. For example, a survey of American adults found that slightly more than half knew how long it takes the Earth to revolve once around the Sun, and fewer than 6 of 10 realized that early humans and dinosaurs didn't live at the same time (ScienceDaily, 2009). Experts suggest that this lack of knowledge imperils our country's future, because it makes us less able to make informed political, economic, and environmental decisions (Romano, 2011).

Similar concerns are being raised at the school level. Evidence indicates that students are sometimes promoted from one grade to the next without mastering essential content and are graduating from high school without the skills needed to succeed in college or the workforce (Greene & Winters, 2006).

In response to concerns about students' lack of knowledge, educators have established academic **standards,** statements that describe what students should know or be able to do at the end of a prescribed period of study. Every state in the nation has developed standards, and currently a movement exists to implement national standards (Gewertz, 2010).

Standards-based education focuses curricula and instruction on these standards, and **accountability** is the process of requiring students to demonstrate that they have met specified standards and making teachers responsible for students' performance.

Standardized Testing

The process of accountability is where standardized testing becomes prominent. (We examine standardized tests in detail in the next section of the chapter.) Standardized testing is the mechanism used to determine if students have met the standards, and its influence is enormous. The fact that students in other industrialized countries, such as Japan and Germany, score higher than American students on these tests has alarmed leaders in our country, and reform movements that began in the early 1980s and continue today are largely due to concerns about low scores on standardized tests (Koretz, 2009).

Standardized testing is controversial (D. D. Johnson, Johnson, Farenga, & Ness, 2008; Popham, 2011a). In a given year, millions of students take state-mandated tests at a cost of more than a billion dollars annually. Many educators and parents—as you saw illustrated in Mrs. Palmer's question to Mike—feel that standardized testing is overemphasized and argue that they detract from a balanced curriculum (Heilig & Darling-Hammond, 2008; Nichols & Berliner, 2008). In addition, beginning teachers often feel inadequately prepared to deal with the new assessment roles required of them by the accountability movement (Stiggins & Chappuis, 2012).

High-Stakes Tests

High-stakes tests are standardized tests used to make important decisions that affect students, teachers, schools, and school districts (Au, 2007; M. D. Miller, Linn, & Gronlund, 2009). High-stakes tests in education are usually created at the state level; they're used to measure the extent to which students have met standards; they're given at designated grade levels, such as 5th, 8th, and 10th; and the results are used to make decisions about promotion and graduation. When students can't move to the next grade level or graduate from high school because they fail a test, for example, the "stakes" are very high, thus the term "high-stakes tests."

High-stakes testing is also controversial. Advocates claim the process helps clarify the goals of school systems, sends clear messages to students about what they should be learning, and provides the public with hard evidence about school effectiveness (Hirsch, 2006; Phelps, 2005). While conceding that teacher preparation, instructional materials, and the tests themselves need to be improved, advocates argue that the tests are the fairest and most effective means of providing a quality education for all students. More than 10 years ago, Hirsch (2000) commented: "They [standards and tests that measure achievement of the standards] are the most promising educational development in half a century" (p. 64). His view continues to summarize advocates' position today.

Critics argue that teachers spend too much class time having students practice for the tests, the curriculum is narrowed to what is being tested, and the tests don't provide a true measure of what students have learned (Nichols & Berliner, 2008). Critics also contend that cutoff scores are arbitrary, and the instruments are too crude to be used in making crucial decisions about students, teachers, and schools. In addition, the tests have had a disproportionately adverse impact on students from minority cultures, particularly those with limited proficiency in English (Viadero, 2009).

Standards. Statements that describe what students should know or be able to do at the end of a prescribed period of study.

Standards-based education. The process of focusing curricula and instruction on predetermined goals or standards.

Accountability. The process of requiring students to demonstrate that they have met specified standards and holding teachers responsible for students' performance.

High-stakes tests. Standardized tests used to make important decisions that affect students, teachers, schools, and school districts.

High-stakes tests and accountability place new pressures on both teachers and their students.

Other issues exist. For instance, because of the "high stakes" and the pressure on schools and teachers, allegations of cheating on the tests have occurred in a number of schools and school districts (Gillum & Bellow, 2011), widespread scandals have occurred (FairTest, 2005), and criminal investigations related to cheating have been conducted (Rankin, Judd, & Vogell, 2010).

These examples don't affect you directly, but other issues may. For instance, a number of states are considering legislation that will tie teacher salaries to their students' scores on high-stakes tests, which could mean that your salary may be linked to your students' test performance. As you would expect, these proposals are highly contentious (FairTest, 2009; Sawchuck, 2010).

This discussion answers the first question that we asked at the beginning of the chapter: "How have standards and accountability changed standardized testing?" The primary change is in the weight placed on standardized test results and the influence these results have on students, teachers, and schools. Students' performance on standardized tests now, or in the near future, may be used to make decisions ranging from whether they're promoted from one grade to another or allowed to graduate from high school to the amount of money you earn. This is significantly different from the way Mike Chavez used the Stanford Achievement Test; he used the results as a basis for making decisions designed to increase his students' learning.

In spite of the criticisms and contentious issues, standardized testing, and particularly high-stakes testing, is widespread and here to stay. It will be a part of your life as a teacher, and it has important implications for you. For instance, you will be expected to interpret standards, align your instruction with them, and prepare your students for high-stakes tests. And, you are likely to be held accountable for your students' performance on them.

Perhaps even more important, you must be well informed about the strengths and limitations of standardized tests. Other than students' parents or other caregivers, you are the person most important in determining the quality of students' education, and the better informed you are, the more able you will be to make the best professional decisions possible.

We turn now to a more detailed discussion of standardized tests.

---

check your understanding

1.1 Describe the relationship between standards-based education, accountability, and standardized testing.

1.2 Describe two arguments for and two arguments against high-stakes testing.

To receive feedback for these exercises, go to Appendix A.

Standardized Tests

Standardized tests. Assessment instruments given to large samples of students under uniform conditions and scored and reported according to uniform procedures.

Standardized tests are assessment instruments given to large samples of students—nationwide in many cases—under uniform conditions and scored and reported according to uniform procedures. These uniform testing conditions and reporting procedures are the source of the term *standardized*. We're all familiar with them. We took achievement tests as we moved through elementary school, and the SAT or ACT is a rite of passage from high school to college. And, with increased emphasis on accountability, standardized testing has become an even more important part of teachers' and students' lives.

And the impact goes beyond accountability and high-stakes testing. For example, the New York City school system decided to use a standardized test to determine who was admitted to gifted programs for kindergarteners. Parents, eager to have their children in the program, spent an average of $1,000 to prepare their children for the test (Winerip, 2010). Books, test-prep materials and $145-an-hour tutoring sessions became hot-selling items—all to pass a standardized test for entrance into a special kindergarten program!

Standardized tests are designed to answer questions that teacher-made assessments alone can't. They include:

- How do the students in my class compare with others across the country?
- How well is our curriculum preparing students for college or future training?
- How does a particular student compare to those of similar ability?
- Are students learning essential knowledge and skills that will prepare them for life as well as subsequent learning? (Nitko & Brookhart, 2011).

To answer these questions, individuals' test scores are compared to the scores of a **norming group,** a representative sample whose scores are compiled for the purpose of national comparisons. The norming group includes students from different geographical regions, private and public schools, boys and girls, and different cultural and ethnic groups (M. D. Miller et al., 2009). **National norms** are scores on standardized tests earned by representative groups from around the nation. Individuals' scores are then compared to the national norms.

Now, let's look at different ways that standardized tests are used.

Functions of Standardized Tests

Standardized tests serve three primary functions (Aiken & Grath-Marnat, 2006):

- Assessment and diagnosis of learning
- Selection and placement
- Program evaluation and accountability

Assessment and Diagnosis of Learning

From your perspective as a teacher, the most important function of standardized testing is to provide an external, objective picture of your students' progress. In Mike's class, for example, David consistently receives A's in reading, but this doesn't tell his parents, Mike and other teachers, or school administrators how he compares to other children at his grade level across the nation. Were his A's due to high achievement or generous grading? Standardized tests help answer this question, and they provide a complete picture of student progress.

Standardized tests also help diagnose student strengths and weaknesses (Popham, 2011). For example, after seeing that David scored relatively low in listening, Mike might arrange to schedule a standardized diagnostic test. These tests are usually administered individually, with the goal of obtaining more detailed information about a student's achievement or even determining whether or not a student has a special learning need.

Selection and Placement

Selecting and placing students in specialized or limited enrollment programs is another function of standardized tests. For instance, students entering a high school may come from "feeder" middle schools, private schools, and schools outside the district, many with different academic programs. Scores from the math section of a standardized test, for example, can help the math faculty place students in classes that will best match their backgrounds and capabilities.

Standardized test results are also used to make decisions about admission to college or placement in advanced programs, such as programs for the gifted. As you already know, the scores students make on the SAT or ACT are important in determining whether they're accepted by the college of their choice.

Program Evaluation and Accountability

Providing information about the quality of instructional programs is a third function of standardized tests. For example, if an elementary school moves from a reading program

Norming group. The representative group of individuals whose standardized test scores are compiled for the purpose of national comparisons.

National norms. Scores on standardized tests earned by representative groups of students from around the nation to which an individual's score is compared.

based on writing and children's literature to one that emphasizes phonics and basic skills, the faculty can use standardized test results to assess the effectiveness of this change. And, as you saw in the first section of the chapter, high-stakes tests are increasingly being used to hold schools and teachers accountable for student learning.

Norm- Versus Criterion-Referenced Standardized Tests

Norm-referenced grading—sometimes called "grading on the curve"—compares a student's performance to that of others in a class, while criterion-referenced systems assign grades based on predetermined standards, such as 90+ = A, 80-90 = B, and so on. Similarly, **norm-referenced standardized tests** compare (reference) a student's performance to the performance of others, while **criterion-referenced standardized tests**—sometimes called *standards-referenced, content-referenced,* or *domain-referenced* tests—compare performance against a set standard. They may even be called *objectives-based* tests when the standards are in the form of learning objectives (Mertler, 2007).

Norm- and criterion-referenced tests differ in the way scores are reported. Norm-referenced scores represent a student's performance compared to peers, so it doesn't tell teachers what students actually know. For instance, David's percentile rank in reading was 70, which only tells Mike that he scored as well as, or better than, 70% of the students who took the test; it doesn't give Mike any information about David's specific reading skills. In contrast, criterion-referenced scores compare students' performance to a standard, so they provide information about mastery of specific learning objectives, such as the ability to add two-digit numbers or identify the main idea in a paragraph.

With the current focus on standards and accountability, increased emphasis is being placed on criterion-referenced tests, especially at the state and district levels. Nationally, norm-referenced tests, such as the Stanford Achievement Test David took, are still popular, because they allow location-to-location comparisons and the general nature of test content allows them to be used in a wide variety of situations. Both are useful and depend on our assessment goals.

Types of Standardized Tests

Four kinds of standardized tests are commonly used in education.

- Achievement tests
- Diagnostic tests
- Intelligence tests
- Aptitude tests

Let's look at them.

Achievement Tests

Achievement tests, the most widely used type of standardized test, are designed to assess how much students have learned in specific content areas, most commonly reading, language arts, and math, but also in areas such as science, social studies, computer literacy, and critical thinking (Hogan, 2007; Mertler, 2007). These areas are then usually broken down into descriptions of more specific skills. For example, David's test results included a Total Reading, Total Math, Science, Listening, and others. Popular achievement tests include the Iowa Test of Basic Skills, the California Achievement Test, the Stanford Achievement Test, the Comprehensive Test of Basic Skills, and the Metropolitan Achievement Test, as well as statewide assessments developed by different states (Nitko & Brookhart, 2011; Stiggins, 2005).

Educators use standardized tests to assess and diagnose learning, to assist in placement decisions, and to help in program evaluation.

Norm-referenced standardized tests. Standardized tests that compare (reference) a student's performance with the performance of others.

Criterion-referenced standardized tests. Standardized tests that compare performance against a set performance standard.

Achievement tests. Standardized tests designed to assess how much students have learned in specified content areas.

Standardized achievement tests typically include batteries of subtests administered over several days. They reflect a curriculum common to most schools, which means they will assess some, but not all, of the goals of an individual school. This is both a strength and a weakness. Because they are designed for a range of schools, they can be used in a variety of locations, but this "one size fits all" approach may not accurately measure achievement for a specific school or classroom.

Diagnostic Tests

Achievement tests measure students' progress in a range of curriculum areas; **diagnostic tests** are designed to provide a detailed description of a learner's strengths and weaknesses in specific skill areas. Their use is most common in the primary grades, where instruction is designed to match the developmental level of the child. Diagnostic tests are usually administered individually, and, compared to achievement tests, they include a larger number of items, use more subtests, and provide scores in more specific areas (Thorndike, 2005). A diagnostic test in reading, for example, might measure letter recognition, word analysis skills, sight vocabulary, vocabulary in context, and reading comprehension. The Detroit Test of Learning Aptitude, the Durrell Analysis of Reading Difficulty, and the Stanford Diagnostic Reading Test are popular diagnostic tests.

Diagnostic tests. Standardized tests designed to provide a detailed description of learners' strengths and weaknesses in specific skill areas.

Intelligence Tests

Intelligence tests are standardized tests designed to measure an individual's capacity to acquire and use knowledge, to solve problems, and accomplish new tasks. The two most widely used intelligence tests in the United States are the Stanford-Binet and the Wechsler Scales (Salvia, Ysseldyke, & Bolt, 2010). Let's look at them more closely.

Intelligence tests. Standardized tests designed to measure an individual's capacity to acquire and use knowledge, to solve problems, and accomplish new tasks.

The Stanford-Binet. The Stanford-Binet is an individually administered intelligence test composed of several subtests. It comes in a kit that includes testing materials, such as manipulatives and pictures, along with a test manual. Earlier versions heavily emphasized verbal tasks, but the most recent edition also includes nonverbal knowledge. Some examples of the types of items on the test include:

- *Nonverbal knowledge,* such as explaining an absurdity like a person in a bathing suit sitting in snow.
- *Verbal knowledge,* for instance, explaining the meaning of common words.
- *Nonverbal working memory,* such as asking a student to reproduce a display of blocks after a short delay.
- *Verbal working memory,* for instance, having students identify key words in sentences after a brief delay (Roid, 2003).

The Stanford-Binet, 5th edition (Roid, 2003), is a technically sound instrument that is second in popularity only to the Wechsler scales (described in the next section). It has been revised and renormed a number of times over the years, most recently in 2003, using 4,800 schoolchildren, stratified by economic status, geographic region, and community size. The U.S. Census was used to ensure proportional representation of White, African American, Hispanic, Asian, and Asian/Pacific Islander subcultures.

The Wechsler Scales. Developed by David Wechsler over a period of 40 years, the Wechsler scales are the most popular intelligence tests in use today (Salvia et al., 2010). The three Wechsler tests, aimed at preschool-primary, elementary, and adult populations, have two main parts: *verbal* and *performance.*

The Wechsler Intelligence Scale for Children—Fourth Edition is an individually administered intelligence test with 13 subtests, of which 6 are verbal and 7 are performance (Wechsler, 2003). (Table 15.1 outlines some sample subtests.) The performance sections

Table 15.1 Sample items from the Wechsler Intelligence Scale for Children

Verbal Section

Subtest	Description/Examples
Information	This subtest taps general knowledge common to American Culture: 1. How many wings does a bird have? 2. How many nickels make a dime? 3. What is steam made of? 4. Who wrote "Tom Sawyer"? 5. What is *pepper*?
Arithmetic	This subtest is a test of basic mathematical knowledge and skills, including counting and addition through division: 1. Sam had three pieces of candy and Joe gave him four more. How many pieces of candy did Sam have altogether? 2. Three women divided eighteen golf balls equally among themselves. How many golf balls did each person receive? 3. If two buttons cost 15¢, what will be the cost of a dozen buttons?
Similarities	This subtest is designed to measure abstract and logical thinking through use of analogies: 1. In what way are a lion and a tiger alike? 2. In what way are a saw and a hammer alike? 3. In what way are an hour and a week alike? 4. In what way are a circle and a triangle alike?

Performance Section

Subtest	Description/Examples
Picture completion	Students are shown a picture with elements missing, which they are required to identify. This subtest measures general knowledge as well as visual comprehension.
Block design	This subtest focuses on a number of abstract figures. Designed to measure visual-motor coordination, it requires students to match patterns displayed by the examiner.

Picture Completion

Block Design

were added in reaction to the strong verbal emphasis of earlier intelligence tests. Like the Stanford-Binet, the Wechsler scales are considered technically sound by testing experts (Salvia et al., 2010).

The Wechsler's two scales, yielding separate verbal and performance scores, are valuable. For example, a substantially higher score on the performance compared with the verbal scale could indicate a language problem related to poor reading or language-based cultural differences. Because performance subtests demand a minimum of verbal ability, these tasks are helpful in studying learners with disabilities, persons with limited educational background, or students who resist school-like tasks.

Aptitude Tests

Although *aptitude* and *intelligence* are often used synonymously, aptitude—the ability to acquire knowledge—is only one characteristic of intelligence. The concept of *aptitude* is intuitively sensible; for example, people will say, "I just don't have any aptitude for math," implying that their potential for learning math is limited.

Aptitude tests are standardized tests designed to predict the potential for future learning and measure general abilities developed over long periods of time. Aptitude tests are commonly used in selection and placement decisions, and they correlate highly with achievement tests (M. D. Miller et al., 2009; Popham, 2011).

The two most common aptitude tests at the high school level are the SAT and ACT, designed to measure a student's potential for success in college. Experience is important, however; classroom-related knowledge, particularly in language and mathematics, is essential for success on the tests. But, because they are reliable, the tests eliminate teacher bias and differences in teachers' grading practices. In this regard, they add valuable information in predicting future college success.

The class of 2006 was the first to write a timed essay as part of the SAT. This component was added to the traditional verbal and math sections, which were also revamped. The writing subtest was added in an attempt to more closely align it with today's high school curriculum and to address concerns among employers and university professors about the quality of student writing.

Readiness Tests

Readiness tests are standardized tests designed to assess the degree to which children are prepared for an academic or pre-academic program (Gullo, 2005). They are most often used to assess children's readiness for academic work in kindergarten or first grade. In this regard, they have qualities of both aptitude and achievement tests. They are similar to aptitude tests in that they are designed to assess a student's potential for future learning. However, most readiness tests measure the extent to which students have mastered basic concepts, such as *up* and *down*, *left* and *right*, or *big* and *small*, which form the foundation for reading and math. This is what makes them similar to achievement tests.

Standardized readiness tests have become controversial for two important reasons. First, poor performance on a readiness test is likely to delay a child's entry into kindergarten or first grade. This delay is a form of grade retention, a practice that can have negative effects on children's later development (Van Horn, 2008). Second, critics also argue that they assess only cognitive factors and ignore important characteristics that influence school success such as motivation and self-regulation (Stipek, 2002).

Aptitude tests. Standardized tests designed to predict the potential for future learning and measure general abilities developed over long periods of time.

Readiness tests. Standardized tests designed to assess the degree to which children are prepared for an academic or pre-academic program.

Readiness tests are designed to assess the degree to which children are prepared for an academic or pre-academic program.

Readiness tests, like other standardized tests, can provide valuable information for educational decision making. They should not, however, be used as the only criterion for assessing a child's readiness for school. Virtually every five- or six-year-old can benefit from school experiences, and observations of a child's ability to function in a school setting should also be a part of the assessment process (Stipek, 2002).

In this section we discussed the various types of standardized test commonly in use in education and also addressed the questions we asked in "Ed Psych and You" at the beginning of the section. Almost certainly, you took a number of standardized achievement tests, such as the Stanford Achievement Test David Palmer took. You probably also took either the SAT or ACT when you applied for admission to college, and you may have taken a high-stakes test in your state that could have influenced whether or not you were allowed to graduate from high school with a standard diploma. The fact that you're in college and taking this course suggests that you performed well on these tests, but this isn't the case for all students. As educators we need to be careful about the decisions we make on the basis of standardized test scores.

Evaluating Standardized Tests: Validity Revisited

Test validity is important to you and other teachers because you're the major consumers of standardized test results. Let's look at how validity can influence your classroom decisions, revisiting Mike Chavez, the teacher in the case study at the beginning of the chapter.

> Mike Chavez has been asked to serve on a district-wide committee to consider a new standardized achievement battery for the elementary grades. His job is to get feedback from the faculty at his school about the California Achievement Test as an option to the Stanford Achievement Test, the test they're now using.
>
> After providing an overview of the tests during a faculty meeting, Mike asks if people have questions.
>
> "How much problem solving does the California Achievement Test cover?" a fifth-grade teacher asks.
>
> "We're moving our language arts curriculum more in the direction of writing. What about it?" a second-grade teacher also asks.
>
> As the discussion continues, a confused colleague wonders, "Which is better? That's really what we're here for. How about a simple answer?"

Mike couldn't offer a simple answer, not because he was unprepared, but instead because he was asked to make judgments about validity, which is the degree to which an assessment actually measures what it is supposed to measure (M. D. Miller et al., 2009). When we create our own tests, we ensure validity by aligning the test with our learning objectives. Standardized tests are already constructed, so you must judge only the suitability of a test for a specific purpose. (A complete review of more than 1,000 standardized tests can be found in *The Eighteenth Mental Measurements Yearbook* [Spies, Carlson, & Geisinger, 2011]). Validity, in this case, involves the appropriate use of a test, not the design of the test itself.

Experts describe three kinds of standardized test validity—*content, predictive,* and *construct*—and each provides a different perspective on the issue of appropriate use.

Content Validity

Content validity. A test's ability to accurately sample the content taught and to measure the extent to which learners understand it.

Content validity refers to a test's ability to accurately sample the content taught and measure learners' understanding of it (Kane, 2006; Webb, 2006). It is determined by comparing test content with curriculum objectives, and it is a primary concern when considering standardized achievement tests (Hogan, 2007). The question Mike was asked about which test was "better" addresses content validity. The "better" test is the one with the closer match between your school's learning objectives and the content of the test.

Predictive Validity

Predictive validity is the measure of a test's ability to gauge future performance (M. D. Miller et al., 2009). It is central to the SAT and ACT, which are designed to measure a student's potential for doing college work, and it is also the focus of tests that gauge students' readiness for academic tasks in the early elementary grades.

Predictive validity is usually quantified by correlating two variables, such as a standardized test score and student grades. For example, a correlation of .47 exists between the SAT and freshman college grades (FairTest, 2008). High school grades are the only predictor that is better (a correlation of .54).

Why isn't the correlation between standardized tests and college performance higher? The primary reason is that the SAT and ACT are designed to predict "general readiness," but other factors such as motivation, study habits, and prior knowledge also affect performance (Popham, 2007).

Predictive validity. The measure of a test's ability to gauge future performance.

Construct Validity

Construct validity is an indicator of the logical connection between a test and what it is designed to measure. The concept of construct validity is somewhat abstract, but it is important in understanding the total concept of validity. It answers the question, "Do these items actually assess the ideas the test is designed to measure?" For instance, many of the items on the SAT are designed to tap the ability to do abstract thinking about words and numbers, tasks that students are likely to face in their college experience. Because of this, the test has construct validity.

Construct validity. An indicator of the logical connection between a test and what it is designed to measure.

---

check your
understanding

2.1 Describe the functions of standardized tests in the total assessment process.

2.2 As a school district examines different standardized math tests, it finds that some provide broad coverage of math concepts and skills, whereas others provide more detailed information about individual student's strengths and weaknesses in math. What two types of standardized tests is the district considering?

2.3 In a committee meeting, teachers express different views about what they want in a test. One com-

ments, "I want to make sure that the test matches our philosophy." "But it also should match the concepts and skills we're supposed to teach," a second adds. A third replies "That's all fine, but it also needs to tell us if our students will succeed in college math." Which of the different forms of validity are the teachers addressing?

To receive feedback for these questions, go to Appendix A.

Understanding and Interpreting Standardized Test Scores

The fact that they're given to thousands of students, which allow comparisons with students across the United States and around the world, is one of the advantages of standardized tests. Because the amount of information these tests provide is enormous, test publishers use statistical methods to summarize results. We examine some of these statistics in the following sections.

Ed Psych and You

When you took the SAT or ACT as part of your application to college, did you make an average, above average, or below average score? What does "average" mean?

Descriptive Statistics

As an introduction to the use of statistics in summarizing information, take a look at Table 15.2, which contains scores made by two classes of 31 students on a 50-item test, both ranked from the highest to lowest score. (As you examine this information, keep in mind that a standardized test would have a sample much larger than 31 students and would contain a larger number of items. We are using a class-size example here for the sake of illustration.)

As you see, a simple array of scores can be cumbersome and not very informative, even when the scores are ranked. We need more efficient ways of summarizing the information.

Frequency Distributions

Frequency distribution. A distribution of test scores that shows a count of the number of people who obtained each score.

A **frequency distribution** is a distribution of test scores that shows a simple count of the number of people who obtained each score. It can be represented in several ways, one of which is a graph with the possible scores on the horizontal (x) axis and the frequency, or the number of students who got each score, on the vertical (y) axis.

The frequency distributions for our two classes are shown in Figure 15.1. Although this information is still in rough form, we already begin to see differences between the two classes. For instance, there is a wider range of scores in the first class than in the second, and the scores are more nearly clustered near the middle of the second distribution. Beyond this qualitative

Table 15.2 Scores of two classes on a 50-item test

Class #1	Class #2
50	48
49	47
49	46
48	46
47	45
47	45
46	44 ⌐
46	44
45	44 mode
45	44
45	44 ⌐
44 ⌐	43
44	43
44 mode	43
44 ⌐	43
43—median	42—median & mean
42—mean	42
41	42
41	42
40	41
40	41
39	41
39	40
38	40
37	39
37	39
36	38
35	38
34	37
34	36
33	35

description, however, the distributions aren't particularly helpful. We need a better way to summarize the information. Measures of central tendency do this.

Measures of Central Tendency

Measures of central tendency—the mean, median, and mode—are quantitative descriptions of a group's performance as a whole. In a distribution of scores, the **mean** is the average score, the **median** is the middle score in the distribution, and the **mode** is the most frequent score.

To obtain a mean, we simply add the scores and divide by the number of scores. As it turns out, both distributions in Table 15.2 have a mean of 42 (1,302/31). The mean is one indicator of how each group performed as a whole.

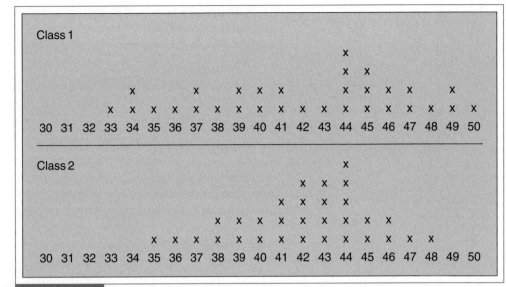

Figure 15.1 Frequency distributions for two classes on a 50-item test

The median for the first distribution is 43, because half the scores (15) fall equal to or above 43, and the other half are equal to or below 43. Using the same process, we find that the median for the second distribution is 42.

The median is useful when extremely high or low scores skew the mean and give a false picture of the sample. For example, you commonly hear or read demographic statistics such as "The median income for families of four in this country went from . . . in 2000 to . . . in 2010." The *median* income is reported because a few multimillion-dollar incomes would make the mean quite high and would give an artificial picture of typical families' standards of living. The median, in contrast, is not affected by these extremes and provides a more realistic picture. The median serves the same function when used with test scores.

Looking once more at the two samples, you can see that the most frequent score for each is 44, which is the mode. Small samples, such as those here, often have more than one mode, resulting in bimodal or even trimodal distributions.

Using our measures of central tendency, we see that the two groups of scores are much alike: They have the same mean, nearly the same median, and the same mode. As you saw from examining the frequency distribution, however, this doesn't give us a complete picture. We also need a measure of their variability, or *spread.*

Measures of Variability

To get a more accurate picture of the samples, we need to see how the scores vary. **Variability** is the degree of spread, or deviation from the mean. One measure of variability is the **range,** the distance between the top and bottom score. The range in the first class is 17, and in the second it's 13, confirming the wider range of scores we saw in the frequency distribution. Although easy to compute, the range is overly influenced by one or more extreme scores.

The **standard deviation,** a statistical measure of the spread of scores, reduces this problem, because a few scores at the outer margins don't overly influence it. For example, if we were to administer an achievement test to an entire high school grade, the standard deviation would be larger than if we administered the same test to an advanced placement class. The variability of scores for the whole grade would be greater.

Measures of central tendency. Quantitative descriptions of a group's performance as a whole.

Mean. The average score in the distribution of a group of scores.

Median. The middle score in the distribution of a group of scores.

Mode. The most frequent score in the distribution of a group of scores.

Variability. The spread of scores, or degree of difference or deviation from the mean.

Range. The distance between the top and bottom score in a distribution of scores.

Standard deviation. A statistical measure of the spread of scores.

With the use of computers, you will be unlikely to calculate a standard deviation manually, but we're briefly describing the procedure here to help you understand the concept. To find the standard deviation:

1. Calculate the mean.
2. Subtract the mean from each of the individual scores.
3. Square each of these values. (This eliminates negative numbers.)
4. Add the squared values.
5. Divide by the total number of scores (31 in our samples).
6. Take the square root.

In our samples, the standard deviations are 4.8 and 3.1, respectively. We saw from merely observing the two distributions that the first was more spread out, and the standard deviation provides a quantitative measure of that spread.

The Normal Distribution

Standardized tests are administered to large (in the hundreds of thousands or even millions) samples of students, and the scores often approximate a *normal distribution*. To understand this concept, look again at our two distributions in Figure 15.1 and then focus specifically on the second one. If we drew a line over the top of the frequency distribution, it would appear as shown in Figure 15.2.

Now imagine a very large sample of scores, such as we would find from a typical standardized test. The curve would approximate the one shown in Figure 15.3. This is a **normal distribution,** a distribution of scores in which the mean, median, and mode are equal and the scores distribute themselves symmetrically in a bell-shaped curve. Many large samples of human characteristics, such as height and weight, tend to distribute themselves this way, as do the results from large samples of most standardized tests.

The sample of scores in Figure 15.2 has both a mean and median of 42, but a mode of 44, so its measures of central tendency don't quite fit the normal distribution. Also, as we see from the normal distribution in Figure 15.3, 68% of all the scores fall within 1 standard deviation from the mean, but in our sample distribution, about 71% of the scores are within 1 standard deviation above and below the mean. Our samples aren't normal distributions, which is typical of the smaller samples found in classrooms.

Interpreting Standardized Test Results

Using our two small samples, we have illustrated techniques that statisticians use to summarize standardized test scores. Again, keep in mind that data gathered from standardized tests come from hundreds of thousands of students instead of the small number in our illustrations. When standardized tests are used, comparing students from different schools, districts, states, and even countries is an important goal. To make these comparisons, and

Normal distribution. A distribution of scores in which the mean, median, and mode are equal and the scores distribute themselves symmetrically in a bell-shaped curve.

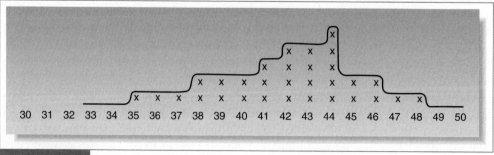

Figure 15.2 Frequency distribution for the second class

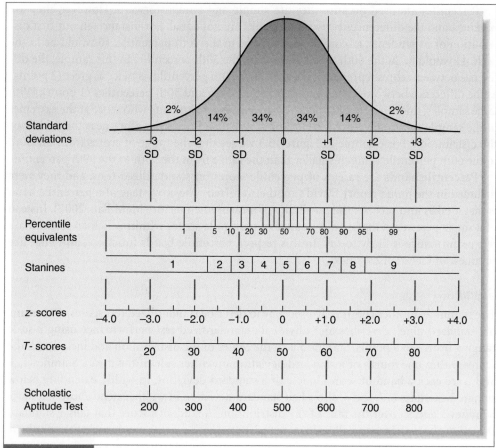

Figure 15.3 Normal distribution

depending on the test, *raw scores, percentile rank, percentile bands, stanines, grade equivalents,* and *standard scores* are used. For example, the home report Mrs. Palmer received included percentile ranks and percentile bands.

We look at these ways of describing test results in the following sections.

Raw Scores

All standardized tests are based on **raw scores,** simply the number of items an individual answered correctly on a standardized test or subtest. For example, the Stanford Achievement Test David took had 80 total items in math, and David answered 56 of them correctly, so his raw score for that subtest is 56. (These results were reported to Mike, as David's teacher, but they weren't sent to David's parents.)

The raw score doesn't tell us much, however, until we compare his score to others. Percentile ranks, stanines, grade equivalents, and standard scores help us do that.

Raw score. The number of items an individual answered correctly on a standardized test or subtest.

Percentile Rank

The **percentile rank (PR)** represents the percentage of students in the norming sample that scored at or below a particular raw score. For instance, David's raw score of 56 in Total Math placed him in the 64th percentile nationally. That means his score was as high as or higher than 64% of the scores of students who took the test across the nation.

Parents and students often confuse percentiles with *percentages.* Percentages reflect the number of correct items compared to the total number possible. Percentile rank, in contrast, is a description that indicates how a student did in comparison to other students taking the test.

Percentile rank (PR). The percentage of students in the norming sample that scored at or below a particular raw score.

Percentiles are used because they are simple and straightforward. However, they are *rankings,* and the differences between the ranks are not equal. For instance, in our first distribution of 31 students, a score of 48 would be in the 90th percentile, 46 would be in the 80th, 44 would be in the 60th, and 43 would be the 50th percentile. In this sample, the difference between scores representing the 90th and 80th percentiles is twice as great (2 points) as the difference between scores representing the 60th and 50th percentiles (1 point). With large samples, this difference is even more pronounced. Students who score at the extremes in the sample vary more from their counterparts than those who score near the middle of the distribution. For example in Figure 15.3 we see that the range of scores from the 50th to the 60th percentile is much smaller than the range from the 90th to the 99th percentile.

Percentile bands are ranges of percentile scores on standardized tests, and they were included in the home report David's mother received. The advantage of a percentile band is that it takes into account the possibility of measurement error (McMillan, 2007). Instead of a single percentile, the band is a range of percentile scores within which an individual's test performance is likely to fall. In this respect, percentile bands function somewhat like stanines, which we discuss next.

Percentile bands. Ranges of percentile scores on standardized tests.

Stanines

The stanine is another commonly used way to describe standardized test scores. A **stanine,** or "standard nine," describes an individual's standardized test performance using a scale ranging from 1 to 9 points. Stanine 5 is in the center of the distribution and includes all the scores within one fourth of a standard deviation on either side of the mean. Stanines 4, 3, and 2 are each a band of scores, one half a standard deviation in width, extending below stanine 5. Stanines 6, 7, and 8, also a half standard deviation in width, extend above stanine 5. Stanines 1 and 9 cover the tails of the distribution. A student's score that falls 1 standard deviation above the mean will be in stanine 7; a student's score 2 standard deviations above the mean will be in stanine 9. Figure 15.3 shows how stanines correspond to other measures we've discussed.

Stanine. A description of an individual's standardized test performance that uses a scale ranging from 1 to 9 points.

Stanines are widely used because they're simple, and they encourage teachers and parents to interpret scores based on a possible range, instead of fine distinctions that may be artificial (McMillan, 2007). For instance, a score in the 57th percentile may be the result of 1 or 2 extra points on a subtest compared to a score in the 52nd percentile, and the student may have guessed the answer correctly, so the difference between the two wouldn't be meaningful. Both scores fall in stanine 5, however. Because it describes performance as a range of possible scores, the stanine is probably a more realistic indicator of performance. Reducing the scores to a 9-point band sacrifices information, however, so it is important to keep the advantages and disadvantages of stanines in mind as you use these to help parents and students interpret standardized test scores.

Grade Equivalents

The **grade equivalent** is a score determined by comparing an individual's score to the scores of students in a particular age group, and it is another common way test results are described. For instance, David's grade equivalent for Total Math was 5.5. That means that he scored as well on the test as the average score for those students taking the test who are in the fifth month of the fifth grade.

Grade-equivalent score. A score that is determined by comparing an individual's score on a standardized test to the scores of students in a particular age group.

This does not imply that David, a fourth grader, should be in the fifth grade. Grade equivalents can be misleading because they oversimplify results and suggest comparisons that aren't necessarily valid (Hogan, 2007). A grade equivalent of 5.5 tells us that David is somewhat advanced in math. It doesn't suggest that he should be promoted to fifth grade, and it doesn't necessarily suggest that he should be working with fifth graders. Because of the possibility of misinterpretation, some standardized tests no longer use grade equivalents (M. D. Miller et al., 2009; Salvia et al., 2010).

Standard Scores

As you saw in our discussion of percentiles, differences in raw scores don't result in comparable differences in the percentile rank. For instance, you saw that it took only a 1-point difference—43 compared with 42—to move from the 50th to the 60th percentile, but it took a 2-point difference—48 compared with 46—to move from the 80th to the 90th percentile in our distribution in Figure 15.2. To deal with this type of discrepancy, standard scores were developed. A **standard score** is a description of performance on a standardized test that uses the standard deviation as the basic unit (McMillan, 2007). Standardized test makers use the mean and standard deviation to report standard scores.

The **z-score,** the number of standard deviation units from the mean, is one type of standard score. A z-score of 2 is 2 standard deviations above the mean, for example, and a z-score of -1 is 1 standard deviation below the mean.

The **t-score** is a standard score that defines the mean as 50 and the standard deviation as 10. A t-score of 70 would be 2 standard deviations above the mean and would correspond to a z-score of 2.

Standard scores such as z-scores and t-scores are useful because they make comparisons convenient. Because they are based on equal units of measurement throughout the distribution, inter-group and inter-test comparisons are possible.

Standard score. A description of performance on a standardized test that uses the standard deviation as the basic unit.

z-score. The number of standard deviation units from the mean.

t-score. A standard score that defines the mean as 50 and the standard deviation as 10.

Standard Error of Measurement

Although standardized tests are technically sophisticated, like all tests they contain measurement error; scores represent only an approximation of a student's "true" score. Hypothetically, if we could give a student the same test over and over, for example, and the student neither gained nor lost any knowledge, we would find that the scores would vary. If we averaged those scores, we would have an estimate of the student's "true" score. A **true score** is the hypothetical average of an individual's scores if repeated testing under ideal conditions were possible. An estimate of the true score is obtained using the **standard error of measurement,** the range of scores within which an individual's true score is likely to fall. This range is sometimes termed the *confidence interval, score band,* or *profile band.* For example, suppose Ben has a raw score of 46 and Kim has a raw score of 52 on a test with a standard error of 4. This means that Ben's true score is between 42 and 50, and Kim's is between 48 and 56. At first glance, Kim appears to have scored significantly higher than Ben, but considering the standard error, their scores may be equal, or Ben's true score may even be higher than Kim's. Understanding standard error is important when we make decisions based on standardized tests. For instance, it would be unwise to place Ben and Kim in different ability groups based solely on the results illustrated here.

In this section we described the different ways that standardized tests are reported, and this section also addresses the questions we asked in "Ed Psych and You" at the beginning of the section. *Average* is often defined in terms of the mean, a measure of central tendency. Average is where most students are—both in terms of intelligence and achievement. However, this single score, or series of scores, fails to capture the many ways that students are unique and different. Keep this in mind as you attempt to interpret the standardized test scores of your students.

True score. The hypothetical average of an individual's scores if repeated testing under ideal conditions were possible.

Standard error of measurement. The range of scores within which an individual's true score is likely to fall.

check your understanding

3.1 Carol is at the 96th percentile rank in number concepts; her friends Marsha and Lenore are at the 86th and 76th, respectively. Is the difference between Carol's and Marsha's scores greater than the difference between Marsha's and Lenore's, or vice versa? Explain.

3.2 A student in our first class (illustrated in Table 15.2 and Figure 15.1) scored 47 on the test. In what

stanine is this score? In what stanine would a score of 47 be for the second class?

3.3 A fourth grader in your class has taken a standardized test, and the summary gives his grade-equivalent score as 6.7. Explain what this means. What implications does this have for your teaching?

To receive feedback for these questions, go to Appendix A.

Classroom connections

Using Standardized Tests Effectively in Classrooms

1. The validity of a standardized achievement test depends on the match between learning objectives and test content. Carefully analyze results to increase instructional alignment.

   - **Elementary:** A fourth-grade team goes over the previous year's test scores to identify areas in the curriculum that need greater attention.

   - **Middle School:** The math teachers in a middle school go over standardized results item by item. Seeing that a large number of students missed a particular item, the teachers plan to place more emphasis on this topic in their instruction.

   - **High School:** English teachers in an urban high school use a scoring rubric to analyze student scores on a statewide writing assessment. They share the rubric with their students and use it to help them improve their writing skills.

2. The value of standardized test scores to consumers depends, in large part, on the extent to which they understand the results. Communicate test results clearly to both students and their caregivers.

   - **Elementary:** Third-grade teachers in an urban elementary school prepare a handout that explains standardized test scores including examples and answers to frequently asked questions. They use the handout in parent–teacher conferences.

   - **Middle School:** A middle school team integrates standardized test scores into a comprehensive packet of assessment materials. When they meet with students and their caregivers, they use the information to identify individual students' areas of strength and those that need improvement.

   - **High School:** During an orientation meeting with parents, members of an English Department first give an overview of tests that students will encounter in high school and describe how scores are reported. During individual meetings with parents, teachers provide specific information about individuals' scores.

Diversity and Standardized Testing

Ed Psych and You

Did you ever take a standardized test where certain parts of the content were unfamiliar to you? Did you ever encounter items on a standardized test that contained vocabulary that you didn't understand? What did these mismatches between test content and you say about you, and what did these mismatches say about the test?

One of the most volatile controversies in standardized testing involves critics' claims that the tests are biased against members of cultural minorities (Freedle, 2010; Santelices & Wilson, 2010). This is particularly true for Hispanic and African American students who, on average, consistently score lower on standardized tests than do White and Asian students (National Assessment of Educational Progress, 2009). And because scoring below established minimums on high-stakes standardized tests can result in grade retention or failure to graduate from high school, the controversy has increased (D. D. Johnson et al., 2008; Popham, 2011). A number of cases have actually gone to the courts, and the validity of tests for cultural minorities and the extent to which students have had the opportunity to learn test content have been key issues (Geisinger, 2005). The essential question is, as standardized tests are increasingly used to make important decisions about students, will members of cultural minorities be treated fairly?

As you would expect, advocates and critics disagree, and two important issues related to standardized testing with minority students remain unresolved. The first is whether the tests are valid and reliable enough to justify using results to make decisions about students' academic careers and lives (D. D. Johnson et al., 2008). The second relates to technical problems involved in testing members of minorities and particularly students who speak English as a second language (Salvia et al., 2010). Significantly, experts and professional organizations including the American Educational Research Association, the American Psychological Association, and the National Council on Measurement in Education are increasingly critical of making decisions about promotion or graduation on the basis of one test score (American Educational Research Association, American Psychological Association, & National Council on Measurement in Education, 1999).

Student Diversity and Assessment Bias

Because of the controversies surrounding standardized testing, increased attention is being focused on the question of whether assessment bias exists. **Assessment bias** is a form of discrimination that occurs when a test or other assessment instrument unfairly penalizes a group of students because of their gender, ethnicity, race, or socioeconomic status (SES).

Measurement experts have identified three types of assessment bias that detract from validity (M. D. Miller et al., 2009):

- Bias in content
- Bias in testing procedures
- Bias in test interpretation and use

As you study these topics, remember that mean differences between groups do not necessarily indicate bias. Underlying causes, such as poverty or inadequate educational opportunities may account for these differences (Nitko & Brookhart, 2011).

Bias in Content

Critics contend that the content of standardized tests is geared to White, middle-class American students, and members of cultural minorities are disadvantaged by this content. For example, the following item is drawn from a standardized science test used to measure the knowledge of sixth graders:

> If you wanted to find out if a distant planet had mountains or rivers on it, which of the following tools should you use?
>
> a. binoculars
> b. microscope
> c. telescope
> d. camera (Popham, 2004, p. 48)

Performance on this item is likely to be influenced by SES and a student's exposure to high-cost items like microscopes and telescopes.

Bias can also occur in word problems (M. D. Miller et al., 2009). For example:

> Alex Rodriguez is batting .310 after 100 trips to the plate. In his next three times at bat, he gets a single, double, and home run. What is his batting average now?

This item requires that students know how batting averages are computed and whether doubles and home runs count more than singles. Word problems can also be biased if students have trouble reading the item because of limited skills with English.

Mismatches between test content and the cultural backgrounds of students can also result in content bias. For example, students from a remote Eskimo community were asked the following question on a standardized vocabulary test: "Which of the following would most likely take you to the hospital if you got hurt?" The "correct" answer was *ambulance*, but Eskimo students replied *airplane* because that is how people in their village receive emergency medical aid (Platt, 2004).

Bias in Testing Procedures

Because students from different cultures respond differently to testing situations, bias can also occur in testing procedures. For example, in one study researchers found that Navajo students were unaware of the consequences of poor test performance, instead treating tests as game-like events (Deyhle, 1987). Other research has found that some minority students *believe* tests will be biased, and as a result they don't try to do well on them (Morgan & Mehta, 2004; Ryan & Ryan, 2005).

Assessment bias. A form of discrimination that occurs when a test or other assessment instrument unfairly penalizes a group of students because of their gender, ethnicity, race, or socioeconomic status.

Teachers should continually guard against bias in test content, procedures, and uses.

Bias in Test Interpretation and Use

Bias can also occur in the ways test results are interpreted and used. Experts are concerned about the adverse effects of testing on minority students' progress through public schools and entrance into college (D. D. Johnson et al., 2008). Evidence suggests that test results are sometimes used in ways that discriminate against members of cultural minorities and those who do not speak English as a first language. For example, a historic study of 812 students classified as being "mentally retarded" found 300% more "Mexican Americans" and 50% more African Americans than would be expected from their numbers in the general population, and, the study population had 40% fewer Anglo Americans than would be expected. Further, people in lower-income brackets were overrepresented, whereas people in the upper brackets were underrepresented (Mercer, 1973). More recent research suggests this problem still exists (Blanchett, 2006).

Standardized Testing and English Learners

Standardized testing poses special challenges for students who are English learners (ELs) and their teachers. Research indicates that students whose first language isn't English consistently score lower than other students on both standardized achievement and intelligence tests (Blanchett, 2006). This isn't surprising to many testing experts, because most standardized tests are developed for native English speakers and depend heavily on English language skills (Geisinger, 2005). This presents a problem for teachers who are asked to use standardized test scores in their work with students who are ELs, because students must be able to read and understand English if a test written in English is to measure performance accurately (Echevarria & Graves, 2011).

The problem of standardized testing with limited-English speakers is not new, but its importance has increased with the emphasis on accountability. The No Child Left Behind legislation has required that all students who are ELs and have been in this country for three consecutive years be tested in reading and language arts using a test written in English (Menken, 2008).

Language is not the only reason for the poor performance of students who are ELs on standardized tests. These students tend to come from lower-SES families, and research consistently demonstrates the adverse affects of poverty on achievement (Macionis, 2009). In addition, students who are ELs typically attend poorer schools, with fewer resources and greater numbers of unqualified or inexperienced teachers (Kozol, 2005).

Researchers have identified additional factors influencing the performance of students who are ELs on standardized tests, all related to the linguistic complexity of the tests. In addition to the fact that the tests are administered in English, the tests contain many technical terms such as *ion, colonization,* and *simile* that aren't commonly used in conversation (Echevarria & Graves, 2011). This puts students who are ELs at a disadvantage, because they acquire language proficiency through everyday conversation. Third, standardized tests are timed, placing an additional cognitive burden on EL test-takers.

Testing Accommodations for English Learners

Accommodations to address these problems focus on either the test itself or testing procedures. For example, attempts to modify the test have either attempted to translate the test into students' first language or simplify vocabulary or sentence structures, such as shortening sentences or converting from passive to active voice (Abedi, 2006). Technical and logistical problems exist with these efforts, however. For example, testing experts question whether the modified and original forms of the test are comparable, which raise questions of validity (Geisinger, 2005), and it isn't economically feasible to translate tests into all the native languages that exist in some urban districts. Even when students speak a common language, cultural differences, such as variations in Spanish dialects spoken in Spain, Mexico, Cuba, and Puerto Rico, make it difficult to construct a test that is culturally and linguistically meaningful (Geisinger, 2005; Solano-Flores & Li, 2006).

Attempts to increase validity through modifications of testing procedures, such as providing regular and bilingual dictionaries and allowing more time for students who are ELs, appear more promising (Abedi & Gandara, 2006). Providing more time, especially when combined with test-specific glossaries, appears to be the most feasible accommodation.

Accommodating Students with Disabilities

In the United States, the Individuals with Disabilities Education Act (IDEA) requires appropriate accommodations for students with disabilities. Many of these testing accommodations are similar to those for students who are ELs. Some accommodations include:

- Modify the presentation format, such as reading questions out loud when reading is an issue.
- Modify the response format (e.g., allow students to dictate their answers when writing is a problem).
- Provide extra time for tests.
- Administer tests in smaller time increments to prevent fatigue or frustration.
- Administer tests in separate, quieter settings free from distractions (American Educational Research Association, et al., 1999).

Modifying standardized assessment procedures can alter the validity of test results, however, so we need to keep this possibility in mind.

Teaching test-taking strategies is a second way to accommodate students with disabilities (Mastropieri & Scruggs, 2010). These strategies include:

- Learn to use separate bubble answer sheets.
- Sort problems by type and difficulty level, and begin with easier ones first.
- Underline key words in problems, and draw diagrams and pictures.
- Eliminate obvious wrong options, and guess where appropriate.

To be effective, these strategies need to be taught through modeling and practiced thoroughly, well before any high-stakes tests are attempted.

This section addresses the questions we asked in "Ed Psych and You" about your experiences with standardized testing. We've all been in testing situations in which we didn't know some of the answers or didn't even understand the question. This may have resulted from our simply not understanding the topic. However, at other times it may have been the result of faulty items that failed to adequately assess our knowledge. Assessment bias exists, and it can negatively influence our students and us. We describe ways to minimize these negative effects in our "Ed Psych and Teaching" feature that follows.

Ed Psych and teaching

Your Role in Standardized Testing

You will play a central role in ensuring that standardized test scores reflect what your students have actually learned. Given current demographic trends in the United States, you almost certainly will have members of cultural minorities in your classes, and some will speak a native language other than English. In addition, you will need to communicate test results to students and their caregivers and use the results to improve your instruction. The following guidelines can assist you in performing these essential functions:

1. Prepare students so that test results accurately reflect what they know and can do.
2. Make accommodations, if possible, for members of cultural minorities and students who are not native English speakers.
3. Administer tests in ways that maximize student performance.
4. Communicate results to students and their caregivers.
5. Use sources of data in addition to standardized test results in making educational decisions.

Let's see how these guidelines operate in classrooms.

Preparing Students

As you saw earlier in the chapter, the validity of standardized tests depends on the match between the test and the purpose for using it. With the present emphasis on district, state, and even nationally mandated tests, it will be your responsibility to ensure that students have learned the content covered on the tests.

Ensuring that students are prepared depends on the effectiveness of instruction. Students should have studied in detail the content covered on the test, and they should have opportunities to practice the skills measured on the test using a format similar to the one they'll encounter on the test (Mertler, 2007). For example, teachers commonly assess spelling by giving quizzes in which students are asked to correctly spell lists of words. However, when spelling is assessed on standardized tests, students are given a list of four closely matched words and asked to select the one spelled correctly. To do well on these items, students need practice with this format.

Students should also be taught general test-taking strategies. These strategies are particularly important for members of cultural minorities, students whose first language isn't English, and students from low-SES backgrounds. Effective test-taking strategies for standardized tests include:

- Read and follow all directions.
- Determine how questions will be scored, such as whether penalties exist for errors in spelling or grammar in written responses, or for guessing on multiple-choice items.
- Eliminate options on multiple-choice items, and make informed guesses with remaining items (if guessing isn't penalized).
- Pace themselves so they have enough time to answer all the questions.
- Answer easier questions first, and go back to check answers if time permits.
- Check to be sure that responses on the answer sheet match the numbers in the test booklet (Nitko & Brookhart, 2011).

Accommodating Members of Minorities and English Learners

As you saw in earlier sections, standardized tests often use technical language that is infrequently used in everyday conversation. Providing concrete examples of technical terms, such as *ion* and *simile* during instruction, and emphasizing the essential characteristics of important concepts can help accommodate differences in background knowledge. This is particularly important for members of cultural minorities and non-native English speakers.

Also, providing dictionaries and allowing extra time for these students are effective accommodations if the testing procedures allow it.

Administering Tests

To ensure that standardized tests yield valid results, they must be uniformly administered. Developers typically provide detailed instructions about how their tests should be administered (Nitko & Brookhart, 2011). Manuals specify the allotted time for each test and subtest—which should be written on the board for students—and provide scripts for introducing and describing the subtests. If scripts and time frames aren't followed precisely, the results can be invalid.

Interpreting Results

Once results are returned, you will be responsible for explaining them to students and their caregivers and using them to improve your instruction. To identify areas that may need improvement, you might compare the scores of one year's class with those in earlier years.

Teachers are responsible for explaining standardized test results to parents and other caregivers and using the results to improve their instruction.

Standardized test scores should be combined with other information about students when communicating results, and you should emphasize that the scores are only approximations of student capabilities. And to the extent possible, avoid technical language in discussing results.

Use Additional Data Sources

Testing experts are clear on the following point: No single test should be used as the basis for educational decisions about individual students (M. D. Miller et al., 2009). At the school level, you can help ensure that alternate data sources such as grades, work samples, and classroom observations are used in making decisions about individual students. At the policy level, you can become an advocate for the use of comprehensive assessment data in making these decisions.

Finally, when making decisions about students, use a variety of sources of data, such as your own quizzes, tests, homework, and informal observations, in addition to standardized test results. This is important for all students, and even more so when working with members of cultural minorities and students who are ELs. These alternate sources help provide a more comprehensive and accurate picture of your students' achievements.

---

check your understanding

4.1 Explain how learner diversity can influence the validity of standardized tests.

4.2 Describe the most effective strategy teachers can use to minimize content bias in the use of standardized tests with their students.

To receive feedback for these questions, go to Appendix A.

Classroom connections

Eliminating Test Bias in Classrooms

1. Test validity can be compromised when cultural factors unfairly affect test performance. Be aware of the potential effects that learner diversity can have on assessment performance.

   ■ **Elementary:** Before any of her students who are non-native English-speaking are referred for special education testing, a first-grade teacher talks with a school psychologist and describes the child's background and language patterns.

   ■ **Middle School:** Before administering a statewide exam, an eighth-grade math teacher explains the purpose and format of the test and gives students practice with the content covered on the test. He reads the directions for taking the test slowly and clearly and writes the amount of time remaining on the board.

   ■ **High School:** A high school English teacher holds sessions after school to help her students with limited English proficiency prepare for a high-stakes test. She explains test purposes and formats and provides the students with timed practice on similar items.

2. Testing procedures can influence student performance and ultimately test validity. Adapt testing procedures to meet the needs of all students.

   ■ **Elementary:** An urban third-grade teacher states positive expectations as her students prepare for a standardized test and carefully monitors them to be sure they stay on task during the test.

   ■ **Middle School:** Before standardized tests are given each year, a middle school language arts teacher takes time to teach test-taking strategies. She models the strategies, discusses them with her students, and provides opportunities to practice them under test-like conditions.

   ■ **High School:** An algebra teacher makes a special effort to ensure that students understand the vocabulary on the state standardized test. Before the test, he carefully reviews important concepts the class has learned during the school year.

Developmentally appropriate practice

Standardized Testing with Learners at Different Ages

Effective assessment with standardized tests requires that teachers take learner development into account. The following sections outline suggestions for accommodating the developmental levels of your students.

Working with Students in Early Childhood Programs and Elementary Schools

The developmental characteristics of young children can have a powerful effect on the validity of standardized tests. Their short attention spans and limited language skills influence their performance, and most won't understand that the tests are important, so they often don't make efforts to perform well. For many young children, a standardized test is just one more worksheet to be completed (Gullo, 2005). They also lack experience with timed tests and multiple-choice formats, which are commonly used on standardized tests. They may not follow directions, and because they tend to be impulsive, they often select the first choice that seems plausible or may rush through the test so they can return to activities they find more enjoyable.

Because of mismatches between testing requirements and students' developmental limitations, teachers of young children should treat standardized test results skeptically, particularly when they're inconsistent with a child's classroom performance. Most importantly, teachers should avoid making long-term predictions about student potential on the basis of standardized test results, and particularly on the basis of these results alone.

Working with Students in Middle Schools

Middle school students are starting to understand the importance of standardized tests, which can have both positive and negative effects; it can increase their motivation to perform well, but it can also result in test anxiety that can decrease their performance.

While generally more test-savvy than younger children in their ability to respond to standardized tests, individual development varies a great deal. Some have acquired the study habits, self-regulatory abilities, and test-taking strategies needed to navigate through timed, standardized test formats successfully, whereas others haven't (Schunk, 2005; Zimmerman, 2005).

To accommodate these differences, middle school teachers should emphasize self-regulation and personal responsibility during tests, teach test-taking strategies, and provide ample practice with formats similar to those students will encounter on standardized tests. Emphasizing that the tests can give them valuable information about their strengths and areas that need more work, stating positive expectations about their performance, and encouraging them to do their best are also helpful with middle school students.

Working with Students in High Schools

By the time they reach high school, students have had a considerable amount of experience with standardized testing. As a result, most are familiar with test formats and procedures, but for students who have had negative experiences with standardized testing, motivation can be a problem (Ryan, Ryan, Arbuthnot, & Samuels, 2007). Motivation can be a special problem for low-performing students, and it often prevents them from performing up to their capabilities. One adolescent facing challenging problems on a test commented,

"I figured I would get them wrong. ... Yeah, because if I know I'm going to get them wrong I just kind of think why bother trying." (Ryan et al., 2007, p. 9)

Teachers of high school students should emphasize that standardized test results exist to provide students with information, and the results don't say anything about their intrinsic worth as human beings or determine whether they will be successful in life. Doing as well as possible is important, however, if the results are to provide the most useful information.

High school students also need help interpreting standardized test scores and how they can be used to make career decisions. Test results can be confusing, and both students and their parents need help understanding and translating them into useful information (Carr, 2008). Caring and understanding teachers are in the best position to help students understand test results because they are familiar with students' classroom performance and can help students make important decisions about their futures.

Summary

1. Describe the relationships between standards-based education, accountability, and standardized testing.
   - Standards-based education is the process of focusing instruction on predetermined goals or standards.
   - Accountability is the process of requiring students to demonstrate that they have met the standards and holding teachers responsible for students' performance. Standardized testing in the form of high-stakes tests are used to determine whether students have met the standards.
   - Advocates of accountability argue that standardized tests efficiently assess the educational achievements of students. Critics counter that misuse of standardized tests discourages innovation, narrows the curriculum, and results in teaching to the test.

2. Describe the functions of standardized tests in the total assessment process.
   - Assessing student academic progress, diagnosing strengths and weaknesses, and placing students in appropriate programs are important functions of standardized tests. Providing information for program evaluation and improvement is also an important function.
   - Achievement tests provide information about student learning; diagnostic tests provide in-depth analysis of specific student strengths and weaknesses; intelligence tests are designed to measure students' ability to acquire and use knowledge, to solve problems, and to accomplish new tasks; and aptitude tests are designed to predict potential for future learning.

   - Validity measures the appropriateness of a test for a specific purpose and includes content, predictive, and construct validity.

3. Interpret standardized test results using statistics and standard scores.
   - Standardized test scores are interpreted by using descriptive statistics to compare an individual's performance to the performance of a norming group.
   - The mean, median, and mode are measures of central tendency, and the range and standard deviation are measures of variability.
   - Percentiles, stanines, grade equivalents, and standard scores all allow a student's score to be compared with the scores of comparable students in a norming group.

4. Explain how learner diversity can influence the validity of standardized tests.
   - Learner diversity can influence the validity of standardized tests if being a member of a cultural minority or a non-native English speaker results in test bias.
   - Content bias occurs when incidental information in items discriminates against certain cultural groups.
   - Bias in testing procedures occurs when groups don't fully understand testing procedures and the implications of time limits.
   - Bias in the use of test results occurs when tests are used in isolation to make important decisions about students.

Understanding Standardized Testing: Preparing for Your Licensure Exam

Your licensure exam will include information related to classroom assessment, and we include the following exercises to help you practice for the exam in your state. This book and these exercises will be a resource for you as you prepare for the exam.

At the beginning of the chapter, you saw how Mike Chavez interpreted standardized test scores for a parent. Let's look now at another situation in which using standardized tests helps answer questions about learning and teaching. Read the case study, and answer the questions that follow.

Peggy Barret looks up from the stack of algebra tests that she is grading as her colleague, Stan Witzel, walks into the teacher's lounge.

"How's it going?" Stan asks.

"Fine . . . I think. I'm scoring tests from my Algebra I class. That's the one where I'm trying to put

more emphasis on problem solving. Quite a few kids are actually getting into the applications now, and they like the problem solving when they do small-group work. The trouble is, some of the others are really struggling. . . . So, I'm not so sure about it all."

"I wish I had your problems. It sounds like your kids are learning, and at least some of them like it," Stan replies.

"Yeah, I know," Peggy nods. "Getting these kids to like any kind of math is an accomplishment, but still I wonder. . . . It's just that I'm not sure if they're getting all that they should. I don't know whether this class is *really* doing better than last year's class or even my other classes this year, for that matter. The tests I give are pretty different in the different classes. I think the kids are doing better on problem solving, but to be honest about it, I see quite a few of them struggling with mechanics. I work on the mechanics, but not as much as in other classes. I'm not sure if I'm putting the right emphasis in the class."

"Good point," Stan shrugs. "I always wonder when I make changes. By emphasizing something more, I wonder if they are missing out on something."

"As important," Peggy continues, "I wonder how they'll do when they go off to college. Quite a few of them in this class will be going. . . . Got any ideas?"

"Good questions, Peggy. I wish I knew, but . . . I guess that's part of teaching."

"Yeah," she replies with her voice trailing off, "it seems as if we should be able to get some better information. I can see that some of the kids just don't seem to get it. I would say their background is weak; they seem to be trying. On the other hand, I checked out

some of their old standardized test results, and their math scores weren't that bad. Maybe it's not background. Maybe they just don't belong in my class."

"Tell me about the kids who are struggling," Stan suggests.

"Well, Jacinta tries really hard. Quan is a whiz at computation but struggles when I ask him to think. Carlos actually seems to do fairly well with mechanics but has a hard time with word problems. For example, I tried to motivate the class the other day with several word problems involving statistics from our basketball team. Most of the class liked them and got them right. Not these three."

"Maybe you ought to talk to Yolanda," Stan suggests. "She's been in this game for awhile and might know about some tests that are available that can help you answer some of your questions."

Questions for Case Analysis

In answering these questions, use information from the chapter, and link your responses to specific information in the case.

1. What type of standardized test would help Peggy determine "whether this class is *really* doing better than last year's class or even my other classes this year"?

2. What type of validity would be the primary concern with this test? Explain.

3. One of Peggy's concerns was the prior knowledge of her students. What type of standardized test might Peggy use to gather data related to this concern?

4. In investigating the problems that her students were having in math, Peggy checked out their overall test scores from past standardized tests. What else might she have done?

To receive feedback for these questions, go to Appendix B.

Your licensure exam will also include multiple-choice questions similar to those your instructor has given you on your quizzes and tests for this course.

Important Concepts

accountability (p. 525)
achievement tests (p. 528)
aptitude tests (p. 531)
assessment bias (p. 541)
construct validity (p. 533)
content validity (p. 532)
criterion-referenced
    standardized tests (p. 528)
diagnostic tests (p. 529)
frequency distribution (p. 534)
grade-equivalent score (p. 538)

high-stakes tests (p. 525)
intelligence tests (p. 529)
mean (p. 535)
measures of central tendency
    (p. 535)
median (p. 535)
mode (p. 535)
national norms (p. 527)
normal distribution (p. 536)
norm-referenced
    standardized tests (p. 528)

norming group (p. 527)
percentile bands (p. 538)
percentile rank (PR) (p. 537)
predictive validity (p. 533)
range (p. 535)
raw score (p. 537)
readiness tests (p. 531)
standard deviation (p. 535)
standard error of
    measurement (p. 539)
standard score (p. 539)

standardized tests (p. 526)
standards (p. 525)
standards-based education
    (p. 525)
stanine (p. 538)
true score (p. 539)
t-score (p. 539)
variability (p. 535)
z-score (p. 539)

Go to the Topic: Assessment in the MyEducationLab (www.myeducationlab.com) for *Educational Psychology: Windows on Classrooms,* where you can:

- Find learning outcomes for Assessment along with the national standards that connect to these outcomes.
- Complete Assignments and Activities that can help you more deeply understand the chapter content.
- Apply and practice your understanding of the core teaching skills identified in the chapter with the Building Teaching Skills and Dispositions learning units.
- Examine challenging situations and cases presented in the IRIS Center Resources.
- Access video clips of CCSSO National Teachers of the Year award winners responding to the question, "Why Do I Teach?" in the Teacher Talk section.
- See video examples included within the Study Plan that provide concrete and real-world illustrations of the topics presented in the chapter.
- Check your comprehension of the content covered in the chapter with the Study Plan. Here you will be able to take a chapter quiz, receive feedback on your answers, and then access Review, Practice, and Enrichment activities to enhance your understanding of chapter content.

MyEducationLab

references

Abe, J. A., & Izzard, C. E. (1999). Compliance, noncompliance strategies, and the correlates of compliance in 5-year-old Japanese and American children. *Social Development, 8,* 1–20.

Abedi, J. (2006). Language issues in item development. In S. Downing, & T. Haladyna (Eds.), *Handbook of test development* (pp. 377–398). Mahwah, NJ: Erlbaum.

Abedi, J., & Gandara, P. (2006). Performance of English language learners as a subgroup in large-scale assessment: Interaction of research and policy. *Educational Measurement: Issues and Practice, 25*(4), 36–46.

Abedi, J., Hofstetter, C., & Lord, C. (2004). Assessment accommodations for English language learners: Implications for policy-based empirical research. *Review of Educational Research, 74*(1), 1–28.

Aboud, F., & Skerry, S. (1984). The development of ethnic identity: A critical review. *Journal of Cross-Cultural Psychology, 15,* 3–34.

Ackerman, P., & Lohman, D. (2006). Individual differences in cognitive function. In P. A. Alexander & P. H. Winne (Eds.), *Handbook of educational psychology* (2nd ed., pp. 139–162). Mahwah, NJ: Erlbaum.

Adams, C. (2006). PowerPoint, habits of mind, and classroom culture. *Journal of Curriculum Studies, 38,* 389–411.

Aiken, L., & Grath-Marnat, G. (2006). *Psychological testing and assessment* (12th ed.). Boston: Pearson.

Aikens, N., & Barbarin, O. (2008). Socioeconomic differences in reading trajectories: The contribution of family, neighborhood, and school contexts. *Journal of Educational Psychology, 100,* 235–251.

Alberto, P. A., & Troutman, A. C. (2009). *Applied behavior analysis for teachers* (8th ed.). Upper Saddle River, NJ: Merrill/Pearson.

Alder, N. (2002). Interpretations of the meaning of care: Creating caring relationships in urban middle school classrooms. *Urban Education, 37*(2), 241–266.

Aldous, J. (2006). Family, ethnicity, and immigrant youths' educational achievements. *Journal of Family Issues, 27,* 1633–1667.

Alexander, J. M., Johnson, K. E., & Leibham, M. E. (2005). Constructing domain-specific knowledge in kindergarten: Relations among knowledge, intelligence, and strategic performance. *Learning and Individual Differences, 15,* 35–52.

Alexander, P. (2003). The development of expertise: The journey from acclimation to proficiency. *Educational Researcher, 32*(8), 10–14.

Alexander, P. (2006). *Psychology in learning and instruction.* Upper Saddle River, NJ: Pearson.

Alexander, P. (2006). *Psychology in learning and instruction.* Upper Saddle River, NJ: Merrill/Pearson.

Alim, H., & Baugh, J. (Eds.). (2007). *Talkin black talk: Language, education, and social change.* New York: Teachers College Press.

Allington, R. L., & McGill-Franzen, A. (2003). The impact of summer setback on the reading achievement gap. *Phi Delta Kappan, 85*(1), 68–71.

Alparsian, C., Tekkaya, C., & Geban, O. (2004). Using the conceptual change instruction to improve learning. *Journal of Biological Education, 37,* 133–137.

Alperstein, J. F. (2005). Commentary on girls, boys, test scores and more. *Teachers College Record,* May 16, 2005. Retrieved from http://tcrecord.org ID Number: 11874

American Association on Intellectual and Developmental Disabilities (AAIDD). (2008). Retrieved from http://www.aaidd.org/content_185.cfm

American Educational Research Association, American Psychological Association, & National Council on Measurement in Education. (1999). *Standards for educational and psychological testing* (2nd ed.). Washington, DC: Author.

Anderman, E. M., & Maehr, M. (1994). Motivation and schooling in the middle grades. *Review of Educational Research, 64,* 287–309.

Anderman, E. M., & Wolters, C. A. (2006). Goals, values, and affect: Influences on motivation. In P. A. Alexander & P. H. Winne (Eds.), *Handbook of educational psychology* (2nd ed., pp. 369–389). Mahwah, NJ: Erlbaum.

Anderman, E., & Murdock, T. (2007). *Psychology of academic cheating.* Burlington, MA: Elsevier Academic Press.

Anderson, D., & Nashon, S. (2007). Predators of knowledge construction: Interpreting students' metacognition in an amusement park physics program. *Science Education, 91,* 298–320.

Anderson, J. R. (2005). *Cognitive psychology and its implications* (6th ed.). New York: Worth.

Anderson, J. R. (2007). Information-processing modules and their relative modality specificity. *Cognitive Psychology, 54*(3), 185–217.

Anderson, K., & Minke, K. (2007). Parent involvement in education: Toward an understanding of parents' decision making. *Journal of Educational Research, 199*(5), 311–323.

Anderson, L., & Krathwohl, D. (Eds.). (2001). *A taxonomy for learning, teaching, and assessing: A revision of Bloom's taxonomy of educational objectives.* New York: Addison Wesley Longman.

Anderson, P. M., & Summerfield, J. P. (2004). Why is urban education different from suburban and rural education? In S. R. Steinberg & J. L. Kinchloe (Eds.), *19 urban questions: Teaching in the city* (pp. 29–39). New York: Peter Lang.

Anderson, R., Nguyen-Jahiel, K., McNurlen, B., Archodidou, A., Kim, S., Reznitskaya, A.,

Tillmanns, M., & Gilbert, L. (2001). The snowball phenomenon: Spread of ways of talking and ways of thinking across groups of children. *Cognition and Instruction, 19*(1), 1–46.

Andrew, L. (2007). Comparison of teacher educators' instructional methods with the constructivist ideal. *The Teacher Educator, 42,* 157–184.

Anfara, V., & Mertens, S. (2008). Do single-sex classes and schools make a difference? *Middle School Journal, 40*(2), 52–57.

Antil, L., Jenkins, J., Wayne, S., & Vadasy, P. (1998). Cooperative learning: Prevalence, conceptualizations, and the relation between research and practice. *American Educational Research Journal, 35*(3), 419–454.

Applebee, A., Langer, J., Nystrand, M., & Gamoran, A. (2003). Discussion-based approaches to developing understanding: Classroom instruction and student performance in middle and high school English. *American Educational Research Journal, 40*(3), 685–730.

Arnett, J. J. (2002). High hopes in a grim world: Emerging adults' view of their futures and of "Generation X." *Youth and Society, 31,* 267–286.

Aronson, E., Wilson, T. D., & Akert, R. D. (2010). *Social psychology* (7th ed.). Upper Saddle River, NJ: Pearson.

Ashiabi, G., & O'Neal, K. (2008). A framework for understanding the association between food insecurity and children's development outcomes. *Child Development Perspectives, 2,* 71–77.

Atkinson, R., & Shiffrin, R. (1968). Human memory: A proposed system and its control processes. In K. Spence & J. Spence (Eds.), *The psychology of learning and motivation: Advances in research and theory* (Vol. 2). San Diego, CA: Academic Press.

Au, K. (1992, April). *"There's almost a lesson here": Teacher and students' purposes in constructing the theme of a story.* Paper presented at the annual meeting of the American Educational Research Association, San Francisco.

Au, W. (2007). High-stakes testing and curricular control: A qualitative metasynthesis. *Educational Researcher, 36*(5), 258–267.

Austin, J. L., Lee, M., & Carr, J. P. (2004). The effects of guided notes on undergraduate students' recording of lecture content. *Journal of Instructional Psychology, 31,* 314–320.

Ausubel, D. P. (1963). *The psychology of meaningful verbal learning.* New York: Grune & Stratton.

Ausubel, D. P. (1968). *Educational psychology: A cognitive view.* New York: Holt, Rinehart & Winston.

Ausubel, D. P. (1977). The facilitation of meaningful verbal learning in the classroom. *Educational Psychologist, 12,* 162–178.

Ayduk, O., Mendoza-Denton, R., Mischel, W., Downey, G., Peake, P. K., & Rodriguez, M. (2000). Regulating the interpersonal self: Strategic self-regulation for coping with rejection sensitivity. *Journal of Personality and Social Psychology, 79*, 776–792.

Babad, E., Bernieri, F., & Rosenthal, R. (1991). Students as judges of teachers' verbal and nonverbal behavior. *American Educational Research Journal, 28*(1), 211–234.

Baddeley, A. (2001). Is working memory still working? *American Psychologist, 56*, 851–864.

Baddeley, A. D. (1986). *Working memory: Theory and practice.* London, UK: Oxford University Press.

Bailey, S. (1993). The current status of gender equity research in American Schools. *Educational psychologist, 28*, 321–339.

Baines, L. (2007). Learning from the world: Achieving more by doing less. *Phi Delta Kappan, 89*, 98–100.

Baker, D. (2006). For Navajo, science and tradition intertwine. *Salt Lake Tribune*, pp. D1, D5.

Baker, D., & Letendre, G. (2005). *National differences, global similarities: World culture and the future of schooling.* Sanford, CA: Stanford University Press.

Baker, S., Gersten, R., Haager, D., & Dingle, M. (2006). Teaching practice and the reading growth of first-grade English learners: Validation of an observation instrument. *Elementary School Journal, 107*(2), 199–220.

Baldwin, J. D., & Baldwin, J. I. (2001). *Behavior principles in everyday life* (4th ed.). Upper Saddle River, NJ: Prentice Hall.

Ball, A. (2010). Cultural studies—Facebook bios—truth or fiction? *New York Times, June 18.* Accessed 6/20/2010 at http://www.nytimes.com/2010/06/20/fashion/20CulturalFacebook.html.

Ball, D. (1992, Summer). Magical hopes: Manipulatives and the reform of math education. *American Educator*, pp. 28–33.

Bandura, A. (1986). *Social foundations of thought and action: A social cognitive theory.* Upper Saddle River, NJ: Prentice Hall.

Bandura, A. (1997). *Self-efficacy: The exercise of control.* New York: Freeman.

Bandura, A. (2001). Social cognitive theory. In *Annual Review of Psychology.* Palo Alto, CA: Annual Review.

Bandura, A. (2004, May). *Toward a psychology of human agency.* Paper presented at the meeting of the American Psychological Society, Chicago.

Banks, J. (2008). *An introduction to multicultural education* (4th ed.). Boston: Allyn & Bacon.

Barkley, R. (Ed.) (2006). *Attention-deficit hyper-activity disorder: A handbook for diagnosis and treatment* (3rd ed.). New York: Guilford.

Barnes, S. P., Torrens, A., & George, V. (2007). The use of portfolios in coordinated school health programs: Benefits and challenges to imple-mentation. *The Journal of School Health, 77*, 171–179.

Barnett, S. M., & Ceci, S. J. (2002). When and where do we apply what we learn? A taxonomy of far transfer. *Psychological Bulletin, 128*, 612–637.

Barr, R., D., & Parrett, W. H. (2001). *Hope fulfilled for at-risk and violent youth* (2nd ed.). Boston: Allyn & Bacon.

Bauerlein, M. (2008). *The dumbest generation: How the digital age stupefies young Americans and jeopardizes our future.* New York: Penguin.

Baum, K., Dinkes, R., Kemp, J. & Snyder, T. D. (2010). *Indicators of school crime and safety: 2009.* Bureau of Justice Statistics. Retrieve from http://bjs.ojp.usdoj.gov/index.cfm?ty=pbdetail&iid=1762

Baumeister, R. F., & DeWall, C. N. (2005). The inner dimension of social exclusion: Intelligent thought and self-regulation among rejected persons. In K. D. Williams, J. P. Forgas, & W. von Hippel (Eds.), *The social outcast: Ostracism, social exclusion, rejection, and bullying* (pp. 53–73). New York: Psychology Press.

Baumeister, R., Campbell, J., Krueger, J., & Vohs, K. (2003). Does high self-esteem cause better performance, interpersonal success, happiness, or healthier lifestyles? *Psychological Science in the Public Interest, 4*, 1–44.

Baumrind, D. (1991). The influence of parenting style on adolescent competence and substance use. *Journal of Early Adolecence, 11*, 56–95.

Begley, S. (2010, June 28 and July 5). This is your brain. Aging. *Newsweek*, 64–68.

Bembenutty, H. (2009). Test anxiety and academic delay of gratification. *College Student Journal, 43*, 10–21.

Bennett, N., & Blundel, D. (1983). Quantity and quality of work in rows of classroom groups. *Educational Psychology, 3*, 93–105.

Benson, P., Scales, P., Hamilton, S., & Sesma, A. (2006). Positive youth development: Theory, research, and applications. In R. Lerner (Vol. Ed.), *Handbook of child psychology: Vol. 1. Theoretical models of human development* (6th ed., pp. 894–941). Hoboken, NJ: John Wiley & Sons, Inc.

Bental, B., & Tirosh, E. (2007). The relationship between attention, executive functions and reading domain abilities in attention deficit hyperactivity disorder and reading disorder: A comparative study. *The Journal of Child Psychology and Psychiatry and Allied Disciplines, 48*, 455–463.

Bereiter, C., & Scardamalia, M. (2006). Education for the knowledge age: Design-centered models of teaching and instruction. In P. A. Alexander & P. H. Winne (Eds.), *Handbook of educational psychology* (2nd ed., pp. 695–714). Mahwah, NJ: Erlbaum.

Berger, K. (2007). Update on bullying at school: Science forgotten? *Developmental Review*, 90–126.

Berk, L. (2010). *Development through the lifespan* (5th ed.). Boston: Allyn & Bacon/Pearson.

Berk, L. (2011). *Infants & children* (7th ed.). Boston: Allyn & Bacon/Pearson.

Berliner, D. C. (2000). A personal response to those who bash education. *Journal of Teacher Educa-tion, 51*, 358–371.

Berliner, D. (2005). Our impoverished view of educational reform. *Teachers College Record,*

August 2. ID Number: 12106. Retrieved from http://www.tcrecord.org

Berliner, D. C. (2006). Educational psychology: Searching for essence throughout a century of influence. In P. A. Alexander & P. H. Winne (Eds.), *Handbook of educational psychology* (2nd ed., pp. 3–42). Mahwah, NJ: Erlbaum.

Berninger, V. (2006). A developmental approach to learning disabilities. In K.A. Renninger & I. Sigel (Vol. Eds.), *Handbook of child psychology: Vol. 4. Child psychology in practice* (6th ed., pp. 420–452). Hoboken, NJ: John Wiley & Sons.

Berrill, D., & Whalen, C. (2007). "Where are the children?" Personal integrity and reflective teaching portfolios. *Teaching and Teacher Education, 23*, 868–884.

Berzonsky, M. D., & Kuk, L. S. (2000). Identity status, identity processing style, and the transition to university. *Journal of Adolescent Research, 15*, 81–98.

Bettis, P., & Adams, N. (Eds.) (2005). *Geographies of girlhood: Identities in-between.* Mahwah, NJ: Lawrence Erlbaum.

Bielenberg, B., & Fillmore, L. W. (2005). The English they need for the test. *Educational Leadership, 62*(4), 45–49.

Biemiller, A. (2005). Addressing developmental patterns in vocabulary. In E. H. Hiebert, & M. L. Kamil (Eds.), *Teaching and learning vocabulary.* Mahwah, NJ: Erlbaum.

Biscaro, M., Broer, K., & Taylor, N. (2004). Self-efficacy, alcohol expectancy and problem-solving appraisal as predictors of alcohol use in college students. *College Student Journal, 38*, 541–555.

Black, P., Harrison, C., Lee, C., Marshall, B., & William, D. (2004). Working inside the black box: Assessment for learning in the classroom. *Phi Delta Kappan, 86*(1), 9–21.

Black, S. (2007). Apprenticeships: A tradition that works. *American School Board Journal, 194*(2), 38–40.

Blakemore, S., & Frith, U. (2005). The learning brain: Lessons for education: A precis. *Developmental Science, 8*, 459–461.

Blanchett, W. (2006). Disproportionate representation of African American students in special education: Acknowledging the role of white privilege and racism. *Educational Researcher, 35*(6), 24–28.

Blatchford, P, Baines, E., Rubie-Davies, C., Bassett, P., & Chowne, A. (2006). The effect of a new approach to group work on pupil–pupil and teacher–pupil interactions. *Journal of Educational Psychology, 98*(4), 750–765.

Bleeker, M. M., & Jacobs, J. E. (2004). Achievement in math and science: Do mothers' beliefs matter 12 years later? *Journal of Educational Psychology, 96*(1), 97–109.

Block, M. (2007). Climate changes lives of whalers in Alaska. All Things Considered. National Public Radio. Retrieved from http://www.npr.org/templates/story/story.php?storyId=14428086

Bloom, B., Englehart, M., Furst, E., Hill, W., & Krathwohl, O. (1956). *Taxonomy of educational* objectives: *The classification of educational goals: Handbook 1. The cognitive domain*. White Plains, NY: Longman.

Bloom, P. (2010). The moral life of babies. *The New York Times Magazine*. Retrieved from http://www.nytimes.com/2010/05/09/magazine/09babies-t.html?_r=1&pagewanted=print.

Blum, R. (2005). A case for school connectedness. *Educational Leadership, 62*(8), 16–19.

Blumenfeld, P., Kempler, T., & Krajcik, J. (2006). Motivation and cognitive engagement in learning environments. In R. K. Sawyer (Ed.), *Cambridge handbook of the learning sciences* (pp. 475–488). Cambridge, MA: Cambridge University Press.

Bogdan W., & Struzynska-Kujalowicz, A. (2007). Power influences self-esteem. *Social Cognition, 25*, 472–494.

Bohn, C. M., Roehrig, A. D., & Pressley, M. (2004). The first days of school in the classrooms of two more effective and four less effective primary-grades teachers. *Elementary School Journal, 104*(4), 269–288.

Bolívar, J. M., & Chrispeels, J. H. (2011). Enhancing parent leadership through building social and intellectual capital. *American Educational Research Journal, 48*, 4–38.

Bonanno, R. A., & Hymel, S. (2010). Beyond hurt feelings: Investigating why some victims of bullying are at greater risk for suicidal ideation. *Merrill-Palmer Quarterly, 56*, 420–440.

Bong, M. (2001). Between- and within-domain relations of academic motivation among middle and high school students: Self-efficacy, task-value, and achievement goals. *Journal of Educational Psychology, 93*, 23–34.

Borko, H., & Putnam, R. (1996). Learning to teach. In D. Berliner & R. Calfee (Eds.), *Handbook of educational psychology* (pp. 673–708). New York: Macmillan.

Borman, G., & Overman, L. (2004). Academic resilience in mathematics among poor and minority students. *Elementary School Journal, 104*(3), 177–196.

Bourne, L. (1982). Typicality effects in logically defined categories. *Memory & Cognition, 10*, 3–9.

Braaksma, M., Rijlaarsdam, G., van den Bergh, H., & van Hout-Wolters, B. (2004). Observational learning and its effects on the orchestration of writing processes. *Cognition & Instruction, 22*(1), 1–36.

Bracey, G. (2005). A nation of cheats. *Phi Delta Kappan, 86*(5), 412–413.

Brady Campaign to Prevent Gun Violence. (2010). *Major school shootings in the United States since 1997*. Retrieved from http://www.bradycampaign.org/xshare/pdf/school-shootings.pdf

Brainerd, C. J. (2003). Jean Piaget, learning research, and American education. In B. Zimmerman & D. Schunk (Eds.), *Educational psychology: A century of contributions* (pp. 251–287). New York: Routledge.

Bransford, J. D., & Schwartz, D. L. (1999). Rethinking transfer: A simple proposal with multiple implications. *Review of Research in Education* (Vol. 24, pp. 61–100). Washington, DC: American Educational Research Association.

Bransford, J., Brown, A., & Cocking, R. (Eds.). (2000). *How people learn: Brain, mind, experience, and school*. Washington, DC: National Academy Press.

Bransford, J., Darling-Hammond, L., & LePage, P. (2005). Introduction. In L. Darling-Hammond & J. Bransford (Eds.), *Preparing teachers for a changing world: What teachers should learn and be able to do* (pp. 1–39). San Francisco: Jossey-Bass/Wiley.

Bransford, J., Derry, S., Berliner, D., Hammerness, K, & Beckett, K. L. (2005). Theories of learning and their roles in teaching. In L. Darling-Hammond & J. Bransford (Eds.), *Preparing teachers for a changing world: What teachers should learn and be able to do* (pp. 40–87). San Francisco: John Wiley & Sons.

Brehmer, Y., & Li, S-C. (2007). Memory plasticity across the life span: Uncovering children's latent potential. *Developmental Psychology, 43*, 465–478.

Brendgen, M., Vitar, F., Boivin, M., Dionne, G., & Perusse, D. (2006). Examining genetic and environmental effects on reactive versus proactive aggression. *Developmental Psychology, 42*(6), 1299–1312.

Bronfenbrenner, U., & Morris, P. (2006). The bioecological model of human development. In R. Lerner (Ed.), *Handbook of child psychology: Vol. 1 Theoretical models of human development* (6th ed., pp. 793–828). Hoboken, NJ: John Wiley & Sons, Inc.

Brookhart, S. (2007/2008). Feedback that fits. *Educational Leadership, 65*(4), 54–59.

Brookhart, S. M., Walsh, J. M., & Zientarski, W. A. (2006). The dynamics of motivation and effort for classroom assessments in middle school science and social studies. *Applied Measurement in Education, 19*, 151–184.

Brooks, D. (2011). *The social animal: The hidden sources of love, character, and achievement*. New York: Random House.

Brophy, J. (2006). History of research on classroom management. In C. M. Evertson & C. S. Weinstein (Eds.), *Handbook of classroom management: Research, practice, and contemporary issues* (pp. 17–43). Mahwah, NJ: Erlbaum.

Brophy, J. (2006a). Graham Nuttall and social constructivist teaching; Research-based cautions and qualifications. *Teaching and Teacher Education, 22*, 529–537.

Brophy, J. (2006b). Observational research on generic aspects of classroom teaching. In P. A. Alexander & P. H. Winne (Eds.), *Handbook of educational psychology* (2nd ed., pp. 755–780). Mahwah, NJ: Erlbaum.

Brophy, J. (2006c). Observational research on generic aspects of classroom teaching. In P. A. Alexander & P. H. Winne (Eds.), *Handbook of educational psychology* (2nd ed., pp. 755–780). Mahwah, NJ: Erlbaum.

Brophy, J. (2010). *Motivating students to learn* (3rd ed.). New York: Routledge.

Brophy, J., & Alleman, J. (2003). Primary-grade students' knowledge and thinking about the supply of utilities (water, heat, and light) to modern homes. *Cognition & Instruction, 21*(1), 79–112.

Brophy, J., & Good, T. (1986). Teacher behavior and student achievement. In M. Wittrock (Ed.), *Handbook of research on teaching* (3rd ed., pp. 328–375). New York: Macmillan.

Brown, A., & Campione, J. (1994). Guided discovery in a community of learners. In K. McGilly (Ed.), *Classroom lessons: Integrating cognitive theory and classroom practice* (pp. 229–270). Cambridge, MA: MIT Press.

Brown, J., Collins, A., & Duguid, P. (1989). Situated cognition and the culture of learning. *Educational Researcher, 18*, 32–42.

Brown-Chidsey, R. (2007). No more "Waiting to fail." *Educational Leadership, 65*(2), 40–46.

Bruner, J. S. (1960). *The process of education*. Cambridge, MA: Harvard University Press.

Bruner, J. S. (1966). *Toward a theory of instruction*. New York: Norton.

Bruner, J. S. (1990). *Acts of meaning*. Cambridge, MA: Harvard University Press.

Bruner, J., Goodenow, J., & Austin, G. (1956). *A study of thinking*. New York: Wiley.

Bruning, R. H., Schraw, G. J., & Norby, M. M. (2011). *Cognitive psychology and instruction* (5th ed.). Upper Saddle River, NJ: Prentice Hall.

Bryan, C. L., & Solmon, M. A. (2007). Self-determination in physical education: Designing class environments to promote active lifestyles. *Journal of Teaching in Physical Education, 26*, 260–278.

Buck, G., Kostin, I., & Morgan, R. (2002). *Examining the relationship of content to gender-based performance difference in advanced placement exams*. (Research Report No. 2002-12). New York: College Board.

Bukowski, W. M., Brendgen, M., & Vitaro, F. (2007). Peers and socialization: Effects on externalizing and internalizing problems. In J. E. Brusec & P. D. Hastings (Eds.), *Handbook of socialization: Theory and research* (pp. 355–381). New York: Guilford Press.

Bulgren, J., Deshler, D., Schumaker, J., & Lenz, B. K. (2000). The use and effectiveness of analogical instruction in diverse secondary content classrooms. *Journal of Educational Psychology, 92*(3), 426–441.

Bullough, R., Jr. (1989). *First-year teacher: A case study*. New York: Teachers College Press.

Bumiller, E. (2010, April 26). We have met the enemy and he is PowerPoint. *New York Times*, p. A1. Retrieved from www.nytimes.com/2010/04/27/world/27powerpoint.html

Burack, J., Flanagan, T., Peled, T., Sutton, J., Zygmuntowicz, C., & Manley, J. (2006). Social perspective-taking skills in maltreated children and adolescents. *Developmental Psychology, 42*, 207–217.

Burbules, N., & Bruce, B. (2001). Theory and research on teaching as dialogue. In V. Richardson (Ed.), *Handbook of research on teaching*

(4th ed., pp. 1102–1121). Washington, DC: America Educational Research Association.

Burke, L. A., Williams, J. M., & Skinner, D. (2007). Teachers' perceptions of thinking skills in the primary curriculum. *Research in Education, 77*, 1–13.

Burns, M. (2005). Looking at how students reason. *Educational Leadership, 63*(3), 26–31.

Bushaw, W. J., & Lopez, S. J. (2010). A time for change: The 42nd annual Phi Delta Kappa/ Gallup Poll of the Public's attitude toward the public schools. *Phi Delta Kappan, 92*, 9–26.

Bushman, B. J., Moeller, S. J., & Crocker. J. (2010). Sweets, sex, or self-esteem? Comparing the value of self-esteem boosts with other pleasant rewards. *Journal of Personality.* "Accepted Article"; doi: 10.1111/j.1467-6494.2010.00712.x

Byars, B. (1970) *Summer of the swans.* New York: Viking.

Byrnes, J. (2007). Some ways in which neuroscientific research can be relevant to education. In D. Coch, J. Fischer, & G. Dawson (Eds.), *Human behavior, learning, and the developing brain: Typical development* (pp. 30–49). New York: Guilford Press.

California State Board of Education. (2008). *Grade ten. History-Social Science Content Standards.* Retrieved from http://www.cde.ca.gov/be/st/ss/ hstgrade10.asp

Cameron, J., Pierce, W. D., & Banko, K. M. (2005). Achievement-based rewards and intrinsic motivation: A test of cognitive mediators. *Journal of Educational Psychology, 97*, 641–655.

Campbell, F., & Burchinal, M. (2008). Early childhood interventions: The Abecedarian Project. In *Extending intelligence: Enhancement and new constructs* (pp. 61–84). New York: Erlbaum/ Taylor & Francis.

Camras, L., Chen, Y., Bakeman, R., Norris, K., & Cain, T. (2006). Culture, ethnicity, and children's facial expressions: A study of European American, Mainland Chinese, Chinese American, and adopted Chinese girls. *Emotion, 6*, 103–114.

Canter, A. (2004). A problem-solving model for improving student achievement. *Principal Leadership, 5*, 11–15.

Canter, L. (1996). First the rapport—then the rules. *Learning, 24*, 12–13.

Card, N., & Hodges, E. V. (2008). Peer victimization among school children: Correlates, causes, consequences, and considerations in assessment and intervention. *School Psychology Quarterly, 23*, 451–461.

Carey, B. (2007, September 4). Bipolar illness soars as a diagnosis for the young. *New York Times*, pp. A1, A15.

Carey, B. (2010). Forget what you know about good study habits. *The New York Times.* Retrieved from http://www.nytimes.com/2010/09/07/ health/views/07mind.html?_r=1&th=&emc=th &pagewanted=print

Carey, B. (2010). Tracing the spark of creative problem-solving. *The New York Times.* Retrieved from http://www.nytimes.com/2010/12/07/ science/07brain.html?_r=1&ref=science

Carnine, D., Silbert, J., Kameenui, E., Tarver, S., & Jongjohann, K. (2006). *Teaching struggling and at-risk readers: A direct instruction approach.* Upper Saddle River, NJ: Merrill/Pearson.

Carr, N. (2008). Is Google making us stupid? *The Atlantic, 301*(6). Retrieved from http://www .theatlantic.com/magazine/archive/2008/07/ is-google-making-us-stupid/6868/

Carr, N. (2008). Talking about test scores. *American School Board Journal, 195*(1), 38–39.

Carr, N. (2010). *The shallows: What the Internet is doing to our brains.* New York: W. W. Norton.

Carter, D. R., & Van Norman, R. K. (2010). Class-wide positive behavior support in preschool: Improving teacher implementation through consultation. *Early Childhood Education Journal, 38*, 279–288.

Carter, K., & Doyle, W. (2006). Classroom management in early childhood and elementary classrooms. In C. M. Evertson & C. S. Weinstein (Eds.), *Handbook of classroom management: Research, practice, and contemporary issues* (pp. 373–406). Mahwah, NJ: Erlbaum.

Carver, S. (2006). Assessing for deep understanding. In R. K. Sawyer (Ed.), *Cambridge handbook of the learning sciences* (pp. 205–224). Cambridge, MA: Cambridge University Press.

Case, R. (1992). *The mind's staircase: Exploring the conceptual underpinnings of children's thought and knowledge.* Hillsdale, NJ: Erlbaum.

Case, R. (1998). The development of central conceptual structures. In D. Kuhn & R. Siegler (Eds.), *Handbook of child psychology: Vol. 2. Cognition, perception, and language* (5th ed., pp. 745–800). New York: Wiley.

Cassady, J. (1999, April). *The effects of examples as elaboration in text on memory and learning.* Paper presented at the annual meeting of the American Educational Research Association, Montreal, Canada.

Cassady, J. C., & Johnson, R. E. (2002). Cognitive anxiety and academic performance. *Contemporary Educational Psychology, 27*, 270–295.

Castagno, A., & Brayboy, B. (2008). Culturally responsive schooling for Indigenous youth: A review of the literature. *Review of Educational Research, 78*, 612–628.

Cattel, R. (1963). Theory of fluid and crystallized intelligence: A critical experiment. *Journal of Educational Psychology, 54*, 1–22.

Cattel, R. (1987). *Intelligence: Its structure, growth, and action.* Amsterdam: North-Holland.

Ceci, S. (2003). Cast in six ponds and you'll reel in something: Looking back on 25 years of research. *American Psychologist, 58*, 855–864.

Centers for Disease Control and Prevention (CDC). (2010a). *Alcohol and drug use.* Retrieved from http://www.cdc.gov/HealthyYouth/alcoholdrug/ index.htm

Centers for Disease Control and Prevention (CDC). (2010b). *Strategies for increasing protective factors among youth.* Retrieved from http://www.cdc .gov/HealthyYouth/AdolescentHealth/ connectedness.htm

Centers for Disease Control and Prevention (CDC). (2010c). Tobacco use. Retrieved from http:// www.cdc.gov/HealthyYouth/tobacco/index.htm

Chaffen, R., & Imreh, G. (2002). Practicing perfection: Piano performance and expert memory. *Psychological Science, 13*, 342–349.

Chao, R. (2001). Extending research on the consequences of parenting style for Chinese American and European Americans. *Child Development, 72*, 1832–1843.

Charles, C., & Senter, G. (2005). *Building classroom discipline* (8th ed.). Boston: Allyn & Bacon.

Charles, C. M., & Senter, G. W. (2012). *Elementary classroom management* (6th ed.). New York: Addison Wesley.

Checkley, K. (1997). The first seven . . . and the eighth. *Educational Leadership, 55*, 8–13.

Chen, J. (2004). Theory of multiple intelligences: Is it a scientific theory? *Teachers College Record, 106*, 17–23.

Chen, X., Anderson, R., Li, W., Hao, M., Wu, X., & Shu, H. (2004). Phonological awareness of bilingual and monolingual Chinese children. *Journal of Educational Psychology, 96*, 142–151.

Chen, X., Wu, H., Chen, H., Wang, L., & Cen, G. (2001). Parenting practices and aggressive behavior in Chinese children. *Parenting: Science and Practice, 1*, 159–184.

Choi, N. (2005). Self-efficacy and self-concept as predictors of college students' academic performance. *Psychology in the Schools, 42*(2), 197–205.

Chomsky, N. (1972). *Language and mind* (2nd ed.). Orlando, FL: Harcourt Brace.

Chomsky, N. (2006). *Language and mind* (3rd ed.). Cambridge, England: Cambridge University Press.

Chomsky, N., & Miller, G. (1958). Finite-state languages. *Information and Control, 1*, 91–112.

Chorzempa, B., & Graham, S. (2006). Primary-grade teachers' use of within-class ability grouping in reading. *Journal of Educational Psychology, 98*(3), 529–541.

Christakis, N. A. & Fowler, J. H. (2009). *Connected: The surprising power of our social networks and how they shape our lives.* New York: Little, Brown and Company.

Christenson, S., & Havsy, L. (2004). Family–school–peer relationships: Significance for social, emotional, and academic learning. In J. Zins, R. Weissberg, M. Wang, & H. Walberg (Eds.), *Building academic success on social and emotional learning* (pp. 59–75). New York: Teachers College Press.

Christenson, S., & Thurlow, M. (2004). School dropouts: Prevention, considerations, interventions, and challenges. *Current Directions in Psychological Science, 13*, 36–39.

Chronicle, E., MacGregor, J., & Ormerod, T. (2004). What makes an insight problem? The roles of heuristics, goal conception, and solution recoding in knowledge-learn problems. *Journal of Experimental Psychology: Learning, Memory, and Cognition, 30*(1), 14–217.

Chumlea, W., Schubert, C., Roche, A., Kulin, H., Lee, P., Himes, J., & Sun, S. (2003). Age at menarche and racial comparisons in U.S. girls. *Pediatrics, 111*(1), 110–113.

Cimera, R. (2006). *Mental retardation doesn't mean "stupid"! A guide for parents and teachers.* New York: Rowman & Littlefield, Lanham.

Ciofalo, J. F., & Wylie, E. G. (2006, January 10). Using diagnostic classroom assessment: One question at a time. *Teachers College Record,* Retrieved from http://www.tcrecord.org/Content.asp.?ContentID=12285

Clark, B. D., Goldberg, E. M., & Rudy, B. (2009). Electrogenic tuning of the axon initial segment. *Neuroscientist 15,* 651–668.

Clark, J., & Paivio, A. (1991). Dual coding theory and education. *Educational Psychology Review, 3,* 149–210.

Clark, K., & Clark, M. (1939). The development of consciousness of self and the emergence of racial identification in Negro preschool children. *Journal of Social Psychology, 10,* 591–599.

Clark, R. C. (2010). *Evidence-based training methods: A guide for training professionals.* Alexandria, VA: ASTD Press.

Clark, R. C., & Mayer, R. E. (2003). *e-learning and the science of instruction: Proven guidelines for consumers and designers of multimedia learning.* San Francisco: Pfeiffer/Wiley.

Clarke, A. (2006). The nature and substance of cooperating teacher reflection. *Teaching and Teacher Education, 22,* 910–921.

Clarke-Stewart, A., & Dunn, J. (Eds.). (2006). *Families count: Effects on child and adolescent development.* New York: Cambridge University Press.

Coffield, F., Moseley, D., Hall, E., & Ecclestone, K. (2004). *Learning styles and pedagogy in post-16 learning: A systematic and critical review.* London: Learning and Skills Research Centre/University of Newcastle upon Tyne.

Cognition and Technology Group at Vanderbilt. (1992). The Jasper Series as an example of anchored instruction: Theory, program description and assessment data. *Educational Psychologist, 27,* 291–315.

Cohen, E. (1994). Restructuring the classroom: Conditions for productive small groups. *Review of Educational Research, 64,* 1–35.

Coiro, J., & Dobler, E. (2007). Exploring the online reading comprehension strategies used by sixth-grade skilled readers to search for and locate information on the Internet. *Reading Research Quarterly, 42,* 214–257.

Colangelo, N., & Davis, G. (Eds.). (2003). *Handbook of gifted education* (3rd ed.). Boston: Allyn & Bacon.

Cole, M., Cole, S. R., & Lightfoot, C. (2005). *The development of children* (5th ed.). New York: W. H. Freeman.

Cole, M., Cole, S. R., & Lightfoot, C. (2009). *The development of children* (6th ed.). New York: W. H. Freeman.

Coles, G. (2004). Danger in the classroom: "Brain glitch" research and learning to read. *Phi Delta Kappan, 85*(5), 344–351.

Coll, C., Bearer, E., & Lerner, R. (Eds.). (2004). *Nature and nurture: The complex interplay of genetic and environmental influences on human behavior and development.* Mahwah, NJ: Erlbaum.

Collins, A. (2006). Cognitive apprenticeship. In R. K. Sawyer (Ed.), *Cambridge handbook of the learning sciences* (pp. 47–60). Cambridge, MA: Cambridge University Press.

Collins, W. A., Maccoby, E. E., Steinberg, L., Hetherington, E. M., & Bornstein, M. H. (2000). Contemporary research on parenting: The case for nature and nurture. *American Psychologist, 55,* 218–232.

Collins, W., & Steinberg, L. (2006). Adolescent development in interpersonal context. In N. Eisenberg (Ed.), *Handbook of child psychology: Vol. 3. Social, emotional, and personality development* (6th ed., pp. 1003–1067). Hoboken, NJ: Wiley.

Colman, D. (2010, July 1). Me, myself and iPhone. *New York Times,* pp. E1, E3.

Common Core State Standards Initiative. (2010a). *Fifty-One States and Territories Join Common Core State Standards Initiative.* Retrieved from http://www.corestandards.org/

Common Core State Standards Initiative. (2010b). Common Core State Standards for Mathematics. Retrieved from http://www.corestandards.org/Files/K12MathStandards.pdf

Common Core State Standards Initiative. (2010c). *Common core state standards for English Language Arts and Literacy in History/Social Studies & Science.* Retrieved from http://www.corestandards.org/Files/K12ELAStandards.pdf

Common Core State Standards Initiative. (2011). *In the states.* Retrieved from http://www.corestandards.org/in-the-states

Comstock, G., & Scharrer, E. (2006). Media and popular culture. In K. Renninger & I. Sigel (Eds.), *Handbook of child psychology: Vol. 4. Child psychology in practice* (6th ed., pp. 817–863). Hoboken, NJ: Wiley.

Comunian, A. L., & Gielan, U. P. (2000). Sociomoral reflection & prosocial & antisocial behavior: Two Italian studies. *Psychological Reports, 87,* 161–175.

Cook, J., & Cook, G. (2009). *Child development: Principles and perspectives* (2nd ed.). Boston: Allyn & Bacon.

Cooper, H. (2006). Research questions and research designs. In P. Alexander & P. Winne (Eds.), *Handbook of educational psychology* (2nd ed., pp. 849–879). Mahwah, NJ: Erlbaum.

Cooper, H., Robinson, J. C., & Patall, E. A. (2006). Does homework improve academic achievement? A synthesis of research, 1987–2003. *Review of Educational Research, 76,* 1–62.

Cooper, J. D., & Kiger, N. (2009). *Literacy: Helping students construct meaning* (7th ed.). Boston: Houghton Mifflin.

Corcoran, C. A., Dershimer, E. L., & Tichenor, M. S. (2004). A teacher's guide to alternative assessment: Taking the first steps. *The Clearing House, 77*(5), 213–216.

Cornelius-White, J. (2007). Learner-centered teacher-student relationships are effective: A meta-analysis. *Review of Educational Research, 77,* 113–143.

Costa, D. S. J., & Boakes, R. A. (2007). Maintenance of responding when reinforcement becomes delayed. *Learning & Behavior, 35,* 95–105.

Côté, J. E., Vaillancourt, T., Barker, E. D., Nagin, D., & Tremblay, R. E. (2007). The joint development of physical and indirect aggression: Predictors of continuity and change during childhood. *Development and Psychopathology, 19,* 37–55.

Council for Exceptional Children. (2005). Retrieved from http://www.CEC.sped.org.IDEALaw&resources

Covington, M. (1992). *Making the grade: A self-worth perspective on motivation and school reform.* Cambridge, MA: Harvard University Press.

Covington, M. (1998). *The will to learn: A guide for motivating young people.* New York: Cambridge University Press.

Covington, M., & Omelich, C. (1987). "I knew it cold before the exam": A test of the anxiety blockage hypothesis. *Journal of Educational Psychology, 79,* 393–400.

Craik, F. I. M. (1979). Human memory. *Annual Review of Psychology, 30,* 63–102.

Crippen, K. J., & Earl, B. L. (2007). The impact of web-based worked examples and self-explanation on performance, problem solving, and self-efficacy. *Computers & Education, 49,* 809–821.

Crosnoe, R. (2005). Double disadvantage or signs of resilience? The elementary school contexts of children from Mexican immigrant families. *American Educational Research Journal, 42*(2), 269–303.

Crosnoe, R., & Huston, A. (2007). Socioeconomic status, schooling, and the developmental trajectories of adolescents. *Developmental Psychology, 43,* 1097–1110.

Cross, T. L., (2001). Gifted children and Erikson's theory of psychosocial development. *Gifted Child Today, 24*(1), 54–55, 61.

Crow, S., R., (2007). Information literacy: What's motivation got to do with it? *Knowledge Quest, 35,* 48–52

Cuban, L. (1993). *How teachers taught: Constancy and change in American classrooms: 1890–1990* (2nd ed). New York: Teachers College Press, Teachers College, Columbia University.

Cuban, L. (2004). Assessing the 20-year impact of multiple intelligences on schooling. *Teachers College Record, 106*(1), 140–146.

Cummins, J. (2000). *Language, power, and pedagogy: Bilingual children in the crossfire.* Clevedon, UK: Multilingual Matters.

Curtindale, L., Laurie-Rose, C., & Bennett-Murphy, L. (2007). Sensory modality, temperament, and the development of sustained attention: A vigilance study in children and adults. *Developmental Psychology, 43*(3), 576–589.

Cushman, K. (2003). *Fires in the bathroom: Advice for teachers from high school students.* New York: The New Press.

D'Amico, A., & Guarnera, M. (2005). Exploring working memory in children with low arithmetical achievement. *Learning and Individual Differences, 15,* 189–202.

Daniels, E., & Leeper, C. (2006). A longitudinal investigation of sports participation, peer acceptance, and self-esteem among adolescent girls and boys. *Sex Roles, 55*, 875–880.

Danner, F., (2008, March). *The effects of perceptions of classroom assessment practices and academic press on classroom mastery goals and high school students' self-reported cheating.* Paper presented at the annual meeting of the American Educational Research Association, New York.

Darden, E. (2007). Autism, the law, and you. *American School Board Journal, 194*(9), 60–61.

Darling-Hammond, L., & Baratz-Snowdon, J. (Eds.). (2005). *A good teacher in every classroom: Preparing the highly qualified teachers our children deserve.* San Francisco: Jossey-Bass/Wiley.

Darling-Hammond, L., & Bransford, J. (Eds.) (2005). *Preparing teachers for a changing world: What teachers should learn and be able to do.* San Francisco: Jossey-Bass.

Davidson, J., & Sternberg, R. (Eds.). (2003). *The psychology of problem solving.* Cambridge: Cambridge University.

Davis, C., & Yang, A. (2005). *Parents and teachers working together.* Turners Falls, MA: Northeast Foundation for Children.

Davis, G. (2003). Identifying creative students, teaching for creative growth. In N. Colangelo & G. Davis (Eds.), *Handbook of gifted education* (3rd ed., pp. 311–324). Boston: Allyn & Bacon.

Davis, G. A., Rimm, S. B., & Siegle, D. (2011). *Education of the gifted and talented* (6th ed.). Upper Saddle River, NJ: Merrill/Pearson.

Davis, S. D., & Piercy, F. P. (2007). What clients of couple therapy model developers and their former students say about change, part I: Model-dependent common factors across three models. *Journal of Marital and Family Therapy, 33*, 318–343.

Davis-Kean, P. E., & Sandler, H. M. (2001). A meta-analysis of measures of self-esteem for young children: A framework for future measurers. *Child Development, 72*, 887–906.

De Corte, E. (2007). Learning from instruction: the case of mathematics. *Learning Inquiry, 1*, 19–30.

De Simone, C. (2007). Applications of concept mapping. *College Teaching, 55*, 33–36.

Deci, E., & Ryan, R. (1987). The support of autonomy and the control of behavior. *Journal of Personality and Social Psychology, 53*, 1024–1037.

Deci, E., & Ryan, R. (2000). The "what" and "why" of goal pursuits: Human needs and the self-determination of behavior. *Psychological Inquiry, 11*, 227–268.

Deci, E., & Ryan, R. (Eds.). (2002). *Handbook of self-determination research.* Rochester, NY: University of Rochester Press.

Deddeh, H., Main, E., & Fulkerson, S. (2010). Eight steps to meaningful grading. *Phi Delta Kappan, 91*(7), 53–58.

Delazer, M., Ischebeck, A., Domahs, F., Zamarian, L., Koppelstaetter, F., Siednetoph, C. et al. (2005). Learning by strategies and learning by drill: Evidence from an fMRI study. *NeuroImage, 25*, 838–849.

della Cava, M. (2010). Attention spans get rewired. *USA Today*, August 4, D1–D2.

Delpit, L. (1995). *Other people's children: Cultural conflict in the classroom.* New York: The New Press.

Demetriou, A., Christou, C., Spanoudis, G., & Platsidou, M. (2002). The development of mental processing: Efficiency, working memory, and thinking. *Monographs of the Society for Research in Child Development* (Serial No. 268, Vol. 67, No. 1). Boston: Blackwell.

Dempster, R., & Corkill, A. (1999). Interference and inhibition in cognition and behavior: Unifying themes for educational psychology. *Educational Psychology Review, 11*, 1–88.

Denig, S. J. (2003, April). *A proposed relationship between multiple intelligences and learning styles.* Paper presented at the annual meeting of the American Educational Research Association, Chicago.

Dennis, T. A., Cole, P. M., Zahn-Waxler, C., & Mizuta, I. (2002). Self in context: Autonomy and relatedness in Japanese and U. S. mother—preschooler dyads. *Child Development, 73*, 1803–1817.

Deyhle, D. (1987). Learning failure: Tests as gatekeepers and the culturally different child. In H. Trueba (Ed.), *Success or failure?* (pp. 85–108). Cambridge, MA: Newbury House.

Deyhle, D., & LeCompte, M. (1999). Cultural differences in child development: Navajo adolescents in middle schools. In R. H. Sheets & E. R. Holins (Eds.), *Racial and ethnic identity in school practices: Aspects of human development* (pp. 123–139). Mahwah, NJ: Erlbaum.

di Sessa, A. (2006). A history of conceptual change research: Threads and fault lines. In R. K. Sawyer (Ed.), *Cambridge handbook of the learning sciences* (pp. 265–282). Cambridge, MA: Cambridge University Press.

Diaz-Rico, L., & Weed, K. (2009). *The crosscultural language and academic development handbook* (4th ed.). Boston: Pearson.

Dickson, S. M. (2004). Tracking concept mastery using a biology portfolio. *The American Biology Teacher, 66*(9), 628–634.

DiMartino, J., & Castaneda, A. (2007). Assessing applied skills. *Educational Leadership, 64*, 38–42.

Ding, M., Li, X., Piccolo, D., & Kulm, G. (2007). Teacher interventions in cooperative-learning mathematics classes. *Journal of Educational Research, 100*(3), 162–176.

Do, S. L., & Schallert, D. L. (2004). Emotions and classroom talk: Toward a model of the role of affect in students' experiences of classroom discussions. *Journal of Educational Psychology, 96*, 619–634

Dolezal, S., Welsh, L., Pressley, M., & Vincent, M. (2003). How nine third-grade teachers motivate student academic engagement. *Elementary School Journal, 103*, 239–268.

Doll, B., Zucker, S., & Brehm, K. (2004). *Resilient classrooms: Creating healthy environments for learning.* New York: Guilford Press.

Donovan, M. S., & Bransford, J. D. (2005). Introduction. In M. S. Donovan & J. D. Bransford (Eds.), *How students learn: History, mathematics, and science in the classroom* (pp. 1–26). Washington, DC: National Academies Press.

Douglas, N. L. (2000). Enemies of critical thinking: Lessons from social psychology research. *Reading Psychology, 21*, 129–144.

Dowson, M., & McInerney, D. (2001). Psychological parameters of students' social and work avoidance goals: A qualitative investigation. *Journal of Educational Psychology, 93*, 35–42.

Doyle, W. (2006). Ecological approaches to classroom management. In C. M. Evertson & C. S. Weinstein (Eds.), *Handbook of classroom management: Research, practice, and contemporary issues* (pp. 97–125). Mahwah, NJ: Erlbaum.

Durbin, D. L., Darling, N., Steinberg, L., & Brown, B. B. (1993). Parenting style and peer group membership in European-American adolescents. *Journal of Research on Adolescents, 3*, 87–100.

Durlak, J. A., Weissberg, R. P., Dymnicki, A. B., Taylor, R. D., & Schellinger, K. B. (2011). The impact of enhancing students' social and emotional learning: A meta-analysis of school-based universal interventions. *Child Development, 82*, 405–432.

Dwairy, M. (2005). Using problem-solving conversation with children. *Intervention in School and Clinic, 40*, 144–150.

Dweck, C. (1975). The role of expectations and attributions in the alleviation of learned helplessness. *Journal of Personality and Social Psychology, 31*, 674–685.

Dweck, C. (1999). Self-theories and goals: Their role in motivation, personality, and development. In R. Dienstbier (Ed.), *Perspectives on motivation: Nebraska symposium on motivation 1990* (Vol. 38, pp. 199–325). Lincoln: University of Nebraska Press.

Dweck, C. (2000). *Self-theories: Their role in motivation, personality, and development.* Philadelphia, PA: Psychology Press.

Dweck, C. S. (2006). *Mindset: The new psychology of success.* New York: Random House.

Dynarski, M., & Gleason, P. (1999, April). *How can we help? What we have learned from evaluations of federal dropout-prevention programs.* Paper presented at the annual meeting of the American Educational Research Association, Montreal, Canada.

Eccles, J. S., Barber, B. L., Stone, M., & Hunt, J. (2003). Extracurricular activities and adolescent development. *Journal of Social Issues, 59*, 865–889.

Eccles, J. S., Wigfield, A., & Schiefele, U. (1998). Motivation to succeed. In W. Damon (Series Ed.) & N. Eisenberg (Vol. Ed.), *Handbook of child psychology: Vol. 3. Social, emotional, and personality development* (5th ed., pp. 1017–1095). New York: Wiley.

Echevarria, J., & Graves, A. (2011). *Sheltered content instruction* (4th ed.). Boston: Allyn & Bacon.

Echevarria, J., Vogt, M., & Short, D. (2004). *Making content comprehensible to English learners: The SIOP model.* Boston: Allyn & Bacon.

Educational Testing Service. (2008). *The Praxis Series™: Principles of Learning and Teaching:*

Grades 7–12 (0524). Retrieved from http://www .ets.org/Media/Tests/PRAXIS/pdf/0524.pdf

Educational Testing Service. (2010a). *The Praxis Series™*. Retrieved from http://www.ets.org/ praxis

Educational Testing Service. (2010b). *About the Praxis Series™ tests*. Retrieved from http://www .ets.org/praxis/about/

Eggen, P., & Kauchak, D. (2002, April). *Synthesizing the literature of motivation: Implications for instruction*. Paper presented at the annual meeting of the American Educational Research Association, New Orleans, LA.

Eggen, P., & Kauchak, D. (2012). *Strategies and models for teachers: Teaching content and thinking skills* (6th ed.). Boston: Pearson.

Eisenberg, N., Fabes, R., & Spinrad, T. (2006). Prosocial development. In N. Eisenberg (Vol. Ed.), *Handbook of child psychology: Vol. 3. Social, emotional, and personality development* (6th ed., pp. 646–718). Hoboken, NJ: John Wiley & Sons.

Eisenman, L. T. (2007). Self-determination interventions: Building a foundation for school completion. *Remedial and Special Education, 28*, 2–8.

Eisenstein, J., O'Connor, B., Smith, N., & Xing, E. (2011). *A latent variable model for geographical lexical variation*. Paper presented at the Linguistic Society of America, Pittsburgh.

Elder, L., & Paul, R. (2007). Critical thinking: The nature of critical and creative thought: Part II. *Journal of Developmental Education, 30*, 36–37.

Elias, M. (2004). Strategies to infuse social and emotional learning into academics. In J. Zins, R. Weissberg, M. Wang, & H. Walberg (Eds.), *Building academic success on social and emotional learning* (pp. 113–134). New York: Teachers College Press.

Elliot, A., & McGregor, H. (2000, April). Approach and avoidance goals and autonomous-controlled regulation: Empirical and conceptual relations. In A. Assor (Chair), *Self-determination theory and achievement goal theory: Convergences, divergences, and educational implications*. Symposium conducted at the annual meeting of the American Educational Research Association, New Orleans.

Elliot, A., & Thrash, T. (2001). Achievement goals and the hierarchical model of achievement motivation. *Educational Psychology Review, 13*, 139–156.

Emerson, M. J., & Miyake, A. (2003). The role of inner speech in task switching: A dual-task investigation. *Journal of Memory and Language, 48*, 148–168.

Emler, N. (1994). Gossip, reputation, and adaptation. In R. F. Goodman & A. Ben-Ze'ev (Eds.), *Good gossip* (pp. 34–46) Lawrence, KS. University of Kansas Press.

Emmer, E. T., & Evertson, C. M. (2009). *Classroom Management for Middle and High School Teachers* (8th ed.). Boston: Allyn & Bacon/Pearson.

Englund, M., Egeland, B., & Collins, W. (2008). Exceptions to high school dropout predictions in a low-income sample: Do adults make a difference? *Journal of Social Issues, 64*, 77–93.

Ennemoser, M., & Schneider, W. (2007). Relations of television viewing and reading: Findings from a 4-year longitudinal study. *Journal of Educational Psychology, 99*, 349–368.

Epstein, J. (2001, April). *School, family, and community partnerships: Preparing educators and improving schools*. Paper presented at the annual meeting of the American Educational Research Association, Seattle.

Ericsson, K. A. (2003). The acquisition of expert performance as problem solving: Construction and modification of mediating mechanisms through deliberate practice. In J. E. Davidson & R. J. Sternberg (Eds.), *The psychology of problem solving* (pp. 31–83). Cambridge, UK: Cambridge University Press.

Erikson, E. (1968). *Identity: Youth and crisis*. New York: Norton.

Erikson, E. (1980). *Identity and the life cycle* (2nd ed.). New York: Norton.

Evans, C., Kirby, U., & Fabrigar, L. (2003). Approaches to learning, need for cognition, and strategic flexibility among university students. *The British Journal of Educational Psychology, 73*, 507–528.

Evans, G., & Kim, P. (2007). Childhood poverty and health: Cumulative risk exposure and stress dysregulation. *Psychological Science, 18*, 953–957.

Evans, L., & Davies, K. (2000). No sissy boys here: A content analysis of the representation of masculinity in elementary school reading texts. *Sex Roles, 42*, 255–270.

Evertson, C. M., & Emmer, E. T. (2009). *Classroom Management for Elementary Teachers* (8th ed.). Boston: Allyn & Bacon/Pearson.

Evertson, C. M., & Weinstein, C. S. (2006). Classroom management as a field of inquiry. In C. M. Evertson & C. S. Weinstein (Eds.), *Handbook of classroom management: Research, practice, and contemporary issues* (pp. 3–15). Mahwah, NJ: Erlbaum.

Exline, R. (1962). Need affiliation and initial communication behavior in problem solving groups characterized by low interpersonal visibility. *Psychological Reports, 10*, 405–411.

Fabiano, G. A., Pelham, W. E., Jr., & Gnagy, E. M. (2007). The single and combined effects of multiple intensities of behavior modification and methylphenidate for children with attention deficit hyperactivity disorder in a classroom setting. *The School Psychology Review, 36*, 195–216.

FairTest. (2005). *Cheating scandal rocks Texas*. Retrieved from http://fairtest.org/cheating-scandal-rocks-texas

FairTest. (2008). SAT I: *A faulty instrument for predicting college success*. FairTest: The National Center for Fair and Open Testing. Retrieved from http://www.fairtest.org.

FairTest. (2009). Paying teachers for student test scores damages schools and undermines learning. Retrieved from http://fairtest.org/ paying-for-student-test-scores-damages-schools

Faris, R., & Felmlee, D. (2011). Status struggle: Network centrality and gender segregation in same- and cross-gender aggression. *American Sociological Review, 76*, 48–73.

Farkas, R. (2003). Effects of traditional versus learning-styles instructional methods on middle school students. *Journal of Educational Research, 97*(1), 42–51.

Fauth, R., Roth, J., & Brooks-Gunn, J. (2007). Does the neighborhood context alter the link between youth's after-school time activities and developmental outcomes? A multilevel analysis. *Developmental Psychology, 43*(3), 760–777.

Feiman-Nemser, S. (2001). From preparation to practice: Designing a continuum to strengthen and sustain teaching. *Teachers College Record, 103*, 1013–1055.

Feldhusen, J. (1998a). Programs and service at the elementary level. In J. VanTassel-Baska (Ed.), *Excellence in educating gifted and talented learners* (3rd ed., pp. 211–223). Denver: Love.

Feldhusen, J. (1998b). Programs and services at the secondary level. In J. VanTassel-Baska (Ed.), *Excellence in educating gifted and talented learners* (3rd ed., pp. 225–240). Denver: Love.

Feldon, D. F. (2007a). Cognitive load and classroom teaching: The double-edged sword of automaticity. *Educational Psychologist, 42*, 123–137.

Ferguson, R. (2003). Teachers' perceptions and expectations and the black–white test score gap. *Urban Education, 38*(4), 460–507.

Fernandez-Berrocal, P., & Santamaria, C. (2006). Mental models in social interaction. *The Journal of Experimental Education, 74*(3), 229–248.

Ferrari, M., & Elik, N. (2003). Influences on intentional conceptual change. In G. M. Sinatra & P. R. Pintrich (Eds.), *Intentional conceptual change* (pp. 21–54). Mahwah, NJ: Erlbaum.

Finn, J., Willert, H., & Marable, M. (2003). Substance use in schools. *Educational Leadership, 60*(6), 80–85.

Fischer, K., & Bidell, T. (2006). Dynamic development of action and thought. In R. Lerner (Vol. Ed.), *Handbook of child psychology: Vol. 1. Theoretical models of human development* (6th ed., pp. 313–399). Hoboken, NJ: John Wiley & Sons.

Fischer, L., Schimmel, D., & Stellman, L. (2006). *Teachers and the law*. New York: Longman.

Fisher, C., Berliner, D., Filby, N., Marliave, R., Cohen, K., & Dishaw, M. (1980). Teaching behaviors, academic learning time, and student achievement: An overview. In C. Denham & A. Lieberman (Eds.), *Time to learn* (pp. 7–32). Washington, DC: National Institute of Education.

Fisher, D. (2006). Keeping adolescents "alive and kickin' it": Addressing suicide in schools. *Phi Delta Kappan, 87*(10), 784–786.

Fishman, B., & Davis, E., (2006). Teacher learning research and the learning sciences. In R. K. Sawyer (Ed.), *Cambridge handbook of the learning sciences* (pp. 535–550). New York: Cambridge University Press.

Flavell, J., Miller, P., & Miller, S. (2002). *Cognitive development* (4th ed.). Upper Saddle River, NJ: Prentice Hall.

Fleming, V., & Alexander, J. (2001). The benefits of peer collaboration: A replication with a delayed posttest. *Contemporary Educational Psychology, 26*, 588–601.

Flores, E., Cicchetti, D., & Rogosch, F. (2005). Predictors of resilience in maltreated and nonmal-treated Latino children. *Developmental Psychology, 41*(2), 338, 351.

Flores, M. M., & Kaylor, M. (2007). The effects of a direct instruction program on the fraction performance of middle school students at-risk for failure in mathematics. *Journal of Instructional Psychology, 34*, 84–94.

Florida Department of Education. (2007). *Grade level expectations for the Sunshine State Standards: Science Grades 6–8*. Retrieved from http://etc.usf.edu/flstandards/sss/pdf/science6.pdf

Flynn, J. (1999). Searching for justice: The discovery of IQ gains over time. *American Psychologist, 54*, 5–20.

Fox, C. L., Elder, T., Gater, J., & Johnson, E. (2010). The association between adolescents' beliefs in a just world and their attitudes to victims of bullying. *The British Journal of Educational Psychology, 80*, 183–198.

Freedle, R. (2010). On replicating ethnic test bias effects: The Santelices & Wilson study. *Harvard Education Review, 80*(30), 394–404.

Freeman, J., McPhail, J., & Berndt, J. (2002). Sixth graders' views of activities that do and do not help them learn. *Elementary School Journal, 102*(4), 335–347.

Freiberg, H. J., & Lamb, S. M. (2009). Dimensions of person-centered classroom management. *Theory into Practice, 48*, 99–105.

Freiberg, J. (1999). Sustaining the paradigm. In J. Freiberg (Ed.), *Beyond behaviorism: Changing the classroom management paradigm* (pp. 164–173). Boston: Allyn & Bacon.

French, D. (2003). A new vision of authentic assessment to overcome the flaws in high-stakes testing. *Middle School Journal, 35*(1), 14–23.

French, S., Seidman, E., Allen, L., & Aber, J. (2006). The development of ethnic identity during adolescence. *Developmental Psychology, 42*, 1–10.

Freng, S., & Webber, D. (2009). Turning up the heat on online teaching evaluations: Does "hotness" matter? *Teaching of Psychology 36*, 189–193.

Frey, B., & Schmitt, V. (2005, April). *Teachers' classroom assessment practices*. Paper presented at the annual meeting of the American Educational Research Association, Montreal, Canada.

Frey, W. H. (2011). A demographic tipping point among America's three-year-olds. *The Brookings Institute*. Retrieved from http://www.brookings.edu/opinions/2011/0207_population_frey.aspx

Friedman, I. A. (2006). Classroom management and teacher stress and burnout. In C. M. Evertson & C. S. Weinstein (Eds.), *Handbook of classroom management: Research, practice, and contemporary issues* (pp. 925–944). Mahwah, NJ: Erlbaum.

Friend, M. (2008). *Special education: Contemporary perspectives for school professionals* (2nd ed.). Boston: Pearson/Allyn & Bacon.

Friend, M. (2011). *Special education: Contemporary perspectives for school professionals* (3rd ed.). Boston: Allyn & Bacon.

Friesen, N. (2011). The lecture as a transmedial pedagogical form: A historical analysis. *Educational Researcher, 40*, 95–102.

Fuchs, D. (2006). Cognitive profiling of children with genetic disorders and the search for a scientific basis of differentiated education. In P. Alexander & P. Winne (Eds.), *Handbook of educational psychology* (2nd ed., pp. 187–206). Mahwah, NJ: Erlbaum.

Fuchs, L. S., Fuchs., D., Prentice, K., Burch, M., Hamlett, C. L., Owen, R., Hosp, M., & Jancek, D. (2003). Explicitly teaching for transfer: Effects on third-grade students' mathematical problem solving. *Journal of Educational Psychology, 95*, 295–305.

Gall, M., Gall, J., & Borg, W. (2010). *Applying educational research: How to read, do, and use research to solve problems of practice* (6th ed.). Boston: Allyn & Bacon/Pearson.

Gao, H., Losh, S. C., Shen, E., Turner, J. E., & Yuan, R. (2007, April). *The effect of collaborative concept mapping on learning, problem solving, and learner attitude*. Paper presented at the annual meeting of the American Educational Research Association, Chicago.

Gardner, H. (1983). *Frames of mind: The theory of multiple intelligences*. New York: Basic Books.

Gardner, H. (1995). Reflections on multiple intelligences: Myths and messages. *Phi Delta Kappan, 77*, 200–209.

Gardner, H., & Hatch, T. (1989). Multiple intelligences go to school. *Educational Researcher, 18*(8), 4–10.

Gardner, H., & Moran, S. (2006). The science of multiple intelligences theory: A response to Lynn Waterhouse. *Educational Psychologist, 41*(4), 227–232.

Garlick, D. (2010). *Intelligence and the brain: Solving the mystery of why people differ in IQ and how a child can be a genius*. Burbank, CA: Aesop Press.

Gaskill, P. J., & Murphy, P. K. (2004). Effects of a memory strategy on second-graders' performance and self-efficacy. *Contemporary Educational Psychology, 29*, 27–49.

Gathercole, S. E., Pickering, S. J., Ambridge, B., & Wearing, H. (2004). The structure of working memory from 4 to 15 years of age. *Developmental Psychology, 49*(2), 177–190.

Gay, G. (2005). Politics of multicultural teacher education. *Journal of Teacher Education, 56*(3), 221–228.

Gay, G. (2006). Connections between classroom management and culturally responsive teaching. In C. Evertson, & C. Weinstein (Eds.), *Handbook of classroom management: Research, practice, and contemporary issues* (pp. 343–370). Mahwah, NJ: Erlbaum.

Gay, L. R., Airasian, P., & Mills, G. E. (2009). *Educational research* (9th ed.). Upper Saddle River, NJ: Pearson Education.

Gazzaniga, M. S. (2008). *Human: The science behind what makes us unique*. New York: HarperCollins.

Ge, X., Jin, R., Natsuaki, M., Frederick, X., Brody, G., Cutrona, C., & Simons, R. (2006). Pubertal maturation and early substance use risks among African American children. *Psychology of Addictive Behaviors, 20*, 404–414.

Geary, D. (2007). An evolutionary perspective on learning disability in mathematics. *Development Neuropsychology, 32*(1), 471–519.

Geisinger, K. (2005). The testing industry, ethnic minorities, and individuals with disabilities. In R. Phelps (Ed.), *Defending standardized testing* (pp. 187–204). Mahwah, NJ: Erlbaum.

Gelman, S., & Kalish, C. (2006). Conceptual development. In W. Damon & R. Lerner (Series Eds.), D. Kuhn & R. Siegler (Vol. Eds.), *Handbook of child psychology: Vol. II. Cognition, perception, and language* (pp. 687–733, 6th ed.). New York: Wiley.

Gentile, J. (1996). Setbacks in the advancement of learning. *Educational Researcher, 25*, 37–39.

Gettinger, M., & Kohler, K. M. (2006). Process–outcome approaches to classroom management and effective teaching. In C. M. Evertson & C. S. Weinstein (Eds.), *Handbook of classroom management: Research, practice, and contemporary issues* (pp. 73–95). Mahwah, NJ: Erlbaum.

Gewertz, C. (2010). Proposed standards go public: Math and English draft elicits kudos and doubts. *Education Week, 29*(25), 1, 14–15.

Gholson, B., & Craig, S. D. (2006). Promoting constructive activities that support vicarious learning during computer-based instruction. *Educational Psychology Review, 18*, 119–139.

Gibbs, J. C. (2010). *Moral development and reality: Beyond the theories of Kohlberg and Hoffman* (2nd ed.). Boston: Pearson Allyn & Bacon.

Gijbels, D., Dochy, F., Van den Bossche, P., & Segers, M. (2005). Effects of problem-based learning: A meta-analysis from the angle of assessment. *Review of Educational Research, 75*(1), 27–61.

Gilligan, C. (1977). In a different voice: Women's conceptions of the self and of morality. *Harvard Educational Review, 47*, 481–517.

Gilligan, C. (1982). *In a different voice: Psychological theory and women's development*. Cambridge, MA: Harvard University Press.

Gilligan, C. (1998). *Minding women: Reshaping the education realm*. Cambridge, MA: Harvard University Press.

Gilligan, C., & Attanucci, J. (1988). Two moral orientations: Gender differences and similarities. *Merrill-Palmer Quarterly, 34*, 223–237.

Gillum, J., & Bellow, M. (2011). When standardized test scores soared in D.C., were the gains real? *USA Today*. Retrieved from http://www.usatoday.com/news/education/2011-03-28-1Aschooltesting28_CV_N.htm

Gimbel, P. (2008). Helping new teachers reflect. *Principal Leadership (High School Ed.), 8*, 6–8.

Ginsberg, A., Shapiro, J., & Brown, S. (2004). *Gender in urban education: Strategies for student achievement*. Portsmouth, NH: Heinemann.

Ginsburg, A., Leinwand, S., & Decker, K. (2009). *Informing grades 1–6 standards development: What can be learned from high-performing Hong Kong, Korea, and Singapore?* Washington, DC: American Institutes for Research.

Gläscher, J., Rudrauf, D., Colom, R., Paul, L., Tranel, D., Damasio, H., & Adolphs, R. (2010). Distributed neural system for general intelligence revealed by lesion mapping. *Proceedings of the National Academy of Sciences of the United States of America, 107,* 4705–4709.

Glassman, M. (2001). Dewey and Vygotsky: Society, experience, and inquiry in educational practice. *Educational Researcher, 30*(4), 3–14.

Glassman, M., & Wang, Y. (2004). On the interconnected nature of interpreting Vygotsky: Rejoinder to Gredler and Shields *Does no one read Vygotsky's words? Educational Researcher, 33*(6), 19–22.

Godley, A., Sweetland, J., Wheeler, R., Minnici, A., & Carpenter, B. (2006). Preparing teachers for dialectally diverse classrooms. *Educational Researcher, 35*(8), 30–37.

Goldstein, R. A. (2004). Who are our urban students and what makes them so different? In S. R. Steinberg & J. L. Kincheloe (Eds.), *19 Urban questions: Teaching in the city* (pp. 41–51). New York: Peter Lang.

Goleman, D. (2006). *Social intelligence.* New York: Westlake Books.

Gollnick, D., & Chinn, P. (2009). *Multicultural education in a pluralistic society* (8th ed.). Upper Saddle River, NJ: Merrill/Pearson Education.

Gonzalez, A., & Wolters, C. (2006). The relation between perceived parenting practices and achievement motivation in mathematics. *Journal of Research in Childhood Education, 21,* 203–217.

Good, T., & Brophy, J. (2008). *Looking in classrooms* (10th ed.). Boston: Allyn & Bacon.

Gootman, E., & Gebeloff, R. (2008, June 19). Poor students lose ground in city's gifted programs. *New York Times,* p. A25.

Gootman, M. E. (1998). Effective in-house suspension. *Educational Leadership, 56*(1), 39–41.

Gordon, T. (1981). Crippling our children with disruption. *Journal of Education, 163,* 228–243.

Graber, J., Brooks-Gunn, J., & Warren, M. (2006). Pubertal effects on adjustment in girls: Moving from demonstrating effects to identifying pathways. *Journal of Youth and Adolescence, 35,* 413–423.

Gragg, C. I. (1940, October 19). Because wisdom can't be told. *Harvard Alumni Bulletin,* 78–84.

Graham, S. (2006). Writing. In P. Alexander, & P. Winne (Eds.), *Handbook of educational psychology* (2nd ed., pp. 457–478). Mahwah, NJ: Erlbaum.

Graham, S. (2010). What educators need to know about bullying behaviors. *Phi Delta Kappan, 92,* 66–69.

Graham, S., & Weiner, B. (1996). Theories and principles of motivation. In D. Berliner & R. Calfee (Eds.), *Handbook of educational psychology* (pp. 63–84). New York: Macmillan.

Grant, L. W. (2006). Persistence and self-efficacy: A key to understanding teacher turnover. *The Delta Kappa Gamma Bulletin, 72*(2), 50–54.

Gray, T., & Fleischman, S. (2005). Successful strategies for English language learners. *Educational Leadership, 62*(4), 84–85.

Green, E. (2010). Building a better teacher. The New York Times Magazine. Retrieved from http://www.nytimes.com/2010/03/07/magazine/07Teachers-t.html?_r=1

Greene, J. A., & Azevedo, R. (2007). A theoretical review of Winne and Hadwin's model of self-regulated learning: New perspectives and directions. *Review of Educational Research, 77,* 334–372.

Greene, J. P., & Winters, M. A. (2006). Getting ahead by staying behind: An evaluation of Florida's program to end social promotion. *Education Next, 6*(2), 65–69.

Greenfield, P., Suzuki, L., & Rothstein-Fish, C. (2006). Cultural pathways through human development. In K. Renninger & I. Sigel (Eds.), *Handbook of child psychology: Vol. 4. Child psychology in practice* (6th ed., pp. 655–699). Hoboken, NJ: Wiley.

Greenfield, P., Trumbull, E., Keller, H., Rothstein-Fisch, C., Suzuki, L. K., & Quiroz, B. (2006). Cultural conceptions of learning and development. In P. Alexander & P. Winner (Eds.), *Handbook of educational psychology* (2nd ed., pp. 675–692). Mahwah, NJ: Erlbaum.

Greeno, J., Collins, A., & Resnick, L. (1996). Cognition and learning. In D. Berliner & R. Calfee (Eds.), *Handbook of educational psychology* (pp. 15–46). New York: Macmillan.

Gronlund, N. (2004). *Writing instructional objectives for teaching and assessment* (7th ed.). Upper Saddle River, NJ: Merrill/Pearson.

Gronlund, N., & Waugh, C. (2009). *Assessing student achievement* (9th ed.). Needham Heights, MA: Allyn & Bacon.

Gruman, D., Harachi, T., Abbott, R., Catalano, R., & Fleming, C. (2008). Longitudinal effects of student mobility on three dimensions of elementary school engagement. *Child Development, 79,* 1833–1852.

Gullo, D. (2005). *Understanding assessment and evaluation in early childhood education* (2nd ed.). New York: Teachers College Press.

Gurian, M., & Stevens, K. (2005). What is happening with boys in school? *Teachers College Record.* Retrieved from http://www.tcrecord.org/Content.asp?ContentID=11854

Guskey, T. (2002, April). *Perspectives on grading and reporting: Differences among teachers, students, and parents.* Paper presented at the annual meeting of the American Educational Research Association, New Orleans.

Hacker, D., Bol, L., Horgan, D., & Rakow, E. (2000). Test prediction and performance in a classroom context. *Journal of Education Psychology, 92,* 160–170.

Hadjioannou, X. (2007). Bringing the background to the foreground: What do classroom environments that support authentic discussions look like? *American Educational Research Journal, 44*(2), 370–399.

Halford, G., & Andrews, G. (2006). Reasoning and problem solving. In D. Kuhn, & R. Siegler (Vol. Eds.), *Handbook of child psychology: Vol. 2. Cognition, perception, and language* (6th ed., pp. 557–608). Hoboken, NJ: John Wiley & Sons.

Hall, T., Strangman, N., & Meyer, A. (2003). *Differentiated instruction and implications for UDL implementation.* Wakefield, MA: National Center on Accessing the General Curriculum. Retrieved from http://aim.cast.org/learn/historyarchive/backgroundpapers/differentiated

Hallahan, D., Kauffman, J., & Pullen, P. (2009). *Exceptional children* (11th ed.). Needham Heights, MA: Allyn & Bacon.

Halpern, D. (2006). Assessing gender gaps in learning and academic achievement. In P. A. Alexander & P. H. Winne (Eds.), *Handbook of educational psychology* (2nd ed., pp. 635–653). Mahwah, NJ: Erlbaum.

Halpern, D. F. (2006). Assessing gender gaps in learning and academic achievement. In P. A. Alexander & P. H. Winne (Eds.), *Handbook of educational psychology* (2nd ed., pp. 635–653). Mahwah, NJ: Erlbaum.

Halpern, D., Benbow, C., Geary, D., Gur, R., Hyde, J., & Gernsbacher, M. (2007). The science of sex differences in science and mathematics. *Psychological Science in the Public Interest, 8,* 1–51.

Hamilton, S. L., Seibert, M. A., Gardner, III, R., & Talbert-Johnson, C. (2000). Using guided notes to improve the academic achievement of incarcerated adolescents with learning and behavior problems. *Remedial and Special Education, 21,* 133–140.

Hancock, D. R. (2001). Effects of test anxiety and evaluative threat on students' achievement and motivation. *The Journal of Educational Research, 94,* 284–290.

Hanish, L. D., Kochenderfer-Ladd, B., Fabes, R. A., Martin, C. L., & Denning, D. (2004). Bullying among young children: The influence of peers and teachers. In D. L. Espelage & S. M. Swearer (Eds.), *Bullying in American schools: A social-ecological perspective on prevention and intervention* (pp. 141–159) Mahwah, NJ: Erlbaum.

Hansbery, L. (1959). *A raisin in the sun.* New York: Random House.

Hanushek, E. E., Rivkin, S. G., & Kain, J. J. (2005). Teachers, schools, and academic achievement. *Econometrica, 73,* 417–458.

Hardman, M. L., Drew, C. J., & Egan, M. W. (2011). *Human exceptionality: School community and family* (10th ed.). Stamford, CT: Cengage.

Harriet, A. W., & Bradley, K. D. (2003). "You can't say you can't play:" Intervening in the process of social exclusion in the kindergarten classroom. *Early Childhood Research Quarterly, 18,* 185–205.

Harry, B., & Klingner, J. (2007). Discarding the deficit model. *Educational Leadership, 64*(5), 16–21.

Hattie, J., & Timperley, H. (2007). The power of feedback. *Review of Educational Research, 77*(1), 81–112.

Hawkins, M. (2004). Researching English language and literacy development in schools. *Educational Researcher, 33*(3), 14–25.

Hebl, M. R., & Mannix, L. M. (2003). The weight of obesity in evaluating others: A mere proximity effect. *Personality and Social Psychology Bulletin, 29,* 28–38.

Heilig, J., & Darling-Hammond, L. (2008). Students in a high-stakes testing context. *Educational Evaluation & Policy Analysis, 30*, 75–110.

Hellmech, N. (2007, March 29). No sugarcoating this: Kids besieged by food ads. *USA Today*, p. 9D.

Henricsson, L., & Rydell, A. M. (2004). Elementary school children with behavior problems: Teacher–child relations and self-perception. A prospective study. *Merrill-Palmer Quarterly, 50*, 111–138.

Herzig, A. (2004). Becoming mathematicians: Women and students of color choosing and leaving doctoral mathematics. *Review of Educational Research, 74*(2), 171–214.

Heward, W. (2009). *Exceptional children* (9th ed.). Upper Saddle River, NJ: Merrill/Pearson.

Hickey, D. T., & Zuiker, S. J. (2005). Engaged participation: A sociocultural model of motivation with implications for educational assessment. *Educational Assessment, 10*, 277–305.

Hicks, M. (2010). *The digital pandemic: Reestabilishing face-to-face contact in the electronic age.* Far Hills, NJ: New Horizon Press.

Hidi, S. (2001). Interest, reading, and learning: Theoretical and practical considerations. *Educational Psychology Review, 13*, 191–209.

Hidi, S., & Renninger, K. A. (2006). The four-phase model of interest development. *Educational Psychologist, 41*(2), 111–127.

Hidi, S., Renninger, K. A., & Krapp, A. (2004). Interest, a motivational variable that combines affecting and cognitive functioning. In D. Dai & R. Sternberg (Eds.), *Motivation, emotion, and cognition: Integrative perspectives on intellectual functioning and development* (pp. 89–155). Mahwah, NJ: Erlbaum.

Hiebert, E. H., & Kamil, M. L. (Eds.). (2005). *Teaching and learning vocabulary.* Mahwah, NJ: Erlbaum.

Higgins, A. T., & Turnure, J. E. (1984). Distractibility and concentration of attention in children's development. *Child Development, 55*, 1799–1810.

Hilbert, T. S., & Renkl, A. (2008). Concept mapping as a follow-up strategy to learning from texts: What characterizes good and poor mappers? *Instructional Science, 36*, 53–73.

Hill, W. F. (2002). *Learning: A survey of psychological interpretations* (7th ed.). Boston: Allyn & Bacon.

Hirsch, E. (2000). The tests we need and why we don't quite have them. *Education Week, 19*(21), 40–41.

Hirsch, E. (2006). *Knowledge deficit: Closing the shocking education gap for American children.* Boston: Hougton Mifflin.

Hmelo-Silver, C. E. (2004). Problem-based learning: What and how do students learn? *Educational Psychology Review, 16*, 236–266.

Hmelo-Silver, C. E., Duncan, R. G., & Chinn, C. A. (2007). Scaffolding and achievement in problem-based and inquiry learning: A response to Kirschner, Sweller, and Clark (2006). *Educational Psychologist, 42*, 99–107.

Hodapp, R., & Dykens, E. (2006). Mental retardation. In K. A. Renninger, & I. Sigel (Vol. Eds.), *Handbook of child psychology: Vol. 4. Child psychology in practice* (6th ed., pp. 453–496). Hoboken, NJ: John Wiley & Sons.

Hogan, T. (2007). *Educational assessment: A practical introduction.* Hoboken, NJ: John Wiley & Sons.

Hogan, T., Rabinowitz, M., & Craven, J. (2003). Representation in teaching: Inference from research on expert and novice teachers. *Educational Psychologist, 38*, 235–247.

Hohn, R. L., & Frey, B. (2002). Heuristic training and performance in elementary mathematical problem solving. *The Journal of Educational Research, 95*, 374–390.

Holland, A. (2004). Plasticity and development. *Brain and Language, 88*, 254–255.

Hong, S., & Ho, H. (2005). Direct and indirect longitudinal effects of parental involvement on student achievement: Second-order latent growth modeling across ethnic groups. *Journal of Educational Psychology, 97*(1), 32–42.

Horn, J. (2008). Spearman, *g*, expertise, and the nature of human cognitive capability. In P. Kyllonen, R. Roberts, & L. Stankov (Eds.), *Extending intelligence: Enhancement and new constructs* (pp. 185–230). New York: Erlbaum/Taylor & Francis.

Horst, S. J., Finney, S. J., & Barron, K. E. (2007). Moving beyond academic achievement goal measures: A study of social achievement goals. *Contemporary Educational Psychology, 32*, 667–698.

Howe, M. L. (2004). The role of conceptual recoding in reducing children's retroactive interference. *Developmental Psychology, 40*, 131–139.

Hoy, W., Tarter, C. J., & Hoy, A. (2006). Academic optimism of schools: A force for student achievement. *American Educational Research Journal, 43*(3), 425–446. http://www.ed.gov/about/bdscomm/list/mathpanel/report/final-report.pdf

Hu, W. (2010, October 1). Making math lessons as easy as 1, pause 2, pause… *New York Times.* Retrieved from http://www.nytimes.com/2010/10/01/education/01math.html

Huan, V. S., Yeo, L. S., & Ang, R. P. (2006). The influence of dispositional optimism and gender on adolescents' perception of academic stress. *Adolescence, 41*, 533–546.

Huber, J. A. (2004). A closer look at SQ3R. *Reading Improvement, 41*, 108–112.

Huguet, P., & Régner, I. (2007). Stereotype threat among schoolgirls in quasi-ordinary classroom circumstances. *Journal of Educational Psychology, 99*, 545–560.

Hyman, I., Kay, B., Tabori, A., Weber, M., Mahon, M., & Cohen, I. (2006). Bullying: Theory, research, and interventions. In C. M. Evertson & C. S. Weinstein (Eds.), *Handbook of classroom management: Research, practice, and contemporary issues* (pp. 855–884). Mahwah, NJ: Erlbaum.

Igo, L. B., Bruning, R., & McCrudden, M. (2005). Exploring differences in students' copy-and-paste decision making and processing: A mixed-methods study. *Journal of Educational Psychology, 97*(1), 103–116.

Igo, L. B., Kiewra, K., & Bruning, R. (2004). Removing the snare from the pair: Using pictures to learn confusing word pairs. *Journal of Experimental Education, 72*(3), 165–178.

Illinois State Board of Education. (2008). *Illinois learning standards: Mathematics, State Goal 6: Number sense.* Retrieved from http://www.isbenet/ils/math/pdf/goal6.pdf

Inan, F. A., Lowther, D. L., Ross, S. M., & Strahl, D. (2010). Pattern of classroom activities during students' use of computers: Relations between instructional strategies and computer applications. *Teaching and Teacher Education, 26*, 540–546.

Ingersoll, R., & Smith, T. (2004). What are the effects of induction and mentoring on beginning teacher turnover? *American Educational Research Journal, 41*(3), 681–714.

Inhelder, B., & Piaget, J. (1958). *The growth of logical thinking from childhood to adolescence* (A. Parsons & S. Milgram, Trans.). New York: Basic Books.

Isaacson, A. (2009). Riding the rails. *The New York Times.* http://travel.nytimes.com/2009/03/08/travel/08amtrak.html

Isseks, M. (2011). How PowerPoint is killing education. *Educational Leadership, 68*, 74–76.

Iyengar, S., & Lepper, M. (1999). Rethinking the role of choice: A cultural perspective on intrinsic motivation. *Journal of Personality and Social Psychology, 76*, 349–366.

Jackson, M. (2009). *Distracted: The erosion of attention and the coming dark age.* Amherst, NY: Prometheus Books.

Jackson, P. (1968). *Life in classrooms.* New York: Holt, Rinehart & Winston.

Jacobs, J. E., Lanza, S., Osgood, D. W., Eccles, J. S., & Wigfield, A. (2002). Changes in children's self-competence and values: Gender and domain differences across grades one through twelve. *Child Development, 73*, 509–527.

Jacobson, L. (2008). Children's lack of playtime seen as troubling health, school issue. *Education Week, 28*(14), 1, 14–15.

Jensen, E. (2005). *Teaching with the brain in mind* (2nd ed.). Alexandria, VA: Association for Supervision and Curriculum Development.

Jitendra, A., Haria, P., Griffin, C., Leh, J., Adams, A., & Kaduvettoor, A. (2007). A comparison of single and multiple strategy instruction on third-grade students' mathematical problem solving. *Journal of Educational Psychology, 99*(1), 115–127.

Johnson, B., & Christensen, L. (2008). *Educational research: Quantitative, qualitative and mixed approaches* (3rd ed.). Los Angeles: Sage.

Johnson, D. D., Johnson, B., Farenga, S., & Ness, D. (2008). *Stop high-stakes testing: An appeal to Americans' conscience.* Lanham, MD: Rowan & Littlefield.

Johnson, D. W., & Johnson, R. (2006). *Learning together and alone: Cooperation, competition, and individualization* (8th ed.). Needham Heights, MA: Allyn & Bacon.

Johnson, J., & Duffett, A. (2002). *When it's your own child: A report on special education and the families who use it.* New York: The Public Agenda.

Johnson, L. (2004). Down with detention. *Education Week, 24*(14), 39–40.

Johnson, S., & Birkeland, S. (2003, April). *Pursuing a "sense of success:" New teachers explain their career decisions.* Paper presented at the annual meeting of the American Educational Research Association, New Orleans, LA.

Johnson, W., & Bouchard, T. (2005). The structure of human intelligence: It is verbal, perceptual, and image rotation (VPR), not fluid and crystallized. *Intelligence, 33,* 393–416.

Jonassen, D., Howland, J., Moore, J., & Marra, R. (2003). *Learning to solve problems with technology* (2nd ed.). Upper Saddle River, NJ: Merrill/Pearson.

Jones, N., Kemenes, G., & Benjamin, P. (2001). Selective expression of electrical correlates of differential appetitive classical conditioning in a feedback network. *Journal of Neurophysiology, 85,* 89–97.

Jones, S., & Dindia, K. (2004). A meta-analytic perspective on sex equity in the classroom. *Review of Educational Research, 74*(4), 443–471.

Jones, V. F., & Jones, L. S. (2010). *Comprehensive classroom management: Creating communities of support and solving problems* (9th ed.). Boston: Allyn & Bacon.

Jones, V., & Jones, L. (2010). *Comprehensive classroom management: Creating communities of support and solving problems* (9th ed.). Upper Saddle River, NJ: Pearson.

Jordan, J. (2006). Relational resilience in girls. In S. Goldstein & R. Brooks (Eds.), *Handbook of resilience in children* (pp. 79–90). New York: Springer-Verlag.

Josephson Institute Center for Youth Ethics. (2010). *The ethics of American youth: 2010.* Retrieved from http://charactercounts.org/programs/reportcard/2010/index.html

Juvonen, J. (2006). Sense of belonging, social bonds, and school functioning. In P. A. Alexander & P. H. Winne (Eds.), *Handbook of educational psychology* (2nd ed., pp. 655–674). Mahwah, NJ: Erlbaum.

Juvonen, J. (2007). Reforming middle schools: Focus on continuity, social connectedness, and engagement. *Educational Psychologist, 42,* 197–208.

Kafai, Y. (2006). Constructionism. In R. K. Sawyer (Ed.), *The Cambridge handbook of the learning sciences* (pp. 35–46). New York: Cambridge University Press.

Kaff, M. S., Zabel, R. H., & Milham, M. (2007). Revisiting cost–benefit relationships of behavior management strategies: What special educators say about usefulness, intensity, and effectiveness. *Preventing School Failure, 51,* 35–45.

Kagitcibasi, C. (2007). *Family, self, and human development across cultures: Theory and applications* (2nd ed.). Mahwah, NJ: Erlbaum.

Kahlenberg, R. (2006). Integration by income. *American School Board Journal, 193*(4), 51–52.

Kahng, S. W., & Iwata, B. A. (1999). Correspondence between outcomes of brief and extended functional analyses. *Journal of Applied Behavior Analysis, 32,* 149–159.

Kakkarainen, O., & Ahtee, M. (2007). The durability of conceptual change in learning the concept of weight in the case of a pulley in balance. *International Journal of Science and Mathematics Education, 5,* 461–482.

Kalb, C., & White, E. (2010, May 24 & 31). What should you really be afraid of? *Newsweek,* p. 84.

Kane, M. (2006). Content-related validity evidence in test development. In S. Dowing & T. Haladyna (Eds.), *Handbook of test development* (pp. 131– 154). Mahwah, NJ: Erlbaum.

Karateken, C. (2004). A test of the integrity of the components of Baddeley's model of working memory in attention-deficit/hyperactivity disorder (ADHD). *The Journal of Child Psychology and Psychiatry and Allied Disciplines, 45*(5), 912–926.

Kartal, G. (2010). Does language matter in multimedia learning? Personalization principle revisited. *Journal of Educational Psychology, 102,* 615–624.

Karten, T. (2005). Inclusion strategies that work: Research-based methods for the classroom. Thousand Oaks, CA: Corwin Press.

Kastens, K., & Liben, L. (2007). Eliciting self-explanations improves children's performance on a field-based map skills task. *Cognition and Instruction, 25*(1), 45–74.

Kastens, K., & Liben, L. (2007). Eliciting self-explanations improves children's performance on a field-based map skills task. *Cognition and Instruction, 25*(1), 45–74.

Kato, T., & Manning, M. (2007). Content knowledge—The real reading crisis. *Childhood Education, 83,* 238–239.

Katzir, T., & Paré-Blagoev, J. (2006). Applying cognitive neuroscience research to education: The case of literacy. *Educational Psychologist, 4,* 53–74.

Kauchak, D., & Eggen, P. (2012). *Learning and teaching: Research-based methods* (6th ed.). Boston: Pearson.

Kaufman, D., & Moss, D. M. (2010). A new look at preservice teachers' conceptions of classroom management and organization: Uncovering complexity and dissonance. *The Teacher Educator, 45,* 118–136.

Kaufman, J. C., & Sternberg, R. J. (2007). Creativity. *Change, 39,* 55–58.

Keating, D. P. (2004). Cognitive and brain development. In R. Lerner & L. Steinberg (Eds.), *Handbook of adolescent psychology* (2nd ed.). New York: Wiley.

Kelly, M. (2011). *School violence: How prevalent is it?* Retrieved from http://712educators.about.com/cs/schoolviolence/a/schoolviolence.htm

Kerman, S. (1979). Teacher expectations and student achievement. *Phi Delta Kappan, 60,* 70–72.

Kibby, M. Y., Marks, W., & Morgan, S. (2004). Specific impairment in developmental reading disabilities: A working memory approach. *Journal of Learning Disabilities, 37*(4), 349–363.

Kidron, Y., & Fleischman, S. (2006). Promoting adolescents' prosocial behavior. *Educational Leadership, 63*(7), 90–91.

Kidron, Y., & Fleischman, S. (2006). Promoting adolescents' prosocial behavior. *Educational Leadership, 63*(7), 90–91.

Kids Health for Parents. (2006). *About teen suicide.* Retrieved from http://www.kidshealth.org/sui_fact.htm

Kim, Y., & Baylor, A. L. (2006). A social-cognitive framework for pedagogical agents as learning companions. *Educational Technology Research and Development, 54,* 569–596.

Kincheloe, J. (2004). Why a book on urban education? In Steinberg, S., & Kincheloe, J. (Eds.), *19 Urban questions: Teaching in the city* (pp. 1–27). New York: Peter Lang.

King-Friedrichs, J., & Browne, D. (2001). Learning to remember. *The Science Teacher, 68,* 44–46.

Kirschner, P. A., Sweller, J., & Clark, R. E. (2006). Why minimal guidance during instruction does not work: An analysis of the failure of constructivist, discovery, problem-based, experiential, and inquiry-based teaching. *Educational Psychologist, 41,* 75–86.

Kirylo, J. D., Thirumurthy, V., & Spezzini, S. (2010). Children were punished: Not for what they said, but for what their teachers heard. *Childhood Education, 86,* 130–131.

Kitayama, S., & Cohen, D. (Eds.). (2007). *Handbook of cultural psychology.* New York: Guilford Press.

Kitsantas, A., Zimmerman, B., & Cleary, T. (2000). The role of observation and emulation in the development of athletic self-regulation. *Journal of Educational Psychology, 92*(4), 811–817.

Knight, J. (2002). Crossing the boundaries: What constructivists can teach intensive-explicit instructors and vice versa. *Focus on Exceptional Children, 35,* 1–14, 16.

Kober, N. (2006). *A public education primer: Basic (and sometimes surprising) facts about the U.S. education system.* Washington, DC: Center on Education Policy.

Kohlberg, L. (1963). The development of children's orientation toward moral order: Sequence in the development of human thought. *Vita Humana, 6,* 11–33.

Kohlberg, L. (1969). Stage and sequence: The cognitive-developmental approach to socialization. In D. Goslin (Ed.), *Handbook of socialization theory and research.* Chicago: Rand McNally.

Kohlberg, L. (1981). *Philosophy of moral development.* New York: Harper & Row.

Kohlberg, L. (1984). *The psychology of moral development: the nature and validity of moral stages.* San Francisco: Harper & Row.

Kohn, A. (1993). *Punished by rewards: The trouble with gold stars, incentive plans, A's, praise, and other bribes.* Boston: Houghton Mifflin.

Kohn, A. (1996). By all available means: Cameron and Pierce's defense of extrinsic motivators. *Review of Educational Research, 66,* 1–4.

Kohn, A. (2004). Challenging students—and how to have more of them. *Phi Delta Kappan, 86*(3), 184–194.

Kohn, A. (2005a). *Unconditional parenting: Moving from rewards and punishments to love and reason.* New York: Atria Books.

Kohn, A. (2005b). Unconditional teaching. *Educational Leadership, 63*(1), 20–24.

Kohn, A. (2006a). *The homework myth: Why our kids get too much of a bad thing.* Cambridge, MA: Da Capo Press.

Kohn, A. (2006b). Abusing research: The study of homework and other examples. *Phi Delta Kappan, 88*, 9–22.

Kohn, A. (2007). Who's cheating whom? *Phi Delta Kappan, 89*(2), 89–97.

Koretz, D. (2009). How do American students measure up? Making sense of international comparison. *Future Child, 19*(1), 37–51.

Kornell, N., Castel, A. D., Eich, T. S., & Bjork, R. A. (2010). Spacing as a friend of both memory and induction in young and older adults. *Psychology and Aging, 25*, 498–503.

Kornhaber, M., Fierros, E., & Veenema, S. (2004). *Multiple intelligences: Best ideas from research and practice.* Boston: Allyn & Bacon.

Kounin, J. (1970). *Discipline and group management in classrooms.* New York: Holt, Rinehart & Winston.

Kozhevnikov, M., Hegarty, M., & Mayer, R. (1999, April). *Students' use of imagery in solving qualitative problems in kinematics.* Paper presented at the annual meeting of the American Educational Research Association, Montreal, Canada.

Kozol, J. (2005). *The shame of the nation: The restoration of apartheid schooling in America.* New York: Crown.

Kraft, M. A. (2010). From ringmaster to conductor: 10 simple techniques that can turn an unruly class into a productive one. *Phi Delta Kappan, 91*, 44–47.

Krajcik, J., & Blumenfeld, P. (2006). Project-based learning. In R. K. Sawyer, (Ed.), *Cambridge handbook of the learning sciences* (pp. 317–334). Cambridge, MA: Cambridge University Press.

Krashen, S. (2005). Skyrocketing scores: An urban legend. *Educational Leadership, 62*(4), 37–39.

Krashen, S., Rolstad, K., & MacSwan, J. (2007). *Bilingual education controversy continues.* Retrieved from http://www.suite101.com/content/us-bilingual-education-controversy-continues-a148086

Kratzig, G., & Arbuthnott, K. (2006). Perceptual learning style and learning proficiency: A test of the hypothesis. *Journal of Educational Psychology, 98*(1), 238–246.

Krebs, D., & Denton, K. (2005). *A guide for establishing prosocial communities.* New York: Springer.

Krebs, S. S., & Roebers, C. M. (2010). Children's strategic regulation, metacognitive monitoring, and control processes during test taking. *The British Journal of Educational Psychology, 80*, 325–340.

Kroesbergen, E. H., & van Luit, E. H. (2002). Teaching multiplication to low math performers: Guided versus structured instruction. *Instructional Science, 30*, 361–378.

Kroger, J. (2000). *Identity development: Adolescence through adulthood.* Thousand Oaks, CA: Sage.

Kuhl, P. (2004). Early language acquisition: Cracking the speech code. *Nature Reviews Neuroscience, 5*, 831–843.

Kuhn, D. (2001). Why development does (and does not) occur: Evidence from the domain of inductive reasoning. In J. L. McClelland & R. S. Seigler (Eds.), *Mechanisms of cognitive development: Behavioral and neural perspectives* (pp. 221–249). Mahwah, NJ: Erlbaum.

Kuhn, D., & Park, S. H. (2005). Epistemological understanding and the development of intellectual values. *International Journal of Educational Research, 43*, 111–124.

Labov, W. (1972). *Language in the inner city: Studies in the "Black" English vernacular.* Philadelphia: University of Pennsylvania Press.

Ladd, G. (2006). Peer rejection, aggressive or withdrawn behavior, and psychological maladjustment from ages 5 to 12: An examination of four predictive models. *Child Development, 77*, 822–846.

Lafee, S. (2005). Another weighty burden. *School Administrator, 62*(9), 10–16.

Laird, R. D., Pettit, G. S., Dodge, K. A., & Bates, J. E. (2005). Peer relationship antecedents of delinquent behavior in late adolescence: Is there evidence of demographic group differences in developmental processes? *Development and psychopathology, 17*, 127–144.

Lalli, J. S., & Kates, K. (1998). The effects of reinforcer preference on functional analysis outcomes. *Journal of Applied Behavior Analysis, 31*, 79–90.

Lam, S-F., & Law, Y-K. (2007). The roles of instructional practices and motivation in writing performance. *The Journal of Experimental Education, 75*, 145–164.

Landrum, T. J., & Kaufman, J. M. (2006). Behavioral approaches to classroom management. In C. M. Evertson & C. S. Weinstein (Eds.), *Handbook of classroom management: Research, practice, and contemporary issues* (pp. 47–71). Mahwah, NJ: Erlbaum.

Landry, S., Smith, K., & Swank, P. (2006). Responsive parenting: Establishing early foundations for social, communication, and independent problem-solving skills. *Developmental Psychology, 42*(4), 627–642.

Langenegger, J. (2011, April). *Changes that stick: The role of sustaining forces.* Paper presented at the annual meeting of the American Educational Research Association, New Orleans.

Lave, J. (1997). The culture of acquisition and the culture of understanding. In D. Kirshner & J. A. Whitson (Eds.), *Situated cognition: Social, semiotic, and psychological perspectives* (pp. 17–35). Mahwah, NJ: Erlbaum.

Leaper, C., & Friedman, C., (2007). The socialization of gender. In J. Grusec & P. Hastings (Eds.), *Handbook of socialization: Theory and research* (pp. 561–587). New York: Guilford Press.

Lee, C. D., & Spratley, A. (2010). *Reading in the disciplines: The challenges of adolescent literacy.* New York: Carnegie Corporation of New York.

Lee, J., & Bowen, N. (2006). Parent involvement, cultural capital, and the achievement gap among elementary school children. *American Educational Research Journal, 43*(2), 193–218.

Lee, J., & Reigeluth, C. M. (2003). Formative research on the heuristic task analysis process. *Educational Technology Research and Development, 51*, 5–24.

Lee, R., Sturmey, P., & Fields, L. (2007). Schedule-induced and operant mechanisms that influence response variability: A review and implications for future investigations. *The Psychological Record, 57*, 429–465.

Lee, V. (2000). Using hierarchical linear modeling to study social contexts: The case of school effects. *Educational Psychologist, 35*, 125–141.

Leinhardt, G. (2001). Instructional explanations: A commonplace for teaching and location for contrast. In V. Richardson (Ed.), *Handbook of research on teaching* (4th ed., pp. 333–357). Washington, DC: American Educational Research Association.

Leinhardt, G., & Steele, M. (2005). Seeing the complexity of standing to the side: Instructional dialogues. *Cognition and Instruction, 23*(1), 87–163.

Lemov, D. (2010). *Teach like a champion: 49 techniques that put students on the path to college.* San Francisco: Jossey-Bass.

Leonard, J. (2008). *Culturally specific pedagogy in the mathematics classroom: Strategies for teachers of diverse students.* New York: Routledge.

Leont'ev, A. (1981). The problem of activity in psychology. In J. Wertsch (Ed.), *The concept of activity in Soviet psychology* (pp. 37–71). Armonk, NY: Sharpe.

LePage, P., Darling-Hammond, L., & Akar, H., with Gutierrez, C., Jenkins-Gunn, E., & Rosebrock, K. (2005). Classroom management. In L. Darling-Hammond & J. Bransford (Eds.), *Preparing teachers for a changing world: What teachers should learn and be able to do* (pp. 327–357). San Francisco: Jossey-Bass/Wiley.

Lepper, M., & Hodell, M. (1989). Intrinsic motivation in the classroom. In C. Ames & R. Ames (Eds.), *Research on motivation in education* (Vol. 3, pp. 73–105). San Diego: Academic Press.

Lerner, R. (2006). Developmental science, developmental systems, and contemporary theories of human development. In W. Damon & R. Lerner (Series Eds.), R. Lerner (Vol. Ed.), *Handbook of child psychology: Vol. I. Theoretical models of human development* (6th ed., 1–17). New York: Wiley.

Leung, A., Maddux, W., Galinsky, A., & Chiu, C. (2008). Multicultural experience enhances creativity: The when and how. *American Psychologist, 63*, 169–181.

Levesque, C., Stanek, L., Zuehlke, A. N., & Ryan, R. (2004). Autonomy and competence in German and American university students: A comparative study based on self-determination theory. *Journal of Educational Psychology, 96*(1), 68–84.

Lew, J. (2006). *Asian Americans in class: Charting the achievement gap among Korean American youth.* New York: Teachers College Press.

Lewis, J. L, & Kim, E. (2008). A desire to learn: African American children's positive attitudes toward learning within school cultures of low expectations, *Teachers College Record*, 110, 1304–1329.

Li, J. (2005). Mind or virtue: Western and Chinese beliefs about learning. *Current Directions in Psychological Science, 14*, 190–194.

Li, Y., Anderson, R., Nguyen-Jahiel, K., Dong, T., Archodidou, A., Kim, I., Kuo, L., Clark, A., Wu, X., Jadallah, M., & Miller, B. (2007). Emergent leadership in children's discussion groups. *Cognition and Instruction, 25*, 75–111.

Lillard, A. (2007). *Montessori: The science behind the genius.* New York: Oxford University Press.

Lillard, A. S. (1997). Other folks' theories of mind and behavior. *Psychological Science, 8*, 268–274.

Lin, J.-R. (2007). Responses to anomalous data obtained from repeatable experiments in the laboratory. *Journal of Research in Science Teaching, 44*(3), 506–528.

Lindfors, K., Elovainio, M., Wickman, S., Vuroinen. R., Sinkkonen, J., Dunkel, L. (2007). Brief report: The role of ego development in psychosocial adjustment among boys with delayed puberty. *Journal of Research on Adolescence, 17*(4), 601–612.

Linn, S. (2009). *Case for make believe: Saving play in a commercialized world.* New York: The New Press.

Linnenbrink, E. A., & Pintrich, P. R. (2003). Achievement goals and intentional conceptual change. In G. M. Sinatra & P. R. Pintrich (Eds.), *Intentional conceptual change* (pp. 347–374). Mahwah, NJ: Erlbaum.

Lohman, D. (2001, April). *Fluid intelligence, inductive reasoning, and working memory: Where the theory of multiple intelligences falls short.* Paper presented at the annual meeting of the American Educational Research Association, Seattle.

Lopes, P., & Salovey, P. (2004). Toward a broader education: Social, emotional, and practical skills. In J. Zins, R. Weissberg, M. Wang, & H. Walberg (Eds.), *Building academic success on social and emotional learning* (pp. 76–93). New York: Teachers College Press.

Loughran, J., Mulhall, P., & Berry, A. (2004). In search of pedagogical content knowledge in science: Developing ways of articulating and documenting professional practice. *Journal of Research in Science Teaching, 41*, 370–391.

Lovelace, M. (2005). Meta-analysis of experimental research based on the Dunn and Dunn Model. *Journal of Educational Research, 98*(3), 176–183.

Luft, P., Brown, C. M., & Sutherin, L. J. (2007). Are you and your students bored with the benchmarks? Sinking under the standards? *Teaching Exceptional Children, 39*, 39–46.

Lumeng, J. C., & Cardinal, T. M. (2007). Providing information about a flavor to preschoolers: Effects on liking and memory for having tasted it. *Chemical Senses, 32*, 505–513.

Luna, B., Garver, K. E., Urban, T. A., Lazar, N. A., & Sweeny, J. A. (2004). Maturation of cognitive processes from late childhood to adulthood. *Child Development, 75*, 1357–1372.

Lundberg, U., Granqvist, M., Hansson, T., Magnusson, M., & Wallin, L. (1989). Psychological and physiological stress responses during repetitive work at an assembly line. *Work & Stress, 3*, 143–153.

Lunenberg, M., Korthagen, F., & Swennen, A. (2007). The teacher educator as a role model. *Teaching and Teacher Education, 23*, 586–601.

Luria, A. R. (1976). *Cognitive development: Its cultural and social foundations.* Cambridge, MA: Harvard University Press.

Luthar, S., & Latendresse, S. (2005). Children of the affluent: Challenges to well-being. *Current Directions in Psychological Science, 14*, 49–53.

Lutz, S., Guthrie, J., & Davis, M. (2006). Scaffolding for engagement in elementary school reading instruction. *Journal of Educational Research, 100*(1), 3–20.

Luyckx, K., Goossens, L., & Soenens, B. (2006). A developmental contextual perspective on identity construction in emerging adulthood: Change dynamics in commitment formation and commitment evaluation. *Developmental Psychology, 42*(2), 366–380.

Maag, J. (2001). Rewarded by punishment: Reflections on the disuse of positive reinforcement in schools. *Exceptional Children, 67*, 173–186.

Maccoby, E. (2002). Gender and group process: A development perspective. *Current Directions in Psychological Science, 11*, 54–58.

Macionis, J. (2009). *Society: The basics* (9th ed.). Upper Saddle River, NJ: Prentice Hall.

Macionis, J., & Parillo, V. (2010). *Cities and urban life* (5th ed.). Upper Saddle River, NJ: Merrill/Pearson Education.

MacNeil, M. S. (2007). Concept mapping as a means of course evaluation. *Journal of Nursing Education, 46*, 232–234.

Macpherson, R., & Stanovich, K. E. (2007). Cognitive ability, thinking dispositions, and instructional set as predictors of critical thinking. *Learning and Individual Differences, 17*, 115–127.

Mager, R. (1962). Preparing instructional objectives. Palo Alto, CA: Featon.

Mager, R. F. (2000). What Every Manager Should Know About Training: An Insider's Guide to Getting Your Money's Worth from Training (2nd ed.). Atlanta: GA: The Center for Effective Performance, Inc.

Maguire, E., Gadian, D., Johnsrude, I., Good, C., Ashburner, J., Frackowiak, R., & Frith, C. (2000). Navigation-related structural change in the hippocampi of taxi drivers. *Proceedings of the National Academy of Science, USA, 97*(8), 4398-4403.

Mahoney, J., Larson, R., & Eccles, J. (2005). *Organized activities as contexts of development: Extracurricular activities.* New York: Routledge.

Manzo, K. (2006). Young adults don't think world knowledge is vital. *Education Week, 25*(36), 8.

Manzo, K. (2008). Researchers propose NAEP look beyond academic measures. *Education Week, 27*(25), 8.

Marchand, G., & Skinner, E. A. (2007). Motivational dynamics of children's academic help-seeking and concealment. *Journal of Educational Psychology, 99*, 65–82.

Marcia, J. (1980). Identity in adolescence. In J. Adelson (Ed.), *Handbook of adolescent psychology.* New York: Wiley.

Marcia, J. (1987). The identity status approach to the study of ego identity development. In T. Honess & K. Yardley (Eds.), *Self and identity: Perspectives across the life span.* London: Routledge & Kegan Paul.

Marcia, J. (1988). Common processes underlying ego identity, cognitive/moral development, and individuation. In D. Lapsley & F. Power (Eds.), *Self, ego, and identity: Integrative approaches* (pp. 211–225). New York: Springer-Verlag.

Marcia, J. (1999). Representational thought in ego identity, psychotherapy, and psychosocial development. In I. E. Sigel (Ed.), *Development of mental representation: Theories and applications.* Mahwah, NJ: Lawrence Erlbaum.

Margolis, J. (2010). What teacher quality is a local issue (and why Race to the Top is a misguided flop). *Teachers College Record.* Retrieved from http://www.tcrecord.org/Content.asp?ContentID=16023

Marinoff, L. (2003). *The big questions: How philosophy can change your life.* New York: Bloomsbury.

Marion, S., & Pellegrino, J. (2006). A validity framework for evaluating the technical quality of alternate assessments. *Educational Measurement: Issues and Practices, 25*(4), 47–57.

Mark, G., Gudith, D., & Klocke, U. (2008). *The cost of interrupted work: More speed and stress.* Proceedings of the twenty-sixth annual SIGCHI conference on human factors in computing systems, Florence, Italy.

Marsh, H., & Ayotte, V. (2003). Do multiple dimensions of self-concept become more differentiated with age? The differential distinctiveness hypothesis. *Journal of Educational Psychology, 95*, 687–706.

Martin, J. (2006). Social cultural perspectives in educational psychology. In P. A. Alexander & P. H. Winne (Eds.), *Handbook of educational psychology* (2nd ed., pp. 595–614). Mahwah, NJ: Erlbaum.

Martone, A., & Sireci, S. G. (2009). Evaluating alignment between curriculum, assessment, and instruction. *Review of Educational Research, 79*, 1332–1361.

Marzano, R. J. (2003). *What works in schools: Translating research into action.* Alexandria VA: Association for Supervision and Curriculum Development.

Marzano, R. J. (2007). *Classroom assessment and grading that work.* Alexandria VA: Association for Supervision and Curriculum Development.

Marzano, R. J., & Pickering, D. J. (2007). Errors and allegations about research on homework. *Phi Delta Kappan, 88,* 507–513.

Maslow, A. (1968). *Toward a psychology of being* (2nd ed.). New York: Van Nostrand.

Maslow, A. (1970). *Motivation and personality* (2nd ed.). New York: Harper & Row. (Original work published 1954)

Maslow, A. H. (1987). *Motivation and personality* (3rd ed.). New York: Harper & Row.

Mason, L. (2007). Introduction: Bridging the cognitive and sociocultural approaches in research on conceptual change: Is it feasible? *Educational Psychologist, 42*(1), 1–8.

Masten, A., & Gewirtz, A. (2006). Vulnerablity and resilience in early child development. In K. McCartney & D. Phillips (Eds.), *Blackwell handbook of early childhood development* (pp. 22–43). Malden, MA: Blackwell.

Masten, A., & Shaffer, A. (2006). How families matter in child development: Reflections from research on risk and resilience. In A. Masten & A. Shaffer (Eds.), *Families count: Effects on child and adolescent development* (pp. 5–25). New York: Cambridge University Press.

Mastropieri, M., & Scruggs, T. (2010). *The inclusive classroom: Strategies for effective differentiated instruction* (4th ed.). Upper Saddle River, NJ: Merrill/Pearson.

Mastropieri, M., Scruggs, T., & Berkeley, S. (2007). Peers helping peers. *Educational Leadership, 64*(5), 54–58.

Math.com. (2010). *Estimating and rounding decimals.* Retrieved from http://www.math.com/school/subject1/practice/S1U1L3/S1U1L3Pract.html

Mawhinney, T., & Sagan, L. (2007). The power of personal relationships. *Phi Delta Kappan, 88*(6), 460–464.

Mayer, R. (2002). *The promise of educational psychology: Volume II. Teaching for meaningful learning.* Upper Saddle River, NJ: Merrill/Pearson.

Mayer, R. (2008). *Learning and instruction* (2nd ed.). Upper Saddle River, NJ: Pearson.

Mayer, R. E. (2002). *The promise of educational psychology: Volume II. Teaching for meaningful learning.* Upper Saddle River, NJ: Merrilll/Pearson.

Mayer, R. E. (2004). Should there be a three-strikes rule against pure discovery learning? *American Psychologist, 59,* 14–19.

Mayer, R. E. (2008). *Learning and instruction* (2nd ed.). Upper Saddle River, NJ: Pearson.

Mayer, R. E., & Wittrock, M. C. (2006). Problem solving. In P. A. Alexander & P. H. Winne (Eds.), *Handbook of educational psychology* (2nd ed., pp. 287–303). Mahwah, NJ: Erlbaum.

Mayer, R., & Massa, L. (2003). Three facts of visual and verbal learners: Cognitive ability, cognitive style, and learning preference. *Journal of Educational Psychology, 95,* 833–846.

Mazur, J. E. (2006). *Learning and behavior* (6th ed.). Upper Saddle River, NJ: Merrill/Pearson.

McCleery, J., Twyman, T., & Tindal, G. (2003, April). *Using concepts to frame history content with explicit instruction.* Paper presented at the annual meeting of the American Educational Research Association, Chicago.

McCoach, D. B., O'Connell, A., & Levitt, H. (2006). Ability grouping across kindergarten using an early childhood longitudinal study. *Journal of Educational Research, 99*(6), 339–346.

McCurdy, B. L., Kunsch, C., & Reibstein, S. (2007). Secondary prevention in the urban school: Implementing the behavior education program. *Preventing School Failure, 51,* 12–19.

McCutchen, D. (2000). Knowledge, processing, and working memory: Implications for a theory of writing. *Educational Psychologist, 35*(1), 13–23.

McDermott, R., Goldman, S., & Varenne, H. (2006). The cultural work of learning disabilities. *Educational Researcher, 35*(6), 12–17.

McDevitt, T. M., & Ormrod, J. E. (2010). *Child development and education* (4th ed.). Upper Saddle River, NJ: Pearson.

McDevitt, T., Spivey, N., Sheehan, E., Lennon, R., & Story, R. (1990). Children's beliefs about listening: Is it enough to be still and quiet? *Child Development, 61,* 713–721.

McDonough, P. (2009). TV viewing among kids at an eight-year high. *Nielsen Wire.* Retrieved from http://blog.nielsen.com/nielsenwire/media_entertainment/tv-viewing-among-kids-at-an-eight-year-high/

McKeachie, W., & Kulik, J. (1975). Effective college teaching. In F. Kerlinger (Ed.), *Review of research in education: Vol. 3* (pp. 24–39). Washington, DC: American Educational Research Association.

McLeod, J., & Yates, L. (2006). *Making modern lives: Subjectivity, schooling, and social change.* Albany, NY: State University of New York Press.

McMahon, S., Rose, D., & Parks, M. (2004). Multiple intelligences and reading achievement; An examination of the Teele Inventory of Multiple Intelligences. *Journal of Experimental Education, 73*(1), 41–52.

McMillan, J. (2007). *Classroom assessment: Principles and practices for effective standards-based instruction* (4th ed.). Boston: Allyn & Bacon.

Md-Yunus, S. (2007). How parents can encourage creativity in children. *Childhood Education, 83,* 236–237.

Medin, D., Proffitt, J., & Schwartz. H. (2000). Concepts: An overview. In A. Kazdin (Ed.), *Encyclopedia of psychology* (Vol. 2, pp. 242–245). New York: Oxford University Press.

Medina, J. (2009, March 11). Boys and girls together, taught separately in public school. *New York Times,* p. A24.

Meek, C. (2006). From the inside out: A look at testing special education students. *Phi Delta Kappan, 88*(4), 293–297.

Meichenbaum, D. (2000). *Cognitive behavior modification: An integrative approach.* Dordrecht, Netherlands: Kluwer Academic.

Meltzer, L., Pollica, L., & Barzillai, M. (2007). Executive function in the classroom: Embedding strategy instruction into daily teaching practices. In L. Meltzer (Ed.), *Executive function in education: From theory to practice* (pp. 165–193). New York: Guilford Press.

Mendle, J., Tukheimer, E., & Emery, R. (2007). Detrimental psychological outcomes associated with early pubertal timing in adolescent girls. *Developmental Review, 27,* 151–171.

Menken, K. (2008). *English learners left behind: Standardized testing as language policy.* Clevedon, England: Multilingual Matters.

Mercer, J. (1973). *Labeling the mentally retarded.* Berkeley: University of California Press.

Merisuo-Storm, T. (2007). Pupils' attitudes towards foreign-language learning and the development of literacy skills in bilingual education. *Teacher & Teacher Education, 23,* 226–235.

Mertler, C. (2007). *Interpreting standardized test scores: Strategies for data-driven instructional decision making.* Los Angeles: Sage.

Midgley, C. (2001). A goal theory perspective on the current status of middle level schools. In T. Urdan & F. Pajares (Eds.), *Adolescence and education* (Vol. I, pp. 33–59). Greenwich, CT: Information Age Publishing.

Midgley, C., Kaplan, A., & Middleton, M. (2001). Performance-approach goals. Good for what, for whom, under what circumstances, and at what cost? *Journal of Educational Psychology, 93,* 77–86.

Miller, G. (1956). The magical number seven, plus or minus two: Some limits on our capacity for processing information. *Psychological Review, 63,* 81–97.

Miller, M. D., Linn, R. L., & Gronlund, N. E. (2009). *Measurement and assessment in teaching* (10th ed.). Upper Saddle River, NJ: Merrill/Pearson.

Miller, P. (2002). *Theories of developmental psychology* (4th ed.). New York: Worth.

Milner, H. R., & Tenore, F. B. (2010). Classroom management in diverse classrooms. *Urban Education, 45,* 560–603.

Milsom, A., & Glanville, J. L. (2010). Factors mediating the relationship between social skills and academic grades in a sample of students diagnosed with learning disabilities and emotional disturbances. *Remedial and Special Education, 31,* 241–251.

Miltenberger, R.G. (2008). *Behavior modification: Principles and procedures* (4th ed.). Belmont, CA: Wadsworth/Cengage.

Mischel, W., Shoda, Y., & Rodriguez, M. (1989). Delay of gratification in children. *Science, 244,* 933–938.

Moffitt, T. E., Arseneault, L., Belsky, D., Dickson, N., Hancox, R. J., Harrington, H., . . . Caspi, A. (2011). A gradient of childhood self-control predicts health, wealth, and public safety. *PNAS.*

Retrieved from http://www.pnas.org/content/early/2011/01/20/1010076108.full.pdf+html

Moore, J. (2007, October). Suicide trends among youths and young adults 10–24 years—United States, 1990–2004. *Youth Today*, p. 29.

Morelli, G. A., & Rothbaum, F. (2007). Situating the child in context: Attachment relationships and self-regulation in different cultures. In S. Kitayama & D. Cohen (Eds.) *Handbook of cultural psychology* (pp. 500–527). New York: Guilford Press.

Moreno, R. (2004). Decreasing cognitive load for novice students: Effects of explanatory versus corrective feedback in discovery-based multimedia. *Instructional Science, 32*, 99–113.

Moreno, R., & Duran, R. (2004). Do multiple representations need explanations: The role of verbal guidance and individual differences in multimedia mathematics learning. *Journal of Educational Psychology, 96*, 492–503.

Moreno, R., & Mayer, R. (2000). Engaging students in active learning: The case for personalized multimedia messages. *Journal of Educational Psychology, 92*(4), 724–733.

Moreno, R., & Mayer, R. (2005). Role of guidance, reflection, and interactivity in an agent-based multimedia game. *Journal of Educational Psychology, 97*(1), 117–128.

Moreno, R., & Valdez, A. (2007). Immediate and delayed effects of using a classroom case exemplar in teacher education: The role of presentation format. *Journal of Educational Psychology, 99*(1), 194–206.

Morgan, P. L., & Fuchs, D. (2007). Is there a bidirectional relationship between children's reading skills and reading motivation? *Exceptional Children, 73*, 165–183.

Morgan, S. L., & Mehta, J. D. (2004). Beyond the laboratory: Evaluating the survey evidence for the disidentification explanation of black–white differences in achievement. *Sociology of Education, 77*(1), 82–101.

Moriarity, A. (2009). Managing confrontations safely and effectively. *Kappa Delta Pi Record, 45*, 78–83.

Murdock, T. B., Miller, A., & Kohlhardt, J. (2004). Effects of classroom context variables in high school students' judgments of the acceptability and likelihood of cheating. *Journal of Educational Psychology, 96*(4), 765–777.

Murdock, T., & Anderman, E. (2006). Motivational perspectives on student cheating: Toward an integrated model of academic dishonesty. *Educational Psychologist, 41*, 129–145.

Murphy, J. C. (2007). Hey, Ms. A! One student teacher's success story. *Kappa Delta Pi Record, 43*, 52–55.

Myers, K. M., & Davis, M. (2007). Mechanisms of fear extinction. *Molecular Psychiatry, 12*, 120–150.

Nasir, N., Rosebery, A., Warren, B., & Lee, C. (2006). Learning as a cultural process: Achieving equity through diversity. In R. K. Sawyer (Ed.), *The Cambridge handbook of the learning sciences* (pp. 489–504). New York: Cambridge University Press.

National Assessment of Educational Progress. (2009). *The nation's report card*. Washington, DC: National Center for Educational Statistics. Retrieved from http://www.nces.ed.gov/nationsreportcard and http://nationsreportcard.gov/reading_2009/nat_g4.asp?subtab_id=Tab_7&tab_id=tab1#tabsContainer

National Center for Education Statistics. (2007). *The reading literacy of U.S. fourth-grade students in an international context*. Washington, DC: Author.

National Council of Young Sports. (2008). *Report on trends and participation in organized youth sports*. Stuart, FL: Author.

National Education Association. (2007). *Status of the American school teacher, 2006–2007*. Washington, DC: Author.

National excellence: A case for developing America's talent. (1993). Washington, DC: U.S. Department of Education, Office of Educational Research and Improvement.

National Federation of State High School Associations. (2008). *2007–2008 high school athletics participation survey*. Retrieved from http://www.nfhs.org/core/contentmanager/uploads/2007-08%20Participation%20Survey.pdf

National Joint Committee on Learning Disabilities. (1994). Learning disabilities: Issues on definition. A position paper of the National Joint Committee in Learning Disabilities. In *Collective perspectives on issues affecting learning disability: Position papers and statements*. Austin, TX: Pro-Ed.

National Poverty Center. (2008). *Poverty facts*. Retrieved from http://www.npc.umich.edu/poverty/

Neisser, U. (1967). *Cognitive psychology*. New York: Appleton-Century-Crofts.

Nelson, C. Thomas, K., & de Haan, M. (2006). Neural bases of cognitive development. In D. Kuhn, R. Siegler (Vol. Eds.), W. Damon, & R. Lerner (Series Eds.), *Handbook of child psychology. Vol. 2: Cognition, perception, and language* (6th ed., pp. 3–57). New York: Wiley.

Nelson, J. A. P., Young, B. J., Young, E. L., & Cox, G. (2010). Using teacher-written praise notes to promote a positive environment in a middle school. *Preventing School Failure, 54*, 119–125.

Nesbit, J., & Adesope, O. (2006). Learning with concept and knowledge maps: A meta-analysis. *Review of Educational Research, 76*(3), 413–448.

Nettelbeck, T., & Wilson, C. (2010). Intelligence and IQ. In K. Wheldall (Ed.), *Developments in educational psychology* (2nd ed, pp. 30–52). New York: Routledge.

New Commission on the Skills of the American Workforce. (2006). *Tough choices or tough time*. Retrieved from http://www.skillscommission.org/executive.htm

Newcombe, N., & Huttenlocher, J. (2006). Development of spatial cognition. In D. Kuhn & R. Siegler (Eds.), *Handbook of child psychology: Vol 2. Cognition, perception, and language* (6th ed., pp. 734–776). Hoboken, NJ: Wiley.

Ngo, B., & Lee, S. (2007). Complicating the image of model minority success: A review of southeast Asian American education. *Review of Educational Research, 77*(4), 415–453.

Nichols, S., & Berliner, D. (2008) Why has high-stakes testing so easily slipped into contemporary American life? *Phi Delta Kappan, 89*, 672–676.

Nilsson, L., & Archer, T. (1989). Aversively motivated behavior: Which are the perspectives? In T. Archer & L. Nilsson (Eds.), *Aversion, avoidance and anxiety*. Hillsdale, NJ: Erlbaum.

Nitko, A., & Brookhart, S. (2011). *Educational assessment of students* (5th ed.). Upper Saddle River, NJ: Merrill/Pearson.

Nitko, A., L., & Brookhart, S. M. (2011). *Educational assessment of students* (6th ed.). Upper Saddle River, NJ: Pearson.

Noddings, N. (1992). *The challenge to care in schools: An alternative approach to education*. New York: Teachers College Press.

Noddings, N. (2001). The caring teacher. In V. Richardson (Ed.), *Handbook of research on teaching* (4th ed., pp. 99–105). Washington, DC: American Educational Research Association.

Noddings, N. (2002). *Educating moral people: A caring alternative approach to education*. New York: Teachers College Press.

Noguera, P. (2003). *City schools and the American dream: Reclaiming the promise of public education*. New York: Teachers College Press.

Norenzayan, A., Choi, I., & Peng, K. (2007). Perception and cognition. In S. Kitayama & D. Cohen (Eds.), *Handbook of cultural psychology* (pp. 569–594). New York: Guilford Press.

Notar, C. E., Zuelke, D. C., Wilson, J. D., & Yunker, B. D. (2004). The table of specifications: Ensuring accountability in teacher made tests. *Journal of Instructional Psychology, 31*(2), 115–129.

Novak, J. D., & Cañas, A. J. (2006). The theory underlying concept maps and how to construct and use them. Retrieved from http://cmap.ihmc.us/Publications/ResearchPapers/TheoryCmaps/TheoryUnderlyingConceptMaps.htm

Nucci, L. (2001). *Education in the moral domain*. Cambridge, England: Cambridge University Press.

Nucci, L. (2006). Classroom management for moral and social development. In C. Evertson & C. Weinstein (Eds.), *Handbook of classroom management: Research, practice, and contemporary issues* (pp. 711–731). Mahwah, NJ: Erlbaum.

Nuthall, G. A. (2000). The role of memory in the acquisition and retention of knowledge in science and social studies units. *Cognition and Instruction, 18*(1), 83–139.

O'Brien, T. (1999). Parrot math. *Phi Delta Kappan, 80*, 434–438.

O'Conner, C., & Fernandez, S. (2006). Race, class, and disproportionality: Reevaluating the relationship between poverty and special education placement. *Educational Researcher, 35*(6), 6–11.

O'Connor, E. E., Dearing, E., & Collins, B. A. (2011). Teacher-child relationship and behavior problem trajectories in elementary school. *American Educational Research Journal, 48,* 120–162.

O'Connor, E., & McCartney, K. (2007). Examining teacher–child relationships and achievement as part of an ecological model of development. *American Educational Research Journal, 44*(2), 340–369.

O'Donnell, A. (2006). The role of peers and group learning. In P. Alexander & P. Winne (Eds.), *Handbook of educational psychology* (2nd ed., pp. 781–802). Mahwah, NJ: Erlbaum.

O'Mara, A., Marsh, H., Craven, R., & Debus, R. (2006). Do self-concept interventions make a difference? A synergistic blend of construct validation and meta-analysis. *Educational Psychologist, 41*(3), 181–206.

O'Meara. J. (2011). *Beyond differentiated instruction.* Thousand Oaks, CA: Corwin Press.

Oakes, J. (2005). *Keeping track: How schools structure inequality* (2nd ed.). New Haven, CT: Yale University Press.

Obradovic, J., Burt, K. B., & Masten, A. S. (2010). Testing a dual cascade model linking competence and symptoms over 20 years from childhood to adulthood. *Journal of Clinical Child and Adolescent Psychology, 39,* 90–102.

Ogbu, J. (1992). Understanding cultural diversity and learning. *Educational Researcher, 21*(8), 5–14.

Ogbu, J. (1999, April). *The significance of minority status.* Paper presented at the annual meeting of the American Educational Research Association, Montreal, Canada.

Ogbu, J. (2003). *Black American students in an affluent suburb: A study of academic disengagement.* Mahwah, NJ: Erlbaum.

Ogbu, J., & Simons, H. (1998). Voluntary and involuntary minorities: A cultural-ecological theory of school performance with some implications for education. *Anthropology & Education Quarterly, 29*(2), 155–188.

Ogden, C., & Carroll, M. (2010). Prevalence of obesity among children and adolescents: United States, trends 1963–1965 through 2007–2008. *Center for Disease Control and Prevention.* Retrieved from http://www.cdc.gov/nchs/data/hestat/obesity_child_07_08/obesity_child_07_08.htm

Okagaki, L. (2006). Ethnicity, learning. In P. A. Alexander & P. H. Winne (Eds.), *Handbook of educational psychology* (2nd ed., pp. 615–634). Mahwah, NJ: Erlbaum.

Owens, R. (2005). *Language development* (6th ed.). Boston: Allyn & Bacon.

Owens, R. (2008). *Language development* (7th ed.). Boston: Allyn & Bacon.

Paas, F., Renkl, A., & Sweller, J. (2004). Cognitive load theory: Instructional implications of the interaction between information structures and cognitive architecture. *Instructional Science, 32*(1), 1–8.

Padilla, A. (2006). Second language learning: Issues in research and teaching. In P. Alexander & P. Winne (Eds.), *Handbook of educational psychology* (2nd ed., pp. 571–592). Mahwah, NJ: Erlbaum.

Padilla-Walker, L. M., Harper, J. M., & Jensen, A. C. (2010). Self-regulation as a mediator between sibling relationship quality and early adolescents' positive and negative outcomes. *Journal of Family Psychology, 24,* 419–428.

Paivio, A. (1986). *Mental representations: A dual-coding approach.* New York: Oxford University.

Paivio, A. (1991). Dual coding theory: Retrospect and current status. *Canadian Journal of Psychology, 45,* 255–287.

Pajares, F., & Valiante, G. (1999, April). *Writing self-efficacy of middle school students: Relation to motivation constructs, achievement, gender, and gender orientation.* Paper presented at the annual meeting of the American Educational Research Association, Montreal, Canada.

Palincsar, A. (1998). Social constructivist perspectives on teaching and learning. *Annual Review of Psychology, 49,* 345–375.

Paris, S. G., & Paris, A. H. (2001). Classroom application of research on self-regulated learning. *Educational Psychologist, 36,* 89–101.

Paris, S. G., Morrison, F. J., & Miller, K. F. (2006). Academic pathways from preschool through elementary school. In P. A. Alexander & P. H. Winne (Eds.), *Handbook of educational psychology* (2nd ed., pp. 61–85). Mahwah, NJ: Erlbaum.

Parker-Pope, T. (2010, July 20). Attention disorders can take a toll on marriage. *New York Times,* p. D5.

Parks, F. R., & Kennedy, J. H. (2007). The impact of race, physical attractiveness, and gender on education majors' and teachers' perceptions of student competence. *Journal of Black Studies, 37,* 936–943.

Pashler, H., & Carrier, M. (1996). Structures, processes, and the flow of information. In E. Bjork & R. Bjork (Eds.), *Memory* (pp. 3–29). San Diego, CA: Academic Press.

Pashler, H., McDaniel, M., Rohrer, D., & Bjork, R. (2008). Learning styles: Concepts and evidence. *Psychological Science in the Public Interest, 9,* 105–119.

Patrick, H., Anderman, L. H., & Ryan, A. M. (2002). Social motivation and the classroom social environment. In C. Midgley (Ed.), *Goals, goal structures, and patterns of adaptive learning* (pp. 85–108). Mahwah, NJ: Erlbaum.

Paul, A. M. (2011, January 31). The roar of the tiger mom. *Time,* 34–40.

Péladeau, N., Forget, J., & Gagné, F. (2003). Effect of paced and unpaced practice on skill application and retention: How much is enough? *American Educational Research Journal, 40*(3), 769–801.

Pellegrini, A. (2005). *Recess: Its role in development and education.* Mahwah, NJ: Erlbaum.

Pellegrini, A. D. (2002). Bullying, victimization, and sexual harassment during the transition to middle school. *Educational Psychologist, 37,* 151–163.

Pellegrino, A. M. (2010). Pre-service teachers and classroom authority. *American Secondary Education, 38,* 62–78.

Pence, K., & Justice, L. (2008). *Language development from theory to practice.* Upper Saddle River, NJ: Merrill/Pearson Education.

Peregoy, S., & Boyle, O. (2008). *Reading, writing, and learning in ESL* (5th ed.). New York: Longman.

Peregoy, S., & Boyle, O. (2009). *Reading, writing, and learning in ESL* (5th ed.). New York: Longman.

Perkins-Gough, D. (2004). A two-tiered education system. *Educational Leadership, 62*(3), 87–88.

Perkins-Gough, D. (2006). Do we really have a "boy crisis"? *Educational Leadership, 64*(1), 93–94.

Perlmutter, D. D. (2004, December 10). Are we grading on the curves? *The Chronicle of Higher Education,* B13–14.

Perry, N. E., Turner, J. C., & Meyer, D. K. (2006). Classrooms as contexts for motivating learning. In P. A. Alexander & P. H. Winne (Eds.), *Handbook of educational psychology* (2nd ed., pp. 327–348). Mahwah, NJ: Erlbaum.

Perry, N. E., Turner, J. C., & Meyer, D. K. (2006). Classrooms as contexts for motivating learning. In P. A. Alexander & P. H. Winne (Eds.), *Handbook of educational psychology* (2nd ed., pp. 327–348). Mahwah, NJ: Erlbaum.

Peverly, S. P., Brobst, K. E., & Graham, M. (2003). College adults are not good at self-regulation: A study on the relationship of self-regulation, note taking, and test taking. *Journal of Educational Psychology, 95,* 335–346.

Peverly, S. Ramaswamy, V., Brown, C., Sumowski, J., Alidoost, M., & Garner, J. (2007). What predicts skill in lecture note taking? *Journal of Educational Psychology, 99*(1), 167–180.

Pew Charitable Trust. (2010). Pew Internet project: Teens and mobile phones. Retrieved from http://www.pewtrusts.org/news_room_detail.aspx?id=58543

Pew Hispanic Center. (2011). *Statistical Portrait of the Foreign-Born Population in the United States, 2008.* Retrieved from http://pewhispanic.org/files/factsheets/foreignborn2008/Table%201.pdf

Pfiffner, L., Rosen, L., & O'Leary, S. (1985). The efficacy of an all-positive approach to classroom management. *Journal of Applied Behavior Analysis, 18,* 257–261.

Phelps, L., McGrew, K., Knopik, S., & Ford, L. (2005). The general (g), broad, and narrow CHC stratum characteristics of the WJ III and WISC-III tests: A confirmatory cross-battery investigation. *School Psychology Quarterly, 20,* 66–88.

Phelps, R. (Ed.) (2005). *Defending standardized testing.* Mahwah, NJ: Erlbaum.

Phye, G. (2005). Transfer and problem solving: A psychological integration of models, metaphors, and methods. In J. Royer (Ed.), *The cognitive revolution in educational psychology* (pp. 249–292). Greenwich, CT: Information Age Publishing.

Piaget, J. (1952). *Origins of intelligence in children.* New York: International Universities Press.

Piaget, J. (1959). *Language and thought of the child* (M. Grabain, Trans.). New York: Humanities Press.

Piaget, J. (1965). The *moral judgment of the child.* New York: Free Press. (Original work published 1932)

Piaget, J. (1970). *The science of education and the psychology of the child.* New York: Orion Press.

Piaget, J. (1977). Problems in equilibration. In M. Appel & L. Goldberg (Eds.), *Topics in cognitive development: Vol. 1. Equilibration: Theory, research, and application* (pp. 3–13). New York: Plenum Press.

Piaget, J. (1980). *Adaptation and intelligence: Organic selection and phenocopy* (S. Eames, Trans.). Chicago: University of Chicago Press.

Piaget, J., & Inhelder, B. (1956). *The child's conception of space.* Boston: Routledge and Kegan-Paul.

Pianta, R., Belsky, J., Houts, R., Morrison, F., & NICHD Early Child Care Research Network. (2007). Opportunities to learn in America's elementary classrooms. *Science, 315,* 1795–1796.

Pierangelo, R., & Guiliani, G. (2006). *Assessment in special education* (2nd ed.). Boston: Allyn & Bacon.

Pinker, S. (2007). *Stuff of thought: Language a window into human nature.* New York: Houghton Mifflin.

Pinker, S. (2010, June 11). Mind over mass media. *New York Times*, p. A27.

Pintrich, P. (2000). Multiple goals, multiple pathways: The role of goal orientation in learning and achievement. *Journal of Educational Psychology, 92,* 544–555.

Pittman, K., & Beth-Halachmy, S. (1997, March). *The role of prior knowledge in analogy use.* Paper presented at the annual meeting of the American Educational Research Association, Chicago.

Plata, M., Trusty, J., & Glasgow, D. (2005). Adolescents with learning disabilities: Are they allowed to participate in activities? *Journal of Educational Research, 98*(3), 136–143.

Platt, R. (2004). Standardized tests: Whose standards are we talking about? *Phi Delta Kappan, 85*(5), 381–382.

Plucker, J. A., Beghetto, R. A., & Dow, G. T. (2004). Why isn't creativity more important to educational psychologists? Potentials, pitfalls, and future directions in creativity research. *Educational Psychologist, 39,* 83–96.

Popham, W. J. (2004). *American's failing schools: How parents and teachers can cope with No Child Left Behind.* New York: Routledge Falmer.

Popham, W. J. (2007). Who should make the test? *Educational Leadership, 65*(1), 80–82.

Popham, W. J. (2011a). *Classroom assessment: What teachers need to know* (6th ed.). Boston: Pearson.

Popham, W. J. (2011b). Combating phony formative assessment – with a hyphen. *Education Week, 30*(21), 35.

Posner, M., & Rothbart, M. (2007). *Educating the human brain.* Washington, DC: American Psychological Association.

Powell, R., & Caseau, D. (2004). *Classroom communication and diversity.* Mahwah, NJ: Erlbaum.

Powers, T. G., Bindler, R. C., Goetz, S., & Daratha, K. B. (2010). Obesity prevention in early adolescence: Student, parent, and teacher views. *Journal of School Health, 80,* 13–19.

Prawat, R. (1989). Promoting access to knowledge, strategy, and disposition in students: A research synthesis. *Review of Educational Research, 59,* 1–41.

Premack, D. (1965). Reinforcement theory. In D. Levine (Ed.), *Nebraska Symposium on Motivation* (Vol. 13, pp. 3–41). Lincoln: University of Nebraska Press.

Pressley, M., & Harris, K. R. (2006). Cognitive strategies instruction: From basic research to classroom instruction. In P. A. Alexander & P. H. Winne (Eds.), *Handbook of educational psychology* (2nd ed., pp. 265–286). Mahwah, NJ: Erlbaum.

Pressley, M., & Hilden, K. (2006). Cognitive strategies. In D. Kuhn & R. Siegler (Eds.), *Handbook of child psychology* (6th ed., Vol. 2, pp. 511–556). Hoboken, NJ: John Wiley & Sons.

Pritchard, R. (1990). The effects of cultural schemata on reading processing strategies. *Reading Research Quarterly, 25,* 273–295.

Programme for International Student Assessment. (2006). *PISA 2006: Science competencies for tomorrow's world.* Retrieved from www.oecd.org

Puntambekar, S., & Hübscher, R. (2005). Tools for scaffolding students in a complex learning environment: What have we gained and what have we missed? *Educational Psychologist, 40*(1), 1–12.

Purdie, N., Hattie, J., & Carrol, A. (2002). A review of the research on interventions for attention deficit hyperactivity disorder: What works best? *Review of Educational Research, 72,* 61–100.

Putnam, R., & Borko, H. (2000). What do new views of knowledge and thinking have to say about research on teacher learning? *Educational Researcher, 29*(1), 4–15.

Putwain, D. (2007). Test anxiety in UK schoolchildren: Prevalence and demographic patterns. *British Journal of Educational Psychology, 77,* 579–503.

Qian, G., & Pan, J. (2002). A comparison of epistemological beliefs and learning from science text between American and Chinese high school students. In B. K Hofer & P. R. Pintrich (Eds), *Personal epistemology: The psychology of beliefs about knowledge and knowing* (pp. 365–385). Mahwah, NJ: Erlbaum.

Quinn, J. M., Pascoe, A., Wood, W., & Neal, D. T. (2010). Can't control yourself? Monitor those bad habits. *Personality and Social Psychology Bulletin, 36,* 499–511.

Quinn, P. C. (2002). Category representation in your infants. *Current Directions in Psychological Science, 11,* 66–70.

Ramirez, G., & Beilock, S. L. (2011, January 14). Writing about testing worries boosts exam performance in the classroom. *Science, 331*(6014), 211–213.

Rankin, B., Judd, A., & Vogell, H. (2010). Fulton DA sees 'clear-cut' evidence of APS test cheating. *The Atlanta Journal-Constitution.* Retrieved from http://www.ajc.com/news/atlanta/fulton-da-sees-clear-759297.html

Raskauskas, J., & Stoltz, A. (2007). Involvement in traditional and electronic bullying among adolescents. *Developmental Psychology, 43*(3), 564–575.

Rathunde, K., & Csikszentmihalyi, M. (2006). The developing person: An experiential perspective. In R. Lerner (Ed.), *Handbook of child psychology* (6th ed., pp. 465–515). New York: John Wiley.

Reichert, M. C. (2010). Hopeful news on regarding the crisis in U.S. education: Exploring the human element in teaching boys. *Education Week, 30*(12), 27.

Reichert, M., & Hawley, R. (2010). Reaching boys teaching boys: Strategies that work—and why. San Francisco: John Wiley and Sons.

Reis, S., Colbert, R., & Hébert, T. (2005). Understanding resilience in diverse, talented students in an urban high school. *Roeper Review, 27*(2), 110–120.

Reisberg, D. (2010). *Cognition: Exploring the science of the mind* (4th ed.). New York: Norton.

Renkl, A., Stark, R., Gruber, H., & Mandl, H. (1998). Learning from worked-out examples: The effects of example variability and elicited self-explanations. *Contemporary Educational Psychology, 23,* 90–108.

Renninger, K. A. (2000). Individual interest and its implications for understanding intrinsic motivation. In J. M. Harackiewicz & C. Sansone (Eds.), *Intrinsic and extrinsic motivation: The search for optimal motivation and performance* (pp. 373–404). San Diego, CA: Academic Press.

Renzulli, J., & Reis, S. (2003). The schoolwide enrichment model: Developing creative and productive giftedness. In N. Colangelo & G. Davis (Eds.), *Handbook of gifted education* (3rd ed., pp. 184–203). Boston: Allyn & Bacon.

Resnick, L., & Klopfer, L. (1989). Toward the thinking curriculum: An overview. In L. Resnick & L. Klopfer (Eds.), *Toward the thinking curriculum: Current cognitive research* (pp. 1–18).

Rest, J., Narvaez, D., Bebeau, M., & Thoma, S. (1999). A neo-Kohlbergian approach: The DIT and schema theory. *Educational Psychology Review, 11,* 291–324.

Reupert, A., & Woodcock, S. (2010). Success and near misses: Pre-service teachers' use, confidence and success in various classroom management strategies. *Teaching and Teacher Education, 26,* 1261–1268.

Reutzel, D., & Cooter, R. (2008). *Teaching children to read: The teacher makes the difference* (5th ed.). Upper Saddle River, NJ: Merrill/Pearson.

Riley, M., Greeno, J., & Heller, J. (1982). The development of children's problem-solving ability in arithmetic. In H. Ginsburg (Ed.), *Development of mathematical thinking.* San Diego, CA: Academic Press.

Rittle-Johnson, B., & Alibali, M. (1999). Conceptual and procedural knowledge of mathematics: Does one lead to the other? *Journal of Educational Psychology, 91*(1), 175–189.

Ritts, V., Patterson, M. L., & Tubbs, M. E. (1992). Expectations, impressions, and judgments of physically attractive students: A Review. *Review of Educational Research, 62,* 413–426.

Ritts, V., Patterson, M. L., & Tubbs, M. E. (1992). Expectations, impressions, and judgments of physically attractive students: A review. *Review of Educational Research, 62,* 413–426.

Rivkin, S. G., Hanushek, E. E., & Kain, J. J. (2001). *Teachers, schools, and academic achievement.* Amherst, MA: Amherst College.

Roberts, S. (2007). *In name count, Garcias are catching up to Joneses.* Retrieved from http://www.nytimes.com/2007/22/17/us/17surnames.html?th&emc=th

Robertson, J. (2000). Is attribution training a worthwhile classroom intervention for K–12 students with learning difficulties? *Educational Psychology Review, 12*(1), 111–134.

Roblyer, M. D., & Doering, A. H. (2010). *Integrating educational technology into teaching* (5th ed.). Boston: Allyn & Bacon/Pearson.

Roediger, III, H. L., & Karpicke, J. D. (2006). Test-enhanced learning: Taking memory tests improves long-term retention. *Psychological Science, 17,* 249–255.

Roeser, R. W., Mariachi, R., & Gehlbach, H. (2002). A goal theory perspective on teachers' professional identities and the contexts of teaching. In C. Midgley (Ed.), *Goals, goal structure, and patterns of adaptive learning* (pp. 205–241). Mahwah, NJ: Erlbaum.

Roeser, R. W., Peck, S. C., & Nasir, N. S. (2006). Self and identity processes in school motivation, learning and achievement.). In P. A. Alexander & P. H. Winne (Eds.), *Handbook of educational psychology* (2nd ed., pp. 391–424). Mahwah, NJ: Erlbaum.

Rogers, C. (1963). Actualizing tendency in relation to motives and to consciousness. In M. Jones (Ed.), *Nebraska Symposium on Motivation* (Vol. 11, pp. 1–24). Lincoln: University of Nebraska Press.

Rogers, C., & Freiberg, H. J. (1994). *Freedom to learn* (3rd ed.). Upper Saddle River, NJ: Merrill/Pearson.

Rogoff, B. (2003). *The cultural context of human development.* Oxford, England: Oxford University Press.

Rohrer, D., & Pashler, H. (2010). Recent research on human learning challenges conventional instructional strategies. *Educational Researcher, 39,* 406–412.

Roid, G. (2003). *Stanford-Binet Intelligence Scales, Fifth Edition.* Itasca, IL: Riverside.

Romano, A. (2011, March 28). How dumb are we? *Newsweek,* 56–60.

Romboy, D., & Kinkead, L. (2005, April 14). Surviving in America. *Deseret Morning News, 155*(303), pp. 1, 11, 12.

Roopnarine, J., & Evans, M. (2007). Family structural organization, mother-child and father-child relationships and psychological outcomes in English-speaking African Caribbean and Indo Caribbean families. In M. Sutherland (Ed.), *Psychological development in the Caribbean.* Kingston, Jamaica: Ian Randle.

Rosen, L., O'Leary, S., Joyce, S., Conway, G., & Pfiffner, L. (1984). The importance of prudent negative consequences for maintaining the appropriate behavior of hyperactive students. *Journal of Abnormal Child Psychology, 12,* 581–604.

Rosenberg, M., Westling, D., & McLesky, J. (2008). *Special education for today's teachers: An introduction.* Upper Saddle River, NJ: Merrill/Pearson.

Rosenfield, P., Lambert, S., & Black, R. (1985). Desk arrangement effects on pupil classroom behavior. *Journal of Educational Psychology, 77,* 101–108.

Rosenshine, B. (1987). Explicit teaching. In D. Berliner & B. Rosenshine (Eds.), *Talks to teachers.* New York: Random House.

Rosenshine, B. (2006). The struggles of the lower-scoring students. *Teaching and Teacher Education, 22,* 555–562.

Roseth, C. J., Johnson, D. W., Johnson, R. T., Fang, F., Hilk, C. L., & Fleming, M. A. (2007, April). *Effects of cooperative learning on elementary school students' achievement: A meta-analysis.* Paper presented at the annual meeting of the American Educational Research Association, Chicago.

Roth, W., & Lee, Y. (2007). "Vygotsky's neglected legacy:" Cultural-historical activity theory. *Review of Educational Research, 77*(2), 186–232.

Rowe, M. (1974). Wait-time and rewards as instructional variables, their influence on language, logic, and fate control: Part I. Wait-time. *Journal of Research in Science Teaching, 11,* 81–94.

Rowe, M. (1986). Wait-time: Slowing down may be a way of speeding up. *Journal of Teacher Education, 37*(1), 43–50.

Rubin, K., Bukowski, W., & Parker, J. (2006). Peer interactions, relationships, and groups. In N. Eisenberg (Vol. Ed,), *Handbook of child psychology: Vol. 3. Social, emotional, and personality development* (6th ed., pp. 571–645). Hoboken, NJ: John Wiley & Sons.

Rubinson, F. (2004). Urban dropouts: Why so many and what can be done? In S. R. Steinberg & J. L. Kincheloe (Eds.), *19 urban questions: Teaching in the city* (pp. 53–67). New York: Peter Lang.

Ruble, D., Martin, C., & Berenbaum, S. (2006). Gender development. In W. Damon & R. Lerner (Series Eds.), N. Eisenberg (Vol. Ed.), *Handbook of child psychology: Vol. III. Social, emotional, and personality development* (6th ed., pp. 858–932). New York: Wiley.

Rudolph, K. D., Caldwell, M. S., & Conley, C. S. (2005). Need for approval and children's well-being. *Child Development, 72,* 309–323.

Runco, M. A. (2004). Creativity as an extracognitive phenomenon. In L. V. Shavinina & M. Ferrari (Eds.), *Beyond knowledge: Extracognitive aspects of developing high ability* (pp. 17–25). Mahwah, NJ: Erlbaum.

Rutter, M., Maughan, B., Mortimore, P., Ousten, J., & Smith, A. (l979). *Fifteen thousand hours. Secondary schools and their effects on children.* Cambridge, MA: Harvard University Press.

Ryan, J. B., Katsiyannis, A., & Peterson, R. (2007). IDEA 2004 and disciplining students with disabilities. *NASSP Bulletin, 91,* 130–140.

Ryan, K. E., & Ryan, A. M. (2005). Psychological processes of stereotype threat and standardized math test performance. *Educational Psychologist, 40*(1), 53–63.

Ryan, K. E., Ryan, A. M., Arbuthnot, K., & Samuels, M. (2007). Students' motivation for standardized math exams. *Educational Researcher, 36*(1), 5–13.

Ryan, R., & Deci, E. (1996). When paradigms clash: Comments on Cameron and Pierce's claim that rewards do not undermine intrinsic motivation. *Review of Educational Research, 66,* 33–38.

Ryan, R., & Deci, E. (2000). Intrinsic and extrinsic motivations: Classic definitions and new directions. *Contemporary Educational Psychology, 25,* 54–67.

Saarni, C., Campos, J., Camras, L., & Witherington, D. (2006). Emotional development: Action, communication, and understanding. In N. Eisenberg (Vol. Ed,), *Handbook of child psychology: Vol. 3. Social, emotional, and personality development* (6th ed., pp. 226–299). Hoboken, NJ: John Wiley & Sons.

Sack-Min, J. (2007). The issues of IDEA. *American School Board Journal, 194*(3), 20–25.

Sadoski, M., & Paivio, A. (2001). *Imagery and text: A dual coding theory of reading and writing.* Mahwah, NJ: Erlbaum.

Safer, N., & Fleischman, S. (2005). How student progress monitoring improves instruction. *Educational Leadership, 62*(5), 81–83.

Sailor, W., & Roger, B. (2005). Rethinking inclusion: Schoolwide applications. *Phi Delta Kappan, 86*(7), 503–509.

Saleh, M., Lazonder, A. W., & Jong, Ton de. (2007). Structuring collaboration in mixed-ability groups to promote verbal interaction, learning, and motivation of average-ability students. *Contemporary Educational Psychology, 32,* 314–331.

Salvia, J., Ysseldyke, J., & Bolt, S. (2010). *Assessment in special and inclusive education* (11th ed.). Boston: Cengage.

Samuels, C. (2009). 'What works' guide gives RTI thumbs up on reading. *Education Week, 28*(23), 7.

Samuels, C. (2009). Recess and behavior. *Education Week, 28*(20), 4.

Samuels, C. (2010). Value of IDEA ratings questioned. *Education Week, 29*(36), 1, 27.

Sanders, J., & Nelson, S. C. (2004). Closing gender gaps in science. *Educational Leadership, 62*(3), 74–77.

Sanders, W. L., & Rivers, J. C. (1996). *Cumulative and residual effects of teachers on student academic achievement.* Knoxville, TN: University of Tennessee Value-Added Research and Assessment Center.

Santa Cruz, N. (2010). Minority population growing in the United States, census estimates show. *Los Angeles Times.* Retrieved from http://articles.latimes.com/2010/jun/10/nation/la-na-census-20100611

Santelices, M., & Wilson, M. (2010). Unfair treatment? The case of Freedle, the SAT, and the standardization approach to differential item functioning. *Harvard Educational Review, 80*(1), 106–133.

Sapon-Shevin, M. (2007). *Widening the circle: The power of inclusive classrooms.* Boston: Beacon Press.

Saulny, S. (2011). Black? White? Asian? More young Americans choose all of the above. *New York Times, January 29.* Retrieved from http://www.nytimes.com/2011/01/30/us/30mixed.html

Sawchuk, S. (2010). Merit-pay model pushed by Duncan shows no achievement edge. *Education Week, 29*(33), 1, 21.

Sawyer, R. K. (2006). Introduction: The new science of learning. In R. K. Sawyer (Ed.), *The Cambridge handbook of the learning sciences* (pp. 1–18). New York: Cambridge University Press.

Schacter, D. (2001). *The seven deadly sins of memory.* Boston: Houghton Mifflin.

Schaffer, M., Clark, S., & Jeglic, E. L. (2009). The role of empathy and parenting style in the development of antisocial behaviors. *Crime & Delinquency, 55,* 586–599.

Schellenberg, S., & Eggen, P. (2008, March). *Educational psychology students' awareness of moral issues in classroom instruction: A developmental analysis.* Paper presented at the annual meeting of the American Educational Research Association, New York.

Schiever, S., & Maker, C. J. (2003). New directions in enrichment and acceleration. In N. Colangelo & G. Davis (Eds.), *Handbook of gifted education* (3rd ed., pp. 163–173). Boston: Allyn & Bacon.

Schlesinger, A. (1992). *The disuniting of America: Reflections on a multicultural society.* New York: Norton.

Schneider, W., & Lockl, K. (2002). The development of metacognitive knowledge in children and adolescents. In T. J. Perfect & B. L. Schwartz (Eds.), *Applied metacognition* (pp. 224–257). Cambridge, UK: Cambridge University Press.

Schoenfeld, A. (1991). On mathematics as sense making: An informal attack on the unfortunate divorce of formal and informal mathematics. In J. Voss, D. Perkind, & J. Segal (Eds.), *Informal reasoning and education* (pp. 311–343). Hillsdale, NJ: Erlbaum.

Schoenfeld, A. H. (2006). Mathematics teaching and learning. In P. A. Alexander & P. H. Winne (Eds.), *Handbook of educational psychology* (2nd ed., pp. 479–510). Mahwah, NJ: Erlbaum.

Schraw, G. (2006). Knowledge structures and processes. In P. A. Alexander & P. H. Winne (Eds.), *Handbook of educational psychology* (2nd ed., pp. 245–263). Mahwah, NJ: Erlbaum.

Schraw, G., & Lehman, S. (2001). Situational interest: A review of the literature and directions for future research. *Educational Psychology Review, 13*(1), 23–52.

Schraw, G., Flowerday, T., & Lehman, S. (2001). Increasing situational interest in the classroom. *Educational Psychology Review, 13*(3), 211–224.

Schunk, D. & Ertmer, P. (2000). Self-regulation and academic learning: Self-efficacy enhancing interventions. In M. Boekaerts, P. Pintrich, & M. Zeidner (Eds.), *Handbook of self-regulation* (pp. 631–649). San Diego: Academic Press.

Schunk, D. (2005). Self-regulated learning: The educational legacy of Paul R. Pintrich. *Educational Psychologist, 40*(2), 85–94.

Schunk, D. (2008). *Learning theories: An educational perspective* (5th ed.). Upper Saddle River, NJ: Merrill/Pearson.

Schunk, D. H., & Ertmer, P. A. (2000). Self regulation and academic learning: Self-efficacy enhancing interventions. In M. Boekaerts, P. R. Pintrich, & M. Zeidner (Eds.), *Handbook of self-regulation* (pp. 631–649). San Diego: Academic Press.

Schunk, D. H., & Pajares, F. (2004). Self-efficacy in education revisited: Empirical and applied evidence. In D. M. McInerney & S. Van Etten (Eds.), *Sociocultural influences on motivation and learning: Vol. 4. Big theories revisited* (pp. 115–138). Greenwich, CT: Information Age.

Schunk, D. H., & Zimmerman, B. J. (2006). Competence and control beliefs: Distinguishing the means and the ends. In P. A. Alexander & P. H. Winne (Eds.), *Handbook of educational psychology* (2nd ed., pp. 349–367). Mahwah, NJ: Erlbaum.

Schunk, D. H., Pintrich, P. R, & Meece, J. L. (2008). *Motivation in education: Theory, research, and applications* (3rd ed.). Upper Saddle River, NJ: Merrill/Pearson.

Schutz, A. (2004, April). *Home is a prison in the global city: A critical review of urban school–community relationships.* Paper presented at the annual meeting of the American Educational Research Association, San Diego.

Schwartz, D., & Heiser, J. (2006). Spatial representations and imagery in learning. In R. K. Sawyer (Ed.), *The Cambridge handbook of the learning sciences* (pp. 283–298). New York: Cambridge University Press.

Schwartz, D., Bransford, J., & Sears, D. (2005). Efficiency and innovation in transfer. In J. Mestre (Ed.), *Transfer of learning from a modern multi-disciplinary perspective* (pp. 1–51). Greenwich, CT: Information Age Publishing.

Schweinle, A., Meyer, D. K., & Turner, J. C. (2006). Striking the right balance: Students' motivation and affect in elementary mathematics. *The Journal of Educational Research, 99,* 271–293.

ScienceDaily. (2009). *American adults flunk basic science.* Retrieved from http://www.sciencedaily.com/releases/2009/03/090312115133.htm

Scott, T. M., Alter, P. J., Rosenberg, M., & Borgmeier, C. (2010). Decision-making in secondary and tertiary interventions of school-wide systems of positive behavior support. *Education and Treatment of Children, 33,* 513–535.

Scott, T. M., Gagnon, J. C., & Nelson, C. M. (2008). School-wide systems of positive behavior support: A framework for reducing school crime and violence. *Journal of Behavior Analysis of Offender and Victim: Treatment and Prevention, 1,* 259–272.

Segall, A. (2004). Revising pedagogical content knowledge: The pedagogy of content/the content of pedagogy. *Teaching and Teacher Education, 20,* 489–504.

Seidman, L. J., Valera, E. M., Makris, N. (2005). Structural brain imaging of adult ADHD. *Biological Psychiatry, 57,* 1263–1272.

Serafino, K., & Cicchelli, T. (2003). Cognitive theories, prior knowledge, and anchored instruction on mathematical problem solving and transfer. *Education and Urban Society, 36*(1), 79–93.

Shah, N. (2011, February). Study punctures stereotypes about social status of bullies. *Education Week, 9*(21), 9.

Shaw, P., & Rapoport, J. (2007). Attention-deficit/hyperactivity disorder is characterized by a delay in cortical maturation. *Proceedings of the National Academy of Sciences, 104*(49), 19649–19654.

Shaywitz, B., Shaywitz, S., Blachman, B., Pugh, K., Fulbright, R., Skudlarski, P., Menci, W., Constable, R., Holahan, J., Marchiono, K., Fletcher, J., Lyon, G., & Gore, J. (2004). Development of left occipitotemporal systems for skilled reading in children after a phonologically-based interaction. *Biological Psychiatry, 55*(9), 926–933.

Shaywitz, S. E., & Shaywitz, B. A. (2004). Reading disability and the brain. *Educational Leadership, 61*(6), 7–11.

Sheldon, S. (2007). Improving student attendance with school, family, and community partnerships. *Journal of Educational Research, 199,* 267–275.

Shelton, J. T., Elliott, E. M., Matthews, R. A., Hill, B. D., & Gouvier, W. D. (2010). The relationships of working memory, secondary memory, and general fluid intelligence: Working memory is special. *Journal of Experimental Psychology. Learning, Memory and Cognition, 36,* 813–820.

Shen, C-Y., & Tsai, H-C. (2009). Design principles of worked examples: A review of the empirical studies. *Journal of Instructional Psychology, 36,* 238–244.

Shepard, L. (2005). Linking formative assessing to scaffolding. *Educational Leadership, 63*(3), 66–71.

Sherer, Y. C., & Nickerson, A. B. (2010). Anti-bullying practices in American schools: Perspectives of school psychologists. *Psychology in the Schools, 47,* 217–229.

Shirin, A. (2007). *Can deaf and hard of hearing students be successful in general education classes?* Retrieved from http://www.tcrecord.org/Content.asp?ContentID=13461

Shuell, T. (1996). Teaching and learning in a classroom context. In D. Berliner & R. Calfee (Eds.), *Handbook of educational psychology* (pp. 726–764). New York: Macmillan.

Shulman, L. (1986). Those who understand: Knowledge growth in teaching. *Educational Researcher, 15*(2), 4–14.

Shulman, L. (1987). Knowledge and teaching: Foundations of the new reform. *Harvard Educational Review, 57,* 1–22.

Shute, V. J. (2008). Focus on formative feedback. *Review of Educational Research, 78,* 153–189.

Siegel, M. (2002, April). *Models of teacher learning: A study of case analyses by preservice teachers.* Paper presented at the annual meeting of the American Educational Research Association, New Orleans.

Siegler, R. (2006). Microgenetic analyses of learning. In D. Kuhn, & R. Siegler (Vol. Eds.), *Handbook of child psychology: Vol. 2. Cognition, perception, and language* (6th ed., pp. 464–510). Hoboken, NJ: John Wiley & Sons.

Siegler, R., & Alibali, M. (2005). *Children's thinking* (4th ed.). Upper Saddle River, NJ: Prentice Hall.

Silver-Pacuilla, H., & Fleischman, S. (2006). Technology to help struggling students. *Educational Leadership, 63*(5), 84–85.

Silvia, P. J., & Sanders, C. E. (2010). Why are smart people curious? Fluid intelligence, openness to experience, and interest. *Learning and Individual Differences, 20*, 242–245.

Simon, H. (2001). Learning to research about learning. In S. M. Carver & D. Klake (Eds.), *Cognition and instruction*. Mahwah, NJ: Erlbaum.

Sinatra, G. M., & Pintrich, P. R. (2003). The role of intentions in conceptual change learning. In G. M. Sinatra & P. R. Pintrich (Eds.), *Intentional conceptual change* (pp. 1–18). Mahwah, NJ: Erlbaum.

Skiba, R. J., Michael, R. S., Nardo, A. C., & Peterson, R. L. (2002). The color of discipline: Sources of racial and gender disproportionality in school punishment. *The Urban Review, 34*, 317–342.

Skinner, B. F. (1953). *Science and human behavior*. New York: Macmillan.

Skinner, B. F. (1954). The science of learning and the art of teaching. *Harvard Educational Review, 24*, 86–97.

Skinner, B. F. (1957). *Verbal behavior*. Upper Saddle River, NJ: Prentice Hall.

Slavin, R. (1987). Ability grouping and student achievement in elementary schools: A best-evidence synthesis. *Review of Educational Research, 57*, 293–336.

Slavin, R. (1995). *Cooperative learning: Theory, research, and practice* (2nd ed.). Needham Heights, MA: Allyn & Bacon.

Slavin, R., & Cheung, A. (2004). *Effective reading programs for English language learners: A best-evidence synthesis. Baltimore: Center for Research on the Education of Students Placed at Risk, Johns Hopkins University.* Retrieved, from www.csos.jhu.edu/crespar/techReports/Report66.pdf

Small, G., & Vorgan, G. (2008). *iBrain: Surviving the technological alteration of the modern mind.* New York: William Morrow.

Smetana, J. G., & Gettman, D. C. (2006). Autonomy and relatedness with parents and romantic development in African American adolescents. *Developmental Psychology, 42*, 1347–1351.

Smith, A., & Bondy, E. (2007). "No! I won't!" Understanding and responding to defiance. *Childhood Education, 83*, 151–157.

Smith, F. (2005). Intensive care. *Edutopia, 1*(9), 47–49.

Smith, J., Brewer, D. M., & Heffner, T. (2003). Using portfolio assessments with young children who are at risk for school failure. *Preventing School Failure, 48*(1), 38–40.

Smith, S. M., Glenberg, A., & Bjork, R. A. (1978). Environmental context and human memory. *Memory & Cognition, 6*, 342–353.

Smith, T. E., Polloway, E. A., Patton, J. R., & Dowdy, C. A. (2008). *Teaching students with special needs in inclusive settings* (5th ed.). Boston: Allyn & Bacon.

Smokowski, P. (1997, April). *What personal essays tell us about resiliency and protective factors in adolescence.* Paper presented at the annual meeting of the American Educational Research Association, Chicago.

Smrtnik-Vitulic, H., & Zupancic, M. (2010). Personality traits as a predictor of academic achievement in adolescents. *Educational Studies.* Retrieved from http://dx.doi.org/10.1080/03055691003729062

Snow, C., & Kang, J. (2006). Becoming bilingual, biliterate, and bicultural. In K. A. Renninger & I. Sigel (Vol. Eds.), *Handbook of child psychology: Vol. 4. Social, emotional, and personality development* (6th ed., pp. 75–102). Hoboken, NJ: John Wiley & Sons.

Snow, C., Griffin, P., & Burns, M. S. (2005). *Knowledge to support the teaching of reading: Preparing teachers for a changing world.* San Francisco: Jossey-Bass.

Solano-Flores, G., & Li, M. (2006). The use of generalizability (G) theory in the testing of linguistic minorities. *Educational Measurement: Issues and Practices, 25*(1), 13–22.

Solley, B. A. (2007). On standardized testing. *Childhood Education, 84*, 31–37.

Solorzano, R. (2008). High stakes testing: Issues, implications, and remedies for English language learners. *Educational Researcher, 78*, 260–329.

Sommers, C. (2008). *The case against Title-Nining the sciences.* Retrieved from http://www.tcrecord.org

Song, J., & Felch, J. (2009). Judging teachers: Much of what you thought you knew is wrong. *Los Angeles Times.* Retrieved from http://latimes blogs.latimes.com/lanow/2009/10/challenging-classroom-myths.html

Southerland, S. A., & Sinatra, G. M. (2003). Learning about biological evolution: A special case of intentional conceptual change. In G. M. Sinatra & P. R. Pintrich (Eds.), *Intentional conceptual change* (pp. 317–345). Mahwah, NJ: Erlbaum.

Spear, L. (2007). Brain development and adolescent behavior. In D. Coch, K. Fischer, & G. Dawson (Eds.), *Human behavior, learning, and the developing brain: Typical development* (pp. 362–396). New York: Guilford Press.

Spearman, C. (1927). *The abilities of man: Their nature and measurement.* New York: Macmillan.

Spector, J. M. (2008). Cognition and learning in the digital age: Promising research and practice. *Computers in Human Behavior, 24*, 249–262.

Spera, C. (2005). A review of the relationship among parent practices, parenting styles, and adolescent school achievement. *Educational Psychology Review, 17*, 125–146.

Spies, R. A., Carlson, J. F., & Geisinger, K. F. (2011). *The eighteenth mental measurements yearbook.* Lincoln, NE: The Buros Institute of Mental Measurements.

Springer, K. (2010). *Educational research: A contextual approach.* Hoboken, NJ: John Wiley and Sons.

Stahl, R., DeMasi, K., Gehrke, R., Guy, C., & Scown, J. (2005, April). *Perceptions, conceptions and misconceptions of wait time and wait time behaviors among pre-service and in-service teachers.* Paper presented at the annual meeting of the American Educational Research Association, Montreal, Canada.

Standage, M., Treasure, D. C., Hooper, K., & Kuczka, K. (2007). Self-handicapping in school physical education: The influence of the motivational climate. *The British Journal of Educational Psychology, 77*, 81–99.

Standen, A. (2007) Gender matters: Educators battle over single-sex schools. *Edutopia, 3*(1), 46–49.

Stanford Achievement Test Series, Tenth Edition. (2011). *Sample home report.* Retrieved from http://www.pearsonassessments.com/hai/Images/dotCom/sat10/sat10_home_report.pdf

Staples, M. (2007). Supporting whole-class collaborative inquiry in a secondary mathematics classroom. *Cognition and Instruction, 25*, 161–217.

Star, J. (2004, April). *The development of flexible procedural knowledge in equation solving.* Paper presented at the annual meeting of the American Educational Research Association, San Diego.

Steinberg, L. (1996). *Beyond the classroom: Why school reform has failed and what parents need to do.* New York: Touchstone.

Sternberg, R. (1998a). Applying the triarchic theory of human intelligence in the classroom. In R. Sternberg & W. Williams (Eds.), *Intelligence, instruction, and assessment* (pp. 1–16). Mahwah, NJ: Erlbaum.

Sternberg, R. (1998b). Metacognition, abilities, and developing expertise: What makes an expert student? *Instructional Science, 26*(1–2), 127–140.

Sternberg, R. (2003a). *Cognitive psychology* (3rd ed.). Belmont, CA: Wadsworth.

Sternberg, R. (2003b). *Wisdom, intelligence, and creativity synthesized.* Cambridge: Cambridge University Press.

Sternberg, R. (2004). Culture and intelligence. *American Psychologist, 59*, 325–338.

Sternberg, R. (2006). Recognizing neglected strengths. *Educational Leadership, 64*(1), 30–35.

Sternberg, R. (2007). Who are bright children? The cultural context of being and acting intelligent. *Educational Researcher, 36*(3), 148–155.

Sternberg, R. (2009). Foreword. In S. Tobias & T. Duffy (Eds.), *Constructivist instruction: Success or failure* (pp. x–xi). New York: Routledge.

Sternberg, R., & Grigorenko, E. (2001). Learning disabilities, schooling, and society. *Phi Delta Kappan, 83*(4), 335–338.

Stiggins, R. (2005). *Student-centered classroom assessment* (4th ed.). Upper Saddle River, NJ: Merrill/Pearson.

Stiggins, R. (2007). Assessment through the student's eyes. *Educational Leadership, 64*(8), 22–26.

Stiggins, R. (2008). *An introduction to student-involved assessment for learning* (5th ed.). Upper Saddle River, NJ: Pearson.

Stiggins, R. J., Arter, J. A., Chappuis, J., & Chappuis, S. (2010). *Classroom assessment for student learning: Doing it right-using it well.* Boston: Allyn & Bacon/Pearson.

Stiggins, R. J., & Chappuis, J. (2012). *Introduction to student-involved assessment FOR learning* (6th ed.). Boston: Allyn & Bacon.

Stinson, D. (2006). African American male adolescents, schooling (and mathematics): Deficiency, rejection, and achievement. *Review of Educational Research, 76*, 477–506.

Stipek, D. (2002). *Motivation to learn* (4th ed.). Boston: Allyn & Bacon.

Stobbe, M. (2007, December 4). Studies suggest online harassment of children is on the rise. *Salt Lake Tribune*, p. E4.

Stock, E., & Fisman, R. (2010). The not-so-simple debate on home computers and achievement. *Education Week, 30*(7), 24–25, 27.

Stross, R. (2010). Computers at home: Educational hope vs. teenage reality. *New York Times, July 21*. Retrieved from http://www.nytimes.com/2010/07/11/business/11digi.html

Stuebing, K., Fletcher, J., LeDoux, J., Lyon, G., Shaywitz, S., & Shaywitz, B. (2002). Validity of IQ-discrepancy classifications of reading disabilities: A meta-analysis. *American Educational Research Journal, 39*(2), 469–518.

Su, A. Y-L. (2007). The impact of individual ability, favorable team member scores, and student perception of course importance on student preference of team-based learning and grading methods. *Adolescence, 42*, 805–826.

Suarez-Orozco, C., Pimentel, A., & Martin, M. (2009). The significance of relationships: Academic engagement and achievement among newcomer immigrant youth. *Teachers College Record Volume, 111*, 712–749. Retrieved from http://www.tcrecord.org/Content.asp?ContentID=15342

Suh, S., Suh, J., & Houston, I. (2007). Predictors of categorical at-risk high school dropouts. *Journal of Counseling & Development, 85*, 196–203.

Sungur, S., & Tekkaya, C. (2006). Effects of problem-based learning and traditional instruction on self-regulated learning. *Journal of Educational Research, 99*(5), 307–318.

SupermarketPage.com. (2010). Supermarket secrets. Retrieved from http://supermarketpage.com/secrets.php

Swanson, T. (2005). Providing structure for children with learning and behavior problems. *Intervention in School and Clinic, 40*, 182–187.

Sweller, J. (2003). Evolution of human cognitive architecture. *The Psychology of Learning and Motivation, 43*, 215–266.

Sweller, J., van Merrienboer, J., & Paas, F. (1998). Cognitive architecture and instructional design. *Educational Psychology Review, 10*, 251–296.

Tamim, R. M., Bernard, R. M., Borokhovski, E., Abrami, P. C., & Schmid, R. F. (2011). What forty years of research says about the impact of technology on learning: A second-order meta-analysis and validation study. *Review of Educational Research, 81*, 4–28.

Tammelen, T., Näyhä, S., Hills, A., & Jarvelin, M. (2003). Adolescent participation in sports and adult physical activity. *American Journal of Preventive Medicine, 24*, 22–28.

Tang, Y., Zhang, W., Chen, K., Feng, S., Ji, Y., Shen, J., Reiman, E., & Liu, Y. (2006). Arithmetic processing in the brain shaped by culture. *Proceedings of the National Academy of Sciences USA, 103*, 10775–10780.

Tannenbaum, A. (2003). Nature and nurture of giftedness. In N. Colangelo, & G. Davis (Eds.), *Handbook of gifted education* (3rd ed., pp. 45–59). Boston: Allyn & Bacon.

Tanner, D., & Tanner, L. (2007). *Curriculum development: Theory into practice* (4th ed.). Upper Saddle River, NJ: Prentice Hall.

Taraban, R., Anderson, E. E., & DeFinis, A. (2007). First steps in understanding engineering students' growth of conceptual and procedural knowledge in an interactive learning context. *Journal of Engineering Education, 96*, 57–68.

Taylor, K., & Rohrer, D. (2010). The effects of interleaved practice. *Applied Cognitive Psychology, 24*, 837–848.

Tenenbaum, H., & Ruck, M. (2007). Are teachers' expectations different for racial minority than for European American students? A meta-analysis. *Journal of Educational Psychology, 99*, 253–273.

Terhune, K. (1968). Studies of motives, cooperation, and conflict within laboratory microcosms. In G. Snyder (Ed.), *Studies in international conflict* (Vol. 4, pp. 29–58). Buffalo, NY: SUNY Buffalo Council on International Studies.

Terman, L., & Oden, M. (1947). The gifted child grows up. In L. Terman (Ed.), *Genetic studies of genius* (Vol. 4). Stanford, CA: Stanford University Press.

Terman, L., & Oden, M. (1959). The gifted group in mid-life. In L. Terman (Ed.), *Genetic studies of genius* (Vol. 5). Stanford, CA: Stanford University Press.

Terman, L., Baldwin, B., & Bronson, E. (1925). Mental and physical traits of a thousand gifted children. In L. Terman (Ed.), *Genetic studies of genius* (Vol. 1). Stanford, CA: Stanford University Press.

Terry, S. (2009). *Learning and memory: Basic principles, process, and procedures* (4th ed.). Boston: Allyn & Bacon.

Texas Education Agency. (2008). *Chapter 111. Texas essential knowledge and skills for mathematics. Grade 3*. Retrieved from http://www.tea.state.tx.us/rules/tac/ch111.html#s11111

Texas Education Agency. (2009). *Texas assessment of knowledge and skills. Grade 3, Mathematics*. Retrieved from http://ritter.tea.state.tx.us/student.assessment/resources/release/tests2009/taks_g03_math.pdf

Thaler, R. H., & Sunstein, C. R. (2008). *Nudge: Improving decisions about health, wealth, and happiness*. New Haven, CT: Yale University Press.

Tharp, R., & Gallimore, R. (1991). *The instructional conversation: Teaching and learning in social activity*. Washington, DC: National Center for Research on Cultural Diversity and Second Language Learning.

Thiede, K. W., & Anderson, M. C. M. (2003). Summarizing can improve metacomprehension accuracy. *Contemporary Educational Psychology, 28*, 129–160.

Thiede, K. W., Anderson, M. C. M., & Therriault, D. (2003). Accuracy of metacognitive monitoring affects learning of texts. *Journal of Educational Psychology, 95*, 66–73.

Thomas, E., & Wingert, P. (2010, March 15). Why we can't get rid of failing teachers. *Newsweek*, 24–27.

Thompson, R. A., & Raikes, H. A. (2003). Toward the next quarter-century: Conceptual and methodological challenges for attachment theory. *Development and Psychopathology, 15*, 691–718.

Thorndike, E. (1924). Mental discipline in high school studies. *Journal of Educational Psychology, 15*, 1–2, 83–98.

Thorndike, R. M. (2005). *Measurement and evaluation in psychology and education* (7th ed.). Upper Saddle River, NJ: Merrill/Pearson.

Tiedt, P., & Tiedt, I. (2010). *Multicultural teaching* (8th ed.). Boston: Allyn & Bacon.

Tillema, H., & Smith, K. (2007). Portfolio appraisal: In search of criteria. *Teaching and Teacher Education, 23*, 442–456.

Toga, A., & Thompson, P. (2005). Genetics of brain structure and intelligence. *Annual Review of Neuroscience, 28*, 1–23.

Tollefson, N. (2000). Classroom applications of cognitive theories of motivation. *Educational Psychology Review, 12*, 63–83.

Tomasello, M. (2006). Acquiring linguistic constructions. In D. Kuhn, & R. Siegler (Vol. Eds.), *Handbook of child psychology: Vol. 2. Cognition, perception, and language* (6th ed., pp. 255–298). Hoboken, NJ: John Wiley & Sons.

Tomlinson, C. A., & McTighe, J. (2006). *Integrating differentiated instruction and understanding by design: Connecting content and kids*. Alexandria, VA: Association for Supervision and Curriculum Development.

Tompkins, G. (2009). *Literacy for the 21st century: A balanced approach* (5th ed.). Upper Saddle River, NJ: Merrill/Pearson.

Trautwein, U., & Ludtke, O. (2007). Students' self-reported effort and time on homework in six school subjects: Between-student differences and within-student variation. *Journal of Educational Psychology, 99*, 432–444.

Trautwein, U., Ludtke, O., & Schnyder, I. (2006). Predicting homework effort: Support for a domain-specific, multilevel homework model. *Journal of Educational Psychology, 98*, 438–456.

Trawick-Smith, J. (2003). *Early childhood development: A multicultural perspective* (3rd ed.). Upper Saddle River, NJ: Merrill/Pearson.

Trzesniewski, K., Donnellan, M., Moffitt, T., Robins, R., Poulton, R., & Caspi, A. (2006). Low self-esteem during adolescence predicts poor health, criminal behavior, and limited economic prospects during adulthood. *Developmental Psychology, 42*(2), 381–390.

Tschannen-Moran, M., Woolfolk Hoy, A., & Hoy, W. (1998). Teacher efficacy: Its meaning and measure. *Review of Educational Research, 68*(2), 202–248.

Tulving, E. (2002). Episodic memory: From mind to brain. *Annual Review of Psychology, 53*, 1–25.

Turiel, E. (2006). The development of morality. In N. Eisenberg (Vol. Ed,), *Handbook of child psychology: Vol. 3. Social, emotional, and personality development* (6th ed., pp. 789–857). Hoboken, NJ: John Wiley & Sons.

Turnbull, A., Turnbull, R. &. Wehmeyer, M. L. (2010). *Exceptional lives: Special education in today's schools* (6th ed.). Upper Saddle River, NJ: Merrill/Pearson.

Twenge, J. M., & Campbell, W. K. (2001). Age and birth cohort differences in self-esteem: A cross temporal meta-analysis. *Journal of Personality and Social Psychology Review, 5,* 321–344.

Tyler, K., Uqdah, A., Dillihunt, M., Beatty-Hazelbaker, R., Connor, T., Gadson, N., et al. (2008). Cultural discontinuity: Toward a quantitative investigation of a major hypothesis in education. *Educational Research, 37,* 280–297.

Tyler, R. (1950). *Basic principles of curriculum and instruction.* Chicago: University of Chicago Press.

U.S. Bureau of Census. (2003). *Statistical abstract of the United States* (123rd ed.). Washington, DC: U.S. Government Printing Office.

U.S. Bureau of Census. (2007). *Income, earnings, and poverty estimates released in American Fact Finder, 8/28/07.* Retrieved from http://factfinder.census.gov/home/saff/main.html?_lang=en

U.S. Bureau of Census. (2010). *Table 232. Children who speak a language other than English at home by region: 2008.* Washington, DC: U.S. Government Printing Office.

U.S. Department of Agriculture. (2007). *Healthy food: Healthy communities.* Retrieved from http://www.csrees.usda.gov/newsroom/news/2007news/cfp_report.pdf

U.S. Department of Education. (2008). *Foundations for success: The final report of the National Mathematics Advisory Council.* Retrieved from http://www.ed.gov/about/bdscomm/list/mathpanel/report/final-report.pdf

U.S. Department of Education. (2009). *Twenty-eighth annual report to Congress on the implementation of the Individuals with Disabilities Education Act.* Washington, DC: U.S. Government Printing Office.

U.S. Department of Health and Human Services, Administration on Children, Youth, and Families. (2009). *Child maltreatment 2007.* Washington, DC: U.S. Government Printing Office.

U.S. English. (2011). *Official English: Why is official English necessary?* Retrieved from http://www.usenglish.org/view/10

Underhill, P. (2009). *Why we buy: The science of shopping.* New York: Simon & Schuster Adult Publishing.

Urdan, T. C., & Maehr, M. L. (1995). Beyond a two-goal theory of motivation and achievement: A case for social goals. *Review of Educational Research, 65,* 213–243.

Uygur, T., & Ozdas, A. (2007). The effect of arrow diagrams on achievement in applying the chain rule. *Primus, 17,* 131–147.

Vacca, R. T., Vacca, J. L., & Mraz, M. E. (2011). *Content area reading: Literacy and learning across the curriculum* (10th ed) Boston: Allyn & Bacon.

van Gelder, T. (2005). Teaching critical thinking: Some lessons from cognitive science. *College Teaching, 53,* 41–46.

Van Horn, R. (2008). *Bridging the chasm between research and practice: A guide to major educational research.* Lanham, MD: Rowman & Littlefield Education.

van Merriënboer, J., Kirschner, P., & Kester, L. (2003). Taking the load off a learner's mind: Instructional design for complex learning. *Educational Psychologist, 38*(1), 5–13.

VanDeWeghe, R. (2007). How does assessment affect creativity? *English Journal, 96,* 91–93.

Vansteenkiste, M., Zhou, M., Lens, W., & Soenens, B. (2005). Experiences of autonomy and control among Chinese learners: Vitalizing or immobilizing. *Journal of Educational Psychology, 97,* 468–483.

Varma, S., McCandliss, B., & Schwartz, D. (2008). Scientific and pragmatic challenges for bridging education and neuroscience. *Education Researcher, 37,* 140–152.

Vaughn, S., & Bos, C. (2009). *Strategies for teaching students with learning and behavior problems* (7th ed.). Boston: Allyn & Bacon.

Vavilis, B., & Vavilis, S. (2004). Why are we learning this? What is this stuff good for, anyway?: The importance of conversation in the classroom. *Phi Delta Kappan, 86*(4), 282–287.

Vedantam, S. (2010). *The hidden brain: How our unconscious minds elect presidents, control markets, wage wars, and save our lives.* New York: Spiegel & Grau.

Veenman, M. V., & Spaans, M. A. (2005). Relation between intellectual and metacognitive skills: Age and task differences. *Learning and Individual Differences, 15,* 159–176.

Veralas, M., & Pappas, C. (2006). Intertextuality in read-alouds of integrated science-literacy units in urban primary classrooms: Opportunities for the development of thought and language. *Cognition and Instruction, 24,* 211–259.

Verdinelli, S., & Gentile, J. R. (2003). Changes in teaching philosophies among in-service teachers after experience mastery learning. *Action in Teach Education, 25,* 56–66.

Verkoeijen, P. P., Rikers, R. M., & Schmidt, H. G. (2005). The effects of prior knowledge on study-time allocation and free recall: Investigating the discrepancy reduction model. *The Journal of Psychology, 139,* 67–79.

Vermeer, H. J., Boekaerts, M., & Seegers, G. (2000). Motivational and gender differences: Sixth-grade students' mathematical problem-solving behavior. *Journal of Educational Psychology, 92,* 308–315.

Viadero, D. (2009). Scholars probe diverse effects of exit exams. *Education Week, 28*(30), 1–10.

Virginia Youth Violence Project. (2010). *Serious violent crime rate in U.S. Schools.* Retrieved from http://youthviolence.edschool.virginia.edu/violence-in-schools/national-statistics.html

VirginiaTech Transportation Institute. (2009). *New data from VTTI provides insight into cell phone use and driving distractions.* Retrieved from http://www.vtti.vt.edu/PDF/7-22-09-VTTI-Press_Release_Cell_phones_and_Driver_Distraction.pdf

Von der Linden, N., & Roebers, C. M. (2006). Developmental changes in uncertainty monitoring during an event recall task. *Metacognition and Learning, 1,* 213–228.

von Károlyi, C., Ramos-Ford, V., & Gardner, H. (2003). Multiple intelligences: A perspective on giftedness. In N. Colangelo & G. Davis (Eds.), *Handbook of gifted education* (3rd ed., pp. 100–112). Boston: Allyn & Bacon.

Vosniadou, S. (2007). The cognitive-situative divide and the problem of conceptual change. *Educational Psychologist, 42*(1), 55–66.

Vygotsky, L. (1978). *Mind in society: The development of higher psychological processes* (M. Cole, V. John-Steiner, S. Scribner, & E. Souberman, Eds. & Trans.). Cambridge, MA: Harvard University Press.

Vygotsky, L. (1986). *Thought and language.* Cambridge, MA: MIT Press.

Wadsworth, B. J. (2004). *Piaget's theory of cognitive and affective development* (5th ed.). Boston: Pearson Education.

Walker, D. (2009). Effectiveness of state anti-bullying laws questioned. *Education Week, 29*(4), 7.

Walker, J. E., Bauer, A. M., & Shea, T. M. (2004). *Behavior management: A practical approach for educators* (8th ed.). Upper Saddle River, NJ: Merrill/Pearson.

Walker, J. M., & Hoover-Dempsey, K. V. (2006). Why research on parents' involvement is important to classroom management. In C. M. Evertson & C. S. Weinstein (Eds.), *Handbook of classroom management: Research, practice, and contemporary issues* (pp. 665–684). Mahwah, NJ: Erlbaum.

Walsh, D., & Bennett, N. (2004). *Why do they act that way?: A survival guide to the adolescent brain for you and your teen.* New York: Free Press.

Ware, H., & Kitsantas, A. (2007). Teacher and collective efficacy beliefs as predictors of professional commitment. *Journal of Educational Research, 100*(5), 303–310.

Waterhouse, L. (2006). Multiple intelligences, the Mozart effect, and emotional intelligence: A critical review. *Educational Psychologist, 41*(4), 217–225.

Watson, M., & Battistich, V. (2006). Building and sustaining caring communities. In C. M. Evertson & C. S. Weinstein (Eds.), *Handbook of classroom management: Research, practice, and contemporary issues* (pp. 253–279). Mahwah, NJ: Erlbaum.

Watson, M., & Ecken, L. (2003). *Learning to trust: Transforming difficult elementary classrooms through developmental discipline.* San Francisco: Jossey-Bass.

Waxman, H., Huang, S., Anderson, L., & Weinstein, T. (1997). Classroom process differences in inner-city elementary schools. *Journal of Educational Research, 91*(1), 49–59.

Waxman, S., & Lidz, J. (2006). Early word learning. In W. Damon & R. Lerner (Series Eds.), D. Kuhn & R. Siegler (Vol. Eds.), *Handbook of child psychology: Vol. II. Cognition, perception, and language* (6th ed., pp. 299–335). New York: Wiley.

Way, N., Reddy, R., & Rhodes, J. (2007). Students' perceptions of school climate during the middle school years: Associations with trajectories of psychological and behavioral adjustment. *American Journal of Community Psychology, 40,* 194–213.

Webb, N. (2006). Indentifying content for student achievement tests. In S. Downing & T. Haladyna (Eds.), *Handbook of test development* (pp. 155–180). Mahwah, NJ: Erlbaum.

Webb, N., Farivar, S., & Mastergeorge, A. (2002). Productive helping in cooperative groups. *Theory Into Practice, 41*(1).

Wechsler, D. (2003). *Wechsler Intelligence Scale for Children* (4th ed.) San Antonio, TX: Psychological Corporation.

Weigel, D., Martin, S., & Bennett, K. (2005). Ecological influences of the home and the child-care center on preschool-age children's literacy development. *Reading Research Quarterly, 40*(2), 204–228.

Weil, E. (2008). Should boys and girls be taught separately? *New Times Magazine, March 2,* 33–45.

Weiland, A., & Coughlin, R. (1979). Self-identification and preferences: A comparison of White and Mexican American first and third graders. *Journal of Social Psychology, 10,* 356–365.

Weiner, B. (1992). *Human motivation: Metaphors, theories, and research.* Newbury Park, CA: Sage.

Weiner, B. (1994). Ability versus effort revisited: The moral determinants of achievement evaluation and achievement as a moral system. *Educational Psychologist, 29,* 163–172.

Weiner, B. (2000). Interpersonal and intrapersonal theories of motivation from an attributional perspective. *Educational Psychology Review, 12,* 1–14.

Weiner, B. (2001). Intrapersonal and interpersonal theories of motivation from an attribution perspective. In F. Salili, C. Chiu, & Y. Hong (Eds.), *Student motivation: The culture and context of learning* (pp. 17–30). New York: Kluer Academic/Plenum.

Weinstein, C. S., Romano, M. E., & Mignano, A. J., Jr. (2011). *Elementary classroom management: Lessons from research and practice* (5th ed.). New York: McGraw-Hill.

Weinstein, R. (2002). *Reaching higher: The power of expectations in schooling.* Cambridge, MA: Harvard University Press.

Weinstock, J. (2007). Don't call my kid smart. *T.H.E. Journal, 34,* 6.

Weiss, H., Mayer, E., Kreider, H., Vaughan, M., Dearing, E., Hencke, R., & Pinto, K. (2003). Making it work: Low-income working mothers' involvement in their children's education. *American Educational Research Journal, 40*(4), 879–901.

Weiss, I., & Pasley, J. (2004). What is high-quality instruction? *Educational Leadership, 61*(5), 24–28.

Weissglass, S. (1998). *Ripples of hope: Building relationships for educational change.* Santa Barbara, CA: Center for Educational Change in Mathematics & Science, University of California.

Wentzel, K. (1996). Social goals and social relationships as motivators of school adjustment. In J. Juvonen & K. Wentzel (Eds.), *Social motivation: Understanding children's school adjustment* (pp. 226–247). Cambridge, England: Cambridge University Press.

Wentzel, K. (1999). Social-motivational processes and interpersonal relationships: Implications for understanding students' academic success. *Journal of Educational Psychology, 91,* 76–97.

Wentzel, K. (2000). What is it that I'm trying to achieve? Classroom goals from a content perspective. *Contemporary Educational Psychology, 25,* 105–115.

Wentzel, K. R. (2002). The contribution of social goal setting to children's school adjustment. In A. Wigfield & J. S. Eccles (Eds.), *Development of achievement motivation* (pp. 221–246). New York: Academic Press.

Wentzel, K. R. (2003). Sociometric status and adjustment in middle school: A longitudinal study. *Journal of Early Adolescence, 23,* 5–28.

Wentzel, K. R., & Wigfield, A. (2007). Motivational interventions that work: Themes and remaining issues. *Educational Psychologist, 42,* 261–271.

Werner, E. (2006). What can we learn about resilience from large-scale longitudinal studies? In S. Goldstein & R. Brooks (Eds.), *Handbook of resilience in children* (pp. 91–105). New York: Springer.

Whitaker S. J., Lowe, P. A., & Lee, S. W. (2007). Significant predictors of test anxiety among students with and without disabilities. *Journal of Learning Disabilities, 40,* 360–376.

White, R. (1959). Motivation reconsidered: The concept of competence. *Psychological Review, 66,* 297–333.

Wigfield, A. (1994). Expectancy-value theory of achievement motivation: A developmental perspective. *Educational Psychology Review, 6,* 49–78.

Wigfield, A., & Eccles, J. (1992). The development of achievement task values: A theoretical analysis. *Developmental Review, 12,* 265–310.

Wigfield, A., & Eccles, J. (2000). Expectancy-value theory of achievement motivation. *Contemporary Educational Psychology, 25,* 68–81.

Wigfield, A., & Eccles, J. S. (2002). The development of competence beliefs, expectancies for success, and achievement values from childhood through adolescence. In A. Wigfield & J. S. Eccles (Eds.), *Development of achievement motivation. A volume in the educational psychology series* (pp. 91–120). San Diego, CA: Academic Press.

Wigfield, A., Byrnes, J., & Eccles, J. (2006). Development during early and middle adolescence. In P. Alexander & P. Winne (Eds.), *Handbook of educational psychology* (2nd ed., pp. 87–114). Mahwah, NJ: Erlbaum.

Wigfield, A., Eccles, J., & Pintrich, P. (1996). Development between the ages of 11 and 25.

In D. Berliner & R. Calfee (Eds.), *Handbook of educational psychology* (pp. 148–185). New York: Macmillan.

Wigfield, A., Guthrie, J., Tonks, S., & Perencevich, K. (2004). Children's motivation for reading: Domain specificity and instructional influences. *Journal of Educational Research, 97*(6), 299–310.

Willard, N. (2006). *Cyberbullying and cyberthreats: Responding to the challenge of online social cruelty, threats and distress.* Eugene, OR: Center for Safe and Responsible Internet Use.

Williams, C., & Zacks, R. (2001). Is retrieval-induced forgetting an inhibitory process? *American Journal of Psychology, 114,* 329–354.

Williams, M. (2009). U.S. bilingual education controversy continues. Retrieved from http://www .suite101.com/content/us-bilingual-education-controversy-continues-a148086

Willingham, D. T. (2006). "Brain-based" learning: More fiction than fact. *American Educator, 30*(3), 27–30, 40–41.

Willingham, D. T. (2007). *Cognition: The thinking animal* (3rd ed.). Upper Saddle River, NJ: Merrill/Pearson.

Willingham, D. T. (2009a). Why don't kids like school. *Teachers College Record,* ID Number 15609. Retrieved from http://www.tcrecord.org

Willingham, D. T. (2009b). *Why don't students like school? A cognitive scientist answers questions about how the mind works and what it means in your classroom.* San Francisco: Jossey-Bass.

Willis, J. (2006). *Research-based strategies to ignite student learning: Insights from a neurologist and classroom teacher.* Alexandria, VA: ASCD.

Willis, J. (2007). Which brain research can educators trust? *Phi Delta Kappan, 88*(9), 697–699.

Willis, S. L., Tennstedt, S. L, Marsiske, M., Ball, K., Elias, J., Koepke, K. M., Morris, J. N., Rebok, G. W., Unverzagt, F. W., Stoddard, A. M., & Wright, E. (2006). Long-term effects of cognitive training on everyday functional outcomes in older adults. *The Journal of the American Medical Association, 296.* Retrieved from http://jama.ama-assn.org/cgi/content/full/296/23/2805#AUTHINFO

Wilson, B. L., & Corbett, H. (2001). *Listening to urban kids: School reform and the teachers they want.* Albany, NY: State University of New York Press.

Winerip, M. (2010, July 26). Equity of test is debated as children compete for gifted kindergarten. *New York Times,* p. A16.

Wing, R. R. & Jeffery, R. W. (1999). Benefits of recruiting participants with friends and increasing social support for weight loss and maintenance. *Journal of Consulting and Clinical Psychology, 67,* 132–138.

Winitzky, N. (1994). Multicultural and main-streamed classrooms. In R. Arends (Ed.), *Learning to teach* (3rd ed., pp. 132–170). New York: McGraw-Hill.

Winsler, A., & Naglieri, J. (2003). Overt and covert verbal problem-solving strategies: Developmental trends in use, awareness, and relations with task performance in children aged 5 to 17. *Child Development, 74,* 659–678.

Wolters, C. (2003). Understanding procrastination from a self-regulated learning perspective. *Journal of Educational Psychology, 95,* 179–187.

Wolz, D. J. (2003). Implicit cognitive processes as aptitudes for learning. *Educational Psychologist, 38,* 95–104.

Wood, M. (2005). *High school counselors say they lack skills to assist gay, lesbian students.* Retrieved from www.bsu.edu/news

Woolfolk Hoy, A., Davis, H., & Pape, S. J. (2006). Teacher knowledge and beliefs. In P. A. Alexander & P. H. Winne (Eds.), *Handbook of educational psychology* (2nd ed., pp. 715–737). Mahwah, NJ: Erlbaum.

Wortham, S. (2004). The interdependence of social identification and learning. *American Educational Research Journal, 41*(3), 715–750.

Wright, W. (2006). A Catch-22 for language learners. *Educational Leadership, 64*(3), 22–27.

Wubbels, T., Brekeimans, M., den Brok, P., & van Tartwijk, J. (2006). An interpersonal perspective on classroom management in secondary classrooms in the Netherlands. In C. M. Evertson & C. S. Weinstein (Eds.), *Handbook of classroom management: Research, practice, and contemporary issues* (pp. 1161–1191). Mahwah, NJ: Erlbaum.

Yeager, M. (2007). Understanding NAEP: Inside the nation's education report card. Retrieved from http://www.educationsector.org/analysis/analysis_show.htm?doc_id=560606

Yell, M. L., Robinson, T. R., & Drasgow, E. (2001). Cognitive behavior modification. In T. J. Zirpoli & K. J. Melloy, *Behavior management: Applications for teachers* (3rd ed., pp. 200–246). Upper Saddle River, NJ: Merrill/Pearson.

Yip, D. Y. (2004). Questioning skills for conceptual change in science instruction. *Journal of Biological Education, 38,* 76–83.

Young, M., & Scribner, J. (1997, March). *The synergy of parental involvement and student engagement at the secondary level: Relationships of consequence in Mexican-American communities.* Paper presented at the annual meeting of the American Educational Research Association, Chicago.

Younger, M., & Warrington, M. (2006). Would Harry and Hermione have done better in single-sex classes? A review of single-sex teaching in coeducational secondary schools in the United Kingdom. *American Educational Research Journal, 43*(4), 579–620.

Zakaria, F. (2011, February). Why it's different this time: The combination of youth and technology is driving a wave of change. Fingers crossed: it may turn out just fine. *Time, 177*(8), 30–31.

Zaragoza, N. (2005). Including families in the teaching and learning process. In J. Kincheloe (Ed.), *Classroom teaching: An introduction.* New York: Peter Lang.

Zeelenberg, R., Wadenmakers, E.-J., & Rotteveel, M. (2006). The impact of emotion on perception: Bias or enhanced processing. *Psychological Science, 17,* 287–291.

Zehr, M. A. (2006). Reacting to reviews, states cut portfolio assessments for ELL students. *Education Week, 26*(12), 7.

Zeldin, A., & Pajares, F. (2000). Against the odds: Self efficacy beliefs of women in mathematical, scientific, and technological careers. *American Educational Research Journal, 37,* 215–246.

Zhou, L., Goff, G., & Iwata, B. (2000). Effects of increased response effort on self-injury and objective manipulation as competing responses. *Journal of Applied Behavioral Analysis, 33,* 29–40.

Zhou, Q., Hofer, C., & Eisenberg, N. (2007). The developmental trajectories of attention focusing, attentional and behavioral persistence, and externalizing problems during school-age years. *Developmental Psychology,* (43), 369–385.

Zimmerman, B. (2005, April). *Integrating cognition, motivation and emotion: A social cognitive perspective.* Paper presented at the annual meeting of the American Educational Research Association, Montreal, Canada.

Zimmerman, B. J., & Schunk, D. H. (2001). *Self-regulated learning and academic achievement: Theoretical perspectives* (2nd ed.). Mahwah, NJ: Erlbaum.

Zimmerman, B. J., & Schunk, D. H. (2004). Self-regulating intellectual processes and outcomes: A social cognitive perspective. In D. Y. Dai & R. J. Sternberg (Eds.), *Motivation, emotion, and cognition: Integrative perspectives on intellectual functioning and development* (pp. 323–350). Mahwah, NJ: Erlbaum.

Zimmerman, B., & Schunk, D. (Eds.). (2001). *Self-regulated learning and academic achievement: Theoretical perspectives* (2nd ed.). Mahwah, NJ: Erlbaum.

Zimmerman, F. J., Christakis, D. A., & Meltzoff, A. N. (2007). Associations between media viewing and language development in children under age 2 years. *The Journal of Pediatrics, 151,* 364–368.

Zins, J., Bloodworth, M., Weissberg, R., & Walberg, H. (2004). The scientific base linking social and emotional learning to school success. In J. Zins, R. Weissberg, M. Wang, & H. Walberg (Eds.), *Building academic success on social and emotional learning* (pp. 3–22). New York: Teachers College Press.

Zirpoli, T. J., & Melloy, K. J. (2001). *Behavior management: Applications for teachers.* Upper Saddle River, NJ: Merrill/Pearson.

Zwiers, J. (2005). The third language of academic English. *Educational Leadership, 62*(4), 60–63.

glossary

Ability grouping. The process of placing students of similar abilities into groups and attempting to match instruction to the needs of these groups.

Academic language proficiency. A level of proficiency in English that allows students to handle demanding learning tasks with abstract concepts.

Acceleration. Programs for students who are gifted and talented that keep the curriculum the same but allow students to move through it more quickly.

Accommodation. The process of creating new schemes or adjusting old ones when they can no longer explain new experiences.

Accountability. The process of requiring students to demonstrate that they have met specified standards and holding teachers responsible for students' performance.

Achievement tests. Standardized tests designed to assess how much students have learned in specified content areas.

Action research. Applied research designed to answer a specific school- or classroom-related question.

Adaptive behavior. A person's ability to perform the functions of everyday living.

Adaptive fit. The degree to which a school environment accommodates the student's needs and the degree to which a student can meet the requirements of a particular school setting.

Algorithm. A specific step or set of steps for finding the solution to a problem.

Alternative assessment. Assessment measures that include projects and performance assessment.

Analogies. Descriptions of relationships between ideas that are similar in some but not all respects.

Antecedents. Stimuli that precede and induce behaviors.

Anxiety. A general uneasiness and feeling of tension relating to a situation with an uncertain outcome.

Applied behavior analysis (ABA). The process of systematically implementing the principles of operant conditioning to change student behavior.

Appropriating understanding. The process of individually internalizing understanding after it has first been socially constructed.

Aptitude tests. Standardized tests designed to predict the potential for future learning and measure general abilities developed over long periods of time.

Assertive discipline. An approach to classroom management that promotes a clear and firm response style with students.

Assessment bias. A form of discrimination that occurs when a test or other assessment instrument unfairly penalizes a group of students because of their gender, ethnicity, race, or socioeconomic status.

Assessment. The process of gathering information and making decisions about students' learning progress.

Assessment *for* learning. Assessment that is a continual, ongoing process designed to support and increase learning.

Assimilation. The process of using existing schemes to interpret new experiences.

Assistive technology. A set of adaptive tools that support students with disabilities in learning activities and daily life tasks.

Attachment. The strong emotional bond that forms between children and caregivers.

Attainment value. The importance an individual attaches to doing well on a task.

Attention deficit hyperactivity disorder (ADHD). A learning problem characterized by difficulties in maintaining attention.

Attention. The process of consciously focusing on a stimulus.

Attribution theory. A cognitive theory of motivation that attempts to systematically describe learners' beliefs about the causes of their successes and failures and how these beliefs influence motivation to learn.

Attributions. Explanations, or beliefs, related to the causes of performance.

Autism spectrum disorder. A description of a cluster of disorders characterized by impaired social relationships and skills and often associated with highly unusual behavior.

Automaticity. The ability to perform mental operations with little awareness or conscious effort.

Autonomous morality. A stage of moral development characterized by the belief that fairness and justice is the reciprocal process of treating others as they would want to be treated.

Autonomy. Independence and the ability to alter the environment when necessary.

Axons. Longer branches that extend from the cell body of neurons and transmit messages to other neurons.

Basic interpersonal communication skills. A level of proficiency in English that allows students to interact conversationally with their peers.

Behavior disorders. Serious and persistent age-inappropriate behaviors that result in social conflict, personal unhappiness, and often school failure.

Behaviorism. A theory that explains learning in terms of observable behaviors and how they're influenced by stimuli from the environment.

Belief preservation. People's tendency to make evidence subservient to belief, rather than the other way around.

Belief. A cognitive idea we accept as true without necessarily having definitive evidence to support it.

Between-class grouping. Divides students in a certain grade into levels, such as high, medium, and low.

Bidialecticism. The ability to switch back and forth between a dialect and Standard English.

Bilingualism. The ability to speak, read, and write in two languages.

Bipolar disorder. A condition characterized by alternative episodes of depressive and manic states.

Blocked practice. The process of practicing one skill extensively and then moving to a different skill.

Bullying. A form of peer aggression that involves a systematic or repetitious abuse of power between students.

Caring. A teacher's empathy and investment in the protection and development of young people.

Case studies. Authentic stories of teaching and learning events in classrooms.

Central executive. A supervisory component of working memory that controls the flow of information to and from the other components.

Centration (centering). The tendency to focus on the most perceptually obvious aspect of an object or event, neglecting other important aspects.

Characteristics. A concept's essential elements.

Checklists. Written descriptions of dimensions that must be present in an acceptable performance of an activity.

Chunking. The process of mentally combining separate items into larger, more meaningful units.

Classical conditioning. A component of behaviorism that explains how we *learn* to display involuntary emotional or physiological responses that are similar to instinctive or reflexive responses.

Classification. The process of grouping objects on the basis of common characteristics.

Classroom assessment. All the processes involved in making decisions about students' learning progress.

Classroom management. "Actions teachers take to create an environment that supports and facilitates both academic and social–emotional learning" (Evertson & Weinstein, 2006, p. 4).

Classroom organization. A professional skill that includes preparing materials in advance, starting classes and activities on time, making transitions quickly and smoothly, and creating well-established routines.

Closure. A summary that occurs at the end of lessons.

Cognitive apprenticeship. The process of having a less-skilled learner work at the side of an expert to develop cognitive skills.

Cognitive behavior modification. A procedure that promotes behavioral change and self-regulation in students through self-talk and self-instruction.

Cognitive constructivism. A view that describes knowledge construction as an individual, internal process.

Cognitive development. Changes in our thinking that occur as a result of maturation and experience.

Cognitive domain. The area of learning that focuses on knowledge and higher cognitive processes, such as applying and analyzing.

Cognitive learning theories. Theories that explain learning in terms of people's thinking and the processes involved in acquiring, organizing, and using knowledge.

Cognitive load. The amount of mental activity imposed on working memory.

Cognitive modeling. The process of performing a demonstration combined with verbalizing the thinking behind the actions.

Cognitive theory. A theory of learning that focuses on changes in behavior that result from observing others.

Cognitive tools. The concepts and symbols (numbers and language) together with the real tools that allow people to think, solve problems, and function in a culture.

Collaborative consultation. The process of general and special education teachers working together to create effective learning experiences for students with exceptionalities.

Collective efficacy. Beliefs that the faculty as a whole in a school can have a positive effect on student learning.

Collective self-esteem. Individuals' perceptions of the relative worth of the groups to which they belong.

Common Core State Standards Initiative (CCSSI). A state-led effort to establish a single set of clear educational standards for English-language arts and mathematics that states can share and voluntarily adopt.

Communication disorders. Exceptionalities that interfere with students' abilities to receive and understand information from others and express their own ideas.

Community of caring and trust. A classroom environment in which learners feel physically and emotionally safe and their needs for belonging and relatedness are met.

Community of learners. A learning environment in which the teacher and students work together to help everyone learn.

Competence. The ability to function effectively in the environment.

Completion. A paper-and-pencil format that includes a question or an incomplete statement that requires the learner to supply the answer.

Comprehension monitoring. The process of checking to see if we understand what we have read or heard.

Concept map. A visual representation of the relationships among concepts that includes the concepts themselves, sometimes enclosed in circles or boxes, together with relationships among concepts indicated by lines linking the concepts.

Concepts. Mental constructs or representations of categories that allow us to identify examples and nonexamples of those categories.

Conceptual hierarchies. Types of concept maps that visually illustrate superordinate, subordinate, and coordinate relationships among concepts.

Conditional knowledge. Knowledge of where and when to use declarative and procedural knowledge.

Conditioned response. A learned physiological or emotional response that is similar to the unconditioned response.

Conditioned stimulus. A formerly neutral stimulus that becomes associated with an unconditioned stimulus.

Confirmation bias. People's tendency to focus only on evidence that supports their beliefs.

Connected discourse. Instruction that is thematic and leads to a point.

Consequences. An event (stimulus) that occurs following a behavior that influences the probability of the behavior recurring.

Conservation. The idea that the "amount" of some substance stays the same regardless of its shape or the number of pieces into which it is divided.

Construct validity. An indicator of the logical connection between a test and what it is designed to measure.

Content validity. A test's ability to accurately sample the content taught and to measure the extent to which learners understand it.

Continuous reinforcement schedule. A schedule of reinforcement in which every desired behavior is reinforced.

Conventional morality. A moral orientation linked to uncritical acceptance of society's conventions about right and wrong.

Cooperative learning. A set of instructional strategies in which students work in mixed-ability groups to reach specific cognitive and social development objectives.

Correlation. A relationship, either positive or negative, between two or more variables.

Correlational research. The process of looking for relationships between variables that enables researchers to predict changes in one variable on the basis of changes in another without implying that one variable causes the other.

Cost. The consideration of what a person must give up to engage in an activity.

Creativity. The ability to produce original works or solutions to problems that are productive.

Crisis. A psychosocial challenge that presents opportunities for development.

Criterion-referenced grading. A grading system in which you make assessment decisions according to a predetermined standard.

Criterion-referenced standardized tests. Standardized tests that compare performance against a set performance standard.

Critical thinking. An individual's ability and inclination to make and assess conclusions based on evidence.

Crystallized intelligence. Culture-specific mental ability, heavily dependent on experience and schooling.

Cultural mismatch. A clash between a child's home culture and the culture of the school that creates conflicting expectations for students' and their behavior.

Culturally responsive classroom management. Classroom management that combines cultural knowledge with teachers' awareness of possible personal biases.

Culturally responsive teaching. An approach to education that attempts to understand the cultures of the students we teach, communicate positive attitudes about cultural diversity, and employ a variety of instructional approaches that build on students' cultural backgrounds.

Culture. The knowledge, attitudes, values, and customs that characterize a social group.

Cyberbullying. The use of electronic media to harass or intimidate other students.

Deaf. A hearing impairment that requires the use of other senses, usually sight, to communicate.

Declarative knowledge. Knowledge of facts, definitions, procedures, and rules.

Deficiency needs. Needs that energize people to meet them if they're unfulfilled.

Delay of gratification. The ability to forgo an immediate pleasure or reward in order to gain a more substantial one later.

Dendrites. Relatively short, branchlike structures that extend from the cell body of neurons and receive messages from other neurons.

Descriptive research. Research that uses tools such as tests, surveys, and observations to describe the status or characteristics of a situation or phenomenon.

Desist. A verbal or nonverbal communication used to stop a behavior.

Development. The changes that occur in human beings as they grow from infancy to adulthood.

Developmental differences. Changes in students' thinking personalities and social skills that result from maturation and experience.

Developmentally appropriate practice. Instruction that matches teacher actions to the capabilities and needs of learners at different developmental levels.

Diagnostic assessment. A form of assessment designed to provide information about students' prior knowledge and misconceptions before beginning a learning activity.

Diagnostic tests. Standardized tests designed to provide a detailed description of learners' strengths and weaknesses in specific skill areas.

Dialect. A variation of Standard English that is associated with a particular regional or social group and is distinct in vocabulary, grammar, or pronunciation.

Differentiating instruction. The process of adapting instruction to meet the needs of students who vary in background knowledge, skills, needs, and motivations.

Direct instruction. A teaching model designed to help students acquire well-defined knowledge and skills needed for later learning.

Disabilities. Functional limitations or an inability to perform a certain act.

Discipline. Teachers' responses to student misbehavior.

Discrepancy model of identification. One method of identifying students with learning problems that focuses on differences between achievement and intelligence tests or subtests.

Discrimination. The process that occurs when a person gives different responses to related but not identical stimuli.

Disorder. A general malfunction of mental, physical, or psychological processes.

Distractors. Incorrect choices in multiple-choice items.

Divergent thinking. The ability to generate a variety of alternate, original solutions to questions or problems.

Drawing analogies. A heuristic that is used to solve unfamiliar problems by comparing them with those already solved.

Dual-coding theory. A theory suggesting that long-term memory contains two distinct memory systems: one for verbal information and one that stores images.

Due process. The guarantee that parents have the right to be involved in identifying and placing their children in special programs, to access school records, and to obtain an independent evaluation if they're not satisfied with the one conducted by the school.

Educational psychology. The academic discipline that focuses on human teaching and learning.

Effective teachers. Teachers who are able to produce more learning in their students than would be expected for the students' background and ability.

Effective teaching. Instruction that promotes as much learning as possible in all students.

Egocentrism. The inability to see objects and events from others' perspectives.

Elaboration. An encoding strategy that increases the meaningfulness of new information by connecting it to existing knowledge.

Elaborative questioning. The process of drawing inferences, identifying examples, and forming relationships.

Emotional intelligence. The ability to understand emotions in ourselves and others.

Emotional self-regulation. The ability to manage our emotions so we can cope with the environment and accomplish goals.

Empathy. The ability to experience the same emotion someone else is feeling.

Emphasis. Verbal and vocal cues that alert students to important information in a lesson.

Encoding. The process of representing information in long-term memory.

English as a second language (ESL) pullout programs. Programs for students who are English learners who receive most of their instruction in general education classrooms but are also pulled out for extra help.

English learners (ELs). Students for whom English is not their first or home language.

Enrichment. Programs for students who are gifted and talented that provide alternate instruction.

Entity view of intelligence. The belief that intelligence is essentially fixed and stable over time.

Episodic memory. Memory for personal experiences.

Equilibrium. A cognitive state in which we're able to explain new experiences by using existing understanding.

Equitable distribution. The process of calling on all the students in a class as equally as possible, whether or not they have their hands raised.

Essay. A paper-and-pencil format that requires students to make extended written responses to questions or problems.

Essential teaching skills. Basic abilities that all teachers, including those in their first year of teaching, should possess to maximize student learning.

Ethnic identity. An awareness of ethnic group membership and a commitment to the attitudes, values, and behaviors of that group.

Ethnicity. A person's ancestry and the way individuals identify with the nation from which they or their ancestors came.

Exemplars. In concept-learning theory, the most highly typical examples of a concept.

Exosystem. In bioecological theory, societal influences that affect both the micro- and mesosystems.

Expectation. A belief about a future outcome. The influence of expectations on motivation is often described using expectancy × value theory.

Expectancy × value theory. A theory that explains motivation by saying that learners will be motivated to engage in a task to the extent that they expect to succeed on a task *times* the value they place on the success.

Experimental research. A type of research that systematically manipulates variables in attempts to determine cause and effect.

Experts. Individuals who are highly knowledgeable or skilled in a specific domain, such as math, history, chess, or teaching.

External morality. A stage of moral development in which individuals view rules as fixed and permanent and enforced by authority figures.

Extinction (classical conditioning). The process that occurs when the conditioned stimulus occurs often enough in the absence of the unconditioned stimulus so that it no longer elicits the conditioned response.

Extinction (operant conditioning). The disappearance of a behavior as a result of nonreinforcement.

Extrinsic motivation. Motivation to engage in an activity as a means to an end.

Feedback. Information teachers provide to students that helps students determine whether or not the knowledge they're constructing is accurate and valid.

Fluid intelligence. The flexible, culture-free mental ability to adapt to new situations and acquire knowledge quickly.

Focus. The essential teaching skill teachers use to capture and maintain students' attention and interest throughout the lesson.

Forgetting. The loss of, or inability to retrieve, information from long-term memory.

Formal assessment. The process of systematically gathering the same kind of information from every student and making decisions based on that information.

Formative assessment. The process of using assessments to provide students with feedback about learning progress, but not using the assessment information to make decisions about grading.

Frequency distribution. A distribution of test scores that shows a count of the number of people who obtained each score.

Functional analysis. The strategy used to identify antecedents and consequences that influence behavior.

Gender-role identity. Beliefs about appropriate characteristics and behaviors of males and females.

General pedagogical knowledge. A type of professional knowledge that involves an understanding of instructional strategies and classroom management that apply to all topics and subject matter areas.

General transfer. The ability to apply knowledge or skills learned in one context to a variety of different contexts.

Generalization. The process that occurs when stimuli similar, but not identical, to a conditioned stimulus elicit the conditioned responses by themselves.

Gifts and talents. Abilities at the upper end of the continuum that require additional support to reach full potential.

Goal. An outcome an individual hopes to attain.

Grade-equivalent score. A score that is determined by comparing an individual's score on a standardized test to the scores of students in a particular age group.

Growth needs. Needs in intellectual achievement and aesthetic appreciation that increase as people have experiences with them.

Guided discovery. A model of instruction that involves teachers' scaffolding students' constructions of concepts and the relationships among them.

Guided notes. Teacher-prepared handouts that "guide" students with cues and space available for writing key ideas and relationships.

Guilt. The uncomfortable feeling people get when they know they've caused distress for someone else.

Handicap. A condition imposed on a person's functioning that restricts the individual's abilities.

Heuristics. General, widely applicable problem-solving strategies.

High-quality examples. Examples that include all the information learners need to understand a topic.

High-stakes tests. Standardized tests used to make important decisions that affect students, teachers, schools, and school districts.

Hostile attributional bias. A tendency to view others' behaviors as hostile or aggressive.

Identity. Individuals' self constructed definition of who they are, what their existence means, and what they want in life.

Ill-defined problem. A problem that has an ambiguous goal, more than one acceptable solution, and no generally agreed-upon strategy for reaching a solution.

Imagery. The process of forming mental pictures of an idea.

I-message. A nonaccusatory communication that addresses a behavior and describes the effects on the sender and the feelings it generates in the sender.

Immersion programs. English language programs that place students who are English learners in general education classrooms without additional assistance to help them learn both English and academic content at the same time.

Implementing instruction. The process of putting decisions made during planning into action.

Inclusion. A comprehensive approach to educating students with exceptionalities that advocates a total, systematic, and coordinated web of services.

Incremental view of intelligence. The belief that intelligence, or ability, is not stable and can be increased with effort.

Individualized education program (IEP). A written statement that provides a framework for delivering a free and appropriate education (FAPE) to every eligible student with a disability.

Informal assessment. The process of gathering incidental information about learning progress and making decisions based on that information.

Information-processing theory. A theory that describes how information enters our memory system, is organized, and finally stored.

Inhibition. A self-imposed restriction on one's behavior.

Instructional alignment. The match between learning objectives, learning activities, and assessments.

Instrumental aggression. An aggressive act aimed at gaining an object or privilege.

Intellectual disability. A disability characterized by significant limitations both in intellectual functioning and in adaptive behavior.

Intelligence. The ability to acquire and use knowledge, solve problems and reason in the abstract, and adapt to new situations in the environment.

Intelligence tests. Standardized tests designed to measure an individual's capacity to acquire and use knowledge, to solve problems, and accomplish new tasks.

Interference. The loss of information because something learned either before or after detracts from understanding.

Intermittent reinforcement schedule. A schedule of reinforcement in which some, but not all, of the desired behaviors are reinforced.

Internalization. The process through which learners incorporate external, society-based activities into internal cognitive processes.

Interpersonal harmony. A stage of moral reasoning in which conclusions are based on loyalty, living up to the expectations of others, and social conventions.

Interspersed practice. The process of mixing the practice of different skills.

Interval schedule of reinforcement. An intermittent reinforcement schedule in which behaviors are reinforced after a predictable (fixed) or unpredictable (variable) time interval.

Intrinsic motivation. Motivation to be involved in an activity for its own sake.

Introductory focus. A lesson beginning that attracts student attention and provides a conceptual framework for the lesson.

Involvement. The extent to which people are actively participating in an activity.

Joplin plan. Homogeneous grouping in reading, combined with heterogeneous grouping in other areas.

Language acquisition device (LAD). A genetically controlled set of processing skills that enables children to understand and use the rules governing language.

Language disorders *(receptive disorders)*. Problems with understanding language or using language to express ideas.

Law and order. A stage of moral reasoning in which conclusions are based on following laws and rules for their own sake.

Learned helplessness. The debilitating belief that one is incapable of accomplishing tasks and has little control of the environment.

Learner diversity. The group and individual differences in our students.

Learners with exceptionalities. Students who need special help and resources to reach their full potential.

Learning (behaviorism). A relatively enduring change in observable behavior that occurs as a result of experience.

Learning (cognitive). A change in mental processes that creates the capacity to demonstrate different behaviors.

Learning disabilities. Difficulty in acquiring and using reading, writing, reasoning, listening, or mathematical abilities.

Learning objective. A statement that specifies what students should know or be able to do with respect to a topic.

Learning styles. Students' personal approaches to learning, problem solving, and processing information.

Least restrictive environment (LRE). A policy that places students in as typical an educational setting as possible while still meeting the students' special needs.

Lecture–discussion. An instructional model designed to help students acquire organized bodies of knowledge.

Logical consequences. Outcomes that are conceptually related to misbehavior; they help learners make sense of an intervention by creating a link between their actions and its consequences.

Long-term memory. The permanent information store in our human memory system.

Macrosystem. Bronfenbrenner's fourth level, which includes cultural influences on development.

Mainstreaming. The practice of moving students with exceptionalities from segregated settings into general education classrooms.

Maintenance EL programs. Programs for students who are English learners (ELs) that build on students' native language by teaching in both languages.

Market exchange. A stage of moral reasoning in which conclusions are based on an act of reciprocity on someone else's part.

Mastery goal. A goal that focuses on accomplishing a task, improving, and increasing understanding.

Mastery learning. A system of instruction that allows students to progress at their own rate through a unit of study.

Mastery-focused classroom. A classroom environment that emphasizes effort, continuous improvement, and understanding.

Matching. A paper-and-pencil format that requires learners to classify a series of examples using the same alternatives.

Maturation. Genetically controlled, age-related changes in individuals.

Mean. The average score in the distribution of a group of scores.

Meaningfulness. The extent to which information in long-term memory is interconnected with other information.

Means–ends analysis. A heuristic that breaks the problem into subgoals and works successively on each.

Measures of central tendency. Quantitative descriptions of a group's performance as a whole.

Median. The middle score in the distribution of a group of scores.

Memory stores. Sensory memory, working memory, and long-term memory repositories that hold information, both in a raw state and in organized, meaningful form.

Mesosystem. In Bronfenbrenner's model, the interactions and connections between the different elements of children's immediate settings.

Meta-attention. Our knowledge of and control over our ability to pay attention.

Metacognition. Our awareness of and control over our cognitive processes.

Metamemory. Knowledge of and control over our memory strategies.

Microsystem. In Bronfenbrenner's bioecological theory, the people and activities in a child's immediate surroundings.

Misconception. A belief that is inconsistent with evidence or commonly accepted explanations.

Mnemonic devices. Memory strategies that create associations that don't exist naturally in the content.

Mode. The most frequent score in the distribution of a group of scores.

Model. A representation that helps us visualize what we can't observe directly.

Modeling. A general term that refers to behavioral, cognitive, and affective changes deriving from observing the actions of others.

Models of instruction. Prescriptive approaches to teaching designed to help students acquire a deep understanding of specific forms of knowledge.

Moral development. Advances in people's conceptions of right and wrong, and prosocial behaviors and traits such as honesty, fairness, and respect for others.

Moral dilemma. An ambiguous, conflicting situation that requires a person to make a moral decision.

Motivation. The "process whereby goal-directed activity is instigated and sustained" (Schunk, Pintrich & Meece, 2008, p. 4).

Motivation to learn. Students' "tendencies to find academic activities meaningful and worthwhile and to try to get the intended learning benefits from them" (Brophy, 2010, p. 11).

Motivational zone of proximal development. The match between a learning activity and learners' prior knowledge and experiences that is close enough to stimulate interest and perceived value in the activity but not so familiar that learners are satiated by it.

Multicultural education. An approach to teaching that examines the influence of culture on learning and attempts to find ways that students' cultures can be used to enhance achievement.

Multiple-choice. A paper-and-pencil format that consists of a question or statement, called a stem, and a series of answer choices that include one correct—or best—answer and a series of distractors.

National norms. Scores on standardized tests earned by representative groups of students from around the nation to which an individual's score is compared.

Nativist theory. A theory of language development that suggests all humans are genetically wired to learn language.

Nature view of intelligence. The assertion that intelligence is essentially determined by genetics.

Need. An internal force or drive to attain or to avoid a certain state or object.

Need for approval. The desire to be accepted and judged positively by others.

Negative reinforcement. The process of increasing behavior by removing or avoiding an aversive stimulus.

Negligence. The failure of teachers or schools to exercise sufficient care in protecting students from injury.

Neo-Piagetian theory. A theory of cognitive development that accepts Piaget's stages but uses the acquisition of specific processing strategies to explain movement from one stage to the next.

Neurons. Nerve cells composed of cell bodies, dendrites, and axons, which make up the learning capability of the brain.

Neutral stimulus. An object or event that doesn't initially impact behavior one way or the other.

Normal distribution. A distribution of scores in which the mean, median, and mode are equal and the scores distribute themselves symmetrically in a bell-shaped curve.

Norming group. The representative group of individuals whose standardized test scores are compiled for the purpose of national comparisons.

Norm-referenced grading. A grading system in which teachers base assessment decisions about an individual's performance on comparisons to the performance of peers.

Norm-referenced standardized tests. Standardized tests that compare (reference) a student's performance with the performance of others.

Nurture view of intelligence. The assertion that emphasizes the influence of the environment on intelligence.

Object permanence. The understanding that objects exist even when out of sight.

Open-ended questions. Questions for which a variety of answers is acceptable.

Operant conditioning. A behaviorist form of learning that occurs when an observable behavior changes in frequency or duration as the result of a consequence.

Order and safety. A learning climate variable that creates a predictable learning environment and supports learner autonomy together with a sense of physical and emotional security.

Organization. An encoding strategy that involves the clustering of related items of content into categories that illustrate relationships.

Organized bodies of knowledge. Topics that connect facts, concepts, and generalizations, and make the relationships among them explicit.

Overgeneralization. A language pattern that occurs when a child uses a word to refer to a broader class of objects than is appropriate.

Overlapping. The ability to intervene in cases of misbehavior without disrupting the flow of a lesson.

Parenting style. General patterns of interacting with and disciplining children.

Partial hearing impairment. An impairment that allows a student to use a hearing aid and to hear well enough to be taught through auditory channels.

Pedagogical content knowledge. An understanding of how to represent topics in ways that make them understandable to learners, as well as an understanding of what makes specific topics easy or hard to learn.

People-first language. Language in which a student's disability is identified after the student is named.

Percentile bands. Ranges of percentile scores on standardized tests.

Percentile rank (PR). The percentage of students in the norming sample that scored at or below a particular raw score.

Perception. The process people use to find meaning in stimuli.

Performance assessments. Direct examinations of student performance on tasks that are relevant to life outside of school.

Performance goal. A goal that focuses on demonstrating ability and competence and how learners compare to others.

Performance-approach goal. A goal that emphasizes looking competent and receiving favorable judgments from others.

Performance-avoidance goal. A goal that emphasizes attempts to avoid looking incompetent and being judged unfavorably.

Performance-focused classroom. A classroom environment that emphasizes high grades, public displays of ability, and performance compared to others.

Personal development. Age-related changes in personality and the ways that individuals react to their environment.

Personal interest. "A person's ongoing affinity, attraction, or liking for a domain, subject area, topic, or activity" (Anderman & Wolters, 2006, p. 374).

Personal teaching efficacy. Teachers' beliefs that they can help all students learn, regardless of their prior knowledge, ability, or personal backgrounds.

Personal, social, and emotional development. Changes in our personality, the ways we interact with others, and our ability to manage our feelings.

Personalization. The process of using intellectually and/or emotionally relevant examples to illustrate a topic.

Perspective taking. The ability to understand the thoughts and feelings of others.

Phonological loop. A short-term storage system for words and sounds in working memory.

Physical aggression. An aggressive act that can cause bodily injury.

Physical development. Changes in the size, shape, and functioning of our bodies.

Portfolio assessment. The process of selecting collections of student work that both students and teachers evaluate using preset criteria.

Positive behavior support. Interventions that replace problem behaviors with appropriate behaviors that serve the same purpose for the student.

Positive learning climate. A classroom climate in which the teacher and students work together as a community of learners to help everyone achieve.

Positive reinforcement. The process of increasing the frequency or duration of a behavior as the result of *presenting* a reinforcer.

Postconventional morality. A moral orientation that views moral issues in terms of abstract and self-developed principles of right and wrong.

Precise language. Teacher language that omits vague terms from explanations and responses to students' questions.

Preconventional morality. An egocentric orientation lacking any internalized standards for right and wrong.

Predictive validity. The measure of a test's ability to gauge future performance.

Premack principle. The principle stating that a more-desired activity can serve as a positive reinforcer for a less-desired activity.

Presentation punishment. The process of decreasing a behavior that occurs when a stimulus (punisher) is presented.

Principles (laws). Statements about an area of study that are generally accepted as true.

Private speech. Self-talk that guides thinking and action.

Proactive aggression. A deliberate aggressive act initiated toward another.

Proactive interference. The loss of new information because of the influence of prior learning.

Problem. The presence of a goal but the absence of an obvious way to achieve it.

Problem-based learning. A teaching strategy that uses problems as the focus for developing content, skills, and self-regulation.

Procedural knowledge. Knowledge of how to perform tasks.

Procedures. Guidelines for accomplishing recurring tasks.

Professional knowledge. The body of information and skills that are unique to a particular area of study.

Prompting. An additional question or statement used to elicit an appropriate student response after a student fails to answer correctly.

Prototype. In concept-learning theory, the best representation of the category.

Puberty. The series of physiological changes that occur during adolescence and lead to reproductive maturation.

Punishers. Consequences that weaken behaviors, or decrease the likelihood of the behaviors' recurring.

Punishment. The process of using punishers to decrease behavior.

Punishment–obedience. A stage of moral reasoning in which conclusions are based on the chances of getting caught and being punished.

Qualitative research. A type of research that attempts to describe a complex educational phenomenon in a holistic fashion using nonnumeric data.

Questioning frequency. Refers to the number of questions teachers ask during a learning activity.

Race. A socially constructed category composed of people who share biologically transmitted traits considered important.

Range. The distance between the top and bottom score in a distribution of scores.

Rating scales. Written descriptions of the dimensions of an acceptable performance and scales of values on which each dimension is rated.

Ratio schedule of reinforcement. An intermittent reinforcement schedule where specific behaviors are reinforced either predictably (fixed) or unpredictably (variable).

Raw score. The number of items an individual answered correctly on a standardized test or subtest.

Reactive aggression. An aggressive act committed in response to frustration or another aggressive act.

Readiness tests. Standardized tests designed to assess the degree to which children are prepared for an academic or pre-academic program.

Reciprocal causation. The interdependence of the environment, behavior, and personal factors in learning.

Reflective practice. The process of conducting a critical self-examination of one's teaching.

Rehearsal. The process of repeating information over and over, either out loud or silently, without altering its form.

Reinforcement schedules. Patterns in the frequency and predictability of reinforcers that have differential effects on behavior.

Reinforcement. The process of applying reinforcers to increase behavior.

Reinforcer. A consequence that increases the likelihood of a behavior recurring.

Relatedness. The feeling of being connected to others in one's social environment and feeling worthy of love and respect.

Relational aggression. An aggressive act that can adversely affect interpersonal relationships.

Reliability. The extent to which assessments are consistent and free from errors of measurement.

Removal punishment. The process of decreasing a behavior that occurs when a stimulus is removed or when an individual cannot receive positive reinforcement.

Research. The process of systematically gathering information in an attempt to answer professional questions.

Resilience. A learner characteristic that, despite adversity, raises the likelihood of success in school and later life.

Resistance cultures. Cultures with beliefs, values, and behaviors that reject the values of mainstream culture.

Response cost. The process of removing reinforcers already given.

Response to intervention model of identification. A method of identifying a learning problem that focuses on the specific classroom instructional adaptations that teachers use and their success.

Retrieval. The process of pulling information from long-term memory into working memory.

Retroactive interference. The loss of previously learned information because of the influence of new learning.

Reversibility. The ability to mentally trace the process of moving from an existing state back to a previous state.

Review. A summary that helps students link what they've already learned to new information in the learning activity.

Rote learning. Learning that involves storing information in isolated pieces, most commonly through memorization.

Rubric. A scoring scale that explicitly describes criteria for grading.

Rules. Descriptions of standards for acceptable behavior.

Satiation. The process of using a reinforcer so frequently that it loses its ability to strengthen behaviors.

Scaffolding. Assistance that helps children complete tasks they cannot complete independently.

Schema activation. An encoding strategy that involves activating relevant prior knowledge so that new knowledge can be connected to it.

Schemas. Cognitive structures that represent the way information is organized in our long-term memory.

Schemes. Mental operations that represent our constructed understanding of the world.

School connectedness. The belief by students that adults and peers in the school care about their learning as well as about them as individuals.

Scripts. Schemas for events that guide behavior in particular situations.

Self-actualization. Reaching one's full potential and becoming all that we are capable of being.

Self-concept. A cognitive assessment of their physical, social, and academic competence.

Self-determination. The need to act on and control one's environment.

Self-efficacy. The belief that one is capable of accomplishing a specific task.

Self-esteem (self-worth). An emotional reaction to, or an evaluation of, the self.

Self-fulfilling prophecy. A phenomenon that occurs when a person's performance results from and confirms beliefs about his or her capabilities.

Self-regulated learning. The process of setting personal goals, combined with the motivation, thought processes, strategies, and behaviors that lead to reaching the goals.

Self-regulation. The ability to direct and control one's own actions and emotions.

Self-worth. An emotional reaction to or an evaluation of the self.

Semantic memory. Memory for concepts, principles, and the relationships among them.

Semantics. A branch of linguistics that examines the meaning of words.

Sensory memory. The memory store that briefly holds incoming stimuli from the environment until they can be processed.

Seriation. The ability to order objects according to increasing or decreasing length, weight, or volume.

Sexual identity. Students' self-constructed definition of who they are with respect to gender orientation.

Sexual orientation. The gender to which an individual is romantically and sexually attracted.

Shame. The painful emotion aroused when people recognize that they have failed to act or think in ways they believe are good.

Shaping. The process of reinforcing successive approximations of a behavior.

Sheltered English. An approach to teaching students who are ELs in academic classrooms that modifies instruction to assist students in learning content.

Short-term memory. Historically, the part of our memory system that temporarily holds information until it can be processed.

Single-gender classes. Classes where boys and girls are segregated for part or all of the day.

Situated cognition. A theoretical position in social constructivism suggesting that learning depends on, and cannot be separated from, the context in which it occurs.

Situational interest. A person's current enjoyment, pleasure, or satisfaction generated by the immediate context.

Social cognitive theory. A theory of learning that focuses on changes in behavior that result from observing others.

Social constructivism. A view of constructivism suggesting that learners first construct knowledge in a social context and then individually internalize it.

Social contract. A stage of moral reasoning in which conclusions are based on socially agreed-upon principles.

Social conventions. Societal norms and ways of behaving in specific situations.

Social development. The advances people make in their ability to interact and get along with others.

Social experience. The process of interacting with others.

Social goals. Goals to achieve particular social outcomes or interactions.

Social problem solving. The ability to resolve conflicts in ways that are beneficial to all involved.

Sociocultural theory. A form of social constructivism that emphasizes the social dimensions of learning, but places greater emphasis on the larger cultural contexts in which learning occurs.

Sociocultural theory of development. A theory of cognitive development that emphasizes the influence of social interactions and language, embedded within a cultural context, on cognitive development.

Socioeconomic status (SES). The combination of parents' income, occupation, and level of education that describes relative standing in society of a family or individual.

Special education. Instruction designed to meet the unique needs of students with exceptionalities.

Specific transfer. The ability to apply information in a context similar to the one in which it was originally learned.

Speech disorders (*expressive disorders*)**.** Problems in forming and sequencing sounds.

Stages of development. General patterns of thinking for children at different ages or with different amounts of experience.

Standard deviation. A statistical measure of the spread of scores.

Standard error of measurement. The range of scores within which an individual's true score is likely to fall.

Standard score. A description of performance on a standardized test that uses the standard deviation as the basic unit.

Standardized tests. Assessment instruments given to large samples of students under uniform conditions and scored and reported according to uniform procedures.

Standards. Statements that describe what students should know or be able to do at the end of a prescribed period of study.

Standards-based education. The process of focusing curricula and instruction on predetermined goals or standards.

Standards-based grading. A grading system that is based on a student's mastery of specific standards.

Stanine. A description of an individual's standardized test performance that uses a scale ranging from 1 to 9 points.

Stem. The beginning part of a multiple-choice item that presents the item as a problem to be solved, a question to be answered, or an incomplete statement.

Stereotype threat. The anxiety felt by members of a group resulting from concern that their behavior might confirm a stereotype.

Strategies. Cognitive operations that exceed the normal activities required to carry out a task.

Structured immersion. A type of immersion English language program that attempts to assist students who are ELs by teaching both English and academic subjects at a slower pace.

Students at risk. Students who fail to complete their education with the skills necessary to succeed in today's society.

Study strategies. Specific techniques students use to increase their understanding of written materials and teacher presentations.

Summarizing. The process of preparing a concise description of verbal or written passages.

Summative assessment. The process of using assessment results for making grading decisions.

Synapses. The tiny spaces between neurons that allow messages to be transmitted from one neuron to another.

Syntax. The set of rules that we use to put words together into meaningful sentences.

Systematic observation. The process of specifying criteria for acceptable performance in an activity and taking notes based on the criteria.

Table of specifications. A matrix that helps teachers organize learning objectives by cognitive level or content area and links instruction and assessment to objectives and standards.

Task analysis. The process of breaking content into component parts and sequencing the parts.

Task comprehension. Learners' awareness of what they are supposed to be learning and an understanding of why the task is important and worthwhile.

Temperament. The relatively stable inherited characteristics that influence the way we respond to social and physical stimuli.

Test anxiety. An unpleasant emotional reaction to testing situations that can lower performance.

Text signals. Elements included in written materials that communicate text organization and key ideas.

Theories. Sets of related patterns, derived from observations, that researchers use to explain and predict events in the world.

Theory of mind. An understanding that other people have distinctive perceptions, feelings, desires, and beliefs.

Timeout. The process of isolating a student from classmates so he or she cannot get positive reinforcement.

Tracking. Placing students in different classes or curricula on the basis of achievement.

Transfer. The ability to apply understanding acquired in one context to a different context.

Transformation. The ability to mentally record the process of moving from one state to another.

Transition signals. Verbal statements indicating that one idea is ending and another is beginning.

Transitional EL programs. English learner (EL) programs that attempt to use the native language as an instructional aid until English becomes proficient.

Transitivity. The ability to infer a relationship between two objects based on knowledge of their relationship with a third object.

True score. The hypothetical average of an individual's scores if repeated testing under ideal conditions were possible.

True–false. A paper-and-pencil format that includes statements that learners judge as being correct or incorrect.

t-score. A standard score that defines the mean as 50 and the standard deviation as 10.

Unconditional positive regard. Treating individuals as if they are innately worthy regardless of their behavior.

Unconditioned response. The instinctive or reflexive (unlearned) physiological or emotional response caused by the unconditioned stimulus.

Unconditioned stimulus. An object or event that causes an instinctive or reflex (unlearned) emotional or physiological response.

Undergeneralization. A language pattern that occurs when a child uses a word too narrowly.

Universal principles stage. A stage of moral reasoning in which conclusions are based on abstract and general principles that transcend or exceed society's laws.

Utility value. The belief that a topic, activity, or course of study will be useful for meeting future goals, including career goals.

Validity. The degree to which an assessment actually measures what it is supposed to measure.

Value. The benefits, rewards, or advantages that individuals believe can result from participating in an activity.

Variability. The spread of scores, or degree of difference or deviation from the mean.

Vicarious learning. The process of observing the consequences of others' actions and adjusting our own behavior accordingly.

Visual handicap. An uncorrectable visual impairment that interferes with learning.

Visual-spatial sketchpad. A short-term storage system for visual and special information in working memory.

Wait-time. A period of silence, both before and after calling on a student that gives students time to think about their answer to a question.

Well-defined problem. A problem that has a clear goal, only one correct solution, and a certain method for finding it.

Within-class grouping. divides students in a single class into groups, typically based on reading and math scores.

Withitness. A teacher's awareness of what is going on in all parts of the classroom at all times and communicating this awareness to students.

Worked examples. Problems with completed solutions that provide students with one way of solving problems.

Working memory. The memory store that holds information as we consciously process and try to make sense of it.

Zone of proximal development. A range of tasks that an individual cannot yet do alone but can accomplish when assisted by the guidance of others.

z-score. The number of standard deviation units from the mean.appendix A

appendix A

Feedback for "Check Your Understanding" Questions

Chapter 1

1.1 The essential difference between effective and ineffective teachers is their level of knowledge and skills. Effective teachers are highly knowledgeable and skilled, more knowledgeable and skilled than their less effective counterparts. Students taught by effective teachers learn much more than those taught by ineffective teachers. Research indicates that, other than the home environment, the quality of the teacher is the single most important influence on student learning.

1.2 One striking example is a widely publicized study involving students in the third, fourth, and fifth grades. Researchers found that students who had highly effective teachers in these grades scored more than 50 percentile points higher on standardized math tests than students who had ineffective teachers in the same three grades!

2.1 Knowledge of content, pedagogical content knowledge, general pedagogical knowledge, and knowledge of learners and learning are four types of knowledge professional teachers possess. Knowledge of content describes teachers' understanding of math, reading, geography, or whatever topic is being taught. Pedagogical content knowledge is the ability to represent the topic in ways that are understandable, such as the folded pieces of paper discussed in this chapter as a way of representing the multiplication of fractions. General pedagogical knowledge refers to the professional abilities necessary to teach in all situations, such as questioning skills, or the ability to organize classrooms. Knowledge of learners and learning refers to factors such as an understanding of how students learn, and how students' motivation influences learning.

2.2 Keith's statement that best indicates that he lacks pedagogical content knowledge is, "I explain the stuff so carefully, but some of the kids just sit with blank looks on their faces." When teachers lack pedagogical content knowledge, they commonly revert to abstract explanations that aren't meaningful to students. We're not implying that teachers shouldn't try to explain topics; rather, we're suggesting that relying on explanations alone often fails to increase learners' understanding as much as a teacher might expect.

2.3 The teacher in this case is using the pieces of bubble wrap to help students visualize the way that cells form tissues. The ability to create this representation is an indicator of the teacher's pedagogical content knowledge. (In this case, the bubble wrap is a model for the formation of tissue; it helps students visualize what they can't observe directly.)

3.1 First, and perhaps most obviously, students learn content, such as the history of our country, and they learn skills, such as the ability to write effectively and solve math problems. As they acquire experience, their knowledge and skills improve, and we say they've developed cognitively. Second, they learn social skills and develop in their ability to relate to, and work with, others. This development includes understanding and respect for people from different ethnic and language backgrounds. Third, they learn to take responsibility for their own actions, set their own goals, and make plans to help them reach the goals–processes involved in self-regulation. Finally, they learn to value content and skills that may not be intrinsically interesting to them, but they realize that these forms of learning are important for their overall development.

3.2 Self-regulation is the ability to direct and control ones own actions and emotions. It includes: self-motivation—taking responsibility for completing tasks and engaging in appropriate activities; delay of gratification—forgoing immediate rewards to gain more substantial ones later; impulse control—resisting urges to display inappropriate behaviors; emotional regulation—expressing emotions in socially appropriate ways; self-socialization—understanding society's standards of behavior and acting in accordance with those standards; self-regulated learning—setting personal learning goals together with the thinking and strategies used to reach the goals.

3.3 Helping you understand each of these forms of learning and development, and how you can promote them in your teaching is the focus of educational psychology. As you study the topic in this book you will realize that your role as a teacher is much more than simply helping students acquire content. It includes helping students develop personally and socially, to respect individuals and groups with different backgrounds, to accept responsibility, and to value learning.

4.1 Many of the ideas in educational psychology are abstract. Because they're abstract, they can be difficult to understand and apply to teaching. The use of case studies provides concrete reference points that make the abstract ideas of educational psychology more meaningful and applicable to the real world that you will face when you begin your career.

4.2 The licensure exams you'll take prior to licensure contain cases similar to the ones you'll encounter in this text. Studying them not only will help you learn the content, but will also prepare you for this type of exam format.

Chapter 2

1.1 *Development* refers to the changes that occur in human beings as they grow from infancy to adulthood. An understanding of development is important for three reasons. First, it provides insights into the thinking and behaviors of the students we teach. Second, it helps us guide and direct development. Third, it reminds us that students may be at different developmental levels when they enter our classrooms, and we should adjust our expectations accordingly.

1.2 All development is based on three principles. First, development depends on both heredity and the environment. While heredity provides the raw materials for development, environmental influences shape development in major ways. Teachers play a major role in providing these experiences and shaping development.

A second basic principle of development is that development proceeds in a relatively orderly and predictable pattern. When teachers understand these patterns, they can better address these developmental strengths and limitations in their instruction.

A third principle of development is that children develop at different rates. Though we typically group children by their chronological age, this does not ensure that they are all at the same stage of development. Understanding this developmental variability makes teachers more sensitive to individual differences and helps them accommodate these differences in their teaching.

1.3 As the brain develops, synaptic connections between neurons are both strengthened and eliminated (synaptic pruning). The direction of these connections influences our cognitive development. Healthy cognitive development is dependent upon a nurturing environment that provides for both physical needs and stimulation from the environment.

The cerebral cortex is the part of the brain involved with higher cognitive processes, such as language and thinking as well as impulse control. The development of the cerebral cortex allows us to plan, problem solve, and make informed and thoughtful decisions.

2.1 Hands-on activities provide the direct experiences that Piaget believed are necessary for development. Experience also helps us understand the statement made in this section, "Although approximate chronological ages are attached to the stages, children pass through them at different rates." Differences in experience, together with differences in maturation, are the two most important reasons why children pass through the stages at different rates.

2.2 First, the children tend to center on the length of the row in the case of the coins and the length of the clay in the case of the flattened piece of clay. The length of the row and the longer, flatter clay are more perceptually obvious than are the number of coins or the amount of clay, so the children conclude that there are more coins in the bottom row and more clay in the flattened piece. Second, because young children lack transformation, they don't mentally record the process of spreading the coins apart in the bottom row, or flattening the clay, so they see each as new and different. Third, since they lack reversibility, they're unable to mentally trace the process of reforming the length of the row to its original state, or mentally trace the process of reforming the flattened clay back into a ball. When lack of transformation and reversibility are combined with their tendency to center, we can see why they conclude that the bottom row has more coins, even though no coins were added or removed, and conclude that the amount of clay is different even though no clay is added or removed.

2.3 You have had a variety of experiences with using the Windows operating system, and you have organized those experiences into an *operating system* scheme. Your scheme has helped you to achieve equilibrium. However, when you encountered Linux, your equilibrium was disrupted, and you were forced to accommodate your scheme. You modified your original *operating system* scheme and constructed a new, *Linux-operating-system* scheme, and your equilibrium was re-established, allowing you to assimilate new operations with it.

3.1 The section entitled "Language and Development" suggests that you should encourage your students to talk about their developing understanding of mathematics. Language is a cognitive tool that allows learners to think about the world and solve problems, and the more practice students get putting their understanding into words, the better their understanding will be, and the more their development will be advanced.

3.2 Language is a cognitive tool kit embedded within each culture. In our culture, ice is a simple idea, something we put in our beverages to cool them off. In the Yu'pik culture, however, ice is a more complex concept, and they have more terms and more ways of describing it. Their language reflects the fact that ice is a more complex and important idea in their culture than it is in ours. Because of its importance to their culture, ice is more important to development in their culture.

3.3 The zone of proximal development is the point in your development where you can benefit from instructional support. So, being able to perform word processing skills with support represents your zone of proximal development. Your friend's zone is somewhere beyond your zone, and it might involve sophisticated presentation skills beyond mere word processing. This would be the point where she would need support to advance her development. These differences suggest that her word processing skills are more fully developed than yours.

4.1 Nativist theory, which asserts that children have a language acquisition device that allows them to produce sentences they haven't heard before, provides the best explanation.

Neither behaviorism nor social cognitive theory can adequately explain this particular misuse of language, because it is unlikely that anyone reinforced the child for using the adjective form, "gooder," and it is also unlikely that anyone has modeled it for the child.

Sociocultural theory, which stresses the learning of language in functional settings, also has difficulty explaining this adjective form, because it isn't viewed as culturally acceptable usage.

4.2 Using "gooder" is an example of overgeneralization. The child is overgeneralizing the rule, "To make a comparative adjective, add *er* to it."

4.3 Vocabulary development involves the acquisition of new word meanings. Syntax, by contrast, involves learning the grammatical rules for combining words into sentences that make sense. Both are essential for successful school learning. Without vocabulary development, the meaning of new terms and ideas suffers; without syntax, students have problems expressing ideas and understanding the ideas of others.

Chapter 3

1.1 The components of the model include the individual, the microsystem, mesosystem, exosystem, and macrosystem. Each influences personal, social, and moral development. The microsystem includes immediate influences, such as parents and peers. The mesosystem describes the extent to which the elements of the microsystem interact effectively, such as home–school collaboration. The ecosystem includes societal forces, such as parents' jobs, which can influence the amount of time parents have to spend with their children. The macrosystem is the larger culture in which the individual lives, and it influences development through the values it communicates and the resources it provides to promote development.

1.2 *Authoritative parents* set high expectations and are warm and responsive. Their children tend to be mature, confident, and successful in school. *Authoritarian parents* have high expectations but tend to be cold and unresponsive. Their children tend to be withdrawn and sometimes lack social skills. *Permissive parents* are warm but hold few expectations for their children, who tend to be immature, compulsive, and unmotivated. *Uninvolved parents* have few expectations for their children and are cold and unresponsive. Their children tend to lack self-control and long-term goals.

1.3 Peers influence development through their attitudes and values, opportunities to practice social skills, and emotional support. If peer groups are academically oriented, for example, they promote achievement. Peers, and especially friends, help adolescents understand that they aren't the only ones going through the sometimes confusing changes that occur during this period.

2.1 Physical development—particularly early and late development in teenagers—can strongly influence personal, social, and moral development, and it often has the opposite effect for girls compared to boys. Early physical and sexual development often has adverse effects on girls' socioemotional development and positive effects on boys'. Early-developing boys tend to be more confident and well-adjusted, while early-developing girls tend to be more anxious about themselves and their bodies. By contrast, late-developing boys tend to be more anxious and less well-adjusted, while late-developing girls seem to benefit from the delay.

2.2 Physical development is important to classroom teachers because it also affects other aspects of development, such as social and emotional growth. Healthy physical development is related to healthy social and emotional development and can also set the stage for healthy physical development later in life.

3.1 Erikson's theory would explain the student's behavior by saying that he hasn't positively resolved the initiative–guilt crisis. This doesn't imply that his industry–inferiority or identity–confusion crises cannot be resolved somewhat satisfactorily, however, as indicated by the fact that "he does a good job on his required work," and he "seems to be quite happy." Erikson's work would suggest that this student simply has a personality "glitch" with respect to initiative. It may never have a significant effect on his personal functioning unless he finds himself in a job in which initiative is needed and valued.

You might respond by encouraging him to take initiative and then reinforcing any initiative that he takes. In addition, creating a classroom environment that deemphasizes competition can also encourage student initiative.

3.2 Based on their comments in the conversation, Taylor is in the state of identity achievement. He stated, "I'm going into nursing," and he appeared to have few doubts about his decision.

Sandy's comments suggest that she is at the state of identity diffusion. She has considered veterinary medicine, and she has also given some thought to teaching, but her thinking is somewhat haphazard.

Ramon is at the state of identity foreclosure. His parents want him to be a lawyer, and he has acquiesced to their wishes.

Nancy's comments, "I'm not willing to decide yet," and "I'm going to think about it a while," indicate that she is at the state of identity moratorium.

3.3 The student's comments reflect his self-concept, which is a cognitive appraisal of one's physical, social, and academic competence. Self-esteem, by contrast, is our emotional evaluation of the self, and we see no evidence of either high or low self-esteem in the comments. Self-concept is more closely related to academic achievement than is self-esteem.

4.1 Perspective taking and social problem solving are the two major components of advancing social development. Perspective taking is the ability to understand the thoughts and feelings of others, and teachers promote it by encouraging students to consider the way others might think or feel. Social problem solving is the ability to resolve conflicts in ways that are beneficial to all involved. Like perspective taking, developing this social skill takes time and opportunities to practice.

4.2 The teacher in this case is trying to develop social problem solving. By asking, "What could we do to make both of you happy?" she was attempting to help the children learn to resolve a conflict in ways that would be beneficial to both.

5.1 A driver reasoning at Stage 3 would be likely to say that everybody else is going 65, so it's okay for me to do the same. At Stage 4, a person would be more likely to say

that the law says 55, so I'm slowing down. I don't care what everyone else is doing.

5.2 Gilligan's work would suggest that a woman would be more likely than a man to interpret this incident from an interpersonal perspective. For example, a woman might reason that whispering is justified because they were helping Gary, whereas a man might be more likely to reason that the assignment was given, and Gary, as with everyone else, should know it. According to Gilligan, the major difference between women and men involves the relative emphasis placed on caring and social problem solving (for women) versus abstract justice (for men).

5.3 Empathy, prosocial behaviors, and emotional regulation are most closely related to Kohlberg's Stage 3. People reasoning at this stage make moral decisions based on their concern for others, which is similar to these factors.

Chapter 4

1.1 *Culture* refers to differences in the knowledge, attitudes, values, customs, and ways of acting that characterize different social groups. *Ethnicity* is a part of cultural diversity, and refers to differences in people's ancestry, the way they identify themselves with the nation from which they or their ancestors come. *Culture* is the broader of the two terms, describing differences in the total sets of attitudes, values, and customs of different groups. *Ethnicity* is narrower, referring specifically to differences in people's ancestral heritage.

Culture and ethnicity influence learning through the cultural attitudes, values, and patterns of interaction that students bring to school.

1.2 A resistance culture is characterized by the tendency of its members to reject the attitudes, values, and ways of acting that are characteristic of the majority culture.

To deal with resistance cultures, experts recommend that teachers help members of cultural minorities adapt to the requirements of schools without losing their cultural identities, a process Ogbu (2003) calls "accommodation without assimilation."

1.3 Competition in classrooms is one way in which classroom organization can clash with the values of students who are members of cultural minorities. Competition poses challenges for some students who are members of a cultural minority because it clashes with values of cooperation that are taught at home. Teachers can deal with this problem by deemphasizing student–student comparisons and by using instructional strategies, such as cooperative learning, that emphasize students working with each other.

2.1 Federal legislation, which ended quotas based on national origin, resulted in more immigrants coming to the United States from a wider variety of places. This resulted in much more cultural, ethnic, and linguistic diversity.

Teachers can accommodate this diversity by first communicating that all cultures are valued and respected, such as Gary Nolan did with his students. Second, teachers should involve all students—regardless of cultural background or language skills—in learning activities. Involving students communicates that you believe each student is important and that you expect all students to participate and learn. Third, represent the topics you teach as concretely as possible. Actual objects are most effective, and when they are unavailable, pictures are an acceptable alternative. Finally, maximize opportunities for students to practice language, placing extra emphasis on important vocabulary. When students struggle with particular terms, or with putting their understanding into words, provide prompts and cues to scaffold their efforts.

2.2 English dialects are variations of Standard English that are distinct in vocabulary, grammar, or punctuation. Teachers sometimes misinterpret students' dialects as substandard English, which can lead to lowered evaluations of student work and lowered expectations for student achievement. Effective teachers accept and build on students' dialects and develop bidialecticism in their students.

2.3 The major approaches to helping students who are English learners (ELs) are immersion, maintenance, transitional, English as a second language (ESL) pull-out, and sheltered English. They are similar in that they all have the goal of teaching English. They differ in the extent to which they emphasize maintaining and building on students' native languages, and the amount of structure and support they provide in learning academic content. For example, maintenance programs have the dual goals of maintaining and developing literacy in the native language and also teaching English literacy skills. Transition programs use the first language as an aid to learning English. Pullout and sheltered English programs adapt instruction in content areas by providing scaffolds that assist content acquisition. Immersion programs place students who are ELs in English-only classrooms.

3.1 Gender can influence learning if either girls or boys adopt gender-stereotyped beliefs, such as believing that math or computer science are male domains, or believing that girls are inherently better at English and writing than boys.

Teachers can attempt to eliminate gender bias by openly discussing gender issues, expecting the same academic behaviors from both boys and girls, and inviting nonstereotypical role models to their classes to discuss gender issues.

3.2 Gender-role identity describes beliefs about appropriate characteristics and behaviors of the two sexes. It is important to teachers because a student's gender-role identity can influence how a student approaches different subjects. For example, when girls believe that math and science are male domains, or when boys believe that nursing is a female domain, they are less likely to take related courses or attempt to excel in them.

3.3 Treating boys and girls as equally as possible during learning activities is an important way to reduce gender bias during learning activities. This means calling on boys and girls as equally as possible, keeping the level of questions similar for both, providing similar detail in feedback, and putting them in leadership roles in the classroom.

4.1 *Socioeconomic status (SES)* is a person's relative standing in society resulting from a combination of family income, parents' occupations, and the level of education parents attain. High-income parents, and parents who are in fields such as medicine, law, education, or engineering and architecture, and level of education, such as earning college degrees, are considered to be high in SES.

SES affects learning in three major ways. The first is in the way students' basic needs are met and the quality of their experiences. Poverty can influence a family's ability to provide adequate housing, nutrition, and medical care. SES can also affect the quality of background experiences that adults offer to children. A second way that SES affects learning is by influencing the level of parental involvement; lower-SES parents tend to be less involved in their children's education. A third way SES influences learning is through attitudes and values. For example, many high-SES parents encourage autonomy, individual responsibility, and self-control, whereas lower-SES parents tend to value obedience and conformity. High-SES parents also have positive expectations for their children and encourage them to graduate from high school and attend college; low-SES parents tend to have lower aspirations for academic advancement.

4.2 When considering a student's SES, you should be careful about stereotyping students based on their SES. You should remember that the research describes group patterns, which may or may not apply to individuals. Many lower-SES families provide rich learning environments for their children and have positive attitudes and values that promote learning.

4.3 Schools that promote resilience have high and uncompromising standards, promote strong personal bonds between teachers and students, have high order and structure, and encourage student participation in after-school activities.

Teachers who are effective in promoting resilience in students at risk form strong personal bonds with their students, interacting with them to get to know their families and lives. They maintain high expectations, use interactive teaching strategies, and emphasize success and mastery of content. They also motivate students through personal contacts and instructional support, and they attempt to link school to students' lives.

Effective teachers promote resilience in their students by creating and maintaining productive learning environments. They also combine high expectations with frequent feedback about learning progress. They use interactive teaching strategies that use high-quality examples; both of these help ensure student success. Finally, they stress student self-regulation and the acquisition of learning strategies.

Chapter 5

1.1 One definition of intelligence suggests that it is the ability to acquire and use knowledge, solve problems and reason in the abstract, and adapt to new situations in the environment. A second perspective simply suggests that intelligence is the characteristic or set of characteristics that intelligence tests measure.

Historical views of intelligence suggest that it is a single trait that influences performance across a myriad of tasks. Gardner and Sternberg, in contrast, argue that it is composed of several dimensions. Gardner suggests that the dimensions are relatively independent. Sternberg believes that the ability to adapt to one's environment is an indicator of intelligence.

1.2 Ability grouping is the process of placing students with similar academic abilities in the same learning environments. Research indicates that, while well-intentioned, it has potential drawbacks that can decrease achievement, such as lowered teacher expectations and poorer instruction for those in lower-ability groups.

Experts recommend that teachers minimize its use in classrooms and constantly be aware of potentials for adverse effects.

1.3 The nature view of intelligence asserts that it is essentially determined by genetics; the nurture view of intelligence emphasizes the influence of the environment. Evidence indicates that it is influenced by both. For example, children exposed to enriched learning experiences, both in preschool and in later schooling, score higher on intelligence tests than those lacking the experiences.

2.1 The Individuals with Disabilities Education Act (IDEA) was passed in 1975 to ensure a free and appropriate public education (FAPE) for all students with disabilities. Its provisions stipulate that these children be educated in a least restrictive environment (LRE) and be protected against discrimination in testing. The provisions further guarantee that parents are involved in the development of each child's individualized education program (IEP).

2.2 Recent amendments to IDEA make states responsible for locating children who need special services and have strengthened requirements for nondiscriminatory assessment, due process, parents' involvement in IEPs, and the confidentiality of school records.

2.3 The free and appropriate public education (FAPE) provision of IDEA asserts that every student can learn and is entitled to a FAPE. Mainstreaming, the practice of moving students with exceptionalities from segregated settings into general education classrooms, was the first attempt to meet the requirements of FAPE. Over time, mainstreaming evolved into inclusion, a comprehensive approach to educating students with exceptionalities that advocates a total, systematic, and coordinated web of services.

3.1 The most common learning problems that teachers in general education classrooms are likely to encounter include learning disabilities, which represent difficulties in specific areas, such as reading; attention deficit hyperactivity disorders, indicated by problems with maintaining attention; communication disorders, including speech and language problems; intellectual disabilities, characterized by limitations in intellectual functioning and adaptive behavior; and behavior disorders, characterized by persistent, age-inappropriate behaviors. Visual and hearing disabilities also may exist.

3.2 Learning disabilities and intellectual disabilities are similar in that both are disabilities that interfere with learning. In addition, both can result from a variety of causes, and they are related to some type of central nervous system dysfunction. They are different in that learning disabilities usually involve students with average intelligence or above and are often limited to a specific area such as math or reading, whereas intellectual disabilities involve a broad range of intellectual functioning.

3.3 Students with behavior disorders display serious and persistent age-inappropriate behaviors that result in social conflict, personal unhappiness, and often school failure. Externalizing behavior disorders are characterized by hyperactivity, defiance, hostility, and failure to respond to typical rules and consequences. Internalizing behavior disorders, by contrast, are characterized by social withdrawal, guilt, depression, and anxiety problems.

3.4 Communication disorders are exceptionalities that interfere with students' abilities to receive and to understand information from others and to express their own ideas or questions. Because much of the information and interactions in classrooms are verbal, communication disorders can disrupt the flow of communication and information.

4.1 Characteristics of students who are gifted and talented commonly include the ability to learn quickly and independently, advanced language and reading skills, effective learning and metacognitive strategies, and high motivation and achievement. Educators have broadened the definition of students who are gifted and talented to encompass not only students who score well on intelligence tests but also students who may have unique talents in specific areas such as art, music, or writing. The broadening of this definition means that teachers play a crucial role in helping to identify these students, whose talents may not show up on standardized tests.

4.2 Gifted and talented students are commonly identified through performance on standardized tests and nominations from teachers. However, because tests depend heavily on language, these scores are not always valid, particularly for cultural minorities. And teachers sometimes confuse conformity, neatness, and good behavior with being gifted and talented. Experts recommend the inclusion of—in addition to test scores and teacher recommendations—more flexible and less culturally dependent methods, such as creativity measures, tests of spatial ability, and peer and parent nominations when attempting to identify gifted and talented students.

4.3 Acceleration and enrichment are the two most common methods used for teaching gifted and talented students. Acceleration keeps the curriculum the same but allows students to move through it more quickly. Because it keeps curriculum the same, it is easier to implement, but it maintains a narrow focus on the general education curriculum and may cause developmental problems when younger students are mixed with older ones.

Enrichment, by contrast, alters curriculum and instruction by providing varied instruction. Though harder to implement, it provides students with more choice and flexibility.

5.1 Teachers are expected to fulfill the following roles when working with students having exceptionalities: First, they modify their instruction in attempts to meet individual students' needs. Second, they collaborate with special education specialists in helping students who may have exceptionalities. Collaborative consultation provides teachers with a team of professionals that helps identify and instruct students with exceptionalities. Third, teachers promote the social integration and development of students with exceptionalities. This includes developing classmates' understanding and acceptance of students with exceptionalities and helping students with exceptionalities develop their own social skills.

5.2 Research indicates that the teaching strategies that are effective for all students are also effective for learners with exceptionalities. This means that you teach in the same way that you teach all students, but you make an even greater effort with your students having exceptionalities to ensure learning success. To do this, you'll need to provide additional instructional scaffolding, such as working with these students one-on-one, to ensure learning progress. You may need to adapt homework, seatwork assignments, and reading. You'll also need to teach these students learning strategies, such as how to monitor their attention, take notes, summarize important points, and organize their time.

5.3 You can promote the social integration and growth of students with exceptionalities in the following ways: First, try to help all students understand and appreciate different forms of diversity, including exceptionalities. Second, help students with exceptionalities learn acceptable ways of acting through direct instruction and modeling. Third, use interactive teaching strategies and peer interaction strategies such as peer tutoring and cooperative learning to promote social interaction and integration.

Chapter 6

1.1 The principles on which cognitive learning theory is based are:

- *Learning and development depend on experience.* This principle is evident in our everyday life. Learning to drive is a simple example. If our only experience with driving involves vehicles with automatic transmissions, our ability to drive is less developed than it would be if we have experiences driving cars with both automatic transmissions and with standard stick shifts.

- *People want their experiences to make sense.* People instinctively strive to understand their experiences. They want the world to make sense, and as a result, they attempt to create understanding that makes sense to them.

- *To make sense of their experiences, learners construct knowledge.* Learners don't behave like tape recorders, keeping an exact copy of what they hear or read in their memories. Instead, they mentally modify the experiences so they make sense. This is consistent with a drive to understand their world, which was explained in the description of the second principle.

- *Knowledge that learners construct depends on what they already know.* People construct understanding based on what they already know. For example, many people believe that summers in the northern hemisphere are warmer than winters because we are closer to sun in the summer. (We, in fact, are slightly farther away, but the sun's rays are more direct.) This idea is based on knowing that as we move closer to an open fire or a hot stove burner we get warmer.

- *Social interaction facilitates learning.* As people discuss ideas, they construct understanding that they wouldn't have acquired on their own. This is consistent with the old adage, "Two heads are better than one."

1.2 This illustrates the principle *social interaction facilitates learning.* You have a problem, you discuss it, and you solve it during the course of the discussion. You can solve the problem because your friend provided you with information—suggesting looking at where the speakers are attached—and you build on her idea.

1.3 The following principles of learning all apply in this example: *People want their experiences to make sense; to make sense of their experiences, people construct knowledge; and the knowledge that people construct depends on what they already know.* Since oil is "thicker" than water, it makes sense that it would also be "heavier." So,

concluding that the side with the oil would go down is a sensible conclusion.

Your friend constructed this conclusion on his own, and he constructed it because it made sense to him. It's unlikely that someone explained it this way or that he read it, since the conclusion is invalid.

In general, "thicker" substances are indeed more dense than those less thick, so your friend constructed this conclusion based on what he already knew, or on the basis of past experiences.

2.1 Cognitive constructivism is based on the view that knowledge construction is an internal, individual process, whereas social constructivism is grounded in the position that knowledge construction first occurs in the social environment and then is appropriated and internalized by individuals.

2.2 Suzanne's thinking better illustrates cognitive constructivism. She had a clear (to her) schema that guided her thinking (her belief that keeping the number of tiles equal on each side of the fulcrum would make the beam balance), and she brought this view to the learning activity. It didn't result from her interaction with her peers.

2.3 This is an example of situated cognition. The teacher presented several examples of diphthongs—*oy, ou, oo,* and *ow.* However, *ou* was used in two different ways—*house* and *could; oo* is used in three different ways—*looks, moon,* and *floor;* and *ow* is used in two different ways—*bowed* and *owl.* The children would have been unable to determine the differences if the examples had not been embedded (situated) in the context of the passage.

3.1 A misconception is a belief that is inconsistent with evidence or commonly accepted explanations. Simply, they occur because people construct them, and the principles of learning discussed at the beginning of the chapter help us understand why. First, people have experience consistent with the misconception, like you saw with the example of the ball in flight, and second, the misconception makes sense to the person who originally constructs it.

3.2 People's prior experiences are the most common source of misconceptions, and many examples exist. For instance, as you saw earlier in the chapter, because 5 is greater than 3, some children believe that 1/5 is greater than 1/3.

Appearances are a second source of misconceptions. For example, because oil appears "thick," some people, until they think about it, believe that it is more dense than water. But, we know it's less dense, since it floats on water.

Society is a third source. For instance, minority youth are often led to believe that professional sports is a realistic career goal as an adult, but statistics indicate that the vast majority of student athletes never make it to the pro ranks.

Finally, language can contribute to misconceptions. The news media will periodically refer to the danger of "heavy metals" such as lead and mercury, when, in fact, any metal can be "heavy" depending on the amount of it that exists.

3.3 First, the original misconception must become dissatisfying. This means that students need convincing evidence that the misconception is invalid, such as Suzanne saw when they tried her solution and it didn't work.

Second, an alternative explanation must become satisfying. When Suzanne could see that the beam would balance if she took both the number of tiles and the distance from the fulcrum into account, the alternative conception became more satisfying.

Third, the new conception must be useful. Suzanne was able to explain the solution to an additional problem using the new conception.

4.1 The suggestions for classroom practice and their connection to the principles of learning are outlined as follows:
- *Provide your students with experiences using high-quality examples.* Examples and other representations are the experiences students use to construct their knowledge. These experiences provide the background knowledge students need to construct their understanding, because the understanding that is constructed depends on the knowledge that students already possess.
- *Connect content to the real world.* Situated cognition suggests that the knowledge students construct depends on the context in which it is constructed. Real-world contexts make knowledge construction more meaningful by showing students how ideas relate to their lives.
- *Promote high levels of social interaction.* The learning principle *social interaction facilitates learning* and social constructivist learning theory both suggest that knowledge is first constructed in a social environment and is later appropriated by individuals.
- *Treat verbal explanations skeptically.* Students construct their own knowledge that makes sense to them. If an explanation doesn't make sense to a student, the student will reconstruct and remember the

information in a way that does make sense. This helps us understand why "wisdom can't be told." Explaining tries to "tell" wisdom, instead of guiding students in the knowledge construction process.
- *Promote learning with assessment.* Because students construct their own knowledge, the knowledge they construct will vary. Ongoing assessment is the only way to determine if their constructions are valid.

4.2 "Connect content to the real world" is the suggestion best illustrated. Studying the rules in the context of a written passage is a more nearly real-world task than studying the rules in the context of isolated sentences. Having the students write their own essays using possessives would also be effective.

4.3 Effective assessments provide teachers with insights into students' thinking. This means that the reasoning students use to arrive at their answers is as important as the answers themselves.

Chapter 7

1.1 The human memory model is the cognitive architecture that can be used to describe how people gather, organize, and store their experiences. It is composed of memory stores, repositories that hold information; cognitive processes that move information from one store to another; and metacognition, which monitors and regulates both the storage and movement of information.

1.2 The arrow and the term *response* are intended to represent the fact that our responses come from working memory. It is the conscious part of our information-processing system.

1.3 These arrows are intended to represent the fact that metacognition regulates the cognitive processes. If, for example, you shut music off while you study because it's distracting you, you are making a conscious effort to control your attention. This is a form of metacognition.

2.1 The characteristics of working memory suggest that students should memorize math facts. If being able to recall the facts is automatic, cognitive load on the students is reduced, and they have more working memory space to devote to problem solving and other complex tasks.

2.2 We can again use the characteristics of working memory to answer this question. 2HEALTH has been chunked into two units, so 2HEALTH imposes a lighter load on working memory than do the numbers 243–2584. Since the load is lighter, the information is easier to encode and remember.

2.3 Procedural knowledge, as with declarative knowledge, is stored in long-term memory. An example in the opening case that illustrates students being required to demonstrate procedural knowledge occurred when David said, "Be sure you write and explain each of your answers," after he presented the students with the questions. Being required to write the answers required the students to use procedural knowledge.

Developing procedural knowledge requires a great deal of practice and also strongly depends on declarative knowledge. In this case, declarative knowledge about the particular aspect of the solar system that they were examining would be required.

3.1 The cognitive processes in the human memory model are:
- *Attention.* Attention is the process of focusing on a particular stimulus or group of stimuli and ignoring the myriad of other stimuli that exist. The idea of "white noise" relates to the concept of attention. We are often not aware of "white noise" such as the whisper of an air conditioner until we're made aware of its existence—until we attend to it.
- *Perception.* Perception is the process of attaching meaning to stimuli. It is illustrated by the fact that we commonly see two people have the same experience but interpret it very differently.
- *Rehearsal.* Rehearsal is the process of repeating information over and over without altering its form, such as memorizing names, dates, and other facts, such as $8 \times 7 = 56$. Elaborative rehearsal, the process of linking information to be learned to existing information, is much more effective than is maintenance rehearsal. When rehearsal moves information to long-term memory, it is a form of encoding.
- *Encoding.* Encoding is the process of representing information in long-term memory. The goal in encoding is to make the information as meaningful as possible by connecting it to knowledge already in long-term memory.
- *Retrieval.* Retrieval is the process of pulling information from long-term memory back into working memory. Retrieval is an essential process, because constructing new knowledge depends on knowledge that already exists in long-term memory.

3.2 When a teacher asks, "What do we mean by plot development?" she is checking her students' perceptions, because she is attempting to determine what the idea means to them. The most effective way of checking students' perceptions is to simply ask them—ask them what they see or notice, or ask them what the information in a picture, term, passage, map, graph, or whatever is displayed means to them.

3.3 The students used *rehearsal* when they practiced with the flash cards. We see no evidence in the description that the students were relating the facts in the flash cards to other information, which would involve elaboration.

When the students compared the problems to problems they had solved in class, they were using *schema activation* and *elaboration* as encoding strategies.

4.1 *Metacognition,* often described as "thinking about thinking," is our awareness of, and control over, our cognitive processes. Metacognition regulates the way we process information. For instance, an individual who is aware that she is not fully comprehending the information she is reading, and who stops periodically to summarize what she has read, is demonstrating metacognition. Because she is metacognitive, she will process the information she is reading more efficiently, and learning will be increased. Learners who are metacognitive recognize when they are using an ineffective strategy and then modify the strategy, or select a new strategy, in order to increase their understanding. The result is higher achievement.

4.2 Yes, stopping and going back to the top of the page and rereading one of the sections is an example of metacognition. You realize that you haven't understood the section (which is knowledge awareness of your memory strategy), and you go back and reread (which is exercising control over your memory strategy).

4.3 You are more metacognitive in your note taking than your friend. You are continually making decisions about what information is most important to write down, which demonstrates knowledge of, and control over, your thinking about note taking. (And, because you're constantly making decisions, you are more cognitively active than your friend.)

Chapter 8

1.1 A concept is a mental class or category constructed in such a way that an individual can identify examples and nonexamples of the category. Young children gradually acquire (construct) concepts by encountering examples and nonexamples of them in their daily experiences. For instance, the child is out with his mother and she points to a car and says, "Car!" After seeing several cars, he begins to say, "Car," when he sees one. Then, if he sees a pickup truck and says, "Car," his mother then says something like, "No, honey, that's a truck." The pickup truck serves as a nonexample for *car,* and this process helps him differentiate between cars and trucks. Gradually, he constructs a concept of each. As he acquires additional experiences, he learns more precise distinctions, such as the difference between a car, truck, and SUV. The same process applies with all the concepts that young children—and people of all ages—learn.

1.2 The concept *noun* is easier to learn than the concept *culture* because it obeys a well-defined rule that says a noun must be the name of a person, place, or thing. Also, its characteristics are more concrete than are the characteristics of the concept *culture*. The rule-driven theory best explains how people learn the concept *noun*. The exemplar theory of concept learning best explains how we construct the concept *culture*.

1.3 Typically, students—and people in general—think that an adverb is a word that ends in "ly," and they likely do so because it's simple and easy to remember. Providing an example of an adverb that does not end in "ly" helps learners realize that some adverbs don't end in "ly," and that they must consider how the word functions in a sentence rather than simply center on the "ly."

2.1 This is an ill-defined problem. Because the problem is ill-defined, the goal is ambiguous. So, to solve it you must first specify your goal or goals. For example, you might define *thinking* as the ability to make conclusions based on evidence. Then, as a strategy you might provide your students with practice in answering questions, the answers for which are not specifically stated in their books. As they attempt to answer these questions, you encourage them to provide evidence for each answer they give. In time, and with extensive practice, the students' thinking will gradually improve.

2.2 In being satisfied with the fact that their answers varied, the students ineffectively applied the *evaluate the results* stage of problem solving. This tendency illustrates a common problem in problem-solving activities. Students tend to be satisfied with their answers whether or not they make sense. Requiring students to justify their thinking by providing reasons for their answers and asking for estimates can increase their metacognition about their problem solving.

2.3 To make your problem solving as meaningful as possible, you should first attempt to solve the problem before you look at the solution. Doing so puts you in a cognitively active role, whereas simply reading the problem and then reading the solution is less cognitively active.

3.1 No, reading the chapter carefully is not strategic learning. Strategic learning is the application of cognitive operations that go beyond the normal activities required to carry out a task. While you are attempting to read carefully and understand the content, you are not applying any strategy that goes beyond the normal activity—reading—required to carry out the task.

3.2 Ruiz's strategy is the most effective, because he is demonstrating the highest level of metacognition in his approach. He is making conscious decisions about what information is most important to highlight. Will's strategy is the least effective, because passive highlighting requires little cognitive effort and is the least metacognitive. (Even though he is physically "active" in highlighting whole chapters, he is cognitively passive, because he isn't thinking about the process.)

3.3 Francisco's comment, "We found a pattern in the data," best illustrates metacognition. He recognized that they had previously found a pattern. Students' being aware of their thought processes is an essential component of critical thinking.

4.1 With respect to transfer, the students are least likely to identify a dolphin as a mammal, because it is least similar to the other examples. Similarity between the two learning situations is the factor that is best illustrated in this case.

4.2 Based on the factors that affect transfer, your efforts were not effective. First, pictures of the mammals, while better than written words, are not as high quality as a live mammal, such as a student's hamster, would be. A combination of one or two live mammals, such as the hamster and the students themselves, combined with pictures, would be much higher quality. Second, the variety of examples is inadequate. Better variety would include a bat, so they see that some mammals fly; a whale, porpoise, or some other aquatic mammal, so the students don't conclude that only fish live in water; and perhaps an egg-laying mammal, such as a duck-billed platypus. Finally, we have no evidence of whether the examples were presented in any realistic context so students could see characteristics of mammals, like warm-blooded and giving live birth, in the examples.

4.3 Choice 2 is the most effective example. It is the only one that actually illustrates the concept. Choice 1 illustrates only a thoughtful look, and the words, "The girl is experiencing internal conflict," provide little critical information. It could even lead to the misconception that whenever people look thoughtful, they're experiencing internal conflict. Choice 3 is only a definition. Definitions are abstract, and often students don't do much more than memorize definitions. Definitions, alone, lead to superficial learning.

Chapter 9

1.1 In Pavlov's experiments, the meat powder was the unconditioned stimulus, in response to which the dogs reflexively salivated as unconditioned (unlearned) responses. The lab assistants became associated with the meat powder, so the lab assistants, which were neutral stimuli before they brought the meat powder, became conditioned stimuli, and the dog's salivation at the sight of the lab assistants were conditioned responses. The dogs *learned* to salivate at the sight of the lab assistants.

1.2 We can explain Tim's nervousness following his bad experience in the following way. Tim failed the algebra quiz and was devastated as a result. The failure was an unconditioned stimulus and the devastation was an unconditioned response. He associated subsequent quizzes with the initial failure, so they became conditioned stimuli, which caused nervousness as conditioned responses. He learned to be nervous in those quizzes. Notice that the conditioned response is similar to the unconditioned response, and both were out of Tim's control, that is, they were involuntary.

Tim's nervousness later decreased because he took additional quizzes (conditioned stimuli) without experiencing failure (the unconditioned stimulus), so his anxiety (the conditioned response) became extinct. (Similarly, and unfortunately, if you continue to hear a song that triggers a romantic feeling, but you don't have a romantic encounter with which the song was originally associated, the song will eventually stop triggering the romantic feeling.)

1.3 In the case of our test anxiety, some event during a test in our past, such as happened in Tim's case, caused us to feel anxiety or an emotion similar to anxiety. The event is the unconditioned stimulus, and the anxiety is the unconditioned response. Subsequent tests became associated with the event, as also was the case with Tim, so the tests became conditioned stimuli, and our test anxiety was the conditioned response. We learned to be anxious in tests.

In the case of learning to fear spiders and snakes, we initially had some frightening experience. The experience (event) was the unconditioned stimulus, and the fear or panic we felt was the unconditioned response. Spiders and snakes became associated with the experience, so they became a conditioned stimulus, and a fear similar to the initial fear was the conditioned response. We learned to fear these.

In the example with the warm feeling when smelling Thanksgiving turkey, the warm feeling is the conditioned response, and the smell is the conditioned stimulus. The unconditioned stimulus is past experience at Thanksgiving, such as being in the company of loving family members, and the unconditioned response is the warm feeling that results from being around family. The smell of turkey is associated with the company of loving family, and we learned to react with a warm feeling at the smell of Thanksgiving turkey.

In the case of the uneasy feeling in a dentist's office, the office is the conditioned stimulus, and the uneasy feeling is the conditioned response. Having dental work done is the unconditioned stimulus, and the discomfort that results is the conditioned response. The dentist's office is associated with having dental work done. We learned to feel uneasy when entering the dentist's office.

1.4 Our reaction to Latin music illustrates the concept *generalization*. Other forms of Latin music are stimuli similar to the initial conditioned stimulus (the song we heard when we had the romantic encounter), so our emotion has generalized to all forms of romantic Latin music. We *discriminate*, however, between Latin and rock music.

2.1 Judy's off-task behavior is increasing; she goes off task sooner the second time you admonish her than she did the first time. You presented her with your admonishment, and her behavior is increasing, so you have (unintentionally) positively reinforced her. We can explain her behavior by saying that she has been positively reinforced for going off task. This possibility has important implications for teachers. You intended to stop the off-task behavior, but your admonishment had the opposite effect.

2.2 We can explain Rick's behavior by saying that he is being punished (with presentation punishment) for the lengths of the tests he gives. His behavior is decreasing—he is decreasing the length of his tests—as a result of being presented with the students' complaints.

We can explain the students' behavior by saying that they are being negatively reinforced for complaining. Their complaining is increasing—they complained sooner each time—and the negative reinforcer is Rick's removing an aversive stimulus—some of the test material.

2.3 Because the beeper depends on time, it is an interval schedule, and because it is unpredictable (the students don't know when the beeper will go off), it is a variable-interval schedule.

2.4 The displayed exercise is the antecedent; it induces the desired behavior. The students' conscientious work is the behavior, and Anita's compliments are the reinforcers.

3.1 The ineffectiveness of this practice can be explained using the nonoccurrence of expected consequences. In cooperative learning groups, some students make a greater contribution than others. Those who make the greater contribution expect to be reinforced by receiving a higher grade than those who contributed less. When all members of the group receive the same grade, the expectation isn't met, so the nonoccurrence of the expected reinforcer can act as a punisher, making a similar contribution in the next cooperative learning activity less likely. The nonoccurrence of the expected reinforcer can also lead to resentment, a problem in some cooperative learning activities (Cohen, 1994).

3.2 Reciprocal causation describes the interdependence of the environment, personal factors (e.g., beliefs and expectations), and behavior. In Mike's case, the environment (the first instructor's class) influenced his behavior (he often drifted off), and his behavior influenced his expectations (he believed he wasn't learning). In turn, his behavior influenced the environment (he switched to Mr. Adams's class); the environment influenced a personal factor (he expected to be called on); and the personal factor influenced his behavior (he paid attention as a result of his expectation).

3.3 The benched player was punished, and being punished explains why that player didn't commit the foul again. The rest of the team was vicariously punished through the benching of the player who committed the foul. They expected to be benched for committing a similar foul, so they avoided doing so.

3.4 Tim was vicariously reinforced through Susan's success, and she was a model for him. He observed the consequences of her study habits, and he changed his behavior accordingly. He sustained his efforts because he expected to be reinforced for imitating Susan's behavior.

4.1 Because the speech was seen on a DVD, it is a form of symbolic modeling. The modeling is likely to be effective because Martin Luther King, Jr., is a high-status model. For African American students, the modeling would be especially effective because of perceived similarity. Assuming that students knew how to be idealistic, the modeling outcome most likely would facilitate existing behaviors. If we assume that the students didn't know how to be idealistic, the outcome could involve learning new behaviors. Emotional arousal is also likely, because of the powerful way he delivered his speech.

4.2 The person who first crossed the street is a direct model. You imitated the behavior of a live person instead of someone you saw on TV, in the movies, or in a book. The model's behavior weakened your inhibition about crossing the street against the red light. The modeling outcome is changing inhibitions instead of facilitating an existing behavior because crossing the street against a red light is socially unacceptable.

4.3 Your self-regulation began with a goal: to answer and understand each of the "Check Your Understanding" questions in the chapter. You monitored your progress by checking off each question that you answered and understood. You completed a self-assessment by checking your answers against the feedback in Appendix A, and you modified your strategy if you answered incorrectly.

Chapter 10

1.1 Motivation is a process whereby goal-directed activity is instigated and sustained. Motivation influences learning by maintaining efforts to reach personal goals.

1.2 Behaviorism describes motivation in the same way that it describes learning. For example, an increase in behavior is viewed as evidence of learning, and it is also viewed as evidence of motivation.

 Cognitive views of motivation describe motivation as people's need to understand and make sense of their experiences. Social cognitive views emphasize the role of beliefs, expectations, and observing the actions of others in their explanations of motivation.

 Sociocultural views of motivation focus on individuals' participating in a learning community. Through participating in a community in which all members help each other learn, individuals' motivation to learn is increased.

 Humanistic views of motivation describe motivation as people's attempts to fulfill their total potential as human beings and to become self-actualized.

2.1 According to Maslow, deficiency needs—survival, safety, belonging, and self-esteem—must be met before students will be motivated to move to growth needs. This suggests, for example, that students must feel safe (both physically and emotionally) in classrooms if they are going to be motivated to learn.

2.2 As learners get evidence that their competence is increasing, their motivation to learn also increases. This explains why praise for genuine accomplishment can increase intrinsic motivation. Similarly, as students' perceptions of autonomy increase, so does their motivation to learn. And when students believe that their teachers are committed to them both as learners and as people, they are motivated to learn, because these teachers help students meet their need for relatedness.

2.3 High ability is strongly valued in our society, so self-worth is linked to perceptions of high ability. Students' motivation to learn often depends on maintaining perceptions of high ability to maintain their sense of self-worth. Teachers can help reduce this inclination by deemphasizing social comparisons and emphasizing the belief that ability can be increased with effort.

3.1 Beliefs are ideas we accept as true without necessarily having definitive evidence to support them. Expectations, for example, are beliefs about future outcomes. If learners believe that they're going to succeed, their motivation to learn is likely to increase. The opposite is true if they don't believe they're going to succeed.

Similarly, if learners believe they can accomplish a specific task (high self-efficacy), they are more likely to persevere on the task than if they don't believe they can. And, if learners believe that accomplishing a task has high attainment or utility value, they are also more likely to persevere.

3.2 This statement best illustrates *utility value.* For the individual, studying algebra has high utility value. He isn't intrinsically interested in algebra, and may not believe that he is particularly good at it, but he believes it will be valuable to him in the future. Utility value is a component of expectancy × value theory.

3.3 Because Armondo attributed his success to luck, his emotional reaction is likely to be neutral. Because luck is external, he won't feel the pride that attributing his success to either ability or effort would cause. (Because he succeeded, he also won't feel the shame that results from failure that is attributed to lack of ability, or guilt that people feel when they attribute failure to lack of effort.) Because his success resulted from luck, he won't expect similar results in the future, his future effort is likely to decrease, and, as a result, his achievement is also likely to decrease.

Ashley's emotional reaction is likely to be frustration or something similar to it, because task difficulty is not controllable. Because she is out of control, she is not likely to expect success in the future, and her motivation and learning will decrease.

4.1 Learners' goals can influence their motivation to learn in several ways. For example, students with mastery goals persist on challenging tasks, accept challenges, and use effective strategies. Students with performance-approach goals may use superficial learning strategies, exert only enough effort to perform on the task, and engage in self-handicapping strategies. Students with performance-avoidance goals emphasize avoiding looking incompetent and being judged unfavorably by others, and to do so, they may avoid the very tasks that can lead to competence. Social goals can either increase or decrease motivation to learn (see the feedback for item 4.2), and work-avoidance goals strongly detract from both motivation and learning.

4.2 The combination of mastery goals and social-responsibility goals results in the highest level of motivation and achievement. Mastery goals focus on understanding and mastery of tasks, and social-responsibility goals emphasize avoiding disappointing others. The combination of the two leads to sustained effort, and with it, increased achievement.

5.1 Connecting topics to the real world, personalizing content, involving students, using concrete examples, and making clear and logical presentations can all increase learner interest. Teachers can also increase interest by giving students choices when opportunities exist.

5.2 The most effective way of capitalizing on emotions to increase motivation to learn is by attempting to increase learner interest, because interesting activities arouse positive emotions. Teachers can also capitalize on emotions to increase motivation to learn by raising questions about moral issues and personal characteristics related to the topics they teach. For instance, beginning a study of the American Revolution by posing questions about the fairness of taxes levied by the British, their rationale for imposing them, and the colonists' reactions can provoke emotional reactions and increased interest.

5.3 Teachers can reduce anxiety in students in several ways, including the following:
- Make clear and specific your expectations about learning and how you will assess students.
- Use instructional strategies that promote understanding, such as providing high-quality examples, promoting student involvement, and providing specific feedback on assessments.
- Provide outside help for students who request it.
- Drop one or two quizzes during a grading period for purposes of assigning grades.

These strategies won't eliminate anxiety in all cases or for all students, but they can be important factors in reducing anxiety for many students.

Chapter 11

1.1 A mastery-focused classroom emphasizes effort, improvement, and deep understanding of the topics being studied. A performance-focused classroom emphasizes high grades, public displays of ability, and performance compared to others.

1.2 Based on the descriptions of mastery-focused and performance-focused classrooms, this is an ineffective comment. The statement, "Excellent job on the last test, everyone. More than half the class got an A or a B," emphasizes high grades and performance instead of effort, improvement, and understanding.

2.1 Teachers who increase students' motivation to learn believe they can increase student learning regardless of their teaching conditions or students' backgrounds (high personal teaching efficacy). They care about their students as people, and they are committed to their students' learning. They model desirable characteristics, demonstrate enthusiasm by communicating their own genuine interest in the topics they teach, and create positive expectations for their students.

2.2 High-efficacy teachers believe that their efforts to help students learn make a difference, whereas low-efficacy teachers believe that their efforts are largely in vain. Because low-efficacy teachers don't believe that they make a difference anyway, trying something new—according to their beliefs—is not likely to matter. As a result, they are not inclined to try new curriculum materials or strategies.

2.3 The most effective way to communicate your enthusiasm to students is to model your own genuine interest in the topics you're teaching. Because people tend to imitate behaviors they observe in others, if students see that you are truly interested in the topics you're teaching, the likelihood that they also will be interested increases.

2.4 Teachers call on students who, they expect, will be able to answer their questions. If they don't believe that a student can answer, they are less likely to call on the student.

 Two factors explain this tendency. First, a student's answering the question is reinforcing for the teacher. Second, if a student can't answer, the teacher should provide prompts or cues that will help the student give an acceptable answer. Thinking of these prompts and cues during the course of a lesson presents a heavy cognitive load for the teacher.

3.1 Classrooms that increase motivation to learn are orderly and safe, students experience success on challenging tasks, and they understand what they're supposed to be learning and why the topic is important (task comprehension).

3.2 Based on the discussion of the climate variables in the Model for Promoting Student Motivation, the teacher's approach would be unlikely to increase students' motivation to learn, even if they succeed. First, the task presents a minimal level of challenge, and no rationale for the task is evident.

3.3 The two variables in the Model for Promoting Student Motivation that the teacher is attempting to address are order and safety and task comprehension. Enforcing a rule that prevents students from making sarcastic or demeaning comments promotes a sense of emotional security, and providing a rationale is consistent with task comprehension.

4.1 Teachers can increase students' motivation to learn when they consciously plan to attract students' *attention* and provide a conceptual umbrella for the lesson (*introductory focus*), *personalize content*, promote high levels of *involvement* in learning activities, and provide informative *feedback* about learning progress.

4.2 The best example of the way DeVonne personalized her lesson was by asking the students if Mrs. Sapp (the school principal) was an arthropod.

4.3 Mastery-oriented feedback provides information about existing understanding or information that teachers use to increase understanding. For instance, "Your paragraph needs to include at least two supporting details for your conclusion. Your second sentence is the only supporting detail in your paragraph" is an example of mastery-oriented feedback about the quality of written paragraphs.

 Performance-oriented feedback describes grades or comparisons among students. Examples include statements such as, "Well done. You got all the points on your essay," or "There were five A's and four B's on the last quiz."

Chapter 12

1.1 The goals of classroom management include: Developing student self-regulation, creating communities of caring and trust, and maximizing time available for learning. The goals are interdependent. For example, as students become self-regulated, and they learn to control their impulses and behave in socially appropriate ways, communities of caring and trust are easier to create, and time available for learning is increased.

1.2 Strategies for promoting learner self-regulation typically involve setting and monitoring goals. Getting students to commit to the goals is an essential aspect of the process. Sam promoted commitment to goals by emphasizing the relationship between personal responsibility and learning, soliciting student input into class procedures, providing examples of responsible and irresponsible behavior, modeling responsibility, and providing a chart that students could use to monitor progress toward their goals.

1.3 Sam recognized that his students would initially be externally regulated, which meant that they would behave responsibly to receive rewards for meeting their responsibility and learning goals and avoid being punished (e.g., spending "quiet time" alone) if they failed to meet their social responsibility goals.

His students would advance in self-regulation if, at a later point in the year, they decided to set and meet social responsibility and learning goals because they believed that meeting the goals would help them get better grades. This would still illustrate extrinsic motivation, but it would be an advance in self-regulation.

1.4 The suggestion to call on all students as equally as possible most closely relates to engaged time. Teachers call on students to involve them in learning activities, or in other words, to engage them. Being called on doesn't ensure that students will succeed, so academic learning time isn't as directly addressed.

2.1 Because their thinking is concrete, children in elementary schools need rules that are clear and concrete. Rules and procedures must be explicitly taught as Martha Oakes did with her first graders. The number of rules should be kept small, because one of the most common reasons for breaking rules in elementary schools is that the children simply forget them.

The influence of peers increases in middle schools, and their needs for belonging, social acceptance, autonomy, and independence increase. Providing reasons for rules, and enforcing rules fairly and consistently, becomes increasingly important with these students.

High school students' behavior tends to stabilize, they communicate more effectively at an adult level, and they respond well to clear rationales for rules and the need to accept personal responsibility.

2.2 As students mature, they are less likely to hit, poke, and otherwise put their hands on other students. As a result, a rule requiring them to keep their hands to themselves is less necessary with older students.

2.3 Examples provide the experiences learners use to construct their understanding of the topics they study. They construct their understanding of rules and procedures in the same way that they construct understanding of any other topic.

3.1 Formal communication with parents includes open houses, interim progress reports, and report cards. Teachers can enhance communication with a beginning-of-school letter to parents expressing a commitment to learning, optimism about the school year, and a general description of class procedures. In addition, some teachers send packets of work home to parents, which are to be signed and returned. Finally, calling or e-mailing parents about both positive and negative events is an important part of the overall communication process.

3.2 First, Jacinta helped develop learner self-regulation by involving students in preparing the letter home. Second, the letter contributed to the creation of a caring, trusting classroom climate by making all students in her class feel welcome and important. Over time, reaching the first two goals would contribute to reaching the third—maximizing time for teaching and learning.

3.3 Time is a unique resource in that everyone has the same amount of it. So, the way people choose to allocate their time is a direct indicator of their priorities. When teachers choose to allocate some of their personal time to calling or e-mailing parents, it communicates to parents that the child is important.

4.1 People's need to make sense of their experiences is the framework on which all cognitive interventions are based. For example, when teachers' verbal and nonverbal behaviors are congruent, the communication makes sense. Also, when a person describes a behavior combined with the impact that the behavior has on others, as is the case with I-messages, the communication also makes sense. And, logical consequences make sense. For example, it made more sense to Allen to have to pick up Alyssia's books when he knocked them out of her hands than serving detention would have.

4.2 First, praising desired behavior is a form of positive reinforcement. The next point, ignoring inappropriate behavior, is an application of extinction, which is the process of not reinforcing a behavior. The next point, using indirect cues capitalizes on vicarious reinforcement. Desists are mild punishers, and applying consequences, such as timeout, is another form of punishment.

4.3 An effective I-message that a teacher could use in responding to a student's talking might be: "Talking interrupts my teaching, this makes me lose my train of thought, and I get annoyed when my train of thought is disrupted." It addressed the behavior (talking), describes the effect on the sender (makes me lose my train of thought), and describes the feelings generated in the sender (annoyance when my train of thought is disrupted).

4.4 Having the student wash the door is the preferred consequence. It is logical; if you spit on the door and make it dirty, you should wash it. Being put in detention is a punishment, but no logical connection exists between the behavior and the consequence.

5.1 You are required by law to intervene in the case of a fight or other aggressive act. Failure to do so can result in being sued for negligence. You are not legally required to break up the fight; immediately reporting it to administrators is acceptable.

5.2 First, you must attempt to stop the fighting or bullying if possible. If a loud noise, such as shouting or slamming a chair on the floor, doesn't stop it, immediately send an uninvolved student for help. Second, you should protect the victim, and third, you should get help if you have not already done so.

5.3 Long-term cognitive approaches to bullying focus on helping students develop social skills, such as self-control, perspective taking, expressing anger verbally instead of physically, and learning to make and defend arguments.

Chapter 13

1.1 The four essential steps involved in planning for instruction consist of the following:
   1. *Identify topics.* Standards, curriculum guides, textbooks, and the teacher's professional knowledge are sources that help make this decision.
   2. *Specify learning objectives.* Though the format for preparing learning objectives varies, the important aspect of preparing learning objectives is clarity about desired learning outcomes.
   3. *Prepare and organize learning activities.* A task analysis can be helpful in this process: identify the components of the topic, sequence them, and prepare and order examples.
   4. *Plan for assessments.* This means that assessments are created during planning instead of after learning activities have been completed.

   As you implement these steps, you should also carefully analyze the relationship between the learning objective(s), learning activity, and assessment to be sure that they are aligned; that is, the learning activity and assessment are consistent with the learning objective and each other.

1.2 When your planning involves standards, interpreting the standard is an additional step, and it precedes the other steps. Descriptions of standards vary; some are very specific, whereas others are quite general. When working with a standard described in general terms, teachers must first make a decision about what the standard means, then follow the rest of the planning steps; that is, plan learning activities and assessments.

1.3 This objective is best classified into the cell where metacognitive knowledge intersects with analyze. The tendency to look for relevant and irrelevant information in all the topics suggests metacognition, and determining what is relevant and irrelevant involves analysis.

2.1 Essential teaching skills are the abilities that all teachers should possess. They are analogous to the basic skills of reading, writing, and math that all people need to function effectively in our world. Essential teaching skills are the abilities that all teachers, regardless of content area, topic, or grade level, should have in order to function effectively in classrooms. They are important because they help promote learning in all students.

2.2 The case studies that introduce each chapter are our attempts to provide focus for the chapters. They are intended to attract your attention by beginning the chapter with a realistic look at classrooms. Then, the cases provide an umbrella under which we develop the content of the chapter.

2.3 The two essential teaching skills that are best illustrated in each chapter are feedback and review and closure. For example, in Appendix A, you receive feedback for all of the "Check Your Understanding" questions. When you go to Appendix B, you receive feedback for all of the "Preparing for Your Licensure Exam" questions that appear at the end of each chapter.

   In the summary of each chapter, you receive a review of the chapter's contents, which are aligned with the learning outcomes.

   We also attempt to model effective, clear communication in our writing. We try to use clear language; to emphasize important points with figures, tables, bulleted lists, and margin definitions; and to develop the chapters in thematic ways that represent connected discourse.

3.1 The introduction phase of direct instruction, lecture–discussion, and guided discovery is important because it capitalizes on focus. Focus attracts students' attention and provides a conceptual umbrella for the lesson.

   We can also explain the need for the introduction phase using the human memory model. Effective processing begins with attention. If learners don't attend to information, it is lost, so attracting and maintaining attention are essential. The introduction phase addresses this need.

3.2 The presentation phase of direct instruction is most important for ensuring successful independent practice, and it is in this phase that we see the most difference between effective and ineffective teachers. If the presentation phase is ineffective, both guided practice and independent practice will be difficult and confusing. Remember, independent practice strengthens earlier understanding; it does not teach the skill. If teachers have to provide a great deal of explanation during independent practice, error rates increase and student achievement decreases.

3.3 Effective instruction requires that the teacher's objectives are clear and the learning activity is aligned with the objectives. Also, the teacher should carefully monitor students' thinking throughout and intervene when necessary to prevent misconceptions, but not so soon that opportunities for constructing understanding are reduced.

3.4 She introduced cooperative learning quite effectively. Her task was short and simple, it was clear and specific: write three differences on paper. These written differences provided a product, which increased accountability, and she monitored students' work.

4.1 First, effective assessments are aligned with a teacher's objectives and learning activity. Second, effective assessments give teachers information about students' thinking, as you saw with Scott's item that asked students to explain what made the papers go together.

4.2 Feedback is the essential teaching skill that teachers must use in conjunction with assessments if the assessments are to increase student learning. This means that teachers should always thoroughly discuss assessment items after scoring and returning them to students, which allows students to revise and elaborate on their thinking.

4.3 The primary problem with the assessment (and the learning activity) is that it is not aligned with his learning objective. His objective was for them to use figurative language in their writing. But we saw no evidence that they practiced writing. Giving them examples, and having them identify examples, is an effective first step, but if the assessment is aligned with the objective, his assessment must require them to write.

Chapter 14

1.1 Assessment *for* learning makes assessment an integral part of the teaching–learning process and is designed to support and increase learning. It includes diagnosing students' current understanding, attempting to increase students' motivation to learn and self-regulation, and measuring student achievement.

To promote learning, all forms of assessment must be valid and reliable. Assessments that are invalid or unreliable don't provide teachers with the accurate information they need to make decisions to promote learning.

1.2 Assuming that the assessment is consistent with his learning objectives, it is valid. Specifying that grammar and punctuation are important and then giving students a score for this component of the essay is a valid procedure.

1.3 Her assessment is not valid. Her learning objective is for students to be able to design experiments, but she assesses their recall of the steps involved. Her assessment isn't aligned with her learning objective, so it is invalid. It is likely that her assessment is reliable, because she will be able to score it consistently.

2.1 Informal assessment is the process of gathering incidental information about students' learning progress or development and making decisions based on that information. Teachers make an enormous number of decisions every day, ranging from which students to call on and when, whether to intervene in a classroom incident, or when to modify a lesson if students seem to be struggling. None of these decisions would be possible without informal assessment.

2.2 Teachers' ability to promote learners' personal, social, and moral development depend largely on informal assessment. When teachers make decisions about students' perspective taking or social problem-solving abilities—both important parts of social development—the decisions are part of informal assessment. Similarly, when teachers make decisions about promoting prosocial behaviors—an important part of moral development—their decisions are also part of informal assessment.

2.3 Because getting consistent information is difficult with informal assessments, they can be unreliable. We need to be aware of the possibility of unreliable information so we don't make decisions that can decrease learning or damage students emotionally.

3.1 Formal assessment is the process of gathering the same kind of systematic information from each student. Quizzes, tests, performance assessments, and homework are all forms of formal assessment.

Formal assessment differs from informal assessment in its systematic nature. Informal assessments don't gather the same information from each student.

3.2 In item 1, forms of the term *circulate* appear in both the stem and the correct answer. In item 2, the correct choice is written in more technical terms than are the distractors. Teachers fall into this trap when they take the correct choice directly from the text and then make up the distractors. Their informal language appears in the distractors, whereas text language appears in the correct answer.

In item 3, the correct choice is significantly longer than the incorrect choices; the teacher gives a similar clue when the correct choice is shorter than the distractors. If one choice is significantly longer or shorter than others, it should be a distractor.

In item 4, choices *a* and *c* are stated in absolute terms, which alerts test-wise students. Absolute terms, such as *all, always, none,* and *never,* are usually associated with incorrect answers. If used, they should be in the correct answer, such as "All algae contain chlorophyll."

The stem in item 5 is stated in negative terms without this fact being emphasized (the word *not* should be underlined). Also, choice *a* is grammatically inconsistent with the stem. One solution to the problem is to end the stem with "a(n)," so grammatical consistency is preserved.

In item 6, choices *a* and *c* are automatically eliminated, because both are gerunds and only one answer can be correct. Also, item 6 uses "all of the above" as a choice; it can't be correct if *a* and *c* are eliminated. That makes *b* the only possible choice. A student could get the item right and have no idea what a participle is.

Preparing valid multiple-choice items requires both thought and care. With effort and practice, however, you can become skilled at it, and when you do, you have a powerful learning and assessment tool.

3.3 You would create a rating scale by first identifying the criteria for effective multiple-choice items. You would then describe each of these criteria in a single statement, which could be rated.

An example might appear as follows:
DIRECTIONS: Assess each of the test items using the following dimensions. For each dimension, circle a 5 for an excellent performance, 4 for a very good performance, 3 for good performance, 2 for fair, and 1 for poor.

5 4 3 2 1	States one clear problem in the stem.
5 4 3 2 1	Each distractor is plausible.
5 4 3 2 1	Wording in the stem and in the correct choice is dissimilar.
5 4 3 2 1	Phrasing in the correct choice and in the distractors is similar.
5 4 3 2 1	The correct choice and distractors are similar in length.
5 4 3 2 1	Negative wording is appropriately emphasized.
5 4 3 2 1	All distractors have different meanings.

3.4 Essay items can be performance assessments to the extent that they tap higher-level thinking in real-life situations. For example, asking students to write an essay on a topic of their choice, using available resources, would be closer to the idea of a performance assessment than a closed-book, timed test, with the teacher specifying the topic.

4.1 Effective assessment practices include careful planning for assessment, preparing students for assessments, creating a positive environment for administering assessments, and analyzing results.

Effective assessment practices increase student learning in the following ways: First, creating assessments during the planning process helps increase validity through instructional alignment. Second, preparing students for assessments provides them with practice responding to items similar to those that will be on the actual assessment, and also allows you to teach test-taking strategies. Both increase learning. Third, creating an environment similar to the one in which the students studied the topics covered on the assessment, and eliminating distractions also increases performance. Finally, analyzing results and providing students with feedback help develop a more accurate and deeper understanding of the topics measured on the assessment.

4.2 The primary purpose of a table of specifications is to ensure that assessments are valid by aligning them with learning objectives. A table of specifications increases validity in two ways: First, by systematically identifying important information, it helps guarantee content coverage. Second, by focusing on the level of the items, it helps ensure that the level of each item on the test matches the level of the objectives and instruction.

To maximize these benefits, tables of specifications should be created during the process of planning for instruction.

4.3 First, DeVonne emphasized reading the directions carefully. Second, she told them to skip a problem if they got stuck. Third, she reminded them not to forget to go back to any problem that they had skipped.

5.1 The components of a total assessment system include preparing specific items such as paper-and-pencil, performance assessment, and portfolio assessments. The components also include preparing students, administering assessments, analyzing results, and assigning grades.

Decisions involved in designing a total assessment system include the following:

- The number of tests and quizzes to be given
- Whether to use performance assessments and/or portfolios and how they will be integrated into the total assessment system
- The level at which assessment items will be written, such as recall of factual knowledge, or application of conceptual knowledge
- How homework will be included in the process of assigning grades
- The assessment and reporting of affective dimensions, such as cooperation and effort

5.2 Formative assessment is an ongoing process that uses informal assessments, homework, and ungraded quizzes and tests to provide students with feedback and to allow teachers to diagnose learning problems. Summative assessment occurs after instruction, and teachers use it for grading purposes. Providing students with detailed feedback about their performance on the assessments is an essential component of both.

5.3 A grading system based on percentages is easier to manage and easier to communicate to students and parents. However, it can provide a distorted picture of learning progress, because percentages for different assignments are usually averaged, which attaches equal weight to assignments that differ in length. A point system may be harder to communicate to students and parents but provides a more accurate picture of learning progress.

Chapter 15

1.1 Standards-based education is the process of focusing instruction on predetermined goals or standards, and accountability is the process of requiring students to demonstrate that they have met the standards and holding teachers responsible for students' performance. Standardized testing in the form of high-stakes tests is used to determine whether students have met the standards.

1.2 Arguments for high-stakes testing include the following: The process identifies important learning outcomes, communicates them to both students and the public, and provides evidence about whether students are acquiring essential knowledge. Advocates also claim that this process improves learning for all students.

Arguments against high-stakes testing suggest that it narrows the curriculum; in essence, what is tested becomes the curriculum. This encourages teachers to ignore areas that aren't tested, such as art and music. Critics also argue that the tests don't provide a true measure of what students have learned, that cutoff scores are arbitrary, and the instruments are too crude to be used in making important decisions about students, teachers, and schools. In addition, the tests have a disproportionately adverse impact on students from minority cultures and particularly those with limited proficiency in English.

2.1 Standardized tests serve three primary functions: (1) assessment and diagnosis of learning, such as how students' achievement compares to the achievement of other students around the nation (or even the world), as well as identification of specific strengths and weaknesses; (2) selection and placement, such as placing students new to a school in a certain class level, a program for the gifted and talented, or admission to college; and (3) program evaluation and accountability, such as assessing a new curriculum and the extent to which a school or district meets state-mandated accountability measures.

2.2 The district is considering both achievement and diagnostic tests. Standardized achievement tests are designed to provide comprehensive coverage of different content areas. Diagnostic tests, in comparison, are designed to provide more specific, detailed information about an individual student's strengths and weaknesses.

2.3 The first teacher is addressing construct validity, a description of the extent to which an assessment accurately measures a characteristic that is not directly observable. The second is addressing content validity, the match between a test's contents and the content of the math curriculum. The third teacher is looking for predictive validity, the test's ability to gauge future performance in college.

3.1 A greater difference exists between the performances of Carol and Marsha than between Marsha and Lenore. Students' percentile ranks at the extremes of a distribution vary more from their counterparts than those who score near the middle of the distribution.

3.2 In the first class, with a standard deviation of 4.8, a score of 47 would be in stanine 7 (slightly more than 1 standard deviation above the mean). In the second distribution, with a standard deviation of 3.1, a score of 47 would be in stanine 8 (more than 1.5 standard deviations above the mean).

3.3 A grade-equivalent score of 6.7 means that he scored as well as the average sixth grader in the seventh month of the sixth grade. It means that the fourth grader is somewhat advanced. (It does not mean that the student should be in the sixth grade, nor does it mean that the student is generally capable of doing sixth-grade work.)

4.1 Learner diversity can influence the validity of standardized tests if bias exists in the content of the tests, testing procedures, or test use. Content bias exists if performance on a test requires knowledge that is not relevant to the concept or skill being tested and is knowledge that learners from diverse backgrounds may not possess. Bias in testing procedures exists if students are not familiar with aspects of the testing process, such as time limits or testing formats that place a burden on the students that detracts from their performance.

Tests can also be biased with respect to use if educators make decisions about students based on the results of a single test.

4.2 Using the most effective strategy teachers have for minimizing content bias is to prepare students as fully as possible for the tests. This includes providing concrete reference points for technical vocabulary, carefully teaching and emphasizing test-taking strategies, aligning instruction with prescribed standards, and providing students with ample practice with formats similar to the formats they will face on the tests. This strategy is important for all students, and it is even more essential for members of cultural minorities and students who are not native English speakers.

appendix B

Feedback for "Questions for Case Analysis"

Chapter 1

1. Rebecca most explicitly demonstrated general pedagogical knowledge in her lesson. The class was orderly, and she used questioning to involve a number of the children in the lesson.

2. Richard demonstrated each of the forms of knowledge, but pedagogical content knowledge and knowledge of learners and learning were most prominent. Using concrete examples such as a starfish and Jason to illustrate different types of symmetry demonstrated his pedagogical content knowledge (his ability to represent abstract concepts in ways that make sense to learners).

   Richard demonstrated knowledge of learners and learning by having Jason go to the front of the room. He understood, for instance, that using a personalized example, such as Jason, increases student interest, and with it, motivation to learn. He also understood that concrete examples, such as the sponge, starfish, and Jason are more effective than abstract examples.

3. Didi clearly understood Charles's Law, which is knowledge of content. Most obviously, she demonstrated pedagogical content knowledge in her lesson. Her ability to represent the relationship between temperature and pressure in a way that made sense to students demonstrated her ability to illustrate an abstract idea (Charles's law) with concrete examples (the balloons).

4. Bob Duchaine primarily demonstrated knowledge of content. He obviously understood the factors surrounding the Vietnam War. However, the fact that he used only lecture as a way of teaching this content suggests that he might not possess as much of the other forms of professional knowledge.

Chapter 2

1. Jenny's students demonstrated characteristics of preoperational learners. For instance, Jessica's reason for the towel staying dry was, "Cause it's inside and the rest is outside," and Anthony concluded that "A water seal," had kept the towel dry. This is perceptually based reasoning, which is characteristic of preoperational learners.

2. Jenny promoted cognitive development by providing direct, concrete experiences for her students. She also allowed her students to experiment with the materials in a follow-up, hands-on activity, which provided even more direct experience.

3. Jenny tipped the glass, so the students *could see* that bubbles escaped from the glass. Since the students were preoperational, which means their thinking was perceptual, it was essential that they could see the bubbles.

4. While we don't have enough evidence to determine if the lesson was conducted in all the students' zones of proximal development, the comments of several indicated that, with Jenny's guidance, they understood the topic. This suggests that the lesson was conducted in their zones.

   Jenny provided scaffolding in the form of questions, prompts, and concrete illustrations, such as tipping the glass to allow the air bubbles to escape.

Chapter 3

1. Based on Erikson's work, we might conclude that Karl hasn't positively resolved the industry–inferiority crisis with respect to English. He says, "I'm no good at English," for example. On the other hand, he presumably feels a sense of accomplishment with respect to basketball, because Helen described him as "poetry in motion."

2. Research indicates that the strongest correlations exist between specific academic self-concepts and achievement. This is corroborated in Karl's case. His self-concept in English is low, but in math and science it appears to be better. Also, his physical self-concept is probably quite high, since, according to Helen, he's very good at basketball.

3. Helen's handling of the cheating problem was ineffective. First, her classroom structure promoted a form of external morality; for example, her comment to Nathan was, "Nathan, remember my first rule?" instead of, "Nathan, why is it important to raise your hand when you want to speak?"

   Second, her comment, "If I catch anyone cheating on Thursday, I'll tear up your quiz and give you a failing grade," was again consistent with external morality. A more effective approach would have been to try to promote autonomous morality by discussing the issue of cheating, and by describing teaching and learning as social contracts. When students take tests, they are in a contract that requires them to do the work on their own. While this orientation won't stop all cheating, it creates a more effective climate for promoting moral development.

4. Several things in Helen's approach to her classroom and her instruction could have been improved. In addition to the emotional climate, as indicated by her response to Nathan and her threat to tear up papers if others were caught cheating, her expectations for students were negative. For example, she commented to them, "You did so poorly on the quiz, and I explained everything so carefully. You must not have studied very hard." While we can't be completely sure, it appears that her instruction is very teacher centered. An approach that involved the students would have been more effective. When students don't have opportunities to interact with each other, opportunities for social development are limited.

Chapter 4

1. The most prominent strategy Teri used to eliminate gender bias was to call on all students—both male and female—equally. Other strategies she might have employed include strategically assigning girls to key roles in small groups, openly talking about the problem in class, and bringing female role models into her class.

2. The overheads that Teri used to illustrate *mercantilism* minimized the role of previous background knowledge by containing all of the essential characteristics.

3. Teri provided challenge by asking her students to find commonalities between the two examples of *mercantilism*. She encouraged success by structuring her questioning strategies so that students were able to construct the concept from the examples.

4. She actively involved her students in two ways. She had them work in groups, and she used questioning to involve them in the whole-group portion of the lesson.

Chapter 5

1. Mike helped create a supportive climate in several ways. Some seem minor, but collectively they were all significant. For example, he smiled at his students, willingly repeated part of the problem for Gwenn, and offered encouragement by telling them in a positive tone that he was going to call on them first in the lesson. He also provided support for other students, such as whispering, "That's terrific," to Todd and giving him a light "thump" on the back and encouraging

Herchel when he said, "I . . . I . . . don't know." While each of these behaviors—alone—is relatively minor, when combined they result in a climate of support and positive expectations.

2. First, Mike was consistently positive with the students, and he stated positive expectations throughout the lesson. Second, he taught the lesson in small steps and prompted students, such as Herchel, whenever they were unable to answer.

3. First, he had the three students with learning disabilities come to class a few minutes early, so he could carefully read his warm-up problem to them and be sure they understood what was asked for in the problem before the rest of the students began. Then he worked with them in a small group while the rest of the students were doing seat work to give them the extra scaffolding they needed to help get them to the point where they could work on their own.

4. He helped Todd develop a system in which Todd would chart his own behavior, with the goal being the development of self-management. He also provided Todd with the emotional support and reinforcement needed to help make the system work.

   We don't have evidence in the case study about support for Horace. This can be a problem, since Horace is shy and withdrawn, and he can become "lost in the shuffle." A relatively simply way to provide support would be to include him in the question-and-answer activity and prompt him if necessary to ensure that he can answer successfully before turning to another student. In this way, he can involve Horace, and hopefully, in time, make significant progress with him.

Chapter 6

1. Scott applied each of the principles of cognitive learning theory in his lesson. First, his lesson, overall, provided students with experiences that helped them understand how to design experiments and control variables.

   Second, the students' tendency to try to solve the problem by changing more than one variable at a time illustrated the following principles: *people want their experiences to make sense*, and *to make sense of their experiences, learners construct knowledge*. Changing two—or even all three—variables made sense to the students.

   The students' tendency to change more than one variable at a time also illustrated the principle *knowledge that learners construct depends on what they already know*. The students knew that they had to manipulate the variables, but they didn't have sufficient prior knowledge or experience to help them understand that the variables had to be changed systematically, varying only one at a time.

The principle *social interaction facilitates learning* was demonstrated in two ways. First, Scott's questions helped them reconsider their procedures, and talking to each other provided different perspectives on ways to identify and isolate key variables.

2. When students said, "Mr. Sowell, we found out that the shorter it is and the heavier it is, the faster it goes," this indicated that they had changed both variables and revealed a misconception about controlling variables. Scott then asked which of the two variables was responsible for the change in the frequency.

When Wensley and Jonathan said simultaneously, "They both changed," Scott responded, "Think about that. You need to come up with a conclusion about length, about weight, and about angle—how each of them influences the frequency of your pendulum." This question challenged their thinking, but probably not directly enough to result in conceptual change. Scott later demonstrated and explained the need to control variables, but whether the explanation would have been effective for promoting conceptual change is uncertain, because we don't know about the results of his subsequent assessments.

Chapter 7

1. Applying the memory model requires that teachers consciously attempt to attract and maintain students' attention, check their perceptions, and promote meaningful encoding without imposing a cognitive load that exceeds their working memory capacities. Sue's lesson was an effective application of the memory model. She helped attract and maintain students' attention by challenging them to find evidence in the book that Dimmesdale was the illicit lover and by using the passage from the book describing Dimmesdale's speech. She also used class discussion as a mechanism to maintain attention. In each instance she used student responses to check their perceptions. Sue avoided imposing too heavy a cognitive load by asking one question at a time and giving them time to consider their answers. She promoted meaningful encoding by encouraging her students to use imagery to gain more insights into Dimmesdale's character. When they wrote in their journals and discussed Hester's reaction to Dimmesdale's speech, they were cognitively active, linking the information in the novel to their background knowledge. Through the discussion they elaborated on each other's understanding. Imagery, activity, and elaboration are all processes that make information meaningful.

2. Encoding was the cognitive process most prominent in her lesson. As we saw in item 1, Sue promoted encoding by encouraging students to use imagery to gain insights into Dimmesdale's character, by putting them in active roles with their journal writing and class discussion, and promoting elaboration in the class discussion.

While encoding was the most significant process, perception was prominent as well. For instance, when the students offered different views of Hester's reaction to Dimmesdale's speech, they were describing their perceptions.

3. Declarative knowledge is knowledge of facts, definitions, procedures, and rules; procedural knowledge involves knowing how to perform tasks. Sue focused on declarative knowledge when she reviewed the novel's plot at the beginning of the lesson. The primary focus of the lesson was on declarative knowledge—helping the students develop an understanding of the characters in the novel. When the students wrote in their journals, they were demonstrating procedural knowledge. Sue could have increased the likelihood of transfer by giving her students some additional information and have them create a bar graph of that information.

Chapter 8

1. Sue did a generally good job of teaching problem solving with young children. She introduced the situation and asked the children how they would solve the problem. In this way she provided practice in identifying the problem and selecting a strategy for solving it. The learning-center work gave the students experience in applying their understanding of graphing to other problems.

Sue did a very good job of presenting her problem in a meaningful context, and she provided considerable scaffolding for the children who had difficulty with the process and the applications.

2. Sue did quite well at promoting critical thinking in her lesson. For example, she asked students to make observations of the information in the graphs, and she asked students to confirm their conclusions with observations (e.g., "How did you solve the problem?" and "Does that work?").

She could have increased the emphasis on critical thinking by giving her students the chance to practice critical thinking in other contexts. For instance, she might have posed questions, such as, "Suppose we went around the school and asked people what their favorite flavor of jelly bean is. What do you think they would say?" After the students predicted, she could ask them for the basis for their prediction (such as the information in their graph), or she could ask them how they could find out what the whole school preferred.

3. Promoting transfer was one of the strengths of Sue's lesson. After she conducted the whole-group activity, she had students work at a series of centers, each of which focused on gathering information and preparing bar graphs in different contexts. In this way, the students had a variety of high-quality experiences, all of which were in realistic contexts.

Chapter 9

1. Helen's comment to Jenny is the best example of classical conditioning in the case study. Getting caught off guard when Mr. Rose sent her to the board was the *unconditioned stimulus* for Helen, and feeling like an idiot was the *unconditioned response*. Going to the board became associated with getting caught off guard, so going to the board became the *conditioned stimulus*, which resulted in her feeling nervous as the *conditioned response*. Feeling nervous is an emotion similar to her original emotion of feeling like an idiot.

   Warren could help extinguish Helen's nervousness by ensuring her success as she worked at the board. This might require some extra scaffolding and emotional support as she worked through the problems.

2. The first example of punishment occurred when Warren reduced his first homework assignment from six to five word problems. The students' complaints were presentation punishers. They presented him with their complaints, and he reduced the length of the assignment.

   The second example occurred when students complained again and he reduced the assignment from five to four problems. While longer homework assignments don't necessarily result in more learning, students need to practice the problem-solving skills Warren was trying to teach. Reducing the homework assignments too much is likely to decrease learning.

3. Warren negatively reinforced students by reducing the length of the homework assignments when they complained. Their behavior increased, as indicated by the fact that they complained about the homework assignment sooner on Friday than they did on Thursday. Taking away some of the homework assignment was the negative reinforcer.

   Warren also negatively reinforced Pamela for not answering his question by removing the question and turning it to Callie. This is likely to result in Pamela's saying she doesn't know more quickly the next time she is called on and is uncertain about the answer.

A more effective move would be to prompt Pamela and then positively reinforce her for her efforts. We want to reinforce students for answering instead of for not answering.

4. Warren's modeling was effective in two ways. First, he demonstrated the solution to a problem, and second, he capitalized on cognitive modeling by articulating his thinking during the demonstration, "Now, . . . the first thing I think about when I see a problem like this one is, 'What does the jacket cost now?' I have to figure out the price, and to do that I will take 25% of the $84. . . . "

   Warren's modeling was ineffective when he said, "I realize that percentages and decimals aren't your favorite topic, and I'm not wild about them either, but they'll be on the state exam, so we might as well buckle down and learn them." Because people tend to imitate behaviors they observe in others, modeling distaste for a topic increases the likelihood that students will decide that the topic is boring.

5. When Cris caught his error and corrected himself, Warren commented, "Good, . . . that's what we're trying to do. We are all going to make mistakes, but if we catch ourselves, we're making progress. Keep it up." His comment reinforced Cris and simultaneously vicariously reinforced the other students. He also used Cris as a model, and, because everyone in the class is similar in that they are all students, Cris was likely to be an effective model because of perceived similarity. (Warren's praise suggested that Cris was also competent, which would further increase his effectiveness as a model.)

Chapter 10

1. Damon's instruction was less than effective for capitalizing on learners' needs to promote motivation. For example, his comment to Clifton, "so that doesn't make sense," detracts from his feelings of safety. Also, the comment communicated that Clifton lacked competence, which is an innate need according to self-determination theory, as did his comment to Jeremy, "I know you have a tough time with written assignments."

   Also, his display of grades and his comment, "Let's give these sharp ones a run for their money," emphasized ability, which would detract from the self-worth of students who didn't perform well on the test.

2. Damon's display of grades and comments promoted a performance orientation, rather than a mastery orientation. A more effective approach would be to deemphasize students' performance, instead emphasizing and modeling effort attributions, as Kathy Brewster did with her students.

3. Personalizing content, using concrete examples, and promoting high levels of involvement increase interest. In contrast with Kathy Brewster, Damon presented facts about the Crusades in a lecture. He used no concrete examples, he made no attempt to personalize the content, and students were generally uninvolved. Further, in making the comment, "I know that learning dates and places isn't the most pleasant stuff, but you might as well get used to it, because that's what history is all about," he modeled disinterest in the topic, which would detract from his students' interest.

Chapter 11

1. The students' enthusiasm can be explained with each of the components of the Model for Promoting Student Motivation. For instance, with respect to teacher qualities, DeVonne was enthusiastic, caring, and had positive expectations for her students. With respect to the climate variables, her class was orderly, and the students felt very safe. In addition, she explained the writing task clearly, which increased task comprehension, and the assignment provided opportunities for both challenge and success. With respect to the instructional variables, the students were highly involved, and displaying their own paragraph strongly capitalized on personalization. Also, they received feedback about the task. The fact that it was public feedback didn't bother the students, probably because of the safety of DeVonne's classroom and the influence of personalization. Development was also likely a factor. High school students, for example, might have been less comfortable with the process.

2. Teachers who are successful with students from diverse backgrounds are enthusiastic, caring, and have high expectations. They also create lessons that connect to students' lives and have high rates of involvement. DeVonne possessed each of these teacher qualities, her lesson connected to students' lives by allowing them to write on a topic of their choice, and they were actively involved throughout the lesson.

Chapter 12

1. Janelle's planning for classroom management was not effective. For example, Janelle's students were expected to sit quietly while she called the roll, went to the file cabinet to get out her transparencies, and finished arranging her materials. The result was lost instructional time for Janelle and "dead" time for students, during which disruptions occurred.

2. Several problems existed in Janelle's management interventions. First, she demonstrated lack of withitness when she admonished Leila for blurting out "Stop it, Damon." Janelle initially caught the wrong one and allowed the incident to disrupt the learning activity. Janelle also allowed her encounter with Howard and Manny to disrupt the momentum of her lesson. Janelle's nonverbal behavior also didn't communicate that she was "in charge," or that she meant it when she intervened. For example, she looked up from her papers to admonish Howard and Manny, and she again looked up in response to a hum of voices around the classroom. Also, requiring Manny to read the rule aloud in front of the class was a form of power play that did nothing to improve the classroom climate, and her comment, "You've been bothering me all week . . ." was inconsistent with recommendations of experts to criticize the behavior and not the student.

3. Janelle's instruction would have been more effective if it had been more interactive and developed with more supporting materials such as maps and globes. This would have allowed her to involve students more, which usually results in fewer management problems. Janelle's management was also less effective than it might have been. She wasn't well-organized, and she didn't communicate as clearly and assertively as she might have to be effective. In addition, she was slightly less withit than what would have been desirable, and she allowed her interventions with the students to disrupt the momentum and smoothness of her lesson, resulting in more problems with management.

   Several suggestions for improvement include the following: First, Janelle would have been more effective if she had been better organized. A beginning-of-class warm-up activity would have helped her better use her time and would also have eliminated dead time at the beginning of the lesson during which management problems can occur. Also, her materials should have been ready and waiting, so she didn't have to spend time arranging them while students were supposed to sit quietly. Ensuring that her verbal and nonverbal communications were congruent would have made her admonishments of the students more credible. Using an I-message with Howard would have been a more effective intervention than saying, "You've been bothering me all week." Finally, keeping her intervention with Howard and Manny brief would have allowed her to maintain the flow of her lesson.

Chapter 13

1. Planning typically involves several decisions. First, Judy had to decide that the topic—identifying relationships between geography and economy of different

geographical regions—was an important topic to study. Second, Judy decided that her learning objective would be for students to describe the effect of geography on the economy of a region. Third, she had to make a decision about how the learning activity would be prepared. She decided that she would have the students gather information about the regions, organize the information in a matrix, and then analyze the information. She also decided that she would use a combination of group work and whole-class discussion in her learning activity.

2. *Alignment* refers to the connections between learning objectives, instructional activities, and assessment. Judy's learning objective was for students to understand the relationships between geography and the economy of different regions in the country. Because her learning activity focused on these relationships, her objective and learning activity were aligned.

3. Judy demonstrated several of the essential teaching skills in her lesson. First, she demonstrated a positive approach to the lesson with appropriately high expectations. She was well organized. She began the lesson immediately after the bell rang, she had the chart already displayed on the wall of her room, and students moved back and forth from small-group to whole-group activities quickly and smoothly.

   Judy's communication was clear. She used clear language, and the lesson was thematic and led to a point (connected discourse). We didn't see explicit transition signals in the lesson, nor was emphasis apparent.

   The chart that Judy and the students had prepared provided an effective form of focus. Judy's questioning was quite good. She called on a variety of students, called on girls and boys about equally, called on students by name, and ensured success with open-ended questions and prompting.

   Because of the way the lesson was organized, much of Judy's feedback was a simple acknowledgment of students' observations, and her closure was quite brief, because the period was nearing an end. She would need to do a careful review the next day to ensure that the students had encoded the information clearly into long-term memory.

Chapter 14

1. Ron's teaching was out of alignment. His learning objective was, ". . . you'll all be able to use pronouns correctly in your writing." This goal was congruent with the second part of his assessment, which asked students to write a passage in which pronoun cases were used correctly. However, his learning activity focused on the sentences in isolation rather than on writing, so it was not congruent with his goal and the second part of his assessment. To make his instruction congruent with his goal, Ron needs to provide students with practice using pronouns correctly in their writing.

2. Effective preparation for testing involves giving students the opportunity to practice on test-like items similar to those they will encounter on the test itself. During preparation, Ron's students responded only to the specific and isolated sentences, and they didn't practice using pronouns in their writing.

   The only problem that existed with his administration of the test was the fact that students were pressed for time, and he may have increased the anxiety of test-anxious students by his repeated reminders of the amount of time remaining. Giving students more time to finish the exam would remedy this problem.

   In discussing the test results, Ron again deemphasized their writing in favor of the specific items, and his feedback was somewhat vague. Unquestionably, providing feedback for every student is very demanding, but he could have written a model response to which the students could have compared their own paragraphs.

3. Ron's instruction for urban learners would have been more effective if he had made his instruction more concrete. For example, he could have prepared a personalized written passage that included examples of pronoun cases, and in this way his content would have been more meaningful for his students.

   Research indicates that learners from diverse backgrounds benefit from explicit test-preparation procedures. Had Ron provided more test-preparation practice, particularly with writing, his assessment would have been more effective and valid.

4. Ron used his time well, his instruction was interactive, he had a clear learning objective for his students, and he provided practice for his students with respect to properly placing the pronoun in specific sentences. These were the strengths of his instruction and assessment.

   His primary weaknesses were the fact that his learning objective, learning activity, and assessment were out of alignment; he didn't provide as much practice for his students as he might have, especially with using pronouns in their writing; and he didn't discuss the test results as thoroughly as he might have.

Chapter 15

1. Standardized achievement tests are specifically designed to provide information about how much students learn in various content areas. To be useful in answering her question, the standardized achievement test would have to be carefully aligned with her objectives.

2. Content validity, or the extent to which a standardized achievement test actually covers important content. This is essentially an issue of alignment.

3. Because of their focus on specific content, standardized diagnostic tests would be most useful here. Diagnostic tests assess more narrowly, but do so more thoroughly, thus providing teachers with more in-depth information about specific topics.

4. The more information that teachers gather in their decision making, the better their decisions. Other possible sources of information include specific subtests within the standardized tests, previous grades in math classes, and observations and evaluations from previous teachers.

appendix C

Using This Text to Practice for the Praxis™ *Principles of Learning and Teaching* Exam

In the United States, most states plus the District of Columbia, Guam, and the U.S. Virgin Islands use Praxis™ exams as part of their teacher licensing requirement. Four *Principles of Learning and Teaching* (PLT) tests, one each for teachers seeking licensure in Early Childhood, or grades K–6, 5–9, and 7–12, are among the Praxis™ exams. *Educational Psychology: Windows on Classrooms* addresses virtually all of the topics covered in the PLT tests.

The *Principles of Learning and Teaching* exam has two parts. One consists of 24 multiple-choice questions organized into two sections of 12 questions each. The multiple-choice questions are similar to those in the test bank that accompanies *Educational Psychology: Windows on Classrooms*. The second part is based on "case histories" (case studies), which you will be asked to read and analyze. The case histories are very similar to the case studies that appear throughout this text.

The case-based part of the Praxis™ *Principles of Learning and Teaching* exam consists of four case histories followed by

three short-answer questions each. The short-answer questions will cover all of the topics identified in the column under "Topics Covered on the Praxis™ Exam" in the table below. Each short-answer question will be scored on a scale of 0–2. Questions require you to "demonstrate understanding of the importance of an aspect of teaching, demonstrate understanding of the principles of learning and teaching underlying an aspect of teaching, or recognize when and how to apply the principles of learning and teaching underlying an aspect of teaching" (Educational Testing Service, 2008b, p. 1). We have designed this text to help you succeed on the Praxis™ *Principles of Learning and Teaching* exam by including case studies at the end of each chapter, which are followed by short-answer questions. The case studies and questions provide you with practice responding to questions similar to those that will appear on the exam. We provide feedback for the short-answer questions in Appendix B of this text.

Topics Covered on the Praxis™ Exam	Chapter Content Aligned with Praxis™ Topics
I. Students as Learners (approximately 33% of total test)	
A. Student Development and the Learning Process	
1. Theoretical foundations about how learning occurs: how students construct knowledge, acquire skills, and develop habits of mind	Chapter 2: Cognitive and Language Development • Brain research and cognitive development (pp. 31–34) • Piaget's theory of cognitive development (pp. 34–44) • Current views of cognitive development (p. 44) • Lev Vygotsky's sociocultural theory of cognitive development (pp. 45–49) Chapter 6: Principles of Cognitive Learning Theory and the Construction of Knowledge (Entire chapter) Chapter 7: Cognitive Learning and Human Memory (Entire chapter) Chapter 8: Complex Cognitive Processes (Entire chapter) Chapter 9: Behaviorism and Social Cognitive Theory (Entire chapter)

2. Human development in the physical, social, emotional, moral, speech/language, and cognitive domains	Chapter 2: Cognitive and Language Development (Entire chapter) Chapter 3: Personal, Social, and Moral Development (Entire chapter) Chapter 7: Cognitive Learning and Human Memory • Metacognition: Knowledge and control of cognitive processes (pp. 239–242) Chapter 8: Complex Cognitive Processes • The strategic learner (pp. 270–276) Chapter 9: Behaviorism and Social Cognitive Theory • Self-regulated learning (pp. 318–320) Chapter 12: Classroom Management: Developing Self-regulated Learners • Developing learners self-regulation (pp. 393–396)

B. Students as Diverse Learners

1. Differences in the ways students learn and perform	Chapter 2: Cognitive and Language Development • Stages of development (pp. 38–43) • Culture and development (pp. 45–46) • Language and development (p. 47) Chapter 4: Learner Diversity • Culture and classrooms (pp. 108–112) • Ed Psych and Teaching: Teaching students in your classes who are culturally and linguistically diverse (pp. 117–118) • Gender differences in classrooms (p. 122) • Ed Psych and Teaching: Responding to your students' gender differences (pp. 123–124) • How SES influences learning (pp. 126–127) Chapter 5: Learners with Exceptionalities • Gardner's theory of multiple intelligences (pp. 141–143) • Learning styles (pp. 145–146)
2. Areas of exceptionality in students' learning	Chapter 5: Learners with Exceptionalities • Learning disabilities (pp. 153–155) • Attention deficit/hyperactivity disorder (pp. 155–156) • Communication disorders (pp. 156–157) • Intellectual disabilities (pp. 157–158) • Behavior disorders (pp. 158–160) • Autism spectrum disorder (pp. 160–161) • Visual disabilities (pp. 161–162) • Hearing disabilities (p. 162)
3. Legislation and institutional responsibilities relating to exceptional students	Chapter 5: Learners with Exceptionalities • Individuals with Disabilities Education Act (pp. 147–150) • Amendments to the Individuals with Disabilities Education Act (p. 148)
4. Approaches for accommodating various learning styles, intelligences, or exceptionalities	Chapter 5: Learners with Exceptionalities • Gardner's theory of multiple intelligences (pp. 141–143) • Ability grouping (pp. 144–145) • Learning styles (pp. 145–146) • Identifying students with exceptionalities (pp. 151–152) • Modifying instruction to meet students' needs (pp. 169–170) • Promoting social integration and development (pp. 171–172) • Developmentally appropriate practice: Teaching students with exceptionalities at different ages (pp. 173–174) Chapter 14: Increasing Learning Through Assessment • Performance assessments (pp. 495–498) • Exploring diversity: Effective assessment practices with learners from diverse backgrounds (p. 515)

5. Process of second language acquisition and strategies to support the learning of students for whom English is not a first language	**Chapter 2: Cognitive and Language Development** • Exploring diversity: Language development for non-native English speakers (p. 57) **Chapter 4: Learner Diversity** • English dialects (pp. 112–113) • English language learners (pp. 113–116) • Ed Psych and Teaching: Teaching students in your classes who are culturally and linguistically diverse (pp. 117–118)
6. Understanding the influence of individual experiences, talents, and prior learning, as well as language, culture, family, and community values on students' learning	**Chapter 2: Cognitive and Language Development (Entire chapter)** **Chapter 3: Personal, Social, and Moral Development** • Bronfenbrenner's bioecological theory of development (pp. 67–75) • Social development (pp. 87–88) **Chapter 4: Learner Diversity** • Culture and classrooms (pp. 108–112) • Linguistic diversity (pp. 112–116) • How SES influences learning (pp. 126–127) **Chapter 6: Principles of Cognitive Learning Theory and the Construction of Knowledge** • Exploring diversity: The impact of diversity on knowledge construction (p. 197) **Chapter 7: Cognitive Learning and Human Memory** • Exploring diversity: The impact of diversity on cognitive (p. 239)

C. Student Motivation and the Learning Environment

1. Theoretical foundations of human motivation and behavior	**Chapter 10: Motivation and Learning** • Behaviorist views of motivation (pp. 332–333) • Cognitive and social cognitive views of motivation (pp. 333–334) • Sociocultural views of motivation (p. 334) • Humanistic views of motivation (pp. 334–336)
2. How knowledge of human motivation and behavior should influence strategies for organizing and supporting individual and group work in the classroom	**Chapter 10: Motivation and Learning** • Ed Psych and Teaching: Using the influence of needs to increase your students' motivation to learn (pp. 340–341) • Ed Psych and Teaching: Using beliefs, goals and interests to increase your students' motivation to learn (pp. 355–356) • Developmentally appropriate practice: Motivation to learn in students at different ages (p. 357) **Chapter 11: A Classroom Model for Promoting Student Motivation** • Creating a mastery-focused classroom (pp. 365–366) • The teacher: Personal qualities that increase motivation to learn (pp. 366–370) • Ed Psych and Teaching: Demonstrating personal qualities that increase your students' motivation to learn (pp. 370–371) • Learning climate: Creating a motivating environment (pp. 372–375) • Instructional variables: Developing interest in learning activities (pp. 376–382) • Ed Psych and Teaching: Applying the climate and instructional variables to increase your students' motivation to learn (pp. 382–383)

3. Factors and situations that are likely to promote or diminish students' motivation to learn, and how to help students become self-motivated	**Chapter 3: Personal, Social, and Moral Development** • Ethnic identity (pp. 85–86) **Chapter 9: Behaviorism and Social Cognitive Theory** • Self-regulated learning (pp. 318–320) **Chapter 10: Motivation and Learning** • Ed Psych and Teaching: Using the influence of needs to increase your students' motivation to learn (pp. 340–341) • Ed Psych and Teaching: Using beliefs, goals and interests to increase your students' motivation to learn (pp. 355–356) **Chapter 11: A Classroom Model for Promoting Student Motivation** • Creating a mastery-focused classroom (pp. 365–366) • The teacher: Personal qualities that increase motivation to learn (pp. 366–370) • Ed Psych and Teaching: Demonstrating personal qualities that increase your students' motivation to learn (pp. 370–371) • Learning climate: Creating a motivating environment (pp. 372–375) • Instructional variables: Developing interest in learning activities (pp. 376–382) • Ed Psych and Teaching: Applying the climate and instructional variables to increase your students' motivation to learn (pp. 382–383) **Chapter 12: Classroom Management: Developing Self-regulated Learners** • Developing learner self-regulation (pp. 393–396) **Chapter 13: Learning and Effective Teaching** • Focus (p. 446)
4. Principles of effective classroom management and strategies to promote positive relationships, cooperation, and purposeful learning	**Chapter 11: A Classroom Model for Promoting Student Motivation** • Creating a mastery-focused classroom (pp. 365–366) • Order and safety: Classrooms as secure places to learn (p. 373) **Chapter 12: Classroom Management: Developing Self-regulated Learners** (Entire chapter) **Chapter 13: Learning and Effective Teaching** • Implementing instruction (pp. 442–452)

II. Instruction and Assessment (approximately 33% of total test)

A. Instructional Strategies

1. Major cognitive processes associated with student learning	**Chapter 2: Cognitive and Language Development** • Ed Psych and Teaching: Applying Piaget's theory with your students (p. 43) • Ed Psych and Teaching: Applying Vygotsky's theory with your students (p. 49) **Chapter 6: Principles of Cognitive Learning Theory and the Construction of Knowledge** (Entire chapter) **Chapter 7: Cognitive Learning and Human Memory** (Entire chapter) **Chapter 8: Complex Cognitive Processes** (Entire chapter) **Chapter 9: Behaviorism and Social Cognitive Theory** • Social cognitive theory (pp. 310–321)

2. Major categories, advantages, and appropriate uses of instructional strategies	Chapter 6: Principles of Cognitive Learning Theory and the Construction of Knowledge • Suggestions for classroom practice (pp. 198–202) • Ed Psych and Teaching: Applying principles of learning in your classroom (pp. 202–203) Chapter 7: Cognitive Learning and Human Memory • Ed Psych and Teaching: Applying the human memory model in your teaching (pp. 244–245) Chapter 8: Complex Cognitive Processes • Ed Psych and Teaching: Applying concept learning theory with your students (pp. 255–256) • Ed Psych and Teaching: Helping your students become better problem solvers (p. 265) • Ed Psych and Teaching: Helping your students become strategic learners (pp. 278–279) Chapter 13: Learning and Effective Teaching • Implementing instruction (pp. 442–452) • Models of instruction (pp. 453–465)
3. Principles, techniques, and methods associated with major instructional strategies	Chapter 13: Learning and Effective Teaching • Direct instruction (pp. 453–457) • Lecture–discussion (pp. 457–460) • Guided discovery (pp. 460–462) • Cooperative learning (pp. 463–465)
4. Methods for enhancing student learning through the use of a variety of resources and materials	Chapter 2: Cognitive and Language Development • Ed Psych and Teaching: Applying Piaget's theory with your students (p. 43) • Ed Psych and Teaching: Applying Vygotsky's theory with your students (p. 49) Chapter 6: Principles of Cognitive Learning Theory and the Construction of Knowledge • Suggestions for classroom practice (pp. 198–202) • Ed Psych and Teaching: Applying principles of learning in your classroom (pp. 202–203) • Technology, learning, and development: Capitalization on technology to promote knowledge construction (p. 202) Chapter 7: Cognitive Learning and Human Memory • Ed Psych and Teaching: Applying the human memory model in your teaching (pp. 244–245) Chapter 8: Complex Cognitive Processes • Technology, learning, and development: Using technology to promote problem solving (pp. 268–269) • Ed Psych and Teaching: Helping your students become strategic learners (pp. 278–279) Chapter 13: Learning and Effective Teaching • Implementing instruction (pp. 442–452) • Direct instruction (pp. 453–457) • Lecture–discussion (pp. 457–460) • Guided discovery (pp. 460–462) • Cooperative learning (pp. 463–465) • Technology, learning, and development: Using PowerPoint effectively (pp. 467–469)

B. Planning Instruction

1. Techniques for planning instruction, including addressing curriculum goals, selecting content topics, incorporating learning theory, subject matter, curriculum development, and student development and interests	**Chapter 13: Learning and Effective Teaching** • Identifying topics (pp. 433–434) • Specifying learning objectives (pp. 434–436) • Preparing and organizing learning activities (p. 437) • Planning for assessment (p. 437) • Instructional alignment (p. 438) • Planning in a standards-based environment (pp. 438–441)
2. Techniques for creating effective bridges between curriculum goals and students' experiences	**Chapter 6: Principles of Cognitive Learning Theory and the Construction of Knowledge** • The origin of misconception (pp. 195–196) • Teaching for conceptual change (p. 196) **Chapter 7: Cognitive Learning and Human Memory** • Imagery (p. 231) • Organization (pp. 231–233) • Schema activation (p. 233) • Elaboration (pp. 233–234) **Chapter 8: Complex Cognitive Processes** • Ed Psych and Teaching: Applying concept learning theory with your students (pp. 255–256) • Ed Psych and Teaching: Helping your students become better problem solvers (p. 265) • Ed Psych and Teaching: Helping your students become strategic learners (pp. 278–279) **Chapter 9: Behaviorism and Social Cognitive Theory** • Modeling (pp. 312–314) **Chapter 13: Learning and Effective Teaching** • Guided practice (p. 456) • Independent practice (p. 456) • Homework (pp. 456–457)

C. Assessment Strategies

1. Types of assessments	**Chapter 6: Principles of Cognitive Learning Theory and the Construction of Knowledge** • Promote learning with assessment (p. 201) **Chapter 10: Motivation and Learning** • Assessment and learning: The role of assessment in self-determination (p. 339) **Chapter 11: A Classroom Model for Promoting Student Motivation** • Assessment and learning: Using feedback to increase interest and self-efficacy (pp. 383–384) **Chapter 13: Learning and Effective Teaching** • Assessment and learning: Using assessment as a learning tool (pp. 471–472) **Chapter 14: Increasing Learning Through Assessment** • Informal assessment (pp. 485–488) • Paper-and-pencil items (pp. 489–494) • Performance assessments (pp. 495–498) • Portfolio assessment: Involving students in the assessment process (p. 499) **Chapter 15: Standardized Testing and Learning** • Types of standardized tests (pp. 528–532)

2. Characteristics of assessments	Chapter 14: Increasing Learning Through Assessment • Validity: Making accurate assessment decisions (p. 484) • Reliability: Consistency in assessment (pp. 484–485) • Paper-and-pencil items (pp. 489–494) • Performance assessments (pp. 495–498) • Portfolio assessment: Involving students in the assessment process (p. 499) Chapter 15: Standardized Testing and Learning • Evaluating standardized tests: Validity revisited (pp. 532–533)
3. Scoring assessments	Chapter 14: Increasing Learning Through Assessment • Using rubrics (pp. 493–494) • Performance assessment (pp. 495–498) • Portfolio assessment: Involving students in alternative assessment (p. 499) • Analyzing results (pp. 507–508) Chapter 15: Standardized Testing and Learning • Understanding and interpreting standardized test scores (pp. 533–539)
4. Uses of assessments	Chapter 13: Learning and Effective Teaching • Planning for assessment (p. 437) • Assessment and learning: Using assessment as a learning tool (pp. 471–472) Chapter 14: Increasing Learning Through Assessment • Effective assessment practices (pp. 502–508) • Grading and reporting: The total assessment system (pp. 509–514) Chapter 15: Standardized Testing and Learning • Accountability and standardized testing (pp. 524–526) • Functions of standardized tests (pp. 527–528) • Understanding and interpreting standardized test results (pp. 533–539) • Diversity and standardized testing (pp. 540–543)
5. Understanding of measurement theory and assessment-related issues	Chapter 14: Increasing Learning Through Assessment • Assessment *for* student learning (pp. 482–483) • Commercially prepared test items (p. 494) • Planning for assessment (pp. 502–503) • Preparing students for assessments (pp. 503–506) • Administering assessments (pp. 506–507) • Designing a grading system (pp. 510–511) • Assigning grades: Increasing learning and motivation (pp. 511–513) Chapter 15: Standardized Testing and Learning • Accountability issues in standardized testing (pp. 524–526) • Student diversity and assessment bias (pp. 541–542) • Standardized testing and English language learners (pp. 542–543)
6. Interpreting and communicating results of assessments	Chapter 14: Increasing Learning Through Assessment • Designing a grading system (pp. 510–511) • Assigning grades: Increasing learning and motivation (pp. 511–513) Chapter 15: Standardized Testing and Learning • Understanding and interpreting standardized test scores (pp. 533–539) • Accountability issues in standardized testing (pp. 524–526) • Diversity and standardized testing (pp. 540–543)

III. Communication Techniques (approximately 11% of total test)

A. Basic, Effective Verbal and Nonverbal Communication Techniques

Chapter 2: Cognitive and Language Development
- Language and development (p. 47)
- Developmentally Appropriate Practice: Promoting language development with learners at different ages (p. 59)

Chapter 3: Personal, Social, and Moral Development
- Social development (pp. 87–88)

Chapter 6: Principles of Cognitive Learning Theory and the Construction of Knowledge
- Social interaction facilitates learning (pp. 185–188)

Chapter 12: Classroom Management: Developing Self-Regulated Learners
- Communicating with parents (pp. 406–409)
- Benefits of communication (pp. 406–407)
- Keep verbal and non-verbal behaviors congruent (pp. 413–414)

Chapter 13: Learning and Effective Teaching
- Communication (p. 451)

B. Effect of Cultural and Gender Differences on Communications in the Classroom

Chapter 4: Learner Diversity
- Culture and classrooms (pp. 108–112)
- Linguistic diversity (pp. 112–116)
- Ed Psych and Teaching: Teaching students in your classes who are culturally and linguistically diverse (pp. 117–118)
- Gender differences in classroom behavior (p. 122)
- Gender stereotypes and perceptions (pp. 122–123)

Chapter 11: A Classroom Model for Promoting Student Motivation
- Exploring diversity: Personalizing content to increase motivation to learning in students from diverse background (p. 379)

Chapter 13: Learning and Effective Teaching
- Exploring diversity: Using cooperative learning to capitalize on your students' diversity (pp. 465–466)

C. Types of Communications and Interactions That Can Stimulate Discussion in Different Ways for Particular Purposes

Chapter 2: Cognitive and Language Development
- Ed Psych and Teaching: Applying Piaget's theory with your students (p. 43)
- Ed Psych and Teaching: Applying Vygotsky's theory with your students (p. 49)

Chapter 6: Principles of Cognitive Learning Theory and the Construction of Knowledge
- Suggestions for classroom practice (pp. 198–202)
- Ed Psych and Teaching: Applying principles of learning in your classroom (pp. 202–203)
- Technology, learning, and development: Capitalizing on technology to promote knowlege construction (p. 202)

Chapter 7: Cognitive Learning and Human Memory
- Ed Psych and Teaching: Applying the human memory model in your teaching (pp. 244–245)

Chapter 8: Complex Cognitive Processes
- Creativity in problem solving (pp. 267–268)
- Ed Psych and Teaching: Helping your students become better problem solvers (p. 265)

Chapter 11: A Classroom Model for Promoting Student Motivation
- Instructional variables: Developing interest in learning activities (pp. 376–379)

Chapter 12: Classroom Management: Developing Self-regulated Learners
- Creating a community of caring and trust (p. 396)

Chapter 13: Learning and Effective Teaching
- Questioning (pp. 446–449)
- Direct instruction (pp. 453–457)
- Lecture–discussion (pp. 457–460)
- Guided discovery (pp. 460–462)

IV. Teacher Professionalism (Profession and Community) (approximately 22% of total test)

A. The Reflective Practitioner

1. Types of resources available for professional development and learning	Chapter 1: Educational Psychology: Understanding Learning and Teaching • The preeminence of teachers (pp. 5–6) • Educational psychology, expert teaching, and professional knowledge (pp. 6–13)
2. Ability to read, understand, and apply articles and books about current research, views, ideas, and debates regarding best teaching practices	Chapter 1: Educational Psychology: Understanding Learning and Teaching • Educational psychology, expert teaching, and professional knowledge (pp. 6–13) • The role of research in acquiring professional knowledge (pp. 14–16)
3. Ongoing personal reflection on teaching and learning practices as a basis for making professional decisions	Chapter 1: Educational Psychology: Understanding Learning and Teaching • Educational psychology, expert teaching, and professional knowledge (pp. 6–13) • Teacher knowledge and reflective practice (p. 12)

B. The Larger Community

1. The role of the school as a resource to the larger community	Chapter 3: Personal, Social, and Moral Development • Ed Psych and Teaching: Supporting your students' identity and self-concept development (p. 84) • Ed Psych and Teaching: Applying an understanding of social development with your students (pp. 88–89) Chapter 12: Classroom Management: Developing Self-regulated Learners • Communicating with parents (pp. 406–409)

2. Factors in the students' environment outside of school (family circumstances, community environments, health and economic conditions) that may influence students' life and learning	Chapter 3: Personal, Social, and Moral Development • Bronfenbrenner's bioecological theory of development (pp. 67–75) Chapter 4: Learner Diversity • Culture and classrooms (pp. 108–112) • How SES influences learning (pp. 126–127)
3. Develop and utilize active partnerships among teachers, parents/guardians, and leaders in the community to support the educational process	Chapter 3: Personal, Social, and Moral Development • Peer aggression (pp. 73–74) Chapter 9: Behaviorism and Social Cognitive Theory • Capitalizing on minority role models (p. 318) Chapter 12: Classroom Management: Developing Self-regulated Learners • Benefits of communication (pp. 406–407) • Strategies for involving parents (pp. 407–409)
4. Major laws related to students' rights and teacher responsibilities	Chapter 5: Learners with Exceptionalities • Individuals with Disabilities Education Act (IDEA) (pp. 147–150) • Amendments to the Individuals with Disabilities Education Act (p. 148) Chapter 12: Classroom Management: Developing Self-regulated Learners • Responding to defiant students (p. 422) • Responding to fighting (pp. 422–423) • Responding to bullying (p. 423)

name index

subject index